To Mary
with love
from Dad.

Christmas. 1952.

ROGET'S THESAURUS

Existence

1

Ens, entity, being, existce — Nonentity, nullity, nihility

Essence, quintessce, quiddity — nonexistce, nothg, nought

Nature, thing, substance, course, world, frame, position, constitution — void, zero, cypher, blank, empty

Reality, (v. truth) actual existce — fact, course of things, under ye sun, extant, present — unsubstantial, Unreal, ideal, imaginary, visionary, fabulous, fictitious, supposititious, absent, shadow, dream, phantom, phantasm

Positive, affirmative, absolute, intrinsic, substantive, inherent — Negative, virtual, extrinsic, potential, adjective

To be, exist, obtain, stand, pass, subsist, prevail, lie — on foot, on ye tapis

to constitute, form, compose — to consist of

State, Mode of existce, condition, nature, constitutn, habit, scope, habitude, temperament

Affection, predicament, situatn, positn, posture, place, contingency

Circumstances, case, plight, trim, tune, — point, degree, juncture, conjuncture, pass, emergency, exigency.

Mode, manner, style, cast, fashion, form, shape, strain, way, degree — tenure, terms, tenor, footing, character, capacity

Relation, -ship, affinity, alliance, analogy, filiatn (v. connectn)

Reference, about, respectg, regardg, concerning, touching, in point of, as to, — pertaining to, belongg, applicable to, relatively, according to

Comparable, commensurate, correspondent, accordant — incompble, incomte -able, irreconcilable, discordant

Facsimile of the first page of the MS. classified catalogue of words completed by Dr. P. M. Roget in 1805, which was the germ of the Thesaurus.

THESAURUS

OF ENGLISH WORDS AND PHRASES

Classified and Arranged so as to Facilitate the Expression of Ideas and to Assist in Literary Composition

by

PETER MARK ROGET, M.D., F.R.S.

Enlarged by

JOHN LEWIS ROGET, M.A.

New Edition Revised and Enlarged by

SAMUEL ROMILLY ROGET, M.A.

1724

LONGMANS, GREEN AND CO

LONDON • NEW YORK • TORONTO

LONGMANS, GREEN AND CO LTD
6 & 7 CLIFFORD STREET LONDON W 1
ALSO AT MELBOURNE AND CAPE TOWN
LONGMANS, GREEN AND CO INC
55 FIFTH AVENUE NEW YORK 3
LONGMANS, GREEN AND CO
215 VICTORIA STREET TORONTO 1
ORIENT LONGMANS LTD
BOMBAY CALCUTTA MADRAS

New Edition . . . July 1936
New Impressions August 1937, January 1939, May 1941, September 1941, February 1942, August 1942, January 1943, October 1944, January 1946, November 1946, February 1949 (Reprint of 1941 Canadian Revision), February 1952

Printed in Great Britain
SPOTTISWOODE, BALLANTYNE & CO. LTD.
London & Colchester

PREFACE
TO
1936 EDITION

In preparing the present edition, the Index (pp. 387–705) upon which the usefulness of the work so largely depends has been checked, line by line, from beginning to end. Not only have a considerable number of corrections been made but the opportunity has been taken to revise the index generally and to add further references. The editor should also acknowledge the kindness of many correspondents who, after expressing their appreciation of the value of the Thesaurus in their work and play, have helped to render it more nearly perfect by their suggestions both as regards the text and the index. After making these corrections in the type, a new set of plates has been made, and it is hoped that the edition now offered will prove of greater utility than any of its many predecessors.

S. R. R.

July 1936

PREFACE
TO
1933 EDITION

As explained in the author's original preface to the Thesaurus, Dr. P. M. Roget made a list in MS. of words classified according to the ideas that they express, for his own use, as long ago as 1805 ; and a facsimile of the first page of this interesting little notebook is given in the frontispiece of the present edition. It was not, however, until he was over seventy years of age that he could spare the time to undertake the colossal task of expanding this into the famous volume which was published by Messrs. Longmans, Brown, Green & Longman in 1852.

This was followed by a second edition in 1853, a 'third and cheaper edition, enlarged and improved' two years later, a fourth edition in the same year, and a fifth edition in 1857. Since then edition has followed edition almost every year, and sometimes two or even three times in one year, until 76 printings have been called for, totalling some two hundred thousand books, and it is worthy of note that after eighty years the Thesaurus is still published by the same firm, and from the same address in Paternoster Row, now as when issued originally.

On Dr. Roget's death at an advanced age in 1869, the work passed into the hands of his son, John Lewis Roget, who completed the further comprehensive revision and enlargement on which Dr. Roget was engaged at the time of his death. This new edition, with its much more extensive index, appeared in 1879, and he continued to revise periodical reprints until his own death in 1908, when it devolved upon the undersigned to carry on the task initiated by his grandfather, and some further enlargement was made in 1925.

In the edition now presented a large number of further new words and phrases have been added throughout the book ; but in very few cases have words been removed, because archaic and even obsolete words are often sought for by authors. A few examples of alternative and obsolete spelling have however been removed, but no alteration whatever has been made in the general arrangement and classification of the categories. In its preparation advantage has been taken of a considerable number of suggestions from both sides of the Atlantic, and the editor wishes particularly to acknowledge the valuable assistance of Mr. Willard Jerome Heggen, to whom a substantial proportion of the additions are due, including some expressions in commoner use in America than in England, the presence of which in the Thesaurus will, it is hoped, extend its general usefulness.

S. R. Roget

October 1933

PREFACE

TO

THE FIRST EDITION

(1852)

It is now nearly fifty years since I first projected a system of verbal classification similar to that on which the present Work is founded. Conceiving that such a compilation might help to supply my own deficiencies, I had, in the year 1805, completed a classed catalogue of words on a small scale, but on the same principle, and nearly in the same form, as the Thesaurus now published.* I had often during that long interval found this little collection, scanty and imperfect as it was, of much use to me in literary composition, and often contemplated its extension and improvement; but a sense of the magnitude of the task, amidst a multitude of other avocations, deterred me from the attempt. Since my retirement from the duties of Secretary of the Royal Society, however, finding myself possessed of more leisure, and believing that a repertory of which I had myself experienced the advantage might, when amplified, prove useful to others, I resolved to embark in an undertaking which, for the last three or four years, has given me incessant occupation, and has, indeed, imposed upon me an amount of labour very much greater than I had anticipated. Notwithstanding all the pains I have bestowed on its execution, I am fully aware of its numerous deficiencies and imperfections, and of its falling far short of the degree of excellence that might be attained. But, in a Work of this nature, where perfection is placed at so great a distance, I have thought it best to limit my ambition to that moderate share of merit which it may claim in its present form; trusting to the indulgence of those for whose benefit it is intended, and to the candour of critics who, while they find it easy to detect faults, can at the same time duly appreciate difficulties.

P. M. Roget

April 29th, 1852

* A facsimile of the first page of this little manuscript book which is the original form of the Thesaurus is given in the frontispiece.

EDITOR'S PREFACE

(1879)

(*Slightly Abridged*)

THE FIRST EDITION of Dr. Roget's Thesaurus was published in the year 1852, and a second in the ensuing spring. On the issue of the third, in 1855, the volume was stereotyped. Since that time until now, the work has been reprinted in the same form and with little alteration, in rapidly succeeding editions, the printing of which has worn out the original plates.

During the last years of the author's life, which closed, at a very advanced age, in the month of September, 1869, he was engaged in the task of collecting additional words and phrases, for an enlarged edition which he had long projected. This he did not live to complete, and it became my duty, as his son, to attempt to carry the design into execution.

The result of the author's labours was embodied in a copy of the Thesaurus, in which the margins and spaces about the letterpress were closely covered with written words and phrases, without any very precise indication of the places in the text where additions or alterations were intended to be made. On a careful examination of these *addenda,* I came to the conclusion that, in order to introduce them with advantage, it would be necessary to make some slight changes; without, however, interfering at all with the framework of the book, and but little with the details of its system. In this proceeding my course has been mainly determined by the following considerations.

Any attempt at a philosophical arrangement under categories of the words of our language must reveal the fact that it is impossible to separate and circumscribe the several groups by absolutely distinct boundary lines. Many words, originally employed to express simple conceptions, are found to be capable, with perhaps a very slight modification of meaning, of being applied in many varied associations. Connecting links, thus formed, induce an approach between the categories; and a danger arises that the outlines of our classification may, by their means, become confused and eventually merged. Were we to disengage these interwoven ramifications, and seek to confine every word to its main or original import, we should find some secondary meaning has become so firmly associated with many words and phrases, that to sever the alliance would be to deprive our language of the richness due to an infinity of natural adaptations.

Were we, on the other hand, to attempt to include, in each category of the Thesaurus, every word and phrase which could by any possibility be appropriately used in relation to the leading idea for which that category was designed, we should impair, if not destroy, the whole use and value of the book. For, in the endeavour to enrich our treasury of expression, we might easily allow ourselves to be led imperceptibly onward by the natural association of one word with another, and to add word after word, until group after group would successively be absorbed under some single heading, and the fundamental divisions of the system be effaced. The small cluster of nearly synonymous words, which had formed the nucleus of a category, would be lost in a sea of phrases, and it would become difficult to recognize those which were peculiarly adapted to express the leading ideas.

These considerations were material in dealing with the new and multitudinous store of words and phrases which the author had accumulated. Many of these were altogether new to the Thesaurus. Many were merely repetitions in new places of words already included in its pages. With reference to cases similar to the latter, the author had declared it to have been a general rule with him 'to place words and phrases which appertain more especially to one head, also under other heads to which they have a relation,' whenever it appeared to him 'that this repetition would suit the convenience of the inquirer and spare him the trouble of turning to other parts of the work.' But, with the now increased mass of words, it became a question, in many cases, whether such repetition would still prove convenient. Where categories might by that course be unduly swollen, or where they might, by reason of their being separated from each other by subtile distinctions or faint lines of demarcation, be thereby too nearly assimilated, I thought it would often be better to confine words of the kind referred to to their primary headings. The necessity of keeping the book within reasonable dimensions had also to be borne in mind.

Under these circumstances, the best method of ensuring the ready accessibility of the multitude of words now to be dealt with, and at the same time preserving unimpaired the unity of the several categories, appeared to me to lie in the copious use of references from one place in the book to another. Relying on this contrivance as a means of opening more widely the resources of the collection, by making the groups of words mutually suggestive, and thereby leading not only to more varied forms of expression, but to kindred ideas, I have added largely to the references already inserted by the author. I have also ventured occasionally to substitute a reference for a group of words, when the identical group existed in another place, and could thus be made immediately available.

In order, at the same time, to make the value of the references more appreciable, I have (whenever it has appeared to me to be necessary) inserted, in a parenthesis, a word indicating the nature of the group or category referred to. Any one using the book will thereby be enabled to judge whether it will be worth his while to turn to the place in question.

The cross references may also be looked upon as indicating in some degree the natural points of connection between the categories, and the ramification of the ideas which they embody. As would be the case under any classification of language, a large proportion of the expressions, to find which recourse is had to the Thesaurus, lie on an ill-defined border land between one category and another; and it is not always easy, even with the aid of a carefully compiled index, to determine under which of several allied headings they should be sought. In the present edition, when the inquirer has once started on his voyage of discovery, the references enable him to pass freely from one division to another without recurring to the Index.

Many new words have also been inserted which were not contained in the author's manuscript.

Except in a very few cases, where distinct ideas were obviously united under one head, I have not had the presumption to meddle with the author's division into categories; but, within each category, I have endeavoured to carry somewhat further the sorting of words according to the ideas which they convey.

With these objects in view, I have supplied the work with a new and elaborate Index, much more complete than that which was appended to the previous editions. Although, in the original design of his work, the author appears to have conceived the process of search for a required expression as one in which the system of classification would be first consulted, and the Index afterwards called in aid if necessary, I believe that almost everyone who uses the book finds it more convenient to have recourse to the Index first.

From the peculiar nature and use of the Thesaurus, its Index will be found to differ, in some of its essential functions, from an alphabetical table of contents. The present Index does not merely afford an indication of the place where every given word or topic occurs or is dealt with in the text; but it is intended as a guide to other expressions which may be found there. The word we look out in this Index is not that which we require, but that which we wish to avoid. It is, therefore, not necessary that every word there given should be a repetition of one in the text. It may even happen that the word selected as a guide, though suggestive of the group wanted, is wholly unfit to be comprised within it.

The new Index contains not only all the *words* in the book (without needless repetition of conjugate forms), but likewise the *phrases*, all of which had been excluded from the Index to the previous editions. It is hoped that these additions, although they increase the bulk of the book, will have the effect of extending its usefulness in at least a corresponding degree.

Some changes of detail have also been made, where the form of the work seemed susceptible of improvement, and there was no reason to suppose that the author would have disapproved of the alteration. In the previous editions, the *phrases* were in general placed in separate paragraphs, under the heading **Phr.**, in each of the subdivisions assigned to the different grammatical parts of speech. In the present edition, *words* and *phrases* are placed together, and the heading **Phr.** is only employed in the case of phrases which have no convenient place in such an arrangement. Much space has been saved, and many repetitions have been avoided, by the use of lines and hyphens, where words or phrases in the same group have syllables or parts in common, and by references from one part of speech to another. These abbreviations may be best explained by examples, of which the following are a few:—

'with -relation, - reference, - respect, - regard- to'; is meant to include the phrases 'with relation to,' 'with reference to,' 'with respect to,' 'with regard to.'

'root –, weed –, grub –, rake- -up, – out;' includes 'root up,' 'root out,' 'weed up,' 'weed out,' 'grub up,' 'grub out,' 'rake up,' 'rake out.'

'away from –, foreign to –, beside- the -purpose, – question, – transaction, – point;' includes 'away from the purpose,' 'foreign to the purpose,' 'beside the purpose,' 'away from the question,' 'foreign to the question,' 'foreign to the transaction,' 'beside the question,' 'away from the point,' 'beside the transaction,' 'foreign to the point,' 'away from the transaction,' 'beside the point.'

'raze – to the ground'; includes 'raze,' and 'raze to the ground.'

'campan-iform, -ulate, -iliform;' includes 'campaniform,' 'campanulate,' and 'campaniliform.'

'goodness &c. *adj.*'; 'badly &c. *adj.*'; 'hindred &c. *v.*'; include all words similarly formed from synonyms of 'good,' 'bad,' and 'hinder,' respectively, given under the headings **Adj.** and **V.** in the same categories where the abbreviations occur.

The participle 'to' before a verb has in all cases been rejected, the heading **V.** being thought sufficiently distinctive; the use of capitals for the initial letters of the first words of paragraphs has been abandoned, as giving those words undue importance; and the title of each category has been kept distinct from the collection of words under its heading.

I should be ungrateful were I not to acknowledge the assistance derived, both by my father and myself, from various suggestions made by well-wishers to the work, some of whom have been personally unknown to either of us; and also to record my thanks to several kind friends, and to Messrs. Spottiswoode and Co.'s careful reader, for valuable aid during the passage of the sheets through the press.

JOHN L. ROGET

March 17th, 1879.

INTRODUCTION

[*Notes within brackets are by the editors.*]

THE present Work is intended to supply, with respect to the English language, a desideratum hitherto unsupplied in any language; namely, a collection of the words it contains and of the idiomatic combinations peculiar to it, arranged, not in alphabetical order as they are in a Dictionary, but according to the *ideas* which they express.* The purpose of an ordinary dictionary is simply to explain the meaning of the words; and the problem of which it professes to furnish the solution may be stated thus:—The word being given, to find its signification, or the idea it is intended to convey. The object aimed at in the present undertaking is exactly the converse of this: namely,—The idea being given, to find the word, or words, by which that idea may be most fitly and aptly expressed. For this purpose, the words and phrases of the language are here classed, not according to their sound or their orthography, but strictly according to their *signification*.

The communication of our thoughts by means of language, whether spoken or written, like every other object of mental exertion, constitutes a peculiar art, which, like other arts, cannot be acquired in any perfection but by long and continued practice. Some, indeed, there are more highly gifted than others with a facility of expression, and naturally endowed with the power of eloquence; but to none is it at all times an easy process to embody, in exact and appropriate language, the various trains of ideas that are passing through the mind, or to depict in their true colours and proportions, the diversified and nicer shades of feeling which accompany them. To those who are unpractised in the art of composition, or unused to extempore speaking, these difficulties present themselves in their most formidable aspect. However distinct may be our views, however vivid our conceptions, or however fervent our emotions, we cannot but be often conscious that the phraseology we have at our command is inadequate to do them justice. We seek in vain the words we need, and strive ineffectually to devise forms of expression which shall faithfully portray our thoughts and sentiments. The appropriate terms, notwithstanding our utmost efforts, cannot be conjured up at will. Like 'spirits from the vasty deep,' they come not when we call; and we are driven to the employment of a set of words and phrases either too general or too

* See note in p. xxi.

limited, too strong or too feeble, which suit not the occasion, which hit not the mark we aim at; and the result of our prolonged exertion is a style at once laboured and obscure, vapid and redundant, or vitiated by the still graver faults of affectation or ambiguity.

It is to those who are thus painfully groping their way and struggling with the difficulties of composition, that this Work professes to hold out a helping hand. The assistance it gives is that of furnishing on every topic a copious store of words and phrases, adapted to express all the recognizable shades and modifications of the general idea under which those words and phrases are arranged. The inquirer can readily select, out of the ample collection spread out before his eyes in the following pages, those expressions which are best suited to his purpose, and which might not have occurred to him without such assistance. In order to make this selection, he scarcely ever need engage in any critical or elaborate study of the subtle distinction existing between synonymous terms; for if the materials set before him be sufficiently abundant, an instinctive tact will rarely fail to lead him to the proper choice. Even while glancing over the columns of this Work, his eye may chance to light upon a particular term, which may save the cost of a clumsy paraphrase, or spare the labour of a tortuous circumlocution. Some felicitous turn of expression thus introduced will frequently open to the mind of the reader a whole vista of collateral ideas, which could not, without an extended and obtrusive episode, have been unfolded to his view; and often will the judicious insertion of a happy epithet, like a beam of sunshine in a landscape, illumine and adorn the subject which it touches, imparting new grace and giving life and spirit to the picture.

Every workman in the exercise of his art should be provided with proper implements. For the fabrication of complicated and curious pieces of mechanism, the artisan requires a corresponding assortment of various tools and instruments. For giving proper effect to the fictions of the drama, the actor should have at his disposal a well-furnished wardrobe, supplying the costumes best suited to the personages he is to represent. For the perfect delineation of the beauties of nature, the painter should have within reach of his pencil every variety and combination of hues and tints. Now, the writer, as well as the orator, employs for the accomplishment of his purposes the instrumentality of words; it is in words that he clothes his thoughts; it is by means of words that he depicts his feelings. It is therefore essential to his success that he be provided with a copious vocabulary, and that he possess an entire command of all the resources and appliances of his language. To the acquisition of this power no procedure appears more directly conducive than the study of a methodized system such as that now offered to his use.

The utility of the present Work will be appreciated more especially by those who are engaged in the arduous process of translating into English a work written in another language. Simple as the operation may appear, on a superficial view, of rendering into English each of its sentences, the task of transfusing, with perfect exactness, the sense of the original, preserving at the same time the style and character of its composition, and reflecting with fidelity the mind and the spirit of the author, is a task of extreme difficulty. The cultivation of this useful department of literature was in ancient times strongly recommended both by Cicero and by Quintilian, as essential to the formation of a good writer and accomplished orator. Regarded simply as a mental exercise, the practice of translation is the best training for the attainment of that mastery of language and felicity of diction, which are the sources of the highest oratory, and are requisite for the possession of a graceful and persuasive eloquence. By rendering ourselves the faithful interpreters of the thoughts and feelings of others, we are rewarded with the acquisition of greater readiness and facility in correctly expressing our own; as he who has best learned to execute the orders of a commander, becomes himself best qualified to command.

In the earliest periods of civilization, translators have been the agents for propagating knowledge from nation to nation, and the value of their labours has been inestimable; but, in the present age, when so many different languages have become the depositories of the vast treasures of literature and of science which have been accumulating for centuries, the utility of accurate translations has greatly increased, and it has become a more important object to attain perfection in the art.

The use of language is not confined to its being the medium through which we communicate our ideas to one another; it fulfils a no less important function as an *instrument of thought*; not being merely its vehicle, but giving it wings for flight. Metaphysicians are agreed that scarcely any of our intellectual operations could be carried on to any considerable extent, without the agency of words. None but those who are conversant with the philosophy of mental phenomena, can be aware of the immense influence that is exercised by language in promoting the development of our ideas, in fixing them in the mind, and in detaining them for steady contemplation. Into every process of reasoning, language enters as an essential element. Words are the instruments by which we form all our abstractions, by which we fashion and embody our ideas, and by which we are enabled to glide along a series of premises and conclusions with a rapidity so great as to leave in the memory no trace of the successive steps of the process; and we remain unconscious how much we owe to this potent auxiliary of the reasoning faculty. It is on this ground, also, that the present Work founds a claim to utility. The review of a catalogue of words of analogous signification, will often suggest by association other trains of thought, which, presenting the subject under new and varied aspects, will vastly expand the sphere of our mental vision. Amidst the many objects thus brought within the range of our contemplation, some striking similitude or appropriate image, some excursive flight or brilliant conception, may flash on the mind, giving point and force to our arguments, awakening a responsive chord in the imagination or sensibility of the reader, and procuring for our reasonings a more ready access both to his understanding and to his heart.

It is of the utmost consequence that strict accuracy should regulate our use of language, and that every one should acquire the power and the habit of expressing his thoughts with perspicuity and correctness. Few, indeed, can appreciate the real extent and importance of that influence which language has always exercised on human affairs, or can be aware how often these are determined by causes much slighter than are apparent to a superficial observer. False logic, disguised under specious phraseology, too often gains the assent of the unthinking multitude, disseminating far and wide the seeds of prejudice and error. Truisms pass current, and wear the semblance of profound wisdom, when dressed up in the tinsel garb of antithetical phrases, or set off by an imposing pomp of paradox. By a confused jargon of involved and mystical sentences, the imagination is easily inveigled into a transcendental region of clouds, and the understanding beguiled into the belief that it is acquiring knowledge and approaching truth. A misapplied or misapprehended term is sufficient to give rise to fierce and interminable disputes; a misnomer has turned the tide of popular opinion; a verbal sophism has decided a party question; an artful watchword, thrown among combustible materials, has kindled the flame of deadly warfare, and changed the destiny of an empire.

In constructing the following system of classification of the ideas which are expressible by language, my chief aim has been to obtain the greatest amount of practical utility. I have accordingly adopted such principles of arrangement as appeared to me to be the simplest and most natural, and which would not require, either for their comprehension or application, any disciplined acumen, or depth of metaphysical or antiquarian lore. Eschewing all needless refinements and subtleties, I have taken as my guide the more obvious characters of the ideas for which expressions were to be tabulated, arranging them under such classes and categories as reflection and experience had taught me would conduct the inquirer most readily and quickly to the object of his search. Commencing with the ideas expressing abstract relations, I proceeded to those which relate to space and to the phenomena of the material world, and lastly to those in which the mind is concerned, and which comprehend intellect, volition, and feeling; thus establishing six primary Classes of Categories.

1. The first of these classes comprehends ideas derived from the more general and ABSTRACT RELATIONS among things, such as *Existence, Resemblance, Quantity, Order, Number, Time, Power.*

2. The second class refers to SPACE and its various relations, including *Motion,* or change of place.

3. The third class includes all ideas that relate to the MATERIAL WORLD; namely, the *Properties of Matter*, such as *Solidity*, *Fluidity*, *Heat*, *Sound*, *Light*, and the *Phenomena* they present, as well as the simple *Perceptions* to which they give rise.

4. The fourth class embraces all ideas of phenomena relating to the INTELLECT and its operations; comprising the *Acquisition*, the *Retention*, and the *Communication of Ideas*.

5. The fifth class includes the ideas derived from the exercise of VOLITION; embracing the phenomena and results of our *Voluntary and Active Powers;* such as *Choice*, *Intention*, *Utility*, *Action*, *Antagonism*, *Authority*, *Compact*, *Property*, &c.

6. The sixth and last class comprehends all ideas derived from the operation of our SENTIENT AND MORAL POWERS; including our *Feelings*, *Emotions*, *Passions*, and *Moral and Religious Sentiments*.*

The further subdivisions and minuter details will be best understood from an inspection of the Tabular Synopsis of Categories prefixed to the Work, in which are specified the several *topics* or *heads of signification*, under which the words have been arranged. By the aid of this table the reader will, with a little practice, readily discover the place which the particular topic he is in search of occupies in the series; and on turning to the page in the body of the Work which contains it, he will find the group of expressions he requires, out of which he may cull those that are most appropriate to his purpose. For the convenience of reference, I have designated each separate group or heading by a particular number; so that if, during the search, any doubt or difficulty should occur, recourse may be had to the copious alphabetical Index of words at the end of the volume, which will at once indicate the number of the required group.†

* It must necessarily happen in every system of classification framed with this view, that ideas and expressions arranged under one class must include also ideas relating to another class; for the operations of the *Intellect* generally involve also those of the *Will*, and *vice versâ;* and our *Affections* and *Emotions*, in like manner, generally imply the agency both of the *Intellect* and of the *Will*. All that can be effected, therefore, is to arrange the words according to the principal or dominant idea they convey. *Teaching*, for example, although a Voluntary act, relates primarily to the Communication of Ideas, and is accordingly placed at No. 537, under Class IV Division (II). On the other hand, *Choice*, *Conduct*, *Skill*, &c., although implying the co-operation of Voluntary with Intellectual acts, relate principally to the former, and are therefore arranged under Class V.

† It often happens that the same word admits of various applications, or may be used in different senses. In consulting the Index the reader will be guided to the number of the heading under which that word, in each particular acceptation, will be found, by means of *supplementary words* printed in Italics; which words, however, are not to be understood as explaining the meaning of the word to which they are annexed, but only as assisting in the required reference. I have also, for shortness' sake, generally omitted words immediately derived from the primary one inserted, which sufficiently represents the whole group of correlative words referable to the same heading. Thus the number affixed to *Beauty* applies to all its derivatives, such as *Beautiful*, *Beauteous*, *Beautifulness*, *Beautifully*, &c., the insertion of which was therefore needless. [In compiling the new Index the editor has adopted this principle as a general rule, from which, however, he has not scrupled to depart where he has deemed it expedient to do so.]

The object I have proposed to myself in this Work would have been put imperfectly attained if I had confined myself to a mere catalogue of words, and had omitted the numerous phrases and forms of expression composed of several words, which are of such frequent use as to entitle them to rank among the constituent parts of the language.* Very few of these verbal combinations, so essential to the knowledge of our native tongue, and so profusely abounding in its daily use, are to be met with in ordinary dictionaries. These phrases and forms of expression I have endeavoured diligently to collect and to insert in their proper places, under the general ideas that they are designed to convey. Some of these conventional forms, indeed, partake of the nature of proverbial expressions; but actual proverbs, as such, being wholly of a didactic character, do not come within the scope of the present Work; and the reader must therefore not expect to find them here inserted.†

For the purpose of exhibiting with greater distinctness the relations between words expressing opposite and correlative ideas, I have, whenever the subject admitted of such an arrangement, placed them in two parallel columns in the same page, so that each group of expressions may be readily contrasted with those which occupy the adjacent column, and constitute their antithesis. By carrying the eye from the one to the other, the inquirer may often discover forms of expression, of which he may avail himself advantageously, to diversify and infuse vigour into his phraseology. Rhetoricians, indeed, are well aware of the power derived from the skilful introduction of antitheses in giving point to an argument, and imparting force and brilliancy to the diction. A too frequent and indiscreet employment of this figure of rhetoric may, it is true, give rise to a vicious and affected style; but it is unreasonable to condemn indiscriminately the occasional and moderate use of a practice on account of its possible abuse.

The study of correlative terms existing in a particular language, may often throw valuable light on the manners and customs of the nations using it. Thus, Hume has drawn important inferences with regard to the state of society among the ancient Romans, from certain deficiencies which he remarked in the Latin language.‡

* For example:—To take time by the forelock;—to turn over a new leaf;—to show the white feather;—to have a finger in the pie;—to let the cat out of the bag;—to take care of number one;—to kill two birds with one stone, &c., &c.

† See Trench, *On the Lessons in Proverbs*.

‡ 'It is an universal observation,' he remarks, 'which we may form upon language, that where two related parts of a whole bear any proportion to each other, in numbers, rank, or consideration, there are always correlative terms invented which answer to both the parts, and express their mutual relation. If they bear no proportion to each other, the term is only invented for the less, and marks its distinction from the whole. Thus, *man* and *woman*, *master* and *servant*, *father* and *son*, *prince* and *subject*, *stranger* and *citizen*, are correlative terms. But the words *seaman*, *carpenter*, *smith*, *tailor*, &c., have no correspondent terms, which express those who are no seamen, no carpenters, &c. Languages differ very much with regard to the particular words where this distinction obtains; and may thence afford very strong inferences concerning the manners and customs of different nations. The military government of the

In many cases, two ideas which are completely opposed to each other, admit of an intermediate or neutral idea, equidistant from both; all these being expressible by corresponding definite terms. Thus, in the following examples, the words in the first and third columns, which express opposite ideas, admit of the intermediate terms contained in the middle column, having a neutral sense with reference to the former.

Identity	*Difference*	*Contrariety*
Beginning	*Middle*	*End*
Past	*Present*	*Future*

In other cases, the intermediate word is simply the negative to each of two opposite positions; as, for example—

Convexity	*Flatness*	*Concavity*
Desire	*Indifference*	*Aversion*

Sometimes the intermediate word is properly the standard with which each of the extremes is compared; as in the case of

Insufficiency	*Sufficiency*	*Redundance*

for here the middle term, *Sufficiency*, is equally opposed, on the one hand to *Insufficiency*, and on the other to *Redundance*.*

These forms of correlative expressions would suggest the use of triple, instead of double, columns, for tabulating this threefold order of words; but the practical inconvenience attending such an arrangement would probably overbalance its advantages.

It often happens that the same word has several correlative terms, according to the different relations in which it is considered. Thus, to the word *Giving* are opposed both *Receiving* and *Taking*; the former

Roman emperors had exalted the soldiery so high that they balanced all the other orders of the state: hence *miles* and *paganus* became relative terms; a thing, till then, unknown to ancient, and still so to modern languages.'—'The term for a slave, born and bred in the family, was *verna*. As *servus* was the name of the genius, and *verna* of the species without any correlative, this forms a strong presumption that the latter were by far the least numerous: and from the same principles I infer that if the number of slaves brought by the Romans from foreign countries had not extremely exceeded those which were bred at home, *verna* would have had a correlative, which would have expressed the former species of slaves. But these, it would seem, composed the main body of the ancient slaves, and the latter were but a few exceptions'.—Hume, *Essay on the Populousness of Ancient Nations.*

The warlike propensity of the same nation may, in like manner, be inferred from the use of the word *hostis* to denote both *a foreigner* and *an enemy.*

* [In the following cases, the intermediate word signifies an imperfect degree of each of the qualities set in opposition—

Light	*Dimness*	*Darkness*
Transparency	*Semitransparency*	*Opacity*
Vision	*Dimsightedness*	*Blindness*]

correlation having reference to the *persons* concerned in the transfer, while the latter relates to the *mode* of transfer. *Old* has for opposite both *New* and *Young*, according as it is applied to *things* or to *living things*. *Attack* and *Defence* are correlative terms; as are also *Attack* and *Resistance*. *Resistance*, again, has for its other correlative *Submission*. *Truth in the abstract* is opposed to *Error*; but the opposite of *Truth communicated* is *Falsehood*. *Acquisition* is contrasted both with *Deprivation* and with *Loss*. *Refusal* is the counterpart both of *Offer* and of *Consent*. *Disuse* and *Misuse* may either of them be considered as the correlative of *Use*. *Teaching* with reference to what is taught, is opposed to *Misteaching*; but with reference to the act itself, its proper reciprocal is *Learning*.

Words contrasted in form do not always bear the same contrast in their meaning. The word *Malefactor*, for example, would, from its derivation, appear to be exactly the opposite of *Benefactor*: but the ideas attached to these two words are far from being directly opposed; for while the latter expresses one who confers a benefit, the former denotes one who has violated the laws.

Independently of the immediate practical uses derivable from the arrangement of words in double columns, many considerations, interesting in a philosophical point of view, are presented by the study of correlative expressions. It will be found, on strict examination, that there seldom exists an exact opposition between two words which may at first sight appear to be the counterparts of one another; for in general, the one will be found to possess in reality more force or extent of meaning than the other with which it is contrasted. The correlative term sometimes assumes the form of a mere negative, although it is really endowed with a considerable positive force. Thus *Disrespect* is not merely the absence of *Respect*; its signification trenches on the opposite idea, namely, *Contempt*. In like manner, *Untruth* is not merely the negative of *Truth*; it involves a degree of *Falsehood*. *Irreligion*, which is properly *the want of Religion*, is understood as being nearly synonymous with *Impiety*. For these reasons, the reader must not expect that all the words which stand side by side in the two columns shall be the precise correlatives of each other; for the nature of the subject, as well as the imperfections of language, renders it impossible always to preserve such an exactness of correlation.

There exist comparatively few words of a general character to which no correlative term, either of negation or of opposition, can be assigned, and which therefore require no corresponding second column. The correlative idea, especially that which constitutes a sense negative to the primary one, may, indeed, be formed or conceived; but, from its occurring rarely, no word has been framed to represent it; for, in language, as in other matters, the supply fails when there is no probability of a demand. Occasionally we find this deficiency provided for by the contrivance of prefixing the syllable *non*; as, for instance, the negatives of *existence, performance, payment*, &c., are expressed by the compound words, *non-existence, non-performance, non-payment*, &c. Functions of a similar kind are performed by the prefixes *dis-**, *anti-*, *contra-*, *mis-*, *in-*, and *un-*.† With respect to all these, and especially the last, great latitude is allowed according to the necessities of the case; a latitude which is limited only by the taste and discretion of the writer.

On the other hand, it is hardly possible to find two words having in all respects the same meaning, and being therefore interchangeable; that is, admitting of being employed indiscriminately, the one or the other, in all their applications. The investigation of the distinctions to be drawn between words apparently synonymous, forms a separate branch of inquiry, which I have not presumed here to enter upon; for the subject has already occupied the attention of much abler critics than myself, and its complete exhaustion would require the devotion of a whole life. The purpose of this Work, it must be borne in mind, is, not to explain the signification of words, but simply to classify and arrange them according to the sense in which they are now used, and which I presume to be already known to the reader. I enter into no inquiry into the changes of meaning they may have undergone in the course of time.‡ I am content to accept them at the value of their present currency, and have no concern with their etymologies, or with the history of their transformations; far less do I venture to thrid the mazes of the vast labyrinth into which I should be led by any attempt at a general discrimination of synonyms. The difficulties I have had to contend with have already been sufficiently great, without this addition to my labours.

The most cursory glance over the pages of a Dictionary will show that a great number of words are used in various senses, sometimes distinguished by slight shades of difference, but often diverging widely from their primary signification, and even, in some cases, bearing to it no perceptible relation. It may even happen that the very same word has two significations quite opposite to one another. This is the case with the verb *to cleave*, which means *to adhere tenaciously*, and also *to separate by a blow*. *To propugn* sometimes expressed *to attack*; at other times *to defend*. *To let* is *to hinder*, as well as *to permit*. *To*

* The words *disannul* and *dissever*, however, have the same meaning as *annul* and *sever*; *to unloose* is the same as *to loose*, and *inebrity* is synonymous with *ebriety*.

† In the case of adjectives, the addition to a substantive of the terminal syllable *less*, gives it a negative meaning: as *taste, tasteless; care, careless; hope, hopeless; friend, friendless; fault, faultless;* &c.

‡ Such changes are innumerable: for instance, the words *tyrant, parasite, sophist, churl, knave, villain*, anciently conveyed no opprobrious meaning. *Impertinent* merely expressed *irrelative*, and implied neither *rudeness* nor *intrusion*, as it does at present. *Indifferent* originally meant *impartial; extravagant* was simply *digressive;* and *to prevent* was properly *to precede* and *assist*. The old translations of the Scriptures furnish many striking examples of the alterations which time has brought in the signification of words. Much curious information on this subject is contained in Trench's *Lectures on the Study of Words*.

ravel means both *to entangle* and *to disentangle*. *Shameful* and *shameless* are nearly synonymous. *Priceless* may either mean *invaluable* or *of no value*. *Nervous* is used sometimes for *strong*, at other times for *weak*. The alphabetical Index at the end of this Work sufficiently shows the multiplicity of uses to which, by the elasticity of language, the meaning of words has been stretched, so as to adapt them to a great variety of modified significations in subservience to the nicer shades of thought, which, under peculiarity of circumstances, require corresponding expression. Words thus admitting of different meanings have therefore to be arranged under each of the respective heads corresponding to these various acceptations. There are many words, again, which express ideas compounded of two elementary ideas belonging to different classes. It is therefore necessary to place these words respectively under each of the generic heads to which they relate. The necessity of these repetitions is increased by the circumstance, that ideas included under one class are often connected by relations of the same kind as the ideas which belong to another class. Thus we find the same relations of *order* and of *quantity* existing among the ideas of *Time* as well as those of *Space*. Sequence in the one is denoted by the same terms as sequence in the other; and the measures of time also express the measures of space. The cause and the effect are often designated by the same word. The word *Sound*, for instance, denotes both the impression made upon the ear by sonorous vibrations, and also the vibrations themselves, which are the cause or source of that impression. *Mixture* is used for the act of mixing, as well as for the product of that operation. *Taste* and *Smell* express both the sensations and the qualities of material bodies giving rise to them. *Thought* is the act of thinking; but the same word denotes also the idea resulting from that act. *Judgment* is the act of deciding, and also the decision come to. *Purchase* is the acquisition of a thing by payment, as well as the thing itself so acquired. *Speech* is both the act of speaking and the words spoken; and so on with regard to an endless multiplicity of words. Mind is essentially distinct from Matter; and yet, in all languages, the attributes of the one are metaphorically transferred to those of the other. Matter, in all its forms, is endowed by the figurative genius of every language with the functions which pertain to intellect; and we perpetually talk of its phenomena and of its powers, as if they resulted from the voluntary influence of one body on another, acting and reacting, impelling and being impelled, controlling and being controlled, as if animated by spontaneous energies and guided by specific intentions. On the other hand, expressions, of which the primary signification refers exclusively to the properties and actions of matter, are metaphorically applied to the phenomena of thought and volition, and even to the feelings and passions of the soul; and in speaking of a *ray of hope*, a *shade of doubt*, a *flight of fancy*, a *flash of wit*, the *warmth of emotion*, or the *ebullitions of anger*, we are scarcely conscious that we are employing metaphors which have this material origin.

As a general rule, I have deemed it incumbent on me to place words and phrases which appertain more especially to one head, also under the other heads to which they have a relation, whenever it appeared to me that this repetition would suit the convenience of the inquirer, and spare him the trouble of turning to other parts of the work; for I have always preferred to subject myself to the imputation of redundance, rather than incur the reproach of insufficiency.* When, however, the divergence of the associated from the primary idea is sufficiently marked, I have contented myself with making a reference to the place where the modified signification will be found.† But in order to prevent needless extension, I have, in general, omitted *conjugate words,* ‡ which are so obviously derivable from those that are given in the same place, that the reader may safely be left to form them for himself. This is the case with adverbs derived from adjectives by the simple addition of the terminal syllable *-ly*; such as *closely, carefully, safely,* &c., from *close, careful, safe,* &c., and also with adjectives or participles immediately derived from the verbs which are already given. In all such cases, an '&c.' indicates that reference is understood to be made to these roots.§ I have observed the same rule in compiling the Index; retaining only the primary or more simple word, and omitting the conjugate words obviously derived from them. Thus I assume the word *short* as the representative of its immediate derivatives *shortness, shorten, shortening, shortened, shorter, shortly,* which would have had the same references, and which the reader can readily supply. ||

The same verb is frequently used indiscriminately either in the active or transitive, or in the neuter or intransitive sense. In these cases, I have generally not thought it worth while to increase the bulk of the Work by the needless repetition of that word; for the reader, whom I suppose

* Frequent repetitions of the same series of expressions, accordingly, will be met with under various headings. For example, the word *Relinquishment* with its synonyms, occurs as a heading at No. 624, where it applies to *intention*, and also at No. 782, where it refers to *property*. The word *Chance* has two significations, distinct from one another: the one implying the *absence of an assignable cause;* in which case it comes under the category of the relation of Causation, and occupies the No. 156: the other, the *absence of design*, in which latter sense it ranks under the operations of the Will, and has assigned to it the place No. 621. I have, in like manner, distinguished *Sensibility, Pleasure, Pain, Taste,* &c., according as they relate to *Physical*, or to *Moral Affections;* the fomer being found at Nos. 375, 377, 378, 390, &c., and the latter at Nos. 822, 827, 828, 850, &c.

† [See Editor's Preface, p. x.]

‡ By '*conjugate* or *paronymous* words is meant, correctly speaking, different parts of speech from the same root, which exactly corresponds in point of meaning.'—*A Selection of English Synonyms*, edited by Archbishop Whately.

§ [The author's practice, in this respect, has been followed in the present edition, and a reference to the group of adjectives, verbs, or other roots, has been added, where such suggestion has been thought expedient.]

|| [See note in p. xvii.]

to understand the use of the words, must also be presumed to be competent to apply them correctly.

There are a multitude of words of a specific character which, although they properly occupy places in the columns of a dictionary, yet, having no relation to general ideas, do not come within the scope of this compilation, and are consequently omitted.* The names of objects in Natural History, and technical terms belonging exclusively to Science or to Art, or relating to particular operations, and of which the signification is restricted to those specific objects, come under this category. Exceptions must, however, be made in favor of such words as admit of metaphorical application to general subjects, with which custom has associated them, and of which they may be cited as being typical or illustrative. Thus, the word *Lion* will find a place under the head of *Courage*, of which it is regarded as the type. *Anchor*, being emblematic of *Hope*, is introduced among the words expressing that emotion; and in like manner, *butterfly* and *weathercock*, which are suggestive of fickleness, are included in the category of *Irresolution*.

With regard to the admission of many words and expressions, which the classical reader might be disposed to condemn as vulgarisms, or which he, perhaps, might stigmatize as pertaining rather to the slang than to the legitimate language of the day, I would beg to observe, that, having due regard to the uses to which this Work was to be adapted, I did not feel myself justified in excluding them solely on that ground, if they possessed an acknowledged currency in general intercourse. It is obvious that, with respect to degrees of conventionality, I could not have attempted to draw any strict lines of demarcation; and far less could I have presumed to erect any absolute standard of purity. My object, be it remembered, is not to regulate the use of words, but simply to supply and to suggest such as may be wanted on occasion, leaving the proper selection entirely to the discretion and taste of the employer.† If a novelist or a dramatist, for example, proposed to delineate some vulgar personage, he would wish to have the power of putting into the mouth of the speaker expressions that would accord with his character; just as the actor, to revert to a former comparison, who had to personate a peasant, would choose for his attire the most homely garb, and would have just reason to complain if the theatrical wardrobe furnished him with no suitable costume.

Words which have, in process of time, become obsolete, are of course

* [The author did not in all cases rigidly adhere to this rule; and the editors have thought themselves justified both in retaining and in adding some words of the specific character here mentioned, which may be occasionally in request by general writers, although in categories of this nature no attempt at completeness has been made.]

† [It may be added that the Thesaurus is an aid not only in the choice of appropriate forms of expression, but in the rejection of those which are unfit; and that a vulgar phrase may often furnish a convenient clue to the group of classic synonyms among which it is placed. Moreover, the slang expressions admitted into the work bear but a small proportion to those in constant use by English writers and speakers.]

rejected from this collection.* On the other hand, I have admitted a considerable number of words and phrases borrowed from other languages, chiefly the French and Latin, some of which may be considered as already naturalized; while others, though avowedly foreign, are frequently employed in English composition, particularly in familiar style, on account of their being peculiarly expressive, and because we have no corresponding words of equal force in our own language.† The rapid advances which are being made in scientific knowledge, and consequent improvement in all the arts of life, and the extension of those arts and sciences to so many new purposes and objects, create a continual demand for the formation of new terms to express new agencies, new wants, and new combinations. Such terms, from being at first merely technical, are rendered, by more general use, familiar to the multitude, and having a well-defined acceptation, are eventually incorporated into the language, which they contribute to enlarge and to enrich. *Neologies* of this kind are perfectly legitimate, and highly advantageous; and they necessarily introduce those gradual and progressive changes which every language is destined to undergo.‡ Some modern writers, however, have indulged in a habit of arbitrarily fabricating new words and a new-fangled phraseology, without any necessity, and with manifest injury to the purity of the language. This vicious practice, the offspring of indolence or conceit, implies an ignorance or neglect of the riches in which the English language already abounds, and which would have supplied them with words of recognized legitimacy, conveying precisely the same meaning as those they so recklessly coin in the illegal mint of their own fancy.

A work constructed on the plan of classification I have proposed might, if ably executed, be of great value, in tending to limit the fluctuations to which language has always been subject, by establishing an authoritative standard for its regulation. Future historians, philologists, and lexicographers, when investigating the period when new words were introduced, or discussing the import given at the present time to the old, might find their labours lightened by being enabled to appeal to such a standard, instead of having to search for data among the scattered writings of the

* [A few apparently obsolete words have nevertheless found their way into the Thesaurus. In justification of their admission, it may be contended that well-known words, though no longer current, give occasional point by an archaic form of expression, and are of value to the novelist or dramatist who has to depict a bygone age.]

† All these words and phrases are printed in Italics. [A few of these expressions, although widely used by writers of English, are of a form which is really incorrect or unusual in their own language, in some more extreme cases of this kind, the more widely used or incorrect form has been given.]

‡ Thus, in framing the present classification, I have frequently felt the want of substantive terms corresponding to abstract qualities or ideas denoted by certain adjectives, and have been often tempted to invent words that might express these abstractions; but I have yielded to this temptation only in the four following instances, having framed from the adjectives *irrelative*, *amorphous*, *sinistral*, and *gaseous*, the abstract nouns *irrelation*, *amorphism*, *sinistrality*, and *gaseity*. I have ventured also to introduce the adjective *intersocial* to express the active voluntary relations between man and man.

age. Nor would its utility be confined to a single language; for the principles of its construction are universally applicable to all languages, whether living or dead. On the same plan of classification there might be formed a French, a German, a Latin, or a Greek Thesaurus, possessing, in their respective spheres, the same advantages as those of the English model.* Still more useful would be a conjunction of these methodized compilations in two languages, the French and English, for instance; the columns of each being placed in parallel juxtaposition. No means yet devised would so greatly facilitate the acquisition of the one language, by those who are acquainted with the other: none would afford such ample assistance to the translator in either language; and none would supply such ready and effectual means of instituting an accurate comparison between them, and of fairly appreciating their respective merits and defects. In a still higher degree would all those advantages be combined and multiplied in a *Polyglot Lexicon* constructed on this system.

Metaphysicians engaged in the more profound investigation of the Philosophy of Language will be materially assisted by having the ground thus prepared for them, in a previous analysis and classification of our ideas; for such classification of ideas is the true basis on which words, which are their symbols, should be classified.† It is by such analysis alone that we can arrive at a clear perception of the relation which these

* [This suggestion has been followed, in French, in a '*Dictionnaire Idéologique*' by T. Robertson (Paris, 1859); and, in German, in a '*Deutscher Sprachschatz*' by D. Sanders (Hamburg, 1878), and '*Deutscher Wortschatz oder Der passende Ausdruck*' by A. Schelling (Stuttgart, 1829).]

† The principle by which I have been guided in framing my verbal classification is the same as that which is employed in the various departments of Natural History. Thus the sectional divisions I have formed, correspond to Natural Families in Botany and Zoology, and the filiation of words presents a network analogous to the natural filiation of plants or animals.

The following are the only publications that have come to my knowledge in which any attempt has been made to construct a systematic arrangement of ideas with a view to their expression. The earliest of these, supposed to be at least nine hundred years old, is the AMERA CÓSHA, or *Vocabulary of the Sanscrit Language*, by Amera Sinha, of which an English translation, by the late Henry T. Colebrooke, was printed at Serampoor, in the year 1808. The classification of words is there, as might be expected, exceedingly imperfect and confused, especially in all that relates to abstract ideas or mental operations. This will be apparent from the very title of the first section, which comprehends '*Heaven, Gods, Demons, Fire, Air, Velocity, Eternity, Much:*' while *Sin, Virtue, Happiness, Destiny, Cause, Nature, Intellect, Reasoning, Knowledge, Senses, Tastes, Odours, Colours*, are all included and jumbled together in the fourth section. A more logical order, however, pervades the sections relating to natural objects, such as *Seas, Earth, Towns, Plants*, and *Animals*, which form separate classes; exhibiting a remarkable effort at analysis at so remote a period of Indian literature.

The well-known work of Bishop Wilkins entitled '*An Essay towards a Real Character and a Philosophical Language*,' published in 1668, had for its object the formation of a system of symbols which might serve as a universal language. It professed to be founded on a 'scheme of analysis of the things or notions to which names were to be assigned'; but notwithstanding the immense labour and ingenuity expended in the construction of this system, it was soon found to be far too abstruse and recondite for practical application.

In the year 1797, there appeared in Paris an anonymous work, entitled 'PASIGRAPHIE, *ou Premiers Eléments du nouvel Art-Science d'écrire et d'imprimer une langue*

symbols bear to their corresponding ideas, or can obtain a correct knowledge of the elements which enter into the formation of compound ideas, and of the exclusions by which we arrive at the abstractions so perpetually resorted to in the process of reasoning, and in the communication of our thoughts.

Lastly, such analysis alone can determine the principles on which a strictly *Philosophical Language* might be constructed. The probable result of the construction of such a language would be its eventual adoption by every civilized nation; thus realizing that splendid aspiration of philanthropists—the establishment of a Universal Language. However utopian such a project may appear to the present generation, and however abortive may have been the former endeavours of Bishop Wilkins and others to realize it,* its accomplishment is surely not beset with greater difficulties than have impeded the progress to many other beneficial objects, which in former times appeared to be no less visionary, and which yet were successfully achieved, in later ages, by the continued and persevering exertions of the human intellect. Is there at the present day, then, any ground for despair, that at some future stage of that higher civilization to which we trust the world is gradually tending, some new and bolder effort of genius towards the solution of this great problem may be crowned with success, and compass an object of such vast and paramount utility? Nothing, indeed, would conduce more directly to bring about a golden age of union and harmony among the several nations and races of mankind than the removal of that barrier to the interchange of thought and mutual good understanding between man and man, which is now interposed by the diversity of their respective languages.

de maniere a etre lu et entendu dans toute autre langue sans traduction,' of which an edition in German was also published. It contains a great number of tabular schemes of categories; all of which appear to be excessively arbitrary and artificial, and extremely difficult of application, as well as of apprehension. [Systems of grouping with relation to ideas are also adopted in an '*Analytical Dictionary of the English Language*' by David Booth (London, 1835), a '*Dictionnaire Analogique de la Langue Française*' by P. Boissière (Paris), and a '*Dictionnaire Logique de la Langue Française*' by L'Abbé Elie Blanc (Paris, 1882).]

* 'The Languages,' observes Horne Tooke, 'which are commonly used throughout the world, are much more simple and easy, convenient and philosophical, than Wilkins' scheme for a *real character;* or than any other scheme that has been at any other time imagined or proposed for the purpose.'—''Επεα Πτερόεντα, p. 125.

PLAN OF CLASSIFICATION

Class	Section	Nos.
I. ABSTRACT RELATIONS	I. Existence	1 to 8
	II. Relation	9— 24
	III. Quantity	25— 57
	IV. Order	58— 83
	V. Number	84— 105
	VI. Time	106— 139
	VII. Change	140— 152
	VIII. Causation	153— 179
II. SPACE	I. Generally	180— 191
	II. Dimensions	192— 239
	III. Form	240— 263
	IV. Motion	264— 315
III. MATTER	I. Generally	316— 320
	II. Inorganic	321— 356
	III. Organic	357— 449
	Division	
IV. INTELLECT	(I.) Formation of Ideas	450— 515
	(II.) Communication of Ideas	516— 599
V. VOLITION	(I.) Individual	600— 736
	(II.) Intersocial	737— 819
	Section	
VI. AFFECTIONS	I. Generally	820— 826
	II. Personal	827— 887
	III. Sympathetic	888— 921
	IV. Moral	922— 975
	V. Religious	976—1000

TABULAR SYNOPSIS OF CATEGORIES

CLASS I. ABSTRACT RELATIONS

I. EXISTENCE

1°. ABSTRACT	1. Existence.	2. Inexistence.
2°. CONCRETE	3. Substantiality.	4. Unsubstantiality.
3°. FORMAL	*Internal.*	*External.*
	5. Intrinsicality.	6. Extrinsicality.
4°. MODAL	*Absolute.*	*Relative.*
	7. State.	8. Circumstance.

II. RELATION

1°. ABSOLUTE	9. Relation.	10. Irrelation.
	11. Consanguinity.	
	12. Correlation.	
	13. Identity.	14. Contrariety.
	15. Difference.	
2°. CONTINUOUS	16. Uniformity.	16*a*. Non-uniformity.
3°. PARTIAL	17. Similarity.	18. Dissimilarity.
	19. Imitation.	20. Non-imitation.
	20*a*. Variation.	
	21. Copy.	22. Prototype.
4°. GENERAL	23. Agreement.	24. Disagreement.

III. QUANTITY

1°. SIMPLE	*Absolute.*	*Relative.*
	25. Quantity.	26. Degree.
2°. COMPARATIVE	27. Equality.	28. Inequality.
	29. Mean.	
	30. Compensation.	
	By Comparison with a Standard.	
	31. Greatness.	32. Smallness.
	By Comparison with a similar Object.	
	33. Superiority.	34. Inferiority.
	Changes in Quantity.	
	35. Increase.	36. Decrease.
3°. CONJUNCTIVE	37. Addition.	38. Non-addition. Subduction.
	39. Adjunct.	40. Remainder.
		40*a*. Decrement.
	41. Mixture.	42. Simpleness.
	43. Junction.	44. Disjunction.
	45. Vinculum.	
	46. Coherence.	47. Incoherence.
	48. Combination.	49. Decomposition.

4°. CONCRETE	50. Whole.	51. Part.
	52. Completeness.	53. Incompleteness.
	54. Composition.	55. Exclusion.
	56. Component.	57. Extraneous.

IV. ORDER

1°. GENERAL	58. Order.	59. Disorder.
	60. Arrangement.	61. Derangement.
2°. CONSECUTIVE	62. Precedence.	63. Sequence.
	64. Precursor.	65. Sequel.
	66. Beginning.	67. End.
	68. Middle.	
	69. Continuity.	70. Discontinuity.
	71. Term.	
3°. COLLECTIVE	72. Assemblage.	73. Non-assemblage. Dispersion.
	74. Focus.	
4°. DISTRIBUTIVE	75. Class.	
	76. Inclusion.	77. Exclusion.
	78. Generality.	79. Speciality.
5°. CATEGORICAL	80. Rule.	81. Multiformity.
	82. Conformity.	83. Unconformity.

V. NUMBER

1°. ABSTRACT	84. Number.	
	85. Numeration.	
	86. List.	
2°. DETERMINATE	87. Unity.	88. Accompaniment.
	89. Duality.	
	90. Duplication.	91. Bisection.
	92. Triality.	
	93. Triplication.	96. Quadruplication.
	94. Trisection.	
	95. Quaternity.	97. Quadrisection.
	98. Five, &c.	99. Quinquesection, &c.
3°. INDETERMINATE	100. Plurality.	100*a*. Fraction.
		101. Zero.
	102. Multitude.	103. Fewness.
	104. Repetition.	
	105. Infinity.	

VI. TIME

1°. ABSOLUTE	106. Time.	107. Neverness.
	Definite.	*Indefinite.*
	108. Period.	109. Course.
	108*a*. Contingent Duration.	
	110. Diuturnity.	111. Transientness.
	112. Perpetuity.	113. Instantaneity.
	114. Chronometry.	115. Anachronism.
2°. RELATIVE — 1. *to Succession*	116. Priority.	117. Posteriority.
	118. Present time.	119. Different time.
	120. Synchronism.	
2°. RELATIVE — 2. *to a Period*	121. Futurity.	122. Preterition.
	123. Newness.	124. Oldness.
	125. Morning.	126. Evening.
	127. Youth.	128. Age.
	129. Infant.	130. Veteran.
	131. Adolescence.	
2°. RELATIVE — 3. *to an Effect or purpose*	132. Earliness.	133. Lateness.
	134. Occasion.	135. Intempestivity.
3°. RECURRENT	136. Frequency.	137. Infrequency.
	138. Periodicity.	139. Irregularity.

VII. CHANGE

1°. Simple	140. Change.	141. Permanence.
	142. Cessation.	143. Continuance.
	144. Conversion.	145. Reversion.
	146. Revolution.	
	147. Substitution.	148. Interchange.
2°. Complex	149. Changeableness.	150. Stability.
	Present.	*Future.*
	151. Eventuality.	152. Destiny.

VIII. CAUSATION

1°. Constancy of Sequence	153. *Constant Antecedent.* Cause.	154. *Constant Sequent.* Effect.
	155. *Assignment of Cause.* Attribution.	156. *Absence of Assignment.* Chance.
2°. Connection between Cause and Effect	157. Power.	158. Impotence.
	Degrees of Power.	
	159. Strength.	160. Weakness.
3°. Power in Operation	161. Production.	162. Destruction.
	163. Reproduction.	
	164. Producer.	165. Destroyer.
	166. Paternity.	167. Posterity.
	168. Productiveness.	169. Unproductiveness.
	170. Agency.	
	171. Energy.	172. Inertness.
	173. Violence.	174. Moderation.
4°. Indirect Power	175. Influence.	175*a*. Absence of Influence.
	176. Tendency.	
	177. Liability.	
5°. Combinations of Causes	178. Concurrence.	179. Counteraction.

Class II. SPACE

I. SPACE IN GENERAL

1°. Abstract Space		180*a*. Inextension.
	180. *Indefinite.* Space.	181. *Definite.* Region.
		182. *Limited.* Place.
2°. Relative Space	183. Situation.	
	184. Location.	185. Displacement.
3°. Existence in Space	186. Presence.	187. Absence.
	188. Inhabitant.	189. Abode.
	190. Contents.	191. Receptacle.

II. DIMENSIONS

1°. General	192. Size.	193. Littleness.
	194. Expansion.	195. Contraction.
	196. Distance.	197. Nearness.
	198. Interval.	199. Contiguity.
2°. Linear	200. Length.	201. Shortness.
	202. Breadth. Thickness.	203. Narrowness. Thinness.
	204. Layer.	205. Filament.
	206. Height.	207. Lowness.
	208. Depth.	209. Shallowness.

2°. Linear—*continued*…	210. Summit.	211. Base.
	212. Verticality.	213. Horizontality.
	214. Pendency.	215. Support.
	216. Parallelism.	217. Obliquity.
	218. Inversion.	
	219. Crossing.	
3°. Centrical — 1. *General*	220. Exteriority.	221. Interiority.
	222. Centrality.	
	223. Covering.	224. Lining.
	225. Investment.	226. Divestment.
	227. Circumjacence.	228. Interjacence.
	229. Circumscription.	
	230. Outline.	
	231. Edge.	
	232. Inclosure.	
	233. Limit.	
2. *Special*	234. Front	235. Rear.
	236. Laterality.	237. Contraposition.
	238. Dextrality.	239. Sinistrality.

III. FORM

1°. General…	240. Form.	241. Amorphism.
	242. Symmetry.	243. Distortion.
2°. Special…	244. Angularity.	
	245. Curvature.	246. Straightness.
	247. Circularity.	248. Convolution.
	249. Rotundity.	
3°. Superficial…	250. Convexity.	252. Concavity.
	251. Flatness.	
	253. Sharpness.	254. Bluntness.
	255. Smoothness.	256. Roughness.
	257. Notch.	
	258. Fold.	
	259. Furrow.	
	260. Opening.	261. Closure.
	262. Perforator.	263. Stopper.

IV. MOTION

1°. Motion in General	264. Motion.	265. Quiescence.
	266. Journey.	267. Navigation.
	268. Traveller.	269. Mariner.
	270. Transference.	
	271. Carrier.	
	272. Vehicle.	273. Ship.
2°. Degrees of Motion	274. Velocity.	275. Slowness.
3°. Conjoined with Force…	276. Impulse.	277. Recoil.
4°. With Reference to Direction…	278. Direction.	279. Deviation.
	280. Precession.	281. Sequence.
	282. Progression.	283. Regression.
	284. Propulsion.	285. Traction.
	286. Approach.	287. Recession.
	288. Attraction.	289. Repulsion.
	290. Convergence.	291. Divergence.
	292. Arrival.	293. Departure.
	294. Ingress.	295. Egress.
	296. Reception.	297. Ejection.
	298. Food.	299. Excretion.
	300. Insertion.	301. Extraction.
	302. Passage.	
	303. Overstep.	304. Shortcoming.

4°. WITH REFERENCE TO DIRECTION—*cont.*..	305. Ascent.	306. Descent.
	307. Elevation.	308. Depression.
	309. Leap.	310. Plunge.
	311. Circuition.	
	312. Rotation.	313. Evolution.
	314. Oscillation.	
	315. Agitation.	

CLASS III. MATTER

I. MATTER IN GENERAL.......	316. Materiality.	317. Immateriality.
	318. World.	
	319. Gravity.	320. Levity.
II. INORGANIC MATTER		
1°. SOLIDS.............	321. Density.	322. Rarity.
	323. Hardness.	324. Softness.
	325. Elasticity.	326. Inelasticity.
	327. Tenacity.	328. Brittleness.
	329. Texture.	
	330. Pulverulence.	
	331. Friction.	332. Lubrication.
2°. FLUIDS 1. *In General*	333. Fluidity.	334. Gaseity.
	335. Liquefaction.	336. Vaporization.
2°. FLUIDS 2. *Specific*...	337. Water.	338. Air.
	339. Moisture.	340. Dryness.
	341. Ocean.	342. Land.
	343. Gulf. Lake.	344. Plain.
	345. Marsh.	346. Island.
2°. FLUIDS 3. *In motion*	347. Stream.	
	348. River.	349. Wind.
	350. Conduit.	351. Air-pipe.
3°. IMPERFECT FLUIDS...	352. Semiliquidity.	353. Bubble.
	354. Pulpiness.	355. Unctuousness.
		356. Oil.
		356*a*. Resin.
III. ORGANIC MATTER		
1°. VITALITY 1. *In General*....	357. Organization.	358. Inorganization.
	359. Life.	360. Death.
		361. Killing.
		362. Corpse.
		363. Interment.
1°. VITALITY 2. *Special*	364. Animality.	365. Vegetability.
	366. Animal.	367. Vegetable.
	368. Zoology.	369. Botany.
	370. Cicuration.	371. Agriculture.
	372. Mankind.	
	373. Man.	374. Woman.

2°. Sensation

- (1) *General*
  - 375. Sensibility. — 376. Insensibility.
  - 377. Pleasure. — 378. Pain.
- (2) *Special*
  - 1. *Touch*
    - 379. Touch.
    - 380. Sensations of Touch. — 381. Numbness.
  - 2. *Heat*
    - 382. Heat. — 383. Cold.
    - 384. Calefaction. — 385. Refrigeration.
    - 386. Furnace. — 387. Refrigerator.
    - 388. Fuel.
    - 389. Thermometer.
  - 3. *Taste*
    - 390. Taste. — 391. Insipidity.
    - 392. Pungency.
    - 393. Condiment.
    - 394. Savouriness. — 395. Unsavouriness.
    - 396. Sweetness. — 397. Sourness.
  - 4. *Odour*
    - 398. Odour. — 399. Inodorousness.
    - 400. Fragrance. — 401. Fetor.
  - 5. *Sound*
    - (i.) *Sound in General.*
      - 402. Sound. — 403. Silence.
      - 404. Loudness. — 405. Faintness.
    - (ii.) *Specific Sounds.*
      - 406. Snap. — 407. Roll.
      - 408. Resonance. — 408*a*. Non-resonance.
      - 409. Sibilation.
      - 410. Stridor.
      - 411. Cry. — 412. Ululation.
    - (iii.) *Musical Sounds.*
      - 413. Melody. Concord. — 414. Discord.
      - 415. Music.
      - 416. Musician.
      - 417. Musical Instruments.
    - (iv.) *Perception of Sound.*
      - 418. Hearing. — 419. Deafness.
  - 6. *Light*
    - (i.) *Light in General.*
      - 420. Light. — 421. Darkness.
      - 422. Dimness.
      - 423. Luminary. — 424. Shade.
      - 425. Transparency. — 426. Opacity.
      - 427. Semitransparency.
    - (ii.) *Specific Light.*
      - 428. Colour. — 429. Achromatism.
      - 430. Whiteness. — 431. Blackness.
      - 432. Gray. — 433. Brown.
      - 434. Redness. — 435. Greenness.
      - 436. Yellowness. — 437. Purple.
      - 438. Blueness. — 439. Orange.
      - 440. Variegation.
    - (iii.) *Perceptions of Light.*
      - 441. Vision. — 442. Blindness.
      - 443. Dimsightedness.
      - 444. Spectator.
      - 445. Optical Instruments.
      - 446. Visibility. — 447. Invisibility.
      - 448. Appearance. — 449. Disappearance.

Class IV. INTELLECT

Division (I.). Formation of Ideas

I. Operations of Intellect in General.....	450. Intellect.	450*a*. Absence of Intellect.
	451. Thought.	452. Incogitancy.
	453. Idea.	454. Topic.
II. Precursory Conditions and Operations......	455. Curiosity.	456. Incuriosity.
	457. Attention.	458. Inattention.
	459. Care.	460. Neglect.
	461. Inquiry.	462. Answer.
	463. Experiment.	
	464. Comparison.	
	465. Discrimination.	465*a*. Indiscrimination.
	466. Measurement.	
III. Materials for Reasoning..........	467. Evidence.	468. Counter-evidence.
	469. Qualification.	
	Degrees of Evidence.	
	470. Possibility.	471. Impossibility.
	472. Probability.	473. Improbability.
	474. Certainty.	475. Uncertainty.
IV. Reasoning Processes .	476. Reasoning.	477. { Intuition. Sophistry.
	478. Demonstration.	479. Confutation.
V. Results of Reasoning .	480. Judgement.	481. Misjudgement.
	480*a*. Discovery.	
	482. Over-estimation.	483. Under-estimation.
	484. Belief.	485. { Unbelief. Doubt.
	486. Credulity.	487. Incredulity.
	488. Assent.	489. Dissent.
	490. Knowledge.	491. Ignorance.
	492. Scholar.	493. Ignoramus.
	494. Truth.	495. Error.
	496. Maxim.	497. Absurdity.
	Faculties.	
	498. { Intelligence. Wisdom.	499. { Imbecility. Folly.
	500. Sage.	501. Fool.
	502. Sanity.	503. Insanity.
		504. Madman.
VI. Extension of Thought — 1°. *To the Past*...	505. Memory.	506. Oblivion.
VI. Extension of Thought — 2°. *To the Future*.	507. Expectation.	508. Inexpectation.
		509. Disappointment.
	510. Foresight.	
	511. Prediction.	
	512. Omen.	
	513. Oracle.	
VII. Creative Thought...	514. Supposition.	
	515. Imagination.	

Division (II.). Communication of Ideas

I. Nature of Ideas Communicated

516. Meaning. — 517. Unmeaningness.
518. Intelligibility. — 519. Unintelligibility.
520. Equivocalness.
521. Metaphor.
522. Interpretation. — 523. Misinterpretation.
524. Interpreter.

II. Modes of Communication

525. Manifestation. — 526. Latency.
527. Information. — 528. Concealment.
529. Disclosure. — 530. Ambush.
531. Publication.
532. News. — 533. Secret.
534. Messenger.
535. Affirmation. — 536. Negation.
537. Teaching. — 538. Misteaching. 539. Learning.
540. Teacher. — 541. Learner.
542. School.
543. Veracity. — 544. Falsehood. 545. Deception. 546. Untruth.
547. Dupe. — 548. Deceiver. 549. Exaggeration.

III. Means of Communication

1°. Natural Means

550. Indication.
551. Record. — 552. Obliteration.
553. Recorder.
554. Representation. — 555. Misrepresentation.
556. Painting.
557. Sculpture.
558. Engraving.
559. Artist.

2°. Conventional Means

1. *Language generally*

560. Language.
561. Letter.
562. Word. — 563. Neology.
564. Nomenclature. — 565. Misnomer.
566. Phrase.
567. Grammar. — 568. Solecism.
569. Style.

Qualities of Style.

570. Perspicuity. — 571. Obscurity.
572. Conciseness. — 573. Diffuseness.
574. Vigour. — 575. Feebleness.
576. Plainness. — 577. Ornament.
578. Elegance. — 579. Inelegance.

2. *Spoken Language*

580. Voice. — 581. Aphony.
582. Speech. — 583. Stammering.
584. Loquacity. — 585. Taciturnity.
586. Allocution. — 587. Response.
588. Interlocution. — 589. Soliloquy.

3. *Written Language*

590. Writing. — 591. Printing.
592. Correspondence. — 593. Book.
594. Description.
595. Dissertation.
596. Compendium.
597. Poetry. — 598. Prose.
599. The Drama.

CLASS V. VOLITION

Division (I.). INDIVIDUAL VOLITION

I. VOLITION IN GENERAL	1°. *Acts*	600. Will.	601. Necessity.
		602. Willingness.	603. Unwillingness.
		604. Resolution.	605. Irresolution.
		604*a*. Perseverance. 606. Obstinacy.	607. Tergiversation.
			608. Caprice.
		609. Choice.	609*a*. Absence of Choice. 610. Rejection.
		611. Predetermination.	612. Impulse.
		613. Habit.	614. Desuetude.
	2°. *Causes*	615. Motive.	615*a*. Absence of Motive. 616. Dissuasion.
		617. Plea.	
	3°. *Objects*	618. Good.	619. Evil.
II. PROSPECTIVE VOLITION	1°. *Conceptional*	620. Intention.	621. Chance.
		622. Pursuit.	623. Avoidance.
			624. Relinquishment.
		625. Business.	
		626. Plan.	
		627. Method.	
		628. Mid-Course.	629. Circuit.
		630. Requirement.	
	2°. *Subservience to Ends*	1. *Actual Subservience.*	
		631. Instrumentality.	
		632. Means.	
		633. Instrument.	
		634. Substitute.	
		635. Materials.	
		636. Store.	
		637. Provision.	638. Waste.
		639. Sufficiency.	
		641. Redundance.	640. Insufficiency.
		2. *Degree of Subservience.*	
		642. Importance.	643. Unimportance.
		644. Utility.	645. Inutility.
		646. Expedience.	647. Inexpedience.
		648. Goodness.	649. Badness.
		650. Perfection.	651. Imperfection.
		652. Cleanness.	653. Uncleanness.
		654. Health.	655. Disease.
		656. Salubrity.	657. Insalubrity.
		658. Improvement.	659. Deterioration.
		660. Restoration.	661. Relapse.
		662. Remedy.	663. Bane.
		3. *Contingent Subservience.*	
		664. Safety.	665. Danger.
		666. Refuge.	667. Pitfall.
		668. Warning.	
		669. Alarm.	
		670. Preservation.	
		671. Escape.	
		672. Deliverance.	

II. PROSPECTIVE VOLITION—*cont.*	3°. *Precursory Measures*	673. Preparation.	674. Non-preparation.
		675. Essay.	
		676. Undertaking.	
		677. Use.	678. Disuse. 679. Misuse.
III. ACTION	1°. *Simple*...	680. Action.	681. Inaction.
		682. Activity.	683. Inactivity.
		684. Haste.	685. Leisure.
		686. Exertion.	687. Repose.
		688. Fatigue.	689. Refreshment.
		690. Agent.	
		691. Workshop.	
	2°. *Complex* .	692. Conduct.	
		693. Direction.	
		694. Director.	
		695. Advice.	
		696. Council.	
		697. Precept.	
		698. Skill.	699. Unskilfulness.
		700. Proficient.	701. Bungler.
		702. Cunning.	703. Artlessness.
IV. ANTAGONISM	1°. *Conditional*....	704. Difficulty.	705. Facility.
	2°. *Active*....	706. Hindrance.	707. Aid.
		708. Opposition.	709. Co-operation.
		710. Opponent.	711. Auxiliary.
		712. Party.	
		713. Discord.	714. Concord.
		715. Defiance.	
		716. Attack.	717. Defence.
		718. Retaliation.	719. Resistance.
		720. Contention.	721. Peace.
		722. Warfare.	723. Pacification.
		724. Mediation.	
		725. Submission.	
		726. Combatant.	
		727. Arms.	
		728. Arena.	
V. RESULTS OF ACTION.....		729. Completion.	730. Non-completion.
		731. Success.	732. Failure.
		733. Trophy.	
		734. Prosperity.	735. Adversity.
		736. Mediocrity.	

Division (II.). INTERSOCIAL VOLITION

I. GENERAL...............	737. Authority.	738. Laxity.
	739. Severity.	740. Lenity.
	741. Command.	
	742. Disobedience.	743. Obedience.
	744. Compulsion.	
	745. Master.	746. Servant.
	747. Sceptre.	
	748. Freedom.	749. Subjection.
	750. Liberation.	751. Restraint.
		752. Prison.
	753. Keeper.	754. Prisoner.
	755. Commission.	756. Abrogation.
		757. Resignation.
	758. Consignee.	
	759. Deputy.	

II. SPECIAL	760. Permission.	761. Prohibition.
	762. Consent.	
	763. Offer.	764. Refusal.
	765. Request.	766. Deprecation.
	767. Petitioner.	
III. CONDITIONAL	768. Promise.	768*a*. Release.
	769. Compact.	
	770. Conditions.	
	771. Security.	
	772. Observance.	773. Non-observance.
	774. Compromise.	
IV. POSSESSIVE RELATIONS		
1°. *Property in General*	775. Acquisition.	776. Loss.
	777. Possession.	777*a*. Exemption.
	778. Participation.	
	779. Possessor.	
	780. Property.	
	781. Retention.	782. Relinquishment.
2°. *Transfer of Property*	783. Transfer.	
	784. Giving.	785. Receiving.
	786. Apportionment.	
	787. Lending.	788. Borrowing.
	789. Taking.	790. Restitution.
	791. Stealing.	
	792. Thief.	
	793. Booty.	
3°. *Interchange of Property*	794. Barter.	
	795. Purchase.	796. Sale.
	797. Merchant.	
	798. Merchandise.	
	799. Mart.	
4°. *Monetary Relations*	800. Money.	
	801. Treasurer.	
	802. Treasury.	
	803. Wealth.	804. Poverty.
	805. Credit.	806. Debt.
	807. Payment.	808. Non-payment.
	809. Expenditure.	810. Receipt.
	811. Accounts.	
	812. Price.	813. Discount.
	814. Dearness.	815. Cheapness.
	816. Liberality.	817. Economy.
	818. Prodigality.	819. Parsimony.

CLASS VI. AFFECTIONS

I. AFFECTIONS GENERALLY	820. Affections.	
	821. Feeling.	
	822. Sensibility.	823. Insensibility.
	824. Excitation.	
	825. Excitability.	826. Inexcitability.

II. PERSONAL

1°. Passive	827. Pleasure.	828. Pain.
	829. Pleasureableness.	830. Painfulness.
	831. Content.	832. Discontent. 833. Regret.
	834. Relief.	835. Aggravation.
	836. Cheerfulness.	837. Dejection.
	838. Rejoicing.	839. Lamentation.
	840. Amusement.	841. Weariness.
	842. Wit.	843. Dulness.
	844. Humorist.	
2°. Discriminative	845. Beauty.	846. Ugliness.
	847. Ornament.	848. Blemish.
		849. Simplicity.
	850. Taste.	851. Vulgarity.
	852. Fashion.	
		853. Ridiculousness.
		854. Fop.
		855. Affectation.
		856. Ridicule.
		857. Laughing-stock.
3°. Prospective	858. Hope.	859. Hopelessness. 860. Fear.
	861. Courage.	862. Cowardice.
	863. Rashness.	864. Caution.
	865. Desire.	866. Indifference.
		867. Dislike.
		868. Fastidiousness.
		869. Satiety.
4°. Contemplative	870. Wonder.	871. Expectance.
	872. Prodigy.	
5°. Extrinsic	873. Repute.	874. Disrepute.
	875. Nobility.	876. Commonalty.
	877. Title.	
	878. Pride.	879. Humility.
	880. Vanity.	881. Modesty.
	882. Ostentation.	
	883. Celebration.	
	884. Boasting.	
	885. Insolence.	886. Servility.
	887. Blusterer.	

III. SYMPATHETIC

1°. Social	888. Friendship.	889. Enmity.
	890. Friend.	891. Enemy.
	892. Sociality.	893. Seclusion.
	894. Courtesy.	895. Discourtesy.
	896. Congratulation.	
	897. Love.	898. Hate.
	899. Favourite.	
		900. Resentment.
		901. Irascibility.
		901*a*. Sullenness.
	902. Endearment.	
	903. Marriage.	904. Celibacy. 905. Divorce.

2°. DIFFUSIVE	906. Benevolence.	907. Malevolence.
		908. Malediction.
		909. Threat.
	910. Philanthropy.	911. Misanthropy.
	912. Benefactor.	913. Evil doer.
3°. SPECIAL	914. Pity.	914*a*. Pitilessness.
	915. Condolence.	
4°. RETROSPECTIVE	916. Gratitude.	917. Ingratitude.
	918. Forgiveness.	919. Revenge.
		920. Jealousy.
		921. Envy.

IV. MORAL

1°. OBLIGATIONS	922. Right.	923. Wrong.
	924. Dueness.	925. Undueness.
	926. Duty.	927. Dereliction. / 927*a*. Exemption.
2°. SENTIMENTS	928. Respect.	929. Disrespect.
		930. Contempt.
	931. Approbation.	932. Disapprobation.
	933. Flattery.	934. Detraction.
	935. Flatterer.	936. Detractor.
	937. Vindication.	938. Accusation.
3°. CONDITIONS	939. Probity.	940. Improbity.
		941. Knave.
	942. Disinterestedness.	943. Selfishness.
	944. Virtue.	945. Vice.
	946. Innocence.	947. Guilt.
	948. Good Man.	949. Bad Man.
	950. Penitence.	951. Impenitence.
	952. Atonement.	
4°. PRACTICE	953. Temperance.	954. Intemperance.
		954*a*. Sensualist.
	955. Asceticism.	
	956. Fasting.	957. Gluttony.
	958. Sobriety.	959. Drunkenness.
	960. Purity.	961. Impurity.
		962. Libertine.
5°. INSTITUTIONS	963. Legality.	964. Illegality.
	965. Jurisprudence.	
	966. Tribunal.	
	967. Judge.	
	968. Lawyer.	
	969. Lawsuit.	
	970. Acquittal.	971. Condemnation.
	973. Reward.	972. Punishment. / 974. Penalty.
		975. Scourge.

V. RELIGIOUS

1°. SUPERHUMAN BEINGS AND REGIONS	976. Deity.	
	977. Angel.	978. Satan.
	979. Jupiter.	980. Demon.
	981. Heaven.	982. Hell.
2°. DOCTRINES	983. Theology.	
	983*a*. Orthodoxy.	984. Heterodoxy.
	985. Revelation.	986. Pseudo-revelation.
3°. SENTIMENTS	987. Piety.	988. Impiety.
		989. Irreligion.

4°. ACTS	990. Worship.	991. Idolatry. 992. Sorcery. 993. Spell. 994. Sorcerer.
5°. INSTITUTIONS	995. Churchdom.	
	996. Clergy.	997. Laity.
	998. Rite.	
	999. Canonicals.	
	1000. Temple.	

ABBREVIATIONS, &c.

Adj. *adj.* Adjectives, Participles, and Words having the power of Adjectives.
Adv. *adv.* Adverbs and Adverbial Expressions.
Int. *int.* Interjections.
Phr. *phr.* Phrases.
V. *v.* Verbs.

The numbers are those of the headings, or Categories.

Words in italics within parentheses are not intended to explain the meanings of the words which precede them, but to indicate the nature of allied group of words under the numbers which follow them.

See also the Editor's Preface, p. **xi.**

THESAURUS

OF

ENGLISH WORDS AND PHRASES

CLASS I

WORDS EXPRESSING ABSTRACT RELATIONS

SECTION I. EXISTENCE

1°. BEING, IN THE ABSTRACT

1. Existence.—N. existence, being, entity, *ens*, *esse*, subsistence, quiddity.

reality, realness, actuality; positiveness &c. *adj.*; fact, matter of fact, sober reality; truth &c. 494; actual existence.

presence &c. (*existence in space*) 186; coexistence &c. 120.

stubborn fact; not a -dream &c. 515; no joke.

substance, essence, prime constituent, hypostatis.

[Science of existence], ontology.

V. exist, be; have -being &c. *n.*; subsist, live, breathe, stand, obtain, be the case; occur &c. (*event*) 151; have place, rank, prevail; find oneself, pass the time, vegetate.

consist in, lie in, reside in, inhere in.

come into -existence &c. *n.*; arise &c. (*begin*) 66; come forth &c. (*appear*) 446.

become &c. (*be converted*) 144; bring into existence &c. 161; coexist, pre-exist, endure &c. 141.

Adj. existing &c. *v.*; existent, subsistent, under the sun; in -existence &c. *n.*; extant; afloat, on foot, current, prevalent, rife, in force, -vogue; undestroyed.

real, actual, positive, absolute; true &c. 494; substan-tial, -tive; self-existing, -ent.

2. Inexistence.—N. inexistence; nonexistence, -subsistence; nonentity, *nil*; negativeness &c. *adj.*; nullity; nihil-ity, -ism; *tabula rasa*, blank; abeyance; absence &c. 187; no such thing &c. 4; nothingness, oblivion, *non esse.*

annihilation; extinction &c. (*destruction*) 162.

V. not -exist &c. 1; have no -existence &c. 1; be null and void; cease to -exist &c. 1; pass away, perish; be –, become-extinct &c. *adj.*; die out; disappear &c. 449; melt away, dissolve, leave not a rack behind, leave no trace; go, be no more; die &c. 360.

annihilate, render null, nullify; abrogate &c. 756; destroy &c. 162; take away; remove &c. (*displace*) 185.

Adj. inexistent, non-existent &c. 1; negative, blank, null and void; missing, omitted; absent &c. 187; visionary &c. 515.

unreal, potential, virtual; baseless, *in nubibus*; unsubstantial &c. 4; vain.

un-born, -created, -begotten, -conceived, -produced, -made.

perished, annihilated &c. *v.*; extinct, exhausted, gone, lost, departed; defunct &c. (*dead*) 360; *spurlos versenkt.*

fabulous, ideal &c. (*imaginary*) 515; supposititious &c. 514.

Adv. negatively, virtually, &c. *adj.*

well-founded, -grounded; un-ideal, -imagined; not -potential &c. 2.

Adv. actually &c. *adj.*; in -fact, - point of fact, - reality; indeed; *de* –, *ipso-facto*.

2°. Being, in the Concrete

3. Substantiality.—**N.** substantiality, *hypostasis*; person, thing, object, article; something, a being, an existence; creature, body, substance, flesh and blood, stuff, *substratum*; matter &c. 316; physical nature.

[Totality of existences], world &c. 318; *plenum*.

Adj. substan-tive, -tial, concrete; hypostatic; personal, bodily; tangible &c. (*material*) 316; real, corporeal, evident.

Adv. substantially &c. *adj.*; bodily, essentially.

4. Unsubstantiality.—**N.** un-, in-substantiality; nothingness, nihility.

nothing, naught, *nil*, nullity, zero, cipher, no one, nobody; never –, ne'er -a one; no such thing, none in the world; nothing -whatever, – at all, – on earth; not a -particle &c. (*smallness*) 32; all -talk, – moonshine, – stuff and nonsense, matter of no import.

thing of naught, man of straw, John Doe and Richard Roe; *nominis umbra*, nonentity, figurehead, lay figure; flash in the pan, *vox et præterea nihil*.

shadow; phantasm, phantom &c. (*fallacy of vision*) 443; dream &c. (*imagination*) 515; *ignis fatuus* &c. (luminary) 423; 'such stuff as dreams are made on'; air, thin air; bubble &c. 353; 'baseless fabric of a vision'; mockery.

hollowness, blank; vacuity, void &c. (*absence*) 187.

inanity, fool's paradise, fatuity, stupidity, emptiness of mind.

V. vanish, evaporate, fade, sink, fly –, die –, melt- away, dissolve, disappear &c. 449, become extinct, become invisible.

Adj. unsubstantial; fleeting; base-, ground-less; ungrounded; without –, having no- foundation.

visionary &c. (*imaginary*) 515; immaterial &c. 317; spectral &c. 980; dreamy; shadowy; ethereal, airy, imponderable, tenuous, vague.

vacant, vacuous; empty &c. 187; eviscerated; blank, hollow; nominal; null; inane.

Phr. there's nothing in it.

3°. Formal Existence

Internal conditions

5. Intrinsicality.—**N.** intrinsicality, inbeing, inherence, inhesion, immanence; subjectiveness; *ego*; essence; essentialness &c. *adj.*; essential part, essential stuff, substance, quintessence, incarnation, quiddity, gist, pith, core, kernel, marrow, sap, life-blood, backbone, heart, soul, life, flower; important part &c. (*importance*) 642.

principle, nature, constitution, character, ethos, type, quality, crasis, *diathesis*.

habit; temper, -ament; spirit, humour, grain, disposition, streak, tendency &c. 176.

External conditions

6. Extrinsicality.—**N.** extrinsicality, objectiveness, *non ego*; extraneousness &c. 57; accident; letter of the law.

Adj. derived from without; objective; extrin-sic, -sical; extraneous &c. (*foreign*) 57; modal, adventitious, additional, supervenient, fortuitous; a-, ad-scititious; incidental, casual, accidental, unessential, non-essential, accessory.

implanted, ingrafted, instilled, inculcated.

outward &c. (*external*) 220.

Adv. extrinsically &c. *adj.*

endowment, capacity; capability &c. (*power*) 157; moods, declensions, features, aspects; peculiarities &c. (*specialty*) 79; idiosyncrasy; idiocrasy; diagnostics.

V. be –, run- in the blood; be born so; be -intrinsic &c. *adj.*

Adj. derived from within, subjective; idiocratic, idiosyncratic, intrin-sic, -sical; fundamental, cardinal, normal; inherent, essential, natural; in-nate, -born, -bred, -dwelling, -grained, -wrought; radical, incarnate, thoroughbred, hereditary, inherited, immanent; congen-ital, -ite; connate, running in the blood; coeval with birth, genetic, ingenerate, -genite; indigenous; in the -grain &c. *n.*; bred in the bone, instinctive; inward, internal &c. 221; to the manner born; virtual.

characteristic &c. (*special*) 79, (*indicative*) 550; invariable, incurable, ineradicable, fixed, settled, constant, unchanging.

Adv. intrinsically &c. *adj.*; at bottom, in the main, in effect, essentially, practically, virtually, substantially, *au fond*; fairly.

4°. Modal Existence

Absolute

7. State.—N. state, condition, category, estate, lot, case, trim, mood, pickle, plight &c. 735; temper; aspect &c. (*appearance*) 448.

constitution, habitude, *diathesis*; frame, fabric &c. 329; stamp, set, fit, mould.

mode, modality, schesis; fettle; form &c. (*shape*) 240.

tone, tenor, turn; trim, guise, fashion, light, complexion, style, character.

V. be in –, possess –, enjoy –, labour under- a -state &c. *n.*; be on a footing, do, fare; come to pass.

Adj. conditional, modal, formal; structural, organic.

Adv. conditionally &c. *adj.*; as -the matter stands, – things are; such being the case &c. 8.

Relative

8. Circumstance.—N. circumstance, situation, phase, position, posture, attitude, place, point; terms; *régime*; footing, standing, status.

occasion, juncture, conjuncture; contingency &c. (*event*) 151.

predicament; emergen-ce, -cy; exigency, crisis, pinch, pass, push; turning point; crossroads.

bearings, how the land lies.

Adj. circumstantial; given, conditional, provisional; critical; modal; contingent, incidental; adventitious &c. (*extrinsic*) 6.

Adv. in the circumstances &c. *n.*, under the conditions &c. 7; thus, in such wise.

accordingly; that –, such- being the case; that being so, since, seeing that.

as matters stand; as -things, – times- go.

conditionally, provided, if, in case; if -so, – so be, – it be so; if it so -happen, – turn out; in the event of; in such a -contingency, – case, – event; provisionally, unless, without.

according to -circumstances, – the occasion; as it may -happen, – turn out, – be; as the -case may be, – wind blows; *pro re natâ.*

Section II. RELATION

1°. Absolute Relation

9. Relation.—N. relation, bearing, reference, connection, apposition, interconnection, concern, cognation; applicability, appositeness; correlation

10. [Want, or absence of relation.] **Irrelation.—N.** irrelation, dissociation; inapplicability; inconnection; multifariousness; disconnection &c. (*dis-*

&c. 12; analogy; similarity &c. 17; affinity, intimacy, friendship; homology, alliance, homogeneity, association, rapport; approximation &c. (*nearness*) 197; filiation &c. (*consanguinity*) 11; interest; relevancy &c. 23; relationship, relative position; relativity; interrelation &c. 12.

comparison &c. 464; ratio, proportion.

link, tie, bond, bond of union.

V. be-related &c. *adj.*; have a relation &c. *n.*; relate –, refer- to; bear upon, regard, concern, touch, affect, have to do with; pertain –, belong –, appertain- to; have respect to; answer to; interest.

bring -into relation with, – to bear upon; connect, associate, draw a parallel; link &c. 43.

Adj. relative; correlative &c. 12; cognate; relating to &c. *v.*; relative to, in relation with, referable *or* referrible to; belonging to &c. *v.*; appurtenant to, in common with.

related, connected; implicated, associated, affiliated, akin, allied to; collateral, cognate, congenial, kindred, affinitive, *en rapport*, in touch with.

approxima-tive, -ting; approaching; proportion-al, -ate, -able; allusive, comparable.

in the same -category &c. 75; like &c. 17; relevant &c. (*apt*) 23.

Adv. relatively &c. *adj.*; pertinently &c. 23.

thereof; as -to, – for, – respects, – regards; about; concerning &c. *v.*; anent; relating –, as relates- to; with -relation, – reference, – respect, – regard- to; in respect of; while speaking –, *à propos*-of; in connection with; by the -way, – by; whereas; for –, in -as much as; in point of, as far as; on the -part, – score- of; *quoad hoc*; *pro re natâ*; under the -head &c. (*class*) 75- of; in the matter of, *in re*.

Phr. 'thereby hangs a tale.'

junction) 44; inconsequence, independence; incommensurability; irreconcilableness &c. (*disagreement*) 24; heterogeneity; unconformity &c. 83; irrelevancy, impertinence, *nihil ad rem*; intrusion &c. 24.

V. have no -relation &c. 9 to, – bearing upon, – concern &c. 9 with, – business with; not -concern &c. 9; have -nothing to do with, – no business there; intrude, &c. 24.

bring –, drag –, haul –, lug- in head and shoulders.

Adj. irrelative, irrespective, unrelated, irrelated; arbitrary; independent, unallied; un-, dis-connected; adrift, isolated, insular; extraneous, strange, alien, foreign, outlandish, exotic.

not comparable, incommensurable, heterogeneous; unconformable &c. 83.

irrelevant; rambling &c. 279; inapplicable; not -pertinent, – to the purpose; impertinent, inapposite, beside the mark, *à propos de bottes*; away from –, foreign to –, beside- the -purpose, – question, – transaction, – point; misplaced &c. (*intrusive*) 24.

remote, far fetched, out of the way, forced, neither here nor there, quite another thing; detached, segregated, segregate.

multifarious; discordant &c. 24.

incidental, parenthetical, *obiter dictum*, episodic.

Adv. parenthetically &c. *adj.*; by the -way, – by; *en passant*, incidentally; irrespectively &c. *adj.*; without reference, – regard- to; in the abstract &c. 87; *a se*.

---

11. [Relations of kindred.] **Consanguinity.—N.** consanguinity, relationship, kindred, blood; parentage &c. (*paternity*) 166; filiation, affiliation; lineage, agnation, connection, cognation, alliance; family -connection, – tie; ties of blood; blood relationship; nepotism.

kins-man, -folk; people; kith and kin; rela-tion, -tive; connection; sib; next of kin; uncle, aunt, nephew, niece; cousin, -german; first –, second- cousin; cousin -once, – twice &c.- removed; near –, distant- relation; brother, sister, one's own flesh and blood.

family, patriarch, matriarch; fraternity; brother-, sister-, cousin-hood.

race, stock, generation; sept &c. 166; stirps, side; strain; breed, clan, tribe.

V. be -related &c. *adj.* – to; claim -relationship &c. *n.*- with.

Adj. related, akin, consanguineous, matrilinear, patrilineal, of the blood, family, allied, collateral; cog-, ag-, con-nate; kindred; affiliated, affine; fraternal, avuncular.

intimately –, nearly –, closely –, remotely –, distantly- related, – allied; german.

12. [Double or reciprocal relation.] **Correlation.—N.** reciprocalness &c. *adj.*; recipro-city, -cality, -cation; mutuality, correlation, correspondence, interdependence; interchange &c. 148; exchange, barter; interrelation, interconnection; alternation, see-saw.

V. reciprocate, alternate; interchange &c. 148; exchange; counterchange; interact, correspond, mutualize, give and take.

Adj. reciprocal, mutual, commutual, correlative; alternate; interchangeable; international; correspondent, complementary, analogous.

Adv. *mutatis mutandis*; *vice versâ*; each other; by turns &c. 148; reciprocally &c. *adj.*; to and fro &c. 314.

13. Identity.—N. identity, sameness, oneness, ditto, homogeneity; unity, coincidence, coalescence; convertibility; equality &c. 27; selfness, self, oneself; identification.

monotony, tautology &c. (*repetition*) 104.

synonym.

fac-simile &c. (*copy*) 21; *alter ego* &c. (*similar*) 17; *ipsissima verba* &c. (*exactness*) 494; same; self –, very –, one and the- same; very –, actual- thing; no other.

V. be -identical &c. *adj.*; match, coincide, coalesce.

treat as –, render- -the same, –identical; identify; recognize the identity of.

Adj. identical; self, ilk; the -same &c. *n.*; self same; synonymous; one and the same.

coincid-, coalesc-ent, -ing; indistinguishable; one; equivalent &c. (*equal*) 27; much -the same, – of a muchness; unaltered.

Adv. identically &c. *adj.*; on all fours; *ibid-*, *-em.*

---

14. [Non-coincidence.] **Contrariety.—N.** contrariety, contrast, foil, antithesis, oppositeness; counterpole; contradiction; antagonism &c. (*opposition*) 708; counteraction &c. 179.

inversion &c. 218; the -opposite, – reverse, – inverse, – converse, – antipodes, – other extreme &c. 237.

antonym.

V. be -contrary &c. *adj.*; contrast with, oppose; differ *toto cœlo.*

invert, reverse, turn the tables &c. 218.

contra-dict, -vene; antagonize &c. 708.

Adj. contrar-y, -ious, -iant; opposite, counter, dead against; ad-, con-, reverse; opposed, antithetical, contrasted, antipodean, antagonistic, opposing; conflicting, inconsistent, contradictory, at cross purposes; negative; hostile &c. 708.

differing *toto cœlo*; diametrically opposite; as opposite as -black and white, – light and darkness, – fire and water, – the poles, as different as chalk from cheese; 'Hyperion to a satyr'; quite the -contrary, – reverse; no such thing, just the other way, *tout au contraire.*

Adv. contrarily &c. *adj.*; *contra*, contrariwise, *per contra*, on the contrary, nay rather; topsy-turvy; *vice versâ*; on the other hand &c. (*in compensation*) 30.

15. Difference.—N. difference, unlikeness; heterogeneity; vari-ance, -ation, -ety; diversity, dissimilarity &c. 18; disagreement &c. 24; disparity &c. (*inequality*) 28; distinction, contradistinction; distinctness; discrepancy, divergence, contrast &c. 18; nonconformity, incompatibility, antithesis.

discord &c. 713.

modification, moods and tenses.

nice –, fine –, delicate –, subtle- distinction; shade of difference, *nuance;* discrimination &c. 465; *differentia.*

different thing, something else, variant, apple off another tree, horse of another colour, another pair of shoes; this that or the other.

V. be -different &c. *adj.*; differ, vary, ablude, mismatch, contrast; diverge –, depart –, deviate- -from; divaricate; differ *-toto cœlo, – longo intervallo.*

disagree &c. 713.

vary, modify &c. (*change*) 140.

discriminate &c. 465.

Adj. differing &c. *v.*; different, diverse, divided, heterogeneous; distinguishable; varied, modified; divergent, incongruous, diversified, various; discrepant, dissentient, differential; divers, all manner of; variform &c. 81; discordant &c. 713.

other, another, not the same; unequal &c. 28; unmatched; widely apart.

distinctive, characteristic; discriminative; distinguishing.

Adv. differently &c. *adj.*

Phr. *il y a fagots et fagots; quot homines tot sententiæ;* one man's meat is another man's poison.

2°. Continuous Relation

16. Uniformity. — **N.** uniformity; homogene-ity, -ousness; continuity, stability, consistency; connatural-ity, -ness; homology; accordance; conformity &c. 82; agreement &c. 23.

regularity, constancy, even tenor, routine; monotony, evenness, sameness, dead level; steadiness, equability, unity.

V. be -uniform &c. *adj.*; accord with &c. 23; run through.

become -uniform &c. *adj.*; conform to &c. 82.

render uniform &c. *adj.*; assimilate, level, smooth, dress.

Adj. uniform; homo-geneous, -logous; of a piece, consistent, steady; connatural; monotonous, changeless, dreary, even, invariable, equable, level, regular, stereotyped, unchanged, unvarying; methodical &c. 60; habitual &c. 613.

Adv. uniformly &c. *adj.*; uniformly with &c. (*conformably*) 82; in harmony with &c. (*agreeing*) 23; in a -rut, – groove.

always, ever &c. 112; invariably, without exception, never otherwise; by clock-work; endlessly &c. 112.

Phr. *ab uno disce omnes.*

16a. [Absence or want of uniformity.] **Non-uniformity.**—**N.** diversity irregularity, unevenness; multiformity &c. 81; unconformity &c. 83; roughness &c. 256; heterogeneity, heteromorphism.

Adj. diversified, varied, irregular, uneven, rough &c. 256; multifarious; multiform &c. 81; of various kinds; all -manner, – sorts, – kinds- of.

Adv. in all manner of ways, here there and everywhere.

3°. Partial Relation

17. Similarity.—**N.** similarity, resemblance, likeness, similitude, sem-

18. Dissimilarity.—**N.** dissimil-arity, -itude; unlikeness, diversity, disparity,

blance; affinity, approximation, parallelism; parity; agreement &c. 23; ana-logy, -logicalness; correspondence, equality &c.

connatural-ness, -ity; brotherhood, family likeness.

alliteration, rhyme, pun.

repetition &c. 104; sameness &c. (*identity*) 13; uniformity &c. 16.

analogue; the like; match, *pendant*, fellow, companion, pair, mate, twin, double, counterpart, brother, sister; one's second self, *alter ego*, chip of the old block, *par nobile fratrum*, *Arcades ambo*, birds of a feather, *et hoc genus omne*.

parallel; simile; type &c. (*metaphor*) 521; image &c. (*representation*) 554; photograph; close –, striking –, speaking –, faithful &c. *adj.* – likeness, – resemblance.

V. be -similar &c. *adj.*; look like, resemble, bear resemblance, favour; savour –, smack- of; approximate; parallel, match, rhyme with; take after; imitate &c. 19; run in pairs.

render -similar &c. *adj.*; assimilate, approximate, bring near; connaturalize, make alike; rhyme, pun.

Adj. similar; resembling &c. *v.*; like, alike; twin.

analog-ous, -ical; parallel, of a piece; such as, so.

connatural, congeneric, allied to; corresponding, cognate; akin to &c. (*consanguineous*) 11.

approximate, much the same, near, close, something like, such like; a show of; mock, *pseudo*, simulating, representing.

exact &c. (*true*) 494; lifelike, faithful, realistic; true to -nature, – the life; the -very image – picture- of; for all the world like, *comme deux gouttes d'eau*; as like as -two peas, – it can stare; *instar omnium*, cast in the same mould, ridiculously like.

Adv. as if, so to speak; as –, as if- it were; *quasi*, just as, *veluti in speculum*.

dissemblance; divergence, inequality, difference &c. 15; novelty; variation, variety, originality, disguise.

V. be -unlike &c. *adj.*; vary &c. (*differ*) 15; bear no resemblance to, differ *toto cœlo*.

render -unlike &c. *adj.*; vary &c. (*diversify*) 140.

Adj. dissimilar, unlike, disparate; of a different kind &c. (*class*) 75; unmatched, unique; new, novel; unprecedented &c. 83; original.

nothing of the kind; no such –, quite another- thing; far from it, other than, cast in a different mould, *tertium quid*, as like a dock as a daisy, 'very like a whale'; as different as -chalk from cheese, – Macedon and Monmouth; *lucus a non lucendo*.

diversified &c. 16*a*.

Adv. otherwise, *alias*.

---

19. Imitation.—N. imitation; copying &c. *v.*; transcription; repetition, mimeograph, mimeotype, duplication, reduplication; quotation; reproduction.

mockery, mimicry, mime, simulation, impersonation; representation &c. 554; semblance, simulacrum; pretence; copy &c. 21; assimilation.

paraphrase, parody &c. 21.

plagiarism; forgery &c. (*falsehood*) 544.

imitator, echo, cuckoo, parrot, ape, monkey, mocking-bird, mimic, impersonator; copyist.

V. imitate, copy, mirror, reflect, reproduce, repeat, borrow; do like, echo, re-echo, catch; transcribe; match, parallel.

20. Non-Imitation.—N. no imitation, genuineness, originality; creativeness.

Adj. unimitated, uncopied; unmatched, unparalleled; inimitable &c. 33; *unique*, original, primordial, primary, pristine, underived, first-hand, archetypal, prototypal.

---

mock, take off, mimic, ape, simulate, personate, impersonate; forge; act &c. (*drama*) 599; represent &c. 554; counterfeit, duplicate; portray, parody, travesty, caricature, burlesque.

follow –, tread- in the- -steps, – footsteps, – wake- of; pattern after, take pattern by; follow -suit, – the example of; walk in the shoes of, take a leaf out of another's book, strike in with; take –, model -after; emulate.

Adj. imitated &c. *v.*; mock, mimic; counterfeit, false, pseudo; modelled after, moulded on, paraphrastic; literal; imitative, apish; second-hand; imitable; sham &c. 545.

Adv. literally, to the letter, strictly, precisely, *verbatim, literatim, sic, totidem verbis,* word for word, *mot à mot.*

Phr. like master like man.

20a. Variation.—N. variation; alteration &c. (*change*) 140; modification, moods and tenses; modulation.

divergency &c. 291; deviation &c. 279; aberration; innovation.

V. vary &c. (*change*) 140; deviate &c. 279; diverge &c. 291.

Adj. varied &c. *v.*; modified; dissimilar &c. 18; diversified &c. 16*a.*

21. [Result of imitation.] **Copy.—N.** copy, fac-simile, counterpart, *effigies,* effigy, symbol, image, form, likeness, similitude, semblance, resemblance, cast, electrotype, stereotype, tracing, ectype; imitation &c. 19; model, representation, adumbration, study; counterfeit presentment, portrait &c. (*representment*) 554.

duplicate; transcript, -ion; reflex, -ion; shadow, echo; chip of the old block; reprint, reproduction, casting, engraving, replica; transfer; second edition &c. (*repetition*) 104; *réchauffé;* apograph, fair copy, revise.

parody, caricature, cartoon, burlesque, travesty, paraphrase.

servile -copy, – imitation; counterfeit &c. (*deception*) 545; *pasticcio.*

Adj. faithful; lifelike &c. (*similar*) 17.

22. [Thing copied.] **Prototype.—N.** prototype, original, model, pattern, founding, precedent, standard, scantling, type, arche-, anti-type; protoplast, copy-book, module, exemplar, example, ensample, specimen; paradigm; guide; templet; lay-figure.

text, copy, manuscript, MS., design; fugleman, keynote.

die, mould; matrix, engraving, last, plasm; pro-, proto-plasm; mint; seal, punch, *intaglio,* negative, stamp.

V. be –, set- an example; set a copy; standardize.

4°. General Relation

23. Agreement. — N. agreement; ac-cord, -cordance; unison, harmony, syntony; concord &c. 714; concordance, concert, understanding, convention, *entente -cordiale, consortium,* consensus of opinion, pact, mutual understanding, unanimity.

conformity &c. 82; conformance; uniformity &c. 16; consonance, consentaneousness, consistency; congruity, -ence; keeping; congeniality; correspondence, concinnity, parallelism, apposition, union.

fitness, aptness &c. *adj.*; relevancy;

24. Disagreement. — N. disagreement; dis-cord, -cordance; disunion, dissonance, dissidence, discrepancy; unconformity &c. 83; incongru-ity, -ence; discongruity, *mésalliance, oxymoron;* jarring &c. *v.*; clash, collision, dissension &c. 713; conflict &c. (*opposition*) 708; controversy &c. 720; falling out, wrangle, argument.

disparity, mismatch, misfit, disproportion; disproportionateness &c. *adj.*; variance, divergence, repugnance.

unfitness &c. *adj.*; inaptitude, impropriety; inapplicability &c. *adj.*; in-

pertinen-ce, -cy; sortance; case in point; aptitude, coaptation, propriety, applicability, admissibility, commensurability, compatibility, suitability; cognation &c. (*relation*) 9.

adaptation, adjustment, arrangement, graduation, accommodation; reconcil-iation -ement; assimilation; attunement.

consent &c. (*assent*) 488; concurrence &c. 178; co-operation &c. 709.

right man in the right place, very thing; quite –, just- the thing.

V. be -accordant &c. *adj.*; agree, accord, harmonize; correspond, tally, respond; meet, suit, fit, befit, do, adapt itself to; fall in –, chime in –, square –, quadrate –, consort –, comport- with; dovetail, assimilate; fit like a glove; fit to a -tittle, – T; match &c. 17; become one.

consent &c. (*assent*) 488.

render -accordant &c. *adj.*; fit, suit, adapt, accommodate; graduate; adjust &c. (*render equal*) 27; dress, regulate, readjust; accord, harmonize, reconcile; fadge, dovetail, square.

Adj. agreeing, suiting &c. *v.*; in accord, accordant, concordant, consonant, congruous, consentaneous, correspondent, corresponding, homologous, congenial; becoming; harmonious, reconcilable, conformable; in -accordance, – harmony, – keeping, – unison, &c. *n.*- with; at one with, of one mind, of a piece; consistent, compatible, proportionate, answerable; commensurate; on all fours.

apt, apposite, pertinent, pat; to the -point, – purpose; happy, felicitous, germane, *ad rem*, in point, bearing upon, applicable, relevant, admissible.

fit, adapted, *in loco*, *à propos*, appropriate, seasonable, sortable, suitable, idoneous, deft; meet &c. (*expedient*) 646.

at home, in one's proper element.

Adv. *à propos of*; pertinently &c. *adj.*; *pro rata.*

Phr. *rem acu tetigisti*, the cap fits.

consistency, inconcinnity; irrelevancy &c. (*irrelation*) 10.

misjoin-ing, -der; syncretism, intrusion, interference; *concordia discors.*

fish out of water.

V. disagree; clash, quarrel, jar &c. (*discord*) 713; interfere, intrude, come amiss; not concern &c. 10; mismatch; *humano capiti cervicem jungere equinam.*

Adj. disagreeing &c. *v.*; discordant, discrepant; at -variance, – war; hostile, antagonistic, repugnant, factious, contradictory, dissentious, incompatible, irreconcilable, inconsistent with; unconformable, exceptional &c. 83; intrusive, incongruous; disproportionate, -ed; unharmonious; unconsonant; divergent, repugnant to.

inapt, unapt, inappropriate, inept, infelicitous, improper; unsuit-ed, -able; inapplicable; un-fit, -fitting, -befitting; unbecoming; ill-timed, ill-adapted, unseasonable, *mal à propos*, inadmissible; inapposite &c. (*irrelevant*) 10.

uncongenial; ill-assorted, -sorted, -matched; mis-matched, -mated, -joined, -placed; unaccommodating, irreducible, uncommensurable, unsympathetic.

out of -character, – keeping, – proportion, – joint, – tune, – place, – season, – its element; at -odds, – variance with.

Adv. in -defiance, – contempt, – spite-of; discordantly &c. *adj.*; *à tort et à travers.*

SECTION III. QUANTITY

1°. SIMPLE QUANTITY

25. [Absolute quantity.] **Quantity.**— **N.** quantity, magnitude; size &c. (*dimensions*) 192; amplitude, mass,

26. [Relative quantity.] **Degree.**— **N.** degree, grade, extent, measure, proportion, amount, ratio, stint, standard, amount, *quantum*, measure, measurement, substance, strength.

[Science of quantity.] Mathematics, Mathesis.

[Definite or finite quantity] arm-, hand-, mouth-, spoon-, thimble-, capful; stock, batch, lot, dose, ration, quotum, quota, pittance, driblet, part, portion &c. 51.

Adj. quantitative, some, any, more or less.

Adv. to the tune of.

height, pitch; reach, amplitude, range, scope, size, calibre; gradation, shade; tenor, compass; sphere, station, rank, standing; rate, way, sort.

point, mark, step, stage &c. (*term*) 71; intensity, strength &c. (*greatness*) 31.

V. compare, graduate, calibrate, measure.

Adj. comparative; gradual, shading off, gradational; within the bounds &c. (*limit*), 233.

Adv. by degrees, gradually, inasmuch, *pro tanto*; how-ever, -soever; step by step, bit by bit, little by little, inch by inch, drop by drop, gradatim; by -inches, – slow degrees, – little and little; in some -degree, – measure; to some extent; just a bit.

2°. Comparative Quantity

27. [Sameness of quantity or degree.] **Equality.—N.** equality, parity, co-extension, symmetry, balance, poise; evenness, monotony, level.

equivalence; equi-pollence, -poise, -librium, -ponderance; par, quits; not a pin to choose; distinction without a difference, six of one and half a dozen of the other; identity &c. 13; similarity &c. 17; isotropism; coequality.

equalization, equation; equilibration, co-ordination, adjustment, readjustment.

drawn -game, -battle, draw, stalemate; neck and neck race; tie, dead heat.

match, peer, compeer, equal, mate, fellow, brother; equivalent.

V. be -equal &c. *adj.*; equal, match, reach, keep pace with, run abreast; come –, amount –, come up-to; be –, lie- on a level with; balance; cope with; come to the same thing; level off.

render -equal &c. *adj.*; equalize, level, dress, balance, equate, handicap, give points, trim, adjust, poise; fit, accommodate; adapt &c. (*render accordant*) 23; strike a balance; establish –, restore- equality, – equilibrium; readjust; stretch on the bed of Procrustes.

Adj. equal, even, level, monotonous, coequal, symmetrical, coordinate; on a -par, – level, – footing- with; up to the mark; equiparent.

equivalent, tantamount; quits; homologous; synonymous &c. 522; resolvable into, convertible, much at one, as broad as long, neither more nor less; much the same –, the same thing –, as good- as; all -one, – the same; equi-pollent, -ponderant, -ponderous, -balanced; equalized &c. *v.*; drawn; half and half; isochronous; isoperimetrical.

28. [Difference of quantity or degree.] **Inequality.—N.** inequality; dis-, im-parity; odds; difference &c. 15; ill-balanced; unevenness; inclination of the balance, partiality; shortcoming; casting – make- weight; superiority &c. 33; inferiority &c. 34.

V. be -unequal &c. *adj.*; countervail; have –, give- the advantage; turn the scale; kick the beam; topple, -over; over-match &c. 33; not come up to &c. 34.

Adj. unequal, uneven, disparate, partial; un-, over-balanced; top-heavy, lop-sided.

Adv. *haud passibus æquis.*

Adv. equally &c. *adj.*; *pari passu, ad eundem, cæteris paribus*; *in equilibrio*; to all intents and purposes.

Phr. it -comes, -adds up, – amounts- to the same thing.

29. Mean.—N. mean, medium, intermedium, average, run of the mill, normal, balance; mediocrity, generality, rule, ordinary -run, -ruck; golden mean &c. (*mid-course*) 628; middle &c. 68; compromise &c. 774; neutrality; middle point, middle course.

V. split the difference; take the -average &c. *n.*; reduce to a -mean &c. *n.*; strike a balance, pair off.

Adj. mean, intermediate; medial; middle &c. 68; average, normal, standard; neutral; middling, moderate.

mediocre, middle-class; *bourgeois*, commonplace &c. (*unimportant*) 643.

Adv. on an average, in the long run; taking -one with another, – all things together, – it for all in all; *communibus annis*, in round numbers.

30. Compensation.—N. compensation, equation; commutation; indemnification; compromise &c. 774; neutralization, nullification; counteraction &c. 179; reaction; measure for measure; retaliation &c. 718; equalization &c. 27; redemption, recoupment, recompense.

set-off, offset; make- casting-weight; counterpoise, equipoise, ballast; indemnity, reparation &c. 790; equivalent, *quid pro quo*; bribe, hush-money, tribute &c. 784; amends &c. (*atonement*) 952; counterclaim, counterbalance, equiponderance, countervail, cross demand.

V. make -amends, – compensation; com-pensate, -pense; indemnify; counter-act, -vail, -poise; equiponderate; balance; out-, over-, counter-balance; set off, offset, cancel; hedge, square, give and take; make up -for, – lee way; cover, fill up, neutralize, nullify; equalize &c. 27; make good; redeem &c. (*atone*) 952; recoup, pay &c. 973.

Adj. compensat-ing, -ory; amendatory, reparative, countervailing &c. *v.*; in the opposite scale; equivalent &c. (*equal*) 27.

Adv. in -return, – consideration; but, however, yet, still, notwithstanding; neverthe-, nath-less; although, though; al-, how-beit; in spite of, despite; maugre; at -all events, – any rate; be that as it may, for all that, even so, on the other hand, at the same time, *quoad minus*, *quand même*, however that may be; after all, – is said and done; taking one thing with another &c. (*average*) 29.

Quantity by Comparison with a Standard

31. Greatness.—N. greatness &c. *adj.*; magnitude; size &c. (*dimensions*) 192; multitude &c. (*number*) 102; immensity, enormity; infinity &c. 105; might, strength, intensity, fulness; importance &c. 642; fame &c. 873.

great quantity, quantity, deal, power, sight, pot, volume, world; mass, heap &c. (*assemblage*) 72; stock &c. (*store*) 636; peck, bushel, load, cargo; cart –, wagon –, car –, truck –, ship- load; flood, spring tide; abundance &c. (*sufficiency*) 639.

principal –, chief –, main –, greater –,

32. Smallness.—N. smallness &c. *adj.*; littleness &c. (*small size*) 193; tenuity; paucity; fewness &c. (*small number*) 103; meanness, insignificance &c. (*unimportance*) 643; mediocrity, moderation.

small quantity, *modicum*, *minimum*; vanishing point; material point, electron, atom, particle, molecule, corpuscle, point, dab, fleck, speck, dot, mote, jot, iota, ace; *minutiæ*, details; look, thought, idea, *soupçon*, whit, tittle, shade, shadow; spark, *scintilla*, gleam; touch, cast; grain, scruple,

major –, best –, essential- part; bulk, mass &c. (*whole*) 50.

V. be -great &c. *adj.*; run high, soar, loom up, tower, bulk large, transcend; rise –, carry- to a great height; know no bounds; scale, overtop, ascend.

enlarge &c. (*increase*) 35, (*expand*) 194.

Adj. great; greater &c. 33; large, considerable, fair, above par; big, massive, huge &c. (*large in size*) 192; ample; abundant &c. (*enough*) 639; Herculean &c. 159; full, intense, strong, sound, passing, heavy, plenary, deep, high; signal, at its height, in the zenith.

world-wide, wide-spread, extensive; wholesale; many &c. 102.

goodly, noble, precious, mighty; sad, grave, serious; far gone, arrant, downright; utter, -most; crass, gross, arch, profound, intense, consummate; rank, unmitigated, red-hot, desperate; glaring, flagrant, stark staring; thorough-paced, -going; roaring, thumping, thundering, strapping, whacking; extraordinary; important &c. 642; unsurpassed &c. (*supreme*) 33; complete &c. 52.

vast, immense, enormous, extreme; inordinate, excessive, extravagant, exorbitant, outrageous, preposterous, unconscionable, swingeing, monstrous, over-grown; towering, stupendous, prodigious, astonishing, incredible; terrific, frightful; marvellous &c. (*wonder*) 870; grand.

unlimited &c. (*infinite*) 105; unapproachable, unutterable, indescribable, ineffable, unspeakable, inexpressible, beyond expression, fabulous.

un-diminished, -abated, -reduced, -restricted.

absolute, positive, stark, decided, unequivocal, essential, perfect, finished.

remarkable, of mark, marked, pointed, veriest; noticeable, uncommon, noteworthy, eminent &c. 873.

Adv. [in a positive degree] truly &c. (*truth*) 494; decidedly, unequivocally, purely, absolutely, seriously, essentially, fundamentally, radically, downright, in all conscience; for the most part, in the main.

[in a complete degree] entirely &c. (*completely*) 52; abundantly, &c. (*suf-*

granule, globule, minim, sup, sip, sop, spice, drop, droplet, sprinkling, dash, smack, tinge, tincture; inch, patch, scantling, dole; scrap, shred, tag, splinter, rag, tatter, cantlet, flitter, gobbet, mite, bit, morsel, crumb, seed, fritter, shive; snip, -pet; snick, snack, snatch, slip, scrag; chip, -ping; shiver, sliver, driblet, clipping, paring, shaving, hair.

nutshell; thimble-, spoon-, hand-, cap-, mouth-ful; fragment; fraction &c. (*part*) 51; drop in the ocean, drop in the bucket.

animalcule &c. 193.

trifle &c. (*unimportant thing*) 643; mere –, next to- nothing; hardly anything; just enough to swear by; the shadow of a shade.

finiteness, finite quantity.

V. be -small &c. *adj.*; lie in a nutshell.

diminish &c. (*decrease*) 36, (*contract*) 195.

Adj. small, little, tiny, weeny; diminutive &c. (*small in size*) 193; minute; minikin, fine, inconsiderable, dribbling, paltry &c. (*unimportant*) 643; faint &c. (*weak*) 160; slender, light, slight, scanty, scant, limited; meagre &c. (*insufficient*) 640; sparing; few &c. 103; low, so-so, middling, tolerable, no great shakes; below –, under-par, – the mark; at a low ebb; half-way; moderate, modest; tender, subtle; petty, shallow, skin-deep.

inappreciable, evanescent, infinitesimal, homœopathic, very small, atomic, molecular, ultra-, -microscopic.

petty, shallow &c. 499.

mere, simple, sheer, stark, bare; near run.

Adv. [in a small degree] to a small extent, on a small scale; a -little, – wee, – tiny bit; slightly &c. *adj.*; imperceptibly; miserably, wretchedly; insufficiently &c. 640; imperfectly; faintly &c. 160; passably, pretty well, well enough.

[in a certain or limited degree] partially, in part; in –, to a certain degree; to a certain extent; comparatively; some, rather; in some -degree, -measure; some-thing, -what; simply, only, purely, merely; at –, at the- -least,

ficiently) 639; widely, far and wide.

[in a great or high degree] greatly &c. *adj.*; much, muckle, well, indeed, very, very much, a deal, no end of, most, not a little; pretty, – well; enough, in a great measure, passing richly; to a -large, – great, – gigantic- extent; on a large scale; so; never –, ever- so; ever so much; by wholesale; mightily, mighty, powerfully; with a witness, *ultra*, in the extreme, extremely, exceedingly, intensely, exquisitely, acutely, indefinitely, immeasurably; beyond -compare, – comparison, – measure, – all bounds; incalculably, infinitely.

[in a supreme degree] pre-eminently, superlatively &c. (*superiority*) 33.

[in a too great degree] immoderately, unduly, monstrously, grossly, preposterously, inordinately, exorbitantly, excessively, enormously, out of all proportion, with a vengeance.

[in a marked degree] particularly, remarkably, singularly, curiously, uncommonly, unusually, peculiarly, notably, signally, strikingly, pointedly, mainly, chiefly; famously, egregiously, prominently, glaringly, emphatically, strangely, wonderfully, amazingly, surprisingly, astonishingly, incredibly, marvellously, awfully, stupendously.

[in an exceptional degree] peculiarly &c. (*unconformity*) 83.

[in a violent degree] furiously &c. (*violence*) 173; severely, desperately, tremendously, extravagantly, confoundedly, deucedly, devilishly, with a vengeance; *à* –, *à toute- outrance*.

[in a painful degree] painfully, sadly, grossly, sorely, bitterly, piteously, grievously, miserably, cruelly, woefully, lamentably, shockingly, frightfully, dreadfully, fearfully, terribly, horribly, distressingly, balefully.

– most; ever so little, as little as may be, *tant soit peu*, in ever so small a degree; thus far, *pro tanto*, within bounds, in a manner, after a fashion.

almost, nearly, well nigh, short of, not quite, all but; near –, close- upon; *peu s'en faut*, near the mark; within an -ace, – inch- of; on the brink of; scarcely, hardly, barely, only just, no more than.

[in an uncertain degree] about, thereabouts, somewhere about, nearly, say; be the same -more, – little more- or less.

[in no degree] no- ways, – wise; not -at all, – in the least, – a bit, – a bit of it, – a whit, – a jot, – a shadow; in no -wise, – respect; by no -means, – manner of means; on no account, at no hand.

Quantity by Comparison with a Similar Object

33. Superiority.—N. supremacy, superiority, majority; greatness &c. 31; advantage, odds, pull; preponderance, -ation; predominance, vantage ground, coign of vantage, prevalence, partiality; personal superiority; sovereignty &c. 737; nobility &c. (*rank*) 875; Triton among the minnows, *primus inter pares, nulli secundus*, superman; captain &c. 745.

supremacy, pre-eminence; primacy, lead, *maximum*; record; climax, crest, top; culmination &c. (*summit*) 210; transcendence; *ne plus ultra*; lion's share, Benjamin's mess; excess; bisque,

34. Inferiority.—N. inferiority, minority, subordinancy; shortcoming, deficiency; handicap; *minimum*; smallness &c. 32; imperfection, shabbiness.

[personal inferiority] commonalty &c. 876; subordinate, substitute, sub.

V. be -inferior &c. *adj.*; fall –, come- short of; not -pass, – come up to; want.

become –, render- smaller &c. (*decrease*) 36, (*contract*) 195; hide its diminished head, retire into the shade, yield the palm, play second fiddle, take a back seat; bow.

Adj. inferior, smaller; small &c. 32;

surplus &c. (*remainder*) 40, (*redundance*) 641.

V. be -superior &c. *adj.*; exceed, excel, transcend; out-do, -balance, -weigh, -rival, -Herod, outrank, pass, surpass, surmount, get ahead of; over-top, -ride, -pass, -balance, -weigh, -match; top, o'er-top, cap, beat, win out, cut out; beat hollow; outstrip &c. 303; eclipse, throw into the shade, take the shine out of, put one's nose out of joint; have the -upper hand, - whip hand of, - advantage; turn the scale, play first fiddle &c. (*importance*) 642; preponderate, predominate, prevail; precede, take precedence, come first; come to a head, culminate; beat &c. all others, bear the palm; break the record, take the cake.

minor, less, lesser, deficient, minus, lower, subordinate, secondary; second-rate &c. (*imperfect*) 651; sub, subaltern; thrown into the shade; weighed in the balance and found wanting; not fit to hold a candle to.

least, smallest &c. (*see* little, small &c. 193); lowest.

diminished &c. (*decreased*) 36; reduced &c. (*contracted*) 195; unimportant &c. 643.

Adv. less; under -, below- -the mark, - par; at -the bottom of the scale, - a low ebb, - a disadvantage; short of, under.

---

become -, render- -larger, &c. (*increase*) 35, (*expand*) 194.

Adj. superior, greater, major, higher; exceeding &c. *v.*; great &c. 31; distinguished, *ultra*; vaulting; more than a match for.

supreme, greatest, maximal, maximum, utmost, paramount, pre-eminent, foremost, crowning; first-rate &c. (*important*) 642, (*excellent*) 648; unrivalled; peer-, match-less; none such, second to none, *sans pareil*; un-paragoned, -paralleled, -equalled, -approached, -surpassed; superlative, inimitable, *facile princeps*, incomparable, sovereign, without parallel, *nulli secundus*, *ne plus ultra*; beyond -compare, - comparison; culminating &c. (*topmost*) 210; transcendent, -ental; *plus royaliste que le Roi.*

increased &c. (*added to*) 35; enlarged &c. (*expanded*) 194.

Adv. beyond, more, over; over -, above- the mark; above par; upwards -, in advance- of; over and above; at the top of the scale, on the crest, at its height.

[in a superior or supreme degree] eminently, egregiously, pre-eminently, surpassing, prominently, superlatively, supremely, above all, of all things, the most, to crown all, *par excellence*, principally, especially, particularly, peculiarly, *a fortiori*, even, yea, still more.

Phr. 'we shall not look upon his like again.'

Changes in Quantity

35. Increase—**N.** increase, augmentation, addition, enlargement, extension; dilatation &c. (*expansion*) 194; multiplication; increment, accretion; accession &c. 37; production &c. 161; development, growth; aggrandizement, aggravation, intensification; rise; ascent &c. 305; anabasis; ex-aggeration, -acerbation; spread &c. (*dispersion*) 73; flood-, spring-, -tide; gain, produce, profit &c. 618; booty, plunder &c. 793.

V. increase, augment, add to, enlarge; dilate &c. (*expand*) 194; grow,

36. Non-Increase, Decrease.—**N.** decrease, diminution; lessening &c. *v.*; subtraction &c. 38; reduction, abatement, declension; shrinkage &c. (*contraction*) 195; coarctation; abridgment &c. (*shortening*) 201; extenuation.

subsidence, catabasis, wane, ebb-, neap-tide, decline; descent &c. 306; decrement, reflux, depreciation; erosion, wear and tear, deterioration &c. 659; anticlimax; mitigation &c. (*moderation*) 174.

V. decrease, diminish, lessen; abridge

wax, mount, swell, get ahead, gain strength; advance; run –, shoot- up; rise; ascend &c. 305; sprout &c. 194.

aggrandize; raise, exalt; deepen, heighten; lengthen; thicken; strengthen; intensify, enhance, inflate, magnify, double, redouble; multiply; aggravate, exaggerate; ex-asperate, -acerbate; add fuel to the flame, *oleum addere camino*, superadd &c. (*add*) 37; spread &c. (*disperse*) 73.

Adj. increased &c. *v.*; on the increase, undiminished; additional &c. (*added*) 37; increasing &c. *v.*; growing, crescent, intensive, cumulative.

Adv. *crescendo*, increasingly.

Phr. *vires acquirit eundo*.

&c. (*shorten*) 201; shrink &c. (*contract*) 195; drop –, fall –, tail- off; fall away, waste, wear, erode; wane, ebb, decline; descend &c. 306; subside; deliquesce, melt –, die -away; retire into the shade, hide its diminished head, fall to a low ebb, run low, languish, decay, crumble, consume away.

bate, abate, dequantitate; discount; depreciate; extenuate, lower, weaken, attenuate, fritter away; mitigate &c. (*moderate*) 174; belittle, minimize; dwarf, throw into the shade; keep down, reduce &c. 195; shorten &c. 201; subtract &c. 38.

Adj. unincreased &c. (*see* increase &c. 35); decreased &c. *v.*; decreasing &c. *v.*; on the -wane &c. *n.*; deliquescent.

Adv. *diminuendo*, *decrescendo*, decreasingly.

3°. Conjunctive Quantity

37. Addition.—N. addition, annexation, adjection; junction &c. 43; super-position, -addition, -junction, -fetation; accession, reinforcement; increase &c. 35; increment, supplement; accompaniment &c. 88; interposition &c. 228; insertion &c. 300; summation &c. 85; adjunct &c. 39.

V. add, annex, adject, affix, attach, superadd, subjoin, superpose; clap –, saddle- on; tack to, postfix, append, tag; ingraft; saddle with; sprinkle; introduce &c. (*interpose*) 228; insert &c. 300.

become added, accrue; ad-, supervene; add up &c. 85.

reinforce, strengthen, swell the ranks of; augment &c. 35.

Adj. added &c. *v.*; additional; supplement, -al, -ary; suppletory, subjunctive; adjec-, adsci-, asci-titious; additive, extra, spare, further, fresh, more, new, ulterior, other, auxiliary, supernumerary, accessory.

Adv. in addition, more, plus, extra; and, also, likewise, too, furthermore, further, item; and -also, – eke; else, besides, to boot, *et cætera*; &c.; and so -on, – forth; into the bargain, *cum multis aliis*, over and above, moreover.

with, withal; including, inclusive, as well as, not to mention, let

38. Non-Addition. Subduction.—N. sub-traction, -duction; deduction, retrenchment; removal; ab-, sub-lation; abstraction &c. (*taking*) 789; garbling &c. *v.*; mutilation, detruncation; amputation, severance; abs-, ex-, re-cision; curtailment &c. 201; minuend, subtrahend; decrease &c. 36; abrasion.

V. sub-tract, -duct; rebate, de-duct, -duce; bate, retrench; remove, withdraw; take -from, – away; detract.

garble, mutilate, amputate, sever, detruncate; cut -off, – away, – out; expurgate; abscind, excise; pare, thin, prune, decimate; abrade, scrape, file; geld, castrate, emasculate, unman, spay, caponize; eliminate.

diminish &c. 36; curtail &c. (*shorten*) 201; deprive of &c. (*take*) 789; weaken.

Adj. subtracted &c. *v.*; subtractive. tailless, acaudal.

Adv. in -deduction &c. *n.*; less; short of; minus, without, except, excepting, with the exception of, barring, bar, save, exclusive of, save and except, with a reservation.

---

alone; together –, along –, coupled –, in conjunction- with; conjointly; jointly &c. 43.

39. [Thing added.] Adjunct.—**N.** adjunct; addit-ion, -ament; *additum*, affix, appendage, annex; augment, -ation; increment, reinforcement, supernumerary, accessory, item; garnish, sauce; accompaniment &c. 88; adjective, *addendum*, accession, complement, supplement; continuation; extension, subscript, tag, appendix, postscript, interlineation, interpolation, insertion.

rider, codicil, off-shoot, episode, side issue, corollary; piece; flap, lapel, label, tab, strip, fold, lappet, apron, skirt, embroidery, trappings, *cortège*; tail, suffix &c. (*sequel*) 65; wing.

Adj. additional &c. 37.

Adv. in addition &c. 37.

---

40. [Thing remaining.] **Remainder**—**N.** remainder, residue; remains, *remanet*, remnant, rest, relic, relict; leavings, heel-tap, odds and ends, cheese-parings, candle ends, orts; *residuum*; dottle, dregs &c. (*dirt*) 653; refuse &c. (*useless*) 645; stubble, result, educt; fag-end, stub; ruins, wreck, skeleton, stump; *alluvium*.

surplus, overplus, excess; balance, complement; superfluity &c. (*redundance*) 641; surviv-al, -ance; afterglow.

V. remain; be -left &c. *adj.*; exceed, survive; leave.

Adj. remaining, left; left -behind, – over; residu-al, -ary; over, odd; unconsumed, sedimentary; surviving; net; exceeding, over and above; outlying, -standing; cast off &c. 782; superfluous &c. (*redundant*) 641.

40a. [Thing deducted.] **Decrement.**—**N.** decrement, discount, rebate, defect, loss, deduction, eduction, tare; drawback; waste, wastage; reprise.

41. [Forming a whole without coherence.] **Mixture.**—**N.** mix-, admix-, commix-ture, -tion, mingling; commixion, immixture, interfusion, intermixture, alloyage, matrimony; junction &c. 43; combination &c. 48; entanglement, interlacing; miscegenation, interbreeding.

impregnation; in-, dif-, suf-, trans fusion; infiltration; seasoning, sprinkling, interlarding; interpolation &c. 228; adulteration, sophistication.

[Thing mixed] tinge, tincture, touch, dash, smack, sprinkling, spice, seasoning, infusion, *soupçon*.

[Compound resulting from mixture] alloy, brass, bronze, pewter &c.; amalgam, *magma*, blend, half-and-half, *mélange*, *tertium quid*, miscellany, *ambigu*, medley, mess, hash, hotchpotch, hodgepodge, *pasticcio*, patchwork, odds and ends, all sorts; jumble &c. (*disorder*) 59; salad, sauce, mash, *omnium gatherum*, gallimaufry, ragout, *olla podrida*, *olio*, salmagundi, *potpourri*, Noah's ark; texture, mingled yarn; mosaic &c. (*variegation*) 440.

half-blood, -caste, -breed, Eurasian; mulatto; terc-, quart-, quinteron &c.; quad-, octo-roon; *griffo*, *zambo*; cross, hybrid, mongrel &c. 83.

42. [Freedom from mixture.] **Simpleness.**—**N.** simpleness &c. *adj.*; purity, homogeneity.

elimination; sifting &c. *v.*; purification &c. (*cleanness*) 652.

V. render -simple &c. *adj.*; simplify.

sift, winnow, bolt, eliminate; narrow down; get rid of, exclude &c. 55; clear; purify &c. (*clean*) 652; disentangle &c. (*disjoin*) 44.

Adj. simple, uniform, of a piece, homogeneous, single, pure, clear, sheer, neat; Attic.

un-mixed, -mingled, -blended, -combined, -compounded; elementary, undecomposed; un-adulterated, -sophisticated, -alloyed, -tinged, -fortified; pure and simple.

free –, exempt- from; exclusive.

Adv. simply &c. *adj.*; only.

V. mix; join &c. 43; combine &c. 48; com-, im-, inter-mix; mix up with, mingle; com-, inter-, be-mingle; shuffle &c. (*derange*) 61; pound together; hash –, stir- up; knead, brew; impregnate with; interlard &c. (*interpolate*) 228; inter-twine, -weave &c. 219; associate with, miscegenate, interbreed.

be mixed &c.; get among, be entangled with.

instil, imbue; in-, suf-, trans-fuse; infiltrate, dash, tinge, tincture, season, sprinkle, besprinkle, attemper, medicate, blend, cross; alloy, amalgamate, compound, adulterate, sophisticate, infect.

Adj. mixed &c. *v.*; implex, composite, half-and-half, linsey-wolsey, hybrid, mongrel, heterogeneous; motley &c. (*variegated*) 440; miscellaneous, promiscuous, indiscriminate; miscible.

Adv. among, amongst, amid, amidst, with; in the midst of, in the crowd.

43. Junction.—N. junction; joining &c. *v.*; joinder, union; con-nection, -junction, -jugation, compendency, annex-ion, -ation, -ment; coalition; astriction, attachment, compagination, vincture, ligation, alligation; accouplement; marriage &c. (*wedlock*) 903; infibulation, inosculation, symphysis, anastomosis, confluence, communication, concatenation; concurrence, meeting, reunion; assemblage &c. 72.

copulation, coition, intercourse.

joint, joining, juncture, chiasma, pivot, hinge, articulation, commissure, seam, suture, gusset, stitch, splice; link &c. 45; mitre, mortise.

closeness, tightness &c. *adj.*; coherence &c. 46; combination &c. 48.

V. join, unite; con-join, -nect; associate; put –, lay –, clap –, hang –, lump –, hold –, piece –, tack –, fix –, bind up- together; embody, re-embody; roll into one.

attach, fix, affix, saddle on, fasten, bind, paste, secure, clinch, twist, make -fast &c. *adj.*; tie, pinion, string, strap, sew, lace, stitch, tack, baste, knit, button, buckle, hitch, lash, truss, bandage, braid, splice, swathe, gird, tether, moor, picket, harness, chain; fetter &c. (*restrain*) 751; lock, latch, belay, brace, hook, grapple, leash, couple, accouple, link, yoke, bracket; marry &c. (*wed*) 903; bridge over, span.

pin, nail, bolt, hasp, clasp, clamp, screw, rivet; impact, solder, braze, cement, set; weld –, fuse- together; wedge, rabbet, mortise, mitre, jam, dovetail, enchase; graft, ingraft, inosculate; en-, in-twine; inter-link, -lace,

44. Disjunction.—N. dis-junction, -connection, -unity, -union, -association, -engagement, -sociation; discontinuity &c. 70; inconnection; abstraction, -edness; isolation; insul-arity, -ation; oasis; separateness &c. *adj.*; severalty; *disjecta membra*; dispersion &c. 73; apportionment &c. 786.

separation; parting &c. *v.*; detachment, segregation; divorce, sejunction, seposition, diduction, diremption, discerption; elision; *cæsura*, division, subdivision, break, fracture, rupture; compartition; dis-memberment, -integration, -location; luxation; sever-, dis-sever-ance; scission; re-, ab-scission; circumcision; lacer-, dilacer-ation; dis-, ab-ruption; avulsion, divulsion; section, resection, cleavage; fission; separability; separatism.

fissure, breach, rent, split, rift, crack, slit, slot, incision.

dissection, anatomy; decomposition &c. 49; cutting instrument &c. (*sharpness*) 253; saw.

V. be -disjoined &c.; come –, fall- -off, – to pieces; peel off; get loose.

dis-join, -connect, -engage, -unite, -sociate, -pair; divorce, part, dispart, detach, uncouple, separate, cut off, rescind, segregate; set –, keep- apart; insulate, isolate; throw out of gear; cut adrift; loose; un-loose, -do, -bind, -tie, -hitch, -chain, -lock &c. (*fix*) 43, -pack, -ravel; disentangle; set free &c. (*liberate*) 750.

sunder, divide, subdivide, sectionalize, sever, dissever, abscind; cut; segment; in-cide, -cise; circumcise; saw, snip, nib, nip, cleave, rive, rend, slit,

-twine, -twist, -weave; entangle; twine round, belay; tighten; trice –, screw-up.

be -joined &c.; hang –, hold- together; cohere &c. 46.

Adj. joined &c. *v.*; joint; con-joint, -junct; corporate, compact; hand in hand.

firm, fast, close, tight, taut, taught, tense, secure, set, intervolved; in-separable, -dissoluble, -secable, -severable.

Adv. jointly &c. *adj.*; in conjunction with &c. (*in addition to*) 37; fast, firmly &c. *adj.*; intimately.

---

split, splinter, chip, crack, snap, break, tear, burst; rend &c. -asunder, – in twain; wrench, rupture, shatter, shiver, cranch, crunch, craunch, chop; rip up; hack, hew, slash; whittle; haggle, hackle, discind, lacerate, scamble, mangle, gash, hash, slice, shave:

cut up, carve, quarter, dissect, anatomize; take –, pull –, pick –, tear- to pieces; tear to tatters, – piecemeal; divellicate; skin &c. 226; dis-integrate, -member, -branch, -band; disperse &c. 73; dis-locate, -joint; break up; mince; comminute &c. (*pulverize*) 330; distribute, apportion &c. 786.

part, – company; separate, leave; alienate, estrange.

Adj. disjoined &c. *v.*; discontinuous &c. 70; bipartite, multipartite, abstract; digitate; disjunctive; isolated &c. *v.*; insular, separate, disparate, discrete, apart, asunder, far between, loose, free; unattached, -annexed, -associated, -connected; distinct; adrift; straggling; rift, reft, cleft, split.

[capable of being divided] scissile, partible, divisible, separable, severable, detachable.

Adv. separately &c. *adj.*; one by one, severally, apart; adrift, asunder, in twain; in the abstract, abstractedly.

45. [Connecting medium.] **Vinculum.—N.** vinculum, link, *nexus*; connec-tive, -tion; junction &c. 43; bond of union, copula, intermedium, hyphen; bracket; bridge, stepping-stone, isthmus.

bond, tendon, tendril; fibre; cord, -age; riband, ribbon, rope, guy, cable, line, halser, hawser, painter, moorings, wire, chain; string &c. (*filament*) 205.

fastening, tie; liga-ment, -ture; strap; bowline, halliard, tackle, lanyard, rigging, shrouds; standing –, running- rigging; traces, harness; yoke; band, -age; brace, roller, fillet; inkle; with, withe, withy; thong, braid; girder, tie-beam; girt, cinch, girth, girdle, cestus, garter, braces, suspenders, halter, noose, lasso, lariat, surcingle, knot, hitch, running knot, frog.

pin, corking pin, nail, brad, tack, skewer, staple, cleat, clamp; cramp, screw, button, buckle, clasp, hasp, hinge, hank, catch, latch, bolt, ring, latchet, pawl, tag; tooth; stud; hook, – and eye; morse, lock, holdfast, padlock, rivet; anchor, grappling-iron, drawbar, coupler, drawhead, coupling, treenail, trennel, stake, pale, pile, post, bollard.

cement, glue, gum, paste, size, wafer, solder, lute, putty, bird-lime, mortar, stucco, plaster, grout.

shackle, rein &c. (*means of restraint*) 752; suspender &c. 214; prop &c. (*support*) 215.

V. bridge over, span; connect &c. 43; hang &c. 214.

46. Coherence.—N. co-, ad-herence, -hesion, -hesiveness; concretion, accretion; con-, ag-glutination, -glomeration; aggregation; consolidation, set, cementation; sticking, soldering &c. *v.*; connection.

47. [Want of adhesion, non-adhesion, immiscibility.] **Incoherence.—N.** non-adhesion; immiscibility; incoherence; looseness &c. *adj.*; laxity; relaxation; loosening &c. *v.*; freedom; disjunction &c. 44; rope of sand.

tenacity, toughness; stickiness &c. 352; insepara-bility, -bleness; bur, remora.

conglomerate, concrete &c. (*density*) 321.

V. cohere, adhere, stick, cling, cleave, hold, take hold of, hold fast, close with, embrace, clasp, hug; grow –, hang- together; twine round &c. (*join*) 43.

stick like -a leech, – wax; stick close; cling like -ivy, – a bur; adhere like -a remora, – Dejanira's shirt.

glue; ag-, con-glutinate; cement, lute, paste, gum; solder, weld; cake, coagulate, consolidate &c. (*solidify*) 321; agglomerate.

Adj. co-, ad-hesive, -hering &c. *v.*; tenacious, tough; sticky &c. 352.

united, unseparated, sessile, inseparable, inextricable, infrangible; compact &c. (*dense*) 321.

V. make -loose &c. *adj.*; loosen slacken, relax; un-glue &c. 46; detach &c. (*disjoin*) 44.

Adj. non-adhesive, immiscible; incoherent, detached, loose, slack, baggy, lax, relaxed, flapping, streaming; dishevelled; segregated, like grains of sand; un-consolidated &c. 321, -combined &c. 48; non-cohesive.

---

48. Combination.—N. combination; mixture &c. 41; alloy; junction &c. 43; union, unification, synthesis, incorporation, amalgamation, embodiment, coalescence, crasis, fusion, blend, blending, absorption, centralization, federation.

compound, amalgam, composition, *tertium quid*; resultant, impregnation.

V. combine, unite, incorporate, alloy, intertwine &c. 41; amalgamate, embody, absorb, re-embody, blend, merge, fuse, melt into one, consolidate, coalesce, centralize, impregnate; put –, lump- together; federate, associate; fraternize; cement a union, marry, wed, couple, pair, ally.

Adj. combined &c. *v.*; conjunctive, conjugate, conjoint, allied, confederate; impregnated with, ingrained, inoculated.

49. Decomposition.—N. decomposition, analysis, diæresis, dissection, resolution, catalysis, electrolysis, hydrolysis, photolysis, dissolution; dispersion &c. 73; disjunction &c. 44; disintegration, decay, rot, putrefaction, putrescence, caries, necrosis, corruption &c. (*uncleanness*) 653.

V. decom-pose, -pound; analyze, disembody, dissolve; resolve –, separate- into its elements; electrolyze; dissect, decentralize, break up; disintegrate; disperse &c. 73; unravel &c. (*unroll*) 313; crumble into dust; decay &c. *n.*; deteriorate &c. 659.

Adj. decomposed &c. *v.*; catalytic, analytical.

4°. Concrete Quantity

50. Whole. [Principal part.]—N. whole, totality, integrity; totalness &c. *adj.*; entirety, *ensemble*, collectiveness; unity &c. 87; completeness &c. 52; indivisibility, indiscerptibility; integration, embodiment; integer, integral.

all, the whole, total, aggregate, one and all, gross amount, sum, sum-total, *tout ensemble*, length and breadth of, Alpha and Omega, 'be all and end all,' lock, stock and barrel.

bulk, mass, lump, tissue, staple, body, torso, *compages*; trunk, bole, hull, hulk, skeleton; greater –, major

51. Part.—N. part, portion; dose; item, particular; aught, any; division, ward; subdivision, section; chapter, verse; article, clause, count, paragraph, passage; phrase; number, volume, book, fascicule; sector, segment; fraction, fragment; cantle, -t; frustum; detachment, parcel, unit, class &c. 75.

piece, lump, bit; cut, -ting; chip, chunk, collop, slice, scale, shard; lamina &c. 204; moiety; small part; morsel, scrap, crumb; particle &c. (*smallness*) 32; instalment, dividend; share &c. (*allotment*) 786.

–, best –, principal –, main- part; essential part &c. (*importance*) 642; lion's share, Benjamin's mess; the long and the short; nearly –, almost- all.

V. form –, constitute- a whole; integrate, embody, amass; aggregate &c. (*assemble*) 72; amount to, come to.

Adj. whole, total, integral, entire; complete &c. 52; one, individual.

un-broken, -cut, -divided, -severed, -clipped, -cropped, -shorn; seamless; undiminished; un-demolished, -dissolved, -destroyed, -bruised.

in-divisible, -dissoluble, -dissolvable, -discerptible.

wholesale, sweeping, comprehensive.

Adv. wholly, altogether; totally &c. (*completely*) 52; entirely, all, all in all, considering all things, in a body, collectively, all put together; in the -aggregate, – lump, – mass, – gross, – main, – long run; *en masse*, on the whole, as a whole, bodily, *en bloc*, *in extenso*, throughout, every inch; substantially.

débris, odds and ends, oddments, *detritus*; *excerpta*; member, limb, lobe, lobule, arm, wing, scion, branch, bough, joint, link, offshoot, ramification, twig, stipule, tendril, bush, spray, sprig; runner; leaf, -let; stump; constituent, ingredient, component part &c. 56.

compartment; department &c. (*class*) 75; county &c. (*region*) 181.

V. part, divide, break &c. (*disjoin*) 44; partition &c. (*apportion*) 786.

Adj. fractional, fragmentary; sectional, aliquot; divided &c. *v.*; in compartments, multifid, incomplete, partial, divided &c. 44.

Adv. partly, in part, partially; piecemeal, part by part; by -instalments, – snatches, – inches, – driblets; bit by bit, inch by inch, foot by foot, drop by drop; in -detail, – lots.

---

52. Completeness.—N. completeness &c. *adj.*; completion &c. 729; integration; integrality.

entirety; universality; totality; perfection &c. 650; solid-ity, -arity; unity; all; *ne plus ultra*, ideal, limit.

complement, supplement, makeweight; filling up &c. *v.*

impletion; satur-ation, -ity; high water; high –, flood –, spring- tide; fill, load, bumper, bellyful; brimmer; sufficiency &c. 639.

V. be -complete &c. *adj.*; come to a head.

render -complete &c. *adj.*; complete &c. (*accomplish*) 729; fill, charge, load, replenish; make-up, – good; piece –, eke- out; supply deficiencies; fill -up, – in, – to the brim, – the measure of; saturate &c. 869.

go the whole -hog, – length, go all lengths.

Adj. complete, entire; whole &c. 50; perfect &c. 650; full, good, absolute, thorough, plenary; solid, undivided; with all its parts.

exhaustive, radical, sweeping, thorough-going; dead.

regular, consummate, unmitigated, sheer, unqualified, unconditional, free; abundant &c. (*sufficient*) 639.

53. Incompleteness.—N. incompleteness &c. *adj.*; deficiency, short -measure, – weight; shortcoming &c. 304; insufficiency &c. 640; imperfection &c. 651; immaturity &c. (*non-preparation*) 674; half measures.

[part wanting] defect, deficit, shortage, ullage, defalcation, omission, *caret*; interval &c. 198; break &c. (*discontinuity*) 70; non-completion &c. 730; missing link.

V. be -incomplete &c. *adj.*; fall short of &c. 304; lack &c. (*be insufficient*) 640; neglect &c. 460.

Adj. incomplete; imperfect &c. 651; unfinished; uncompleted &c. (*see* complete &c. 729); defective, deficient, wanting; failing; in -default, – arrear; short, – of; hollow, meagre, lame, half-and-half, perfunctory, sketchy; crude &c. (*unprepared*) 674.

mutilated, garbled, mangled, docked, lopped, truncated; bobtailed, cropped, bobbed, shingled.

in -progress, – hand; going on, proceeding.

Adv. incompletely &c. *adj.*; by halves.

Phr. *cætera desunt*; *caret*.

---

brimming; brim-, top-ful; chock –, choke- full; as full as -an egg is of meat, – a vetch, – a tick; saturated, crammed; replete &c. (*redundant*) 641; fraught, laden; full-laden, -fraught, -charged; heavy laden.

completing &c. *v.*; supplement-al, -ary; ascititious.

Adv. completely &c. *adj.*; altogether, outright, wholly, totally, *in toto*, quite; over head and ears; effectually, for good and all, nicely, fully, through thick and thin, head and shoulders; neck and -heel, – crop; all out; in -all respects, – every respect; at all points, out and out, to all intents and purposes; *toto cœlo*; utterly, clean, – as a whistle; to the -full, – utmost, – backbone; hollow, stark; heart and soul, root and branch; down to the ground.

to the top of one's bent, as far as possible, *à outrance*.

throughout; from -first to last, – beginning to end, – end to end, – one end to the other, – Dan to Beersheba, – head to foot, – head to heels, – top to toe, – top to bottom; *de fond en comble*; *à fond*, *a capite ad calcem*, *ab ovo usque ad mala*, fore and aft; every -whit, – inch; *cap-à-pie*, to the end of the chapter; up to the -brim, – ears, – eyes; as . . . as can be.

on all accounts; *sous tous les rapports*; with a -vengeance, – witness.

54. Composition.—**N.** composition, constitution, crasis, synthesis; make-up; combination &c. 48; inclusion, admission, comprehension, reception; embodiment, formation, conformation, production.

compilation &c. 72; (*musical*) composition &c. 415; painting &c. 556; writing &c. 590; typography &c. 591.

V. be -composed, – made, – formed, – made up- of; consist of, be resolved into.

include &c. (*in a class*) 76; subsume; synthesize; contain, hold, comprehend, take in, admit, embrace, embody; involve; implicate, drag into.

compose, constitute, form, make; make –, fill –, build- up; weave, construct, fabricate; compile; write, draw; set up (*printing*); enter into the composition of &c. (*be a component*) 56.

Adj. containing, constituting &c. *v.*

---

55. Exclusion.—**N.** exclusion, non-admission, omission, exception, rejection, repudiation; exile &c. (*seclusion*) 893; preclusion, lock out, ostracism, prohibition; disbarment, expulsion, ban.

separation, segregation, seposition, elimination, coffer-dam.

V. be excluded from &c.

exclude, bar, ban; leave –, shut –, thrust –, bar- out; reject, repudiate, spurn, blackball; ostracize, boycott; lay –, put –, set -apart, – aside; relegate, segregate; throw overboard; strike -off, – out; neglect &c. 460; banish &c. (*seclude*) 893; separate &c. (*disjoin*) 44.

pass over, omit; garble; eliminate, weed, winnow.

Adj. excluding &c. *v.*; exclusive.

excluded &c. *v.*; unrecounted, not included in; inadmissible; preventive, interdictive.

Adv. exclusive of, barring; except; with the exception of; save, bating.

56. Component.—**N.** component; component –, integral –, integrant- part; element, constituent, ingredient, leaven, part and parcel; contents; appurtenance; feature; member &c. (*part*) 51; personnel.

V. enter into, – the composition of; be a -component &c. *n.*; be –, form- part of; merge –, be merged- in; be

57. Extraneousness.—**N.** extraneousness &c. *adj.*; extrinsicality &c. 6; exteriority &c. 220; alienism.

foreign -body, – substance, – element; alien, stranger, intruder, interloper, foreigner, tramontane, *novus homo*, new comer, immi-, emi-grant; creole, Afrikander; outsider, outlander, tenderfoot.

implicated in; share in &c. (*participate*) 778; belong –, appertain- to.

form, make, constitute, compose.

Adj. forming &c. *v.*; inclusive; inherent &c. 5.

Adj. extraneous, foreign, alien, ulterior; exterior, external, outside, outlandish; oversea; tra-, ultra-montane.

excluded &c. 55; inadmissible; exceptional.

Adv. in foreign -parts, – lands; abroad, beyond seas, overseas.

SECTION IV. ORDER

1°. ORDER IN GENERAL

58. Order.—N. order, regularity &c. 80; uniformity, symmetry, *lucidus ordo*; harmony, music of the spheres.

gradation, progression; series &c. (*continuity*) 69.

subordination; course, even tenor, routine; method, disposition, arrangement, array, system, economy, discipline; orderliness &c. *adj.*

rank, place, &c. (*term*) 71.

V. be –, become- in order &c. *adj.*; form, fall in, draw up; arrange –, range –, place- itself; adjust; fall into –, take- -one's place, – rank; rally round; arrange &c. 60.

Adj. orderly, regular; in -order, – trim, – apple-pie order, according to Cocker, – its proper place, neat, neat as a pin, tidy, *en règle*, well regulated, correct, methodical, uniform, symmetrical, ship-shape, business-like, systematic; habitual; unconfused &c. (*see* confuse &c. 61) arranged &c. 60.

Adv. in order; methodically &c. *adj.*; in -turn, – its turn; step by step; by regular -steps, – gradations, – stages, – intervals; *seriatim*, systematically, by clockwork, *gradatim*; at stated periods &c. (*periodically*) 138; O.K.

59. [Absence, or want of Order, &c.] **Disorder.—N.** disorder; derangement &c. 61; irregularity; anomaly &c. (*unconformity*) 83; anar-chy, -chism; want of method; dishevelment, untidiness &c. *adj.*; disunion; discord &c. 24.

confusion; confusedness &c. *adj.*; disarray, jumble, mix-up, huddle, litter, lumber; *cahotage*; farrago; mess, muss, mash, muddle, hash; hotchpotch; *imbroglio*, chaos, *omnium gatherum*, medley; mere -mixture &c. 41; fortuitous concourse of atoms, *disjecta membra*, *rudis indigestaque moles*.

complexity; complexness &c. *adj.*; com-, im-plication; intri-cacy, -cation; perplexity; network, maze, labyrinth; wilderness, jungle; involution, ravelling, entanglement; coil &c. (*convolution*) 248; sleave, tangled skein, knot, Gordian knot, kink, web; wheels within wheels.

turmoil; ferment, &c. (*agitation*) 315; to do, trouble, pudder, pother, row, disturbance, convulsion, tumult, pandemonium, uproar, riot, rumpus, stour, scramble, *fracas*, embroilment, *mêlée*, spill and pelt, rough and tumble; whirlwind &c. 349; bear garden, Babel, Saturnalia, Donnybrook Fair, confusion worse confounded, most admired disorder, *concordia discors*; Bedlam –, hell- broke loose; bull in a china shop; all the fat in the fire, *diable à quatre*, Devil to pay; pretty kettle of fish; pretty piece of -work, – business.

slattern, slut, sloven, draggle-tail.

V. be -disorderly &c. *adj.*; ferment, play at cross purposes.

put out of order; derange &c. 61; ravel &c. 219; ruffle, rumple; bungle, botch.

Adj. disorderly, orderless; out of -order, – place, – gear, – whack; irregular, desultory; anomalous &c. (*unconformable*) 83; acephalous, disorganized, straggling; un-, im-methodical; unsymmetric; unsystematic; untidy, slovenly, bedraggled, messy; dislocated; out of sorts; promiscuous, indiscriminate; chaotic, anarchical, lawless; unarranged &c. 60; confused, tumultuous, turbulent, tempestuous; deranged &c. 61; topsy turvy &c. (*inverted*) 218; shapeless &c. 241; disjointed, out of joint.

com-plex, -plexed; intricate, complicated, perplexed, involved, ravelled, entangled, knotted, tangled, inextricable; irreducible.

troublous; riotous &c. (*violent*) 173.

Adv. irregularly &c. *adj.*; by fits and -snatches, – starts; pell-mell; higgledy-piggledy; helter-skelter, harum-scarum; in a ferment; at -sixes and sevens, – cross purposes; upside down &c. 218.

Phr. the cart before the horse, chaos is come again.

60. [Reduction to Order.] **Arrangement.—N.** arrangement; plan &c. 626; preparation &c. 673; dispos-al, -ition; col-, al-location; distribution; sorting &c. *v.*; assortment, allotment; grouping; apportionment, *taxis*, taxonomy, *syn-taxis*, graduation, organization, grading; re-organization, rationalization.

analysis, classification, division, digestion; systematism.

[Result of arrangement] order, orderliness, form, array; digest, synopsis &c. (*compendium*) 596; *syntagma*, table, atlas; register &c. (*record*) 551; score &c. 415; cosmos, organism, architecture.

[Instrument for sorting] sieve &c. 260; file, card index.

V. reduce to –, bring into- order; introduce order into; rally.

arrange, dispose, place, form; put –, set –, place- in order; straighten up, tidy up; set out, collocate, allocate, pack, marshal, range, size, rank, array, group, parcel out, allot, space, distribute, deal; cast –, assign- the parts; dispose of, assign places to; assort, sort; sift, riddle; put –, set- -to rights, – into shape, – in trim, – in array.

class, -ify; divide; file, string together, thread; register &c. (*record*) 551; list, catalogue, tabulate, index, alphabeticize, graduate, digest, grade, codify; orchestrate, score.

methodize, regulate, systematize, standardize, co-ordinate, organize, settle, fix, apportion.

unravel, disentangle, ravel, card; disembroil.

Adj. arranged &c. *v.*; embattled, in battle array; cut and dried; methodical, orderly, regular, systematic, tabular.

61. [Subversion of Order; bringing into disorder.] **Derangement.—N.** derangement &c. *v.*; disorder &c. 59; evection, discomposure, disturbance; dis-, de-organization; involvement; dislocation; perturbation, interruption; shuffling &c. *v.*; inversion &c. 218; corrugation &c. (*fold*) 258; insanity &c. 503.

V. derange; dis-, mis-arrange; dis-, mis-place; mislay, discompose, disorder, de-, dis-organize; embroil, unsettle, disturb, confuse, trouble, perturb, jumble, tumble; huddle, shuffle, muddle, toss, hustle, fumble, riot; bring –, put –, throw- into -disorder &c. 59; break the ranks, disconcert, convulse; break in upon.

unhinge, dislocate, put out of joint, throw out of gear.

turn topsy-turvy &c. (*invert*) 218; bedevil; complicate, involve, perplex, confound; im-, em-brangle; tangle, en-tangle, ravel, tousle, dishevel, ruffle, rumple &c. (*fold*) 258; dement.

litter, scatter; mix &c. 41.

Adj. deranged &c. *v.*; syncre-tic, -tistic.

2°. Consecutive Order

62. Precedence.—**N.** precedence; coming before &c. *v.*; the lead, *le pas*; superiority &c. 33; importance &c. 642; anteced-ence, -ency; anteriority &c. (*front*) 234; precursor &c. 64; priority &c. 116; precession &c. 280; anteposition, preference.

V. precede; come -before, – first; forerun, head, lead, take the lead; lead the -way, – dance; introduce, usher in; have the *pas*; set the fashion &c. (*influence*) 175; lead off, kick off, open the ball; take –, have- precedence; outrank; have the start &c. (*get before*) 280.

place before; prefix; premise, prelude, preface.

Adj. preceding &c. *v.*; pre-, antecedent; anterior; prior &c. 116; before; former, foregoing; before-, above-mentioned; aforesaid, said; precurs-ory, -ive; prevenient, preliminary, prefatory, introductory; prelus-ive, -ory; proemial, preparatory.

Adv. before; in advance &c. (*precession*) 280.

Phr. *seniores priores.*

63. Sequence.—**N.** sequence, coming after; going after &c. (*following*) 281; consecution, succession; posteriority &c. 117.

continuation; prolongation, order of succession; successiveness; Elijah's mantle.

secondariness; subordinancy &c. (*inferiority*) 34.

V. succeed; come -after, – on, – next; follow, ensue, step into the shoes of; alternate.

place after, suffix, append.

Adj. succeeding &c. *v.*; sequent; sub-, con-sequent; sequacious, proximate, next; consecutive &c. (*continuity*) 69; alternate, amœbæan.

latter; posterior &c. 117.

Adv. after, subsequently; behind &c. (*rear*) 235.

---

64. Precursor.—**N.** precursor, antecedent, precedent, predecessor; forerunner, van-courier, *avant-coureur*, pioneer, prodrome, *prodromos*, outrider; leader, bell-wether; herald, harbinger; dawn.

prelude, preamble, preface, prologue, foreword, *avant-propos*, *protasis*, prolusion, proem, *prolepsis*, *prolegomena*, prefix, introduction; lead, heading, frontispiece, groundwork; preparation &c. 673; overture, voluntary, *exordium*, symphony, *ritornello*; premises.

prefigurement &c. 511; omen &c. 512.

Adj. precursory; prelu-sive, -sory, -dious; proemial, introductory, prefatory, prodromous, inaugural, preliminary; precedent &c. (*prior*) 116.

65. Sequel.—**N.** sequel, suffix, successor; tail, queue, train, wake, trail, rear; retinue, suite; appendix, postscript, subscript; epilogue; conclusion; peroration; codicil; continuation, *sequela*; appendage &c. 39; tail –, heel-piece; tag, more last words; colophon, *feliciter explicit.*

follower, after-glow, -growth, -crop, -taste, -math.

after-part, -piece, -course, -thought, -game; *arrière pensée*, second thoughts.

---

66. Beginning.—**N.** beginning, commencement, opening, outset, incipience, inception, inchoation; introduction &c. (*precursor*) 64; *alpha*; initial; foundation; inauguration, *début*, *le premier pas*, embarcation, rising of the curtain; zero hour; exordium, curtain raiser; maiden speech; prelude; outbreak, onset, brunt; initiative, move, first move; gambit, narrow –, thin-

67. End.—**N.** end, close, termination; desinence, conclusion, *finis*, *finale*, period, term, *terminus*, last, *omega*; extreme, -tremity; gable –, butt –, fag-end; tip, nib, point; tail &c. (*rear*) 235; verge &c. (*edge*) 231; tag, epilogue, peroration; *bonne bouche*; bitter end, tail end; terminal; *apodosis*; appendix.

consummation, *dénouement*; finish &c. (*completion*) 729; fate; doom, -sday;

end of the wedge; fresh start, new departure; forefront.

origin &c. (*cause*) 153; source, rise; bud, germ &c. 153; egg, rudiment; genesis, birth, nativity, cradle, infancy, incunabula; start, starting-point &c. 293; dawn &c. (*morning*) 125.

title-page; head, -ing, caption; van &c. (*front*) 234, *feliciter incipit.*

en-trance, -try; inlet, orifice, mouth, chops, lips, porch, portal, portico, *propylon*, door; gate, -way; postern, wicket, threshold, vestibule; skirts, border &c. (*edge*) 231; tee.

first -stage, – blush, – glance, – impression, – sight.

rudiments, elements, outlines, *principia*, grammar, *protasis*; alphabet, ABC.

V. begin, commence, inchoate, rise, arise, originate, institute, conceive, initiate, open, dawn, set in, take its rise, enter upon, start; enter; set out &c. (*depart*) 293; embark in.

usher in; lead -off, – the way; take the -lead, – initiative; inaugurate, head; stand -at the head, – first, – for; lay the foundations &c. (*prepare*) 673; found &c. (*cause*) 153; set -up, – on foot, – agoing, – abroach, – the ball in motion; apply the match to a train; launch, broach; open -up, – the door to; set -about, – to work; make a -beginning, – start; handsel; take the first step, lay the first stone, cut the first turf; break -ground, – the ice, – cover; pass –, cross- the Rubicon; open -fire, – the ball; ventilate, air; undertake &c. 676.

come into -existence, – the world; make one's *début*, take birth; burst forth, break out; spring –, crop- up.

begin -at the beginning, – *ab ovo*, – again, – *de novo*; start afresh, make a fresh start, shuffle the cards, resume, recommence.

Adj. beginning &c. *v.*; initi-al, -atory, -ative; inceptive, introductory, incipient; proemial, inaugural; incho-ate, -ative; embryonic, rudimental; primogenial; primeval &c. (*old*) 124; rudimentary, aboriginal; natal, nascent.

first, foremost, front, leading, head; maiden.

begun &c. *v.*; just -begun &c. *v.*

Adv. at –, in- the beginning &c. *n.*; first, in the first place, *imprimis*, first and foremost; *in limine*; in -the bud, – embryo, – its infancy; from -the beginning, – its birth; *ab -initio*, – *ovo*, – *incunabulis*, primarily, originally.

crack of doom, day of Judgement, fall of the curtain, wind-up; goal, destination; limit, stoppage, end all, determination; expiration, expiry; death &c. 360; end of all things; finality; eschatology.

break up, *commencement de la fin*, last stage, turning point; *coup de grâce*, death-blow; knock-out.

V. end, close, finish, terminate, conclude, be all over; expire; die &c. 360; come –, draw- to a -close &c. *n.*; have run its course; run out, pass away.

bring to an -end &c. *n.*; put an end to, make an end of; determine; get through; achieve &c. (*complete*) 729; stop &c. (*make to cease*) 142; shut up shop.

Adj. ending &c. *v.*; final, terminal, definitive, conclusive; crowning &c. (*completing*) 729; last, ultimate; hindermost; rear &c. 235; caudal.

contermin-ate, -ous, -able.

ended &c. *v.*; at an end; settled, decided, over, played out, set at rest.

penultimate; last but -one, – two, &c.

unbegun, uncommenced; fresh.

Adv. finally &c. *adj.*; in fine; at the last; once for all.

---

68. Middle.—**N.** middle, midst, mediety; mean &c. 29; medium, middle term; centre &c. 222, mid-course &c. 628; *mezzo termine*; *juste milieu* &c. 628; half-way house, nave, navel, omphalos; nucle-us, -olus.

equidistance, bisection, half-distance; middle-distance, equator, diaphragm, midriff; interjacence &c. 228.

Adj. middle, medial, mesial, mean, mid; middle-, mid-most; middling; mediate; intermediate &c. (*interjacent*) 228; equidistant; central &c. 222; mediterranean, equatorial.

Adv. in the middle; in the thick; mid-, half-way; midships, *in medias res.*

69. [Uninterrupted sequence.] **Continuity.—N.** continuity; consecu-tion, -tiveness &c. *adj.*; succession, round, suite, progression, series, train, chain; cat-, concat-enation; catena; scale; gradation, course, constant flow, perpetuity.

procession, column; retinue, *cortège*, cavalcade, rank and file, line of battle, array.

pedigree, genealogy, lineage, race &c. 166.

rank, file, line, row, range, tier, string, thread, team; suit; colonnade.

V. follow in –, form- a series &c. *n.*; fall in.

arrange in a -series &c. *n.*; string together, catenate, file, thread, graduate, tabulate.

Adj. continu-ous, -ed; consecutive; progressive, gradual; serial, successive; immediate, unbroken, entire; linear; in a -line, – row &c. *n.*; uninter-rupted, -mitting; unremitting; perennial, evergreen; constant.

Adv. continuously &c. *adj.*; *seriatim*; in a -line &c. *n.*; in -succession, – turn; running, gradually, step by step, *gradatim*, at a stretch; in -file, – column, – single file, – Indian file.

70. [Interrupted sequence.] **Discontinuity.—N.** discontinuity; disjunction &c. 44; anacoluthon, *non sequitur*; interruption, break, fracture, flaw, fault, split, crack, cut; gap &c. (*interval*) 198; solution of continuity, *cæsura*; broken thread; parenthesis, episode; rhapsody, patchwork; intermission; alternation &c. (*periodicity*) 138; dropping fire.

V. be -discontinuous &c. *adj.*; alternate, intermit.

discontinue, pause, interrupt; intervene; break, – in upon; interpose &c. 228; break –, snap- the thread; disconnect &c. (*disjoin*) 44.

Adj. discontinuous, unsuccessive, broken, interrupted, *décousu*; dis-, un-connected, discrete, disjunctive; fitful &c. (*irregular*) 139; spasmodic, desultory, intermit-ting &c. *v.*, -tent; alternate; recurrent &c. (*periodic*) 138; few and far between.

Adv. at intervals; by -snatches, – jerks, – skips, – catches, – fits and starts; skippingly, *per saltum*; *longo intervallo*.

---

71. Term.—N. term, rank, station, stage, step; degree &c. 26; scale, remove, grade, link, peg, round –, rung- of the ladder, *status*, position, place, point, mark, *pas*, period, pitch; stand, -ing; footing, range.

V. hold –, occupy –, fall into- a place &c. *n.*

3°. Collective Order

72. Assemblage.—N. assemblage; col-lection, -location, -ligation; compilation, levy, gathering, ingathering, mobilization, meet, foregathering, muster, *attroupement*; con-course, -flux, -gregation, -tesseration, -vergence &c. 290; meeting, *levée*, *réunion*, drawing room, at home; conversazione &c. (*social gathering*) 892; assembly, congress, eisteddfod; conven-tion, -ticle;

73. Non-assemblage. Dispersion.—N. dispersion; disjunction &c. 44; divergence &c. 291; scattering &c. *v.*; dissemination, broadcasting, diffusion, dissipation, distribution; apportionment &c. 786; spread, respersion, circumfusion, interspersion, spargefaction.

waifs and estrays, flotsam and jetsam, *disjecta membra*.

V. disperse, scatter, sow, dissemi-

gemote; conclave, &c. (*council*) 696; posse, *posse comitatûs*; Noah's ark.

miscellany, *collectanea*, symposium; museum, menagerie, &c. (*store*) 636.

crowd, throng, multitude; flood, rush, deluge; rout, rabble, mob, press, crush, *cohue*, jam, horde, body, tribe; crew, gang, knot, squad, band, party; swarm, shoal, school, covey, flock, herd, drove, kennel; array, bevy, galaxy; *corps*, company, troop, *troupe*; army, force, regiment, &c. (*combatants*) 726; host &c. (*multitude*) 102; populousness.

clan, brotherhood, association &c. (*party*) 712.

volley, shower, storm, cloud.

group, cluster, Pleiades, clump, pencil; set, batch, lot, pack; budget, *dossier*, assortment, bunch; parcel; pack-et, -age; bundle, *fasciculus*, fascine, bale; ser-on, -oon; faggot, wisp, truss, tuft; shock, rick, fardel, stack, sheaf, swath, gavel, haycock, stook.

accumulation &c. (*store*) 636; congeries, heap, lump, pile, *rouleau*, tissue, mass, pyramid; drift; snow-ball, -drift; acervation, cumulation, amassment, glom-, agglom-eration; conglobation; conglomeration, -ate; coacervation, coagmentation, aggregation, concentration, congestion, *omnium gatherum*, *spicilegium*, black hole of Calcutta; quantity &c. (*greatness*) 31.

collector, gatherer; whip, -per in.

V. [be or come together] assemble, collect, muster; meet, unite, join, rejoin; cluster, flock, swarm, surge, stream, herd, crowd, throng, associate; con-gregate, -glomerate, -centrate; centre round, *rendezvous*, resort; come –, flock –, get –, pig- together; forgather; huddle; reassemble.

[get or bring together] assemble, muster, mobilize; bring –, get –, put –, draw –, scrape –, lump- together; col-lect, -locate, -ligate; get –, whip- in; gather; hold a meeting; con-vene, -voke, -vocate; rake up, dredge; heap, mass, pile; pack, put up, truss, cram; acervate; ag-glomerate, -gregate; compile; group, aggroup, concentrate, unite; collect –, bring- into a focus; amass, accumulate &c. (*store*) 636; collect in a drag-net; heap Ossa upon Pelion.

Adj. assembled &c. *v.*; closely packed, dense, serried, crowded to suffocation, teeming, swarming, populous; as thick as hops; all of a heap, fasciculated; cumulative.

Phr. the plot thickens.

nate, radiate, diffuse, shed, spread, ted, bestrew, overspread, dispense, disband, disembody, demobilize, dismember, distribute; apportion &c. 786; blow off, let out, dispel, cast forth, draught off; strew, straw, strow; spirtle, cast, sprinkle, spatter; issue, deal out, retail, utter; re-, inter-sperse; set abroach, circumfuse.

turn –, cast- adrift; scatter to the winds; sow broadcast.

spread like wildfire, disperse themselves.

Adj. unassembled &c. (*see* assemble &c. 72); dispersed &c. *v.*; sparse, dispread, broadcast, sporadic, widespread; far-flung; epidemic &c. (*general*) 78; adrift, stray; dishevelled, streaming.

Adv. *sparsim*, here and there, *passim*.

---

74. [Place of meeting.] **Focus.—N.** focus; point of- convergence &c. 290; corradiation; centre &c. 222; gathering-place, resort; haunt; retreat; *venue*, *rendezvous*; rallying point, headquarters, home, club; *dépôt* &c. (*store*) 636; tryst, trysting-place; place of -meeting, – resort, – assignation; *point de* –, *lieu de- réunion*; issue.

V. bring to- a point, – a focus, – an issue; focus.

4°. DISTRIBUTIVE ORDER

75. **Class.—N.** class, category, *categorema*, head, order, sec-

tion; division, subdivision; department, province, domain, sphere.
kind, sort, genus, species, variety, branch, family, race, tribe, caste, sept, clan, breed; *clique, coterie*; type, kit, sect, set; assortment; feather, kidney; suit; range; gender, sex, kin.
manner, description, denomination, persuasion, connection, designation, character, stamp; predicament; conviction &c. 484.
similarity &c. 17.

76. Inclusion. [Comprehension under, or reference to a class.]—**N.** inclusion, admission, incorporation, comprehension, reception.
composition &c. (*inclusion in a compound*) 54.
V. be -included in &c.; come –, fall –, range- under; belong –, pertain- to; range with; merge in.
include, compromise, comprehend, contain, admit, embrace, receive; enclose &c. (*circumscribe*) 229; incorporate, cover, embody, encircle.
reckon –, enumerate –, number- among; refer to; place –, arrange- under, – with; take into account.
Adj. includ-ed, -ing &c. *v.*; inclusive; comprehensive, all-embracing; congen-er, -erous: of the same -class &c. 75.
Phr. *et hoc genus omne,* &c.; *et cætera.*

77. Exclusion.*—**N.** exclusion &c. 55.

78. Generality. — **N.** general-ity, -ization; universality; catholic-ity, -ism; miscel-lany, -laneousness; drag-net.
every-one, -body; all hands, all the world and his wife; any body, N or M, all sorts; *tout le monde.*
prevalence, run.
V. be -general &c. *adj.*; prevail, obtain, be going about, stalk abroad.
render -general &c. *adj.*; generalize; spread, broadcast.
Adj. general, usual, current, generic, collective; broad, comprehensive, sweeping; encyclopedical, panoramic, widespread &c. (*dispersed*) 73.
universal; catho-lic, -lical; common, world-wide; œ-, e-cumenical; transcendental; prevalent, prevailing, rife, epidemic, besetting; all over, covered with.
every, all; indeterminate, indefinite, unspecified, impersonal.
customary &c. (*habitual*) 613.
Adv. what-ever, -soever; to a man, one and all, without exception.
generally &c. *adj.*; always, for better

79. Speciality.—**N.** speciality, *spécialité*; individ-uality, -uity; particularity, peculiarity; idiocrasy &c. (*tendency*) 176; personality, characteristic, mannerism, idiosyncrasy, attribute, specificness &c. *adj.*; singularity &c. (*unconformity*) 83; reading, version, lection; state; *trait*; distinctive feature; technicality; *differentia.*
particulars, details, minutiæ, items, counts.
I, self, I myself, *ego*; my-, him-, her-, it-self.
V. specify, particularize, individualize, realize, specialize, designate, differentiate, determine, define, denote, indicate, itemize, detail.
descend to particulars, enter into detail, come to the point.
Adj. special, particular, individual, specific, proper, personal, intimate, original, private, respective, definite, concrete, determinate, especial, certain, esoteric, endemic, partial, party, peculiar, marked, appropriate, several, characteristic, diagnostic, exact, exclusive; singular &c. (*exceptional*) 83;

* The same set of words is used to express *Exclusion from a class* and *Exclusion from a compound.* Reference is therefore made to the former at 55. This identity does not occur with regard to *Inclusion*, which therefore constitutes a separate category.

for worse; in general, generally speaking; speaking generally; for the most part; in the long run &c. (*on an average*) 29.

---

idiomatic; typical, representative, distinctive.

this, that; yon, -der.

Adv. specially &c. *adj.*; in particular, *in propriâ personâ*; *ad hominem*; for my part.

each, apiece, one by one; severally, respectively, each to each; *seriatim*, in detail, bit by bit; *pro hac vice*, – *re natâ*.

namely, that is to say, *videlicet*, viz.; to wit; i.e., e.g.

5°. Order as regards Categories

80. Rule.—N. regularity, uniformity &c. 16; clock-work precision; punctuality &c. (*exactness*) 494; routine &c. (*custom*) 613; formula; system; rut; canon, convention, maxim; rule &c. (*form, regulation*) 697; key-note, standard, model; precedent &c. (*prototype*) 22; conformity &c. 82.

nature, principle; law; order of things; normal –, natural –, ordinary –, model- -state, – condition; standing -dish, – order; normality; Procrustean law; law of the Medes and Persians; hard and fast rule.

Adj. regular, uniform, symmetrical, constant, steady; according to rule &c. (*conformable*) 82; customary &c. 613; orderly &c. 58.

81. Multiformity.—N. multi-, omniformity; variety, diversity; multifariousness &c. *adj.*

Adj. multi-form, -fold, -farious, -generous; multiplex, variform, manifold, many-sided, multiplicate; omni-form, -genous, -farious; polymorphic; protean; heterogeneous, motley, mosaic; epicene, indiscriminate, desultory, irregular, diversified, different, divers; all manner of; of -every description, – all sorts and kinds; *et hoc genus omne*; and what not? *de omnibus rebus et quibusdam aliis*.

---

82. Conformity.—N. conform-ity, -ance; observance.

naturalization; conventionality &c. (*custom*) 613; agreement &c. 23.

example, instance, specimen, sample, quotation; exemplification, illustration, case in point; object lesson.

conventionalist, formalist, Philistine.

pattern &c. (*prototype*) 22.

V. conform to, – rule; accommodate –, adapt- oneself to; rub off corners.

be -regular &c. *adj.*; move in a groove; follow –, observe –, go by –, bend to –, obey- -rules, – precedents; comply –, tally –, chime in –, fall in- with; be -guided, – regulated- by; fall into a -custom, – usage; follow the -fashion, – multitude; pass muster, do as others do, *hurler avec les loups*; do at Rome as the Romans do; go –, swim- with the -stream, – current, – tide; tread the beaten track &c. (*habit*) 613; rubber-stamp; keep one in countenance.

exemplify, illustrate, cite, quote, put

83. Unconformity.—N. non-conformity &c. 82; un-, dis-conformity; unconventionality, informality, abnormity, anomaly; anomalousness &c. *adj.*; exception, peculiarity, &c. 79; infraction –, breach –, violation –, infringement- of -law, – custom, – usage; eccentricity, *bizarrerie*, oddity, *je ne sais quoi*, monstrosity, rarity; freak of Nature.

individuality, idiosyncrasy, singularity, originality, mannerism.

aberration; irregularity; variety; singularity; exemption; salvo &c. (*qualification*) 469.

nonconformist; nondescript, character, original, nonsuch, monster, prodigy, wonder, miracle, curiosity, missing link, flying fish, black swan, *lusus naturæ*, *rara avis*, queer fish; mongrel; half-caste, -blood, -breed; *métis*, cross breed, hybrid, mule, mulatto, sacatra, marabou; *tertium quid*, hermaphrodite, gynander, androgyn.

phœnix, chimera, hydra, sphinx, minotaur; griff-in, -on; centaur; hippo-

a case; produce an- instance &c. *n.*

Adj. conformable to rule, adaptable, compliant, consistent, agreeable; regular &c. 80; according to -regulation, - rule, - Cocker; *en règle, selon les règles*, well regulated, orderly; symmetric &c. 242.

conventional, commonplace &c. (*customary*) 613; of -daily, - every day-occurrence; in the natural order of things; ordinary, common, - or garden, prosaic, habitual, usual.

in the order of the day; naturalized.

typical, normal, formal; canonical, orthodox, sound, strict, rigid, positive, uncompromising, Procrustean; point device.

secundum artem, ship-shape, technical.

exemplary, illustrative, in point.

Adv. conformably &c. *adj.*; by rule; agreeably to; in -conformity, - accordance, - keeping- with; according to; consistently with; as usual, *ad instar, instar omnium; more -solito, - majorum.*

for the sake of conformity; of -, as a matter of- course; *pro formâ*, for form's sake, by the card; according to plan.

invariably &c. (*uniformly*) 16.

for -example, - instance; *exempli gratiâ; e.g.; inter alia.*

Phr. *cela va sans dire; ex pede Herculem, noscitur a sociis.*

---

griff, -centaur; sagittary; kraken, cockatrice, wyvern, roc, liver, dragon, sea-serpent; mermaid; unicorn; Cyclops, 'men whose heads do grow beneath their shoulders'; Teratology.

fish out of water; neither -one thing nor another, - fish flesh nor fowl nor good red herring; one in a -way, - thousand; out-cast, -law; Ishmael, pariah; oasis.

V. be -unconformable &c. *adj.*; leave the beaten -track, - path; infringe -, break -, violate- a -law, - habit, - usage, - custom; drive a coach and six through; stretch a point; have no business there; baffle -, beggar- all description.

Adj. unconformable, exceptional; abnorm-al, -ous; anomal-ous, -istic; out of -order, - place, - keeping, - tune, - one's element; irregular, arbitrary; lawless, informal, aberrant, stray, wandering, wanton; peculiar, exclusive, unnatural, eccentric, crotchety, egregious; out of the -beaten track, - common, - common run, - pale of; misplaced; funny.

un-usual, -accustomed, -customary, -wonted, -common; rare, singular, unique, curious, odd, extraordinary, strange, monstrous; wonderful &c. 870; unexpected, unaccountable; *outré*, out of the way, remarkable, noteworthy; queer, quaint, nondescript, none such, *sui generis*; original, unconventional, Bohemian, unfashionable; un-described, -precedented, -paralleled, -exampled, -heard of, -familiar; fantastic, new-fangled, grotesque, *bizarre*; outlandish, exotic, *tombé des nues*, preternatural; denaturalized.

heterogeneous, heteroclite, amorphous, mongrel, amphibious, epicene, half-blood, hybrid; androgyn-ous, -al; unsymmetric &c. 243.

qualified &c. 469.

Adv. unconformably &c. *adj.*; except, unless, save, barring, beside, without, save and except, let alone.

however, yet, but.

Int. what -on earth! - in the world!

Phr. never was -seen, - heard, - known- the like.

Section V. NUMBER

1°. Number, in the Abstract

84. Number.—N. number, symbol, numeral, figure, cipher, digit, integer; counter; round number; formula; function; series.

sum, total, aggregate, difference, complement, subtrahend; product; multipli-cand, -er, -cator; coefficient, multiple; dividend, divisor, factor, quotient, sub-multiple, fraction; mixed number; numerator, denominator; decimal, circulating decimal, repetend; common measure, aliquot part; reciprocal; prime number; totitive, totient.

permutation, combination, variation; election.

ratio, proportion; progression; arithmetical –, geometrical –, harmonical- progression; percentage.

figurate –, pyramidal –, polygonal- numbers.

power, root, exponent, index, logarithm, antilogarithm; modulus.

differential, integral, fluxion, fluent.

Adj. numeral, complementary, divisible, aliquot, reciprocal, prime, fractional, decimal, figurate, incommensurable.

proportional, exponential, logarithmic, logometric, differential, fluxional, integral.

positive, negative; rational, irrational; surd, radical, real, imaginary, impossible.

85. Numeration.—N. numeration; numbering &c. *v.*; pagination; tale, tally, recension, enumeration, summation, reckoning, computation, supputation; calcu-lation, -lus; algorithm, rhabdology, dactylonomy; measurement &c. 466; statistics.

arithmetic, analysis, algebra, fluxions; differential –, integral –, infinitesimal- calculus; calculus of differences.

[Statistics] dead reckoning, muster, poll, census, capitation, roll-call, recapitulation; account &c. (*list*) 86.

[Operations] notation, addition, subtraction, multiplication, division, proportion, rule of three, practice, equations, extraction of roots, reduction, involution, evolution, approximation, interpolation, differentiation, integration.

[Instruments] abacus, swan-pan, logometer, sliding –, slide- rule, tallies, Napier's bones, calculating –, adding- machine, difference engine; cash register.

arithmetician, calculator, abacist; mathematician, actuary, statistician, surveyor, geodesist.

V. number, count, tell; call –, run- over, take an account of, enumerate, call the roll, muster, poll, recite, recapitulate; sum; sum –, cast- up; tell off, score, cipher, compute, calculate, set a price, reckon, – up, estimate; suppute, add, subtract, multiply, divide, extract roots.

check, prove, demonstrate, balance, audit, overhaul, take stock; affix numbers to, page, foliate, paginate.

amount –, come- to.

Adj. numer-al, -ical; arithmetical, analytic, algebraic, statistical, numerable, computable, calculable; commensur-able, -ate; incommensur-able, -ate.

86. List.—N. list, catalogue, enumeration, inventory, schedule; register &c. (*record*) 551; account; bill, – of costs; syllabus; terrier, tally, file; almanac, calendar, index, table, atlas, contents, card index; rota, ticket; book, ledger; synopsis, *catalogue raisonné*; *tableau*; scroll, manifest, invoice, bill of lading; prospectus, *programme*; bill of fare, *menu*, *carte*; score, census, statistics, returns; Red –, Blue –, Domesday- book; *cadastre*; directory, gazetteer, dictionary, glossary, lexicon, thesaurus, gradus.

roll; check –, chequer –, bead- roll, – of honour; muster -roll, – book; roster, panel; cartulary, diptych.

V. list, enrol, schedule, register &c. *n.*; indent, post, docket; matriculate.

Adj. cadastral, listed &c. *v.*

2°. Determinate Number

87. Unity.—N. unity; oneness &c. *adj.*; individuality; solitude &c. (*seclusion*) 893; isolation &c. (*disjunction*) 44; unification &c. 48.

one, unit, ace; item; individual; solo, none else, no other, naught beside.

V. be -one, – alone &c. *adj.*; dine with Duke Humphrey.

isolate &c. (*disjoin*) 44.

render one; unite &c. (*join*) 43, (*combine*) 48.

Adj. one, sole, single, solitary, only-begotten; individual, apart, alone; kithless.

un-accompanied, -attended; *solus*, single-handed; singular, odd, unique, unrepeated, azygous, first and last; isolated &c. (*disjoined*) 44; insular; unitary.

lone; lone-ly, -some; desolate, dreary.

in-secable, -severable, -discerptible; compact, irresolvable.

Adv. singly &c. *adj.*; alone, by itself, *per se*, only, apart, in the singular number, in the abstract; one -by one, – at a time; simply; one and a half, *sesqui-*.

Phr. *natura il fece, e poi roppe la stampa.*

88. Accompaniment.—N. accompaniment; appurtenance, adjunct &c. 39; context.

coexistence, concomitance, company, association, companionship; part-, co-part-nership; coefficiency.

concomitant, accessory, coefficient; companion, attendant, fellow, associate, consort, spouse, colleague, *fidus Achates*; part-, co-part-ner; satellite, hanger on, shadow; escort, *entourage*, suite, *cortège*; convoy, follower &c. 65; attribute.

V. accompany, coexist, attend, convoy, chaperon; hang –, wait- on; go hand in hand with; synchronize &c. 120; bear –, keep- company; row in the same boat; bring in its train, associate –, couple- with.

Adj. accompanying &c. *v.*; concomitant, fellow, twin, joint; associated –, coupled- with; accessory, attendant, *obbligato*.

Adv. with, withal; together –, along –, in company- with; hand in hand, side by side; cheek by -jowl, – jole; arm in arm; there-, here-with; and &c. (*addition*) 37.

together, in a body, collectively.

---

89. Duality.—N. dual-ity, -ism; duplicity; bi-plicity, -formity; span, polarity.

two, deuce, couple, couplet, doublet, brace, pair, cheeks, twins, Castor and Pollux, *gemini*, Siamese twins; fellows; yoke, conjugation, dyad, distich.

V. [unite in pairs] pair, couple, bracket, yoke; conduplicate, mate.

Adj. two, twain; dual, -istic; binary, binomial; twin, biparous; dyadic; conduplicate; duplex &c. 90; *tête-à-tête*; paired; dihedral.

coupled &c. *v.*; conjugate.

both, – the one and the other.

90. Duplication.—N. duplication; doubling &c. *v.*; gemi-, ingemi-nation; reduplication; iteration &c. (*repetition*) 104; renewal.

V. double; re-double, -duplicate; geminate; repeat &c. 104; renew &c. 660; duplicate, copy &c. 21.

Adj. double; doubled &c. *v.*; bicameral, bicapital, bi-fold, -form, -lateral,

91. [Division into two parts.] **Bisection.—N.** bi-section, -partition; di-, subdi-chotomy; halving &c. *v.*; dimidiation; *hendiadys*.

bifurcation, forking, branching, furcation, ramification, divarication; fork, prong; fold.

half, moiety.

V. bisect, halve, divide, split, cut in

-farious, -facial; two-fold, -sided, -headed, -edged &c.; duplex; double-faced; twin, duplicate, ingeminate; second; dual &c. 89.

Adv. twice, once more; over again &c. (*repeatedly*) 104; as much again, twofold.

secondly, in the second place, again.

two, cleave, dimidiate, dichotomize, divaricate.

go halves, divide with.

separate, fork, bifurcate; branch -off, ~ out; ramify.

Adj. bisected &c. *v.*; cloven, cleft; bipartite, biconjugate, bicuspid, bifid; bifur-cous, -cate, -cated; semi-, demi- hemi-.

92. Triality.—**N.** triality, trinity,* triplicity.

three, triad, triplet, trey, trio, ternion, trinomial, leash; tierce; triennium; trefoil, triangle, trident, tripod, triumvirate, *troika.*

third power, cube.

Adj. three; tri-form, -nal, -nomial; tertiary; triune.

93. Triplication.—**N.** tripli-cation, -city; trebleness, trine, trilogy.

V. treble, triple, triplicate, cube.

Adj. treble, triple; tern, -ary; triplex, triplicate, threefold, trilogistic; third; trinal; trihedral.

Adv. three -times, – fold; thrice, in the third place, thirdly; trebly &c. *adj.*

94. [Division into three parts.] **Trisection.** — **N.** tri-section, -partition, -chotomy; third, – part.

V. trisect, divide into three parts, trifurcate.

Adj. trifid; trisected &c. *v.*; tri-partite, -chotomous, -sulcate.

---

95. Quaternity.—**N.** quaternity, four, tetrad, quartet, quaternion, square, quadrature, quarter, quadruplet; quadrilateral, quadrangle, quatrefoil; *quadriga.*

V. reduce to a square, square.

Adj. four; quat-ernary, -ernal; quadratic; quartile, quartic, tetractic, tetrad, tetrahedral; quadrennial; quadrivalent.

96. Quadruplication.—**N.** quadruplication.

V. multiply by four, quadruplicate, biquadrate.

Adj. fourfold; quad-ruple, -ruplicate, -rible; quadruplex; fourth.

Adv. four times; in the fourth place, fourthly.

---

97. [Division into four parts.] **Quadrisection.**—**N.** quadri-section, -partition; quartering &c. *v.*; fourth; quart, -er, -ern; farthing (*i.e.* fourthing); quarto.

V. quarter, divide into four parts, quadrisect.

Adj. quartered &c. *v.*; quadri-fid, -partite.

98. Five, &c.—**N.** five, cinque, quint, quincunx, quintuplet, quintet, pentagon, pentameter, Pentateuch; six, half-a-dozen, sextet, hexagon, hexameter; seven, Heptarchy; eight, octet, octagon, octave; nine, three times three; ten, decade; eleven; twelve, dozen; thirteen; long –, baker's- dozen.

twenty, score; twenty-four, four and twenty, two dozen; twenty-five, five and twenty, quarter of a hundred; forty, two score; fifty, half a hundred; sixty, three score, sexagenarian; seventy, three score and ten, septuagenarian; eighty, four score, octogenarian; ninety, four score and ten, nonagenarian.

99. Quinquesection, &c.—**N.** division by -five &c. 98; quinquesection &c.; fifth &c.; decimation.

V. decimate, quinquesect.

Adj. quinque-fid, -partite; quinquarticular; octifid; decimal, tenth, tithe, teind; duodecimal, twelfth; sexa-gesimal, -genary; hundredth, centesimal; millesimal &c.

---

* *Trinity* is hardly ever used except in a theological sense; *see* Deity 976.

hundred, centenary, hecatomb, century; hundredweight, cwt.; one hundred and forty-four, gross; bicentenary, tercentenary &c.

thousand, chiliad; myriad, millennium, ten thousand; lac, lakh, one hundred thousand, plum; million; thousand million, *milliard*.

billion, trillion &c.

V. centuriate.

Adj. five, quinary, quintuple; fifth; senary, sextuple; sixth; seventh; octuple; eighth; ninefold, ninth; tenfold, decimal, denary, decuple, tenth; eleventh; duo-denary, -denal; twelfth; in one's 'teens, thirteenth.

vices-, viges-imal; twentieth; twenty-fourth &c. *n.*

cent-uple, -uplicate, -ennial, -enary, -urial; secular, hundredth; thousandth; millenary &c.

3°. Indeterminate Number

100. [More than one.] **Plurality.—N.** plurality; a -number, – certain number; one or two, two or three &c.; a few, several; multitude &c. 102.

Adj. plural, more than one, upwards of, some, certain; not -alone &c. 87.

Adv. *et cætera*, &c., etc.

Phr. *non deficit alter.*

100a. [Less than one.] **Fraction.—N.** fraction, fractional part, fragment; part &c. 51.

Adj. fractional, fragmentary, partial.

101. Zero.—N. zero, nothing naught, nought, duck's egg, goose egg; cipher, none, nobody; not a soul; *âme qui vive*; absence &c. 187; unsubstantiality &c. 4.

Adj. not -one, – any.

102. Multitude.—N. multitude; numerousness &c. *adj.*; numer-osity, -ality; multiplicity; profusion &c. (*plenty*) 639; legion, host; great –, large –, round –, enormous- number; a quantity, numbers, array, sight, army, sea, galaxy; scores, peck, bushel, school, shoal, swarm, draft, bevy, cloud, flock, herd, drove, flight, covey, hive, brood, litter, farrow, fry, nest; mob, crowd &c. (*assemblage*) 72; lots, loads, heaps; all the world and his wife.

[Increase of number] greater number, majority; multiplication, multiple.

V. be -numerous &c. *adj.*; swarm –, teem –, crawl –, creep -with; crowd, swarm, come thick upon; outnumber, multiply; people; swarm like -locusts, – bees; be alive with.

Adj. many, several, sundry, divers, various, not a few; a -hundred, – thousand, – myriad, – million, – thousand and one; some -ten or a dozen, – forty or fifty &c.; half a -dozen, – hundred &c.; very –, full –, ever so- many; numer-ous, -ose; profuse, in profusion; manifold, multiplied, multitudinous, multiferous, multiple, multinomial, teeming, crawling, populous, peopled, crowded, thick, studded; galore.

thick coming, many more, more than one can tell, a world of; no end -of, – to; *cum multis aliis*; thick as -hops, – hail; plenty as blackberries; numerous as the -stars in the firmament, – sands on

103. Fewness.—N. fewness &c. *adj.*; paucity, small number; small quantity &c. 32; scarcity, sparsity; rarity; infrequency &c. 137; handful; maniple; minority, exiguity.

[Diminution of number] reduction; weeding &c. *v.*; elimination, sarculation, decimation.

V. be -few &c. *adj.*

render -few &c. *adj.*; reduce, diminish the number, weed, eliminate, thin decimate.

Adj. few; scarce; scant, -y; thin, rare, thinly scattered, few and far between; exiguous; infrequent &c. 137; *rari nantes*; hardly –, scarcely- any; to be counted on one's fingers; reduced &c. *v.*; unrepeated.

Adv. here and there.

the sea-shore, – hairs on the head; and -what not, – heaven knows what; endless &c. (*infinite*) 105.

Phr. their name is 'Legion.'

104. Repetition.—N. repetition, iteration, reiteration, duplication, ding-dong, alliteration; *epistrophe*; harping, recurrence, succession, run; batto-, tauto-logy; monotony, tautophony; rhythm &c. 138; pleonasm, redundancy, diffuseness.

chimes, repetend, echo, *ritornello*, burden of a song, *refrain*; rehearsal; encore; *réchauffé*, *rifacimento*, recapitulation.

cuckoo &c. (*imitation*) 19; reverberation &c. 408; drumming &c. (*roll*) 407; renewal &c. (*restoration*) 660.

twice-told tale; old -story, – song, chestnut; second –, new- edition; reprint, new impression; return game, return match, reappearance, reproduction; periodicity &c. 138.

V. repeat, iterate, reiterate, reproduce, parrot, echo, re-echo, drum, harp upon, battologize, hammer, redouble.

recur, revert, return, reappear; renew &c. (*restore*) 660.

rehearse; do –, say- over again; ring the changes on; harp on the same string; din –, drum- in the ear; conjugate in all its moods, tenses and inflexions, begin again, go over the same ground, go the same round, never hear the last of; resume, return to, recapitulate, reword.

Adj. repeated &c. *v.*; repetition-al, -ary; recur-rent, -ring; ever recurring, thick coming; frequent, incessant, redundant, pleonastic, tautological.

monotonous, harping, iterative; mocking, chiming; retold; aforesaid, -named; above-mentioned, said; habitual &c. 613; another.

Adv. repeatedly, often, again, afresh, anew, over again, once more; ditto, *encore*, *de novo*, *bis*, *da capo*.

again and again; over and over, – again; many times over; time- and again, – after time; year after year; day by day &c.; many –, several –, a number of- times; many –, full many- a time; times out of number, year in and year out, morning, noon and night; frequently &c. 136.

Phr. *ecce iterum Crispinus*, *toujours perdrix*, cut and come again; 'tomorrow and tomorrow.'

105. Infinity.—N. infini-ty, -tude, -teness &c. *adj.*; perpetuity &c. 112.

V. be -infinite &c. *adj.*; know –, have- no -limits, – bounds; go on for ever.

Adj. infinite; immense; number-, count-, sum-, measure-less; innumer-, immeasur-, incalcul-, illimit-, intermin-, unfathom-, unapproach-able; exhaustless, inexhaustible, indefinite; without -number, – measure, – limit, – end; incomprehensible; limit-, end-, bound-, termless; un-told, -numbered, -measured, -bounded, -limited; illimited; perpetual &c. 112.

Adv. infinitely &c. *adj.*; *ad infinitum*.

Section VI. TIME

1°. Absolute Time

106. Time.—N. time, duration; period, term, stage, space, span, spell, season; the whole -time, – period; course &c. 109.

107. Neverness.*—N. 'neverness'; absence of time, no time; *dies non*; Tib's eve; Greek Kalends.

Adv. never; at no -time, – period;

* A term introduced by Bishop Wilkins.

intermediate time, while, *interim*, interval, bit, pendency; inter-vention, -mission, -mittence, -regnum, -lude; respite.

era, epoch, æon, cycle; time of life, age, year, date; decade &c. (*period*) 108; moment, &c. (*instant*) 113; reign &c. 737.

glass –, ravages –, whirligig –, noiseless foot- of time; scythe.

V. continue, last, endure, go on, hold out, remain, stay, persist, abide, run; intervene; elapse &c. 109.

take –, take up –, fill –, occupy- time.

pass –, pass away –, spend –, while away –, consume –, talk against –, kill- time; tide over; use –, employ- time; tarry &c. 110; seize an opportunity &c. 134; waste time &c. (*be inactive*) 683.

Adj. continuing &c. *v.*; on foot; permanent &c. (*durable*) 110.

Adv. while, whilst, during, pending; during the -time, – interval; in the course of; for the time being, day by day; in the time of, when; mean-time, -while; in the -meantime, – *interim*; *ad interim*, *pendente lite*; *de die in diem*; from -day to day, – hour to hour &c.; hourly, always; for a -time, – season; till, until, up to, yet; the whole –, all the- time; all along; throughout &c. (*completely*) 52; for good &c. (*diuturnity*) 110.

here-, there-, where-upon; then; *anno*, – *Domini*; A.D.; *ante Christum*; A.C.; before Christ; B.C.; *anno urbis conditæ*; A.U.C.; *anno regni*; A.R.; once upon a time, one fine morning.

Phr. time -runs, – runs against; *tempus fugit*.

on no occasion, never in all one's born days, nevermore, *sine die*.

---

108. [Definite duration, or portion of time.] **Period.**—**N.** period; second, minute, hour, day, week, sennight, octave, month, moon, quarter, semester, year, *lustrum*, *quinquennium*, decade, *decennium*, indiction, lifetime, generation, epoch, era, cycle.

century, age, *millennium*; *annus magnus*.

Adj. horary; hourly, annual &c. (*periodical*) 138.

108a. Contingent Duration.—**Adv.** during -pleasure, – good behaviour; *quamdiu se bene gesserit*.

---

109. [Indefinite duration.] **Course.**—**N.** course –, progress –, process –, succession –, lapse –, flow –, flux –, effluxion, stream –, tract –, current –, sweep –, tide –, march –, step –, flight- of time; duration &c. 106.

[Indefinite time] aorist.

V. elapse, lapse, flow, run, proceed, advance, pass; roll –, wear –, press –, drag- on; flit, fly, slip, slide, glide, crawl; run -its course.

out; expire; go –, pass- by; be -past &c. 122.

Adj. elapsing &c. *v.*; aoristic; progressive, transient &c. 111.

Adv. in due -time, – season; in -course, – process, – the fulness- of time; in time.

Phr. *labitur et labetur*; *truditur dies die*; *fugaces labuntur anni*; 'tomorrow and tomorrow and tomorrow creeps in this petty pace from day to day.'

110. [Long duration.] **Diuturnity.**—**N.** diuturnity; a -long –, length of- time; an age, a century, an eternity,

111. [Short duration.] **Transientness.**—**N.** transientness &c. *adj.*; evanescence, impermanence, fugacity, transi-

æons; slowness &c. 275; perpetuity &c. 112; blue moon.

dura-bleness, -bility; persistence, lastingness &c. *adj.*; continuance, assiduity, endurance, standing; permanence &c. (*stability*) 150; survi-val, -vance; longevity &c. (*age*) 128; distance of time.

protraction –, prolongation –, extension- of time; delay &c. (*lateness*) 133.

V. last, endure, stand, remain, abide, continue, brave a thousand years.

tarry &c. (*be late*) 133; drag -on, – its slow length along, – a lengthening chain; protract, prolong; spin –, eke –, draw –, lengthen- out; temporize; gain –, make –, talk against- time.

out-last, -live; survive; live to fight again.

Adj. durable; perdurable; lasting &c. *v.*; of long -duration, – standing; permanent, chronic, long-standing; intransi-ent, -tive; intransmutable, persistent; life-, live-long; longeval, long-lived, macrobiotic, diuturnal, sempervirent, evergreen, perennial; unin-, ter-, unre-mitting; perpetual &c. 112.

lingering, protracted, prolonged, spun out &c. *v.*; long-pending, -winded; slow &c. 275.

Adv. long; for -a long time, – an age, – ages, – ever so long, – many a long day; long ago &c. (*in a past time*) 122; *longo intervallo.*

all the -day long, – year round; the livelong day, as the day is long, morning, noon and night; hour after hour, day after day, &c.; for good; permanently &c. *adj.*

112. [Endless duration.] **Perpetuity.** —**N.** perpetuity, eternity, timelessness; everness,* aye, sempiternity, immortality, athanasia; everlastingness &c. *adj.*; perpetuation; infinite duration.

V. last –, endure –, go on- for ever; have no end.

eternize, eternify, perpetuate, immortalize.

Adj. perpetual, eternal, eterne; everlasting, -living, -flowing; continual, constant, sempiternal; co-eternal; endless, unending; ceaseless, incessant, uninterrupted, indesinent, unceasing; interminable, having no end; unfadtoriness, volatility, caducity, mortality, span; flash in the pan, nine days' wonder, bubble, May-fly; spurt; temporary arrangement, interregnum.

velocity &c. 274; suddenness &c. 113; changeableness &c. 149.

V. be -transient &c. *adj.*; flit, pass away, fly, gallop, vanish, fade, fleet, melt away, evaporate; pass away like a -cloud, – summer cloud, – shadow, – dream.

Adj. transi-ent, -tory, -tive; passing, evanescent, fleeting; flying &c. *v.*; fug-acious, -itive; shifting, slippery; spasmodic.

tempor-al, -ary; provis-ional, -ory; cursory, short-lived, ephemeral, deciduous; perishable, mortal, precarious; impermanent.

brief, quick, brisk; cometary, meteoric, extemporaneous, summary; pressed for time &c. (*haste*) 684; sudden, momentary &c. (*instantaneous*) 113.

Adv. temporarily &c. *adj.*; *pro tempore*; for -the moment, – a time; awhile, *en passant, in transitu*; in a short time; soon &c. (*early*) 132; briefly &c. *adj.*; at short notice; on the -point, – eve -of; *in articulo*; between cup and lip.

Phr. one's days are numbered; the time is up; here to-day and gone to-morrow; *non semper erit æstas; eheu! fugaces labuntur anni; sic transit gloria mundi.*

---

113. [Point of time.] **Instantaneity.** —**N.** instantane-ity, -ousness; sudden-, abrupt-ness.

moment, instant, second, minute; twinkling, trice, flash, breath, crack, jiffy, *coup*, burst, flash of lightning, stroke of time.

epoch, time; time of -day, – night; hour, minute; very -minute &c., – time, – hour; present –, right –, true –, exact –, correct- time.

V. be -instantaneous &c. *adj.*; twinkle, flash.

Adj. instantaneous, momentary, extempore, sudden, instant, abrupt;

* Bishop Wilkins.

ing, evergreen, amaranthine; never-ending, -dying, -fading; deathless, immortal, undying, imperishable.

Adv. perpetually &c. *adj.*; always, ever, evermore, aye; for -ever, – aye, – evermore, – ever and a day, – ever and ever; in all ages, from age to age; without end; world –, time- without end; *in sæcula sæculorum*; to the -end of time, – crack of doom, – 'last syllable of recorded time'; till doomsday; constantly &c. (*very frequently*) 136.

Phr. *esto perpetua!; labitur et labetur in omne volubilis ævum.*

---

subitaneous, hasty; quick as -thought,* – lightning, – a flash; rapid as electricity.

Adv. instantaneously &c. *adj.*; in –, in less than- no time; *presto, subito, instanter*, suddenly, at a stroke, like- a shot, – greased lightning; in a trice, in a moment &c. *n.*; eftsoons, in the twinkling of -an eye, – a bed post; at one jump, in the same breath, *per saltum, uno saltu*; at –, all at- once; in one's tracks; plump, slap; 'at one fell swoop'; at the same -instant &c. *n.*; immediately &c. (*early*) 132; extempore, on the -spot, – spur of the moment, – dot; just then; slap- dash &c. (*haste*) 684; before you could -turn round, – say -knife, – Jack Robinson.

Phr. touch and go; no sooner said than done.

114. [Estimation, measurement, and record of time.] **Chronometry.—N.** chrono-, horo-metry, -logy; date, epoch; style, era, age.

almanac, calendar, ephemeris; register, -try; chronicle, annals, journal, diary, chronogram.

[Instruments for the measurement of time] clock, watch; chrono-meter, -scope, -graph; repeater, alarum; time-keeper, -piece; dial, sun-dial, *gnomon, pendule*, horologe, pendulum, hour-glass, water clock, clepsydra.

mean –, Greenwich –, solar –, sidereal –, local –, summer- time; daylight saving.

chrono-grapher, -loger, -logist; annalist.

V. fix –, mark- the time; date, register, chronicle; measure –, beat –, mark- time; bear date.

Adj. chrono-logical, -metrical, -grammatical; isochronal.

Adv. o'clock; *a.m., p.m.*

115. [False estimate of time.] **Anachronism.—N.** ana-, meta-, para-, prochronism; *prolepsis*, misdate; anticipation, antichronism.

disregard –, neglect –, oblivion- of time.

intempestivity &c. 135.

V. mis-, ante-, post-, over-date; anticipate; take no note of time.

Adj. misdated &c. *v.*; undated; overdue; out of date; anachronous &c. *n.*

2°. Relative Time

1. *Time with reference to Succession*

116. Priority.—N. priority, antecedence, anteriority, pre-existence, precedence &c. 62; precession &c. 280; precursor &c. 64; the past &c. 122; premises.

V. precede, come before; forerun; antecede, go before &c. (*lead*) 280; pre-exist; dawn; premise, presage &c. 511.

be -beforehand &c. (*be early*) 132;

117. Posteriority.—N. posteriority; succession, sequence; following &c. 281; subsequence, supervention; futurity &c. 121; successor; sequel &c. 65; remainder, reversion.

V. follow &c. 281 –, come –, go- after; ensue, result; succeed, supervene; step into the shoes of.

Adj. subsequent, posterior, following, after, later, succeeding, postliminious,

* See note on 264.

steal a march upon, anticipate, forestall; have –, gain- the start.

Adj. prior, previous; preced-ing, -ent; anterior, antecedent; pre-existing, -existent; foresighted; former, foregoing; afore –, before-, above-mentioned; aforesaid, said; introductory &c. (*precursory*) 64; pre-war.

Adv. before, prior to; earlier; previously &c. *adj.*; afore, ere, theretofore, erewhile; ere –, before- -then, – now; erewhile, already, yet, beforehand; aforetime, on the eve of, in anticipation.

postnate; successive &c. 63; postdiluvial, -an; *puisné*; posthumous; post-war, future &c. 121.

Adv. subsequently, after, afterwards, since, later; at a -subsequent, – later- period; next, in the sequel, close upon, thereafter, thereupon, upon which, eftsoons; from that -time, – moment; after a -while, – time; in process of time.

postcenal, postcibal, postprandial, after-dinner.

118. The Present Time.—N. the present -time, – day, – moment, – juncture, – occasion; the times, existing time, time being; twentieth century; nonce, crisis, epoch, day, hour.

age, time of life.

Adj. present, actual, instant, current, latest, existing, that is.

Adv. at this -time, – moment &c. 113; at the -present time &c. *n.*; now, at present.

at this time of day, to-day, now-a-days; already; even –, but –, just-now; on the present occasion; for the -time being, – nonce; *pro hâc vice*; on the -nail, – spot; on the spur of the -moment, – occasion.

until now; to -this, – the present day.

119. [Time different from the present.] **Different Time.—N.** different –, other- time.

[Indefinite time] aorist.

Adj. aoristic.

Adv. at that –, at which- -time, – moment, – instant; then, on that occasion, upon.

when; when-ever, -soever; upon which, on which occasion; at -another, – a different, – some other, – any- time; at various times; some –, one- -of these days, – fine morning, – day; sooner or later; some time or other; once upon a time, once.

120. Synchronism.—N. synchronism; coexistence, coincidence; simultaneousness &c. *adj.*; concurrence, concomitance, unity of time, interim.

[Having equal times] isochronism, syntony.

contemporary, coetanian.

V. coexist, concur, accompany, go hand in hand, keep pace with; synchronize, isochronize.

Adj. synchron-ous, -al, -ical, -istical; simultaneous, coexisting, coincident, concomitant, concurrent; coev-al, -ous; contempora-ry, -neous; coetaneous; coterminous, coeternal; isochronous.

Adv. at the same time; simultaneously &c. *adj.*; together, in concert, during the same time; in the same breath; *pari passu*; in the interim.

at the -very moment &c. 113; just as, as soon as; meanwhile &c. (*while*) 106.

121. [Prospective time.] **Futurity. —N.** futur-ity, -ition; future, hereafter, time to come; approaching –, coming –, after- -time, – age, – days, – hours, – years, – ages, – life; morrow, to-morrow, by and by; millennium, doomsday, day of judgment, crack of doom, remote future.

122. [Retrospective time.] **Preterition.—N.** preterition; priority &c. 116; the past, past time; days –, times- -of yore, – of old, – past, – gone by; bygone days, good old days; old –, ancient –, former -times; fore time; yesterdays; the olden –, good old-time; auld lang syne; eld.

approach of time, advent, time drawing on, womb of time; destiny &c. 152; eventuality.

heritage, heirs, posterity, descendants.

prospect &c. (*expectation*) 507; foresight &c. 510.

V. look forwards; anticipate &c. (*expect*) 507, (*foresee*) 510; forestall &c. (*be early*) 132.

come –, draw- on; draw near; approach, await, threaten; impend &c. (*be destined*) 152.

Adj. future, to come; coming &c. (*impending*) 152; next, near; near –, close- at hand; eventual, ulterior; expectant, prospective, in prospect &c. (*expectation*) 507.

Adv. prospectively, hereafter, on the knees of the gods, in future; to-morrow, the day after to-morrow; in -course, – process, – the fulness- of time; eventually, ultimately, sooner or later; *proximo*; *paulo post futurum*; in after time; one of these days; after a -time, – while.

from this time; hence-forth, -forwards; thence; thence-forth, -forward; whereupon, upon which.

soon &c. (*early*) 132; on the -eve, – point, – brink- of; about to; close upon.

---

antiquity, antiqueness, *status quo*; time immemorial; distance of time; remote -age, – time; ancient history; remote past; rust of antiquity; ancientness.

pale-ontology, -ography, -ology; palætiology,* archæology; archaism, antiquarianism, mediævalism, pre-Raphaelitism; retrospection, looking back, memory &c. 505.

laudator temporis acti; mediævalist, pre-Raphaelite; antiqu-ary, -arian; archæologist &c.; Oldbuck, Dryasdust.

ancestry &c. (*paternity*) 166.

V. be -past &c. *adj.*; have -expired &c. *adj.*, – run its course, – had its day; pass; pass –, go- -by, – away, – off; lapse, blow over.

look –, trace –, cast the eyes- back; exhume.

Adj. past, gone, gone by, over, passed away, bygone, foregone; elapsed, lapsed, preterlapsed, expired, no more, run out, blown over, that has been, whilom, extinct, never to return, exploded, forgotten, irrecoverable; obsolete &c. (*old*) 124; extinct as the dodo.

former, pristine, *quondam*, *ci-devant*, late; ancestral.

foregoing; last, latter; recent, overnight; past, preterite, preter-perfect, -pluperfect, past perfect.

looking back &c. *v.*; retro-spective, -active; archæological &c. *n.*

Adv. formerly; of -old, – yore; erst, whilom, erewhile, time was, ago, over; in -the olden time &c. *n.*; anciently, long -ago, – since; a long -while, – time- ago; years –, ages- ago; some time -ago, – since, – back.

yesterday, the day before yesterday; last -year, – season, – month &c.; *ultimo*; lately &c. (*newly*) 123.

retrospectively; ere –, before –, till- now; hitherto, heretofore; no longer; once, – upon a time; from time immemorial; in the memory of man; time out of mind; already, yet, up to this time; *ex post facto*.

Phr. time was; the time -has, – hath- been.

2. *Time with reference to a particular Period*

123. Newness.—N. newness &c. *adj.*; neologism, neoterism; novelty, recency; immaturity; youth &c. 127; gloss of novelty.

124. Oldness.—N. oldness &c. *adj.*; age, antiquity; cobwebs of antiquity.

maturity, ripeness; decline, decay; senility &c. 128.

* Whewell.

innovation; renovation &c. (*restoration*) 660.

modernist, neologist, neoteric.

modernism, modernity; mushroom; latest fashion, *dernier cri.*

upstart, *parvenu, nouveau riche.*

V. renew &c. (*restore*) 660; modernize.

Adj. new, novel, recent, fresh, green; young &c. 127; evergreen; raw, immature; virgin; un-tried, -handseled, -used, -trodden, -beaten; fledgling.

late, modern, neoteric; new-born, -fashioned, -fangled, -fledged; of yesterday; just out, brand –, span-new, up to date, topical; vernal, renovated; innovatory.

fresh as -a rose, – a daisy, – paint; spick and span.

Adv. newly &c. *adj.*; afresh, anew, lately, just now, only yesterday, the other day; latterly, of late.

not long –, a short time- ago.

---

seniority, eldership, primogeniture.

archaism &c. (*the past*) 122; thing –, relic- of the past; megatherium.

tradition, prescription, custom, folklore, immemorial usage, common law.

V. be -old &c. *adj.*; have -had, – seen- its day; become -old &c. *adj.*; age, fade.

Adj. old, olden, ancient, antique; of long standing, time-honoured, venerable; eld-er, -est; first-born.

prime; prim-itive, -eval, -igenous; primordi-al, -nate; aboriginal &c. (*beginning*) 66; diluvian, antediluvian; pre-historic; patriarchal, preadamite; palæocrystic; fossil, paleozoic, preglacial, ante-mundane; archaic, classic, mediæval, pre-Raphaelite, ancestral, black-letter.

immemorial, traditional, prescriptive, customary, whereof the memory of man runneth not to the contrary; inveterate, rooted.

antiquated, of other times, rococo, of the old school, after-age, obsolete; fusty, moth-eaten; out of -date, – fashion; stale, old-fashioned, behind the -age, – times; exploded; gone out, – by; *passé*, outworn, run out; disused; senile &c. 128; time-worn; crumbling &c. (*deteriorated*) 659; second-hand.

old as -the hills, – Methuselah, – Adam, – history; Anno Domini.

Adv. since the -world was made, – year one, – days of Methuselah.

125. Morning. [Noon.]—**N.** morning, morn, matins, forenoon, *a.m.*, prime, dawn, daybreak, daylight, sun-up, peep –, break- of day; aurora, Eos; first blush –, prime- of the morning; twilight, crepuscule, sunrise, cockcrow.

spring; vernal equinox.

noon; mid-, noon-day; noontide, meridian, prime.

summer, midsummer; summer solstice.

Adj. matin, matutinal; vernal, æstival.

Adv. at -sunrise &c. *n.*; with the lark, when the morning dawns.

126. Evening. [Midnight.]—**N.** evening, eve; decline –, fall –, close- of day; eventide, evensong, vespers; candlelight; nightfall, curfew, dusk, twilight, blind man's holiday; eleventh hour; sun-set, -down; going down of the sun, cock-shut, dewy eve, gloaming, bed-time.

afternoon, *post meridiem, p.m.*

autumn; fall, – of the leaf; autumnal equinox, Indian summer, harvest-time.

midnight; dead –, witching time- of night; winter, – solstice.

Adj. vespertine, autumnal, nocturnal, wintry, brumal, hiemal.

127. Youth.—**N.** youth; juven- -ility, -escence; juniority; infancy; baby-, child-, boy-, girl-, youth-hood; *incunabula*; minority, immaturity, nonage, teens, tender age, bloom.

cradle, nursery, leading-strings, pupilage, puberty, *pucelage.*

128. Age.—**N.** age; oldness &c. *adj.*; old –, advanced- age; sen-ility, -escence; years, anility, grey hairs, climacteric, grand climacteric, declining years, decrepitude, hoary age, caducity, superannuation; second childhood, -ishness; dotage; vale of years,

prime –, flower –, spring-tide –, seed-time –, golden season- of life; heyday of youth, school days; rising generation, younger generation.

Adj. young, youthful, juvenile, green, callow, budding, sappy, *puisné*, beardless, unfledged, unripe, under age, in one's teens; *in statu pupillari*; younger, junior.

---

decline of life, 'sear and yellow leaf'; three-score years and ten; green old age, ripe old age; longevity; time of life.

seniority, eldership; elders &c. (*veteran*) 130; firstling; *doyen*, dean, father; primogeniture; nostology.

V. be -aged &c. *adj.*; grow –, get-old &c. *adj.*; age; decline, wane.

Adj. aged; old &c. 124; elderly, senile; matronly, anile; in years; ripe, mellow, run to seed, declining, waning, past one's prime; grey, -headed; hoar, -y; venerable, time-worn, antiquated, *passé*, effete, doddering, decrepit, superannuated; advanced in -life, – years; stricken in years; wrinkled, marked with the crow's foot; having one foot in the grave; doting &c. (*imbecile*) 499.

old-, eld-er, -est; senior; first-born.

turned of, years old; of a certain age, no chicken, old as Methuselah; gerontic; ancestral; patriarchal &c. (*ancient*) 124.

129. Infant.—**N.** infant, babe, baby; nurse-, suck-, year-, wean-ling; *papoose*, *bambino*.

child, bairn, little- one, – tot, – mite, chick, brat, chit, pickaninny, kid, urchin; bant-, brat-ling; elf.

youth, boy, lad, slip, sprig, stripling, youngster, cub, unlicked cub, younker, callant, whipster, whipper-snapper, schoolboy, hobbledehoy, hopeful, cadet, minor, master.

scion; sap-, seed-ling; tendril, olive-branch, nestling, chicken, duckling; larva, caterpillar, chrysalis, cocoon; tadpole, whelp, cub, pullet, fry, callow; codlin, -g; *fœtus*, calf, colt, pup, foal, kitten; lamb, -kin.

girl; lass, -ie; wench, miss, damsel, *demoiselle*, damozel; maid, -en; virgin; nymph; colleen; minx, baggage, school-girl; tomboy, flapper, hoyden.

Adj. infant-ine, -ile; puerile; boy-, girl-, child-, baby-, kitten-ish; baby; new-born, unfledged, new-fledged, callow.

in -the cradle, – swaddling clothes, – long clothes, – arms, – leading strings; at the breast; in one's teens; young &c. 127.

130. Veteran.—**N.** veteran, old man, seer, patriarch, greybeard, dugout, grand-father, -sire; grandam, beldam; gaffer, gammer; hag, crone; pantaloon; sexage-, octoge-, nonage-, cente-narian; old stager; dotard &c. 501.

preadamite, Methuselah, Nestor, Rip van Winkle, old Parr; elders; forefathers &c. (*paternity*) 166.

---

131. Adolescence.—**N.** adolescence, pubescence, majority; adultness &c. *adj.*; manhood, virility, maturity; flower of age; prime –, meridian- of life.

man &c. 373; woman &c. 374; adult, no chicken.

V. come -of age, – to man's estate, – to years of discretion; attain majority, assume the *toga virilis*; have -cut one's eye-teeth, – sown one's wild oats, settle down.

Adj. adolescent, pubescent, of age; of -full, – ripe- age; out of one's teens, grown up, mature, full- blown, – grown, in one's prime, in full bloom, manly, virile, adult; womanly, matronly; marriageable, nubile.

3. *Time with reference to an Effect or Purpose*

132. Earliness.—N. earliness &c. *adj.*; morning &c. 125.

punctuality; promptitude &c. (*activity*) 682; haste &c. (*velocity*) 274; suddenness &c. (*instantaneity*) 113.

prematurity, precocity, precipitation, anticipation; prevenience, a stitch in time.

V. be -early &c. *adj.*, – beforehand &c. *adv.*; keep time, take time by the forelock, anticipate, forestall; have –, gain- the start; steal a march upon; gain time, draw on futurity; bespeak, secure, engage, pre-engage.

accelerate; expedite &c. (*quicken*) 274; make haste &c. (*hurry*) 684.

Adj. early, prime, timely, in time, punctual, forward; prompt &c. (*active*) 682; summary.

premature, precipitate, precocious; prevenient, anticipatory; rathe.

sudden &c. (*instantaneous*) 113; unexpected &c. 508; impending, imminent; near, – at hand; immediate.

Adv. early, soon, anon, betimes, rathe; eft, -soons; ere –, before- long; punctually &c. *adj.*; to the minute; in time; in -good, – military, – pudding, – due- time; time enough.

beforehand; prematurely &c. *adj.*; precipitately &c. (*hastily*) 684; too soon; before -its, – one's- time; in anticipation; unexpectedly &c. 508.

suddenly &c. (*instantaneously*) 113; before one can say 'Jack Robinson,' at short notice, extempore; on the spur of the -moment, – occasion; at once; on the -spot, – instant; at sight; off –, out of- hand; *à vue d'œil*; straight, -way, -forth; forthwith, incontinently, summarily, instanter, immediately, briefly, shortly, quickly, speedily, apace, before the ink is dry, almost immediately, presently, at the first opportunity, in no long time, by and by, in a while, directly.

Phr. touch and go, no sooner said than done.

133. Lateness.—N. lateness &c. *adj.*; tardiness &c. (*slowness*) 275.

de-lay, -lation; cunctation, procrastination; detention; deferring &c. *v.*; filibuster, postponement, adjournment, prorogation, retardation, respite, reprieve, stay; protraction, prolongation, moratorium; contango; demurrage; remand; Fabian policy, *médecine expectante*, chancery suit; leeway; high time.

V. be -late &c. *adj.*; tarry, wait, stay, bide, take time; dawdle &c. (*be inactive*) 683; linger, loiter, saunter, lag behind; bide –, take- one's time; hang -about, – around, – back, – in the balance; gain time; hang fire; stand –, lie-over.

put off, defer, delay, lay over, suspend; shift –, stave- off; waive, retard, remand, postpone, adjourn; procrastinate; dally; prolong, protract; spin –, draw –, lengthen- out; prorogue; keep back; tide over; push –, drive- to the last; let the matter stand over; reserve &c. (*store*) 636; temporize; consult one's pillow, sleep upon it.

shelve, table, lay on the table.

lose an opportunity &c. 135; be kept waiting, dance attendance; kick –, cool- one's heels; *faire antichambre*; wait impatiently; await &c. (*expect*) 507; sit up, – at night.

Adj. late, tardy, slow, behindhand, belated, postliminious, posthumous, backward, unpunctual; dilatory &c. (*slow*), overdue 275; delayed &c. *v.*; in abeyance.

Adv. late; late-, back-ward; late in the day; at -sunset, – the eleventh hour, – length, – last, – long; ultimately; after –, behind- time; too late; too late for &c. 135.

slowly, leisurely, deliberately, at one's leisure; *ex post facto*; *sine die*.

Phr. *nonum prematur in annum*.

---

134. Occasion.—N. occasion, opportunity, opening, room, scope, field; suitable –, proper- -time, – season; high time; opportuneness &c. *adj.*; tempestivity.

135. Intempestivity.—N. intempestivity; unseasonableness; unsuitable –, improper-time; unreasonableness &c. *adj.*; evil hour; *contretemps*; intrusion; anachronism &c. 115.

crisis, turn, juncture, emergency, conjuncture; turning point, given time.

nick of time; golden –, well-timed –, fine –, favourable- opportunity; clear stage, fair field; *mollia tempora*; *fata Morgana*; spare time &c. (*leisure*) 685.

V. seize &c. (*take*) 789 –, use &c. 677 –, give &c. 784- an -opportunity, – occasion; improve the occasion.

suit the occasion &c. (*be expedient*) 646.

strike the iron while it is hot, *battre le fer sur l'enclume*, make hay while the sun shines, take time by the forelock, *prendre la balle au bond*.

Adj. opportune, timely, well-timed, timeous, timeful, seasonable.

providential, lucky, fortunate, happy, favourable, propitious, auspicious, critical; suitable &c. 23; *obiter dicta*.

Adv. opportunely &c. *adj.*; in -proper, – due- -time, – course, – season; for the nonce; in the -nick, – fulness- of time; all in good time; just in time, at the eleventh hour, now or never.

by the -way, – by; *en passant*, *à propos*; *pro -re natâ*, – *hac vice*; *par parenthèse*, parenthetically, by way of parenthesis; while -speaking of, – on this subject; extempore; on the spur of the -moment, – occasion; on the spot &c. (*early*) 132.

Phr. *carpe diem*; *occasionem cognosce*; one's hour is come, the time is up; that reminds me.

V. be -ill timed &c. *adj.*; mistime, intrude, come amiss, break in upon; have other fish to fry; be -busy, – engaged, – tied up, – occupied.

lose –, throw away –, waste –, neglect &c. 460- an opportunity; allow –, suffer- the -opportunity, – occasion- to -pass, – slip, – go by, – escape, – lapse; waste time &c. (*be inactive*) 683; let slip through the fingers, lock the stable door when the steed is stolen.

Adj. ill-, mis-timed; untimely, intrusive, unseasonable; out of -date, – season; inopportune, timeless, untoward, *mal à propos*, unlucky, inauspicious, unpropitious, unfortunate, unfavourable; unsuited &c. 24; inexpedient &c. 647.

unpunctual &c. (*late*) 133; too late for; premature &c. (*early*) 132; too soon for; wise after the event.

Adv. inopportunely &c. *adj.*; as ill luck would have it, in an evil hour, the time having gone by, a day after the fair.

Phr. after meat mustard, after death the doctor.

3°. Recurrent Time

136. Frequency.—**N.** frequency, oftness; repetition, &c. 104.

V. recur &c. 104; do nothing but; keep, – on.

Adj. frequent, many times, not rare, thickcoming, incessant, perpetual, continual, constant, recurrent, repeated &c. 104; habitual &c. 613; hourly, &c. 138.

Adv. often, often to be met with, oft; oft-, often-times; frequently; repeatedly &c. 104; unseldom, not unfrequently; in -quick, – rapid- succession; many a time and oft; daily, hourly &c.; every -day, – hour, – moment &c.

perpetually, continually, constantly, incessantly, without ceasing, at all times, daily and hourly, night and day,

137. Infrequency.—**N.** infrequency, infrequence, rareness, rarity; fewness &c. 103; seldomness, uncommonness.

V. be -rare &c. *adj.*

Adj. un-, in-frequent; uncommon, sporadic, rare, – as a blue diamond; few &c. 103; scarce; almost unheard of, unprecedented, which has not occurred within the memory of the oldest inhabitant, not within one's previous experience.

Adv. seldom, rarely, scarcely, hardly; not often, unfrequently, infrequently, unoften; scarcely –, hardly- ever; once in a blue moon.

once; once -for all, – in a way; *pro hac vice*; like angels' visits, few and far between.

---

day and night, day after day, morning noon and night, ever and anon.

most often; commonly &c. (*habitually*) 613.

sometimes, occasionally, at times, now and then, from time to time, there being times when, *toties quoties*, often enough, again and again &c. 104.

138. Regularity of recurrence. Periodicity.—N. periodicity, intermittence; beat; oscillation &c. 314; pulse, pulsation; rhythm; alter-nation, -nateness, -nativeness, -nity.

bout, round, revolution, rotation, turn.

anniversary, birthday, jubilee, centenary, bi-, ter-centenary.

[Regularity of return] rota, cycle, period, stated time, routine; days of the week; Sunday, Monday &c.; months of the year; January &c.; feast, fast, saint's day &c.; Christmas, Easter, New Year's Day &c. 998; quarter-, Lady-, Midsummer-, Michaelmas-day; May Day, the King's Birthday; leap year; seasons.

punctuality, regularity, steadiness.

V. recur in regular -order, – succession; return, revolve, rotate; come -again, – in its turn; come round, – again; beat, pulsate; alternate; intermit.

Adj. periodic, -al; serial, recurrent, cyclic-, -al, rhythmic-, -al, even; recurring &c. *v.*; inter-, re-mittent; alternate, every other.

hourly; diurnal, daily; quotidian, tertian, weekly; hebdomad-al, -ary; bi-weekly, fortnightly; monthly, menstrual, catamenial; yearly, annual; biennial, triennial, &c.; bissextile; centennial, secular; paschal, lenten, &c.

regular, steady, punctual, constant, methodical, regular as clockwork.

Adv. periodically &c. *adj.*; at -regular intervals, – stated times; at -fixed, – established- periods; punctually &c. *adj.*; *de die in diem*; from day to day, day by day.

by turns; in -turn, – rotation; alternately, every other day, off and on, ride and tie, round and round.

139. Irregularity of recurrence.—N. irregularity, uncertainty, unpunctuality; fitfulness &c. *adj*.

Adj. irregular, uneven, uncertain, unpunctual, capricious, erratic, desultory, fitful, flickering; rambling, rhapsodical; spasmodic, unsystematic, unequal, variable, halting.

Adv. irregularly &c. *adj.*; by fits and starts &c. (*discontinuously*) 70.

Section VII. CHANGE

1°. Simple Change

140. [Difference at different times.] Change.—N. change, alteration, mutation, permutation, variation, modification, modulation, inflexion, mood, qualification, innovation, *metastasis*, deviation, shift, turn; diversion; break.

transformation, transfiguration; metamorphosis; metabolism; transmutation; transubstantiation; metagenesis, transanimation, transmigration, me-

141. [Absence of change.] Permanence.—N. stability &c. 150; quiescence &c. 265; obstinacy &c. 606.

permanence, -cy, persistence, fixity, fixity of purpose, endurance, durability; standing, *status quo*; maintenance, preservation, conservation; conservatism; *laissez-faire*; law of the Medes and Persians; standing dish.

V. let -alone, – be; persist, remain,

tempsychosis; **version**; metathesis; transmogrification; catalysis; *avatar*; alterative.

conversion &c. (*gradual change*) 144; revolution &c. (*sudden or radical change*) 146; inversion &c. (*reversal*) 218; displacement &c. 185; transference &c. 270.

changeableness &c. 149; tergiversation &c. (*change of mind*) 607.

V. change, alter, vary, wax and wane; modulate, diversify, qualify, tamper with; turn, shift, veer, jibe, tack, chop, shuffle, swerve, dodge, warp, deviate, turn aside, evert, intervert; pass to, take a turn, turn the corner, resume.

work a change, modify, vamp, revamp, superinduce; trans-form, -mute, -ume, -figure &c. *n.*; metamorphose, ring the changes; convert, resolve; revolutionize; chop and change; patch, re-shape.

innovate, introduce new blood, shuffle the cards, spin the wheel; give a -turn, – colour- to; influence, turn the scale; shift the scene, turn over a new leaf.

recast &c. 146; reverse &c. 218; disturb &c. 61; convert into &c. 144.

Adj. changed &c. *v.*; new-fangled; changeable &c. 149; transitional; modifiable; alterative.

Adv. *mutatis mutandis.*

Int. *quantum mutatus!*

Phr. 'a change came o'er the spirit of my dream'; *nous avons changé tout cela*; *tempora mutantur et nos mutamur in illis*; *non sum qualis eram.*

stay, tarry, rest; hold, – on; last, endure, bide, abide, aby, dwell, maintain, keep; stand, – still, – fast; subsist, live, outlive, survive; hold –, keep- one's -ground, – footing; hold good.

Adj. stable &c. 150; persisting &c. *v.*; permanent; established, fixed; durable; unchanged &c. (change &c. 140); unrenewed; intact, inviolate; persistent; monotonous, uncheckered; unfailing.

un-destroyed, -repealed, -suppressed; conservative, *qualis ab incepto*; prescriptive &c. (*old*) 124; stationary &c. 265.

Adv. *in statu quo*; for good, finally; at a stand, -still; *uti possidetis*; without a shadow of turning.

Phr. as you were!; *j'y suis j'y reste*; *esto perpetua*; *nolumus leges Angliæ mutari*; let sleeping dogs lie.

---

142. [Change from action to rest.] **Cessation.—N.** cessation, discontinuance, desistance, desinence.

inter-, re-mission; sus-pense, -pension; interruption, hitch; hartal; stop; stopping &c. *v.*; closure, stoppage, halt; arrival &c. 292.

pause, rest, lull, respite, truce, armistice, drop; interregnum, abeyance.

closure &c. 261.

dead -stop, – stand, – lock; checkmate; comma, colon, semicolon, period, full stop; end &c. 67; death &c. 360; *cæsura.*

V. cease, discontinue, desist, stay; break –, leave- off; hold, stop, pull up, stall, stop short, check; stick, deadlock, hang fire; halt; pause, rest.

have done with, give over, surcease,

143. Continuance in action.—N. continu-ance, -ation; run; extension, prolongation; maintenance, perpetuation; persistence &c. (*perseverance*) 604*a*; repetition &c. 104.

V. continue, persist; go –, jog –, keep –, carry –, run – hold- on; abide, keep, pursue, stick to; endure; take –, maintain- its course; keep up.

sustain, uphold, hold up, keep on foot; follow up, perpetuate, prolong; maintain; preserve &c. 604*a*; harp upon &c. (*repeat*) 104.

keep -going, – alive, – at it, – the pot boiling, – the ball rolling, – up the ball; plod-, plug- along; slog on; die in harness; hold on –, pursue- the even tenor of one's way.

let be; *stare super antiquas vias*;

shut up shop; give up &c. (*relinquish*) 624.

hold –, stay- one's hand; rest on one's oars, repose on one's laurels.

come to a -stand, – standstill, – dead lock, – full stop; arrive &c. 292; go out, die away, peter out; wear -away, – off; pass away &c. (*be past*) 122; be at an end.

intromit, interrupt, suspend, interpel; inter-, re-mit; put -an end, – a stop, – a period- to; bring to a stand, -still; stop, cut out, cut short, arrest, avast; stem the -tide, – torrent; pull the check string; switch off.

Int. halt! hold! stop! enough! avast! have done! a truce to! soft! leave off! shut up! give over! chuck it!

quieta non movere; let things take their course.

Adj. continuing &c. *v.*; uninterrupted, unintermitting, unremitting, unvarying, unshifting; unreversed, unstopped, unrevoked, unvaried; sustained; undying &c. (*perpetual*) 112; inconvertible.

follow-up.

Int. carry on! right away!

Phr. *vestigia nulla retrorsum*; *labitur et labetur*.

---

144. [Gradual change to something different.] **Conversion.—N.** conversion, reduction, transmutation, transformation, development, resolution, assimilation; assumption; naturalization.

chemistry, alchemy; progress, growth, lapse, flux.

passage; transit, -ion; transmigration, shifting &c. *v.*; conjugation; convertibility.

crucible, alembic, caldron, retort, test tube &c.

convert, neophyte, proselyte, pervert, renegade, deserter, apostate, turncoat.

V. be converted into; become, get, wax; come –, turn- -to, – into; turn out, lapse, shift; run –, fall –, pass –, slide –, glide –, grow –, ripen –, open –, resolve itself –, settle –, merge- into; melt, grow, come round to, mature, mellow; assume the -form, – shape, – state, – nature, – character- of; illapse; assume a new phase, undergo a change.

convert –, resolve- into; make, render; mould, form &c. 240; remodel, new model, refound, reform, reorganize; assimilate –, bring –, reduce- to; transform.

Adj. converted into &c. *v.*; convertible, resolvable into; transitional; naturalized.

Adv. gradually &c. (*slowly*) 275; *in transitu* &c. (*transference*) 270.

145. Reversion.—N. reversion, return; revulsion; reaction.

turning point, turn of the tide; *status quo ante bellum*; calm before a storm.

alternation &c. (*periodicity*) 138; inversion &c. 218; recoil &c. 277; regression &c. 283; restoration &c. 660; relapse &c. 661; vicinism, atavism, throwback.

V. revert, turn back, return; relapse &c. 661; recoil &c. 277; retreat &c. 283; restore &c. 660; undo, unmake; turn the -tide, – scale; escheat.

Adj. reverting &c. *v.*; revulsive, reactionary.

Adv. *à rebours*, wrong side out.

146. [Sudden or violent change.] **Revolution.—N.** revolution, *bouleversement*, subversion, break up; destruction &c. 162; sudden –, radical –, sweeping –, organic- change; clean sweep, *coup d'état*, overthrow, *débâcle*; counter-revolution, rebellion &c. 742.

transilience, jump, leap, plunge, jerk, start; explosion; spasm, convulsion, throe, revulsion; storm, earthquake, eruption, upheaval, cataclysm;

legerdemain &c. (*trick*) 545.

V. revolutionize; new model, remodel, recast; strike out something new, break with the past; change the face of, unsex; revert &c. 742.

Adj. unrecognizable.

Revolutionary, Bolshevik &c. 742.

147. [Change of one thing for another.] **Substitution.—N.** substitution, subrogation, commutation; supplanting &c. *v.*, supersession, metonymy &c. (*figure of speech*) 521.

[Thing substituted] substitute, *succedaneum*, make-shift, temporary expedient, shift, *pis aller*, stop-gap, jury-mast, *locum tenens*, warming-pan, dummy, goat, scape-goat; double; changeling; *quid pro quo*, alternative; remount; representative &c. (*deputy*) 759; palimpsest.

price, purchase-money, consideration, equivalent.

V. substitute, put in the place of, change for; make way for, give place to; supply –, take- the place of; supplant, supersede, replace, cut out, serve as a substitute; step into –, stand in- the shoes of; make a shift –, put up- with; borrow of Peter to pay Paul; commute, redeem, compound for.

Adj. substituted &c. *v.*; vicarious, subdititious; substitutional.

Adv. instead; in -place, – lieu, – the stead, – the room- of; *faute de mieux.*

148. [Double or mutual change.] **Interchange.—N.** inter-, ex-change; com-, per-, inter-mutation; reciprocation, transposal, transposition, shuffling; reciprocity, castling [at chess]; hocus-pocus.

interchange-ableness, -ability.

barter &c. 794; tit for tat &c. (*retaliation*) 718; cross fire, battledore and shuttlecock; *quid pro quo*.

V. inter-, ex-, counter-change; bandy, transpose, shuffle, change hands, swap, trade, permute, reciprocate, commute; give and take, return the compliment; play at -puss in the corner, – battledore and shuttlecock; retaliate &c. 718; barter &c. 794.

Adj. interchanged &c. *v.*; reciprocal, mutual, commutative, interchanged &c. *v.*; interchangeable, intercurrent.

Adv. in exchange, *vice versâ*, *mutatis mutandis*, backwards and forwards, by turns, turn and turn about, turn about; each –, every one- in his turn.

2°. Complex Change

149. Changeableness.—N. changeableness &c. *adj.*; mutability, inconstancy; versatility, mobility; instability, unstable equilibrium; vacillation &c. (*irresolution*) 605; fluctuation, vicissitude; alternation &c. (*oscillation*) 314.

restlessness &c. *adj.*; fidgets, disquiet; dis-, in-quietude; unrest; agitation &c. 315.

moon, Proteus, chameleon, kaleidoscope, quicksilver, shifting sands, weathercock, harlequin, Cynthia of the minute, April showers; wheel of Fortune; transientness &c. 111.

V. fluctuate, vary, waver, flounder, flicker, flitter, flit, flutter, shift, shuffle, shake, totter, tremble, vacillate, wamble, turn and turn about, ring the changes; sway –, shift- to and fro; change and change about; oscillate

150. Stability.—N. stability; immutability &c. *adj.*; unchangeableness &c. *adj.*; constancy; stable equilibrium, immobility, soundness, vitality, stabiliment, stabilization, stiffness, ankylosis, solidity, *aplomb*.

establishment, fixture; rock, pillar, tower, foundation, leopard's spots, Ethiopian's skin, law of the Medes and Persians.

stabilimeter, stabilizator.

permanence &c. 141; obstinacy &c. 606.

V. be -firm &c. *adj.*; stick fast; stand –, keep –, remain- firm; weather the storm.

settle, establish, stablish, ascertain, fix, set, stabilitate, stabilize; retain, stet, keep hold; make -good, – sure; fasten &c. (*join*) 43; set on its legs, float; perpetuate.

&c. 314; vibrate –, oscillate- between two extremes; alternate; have as many phases as the moon.

Adj. change-able, -ful; changing &c. 140; mutable, variable, checkered, ever changing, kaleidoscopic, prote-an, -iform; versatile.

unstaid, inconstant; un-steady, -stable, -fixed, -settled; fluctuating &c. *v.*; restless; mercurial; agitated &c. 315; erratic, fickle; irresolute &c. 605; capricious &c. 608; touch-and-go; inconsonant, fitful, spasmodic; vibratory; vagrant, wayward, wavering; desultory; afloat; alternating; alterable, plastic, mobile; fleeting, transient &c. 111.

Adv. see-saw &c. (*oscillation*) 314; off and on.

---

settle down; strike –, take- root; take up one's abode &c. 184; build one's house on a rock.

Adj. unchangeable, immutable; unalter-ed, -able; not to be changed, constant; permanent &c. 141; invariable, undeviating; stable, durable; perennial &c. (*diuturnal*) 110.

fixed, steadfast, firm, fast, steady, balanced; confirmed, valid, fiducial, immovable, irremovable, riveted, rooted; settled, established &c. *v.*; vested; incontrovertible, stereotyped, indeclinable.

tethered, anchored, moored, at anchor, on a rock, firm as a rock; firmly -seated, – established &c. *v.*; deep-rooted, ineradicable; inveterate; obstinate &c. 606.

transfixed, stuck fast, aground, high and dry, stranded.

indefeasible, irretrievable, intransmutable, incommutable, irresoluble, irrevocable, irreversible, reverseless, inextinguishable, irreducible; indissol-uble, -vable; indestructible, undying, imperishable, indelible, indeciduous; insusceptible, – of change.

Int. *stet.*

Present Events

151. Eventuality.—**N.** eventuality, event, occurrence, incident, affair, transaction, proceeding, fact; matter of –, naked- fact; phenomenon; advent.

business, concern; circumstance, particular, casualty, happening, accident, adventure, passage, crisis, pass, emergency, contingency, consequence &c. 154.

the world, life, things, doings, affairs, matters; things –, affairs- in general; the times, state of affairs, order of the day; course –, tide –, stream –, current –, run –, march- of -things, – events; ups and downs of life; chapter of accidents &c. (*chance*) 156; situation &c. (*circumstances*) 8.

V. happen, occur; take -place, – effect; come, become of; come -off, – about, – round, – into existence, – forth, – to pass, – on; pass, present itself; fall; fall –, turn- out; run, be on foot, fall in; be-fall, -tide, -chance; prove, eventuate, draw on; turn –, crop –, spring –, cast- up; super-, sur-vene; issue, emanate, arrive, ensue,

Future Events

152. Destiny.—**N.** destiny &c. (*necessity*) 601; hereafter, future –, post-existence; future state, next world, world to come, after life; futurity &c. 121; everlasting -life, – death; prospect &c. (*expectation*) 507.

V. impend; hang –, lie –, hover-over; threaten, loom, await, come on, approach, stare one in the face; fore-, pre-ordain; predestine, doom, foredoom, foreshadow, have in store for.

Adj. impending &c. *v.*; destined; about to -be, – happen; coming, in store, to come, going to happen, instant, at hand, near; near –, close- at hand; overhanging, hanging over one's head, imminent; brewing, preparing, forthcoming; in the wind, on the cards, in reserve; that -will, – is to- be; in prospect &c. (*expected*) 507; looming in the -distance, – horizon, – future; unborn, in embryo; in the womb of -time; – futurity; on the knees of the gods; pregnant &c. (*producing*) 161.

Adv. in -time, – the long run; all in good time; eventually &c. 151; what-

arise, start, hold, take its course; pass off &c. (*be past*) 122.

meet with; experience; fall to the lot of; be one's -chance, - fortune, - lot; find; encounter, undergo; pass -, go- through; endure &c. (*feel*) 821.

Adj. happening &c. *v.*; going on, doing, current; in the wind, afloat; on -foot, - the *tapis*; at issue, in question; incidental.

eventful, momentous, signal; stirring, bustling, full of incident.

Adv. eventually, ultimately, in -the event of, - case; in the course of things; in the -natural, - ordinary- course of things; as -things, - times- go; as the world -goes, - wags; as the -tree falls, - cat jumps; as it may -turn out, - happen.

Phr. the plot thickens.

ever may happen &c. (*certainly*) 474; as -chance &c. 156- would have it.

Section VIII. CAUSATION

1°. Constancy of Sequence in Events

153. [Constant antecedent.] Cause. —**N.** cause, origin, source, principle, element; occasioner, prime mover, engine, turbine, motor, *primum mobile*; *vera causa*; author &c. (*producer*) 164; main-spring, agent; dynamo, generator, battery (electric); leaven; groundwork, foundation &c. (*support*) 215.

spring, fountain, well, font; fountain -, spring- head; *fons et origo*, genesis; descent &c. (*paternity*) 166; remote cause; influence.

pivot, hinge, turning-point, lever; key; kernel, core; proximate cause, *causa causans*; last straw that breaks the camel's back.

ground; reason, - why; why and wherefore, rationale, occasion, derivation; final cause &c. (*intention*) 620; *le dessous des cartes*; undercurrents.

rudiment, egg, germ, embryo, fœtus bud, root, *radix*, radical, etymon, nucleus, seed, stem, stalk, stock, *stirps*, trunk, tap-root; latent organism.

nest, cradle, nursery, womb, *nidus*, birth-, breeding-place, hot-bed.

caus-ality, -ation; origination; production &c. 161.

V. be the -cause &c. *n.*- of; originate; give -origin, - rise, - occasion- to; cause, occasion, sow the seeds of, kindle, suscitate; bring -on, - to pass, - about; produce; create &c. 161; set -up, - afloat, - on foot; found, broach,

154. [Constant sequent.] Effect.—**N.** effect, consequence, sequela; derivative, -tion; result; result-ant, -ance; upshot, issue, *dénouement*; outcome; termination, end &c. 67; development, outgrowth, fruit, crop, harvest, product, bud, blossom, florescence, ear.

production, produce, product, finished product, work, handiwork, fabric, performance; creature, creation; offspring, -shoot; first-fruits, -lings; *prémices*.

V. be the -effect &c. *n.*- of; be -due, - owing- to; originate -in, - from; rise -, arise -, take its rise -, spring -, proceed -, emanate -, come -, grow -, bud -, sprout -, germinate -, issue -, flow -, result -, follow -, derive its origin -, accrue- from; come -to, - of, - out of; depend -, hang -, hinge -, turn- upon.

take the consequences, sow the wind and reap the whirlwind.

Adj. owing to; resulting from &c. *v.*; resultant; derivable from; due to; caused &c. by, 153; dependent upon; derived -, evolved- from; derivative; hereditary.

Adv. of course, it follows that, naturally, consequently; as a -, in- consequence; through all, all along of, necessarily, eventually.

Phr. *cela va sans dire*, thereby hangs a tale.

---

institute, lay the foundation of, inaugurate; lie at the root of.

procure, induce, draw down, open the door to, superinduce, evoke, entail, operate; elicit, provoke.

conduce to &c. (*tend to*) 176; contribute; promote; have a -hand in, - finger in- the pie; determine, decide, turn the scale, give the casting vote; have a common origin; derive its origin &c. (*effect*) 154.

Adj. caused &c. *v.*; causal, original; prim-ary, -itive, -ordial; aboriginal; radical; inceptive, embry-onic, -otic; *in -embryo, - ovo*; seminal, germinal; formative, productive &c. 168; at the bottom of; connate, having a common origin.

Adv. because &c. 155; behind the scenes.

155. [Assignment of cause.] **Attribution.—N.** attribution, theory, etiology, ascription, reference to, rationale; accounting for &c. *v.*; palaetiology,* imputation, derivation from.

fil-, affil-iation; pedigree &c. (*paternity*) 166.

explanation &c. (*interpretation*) 522; reason why &c. (*cause*) 153.

V. attribute -, ascribe -, impute -, refer -, lay -, point -, trace -, bring home- to; put -, set- down- to; charge -, ground- on; invest with, assign as cause, charge with, blame, lay at the door of, father upon; saddle with; affiliate; account for, derive from, point out the -reason &c. 153; theorize; tell how it comes; put the saddle on the right horse.

Adj. attributed &c. *v.*; attributable &c. *v.*; refer-able, -rible; due to, derivable from; owing to &c. (*effect*) 154; putative.

Adv. hence, thence, therefore, for, since, on account of, because, owing to; on that account; from -this, - that- cause; thanks to, forasmuch as; whence, *propter hoc.*

why? wherefore? whence? how -comes, - is, - happens- it? how does it happen?

in -some, - some such- way; somehow, - or other.

Phr. that is why; *hinc illæ lachrymæ*; *cherchez la femme.*

156. [Absence of assignable cause.] **Chance.†—N.** chance, indetermination, accident, fortune, hazard, hap, haphazard, chance-medley, random, luck, *raccroc*, casualty, fortuity, contingence, coincidence, adventure, hit; fate &c. (*necessity*) 601; equal chance; lottery, raffle, tombola, sweepstake; toss up &c. 621; turn of the -table, - cards; hazard of the die, chapter of accidents; cast -, throw- of the dice; heads or tails, wheel of Fortune, whirligig of chance; *sortes, - Virgilianæ, -biblicæ.*

probability, possibility, contingency, odds, long odds, run of luck; main-chance.

theory of -probabilities, - chances; book-making; assurance; speculation, gamble, gaming &c. 621.

V. chance, hap, turn up; fall to one's lot; be one's -fate &c. 601; stumble on, light -, blunder -, hit- upon; take one's chance &c. 621.

Adj. casual, fortuitous, accidental, haphazard, random, stray, adventitious, adventive, causeless, incidental. contingent, uncaused, undetermined, indeterminate; possible &c. 470; unintentional &c. 621.

Adv. by -chance, - accident; casually; perchance &c. (*possibly*) 470; for aught one knows; as -good, - bad, - ill-luck &c. *n.*- would have it; as it may -be, - chance, - turn up, - happen; as the case may be.

2°. Connection between Cause and Effect

157. Power.—N. power; poten-cy, -tiality; puissance, might, force; energy &c. 171; dint; right -hand, - arm;

158. Impotence.—N. impotence; in-, dis-ability; disablement, impuissance, imbecility, caducity; incapa-city,

* Whewell, 'History of the Inductive Sciences,' book xviii, vol. iii., p. 397 (3rd edit.).

† The word *Chance* has two distinct meanings: the first, the absence of assignable *cause*, as above; and the second, the absence of *design*—for the latter see 621.

ascendency, sway, control; pre-potency, -pollence; almightiness, omnipotence; authority &c. 737; strength &c. 159.

ability; ableness &c. *adj.*; competency; effi-ciency, -cacy; validity, cogency; enablement; vantage ground; influence &c. 175; horse power; dynamometer.

pressure; elasticity; gravity, electricity, magnetism, galvanism, voltaic electricity, voltaism, electro-magnetism, electrostatics, electrification, electric current &c.; attraction, repulsion; *vis -inertiæ, – mortua, – viva*; potential –, dynamic –, kinetic –, electrical –, chemical –, atomic- energy; friction, suction.

capability, capacity; *quid valeant humeri quid ferre recusent*; faculty, quality, attribute, endowment, virtue, gift, property, qualification, susceptibility.

V. be -powerful &c. *adj.*; gain -power &c. *n.*

belong –, pertain- to; lie –, be- in one's power; can.

give –, confer –, exercise- power &c. *n.*; empower, enable, invest; in-, en-due; endow, arm; strengthen &c. 159; compel &c. 744.

Adj. powerful, puissant; potent, -ial; capable, able; equal –, up- to; cogent, valid; effect-ive, -ual; efficient, efficacious, adequate, competent; multi-, pleni-, omni-, armi- potent; mighty, ascendent; almighty.

electric, electrical &c.

forcible &c. *adj.* (*energetic*) 171; influential &c. 175; productive &c. 168.

Adv. powerfully &c. *adj.*; by -virtue, – dint- of.

-bility, inapt-, inept-itude; indocility; invalidity, inefficiency, incompetence, disqualification.

telum imbelle, brutum fulmen, blank cartridge, flash in the pan, *vox et præterea nihil*, dead letter, bit of waste paper, dummy; scrap of paper.

inefficacy &c. (*inutility*) 645; failure &c. 732.

helplessness &c. *adj.*; prostration, paralysis, palsy, ataxia, apoplexy, syncope, sideration, *deliquium*, collapse, exhaustion, softening of the brain, emasculation, inanition, senility &c. 128; castrato, eunuch.

cripple, old woman, muff, mollycoddle, milksop.

V. be -impotent &c. *adj.*; not have a leg to stand on.

vouloir -rompre l'anguille au genou, – prendre la lune avec les dents.

collapse, faint, swoon, fall into a swoon, drop; go by the board; end in smoke &c. (*fail*) 732.

render -powerless &c. *adj.*; deprive of power; decontrol; dis-able, -enable; disarm, incapacitate, disqualify, unfit, invalidate, undermine, deaden, cramp, tie the hands; double up, prostrate, paralyze, muzzle, cripple, becripple, maim, lame, hamstring, draw the teeth of; throttle, strangle, *garrotte*; ratten, silence, sprain, clip the wings of, render *hors de combat*, spike the guns; take the wind out of one's sails, scotch the snake, put a spoke in one's wheel; break the -neck, – back; un-hinge, -fit; put out of gear.

unman, unnerve, devitalize, attenuate, enervate; emasculate, spay, caponize, castrate, geld; effeminize.

shatter, exhaust; weaken &c. 160.

Adj. powerless, impotent, unable, incapable, incompetent; ineff-icient, -ective; inept; un-fit, -fitted; un-, dis-qualified; unendowed; in-, un-apt; crippled, decrepit, disabled &c. *v.*; armless.

harmless, unarmed, weaponless, defenceless, *sine ictu*, unfortified, indefensible, vincible, pregnable, untenable.

para-lytic, -lyzed; palsied, imbecile; nerve-, sinew-, marrow-, pith-, lust-less; emasculate, disjointed; out of -joint, – gear; un- -nerved, -hinged; water-logged, on one's beam ends, rudderless; laid on one's back; done up, dead beat, exhausted, shattered, demoralized; gravelled &c. (*in difficulty*) 704; helpless, unfriended, fatherless; without a leg to stand on, *hors de combat*, laid on the shelf;

null and void, nugatory, inoperative, good for nothing; dud; invertebrate; ineffectual &c. (*failing*) 732; inadequate &c. 640; inefficacious &c. (*useless*) 645.

159. [Degree of power.] Strength. —**N.** strength; power &c. 157; energy &c. 171; vigour, force; main –, physical –, brute- force; spring, elasticity, tone, tension, tonicity.

stoutness &c. *adj*; lustihood, stamina, nerve, muscle, sinew, thews and sinews, *physique*; pith, -iness; virility, vitality.

athlet-ics, -icism; gymnastics, feats of strength.

adamant, steel, iron, oak, heart of oak; iron grip; grit, bone.

athlete, gymnast, tumbler, acrobat; Atlas, Hercules, Antæus, Samson, Cyclops, Goliath, Titan; tower of strength; giant refreshed.

strengthening &c. *v.*; invigoration, refreshment, refocillation.

[Science of forces] dynamics, statics.

V. be -strong &c. *adj.*, – stronger; overmatch.

render -strong &c. *adj.*; give -strength &c. *n.*; strengthen, invigorate, brace, nerve, fortify, buttress, sustain, harden, case-harden, steel; gird; screw –, wind –, set- up; gird –, brace- up one's loins; recruit, set on one's legs; vivify; refresh &c. 689; refect; reinforce &c. (*restore*) 660.

Adj. strong, mighty, vigorous, forcible, hard, adamantine, stout, robust, sturdy, hardy, powerful, potent, puissant, valid.

resistless, irresistible, invincible, proof against, impregnable, unconquerable, indomitable, inextinguishable, unquenchable; incontestable; more than a match for; over-powering, -whelming; all-powerful; sovereign.

able-bodied; athletic, gymnastic; Herculean, Cyclopean, Atlantean; muscular, husky, brawny, wiry, well-knit, broad-shouldered, sinewy, strapping, stalwart, gigantic.

man-ly, -like, -ful; masculine, male, virile, in the prime of manhood.

un-weakened, -allayed, -withered, -shaken, -worn, -exhausted; in full -force, – swing; in the plenitude of power.

160. Weakness.—**N.** weakness &c. *adj.*; debility, atony, relaxation, languor, enervation; impotence &c. 158; infirmity; effeminancy, feminality; fragility, flaccidity; inactivity &c. 683.

declension –, loss –, failure- of strength; delicacy, invalidation, decrepitude, asthenia, adynamy, cachexy, *cachexia*, anæmia, bloodlessness, sprain, strain.

reed, thread, rope of sand, broken reed, house -of cards, – built on sand.

soft-, weak-ling; infant &c. 129; youth &c. 127.

V. be -weak &c. *adj.*; drop, crumble, give way, totter, tremble, shake, halt, limp, fade, languish, decline, flag, fail, have one foot in the grave.

render -weak &c. *adj.*; weaken, enfeeble, debilitate, shake, deprive of strength, relax, enervate; un-brace, -nerve; cripple, unman, &c. (*render powerless*) 158; cramp, reduce, sprain, strain, blunt the edge of; dilute, impoverish; decimate; extenuate; reduce -in strength, – the strength of; invalidate; *mettre de l'eau dans son vin.*

Adj. weak, feeble, debile; impotent &c. 158; relaxed, unnerved &c. *v.*; sap-, strength-, power-less; weakly, unstrung, flaccid, adynamic, asthenic; nervous.

soft, effeminate, feminate, womanish.

frail, fragile, shattery, frangible, brittle &c. 328; flimsy, unsubstantial, gimcrack, gingerbread; rickety, cranky; creachy; drooping, tottering &c. *v.*; broken, lame, halt, game, withered, shattered, shaken, crazy, shaky, tumble-down; palsied &c. 158; decrepit; C3.

languid, poor, poorly, infirm; faint, -ish; sickly &c. (*disease*) 655; dull, slack, evanid, spent, short-winded, effete; weatherbeaten; decayed, rotten, worn, seedy, languishing, wasted, washy, wishy-washy, laid low, pulled down, the worse for wear.

un-strengthened &c. 159, -supported, -aided, -assisted; aidless, defenceless &c. 158.

stubborn, thick-ribbed, made of iron, deep-rooted; strong as -a lion, – a horse, – brandy; sound as a roach; in -fine, – high- feather; in fine fettle; like a giant refreshed.

Adv. strongly &c. *adj.*; by -force &c. *n.*; by main force &c. (*by compulsion*) 744.

Phr. 'our withers are unwrung.'

on its last legs; weak as a -child, – baby, – chicken, – cat, – rat; weak as -water, – water gruel, – gingerbread, – milk and water; colourless &c. 429.

Phr. *non sum qualis eram.*

3°. Power in Operation

161. Production.—N. production, creation, construction, formation, fabrication, manufacture; building, architecture, erection, edification; coinage; organization; *nisus formativus*; putting together &c. *v.*; establishment; workmanship, performance; achievement &c. (*completion*) 729; effect &c. 154.

flowering, fructification, fruition.

bringing forth &c. *v.*; parturition, birth, birth-throe, child-birth, delivery, confinement, *accouchement*, travail, labour, midwifery, obstetrics; geniture; gestation &c. (*maturation*) 673; evolution, development, growth; genesis, fertilization, breeding, conception, germination, generation, *epigenesis*, pro-creation, -generation, -pagation; fecundation, impregnation; spontaneous generation; *arche-genesis, -biosis; bio-, abio-, homo-, xeno-genesis.**

authorship, publication; works, *œuvre, opus.*

edifice, building, structure, fabric, erection, pile, tower, flower, fruit.

V. produce, perform, operate, do, make, gar, form, construct, fabricate, frame, contrive, manufacture; weave, forge, coin, carve, chisel; build, raise, edify, rear, erect, put together; set –, run- up; establish, constitute, compose, organize, institute, get up; achieve, accomplish &c. (*complete*) 729.

flower, sprout, blossom, burgeon, bear fruit, fructify, spawn, teem, ean, yean, farrow, drop, calf, pup, whelp, kitten, kindle; bear, lay, bring forth, give birth to, lie in, be brought to bed of, evolve, pullulate, usher into the world.

make productive &c. 168; create; beget, conceive, get, generate, fecun-

162. [Non-production.] **Destruction. —N.** destruction; waste, dissolution, breaking up; di-, dis-ruption; consumption; disorganization.

fall, downfall, ruin, perdition, crash, smash, havoc, *délabrement, débâcle*; break -down, – up; prostration; desolation, *bouleversement*, wreck, crack-up, crash, wrack, shipwreck, cataclysm; Caudine Forks, Sedan.

extinction, annihilation; destruction of life &c. 361; knock-out, knock-down blow; doom, crack of doom.

destroying &c. *v.*; demo-lition, -lishment; biblioclasm; overthrow, subversion, suppression; abolition &c. (*abrogation*) 756; sacrifice; ravage, devastation, *sabotage, razzia*; incendiarism; revolution &c. 146; extirpation &c. (*extraction*) 301; *commencement de la fin*, road to ruin; dilapidation &c. (*deterioration*) 659.

V. be -destroyed &c.; perish; fall, – to the ground; tumble, topple; go –, fall- to pieces; break up; crumble, – to dust; go to -the dogs, – the wall, – smash, – shivers, – wreck, – pot, – wrack and ruin; go -by the board, – all to smash, – to pieces, – under; be all -over, – up- with; totter to its fall.

destroy; do –, make- away with; nullify; annul &c. 756; sacrifice, demolish; tear up; over-turn, -throw, -whelm; upset, subvert, put an end to; seal the doom of, do for, dish, undo; break –, cut- up; break –, cut –, pull –, mow –, blow –, beat- down; suppress, quash, put down; cut short, take off, blot out; dispel, dissipate, dissolve; consume; abolish.

smash, – to smithereens, quell, squash, squelch, crumple up, shatter,

* Huxley.

date, impregnate; pro-create, -generate, -pagate; engender; bring –, call- into -being, – existence; breed, hatch, develop, bring up.

induce, superinduce; suscitate; cause &c. 153; acquire &c. 775.

Adj. produc-ed, -ing &c. *v.*; productive of; prolific &c. 168; creative; formative; gen-etic, -ial, -ital; fertile, pregnant; *enceinte*, big –, fraught-with; with child, in the family way, teeming, parturient, in the straw, brought to bed of; puerper-al, -ous.

architectonic; constructive.

---

shiver; batter; tear –, crush –, cut –, shake –, pull –, pick- to pieces; nip; tear to -rags, – tatters; crush –, knock- to atoms; pulverize; ruin; strike out; throw –, knock- -down, – over; lay by the heels; fell, sink, swamp, scuttle, wreck, crash, shipwreck, engulf, submerge; lay in -ashes, – ruins; sweep away, erase, expunge, strike out, delete, efface, raze; level, – with the -ground, – dust.

deal destruction, lay waste, ravage, gut; disorganize; dismantle &c. (*render useless*) 645; devour, swallow up, desolate, devastate, sap, mine, blast, confound; exterminate, extinguish, quench, annihilate; snuff –, put –, stamp –, trample- out; lay –, trample- in the dust; prostrate; tread –, crush –, trample- under foot; lay the axe to the root of; make -short work, – a clean sweep, – mince-meat- of; cut up root and branch; fling –, scatter- to the winds; throw overboard; strike at the root of, sap the foundations of, spring a mine, blow up; ravage with fire and sword; cast to the dogs; eradicate &c. 301.

Adj. destroyed &c. *v.*; perishing &c. *v.*; trembling –, nodding –, tottering- to its fall; in course of -destruction &c. *n.*; extinct.

destructive, subversive, ruinous, incendiary, deletory; destroying &c. *v.*; suicidal; deadly &c. (*killing*) 361.

Adv. with -crushing effect, – a sledge-hammer.

Phr. *delenda est Carthago.*

163. Reproduction.—**N.** reproduction, renovation; restoration &c. 660; renewal; new edition, reprint &c. 21; revival, regeneration, palingenesia, revivification; apotheosis; resuscitation, reanimation, resurrection, resurgence, reappearance, atavism; Phœnix; reincarnation.

generation &c. (*production*) 161; multiplication.

V. reproduce; restore &c. 660; revive, renovate, renew, regenerate, revivify, resuscitate, reanimate, refashion, stir the embers, put into the crucible; multiply, repeat, resurge.

crop up, spring up like mushrooms.

Adj. reproduced &c. *v.*; renascent, reappearing; reproductive; resurgent; progenitive; Hydra-headed.

164. Producer.—**N.** producer, creator, deviser, designer, originator, inventor, author, founder, generator, mover, architect; grower, constructor, maker &c. (*agent*) 690.

165. Destroyer.—**N.** destroyer &c. (destroy &c. 162); cankerworm &c. (*bane*) 663; iconoclast; assassin &c. (*killer*) 361; executioner &c. (*punish*) 975; Hun, Vandal, nihilist, anarchist.

166. Paternity.—**N.** paternity; parentage; fatherhood; consanguinity &c. 11.

parent, father, sire, dad, daddy, papa, governor, *pater*, *paterfamilias*, *abba*; genitor, progenitor, procreator, begetter; ancestor; grand-sire, -father; great-grandfather.

167. Posterity.—**N.** posterity, progeny, breed, issue, offspring, brood, litter, seed, farrow, spawn, spat; family, children, grandchildren, heirs; great-grandchild.

child, son, daughter; kid; infant &c. 129; bantling, scion; shoot, sprout, olive branch, sprit, branch; off-shoot,

house, stem, trunk, tree, stock, *stirps*, pedigree, lineage, line, family, tribe, sept, race, clan; genealogy, descent, extraction, birth, ancestry; forefathers, forbears, patriarchs.

motherhood, maternity; mother, dam, mamma, *materfamilias*; grandmother; matriarch.

Adj. paternal, parental; maternal; family, ancestral, linear, matrilinear, patrilineal, patriarchal.

-set; ramification; descendant; heir, -ess; heir -apparent, – presumptive; chip of the old block; heredity; rising generation.

straight descent, sonship, line, lineage, filiation, primogeniture.

Adj. filial.

168. Productiveness.—N. productiveness &c. *adj.*; fecundity, fertility, luxuriance, uberty.

pregnancy, pullulation, fructification, multiplication, propagation, procreation; superfetation.

milch cow, rabbit, hydra, warren, seed-plot, land flowing with milk and honey; second crop, after-crop, -growth, -math; fertilization.

V. make -productive &c. *adj.*; fructify; procreate, generate, fertilize, spermatize, impregnate; fecund-ate, -ify; teem, pullulate, multiply; produce &c. 161; conceive.

Adj. productive, prolific; teem-ing, -ful; fertile, fruitful, frugiferous, fruit-bearing; fructiferous; fecund, luxuriant; pregnant, uberous.

procre-ant, -ative; generative, life-giving, spermatic; originative; multiparous; omnific; propagable.

parturient &c. (*producing*) 161; profitable &c. (*useful*) 644.

169. Unproductiveness.—N. unproductiveness &c. *adj.*; infertility, sterility, infecundity; impotence &c. 158-unprofitableness &c. (*inutility*) 645.

waste, desert, Sahara, wild, wilderness, howling wilderness.

V. be -unproductive &c. *adj.*; hang fire, flash in the pan, come to nothing.

Adj. unproductive, inoperative, barren, addle, unfertile, unprolific, arid, sterile, unfruitful, acarpous, infecund; *sine prole*; fallow; teem-, issue-, fruitless; unprofitable &c. (*useless*) 645; null and void, of no effect.

170. Agency.—N. agency, operation, force, working, strain, function, office, maintenance, exercise, work, swing, play; inter-working, -action, procuration, procurement.

causation &c. 153; instrumentality &c. 631; influence &c. 175; action &c. (*voluntary*) 680; *modus operandi* &c. 627.

quickening –, maintaining- power; home stroke.

V. be -in action &c. *adj.*; operate, work; act, – upon; perform, play, support, sustain, strain, maintain, take effect, quicken, strike.

come –, bring- into -operation, – play; have -play, – free play; bring to bear upon.

Adj. operative, efficient, efficacious, practical, effectual.

at work, on foot; acting &c. (*doing*) 680; in -operation, – force, – action, – play, – exercise; acted –, wrought- upon.

Adv. by the -agency &c. *n.*- of; through &c. (*instrumentality*) 631; by means of &c. 632.

171. Physical Energy.—N. energy, physical energy, force; keenness &c. *adj.*; intensity, vigour, strength, elasticity; go; pep, live wire, high pressure; backbone, mettle, fire, vim.

acri-mony, -tude, -dity; causticity,

172. Physical Inertness.—N. inertness, dulness &c. *adj.*; inertia, *vis inertiæ*, inertion, inactivity, torpor, languor; dormancy, quiescence &c. 265; latency, inaction, passivity.

mental inertness; sloth &c. (*inac*

virulence, poignancy; harshness &c. *adj.*; severity, edge, point; pungency &c. 392.

cantharides; Spanish fly; seasoning &c. (*condiment*) 393, stimulant, excitant.

activity, agitation, effervescence; ferment, -ation; ebullition, splutter, perturbation, stir, bustle; voluntary energy &c. 682; quicksilver.

resolution &c. (*mental energy*) 604; exertion &c. (*effort*) 686; excitation &c. (*mental*) 824.

V. give -energy &c. *n.*; energize, stimulate, kindle, excite, activate, exert; sharpen, pep up, intensify; inflame &c. (*render violent*) 173; wind up &c. (*strengthen*) 159.

strike, – into, – hard, – home; make an impression.

Adj. strong, energetic, forcible, active; strenuous, forceful, mettlesome, enterprising, go ahead; intense, deep-dyed, severe, keen, vivid, sharp, acute, incisive, trenchant, brisk, vigorous, live.

rousing, irritating; poignant; virulent, caustic, corrosive, mordant, harsh, stringent; double-edged, – shotted, – distilled; drastic, escharotic; racy &c. (*pungent*) 392; sarcastic &c. 932; irenic.

potent &c. (*powerful*) 157; radio-active.

Adv. strongly &c. *adj.*; *fortiter in re*; with telling effect.

Phr. the steam is up; *vires acquirit eundo.*

172. Inertness.—**N.** inertness, inertia, vis inertiæ, inertion, inactivity &c. (*inaction*) 681; (*passivity*) 862; inexcitability &c. 826; irresolution &c. 605; obstinacy &c. 606; permanence &c. 141.

V. be -inert &c. *adj.*; hang fire, smoulder.

Adj. inert, inactive, passive, pacific; torpid &c. 683; sluggish, stagnant, dull, heavy, flat, slack, tame, slow, blunt; lifeless, dead, uninfluential.

latent, dormant, smouldering, unexerted.

Adv. inactively &c. *adj.*; in -suspense, -abeyance.

173. Violence.—**N.** violence, inclemency, vehemence, might, impetuosity; boisterousness &c. *adj.*; effervescence, ebullition; turbulence, bluster; uproar, riot, row, rumpus, *le diable à quatre*, devil to pay, all the fat in the fire.

severity &c. 739; ferocity, rage, berserk, fury; exacerbation, exasperation, malignity; fit, paroxysm, orgasm; force, brute force; outrage; *coup de main*; strain, shock, shog; spasm, convulsion, throe; hysterics, passion &c. (*state of excitability*) 825.

out-break, -burst; burst, bounce, dissilience, discharge, volley, explosion, blow up, blast, detonation, rush, eruption, displosion, torrent.

turmoil &c. (*disorder*) 59; ferment &c. (*agitation*) 315; storm, tempest, rough weather; squall &c. (*wind*) 349; earthquake, volcano, thunderstorm.

fury, dragon, demon, tiger, beldame, Tisiphone, Megæra, Alecto, madcap, wild beast; fire-eater &c. (*blusterer*) 887.

V. be -violent &c. *adj.*; run high; ferment, effervesce; romp, rampage; **run -wild, - riot;** break the peace;

174. Moderation.—**N.** moderation; lenity &c. 740; temperance, temperateness, gentleness &c. *adj.*; sobriety; quiet; mental calmness &c. (*inexcitability*) 826.

moderating &c. *v.*; relaxation, remission, mitigation &c. 834; tranquillization, alleviation, assuagement, appeasement, contemporation, pacification.

measure, *juste milieu*, golden mean &c. 29.

moderator; lullaby, sedative, lenitive, demulcent, rose-water, balm, soothing syrup, poppy, opiate, anodyne, milk, opium, laudanum, 'poppy or mandragora'; wet blanket; palliative, calmative.

V. be -moderate &c. *adj.*; keep within -bounds, – compass; sober –, settle- down; keep the peace, remit, relent; shorten sail.

moderate, soften, mitigate, temper, accoy; at-, con-temper; mollify, lenify, dull, take off the edge, blunt, obtund, sheathe, subdue, chasten; sober –, tone –, smooth- down; censor, blue-

rush, tear; rush head-long, -foremost; run amuck, raise a storm, make a riot; make –, kick up- a row, – a fuss; bluster, rage, roar, riot, storm; boil, – over; fume, foam, come in like a lion, wreak, bear down, ride rough-shod, out-Herod Herod; spread like wildfire.

break –, fly –, burst- out; bounce, shock, strain; break-, pry-, force-, prize- open.

render -violent &c. *adj.*; sharpen, stir up, quicken, excite, incite, urge, lash, stimulate; irritate, inflame, exacerbate, kindle, suscitate, foment; accelerate, aggravate, exasperate, convulse, infuriate, madden, lash into fury; fan –, add fuel to- the flame; *oleum addere camino.*

explode, go off, displode, fly, detonate, thunder, blow up, flash, flare, erupt, burst; let -off, – fly; discharge, detonize, fulminate.

Adj. violent, vehement, forcible; warm; acute, sharp; rough, rude, un gentle, bluff, boisterous, wild, vicious; brusque, abrupt, waspish; impetuous; rampant.

turbulent; disorderly; blustering, raging &c. *v.*; troublous, riotous; tumultu-ary, -ous; obstreperous, uproarious; extravagant, unmitigated; ravening, tameless; frenzied &c. (*insane*) 503; desperate &c. (*rash*) 863; infuriate, towering, furious, outrageous, frantic, hysteric, in hysterics.

fiery, flaming, scorching, hot, red-hot, ebullient.

savage, fierce, ferocious, fierce as a tiger.

excited &c. *v.*; un-quelled, -quenched, -extinguished, -repressed, -bridled, -ruly; headstrong; un-governable, -appeasable, -mitigable; un-, in-controllable; insup-, irre-pressible.

spasmodic, convulsive, explosive; detonating &c. *v.*; volcanic, meteoric; stormy &c. (*wind*) 349.

Adv. violently &c. *adj.*; amain; by -storm, – force, – main force; with might and main; tooth and nail, *vi et armis*, at the point of the -sword, – bayonet; at one fell swoop; with a high hand, through thick and thin; in desperation, with a vengeance; *à –, à toute-outrance*; head-long, -foremost, -first; like a bull at a gate.

pencil, weaken &c. 160; lessen &c. (*decrease*) 36; check; palliate.

tranquillize, assuage, appease, dulcify, swage, lull, soothe, compose, still, calm, cool, quiet, hush, quell, sober, pacify, tame, damp, lay, allay, rebate, slacken, smooth, alleviate, rock to sleep, deaden, smother; throw -cold water on, – a wet blanket over; slake; curb &c. (*restrain*) 751; tame &c. (*subjugate*) 749 ; smooth over; pour oil on the -waves, – troubled waters; pour balm into, *mettre de l'eau dans son vin.*

go out like a lamb, 'roar you as gently as any sucking dove.'

Adj. moderate; lenient &c. 740; gentle, mild; cool, sober, temperate, reasonable, measured; tempered &c. *v.*; calm, unruffled, quiet, tranquil, still; slow, smooth, untroubled; tame; peaceful, -able; pacific, halcyon.

un-exciting, -irritating; soft, bland, oily, demulcent, lenitive, anodyne; hypnotic &c. 683; sedative; assuaging.

mild as mother's milk; milk and water; gentle as a lamb.

Adv. moderately &c. *adj.*; gingerly; *piano*; under easy sail, at half speed; within -bounds, – compass; in reason.

Phr. *est modus in rebus.*

4°. Indirect Power

175. Influence.—N. influence; importance &c. 642; weight, pressure, preponderance, prevalence, sway, pull; predomi-nance, -nancy; ascendency; control, dominance, reign; authority

175a. Absence of Influence.—N. impotence &c. 158; inertness &c. 172; irrelevancy &c. 10.

V. have no -influence &c. 175.

Adj. uninfluential; unconduc-ing,

&c. 737; capability &c. (*power*) 157; interest; spell, magic, magnetism.

footing; purchase &c. (*support*) 215; play, leverage, vantage ground.

tower of strength, host in himself; protection, patronage, auspices.

V. have -influence &c. *n.*; be -influential &c. *adj.*; carry weight, actuate, sway, bias, weigh, tell; have a hold upon, magnetize, bear upon, gain a footing, work upon; take -root, – hold; strike root in.

run through, pervade; prevail, dominate, predominate, subject; out-, over-weigh; over-ride, -bear, – come; gain head; rage; be -rife &c. *adj.*; spread like wildfire; have –, get –, gain- -the upper hand, – full play.

be -recognized – listened to; make one's voice heard, gain a hearing; play a -part, – leading part- in; lead, control, rule, master; get the mastery over; make one's influence felt, cut ice with; take the lead, pull the strings; turn –, throw one's weight into- the scale; set the fashion, lead the dance.

Adj. influential; important &c. 642; weighty; prevailing &c. *v.*; prevalent, rife, rampant, dominant, regnant, predominant, in the ascendant, hegemonical; authoritative, recognized, telling, with authority.

Adv. with telling effect.

-ive, -ting to; powerless &c. 158; irrelevant &c. 10.

---

176. Tendency.—N. tendency; apt-ness, -itude; proneness, proclivity, bent, turn, tone, bias, set, warp, leaning to, predisposition, inclination, conatus, propensity, susceptibility, liability &c. 177; quality, nature, temperament; characteristic, idio-crasy, -syncrasy-; cast, vein, grain; humour, mood; drift &c. (*direction*) 278; con-duciveness, -ducement; applicability &c. (*utility*) 644; subservience &c. (*instrumentality*) 631.

V. tend, contribute, conduce, lead, dispose, incline, verge, bend to, warp, turn, trend, affect, carry, redound to, bid fair to, gravitate towards; promote &c. (*aid*) 707.

Adj. tending &c. *v.*; conducive, working towards, in a fair way to, calculated to; liable &c. 177; subservient &c. (*instrumental*) 631; useful &c. 644; subsidiary &c. (*helping*) 707.

Adv. for, whither.

177. Liability.—N. lia-bility, -bleness; possibility, contingency; suscepti-vity, -bility.

V. be -liable &c. *adj.*; incur, lay oneself open to; run the –, stand a- chance; lie under, expose oneself to, open a door to.

Adj. liable, subject; in danger &c. 665; open –, exposed –, obnoxious- to; answerable, responsible, accountable, amenable; unexempt from; apt to; dependent on; incident to.

contingent, incidental, possible, on the cards, within range of, at the mercy of.

5°. Combinations of Causes

178. Concurrence.—N. concurrence, co-operation, coagency; coincidence, consilience; union; agreement &c. 23; consent &c. (*assent*) 488; alliance; concert &c. 709; partnership &c. 712; collaboration, conformity.

V. con-cur, -duce, -spire, -tribute;

179. Counteraction.—N. counteraction, opposition; contrariety &c. 14; antagonism, polarity; clashing &c. *v.*: collision, interference, resistance, renitency, friction; reaction; retroaction; repercussion &c. (*recoil*) 277; counterblast; neutralization &c. (*compensa-*

agree, unite, harmonize; hang –, pull- together &c. (*co-operate*) 709; help to &c. (*aid*) 707.

keep pace with, run parallel to; go –, go along –, go hand in hand- with.

Adj. concurring &c. *v.*; concurrent, conformable, joint, co-operative, concordant, coincident, concomitant, harmonious; in alliance with, banded together, of one mind, at one with; parallel.

Adv. with one consent.

tion) 30; *vis inertiæ*; check &c. (*hindrance*) 706.

voluntary -opposition &c. 708, – resistance &c. 719; repression &c. (*restraint*) 751.

V. counteract; run counter, clash, cross; interfere –, conflict- with; jostle; go –, run –, beat–, militate- against; stultify; antagonize, frustrate, oppose &c. 708; withstand &c. (*resist*) 719; hinder &c. 706; repress &c. (*restrain*) 751; react &c. (*recoil*) 277.

undo, neutralise, cancel; counterpoise &c. (*compensate*) 30; overpoise.

Adj. counteracting &c. *v.*; antagonistic, conflicting, retroactive, renitent, reactionary; contrary &c. 14.

Adv. although &c. 30; in spite of &c. 708; *malgré*; against.

CLASS II

Words Relating to SPACE

Section I. SPACE IN GENERAL

1°. Abstract Space

180. (Indefinite space.) Space.—**N.** space, extension, extent, superficial extent, expanse, stretch; capacity, room, accommodation, scope, range, latitude, field, way, expansion, compass, sweep, play, swing, spread.

spare –, elbow –, house- room; stowage, roomage, margin; opening, sphere, arena; lee-, sea-, head-way.

open –, free- space; wide open spaces; void &c. (*absence*) 187; waste; wild-, wilder-ness; up-, bottom-, moor -land; *campagna, veld,* prairie, steppe.

abyss &c. (*interval*) 198; unlimited space; infinity &c. 105; world, wide world; ubiquity &c. (*presence*) 186; length and breadth of the land.

proportions, acreage; acres, – roods and perches; square -inches, – yards &c.

Adj. spacious, roomy, extensive, expansive, capacious, ample; wide-spread, vast, world-wide, uncircumscribed; boundless &c. (*infinite*) 105; shore-, track-, path-less; large &c. 192.

Adv. extensively &c. *adj.*; wherever; everywhere; far and -near, – wide; right and left, all over, all the world over; throughout the -world, – length and breadth of the land; under the sun, in every quarter; in all -quarters, – lands; here, there and everywhere; from -pole to pole, – China to Peru, – Indus to the pole, – Dan to Beersheba, – end to end; on the face of the earth, in the wide world, from all points of the compass; to the -four winds, – uttermost parts of the earth.

180a. Inextension.—N. in-, non-extension; point; atom &c. (*smallness*) 32; pinprick; limitation &c. 229.

181. (Definite space.) **Region.—N.** region, sphere, sphere of influence, corridor, ground, soil, area, realm, hemisphere, quarter, district, beat, orb, circuit, circle; pale &c. (*limit*) 233; com-, de-partment; domain, tract, territory, terrain, country, canton, county, shire, province, *arrondissement,* diocese, parish, township, borough, constituency, *commune,* ward, wapentake, hundred, riding, lathe, garth, soke, tithing, bailiwick; empire, kingdom, principality, duchy, grand –, arch- duchy, palatinate; republic, commonwealth, dominion, colony, state, island.

arena, precincts, *enceinte,* walk, march; patch, plot, enclosure, &c. 232; close, *enclave,* field, court; street &c. (*abode*) 189.

clime, climate, zone, meridian, latitude.

Adj. territorial, local, parochial, provincial, insular.

182. (Limited space.) **Place.—N.** place, lieu, spot, point, dot; niche, nook, &c. (*corner*) 244; hole; pigeonhole &c. (*receptacle*) 191; compartment; premises, precinct, station, confine; area, court, yard, court-yard, quadrangle, square, compound; abode &c. 189; locality &c. (*situation*) 183.

ins and outs; every hole and corner.

Adv. somewhere, in some place, wherever it may be, here and there, in various places, *passim.*

2°. Relative Space

183. Situation.—N. situation, position, locality, *locale*, *status*, latitude and longitude; footing, standing, standpoint, post; stage; aspect, attitude, posture, *pose*.

place, site, base, station, seat, *venue*, whereabouts, environment, neighbourhood; bearings &c. (*direction*) 278; spot &c. (*limited space*) 182.

top- ge, chor-ography; map &c. 554.

V. be -situated, – situate; lie; have its seat in.

Adj. situ-ate, -ated; local, topical, topographical &c. *n.*

Adv. *in -situ*, – *loco*; here and there, *passim*; here-, there-, whereabouts; in place, here, there.

in –, amidst- such and such- -surroundings, – *environs*, – *entourage*.

184. Location.—N. loca-tion, -lization; lodgment; de-, re-position; stow-, pack-age; collocation; packing, lading; establishment, settlement, installation; fixation; insertion &c. 300.

anchorage, roadstead, mooring, mooring mast, encampment, camp, bivouac.

plantation, colony, settlement, cantonment, encampment, reservation; colonization, domestication, situation; habitation &c. (*abode*) 189; cohabitation; 'a local habitation and a name'; idenization, naturalization.

V. place, situate, locate, localize, make a place for, put, lay, set, seat, station, lodge, quarter, post, install; store, house, stow; establish, fix, pin, root; graft; plant &c. (*insert*) 300; shelve, pitch, camp, lay down, deposit, reposit; cradle; moor, tether, picket; pack, tuck in; embed; vest, invest in.

billet on, quarter upon, saddle with; load, lade, freight; pocket, put up, bag.

inhabit &c. (*be present*) 186; domesticate, colonize, populate, people; take –, strike- root; anchor; cast –, come to an- anchor; sit –, settle-down; settle; take up one's -abode, – quarters; plant –, establish –, locate- oneself; squat, perch, hive, *se nicher*, bivouac, burrow, get a footing; encamp, pitch one's tent; put up -at, – one's horses at; keep house.

indenizen, naturalize, adopt.

put back, replace &c. (*restore*) 660.

Adj. placed &c. *v.*; situate, posited, ensconced, embedded, embosomed, rooted; domesticated; vested in, unremoved.

moored &c. *v.*; at anchor.

185. Displacement.—N. displacement, elocation, transposition.

ejectment &c. 297; exile &c. (*banishment*) 893; removal &c. (*transference*) 270; unshipment.

misplacement, dislocation &c. 61; fish out of water.

V. dis-place, -plant, -lodge, -nest, -establish; misplace, unseat, disturb; exile &c. (*seclude*) 893; ablegate, set aside, remove; take –, cart- away; rake –, draft- off; lade &c. 184, unship.

unload, empty &c. (*eject*) 297; transfer &c. 270; dispel.

vacate; depart &c. 293.

Adj. displaced &c. *v.*; un-placed, -housed, -harboured, -established, -settled; house-, home-less; out of place, – a situation.

misplaced, out of its element.

3°. Existence in Space

186. Presence.—N. presence; occupancy, -ation; attendance; whereness.

permeation, pervasion; diffusion &c. (*dispersion*) 73.

187. [Nullibiety. *] **Absence.** — N. absence; inexistence &c. 2; non-residence, absenteeism; non-attendance, *alibi*.

* Bishop Wilkins.

ubi-ety, -quity, -quitariness; omnipresence.

bystander &c. (*spectator*) 444.

V. exist in space, be -present &c. *adj.* assist at; make one -of, – at; look on, attend, remain; find –, present- oneself; show one's face; fall in the way of, occur in a place; lie, stand; occupy.

people; inhabit, dwell, reside, stay, sojourn, live, room, abide, bunk, lodge, nestle, roost, perch; take up one's abode &c. (*be located*) 184; tenant, occupy.

resort to, frequent, haunt; revisit.

fill, pervade, permeate; be -diffused, – disseminated -through; over-spread, -run; run through; meet one at every turn.

Adj. present; occupying, inhabiting &c. *v.*; moored &c. 184; residential, resi-ant, -dent, -dentiary; domiciled.

ubiquit-ous, -ary; omnipresent.

peopled, populous, full of people, inhabited.

Adv. here, there, where, everywhere, aboard, on board, at home, afield; on the spot; here, there and everywhere &c. (*space*) 180; in presence of, before; under the -eyes, – nose- of; in the face of; *in propriâ personâ.*

emptiness &c. *adj.*; void, *vacuum*; vac-uity, -ancy; *tabula rasa*; exemption; *hiatus* &c. (*interval*) 198; no man's land.

truant, absentee.

nobody; nobody -present, – on earth; no one; not a soul; *âme qui vive.*

V. be -absent &c. *adj.*; keep -away, – out of the way; play truant, absent oneself, stay away.

withdraw, make oneself scarce, vacate; go away, slip out, slip away, retreat &c. 293.

Adj. absent, not present, away, nonresident, gone, from home; missing; lost; wanted, wanting; omitted; nowhere to be found; inexistent &c. 2.

empty, void; blank, vac-ant, -uous; untenanted, -occupied, -inhabited; tenantless; desert, -ed; devoid; un-, uninhabitable.

exempt from, not having.

Adv. without, *minus*, nowhere; elsewhere; neither here nor there; in default of; *sans*; behind one's back.

Phr. the bird has flown, *non est inventus.*

---

188. Inhabitant. — N. inhabitant; habitant, resident, -iary; dweller, indweller; occup-ier, -ant, farmer, planter; householder, lodger, boarder, paying guest; inmate, tenant, renter, incumbent, sojourner, *locum tenens*, commorant; settler, squatter, backwoodsman, colonist; islander; denizen, citizen; burgher, oppidan, cockney, cit, townsman, burgess; villager; cot-tager, -tier, -ter; compatriot.

native, indigene, aboriginal, aborigines, autochthones; Briton, Englishman, John Bull; new comer &c. (*stranger*) 57.

garrison, crew; population; people &c. (*mankind*) 372; colony, settlement; household.

V. inhabit &c. (*be present*) 186; indenizen &c. (*locate oneself*) 184.

Adj. indigenous; enchorial; national, nat-ive, -al; autochthonous; British, English; colonial; domestic; domicil-

189. [Place of habitation, or resort.] **Abode.**—N. abode, dwelling, lodging. -s; diggings, domicile, residence, address, habitation, where one's lot is cast, local habitation, berth, seat, lap, sojourn, housing, quarters, headquarters, resiance, tabernacle, throne, ark.

home, fatherland, mother country, country &c. 181; home-stead, -stall; fireside, chimney corner; hearth, – stone; household gods, *lares et penates*, roof, household, housing, *dulce domum*, paternal domicile; native -soil, – land, blighty.

nest, *nidus*, snuggery; arbour, bower &c. 191; lair, den, cave, hole, hiding-place, cache, cell, *sanctum sanctorum* aerie, eyry, rookery, hive; *habitat*, haunt, covert, resort, retreat, perch, roost; nidification.

bivouac, camp, encampment, cantonment, castrametation; barrack, casemate, casern.

iated, -ed; naturalized, vernacular, domesticated; domiciliary.

in the occupation of; garrisoned –, occupied- by.

———————

tent &c. (*covering*) 223; building &c. (*construction*) 161; chamber &c. (*receptacle*) 191.

tenement, messuage, farm, farm-house, grange, *hacienda*.

cot, cabin, log cabin, shack, hut, *châlet*, croft, shed, booth, stall, hovel, bothy, shanty, igloo, tepee, wigwam; pen &c. (*inclosure*) 232; barn, bawn; kennel, sty, dog-hole, cote, coop, hutch, byre; cow-house, -shed; stable, dove-cote, shippen.

house, mansion, place, villa, cottage, box, lodge, hermitage, *rus in urbe*, folly, rotunda, tower, *château*, castle, pavilion, hotel, court, manor-house, capital messuage, hall, palace, alcazar; country seat; kiosk, bungalow; temple &c. 1000; home of rest, alms-, poor-, work-house, asylum; boarding-, lodging-house; flat, maisonette, duplex, penthouse, suite of rooms, apartments, rooms, room, building &c. 161; Mansion House, town hall, Capitol.

assembly-room, auditorium, coliseum, meeting-house, pump-room, spa, health resort, watering-place; club; theatre &c. 840; drill hall, gymnasium, church &c. 1000; Houses of Parliament &c. 696; school &c. 542; inn; hostel, -ry; hotel, tavern, caravansary, khan, hospice; public-, ale-, pot-, mug-house; gin-palace, gin-mill; coffee-, eating-house; canteen, *restaurant*, *rôtisserie*, cafetaria, grill-room, *buffet*, *café*, *estaminet*, *posada*, *bodega*; bar; saloon, speakeasy, shebeen.

hamlet, village, thorp, dorp, ham, kraal; borough, burgh, town, county-seat, – town, city, capital, metropolis; suburb, quarter, parish &c. 181; ghetto; province, country.

street, place, terrace, parade, esplanade, promenade, pier, embankment, road, villas, row, walk, lane, alley, court, quadrangle, quad, wynd, close, yard, passage, rents, mansions, buildings, mews.

square, polygon, circus, crescent, mall, *piazza*, arcade, colonnade, peristyle, cloister; gardens, grove, residences; block of buildings, market-place, *place*.

anchorage, roadstead, roads; dock, basin, wharf, quay, port, harbour; dry-, graving-, floating-dock.

garden, park, pleasure-ground, pleasance, demesne.

V. take up one's abode &c. (*locate oneself*) 184; inhabit &c. (*be present*) 186.

Adj. urban, oppidan, metropolitan; suburban provincial, rural, rustic; countrified; regional, parochial, domestic; cosmopolitan; palatial.

190. [Things contained.] **Contents.—N.** contents; cargo, lading, freight, shipment, load, bale, burden; cart-, ship-load; cup –, basket –, &c. (*receptacle*) 191- of; inside &c. 221; stuffing, ullage.

V. load, lade, ship, charge, fill, stuff.

191. Receptacle.—N. receptacle, container; inclosure &c. 232; recipient, receiver, reservatory.

compartment; cell, -ule; follicle; hole, corner, niche, recess, nook; crypt, stall, pigeon-hole, cove, oriel; cave &c. (*concavity*) 252.

capsule, vesicle, cyst, pod, calyx, *cancelli*, utricle, bladder, udder.

stomach, paunch, *venter*, abdomen, ventricle, crop, craw, ingluvies, maw, gizzard, bread-basket, belly, little Mary; mouth.

pocket, pouch, fob, sheath, scabbard, socket, bag, vanity bag, compact, sac, sack, saccule, despatch –, attaché-, tachy- case, wallet, scrip, card-, note- case, billfold, poke, kit, knap-, haver-, ruck-sack, sachel, satchel, reticule, budget, net; ditty-, -box, -bag, kitbag; portfolio; saddlebags, holster; quiver &c. (*magazine*) 636.

chest, box, coffer, caddy, case, casket, pyx, pix, *caisson*, desk, *bureau*, reliquary, shrine; trunk, portmanteau, band-box, *valise*, suitcase, hand-, traveling-, overnight-, Gladstone-, carpet-bag, brief case; boot, imperial; *vache*; cage, manger, rack.

vessel, vase, bushel, barrel; canister, jar; pottle, basket, punnet, pannier, buck-basket, hopper, maund, creel, cran, crate, cradle, bassinet, wisket, whisket, *jardinière*, *corbeille*, hamper, wastepaper basket, dosser, dorser, tray, hod, scuttle, utensil, spittoon, cuspidor.

[For liquids] cistern &c. (*store*) 636; vat, caldron, barrel, cask, puncheon, keg, rundlet, tun, butt, firkin, hogshead, kilderkin, carboy, amphora, ampulla, bottle, jar, leather bottle, decanter, ewer, cruse, carafe, crock, kit, canteen, flagon; demijohn; flask, -et; stoup, noggin, vial, phial, *ampoule*, cruet, caster; gourd; urn, *épergne*, salver, *patella*, *tazza*, *patera*; pig-, big-gin; tea-, coffee-pot, percolator, *samovar*; tyg, nipperkin, pocket-pistol; tub, bucket, pail, skeel, pot, tankard, jug, pitcher, toby, mug, pipkin; gal-, gall-ipot, pannikin; matrass, receiver, retort, alembic, bolthead, can, kettle; bowl, basin, jorum, punch-bowl, cup, goblet, chalice, tumbler, glass, wineglass, rummer, beaker, tass, horn, saucepan, skillet, posnet, tureen, terrine, *casserole*, sauce-, gravy-boat.

plate, platter, paten, dish, vegetable –, *entrée*- dish, trencher, calabash, porringer, potager, saucer, pan, crucible.

shovel, trowel, spoon; table-, dessert-, tea-, egg-, salt-spoon; spatula, ladle; dipper; baler; watch-glass, thimble.

closet, commode, cupboard, cellaret, *chiffonnière*, locker, bin, bunker, *buffet*, press, safe, sideboard, drawer, chest of drawers, till, *scrutoire*, *secrétaire*, *éscritoire*, davenport, book-case, cabinet, canterbury; corner cupboard, wardrobe.

chamber, apartment, room, cabin; office, court, hall, atrium; suite of rooms, flat, story; saloon, *salon*, parlour; presence-chamber; sitting-, drawing-, reception-, state-, living-, work-room; gallery, cabinet, closet, cubicle; pew, box; *boudoir*; *adytum*, *sanctum*; bed-room, dormitory, dressing-room; refectory, dining-room, *salle-à-manger*; nursery, school-room; library, study; studio; billiard-, bath-, smoking-room; den, canteen, mess, officers' mess; gun-, ward-, mess-room.

attic, loft, garret, cockloft, clerestory; cellar, vault, hold, cockpit; *entresol*; mezzanine floor; ground-floor, *rez-de-chaussée*; basement, kitchen, cook-house, galley, pantry, scullery, offices; store-room &c. (*depository*) 636; lumber-room; dust-hole, -bin; dairy, laundry, coach-house; *garage*; *hangar*; out-, pent-house; lean-to.

portico, porch, piazza, verandah, lobby, court, hall, vestibule, corridor, passage; ante-room, -chamber; lounge; *foyer*, *loggia*.

conservatory, green-house, glass-house, vinery, bower, arbour, summer-house, alcove, grotto, hermitage, pergola.

lodging &c. (*abode*) 189; bed &c. (*support*) 215; carriage &c. (*vehicle*) 272.

Adj. capsular; saccu-lar, -lated; recipient; ventricular, cystic, vascular, vesicular, cellular, camerated, locular, multilocular, poly-gastric; marsupial; siliqu-ose, -ous.

Section II. DIMENSIONS

1°. General Dimensions

192. Size.—N. size, magnitude, dimension, bulk, volume; largeness &c. *adj.*; greatness &c. (*of quantity*) 31; expanse &c. (*space*) 180; amplitude, mass; proportions.

capacity; ton-, tun-nage; calibre, scantling.

turgidity &c. (*expansion*) 194; corpulence, obesity; plumpness, &c. *adj.*; *embonpoint*, corporation, flesh and blood, lustihood.

hugeness &c. *adj.*; enormity, immensity, monstrosity.

giant, Brobdingnagian, Antæus, Goliath, Gog and Magog, Gargantua, monster, mammoth, Cyclops; whale, porpoise, behemoth, leviathan, elephant, hippopotamus; colossus; tun, lump, bulk, block, loaf, mass, clod, nugget, bushel, thumper, whopper, spanker, strapper; Triton among the minnows.

mountain, mound; heap &c. (*assemblage*) 72.

largest portion &c. 50; full-, life-size.

V. be- large &c. *adj.*; become -large &c. (*expand*) 194.

Adj. large, big; great &c. (*in quantity*) 31; considerable, bulky, voluminous, ample, massive, massy; capacious, comprehensive; spacious &c. 180; mighty, towering, fine, magnificent.

corpulent, stout, fat, plump, squab, full, lusty, strapping, bouncing; portly, burly, well-fed, full-grown; stalwart, brawny, fleshy; goodly; in good -case, – condition; in condition; chopping, jolly; chub-, chubby-faced.

lubberly, hulky, unwieldy, lumpish, gaunt, spanking, whacking, whopping, thumping, thundering, hulking; overgrown; puffy &c. (*swollen*) 194.

huge, immense, enormous, mighty; vast, -y; amplitudinous, stupendous; monst-er, -rous; gigantic, elephantine;

193. Littleness.—N. littleness &c. *adj.*; smallness &c. (*of quantity*) 32; exiguity, inextension; parvi-tude, -ty; duodecimo; Elzevir edition, epitome, microcosm; rudiment; vanishing point; thinness &c. 203.

dwarf, pigmy, atomy, Liliputian, midget, chit, pigwidgeon, urchin, elf; doll, puppet; Tom Thumb, Hop-o'-my thumb, Humpty-dumpty; man-, mannikin; *homunculus*, dapperling, fingerling, dandiprat, cock-sparrow, scalawag.

animalcule, monad, mite, insect, emmet, fly, midge, gnat, shrimp, minnow, worm, maggot, entozoon; *bacillus*, microbe, micro-organism, *bacteria*; *infusoria*; microbe; grub; tit, tomtit, runt, mouse, small fry; millet-, mustard-seed; barley-corn; pebble, grain of sand; mole-hill, button, bubble.

point; atom &c. (*small quantity*) 32; fragment &c. (*small part*) 51; powder &c. 330; point of a pin, mathematical point; *minutiæ* &c. (*unimportance*) 643.

micro-graphy, -meter, -scope; vernier; scale.

V. be -little &c. *adj.*; lie in a nutshell; become small &c. (*decrease*) 36, (*contract*) 195.

Adj. little; small &c. (*in quantity*) 32; minute, diminutive, microscopic; inconsiderable &c. (*unimportant*) 643; exiguous, puny, tiny, wee, petty, minikin, miniature, pigmy, elfin; under sized; dwarf, -ed, -ish; spare, stunted, limited; cramp, -ed; pollard, Liliputian, dapper, pocket; port-ative, -able; duodecimo; dumpy, squat; compact, handy; short &c. 201.

impalpable, intangible, evanescent, imperceptible, invisible, inappreciable, infinitesimal, homœopathic; atomic, corpuscular, molecular; rudiment-ary, -al; embryonic.

weazen, scant, scraggy, scrubby;

giant, -like; colossal, Cyclopean, Brobdingnagian, Gargantuan, Titanic; infinite &c. 105.

large as life; plump as a -dumpling, – partridge; fat as -a pig, – a quail, – butter, – brawn, – bacon.

194. Expansion. — N. expansion; increase &c. 35 -of size; enlargement, extension, augmentation; ampli-fica-tion, -ation; aggrandizement, spread, increment, growth, development, pullulation, swell, dilation, dilatation, rarefaction; turg-escence, -idness, -idity; obesity &c. (*size*) 192; dropsy, tumefaction, intumescence, swelling, tumour, *diastole*, distension; puff-ing, -iness; inflation; pandiculation.

dilatability, expansibility.

germination, growth, upgrowth; accretion &c. 35.

over-growth, -distension; hypertrophy, tympany.

bulb &c. (*convexity*) 250; plumper; superiority of size.

V. become -larger &c. (large &c. 192); expand, widen, enlarge, extend, grow, increase, incrassate, swell, gather; fill out; deploy, take open order, dilate, stretch, spread; mantle, wax; grow –, spring- up; bud, bourgeon, shoot, sprout, germinate, put forth, vegetate, pullulate, open, burst forth, flower, blow &c. 734; gain –, gather- flesh; outgrow; spread like wildfire, overrun.

be larger than; surpass &c. (*be superior*) 33.

render -larger &c. (large &c. 192); expand, spread, extend, aggrandize, distend, develop, amplify, spread out, widen, magnify, rarefy, inflate, puff, puff out, blow up, stuff, pad, cram; exaggerate; fatten; bloat, augment.

Adj. expanded &c. *v.*; larger &c. (large &c. 192); swollen; expansive; wide-open, -spread; fan-shaped; flabelliform; overgrown, exaggerated, bloated, fat, turgid, tumid, hypertrophied, dropsical; pot-, swag-bellied; œdematous, obese, puffy, pursy, blowzy, distended; patulous; bulbous &c. (*convex*) 250; full-blown, -grown, -formed; big &c. 192.

thin &c. (*narrow*) 203; granular &c. (*powdery*) 330; shrunk &c. 195.

Adv. in a -small compass, – nutshell; on a small scale.

---

195. Contraction.—N. contraction, reduction, diminution; decrease &c. 36-of size; defalcation, decrement; lessening, shrinkage; collapse, emaciation, attenuation, tabefaction, consumption, marasmus, atrophy; systole, neck, hour-glass.

condensation, compression, constraint, compactness; compendium &c. 596; squeezing &c. *v.*; strangulation; corrugation; astringency, constringency; astringents, sclerotics; contractility, compressibility; coarctation.

inferiority in size.

V. become -small, – smaller; lessen, decrease &c. 36; grow less, dwindle, shrink, contract, narrow, shrivel, collapse, wither, lose flesh, wizen, fall away, waste, wane, ebb; decay &c. (*deteriorate*) 659.

be smaller than, fall short of; not come up to &c. (*be inferior*) 34.

render smaller, lessen, diminish, contract, draw in, narrow, coarctate; constrict, constringe; condense, compress, boil down, deflate, exhaust, empty; squeeze, corrugate, crush, crumple up, warp, purse up, pack, stow; pinch, tighten, strangle; cramp; dwarf, bedwarf; shorten &c. 201; circumscribe &c. 229; restrain &c. 751; fold &c. 258.

pare, reduce, attenuate, rub down, scrape, file, grind, chip, shave, shear.

Adj. contracting &c. *v.*; astringent; shrunk, contracted &c. *v.*; strangulated, tabid, wizened, stunted; tabescent; marasmic; waning &c. *v.*; neap; compact.

unexpanded &c. (expand &c. 194); inswept; contractile; compressible; smaller &c. (small &c. 193).

---

196. Distance.—N. distance; space &c. 180; remoteness, farness; far- cry

197. Nearness.—N. nearness &c. *adj.*; proximity, propinquity; vicinity,

to; longinquity, elongation; offing, background; removedness; parallax; reach, span, stride; drift.

out-post, -skirt; horizon, sky-line; aphelion; foreign parts, *ultima Thule*, *ne plus ultra*, antipodes; long range, giant's stride.

dispersion &c. 73.

V. be -distant &c. *adj.*; extend –, stretch –, reach –, spread –, go –, get –, stretch away- to; range, outrange, outreach.

remain at a distance; keep –, stand- -away, – off, – aloof, – clear of.

Adj. distant; far -off, – away; remote, telescopic, distal, wide of; stretching to &c. *v.*; yon, -der; ulterior; trans-marine, -pontine, -atlantic, -alpine; tramontane; ultra-montane, -mundane; hyperborean, antipodean; inaccessible, out of the way; unapproach-ed, -able; incontiguous.

Adv. far -off, – away; afar, -off; off; away; a -long, – great, – good- way off; wide away, aloof; wide –, clear- of; out of -the way, – reach; abroad, yonder, farther, further, beyond; *outre mer*, over the border, far and wide, over the hills and far away; from pole to pole &c. (*over great space*) 180; to the -uttermost parts, – ends- of the earth; out of -hearing, – range, nobody knows where, *à perte de vue*, out of the sphere of, wide of the mark; a far cry to.

apart, asunder; wide -apart, – asunder; *longo intervallo*; at arm's length.

-age; neighbourhood, adjacency; contiguity &c. 199.

short -distance, – step, – cut; earshot, close quarters, stone's throw; bow –, gun –, pistol- shot; hair's breadth, span; close-up.

purlieus, neighbourhood, vicinage, *environs*, *alentours*, suburbs, confines, *banlieue*, borderland; whereabouts.

bystander; neighbour, borderer.

approach &c. 286; convergence &c. 290; perihelion.

V. be -near &c. *adj.*; adjoin, hang about, trench on; border –, verge upon; stand by, approximate, tread on the heels of, cling to, clasp, hug; cuddle, huddle; hang upon the skirts of, hover; burn; abut.

bring –, draw- -near &c. 286; converge &c. 290; crowd &c. 72; place -side by side &c. *adv.*

Adj. near, nigh; close –, near- at hand; close, neighbouring, propinquent, bordering upon; adjacent, adjoining, limitrophe; proxim-ate, -al; at hand, handy; near the mark, near run; home, intimate.

Adv. near, nigh; hard –, fast- by; close -to, – upon, – up; at the point of; next door to; within -reach, – call, – hearing, – earshot, – range; within an ace of; but a step, not far from, at no great distance; on the -verge, – brink, – skirts- of; in the -environs &c. *n.*; at one's -door, – feet, – elbow, – finger's end, – side; on the tip of one's tongue; under one's nose; within a -stone's throw &c. *n.*; in -sight, – presence- of; at close quarters; cheek by -jole, – jowl; beside, alongside, side by side, *tête-à-tête*; in juxtaposition &c. (*touching*) 199; yard-arm to yard-arm; at the heels of; on the confines of, at the threshold, bordering upon, verging to; in the way.

about; here-, there-abouts; roughly, in round numbers; approxim- -ately, -atively; as good as, well nigh.

198. Interval.—**N.** interval, interspace; separation &c. 44; break, gap, opening; hole &c. 260; chasm, *hiatus*, cæsura; inter-ruption, -regnum; interstice, *lacuna*, cleft, mesh, crevice, chink, rime, creek, cranny, crack, chap, slit, slot, fissure, scissure, rift, flaw, breach, fracture, rent, gash, cut, leak, dike, ha-ha.

199. Contiguity.—**N.** contiguity, contact, proximity, apposition, juxtaposition, touching &c. *v.*; abutment, osculation; meeting, appulse, appulsion, *rencontre*, rencounter, syzygy, coincidence, conjunction, coexistence; adhesion &c. 46.

border-land; frontier &c. (*limit*) 233; tangent.

gorge, defile, ravine, cañon, *crevasse*, abyss, abysm; gulf; inlet, frith, strait, gully, gulch, nullah; pass; notch; furrow &c. 259; yawning gulf; *hiatus -maxime, – valde- deflendus*; parenthesis &c. (*interjacence*) 228; void &c. (*absence*) 187; incompleteness &c. 530.

V. gape &c. (*open*) 260.

Adj. with an interval, far between.

Adv. at intervals &c. (*discontinuously*) 70; *longo intervallo*.

V. be -contiguous &c. *adj.*; join, adjoin, abut on, march with, border; tick, graze, touch, meet, osculate, kiss, come in contact, coincide; coexist; adhere &c. 46.

Adj. contiguous; touching &c. *v.*; in -contact &c. *n.*; conterminous, end to end, osculatory; pertingent; tangential.

hand to hand; close to &c. (*near*) 197; with no -interval &c. 198.

2°. Linear Dimensions

200. Length.—N. length, longitude, span, extent, mileage.

line, bar, rule, stripe, streak, spoke, radius.

lengthening &c. *v.*; pro-longation, -duction, -traction; ten-sion, -sure; extension.

[Measures of length] line, nail, inch, hand, palm, foot, cubit, yard, ell, fathom, rod, pole, perch, furlong, mile, league; chain, metre, kilo-, centi-, milli- &c. -metre.

pedometer, perambulator, odometer, odograph, speedometer, cyclometer, log, telemeter, range finder; scale &c. (*measurement*) 466.

V. be -long &c. *adj.*; stretch out, sprawl; extend –, reach –, stretch- to; make a long arm, 'drag its slow length along.'

render -long &c. *adj.*; lengthen, extend, elongate; stretch; pro-long, -duce, -tract; let –, pay –, draw –, spin- out; drawl.

enfilade, look along, view in perspective.

Adj. long, -some; lengthy, lank, wiredrawn, outstretched; lengthened &c. *v.*; sesquipedalian &c. (*words*) 577; interminable, no end of.

line-ar, -al; longitudinal, oblong.

as long as -my arm, – to-day and to-morrow; unshortened &c. (shorten &c. 201).

Adv. lengthwise, at length, longitudinally, endlong, along; *tandem*; in a line &c. (*continuously*) 69; in perspective.

from -end to end, – stem to stern, – head to foot, – the crown of the head to the sole of the foot, – top to toe, – head to heels; fore and aft.

201. Shortness.—N. shortness &c. *adj.*; brevity; littleness &c. 193; a span.

shortening &c. *v.*; abbrevia-tion, -ture; abridgment, concision, retrenchment, curtailment, decurtation; reduction &c. (*contraction*) 195; epitome &c. (*compendium*) 596.

abridger, abstractor, epitomiser.

elision, ellipsis; conciseness &c. (*in style*) 572.

V. be -short &c. *adj.*; render -short &c. *adj.*; shorten, curtail, abridge, abbreviate, take in, reduce; compress &c. (*contract*) 195; epitomize &c. 596.

retrench, cut short, obtruncate; scrimp, cut, chop up, hack, hew; cut –, pare- down; clip, snip, dock, lop, prune; shear, shave, mow, reap, crop; snub; truncate, pollard, stunt, nip, nip in the bud, check the growth of; [in drawing] foreshorten.

Adj. short, brief, curt; compendious, compact; stubby, scrimp; shorn, stubbed; stumpy, thickset, podgy, stocky, pug; squab, -by; squat, dumpy; little &c. 193; curtailed of its fair proportions; short by; oblate; concise &c. 572; summary.

Adv. shortly &c. *adj.*; in short &c. (*concisely*) 572.

202. Breadth. Thickness.—**N.** breadth, width, latitude, amplitude; diameter, bore, calibre, radius; superficial extent &c. (*space*) 180.

thickness, crassitude; corpulence &c. (*size*) 192; dilatation &c. (*expansion*) 194.

V. be -broad &c. *adj.*; become –, render- -broad &c. *adj.*; expand &c. 194; thicken, widen.

Adj. broad, wide, ample, extended; discous; fan-like; out-spread, -stretched; wide as a church-door.

thick, dumpy, squab, squat, thickset, tubby; thick as a rope, stubby &c. 201.

---

203. Narrowness. Thinness. —**N.** narrowness &c. *adj.*; closeness, exility; exiguity &c. (*little*) 193.

line; hair's –, finger's -breadth; strip, streak, vein.

thinness &c. *adj.*; tenuity; emaciation, macilency, *marcor.*

shaving, slip &c. (*filament*) 205; threadpaper, skeleton, shadow, scrag, anatomy, spindle-shanks, barebones, lantern jaws, mere skin and bone.

middle constriction, stricture, neck, waist, isthmus, wasp, hour-glass; ridge, *ghaut*, pass; ravine &c. 198.

narrowing, coarctation, angustation, tapering; contraction &c. 195.

V. be -narrow &c. *adj.*; narrow, taper, contract &c. 195; render -narrow &c. *adj.*

Adj. narrow, close; slender, thin, fine; *svelte*; thread-like &c. (*filament*) 205; finespun, taper, slim, gracile, slight, slight-made; scant, -y; spare, delicate, incapacious; contracted &c. 195; unexpanded &c. (expand &c. 194); slender as a thread, capillary.

emaciated, lean, meagre, gaunt, macilent; lank, -y; weedy, skinny, scrawny, scraggy; starv-ed, -eling; attenuated, shrivelled, wizened, pinched, peaky, skeletal, spindling, spindle- -legged, -shanked; extenuated, tabid, marcid, bare-bone, raw-boned; herring-gutted; worn to a shadow, lean as a rake; thin as a -lath, – whipping post, – wafer; hatchet-faced; lantern-jawed.

204. Layer.—**N.** layer, stratum, course, bed, zone, *substratum*, floor, flag, stage, story, tier, slab, escarpment, table, tablet, panel, plaque; board, plank; trencher, platter.

plate; lam-ina, -ella; sheet, flake, foil, wafer, scale, coat, peel, pellicle, ply, thickness, membrane, film, leaf, slice, shive, cut, rasher, shaving, integument &c. (*covering*) 223.

stratification, lamination, scaliness, nest of boxes, coats of an onion.

V. slice, shave, pare, peel; plate, coat, veneer; cover &c. 223.

Adj. lamell-ar, -ated, -iform; laminated, -iferous; micaceous; schist-ose, -ous; scaly, filmy, membranous, flaky, squamous; folia-ted, -ceous; stratified, -form; tabular, discoid, spathic.

205. Filament.—**N.** filament, line; fibre, fibril; funicle, vein, hair, capillament, *cilium*, tendril, gossamer; hairstroke; harl.

wire, string, thread, packthread, cotton, sewing-silk, twine, twist, whipcord, cord, rope, cable, yarn, hemp, oakum, jute, wool, worsted.

strip, shred, slip, spill, list, band, fillet, *fascia*, ribbon, riband, tape, roll, lath, slat, strake, splinter, shiver, shaving.

beard &c. (*roughness*) 256; ramification; strand.

Adj. fil-amentous, -aceous, -iform; fibr-ous, -illous; thread-like, wiry, stringy, ropy; capill-ary, -iform; funicular, wire-drawn; anguilliform; flagelliform; hairy &c. (*rough*) 256; ligulate.

---

206. Height.—**N.** height, altitude, elevation, ceiling; eminence. pitch; loftiness &c. *adj.*; sublimity.

tallness &c. *adj.*; stature, procerity; prominence &c. 250.

207. Lowness.—**N.** lowness &c. *adj.*; debasement, depression; prostration &c. (*horizontal*) 213; depression &c. (*concave*) 252.

molehill; lowlands; bottomlands;

colossus &c. (*size*) 192; giant, grenadier, giraffe.

mount, -ain; hill, butte, monticle, fell, knap; cape; head-, fore-land; promontory; ridge, hog's back, dune; rising –, vantage- ground; down; moor, -land; Alp; up-, high-lands; heights &c. (*summit*) 210; knoll, hummock, hillock, barrow, mound, mole, *kopje*; steeps, bluff, cliff, craig, tor, peak, pike, clough; escarpment, edge, ledge, brae; dizzy height.

tower, pillar, column, pylon, obelisk, monument, steeple, spire, minaret, *campanile*, belfry, turret, roof, dome, cupola, pagoda, pyramid; sky scraper; Eiffel tower.

pole, pikestaff, maypole, flagstaff; mast, top –, topgallant- mast.

ceiling &c. (*covering*) 223.

high water; high –, flood –, spring- tide.

altimetry &c. (*angle*) 244; altimeter, height-finder, hypsometer, barograph.

V. be -high &c. *adj.*; tower, soar. command; hover; cap, culminate; overhang, hang over, impend, beetle; bestride, ride, mount; perch, surmount; cover &c. 223; overtop &c. (*be superior*) 33; stand on tiptoe.

become -high &c. *adj.*; grow, – higher, – taller; upgrow; rise &c. (*ascend*) 305.

render -high &c. *adj.*; heighten &c. (*elevate*) 307.

Adj. high, elevated, eminent, exalted, lofty, supernal; tall; gigantic &c. (*big*) 192; Patagonian; towering, beetling, soaring, hanging [gardens]; elevated &c. 307; upper; highest &c. (*topmost*) 210; monticolous, perchiug, hill-dwelling.

up-, moor-land; hilly, mountainous, alpine, sub-alpine, heaven-kissing; cloud-topt, -capt, -touching; aerial.

overhanging &c. *v.*; incumbent, overlying; super-incumbent, -natant, -imposed; prominent &c. 250.

tall as a -maypole, – poplar, – steeple; lanky &c. (*thin*) 203.

Adv. on high, high up, aloft, up, above, aloof, overhead; up –, above- stairs; in the clouds; on -tiptoe, – stilts, – the shoulders of; over head and ears; breast high.

over, upwards; from top to bottom &c. (*completely*) 52.

basement, ground-floor; *rez-de-chaussée* &c. 211; hold; feet, heels.

low water; low –, ebb –, neap –, spring- tide.

V. be -low &c. *adj.*; lie -low, – flat; underlie; crouch, slouch, wallow, grovel; lower &c. (*depress*) 308.

Adj. low, neap, debased; nether, -most; flat, level with the ground; lying low &c. *v.*; crouched, subjacent, squat, prostrate &c. (*horizontal*) 213.

Adv. under; be-, under-neath; below; down, -wards; adown, at the foot of; under-foot, -ground; down –, below-stairs; at a low ebb; below par.

---

208. Depth.—N. depth; deepness &c. *adj.*; profundity, depression &c. (*concavity*) 252.

hollow, pit, shaft, well, crater, abyss; gulf &c. 198; bowels of the earth, bottomless pit, hell.

soundings, depth of water, water, draught, submersion; plummet, sound, probe; sounding -rod, – line, – machine; lead; submarine, diving bell, bathysphere; diver.

V. be -deep &c. *adj.*; render -deep &c. *adj.*; deepen.

plunge &c. 310; sound, heave the lead, take soundings; dig &c. (*excavate*) 252.

209. Shallowness.—N. shallowness &c. *adj.*; shoals; mere scratch.

Adj. shallow, superficial; skin –, ankle –, knee- deep; just enough to wet one's feet; shoal, -y

---

Adj. deep, -seated; profound, sunk, buried; submerged &c. 310; sub-aqueous, -marine, -terranean, -terrene; underground.

bottom-, sound-, fathom-less; unfathom-ed, -able; abysmal; deep as a well, deep-sea.

knee-, ankle-deep.

Adv. beyond –, out of- one's depth; over head and ears, over one's head.

210. Summit.—N. summit, -y; top, vertex, apex, zenith, pinnacle, acme, acropolis, culmination, meridian, utmost height, *ne plus ultra*, height, pitch, maximum, climax, apogee; culminating –, crowning –, turning- point; turn of the tide, fountain head; water-shed, -parting; sky, pole.

tip, -top; crest, crow's nest, cap, truck, peak, nib; end &c. 67; crown, brow; head, nob, noddle, pate.

high places, heights.

top-, top-gallant mast, sky scraper; quarter –, hurricane- deck.

architrave, frieze, cornice, coping, coping-stone, zoophorus, capital, headpiece, capstone, epistyle, sconce, pediment, entablature; tympanum; ceiling &c. (*covering*) 223.

attic, loft, garret, house-top, upper story, roof.

V. culminate, cap, crown, top; overtop &c. (*be superior to*) 33.

Adj. highest &c. (high &c. 206); top; top-, upper-most; tip-top; culminating &c. *v.*; meridi-an, -onal; capital, head, polar, supreme, supernal, top-gallant.

Adv. a-top, at the top of – the tree, – the heap.

211. Base.—N. base, -ment; plinth, dado, wainscot, baseboard; foundation &c. (*support*) 215; substructure, *substratum*, sump, ground, earth, pavement, floor, paving, flag, carpet, ground-floor, deck; footing, groundwork, basis; hold, bilge, orlop deck.

bottom, nadir, foot, sole, toe, hoof, keel, kelson, root.

Adj. bottom; under-, nether-most; fundamental; founded –, based –, grounded –, built- on.

---

212. Verticality. — N. verticality; erectness &c. *adj.*; perpendicularity; right angle, normal; azimuth circle.

wall, palisade, precipice, cliff, steep, bluff.

elevation, erection; square, plumbline, plummet.

V. be -vertical &c. *adj.*; stand -up, – on end, – erect, – upright; stick –, cock-up.

render -vertical &c. *adj.*; set –, stick –, raise –, cock- up; erect, rear, raise, pitch, raise on its legs.

Adj. vertical, upright, erect, perpendicular, normal, plumb, straight, bolt upright; rampant; straight –, standing-up &c. *v.*; rectangular, orthogonal.

Adv. vertically &c. *adj.*; up, on end; up –, right- on end; *à plomb*, endwise; on one's legs; at right angles.

---

213. Horizontality.—N. horizontality; flatness; level, plane; stratum &c. 204; dead -level, – flat; level plane.

recumbency; lying down &c. *v.*; reclination, decumbence; de-, discumbency; proneness &c. *adj.*; accubation, supination, resupination, prostration; azimuth.

plain, floor, platform, bowling-green; cricket-ground; court; gridiron; baseball diamond; hockey rink; tennis-, croquet-ground, – lawn; billiard table; terrace, estrade, esplanade, *parterre*, table-land, *plateau*, ledge.

spirit-, level; T-square.

V. be -horizontal &c. *adj.*; lie, recline, couch; lie -down, – flat, – prostrate; sprawl, loll; sit down.

render -horizontal &c. *adj.*; lay, – down, – out; level, flatten, even, raze, equalize, smooth, align; prostrate, knock down, floor, fell, ground.

Adj. horizontal, level, even, plane;

flat &c. 251; flat as a -billiard table, – bowling green; alluvial; calm, – as a mill-pond; smooth, – as glass.

re-, de-, pro-, ac-cumbent; lying &c. *v.*; prone, supine, couchant, jacent, prostrate.

Adv. horizontally &c. *adj.*; on -one's back. – all fours, – its beam ends.

214. Pendency.—N. pend-, dependency; suspension, hanging &c. *v.*

pendant, drop, tippet, tassel, lobe, tail, train, flap, lappet, skirt, pig-tail, queue, pendulum.

peg, knob, button, hook, nail, stud, ring, staple, tenterhook; davit; fastening &c. 45; spar, horse.

chande-, gase-, electro-lier.

V. be -pendent &c. *adj.*; hang, depend, swing, dangle, droop, sag; swag; daggle, flap, trail, flow.

suspend, hang, sling, hook up, hitch, fasten to, append.

Adj. pend-ent, -ulous; pensile; hanging &c. *v.*; dependent; suspended &c. *v.*; lowering, overhanging, beetling, decumbent; loose, flowing.

having a -peduncle &c. *n.*; pedunculate, tailed, caudate.

---

215. Support.—N. support, ground, foundation, base, basis; *terra firma*; bearing, fulcrum, *point d'appui*, caudex, purchase, footing, hold, -*locus standi*; landing, – stage, – place; stage, platform; block; rest, resting-place; groundwork, *substratum*, sustentation, subvention; floor &c. (*basement*) 211.

supporter; aid &c. 707; prop, stand, anvil, fulciment; hod, stay, shore, skid, rib, sprag, truss, bandage; sleeper; stirrup, stilts, shoe, sole, heel, splint, lap; bar, rod, boom, sprit, outrigger.

staff, stick, crutch, alpenstock, bourdon; *bâton*, maulstick, colstaff, cowlstaff, staddle; stalk, ped-icel, -icle, – uncle.

post, pillar, shaft, column, pilaster; pediment, pedestal; plinth, shank, leg, socle, zocle; buttress, jamb, mullion, abutment; pile, baluster, banister, stanchion, king post; balustrade.

frame, -work, body, *chassis*, *fuselage*; scaffold, skeleton, beam, rafter, girder, lintel, joist, cantilever, travis, trave, corner-stone. summer, transom; rung, round, step, sill.

columella, back-bone; key-stone; axle, -tree; axis; arch, ogive, mainstay.

trunnion, pivot, rowlock; peg &c. (*pendency*) 214; tie-beam &c. (*fastening*) 45; thole pin.

board, ledge, shelf, hob, bracket, trevet, trivet, arbor, rack, hatrack; mantel, -piece, -shelf; slab, console; counter, dresser; flange, corbel; table, trestle, teapoy; shoulder; perch; horse; easel, desk; retable, predella.

seat, throne, dais; divan, musnud; chair, bench, form, stool, camp-stool, sofa, settee, davenport, stall, miserere, arm –, easy –, elbow –, rocking- chair; couch, day bed, *fauteuil*, woolsack, ottoman, settle, squab, bench, box, dicky; saddle, pannel, pillion; side –, pack- saddle; pommel.

bed, berth, pallet, tester, crib, cot, bassinet, hammock, shakedown, camp bed, bunk, truckle-bed, cradle, litter, stretcher, bedstead; four-poster, French bed; bedding, mattress, *paillasse*; pillow, bolster; mat, rug, cushion.

stool, footstool, hassock, faldstool, *prie-dieu*; tabouret; tripod. Atlas, Persides, Atlantes, Caryatides, Hercules.

V. be -supported &c.; lie –, sit –, recline –, lean –, loll –, rest –, stand –, step –, repose –, abut –, bear –, be based &c.- on; have at one's back; be-stride, -straddle.

support, bear, carry, hold, sustain, shoulder; hold –, back –, bolster –, shore- up; up-hold, -bear; prop; under-prop, -pin, -set; bandage, &c. 43; brace, truss; cradle, pillow.

give –, furnish –, afford –, supply –, lend- -support, – foundations; bottom, found, base, ground, embed.

maintain, keep on foot; aid &c. 707.

Adj. support-ing, -ed, &c. *v.*; atlantean, columellar; sustentative, fundamental, basal.

Adv. astride on, astraddle; pick-a-back.

216. Parallelism.—N. parallelism; coextension, concentricity, collimation.

V. be –, lie- parallel to; collimate.

Adj. parallel; coextensive, collateral, concentric, concurrent.

Adv. alongside, abreast &c. (*laterally*) 236.

---

217. Obliquity.—N. obliquity, inclination, skew, slope, slant; crookedness &c. *adj.*; slopeness; leaning &c. *v.*; bevel, bezel, ramp, tilt; bias, list, twist, swag, cant, lurch; distortion &c. 243; bend &c. (*curve*) 245; tower of Pisa.

acclivity, rise, ascent, grade, gradient, *glacis*, rising ground, hill, bank, declivity, downhill, dip, fall, devexity; gentle –, rapid- slope; easy -ascent, – descent; shelving beach; *talus*; *montagne Russe*; *facilis descensus Averni.*

steepness &c. *adj.*; cliff, precipice &c. (*vertical*) 212; escarpment, scarp.

[Measure of inclination] clinometer, theodolite, level, sextant, quadrant, protractor; angle, sine, cosine, tangent &c. hypothenuse:

diagonal; zigzag, chevron.

V. be -oblique &c. *adj.*; slope, slant, lean, incline, shelve, stoop, decline, descend, bend, heel, careen, sag, swag, seel, slouch, cant, sidle.

render -oblique &c. *adj.*; sway, bias; slope, slant; incline, bend, crook; cant, tilt; distort &c. 243.

Adj. oblique, inclined; sloping &c. *v.*; tilted &c. *v.*; recumbent, clinal, skew, askew, slant, aslant, bias, plagiedral, indirect, wry, awry, ajee, crooked; knock-kneed &c. (*distorted*) 243; bevel, out of the perpendicular.

uphill, rising, ascending, acclivous; downhill, falling, descending; declining, declivous, devex, anticlinal; steep, abrupt, precipitous, break-neck.

diagonal; trans-verse, -versal; athwart, antiparallel; curved &c. 245.

Adv. obliquely &c. *adj.*; on –, all on- one side; askew, askant, askance, aslope, asquint, edgewise, at an angle; side-long, -ways; slope-, slant-wise; by a side wind.

218. Inversion.—N. in-, e-, sub-, re-, retro-, intro-version; contraposition &c. 237; contrariety &c. 14; reversal; turn of the tide.

overturn; somer-sault, -set; summerset; *culbute*; revulsion; *pirouette.*

transposition, transposal, anastrophy, *metastasis*, *hyperbaton*, *anastrophe*, *hysteron-proteron*, hypallage, *synchysis*, *tmesis*, parenthesis; *metathesis*; palindrome; Spoonerism.

pronation and supination.

V. be -inverted &c.; turn –, go –, wheel- -round, – about, – to the right about; turn –, go –, tilt –, topple-over; capsize, turn turtle.

in-, sub-, retro-, intro-vert; reverse; up-, over-turn, -set; turn -topsy turvy &c. *adj.*; *culbuter*; transpose, put the cart before the horse, turn the tables.

Adj. inverted &c. *v.*; wrong side -out, – up; inside out, upside down; bottom –, keel- upwards; supine, on one's head, topsy turvy, *sens dessus sens dessous.*

inverse; reverse &c. (*contrary*) 14; opposite &c. 237.

topheavy, unstable.

Adv. inversely &c. *adj.*; hirdie-girdie; heels over head, head over heels.

219. Crossing.—**N.** crossing &c. *v.*; inter-section, – lacement, – twinement, -digitation; decussation, transversion; convolution &c. 248.

reticulation, meshwork, network; inosculation, anastomosis, intertexture, mortise.

net, *plexus*, web, mesh, twill, skein, sleeve, felt, lace; wicker; mat, -ting; plait, trellis, wattle, lattice, grating, *grille*, gridiron, tracery, fretwork, filigree, reticle; tissue, netting, mokes.

cross, crucifix, rood, crisscross, crux; chain, wreath, braid, cat's cradle, knot; entanglement &c. (*disorder*) 59.

[woven fabrics] cloth, linen, muslin, cambric, drill, homespun, tweed, broadcloth &c.

V. cross, decussate; inter-sect, -lace, -twine, -twist, -weave, -digitate, -link.

twine, entwine, weave, inweave, twist, wreathe; anastomose, inosculate, dovetail, splice, link.

mat, plait, plat, braid, felt, twill; tangle, entangle, ravel; net, knot; dishevel, raddle.

Adj. crossing &c. *v.*; crossed, matted &c. *v.*; transverse.

cross, cruciform, crucial; reti-form, -cular, -culated; areolar, cancellated, mullioned, latticed, grated, barred, streaked; textile, secant, plexal; interfretted.

Adv. across, thwart, athwart, transversely, crosswise.

3°. Centrical Dimensions*

1. *General*

220. Exteriority. — **N.** exteriority; outside, exterior; surface, superficies; skin &c. (*covering*) 223; *superstratum*; disk, disc; face, facet.

excentricity; circumjacence &c. 227.

V. be -exterior &c. *adj.*; lie around &c. 227.

place -exteriorly, – outwardly, – outside; put –, turn- out.

Adj. exter-ior, -nal; extraneous, outer, -most; out-ward, -lying, -side, -door; round about &c. 227; extramural.

superficial, skin-deep; frontal, discoid.

extraregarding; eccentric; outstanding; extrinsic &c. 6.

Adv. externally &c. *adj.*; out, without, over, outwards, *ab extra*, out of doors; *extra muros.*

221. Interiority.—**N.** interiority; inside, interior, endocrine; interspace, subsoil, *substratum.*

contents &c. 190; substance, pith, marrow; backbone &c. (*centre*) 222; heart, bosom, breast, abdomen; vitals, viscera, entrails, bowels, belly, intestines, guts, chitterlings, womb, lap; gland, cell; internal organs, *penetralia*, recesses, innermost recesses; cave &c. (*concavity*) 252.

inhabitant &c. 188.

V. be -inside &c. *adj.*, – within &c. *adv.*

place –, keep- within; enclose &c. (*circumscribe*) 229; intern; embed &c. (*insert*) 300.

Adj. inter-ior, -nal; inner, inside, intimate, inward, intraregarding; in-, inner-most; deep-seated; visceral, intes-

* That is, Dimensions having reference to a centre.

in the open air; *sub* -*Jove*, – *dio*; *à la belle étoile*, *al fresco*.

———

tine, -tinal; inland; subcutaneous; interstitial &c. (*interjacent*) 228; inwrought &c. (*intrinsic*) 5; enclosed &c. *v*.

home, domestic, indoor, intramural, vernacular; endemic.

Adv. internally &c. *adj*.; inwards, within, in, inly; here-, there-, where-in; *ab intra*, withinside; in –, within- doors; at home, in the bosom of one's family.

222. Centrality.—N. centrality, centricalness, centre; middle &c. 68; focus &c. 74.

core, kernel; nucleus, nucleolus; heart, pole, axis, pivot, fulcrum, bull's eye; hub, nave, navel; *umbilicus*, spine, backbone, marrow, pith; hot-bed; concentration &c. (*convergence*) 290; centralization; symmetry.

centre of -gravity, – pressure, – percussion, – oscillation, – buoyancy &c. metacentre.

V. be -central &c. *adj*.; converge &c. 290.

render central, centralize, concentrate; bring to a focus.

Adj. centr-al, -ical; middle &c. 68; axial, pivotal, focal, umbilical, concentric; middlemost, nuclear, centric, centraidal; spinal, vertebral.

Adv. middle; midst; centrally &c. *adj*.

223. Covering.—N. covering, cover; canopy, tilt, awning, baldachin, tent, marquee, *tente d'abri*, umbrella, parasol, sunshade; veil (*shade*) 424; shield &c. (*defence*) 717; pall.

roof, dome, cupola, mansard roof; ceiling; thatch, tile; pan-, pen-tile; tiling, shingles, slates, slating, leads; shed &c. (*abode*) 189.

top, lid, covercle, door, *operculum*, eyelid, blind, curtain.

bandage, plaster, lint, wrapping, dossil, finger stall.

coverlet, counterpane, sheet, quilt, comforter, eiderdown; tarpaulin, blanket, rug, drugget, linoleum, oilcloth; housing.

in-, tegument; skin, pellicle, fleece, fell, fur, ermine, miniver, sable, sealskin &c.; leather, morocco, calf, pigskin, elk, kid, cowhide &c.; shagreen, hide; pelt, -ry; cuticle, *dermis*, scarf-skin, *epidermis*.

clothing &c. 225; mask &c. (*concealment*) 530.

peel, crust, bark, rind, *cortex*, husk, shell, coat.

capsule; ferrule; sheath, -ing; pod, cod; casing, case, theca, *elytron*; *involucrum*; wrapp-ing, -er, envelope, vesicle; dermatology, conchology.

armour, -plate, armouring; veneer, facing; pavement; scale &c. (*layer*) 204; coating, paint, stain; varnish &c. (*resin*) 356*a*; anointing &c. *v*.; inunction; incrustation, superposition, obduction, ground, enamel, whitewash, plaster, stucco, rough cast, pebble dash, compo; rendering; cerement; ointment &c. (*grease*) 356.

V. cover; super-pose, -impose; over-lay, -spread; wrap &c. 225; incase; face, case, veneer, pave, paper; tip, cap, bind, revet.

coat, paint, varnish, pay, incrust, stucco, cement, dab, plaster, tar; wash; be-, smear; be-, daub; anoint, do over; gild, plate,

224. Lining.—N. lining, inner coating; coating &c. (*covering*) 223; stalactite, -agmite.

filling, stuffing, wadding, padding, bushing.

wainscot, *parietes*, wall, brattice.

V. line, stuff, incrust, wad, pad, fill.

Adj. lined &c. *v*.

———

electroplate, japan, lacquer, lacker, enamel, whitewash; lay it on thick.

over-lie, -arch; conceal &c. 528.

Adj. covering &c. *v.*; cutaneous, dermal, cortical, cuticular, tegumentary, skinny, scaly, squamous; covered &c. *v.*; imbricated, loricated, armour-plated, iron-clad; under cover, hooded, cloaked, cowled.

225. Investment.—N. investment; covering &c. 223; dress, clothing, raiment, drapery, costume, attire, guise, toilet, *toilette*, trim; habiliment; vesture, -ment; garment, garb, palliament, apparel, wardrobe, wearing apparel, clothes, things.

array; tailoring, millinery; best bib and tucker; finery &c. (*ornament*) 847; full dress &c. (*show*) 882; garniture; theatrical properties.

outfit, equipment, *trousseau*; uniform, khaki, regimentals; academicals, canonicals &c. 999; livery, gear, harness, turn out, accoutrement, caparison, suit, rigging, trappings, traps, slops, togs, toggery; masquerade.

dishabille, morning dress, lounge suit, tea-gown, *kimono*, *négligé*, dressing-gown, *peignoir*, wrapper, undress; shooting-coat; smoking-jacket, mufti; rags, tatters, old clothes; mourning, weeds; duds; slippers.

robe, tunic, dolman, *paletot*, habit, gown, coat, coatee, frock, blouse, middy, sagum, *toga*, smock-frock; frock-, dress-, morning-, tail-coat; dress-suit, – clothes, swallow-tail coat, dinner-, Eton-jacket.

cloak, pall; mantle, mantlet, mantua, shawl, *pelisse*, veil, yashmak; cape, tippet, kirtle, plaid, muffler, comforter, Balaclava helmet, haik, huke, chlamys, mantilla, tabard, housing, horse-cloth, burnous, *roquelaure*; *houppelande*; sur-, top-, over-, great-coat; *surtout*, spencer, cardigan, sweater, blazer; mackintosh, waterproof, slicker, raincoat, oilskin, trench coat, ulster, monkey-, pea-, pilot-jacket, redingote; wraprascal, poncho, cardinal, pelerine, talma.

jacket, jumper, vest, jerkin, waistcoat, doublet, *camisole*, gabardine; stays, *corsage*, corset, corselet, bodice; stomacher; skirt, petticoat, slip, farthingale, kilt, jupe, crinoline, bustle, hobble skirt, *panier*, apron, pinafore; loin cloth.

trousers; breeches, trews, pantaloons, unmentionables, inexpressibles, overalls, pyjamas, smalls, small-clothes; tights, pants, shorts, drawers; knickerbockers, knickers, plus fours, bloomers, divided skirt; phil-, fill-ibeg.

226. Divestment.—N. divestment; taking off &c. *v.*

nudity; bareness &c. *adj.*; undress; dishabille &c. 225, altogether; nu-, denu-dation; decortication, depilation, excoriation, desquamation; moulting; exfoliation.

baldness, alopecia, acomia.

V. divest; uncover &c. (*cover* &c. 223); denude, bare, strip; undress, unclothe, disrobe &c. (dress, enrobe, &c. 225); uncoif; dismantle; uncase; put –, take –, cast- off; shed, doff; husk, peel, pare, decorticate, desquamate, excoriate, skin, scalp, flay, bark, expose, lay open; exfoliate, moult, mew; cast the skin.

Adj. divested &c. *v.*; bare, naked, nude; un-dressed, -draped, -clad, -clothed, -appareled; exposed; in dishabille; *décolleté*; bald, threadbare, ragged, callow, roofless.

in -a state of nature, – nature's garb, – buff, – native buff, – birthday suit; *in puris naturalibus*; with nothing on, stark naked; bald as a coot, bare as the back of one's hand; out at elbows; barefoot; bareback; leaf-, nap-, hairless, shaved, clean shaven, tonsured, beardless, bald-headed, acomous.

head-dress, -gear; cap, *béret*, tam o' shanter, glengarry, topee, sombrero; hat; cocked –, high –, tall –, top –, silk –, opera –, crush -hat, *gibus*, beaver, castor, bonnet, tile, wideawake, billy-cock; bowler; soft felt –, straw –, leghorn -hat, panama; toque; wimple; night-, mob-, skull-cap, biretta; hood, cowl, coif; capote, calach; scull-cap; kerchief, snood; head, *coiffure*; crown &c. (*circle*) 247; *chignon*, pelt, wig, front, peruke, periwig; caftan, turban, fez, *tarboosh*, taj, shako, csako, busby; *képi*, forage cap, bearskin; helmet &c. 717; mask, domino.

body clothes; linen; shirt, sark, smock, shift, *chemise, lingerie*; night-gown, -shirt; bed-gown, *sac de nuit*; jersey, guernsey; underwear, undies, underclothing, -waistcoat.

neck-erchief, -cloth; tie, ruff, collar, cravat, stock, handkerchief, bandana, scarf; bib, tucker; dicky; boa; girdle &c. (*circle*) 247; cummerbund.

shoe, pump, brogue, boot, slipper, sandal, galoche, goloshes, arctics, rubber boots, overshoes, patten, clog, sabot; high-low; Blücher –, Wellington –, Hessian –, jack –, top- boot; Balmoral; legging, puttee, buskin, greave, galligaskin, moccasin, *gamache*, gambado, gaiter, spatter-dash, spat, antigropelos; stocking, hose, gaskins, trunk-hose, sock, hosiery.

glove, gauntlet, mitten, cuff, muffettee, wristband, sleeve.

swaddling cloth, baby-linen, *layette*; pocket-handkerchief.

shroud &c. 363.

clothier, tailor, milliner, *costumier*, sempstress, seamstress, snip; dress-, habit-, breeches-, shoe-maker; cordwainer, cobbler, Crispin, hosier, hatter; draper, linendraper, haberdasher, mercer.

V. invest; cover &c. 223; envelop, lap, involve; in-, en-wrap; wrap; fold –, wrap –, lap –, muffle- up; overlap; sheathe, swathe, swaddle, roll up in, shroud, circumvest.

vest, clothe, array, dress, dight, drape, robe, enrobe, attire, tire, garb, habilitate, apparel, accoutre, rig, fit out; bedizen, deck &c. (*ornament*) 847; perk; equip, harness, caparison; dress up.

wear; don; put –, huddle –, slip- on; mantle.

Adj. invested &c. *v.*; habited; dight, -ed; clad, *costumé*, shod, *chaussé*; *en grande tenue* &c. (*show*) 882.

sartorial.

227. Circumjacence.—N. circumjacence, -ambience; environment, encompassment; atmosphere, medium; surroundings, *entourage*.

outpost; border &c. (*edge*) 231; girdle &c. (*circumference*) 230; outskirts, *boulevards*, suburbs, purlieus, precincts, *faubourgs*, *environs*, *banlieue*, neighbourhood, vicinity.

V. lie -around &c. *adv.*; surround, beset, compass, encompass, environ, inclose, enclose, encircle, circle, embrace, circumvent, lap, gird; begird, girdle, engird; skirt, twine round; hem in &c. (*circumscribe*) 229; besiege, invest, blockade.

Adj. circum-jacent, -ambient, -fluent;

228. Interjacence.—N. inter-jacence, -currence, -venience, -location, -digitation, -penetration; permeation.

inter-jection, -polation, -lineation, -spersion, -calation; embolism.

inter-vention, -ference, -position; in-, ob-trusion; insinuation; insertion &c. 300; dovetailing; infiltration; intromission.

intermedi-um, -ary; go-between, agent, middleman, medium, bodkin, intruder, interloper; parenthesis, episode; fly-leaf.

partition, *septum*, diaphragm, midriff; party-wall, panel, vail, bulkhead, brattice, *cloison*; half-way house.

V. lie –, come –, get- between; inter-

ambient; surrounding &c. *v.*; circumferential, surburban.

Adv. around, about; without; on -every side, - all sides; right and left, all round, round about; in the neighbourhood.

---

vene, slide in, interpenetrate, permeate.

put between, introduce, intromit, import; throw –, wedge –, edge –, jam –, worm –, foist –, run –, plough –, work- in; inter-pose, -ject, -calate, -polate, -line, -leave, -sperse, -weave, -lard, -digitate; let in, dovetail, splice, mortise; insinuate, smuggle; infiltrate, ingrain.

interfere, put in an oar, thrust one's nose in; intrude, obtrude; have a finger in the pie; introduce the thin end of the wedge; thrust in &c. (*insert*) 300.

Adj. inter-jacent, -current, -venient, -vening &c. *v.*, -mediate, -mediary, -calary, -stitial, -costal, -mural, -planetary, -stellar; embolismal.

parenthetical, episodic; mediterranean; intrusive; embosomed; merged, mean, middle, medium, median.

Adv. between, betwixt; 'twixt; among, -st; amid, -st; 'mid, -st; in the thick of; betwixt and between; sandwich-wise; parenthetically, *obiter dictum.*

229. Circumscription.—N. circumscription, limitation, inclosure; confinement &c. (*restraint*) 751; circumvallation, encincture; envelope &c. 232.

V. circumscribe, limit, bound, confine, enclose; surround &c. 227; compass about; imprison &c. (*restrain*) 751; hedge –, wall –, rail- in; fence –, hedge- round; embar; picket, corral.

enfold, bury, incase, pack up, enshrine, inclasp; wrap up &c. (*invest*) 225; embosom.

Adj. circumscribed &c. *v.*; begirt, lapt; circumambient; buried –, immersed- in; embosomed, in the bosom of, imbedded, encysted, mewed up; imprisoned &c. 751; land-locked, in a ring fence.

230. Outline.—N. outline, circumference; peri-meter, -phery; ambit, circuit, lines, *tournure, contour*, profile, *silhouette*, lineaments; bounds, coastline.

zone, belt, girth, band, baldric, zodiac, girdle, tire, cingle, clasp, girt; *cordon* &c. (*inclosure*) 232; circlet &c. 247.

V. outline, delineate, *silhouette*, circumscribe &c. 229; profile, block out.

Adj. outlined &c. *v.*; circumferential, perimetric, peripheral.

231. Edge.—N. edge, verge, brink, brow, brim, margin, border, confines, skirt, rim, felloe, felly, flange, side, mouth; jaws, chops, chaps, *fauces*; lip, muzzle.

threshold, door, porch; portal &c. (*opening*) 260; coast, shore, strand, beach, bank, wharf, quay, dock.

frame, fringe, flounce, frill, list, trimming, edging, skirting, hem, selvedge, welt; furbelow, valance, exergue.

Adj. border, marginal, skirting; labial, labiated, marginated.

232. Inclosure.—N. inclosure, enclosure, envelope; case &c. (*receptacle*) 191; wrapper; girdle &c. 230.

pen, fold, croft, sty; pen-, in-, sheep-fold; paddock, pound, corral, kraal; yard, compound; net, seine net.

wall; hedge, -row; *espalier*; fence &c. (*defence*) 717; pale, paling, balustrade, rail, railing, gunwale; quickset hedge, park paling, circumvallation, *enceinte*, ring fence.

barrier, barricade; gate, -way; door, hatch, *cordon*; prison &c. 752.

dike, dyke, ditch, fosse, moat, trench.

V. inclose; circumscribe &c. 229.

233. Limit.—**N.** limit, boundary, bounds, confine, *enclave*, term, bourn, verge, kerb-stone, curbstone, but, pale; termin-ation, -us; stint, frontier, precinct, marches.

boundary line, landmark, benchmark; line of -demarcation, - circumvallation; pillars of Hercules; Rubicon, turning-point; *ne plus ultra*; sluice, flood-gate.

V. limit, bound, confine, define, circumscribe, demarcate, delimit, encompass.

Adj. definite; contermin-ate, -able, terminable, limitable; terminal, frontier, border, bordering, boundary.

Adv. thus far, - and no further.

2. *Special*

234. Front.—**N.** front; fore, - part; foreground; forefront, face, disk, disc, frontage, *façade*, *proscenium*, facia, frontispiece; priority, anteriority; obverse [of a medal].

fore -, front- rank, first line; van, -guard; advanced guard; outpost, scout.

brow, forehead, visage, physiognomy, phiz, features, countenance, map, mug; rostrum, beak, bow, stem, prow, prore, jib, bowsprit; forecastle.

pioneer &c. (*precursor*) 64; metoposcopy.

V. be -, stand- in front &c. *adj.*; front, face, confront, breast, brave; bend forwards; come to the -front, - fore.

Adj. fore, forward, anterior, front, frontal.

Adv. before; in -front, - the van, - advance; ahead, right ahead; fore-, head-most; in the foreground; before one's -face, - eyes; face to face, *vis-à-vis*.

235. Rear.—**N.** rear, back, posteriority; rear -rank, - guard; background, *hinterland*.

occiput, nape, scruff, chine; heels; tail, rump, croup, buttock, posteriors, bottom, seat, backside, scut, breech, *dorsum*, loin; dorsal -, lumbar- region; hind quarters.

stern, poop, after-part, counter; postern, heel-, tail-piece, crupper.

wake; train &c. (*sequence*) 281.

reverse; other side of the shield.

V. be -behind &c. *adv.*; fall astern; bend backwards; bring up the rear; follow &c. 622; tail, shadow.

Adj. back, rear; hind, -er, -most, -ermost; post-ern, -erior; dorsal, after; caudal, lumbar; mizzen.

Adv. behind; in the -rear, - ruck, - back-ground; behind one's back; at the -heels, - tail, - back- of; back to back.

after, -most, aft, abaft, astern, sternmost, aback, rear-, hind-, back-ward.

236. Laterality.—**N.** laterality; side, flank, beam, quarter, lee; hand; cheek, jowl, jole, wing; profile; temple, *parietes*, loin, haunch, hip.

gable, -end; broadside; lee side.

points of the compass; East, Orient, Levant; West, occident; orientation.

V. be -on one side &c. *adv.*; flank, outflank; sidle; skirt, border.

Adj. lateral, sidelong; collateral;

237. Contraposition.—**N.** contraposition, opposition; polarity; inversion &c. 218; opposite side; antithesis; reverse, inverse; counterpart; antipodes; opposite poles, North and South.

V. be -opposite &c. *adj.*; subtend.

Adj. opposite; reverse, inverse; antipodal, subcontrary; fronting, facing, diametrically opposite.

Northern, Septentrional, Boreal, arc

parietal, flanking, skirting; flanked; sideling.

many-sided; multi-, bi-, tri-, quadrilateral.

East-ern, -ward, -erly; orient, -al, auroral, Levantine; West-ern, -ward, -erly; occidental, Hesperian; equatorial.

tic; Southern, Austral, antarctic, polar.

Adv. over, - the way, - against; against; face to face, *vis-à-vis*; as poles asunder.

Adv. side-ways, -long; broadside on; on one side, abreast, abeam, alongside, beside, aside; by, – the side of; side by side; cheek by jowl &c. (*near*) 197; to -windward, – leeward; laterally &c. *adj.*; right and left; on her beam ends.

238. Dextrality. — **N.** dextrality; right, - hand; dexter, offside, starboard.

Adj. dextral, right-handed; ambidextral, dexterous, dextrorsal &c.

239. Sinistrality.—**N.** sinistrality; left, - hand; *sinister*, nearside, larboard, port.

Adj. sinistral, sinister, sinistrorsal &c., left-handed, sinistromanual, sinistrous.

Section III. FORM

1°. General Form

240. Form.—**N.** form, figure, shape; con-formation, -figuration; make, formation, frame, construction, design, cut, set, build, trim, cut of one's jib; stamp, type, cast, mould; fashion; contour &c. (*outline*) 230; structure &c. 329.

feature, lineament, outline, turn; phase &c. (*aspect*) 448; posture, attitude, *pose*.

[Science of form] morphology.

[Similarity of form] isomorphism.

forming &c. *v.*; form-, figur-, efformation; sculpture.

V. form, shape, figure, fashion, efform, carve, cut, chisel, hew, cast; rough-hew, -cast; sketch; block –, hammer- out; trim; lick –, put- into shape; model, knead, work up into, set, mould, sculpture; cast, stamp; build &c. (*construct*) 161.

Adj. formed &c. *v.*

[Receiving form] plastic, fictile, full-fashioned &c.

[Giving form] plasmic &c.

[Similar in form] isomorphous &c.

241. [Absence of form.] **Amorphism.** —**N.** amorphism, informity, uncouthness; unlicked cub, rough diamond; *rudis indigestaque moles*; disorder &c. 59; deformity &c. 243.

disfigure-, deface-ment, deformation; mutilation.

V. [Destroy form] deface, disfigure, deform, mutilate, truncate; derange &c. 61.

Adj. shapeless, amorphous, malformed, formless; un-formed, -hewn, -fashioned, -shapen; rough, rude, Gothic, barbarous, rugged, in the rough; misshapen &c. 243.

---

242. [Regularity of form.] **Symmetry.** —**N.** symmetry, shapeliness, finish; beauty &c. 845; proportion, eurythmy, eurythmic, uniformity, parallelism; bi-, tri-, multi-lateral symmetry; centrality &c. 222.

243. [Irregularity of form.] **Distortion.**—**N.** dis-, de-, con-tortion; knot, mop, warp, buckle, screw, twist; crookedness &c. (*obliquity*) 217; grimace; deformity; mal-, malcon-formation; monstrosity, misproportion, want

arborescence, branching, ramification.

Adj. symmetrical, shapely, well set, finished; beautiful &c. 845; classic, chaste, severe.

regular, uniform, balanced; equal &c. 27; parallel, coextensive.

arbor-escent, -iform; dendr-iform, -oid; branching; ramous, ramose.

---

of symmetry, *anamorphosis*; ugliness &c. 846; teratology.

V. distort, contort, twist, warp &c. *n.*; wrest, writhe, make faces, deform, misshape.

Adj. distorted &c. *v.*; out of shape, irregular, unsymmetric, awry, wry, askew, crooked, sinuous; anamorphous; not -true, – straight; on one side, crump, deformed; mis-shapen, -begotten; mis-, ill-proportioned; ill-made; grotesque, crooked as a ram's horn; hump-, hunch-, bunch-, crook-backed; bandy; bandy-, bow-legged; bow-, knock-kneed; splay-, club-footed; taliped; round-shouldered; snub-nosed; curtailed of one's fair proportions; scalene, stumpy &c. (*short*) 201; gaunt &c. (*thin*) 203; bloated &c. 194.

Adv. all manner of ways.

2°. Special Form

244. Angularity.—N. angular-ity, -ness; aduncity; angle, cusp, bend; fold &c. 258; notch &c. 257; fork, bifurcation.

elbow, knee, knuckle, ankle, groin, crotch, crutch, crane, fluke, scythe, sickle, zigzag, kimbo.

corner, nook, recess, niche, oriel.

right angle &c. (*perpendicular*) 212; obliquity &c. 217; angle of 45°, mitre; acute –, obtuse –, salient –, re-entrant –, spherical –, solid –, dihedral- angle.

angular -measurement, – elevation, – distance, – velocity; trigon-, goni-ometry; altimetry; clin-, graph-, goni-ometer; theodolite; transit circle; sextant, quadrant; dichotomy.

triangle, trigon, wedge; rectangle, square, lozenge, diamond; rhomb, -us; quadr-angle, -ilateral; parallelogram; quadrature; poly-, penta-, hexa-, hepta-, octa-, deca-gon.

Platonic bodies; cube, rhomboid; tetra-, penta-, hexa-, octa-, dodeca-, icosa-hedron; prism, pyramid; parallelopiped.

V. bend, fork, bifurcate, crinkle, divaricate, branch, ramify.

Adj. angular, bent, crooked, aduncous, uncinated, aquiline, jagged, serrated; falc-iform, -ated; furcular, furcated, forked, bifurcate, crotched; zigzag; dovetailed; knock-kneed, crinkled, akimbo, kimbo, geniculated; oblique &c. 217.

fusiform, wedge-shaped, cuneiform; tri-angular, -gonal, -lateral; quadr-angular, -ilateral; rectangular, square, foursquare, multilateral; polygonal &c. *n.*; cubical, rhomboidal, pyramidal.

245. Curvature.—N. curv-ature, -ity, -ation; incurv-ity, -ation; bend; flexure, -ion; conflexure; crook, hook, bought, bending; de-, inflexion; arcuation, devexity, turn; deviation, *détour*, sweep; curl, -ing; bough; recurv-ity, -ation; sinuosity &c. 248; aduncity.

curve, arc, arch, arcade, vault, dome, bow, crescent, *meniscus*, half-moon, lunule, horse-shoe, loop, crane-neck;

246. Straightness.—N. straightness, rectilinearity, directness; inflexibility &c. (*stiffness*) 323; straight –, right –, direct-, bee- line; short cut.

V. be -straight &c. *adj.*; have no turning; not -incline, – bend, – turn, – deviate- to either side; go straight; steer for &c. (*direction*) 278.

render straight, straighten, rectify; set –, put- straight; un-bend, -fold,

para-, hyper-bola; catenary, festoon; conch-, cardi-oid; caustic, instep; tracery.

V. be -curved &c. *adj.*; sweep, swag, sag; deviate &c. 279; turn; re-enter.

render -curved &c. *adj.*; bend, curve, incurvate; de-, in-flect; crook; turn, round, arch, arcuate, arch over, loop the loop, concamerate; bow, coil, curl, recurve, frizzle.

Adj. curved &c. *v.*; curvi-form, -lineal, -linear; devex, devious; recurv-ed, -ous; *retroussé*; crump; bowed &c. *v.*; vaulted; hooked; falc-iform, -ated; semicircular, crescentic; lun-iform, -ular; semi-lunar, meniscal; conchoidal; cord-iform, -ated; cardioid; heart-, bell-, pear-, fig-shaped; reniform; lenti-form, -cular; bow-legged &c. (*distorted*) 243; oblique &c. 217; circular &c. 247.

-curl &c. 248, -ravel &c. 219, -wrap.

Adj. straight; rectiline-ar, -al; direct, even, right, true, in a line; unbent &c. *v.*; un-deviating, -turned, -distorted, -swerving; straight as an arrow &c. (*direct*) 278; inflexible &c. 323.

---

247. [Simple circularity.] **Circularity.**—**N.** circularity, roundness; rotundity &c. 249.

circle, circlet, clasp, ring, washer, areola, hoop, roundlet, *annulus*, amulet, bracelet, armlet, armilla; ringlet; eye, loop, wheel; cycle, orb, orbit, rundle, zone, belt, *cordon*, band; sash, girdle, cestus, cincture, baldric, fillet, *fascia*, wreath, garland; crown, corona, coronet, chaplet, snood, necklace, collar; noose, lasso, lariat.

ellipse, oval, ovule; ellipsoid, cycloid; epi-cycloid, -cycle; semi-circle; quadrant, sextant, sector.

V. make -round &c. *adj.*; round.

go round; encircle &c. 227; describe a circle &c. 311.

Adj. round, rounded, circular, annular, orbicular; oval, ovate; elliptic, -al; ovoid, egg-shaped; pear-shaped &c. 245; cycloidal &c. *n.*; spherical &c. 249.

---

248. [Complex circularity.] **Convolution.**—**N.** winding &c. *v.*; con-, in-, circum-volution; wave, undulation, tortuosity, anfractuosity; sinu-osity, -ation, sinuousness; meandering, circuit, circumbendibus, twist, twirl, windings and turnings, *ambages*; torsion; inosculation; reticulation &c. (*crossing*) 219.

coil, roll, curl, buckle, spire, spiral, helix, corkscrew, worm, volute, whorl, rundle; tendril; scollop, scallop, escalop; kink.

serpent, snake, eel, maze, labyrinth.

V. be -convoluted &c. *adj.*; wind, twine, turn and twist, twirl; wave, undulate, meander; inosculate; entwine, intwine; twist, coil, roll; wrinkle, curl, crisp, twill; frizz, -le; crimp, crape, indent, scollop, scallop; wring, intort; contort; wreathe &c. (*cross*) 219.

Adj. convoluted; winding, twisted &c. *v.*; tortile, tortive; wavy; und-ated, -ulatory; circling, snaky, snake-like, serpentine; serpent-, anguill-, verm-iform; vermicular; mazy, tortuous, anfractuous, sinuous, flexuous, wavy, sigmoidal.

involved, intricate, complicated, perplexed; labyrinth-ic, -ian, -ine; circuitous; peristaltic; dædalian, curly.

wreathy, frizzly, crapy, buckled; ravelled &c. (*in disorder*) 59.

spiral, coiled, helical, turbinated.

Adv. in and out, round and round.

249. Rotundity.—**N.** rotundity; roundness &c. *adj.*; cylindricity; spher-icity, -oidity; globosity.

cylin-der, -droid; barrel, drum; roll, -er; *rouleau*, column, rolling-pin, rundle; chimney-pot, drain-pipe.

cone, conoid; pear-, egg-, bell-shape.

sphere, globe, ball, boulder, bowlder; spher-, ellips-, ge-, glob-oid, oblong –, oblate- spheroid; drop, spherule, globule, vesicle, bulb, bullet, pellet, *pelote*, clew, pill, marble, pea, knob, pommel, knot.

V. render -spherical &c. *adj.*; form into a sphere, sphere, roll into a ball; give -rotundity &c. *n.*; round.

Adj. rotund; round &c. (*circular*) 247; cylindr-ic, -ical, -oid; columnar, lumbriciform; conic, -al; spher-ical, -oidal; glob-ular, -ated, -ous, -ose; egg-, bell-, pear-shaped; ov-oid, -iform; gibbous; campaniform, -ulate, -iliform; fungiform, bead-like, moniliform, pyriform, bulbous; *teres atque rotundus*; round as -an orange, – an apple, – a ball, – a billiard ball, – a cannon ball.

3°. Superficial Form

250. Convexity. — N. convexity, prominence, projection, swelling, gibbosity, bilge, bulge, protuberance, protrusion; excrescency, camber.

intumescence; tumour, tumor; tubercle, -osity; excrescence; hump, hunch, bunch, gnarl, lump.

tooth, knob, elbow, process, *apophysis*, condyle, bulb, node, nodule, nodosity, tongue, *dorsum*, boss, embossment, bump, clump; sugar-loaf &c. (*sharpness*) 253; bow; mamelon.

pimple, wen, wheal, *papula*, postule, pock, proud flesh, growth, goitre, *sarcoma*, carbuncle, corn, bunion, wart, furnuncle, polypus, adenoid, fungus, fungosity, *exostosis*, bleb, blister, blain; boil &c. (*disease*) 655; bubble, blob.

papilla, nipple, teat, pap, breast, dug, mammilla; proboscis, nose, neb, beak, snout, nozzle, snozzle; Adam's apple; belly, paunch, corporation; withers, back, shoulder, lip, flange.

peg, button, stud, ridge, rib, jutty, trunnion, snag.

cupola, dome, bee-hive; arch, balcony, eaves; pilaster.

relief, relievo, *cameo*; *basso-*, *mezzo-*, *alto-rilievo*; low-, bas-, high-relief.

hill &c. (*height*) 206; cape, promontory, mull; fore-, head-land; point of land, naze, ness, mole, jetty, hummock, ledge, spur.

V. be -prominent &c. *adj.*; project, bulge, protrude, bag, belly, pout, bouge, bunch; jut –, stand –, stick –, poke- out; stick –, bristle –, start –, cock –, shoot- up; swell –, hang –, bend- over; beetle.

render -prominent &c. *adj.*; raise 307; emboss, chase.

251. Flatness.—N. flatness &c. *adj.*; smoothness &c. 255.

plane; level &c. 213; plate, platter, table, tablet, slab.

V. render flat, flatten, squash; level &c. 213.

Adj. flat, plane, even, flush, scutiform, discoid; level &c. (*horizontal*) 213; smooth; flat as -a pancake, – a fluke, – a flounder, – a board, – my hand.

252. Concavity.—N. concavity, depression, dip; hollow, -ness; indentation, *intaglio*, cavity, antrum, dent, dint, dimple, follicle, pit, *sinus*, *alveolus*, *lacuna*; excavation, trench, sap, mine, tunnel, burrow; trough &c. (*furrow*) 259; honeycomb.

cup, basin, crater, punch-bowl; cell &c. (*receptacle*) 191; socket, faucet.

valley, vale, dale, dell, gap, dingle, combe, bottom, slade, strath, glade, grove, glen, cave, cavern, cove; grot, -to; alcove, *cul-de-sac*, blind alley; gully &c. 198; arch &c. (*curve*) 245; bay &c. (*of the sea*) 343.

excavator, sapper, miner.

V. be -concave &c. *adj.*; retire, cave in.

render -concave &c. *adj.*; depress, hollow; scoop, – out; gouge, dig, delve, excavate, dent, dint, mine, sap, undermine, burrow, tunnel, stave in.

Adj. depressed &c. *v.*; concave, hollow, stove in; dished; spoon-like; retiring; retreating; cavernous; porous &c. (*with holes*) 260; cellular, spongy, spongious; honeycombed, alveolar; infundibul-ar, -iform; funnel-, bell-shaped; campaniform, capsular; vaulted, arched.

Adj. convex, prominent, protuberant, underhung, undershot; projecting &c. *v.*; bossed, bossy, nodular, bunchy; clav-ate, -ated; hummocky, *moutonné*, mammiform; papul-ous, -ose; hemispheric, bulbous; bowed, arched; bold; bellied; tuber-ous, -culous; tumorous; cornute, knobby, odontoid; lenti-form, -cular; gibbous.

salient, in relief, raised, *repoussé*; bloated &c. (*expanded*) 194.

253. Sharpness.—**N.** sharpness &c. *adj.*; acuity, acumination; spinosity.

point, spike, spine, *spiculum*, tine; needle, pin; tack, nail; prick, -le; spur, rowel, barb; spit, cusp; horn, antler; snag; tag; thorn, bristle.

nib, tooth, incisor, tusk; spoke, cog, ratchet.

crag, crest, *arête*, cone, peak, sugar-loaf, pike, *aiguille*; spire, pyramid, steeple.

beard, *chevaux de frise*, porcupine, hedgehog, brier, bramble, thistle; comb, awn, bur.

wedge; knife-, cutting- edge; blade, edge-tool, cutlery, knife, penknife, whittle, razor; scalpel, bistoury, lancet; chisel; ploughshare, coulter; hatchet, axe, pick-axe, mattock, pick, adze, bill; bill-hook, cleaver, cutter; skiver; scythe, sickle, scissors, shears; sword &c. (*arms*) 727; bodkin &c. (*perforator*) 262.

sharpener, hone, strop; grind-, whet-stone; steel, emery.

V. be -sharp &c. *adj.*; taper to a point; bristle with.

render -sharp &c. *adj.*; sharpen, point, aculeate, acuminate, whet, barb, spiculate, set, strop, grind.

cut &c. (*sunder*) 44.

Adj. sharp, keen; acute; aci-cular, -form; acu-leated, -minated; pointed; tapering; conical, pyramidal; mucron-ate, -ated; spindle-, needle-shaped; spiked, spiky, ensiform, peaked, salient, cusp-ed; -idate, -idated; corn-ute, -uted, -iculate; prickly; spiny, spinous; thorny, bristling, muricated, pectinated, studded, thistly, briery; craggy &c. (*rough*) 256; snaggy; digitated, two-edged, fusiform; denti-form, -culated; toothed; odontoid; star-like; stell-ated, -iform; arrow-headed; arrowy, barbed, spurred, sagittal; spear-shaped, hastate; horned; conical.

cutting; sharp-, knife-edged; sharp –, keen- as a razor; sharp as a needle; sharpened &c. *v.*; set.

254. Bluntness.—**N.** bluntness &c. *adj.*

V. be –, render- blunt &c. *adj.*; obtund, dull; take off the -point, – edge; turn.

Adj. blunt, obtuse, dull, bluff.

255. Smoothness.—**N.** smoothness &c. *adj.*; polish, gloss; lubric-ity, -ation.

down, velvet, silk, satin; slide; bowling green &c. (*level*) 213; glass, ice; asphalt, pavement, flags.

roller, steam-roller; iron, flat-iron, tailor's goose; sand-, emery-paper; burnisher, turpentine and bees-wax.

V. smooth, -en; plane; file; mow, shave; level, roll; macadamize; polish, burnish, planish, levigate, calender, glaze; iron, hot-press, mangle; lubricate &c. (*oil*) 332.

256. Roughness.—**N.** roughness &c. *adj.*; tooth, grain, texture, ripple; asperity, rugosity, salebrosity, corrugation, nodosity; arborescence &c. 242.

brush, hair, beard, shag, mane, whisker, mutton-chops, *moustache*, *mustachio*, imperial, Van Dyke, tress, lock, curl, ringlet, *fimbriæ*, *cilia*, *villi*; eyelashes, eye-brows, love-lock.

plum-age, -osity; plume, *panache*, crest; feather, tuft, tussock, fringe, toupee.

wool, velvet, plush, nap, pile, floss,

Adj. smooth; polished &c. *v.*; even; level &c. 213; plane &c. (*flat*) 251; sleek, glossy; silken, silky; lanate, downy, velvety; glabrous, slippery, glassy, lubricous, oily, soft; unwrinkled; smooth as -glass, – ice, – velvet, – oil; slippery as an eel; woolly &c. (*feathery*) 256.

fluff, fur, down; byssus, moss, bur.

V. be -rough &c. *adj.*; go against the grain.

render -rough &c. *adj.*; roughen, rough cast, knurl; ruffle, crisp, crumple, crinkle, corrugate, engrail; set on edge, stroke –, rub- the wrong way, rumple.

Adj. rough, uneven; scabrous, knotted; nodular; rug-ged, -ose, -ous; asperous, crisp, salebrous, gnarled, unpolished, unsmooth, rough-hewn; knurled, cross-grained, crag-gy, -ged; crankling, scraggy, jagged, unkempt, prickly &c. (*sharp*) 253; arborescent &c. 242; leafy, well-wooded; feathery; plum-ose, -igerous; tufted, fimbriated, hairy, bristly, ciliated, filamentous, hirsute; crin-ose, -ite; bushy, hispid, villous, pappous, bearded, pilous, shaggy, shagged; fringed, befringed; set-ous, -ose, -aceous; 'like quills upon the fretful porcupine'; rough as a -nutmeg grater, – bear.

downy, velvety, flocculent, woolly; lan-ate, -ated; lanugin-ous. -ose; tomentous.

Adv. against the grain, in the rough, on edge.

257. **Notch.**—N. notch, dent, nick, cut; indent, -ation; serration; dimple.

embrasure, battlement, machicolation; saw, tooth, crenelle, scallop, scollop, vandyke.

V. notch, nick, cut, pink, mill, score, dent, indent, jag, scarify, scotch, crimp, scollop, crenulate, vandyke.

Adj. notched &c. *v.*; crenate, -d; dentate, -d; denticulate, -d; toothed, palmated, serrated.

258. **Fold.**—N. fold, plicature, pleat, plait, ply, crease; tuck, gather; flexion, flexure, joint, elbow, doubling, duplicature, wrinkle, rimple, crinkle, crankle, crumple, rumple, rivel, ruck, ruffle, dog's ear, corrugation, frounce, flounce, lapel; pucker, crow's feet.

V. fold, double, plicate, pleat, plait, crease, wrinkle, crinkle, crankle, curl, smock, cockle up. crocker, rimple, rumple, frizzle, frounce, rivel, twill, corrugate, ruffle, crimple, crumple, pucker; turn –, double- -down, – under; tuck, ruck, hem, gather.

Adj. folded &c *v.*

259. **Furrow.**—N. furrow, groove, rut, *sulcus*, scratch, streak, *striæ*, crack, score, incision, slit; chamfer, fluting.

channel, gutter, trench, ditch, dike, dyke, moat, fosse, trough, kennel; ravine &c. (*interval*) 198.

V. furrow &c. *n.*; flute, groove, carve, corrugate, plough, incise, chase, enchase, grave, engrave, etch, bite in, cross-hatch.

Adj. furrowed &c. *v.*; ribbed, striated, sulcated, fluted, canaliculated; bisulc-ous, -ate; trisulcate; corduroy.

260. **Opening.**—N. hole, foramen; puncture, blow-out, perforation; pin-, key-, loop-, port-, peep-, mouse-, pigeon-hole; eye, – of a needle; eyelet; slot.

opening; apert-ure, -ness; hiation,

261. **Closure.**—N. closure, occlusion, blockade; shutting up &c. *v.*; obstruction &c. (*hindrance*) 706; gag; embolism; contraction &c. 195; infarction; con-, ob-stipation; blind -alley, – corner; *cul-de-sac*, *cæcum*; imper-foration,

yawning, oscitancy, dehiscence, patefaction, pandiculation; gap, chasm &c. (*interval*) 198.

embrasure, window, casement, light; sky-, fan-light; lattice; bay-, bow-window; oriel; dormer, lantern, *abat-jour*.

out-, in-let; vent, vomitory; *embouchure*; orifice, mouth, sucker, muzzle, throat, gullet, placket, weasand, wizen, nozzle, *œsophagus*.

portal, porch, gate, ostiary, postern, wicket, trap-door, hatch, door; arcade; gate-, door-, hatch-, gang-way; lich-gate.

way, path &c. 627; thoroughfare; channel, passage, tube, pipe; water-pipe &c. 350; air-pipe &c. 351; vessel, tubule, canal, gut, fistula; adjutage, ajutage; chimney, smoke stack, flue, tap, funnel, gully, tunnel, main; mine, pit, adit, shaft, gallery.

alley, aisle, glade, lane, vista.

bore, calibre; pore; blind orifice.

por-ousness, -osity; sieve, cullender, colander; grater, shredder; cribble, riddle, screen; honeycomb.

apertion, perforation; piercing &c. *v.*; terebration, empalement, pertusion, puncture, acupuncture, penetration.

opener, key, master-key, *passe-partout*.

V. open, ope, gape, dehisce, yawn, bilge; fly open.

perforate, pierce, empierce, tap, bore, drill; mine &c. (*scoop out*) 252; tunnel; trans-pierce, -fix; enfilade, impale, spike, spear, gore, spit, stab, pink, puncture, lance. trepan, trephine, stick, prick, riddle, punch; stave in.

cut a passage through; make -way, – room- for.

un-cover, -close, -rip; lay –, cut –, rip –, throw- open.

Adj. open; perforated &c. *v.*; perforate; wide open, agape, ajar; un-closed, -stopped; oscitant, gaping, yawning; patent.

tubular, cannular, fistulous; per-vious, -meable; foraminous; vesi-, vas-cular; porous, follicular, cribriform, honeycombed, infundibular, riddled; tubul-ous, -ated, piped.

opening &c. *v.*; aperient.

Int. *open sesame!*

262. Perforator. — N. perforator, piercer, borer, auger, gimlet, stylet, drill, wimble, awl, bradawl, scoop, terrier, corkscrew, dibble, trocar, trepan, trephine, probe, bodkin, needle, stiletto, broach, reamer, rimer, warder, lancet; punch, -eon; spikebit, gouge; spear &c. (*weapon*) 727.

-viousness &c. *adj.*, -meability; stopper &c. 263; *operculum*.

V. close, occlude, plug; block –, stop –, fill –, bung –, cork –, button –, stuff –, shut –, dam- up, obturate; blockade; obstruct &c. (*hinder*) 706; bar, bolt, stop, seal, plumb; choke, throttle; ram down, tamp, dam, cram; trap, clinch; put to –, shut- the door; batten down the hatches.

Adj. closed &c. *v.*; shut, operculated; unopened.

unpierced, imporous, cæcal; imperforate, -vious, -meable; impenetrable; un-, im-passable; invious; path-, way-less; untrodden.

unventilated; air-, water-tight; hermetically sealed; tight, snug.

---

263. Stopper.—N. stopper, stopple; plug, cork, bung, spike, spill, stop-cock, tap; rammer; ram, -rod; piston; stop-gap; wadding, stuffing, padding, stopping, dossil, pledget, tompion, tourniquet. obturator; wad.

cover &c. 223; valve, slide valve; vent-peg, spigot.

janitor, door –, gate- keeper, porter, commissionaire, *concierge*, warder, beadle, Cerberus, usher, guard, sentry, sentinel; ostiary.

Section IV. MOTION

1°. Motion in General

264. [Successive change of place.*] **Motion.**—**N.** motion, movement, move; motivity, motility, going &c. *v.*; unrest.

stream, current, flow, flux, run, course, stir; conduction, evolution; kinematics.

step, rate, pace, tread, stride, gait, clip, port, footfall, cadence, carriage, velocity, angular velocity; progress, locomotion; journey &c. 266; voyage &c. 267; transit &c. 270.

restlessness &c. (*changeableness*) 149; mobility; movableness, motive power; laws of motion; mobilization.

V. be -in motion &c. *adj.*; move, go, hie, gang, budge, stir, pass, flit; hover -round, – about; shift, slide, slither, glide; roll, – on; flow, stream, run, drift, sweep along; wander &c. (*deviate*) 279; walk &c. 266; change –, shift- one's -place, – quarters; dodge; keep -going, – moving.

put –, set- in motion; move; impel &c. 276; propel &c. 284; render movable, mobilize.

Adj. moving &c. *v.*; in motion; motile, transitional; motory, motive; shifting, movable, mobile, mercurial, unquiet; restless &c. (*changeable*) 149; nomadic &c. 266; erratic &c. 279.

Adv. under way; on the -move, – wing, – tramp, – march.

265. Quiescence.—**N.** rest; stillness &c. *adj.*; quiescence; stag-nation, -nancy; fixity, immobility, catalepsy; indisturbance; quietism.

quiet, tranquillity, calm; repose &c. 687; peace; dead calm, anticyclone; statue-like repose; silence &c. 403; not a -breath of air, – mouse stirring; sleep &c. (*inactivity*) 683.

pause, lull &c. (*cessation*) 142; stand, – still; standing still &c. *v.*; lock; dead -lock, – stop, – stand; full stop; fix; embargo.

resting-place; bivouac; home &c. (*abode*) 189; pillow &c. (*support*) 215; haven &c. (*refuge*) 666; goal &c. (*arrival*) 292.

V. be -quiescent &c. *adj.*; stand –, lie- still; keep quiet, repose, hold the breath.

remain, stay; stand, lie to, ride at anchor, remain *in situ*, mark time, tarry; bring –, heave –, lay- to; pull –, draw- up; hold, halt; stop, – short; rest, pause, anchor; cast –, come to an- anchor; rest on one's oars; repose on one's laurels, take breath; stop &c. (*discontinue*) 142.

stagnate, vegetate; *quieta non movere*; let -alone, – well alone; abide, rest and be thankful; keep within doors, stay at home, go to bed.

dwell &c. (*be present*) 186; settle &c. (*be located*) 184; alight &c. (*arrive*) 292.

stick, – fast; stand, – like a post; not stir a -peg, – step; be at a -stand &c. *n.*

quell, becalm, hush, stay, lull to sleep, lay an embargo on; put the brake on.

Adj. quiescent, still; motion-, move-less; fixed; stationary; at -rest, – a stand, – a stand-still, – anchor; stock-still; immotile; standing still &c. *v.*; sedentary, untravelled, stay-at-home; becalmed, stagnant, quiet; un-moved, -disturbed, -ruffled; calm, restful; cataleptic; immovable &c. (*stable*) 150; sleeping &c. (*inactive*) 683; silent &c. 403; still as -a statue, – a post, – a mouse, – death.

Adv. at a stand &c. *adj.*; *tout court*; at the halt.

Int. stop! stay! avast! halt! hold, – hard! whoa!

Phr. *requiescat in pace.*

* A thing cannot be said to *move* from one place to another, unless it passes in succession through every intermediate place; hence motion is only such a change of place as is *successive*. 'Rapid, swift, &c., as thought' are therefore incorrect expressions.

266. [Locomotion by land.] **Journey.**—**N.** travel; travelling &c. *v.*; wayfaring, campaigning.

journey, excursion, expedition, tour, trip, grand tour, circuit, peregrination, discursion, ramble, pilgrimage, *trek*, course, ambulation, march, walk, hike, promenade, constitutional, stroll, saunter, tramp, jog-trot, turn, stalk, perambulation; noctambulation; somnambulism, sleep walking; outing, ride, drive, airing, jaunt.

equitation, horsemanship, riding, *manège*, ride and tie.

roving, vagrancy, pererration; marching and countermarching; nomadism; vagabond-ism, -age; gadding; flit, -ting; migration; e-, im-, de-, inter-migration.

plan, itinerary, guide; hand-, road-book; Baedeker, Murray, Bradshaw, time table.

procession, parade, cavalcade, caravan, file, *cortège*, column.

[Organs and instruments of locomotion] vehicle &c. 272; locomotive &c. 271; legs, feet, pegs, pins, trotters.

traveller &c. 268.

V. travel, journey, course; tour; take –, go- a journey; take –, go out for- -a walk &c. *n.*; have a run; take the air.

flit, take wing; migrate, emigrate, *trek*; rove, prowl, roam, range, patrol, pace up and down, traverse; scour –, traverse- the country; peragrate; per-, circum-ambulate; nomadize, wander, ramble, stroll, saunter, hover, go one's rounds, straggle; gad, – about; expatiate.

walk, march, step, tread, pace, plod, wend; promenade; trudge, tramp; stalk, stride, straddle, strut, foot it, stump, bundle, bowl along, toddle; paddle; tread –, follow –, pursue- a path.

take horse, ride, drive, trot, amble, canter, prance, fisk, frisk, *caracoler*; gallop &c. (*move quickly*) 274; motor, cycle, taxi; go by -car, – train, – tram, – bus, – plane.

peg –, jog –, wag –, shuffle- on; stir one's stumps; bend one's -steps, – course; make –, find –, wend –, pick –, thread –, plough- one's way; coast, slide, glide, skim, skate, ski; march in procession, file off, defile.

go –, repair –, resort –, hie –, betake oneself- to.

Adj. travelling &c. *v.*; ambulatory, itinerant, peripatetic, peram-

267. [Locomotion by water, or air.] **Navigation.**—**N.** navigation; aquatics; boating, cruising, yachting; ship &c. 273; oar, scull, sweep, punt-pole, paddle, – wheel, screw, propeller, stern wheel, sail, canvas.

natation, swimming; fin, flipper; fish's tail.

aerial navigation, air service, airways, airmanship, aero-donetics, -dynamics, -mechanics, -station, -statics, -nautics; ballooning, balloonry; balloon &c. 273; flying, flight, aviation, volitation; wing, pinion, *aileron*.

voyage, sail, cruise, passage, circumnavigation, *periplus*; head-, stern-, lee-way.

mariner, aeronaut &c. 269.

V. sail; put to sea &c. (*depart*) 293; take ship, get under way; spread -sail, – canvas; gather way, have way on; make –, carry- sail; plough the -waves, – deep, – main, – ocean; walk the waters.

navigate, warp, luff, scud, boom, kedge; drift, course, cruise, coast; hug the -shore, – land; circumnavigate.

ply the oar, row, paddle, pull, scull, punt, steam.

swim, float; buffet the waves, ride the storm, skim, *effleurer*, dive, wade.

fly, aviate, be wafted, hover, soar, drift, glide, plane, sideslip, *volplane*, pique, dive, spin, roll, loop, flutter; take -wing, – a flight; wing one's -flight, – way.

Adj. sailing &c. *v.*; seafaring, nautical, maritime, naval; sea-going, coasting; afloat; navigable, aquatic, natatory.

volitant, volant, aerostatic, aerial, aeronautic; alar, alate, pennate.

Adv. under -way, – sail, – canvas, – steam; on the wing.

bulatory, roving, rambling, gadding, discursive, vagrant, migratory, nomadic; circumforane-an, -ous; somnambular, nocti-, mundivagant; locomotive, automotive, self-moving.

way-faring, -worn; travel-stained.

Adv. on -foot, – horseback, – Shanks's mare; by the Marrowbone stage; *in transitu* &c. 270; *en route* &c. 282.

Int. come along!

268. Traveller.—N. traveller, wayfarer, voyager, itinerant, passenger.

tourist, excursionist, globe-trotter; explorer, adventurer, mountaineer, Alpine Club; peregrinator, wanderer, rover, straggler, rambler; bird of passage; gad-about, -ling; vagrant, scatterling, landloper, waifs and estrays, wastrel, stray; loafer; tramp, -er, hobo, beachcomber, vagabond, nomad, Bohemian, gipsy, Arab, Wandering Jew, Hadji, pilgrim, palmer; peripatetic; somnambulist, sleep walker, noctambulist; emigrant, fugitive, refugee, *émigré*.

runner, courier, King's messenger; Mercury, Iris, Ariel, comet.

pedestrian, walker, foot-passenger; cyclist; wheelman.

rider, horseman, equestrian, cavalier, jockey, rough rider, trainer, breaker, huntsman.

driver, coachman, whip, Jehu, charioteer, postilion, post-boy, carter, wagoner, drayman, truckman; cab-man, -driver; *voiturier*, *vetturino*, *condottiere*; engine-driver; stoker, fireman, guard, brakeman, conductor; chauffeur, automobilist, motorist, motor –, truck –, taxi- driver.

269. Mariner.—N. sailor, mariner, navigator, argonaut; sea-man, -farer, -faring man; yachtsman; tar, jack tar, salt, gob, sea-dog, shellback, able seaman, A.B.; man-of-war's man, bluejacket, marine, jolly; midshipman, middy, reefer; captain, commander, master mariner, skipper, mate; ship-, boat-, ferry-, water-, lighter-, barge-, longshore- man, hoveller; bargee, gondolier; oar-, -sman; rower; boat-, cock-swain; coxswain; steersman, helmsman, pilot; crew; lascar.

aerial navigator, aeronaut, balloonist, Icarus, aviator, pilot, observer, flyer, airman.

270. Transference.—N. transfer, -ence; trans-, e-location; displacement; *meta-stasis*, *-thesis*; removal; re-, a-motion; relegation; de-, as-portation; extradition, conveyance, draft; carrying, carriage; convection, -duction, -tagion, infection; transfusion; transfer &c. (*of property*) 783.

transit, transition; passage, ferry, gestation; portage, porterage, carting, cartage; shovelling &c. *v.*; vect-ion, -ure, -itation; shipment, freight, wafture; trans-mission, -port, -portation, -umption, -plantation, -lation; shift-, dodg-ing; dispersion &c. 73; transposition &c. (*interchange*) 148; traction &c. 285.

[Thing transferred] drift, alluvium, detritus, *moraine*; gift, legacy, bequest, lease; freight, mails, cargo, luggage, baggage, goods.

V. trans-fer, -mit, -port, -place, -plant; convey, assign, carry, bear, fetch and carry; carry –, ferry- over; hand, pass, forward; shift; conduct, convoy, bring, fetch, reach.

send, delegate, consign, mail, post, relegate, turn over to, pass the buck, deliver; ship, embark; waft; switch, shunt; transpose &c. (*interchange*) 148; displace &c. 185; throw &c. 284; drag &c. 285.

shovel, lade, dip, ladle, bale, decant, draft off, transfuse.

Adj. transferred &c. *v.*; drifted; movable; port-able, -ative; conductive; contagious, infectious.

transferable, assignable, conveyable, devisable, negotiable, transmissible.

Adv. from -hand to hand, – pillar to post.

on –, by- the way; on the -road, – wing; as one goes; *in transitu, en route, chemin faisant, en passant,* in mid-progress.

271. Carrier.—**N.** carrier, porter, red cap, bearer, messenger, postman, tranter, conveyer; stevedore; coolie; conductor, locomotive, tractor, caterpillar tractor, motor.

beast of burden, cattle, horse, steed, nag, palfrey, Arab, blood horse, thorough-bred, galloway, charger, courser, racer, hunter, jument, pony, filly, colt, foal, barb, roan, jade, hack, *bidet,* pad, cob, tit, punch, roadster, goer; race-, pack-, draft-, cart-, dray-, post-horse, mount; Shetland pony, sheltie; garran; jennet, genet, bayard, mare, stallion, gelding; stud.

Pegasus, Bucephalus, Rozinante.

ass, donkey, jackass, mule, hinny; sumpter -horse, – mule; reindeer; camel, dromedary, mehari, llama, elephant; carrier pigeon.

carriage &c. (*vehicle*) 272; ship &c. 273.

Adj. equine, asinine.

272. Vehicle.—**N.** vehicle, conveyance, carriage, car, caravan, van, furniture van, pantechnicon; wagon, wain, dray, cart, lorry.

carriole; sledge, sled, sleigh, bobsleigh, toboggan, *luge,* truck, tram; limber, tumbrel, pontoon; barrow; wheel-, hand- -barrow, – cart, trolley; perambulator; Bath –, wheel –, sedan-chair, jinriksha, rickshaw; ekka; chaise; palan-keen, -quin; litter, horse-litter, brancard, crate, hurdle, stretcher, ambulance; velocipede, hobby-horse, coaster, scooter, go-cart; cycle; bi-, tri-, quadri-cycle; tandem, safety; skate, roller skate; ski, snow-shoe.

equipage, turn-out; coach, chariot, *quadriga,* chaise, phaëton, break, brake, mail-phaëton, wagonette, drag, curricle, tilbury, whisky, landau, *barouche,* victoria, brougham, clarence, calash, *calèche,* britzska, *araba,* kibitka; berlin; sulky, *désobligeant,* sociable, *vis-à-vis, dormeuse*; jaunting –, outside- car; *tarantass*; runabout; shay.

post-chaise; diligence, stage; stage –, mail –, hackney –, glass- coach; stage-wagon; car, omnibus, bus, fly, *cabriolet,* cab, hansom, shofle, four-wheeler, growler, *droshki,* drosky.

dog-cart, trap, gig, whitechapel, buggy, four-in-hand, unicorn, random, tandem; shandredhan, *char-à-banc.*

automobile, motor-, auto-, touring-, racing-, cycle-, side-, steam-, electric-

273. Ship.—**N.** ship, vessel, sail; craft, bottom.

navy, marine, fleet, flotilla, squadron; shipping.

man of war &c. (*combatant*) 726; transport, tender, store-ship; merchant ship, merchantman; packet, liner; whaler, slaver, collier, coaster, tanker, freighter, freight steamer, cargo boat, lighter; fishing-, pilot- boat; trawler, drifter; cable ship; hulk; yacht; floating palace, ocean greyhound.

ship, bark, barque, brig, snow, hermaphrodite brig; brigantine, barquentine; schooner; topsail –, fore and aft –, three masted- schooner; *chasse-marée*; sloop, cutter, corvette, clipper, foist, yawl, dandy, ketch, smack, lugger, barge, hoy, cat-, -boat, buss; sail-er, -ing vessel, wind-jammer; steam-er, -boat, -ship; mail –, paddle –, screw –, sternwheel- steamer; tug; train-ferry; line of steamers &c.

boat, pinnace, launch, motor-boat, picket-boat; hydroplane; life-, long-, jolly-, bum-, fly-, cock-, ferry-, canal-boat, dory, dugout, galliot; shallop, gig, funny, skiff, dingy, scow, cockle-shell, wherry, coble, punt, cog, lerret; eight-, four-, pair- oar; randan; outrigger; float, raft, pontoon; prame, ice-yacht.

state barge, bucentaur.

catamaran, coracle, gondola, carvel, caravel; felucca, caique, canoe; trireme;

car; motor-, -omnibus, - bus, - cab, - cycle; limousine, landaulette, cabriolet, *coupé*, *voiturette*, runabout, electromobile, taxi, -cab.

train; passenger -, express -, freight -, subway -, special -, corridor -, parliamentary -, luggage -, goods-train, *train de luxe*; 1st-, 2nd-, 3rd-class- -train, - carriage, - compartment; Pullman -, sleeping-, club-, observation-, dining-, restaurant-car; mail-, luggage-, brake-van, coach, car, carriage; rolling stock; horse-box, cattle-truck.

tramcar, trolley-omnibus, trackless trolley.

shovel, spoon, spatula, ladle, hod, hoe; spade, spaddle, loy; spud; pitch-fork.

Adj. vehicular.

---

galley, - foist; bilander, dogger, hooker, howker; argosy, carack; galliass, galleon; galliot, polacca, polacre, corsair, tartane, junk, lorcha, praam, proa, prahu, saick, sampan, xebec, dhow; dahabeah; nuggar, cayak, pirogue.

submarine, submersible.

aircraft (*combatant*) &c. 726; flying machine, air mail, aero-, air-, mono-, bi-, tri-, hydroplane, plane, cabin plane, transport plane, *avion*, flying boat, glider, *aviette*, helicopter; balloon, air-, fire-, gas-, Mongolfier-, pilot-, captive-, free-, kite-, dirigible- balloon, air-ship, *Zeppelin*, blimp; kite, parachute.

nacelle, car, gondola, aileron; hangar, airport, landing field, airdrome; cat-walk, controls, rudder, tail.

Adj. marine, maritime, naval, nautical, seafaring, sea-, ocean-going, sea-worthy.

aerial, aeronautical, air-worthy, flying &c. *n.*

Adv. afloat, aboard; on -board, - ship board, - board ship.

2°. Degrees of Motion

274. Velocity.—N. velocity, speed, celerity; swiftness &c. *adj.*; rapidity, eagle speed; expedition &c. (*activity*) 682; pernicity; acceleration; haste &c. 684.

spurt, rush, dash, race, steeplechase; smart -, lively -, swift &c. *adj.* -, rattling -, spanking -, strapping- -rate, - pace; round pace; flying, flight.

gallop, canter, trot, round trot, run, scamper; hand -, full- gallop; swoop.

lightning, light, electricity, wind; cannon-ball, rocket, arrow, dart, quick-silver; telegraph, express train; torrent; swallow flight.

eagle, antelope, courser, race-horse, gazelle, greyhound, hare, doe, squirrel.

Mercury, Ariel, Camilla, Harlequin.

[Measurement of velocity] speed-ometer, log, -line, tachometer.

V. move quickly, trip, fisk; speed, hie, hasten, sprint, spurt, post, spank, scuttle; scud, -dle, scurry; scour, - the plain; scamper; run, - like mad; fly, race, run a race, cut away, cut and run, shoot, tear, whisk, whiz, sweep, skim, brush; cut -, bowl- along; rush

275. Slowness.—N. slowness &c. *adj.*; languor &c. (*inactivity*) 683; drawl; creeping &c. *v.*, lentor.

retardation; slackening &c. *v.*; delay &c. (*lateness*) 133; claudication.

jog-, dog-trot, walk; mincing steps; slow -march, - time.

slow -goer, - coach, - back; lingerer, loiterer, sluggard, tortoise, snail; dawdle &c. (*inactive*) 683.

V. move -slowly, &c. *adv.*; creep, crawl, lag, slug, walk, drawl, linger, loiter, saunter; plod, trudge, stump along, lumber; trail; drag; dawdle &c. (*be inactive*) 683; grovel, worm one's way, steal along; jog -, rub -, bundle-on; toddle, waddle, wabble, slug; traipse, slouch, shuffle, halt, hobble, limp, claudicate, shamble; flag, falter, totter, stagger; mince, step short; march in -slow time, - funeral procession; take one's time; hang fire &c. (*be late*) 133.

retard, relax; slacken, check, moderate, rein in, curb; reef; strike -, shorten -, take in- sail; put on the drag, apply the brake; clip the wings; reduce the

&c. (*be violent*) 173; dash -on, – off, – forward; bolt; trot, gallop, bound, flit, spring, dart, boom; march in double-time; ride hard, get over the ground, scorch.

hurry &c. (*hasten*) 684; accelerate, put on; quicken; quicken –, mend- one's pace; clap spurs to one's horse; make -haste, – rapid strides, – forced marches, – the best of one's way; put one's best leg foremost, stir one's stumps, wing one's way, set off at a score; carry –, crowd- sail; go off like a shot, go ahead, gain ground; outstrip the wind, fly on the wings of the wind.

keep -up, – pace- with; outstrip &c. 303.

Adj. fast, speedy, swift, rapid, quick, fleet; nimble, agile, expeditious; express; active &c. 682; flying, galloping &c. *v.*; light-, nimble-footed; winged, eagle-winged, mercurial, electric, telegraphic; light-legged, light of heel; swift as -an arrow &c. *n.*; quick as -lightning &c. *n.*, – thought.*

Adv. swiftly &c. *adj.*; with -speed &c. *n.*; apace; at -a great rate, – full speed, – railway speed; full -drive, – gallop; post-haste, in full sail, tantivy; trippingly; instantaneously &c. 113; like a shot.

under press of -sail, – canvas, – sail and steam; *velis et remis*, on eagle's wing, in double quick time; with -rapid, – giant- strides; *à pas de géant*; in seven league boots; whip and spur; *ventre à terre*; as fast as one's -legs, – heels- will carry one; as fast as one can lay feet to the ground, at the top of one's speed; by leaps and bounds; with haste &c. 684; in- high – gear, – speed.

Phr. *vires acquirit eundo.*

speed, decelerate; slacken -speed, – one's pace, lose ground; back -water, – pedal, put the engines astern, throttle down.

Adj. slow, slack; tardy; dilatory &c. (*inactive*) 683; gentle, easy; leisurely; deliberate, gradual; insensible, imperceptible; languid, sluggish, apathetic, phlegmatic, slow-paced, tardigrade, snail-like; creeping &c. *v.*

Adv. slowly &c. *adj.*; leisurely; *piano, adagio*; *largo, larghetto*; at half speed, under easy sail; at a -foot's, – snail's, – funeral- pace; slower than molasses in January; in slow time; with -mincing steps, – clipped wings; *haud passibus æquis*; in- low –, gear, – speed.

gradually &c. *adj.*; *gradatim*; by -degrees, – slow degrees, – inches, – little and little; step by step; inch by inch, bit by bit, little by little, *seriatim*; consecutively.

3°. Motion Conjoined with Force

276. Impulse.—N. impulse, impulsion, impetus; momentum; push, pulsion, thrust, shove, jog, jolt, brunt, booming, boost, throw; explosion &c. (*violence*) 173; propulsion &c. 284.

percussion, concussion, collision, occursion, clash, encounter, cannon, *carambole*, appulse, shock, crash, bump; impact; *élan*; charge &c. (*attack*) 716; beating &c. (*punishment*) 972.

blow, dint, stroke, knock, tap, rap, slap, smack, pat, dab; fillip; slam, bang; hit, whack, thwack, clout; cuff &c. 972; squash, dowse, whap, swap, punch, thump, swipe, jab, pelt, kick, punce, calcitration; *ruade*; arietation; cut, thrust, lunge, yerk.

277. Recoil.—N. recoil; re-, retro- action; revulsion; rebound, *ricochet*; re-percussion, -calcitration; kick, *contrecoup*; springing back &c. *v.*; elasticity &c. 325; reflection, reflex, reflux; reverberation &c. (*resonance*) 408; rebuff, repulse; return.

ducks and drakes; boomerang; spring; reactionist, reactionary.

V. recoil, resile, react; spring –, fly –, bound- back; rebound, reverberate, repercuss, recalcitrate, echo, *ricochet.*

Adj. recoiling &c. *v.*; re-fluent, -percussive, -calcitrant, -actionary; retroactive.

Adv. on the -recoil &c. *n.*

* See note on 264.

hammer, sledge-hammer, mall, maul, mallet, flail; ram, -mer; battering-ram, monkey, pile-driver, punch, bat, tamper, tamping iron; cudgel &c. (*weapon*) 727; axe &c. (*sharp*) 253.

[Science of mechanical forces] mechanics, dynamics &c.

V. give an -impetus &c. *n.*; impel, push; start, give a start to, set going; drive, urge, boom; thrust, prod, foin; cant; elbow, shoulder, jostle, justle, hustle, hurtle, shove, jog, jolt, bean, encounter; run –, bump –, butt- against; knock –, run- one's head against; impinge.

strike, knock, hit, bash, tap, rap, bat, slap, flap, dab, pat, thump, beat, bang, slam, dash; punch, thwack, whack; hit –, strike- hard; swap, batter, dowse, baste; pelt, patter, skelter, buffet, belabour, tamp; fetch one a blow, swat; poke at, pink, lunge, yerk; kick, calcitrate; butt; strike at &c. (*attack*) 716; whip &c. (*punish*) 972; propel &c. 284.

come –, enter- into collision; collide; foul; fall –, run- foul of.

throw &c. (*propel*) 284.

Adj. impelling &c. *v.*; im-pulsive, -pellent; booming; dynamic, -al; impelled &c. *v.*

4°. Motion with Reference to Direction

278. Direction.—N. direction, bearing, course, set, drift, tenor; tendency &c. 176; incidence; bending, trending &c. *v.*; dip, tack, aim, collimation; steer-ing, -age.

point of the compass, cardinal –, half –, quarter- points; North, East, South, West; N by E, ENE, NE by N, NE &c.; rhumb, azimuth, line of collimation.

line, path, road, range, quarter, line of march; alignment; straight shot, bee-line.

V. tend –, bend –, point- towards; conduct –, go- to; point -to, – at; bend, trend, verge, incline, dip, determine.

steer –, make- -for, – towards; aim –, level- at; take aim; keep –, hold- a course; be bound for; bend one's steps towards; direct –, steer –, bend –, shape- one's course; align –, one's march; go straight, – to the point; march -on, – on a point.

ascertain one's -direction &c. *n.*; *s'orienter*, see which way the wind blows; box the compass.

Adj. directed &c. *v.*, – towards; pointing towards &c. *v.*; bound for; aligned –, alligned- with; direct, straight; un-deviating, -swerving; straightforward; North, -ern, -erly, &c. *n.*

directable &c. *v.*

Adv. towards; on the -road, – high

279. Deviation. — N. deviation; swerving &c. *v.*; obliquation, warp, refraction; flection, flexion; sweep; de-flection, -flexure; declination.

diversion, digression, departure from, aberration, drift, sheer; divergence &c. 291; zigzag; *détour* &c. (*circuit*) 629.

[Desultory motion] wandering &c. *v.*; vagrancy, evagation; by-paths and crooked ways.

[Motion sideways, oblique motion] sidling &c. *v.*; *échelon*, leeway; knight's move (at chess).

V. alter one's course, deviate, depart from, turn, trend; bend, curve &c. 245; swerve, heel, bear off.

intervert; deflect; divert, – from its course; put on a new scent, shift, shunt, switch, wear, draw aside, crook, warp short circuit.

stray, straggle; sidle, edge; diverge &c. 291; tralineate, digress, divagate, wander; wind, twist, meander, meander around Robin Hood's barn; veer, tack, sheer; turn -aside, – a corner, – away from; wheel, steer clear of; ramble, rove, drift; go -astray, – adrift; yaw, dodge; step aside, ease off, make way for, shy.

fly off at a tangent; glance off; turn, wheel –, face- about; turn –, face- to the right about; wabble &c. (*oscillate*) 314; go out of one's way &c. (*perform a circuit*) 629; lose one's way.

road- to; *versus*, to; hither, thither, whither; directly; straight, – forwards, – as an arrow; point blank; in a -direct, – straight- line -to, – for, – with; in a line with; full tilt at, as the crow flies.

before –, near –, close to –, against- the wind; windwards, in the wind's eye.

through, *via*, by way of; in all -directions, – manner of ways; *quaquaversum*, from the four winds.

Adj. deviating &c. *v.*; aberrant, errant; ex-, dis-cursive; devious, desultory, loose; rambling; stray, erratic, vagrant, undirected; circuitous, indirect, zigzag; crab-like.

Adv. astray from, round about, wide of the mark; to the right about; all manner of ways; circuitously &c. 629.

obliquely, sideling, like the move of the knight on a chessboard.

---

280. [Going before.] **Precession.—N.** precession, leading, heading; precedence &c. 62; priority &c. 116; the lead, *le pas*; van &c. (*front*) 234; precursor &c. 64.

V. go -before, – ahead, – in the van, – in advance; precede, forerun; usher in, introduce, herald, head, take the lead; lead, – the way, – the dance; get –, have- the start; steal a march; get -before, – ahead, – in front of; outstrip &c. 303; take precedence &c. (*first in order*) 62.

Adj. foremost, first, leading &c. *v.*

Adv. in advance, before, ahead, in the van; fore-, head-most; in front.

Phr. *seniores priores.*

281. [Going after.] **Sequence.—N.** sequence, run; coming after &c. (*order*) 63; (*time*) 117; following; pursuit &c. 622.

follower, attendant, satellite, shadow, dangler, train.

V. follow; pursue &c. 622; go –, fly- after.

attend, beset, dance attendance on, dog, be-dog; tread -in the steps of, – close upon; be –, go –, follow- in the -wake, – trail, – rear- of; trail, follow as a shadow, hang on the skirts of; tread –, follow- on the heels of, tag after.

lag, get behind.

Adj. following &c. *v.*

Adv. behind; in the -rear &c. 235, – train of, wake of; after &c. (*order*) 63, (*time*) 117.

---

282. [Motion forwards; progressive motion.] **Progression.—N.** progress, -ion, -iveness; advancing &c. *v.*; advance, -ment; ongoing; flood-tide, headway; march &c. 266; rise; improvement &c. 658.

V. advance; proceed, progress; get -on, – along, – over the ground; gain ground; jog –, rub –, wag- on; go with the stream; keep –, hold on- one's course; go –, move –, come –, get –, pass –, push –, press- -on, – forward, – forwards, – ahead; press onwards, step forward; make –, work –, carve –, push –, force –, edge –, elbow- one's way; make -progress, – head, – way, – headway, – advances, – strides, – rapid strides &c. (*velocity*) 274; go –, shoot- ahead; distance; make up leeway.

Adj. advancing &c. *v.*; pro-gressive, -fluent; advanced.

283. [Motion backwards.] **Regression.—N.** regress, -ion; retro-cession, -gression, -gradation, -action; *reculade*; retreat, withdrawal, retirement, remigration; recession &c. (*motion from*) 287; recess; crab-like motion.

re-fluence, -flux; backwater, regurgitation, ebb, return; resilience; reflexion (*recoil*) 277; *volte-face.*

counter -motion, – movement, – march; veering, tergiversation, recidivation, backsliding, fall, relapse; deterioration &c. 659.

turning-point &c. (*reversion*) 145.

V. re-cede, -grade, -turn, -vert, -treat, -tire; retro-grade, -cede; back, – down, – out, crawl; withdraw; rebound &c. 277; go –, come –, turn –, hark –, draw –, fall –, get –, put –, run- back; lose ground; fall –, drop- astern; back water, put about; veer, – round; double,

Adv. forward, onward; forth, on ahead, under way, *en route* for, on -one's way, – the way, – the road, – the high road- to; in -progress, – mid progress; *in transitu* &c. 270.

Int. Forward, march!

Phr. *vestigia nulla retrorsum.*

wheel, counter-march; ebb, regurgitate; jib, shrink, shy.

turn -tail, – round, – upon one's heel, – one's back upon; retrace one's steps, dance the back step; sound –, beat- a retreat; go home.

Adj. receding &c. *v.*; retro-grade, -gressive; re-gressive, -fluent, -flex, -cidivous, -silient; crab-like; reactionary &c. 277; counter-clockwise.

Adv. back, -wards; reflexively, to the right about; *à reculons, à rebours.*

Phr. *revenons à nos moutons*, as you were.

284. [Motion given to an object situated in front.] **Propulsion.—N.** pro-pulsion, -jection; *vis a tergo*; push &c. (*impulse*) 276; e-, jaculation; ejection &c. 297; throw, fling, toss, shot, discharge, shy.

[Science of propulsion] gunnery, ballistics, archery.

missile, projectile, ball, *discus*, javelin, hammer, quoit, brickbat, shot, bullet; arrow, shaft; gun &c. (*arms*) 727.

shooter, shot; gunner, gun-layer; archer, toxophilite; bow-, rifle-, marksman; good –, crack- shot; sharpshooter &c. (*combatant*) 726.

V. propel, project, throw, fling, cast, pitch, chuck, toss, jerk, heave, shy, hurl; flirt, fillip.

dart, lance, tilt; e-, jaculate; fulminate, bolt, drive, sling, pitchfork.

send; send –, let –, fire- off; discharge, shoot; launch, send forth, let fly; dash.

put –, set- in motion; set agoing, start; give -a start, – an impulse- to; push, impel &c. 276; trundle &c. (*set in rotation*) 312; expel &c. 297.

carry one off one's legs; put to flight.

Adj. propelled &c. *v.*; propelling &c. *v.*; pro-pulsive, -jectile.

285. [Motion given to an object situated behind.] **Traction.—N.** traction; drawing &c. *v.*; draught, pull, haul; rake; 'a long pull, a strong pull and a pull all together'; towage, haulage.

V. draw, pull, haul, lug, rake, drag, draggle, tug, tow, trail, trawl, train; take in tow.

wrench, jerk, twitch.

Adj. drawing &c. *v.*; tractive, tractile; ductile.

286. [Motion towards.] **Approach.—N.** approach, approximation, appropinquation; access; appulse; afflux, -ion; advent &c. (*approach of time*) 121; pursuit &c. 622; convergence &c. 290.

V. approach, approximate; near; get –, go –, draw- near; come, – near, – to close quarters; move –, set- towards; drift; make up to; gain upon; pursue &c. 622; tread on the heels of; bear up; make the land; hug the -shore, -coast, – land.

Adj. approaching &c. *v.*; approximative; convergent; affluent; impending, imminent &c. (*destined*) 152.

287. [Motion from.] **Recession.—N.** recession, retirement, withdrawal; retreat; retrocession &c. 283; departure &c. 293; recoil &c. 277; flight &c. (*avoidance*) 623.

V. recede, go, move from, retire, ebb, withdraw, shrink; come –, move –, go –, get –, drift- away; depart &c. 293; retreat &c. 283; move –, stand –, sheer- off; swerve from; fall back, stand aside; run away &c. (*avoid*) 623.

remove, shunt, side track, switch off.

Adj. receding &c. *v.*

Adv. on the road.

Int. come hither! approach! here! come! come near!

288. [Motion towards, actively.] **Attraction.—N.** attract-ion, -iveness; pull; drawing to, pulling towards, adduction, magnetism, gravity, attraction of gravitation; lure, bait, decoy.

loadstone, -star; magnet, siderite, magnetite.

V. attract; draw –, pull –, drag- towards; adduce.

lure, bait, decoy.

Adj. attracting &c. *v.*; attrahent, attractive, adducent, adductive.

289. [Motion from, actively.] **Repulsion.—N.** repulsion; driving from &c. *v.*; repulse; abduction.

V. repel; push –, drive – &c. 276. from; chase, dispel; retrude; abduce, abduct; send away, repulse, dismiss.

keep at arm's length, turn one's back upon, give the cold shoulder; send packing; send -off, – away- with a flea in one's ear, – about one's business.

Adj. repelling &c. *v.*; repellant, repulsive; abducent, abductive.

290. [Motion nearer to.] **Convergence.—N.** con-vergence, -fluence, -course, -flux, -gress, -currence, -centration; appulse, meeting; corradiation.

assemblage &c. 72; resort &c. (*focus*) 74; asymptote.

V. converge, concur; come together, unite, meet, fall in with; close -with, – in upon; centre -round, – in; enter in; pour in.

gather together, unite, concentrate, bring into a focus.

Adj. converging &c. *v.*; con-vergent, -fluent, -current; centripetal; asymptotical.

291. [Motion further off.] **Divergence.—N.** diverg-ence, -ency; divarication, ramification, radiation; separation &c. (*disjunction*) 44; dispersion &c. 73; deviation &c. 279; aberration, declination.

V. diverge, divaricate, radiate; ramify; branch –, glance –, file- off; fly off, – at a tangent; spread, scatter, disperse &c. 73; deviate &c. 279; part &c. (*separate*) 44; splay apart.

Adj. diverging &c. *v.*; divergent, radiant, centrifugal; aberrant.

292. [Terminal motion at.] **Arrival.—N.** arrival, advent; landing; de-, disem-barkation; reception, welcome, *vin d'honneur*.

home, goal, bourn; landing-place, -stage; resting –, stopping -place; destination, harbour, haven, port; terminal, terminus, railway station, depot, airport; halt, halting -place, – ground; anchorage &c. (*refuge*) 666.

return, recursion, remigration; meeting; ren-, en-counter.

completion &c. 729.

V. arrive; get to, come to; come; reach, attain; come up, – with, – to; overtake; make, fetch; complete &c. 729; join, rejoin.

light, alight, dismount; land, go ashore; debark, disembark; put -in, – into; visit, cast anchor, pitch one's tent; sit down &c. (*be located*) 184; get to one's journey's end; make the

293. [Initial motion from.] **Departure.—N.** departure, decession, decampment; embarkation; take-off; outset, start; removal; exit &c. (*egress*) 295; exodus, Hejira, flight.

leave-taking, *congé*, valediction, valedictory, adieu, farewell, good-bye, stirrup-cup.

starting -point, – post; point –, place- of -departure, – embarkation; port of embarkation.

V. depart; go, – away; take one's departure, set out; set –, march –, put –, start –, be –, move –, get –, whip –, pack –, go –, take oneself- off; start, issue, march out, debouch; go –, sally- forth; sally, set forward; be gone.

leave a place, quit, vacate, evacuate, abandon; go off the stage, make one's exit; retire, withdraw, remove; go -one's way, – along, – from home; take -flight, – wing; spring, fly, flit, wing

land; be in at the death; come –, get- -back, – home; return; come in &c. (*ingress*) 294; make one's appearance &c. (*appear*) 446; drop in; detrain; outspan.

come to hand; come -at, – across; hit; come –, light –, pop –, bounce –, plump –, burst –, pitch- upon; meet; en- ren-counter; come in contact.

Adj. arriving &c. *v.*; homeward-bound; terminal.

Adv. here, hither.

Int. welcome! hail! all hail! good-day, – morrow; greetings! hullo! well!

---

one's flight; fly –, whip- away; take off, hop off; embark; go -on board, – aboard; set sail; put –, go- to sea; sail, take ship; hoist blue Peter; get under way, weigh anchor; strike tents, break camp, decamp; walk one's chalks, make tracks, cut one's stick; cut and run; take leave; say –, bid- -good-bye &c. *n.*; disappear &c. 449; abscond &c. (*avoid*) 623; entrain, saddle –, harness –, hitch- up; inspan.

Adj. departing &c. *v.*; valedictory; outward bound.

Adv. whence, hence, thence; with a foot in the stirrup; on the -wing, – move.

Int. begone! &c. (*ejection*) 297; to horse! all aboard! farewell! adieu! good-bye, – day! *au revoir! auf Wiedersehen!* fare you well! so long! God -bless you, – speed! *bon voyage!*

294. [Motion into.] **Ingress.**—**N.** ingress; entrance, entry; introgression; influx; intrusion, inroad, incursion, invasion, irruption; pene-, interpenetration; illapse, import, importation, infiltration; immigration; admission &c. (*reception*) 296; insinuation &c. (*interjacence*) 228; insertion &c. 300.

inlet; way in; mouth, door &c. (*opening*) 260; path &c. (*way*) 627; conduit &c. 350; immigrant, visitor, incomer, newcomer, colonist.

V. have the *entrée*; enter; go –, come –, pour –, flow –, creep –, slip –, pop –, break –, burst- -into, – in; set foot on; burst –, break- in upon; invade, intrude, butt in, horn in, crash; insinuate itself; inter-, penetrate; infiltrate; find one's way –, wriggle –, worm oneself- into.

give entrance to &c. (*receive*) 296; insert &c. 300.

Adj. incoming, ingressive &c. *n.*; inward bound.

Adv. inward.

---

295. [Motion out of.] **Egress.**—**N.** egress, exit, issue; emer-sion, -gence; disemboguement; out-break, -burst; e-, pro-ruption; emanation; evacuation; ex-, trans-udation; extravasation, perspiration, sweating, leakage, percolation, distillation, oozing; gush &c. (*water in motion*) 348; outpour, -ing; effluence, effusion; efflux, -ion; drain; dribbling &c. *v.*; defluxion; drainage; out-come, -put; discharge &c. (*excretion*) 299.

export; expatriation; e-, re-migration; *débouche*; exodus &c. (*departure*) 293; emigrant, migrant, *émigré*, colonist.

outlet, vent, spout, tap, sluice, floodgate; pore; vomitory, out-gate, sallyport; way out; mouth, door &c. (*opening*) 260; path &c. (*way*) 627; conduit &c. 350; air-pipe &c. 351.

V. emerge, emanate, issue; go –, come –, move –, pass –, pour –, flow- out of; pass off, evacuate; migrate.

ex-, trans-ude; leak; run, – out, – through; per-, trans-colate; seep; strain, distil; perspire, sweat, drain, ooze; filter, filtrate; dribble, gush, spout, flow out; well, – out; pour, trickle &c. (*water in motion*) 348; effuse, extravasate, disembogue, discharge itself, debouch; come –, break- forth; burst- out, – through; find vent, escape &c. 671.

Adj. effused &c. *v.*; outgoing, outward bound.

Adv. outward.

296. [Motion into, actively.] **Reception.**—**N.** reception; admission, admittance, *entrée*, importation; initiation; intro-duction, -mission, -ception; immission, ingestion, imbibition, absorption, ingurgitation, inhalation; suction, sucking; eating, drinking &c. (*food*) 298; insertion &c. 300; interjection &c. 228.

V. give -entrance to, – admittance to, – the *entrée*; intro-duce, -mit; usher, admit, receive, import, initiate, bring in, open the door to, throw open, ingest, absorb, imbibe, inhale, infiltrate; let –, take –, suck- in; re-admit, -sorb, -absorb; snuff up; swallow, ingurgitate; engulf, engorge; gulp; eat, drink &c. (*food*) 298.

Adj. admit-ting &c. *v.*, -ted &c. *v.*; admissible; absorbent; introductory, introceptive, intromittent, initiatory.

---

297. [Motion out of, actively.] **Ejection.**—**N.** ejection, emission, effusion, rejection, expulsion, eviction, extrusion, trajection; discharge.

egestion, evacuation, vomition, disgorgement, voidance, eruption, eruptiveness; ruc-, eruc-tation, blood-letting, venesection, phlebotomy, paracentesis; tapping, drainage; clear-ance, -age, voidance; vomiting, excretion &c. 299.

deportation; banishment &c. (*punishment*) 972; rogue's march; relegation, extradition; dislodgment.

V. give -exit, – vent- to; let –, give –, pour –, send- out; des-, dis-patch; exhale, excern, excrete, disembogue, secrete, secern; extravasate, shed, void, evacuate, egest, emit; open the -sluices, – floodgates; turn on the tap; extrude, detrude; effuse, spend, expend; pour forth; squirt, spirt, spill, slop; perspire &c. (*exude*) 295; breathe, blow &c. (*wind*) 349.

tap, draw off; bale –, lade- out; let blood, broach.

eject, reject; expel, discard; cut, send to Coventry, boycott, ostracize; *chasser*; banish &c. (*punish*) 972; throw &c. 284 -out, – up, – off, – away, – aside; push &c. 276 -out, – off, – away, – aside; shovel –, sweep- -out, – away; brush –, whisk –, turn –, send- -off, – away; discharge; send –, turn –, cast- adrift; turn –, bundle- out; throw overboard; give the sack to; send -packing, – about one's business, – to the right about; strike off the roll &c. (*abrogate*) 756; turn out- neck and heels, – head and shoulders, – neck and crop; pack off; send away with a flea in the ear; send to Jericho; bow out, show the door to, dismiss, fire, sack.

turn out of -doors, – house and home; evict, oust; exorcise, un-house, -kennel; dislodge; un-, dis-people; depopulate; relegate, deport.

empty; drain, – to the dregs; sweep off; clear, – off, – out, – away; suck, draw off, extract; clean out, make a clean sweep of, clear decks, purge.

em-, dis-, disem-bowel; eviscerate, gut; unearth, root -out, – up; averruncate; weed –, get out; eliminate, get rid of, do away with, shake off; exenterate.

vomit, spew, puke, keck, retch; belch, – out, eruct, eructate; cast –, bring- up; disgorge; expectorate, salivate, clear the throat, hawk, spit, sputter, splutter, slobber, drool, drivel, slaver, slabber.

unpack, unlade, unload, unship; break bulk.

be let out; ooze &c. (*emerge*) 295.

Adj. emitt-ing, -ed &c. *v.*

Int. begone! get you gone! get –, go- -away, – along, – along with you! go your way! away, – with! off with you! go, – about your business! be off! avaunt! aroynt! get out! beat it!

298. [Eating.] **Food.—N.** eating &c. *v.*; deglutition, gulp, epulation, mastication, manducation, rumination, gastronomy, gastrology; panto-, hippo-, ichthyo-phagy &c.; gluttony &c. 957; carnivorousness, vegetarianism.

mouth, jaws, mandible, mazard, chops.

drinking &c. *v.*; potation, draught, libation; carousal &c. (*amusement*) 840; drunkenness &c. 959.

food, *pabulum*; aliment, nourishment, nutriment; susten-ance, -tation; nurture, subsistence, provender, feed, fodder, provision, ration, keep, commons, board; commissariat &c. (*provision*) 637; prey, forage, pasture, pasturage; fare, cheer; diet, -ary; regimen; belly timber, staff of life; bread, -and cheese; proteins, carbohydrates, vitamines.

comestibles, eatables, victuals, edibles, *ingesta*; grub, prog, tack, hard tack, meat; bread, -stuffs; cereals; viands, cates, delicacy, dainty, creature comforts, contents of the larder, flesh-pots; festal board; ambrosia; good -cheer, – living.

hors-d'œuvre; soup, pottage, *potage*, broth, *bouillon*, *consommé*, *purée*, *borsch*, stock, skilly, gumbo; fish, – cakes, – pie; joint, *rôti*, *pièce de résistance*, *relevé*, hash, *réchauffé*, stew, *ragoût*, fricassee, mince, *salmi*, *goulash*, *bouillabaisse*, remove, *entrée*, *croquette*, *rissole*, sausage, curry, bubble and squeak; haggis, collops, giblets; poultry, game &c.; biscuit, bun, scone, rusk, pancake, pie, pastry, pasty, patty, *patisserie*, tart, turnover, *vol-au-vent*, *soufflé*, dumpling, pudding, duff, *compote*, fritters, cake, napoleon, *blancmange*, custard, jelly, jam, sweets &c. 396; *entremet*; oatmeal, porridge, hasty pudding, gruel; eggs, omelet, cheese, matzoon, savoury; vegetable, salad, *mayonnaise*, fruit; sauce, condiment &c. 393; kickshaws.

table, *cuisine*, bill of fare, *menu*, *prix fixe*, ordinary, *à la carte*; cover.

meal, repast, feed, spread; mess; dish, plate, course, side dish; regale; regale-, refresh-, entertain-ment; refection, collation, picnic, feast, banquet, junket; breakfast; lunch, -eon; *déjeuner*, bever, tiffin, tea, dinner, supper, snack, whet, bait, dessert; pot-luck, *table d'hôte*, *déjeuner à la fourchette*; hearty –, square –, substantial –, full- -meal; blow out; light refreshment; pemmican.

mouthful, bolus, gobbet, tit-bit, morsel, sop, sippet.

drink, beverage, liquor, broth, soup; potion, dram, draught, drench, swill; nip, peg, sip, sup, gulp.

wine, champagne, spirits, *liqueur*, beer, porter, stout, ale, malt liquor, julep, Sir John Barleycorn, stingo, heavy wet, bitter, lager-beer, cider; grog, toddy, flip, purl, punch, negus, cup, bishop, posset, wassail; bitters, *apéritif*, high-ball, cocktail; whisky, rum, absinthe; gin &c. (*intoxicating liquor*) 959; coffee, chocolate, cocoa, tea, *maté*, the cup that cheers but not inebriates.

eating-house &c. 189.

299. **Excretion.—N.** excretion, discharge, emanation; ejection &c. 297; exhalation, extrusion, secretion, effusion, extravasation, *ecchymosis*, evacuation, cacation, defecation, dysentery, dejection, *fæces*, excrement; perspiration, sweat; sud-, exud-ation; *diaphoresis*; sewage.

saliva, spittle, rheum; ptyalism, salivation, catarrh, diarrhœa; *ejecta*, *egesta*, *sputum*, *sputa*; *excreta*; lava; *exuviæ* &c. (*uncleanness*) 653.

hemorrhage, bleeding; catamenia, menses; outpouring &c. (*egress*) 295; leucorrhea.

V. excrete &c. (*eject*) 297; emanate &c. (*come out*) 295.

Adj. excretory, fæcal, secretory; ejective, eliminant.

V. eat, feed, fare, devour, swallow, take; gulp, bolt, snap; fall to; despatch, dispatch; discuss; take –, get –, gulp-down; lay –, tuck- in; lick, pick, peck; gormandize &c. 957; bite, champ, munch, cranch, craunch, crunch, chew, masticate, nibble, gnaw, mumble.

live on; feed –, batten –, fatten –, feast- upon; browse, graze, crop, regale; carouse &c. (*make merry*) 840; eat heartily, do justice to, play a good knife and fork, banquet.

break -bread, – one's fast; breakfast, lunch, dine, take tea, sup.

drink, – in, – up, – one's fill; quaff, sip, sup; suck, – up; lap; swig; swill, tipple &c. (*be drunken*) 959; empty one's glass, drain the cup; toss -off, – one's glass; wash down, crack a bottle, wet one's whistle.

cater, purvey &c. 637.

Adj. eatable, edible, esculent, comestible, alimentary; cereal, cibarious; dietetic; culinary; nutri-tive, -tious; succulent; drinkable, pot-able, -ulent; bibulous.

omn-, carn-, herb-, frug-, gran-, gramin-, phyt-ivorus; ichthyophagous.

prandial.

300. [Forcible ingress.] **Insertion.**— **N.** insertion, implantation, intercalation, embolism, introduction; interpolation, insinuation &c. (*intervention*) 228; planting &c. *v.*; injection, inoculation, importation, infusion; forcible -ingress &c. 294; immersion; submersion, -gence; dip, plunge; bath &c. (*water*) 337; interment &c. 363.

V. insert; intro-duce, -mit; put –, run- into; import; inject; interject &c. 228; infuse, instil, inoculate, impregnate, imbue, imbrue.

graft, ingraft, bud, plant, implant; dovetail.

obtrude; thrust –, stick –, ram –, stuff –, tuck –, press –, drive –, pop –, whip –, drop –, put- in; impact; empierce &c. (*make a hole*) 260.

embed; immerse, immerge, merge; bathe, soak &c. (*water*) 337; dip, plunge &c. 310.

bury &c. (*inter*) 363.

insert &c.- itself; plunge ***in medias res.***

Adj. inserted &c. *v.*

301. [Forcible egress.] **Extraction.**— **N.** extraction; extracting &c. *v.*; removal, elimination, extrication, eradication, evolution.

evulsion, avulsion; wrench; expression, squeezing; extirpation, extermination; ejection &c. 297; export &c. (*egress*) 295; distillation.

extractor, corkscrew, forceps, pliers.

V. extract, draw, pit; take –, draw –, pull –, tear –, pluck –, pick –, get- out; wring from, wrench; extort; root –, weed –, grub –, rake- up, – out; eradicate; pull –, pluck- up by the roots; averruncate; unroot; uproot, pull up, extirpate, dredge.

remove; educe, elicit; evolve, extricate; eliminate &c. (*eject*) 297; eviscerate &c. 297.

express, squeeze –, press- out; distil.

Adj. extracted &c. *v.*

---

302. [Motion through.] **Passage.**—**N.** passage, transmission; permeation; pene-, interpene-tration; transudation, infiltration; *osmosis*, osmose, endos-, exos-mose; intercurrence; ingress &c. 294; egress &c. 295; path &c. 627; conduit &c. 350; opening &c. 260; journey &c. 266; voyage &c. 267.

V. pass, – through; perforate &c. (*hole*) 260; penetrate, permeate, thread, thrid, enfilade; go -through, – across; go –, pass- over; cut across; ford, cross; pass and repass, work; make –, thread –, worm –, force- one's way; make –, force- a passage; cut one's way through;

find its -way, – vent; transmit, make way, clear the course; traverse, go over the ground.

Adj. passing &c. *v.*; intercurrent; osmotic &c. *n.*

Adv. *en passant* &c. (*transit*) 270.

303. [Motion beyond.] **Overstep.— N.** trans-cursion, -ilience, -gression; infraction, intrusion; trespass; en-croach-, infringe-ment; extravagation, transcendence; redundance &c. 641; ingress &c. 294.

V. transgress, surpass, pass; go- beyond, – by; show in –, come to the- front; shoot ahead of; steal a march –, gain- upon.

over-step, -pass, -reach, -go, -ride, -leap, -jump, -skip, -lap, -shoot the mark; out-strip, -leap, -jump, -go, -step, -run, -ride, -rival, -do; beat, – hollow; distance; leave in the -lurch, – rear; go one better, throw into the shade; exceed, transcend, surmount; soar &c. (*rise*) 305.

encroach, intrude, trespass, infringe, invade, trench upon, intrench on; strain; stretch –, strain- a point; pass the Rubicon.

Adj. surpassing &c. *v.*

Adv. beyond the mark, ahead.

304. [Motion short of.] **Shortcoming. —N.** shortcoming, failure; delinquency; falling short &c. *v.*; de-fault, -falcation; leeway; labour in vain, no go.

incompleteness &c. 53; imperfection &c. 651; insufficiency &c. 640; non-completion &c. 730; failure &c. 732.

V. come –, fall –, stop- -short, – short of; not reach; want; keep within -bounds, – the mark, – compass.

break down, stick in the mud, collapse, come to nothing; fall -through, – to the ground, – down; cave in, end in smoke, fizzle out, miss the mark, fail; lose ground; miss stays, slump.

Adj. unreached; deficient; short, – of; *minus*; out of depth; perfunctory &c. (*neglect*) 460.

Adv. within -the mark, – compass, – bounds; behindhand; *re infectâ*; to no purpose; far from it.

Phr. the bubble burst.

---

305. [Motion upwards.] **Ascent.—N.** ascent, ascension; rising &c. *v.*; rise, upgrowth; leap &c. 309; acclivity, hill &c. 217; stair, stairs, stair-case, -way, flight of -steps, – stairs; ladder, companion, – way; lift, elevator &c. 307.

rocket, lark; sky-rocket, -lark; Alpine Club.

V. ascend, rise, mount, arise, uprise; go –, get –, work one's way –, start –, spring –, shoot- up; zoom; aspire.

climb, clamber, ramp, scramble, swarm, *escalade*, surmount; scale, – the heights.

tower, soar, hover, spire, plane, swim, float, surge; leap &c. 309.

Adj. rising &c. *v.*; scandent, buoyant; super-natant, -fluitant; excelsior.

Adv. uphill.

---

306. [Motion downwards.] **Descent. —N.** descent, descension, declension, declination; fall; falling &c. *v.*; drop, cadence; subsidence, lapse; come-down, downfall, tumble, slip, tilt, trip, lurch; cropper, *culbute*; titubation, stumble; fate of Icarus; dive, nose-dive, *volplane*.

avalanche, *débâcle*, land-slip, -slide.

declivity, dip, hill; decline, drop.

V. descend; go –, drop –, come- down; fall, gravitate, drop, slip, slide, glissade, dive, plunge, settle; decline, slump, set, sink, droop, come down a peg.

dismount, alight, light, get down; swoop; stoop &c. 308; fall prostrate, precipitate oneself; let fall &c. 308.

tumble, trip, stumble, titubate, lurch, pitch, swag, topple; topple –, tumble- -down, – over; tilt, sprawl, plump down, come a cropper.

Adj. descending &c. *v.*; descendent, declivitous; downcast; decur-rent, -sive; labent, deciduous; nodding to its fall.

Adv. down, -hill, -wards.

307. Elevation.—N. elevation; raising &c. *v.*; erection, lift; sublevation, upheaval; sublimation, exaltation; prominence &c. (*convexity*) 250.

lever &c. 633; crane, derrick, windlass, capstan, winch, dredger, lift, elevator, escalator, dumb waiter.

V. heighten, elevate, raise, lift, erect; set –, stick –, perch –, perk –, tilt- up; rear, hoist, heave; up-lift, -raise, -rear, -bear, -cast, -hoist, -heave; buoy, weigh, mount, give a lift; exalt, sublimate; place –, set- on a pedestal.

take –, drag –, fish- up; dredge.

stand –, rise –, get –, jump- up; spring to one's feet; hold -oneself, – one's head- up; draw oneself up to his full height.

Adj. elevated &c. *v.*; standing up; stilted, attollent, rampant.

Adv. on -stilts, – the shoulders of, – one's legs, – one's hind legs.

308. Depression.—N. lowering &c. *v.*; depression; dip &c. (*concavity*) 252; abasement; detrusion; reduction.

over-throw, -set, -turn; upset; prostration, subversion, precipitation.

bow; courtesy, curtsy; genuflexion, *kowtow*, obeisance, *salaam*.

V. depress, lower; let –, take- -down, – down a peg; cast; let -drop, – fall; sink, debase, bring low, abase, slash, reduce, detrude, pitch, precipitate.

over-throw, -turn, -set; upset, subvert, prostrate, level, fell; cast –, take –, throw –, fling –, dash –, pull –, cut –, knock –, hew- down; raze, – to the ground; humiliate, trample in the dust, pull about one's ears.

sit, – down; couch, squat, crouch, stoop, bend, bow, courtsey, curtsy; bob, duck, dip, genuflect, kneel; *kowtow*, *salaam*, make obeisance, prostrate oneself; bend, bow- the -head, – knee; incline the head; bow down; cower; recline &c. (*be horizontal*) 213.

Adj. depressed &c. *v.*; at a low ebb; prostrate &c. (*horizontal*) 213; detrusive.

---

309. Leap.—N. leap, jump, hop, spring, bound, vault, saltation.

dance, caper, gambol; curvet, caracole; *gam-bade*, *-bado*; capriole, demivolt; buck, – jump; hop, skip and jump.

kangaroo, jerboa, chamois, goat, frog, grasshopper, flea.

V. leap; jump -up, – over the moon; hop, spring, bound, vault, ramp, cut capers, gambol, trip, skip, dance, caper; curvet, *caracole*; foot it, bob, bounce, flounce, start, frisk &c. (*amusement*) 840; jump about &c. (*agitation*) 315; trip it on the light fantastic toe, dance oneself off one's legs.

Adj. leaping &c. *v.*; saltatory, frisky.

Adv. on the light fantastic toe.

310. Plunge.—N. plunge, dip, dive, header; ducking &c. *v.*; submergence, immersion, diver.

V. plunge, dip, souse, duck; dive, plump; take a -plunge, – header, make a plunge; bathe &c. (*water*) 337.

sub-merge, -merse; immerse, douse, sink, engulf, send to -the bottom, – Davy Jones' locker.

get out of one's depth; go -to the bottom, – down like a stone; founder, welter, wallow.

---

311. [Curvilinear motion.] **Circuition.—N.** circuition, circulation; turn, curvet; excursion; circum-vention, -navigation, -ambulation; north-west passage; ambit, gyre, lap, circuit &c. 629.

turning &c. *v.*; wrench; evolution; coil, helix, spiral; corkscrew.

V. turn, bend, wheel; go –, put- about; heel; go –, turn -round, – to the right about; turn on one's heel; make –, describe- a -circle, – complete circle; encircle; go –, pass- through -180°, – 360°.

circum-navigate, -aviate, -ambulate, -vent; put a girdle round the earth, go the round, make the round of.

turn –, round- a corner; double a point.

wind, circulate, meander; whisk, twirl; twist &c. (*convolution*) 248; make a *détour* &c. (*circuit*) 629.

Adj. turning &c. *v.*; circuitous; circum-foraneous, -fluent; devious, roundabout, circum-ambient, -flex, -navigable.

Adv. round about.

312. [Motion in a continued circle.] **Rotation.—N.** rotation, revolution, gyration, circulation, roll; circum-rotation, -volution, -gyration; volutation, circination, turbination, *pirouette*, convolution.

verticity; whir, whirl, swirl, eddy, vortex, whirlpool, gurge; cyclone, tornado; surge; *vertigo*, dizzy round; Maelstrom, Charybdis; Ixion; wheel of Fortune.

wheel, screw, propeller, whirligig, rolling stone, windmill; top, teetotum, merry-go-round; roller; cog-, fly-wheel, spit; jack; caster.

axis, axle, spindle, spool, pivot, pin, hinge, pole, swivel, gimbals, arbor, bobbin, mandrel, shaft.

[Science of rotatory motion] trochilics, gyrostatics.

V. rotate; roll, – along; revolve, spin; turn, – round; circumvolve; circulate, gyre, gyrate, wheel, whirl, swirl, twirl, trundle, troll, bowl; slew round.

roll up, furl; wallow, welter; box the compass; spin like a -top, – teetotum.

Adj. rotating &c. *v.*; rota-tory, -ry; circumrotatory, trochilic, vertiginous, gyratory; vortic-al, -ose.

Adv. head over heels, round and round, like a horse in a mill.

313. [Motion in a reverse circle.] **Evolution.—N.** evolution, unfolding, development; eversion &c. (*inversion*) 218.

V. evolve; un-fold, -roll, -wind, -coil, -twist, -furl, -twine, -ravel; disentangle; develop.

Adj. evolving &c. *v.*; evolved &c. *v.*

---

314. [Reciprocating motion, motion to and fro.] **Oscillation.—N.** oscillation; vibration, libration; motion of a pendulum; nutation; undulation; pulsation; pulse; throb; seismic disturbance.

alternation; coming and going &c. *v.*; ebb and flow, flux and reflux, ups and downs; wave, vibratiuncle, swing, beat, shake, wag, see-saw, dance, lurch, dodge; fluctuation; vacillation &c. (*irresolution*) 605.

seismometer, vibroscope, seismograph.

V. oscillate; vi-, li-brate; alternate, undulate, wave; sway, rock, swing; pulsate, beat; wag, -gle; nod, bob, courtesy, curtsy; tick; play; chatter, wamble, wabble; teeter, dangle, swag.

fluctuate, dance, curvet, reel, quake; quiver, quaver, shake, flicker; wriggle; roll, toss, pitch; flounder, stagger, totter, waddle; move –, bob- up and down &c. *adv.*; pass and repass, ebb and flow, come and go, shuttle; vacillate &c. 605.

brandish, shake, flourish.

Adj. oscillating &c. *v.*; oscill-, undul-, puls-, libr-atory; vibrat-ory, -ile; pendulous, shutterwise, seismic.

Adv. to and fro, up and down, backwards and forwards, see-saw, zigzag, wibble-wabble, in and out, from side to side, like buckets in a well.

315. [Irregular motion.] **Agitation.—N.** agitation, stir, tremor, shake, ripple, jog, jolt, jar, jerk, shock, succussion, trepidation, quiver, quaver, dance; jactit-ation, -ance; shuffling &c. *v.*; twitter, flicker, flutter.

disquiet, perturbation, commotion, turmoil, turbulence; tumult, -uation; hubbub, rout, bustle, fuss, racket, *subsultus*, staggers, megrims, epilepsy, fits, twitching, vellication, St. Vitus' dance.

spasm, throe, throb, palpitation, convulsion, paroxysm; tetanus.

disturbance &c. (*disorder*) 59; restlessness &c. (*changeableness*) 149.

ferment, -ation; ebullition, effervescence, hurly-burly, *cahotage*; tempest, storm, ground swell, heavy sea, whirlpool, vortex &c. 312; whirlwind &c. (*wind*) 349.

V. be -agitated &c.; shake; tremble, – like an aspen leaf; quiver, quaver, quake, shiver, twitter, twire, dither, dodder; twitch, writhe, toss, shuffle, tumble, stagger, bob, reel, sway; wag, -gle, wiggle; wriggle, – like an eel; squirm; dance, stumble, shamble, flounder, totter, flounce, flop, curvet, prance.

throb, pulsate, beat, palpitate, go pit-a-pat; flutter, flitter, flicker, bicker; bustle.

ferment, effervesce, foam; boil, – over; bubble, – up; simmer.

toss –, jump- about; jump like a parched pea; shake to its -centre, – foundations; be the sport of the winds and waves; reel to and fro like a drunken man; move –, drive- from post to pillar and from pillar to post; keep between hawk and buzzard.

agitate, shake, convulse, toss, tumble, bandy, wield, brandish, flap, flourish, whisk, jerk, hitch, jolt; jog, -gle; jostle, buffet, hustle, disturb, stir, shake up, churn, jounce, wallop, whip, vellicate.

Adj. shaking &c. *v.*; agitated, tremulous; de-, sub-sultory; shambling; giddy-paced, saltatory, convulsive, jerky, unquiet, restless, all of a twitter.

Adv. by fits and starts; subsultorily &c. *adj.*; *per saltum*; hop, skip and jump; in -convulsions, – fits, pit-a-pat.

CLASS III

Words relating to MATTER

Section I. MATTER IN GENERAL

316. Materiality.—N. material-ity, -ness; materialization; corpor-eity, -ality; substantiality, material existence, incarnation, flesh and blood, *plenum*; physical condition.

matter, body, substance, brute matter, stuff, element, principle, protoplasm, plasma, *parenchyma*, material, *substratum*, hyle, *corpus*, *pabulum*; frame.

object, article, thing, something; still life; stocks and stones; materials &c. 635.

[Science of matter] physics; somatology, -ics; natural –, experimental- philosophy; physical science, *philosophie positive*, materialism, hylism; materialist, physicist.

V. materialize, incorporate, incarnate, substantiate, embody.

Adj. material, bodily; corpor-eal, -al; physical; somat-ic, -oscopic; sensible, tangible, ponderable, palpable, substantial; fleshly incarnate.

objective, impersonal, neuter, unspiritual, materialistic.

317. Immateriality.—N. immateriality, -ness; incorporeity, dematerialization, unsubstantiality, spirituality; inextension; astral plane.

personality; I, myself, me; *ego*, spirit &c. (*soul*) 450; astral body; immaterialism; spiritual-ism, -ist; subliminal –, subconscious- self.

V. disembody, spiritualize, dematerialize.

Adj. immateri-al, -ate; incorpor-eal, -al; asomatous, unextended; un-, disembodied; extramundane, supersensible, unearthly; pneumatoscopic; spiritual &c. (*psychical*) 450; aery.

personal, subjective.

---

318. World.—N. world, creation, nature, universe; earth, globe, wide world; *cosmos*; terraqueous globe, sphere; macro-, mega-cosm; music of the spheres.

heavens, sky, welkin, empyrean; starry -heaven, – host; firmament; vault –, canopy- of heaven; celestial spaces.

heavenly bodies, stars, luminaries, nebulæ; galaxy, milky way, galactic circle, *via lactea*.

sun, orb of day, Apollo, Phœbus; photo-, chromo-sphere; solar system; planet, -oid, asteroid; comet; satellite; moon, orb of night, Diana, Luna; aerolite, meteor; falling –, shooting- star; meteorite.

constellation, zodiac, signs of the zodiac, Charles's wain, Great Bear, Southern Cross, Orion's belt, Cassiopeia's chair, Pleiades &c.

colures, equator, ecliptic, orbit.

[Science of heavenly bodies] astronomy; urano-graphy, -logy; cosmo-logy, -graphy, -gony; *eidouranion*, orrery; geography; geodesy

&c. (*measurement*) 466; star-gazing, -gazer; astronomer; cosmogonist, geodesist, geographer; observatory.

Adj. cosmic, cosmical, mundane; terr-estrial, -estrious, -aqueous, -ene, -eous; telluric, earthly, geotic, geodetic, cosmogonal, under the sun; sub-lunary, -astral.

solar, heliacal; lunar; celestial, heavenly, empyreal, sphery; starry, stellar; sider-eal, -al; astral; nebular.

Adv. in all creation, on the face of the globe, here below, under the sun.

319. Gravity.—N. gravi-ty, -tation; weight; heaviness &c. *adj.*; specific gravity; ponderosity, pressure, load; bur-den, -then; ballast, counterpoise; lump –, mass –, weight- of.

lead, millstone, mountain, Ossa on Pelion.

weighing, ponderation, trutination; weights; avoirdupois –, troy –, apothecaries'- weight; grain, scruple, drachm, ounce, pound, lb., load, stone, hundredweight, cwt., ton, quintal, carat, pennyweight, tod, gramme, kilogramme &c.

[Weighing instrument] balance, scales, steelyard, beam, weighbridge, spring balance, weighing machine.

[Science of gravity] statics.

V. be -heavy &c. *adj.*; gravitate, weigh, press, cumber, load.

[Measure the weight of] weigh, poise.

Adj. weighty; weighing &c. *v.*; heavy, – as lead; ponder-ous, -able; lump-ish, -y; cumber-, burden-some; cumbrous, unwieldy, massive.

in-, superin-cumbent.

320. Levity.—N. levity; lightness &c. *adj.*; imponderability, imponderableness, buoyancy, volatility.

feather, dust, mote, down, thistledown, flue, cobweb, gossamer, straw, cork, bubble; float, buoy; ether, air.

leaven, ferment, barm, yeast, enzyme.

V. be -light &c. *adj.*; float, swim, be buoyed up.

render -light &c. *adj.*; lighten, levitate; leaven.

Adj. light, subtile, subtle, airy; imponder-ous, -able; astatic, weightless, ethereal, sublimated; uncompressed, volatile; buoyant, floating &c. *v.*; barmy, frothy; portable.

light as -a feather, – thistle down, – air.

fermenting &c. *n.*

SECTION II. INORGANIC MATTER

1°. SOLID MATTER

321. Density.—N. density, solidity; solidness &c. *adj.*; impenetra-, impermea-bility; incompressibility; imporosity; cohesion &c. 46; constipation, consistence, spissitude.

specific gravity; hydro-, areo-meter.

condensation; solid-ation, -ification; consolidation; concretion, caseation, coagulation; petrifaction &c. (*hardening*) 323; crystallization, precipitation; deposit, precipitate, silt; inspissation; thickening &c. *v.*

indivisibility, indiscerptibility, indissolvableness.

solid body, mass, block, knot, lump; con-cretion, -crete, -glomerate; cake,

322. Rarity.—N. rarity; tenuity; absence of -solidity &c. 321; subtility; sponginess, compressibility.

rarefaction, expansion, dilatation, inflation, subtilization.

ether &c. (*gas*) 334.

V. rarefy, expand, dilate, subtilize, attenuate, thin.

Adj. rare, subtile, thin, fine, tenuous, compressible, flimsy, slight; light &c. 320; cavernous, spongy &c. (*hollow*) 252.

rarefied &c. *v.*; unsubstantial; uncom-pact, -pressed.

clot, stone, curd, coagulum, grume; bone, gristle, cartilage.

V. be -dense &c. *adj.*; become –, render- solid &c. *adj.*; solid-ify, -ate; concrete, set, take a set, consolidate, congeal, coagulate; curd, -le; fix, clot, cake, candy, precipitate, deposit, cohere, crystallize; petrify &c. (*harden*) 323.

condense, thicken, inspissate, incrassate; compress, squeeze, ram down, constipate.

Adj. dense, solid; solidified &c. *v.*; cohe-rent, -sive &c. 46; compact, close, serried, thickset; substantial, massive, lumpish; impenetrable, impermeable, imporous; incompressible; constipated; concrete &c. (*hard*) 323; knot-ted, -ty; gnarled; crystal-line, -lizable; thick, grumous, stuffy.

un-dissolved, -melted, -liquefied, -thawed.

in-divisible, -discerptible, -frangible, -dissolvable, -dissoluble, -soluble, -fusible.

323. Hardness.—**N.** hardness &c. *adj.*; rigidity, renitence, inflexibility, temper, callosity, durity.

induration, petrifaction; lapid-ification, -escence; vitri-, ossi-, corni-fication; crystallization.

stone, pebble, flint, marble, rock, fossil, crag, crystal, quartz, granite, adamant; bone, cartilage; heart of oak, block, board, deal board; iron, steel; cast –, wrought- iron; nail; brick, concrete; cement.

V. render -hard &c. *adj.*; harden, stiffen, indurate, petrify, temper, ossify, vitrify.

Adj. hard, rigid, stubborn, stiff, firm; starch, -ed; stark, unbending, unlimber, unyielding; inflexible, tense; indurate, -d; gritty, proof.

adamant-ine, -ean; concrete, stony, rocky, lithic, granitic, vitreous; crystalline; horny, corneous; bony; oss-eous, -ific; cartilaginous; hard as a -stone &c. *n.*; stiff as -buckram, – a poker.

324. Softness.—**N.** softness, pliableness &c. *adj.*; flexibility; pli-ancy, -ability; sequacity, malleability; flabbiness; duct-, tract-ility; extend-, extensibility; plasticity; inelasticity, flaccidity, laxity.

clay, wax, butter, dough, pudding; cushion, pillow, feather-bed, pad, down, padding, wadding.

mollification; softening &c. *v.*

V. render -soft &c. *adj.*; soften, mollify, mellow, relax, temper; mash, knead, squash, *massage*.

bend, yield, relent, relax, give.

Adj. soft, tender, supple; pli-ant, -able; flex-ible, -ile; lithe, -some; lissom, limber, plastic; ductile; tract-ile, -able; malleable, extensile, sequacious, inelastic, mollient.

yielding &c. *v.*; flabby, limp, flimsy.

flaccid, flocculent, downy; spongy, œdematous, medullary, doughy, argillaceous, mellow.

soft as -butter, – down, – silk; yielding as wax; tender as a chicken.

325. Elasticity. — **N.** elasticity, springiness, spring, resilience, renitency, buoyancy.

india-rubber, caoutchouc, gutta-percha, whalebone, gum elastic.

V. be -elastic &c. *adj.*; spring back &c. (*recoil*) 277.

Adj. elastic, tensile, springy, ductile, resilient, renitent, buoyant.

326. Inelasticity.—**N.** want of –, absence of- elasticity &c. 325; inelasticity &c. (*softness*) 324.

Adj. inelastic &c. (*soft*) 324.

---

327. Tenacity.—**N.** tenacity, toughness, strength; cohesion &c. 46; sequacity; stubbornness &c. (*obstinacy*) 606; viscidity &c. 352.

leather; gristle, cartilage.

328. Brittleness.—**N.** brittleness &c. *adj.*; frag-, friab-, frangib-, fiss-ility; frailty; house of -cards, – glass.

V. be -brittle &c. *adj.*; live in a glass house.

V. be -tenacious &c. *adj.*; resist fracture.

Adj. tenacious, tough, cohesive, adhesive, strong, resisting, sequacious, stringy, gristly, cartilaginous, leathery, coriaceous, tough as whit-leather; stubborn &c. (*obstinate*) 606.

break, crack, snap, split, shiver, splinter, crumble, break short, burst, fly, give way; fall to pieces; crumble -to, – into- dust.

Adj. breakable, brittle, frangible, fragile, frail, friable, delicate, gimcrack, shivery, fissile; splitting &c. *v.*; lacerable, splintery, crisp, crimp, short. brittle as glass.

---

329. [Structure.] **Texture.—N.** structure, organization, anatomy, frame, mould, fabric, construction; frame-work, carcass, architecture; stratification, cleavage.

substance, stuff, *compages*, *parenchyma*; constitution, staple, organism.

[Science of structures] organ-, oste-, my-, splanchn-, neur , angi-, aden-ology; angi-, aden-ography.

texture; inter-, con-texture; tissue, grain, web, surface; warp and -woof, – weft; tooth, nap &c. (*roughness*) 256; fineness –, coarseness- of grain.

[Science of tissues] histology.

Adj. structural, organic; anatomic, -al.

text-ural, -ile; fine-, coarse-grained; fine, delicate, subtile, gossamery, filmy; coarse; home-spun; linsey-woolsey.

330. Pulverulence.—N. [State of powder.] pulverulence; sandiness &c. *adj.*; efflorescence; friability.

powder, dust, sand, shingle; sawdust; grit; attrition; meal, bran, flour, *farina*, spore, sporule; crumb, seed, grain; particle &c. (*smallness*) 32; thermion; limature, filings, *débris*, *detritus*, scobs, magistery, fine powder; *flocculi*.

smoke; cloud of -dust, – sand, – smoke; puff –, volume -of smoke; sand –, dust- storm.

[Reduction to powder] pulverization, comminution, attenuation, granulation, disintegration, subaction, contusion, trituration, levigation, abrasion, detrition, multure; limation; filing &c. *v.*

[Instruments for pulverization] mill, millstone, grater, rasp, file, pestle and mortar, nutmeg-grater, teeth, molar, grinder, chopper, grindstone, kern, quern, muller.

V. come to dust; be -disintegrated, – reduced to powder &c.

reduce –, grind- to powder; pulverize, comminute, granulate, triturate, levigate; scrape, file, abrade, rub down, grind, grate, rasp, pound, bray, bruise; con-tuse, -tund; beat, crush, cranch, craunch, crunch, muller, scranch, crumble, disintegrate; attenuate &c. 195.

Adj. powdery, pulverulent, granular, mealy, floury, farinaceous, branny, furfuraceous, flocculent, dusty, sandy, sabulous; aren-ose, -arious, -aceous; gritty; efflorescent, impalpable.

pulverizable; friable, crumbly, shivery; pulverized &c. *v.*; attrite; in pieces.

331. Friction.—N. friction, attrition; rubbing &c. *v.*; erasure; con-frication, -trition; affriction, abrasion, arrosion, limature, frication, rub; elbow-grease; rosin; massage.

V. rub, scratch, abrade, scrape, scrub,

332. [Absence of friction. Prevention of friction.] **Lubrication.—N.** smoothness &c. 255; unctuousness &c. 355.

lubri-cation, -fication; anointment; oiling &c. *v.*

fray, rasp, graze, curry, scour, polish, rub out, erase, gnaw; file, grind &c. (*reduce to powder*) 330; *massage*.

set one's teeth on edge; rosin.

Adj. anatriptic, abrasive.

synovia; lubricant, graphite, glycerine, oil &c. 356; saliva; lather.

V. lubri-cate, -citate; oil, grease, lather, soap; wax.

Adj. lubricated &c. *v.*

2°. Fluid Matter

1. *Fluids in General*

333. Fluidity.—N. fluidity, liquidity; liquidness &c. *adj.*; gaseity &c. 334; liquefaction &c. 334.

fluid, inelastic fluid; liquid, liquor; lymph, humour, juice, sap, serum, blood, serosity, gravy, rheum, ichor, sanies.

solu-bility, -bleness.

[Science of liquids] hydro-logy, -statics, -dynamics, hydraulics &c.

V. be -fluid &c. *adj.*; flow &c. (*water in motion*) 348; liquefy &c. 335.

Adj. liquid, fluid, serous, juicy, succulent, sappy; fluent &c. (*flowing*) 348.

liquefied &c. 335; uncongealed; soluble, hydrostatic &c. *n.*

334. Gaseity.—N. gaseity, gaseousness; vapourousness &c. *adj.*; flatulence, -lency; volatility, aeration, gasification.

elastic fluid, gas, air, vapour, ether, steam, fume, reek, *effluvium*, *flatus*; cloud &c. 353.

[Science of elastic fluids] pneumat-ics, -ostatics; aero-statics, -dynamics &c.

gas-, gaso-meter.

V. gassify, aerate, aerify; emit vapour &c. 336.

Adj. gaseous, aeriform, ethereal, aerial, airy, vaporous, volatile, evaporable; flatulent; aerostatic &c. *n.*

335. Liquefaction.—N. liquefaction; liquescen-ce, -cy, deliquescence; melting &c. (*heat*) 384; colliqu-ation, -efaction; thaw; de-, liquation; lixiviation, dissolution.

solution, apozem, lixivium, infusion, decoction, flux.

solvent, diluent, menstruum, alkahest, *aqua fortis*.

V. render -liquid &c. 333; liquefy, run, deliquesce; melt &c. (*heat*) 384; solve; dissolve, resolve; liquate; hold in solution; leach, lixiviate.

Adj. lique-fied &c. *v.*, -scent, -fiable; deliquescent, soluble, colliquative; solvent.

336. Vaporization. — N. vapor-, volatil-ization; gasification; e-, vaporation; distillation, cohobation, sublimation, exhalation; volatility.

vaporizer, still, retort, spray, atomizer; fumigation, steaming.

V. render -gaseous &c. 334; vaporize, volatilize; distil, sublime; evaporate, exhale, smoke, transpire, emit vapour, fume, reek, steam, fumigate.

Adj. volatilized &c. *v.*; reeking &c. *v.*; volatile; evaporable, vaporizable.

---

2. *Specific Fluids*

337. Water.—N. water; serum, serosity; lymph; rheum; diluent.

dilution, maceration, lotion; washing &c. *v.*; im-, mersion; humectation, infiltration, spargefaction, affusion, irrigation, *douche*, balneation, bath.

deluge &c. (*water in motion*) 348; high water, flood-, spring-tide.

338. Air.—N. air &c. (*gas*) 334; common –, atmospheric- air; atmosphere, stratosphere, isothermal layer, troposphere, Heaviside layer.

open, – air; sky, welkin; blue, – sky; cloud &c. 353.

weather, climate, rise and fall of the barometer, isobar.

V. be -watery &c. *adj.*; reek.

add water, water, wet; moisten &c. 339; dilute, dip, immerse; merge; im-, sub-merge; plunge, souse, duck, drown; soak, steep, macerate, pickle, wash, sprinkle, sparge, lave, bathe, affuse, splash, swash, douse, slosh, drench; dabble, slop, slobber, irrigate, inundate, deluge; syringe, inject, gargle; infiltrate, percolate.

Adj. watery, aqueous, aquatic, lymphatic; balneal, diluent; drenching &c. *v.*; diluted &c. *v.*; weak; wet &c. (*moist*) 339.

Phr. the waters are out.

[Science of air] pneumatics, aero-logy, -scopy, -graphy; meteorology, climatology; eudio-, baro-, aero-meter; aneroid, baro-graph, -scope; weather-gauge, -glass, -cock.

exposure to the -air, – weather; ventilation; aero-station, -nautics, -naut &c. 267 and 269.

V. air, ventilate; fan &c. (*wind*) 349.

Adj. containing air, flatulent, effervescent; windy &c. 349.

atmospheric, airy; aeri-al, -form; pneumatic; meteorological; weather-wise.

Adv. in the open air, out of doors, *à la belle étoile, al fresco*; *sub -Jove, – dio.*

339. Moisture.—**N.** moisture; moistness &c. *adj.*; hum-idity, -ectation; madefaction, dew; *serein*; marsh &c. 345; Hygromet-ry, -er.

V. moisten, wet; humect, -ate; sponge, damp, dampen, bedew; imbue, imbrue, infiltrate, saturate; seethe, sop; soak, drench &c. (*water*) 337.

be -moist &c. *adj.*; not have a dry thread; perspire &c. (*exude*) 295.

Adj. moist, damp; watery &c. 337; undried, humid, wet, dank, muggy, dewy; roric; roscid; juicy.

wringing wet; wet -through, – to the skin; saturated &c. *v.*

swashy, soggy, dabbled; reeking, seething, dripping, soaking, soft, sodden, sloppy, muddy; swampy &c. (*marshy*) 345; irriguous.

340. Dryness.—**N.** dryness &c. *adj.*; siccity, aridity, drought, ebb-, neap-tide, low water.

drying, ex-, de-siccation; evaporation; dehydration; arefaction, dephlegmation, drainage.

drier, desiccator.

V. be -dry &c. *adj.*; render -dry &c. *adj.*; dry; dry –, soak- up; sponge, swab, wipe; ex-, de-siccate, dehydrate, anhydrate; drain, parch.

be fine, hold up.

Adj. dry, anhydrous, arid, waterless; dried &c. *v.*; undamped; juice-, sapless; sear; husky; rainless, without rain, fine; dry as -a bone, – dust, – a stick, – a mummy, – a biscuit; desiccated; dehydrated; water-proof, -tight.

341. Ocean.—**N.** sea, ocean, main, deep, brine, salt water, waters, waves, billows, high seas, offing, great waters, watery waste, 'vasty deep,' briny ocean, herring pond, steamer track, the seven seas; wave, tide &c. (*water in motion*) 348.

hydrograph-y, -er, oceanography; Neptune, Thetis, Triton, Naiad, Nereid; sea-nymph, Siren, mer-maid, -man; trident, dolphin.

Adj. oceanic; mar-ine, -itime; pelagic, -ian; sea-going, -worthy; hydrographic.

Adv. at –, on- sea; afloat, on the high seas.

342. Land.—**N.** land, earth, ground, dry land, *terra firma.*

continent, mainland, peninsula, delta; tongue –, neck- of land; isthmus; oasis; promontory &c. (*projection*) 250; highland &c. (*height*) 206.

coast, shore, scar, strand, beach; bank, lea; sea- board, -side, -shore, -bank, -coast, -beach; rock-, iron-bound coast; loom of the land; derelict; innings; *alluvium*, alluvion.

soil, glebe, clay, loam, marl, cledge, chalk, gravel, mould, subsoil, clod, clot; rock, crag, cliff.

acres; real estate &c. (*property*) 780; landsman, land-lubber, farmer.

geography &c. 318; agriculture &c. 371.

V. land, come to land; set foot on -the soil, - dry land; come -, go- ashore.

Adj. earthy; continental, midland; littoral, riparian, ripuarian; alluvial; terrene &c. (*world*) 318; landed, predial, territorial.

Adv. ashore; on -shore, - land.

343. Gulf. Lake.—**N.** land covered with water, gulf, gulph, bay, inlet, bight, estuary, arm of the sea, fiord, armlet; frith, firth, ostiary, mouth; lagune, lagoon; indraught; cove, creek; natural harbour; roads; strait, narrows; Euripus; sound, belt, gut, kyles.

lake, loch, lough, mere, tarn, plash, broad, pond, pool, lin, puddle, well, artesian well, tank, sump; standing -, dead -, sheet of- water; fish -, mill-pond; race; ditch, dike, dyke, dam; reservoir &c. (*store*) 636.

Adj. lacustrine; land locked.

344. Plain.—**N.** plain, table land, mesa, face of the country; open -, country; basin, downs, waste, weary waste, desert, tundra, wild, steppe, pampas, savanna, prairie, champaign, heath, common, wold, veld; moor, -land, uplands, fell; bush; *plateau* &c. (*level*) 213; *campagna*.

meadow, mead, haugh, pasturage, park, field, lawn, green, plat, plot, grass-plat, greensward, sward, grass, turf, sod, heather; lea, ley, lay; grounds.

Adj. campestrian, champaign, alluvial.

345. Marsh.—**N.** marsh, swamp, morass, marish, moss, fen, bog, quagmire, slough, sump, wash; mud, squash, slush.

Adj. marsh, -y; swampy, boggy, plashy, poachy, quaggy, soft; muddy, sloppy, squashy, spongy; paludal; moor-ish, -y; fenny.

346. Island.—**N.** island, isle, islet, eyot, ait, holm, reef, atoll, breaker; archipelago; islander.

Adj. insular, sea-girt.

3. *Fluids in Motion*

347. [Fluid in motion.] **Stream.**—**N.** stream &c. (*of water*) 348, (*of air*) 349.

V. flow &c. 348; blow &c. 349.

348. [Water in motion.] **River.**—**N.** running water.

jet, spirt, squirt, spout, splash, swash, rush, gush, *jet d'eau*; sluice, chute.

water-spout, -fall; fall, cascade, force, foss; lin, -n; ghyll, Niagara; cata-ract, -dupe, -clysm; *débâcle*, inundation, deluge.

rain, -fall; *serein*; shower, scud; downpour, cloud burst; driving -, pouring -, drenching- rain; hyeto-logy, -graphy; rainy season, monsoon; predominance of Aquarius, reign of St. Swithin; mizzle, drizzle, *stillicidium*, plash; dropping &c. *v.*

stream, course, flux, flow, profluence; effluence &c. (*egress*) 295; defluxion; flowing &c. *v.*; current, tide, race.

spring; fount, -ain; rill, rivulet, gill,

349. [Air in motion.] **Wind.**—**N.** wind, draught, *flatus*, *afflatus*, air; breath, - of air; puff, whiff, zephyr; blow, drift; *aura*; stream, current; under-current.

gust, blast, breeze, squall, gale, half a gale, storm, tempest, hurricane, whirlwind, tornado, samiel, cyclone, typhoon; simoon; harmattan, monsoon, trade wind, sirocco, *mistral*, *bise*, *föhn*, tramontane, levanter; capful of wind; fresh -, stiff- breeze; keen blast; blizzard.

windiness &c. *adj.*; ventosity; rough -, dirty -, ugly -, stress of- weather; dirty-, windy-, mackerel- sky; mare's tail; thick -, black -, white- squall.

anemography, aerodynamics; wind-gauge, anemometer, weather-cock, vane.

gullet, rillet; stream-, brook-let; runnel, sike, burn, beck, brook, stream, river; reach; tributary.

body of water, torrent, rapids, flush, flood, swash, spate; spring –, high –, full-tide; bore; eagre, *hygre*; fresh, -et; undertow, indraught, reflux, undercurrent, eddy, vortex, gurge, whirlpool, Maelstrom, regurgitation, overflow; confluence, corrivation.

wave, billow, surge, swell, ripple; roller, ground swell, surf, breaker, white horses; comber, beach-comber; rough –, heavy –, cross –, long –, short –, chopping –, choppy- sea, choppiness; tidal wave.

[Science of fluids in motion] Hydrodynamics; Hydraul-ics &c.; rain-gauge &c.

water-bearer, – carrier, Aquarius.

irrigation &c. (*water*) 337; pump; watering-pot, – cart; hydrant, standpipe, hose, sprinkler, drencher; fire-engine, squirt, syringe.

V. flow, run; meander; gush, pour, spout, roll, jet, well, issue; drop, drip, dribble, plash, squirt, spurt, spirtle, trill, trickle, distil, percolate; stream, overflow, inundate, deluge, flow over, splash, swash; guggle, murmur, babble, bubble, purl, gurgle, sputter, regurgitate; ooze, flow out &c. (*egress*) 295.

rain, – hard, – in torrents, – cats and dogs, – pitchforks; come down in sheets; pour with rain, drizzle, mizzle, spit, sprinkle, set in.

flow –, fall –, open –, drain- into; discharge itself, disembogue.

[Cause a flow] pour; pour out &c. (*discharge*) 297; shower down; irrigate, drench &c. (*wet*) 337; spill, splash.

[Stop a flow] stanch; dam, -up &c. (*close*) 261; obstruct &c. 706.

Adj. fluent; dif-, pro-, af-fluent; tidal; flowing &c. *v.*; meand-ering, -ry, -rous; fluvi-al, -atile; streamy, showery, rainy, drizzly, drizzling, pluvial, pluviose, stillicidous.

suf-, insuf-, per-, in-, af-flation; blowing, fanning &c. *v.*; ventilation.

sneezing &c. *v.*; sternutation; hiccup, -cough; catching of the breath; breathing &c.

Eolus, Eurus, Boreas, Zephyr, cave of Eolus.

air-pump, lungs, bellows, blow-pipe, fan, blower; pulmotor, ventilator, punkah, aspirator, exhauster, ejector.

V. blow, waft; blow -hard, – great guns, – a hurricane &c. *n.*; whistle, roar, howl, ring in the shrouds; stream, issue.

respire, breathe, in-, ex-hale, puff; whif, -fle; gasp, wheeze; snuff, -le; sniff, -le; sneeze, cough, belch.

fan, ventilate; in-, per-flate; blow –, pump- up.

Adj. blowing &c. *v.*; windy, airy, æolian, flatulent; breezy, gusty, squally; stormy, tempestuous, blustering; boisterous &c. (*violent*) 173.

pulmon-ic, -ary.

---

350. [Channel for the passage of water.] **Conduit.**—**N.** conduit, channel, duct, watercourse, race; head –, tail-race; adit, aqueduct, canal, trough, flume, gutter, pantile; dike, canyon, ravine, gorge, hollow, main, gully, moat, ditch, drain, sewer, culvert, *cloaca*, sough, kennel, siphon, *piscina*; pipe &c. (*tube*) 260; funnel; tunnel &c. (*passage*) 627; water –, waste- pipe; emunctory, gully-hole, artery, aorta, vein, blood vessel; lymphatic; throat, alimentary canal, intestine; pore, spout, scupper; ad-, a-jutage;

351. [Channel for the passage of air.] **Air-pipe.**—**N.** air-pipe, – shaft, – way, – passage, – tube; shaft, flue, chimney, funnel, vent, blow-hole, nostril, nozzle, throat, weasand, *trachea*; *bronch-us, -ia*; larynx, tonsils, wind-pipe, spiracle; venti-duct, -lator; louvre, blow-pipe &c. (*wind*) 349; pipe &c. (*tube*) 260.

---

hose; gar-, gur-goyle; penstock, weir; flood-, water-gate; sluice, lock, valve; rose; waterworks.

Adj. vascular &c. (*with holes*) 260.

3°. Imperfect Fluids

352. Semiliquidity.—N. semiliquidity; stickiness &c. *adj.*; visc-idity, -osity; gumm-, glutin-, muc-osity; spiss-, crass-itude; lentor; adhesiveness &c. (*cohesion*) 46.

inspiss-, incrass-ation; thickening, coagulation.

jelly, aspic, mucilage, gelatin, isinglass; colloid, mucus, phlegm; pituite, lava; glair, starch, gluten, albumen, milk, cream, protein; syrup, treacle; gum, size, glue, paste; wax, bee's-wax; emulsoid, emulsion, soup; squash, mud, slush, slime, ooze; moisture &c. 339; marsh &c. 345.

V. inspiss-, incrass-ate; coagulate, gelatinize, gelatinify, gel, jell, emulsify, thicken; mash, squash, churn, beat up.

Adj. semi-fluid, -liquid; half-melted, -frozen; milky, muddy &c. *n.*; lact-eal, -ean, -eous, -escent, -iferous; emulsive, curdled, thick, succulent, uliginous.

gelat-, album-, mucilag-, glut-inous; gelatine, mastic, amylaceous, ropy, clammy, clotted; vis-cid, -cous; sticky, tacky; slab, -by; lentous, pituitous; mu-cid, -culent, -cous.

353. [Mixture of air and water.] Bubble. [Cloud.]—**N.** bubble; foam, froth, head, fume, spume, lather, suds, spray, surf, yeast, barm, spindrift.

cloud, vapour, fog, mist, haze, steam; scud, rack, *nimbus*; *cumulus*, woolpack, *cirrus*, *stratus*; *cirro-*, *cumulo-stratus*; *cirro-cumulus*; mackerel sky, mare's tail, dirty sky.

[Science of clouds] nephelognosy, nephology.

effervescence, fermentation; bubbling &c. *v.*

nebula; cloudiness &c. (*opacity*) 426; nebulosity &c. (*dimness*) 422.

V. bubble, boil, foam, froth, spume, mantle, sparkle, guggle, gurgle; effervesce, ferment, fizzle; aerate; cloud, overcast, befog.

Adj. bubbling &c. *v.*; frothy, nappy, effervescent, sparkling, *mousseux*, up, fizzy, with a head on.

cloudy &c. *n.*; vaporous, nebulous, overcast; nubiferous, nephological; foggy, brumous.

---

354. Pulpiness.—N. pulpiness &c. *adj.*; pulp, paste, dough, sponge, curd, pap, rob, jam, pudding, mush, fool, poultice, grume, *papier mâché*.

Adj. pulpy &c. *n.*; pultaceous, grumous.

V. pulp, pulpify, mash.

355. Unctuousness.—N. unctuousness &c. *adj.*; unctuosity, lubricity; ointment &c. (*oil*) 356; anointment; lubrication &c. 332.

V. oil &c. (*lubricate*) 332.

Adj. unctuous, oily, oleaginous, adipose, sebaceous; fat, -ty; greasy; waxy, butyraceous, soapy, saponaceous, pinguid, lardaceous; slippery.

---

356. Oil.—N. oil, fat, butter, cream, grease, tallow, suet, lard, dripping, margarine, oleomargarine, exunge, blubber; glycerine, stearine, elaine, oleagine; soap; soft soap, wax, cerement; paraffin, spermaceti, adipocere; petroleum, mineral –, rock –, crystal- oil, kerosene, vegetable –, colza –, olive –, linseed –, cotton seed –, rape –, nut –, fusel- oil; animal –, neat's foot –, signal –, train- oil; ointment, unguent, liniment, salve, pomade, pomatum, brilliantine, spike –, nard.

356a. Resin.—N. resin, rosin, colophony; gum; lac, shellac, sealing-wax; amber, -gris; bitumen, pitch, tar, asphalt, -e, -um; varnish, copal, mastic, magilp, lacquer, japan.

V. varnish &c. (*overlay*) 223.

Adj. resinous, bituminous, pitchy, tarry.

SECTION III. ORGANIC MATTER

1°. VITALITY

1. *Vitality in general*

357. Organization.—N. organized -world, – nature; living –, animated-nature; living beings; organic remains, organism; fossils; animal and vegetable kingdom, *fauna* and *flora*, biota.

prot-oplasm, -ein; albumen; structure &c. 329; organ-ization, -ism.

[Science of living beings] biology; natural history,* organic –, bio-chemistry, anatomy, physiology, embryology, morphology, evolution, Darwinism, Lamarkism, zoology &c. 368; botany &c. 369; naturalist, biologist &c.

Adj. organ-ic, -ized.

358. Inorganization. — N. mineral -world, – kingdom; unorganized –, inorganic –, brute –, inanimate- matter.

[Science of the mineral kingdom] mineralogy; geo-logy, -gnosy, -scopy; metall-urgy, -ography; lithology; orycto-logy, -graphy.

V. turn to dust, pulverize.

Adj. in-organic, -animate; unorganized; azoic; mineral.

---

359. Life.—N. life; vi-tality, -ability; animation; vital -spark, – flame, – force.

respiration, wind; breath -of life, – of one's nostrils; life-blood; Archeus; existence &c. 1.

vivification, vitalization; revivification &c. 163; Prometheus; life to come &c. (*destiny*) 152.

[Science of life] physiology, etiology, embryology, biology; animal economy.

nourishment, staff of life &c. (*food*) 298.

V. be -alive &c. *adj.*; live, breathe, respire; subsist &c. (*exist*) 1; walk the earth; strut and fret one's hour upon a stage; be spared.

see the light, be born, come into the world; fetch –, draw- -breath, – the breath of life; quicken; revive; come to, – life.

give birth to &c. (*produce*) 161; bring to life, put life into, vitalize; vivi-fy, -ficate; reanimate &c. (*restore*) 660; keep -alive, – body and soul together, – the wolf from the door; support life.

have nine lives like a cat.

360. Death.—N. death, dying &c. *v.*; de-cease, -mise; dissolution, departure, *obit*, release, rest, *quietus*, fall; loss, bereavement.

end &c. 67 –, cessation &c. 142 –, loss –, extinction –, ebb- of -life &c. 359.

death-warrant, -watch, -rattle, -bed; stroke –, agonies –, shades –, valley of the shadow –, jaws –, hand- of death; last -breath, – gasp, – agonies; dying -day, – breath, – agonies; swan song, *chant du cygne*; *rigor mortis*; Stygian shore; crossing the bar, the great adventure.

King -of terrors, – Death; Death, Angel of Death; mortality; doom &c. (*necessity*) 601.

euthanasia; happy release; break up of the system; natural -death, – decay; sudden –, violent- death; untimely end, watery grave; suffocation, *asphyxia*; heart failure; fatal disease &c. (*disease*) 655; death-blow &c. (*killing*) 361.

necrology, bills of mortality, obituary; death-song &c. (*lamentation*) 839.

V. die, expire, perish; meet one's -death, – end; pass away, be taken; yield –, resign- one's breath; resign

* The term *Natural History* is also used as relating to all the objects in Nature whether organic or inorganic, and including therefore *Mineralogy*, *Geology*, *Meteorology*, &c.

Adj. living, alive; in -life, – the flesh, – the land of the living; on this side of the grave, above ground, breathing, quick, animated, viable; lively &c. (*active*) 682; alive and kicking; tenacious of life.

vital; vivi-fying, -fied &c. *v.*; Promethean.

Adv. *vivendi causâ.*

---

one's -being, – life; end one's -days, – life, – earthly career; breathe one's last; cease to -live, – breathe; depart this life; be -no more &c. *adj.*; go –, drop –, pop -off; lose –, lay down –, relinquish –, surrender- one's life; drop –, sink- into the grave; close one's eyes; fall –, drop- dead, – down dead; break one's neck; give –, yield- up the ghost; be all over with one.

pay the debt to nature, shuffle off this mortal coil, take one's last sleep; go the way of all flesh; join the -greater number, – majority, – choir invisible; awake to life immortal; come –, turn- to dust; cross the Stygian ferry; go to -one's long account, – one's last home, – Davy Jones's locker, – the wall; receive one's death warrant, make one's will, die a natural death, go out like the snuff of a candle; come to an untimely end; catch one's death; go off the hooks, kick the bucket, peg out; go West; hop the twig, turn up one's toes; die a violent death &c. (*be killed*) 361; make the supreme sacrifice.

Adj. dead, lifeless; deceased, demised, departed, defunct; late, gone, no more; ex-, in-animate; out of the world, taken off, released; departed this life &c. *v.*; dead and gone; bereft of life, stone dead, dead as -a door nail, – a door post, – mutton, – a herring, – nits; launched into eternity, gathered to one's fathers, numbered with the dead, gone to a better land, behind the veil, beyond the grave, – mortal ken.

dying &c. *v.*; mori-bund, -ent, Acherontic; hippocratic; *in -articulo, – extremis*; in the -jaws, – agony- of death; going, – off; *aux abois*; on one's -last legs, – death bed; at -the point of death, – death's door, – the last gasp; near one's end, given over, booked, fey; with one foot in –, tottering on the brink of- the grave.

still-born; mortuary; deadly &c. (*killing*) 361.

Adv. *post -obit, – mortem.*

Phr. life -ebbs, – fails, – hangs by a thread; one's -days are numbered, – hour is come, – race is run, – doom is sealed; Death -knocks at the door, – stares one in the face; the breath is out of the body; the grave closes over one; *sic itur ad astra.*

361. [Destruction of life; violent death.] **Killing.—N.** killing &c. *v.*; homicide, manslaughter, murder, assassination, trucidation, occision; lynching, effusion of blood; blood, -shed; gore, slaughter, carnage, butchery; *battue*, gladiatorial combat.

massacre; *fusillade, noyade, pogrom*; Thuggee, thuggism.

death blow, finishing stroke, *coup de grâce, quietus*; execution &c. (*capital punishment*) 972; judicial murder; martyrdom.

butcher, slayer, murderer, Cain, assassin, cut-throat, garrotter, *bravo*, thug, racketeer, gunman, mobster, gangster, Moloch, *matador, sabreur*; *guet-à-pens*; gallows, executioner &c. (*punishment*) 975; man-eater.

regicide, parricide, fratricide, infanticide, aborticide &c.

suicide, *felo-de-se, suttee, hara-kiri*, Juggernaut; immolation, holocaust.

suffocation, strangulation, garrotte; hanging &c. *v.*

deadly weapon &c. (*arms*) 727; Aceldama; the potter's field, the field of blood.

fatal accident, violent death, casualty.

[Destruction of animals] slaughtering; phthiozoics;* sport, -ing; the chase, venery; hunting, coursing, shooting, fishing; pig-sticking; sports-, hunts-, fisher-man; hunter, Nimrod; slaughterer, knacker, slaughter-house, shambles, *abattoir*.

V. kill, put to death, slay, shed blood; murder, assassinate, butcher, slaughter; victimize, immolate; massacre; take away –, deprive of- life; make away with, put an end to; despatch, decimate; burke, settle, do, – to death, – for:

strangle, garrotte, hang, lynch, throttle, choke, stifle, suffocate, stop the breath, smother, asphyxiate, drown.

sabre; cut -down, – to pieces, – the throat; jugulate; stab, run through the body, bayonet; put to the -sword, – edge of the sword.

shoot, – dead; blow one's brains out; brain, knock on the head; stone, lapidate; give –, deal- a death blow; give a *-quietus*, – *coup de grâce*.

behead, bowstring &c. (*execute*) 972.

hunt, shoot &c. *n.*

cut off, nip in the bud, launch into eternity, send to one's last account, bump off, rub out, sign one's death warrant, strike the death knell of.

give no quarter, pour out blood like water; run amuck, wade knee-deep –, imbrue one's hands- in blood.

die a violent death, welter in one's blood; dash –, blow- out one's brains; commit suicide; kill –, -make away with –, put an end to- oneself.

Adj. killing &c. *v.*; murd-, slaught-erous; sanguin-ary, -olent; blood-stained, -thirsty; homicidal, red-handed; bloody, -minded; ensanguined, gory, sanguineous.

mortal, fatal, lethal; dead-, death-ly; mort-, leth-iferous; unhealthy &c. 657; internecine; suicidal.

sporting; piscator-ial, -y.

Adv. in at the death.

362. Corpse.—N. corpse, corse, carcass, bones, skeleton, dry-bones; defunct, relics, *reliquiæ*, remains, mortal remains, dust, ashes, earth, clay; mummy; carrion; food for- worms, – fishes; tenement of clay, this mortal coil.

shade, ghost, *manes*, apparition &c. 980.

organic remains, fossils.

Adj. cadaverous, corpse-like; unburied &c. 363.

363. Interment.—N. interment, burial, sepulture, entombment; in-, humation; obs-, ex-equies; funeral, wake, pyre, funeral pile; cremation.

funeral -rite, – solemnity; knell, passing bell, tolling; dirge &c. (*lamentation*) 839; cypress; *obit*, dead march, muffled drum; coroner, mortician, undertaker, mute, mourner, professional mourner, pall-bearer; elegy; funeral -oration, – sermon; epitaph.

grave clothes, shroud, winding-sheet, cere-cloth; cerement.

coffin, shell, sarcophagus, urn, pall, bier, hearse, catafalque, cinerary urn.

grave, pit, sepulchre, tomb, vault, crypt, catacomb, mausoleum, *Golgotha*, house of death, narrow house, long home; cemetery, necropolis, boneyard; burial-place, -ground; grave-, church-yard; God's acre; mortuary, tope, cromlech, dolmen, menhir, barrow, tumulus, cairn;

* Bentham, 'Chrestomathia.'

ossuary; bone-, charnel-, dead-house; *morgue*; lich-gate; crematorium.
sexton, grave-digger.
monument, memorial, cenotaph, shrine; grave-, head-, tomb-stone; *memento mori*; hatchment, stone, cross.
exhumation, disinterment; necropsy, autopsy, *post-mortem* examination.
V. inter, bury; lay in –, consign to- the -grave, – tomb; en-, in-tomb; inhume; lay out, prepare for burial, embalm, mummify; conduct a funeral, hold services; toll the knell; put to bed with a shovel.
exhume, disinter, unearth.
Adj. buried &c. *v.*; burial; fune-real, -brial; mortuary, sepulchral, cinerary; elegiac; necroscopic.
Adv. *in memoriam*; *post-obit*, *-mortem*; beneath –, under- the sod.
Phr. *hic jacet*, *ci-gît*, *requiescat in pace*.

2. *Special Vitality*

364. Animality.—**N.** animal life; anima-tion, -lity, -lization; breath.
flesh, – and blood; corporeal nature; *physique*; strength &c. 159.
V. animalize, incorporate.
Adj. fleshly, incarnate, carnal, corporeal, human.

365. Vegetability.—**N.** vegetable life; vegeta-tion, -bility; herbage.
V. vegetate, germinate, sprout, shoot; cultivate.
Adj. vegetable &c. 367; rank, lush.

---

366. Animal.*—**N.** animal, – kingdom; *fauna*; brute creation.
beast, brute, creature, created being; creeping –, living- thing; dumb -animal, – creature.
flocks and herds, live stock; domestic –, wild- animals; game, *feræ naturæ*; beasts of the field, fowls of the air, denizens of the day.
vertebrate, bi-, quadru-ped, mammal, marsupial, bird, reptile, batrachian, amphibian, fish, crustacean, shell fish, articulate, mollusc, worm, insect, zoophyte; protozoon, animalcule &c. 193.
horse &c. (*beast of burden*) 271; cattle, kine, ox; bull, -ock; steer, stot; cow, milch cow, calf, heifer, shorthorn; sheep; lamb, -kin; ewe –, pet- lamb; ewe, ram, tup; pig, swine, boar, hog, shoat, sow; tag, teg, wether.
dog, bitch, hound; pup, -py; whelp, cur, mutt, mongrel; house-, watch-, sheep-, shepherd's-, sporting-, fancy-, lap-, toy-, bull-, badger-dog; mastiff; blood-, grey-, stag-, deer-, fox-, otter-hound; harrier, beagle, spaniel, pointer,

367. Vegetable.*— **N.** vegetable – kingdom; *flora*, verdure.
plant; tree, shrub, bush; creeper; vine; herb, -age; grass.
annual; per-, bi-, tri-ennial; exotic.
timber; primeval –, virgin- forest; wood, -lands; hurst, frith, holt, weald, park, chase, greenwood, brake, grove, copse, coppice, *bocage*, *tope*, clump of trees, thicket, spinet, spinney; under-, brush-wood; boscage, scrub; the oak and the ash and the bonny ivy tree.
bush, jungle, prairie; heath, -er; fern, bracken; furze, gorse, whin broom; grass, turf, grassland, greensward, green, lawn, meadow; pas-ture, -turage; turbary; sedge, rush, weed; fungus, mushroom, toadstool; lichen, moss, conferva, mould; seaweed &c.; growth, crop.
foliage, leafage, branch, bough, ramage; spray &c. 51; leaf, frond, flag, petal, shoot, tendril.
flower, blossom, bud, bloom, bine; flowering plant; tree, sapling, pollard; timber-, fruit-tree; palm-, gum-tree; pulse, legume.

* Extended lists of names of specific varieties of animals, vegetables, &c., are beyond the scope of this work; see Introduction, p. xxv.

setter, retriever; Newfoundland; water -dog, – spaniel; pug, poodle; dachshund; Pinscher; turnspit; terrier; fox –, Skye-terrier; Dandie Dinmont; collie.

cat; puss, -y; kitten; grimalkin; gib-, tom-cat; mouser; fox, Reynard, vixen, stag, deer, hart, buck, doe, roe, antelope.

bird; poultry, fowl, cock, hen, chicken, chanticleer, partlet, rooster, dunghill cock, barn-door fowl; feathered -tribes, – songster; singing –, dicky- bird; canary; finch; auk, dodo, moa, roc, phœnix.

snake, serpent, viper, adder; newt, eft; asp, vermin.

Adj. animal, zoological.

equine, bovine, vaccine, canine, feline; fishy; piscator-y, -ial; molluscous, porcine, vermicular.

Adj. veget-able, -ous; herb-aceous, -al; botanic; sylvan, silvan; arbor- ary, -eous, -escent, -ical; dendritic, dendriform; woody, grassy; ver-dant, -durous; floral, mossy; lign-ous, -eous; wooden, leguminous; end-, ex-ogenous.

---

368. [The science of animals.] **Zoology.**—**N.** zoo-logy, -nomy, -graphy, -tomy; anatomy; comparative anatomy; animal –, comparative- physiology; morphology.

anthrop-, ornith-, ichthy-, herpet-, ophi-, malac-, helminth-, entom-, oryct-, paleont-ology; ichthy- &c. -otomy; taxidermy.

zo- &c. -ologist.

Adj. zoological &c. *n.*

369. [The science of plants.] **Botany.**—**N.** botany; phyto-graphy, -logy, -tomy; vegetable physiology, herborization, dendr-, myc-, fung-, alg-ology; flora, pomona; botanist &c.; botanic garden &c. (*garden*) 371; *hortus siccus, herbarium*, herbal.

herb-ist, -arist, -alist, -orist, -arian &c.

V. botanize, herborize.

Adj. botanical &c. *n.*

370. [The economy or management of animals.] **Cicuration.**—**N.** taming &c. *v.*; cicuration, zoohygiantics; domestication, -ity; *manège*; veterinary art; breeding, pisciculture, apiculture &c.

menagery, vivarium, zoological garden, zoo; bear-pit; aviary, apiary, hive; aquarium, fishery, fish hatchery; duck-, fish-pond; stud-farm; stock farm, dairy.

[Destruction of animals] phthisozoics* &c. (*killing*) 361.

neat-, cow-, shep-herd, shepherdess; grazier, drover, cowboy, cowkeeper; trainer, breeder, groom, ostler &c. 746; veterinary surgeon, vet, horse doctor; farrier; keeper; gamekeeper.

cage &c. (*prison*) 752; hen-coop, bird-cage, cauf; sheep-fold &c. (*inclosure*) 232.

V. tame, domesticate, acclimatize, breed, tend, break in, train, corral, round up; cage, bridle &c. (*restrain*) 751; ride &c. 266.

drive, yoke, harness, hitch; groom,

371. [The economy or management of plants.] **Agriculture.**—**N.** agriculture, cultivation, husbandry, farming; georgics, geoponics; tillage, tilth, agronomy, gardening, spade husbandry, vintage; hort-, arbor-, silv-, citr-, vit-, flor-iculture; intensive culture; landscape gardening; forestry, afforestation.

husbandman, horticulturist, citriculturist, gardener, florist; agricult-or, -urist; yeoman, farmer, cultivator, tiller of the soil, ploughman, sower, reaper; woodcutter, backwoodsman, forester; vine grower, vintager; Boer; Triptolemus.

field, meadow, garden; botanic –, winter –, ornamental –, flower –, kitchen –, truck –, market –, hop- garden; nursery; green-, hot-, glass-house; conservatory, cucumber frame, *cloche*, bed, border, seed-plot; grass-plat, lawn; park &c. (*pleasure ground*) 840; *parterre*, shrubbery, plantation, avenue,

* Bentham.

curry-comb; milk; shear; hatch; incubate.

Adj. pastoral, bucolic; tame, domestic, domesticated, broken in, gentle, docile.

---

arboretum, pinery, *pinetum*, orchard; vineyard, vinery; orangery; farm &c. (*abode*) 189.

V. cultivate; till, – the soil; farm, garden; sow, plant; reap, mow, cut; manure, dress the ground, dig, delve, dibble, hoe, plough, plow, harrow, rake, weed, lop and top, force, transplant, thin out, bed out, prune, graft.

Adj. agr-icultural, -arian, -estic.

arable; predial, rural, rustic, country, bucolic, Bœotian; horticultural.

372. Mankind.—N. man, -kind; human -race, – species, – nature; humanity, mortality, flesh, generation.

[Science of man] anthropo-logy, -graphy, -sophy; ethno-logy, -graphy; humanitarianism.

human being; person, -age; individual, creature, fellow creature, mortal, body, somebody, one; such a –, some- one; soul, living soul; earthling; party, head, hand; *dramatis personæ*.

people, persons, folk, public, society, world; community, – at large; general public; nation, -ality; state, realm; common-weal, -wealth; republic, body politic; million &c. (*commonalty*) 876; population &c. (*inhabitant*) 188.

cosmopolite; lords of the creation; ourselves.

Adj. human, mortal, personal, individual, national, civic, public, cosmopolitan; anthropoid.

373. Man.—N. man, male, he; manhood &c. (*adolescence*) 131; gentleman, sir, master; yeoman, wight, swain, fellow, guy, blade, *beau*, chap, gaffer, goodman; husband &c. (*married man*) 903; Mr., mister, *monsieur*, *sahib*, *Herr*, *señor*, *signor*; boy &c. (*youth*) 129; Adonis.

[Male animal] cock, drake, gander, dog, boar, stag, hart, buck, horse, entire horse, stallion; gib-, tom-cat; he-, Billy-goat; ram, tup; bull, -ock; capon, ox, gelding; steer, stot.

Adj. male, he, masculine; manly, virile; un-womanly, -feminine.

---

374. Woman.—N. woman, she, female, petticoat, skirt, moll, broad.

feminality, feminity, muliebrity; womanhood &c. (*adolescence*) 131; feminism; gynecology, gyniatrics, gynics.

womankind; the -sex, – fair; fair –, softer- sex; weaker vessel; the distaff side.

dame, madam, *madame*, mistress, Mrs., lady, *mem-sahib*, *Frau*, *señora*, *signora*, *donna*, *belle*, matron, dowager, goody, gammer; good -woman, – wife; squaw; wife &c. (*marriage*) 903; matron-age, -hood.

Venus, nymph, wench, *grisette*; little bit of fluff; girl &c. (*youth*) 129.

inamorata (love) &c. 897; courtesan &c. 962.

spinster, old maid, virgin, bachelor girl, new woman, Amazon.

[Female animal] hen, slut, bitch, sow, doe, roe, mare; she-, Nanny-goat; ewe, cow; lioness, tigress; vixen.

gynecæum, harem, *seraglio*, *zenana*, *purdah*.

Adj. female, she; feminine, womanly, ladylike, matronly, maidenly; womanish, effeminate, unmanly, gynecic.

2°. Sensation

(1.) *Sensation in general*

375. Physical Sensibility.—N. sensibility; sensitiveness &c. *adj.*; physical sensibility, feeling, perceptivity, anaphylaxis, susceptibility, æsthetics; moral sensibility &c. 822.

sensation, impression, effect; consciousness &c. (*knowledge*) 490.

external senses.

V. be -sensible &c. *adj.* -of; feel, perceive.

render, -sensible &c. *adj.*; excite, stir, sharpen, cultivate, tutor.

cause sensation, impress; excite –, produce- an impression.

Adj. sens-ible, -itive, -uous; æsthetic, perceptive, sentient; conscious &c. (*aware*) 490; impressionable, responsive, alive to.

acute, sharp, keen, vivid, lively, impressive, thin-skinned.

Adv. to the quick.

376. Physical Insensibility.—N. insensibility, physical insensibility; obtuseness &c. *adj.*; palsy, paralysis, *anæsthesia*, *analgesia*, *narcosis*, *hypnosis*, twilight sleep, stupor, coma, trance, catalepsy; sleep &c. (*inactivity*) 683; moral insensibility &c. 823; numbness &c. 381.

anæsthetic agent, general –, local- anæsthetic, opium, ether, chloroform, cocaine, novocaine, chloral; nitrous oxide, laughing gas; refrigeration.

V. be -insensible &c. *adj.*; have a -thick skin, – rhinoceros hide.

render -insensible &c. *adj.*; blunt, pall, obtund, benumb, deaden, paralyze; anæsthetize, drug, dope; put under the influence of -chloroform &c. *n.*; hypnotize; stupefy, stun, narcotize.

Adj. insensible, unfeeling, senseless, comatose, dazed, impercipient, callous, thick-skinned, pachydermatous; hard, -ened; case-hardened; proof; obtuse, dull; anæsthetic; paralytic, palsied, numb, dead.

377. Physical Pleasure.—N. pleasure; physical –, sensual –, sensuous- pleasure; bodily enjoyment, animal gratification, sensuality; hedonism, luxuriousness &c. *adj.*; dissipation, round of pleasure; titillation, *gusto*, creature comforts, comfort, ease; pillow &c. (*support*) 215; luxury, lap of luxury; purple and fine linen; bed of -down, – roses; velvet, clover; cup of Circe &c. (*intemperance*) 954.

treat; diversion, divertisement, entertainment; refreshment, regale; feast; *délice*; dainty &c. 394; *bonne bouche*.

source of pleasure &c. 829; happiness &c. (*mental enjoyment*) 827.

V. feel –, experience –, receive- pleasure; enjoy, relish; luxuriate –, revel –, riot –, bask –, swim –, wallow- in; feast on; gloat -over, – on; smack the lips.

live -on the fat of the land, – in comfort &c. *adv.*; bask in the sunshine, *faire ses choux gras*.

give pleasure &c. 829.

378. Physical Pain.—N. pain; suffering, -ance; bodily – physical- -pain, – suffering; mental suffering &c. 828; dolour, ache; aching &c. *v.*; smart; shoot, -ing; twinge, twitch, gripe, head-, ear-, tooth-ache; *migraine*, neuralgia, neuritis, lumbago, gout, sciatica; hurt, cut; sore, -ness; discomfort, *malaise*; *tic douloureux*.

spasm, cramp; nightmare, *ephialtes*; crick, stitch, kink; thrill, convulsion, throe; throb &c. (*agitation*) 315; pang.

sharp –, piercing –, throbbing –, shooting –, gnawing –, burning- pain; anguish, agony.

torment, torture; rack; cruci-ation, -fixion; martyrdom; martyr, toad under a harrow, vivisection.

V. feel –, experience –, suffer –, undergo- pain &c. *n.*; suffer, ache, smart, bleed; tingle, shoot; twinge, twitch, lancinate; writhe, wince, make a wry face; sit on -thorns, – pins and needles.

give –, inflict- pain; pain, hurt, chafe, sting, bite, gnaw, gripe, stab, grind;

Adj. enjoying &c. *v.*; luxurious, voluptuous, sensual, hedonistic, comfortable, cosy, snug, in comfort, at ease.

agreeable &c. 829; grateful, refreshing, comforting, cordial, genial; sensuous; palatable &c. 394; sweet &c. (*sugar*) 396; fragrant &c. 400; melodious &c. 413; lovely &c. (*beautiful*) 845.

Adv. in -comfort &c. *n.*; on -a bed of roses &c. *n.*; at one's ease.

pinch, tweak; grate, gall, fret, prick, pierce, wring, convulse; torment, torture; rack, agonize; crucify; ex-, cruciate; break on the wheel, put to the rack; flog &c. (*punish*) 972; grate on the ear &c. (*harsh sound*) 410.

Adj. in -pain &c. *n.*, – a state of pain; pained &c. *v.*

painful; aching &c. *v.*; biting, poignant; sore, raw, tender, with exposed nerve.

(2.) *Special Sensation*

1. *Touch*

379. [Sensation of pressure.] **Touch.—N.** touch; tact, -ion, -ility; feeling; palp-ation, -ability; manipulation; brush, tick, graze, contact &c. 199.

[Organ of touch] hand, finger, fore-finger, thumb, paw, feeler, *antenna*.

V. touch, feel, handle, finger, thumb, paw, fumble, grope, grabble; twiddle, tweedle; pass –, run- the fingers over, massage, rub, knead; palpate, stroke, manipulate, wield; throw out a feeler.

Adj. tact-ual, -ile; tangible, palpable; lambent.

380. Sensations of Touch.—N. itching &c. *v.*; titillation, formication, *aura*.

V. itch, tingle, creep, thrill, sting; prick, -le; tickle, titillate.

Adj. itching &c. *v.*

381. [Insensibility to touch.] **Numbness.—N.** numbness &c. (*physical insensibility*) 376; pins and needles.

local anæsthetic, cocaine, novocaine &c.; morphia.

V. benumb &c. 376; freeze, dull, deaden.

Adj. numb; benumbed &c. *v.*; intangible, impalpable.

2. *Heat*

382. Heat.—N. heat, caloric; temperature, warmth, fervour, calidity; incal-, incand-, recal-, decal-escence; glow, flush, blush; fever, hectic.

phlogiston; fire, spark, scintillation, flash, flame, blaze; arc; bonfire; firework, pyrotechny; wild-fire; sheet of fire, lambent flame; devouring element; conflagration.

summer, dog-days, canicule; baking &c. 384 –, white –, tropical –, Afric –, Bengal –, summer –, blood- heat; heat wave, sirocco, simoon; broiling sun; isolation; warming &c. 384.

sun &c. (*luminary*) 423; fire worshipper &c. 991; furnace &c. 386.

geyser, hot spring, volcano.

[Science of heat] pyrology; therm-

383. Cold.—N. cold, -ness &c. *adj.*; frigidity, gelidity, algidity, inclemency, *fresco*.

winter; depth of –, hard- winter; Siberia, Nova Zembla; Ant-, arctic, North –, South- Pole.

ice; snow, – flake, – crystal, – drift; sleet; hail, -stone; rime, frost; hoar –, white –, hard –, sharp- frost; icicle, thick-ribbed ice; fall of snow, snow storm, heavy fall, *avalanche*; ice-berg, -floe; floe, berg; *glacier*; *névé*, *serac*.

[Sensation of cold] chilliness &c. *adj.*; chill; shivering &c. *v.*; goose-skin, -flesh; *rigor*, horripilation, chattering of teeth; frostbite, chilblain.

V. be -cold &c. *adj.*; shiver, starve, quake, shake, tremble, shudder, didder,

ology, -otics; thermometer &c. 389.

V. be -hot &c. *adj.*; glow, incandesce, flush, sweat, swelter, bask, smoke, reek, stew, simmer, seethe, boil, burn, singe, scorch, scald, grill, broil, blaze, flame; smoulder; parch, fume, pant.

heat &c. (*make hot*) 384; thaw, fuse, melt, give.

Adj. hot, heated, warm, mild, genial, tepid, lukewarm, unfrozen; therm-al, -ic; calorific; ferv-ent, -id; ardent; aglow.

sunny, torrid, tropical, estival, canicular; close, sultry, stifling, stuffy, suffocating, oppressive; reeking &c. *v.*; baking &c. 384.

red –, white –, smoking –, burning &c. *v.* –, piping- hot; like -a furnace, – an oven; hot as -fire, – pepper; hot enough to roast an ox.

fiery; incand-, incal-escent; candent, ebullient, glowing, smoking; on fire; blazing &c. *v.*; in -flames, – a blaze; alight, afire, ablaze; un-quenched, -extinguished; smouldering; in a -heat, – glow, – fever, – perspiration, – sweat; sudorific; swelter-ing, -ed; blood-hot, -warm; warm as -a toast, – wool; recalescent, thermogenic, pyrotechnic, feverish, febrile, inflamed.

volcanic, plutonic, igneous; isother-mal, -mic, -al.

Phr. Not a breath of air.

383. ... quiver; perish with cold; chill &c. (*render cold*) 385.

Adj. cold, cool; chill, -y; gelid, frigid, algid; fresh, keen, bleak, raw, inclement, bitter, biting, niveous, cutting, nipping, piercing, pinching; clay-cold; starved &c. (*made cold*) 385; shivering &c. *v.*; aguish, *transi de froid*; frost-bitten, -bound, -nipped.

cold as -a stone, – marble, – lead, – iron, – a frog, – charity, – Christmas; cool as -a cucumber, – custard.

icy, glacial, frosty, freezing, wintry, brumal, hibernal, boreal, arctic, antarctic, polar, Siberian, hyemal; hyperbore-an, -al; ice-bound; frozen out.

un-warmed, -thawed, -heated; isocheimal, -chimenal.

Adv. coldly, bitterly &c. *adj.*; *à pierre fendre*.

---

384. Calefaction.—N. increase of temperature; heating &c. *v.*; cale-, tepe-, torre-faction; melting, fusion; liquefaction &c. 335; burning &c. *v.*; kindling, combustion; in-, ac-cension; con-, cremation; scorification; cauter-y, -ization; ustulation, calcination; in-, cineration; cupellation; carbonization.

ignition, inflammation, adustion, flagration; de-, con-flagration; empyrosis, incendiarism; arson; *auto-da-fé*; suttee.

boiling &c. *v.*; coction, ebullition, estuation, elixation, decoction.

furnace &c. 386; blanket, flannel, fur, muffler, wrap; wadding &c. (*lining*) 224; clothing &c. 225.

match &c. (*fuel*) 388; incendiary, pyromaniac; *pétroleur, pétroleuse*; cauterant, caustic, lunar caustic, apozem, moxa.

sunstroke, *coup de soleil*; insolation, sunburn.

pottery, ceramics, crockery, porcelain, china; earthen-, stone-ware; pot,

385. Refrigeration.—N. refrigeration, infrigidation, reduction of temperature; cooling &c. *v.*; con-gelation, -glaciation; ice &c. 383; solidification &c. (*density*) 321; refrigerator &c. 387.

V. cool, fan, refrigerate, refresh, ice; congeal, freeze, glaciate; benumb, starve, pinch, chill, petrify, chill to the marrow, nip, cut, pierce, bite, make one's teeth chatter; damp.

Adj. cooled &c. *v.*; frozen out; cooling &c. *v.*; frigorific.

Extinction.—N. *extincteur*; fire, – engine, – extinguisher, – annihilator, – brigade, – man; sprinkler, hose, hydrant, standpipe.

incombusti-bility, -bleness &c. *adj.*

V. Quench, damp; blow-, put –, stamp – out; extinquish.

go –, burn-out.

Adj. incombustible; un-, unin-flammable; fire-proof.

---

mug, *terra-cotta*, brick, clinker; cinder, ash, *scoriæ*; embers, dross, slag, products of combustion, coke, carbon, charcoal.

inflamma-, combusti-bility.

[Transmission of heat] diathermancy, transcalency.

V. heat, warm, chafe, stive, foment; make -hot &c. 382; sun oneself, bask in the sun.

fire; set -fire to, – on fire; kindle, enkindle, light, ignite, strike a light; apply the -match, – torch- to; re-kindle, -lume; fan –, add fuel to- the flame; poke –, stir –, blow- the fire; make a bonfire of; burn at the stake.

melt, thaw, fuse; liquefy &c. 335.

burn, inflame, roast, toast, fry, grill, singe, parch, bake, torrefy, scorch; brand, cauterize, sear, burn in; corrode, char, carbonize, calcine, incinerate; smelt, cupel, scorify; reduce to ashes; burn to a cinder; commit –, consign- to the flames.

boil, digest, stew, cook, seethe, scald, parboil, simmer; do to rags.

take –, catch- fire; blaze &c. (*flame*) 382.

Adj. heated &c. *v.*; molten, sodden; *réchauffé*; heating &c. *v.*

inflammable, burnable, inflammatory, combustible; diatherm-al -anous; burnt &c. *v.*; volcanic.

386. Furnace.—**N.** furnace, blast furnace, fire-box, stove, incinerator, destructor, crematorium, crematory, kiln, oven, oast-house; hot-, bake-, wash-house; laundry; conservatory; hearth, focus; athanor, hypocaust, reverberatory; volcano; forge, fiery furnace; *tuyère*, brasier, salamander, heater, warming-pan, foot-warmer, hot-water bottle; radiator; boiler, geyser, caldron, seething caldron, pot; urn, kettle; chafing-dish; retort, crucible, alembic, still; saggar.

fire-place, -dog, -irons; hearth, ingle, grate, range, kitchener; kitchen range; oil-, gas-, electric, -cooker, -stove; fireless cooker; fire; galley; ca-, cam-boose; poker, tongs, shovel, hob, trivet; and-, grid-iron; frying-, stew-pan &c.

hot –, Turkish –, Russian –, vapour –, shower –, warm- bath; *calidarium*, *tepidarium*, *sudatorium*, sudatory; *hammam*.

387. Refrigerator.—**N.** refrigerator, -y; *frigidarium*; cold storage; refrigerating-plant, – machine; ice-house, -pail, -bag, -chest, -pack; cooler, damper; wine-cooler, freezing mixture.

See 385.

388. Fuel.—**N.** fuel, firing, combustible, coal, wallsend, anthracite, bituminous coal, slack, culm, cannel coal, lignite, briquette, coke, carbon, charcoal; turf, peat, fire-wood, bobbing, faggot, log, Yule log, ember, cinder &c. (*products of combustion*) 384; kindling wood, tinder, touch-wood; fumigator, sulphur, brimstone; incense; port-fire; fire-barrel, -ball, -brand.

fuel oil, gas, gasoline.

brand, torch, fuse; wick; spill, match, safety match, light, lucifer, congreve, vesuvian, vesta, fusee, locofoco; linstock; illuminant.

candle &c. (*luminary*) 423; oil &c. (*grease*), 356; petrol, gasoline, methylated –, spirit; gas, acetylene.

Adj. carbonaceous; combustible, inflammable.

V. stoke, fire, feed, add fuel to the flames.

389. Thermometer.—**N.** thermo-meter, -scope, -stat, -pile, differential thermometer; pyro-, calori-meter; radio micrometer &c.

3. *Taste*

390. Taste.—N. taste, flavour, gust, *gusto*, relish, savour; sapor, sapidity; twang, smack, smatch; after-taste, tang.

tasting; de-, gustation.

palate, tongue, tooth, stomach.

V. taste, savour, smatch, smack, flavour, twang; tickle the palate &c. (*savoury*) 394; smack the lips.

Adj. sapid, saporific; gusta-ble, -tory; strong; flavoured, spiced, savoury; palatable &c. 394.

391. Insipidity.—N. insipidity; tastelessness &c. *adj.*

V. be -tasteless &c. *adj.*

Adj. void of -taste &c. 390; insipid; jejune; taste-, gust-, savour-less; ingustible, mawkish, milk and water, weak, stale, flat, vapid, *fade*, wishy-washy, mild; untasted.

---

392. Pungency.—N. pungency, piquancy, poignancy, *haut-goût*, strong taste, twang, race, tang.

sharpness &c. *adj.*; acrimony, acridity; roughness &c. (*sour*) 397; unsavouriness &c. 395.

nitre, saltpetre; mustard, cayenne, caviare; seasoning &c. (*condiment*) 393; brine.

dram, cordial, nip, pick-me-up, bracer, potion.

nicotine, tobacco, snuff, quid; segar; cigar, -ette, gasper, fag; cheroot; weed; fragrant –, Indian- weed; pipe, clay pipe, churchwarden, brier, meerschaum, hookah, hubble-bubble.

V. be -pungent &c. *adj.*; bite the tongue.

render -pungent &c. *adj.*; season, spice, salt, pepper, pickle, brine, devil, curry.

smoke, chew, take snuff.

Adj. pungent, strong; high-, full-flavoured; high-tasted, -seasoned; gamy; sharp, stinging, rough, *piquant*, racy; biting, mordant; spicy; seasoned &c. *v.*; hot, – as pepper; peppery, vellicating, escharotic, meracious; acrid, acrimonious, bitter; rough &c. (*sour*) 397; unsavoury &c. 395.

salt, saline, brackish, briny; salt as -brine, – a herring, – Lot's wife.

393. Condiment.—N. condiment, flavouring, salt, mustard, pepper, cayenne, curry, seasoning, sauce, spice, cinnamon, chillies, relish, *sauce piquante*, caviare, pot-herbs, onion, garlic, pickle, chutney, nutmeg &c.

V. season &c. (*render pungent*) 392.

394. Savouriness.—N. savouriness &c. *adj.*; relish, zest.

tit-bit, dainty, delicacy, ambrosia, nectar, *bonne bouche*; game, turtle, venison.

V. taste good, be -savoury &c. *adj.*; tickle the -palate, – appetite; flatter the palate.

render -palatable &c. *adj.*

relish, like, smack the lips.

Adj. savoury, well-tasted, to one's taste, tasty, good, palatable, nice, dainty, delectable; tooth-ful, -some;

395. Unsavouriness.—N. unsavouriness &c. *adj.*; amaritude; acri-mony, -tude; roughness &c. (*sour*) 397; acerbity, austerity; gall and worm-wood, rue, quassia, aloes; sickener.

V. be -unpalatable &c. *adj.*; sicken, disgust, nauseate, pall, turn the stomach.

Adj. un-savoury, -palatable, -sweet; ill-flavoured, un-appetizing, -eatable, inedible; bitter, – as gall; acrid, acrimonious; rough.

offensive, repulsive, nasty; sickening

gustful, appetizing, lickerish, delicate, delicious, exquisite, rich, luscious, ambrosial.

Adv. *per amusare la bocca.*

Phr. *cela se laisse manger.*

&c. *v.*; nauseous; loath-, ful-some; unpleasant &c. 830.

---

396. Sweetness.—**N.** sweetness, dulcitude, saccharinity.

sugar, cane-, beet-sugar; saccharine, glucose, syrup, treacle, molasses, honey, manna; confection, -ery; sweets, grocery, conserve, preserve, *confiture*, jam, marmalade, julep; sugar-candy, -plum; licorice, liquorice, plum, lollipop, *bonbon, jujube*, comfit, sweetmeat, caramel, toffee, butterscotch.

nectar; hydromel, mead, metheglin, honeysuckle, *liqueur*, sweet wine.

pastry, pie, tart, puff, pudding, cake.

dulc-ification, -oration.

V. be -sweet &c. *adj.*

render -sweet &c. *adj.*; sugar, saccharize, sweeten; edulcorate; dulc-orate, -ify; candy; mull.

Adj. sweet, sugary; sacchar-ine, -iferous; dulcet, honied, candied, luscious, nectarious, melliferous; sweetened &c. *v.*

sweet as -a nut, – sugar, – honey.

397. Sourness.—**N.** sourness &c. *adj.*; acid, -ity; acetous fermentation; acerbity.

vinegar, verjuice, crab, alum.

V. be –, turn- -sour &c. *adj.*; set the teeth on edge.

render -sour &c. *adj.*; acid-ify, -ulate.

Adj. sour; acid, -ulous, -ulated; acerb; tart, crabbed; acet-ous, -ose; sour as vinegar, sourish, acescent, sub-acid; styptic, hard, rough; unripe, green.

---

4. *Odour*

398. Odour.—**N.** odour, smell, odorament, scent, effluvium; eman-, exhal-ation; fume, essence, trail, nidor, redolence.

sense of smell; scent; act of -smelling &c. *v.*

V. have an -odour &c. *n.*; smell, – of, – strong of; exhale; give out a -smell &c. *n.*; scent.

smell, scent; snuff, – up; sniff, nose, inhale.

Adj. odor-ous, -iferous; smelling, strong-scented; redolent, graveolent, nidorous, pungent.

[Relating to the sense of smell] olfactory, quick-scented.

399. Inodorousness.—**N.** inodorousness; absence –, want- of smell.

V. be -inodorous &c. *adj.*; not smell.

deodorize.

Adj. inodor-ous, -ate; scentless; without –, wanting- smell &c. 398.

deodoriz-ed, -ing.

---

400. Fragrance. — **N.** fragrance, aroma, redolence, perfume, *bouquet*; sweet smell, aromatic perfume.

perfumery; incense; musk, frankincense; pastil, -le; myrrh, perfumes of Arabia, chypre; otto, ottar, attar; bergamot, balm, civet, *pot-pourri*, pulvil; nosegay, *boutonnière*; scent, -bag; *sachet*, scent-bottle, smelling bottle, *vinaigrette*; toilet water, *eau de Cologne*; thurible, censer, thurification.

perfumer; incense bearer.

401. Fetor.—**N.** fetor, fetidness; bad &c. *adj.*; -smell, – odour; stench, stink; mephitis, foul –, mal- odour; *empyreuma*; mustiness &c. *adj.*; rancidity; foulness &c. (*uncleanness*) 653.

stoat, polecat, skunk; assafœtida; fungus, garlic; stink-pot, -bomb.

V. have a -bad smell &c. *n.*; smell; stink, – in the nostrils, – like a polecat; smell -strong &c. *adj.*, – offensively.

Adj. fetid; strong-smelling; high, bad, strong, fulsome, offensive, noisome, rank, rancid, reasty, tainted, musty,

V. be -fragrant &c. *adj.*; have a -perfume &c. *n.*; smell sweet, scent, perfume, thurify, embalm.

Adj. fragrant, aromatic, redolent, spicy, balmy, scented; sweet-smelling, -scented; perfum-ed, -atory; thuriferous; fragrant as a rose, muscadine, ambrosial.

fusty, frouzy; olid, -ous; nidorous; smelling, stinking; putrid &c. 653; suffocating, mephitic; empyreumatic.

---

5. *Sound*

(i.) Sound in General

402. Sound.—N. sound, noise, strain; accent, twang, intonation, tone, tune; cadence; sonority, sonorousness &c. *adj.*; audibility; resonance &c. 408; voice &c. 580.

[Science of sound] acou-, acu-stics; catacoustics, cataphonics; phon-ics, -etics, -ology, -ography; dia-coustics, -phonics.

telephone, phonograph &c. 418.

V. produce sound; sound, make a noise; give out –, emit- sound; phonetize, phonate; resound &c. 408.

Adj. sounding; soniferous; sonorific; resonant, audible, acoustic, auditory, distinct; stertorous; phonic, sonant; phonetic.

---

403. Silence.—N. silence; stillness &c. (*quiet*) 265; peace, hush, lull, rest; muteness &c. 581; solemn –, awful –, dead –, deathlike- silence.

V. be -silent &c. *adj.*; hold one's tongue &c. (*not speak*) 585.

render -silent &c. *adj.*; silence, still, hush; stifle, muffle, gag, stop; muzzle, put to silence &c. (*render mute*) 581.

Adj. silent; still, -y; calm, quiet; noise-, sound-, speech-less; hushed &c. *v.*; mute &c. 581; aphonic.

soft, solemn, awful, deathlike, silent as the grave; inaudible &c. (*faint*) 405.

Adv. silently &c. *adj.*; *sub silentio*; in perfect silence.

Int. hush! 'sh! silence! soft! whist! tush! chut! tut! *pax!* mum's the word! hold your tongue! shut up! be silent! be quiet! stop that noise! hold your row! dry up! peace, be still!

Phr. one might hear a -feather, – pin- drop.

404. Loudness.—N. loudness, power; loud noise, din; clang, -or; clatter, noise, bombilation, roar, uproar, racket, static, grinders, hubbub, *fracas, charivari,* trumpet blast, blare, flourish of trumpets, fanfare, *tintamarre,* peal, swell, blast, alarum, boom; resonance &c. 408.

vociferation; pandemonium, hullaballoo &c. 411; lungs; Stentor; megaphone; siren.

artillery, cannon, gunfire, shellburst, bomb; thunder.

V. be -loud &c. *adj.*; peal, swell, clang, boom, thunder, fulminate, roar; resound &c. 408; speak up, shout &c. (*vociferate*) 411; bellow &c. (*cry as an animal*) 412; give tongue.

rend the -air, – skies; fill the air; din –, ring –, thunder- in the ear;

405. Faintness.—N. faintness &c. *adj.*; faint sound, whisper, breath; under-tone, -breath; murmur, hum, rustle, buzz, purr; plash; sough, moan, sigh, susurration; tinkle; 'still small voice.'

hoarseness &c. *adj.*; raucity.

silencer, soft pedal, damper, mute, *sourdine.*

V. whisper, breathe, murmur, purl, hum, gurgle, ripple, babble, flow; tinkle; mutter &c. (*speak imperfectly*) 583.

steal on the ear; melt in –, float on- the air.

muffle, mute, deaden, damp, stifle.

Adj. inaudible; scarcely –, just- audible; low, dull; stifled, muffled; hoarse, husky; gentle, soft, faint; floating; purling, flowing &c. *v.*;

pierce –, split –, rend- the -ears, – head; deafen, stun; *faire le diable à quatre*; make one's windows shake; awaken –, startle- the echoes; make the welkin ring.

Adj. loud, sonorous; high-, big-sounding; blatant; deep, full, powerful, noisy, clangorous, multisonous, *fortissimo*; thundering, deafening &c. *v.*; trumpet-tongued; ear-splitting, -rending, -deafening; piercing; obstreperous, rackety, uproarious; enough to wake the -dead, – seven sleepers.

shrill &c. 410; clamorous &c. (*vociferous*) 411; stentor-ian, -ophonic.

Adv. loudly &c. *adj.*; aloud; at the top of one's voice, lustily, in full cry.

Phr. the air rings with.

whispered &c. *v.*; liquid; soothing; dulcet &c. (*melodious*) 413.

Adv. in a whisper, with bated breath, *sotto voce*, between the teeth, aside; *pian-o, -issimo*; *à la sourdine*; *con sordine*; out of earshot, inaudibly &c. *adj.*

(ii.) Specific Sounds*

406. [Sudden and violent sounds.] **Snap.**—**N.** snap &c. *v.*; rapping &c. *v.*; de-, crepitation; smack, clap, report; thud; burst, explosion, discharge, detonation, blow-out, back-fire, firing, salvo, volley, pistol-shot.

squib, cracker, gun, rifle, pop-gun.

V. rap, snap, tap, knock; click; clash; crack, -le; crash; pop; slam, bang, clap, thump, plump; toot; back-fire, explode, burst on the ear.

Adj. rapping &c. *v.*

Int. crash! bang!

407. [Repeated and protracted sounds.] **Roll.**—**N.** roll &c. *v.*; drumming &c. *v.*; tattoo; ding-dong; tantara; rataplan; whirr; rat-a-tat; rub-a-dub; pit-a-pat; quaver, clutter, *charivari*, racket; cuckoo; repetition &c. 104; peal of bells, devil's tattoo; reverberation &c. 408.

drumfire, barrage.

machine gun.

V. roll, drum, rumble, rattle, clatter, rustle, roar, drone, patter, clack.

hum, trill, shake; chime, peal, toll; tick, beat.

drum –, din- in the ear.

Adj. rolling &c. *v.*; monotonous &c. (*repeated*), 104; like a bee in a bottle.

408. Resonance.—**N.** resonance; ring &c. *v.*; ringing &c. *v.*; tintinnabulation; reflection, reverberation, clangor.

low –, base –, bass –, flat –, grave –, deep –, pedal- note; bass; *basso, – profondo*; bari-, bary-tone; *contralto*.

V. re-sound, -verberate, -echo; ring, ding, sing, jingle, gingle, chink, clink; tink, -le; chime; gurgle &c. 405; plash, guggle, echo, ring in the ear.

Adj. resounding &c. *v.*; resonant, tinnient, tintinnabulary; deep-toned, -sounding, -mouthed; hollow, sepulchral; gruff &c. (*harsh*) 410.

408a. Non-resonance. — **N.** thud, thump, dead sound; non-resonance; muffled drums, cracked bell; silencer, damper; mute, *sourdine*.

V. sound dead; stop –, damp- the -sound, – reverberations; deaden, muffle.

Adj. non-resonant, dead, muted. muffled.

409. [Hissing sounds.] **Sibilation.**—**N.** sibilation; hiss &c. *v.*; sternutation; high note &c. 410.

goose, serpent, snake.

* [The author's classification of sounds has been retained, though it does not entirely accord with the theories of modern science.—Ed.]

V. hiss, buzz, whiz, rustle; fizz, -le, sizzle, swish; wheeze, whistle, snuffle; squash; sneeze.

Adj. sibilant; hissing &c. *v.*; wheezy.

410. [Harsh sounds.] **Stridor.—N.** creak &c. *v.*; creaking &c. *v.*; discord &c. 414; stridor; harshness, roughness, sharpness &c. *adj.*; cacophony.

acute –, high- note; *soprano*, treble, tenor, *alto*, falsetto, *voce di testa*; shriek, cry &c. 411.

piccolo, fife, penny -whistle, – trumpet.

V. creak, grate, jar, burr, pipe, twang, jangle, clank, clink; scream &c. (*cry*) 411; yelp &c. (*animal sound*) 412; buzz &c. (*hiss*) 409.

set the teeth on edge, *écorcher les oreilles*; pierce –, split- the -ears, – head; offend –, grate upon –, jar upon- the ear.

Adj. creaking &c. *v.*; strident, stridulous, harsh, coarse, hoarse, horrisonous, raucous, metallic, rough, gruff, grum, sepulchral.

sharp, high, acute, shrill, high-pitched; trumpet-toned; piercing, ear-piercing; cracked; discordant &c. 414; cacophonous.

411. Cry.—N. cry &c. *v.*; voice &c. (*human*) 580; bark &c. (*animal*) 412.

vociferation, outcry, hullaballoo, chorus, clamour, hue and cry, plaint; lungs; stentor.

V. cry, roar, shout, bawl, brawl, halloo, halloa, hail, hoop, whoop, yell, bellow, howl, scream, screech, screak, shriek, shrill, squeak, squeal, squall, whine, whinny, pule, pipe, yaup.

cheer, hurrah; hoot; grumble, moan, groan.

snore, snort; grunt &c. (*animal sounds*) 412.

vociferate; raise –, lift up- the voice; call –, sing –, cry- out; exclaim; rend the air; thunder –, shout- at the -top of one's voice, – pitch of one's breath; *s'égosiller*; strain the -throat, – voice, – lungs; give a -cry &c.

Adj. crying &c. *v.*; clam-ant, -orous; vociferous; stentorian &c. (*loud*) 404; open-mouthed.

412. [Animal sounds.] **Ululation.—N.** cry &c. *v.*; crying &c. *v.*; ululation, latration, belling; reboation; call, note; bark, howl, yelp; twittering, woodnote; insect cry, fritinancy, drone; screech; cuckoo.

V. cry, ululate, howl, roar, bellow, blare, rebellow, bark, yelp; bay, – the moon; yap, growl, yarr, yawl, snarl, howl; grunt, -le; snort, squeak; neigh, bray; mew, mewl; purr, caterwaul, pule; bleat, low, moo; troat, croak, crow, screech, caw, coo, gobble, quack, cackle, gaggle, guggle; chuck, -le; cluck; clack; cheep, chirp, chirrup, twitter, sing, cuckoo; pout, wail, hum, buzz; hiss, blatter; hoot.

Adj. crying &c. *v.*; blatant, latrant; re-, mugient; deep-, full-mouthed.

Adv. in full cry.

(iii.) Musical Sounds

413. Melody. Concord.—N. melody, rhythm, measure; rhyme &c. (*poetry*) 597.

pitch, *timbre*, intonation, tone, overtone.

scale, gamut; diapason; diatonic –, chromatic –, enharmonic- scale; key, clef, chords,

modulation, temperament, syncope, syncopation, preparation, suspension, resolution.

414. Discord.—N. discord, -ance; dissonance, cacophony, caterwauling; harshness &c. 410; consecutive fifths.

[Confused sounds] Babel, pandemonium; Dutch –, cat's- concert; marrow-bones and cleavers.

V. be -discordant &c. *adj.*; jar &c. (*sound harshly*) 410.

Adj. discordant; dis-, ab-sonant; out of tune, tuneless; un-musical, -tunable; un-, im-melodious; un-, in-harmonious;

staff, stave, line, space, brace; bar, rest; *appogia-to, -tura*; *acciaccatura*, shake, *arpeggio*.

note, musical note, notes of a scale; sharp, flat, natural; high note &c. (*shrillness*) 410; low note &c. 408; interval; semitone; second, third, fourth &c.; diatessaron.

breve, semibreve, minim, crotchet, quaver; semi-, demisemi-quaver; sustained note, drone, burden.

tonic; key-, leading-, fundamental- note; supertonic, mediant, dominant; sub-mediant, -dominant, organ-, pedal-point; octave, tetrachord; major –, minor- -mode, – scale, – key; Doric mode, passage, phrase.

concord, harmony; unison, -ance; chime, homophony; euphon-y, -ism; tonality; consonance; concent; part.

orchestration, harmonization, – phrasing.

[Science of harmony] harmon-y, -ics; thorough-, fundamental-bass; counterpoint; faburden.

piece of music &c. 415; composer, harmonist, contrapuntist.

V. be -harmonious &c. *adj.*; harmonize, chime, symphonize, transpose; put in tune, tune, accord, string; score, arrange, orchestrate.

Adj. harmoni-ous, -cal; in -concord &c. *n.*, – tune, – concert; unisonant, concentual, symphonizing, isotonic, homophonous, assonant, consonant.

measured, rhythmical, diatonic, chromatic, enharmonic.

melodious, musical; tuneful, tunable; sweet, dulcet, canorous; mell-ow, -ifluous; soft; clear, – as a bell; silvery; euphon-ious, -ic, -ical; symphonious; enchanting &c. (*pleasure-giving*) 829; fine-, full-, silver-toned.

Adv. harmoniously &c. *adj.*

sing-song; cacophonous; jarring, harsh &c. 410.

---

415. Music.—N. music, classical –, modern –, descriptive- music; concert, recital; strain, tune, air, *motif*; melody &c. 413; *aria*, *arietta*; piece of music, *sonata*; *rond-o, -eau*; *pastorale*, *cavatina*, roulade, *fantasia*, *toccata*, *concerto*, overture, symphony, symphonic poem, tone poem, prelude, voluntary, *intermezzo*, variations, *cadenza*; cadence; fugue, canon, serenade, *nocturne*, *notturno*, rhapsody, romance, *aubade*, dithyramb; opera, operetta; oratorio; composition, movement; stave.

instrumental music; full-, orchestral- score; minstrelsy, tweedle-dum and tweedledee, band, orchestra &c. 416; concerted piece, *pot-pourri*, medley, *capriccio*, incidental music; improvisation; peal.

vocal music, vocalism; chaunt, chant; psalm, -ody; hymn; song &c. (*poem*) 597; canticle, canzonet, *cantata*, *bravura*, *coloratura*; lay, ballad, ditty, carol, barcarolle, pastoral, recitative, *recitativo*, *solfeggio*, tonic sol-fa.

Lydian measures; slow -music, – movement; *adagio* &c. *adv.*; minuet; siren strains, soft music, lullaby; *berceuse*, cradle song, dump; dirge &c. (*lament*) 839; pibroch; martial music, march, funeral-, dead- march; dance music; waltz &c. (*dance*) 840; rag-time, syncopation, jazz.

solo, duet, *duo*, *trio*; quartet; quintet, sextet, septet; part song, descant, glee, madrigal, catch, round, chorus, *chorale*; antiphon, -y; accompaniment, second –, alto –, tenor –, bass- part; score, thorough bass; counterpoint.

composer &c. 413; musician &c. 416.

V. compose, perform &c. 416; attune.

Adj. musical; instrumental, orchestral, vocal, choral, lyric, operatic; harmonious &c. 413.

Adv. *adagio*; *largo, larghetto, andan-te, -tino*; *alla capella*; *maestoso, moderato*; *allegr-o, -etto*; *spiritoso, vivace, veloce*; *prest-o, -issimo*; *pian-o, -issimo, fort-e, -issimo, sforzando*; *con brio*; *capriccioso*; *scherz-o, -ando*; *legato, sostenuto, staccato, crescendo, diminuendo, rallentando, affettuoso, arioso*; *parlante, cantabile*; *obbligato*; *pizzicato, tremolo, vibrato.*

416. Musician. [Performance of Music.]—**N.** musician, *artiste, virtuoso,* performer, player, minstrel; bard &c. (*poet*) 597; instrumental-, organ-, accompan-, pian-, violin-, flaut-, harp-ist; harper, fiddler, fifer, trumpeter, piper, drummer; catgut scraper.

band, orchestra, waits.

vocal-, melod-ist; singer, warbler; songst-, chaunt-er, -ress; *diva, cantatrice,* coloratura, soprano, mezzo-soprano, alto, contralto, tenor, baritone, bass, *basso, -profondo.*

choir, quire, chorister; chorus, – singer; choral society, festival, *eisteddfod.*

nightingale, philomel, thrush; siren; Orpheus, Apollo, the Muses, Erato, Euterpe, Terpsichore; tuneful -nine, – quire.

composer &c. 413.

performance, virtuosity, execution, touch, expression, solmization.

V. play, pipe, strike –, tune- up, sweep the chords, tickle –, paw- the ivories, vamp, tweedle, fiddle; strike the lyre, beat the drum; blow –, sound –, wind- the horn; grind the organ; touch the -guitar &c. (*instruments*) 417; thrum, strum, twang, drum, beat –, keep- time, conduct.

execute, perform; accompany; sing –, play- a second; compose, write music, set to music, arrange, harmonize, orchestrate.

sing, chaunt, chant, hum, warble, carol, chirp, chirrup, lilt, purl, quaver, trill, shake, twitter, whistle; sol-fa; intone.

have -an ear for music, – a musical ear, – a correct ear, – absolute pitch.

Adj. playing &c. *v.*; musical, lyric.

Adv. *adagio, andante* &c. (*music*) 415.

417. Musical Instruments.—**N.** musical instruments; band; string-, brass-, drum and fife-, military-, bugle-, German-, dance-, jazz-band; orchestra, string quartet; orchestrion, orchestrelle.

[Stringed instruments] mono-, poly-chord; harp, lyre, lute, archlute, theorbo; mandol-a, -in, -ine; guitar; *ukulele*; psaltery, zither; bandore, cither, -n; gittern, rebeck, *bandurria,* banjo, zither banjo, *balalaika, samisen*; plectrum.

viol, -in, Cremona, Stradivarius; fiddle, kit; *vielle, viola, – d'amore, – di gamba*; tenor, *violoncello,* cello; bass, bass-, base-viol; double-bass, *contrabasso, violone,* hurdy-gurdy; strings, catgut; bow, fiddlestick.

piano, -forte; grand –, concert grand –, baby –, upright –, cottage-piano; pianino, pianette; harpsi-, clavi-, clari-, mani-chord; *clavier,* spinet, virginals; dulcimer, *cymbalo*; Eolian harp; piano-organ, -player, electric piano, player-piano, pianola.

[Wind instruments] organ, church –, pipe –, American- organ; harmoni-um, -phon; accordion, seraphina, concertina; melodeon; barrel-organ; humming top.

flute, fife, piccolo, flageolet, penny-whistle, reed instrument; clari-net, -onet; bass clarionet; saxophone; basset horn, *corno di bassetto*; musette, shawm, oboe, hautboy, *cor Anglais, corno Inglese*, bassoon, double bassoon, *contrafagotto*; bag-, union-pipes; ocarina, Pandean pipes; calliope; sirene, pipe, pitch-pipe; sourdet; whistle, catcall.

horn, bugle, key bugle, cornet, *cornet-à-pistons*, cornopean, clarion, trumpet, trombone, ophicleide, serpent; English-, French-, bugle-, sax-, flugel-, alt-, helicon-, post-horn; sackbut, euphonium, bombardon, tuba, bass tuba.

[Vibrating surfaces] cymbal, bell, gong, peal of bells, *carillon*; tambour, -ine; drum, tom-tom, tab-or, -ret, -ourine, -orin; *sistrum*; *grande caisse*, bass-, big-, side-, kettle-drum; *tympani*; war drums; tymbal, timbrel, castanet, bones; musical-glasses, -stones; harmonica, sounding-board, rattle; gramophone, phonograph.

[Vibrating bars] reed, tuning-fork, triangle, Jew's harp, musical box, harmonicon, xylophone, marimba, *celeste*.

sord-ine, -et; *sourd-ine, -et*; mute.

(iv.) Perception of Sound

418. [Sense of sound.] **Hearing.—N.** hearing &c. *v.*; audition, auscultation; eavesdropping; audibility; acoustics &c. 402.

acute –, nice –, delicate –, quick –, sharp –, correct –, musical -ear; ear for music.

ear, auricle, lug, acoustic organs, auditory apparatus, ear-drum, tympanum; ear-, speaking-trumpet, megaphone; telephone, radiophone, stethoscope, phonograph, gramophone, microphone.

hearer, auditor, listener, eavesdropper; audi-tory, -ence.

V. hear, overhear; hark, -en; list, -en; give –, lend –, bend- an ear; give attention; catch a sound, prick up one's ears; give -a hearing, – audience- to.

hang upon the lips of, be all ear, listen with both ears.

become audible; meet –, fall upon –, catch –, reach- the ear; be heard; ring in the ear &c. (*resound*) 408.

Adj. hearing &c. *v.*; auditory, auricular, aural, auditive, acoustic.

Adv. *arrectis auribus*.

Int. hark, – ye! hear! list, -en! *Oyez!* attention! lend me your ears!

419. Deafness.—N. deafness, hardness of hearing, surdity; inaudibility.

V. be -deaf &c. *adj.*; have no ear; shut –, stop –, close- one's ears; turn a deaf ear to.

render deaf, stun, deafen.

Adj. deaf, earless, surd; hard –, dull- of hearing; deaf-mute, stunned, deafened; stone deaf; deaf as -a post, – an adder, – a beetle, – a trunk-maker.

inaudible &c. 405; out of hearing.

6. *Light*

(i.) Light in General

420. Light.—N. light, ray, beam, stream, gleam, streak, pencil; sun-, moon-beam; dawn, aurora.

day; sunshine; light of -day, – heaven; sun &c. (*luminary*) 423, day-, broad day-, noontide- light; noon-tide, -day; glare.

421. Darkness.—N. darkness &c. *adj.*; blackness &c. (*dark colour*) 431; obscurity, gloom, murk; dusk &c. (*dimness*) 422; tenebrosity, umbrageousness.

Cimmerian –, Stygian –, Egyptian- darkness; night; midnight; dead of –,

glow &c. *v.*; afterglow, sunset; glimmering &c. *v.*; glint; play –, flood- of light; phosphorescence, lambent flame.

flush, halo, glory, nimbus, aureole, *aureola.*

spark, *scintilla*; *facula*; sparkling &c. *v.*; emication, scintillation, flash, blaze, coruscation, fulguration; flame &c. (*fire*) 382; lightning, *ignis fatuus*, &c. (*luminary*) 423, radio-activity.

lustre, sheen, shimmer, reflection; gloss, tinsel, spangle, brightness, brilliancy, splendour; ef-, re-fulgence; ful-gor, -gidity; dazzlement, resplendence, transplendency; luminousness &c. *adj.*; luminosity; lucidity; renitency; radi-ance, -ation; irradiation, illumination, phosphorescence, luminescence.

radiation, radiant heat, infra-red rays, visible radiation, ultra-violet –, actinic- rays, actinism; X –, Roentgen-rays; phot-, heli-ography; optical instruments &c. 445.

[Science of light] optics; photo-logy, -metry; di-, cat-optrics.

[Distribution of light] *chiaroscuro*, *clair-obscur*, clear-obscure, breadth, light and shade, black and white, tonality, half-tone, mezzotint.

reflection, refraction, dispersion, double refraction, polarization, diffraction, interference.

illuminant &c. 423.

V. shine, glow, glitter, phosphoresce; glis-ter, -ten; twinkle, gleam; flare, – up; glare, beam, shimmer, glimmer, flicker, sparkle, scintillate, coruscate, flash, fulgurate, blaze; be -bright &c. *adj.*; reflect light, daze, dazzle, bedazzle, radiate, shoot out beams.

clear up, brighten.

lighten, enlighten; light, – up; irradiate, shine upon; give –, hang out- a light; cast –, throw –, shed- -lustre, – light- upon; illum-e, -ine, -inate; relume, strike a light; kindle &c. (*set fire to*) 384.

Adj. shining &c. *v.*; lumin-ous, -iferous; luc-id, -ent, -ulent, -ific, -iferous; illuminating, light, -some; bright, vivid, splendent, nitid, lustrous, shiny, brilliant, beamy, scintillant, radiant, lambent; sheen, -y; glossy, witching time of night; blind man's holiday; darkness -visible, – that can be felt; palpable, obscure; Erebus.

shade, shadow, umbra, penumbra; sciagraphy; *silhouette*; radiograph, skiagraph.

obscuration; ad-, ob-umbration; obtenebration, offuscation, caligation; extinction; eclipse, total eclipse; gathering of the clouds.

shading; distribution of shade; *chiaroscuro* &c. (*light*) 420.

noctivagation, noctograph, noctuary; obscurantist.

V. be -dark &c. *adj.*

darken, obscure, shade; dim; tone down, lower; over-cast, -shadow; cloud, eclipse; ob-, of-fuscate; ob-, ad-umbrate, cast into the shade; be-cloud, -dim, -darken; cast –, throw –, spread- a -shade, – shadow, – gloom.

extinguish; put –, blow –, snuff- out; doubt.

Adj. dark, -some, -ling; obscure, tenebrous, tenebrious, sombrous, pitch dark, pitchy; caliginous; black &c. (*in colour*) 431.

sunless, lightless &c. (*see* sun, light, &c. 423); sombre, dusky; unilluminated &c. (*see* illuminate &c. 420); nocturnal; dingy, lurid, gloomy; murk-y, -some; shady, umbrageous; overcast &c. (*dim*) 422; cloudy &c. (*opaque*) 426; darkened &c. *v.*

dark as -pitch, – a pit, – Erebus.

benighted; noctivag-ant, -ous.

Adv. in the -dark, – shade; at night.

422. Dimness.—N. dimness &c. *adj.*; darkness &c. 421; paleness &c. (*light colour*) 429.

half-light, *demi-jour*; partial -shadow, – eclipse; shadow of a shade; glimmer, -ing; nebulosity; cloud &c. 353; eclipse.

aurora, dusk, twilight, gloaming, blind man's holiday, shades of evening, crepuscule, cockshut time; break of day, daybreak, dawn.

moon-light, -beam, -shine; star-, owl's-, candle-, rush-, fire-light; farthing candle.

V. be –, grow- -dim &c. *adj.*; flicker, twinkle, glimmer; loom, lower; fade; darken; pale, – its ineffectual fire.

burnished, glassy, sunny, orient, meridian; noon-day, -tide; cloudless, clear; un-clouded, -obscured.

garish; re-, tran-splendent; re-, effulgent; ful-gid, -gent; relucent, splendid, blazing, in a blaze, ablaze, rutilant, meteoric, phosphorescent; aglow.

bright as silver; light –, bright- as -day, – noonday, – the sun at noonday.

optical, actinic; photo-genic, -graphic; heliographic, radioactive.

render -dim &c. *adj.*; dim, bedim, obscure.

Adj. dim, dull, lack-lustre, dingy, darkish, shorn of its beams; dark 421.

faint, shadowed forth; glassy; bleary; cloudy; misty &c. (*opaque*) 426; muggy, fuliginous; nebul-ous, -ar; obnubilated, overcast, crepuscular, twilight, muddy, lurid, leaden, dun, dirty; looming &c. *v.*

pale &c. (*colourless*) 429; confused &c. (*invisible*) 447.

---

423. [Source of light &c.] **Luminary.** —**N.** luminary; light &c. 420; flame &c. (*fire*) 382.

spark, *scintilla*; phosphorescence.

sun, orb of day, day star, Phœbus, Apollo, Helios, Phaethon, Hyperion, Ra, Aurora; star, orb, meteor; falling –, shooting- star; blazing –, dog- star; Sirius, canicula, Aldebaran; morning star, Lucifer, Phosphor, evening star; Hesperus, Venus, planet, moon &c. 318; constellation, galaxy; northern light, *aurora -borealis*, – *australis*, zodiacal light; mock sun, parhelion.

lightning; fork –, sheet –, summer- lightning, St. Elmo's fire; phosphorus; *ignis fatuus*; Jack o' –, Friar's- lantern; Will o' the wisp, fire-drake, *Fata Morgana*.

glow-worm, fire-fly.

radium, luminous paint.

[Artificial light] gas; gas –, lime –, electric –, head –, search –, spot –, flash –, flood –, foot-light; lamp, oil –, gas –, arc –, incandescent- lamp; flare; lant-ern, -horn; dark lantern, bull's eye, projector; candle, *bougie*, tallow –, wax- candle; dip, farthing dip; taper, rush-light; oil &c. (*grease*) 356; wick, burner; Argand, moderator, duplex; torch, *flambeau*, link, brand; cresset; gase-, chande-, electro-lier; candelabrum, *girandole*, sconce, lustre, candle-stick.

firework, fizgig; pyrotechnics; Roman candle, Véry light, star shell, parachute light; rocket, lighthouse &c. (*signal*) 550.

V. illuminate &c. (*light*) 420.

Adj. self-luminous, incandescent; phosphor-ic, -escent; luminescent, fluorescent, radiant &c. (*light*) 420.

424. Shade.—**N.** shade; awning &c. (*cover*) 223; parasol, sunshade, umbrella; screen, curtain, shutter, blind, gauze, veil, mantle, mask; cloud, mist, gathering of clouds; smoke screen; smoked glasses, coloured spectacles; blinkers, blinders.

umbrage, glade; shadow &c. 421.

V. draw a curtain; put up –, close- a shutter; veil &c. *v.*; cast a shadow &c. (*darken*) 421; screen, obstruct the view.

Adj. shady, umbrageous, bowery.

---

425. Transparency. — **N.** transparen-ce, -cy; translucen-ce, -cy; diaphaneity; luc-, pelluc-, limp-idity.

transparent medium, glass, crystal, mica; lymph, water.

V. be -transparent &c. *adj.*; transmit light.

Adj. transparent, pellucid, lucid, diaphanous; trans-, tra-lucent; limpid, clear, serene, crystalline, clear as crys-

426. Opacity.—**N.** opacity; opaqueness &c. *adj.*

film; cloud &c. 353.

V. be -opaque &c. *adj.*; obstruct the passage of light; ob-, of-fuscate.

Adj. opaque, impervious to light.

dim &c. 422; turbid, thick, muddy, opacous, obfuscated, fuliginous, cloudy, hazy, foggy, vaporous, nubiferous, muggy.

tal, vitreous, transpicuous, glassy, hyaline.

smoky, fumid, murky, dirty.

---

427. Semitransparency.—N. semitransparency, opalescence, milkiness, pearliness; gauze, muslin; film; mist &c. (*cloud*) 353; frosted glass.

Adj. semi-transparent, -pellucid, -diaphanous, -opacous, -opaque; opal-escent, -ine; pearly, milky, frosted, mat; misty.

(ii.) Specific Light

428. Colour.—N. colour, hue, tint, tinge, dye, complexion, shade, tincture, cast, livery, coloration, chromatism, glow, flush; tone, key.

pure –, positive –, primary –, primitive –, complementary- colour; three primaries; spectrum, chromatic dispersion; broken –, secondary –, tertiary- colour.

local colour, colouring, keeping, tone, value, aerial perspective.

[Science of colour] chromatics, spectrum analysis; prism, spectroscope.

pigment, colouring matter, paint, dye, wash, distemper, stain; medium; mordant; oil-paint &c. (*painting*) 556.

V. colour, dye, tinge, stain, tint, tinct, tone, paint, wash, ingrain, grain, illuminate, emblazon, imbue; paint &c. (*fine art*) 556; daub.

Adj. coloured &c. *v.*; colorific, tingent, tinctorial; chromatic, prismatic; full-, high-, deep-coloured; doubly-dyed; polychromatic.

bright, vivid, intense, deep; fresh, unfaded; rich, gorgeous; highly coloured; gay; variegated &c. 440.

gaudy, florid; garish; showy, flaunting, flashy; raw, crude; glaring, flaring; discordant, inharmonious.

mellow, harmonious, pearly, sweet, delicate, tender, refined.

429. [Absence of colour.] **Achromatism.—N.** achromatism; de-, discoloration; pall-or, -idity; paleness &c. *adj.*; etiolation; neutral tint, monochrome, black-and-white.

V. lose -colour &c. 428; fade, fly, go; become -colourless &c. *adj.*; turn pale, pale, whiten.

deprive of colour, decolorize, bleach, tarnish, achromatize, blanch, etiolate, wash out, tone down.

Adj. uncoloured &c. (*see* colour &c. 428); colourless, achromatic, hueless, pale, pallid; pale-, tallow-faced; faint, dull, cold, muddy, leaden, dun, wan, sallow, dead, dingy, ashy, ashen, ghastly, cadaverous, glassy, lack-lustre; discoloured &c. *v.*

light-coloured, fair, *blond*; white &c. 430.

pale as -death, – ashes, – a witch, – a ghost, – a corpse.

---

430. Whiteness.—N. whiteness &c. *adj.*; argent.

albification, albescence, albinism, etiolation.

snow, paper, chalk, milk, lily, ivory, silver, alabaster; white lead, chinese –, flake –, ivory –, zinc- white, white-wash, -ning, whiting.

V. be -white &c. *adj.*

render -white &c. *adj.*; whiten- bleach, blanch, etiolate, whitewash, silver, frost.

Adj. white; milky, milk-, snow-white; snowy, niveous, candid, chalky; hoar,

431. Blackness.—N. blackness &c. *adj.*; darkness &c. (*want of light*) 421; swarthness, lividity, dark colour, tone, colour; *chiaroscuro* &c. 420.

nigrification, infuscation, denigration.

jet, ink, ebony, coal, pitch, soot, smudge, charcoal, sloe, raven, crow; negro, blackamoor, man of colour, nigger, darky, Ethiopian, black.

[Pigments] lamp –, ivory –, blue-black; writing –, printing –, printer's –, Indian- ink.

V. be -black &c. *adj.*

-y; frosted, silvery; argent, -ine; canescent.

whitish, creamy, pearly, ivory, fair, *blond*, ash-blond, platinum blond; blanched &c. *v.*; high in tone, light.

white as -a sheet, – driven snow, – a lily, – silver; like -ivory &c. *n.*

---

render -black &c. *adj.*; blacken, infuscate, denigrate; blot, -ch; smutch; smirch; darken &c. 421.

Adj. black, sable, swarthy, sombre, dark, inky, ebon, atramentous, jetty; coal-, jet-black; fuliginous, pitchy, sooty, swart, dusky, dingy, murky, Ethiopic; low-toned, low in tone; of the deepest dye.

black as -jet &c. *n.*, – my hat, – a shoe, – a tinker's pot, – November, – thunder, – midnight; nocturnal &c. (*dark*) 421; nigrescent; gray &c. 432; obscure &c. 421.

Adv. in mourning.

432. Gray.—**N.** gray &c. *adj.*; neutral tint, silver, pepper and salt, *chiaroscuro, grisaille*, grayness.

[Pigments] Payne's gray; black &c. 431.

Adj. gray, grey; steel –, iron- gray, dun, drab, dingy, leaden, livid, sombre, sad, pearly; silver, -y, -ed; ash-en, -y; ciner-eous, -itious; grizzl-y, -ed; dove-, slate-, stone-, mouse-, ash-coloured; mole; cool.

---

433. Brown.—**N.** brown &c. *adj.*

[Pigments] bistre, ochre, sepia, Vandyke brown.

Adj. brown, adust, bay, dapple, auburn, chestnut, nutbrown, cinnamon, hazel, fawn, puce, *écru*, russet, tawny, fuscous, chocolate, maroon, foxy, tan, brunette, whitey-brown; snuff-, liver-coloured; brown as -a berry, – mahogany; reddish brown; copper-, rust- coloured; henna, bronze, khaki; roan, sorrel.

sun-burnt; tanned &c. *v.*

V. render -brown &c. *adj.*; tan, embrown, bronze.

*Primitive Colours**

434. Redness.—**N.** red, scarlet, vermilion, cardinal, Post Office red, carmine, crimson, pink, lake, *cerise*, cherry red, maroon, carnation, *couleur de rose, rose du Barry*; magenta, damask; flesh -colour, – tint; colour; fresh –, high-colour; warmth; gules.

ruby, garnet, carbuncle; rose; rust, iron-mould.

[Dyes and pigments] cinnabar, cochineal; fuchsine; ruddle, madder, red-lead; Indian –, light –, Venetian- red; red ink, annotto.

redness &c. *adj.*; rub-escence, -icundity, -ification; erubescence, blush.

Complementary Colours

435. Greenness.—**N.** green &c. *adj.*; blue and yellow; vert.

emerald, verd antique, verdigris, malachite, beryl, aquamarine, reseda.

[Pigments] *terre verte*, verditer, bice, chlorophyl.

greenness, verdure, verdancy; viridity, -escence.

Adj. green, verdant; glaucous, olive; porraceous; green as grass.

emerald –, pea –, grass –, apple –, sea –, olive –, bottle –, leaf- green.

greenish; vir-ent, -escent.

V. be –, become- -red &c. *adj.*; blush, flush, colour up, mantle, redden.

render -red &c. *adj.*; redden, rouge; rub-ify, -ricate; incarnadine; ruddle.

Adj. red &c. *n.*, -dish; rufous, ruddy, florid, incarnadine, sanguine, bloody, gory; ros-y, -eate; blowz-y, -ed; burnt; rubi-cund, -form;

* The author's classification of colours has been retained, though it does not entirely accord with the theories of modern science. Complete lists of shades or pigments are beyond the scope of this work.

lurid, stammel, blood-red; russet, murrey, carroty, sorrel, lateritious.

rose-, ruby-, cherry-, claret-, wine-, plum-, flame-, flesh-, peach-, salmon-, brick-, brickdust-coloured, reddish brown &c. 433.

blushing &c. *v.*; erubescent; reddened &c. *v.*

red as -fire, – blood, – scarlet, – a turkeycock, – a lobster; warm, hot; foxy.

436. Yellowness.—**N.** yellow &c. *adj.*; or.

[Pigments] gamboge; cadmium –, chrome –, Indian –, lemon- yellow; orpiment, yellow ochre, Claude tint, aureolin.

crocus, saffron, topaz, gold.

jaundice; London fog; yellowness &c. *adj.*

Adj. yellow, aureate, gold, golden, gilt, gilded, flavous, citrine, fallow; fulv-ous, -id; sallow, luteous, tawny, creamy, sandy; xanth-ic, -ous; jaundiced.

gold-, citron-, saffron-, lemon-, sulphur-, amber-, straw-, primrose-, cream-coloured; flaxen, yellowish, buff.

yellow as a -quince, – guinea, – crow's foot.

437. Purple.—**N.** purple &c. *adj.*; blue and red, bishop's purple; aniline dyes, gridelin, amethyst; purpure.

livid-ness, -ity.

V. empurple.

Adj. purple, violet, plum-coloured, lavender, lilac, puce, *mauve*; livid.

438. Blueness.—**N.** blue &c. *adj.*; garter-blue; watchet.

[Pigments] ultramarine, smalt, cobalt, cyanogen; Prussian –, syenite-blue; bice, indigo, woad.

lapis lazuli, sapphire, turquoise.

blue-, bluish-ness; bloom.

Adj. blue, azure, cerulean; sky-blue, -coloured, -dyed; navy-blue, aquamarine, electric blue, royal blue, cyanic; bluish; atmospheric, retiring; cold.

439. Orange.—**N.** orange, red and yellow; gold; or; flame &c. colour, *adj.*

[Pigments] ochre, Mars orange, cadmium.

V. gild, warm.

Adj. orange; ochreous; orange-, gold-, flame-, copper-, brass-, apricot-coloured; warm, hot, glowing.

440. Variegation.—**N.** variegation; di-, tri-chroism; iridescence, irisation, play of colours, polychrome, maculation, spottiness, striæ.

spectrum, rainbow, iris, tulip, peacock, chameleon, butterfly, tortoise-shell; mackerel, – sky; zebra, leopard, mother-of-pearl, nacre, opal, marble, batik.

check, plaid, tartan, patchwork; mar-, par-quetry; mosaic, *tesseræ*, tesselation, chess-board, checkers, chequers; harlequin; Joseph's coat; tricolour; patches, bands, stripes, spots &c. of colour.

V. be -variegated &c. *adj.*; variegate, stripe, streak, checker, chequer; be-, speckle, fleck; be-, sprinkle; stipple, maculate, dot, bespot; tattoo, inlay, tesselate, damascene; embroider, braid, quilt.

Adj. variegated &c. *v.*; many-coloured, -hued; divers-, parti-coloured; di-, poly-chromatic; bi-, tri-, versi-colour; of all -the colours of the rainbow, – manner of colours; kaleidoscopic.

iridescent; opal-ine, -escent; prismatic, nacreous, pearly, shot, *gorge de pigeon*, *chatoyant*, irisated.

pied, piebald, skewbald; motley; mottled, marbled; pepper and salt, paned, dappled, clouded, cymophanous.

mosaic, tesselated, chequered, plaid; tortoiseshell &c. *n.*

spott-ed, -y; punctated, powdered; speckled &c. *v.*; freckled, flea-bitten, studded; fleck-ed, -ered; striated, barred, veined; brind-ed, -led; tabby; watered; grizzled; listed; embroidered &c. *v.*; dædal.

(iii.) Perceptions of Light

441. Vision.—N. vision, sight, optics, eye-sight.

view, look, espial, glance, ken, *coup d'œil*; glimpse, peep, glint; gaze, stare, leer; perlustration, contemplation; conspect-ion, -uity; regard, survey; in-, intro-spection; *reconnaissance*, speculation, watch, espionage, *espionnage*, autopsy; ocular -inspection, - demonstration; sight-seeing.

macrography, micrography.

point of view; view-, stand-point; gazebo, loop-hole, *belvedere*, watch-tower.

field of view; theatre, amphitheatre, arena, vista, horizon; commanding –, bird's eye –, panoramic- view; periscope.

visual organ, organ of vision; eye; naked –, unassisted- eye; eye-ball, retina, pupil, iris, cornea, white; optics, orbs; saucer –, goggle –, gooseberry- eyes.

short sight &c. 443; clear –, sharp –, quick –, eagle –, piercing –, penetrating- -sight, – glance, – eye; perspicacity, discernment; catopsis.

eagle, hawk; cat, lynx; Argus.

evil eye; basilisk, cockatrice.

spectacles, telescope &c. 445.

V. see, behold, discern, perceive, have in sight, descry, sight, make out, discover, distinguish, recognize, spy, espy, ken; get –, have –, catch- a -sight, – glimpse- of; command a view of; witness, contemplate, speculate; cast –, set- the eyes on; be a -spectator &c. 444- of; look on &c. (*be present*) 186; see sights &c. (*curiosity*) 455; see at a glance &c. (*intelligence*) 498.

look, view, eye; lift up the eyes, open one's eye; look -at, – on, – upon, – over, – about one, – round; survey, scan, inspect; run the eye -over, – through; reconnoitre, glance -round, – on, – over; turn –, bend- one's looks upon; direct the eyes to, turn the eyes on, cast a glance, make eyes at.

observe &c. (*attend to*) 457; watch &c. (*care*) 459; see with one's own eyes; watch for &c. (*expect*) 507; peek, peep, peer, pry, take a peep; play at bo-peep.

look -full in the face, – hard at, – intently; strain one's eyes; fix –, rivet- the eyes upon; stare, gaze; pore over, gloat -over, – on; leer, ogle, glare; goggle; cock the eye, squint, gloat, look askance; give the glad eye.

Adj. seeing &c. *v.*; visual, ocular, -al; ophthalmic.

far-, clear-sighted &c. *n.*; eagle-, hawk-, lynx-, keen-, Argus-eyed.

visible &c. 446.

442. Blindness.—N. blindness, anopsia, cecity, excecation, *amaurosis*, cataract, ablepsy, prestriction; dim-sightedness &c. 443.

V. be -blind &c. *adj.*; not see; lose sight of; have the eyes bandaged; grope in the dark.

not look; close –, shut –, turn away –, avert- the eyes; look another way; wink &c. (*limited vision*) 443; shut the eyes –, be blind- to; wink –, blink- at.

render -blind &c. *adj.*; blind, -fold; hoodwink, dazzle; put one's eyes out; throw dust into one's eyes; *jeter de la poudre aux yeux*; screen from sight &c. (*hide*) 528.

Adj. blind; eye-, sight-, vision-less; dark; stone-, sand-, stark-blind; undiscerning; dim-sighted &c. 443.

blind as -a bat, – a buzzard, – a beetle, – a mole, – an owl; wall-eyed.

blinded &c. *v.*

Adv. blind-ly, -fold; darkly.

Adv. visibly &c. 446; in sight of, with one's eyes open.
at -sight, – first sight, – a glance, – the first blush; *primâ facie.*
Int. look! &c. (*attention*) 457.
Phr. the scales falling from one's eyes.

443. [Imperfect vision.] **Dim-sightedness.** [Fallacies of vision.]—**N.** dim –, dull –, half –, short –, near –, long –, double –, astigmatic –, failing- sight; dim &c. -sightedness; snow blindness; purblindness, lippitude; my-, presby-opia; confusion of vision; astigmatism, nystagmus; colour-blindness, dichromism, chromato-pseudo-blepsis, Daltonism; nyctalopy; *strabismus*, strabism, squint, cast in the eye, swivel eye, goggle eyes; obliquity of vision.

winking &c. *v.*; nictitation; blinkard, albino.

dizziness, swimming, scotomy; cataract; ophthalmia.

[Limitation of vision] eye shade, blinker, blinder; screen &c. (*hider*) 530.

[Fallacies of vision] *deceptio visûs*; refraction, distortion, illusion, false light, *anamorphosis*, virtual image, *spectrum*, *mirage*, looming, phasma; phant-asm, -asma, -om; vision; spectre, apparition, ghost; *ignis fatuus* &c. (*luminary*) 423; spectre of the Brocken; magic mirror; magic lantern &c. (*show*) 448; mirror, lens &c. (*instrument*) 445.

V. be -dim-sighted &c. *n.*; see double; have a -mote in the eye, – mist before the eyes, – film over the eyes; see through a -prism, – glass darkly; wink, blink, nictitate; squint; look ask-ant, -ance; screw up the eyes, glare, glower.

dazzle, glare, blur, swim, loom.

Adj. dim-sighted &c. *n.*; my-, presby-opic; astigmatic; moon-, mope-, blear-, goggle-, gooseberry-, one-eyed; blind of one eye, monoculous; half-, pur-, colour-blind; dichromatic.

blind as a bat &c. (*blind*) 442; winking &c. *v.*

444. Spectator.—**N.** spectator, beholder, observer, inspector, viewer, looker-on, onlooker, witness, eye-witness, bystander, passer by; sight-seer.

spy, scout; sentinel &c. (*warning*) 668.

V. witness, behold &c. (*see*) 441; look on &c. (*be present*) 186.

445. Optical Instruments.—**N.** optical instruments; lens, meniscus, magnifier, reading –, burning- glass; micro-, mega-, teino-scope; spectacles, glasses, barnacles, goggles, giglamps, eyeglass, *pince-nez*, monocle; periscopic lens; telescope, glass, lorgnette, binocular; spy-, opera-, field-glass, periscope, range finder.

mirror, reflector, speculum; looking-, pier-, cheval-, hand-glass.

prism; camera, *camera-lucida*, *-obscura*; projector, stereopticon, magic lantern &c. (*show*) 448; chro-, thau-matrope; stereo-, pseudo-, poly-, kaleido-scope.

photo-, opto-, erio-, actino-, luci-, radio-, spectro-meter; polari-, polemo-, spectro-scope, diffraction grating.

optics, optician, optometry, optometrist; microscop-y, -ist; photometry, photography; photographer.

446. Visibility.—**N.** visibility, perceptibility; conspicuousness, distinctness &c. *adj.*; conspicuity; appearance &c. 448; exposure; manifestation &c. 525; ocular -proof, – evidence, – demonstration; field of view &c. (*vision*) 441.

447. Invisibility.—**N.** invisibility, non-appearance, imperceptibility; indistinctness &c. *adj.*; mystery, delitescence.

concealment &c. 528; latency &c. 526.

V. be –, become- -visible &c. *adj.*; appear, emerge, open to the view; meet –, catch- the eye; present –, show –, manifest –, produce –, discover –, reveal –, expose –, betray- itself; stand -forth, – out; show; arise; peep –, peer –, crop- out; start –, spring –, show –, turn –, crop- up; glimmer, glitter, glow, loom; glare; burst forth, scintillate; burst upon the -view, – sight; heave in sight; come -in sight, – into view, – out, – forth, – forward; see the light of day; break through the clouds; make its appearance, show its face, materialize, appear to one's eyes, come upon the stage, enter; float before the eyes, speak for itself &c. (*manifest*) 525; attract the attention &c. 457; reappear; live in a glass house.

expose to view &c. 525.

Adj. visible, perceptible, perceivable, discernible, apparent; in -view, – full view, – sight; exposed to view, *en évidence*; unclouded.

obvious &c. (*manifest*) 525; plain, clear, distinct, definite; well-defined, -marked; in focus; recognizable, palpable, autoptical; glaring, staring, conspicuous; stereoscopic; in -bold, – strong, – high- relief.

periscopic, panoramic.

before –, under- one's eyes; before one, *à vue d'œil,* in one's eye, *oculis subjecta fidelibus.*

Adv. visibly &c. *adj.*; in sight of; before one's eyes &c. *adj.*; *veluti in speculum.*

V. be -invisible &c. *adj.*; be hidden &c. (*hide*) 528; lurk &c. (*lie hidden*) 526; escape notice.

render -invisible &c. *adj.*; conceal &c. 528; put out of sight.

not see &c. (*be blind*) 442; lose sight of.

Adj. invisible, imperceptible; un-, in-discernible; un-, non-apparent; out of –, not in- sight; *à perte de vue*; behind the -scenes, – curtain; view-, sight-less; in-, un-conspicuous; unseen &c. (*see* see &c. 441); covert &c. (*latent*) 526; eclipsed, under an eclipse.

dim &c. (*faint*) 422; mysterious, dark, obscure, confused; indistin-ct, -guishable; shadowy, indefinite, undefined; ill-defined, -marked; blurred, fuzzy, out of focus; misty &c. (*opaque*) 426; veiled &c. (*concealed*) 528; delitescent.

---

448. Appearance.—N. appearance, phenomenon, sight, spectacle, show, premonstration, scene, species, view, *coup d'œil*; look-out, out-look, prospect, vista, perspective, bird's-eye view, scenery, landscape, picture, *tableau*; display, exposure, *mise en scène*; scenery, *décor*; rising of the curtain.

phant-asm, -om &c. (*fallacy of vision*) 443.

pageant, *spectacle*; peep-, raree-, gal-lanty-show; *ombres chinoises*; projector, optical –, magic- lantern, phantasmagoria, dissolving views; cinema, -tograph; bio-scope. -graph; moving pictures, movies, film, screen &c.; pan-, di-, cosm-, ge-orama; *coup –, jeu- de théâtre*; pageantry &c. (*ostentation*) 882; insignia &c. (*indication*) 550.

aspect, phase, *phasis*, seeming; shape &c. (*form*) 240; guise, look,

449. Disappearance.—N. disappearance, evanescence, eclipse, occultation.

departure &c. 293; exit, vanishing point; dissolving views.

V. disappear, vanish, dissolve, fade, melt away, pass, go, avaunt; be -gone &c. *adj.*; leave -no trace, – 'not a rack behind'; go off the stage &c. (*depart*) 293; suffer –, undergo- an eclipse; be lost to –, retire from- -sight, – view.

lose sight of.

efface &c. 552.

Adj. disappearing &c. *v.*; evanescent; missing, lost; lost to -sight, – view; gone; *spurlos versenkt.*

Int. vanish! disappear! avaunt! &c. (*ejection*) 297.

---

complexion, colour, image, mien, air, cast, carriage, port, demeanour; presence, expression, first blush, face of the thing; point of view, light.

lineament, feature, trait, lines; out-line, -side; contour, *silhouette*, face, countenance, physiognomy, visage, phiz, mug, cast of countenance, profile, *tournure*, cut of one's jib, metoposcopy; outside &c. 220.

V. appear; be –, become- visible &c. 446; seem, look, show; present –, wear –, carry –, have –, bear –, exhibit –, take –, take on –, assume- the -appearance, – semblance- of; look like; cut a figure, figure; present to the view; show &c. (*make manifest*) 525.

Adj. apparent, seeming, ostensible; on view.

Adv. apparently; to all -seeming, – appearance; ostensibly, seemingly, as it seems, on the face of it, *primâ facie*; at the first blush, at first sight; in the eyes of; to the eye.

CLASS IV

Words relating to the INTELLECTUAL FACULTIES

Division (I.) FORMATION OF IDEAS

Section I. Operations of Intellect in General

450. Intellect.—**N.** intellect, mind, understanding, reason, thinking principle; rationality; cogitative –, cognitive –, intellectual- faculties; faculties, senses, consciousness, observation, percipience, apperception, mentality, intelligence, intellection, intuition, association of ideas, instinct, flair, conception, judgement, wits, parts, capacity, intellectuality, reasoning power, brains, genius; wit &c. 498; ability &c. (*skill*) 698; wisdom &c. 498.

soul, spirit, ghost, inner man, heart, breast, bosom, *penetralia mentis, divina particula auræ,* heart's core; ego, psyche, pneuma, subconsciousness, subconscious, subliminal self; dual personality.

organ –, seat- of thought; *sensorium,* sensory, brain, gray matter; head, -piece; pate, noddle, skull, scull, *pericranium, cerebrum, cranium,* brain-pan, -box; sconce, upper story.

[Science of mind] metaphysics; psychics, psycho-logy, -metry, -genesis, -analysis, -physics, psychi-atry, -cal research, thought reading &c. 992; ideology; mental –, moral- philosophy; philosophy of the mind; pneumat-, phren-ology; no –, cranio-logy, -scopy.

ideal-ity, -ism; transcendental-, spiritual-ism; immateriality &c. 317.

metaphysician, psychologist &c.

V. note, notice, mark; take -notice, – cognizance- of; be -aware, – conscious- of; realize; appreciate; ruminate &c. (*think*) 451; fancy &c. (*imagine*) 515; conceive, reason, understand.

Adj. [Relating to intellect] intellectual, mental, rational, subjective, metaphysical, nooscopic, spiritual; ghostly; psych-ical, -ological; cerebral.

immaterial &c. 317; endowed with reason.

Adv. *in petto.*

450a. Absence or want of Intellect.—**N.** absence –, want- of -intellect &c. 450; imbecility &c. 499; brutality; brute -instinct, – force.

Adj. unendowed with reason.

---

451. Thought.—**N.** thought; exercitation –, exercise- of the intellect; reflection, cogitation, consideration, meditation, study, lucubration, speculation, deliberation, pondering; head-,

452. [Absence or want of thought.] **Incogitancy.**—**N.** incogitancy, vacancy, inunderstanding; inanity, fatuity &c. 499; thoughtlessness &c. (*inattention*) 458.

brain-work; cerebration; mentation, deep reflection; close study, application &c. (*attention*) 457.

abstract thought, abstraction, contemplation, musing; brown study &c. (*inattention*) 458; reverie, Platonism; depth of thought, workings of the mind, thoughts, inmost thoughts; self-counsel, -communing, -consultation.

association –, succession –, flow –, train –, current- of -thought, – ideas.

after –, mature- thought; reconsideration, second thoughts; retrospection &c. (*memory*) 505; excogitation; examination &c. (*inquiry*) 461; invention &c. (*imagination*) 515.

thoughtfulness &c. *adj.*

V. think, reflect, reason, cogitate, excogitate, consider, deliberate; bestow -thought, – consideration- upon; speculate, contemplate, meditate, ponder, muse, dream, ruminate; brood –, con- over; animadvert, study; bend –, apply- the mind &c. (*attend*) 457; digest, discuss, hammer at, weigh, perpend; realize, appreciate; fancy &c. (*imagine*) 515; trow.

take into consideration; take counsel &c. (*be advised*) 695; commune with –, bethink- oneself; collect one's thoughts; revolve –, turn over –, run over- in the mind; chew the cud –, sleep- upon; take counsel of –, advise with- one's pillow.

rack –, ransack –, crack –, beat –, cudgel- one's brains; set one's -brain, – wits- to work.

harbour –, entertain –, cherish –, nurture- an -idea &c. 453; take into one's head; bear in mind; reconsider.

occur; present –, suggest- itself; come –, get- into one's head; strike one, flit across the view, come uppermost, run in one's head; enter –, pass in –, cross –, flash on –, flash across –, float in –, fasten itself on –, be uppermost in –, occupy- the mind; have in one's mind.

make an impression; sink –, penetrate- into the mind; engross the thoughts.

Adj. thinking &c. *v.*; thoughtful, pensive, meditative, reflective, cogitative, museful, wistful, contemplative, speculative, deliberative, studious, sedate, introspective, Platonic, philosophical.

lost –, engrossed –, rapt –, absorbed- in thought &c. (*inattentive*) 458; deep musing &c. (*intent*) 457.

in the mind, under consideration, in contemplation.

Adv. all things considered; taking everything into account.

Phr. the mind being on the stretch; the -mind, – head- -turning, – running- upon.

V. not -think &c. 451; not think of; dismiss from the -mind, – thoughts &c. 451.

indulge in reverie &c. (*be inattentive*) 458.

put away thought; unbend –, relax –, divert- the mind.

Adj. vacant, unintellectual, unideal, unoccupied, unthinking, inconsiderate, thoughtless; absent &c. (*inattentive*) 458; diverted; irrational &c. 499; narrow-minded &c. 481.

un-thought of, -dreamt of, -considered; off one's mind; incogitable, not to be thought of, inconceivable.

453. [Object of thought.] **Idea.—N.** idea, notion, conception, thought, apprehension, impression, perception, image, sentiment, reflection, observation, consideration; abstract idea, principle; archetype.

view &c. (*opinion*) 484; theory &c.

454. [Subject of thought.] **Topic.—N.** subject of –, material for- thought; food for the mind, mental *pabulum*.

subject, -matter; matter, theme, topic, what it is about, *thesis*, text, business, affair, matter in hand, argument; motion, resolution; head, chap-

514; conceit, fancy; phantasy &c. (*imagination*) 515.

point of view &c. (*aspect*) 448; field of view.

ter; case, point; proposition, theorem; field of inquiry; moot point, problem, &c. (*question*) 461.

V. float –, pass- in the mind &c. 451.

Adj. thought of; uppermost in the mind; *in petto*.

Adv. under -discussion, – consideration, – advisement; in -question, – the mind; on -foot, – the carpet, – the *tapis*; before the house, relative to &c. 9.

Section II. Precursory Conditions and Operations

455. [The desire of knowledge.] **Curiosity.** — **N.** interest, thirst for knowledge; curi-osity, -ousness; inquiring mind; inquisitiveness.

sight-seer, quidnunc, newsmonger, Paul Pry, peeping Tom, eavesdropper; gossip &c. (*news*) 532; questioner, *enfant terrible*.

V. be -curious &c. *adj.*; take an interest in, stare, gape; prick up the ears, see sights, lionize; pry, speer; dig up.

Adj. curious, inquisitive, burning with curiosity, overcurious, nosey; inquiring &c. 461; prying; inquisitorial; agape &c. (*expectant*) 507; attentive &c. 457.

Phr. what's the matter? what next?

456. [Absence of curiosity.] **Incuriosity.**—**N.** incuriosity; incuriousness &c. *adj.*; *insouciance* &c. 866; indifference, apathy.

V. be -incurious &c. *adj.*; have no -curiosity &c. 455; take no interest in &c. 823; mind one's own business.

Adj. incurious, uninquisitive, uninterested, indifferent, bored; impassive &c. 823.

457. Attention.—**N.** attention; mindfulness &c. *adj.*; intent-ness, -iveness; thought &c. 451; adverten-ce, -cy; observ-ance, -ation; consideration, reflection, perpension; heed; particularity; notice, regard &c. *v.*; circumspection &c. (*care*) 459; study, scrutiny, once-over; in-, intro-spection; revision, -al.

active –, diligent –, exclusive –, minute –, close –, intense –, deep –, profound –, abstract –, laboured –, deliberate- -thought, – attention, – application, – study.

minuteness, attention to detail &c. 459.

absorption of mind &c. (*abstraction*) 458.

indication, calling attention to &c. *v.*

V. be -attentive &c. *adj.*; attend, advert to, observe, look, see, view, remark, notice, regard, take notice, mark; give –, pay- -attention, – heed- to; listen in, incline –, lend- an ear to; trouble one's head about; give a

458. Inattention.—**N.** in-attention, -consideration; inconsiderateness &c. *adj.*; oversight; inadverten-ce, -cy; non-observance, disregard.

supineness &c. (*inactivity*) 683; *étourderie*; want of thought; heedlessness &c. (*neglect*) 460; *insouciance* &c. (*indifference*) 866.

abstraction; absence –, absorption- of mind; preoccupation, distraction, reverie, brown study, deep musing, fit of abstraction, woolgathering.

V. be -inattentive &c. *adj.*; overlook, disregard; pass by &c. (*neglect*) 460; not -observe &c. 457; think little of.

close –, shut- one's eyes to; wink at; pay no attention to; dismiss –, discard –, discharge- from one's -thoughts, – mind; drop the subject, think no more of; set –, turn –, put- aside; turn -away from, – one's attention from, – a deaf ear to, – one's back upon.

abstract oneself, dream, indulge in reverie.

escape -notice, – attention; come in

thought –, animadvert- to; occupy oneself with; contemplate &c. (*think of*) 451; look -at, – to, – after, – into, – over; see to; turn –, bend –, apply –, direct –, give- the -mind, – eye, – attention- to; have -an eye to, – in one's eye; bear in mind; take into -account, – consideration; keep in -sight, – view; have regard to, heed, mind, take cognizance of, be engaged in, entertain, recognize; make –, take- note of; note.

examine cursorily; glance -at, – upon, – over; cast –, pass- the eyes over; run over, turn over the leaves, dip into, perstringe; skim &c. (*neglect*) 460; take a cursory view of.

examine, – closely, – intently; scan, scrutinize, consider; give –, bend- one's mind to; overhaul, revise, pore over; inspect, review, pass under review; take stock of; fix –, rivet –, focus –, devote- the -eye, – mind, – thoughts, – attention- on *or* to; hear –, think- out; mind one's business.

revert –, hark back- to; watch &c. (*expect*) 507, (*take care of*) 459; hearken –, listen- to; prick up the ears; have –, keep- the eyes open; come to the point.

meet with attention; fall under one's -notice, – observation; be -under consideration &c. (*topic*) 454.

catch –, strike- the eye; attract notice; catch –, awaken –, wake –, invite –, solicit –, attract –, claim –, excite –, engage –, occupy –, strike –, arrest –, fix –, engross –, absorb –, rivet- the- attention, – mind, – thoughts; be -present to, – uppermost in- the mind.

bring under one's notice; point -out, – to, – at, – the finger at; lay the finger on, indigitate, indicate; direct –, call- attention to; show; put a -mark &c. (*sign*) 550- upon; call soldiers to 'attention'; bring forward &c. (*make manifest*) 525.

Adj. attentive, mindful, heedful, observant, regardful; alive –, awake- to, alert; observing &c. *v.*; taken up –, occupied- with; engaged –, engrossed –, interested –, wrapped- in; absorbed, rapt; breathless; pre-occupied &c. (*inattentive*) 458; watchful &c. (*careful*) 459; intent on, open-eyed, undistracted, upon the stretch; on the watch &c. (*expectant*) 507.

steadfast.

Int. see! look, – here, – out, – alive, – you, – to it! mark! lo!

at one ear and go out at the other; forget &c. (*have no remembrance*) 506.

call off –, draw off –, call away –, divert –, distract- the -attention, – thoughts, – mind; put out of one's head; dis-concert, -compose; put out, confuse, perplex, bewilder, moider, fluster, muddle, dazzle; throw a sop to Cerberus.

Adj. inattentive; un-observant, -mindful, -heeding, -discerning; inadvertent; mind-, regard-, respect-less; listless &c. (*indifferent*) 866; blind, deaf; flighty, hand over head; cur-, percur-sory; giddy-, scatter-, hare-brained; unreflecting, *écervelé*, inconsiderate, off-hand, thoughtless, dizzy, muzzy, brainsick; giddy, – as a goose; wild, harum-scarum, rantipole, high-flying; heed-, care-less &c. (*neglectful*) 460.

absent, absent-minded, abstracted, *distrait*; lost; lost –, wrapped- in thought, woolgathering; rapt, in the clouds, bemused; dreaming –, musing- on other things; pre-occupied; engrossed &c. (*attentive*) 457; in a -reverie &c. *n.*; off one's guard &c. (*inexpectant*) 508; napping; dreamy.

disconcerted, put out &c. *v.*; rattled.

Adv. inattentively, inadvertently &c. *adj.*; *per incuriam, sub silentio.*

Int. stand -at ease, – easy!

Phr. the attention wanders; one's wits gone a -woolgathering, – bird's nesting; it never entered into one's head; the mind running on other things; one's thoughts being elsewhere; had it been a bear it would have bitten you.

---

behold! soho! hark, – ye! mind! halloo! observe! lo and behold! attention! *nota bene*; N.B.; *, †; I'd have you to know; notice! take notice! O yes! *Oyez!*

Phr. this is –, these are- to give notice.

459. Care. [Vigilance.]—**N.** care, solicitude, heed; heedfulness &c. *adj.*; scruple &c. (*conscientiousness*) 939.

watchfulness &c. *adj.*; vigilance, *surveillance*, eyes of Argus, watch, vigil, look out, watch and ward, *l'œil du maître*.

alertness &c. (*activity*) 682; attention &c. 457; prudence &c., circumspection &c. (*caution*) 864; forethought &c. 510; precaution &c. (*preparation*) 673; tidiness &c. (*order*) 58, (*cleanliness*) 652; accuracy &c. (*exactness*) 494; minuteness, attention to detail; meticulousness, nicety, circumstantiality.

V. be -careful &c. *adj.*; reck; take care &c. (*be cautious*) 864; pay attention to &c. 457; take care of; look –, see- -to, – after; keep -an eye, – a sharp eye- upon; keep -watch, – watch and ward; mount guard, set watch, watch; keep in -sight, – view; chaperon, play gooseberry; mind, – one's business.

look -sharp, – about one; look with one's own eyes; keep a -good, – sharp- look-out; have all one's -wits, – eyes- about one; watch for &c. (*expect*) 507; stand to; keep one's eyes –, have the eyes –, sleep with one eye- open.

take precautions &c. 673; protect &c. (*render safe*) 664.

do one's best &c. 682; mind one's Ps and Qs, speak by the card, pick one's steps.

Adj. care-, regard-, heed-ful; taking care &c. *v.*; particular; prudent &c. (*cautious*) 864; considerate; thoughtful &c. (*deliberative*) 451; provident &c. (*prepared*) 673; alert &c. (*active*) 682; sure-footed.

guarded, on one's guard; on the -*qui vive*, – alert, – watch, – look-out; awake, broad awake, vigilant; watch-, wake-, wist-ful; Argus-, lynx- eyed; wide awake &c. (*intelligent*) 498; on the watch for &c. (*expectant*) 507.

tidy &c. (*orderly*) 58, (*clean*) 652; accurate &c. (*exact*) 494; scrupulous

460. Neglect.—**N.** neglect; carelessness &c. *adj.*; trifling &c. *v.*; negligence; omission, laches, default; remissness, slackness, procrastination; supineness &c. (*inactivity*) 683; inattention &c. 458; *nonchalance* &c. (*insensibility*) 823; imprudence, recklessness &c. 863; slovenliness &c. (*disorder*) 59, (*dirt*) 653; improvidence &c. 674; non-completion &c. 730; inexactness &c. (*error*) 495.

paraleipsis [in rhetoric]:

trifler, slacker, waster, waiter on Providence; Micawber.

V. be -negligent &c. *adj.*; take no care of &c. (take care of &c. 459); neglect; let -slip, – go; lay –, set –, cast –, put- aside; keep –, leave- out of sight; lose sight of.

overlook, disregard; pass -over, – by; let pass; blink; wink –, connive- at; gloss over; take no -note, – notice, – thought, – account- of; pay no regard to; *laisser aller*; allow to lie on the table.

scamp; trifle, fribble; do by halves; skimp; cut; slight &c. (*despise*) 930; play –, trifle- with; slur; skim, – the surface; *effleurer*; take a cursory view of &c. 457.

slur –, slip –, skip –, jump- over; pretermit, miss, skip, jump, omit, give the go-by to, push aside, throw into the background, shelve, sink; ignore, shut one's eyes to, refuse to hear, turn a deaf ear to; leave out of one's calculation; not -attend to &c. 457, – mind; not trouble -oneself, – one's head- -with, – about; forget &c. 506; be caught napping &c. (*not expect*) 508; leave a loose thread; let the grass grow under one's feet.

render -neglectful &c. *adj.*; put –, throw- off one's guard.

Adj. neglecting &c. *v.*; unmindful, negligent, neglectful; heedless, careless, thoughtless; perfunctory, remiss, slack.

inconsiderate; un-, in-circumspect;

&c. (*conscientious*) 939; *cavendo tutus* &c. (*safe*) 664.

Adv. carefully &c. *adj.*; with care, gingerly.

Phr. *quis custodiet ipsos custodes?*

---

off one's guard; un-wary, -watchful, -guarded; offhand.

supine &c. (*inactive*) 683; inattentive &c. 458; *insouciant* &c. (*indifferent*) 823; imprudent, reckless &c. 863; slovenly &c. (*disorderly*) 59, (*dirty*) 653; inexact &c. (*erroneous*) 495; improvident &c. 674.

neglected &c. *v.*; un-heeded, -cared for, -perceived, -seen, -observed, -noticed, -noted, -marked, -attended to, -thought of, -regarded, -remarked, -missed; shunted, shelved.

un-examined, -studied, -searched, -scanned, -weighed, -sifted, -explored.

abandoned; buried in a napkin, hid under a bushel.

Adv. negligently &c. *adj.*; hand over head, anyhow; in an unguarded moment &c. (*unexpectedly*) 508; *per incuriam*.

Int. never mind, no matter, let it pass; it will be all the same a hundred years hence.

461. Inquiry. [Subject of Inquiry. Question.]—**N.** inquiry; request &c. 765; search, research, quest; pursuit &c. 622.

examination, review, scrutiny, investigation, indagation; per-quisition, -scrutation, -vestigation; inqu-est, -isition; exploration; *exploitation*, ventilation.

sifting; calculation, analysis, dissection, resolution, induction; Baconian method.

strict –, close –, searching –, exhaustive- inquiry; narrow –, strict- search; study &c. (*consideration*) 451.

scire facias, ad referendum; trial.

questioning &c. *v.*; interroga-tion, -tory; third degree; interpellation; challenge, examination, cross-examination, catechism; feeler, Socratic method, zetetic philosophy; leading question; discussion &c. (*reasoning*) 476; questionnaire, questionary.

reconnoitering, *reconnaissance*; prying &c. *v.*; espionage, *espionnage*; domiciliary visit, peep behind the curtain; lantern of Diogenes.

question, query, problem, *desideratum*, point to be solved, porism; subject –, field- of -inquiry, – controversy; point –, matter- in dispute; moot-point; issue, question at issue; bone of contention &c. (*discord*) 713; plain –, fair –, open- question; enigma &c. (*secret*) 533; knotty point &c. (*difficulty*) 704; *quodlibet*; threshold of an inquiry.

inquirer, investigator, experimenter, inquisitor, inspector, querist,

462. Answer.—**N.** answer, response, reply, replication, *riposte*, rejoinder, surrejoinder, rebutter, surrebutter, counter-evidence &c. 468, counter-charge, defence, plea; retort, repartee; contradiction &c. 536; rescript, -ion; antiphon, -y; acknowledgment; pass-word; echo.

discovery &c. 480*a*; solution &c. (*explanation*) 522; rationale &c. (*cause*) 153; clue &c. (*indication*) 550.

Œdipus; oracle &c. 513; return &c. (*record*) 551.

V. answer, respond, reply, rebut, retort, rejoin; give –, return- answer; acknowledge, echo.

explain &c. (*interpret*) 522; solve &c. (*unriddle*) 522; discover &c. 480*a*; fathom, hunt out &c. (*inquire*) 461; satisfy, set at rest, determine.

Adj. answering &c. *v.*; respon-sive, -dent; oracular; antiphonal; conclusive.

Adv. because &c. (*cause*) 153; on the -scent, – right scent.

Int. *eureka!*

---

examiner, catechist; scrut-ator, -ineer; analyst; quidnunc &c. (*curiosity*) 455.

V. make -inquiry &c. *n.*; inquire, seek, search, frisk, speer, look -for, – about for – out for; scan, reconnoitre, explore, sound, rummage, ransack, pry, peer, look round; look –, go- -over, – through; spy, over-haul.

scratch the head, slap the forehead.

look –, peer–, pry- into every hole and corner; look behind the scenes; trace up; hunt –, fish –, dig –, ferret-out; unearth; leave no stone unturned.

seek a -clue, – clew; hunt, track, trail, shadow, mouse, dodge, trace; follow the -trail, – scent; pursue &c. 622; beat up one's quarters; fish for; feel for &c. (*experiment*) 463.

investigate; take up –, institute –, pursue –, follow up –, conduct –, carry on –, prosecute- -an inquiry &c. *n.*; look -at, – into; pre-examine; discuss, canvass, agitate.

examine, study, consider, calculate; dip –, dive –, delve –, go deep- into; make sure of, probe, sound, fathom; probe to the -bottom, – quick; scrutinize, analyze, anatomize, dissect, parse, resolve, sift, winnow; view –, try- in all its phases; thresh out.

bring in question, subject to examination; put to the proof &c. (*experiment*) 463; audit, tax, pass in review; take into consideration &c. (*think over*) 451; take counsel &c. 695.

ask, question, demand; put –, pop –, propose –, propound –, moot –, start –, raise –, stir –. suggest –, put forth –, ventilate –, grapple with –, go into- a question.

put to the question, interrogate, catechize, pump, grill; cross-question, -examine; dodge; require an answer; pick –, suck- the brains of; feel the pulse.

be -in question &c. *adj.*; undergo examination.

Adj. inquiring &c. *v.*; inquisitive &c. (*curious*) 455; requisit-ive, -ory; catechetical, inquisitorial, analytic; in -search, – quest- of; on the look-out for, interrogative, zetetic; all-searching.

un-determined, -tried, -decided; in -question, – dispute, – issue, – course of inquiry; under -discussion, – consideration, – investigation &c. *n.*, *sub judice*, moot, proposed; doubtful &c. (*uncertain*) 475.

Adv. what? why? wherefore? whence? whither? where? *quære?* how -comes, – happens, – is- it? what is the reason? what's -the matter, – up, – in the wind? what on earth? when? who?

463. Experiment.—N. experiment; essay &c. (*attempt*) 675; research &c. (*investigation*) 461; trial, tentative method, *tâtonnement.*

verification, probation, *experimentum crucis*, proof, criterion, diagnostic, test, tryout, crucial test, acid test.

crucible, reagent, check, touchstone, pix; assay, ordeal; ring.

empiricism, rule of theumb.

feeler; pilot –, messenger- balloon, *balloon d'essai*; pilot engine; scout; straw to show the wind.

speculation, random shot, leap in the dark.

analy-zer, -st; adventurer, explorer, sourdough, prospector; experiment-er, -ist, -alist; assayer.

V. experiment; essay &c. (*endeavour*) 675; try, assay, sample; make –an experiment, – trial of; give a trial to; put upon –, subject to– trial; experiment upon; rehearse; put –, bring –, submit- to the -test, – proof; prove, verify, test, touch, practise upon, try one's strength.

grope; feel –, grope- -for, – one's way; fumble; *tâtonner, aller à tâtons*; put –, throw- out a feeler; send up a pilot balloon; see how the -land lies, – wind blows; consult the barometer; feel the pulse; fish –, bob- for; cast –, beat- about for; angle, trawl, cast one's net, beat the bushes.

venture, try one's fortune &c. (*adventure*) 675; explore &c. (*inquire*) 461.

Adj. experimental; probat-ive, -ory, -ionary; analytic, docimastic; tentative; empirical; speculative.

under probation, on one's trial, on trial, on approval.

464. Comparison.—**N.** comparison, collation, contrast; identification.

sim-ile, -ilitude; allegory &c. (*metaphor*) 521.

V. compare -to, – with; collate, confront; place side by side &c. (*near*) 197; set –, pit- against one another; contrast, balance.

identify, draw a parallel, parallel.

compare notes; institute a comparison; *parva componere magnis.*

Adj. comparative, relative; metaphorical &c. 521.

compared with &c. *v.*; comparable.

Adv. relatively &c. (*relation*) 9; as compared with &c. *v.*

465. Discrimination.—**N.** discrimination, distinction, differentiation, diagnosis, diorism; nice perception; perception –, appreciation- of difference; acuteness; estimation &c. 466; nicety, refinement; taste &c. 850; *critique*, judgement, tact; insight, discernment &c. (*intelligence*) 498; *nuances*.

V. discriminate, distinguish, differentiate, severalize; separate; draw the line, sift; separate –, winnow- the chaff from the wheat; split hairs.

estimate &c. (*measure*) 466; know -which is which, – one's stuff, – one's way about, – what is what, – 'a hawk from a handsaw.'

take into -account, – consideration; give –, allow- due weight to; weigh carefully.

Adj. discriminating &c. *v.*; dioristic, discriminative, critical, distinctive; nice.

Phr. *il y a fagots et fagots*; *rem acu tetigisti.*

465a. Indiscrimination.—**N.** indiscrimination; promiscuity; indistinctness, -ion; uncertainty &c. (*doubt*) 475; obtuseness.

V. not -indiscriminate &c. 465; overlook &c. (*neglect*) 460- a distinction; con-found, -fuse, jumble; swallow whole.

Adj. indiscriminate, undiscriminating, promiscuous; undistinguish-ed, -able, -ing; unmeasured.

466. Measurement.—**N.** measurement, admeasurement, mensuration, survey, valuation, appraisement, assessment, assize; estim-ate, -ation; dead reckoning; reckoning &c. (*numeration*) 85; gauging &c. *v.*

metrology, weights and measures, compound arithmetic.

measure, yard measure, standard, rule, foot-rule, chain, tape, staff, compass, callipers; dividers; gage, gauge, planimeter; meter, line, rod, check.

volt, kilowatt, ampere, candle power; horse power; axle load; foot pound.

flood –, high water- mark; Plimsoll mark; index &c. 550.

scale; gradu-ation, -ated scale; nonius; vernier &c. (*minuteness*) 193; pedo (*length*)- 200, sounding line &c. (*depth*)- 208, thermo (*heat* &c. 389)-, baro (*air* &c. 338)-, dynamo (*power*)- 276, anemo (*wind* 349)-, gonio (*angle* 244)- meter; landmark &c. (*limit*) 233; balance &c. (*weight*) 319; optical instruments &c. 445.

co-ordinates, ordinate and abscissa, polar co-ordinates, latitude and longitude, declination and right ascension, altitude and azimuth.

geo-, stereo-, hypso-metry; metage; surveying, land surveying; geo-desy, -detics, -desia; ortho-, alti-metry; *cadastre.*

astrolabe, armillary sphere.

land, -surveyor; geometer, topographer, cartographer, hydrographer.

V. measure, meter, mete; value, assess, rate, appraise, estimate, form an estimate, set a value on; appreciate; standardize.

span, pace, step; apply the -compass &c. *n.*; gauge, plumb, probe, calliper, sound, fathom &c. 208; heave the -log, – lead; weigh &c. 319; survey.

take an average &c. 29; graduate.

Adj. measuring &c. *v.*; metric, -al; measurable; geodetical, cadastral, topographical.

Section III. Materials for Reasoning

467. Evidence [on one side.]—**N.** evidence; facts, premises, *data*, *præcognita*, grounds.

indication &c. 550; criterion &c. (*test*) 463.

testi-mony, -fication; attestation; deposition &c. (*affirmation*) 535; examination.

admission &c. (*assent*) 488; authority, warrant, credential, diploma, voucher, certificate, docket; record &c. 551; document, muniments; *pièce justificative*; deed, warranty &c. (*security*) 771; signature, seal &c. (*identification*) 550; exhibit, citation, reference.

witness, indicator; eye-, ear-witness; deponent; sponsor.

oral –, documentary –, hearsay –, external –, extrinsic –, internal –, intrinsic –, circumstantial –, cumulative –, *ex parte* –, presumptive –, collateral –, constructive- evidence; proof &c. (*demonstration*) 478; evidence in chief; finger prints, dactylogram.

secondary evidence; confirmation, corroboration, adminicle, support; ratification &c. (*assent*) 488; authentication, verification; compurgation, wager of law, comprobation.

citation, reference.

V. be -evidence &c. *n.*; evince, show, betoken, tell of; indicate &c. (*denote*) 550; imply, involve, argue, bespeak, breathe.

have –, carry- weight; tell, speak

468. [Evidence on the other side, on the other hand.] **Counter-evidence.**—**N.** counter-evidence; evidence on the other -side, – hand; disproof; refutation &c. 479; negation &c. 536; conflicting evidence.

plea &c. 617; vindication &c. 937; counter-protest; *tu quoque* argument; other side –, reverse- of the shield.

V. countervail, oppose; run counter; rebut &c. (*refute*) 479; subvert &c. (*destroy*) 162; check, weaken; contravene; contradict &c. (*deny*) 536; tell another story, turn the -tables, – scale; alter the case; cut both ways; prove a negative.

audire alteram partem.

Adj. countervailing &c. *v.*; contradictory, in rebuttal.

un-attested, -authenticated, -supported by evidence; supposititious, trumped up.

Adv. *per contra*, conversely, on the other hand.

469. Qualification.—**N.** qualification, limitation, modification, colouring.

allowance, grains of allowance, consideration, extenuating circumstances.

condition, proviso, exception; exemption; salvo, saving clause; discount &c. 813.

V. qualify, limit, modify, affect, temper, leaven, give a colour to, introduce new conditions.

allow –, make allowance- for; ad-

volumes; speak for itself &c. (*manifest*) 525.

rest –, depend- upon; repose on.

bear -witness &c. *n.*; give -evidence &c. *n.*; testify, depose, witness, vouch for; sign, seal, undersign, set one's hand and seal, sign and seal, deliver as one's act and deed, certify, attest; acknowledge &c. (*assent*) 488.

make absolute, confirm, ratify, corroborate, endorse, countersign, support, bear out, vindicate, uphold, warrant.

adduce, attest, cite, quote; refer –, appeal- to; call, – to witness; bring -forward, – into court; allege, plead; produce –, confront- witnesses; collect –, bring together –, rake up- evidence.

have –, make out- a case; establish, circumstantiate, authenticate, substantiate, verify, make good, quote chapter and verse; bring -home to, – to book.

Adj. showing &c. *v.*; evidential, indica-tive, -tory; deducible &c. 478; grounded –, founded –, based- on; first hand, authentic, verifiable; corroborative, confirmatory; significant, conclusive.

Adv. by inference; according to, witness, *a fortiori*; still -more, – less; *raison de plus*; in corroboration &c. *n.* of; *valeat quantum*; under -seal, – one's hand and seal.

mit exceptions, take into account; take exception, object.

Adj. qualifying &c. *v.*; conditional; extenuatory; exceptional &c. (*unconformable*) 83.

hypothetical &c. (*supposed*) 514; contingent &c. (*uncertain*) 475.

Adv. provided, – always; if, unless, but, yet; according as; conditionally, admitting, supposing; on the supposition of &c. (*theoretically*) 514; with the understanding, even, although, though, for all that, after all, at all events.

with grains of allowance, *cum grano salis*; *exceptis excipiendis*; wind and weather permitting; if possible &c. 470.

subject to; with this -proviso &c. *n.*

Degrees of Evidence

470. Possibility.—N. possibility, potentiality; what -may be, – is possible &c. *adj.*; compatibility &c. (*agreement*) 23.

practicability, feasibility; practicableness &c. *adj.*

contingency, chance &c. 156.

V. be -possible &c. *adj.*; stand a chance, have a leg to stand on; admit of, bear.

render -possible &c. *adj.*; put in the way of.

Adj. possible; on the -cards, – dice; *in posse*, within the bounds of possibility, conceivable, credible, imaginable; compatible &c. 23.

practicable, feasible, workable, performable, achievable; within -reach, – measurable distance; accessible, superable, surmountable; at-, ob-tainable; contingent &c. (*doubtful*) 475.

Adv. possibly, by possibility; perhaps, -chance, -adventure; may be, haply, mayhap.

471. Impossibility.—N. impossibility &c. *adj.*; what -cannot, – can never- be; sour grapes; infeasibility, impracticability, hopelessness &c. 859.

V. be -impossible &c. *adj.*; have no chance whatever.

attempt impossibilities; square the circle; discover the -philosopher's stone, – elixir of life, – secret of perpetual motion; wash a blackamoor white; skin a flint; make -a silk purse out of a sow's ear, – bricks without straw; have nothing to go upon; weave a rope of sand, build castles in the air, *prendre la lune avec les dents*, extract sunbeams from cucumbers, set the Thames on fire, milk a he-goat into a sieve, catch a weasel asleep, *rompre l'anguille au genou*, be in two places at once.

Adj. impossible; not -possible &c. 470; absurd, contrary to reason; unlikely, at variance with facts; unreasonable &c. 477; incredible &c. 485; beyond the bounds of -reason, – possi-

if possible, wind and weather permitting, God willing, *Deo volente*, D.V.

---

bility; from which reason recoils; visionary; inconceivable &c. (*improbable*) 473; prodigious &c. (*wonderful*) 870; un-, in-imaginable, unthinkable, not a Chinaman's chance.

impracticable, unachievable; un-, in-feasible; insuperable; un-, in-surmountable; unat-, unob-tainable; out of -reach, – the question; not to be -had, – thought of; beyond control; desperate &c. (*hopeless*) 859; incompatible &c. 24; inaccessible, uncomeatable, impassable impervious, innavigable, inextricable.

out of –, beyond- one's -power, – depth, – reach, – grasp; too much for; *ultra crepidam.*

Phr. the grapes are sour; *non possumus*; *non nostrum tantas componere lites.*

472. Probability. — **N.** probability, likelihood; likeliness &c. *adj.*

vraisemblance, verisimilitude, plausibility; colour, semblance, show of; presumption; presumptive –, circumstantial- evidence; credibility.

reasonable –, fair –, good –, favourable- -chance, – prospect; prospect, well-grounded hope; chance &c. 156.

V. be -probable &c. *adj.*; give –, lend- colour to; point to; imply &c. (*evidence*) 467; bid fair &c. (*promise*) 511; stand fair for; stand –, run- a good chance.

presume, infer, suppose, take for granted.

think likely, dare say, flatter oneself; expect &c. 507; count upon &c. (*believe*) 484.

Adj. probable, likely, hopeful, to be expected, in a fair way.

plausible, specious, ostensible, colourable, *ben trovato*, well-founded, reasonable, credible, easy of belief, presumable, presumptive, apparent.

Adv. probably &c. *adj.*; belike; in all -probability, – likelihood; very –, most- likely; as likely as not; like enough; ten &c. to one; apparently, seemingly, according to every reasonable expectation; *primâ facie*; to all appearance &c. (*to the eye*) 448.

Phr. the -chances, – odds- are; appearances –, chances- are in favour of; there is reason to -believe, – think, – expect; I dare say; all Lombard Street to a China orange.

473. Improbability.—**N.** improbability, unlikelihood; unfavourable –, bad –, little –, small–, poor –, scarcely any –, no –, not a ghost of a– chance; bare possibility; long odds; incredibility &c. 485.

V. be -improbable &c. *adj.*; have a -small chance &c. *n.*

Adj. improbable, unlikely, contrary to all reasonable expectation, implausible.

rare &c. (*infrequent*) 137; unheard of, inconceivable; un-, in-imaginable; incredible &c. 485; more than doubtful.

Int. not likely! no fear!

Phr. the chances are against.

---

474. Certainty.—**N.** certainty; necessity &c. 601; certitude, certainness, surety, assurance, sureness; dead –, moral– certainty; infallibleness &c. *adj.*; infallibility, reliability.

gospel, scripture, church, pope, court of final appeal; *res judicato*, *ultimatum.*

positiveness; dogmat-ism, -ist, -izer; *doctrinaire*, know-all, bigot, -ry; opin-

475. Uncertainty.—**N.** uncertainty, incertitude, doubt; doubtfulness &c. *adj.*; dubi-ety, -tation, -tancy, -ousness.

hesitation, suspense; perplexity, embarrassment, dilemma, quandary, Morton's fork, bewilderment; timidity &c. (*fear*) 860; indecision, vacillation &c. 605; *diaporesis*, indetermination.

vagueness &c. *adj.*; haze, fog; ob-

ionist, Sir Oracle; *ipse dixit*; zealot.

fact; positive –, matter of- fact; *fait accompli.*

V. be -certain &c. *adj.*; stand to reason.

render -certain &c. *adj.*; in-, en-, assure; clinch, make sure; determine, decide, set at rest, 'make assurance double sure'; know &c. (*believe*) 484; dismiss all doubt.

dogmatize, lay down the law.

Adj. certain, sure; assured &c. *v.*; solid, well-founded.

unqualified, absolute, positive, determinate, definite, clear, unequivocal, categorical, unmistakable, decisive, decided, ascertained.

inevitable, unavoidable, ineluctable, avoidless.

unerring, infallible; unchangeable &c. 150; to be depended on, trustworthy, reliable, bound.

un-impeachable, -deniable, -questionable; in-disputable, -contestable, -controvertible, -defeasible, -dubitable; irrefutable &c. (*proven*) 478; conclusive, without power of appeal, final.

indubious; without –, beyond a –, without a shade or shadow of- -doubt – question; past dispute; beyond all -question, – dispute; un-doubted, -contested, -questioned, -disputed; question-, doubt-less.

bigoted, fanatical, dogmatic, opinionat-ed, -ive, *doctrinaire.*

authoritative, authentic, official.

sure as -fate, – death and taxes, – a gun.

evident, self-evident, axiomatic; clear, – as day, – as the sun at noonday; obvious.

Adv. certainly &c. *adj.*; for certain, certes, sure, no doubt, doubtless, and no mistake, *flagrante delicto*, sure enough, to be sure, of course, as a matter of course, *à coup sur*, to a certainty, undoubtedly; in truth &c. (*truly*) 494; at -any rate, – all events; without fail; *coûte que coûte*; whatever may happen, if the worst come to the worst; come –, happen- what -may, – will; sink or swim; rain or shine.

Phr. *cela va sans dire*; there is -no question, – not a shadow of doubt; scurity &c. (*darkness*) 421; ambiguity &c. (*double meaning*) 520; contingency, double contingency, possibility upon a possibility; conjecture; open question &c. (*question*) 461; *onus probandi*; blind bargain, pig in a poke, leap in the dark, something or other; needle in a bottle of hay; roving commission.

fallibility, unreliability, untrustworthiness, precariousness.

V. be -uncertain &c. *adj.*; wonder whether.

lose the -clue, – clew, – scent; miss one's way.

not know -what to make of &c. (*unintelligibility*) 519, – which way to turn, – whether one stands on one's head or one's heels; float in a sea of doubt, hesitate, flounder; lose -oneself, – one's head, – one's way, wander aimlessly; muddle one's brains.

render -uncertain &c. *adj.*; put out, pose, puzzle, perplex, embarrass; confuse, -found; bewilder, mystify, bother, moider, nonplus, addle the wits, throw off the scent; *spargere voces in vulgum ambiguas*; keep in suspense.

doubt &c. (*disbelieve*) 485; hang –, tremble- in the balance; depend.

Adj. uncertain; casual; random &c. (*aimless*) 621; changeable &c. 149.

doubtful, dubious; indecisive; unsettled, -decided, -determined; in suspense, open to discussion; controvertible; in question &c. (*inquiry*) 461; insecure, unstable.

vague; in-determinate, -definite; ambiguous, equivocal; undefin-ed, -able; confused &c. (*indistinct*) 447; mystic, mysterious, veiled, obscure, cryptic, oracular.

perplexing &c. *v.*; enigmatic, paradoxical, apocryphal, problematical, hypothetical; experimental &c. 463.

fallible, questionable, precarious, slippery, ticklish, debatable, disputable; un-reliable, -trustworthy.

contingent, – on, dependent on; subject to; dependent on circumstances; occasional; provisional.

unauth-entic, -enticated, -oritative; un-ascertained, -confirmed; undemonstrated; un-told, -counted.

in a -state of uncertainty, – cloud,

the die is cast &c. (*necessity*) 601.

– maze; ignorant &c. 491; on the horns of a dilemma; afraid to say; out of one's reckoning, astray, adrift; at -sea, – fault, – a loss, – one's wit's end, – a *nonplus*; puzzled &c. *v.*; lost, abroad, *désorienté*; dis-tracted, -traught.

Adv. *pendente lite*; *sub spe rati.*

Phr. Heaven knows; who can tell? who shall decide when doctors disagree?

Section IV. Reasoning Processes

476. Reasoning. — **N.** reasoning; ratio-cination, -nalism; dialectics, induction, generalization.

discussion, comment; ventilation; inquiry &c. 461.

argumentation, controversy, debate; polemics, wrangling; contention &c. 720; logomachy; dis-putation, -ceptation; paper war.

art of reasoning, logic.

process –, train –, chain- of reasoning; de-, in-duction; synthesis, analysis.

argument; case, plea, *plaidoyer*, opening; *lemma*, proposition, terms, premises, postulate, *data*, starting point, principle; inference &c. (*judgment*) 480.

pro-, syllogism; enthymeme, sorites, dilemma, *perilepsis*, *a priori* reasoning, *reductio ad absurdum*, horns of a dilemma, *argumentum ad hominem*, comprehensive argument.

reasoner, logician, dialectician; disputant; controver-sialist, -tist; wrangler, arguer, debater, polemic, casuist, rationalist; scientist.

logical sequence; good case; correct –, just –, sound –, valid –, cogent –, logical –, forcible –, persuasive –, persuasory –, consectary –, conclusive &c. 478 –, subtle- reasoning; force of argument; strong -point, – argument.

arguments, reasons, pros and cons.

V. reason, argue, discuss, debate, dispute, wrangle; bandy -words, – arguments; chop logic; hold –, carry on- an argument; controvert &c. (*deny*) 536; canvass; comment –, moralize- upon; consider &c. (*examine*) 461.

open a -discussion, – case; join –, be at- issue; moot; come to the point; stir –, agitate –, ventilate –, torture- a question; try conclusions; take up a -side, – case.

477. [The absence of reasoning.] **Intuition.** [False or vicious reasoning; show of reason.] **Sophistry.**—**N.** intuition, instinct, association; presentiment; rule of thumb.

sophistry, paralogy, perversion, casuistry, jesuitry, equivocation, evasion, mental reservation; chicane, -ry; quiddit, quiddity; mystification; special pleading; speciousness &c. *adj.*; nonsense &c. 497; word-, tongue-fence.

false –, vicious- reasoning; *petitio principii*, *ignoratio elenchi*; *post hoc ergo propter hoc*; *non sequitur*, *ignotum per ignotius*.

misjudgment &c. 481; false teaching &c. 538.

sophism, solecism, paralogism; quibble, quirk, *elenchus*, elench, fallacy, *quodlibet*, subterfuge, subtlety, quillet; inconsistency, antilogy; 'a mockery, a delusion and a snare'; claptrap, mere words; 'lame and impotent conclusion.'

meshes –, cobwebs- of sophistry; flaw in an argument; weak point, bad case.

over-refinement; hair-splitting &c. *v.*

sophist, casuist, paralogist.

V. judge -intuitively, – by intuition; hazard a proposition, talk at random.

reason -ill, – falsely &c. *adj.*; paralogize; misjudge &c. 481.

pervert, quibble; equivocate, mystify, evade, elude; gloss over, varnish; misteach &c. 538; mislead &c. (*error*) 495; cavil, refine, subtilize, split hairs; misrepresent &c. (*lie*) 544.

beg the question, reason in a circle, cut blocks with a razor, beat about the bush, play fast and loose, blow hot and cold, prove that black is white and white black, travel out of the record, *parler à tort et à travers*, put oneself out of court, not have a leg to stand on.

Adj. intuitive, instinctive, impulsive;

contend, take one's stand upon, insist, lay stress on; infer &c. 480.

follow from &c. (*demonstration*) 478.

Adj. rational; reasoning &c. *v.*; rationalistic; argumentative, controversial, dialectic, polemical; discursory, -ive; disputatious.

debatable, controvertible.

logical; in-, de-ductive; synthetic, analytic; relevant &c. 23.

Adv. for, because, hence, whence, seeing that, since, sith, then, thence, so; for -that, – this, – which- reason; for-, inasmuch as; whereas, *ex concesso*, considering, in consideration of; there-, where-fore; consequently, *ergo*, thus, accordingly; *a fortiori*.

in -conclusion, – fine; finally, after all, *au bout du compte*, on the whole, taking one thing with another.

rationally &c. *adj.*

independent of –, anterior to- reason; gratuitous, hazarded; unconnected.

unreasonable, illogical, false, unsound, invalid; unwarranted, not following; inconsequent, -ial; inconsistent, incongruous; abson-ous, -ant; unscientific; untenable, inconclusive, incorrect; fall-acious, -ible; groundless, unproved.

deceptive, sophistical, sophisticated, casuistical, jesuitical; illus-ive, -ory; specious, hollow, plausible, *ad captandum*, evasive; irrelevant &c. 10.

weak, feeble, poor, flimsy, loose, vague, irrational; nonsensical &c. (*absurd*) 497; foolish &c. (*imbecile*) 499; frivolous, pettifogging, quibbling; fine-spun, over-refined.

at the end of one's tether, *au bout de son latin.*

Adv. intuitively &c. *adj.*; by intuition; illogically &c. *adj.*

Phr. *non constat*; that goes for nothing.

---

478. Demonstration.—N. demonstration, proof; conclusiveness &c. *adj.*; *apodixis*, probation, comprobation.

logic of facts &c. (*evidence*) 467; *experimentum crucis* &c. (*test*) 463; argument &c. 476; irrefragability.

V. demonstrate, prove, establish, make good; show; evince &c. (*be evidence of*) 467; verify &c. 467; settle the question, reduce to demonstration, set the question at rest.

make out, – a case; prove one's point, have the best of the argument; draw a conclusion &c. (*judge*) 480.

follow, – of course; stand to reason; hold -good, – water.

Adj. demonstra-ting &c. *v.*, -tive, -ble; probative, unanswerable, conclusive; apodictic, -al; irre-sistible, -futable, -fragable, undeniable.

categorical, decisive, crucial.

demonstrated &c. *v.*; proven; unconfuted, -answered, -refuted; evident &c. 474.

deducible, consequential, consectary, inferential, following.

Adv. of course, in consequence, consequently, as a matter of course.

Phr. *probatum est*; there is nothing more to be said, Q.E.D., it must follow.

479. Confutation.—N. con-, re-futation; answer, complete answer; disproof, conviction, redargution, invalidation; expos-ure, -ition; clincher; retort; *reductio ad absurdum*; knock down –, *tu quoque*- argument.

V. con-, re-fute; parry, negative, disprove, redargue, expose, show the fallacy of, rebut, defeat; demolish &c. (*destroy*) 162; over-throw, -turn; scatter to the winds, explode, invalidate; silence; put –, reduce- to silence; clinch -an argument, – a question; give one a set down, stop the mouth, shut up; have, – on the hip; get the better of; confound, convince.

not leave a leg to stand on, cut the ground from under one's feet.

be confuted &c.; fail; expose –, show- one's weak point.

Adj. confut-ing, -ed &c. *v.*; capable of refutation; re-, con-futable.

condemned -on one's own showing, – out of one's own mouth.

Phr. the argument falls to the ground, *cadit quæstio*, it does not hold water, '*suo sibi gladio hunc jugulo.*'

Section V. Results of Reasoning

480. Judgement. [Conclusion.]—**N.** result, conclusion, upshot; deduction, inference, ergotism, illation; corollary, porism; moral.

estimation, valuation, appreciation, judication; di-, ad-judication; arbitrament, -ement, -ation; assessment, ponderation.

award, estimate; review, criticism, *critique*, notice, report.

decision, determination, judgment, finding, verdict, sentence, decree, – nisi, – absolute, – interlocutory; *dictum*; *res judicata*.

plébiscite, referendum, voice, casting vote; vote &c. (*choice*) 609; opinion &c. (*belief*) 484; good judgment &c. (*wisdom*) 498.

judge, jurist, umpire; arbi-ter, -trator; assessor, referee; censor, reviewer, critic; *connoisseur*; commentator &c. 524; inspector, inspecting officer.

V. judge, conclude; come to –, draw –, arrive at- a conclusion; ascertain, determine, make up one's mind.

deduce, derive, gather, collect, draw an inference, make a deduction, weet, ween.

form an estimate, estimate, size up, appreciate, value, count, assess, rate, rank, account; regard, consider, think of; look upon &c. (*believe*) 484.

settle; pass –, give- an opinion; decide, try, pronounce, rule; pass -judgment, – sentence; sentence, doom; find; give –, deliver- judgment; adjud-ge, -icate; arbitrate, award, report; bring in a verdict; make absolute, set a question at rest; confirm &c. (*assent*) 488.

comment, criticize; review, pass under review &c. (*examine*) 457; investigate &c. (*inquire*) 461.

hold the scales, sit in judgment; try –, hear- a cause.

Adj. judging &c. *v.*; judicious &c. (*wise*) 498; determinate, conclusive, censorious, critical &c. 932.

Adv. on the whole, all things considered.

481. Misjudgment. — **N.** misjudgment, obliquity of –, warped- judgment; mis-calculation, -computation, -conception &c. (*error*) 495; hasty conclusion.

prejud-gment, -ication, -ice; foregone conclusion; pre-notion, -vention, -conception, -dilection, -possession, -apprehension, -sumption, -sentiment; fixed –, preconceived- idea; *idée fixe*; *mentis gratissimus error*; fool's paradise.

esprit de corps, party spirit, race –, class- prejudice, partisanship, clannishness, *prestige*.

bias, warp, twist; hobby, fad, whim, craze, quirk, crotchet, partiality, infatuation, blind side, mote in the eye.

one-sided –, partial –, narrow –, confined –, superficial- -views, – ideas, – conceptions, – notions; narrow mind; bigotry &c. (*obstinacy*) 606; *odium theologicum*; pedantry; hypercriticism.

doctrinaire &c. (*positive*) 474.

V. mis-judge, -estimate, -think, -conjecture, -conceive &c. (*error*) 495; fly in the face of facts; mis-calculate, -reckon, -compute.

overestimate &c. 482; underestimate &c. 483.

pre-, fore-judge; pre-suppose, -sume, -judicate; dogmatize; have a -bias &c. *n.*; have only one idea; *jurare in verba magistri*, run away with the notion; jump –, rush- to a conclusion; look only at one side of the shield; view -with jaundiced eye, – through distorting spectacles; not see beyond one's nose; *dare pondus fumo*; get the wrong sow by the ear &c. (*blunder*) 699.

give a -bias, – twist; bias, warp, twist; pre-judice, -possess.

Adj. misjudging &c. *v.*; ill-judging, wrong-headed; prejudiced, prejudicial, &c. *v.*; jaundiced; short-sighted, purblind; partial, one-sided, superficial.

narrow-minded; confined, insular, provincial, parochial, illiberal, intolerant, narrow, besotted, infatuated, fanatical, cracked, warped, *entêté*, positive, dogmatic, dictatorial; conceited; opin-, opini-ative; opinion-ed, -ate, -ative, -ated; self-opinioned, wedded to an opinion, *opiniâtre*; bigoted &c. (*obstinate*) 606; crotchety, fussy, impracticable; unreason-able, -ing; stupid &c. 499; credulous &c. 486.

misjudged &c. *v.*

Adv. *ex parte.*

Phr. nothing like leather; the wish the father to the thought.

480a. [Result of search or inquiry.] **Discovery.—N.** discovery, invention, detection, disenchantment, disclosure, find, ascertainment, revelation.

trover &c. 775.

V. discover, find, determine, evolve; fix upon; find –, trace –, make –, hunt –, fish –, worm –, ferret –, root- out; fathom; bring –, draw- out; educe, elicit, bring to light, invent; dig –, grub –, fish- up; unearth, disinter.

solve, resolve; un-riddle, -ravel, -lock; pick –, open- the lock; find a -clue, – clew- to; interpret &c. 522; disclose &c. 529.

trace, get at; hit it, have it; lay one's -finger, – hands- upon; spot; get –, arrive- at the -truth &c. 494; put the saddle on the right horse, hit the right nail on the head.

be near the truth. burn; smoke, scent, sniff, smell a rat.

open the eyes to; see -through, – daylight, – in its true colours, – the cloven foot; detect; catch, – tripping.

pitch –, fall –, light –, hit –, stumble –, pop- upon; come across; meet –, fall in- with.

recognize, realize, verify, make certain of, identify.

Int. *eureka!*

482. Overestimation.—N. overestimation &c. *v.*; exaggeration &c. 549; vanity &c. 880; optim-, pessim-ism, -ist; megalomania.

much -cry and little wool, – ado about nothing; storm in a teacup; fine talking, rodomontade, gush, hot air, gas, bombast.

egotism &c. 880; boasting &c. 884.

V. over-estimate, -rate, -value, -prize, -weigh, -reckon, -strain, -praise; estimate too highly, attach too much importance to, make mountains of molehills, catch at straws; strain, magnify; exaggerate &c. 549; set too high a value upon; think –, make- -much, – too much- of; outreckon.

extol, – to the skies; make the -most, – best, – worst- of, eulogize, panegyrize, gush, puff, boost; make two bites of a cherry.

have too high an opinion of oneself &c. (*vanity*) 880.

Adj. overestimated &c. *v.*; oversensitive &c. (*sensibility*) 822; inflated, puffed up, exaggerated &c. 549.

Phr. all his geese are swans; *parturiunt montes.*

483. Underestimation.—N. underestimation; depreciation &c. (*detraction*) 934; pessim-ism, -ist; undervaluing &c. *v.*; modesty &c. 881.

V. under-rate, -estimate, -value, -reckon; depreciate; disparage &c. (*detract*) 934; not do justice to; mis-, dis-prize; ridicule &c. 856; slight &c. (*despise*) 930; neglect &c. 460; slur over, under-state.

make -light, – little, – nothing, – no account- of; minimize, belittle, run down, think nothing of; set -no store by, – at naught; shake off as dewdrops from the lion's mane.

Adj. depreciat-ing, -ed, -ive, -ory, &c. *v.*; un-appreciated, -valued, -prized; pejorative.

484. Belief.—**N.** belief; credence; credit; assurance; faith, trust, troth, confidence, presumption, sanguine expectation &c. (*hope*) 858; dependence on, reliance on.

persuasion, conviction, convincement, plerophory, self-conviction; certainty &c. 474; opinion, mind, view; conception, thinking; impression &c. (*idea*) 453; surmise &c. 514; conclusion &c. (*judgment*) 480.

tenet, dogma, principle, way of thinking; popular belief &c. (*assent*) 488.

firm –, implicit –, settled –, fixed –, rooted –, deep-rooted –, staunch –, unshaken –, steadfast –, inveterate –, calm –, sober –, dispassionate –, impartial –, well-founded- -belief, – opinion &c.; *uberrima fides*.

system of opinions, school, doctrine, articles, canons; declaration –, profession- of faith; tenets, *credenda*, creed; thirty-nine articles &c. (*orthodoxy*) 983*a*; catechism; assent &c. 488; *propaganda* &c. (*teaching*) 537.

credibility &c. (*probability*) 472.

V. believe, credit; give -faith, – credit, – credence- to; see, realize; assume, receive; set down –, take- for; have –, take- it; consider, esteem, presume.

count –, depend –, calculate –, pin one's faith –, reckon –, lean –, build –, rely –, rest- upon; lay one's account for; make sure of.

make oneself easy -about, – on that score; take on -trust, – credit; take for -granted, –gospel; allow –, attach- some weight to.

know, – for certain; have –, make- no doubt; doubt not; be – rest- -assured &c. *adj.*; persuade –, assure –, satisfy- oneself; make up one's mind.

give one credit for; confide –, believe –, put one's trust- in; place –, repose- implicit confidence in; take -one's word for, – at one's word; place reliance on, rely upon, swear by, pay regard to.

think, hold; take, – it; opine, be of opinion, conceive, trow, ween, fancy, apprehend; have –, hold –, possess –, entertain –, adopt –, imbibe –, embrace

485. Unbelief. Doubt.—**N.** un-, dis-, mis-belief; discredit, miscreance; infidelity &c. (*irreligion*) 989; dissent &c. 489; change of -opinion &c. 484; retraction &c. 607.

doubt &c. (*uncertainty*) 475; skepticism, misgiving, demur; dis-, mis-trust; misdoubt, suspicion, jealousy, scruple, qualm; *onus probandi*.

incredib-ility, -leness; incredulity; unbeliever &c. 487.

V. dis-believe, -credit; not -believe &c. 484; misbelieve; refuse to admit &c. (*dissent*) 489; refuse to believe &c. (*incredulity*) 487.

doubt; be -doubtful &c. (*uncertain*) 475; doubt the truth of; be -skeptical as to &c. *adj.*; diffide; dis-, mis-trust; suspect, smoke, scent, smell a rat; have –, harbour –, entertain- -doubts, – suspicions; have one's doubts.

demur, stick at, pause, hesitate, scruple, waver, stop and consider.

hang in -suspense, – doubt.

throw doubt upon, raise a question; bring –, call- in question; question, challenge, query; dispute; deny &c. 536; cavil; cause –, raise –, start –, suggest –, awake- a -doubt, – suspicion; ergotize.

startle, stagger; shake –, stagger- one's faith, – belief.

Adj. unbelieving; incredulous –, skeptical- as to; distrustful –, shy –, suspicious- of; doubting &c. *v.*

doubtful &c. (*uncertain*) 475; disputable; unworthy –, undeserving- of -belief &c. 484; questionable; sus-pect, -picious; open to -suspicion, – doubt; staggering, hard to believe, incredible, not to be believed, inconceivable.

fallible &c. (*uncertain*) 475; undemonstrable; controvertible &c. (*untrue*) 495.

Adv. *cum grano salis.*

Phr. *fronti nulla fides*; *nimium ne crede colori*; '*timeo Danaos et dona ferentes*'; *credat Judæus Apella*; let those believe who may.

–, get hold of –, hazard –, foster –, nurture –, cherish- -a belief, – an opinion &c. *n.*

view –, consider –, take –, hold –, conceive –, regard –, esteem –, deem –, look upon –, account –, set down- as; surmise &c. 514.

get –, take- it into one's head; come round to an opinion; swallow &c. (*credulity*) 486.

cause to -be believed &c. *v.*; satisfy, persuade, have the ear of, gain the confidence of, assure; con-vince, -vict, -vert; put across, sell; wean, bring round; bring –, put –, win- over; indoctrinate &c. (*teach*) 537; cram down the throat; produce –, carry- conviction; bring –, drive- home to.

go down, find credence, pass current; be -received &c. *v.*, – current &c. *adj.*; possess –, take hold of –, take possession of- the mind.

Adj. believing &c. *v.*; certain, sure, assured, positive, cocksure, satisfied, confident, unhesitating, convinced, secure.

under the impression; impressed –, imbued –, penetrated- with.

confiding, trustful, suspectless; unsusp-ecting, -icious; void of suspicion; credulous &c. 486; wedded to.

believed &c. *v.*; accredited, putative; unsuspected.

worthy of –, deserving of –, commanding- -belief, – confidence; credible, reliable, trusted, trustworthy, to be depended on, undoubted; satisfactory; probable &c. 472; fiduci-al, -ary; persuasive, impressive.

relating to belief, doctrinal.

Adv. in the -opinion, – eyes- of; *me judice*; me-seems, -thinks; to the best of one's belief; I -dare say, – doubt not, – have no doubt, – am sure; in my opinion; sure enough &c. (*certainty*) 474; depend –, rely- upon it; be –, rest- assured; I'll warrant you &c. (*affirmation*) 535.

486. Credulity.—**N.** credul-ity, -ousness &c. *adj.*; gull-, cull-ibility; gross credulity, infatuation; self-delusion, -deception; blind reasoning; superstition; one's blind side; bigotry &c. (*obstinacy*) 606; hyper-orthodoxy &c. 984; misjudgment &c. 481.

credulous person &c. (*dupe*) 547.

V. be -credulous &c. *adj.*; *jurare in verba magistri*; follow implicitly; swallow, – whole, gulp down; take on trust; take for -granted, – gospel; run away with -a notion, – an idea; jump –, rush- to a conclusion; think the moon is made of green cheese; take –, grasp- the shadow for the substance; catch at straws.

impose upon &c. (*deceive*) 545.

Adj. credulous, gullible; easily -deceived &c. 545; simple, green, soft, childish, silly, stupid; over-credulous, -confident; infatuated, superstitious; confiding &c. (*believing*) 484.

Phr. the wish the father to the thought; *credo quia impossibile.*

487. Incredulity.—**N.** incredul-ousness, -ity; skepticism, pyrrhonism; want of faith &c. (*irreligion*) 989.

suspiciousness &c. *adj.*; scrupulosity; suspicion &c. (*unbelief*) 485; dissent &c. 489.

unbeliever, skeptic, aporetic; atheist, agnostic, infidel, disbeliever, misbeliever, pyrrhonist &c. 989; heretic &c. (*heterodox*) 984.

V. be -incredulous &c. *adj.*; distrust &c. (*disbelieve*) 485; refuse to believe; shut one's -eyes, – ears- to; turn a deaf ear to; hold aloof; ignore; *nullius jurare in verba magistri.*

Adj. incredulous, skeptical, unbelieving, inconvincible; hard –, shy- of belief; suspicious, scrupulous, distrustful, heterodox &c. 984.

488. Assent.—**N.** assent, -ment; acquiescence, admission; nod; ac-, con-cord, -cordance; agreement &c. 23; affirm-ance, -ation; recognition, acknowledgment, avowal; confession, – of faith.

unanimity, common consent, *consensus*, acclamation, chorus, *vox populi*; popular –, current- -belief, – opinion; public opinion; concurrence &c. (*of causes*) 178; co-operation &c. (*voluntary*) 709.

ratification, confirmation, corroboration, approval, acceptance, *visa*; indorsement, &c. (*record*) 551; O.K.

consent &c. (*compliance*) 762.

affirmant, consenter, covenanter, subscriber, endorser, upholder.

V. assent; give –, yield –, nod- assent; acquiesce; agree &c. 23; receive, accept, accede, accord, concur, lend oneself to, consent, coincide, reciprocate, go with; be -at one with &c. *adj.*; go along –, chime in –, strike in –, close- with; echo, enter into one's views, agree in opinion; vote –, give one's voice- for; recognize; subscribe –, conform –, defer- to; say -yes, – ditto, – amen, – aye- to; to O.K.

acknowledge, own, admit, allow, avow, confess; concede &c. (*yield*) 762; come round to; abide by; permit &c. 760.

come to –, arrive at- -an understanding, – terms, – an agreement.

con-, af-firm; ratify, approve, endorse, countersign; visa; corroborate &c. 467.

go –, swim- with the stream, float with the current; be in the fashion, join in the chorus; be in every mouth.

Adj. assenting &c. *v.*; of one -accord, – mind; of the same mind, at one with, agreed, acquiescent, content; willing &c. 602.

un-contradicted, -challenged, -questioned, -controverted.

carried –, agreed- -*nem. con.* &c. *adv.*; unanimous; agreed on all hands, carried by acclamation.

affirmative &c. 535.

Adv. yes, yea, ay, aye, true; good; well; very -well, – true; well and good; granted; *placet*; even –, just- so; to be sure, surely, 'thou hast said'; truly, exactly, precisely,

489. Dissent.—**N.** dissent; discordance &c. (*disagreement*) 24; difference –, diversity- of opinion.

non-conformity &c. (*heterodoxy*) 984; protestantism, recusancy, schism; disaffection; secession &c. 624; recantation &c. 607.

dissension &c. (*discord*) 713; discontent &c. 832; cavilling.

protest; contradiction &c. (*denial*) 536; non-compliance &c. (*rejection*) 764; disapprobation &c. 932; hartal.

dissent-ient, -er; non-juror, -content; recusant, sectary, schismatic, protestant, non-conformist, separatist, non-co-operator, conscientious objector, passive resister.

V. dissent, demur; call in question &c. (*doubt*) 485; differ in opinion, disagree; say -no &c. 536; refuse -assent, – to admit; cavil, protest, raise one's voice against, make bold to differ; repudiate; contradict &c. (*deny*) 536; agree to differ.

have no notion of, differ *toto cœlo*; revolt -at, – from the idea.

shake the head, shrug the shoulders; look -askance, – askant.

secede; recant &c. 607.

Adj. dissenting &c. *v.*; negative &c. 536; diss-ident, -entient; unconsenting &c. (*refusing*) 764; non-content, -juring; protestant, recusant; uncon-vinced, -verted.

unavowed, unacknowledged; out of the question.

discontented &c. 832; unwilling &c. 603; extorted.

sectarian, denominational, schismatic, heterodox, intolerant.

Adv. no &c. 536; at -variance, – issue- with; under protest; *non placet*.

Int. God forbid! not for the world; not on your life; I beg to differ; I'll be hanged if; never tell me; your humble servant, pardon me; tell that to the marines.

Phr. many men many minds; *quot homines tot sententiæ*; *tant s'en faut*; *il s'en faut bien*.

that's just it, indeed, certainly, certes, *ex concesso*; of course, unquestionably, assuredly, no doubt, doubtless, undoubtedly.

be it so; so -be it, – let it be, so mote it be; amen; with all my heart; willingly &c. 602.

affirmatively, in the affirmative.

with one -consent, – voice, – accord; unanimously, *unâ voce*, by common consent, in chorus, to a man, *nem. con.*; *nemine -contradicente, – dissentiente*; without a dissentient voice; as one man, one and all, on all hands.

490. Knowledge.—N. knowledge; cogn-izance, -ition, -oscence; acquaintance, experience, ken, privity, insight, familiarity; com-, ap-prehension; recognition; appreciation &c. (*judgment*) 480; intuition; consci-ence, -ousness; perception, precognition; acroamatics.

light, enlightenment; glimpse, inkling; side light; glimmer, -ing; dawn; scent, suspicion; impression &c. (*idea*) 453; discovery &c. 480*a*.

system –, body- of knowledge; science, philosophy, pansophy; theory, etiology; circle of the sciences; pandect, doctrine, body of doctrine; cy-, ency-clopædia; school &c. (*system of opinions*) 484.

tree of knowledge; republic of letters &c. (*language*) 560.

erudition, learning, lore, scholarship, reading, letters; literature; book-learning, bookishness; biblio-mania, -latry; information, general information; store of -knowledge &c.; education &c. (*teaching*) 537; culture, attainments; acqui-rements, -sitions; accomplishments, proficiency; practical knowledge &c. (*skill*) 698; higher education, liberal education; dilettantism; rudiments &c. (*beginning*) 66.

deep –, profound –, solid –, accurate –, acroatic –, acroamatic –, vast –, extensive –, encyclopædical- -knowledge, – learning; omniscience, pantology.

march of intellect; progress –, advance- of -science, – learning; schoolmaster abroad.

V. know, ken, scan, wot; wot –, be aware &c. *adj.*- of; ween, weet, trow, have, possess.

conceive; ap-, com-prehend; take, realize, understand, appreciate; fathom, make out; recognize, discern, perceive, see, get a sight of, experience.

491. Ignorance. — N. ignorance, nescience, *tabula rasa*, crass ignorance, *ignorance crasse*; unacquaintance; unconsciousness &c. *adj.*; dark-, blindness; incomprehension, inexperience, simplicity.

unknown quantities, x, y, z.

sealed book, *terra incognita*, virgin soil, unexplored ground; dark ages.

[Imperfect knowledge] smattering, superficiality, half-learning, sciolism, glimmering; bewilderment &c. (*uncertainty*) 475; incapacity.

[Affectation of knowledge] pedantry; charlatan-ry, -ism.

V. be -ignorant &c. *adj.*; not -know &c. 490; know -not, – not what, – nothing of; have no -idea, – notion, – conception; not have the remotest idea; not know chalk from cheese.

ignore, be blind to; keep in ignorance &c. (*conceal*) 528.

see through a glass darkly; have a -film over the eyes, – glimmering &c. *n.*; wonder whether; not know what to make of &c. (*unintelligibility*) 519; not pretend –, not take upon oneself- to say.

Adj. ignorant, nescient; un-knowing, -aware, -acquainted, -apprized, -witting, -weeting, -conscious; wit-, weetless; a stranger to; unconversant.

un-informed, -cultivated, -versed, -instructed, -taught, -initiated, -tutored, -schooled, -guided, -enlightened; Philistine; behind the age.

shallow, superficial, green, rude, empty, half-learned, illiterate; un-read, -informed, -educated, -learned, -lettered, -bookish; empty-headed; lowbrow; pedantic.

in the dark; be-nighted, -lated; blind-ed, -fold; hoodwinked; misinformed; *au bout de son latin*, at the

know full well; have –, possess- some knowledge of; be -*au courant* &c. *adj.*; have -in one's head, – at one's fingers' ends; know by -heart, – rote; be master of; *connaître le dessous des cartes*, know what's what &c. 698.

see one's way; learn, discover &c. 480*a*.

come to one's knowledge &c. (*information*) 527.

Adj. knowing &c. *v.*; cognitive; acroamatic.

aware –, cognizant –, conscious- of; acquainted –, made acquainted- with; privy –, no stranger- to; *au -fait*, – *courant*; in the secret; up –, alive- to; sensible of; behind the -scenes, – curtain; let into; apprised –, informed- of; undeceived.

proficient –, versed –, read –, forward –, strong –, at home- in; conversant –, familiar- with.

erudite, instructed, learned, lettered, educated; high-brow; well-conned, -informed, -read, -grounded, -educated; enlightened, shrewd, insightful, *savant*, blue, bookish, scholastic, solid, profound, deep-read, book-learned; accomplished &c. (*skilful*) 698; omniscient; self-taught, -educated.

known &c. *v.*; ascertained, well-known, recognized, received, notorious, noted; proverbial; familiar, – as household words, to every schoolboy; hackneyed, trite, commonplace.

knowable, cogn-oscible, -izable.

Adv. to –, to the best of- one's knowledge.

Phr. one's eyes being opened &c. (*disclosure*) 529.

end of his tether; at fault; at sea &c. (*uncertain*) 475; caught tripping.

un-known, -apprehended, -explained, -ascertained, -investigated, -explored, -heard of, -perceived; concealed &c. 528; novel.

Adv. ignorantly &c. *adj.*; unawares; for -anything, – aught- one knows; not that one knows.

Int. God –, Heaven –, the Lord –, nobody- knows.

Phr. a little learning is a dangerous thing.

---

492. Scholar—N. scholar, *connoisseur*, *savant*, pundit, schoolman, professor, graduate, wrangler, moonshee; academ-ician, -ist; fellow, don, post graduate, advanced student; master –, bachelor- of arts; doctor, licentiate, gownsman; philo-sopher, -math; scientist, clerk; soph, -ist, -ister; linguist, classicist; glosso-, etymo-, philologist; philologer; lexico-, glosso-grapher; scholiast, commentator, annotator, grammarian; *littérateur*, *literati*, *dilettanti*, *illuminati*; Mezzofanti, admirable Crichton, Mæcenas.

book-worm, *helluo librorum*, biblio-phile, -maniac; blue-stocking, *bas-bleu*; big-wig, learned Theban.

learned –, literary- man; *homo multarum literarum*; man of -learning, – letters, – education; high-brow, intelligentsia.

antiquar-ian, -y; archæologist; sage &c. (*wise man*) 500.

pedant, *doctrinaire*; pedagogue, Dr. Pangloss; pantologist.

teacher &c. 540; schoolboy &c. (*learner*) 541.

Adj. learned &c. 490; brought up at the feet of Gamaliel.

493. Ignoramus.—N. ignoramus, illiterate, moron, dunce, numskull; wooden spoon; no scholar.

sciolist, smatterer, dabbler, half-scholar; *charlatan*; wiseacre.

novice, griffin; greenhorn &c. (*dupe*) 547; tyro &c. (*learner*) 541.

lubber &c. (*bungler*) 701; fool &c. 501; pedant &c. 492.

Adj. bookless, shallow, simple, dense, dumb, thick, dull, ignorant &c. 491.

---

494. [Object of knowledge.] **Truth.** —**N.** fact, reality &c. (*existence*) 1; plain matter of fact; nature &c. (*principle*) 5; truth, verity; gospel; orthodoxy &c. 983*a*; authenticity; veracity &c. 543.

accuracy, exactitude; exact-, precise-ness &c. *adj.*; precision, delicacy; rigour, mathematical precision, punctuality; clockwork precision &c. (*regularity*) 80.

orthology; *ipsissima verba;* letter of the law, realism.

plain –, honest –, sober –, naked –, unalloyed –, unqualified –, stern –, exact –, intrinsic- truth; *nuda veritas*; the very thing; not an -illusion &c. 495; real Simon Pure; unvarnished tale; the truth, the whole truth and nothing but the truth; just the thing.

V. be -true &c. *adj.*, – the case; stand the test; have the true ring; hold -good, – true, – water; conform to rule.

render –, prove- -true &c. *adj.*; substantiate &c. (*evidence*) 467.

get at the truth &c. (*discover*) 480*a*.

Adj. real, actual &c. (*existing*) 1; veritable, true; certain &c. 474; substantially –, categorically- true &c.; true -to the letter, – to life, – to scale, – the facts, – as gospel; unimpeachable; veracious &c. 543; unre-, uncon-futed; un-ideal, -imagined; realistic.

exact, accurate, definite, precise, well defined, just, right, correct, strict, severe; close &c. (*similar*) 17; literal; rigid, rigorous; scrupulous &c. (*conscientious*) 939; religiously exact, punctual, mathematical, scientific; faithful, constant, unerring; curious, particular, punctilious, meticulous, nice, delicate, fine.

genuine, authentic, legitimate, pukka; orthodox &c. 983*a*; official, *ex officio.*

pure, natural, sound, sterling; unsophisticated, -adulterated, -varnished, -coloured; in its true colours.

well-grounded, -founded; solid, substantial, tangible, valid; undis-torted, -guised; un-affected, -exaggerated, -romantic, -flattering.

Adv. truly &c. *adj.*; verily, indeed, in reality; as a matter of fact; beyond

495. Error.—**N.** error, fallacy; misconception, -apprehension, -understanding; inexactness &c. *adj.*; laxity; misconstruction &c. (*misinterpretation*) 523; miscomputation &c. (*misjudgment*) 481; *non-sequitur* &c. 477; misstatement, -report; anachronism; malapropism.

mistake; miss, fault, blunder, boner, bloomer, howler, *quid pro quo,* cross purposes, oversight, misprint, *erratum, corrigendum,* slip, blot, flaw, loose thread; trip, stumble &c. (*failure*) 732; botchery &c. (*want of skill*) 699; slip of the -tongue, – pen; *lapsus -linguæ, – calami,* clerical error; bull &c. (*absurdity*) 497.

il-, de-lusion; false -impression, – idea; bubble; self-deceit, -deception; warped notion; mists of error; superstition, exploded notion.

heresy &c. (*heterodoxy*) 984; hallucination &c. (*insanity*) 503; false light &c. (*fallacy of vision*) 443; dream &c. (*fancy*) 515; fable &c. (*untruth*) 546; bias &c. (*misjudgment*) 481; misleading &c. *v.*

V. be -erroneous &c. *adj.*

cause error; mis-lead, -guide; lead -astray, – into error; beguile, misinform &c. (*misteach*) 538; delude; give a false -impression, – idea; falsify, garble, misstate; deceive &c. 545; lie &c. 544.

err; be -in error &c. *adj.*, – mistaken &c. *v.*; be deceived &c. (*duped*) 547; mistake, receive a false impression, deceive oneself; fall into –, lie under –, labour under- -an error &c. *n.*; be in the wrong, blunder; mis-apprehend, -conceive, -understand, -reckon, -count, -calculate &c. (*misjudge*) 481.

play –, be- at cross purposes &c. (*misinterpret*) 523.

trip, stumble; lose oneself &c. (*uncertainty*) 475; go astray; fail &c. 732; take the wrong sow by the ear &c. (*mismanage*) 699; put the saddle on the wrong horse; reckon without one's host; take the shadow for the substance &c. (*credulity*) 486; dream &c. (*imagine*) 515.

Adj. erroneous, untrue, false, devoid of truth, fallacious, faulty, apocryphal,

-doubt, – question; with truth &c. (*veracity*) 543; certainly &c. (*certain*) 474; actually &c. (*existence*) 1; in effect &c. (*intrinsically*) 5.

exactly &c. *adj.*; *ad amussim*; *verbatim*, – *et literatim*; word for word, literally, *literatim*, *totidem verbis*, *sic*, to the letter, chapter and verse, *ipsissimis verbis*; *ad unguem*; to an inch; to a -nicety, – hair, – tittle, – turn, – T; *au pied de la lettre*; neither more nor less; in -every respect, – all respects; *sous tous les rapports*; at -any rate, – all events; strictly speaking.

Phr. the -truth, – fact- is; *rem acu tetigisti*.

unreal, ungrounded, groundless; unsubstantial &c. 4; heretical &c. (*heterodox*) 984; unsound; illogical &c. 477; wrong.

in-, un-exact; in-accurate, -correct; indefinite &c. (*uncertain*) 475.

illus-ive, -ory; delusive; mock; ideal &c. (*imaginary*) 515; spurious &c. 545; deceitful &c. 544; perverted.

controvertible, unsustain-able, -ed; unauthenticated, untrustworthy.

exploded, refuted, discarded.

in –, under an- error &c. *n.*; mistaken &c. *v.*; tripping &c. *v.*; out, – in one's reckoning; aberrant; beside –, wide of the- -mark, – truth; astray &c. (*at fault*) 475; on -a false, – the wrong-scent; in the wrong box; at cross purposes, all in the wrong, all abroad, at sea.

Adv. more or less.

496. Maxim.—N. maxim, aphorism; apo-, apoph-thegm; *dictum*, saying, gnome, adage, saw, proverb, epigram; sentence, *mot*, motto, word, by-word, precept, moral, phylactery, *protasis*, brocard.

axiom, postulate, theorem, *scholium*, truism.

reflection &c. (*idea*) 453; conclusion &c. (*judgment*) 480; golden rule &c. (*precept*) 697; principle, *principia*; profession of faith &c. (*belief*) 484; formula.

wise –, sage –, received –, admitted –, recognized- maxim &c.; true –, common –, hackneyed –, trite –, commonplace- saying &c.

Adj. aphoristic, proverbial, phylacteric; axiomatic, gnomic.

Adv. as -the saying is, – they say.

497. Absurdity.—N. absurd-ity, -ness &c. *adj.*; imbecility &c. 499; alogy, nonsense, paradox, inconsistency; stultiloqu-y, -ence, futility.

blunder, muddle, bull; Irish-, Hibernic-ism; slip-slop; anticlimax, bathos; sophism &c. 477.

farce, burlesque, *galimatias*, *amphigouri*, rhapsody; farrago &c. (*disorder*) 59; extravagance, romance; sciomachy.

joke, catch, sell, pun, verbal quibble, macaronic.

jargon, fustian, twaddle &c. (*no meaning*) 517; exaggeration &c. 549; moonshine, stuff; mare's nest.

vagary, tomfoolery, mummery, monkey trick, practical joke, *boutade*, *escapade*.

V. play the fool &c. 499; stultify, blunder, muddle; joke; talk nonsense, *parler à tort et à travers*; *battre la campagne*; be -absurd &c. *adj.*

Adj. absurd, nonsensical, preposterous, egregious, senseless, farcical, inconsistent, ridiculous, extravagant, quibbling, futile; macaronic, punning, paradoxical.

foolish &c. 499; sophistical &c. 477; unmeaning &c. 517; without rhyme or reason; fantastic.

Int. fiddle-de-dee! pish! pish and tush! pho! stuff and nonsense! rubbish! rot! bosh! in the name of the Prophet—figs!

Phr. *credat Judæus Apella*; tell it to the marines.

Faculties

498. Intelligence. Wisdom.—N. intelligence, capacity, comprehension,

499. Imbecility. Folly.—N. want of -intelligence &c. 498, – intellect &c.

understanding; intellect &c. 450; nous, parts, sagacity, mother wit, wit, *esprit*, gumption, quick parts, grasp of intellect; acuteness &c. *adj.*; acumen, subtlety, penetration; perspica-cy, -city; discernment, long-headedness, due sense of, good judgement; discrimination &c. 465; craftiness, cunning &c. 702; refinement &c. (*taste*) 850.

head, brains, gray matter, headpiece, upper story, long head; eagle -eye, – glance; eye of a -lynx, – hawk.

wisdom, sapience, sense; good –, common –, plain –, horse- sense; clear thinking; rationality, reason; reasonableness &c. *adj.*; judgement; solidity, depth, profundity, calibre; enlarged views; reach –, compass- of thought; enlargement of mind.

genius, inspiration, *Geist*, fire of genius, heaven-born genius, soul; talent &c. (*aptitude*) 698.

[Wisdom in action] prudence &c. 864; vigilance &c. 459; tact &c. 698; foresight &c. 510; sobriety, self-possession, *aplomb*, ballast, mental -poise, – balance.

a bright thought, inspiration, brainwave, not a bad idea.

V. be -intelligent &c. *adj.*; have all one's wits about one; understand &c. (*intelligible*) 518; catch –, take in- an idea; take a -joke, – hint.

see -through, – at a glance, – with half an eye, – far into, – through a millstone; penetrate; discern &c. (*descry*) 441; foresee &c. 510.

discriminate &c. 465; know what's what &c. 698; listen to reason.

Adj. [Applied to persons] intelligent, quick of apprehension, keen, acute, alive, brainy, awake, bright, quick, sharp; quick-, keen-, clear-, sharp- -eyed, -sighted, -witted; wide awake; canny, shrewd, astute; clear-headed; far-sighted &c. 510; discerning, perspicacious, penetrating, piercing; argute; nimble-, needle-witted; sharp as a needle; alive to &c. (*cognizant*) 490; clever &c. (*apt*) 698; arch &c. (*cunning*) 702; *pas si bête* &c. 682.

wise, sage, sapient, sagacious, reasonable, rational, sound, in one's right

450; shallow-, silli-, foolish-ness &c. *adj.*; imbecility, incapacity, vacancy of mind, poverty of intellect, clouded perception, poor head, apartments to let; stup-, stol-idity; hebetude, dull understanding, meanest capacity; short-sightedness; incompetence &c. (*unskilfulness*) 699.

one's weak side; bias &c. 481; infatuation &c. (*insanity*) 503.

simplicity, puerility, babyhood; dotage, anility, second childishness, senile dementia, fatuity; idio-cy, -tism; drivelling.

folly, frivolity, desipience, irrationality, trifling, ineptitude, nugacity, inconsistency, lip-wisdom, conceit; sophistry &c. 477; giddiness &c. (*inattention*) 458; eccentricity &c. 503; extravagance &c. (*absurdity*) 497; rashness &c. 863.

act of folly &c. 699.

V. be -imbecile &c. *adj.*; have no -brains, – sense &c. 498.

trifle, drivel, *radoter*, dote; ramble &c. (*madness*) 503; play the -fool, – monkey, – goat, take leave of one's senses; not see an inch beyond one's nose; stultify oneself &c. 699; talk nonsense &c. 497.

Adj. [Applied to persons] un-intelligent, -intellectual, -reasoning; mind-, wit-, reason-, brain-less; having no -head &c. 498; not -bright &c. 498; inapprehensible.

weak-, addle-, puzzle-, blunder-, muddle-, muddy-, pig-, beetle-, maggoty-, gross-headed; beef-, fat- -witted, -headed.

weak-, feeble-minded; dull-, shallow-, rattle-, lack-brained; half-, nit-, short-, dull-, blunt-witted; shallow-, clod-, addle-pated; dim-, short-sighted; thick-skulled; weak in the upper story.

shallow, *borné*, weak, wanting, soft, nutty, sappy, spoony; dull, – as a beetle; stupid, heavy, insulse, obtuse, blunt, stolid, doltish, asinine; inapt &c. 699; prosaic &c. 843.

child-ish, -like; infant-ine, -ile; baby-, bab-ish; puerile, anile; simple &c. (*credulous*) 486.

fatuous, idiotic, imbecile, moronic,

mind, sensible, *abnormis sapiens*, judicious, strong-minded.

un-prejudiced, -biassed, -bigoted, -prepossessed; un-dazzled, -perplexed; of unwarped judgment, impartial, equitable, fair, broad-minded.

cool; cool-, long-, hard-, strong-headed; long-sighted, calculating, thoughtful, reflecting; solid, deep, profound.

oracular; heaven-directed, -born.

prudent &c. (*cautious*) 864; sober, staid, solid; considerate, politic, wise in one's generation; watchful &c. 459; provident &c. (*prepared*) 673; in advance of one's age; wise as -a serpent, – Solomon, – Solon.

[Applied to actions] wise, sensible, reasonable, judicious; well-judged, -advised; prudent, politic; expedient &c. 646.

---

500. Sage.—N. sage, wise man; pundit; master -mind, – spirit of the age; longhead, thinker, philosopher.

authority, oracle, mentor, luminary, shining light, *esprit fort*, *magnus Apollo*, Solon, Solomon, Nestor, Magi, 'second Daniel.'

man of learning &c. 492; expert &c. 700; wizard &c. 994.

[Ironically] wiseacre, bigwig.

Adj. wise, learned; authoritative, oracular; erudite &c. 490; venerable, reverenced, revered, *emeritus*.

---

drivelling; blatant, babbling; vacant; sottish; bewildered &c. 475.

blockish, unteachable; Bœot-ian, -ic; bovine; un-gifted, -discerning, -enlightened, -wise, -philosophical; apish.

foolish, silly, senseless, irrational, insensate, nonsensical, inept; maudlin.

narrow-minded &c. 481; bigoted &c. (*obstinate*) 606; giddy &c. (*thoughtless*) 458; rash &c. 863; eccentric &c. (*crazed*) 503.

[Applied to actions] foolish, unwise, indiscreet, injudicious, improper, unreasonable, without reason, ridiculous, silly, stupid, asinine; ill-imagined, -advised, -judged, -devised; inconsistent, irrational, unphilosophical; extravagant &c. (*nonsensical*) 497; sleeveless, idle; useless &c. 645; inexpedient &c. 647; frivolous &c. (*trivial*) 643; absurd &c. 497.

Phr. *Davus sum non Œdipus.*

501. Fool.—N. fool, idiot, tomfool, wiseacre, simpleton, Simple Simon, nit-wit, witling, dizzard, donkey, ass; ninny, -hammer; moron, dolt, booby, Tom Noddy, looby, hoddy-doddy, noddy, nonny, noodle, nizy, owl; goose, -cap; *imbécile*; gaby, *radoteur*, nincompoop, *badaud*, zany; trifler, babbler; pretty fellow; natural, *niais*.

child, baby, infant, innocent, milksop, sop.

oaf, lout, loon, lown, dullard, doodle, calf, colt, buzzard, block, put, stick, stock, numps, tony.

bull-, dunder-, addle-, block-, dull-, logger-, jolt-, jolter-, beetle-, gross-, thick-, giddy-head; num-, thick-skull; lack-, shallow-brain; half-, lack-wit; dunder-pate; fat-head, poor stick.

sawney, gowk; clod, -hopper; clod-, clot-poll, -pate; bull-calf; men of Bœotia, wise men of Gotham.

un sot à triple étage, sot; jobbernowl, changeling, mooncalf, *gobemouche*.

dotard, driveller; old -fogey, – woman; crone, grandmother.

greenhorn &c. (*dupe*) 547; dunce &c. (*ignoramus*) 493; lubber &c. (*bungler*) 701; madman &c. 504.

one who -will not set the Thames on fire, – did not invent gunpowder; *qui n'a pas inventé la poudre*; no conjuror.

502. Sanity.—N. sanity; soundness &c. *adj.*; rationality, normality, sobriety, lucidity, lucid interval; senses, sober senses, sound mind, *mens sana*.

503. Insanity.—N. disordered -reason, – intellect; diseased –, unsound –, abnormal- mind; derangement, unsoundness.

V. be -sane &c. *adj.*; retain one's senses, – reason.

become -sane &c. *adj.*; come to one's senses, sober down.

render -sane &c. *adj.*; bring to one's senses, sober.

Adj. sane, rational, reasonable, *compos mentis*, of sound mind; sound, -minded.

self-possessed; sober, -minded.

in one's -sober senses, – right mind; in possession of one's faculties.

Adv. sanely &c. *adj.*

---

insanity, lunacy; madness &c. *adj.*; mania, *rabies*, *furor*, mental alienation, paranoia, aberration; *amentia*, dementation, -tia, -cy; *dementia præcox*; *morosis*, idiocy, phrenitis, frenzy, raving, incoherence, wandering, delirium, calenture of the brain, delusion, hallucination; lycanthropy, brain storm, *delirium tremens*, D.T's.

vertigo, dizziness, swimming; sunstroke, *coup de soleil*, siriasis.

fanaticism, infatuation, craze; oddity, eccentricity, twist, monomania; klepto-, dipso-mania; hypochondriasis &c. (*low spirits*) 837; *melancholia*, hysteria.

screw –, tile –, slate- loose; bee in one's bonnet, rats in the upper story.

dotage &c. (*imbecility*) 499.

V. be –, become- -insane &c. *adj.*; lose one's senses, – reason, – faculties, – wits; go –, run- mad, run amuck; rave, dote, ramble, wander; drivel &c. (*be imbecile*) 499; have a -screw loose &c. *n.*, – devil; *avoir le diable au corps*; lose one's head &c. (*be uncertain*) 475.

derange, render –, drive- -mad &c. *adj.*; madden, dementate, addle the wits, derange the head, infatuate, befool; turn -the brain, – one's head.

Adj. insane, mad, lunatic; crazy, crazed, ***aliéné, non compos mentis***; not right, cracked, touched; bereft of reason; unhinged, deranged, unsettled in one's mind; insensate, reasonless, beside oneself, demented, daft; phren-, fren-zied, -etic; possessed, – with a devil; far gone, maddened, moonstruck; shatterpated; barmy; mad-, scatter-, shatter-, crack-brained; off one's head; bug-house, *loco*.

maniacal; manic, manic-depressive; delirious, light-headed, incoherent, rambling, doting, wandering; frantic, raving, stark staring mad, amok, amuck, berserk.

corybantic, dithyrambic; rabid, giddy, vertiginous, dizzy, wild, haggard, mazed; flighty; distr-acted, -aught; bewildered &c. (*uncertain*) 475.

mad as a -March hare, – hatter; of -unsound mind &c. *n.*; touched –, wrong –, not right- in one's -head, – mind, – wits, – upper story; out of one's -mind, – senses, – wits; not in one's right mind.

fanatical, infatuated, odd, eccentric; hipp-ed, -ish.

imbecile, silly &c. 499.

Adv. like one possessed.

Phr. the mind having lost its balance; the reason under a cloud; *tête -exaltée, -montée.*

504. Madman.—N. madman, lunatic, maniac, bedlamite, candidate for Bedlam, raver, madcap; energumen; paranoiac; auto-, mono-, pyro-, megalo-, dipso-, klepto-maniac; hypochondriac &c. (*low spirits*) 837.

dreamer &c. 515; rhapsodist, seer, high-flier, enthusiast, crank, eccentric, nut, fanatic, *fanatico*; *exalté*; knight errant, Don Quixote.

idiot &c. 501.

Section VI. Extension of Thought

1°. *To the Past*

505. Memory.—N. memory, remembrance; reten-tion, -tiveness; tenacity; *veteris vestigia flammæ*; tablets of the memory; readiness.

reminiscence, recognition, recurrence, recollection, rememoration; retrospect, -ion; after-thought.

suggestion &c. (*information*) 527; prompting &c. *v.*; hint, reminder, token of remembrance, *memento*, *souvenir*, keepsake, relic, *memorandum*; remembrancer, flapper; memorial &c. (*record*) 551; commemoration &c. (*celebration*) 883.

things to be remembered, *memorabilia*.

art of –, artificial- memory; *memoria technica*; mnemo-nics, -technics; phrenotypics; Mnemosyne; memorandum-, note-, engagement-, prompt-book.

retentive –, tenacious –, green –, trustworthy –, capacious –, faithful –, correct –, exact –, ready –, prompt- memory.

V. remember, mind; retain the -memory, – remembrance- of; keep in view.

have –, hold –, bear –, carry –, keep –, retain- in *or* in the -thoughts, – mind, – memory, – remembrance; be in –, live in –, remain in –, dwell in –, haunt –, impress- one's -memory, – thoughts, – mind.

sink in the mind; run in the head; not be able to get it out of one's head; be deeply impressed with; rankle &c. (*revenge*) 919.

recur to the mind; flash -on the mind, – across the memory.

recognize, recollect, bethink oneself, recall, call up, conjure up, retrace; look –, trace- -back, – backwards; think –, look back- upon; review; call –, recall –, bring- to mind; remembrance; carry one's thoughts back; rake up the past.

suggest &c. (*inform*) 527; prompt; put –, keep- in mind; remind; fan the embers; call –, summon –, rip- up; renew; *infandum renovare dolorem*; task –, tax –, jog –, flap –, refresh –, rub up –, awaken- the memory; pull by the sleeve; bring back to the memory, put in remembrance, memorialize.

get –, have –, learn –, know –, say –, repeat- by -heart – rote; drive –, get- into -one's head; say one's lesson; repeat, – as a parrot; have at one's fingers' ends.

506. Oblivion.—N. oblivion; forgetfulness &c. *adj.*; obliteration &c. 552, of –, insensibility &c. 823 to- the past.

short –, treacherous –, loose –, slippery –, failing- memory; decay –, failure –, lapse- of memory; memory like a sieve; waters of -Lethe, – oblivion, *amnesia*.

pardon, acquittal, amnesty, oblivion; absolution.

V. forget; be -forgetful &c. *adj.*; fall –, sink- into oblivion; have -a short memory &c. *n.*, – no head.

forget one's own name, have on the tip of one's tongue, come in at one ear and go out at the other.

slip –, escape –, fade from –, die away from- the memory; lose, – sight of.

unlearn; efface &c. 552 –, discharge- from the memory; consign to -oblivion, – the tomb of the Capulets; think no more of &c. (*turn the attention from*) 458; cast behind one's back, wean one's thoughts from; let bygones be bygones &c. (*forgive*) 918.

Adj. forgotten &c. *v.*; unremembered, past recollection, bygone, out of mind; buried –, sunk- in oblivion; clean forgotten; gone out of one's -head, – recollection.

forgetful, oblivious, mindless, heedless, Lethean; insensible &c. 823- to the past.

Phr. *non mi ricordo*; the memory -failing, – deserting one, – being at (*or* in) fault.

commit to memory; memorize; con, – over; fix –, rivet –, imprint –, impress –, stamp –, grave –, engrave –, store –, treasure up –, bottle up –, embalm –, enshrine- in the memory; load –, store –, stuff –, burden- the memory with.

redeem from oblivion; keep the memory -alive, – green; *tangere ulcus*; keep up the memory of; commemorate &c. (*celebrate*) 883.

make a note of &c. (*record*) 551.

Adj. remember-ing, -ed &c. *v.*; mindful, reminiscential; retained in the memory &c. *v.*; pent up in one's memory; fresh; green, – in remembrance, still vivid; unforgotten, present to the mind; within one's -memory &c. *n.*; indelible; not to be forgotten, unforgettable, enduring; uppermost in one's thoughts; memorable &c. (*important*) 642.

Adv. by -heart, – rote; without book, *memoriter*.

in memory of; *in memoriam*; suggestive.

Phr. *manet altâ mente repostum*; *forsan et hæc olim meminisse juvabit.*

2°. *To the Future*

507. Expectation.—N. expect-ation, -ance, -ancy; anticipation, reckoning, calculation; contingency; foresight &c. 510.

contemplation, prospection, look out; prospect, perspective, horizon, vista; destiny &c. 152.

suspense, waiting, abeyance; curiosity &c. 455; anxious –, ardent –, eager –, breathless –, sanguine- expectation; torment of Tantalus.

presumption, hope &c. 858; trust &c. (*belief*) 484; prognostication, auspices &c. (*prediction*) 511.

V. expect; look -for, – out for, – forward to; hope for, anticipate; have in -prospect, – contemplation; keep in view; contemplate, promise oneself; not -wonder &c. 870 -at, – if.

wait –, tarry –, lie in wait –, watch –, bargain- for; keep a -good, – sharp- look-out for; await; stand at 'attention,' abide, bide one's –, mark- time, watch.

foresee &c. 510; prepare for &c. 673; forestall &c. (*be early*) 132; count upon &c. (*believe in*) 484; think likely &c. (*probability*) 472; make one's mouth water.

lead one to expect &c. (*predict*) 511; have in store for &c. (*destiny*) 152.

prick up one's ears, hold one's breath.

Adj. expectant; expecting &c. *v.*; in -expectation &c. *n.*; on the watch &c. (*vigilant*) 459; open -eyed, -mouthed;

508. Inexpectation.—N. in-, non-expectation; false expectation &c. (*disappointment*) 509; miscalculation &c. 481; unforeseen contingency, the unforeseen, the unexpected.

surprise, sudden burst, thunderclap, blow, shock; bolt out of the blue; eye-opener; wonder &c. 870.

V. not -expect &c. 507; be taken by surprise; start; miscalculate &c. 481; not bargain for; come –, fall- upon.

be -unexpected &c. *adj.*; come -unawares &c. *adv.*; turn up, pop, drop from the clouds; come –, burst –, flash –, bounce –, steal –, creep- upon one; come –, burst- like a thunderclap, -bolt; take –, catch- -by surprise, – unawares, – napping.

pounce –, spring a mine- upon.

surprise, startle, take aback, electrify, stun, stagger, take away one's breath, throw off one's guard; astonish &c. (*strike with wonder*) 870.

Adj. non-expectant; surprised &c. *v.*; un-warned, -aware; off one's guard; inattentive &c. 458.

un-expected, -anticipated, -prepared for, -looked for, -foreseen, -hoped for; dropped from the clouds; beyond –, contrary to –, against- expectation; out of one's reckoning; unheard of &c. (*exceptional*) 83; startling; sudden &c. (*instantaneous*) 113.

Adv. abruptly, unexpectedly, plump, pop, *à l'improviste*, unawares; without

agape, gaping, all agog; on -tenter-hooks, – tiptoe, – the tiptoe of expectation; *aux aguets*; ready; curious &c. 455; looking forward to; prepared for; on the rack.

expected &c. *v.*; long expected, fore-seen; in prospect &c. *n.*; prospective; in -one's eye, – view, – the horizon; impending &c. (*destiny*) 152.

Adv. expectantly; in the event of; on the watch &c. *adj.*; with -breathless expectation &c. *n.*, – bated breath, – eyes, – ears strained; *arrectis auribus*; on edge.

Phr. we shall see; *nous verrons*.

-notice, – warning, – saying 'by your leave'; like a -thief in the night, – thunderbolt; in an unguarded moment; suddenly &c. (*instantaneously*) 113.

Int. heyday! &c. (*wonder*) 870.

Phr. little did one -think, – expect; nobody would ever -suppose, – think, – expect; who would have thought?

509. [Failure of expectation.] **Disappointment.—N.** disappointment, disillusionment; blighted hope, balk; blow; slip 'twixt cup and lip; non-fulfilment of one's hopes; sad –, bitter- disappointment; trick of fortune; afterclap; false –, vain- expectation; miscalculation &c. 481; fool's paradise; much cry and little wool.

V. be disappointed; look -blank, – blue; look –, stand- -aghast &c. (*wonder*) 870; find to one's cost; laugh on the wrong side of one's mouth; find one a false prophet.

disappoint; crush –, dash –, balk –, disappoint –, blight –, falsify –, defeat –, not realize- one's -hope, – expectation; balk, jilt, bilk; play one -false, – a trick; dash the cup from the lips; tantalize; dumb-found, -founder; disillusion, -ize; dissatisfy, disgruntle.

Adj. disappointed &c. *v.*; disconcerted, aghast; out of one's reckoning; disgruntled.

Phr. the mountain brought forth a mouse; *nascitur ridiculus mus*; *parturiunt montes*; *dis aliter visum*, the bubble burst; one's countenance falling.

510. Foresight.—N. foresight, prospicience, prevision, longsightedness; anticipation; providence &c. (*preparation*) 673.

fore-thought, -cast; pre-deliberation, -surmise; foregone conclusion &c. (*prejudgment*) 481; prudence &c. (*caution*) 864.

foreknowledge; *prognosis*; pre-cognition, -science, -notion, -sentiment; second sight; sagacity &c. (*intelligence*) 498.

prospect &c. (*expectation*) 507; foretaste; prospectus &c. (*plan*) 626.

V. foresee; look -forwards to, – ahead, – beyond; scent from afar; feel in one's bones; look –, pry –, peep- into the future.

see one's way; see how the -land lies, – wind blows, – cat jumps.

anticipate; expect &c. 507; be beforehand &c. (*early*) 132; predict &c. 511; fore-know, -judge, -cast; surmise; have an eye to the -future, – main chance; *respicere finem*; keep a sharp look-out &c. (*vigilance*) 459; forewarn &c. 668.

Adj. foreseeing &c. *v.*; prescient; anticipatory; far-seeing, -sighted; sagacious &c. (*intelligent*) 498; weather-wise; provident &c. (*prepared*) 673; prospective &c. 507.

Adv. against the time when.

511. Prediction.—N. prediction, announcement; program, programme &c. (*plan*) 626; premonition &c. (*warning*) 668; *prognosis*, prophecy, vaticination, mantology, prognostication, premonstration, augur-y, -ation; a-, ha-riolation; fore-, a-boding; bode-, abode-ment; omin-ation,

-ousness; auspices, forecast; sign, presage, prognostic; omen &c. 512; horoscope, nativity; sooth, -saying; fortune-telling; divination; crystal gazing, necromancy &c. 992; prophet &c. 512.

[Divination by the stars] astrology, horoscopy, astromancy, judicial astrology.*

[Place of prediction] *adytum*.

prefigur-ation, -ement; prototype, type.

V. predict, prognosticate, prophesy, vaticinate, divine, foretell, soothsay, augurate, tell fortunes; cast a -horoscope, – nativity; advise; forewarn &c. 668.

presage, augur, bode; a-, fore-bode, -cast; fore-, be-token; prefigure, -show; portend; fore-show, -shadow, shadow forth, typify, ominate, signify, point to, precurse.

usher in, herald, premise, announce; lower.

hold out –, raise –, excite- -expectation, – hope; bid fair, promise, lead one to expect; be the -precursor &c. 64.

Adj. predicting &c. *v.*; predictive, prophetic, fatidical, vaticinal, oracular, Sibylline, haruspical, weatherwise.

ominous, presageful, portentous; augur-ous, -al, -ial; auspici-al, -ous; prescious, monitory, extispicious, premonitory, precursory, significant of, pregnant with, big with the fate of.

Phr. 'coming events cast their shadows before.'

512. Omen.—**N.** omen, portent, presage, prognostic, augury, auspice; sign &c. (*indication*) 550; herald, forerunner, harbinger &c. (*precursor*) 64.

bird of ill omen; signs of the times; gathering clouds; warning &c. 668.

prefigurement &c. 511.

513. Oracle.—**N.** oracle; prophet, -ess; seer, soothsayer, augur, fortune-teller, palmist, medium, clairvoyant, crystal gazer, witch, geomancer, *aruspex*; a-, ha-ruspice; Sibyl; Python, -ess; Pythia; Pythian –, Delphian- oracle; Monitor, Sphinx, Tiresias, Cassandra, Sibylline leaves; Zadkiel, Old Moore; sorcerer &c. 994; interpreter &c. 524.

Section VII. Creative Thought

514. Supposition.—**N.** supposition, assumption, postulation, condition, pre-supposition, hypothesis, postulate, *postulatum*, theory, *data*; pro-, position; *thesis*, theorem; proposal &c. (*plan*) 626.

* The following terms, expressive of different forms of divination, have been collected from various sources, and are here given as a curious illustration of bygone superstitions:

Divination *by oracles*, Theomancy; *by the Bible*, Bibliomancy; *by ghosts*, Psychomancy; *by spirits seen in a magic lens*, Cristallomantia; *by shadows or manes*, Sciomancy; *by appearances in the air*, Aeromancy, Chaomancy; *by the stars at birth*, Genethliacs; *by meteors*, Meteoromancy; *by winds*, Austromancy; *by sacrificial appearances*, Aruspicy (*or* Haruspicy), Hieromancy, Hieroscopy; *by the entrails of animals sacrificed*, Hieromancy; *by the entrails of a human sacrifice*, Anthropomancy; *by the entrails of fishes*, Ichthyomancy; *by sacrificial fire*, Pyromancy; *by red-hot iron*, Sideromancy; *by smoke from the altar*, Capnomancy; *by mice*, Myomancy; *by birds*, Orniscopy, Ornithomancy; *by a cock picking up grains*, Alectryomancy (*or* Alectoromancy); *by fishes*, Ophiomancy; *by herbs*, Botanomancy; *by water*, Hydromancy; *by fountains*,

bare –, vague –, loose- -supposition, – suggestion; conceit; conjecture; guess, – work; rough guess, shot; conjecturality; surmise, suspicion, inkling, suggestion, suggestiveness, association of ideas, hint; presumption &c. (*belief*) 484; divination, speculation.

theorist, speculator, doctrinarian, hypothesist.

V. suppose, conjecture, surmise, suspect, guess, divine; theorize; pre-sume, -surmise, -suppose; assume, fancy, wis, take it; give a guess, speculate, believe, dare say, take it into one's head, take for granted.

put forth; pro-pound, -pose; moot; hypothesize; start, put a case, submit, move, make a motion; hazard –, throw out –, put forward- a - suggestion, – conjecture.

allude to, suggest, hint, put it into one's head.

suggest itself &c. (*thought*) 451; run in the head &c. (*memory*) 505; marvel –, wonder- -if, – whether.

Adj. supposing &c. *v.*; given, mooted, postulatory; assumed &c. *v.* supposit-ive, -itious; gratuitous, speculative, conjectural, hypothetical, suppositional, theoretical, academic, supposable, presumptive, putative.

suggestive, allusive, stimulating.

Adv. if, – so be; an; on the -supposition &c. *n.*; *ex hypothesi*; in -case, – the event of; *quasi*, as if, provided; perhaps &c. (*by possibility*) 470; for aught one knows.

515. Imagination.—N. imagination; originality; invention; fancy; inspiration; *verve*; empathy.

warm –, heated –, excited –, sanguine –, ardent –, fiery –, boiling –, wild –, bold –, daring –, playful –, lively –, fertile- -imagination, – fancy.

'mind's eye'; 'such stuff as dreams are made of.'

ideal ity, -ism; romanticism, utopianism, castle-building; dreaming; frenzy; ecs-, ex-tasy; calenturo &c. (*delirium*) 503; reverie, brown study, trance; somnambulism.

conception, *vorstellung*, excogitation, 'a fine frenzy,' poetic frenzy, divine afflatus; cloud-, dream-land; flight –, fumes- of fancy; 'thick-coming fancies'; creation –, coinage- of the brain; imagery, word painting.

conceit, maggot, figment, myth, dream, vision, shadow, chimera; phan-tasm, -tasy; fantasy, fancy; whim, -sey; vagary, rhapsody, romance, *extravaganza*; air-drawn dagger, bugbear, nightmare; flying Dutchman, great sea-serpent, man in the moon, castle in the air, *châteaux en Espagne*; Utopia, Atlantis, happy valley, millennium, fairy land; land of Prester John, kingdom of Micomicon; work of fiction &c. (*novel*) 594; poetry &c. 597; drama &c. 599; Arabian nights; *le pot au lait*; dream of Alnaschar &c. (*hope*) 858; day –, golden- dream.

illusion &c. (*error*) 495; phantom &c. (*fallacy of vision*) 443; *Fata*

Pegomancy; *by a wand*, Rhabdomancy; *by dough of cakes*, Crithomancy; *by meal*, Aleuromancy, Alphitomancy; *by salt*, Halomancy; *by dice*, Cleromancy; *by arrows*, Belomancy; *by a balanced hatchet*, Axinomancy; *by a balanced sieve*, Coscinomancy; *by a suspended ring*, Dactyliomancy; *by dots made at random on paper*, Geomancy; *by precious stones*, Lithomancy; *by pebbles*, Pessomancy; *by pebbles drawn from a heap*, Psephomancy; *by mirrors*, Catoptromancy; *by writings in ashes*, Tephramancy; *by dreams*, Oneiromancy; *by the hand*, Palmistry, Chiromancy; *by nails reflecting the sun's rays*, Onychomancy; *by finger rings*, Dactylomancy; *by numbers*, Arithmancy; *by drawing lots*, Sortilege; *by passages in books*, Stichomancy; *by the letters forming the name of the person*, Onomancy, Nomancy; *by the features*, Anthroposcopy; *by the mode of laughing*, Geloscopy; *by ventriloquism*, Gastromancy; *by walking in a circle*, Gyromancy; *by dropping melted wax into water*, Ceromancy; *by currents*, Bletonism.

Morgana &c. (*ignis fatuus*) 423; vapour &c. (*cloud*) 353; stretch of the imagination &c. (*exaggeration*) 549.

idealist, romanticist, visionary; mopus; romancer, dreamer; somnambulist; rhapsodist &c. (*fanatic*) 504.

V. imagine, fancy, conceive; ideal-, real-ize; dream, – of; 'give to airy nothing a local habitation and a name.'

create, originate, devise, invent, coin, fabricate; improvise, strike out something new.

set one's wits to work; strain –, crack- one's invention; rack –, ransack –, cudgel- one's brains; excogitate.

give -play, – the reins, – a loose- to the -imagination, – fancy; empathize; indulge in reverie.

conjure up a vision; fancy –, represent –, picture –, figure- to oneself; envisage.

float in the mind; suggest itself &c. (*thought*) 451.

Adj. imagined &c. *v.*; *ben trovato*; air-drawn, -built.

imagin-ing &c. *v.*, -ative; original, inventive, creative, fertile, productive; ingenious.

romantic, high-flown, flighty, extravagant, fanatic, enthusiastic, Utopian, Quixotic; preposterous, rhapsodical.

ideal, unreal; in the clouds, *in nubibus*; unsubstantial &c. 4; illusory &c. (*fallacious*) 495; fictitious, theoretical, hypothetical.

fabulous, legendary; myth-ic, -ological; chimerical; imagin-, visionary; notional; fan-cy, -ciful, -tastic, -tastical; whimsical; fairy, -like.

dreamy, entranced, vaporous.

Division (II.) COMMUNICATION OF IDEAS

Section I. Nature of Ideas Communicated

516. [Idea to be conveyed.] **Meaning.** [Thing signified.]—**N.** meaning; signific-ation, -ance; sense, expression; im-, pur-port; drift, tenor, implication, connotation, essence, force, spirit, bearing, colouring; scope.

matter; subject, -matter; argument, text, sum and substance; gist &c. 5.

general –, broad –, substantial –, colloquial –, literal –, plain –, simple –, accepted –, natural –, unstrained –, true &c. (*exact*) 494 –, honest &c. 543 –, *primâ facie* &c. (*manifest*) 525- meaning.

literality; literal interpretation; after acceptation; allusion &c. (*latency*) 526; suggestion &c. (*information*) 527; synonym; figure of speech &c. 521; acceptation &c. (*interpretation*) 522.

V. mean, signify, express, connote, denote; im-, pur-port; convey, imply, breathe, indicate, bespeak, bear a sense; tell –, speak- of; touch on; point –, allude- to; drive at; involve &c. (*latency*) 526; declare &c. (*affirm*) 535.

517. [Absence of meaning.] **Unmeaningness.**—**N.** unmeaningness &c. *adj.*; scrabble, scribble, scrawl, daub, (*painting*), strumming (*music*).

empty sound, dead letter, *vox et præterea nihil*; 'a tale told by an idiot, full of sound and fury, signifying nothing'; 'sounding brass and a tinkling cymbal.'

nonsense, jargon, gibberish, jabber, mere words, hocus-pocus, fustian, rant, bombast, balderdash, palaver, patter, flummery, verbiage, babble, *bavardage*, *baragouin*, platitude, *niaiserie*; inanity; rigmarole, rodomontade; truism; *nugæ canoræ*; twaddle, twattle, fudge, trash; stuff, – and nonsense; bosh, rubbish, rot, drivel, moonshine, wish-wash, fiddle-faddle, flapdoodle; absurdity &c. 497; vagueness &c. (*unintelligibility*) 519.

V. mean nothing; be -unmeaning &c. *adj.*; twaddle, quibble, rant, gabble, scrabble &c. *n.*

Adj. unmeaning; meaning-, sense-less;

understand by &c. (*interpret*) 522.

Adj. meaning &c. *v.*; expressive, suggestive, meaningful, allusive; signific-ant, -ative, -atory; pithy; full of –, pregnant with- meaning.

declaratory &c. 535; intelligible &c. 518; literal, metaphrastic; synonymous; tantamount &c. (*equivalent*) 27; implied &c. (*latent*) 526; explicit &c. 525; literal &c. 562.

Adv. to that effect; that is to say &c. (*being interpreted*) 522.

literally; evidently, from the context.

nonsensical; void of -sense &c. 516.

in-, un-expressive; vacant, fatuous; not significant; insignificant.

trashy, washy, inane, vague, trumpery, trivial, fiddle-faddle, twaddling, quibbling.

unmeant, not expressed; tacit &c. (*latent*) 526.

inexpressible, undefinable, incommunicable.

Int. rubbish! &c. 497.

---

518. Intelligibility.—N. intelligibility, clearness, clarity, explicitness &c. *adj.*; lucidity, perspicuity; legibility, plain speaking &c. (*manifestation*) 525; precision &c. 494; a word to the wise.

V. be -intelligible &c. *adj.*; speak -for itself, – volumes; tell its own tale, lie on the surface.

render -intelligible &c. *adj.*; popularize, simplify, clear up; elucidate &c. (*explain*) 522.

understand, comprehend; take, – in; catch, grasp, recognize, follow, collect, master, make out; see -with half an eye, – daylight, – one's way; enter into the ideas of; come to an understanding.

Adj. intelligible; clear, – as -day, – crystal, – noonday; lucid; per-, transpicuous; luminous, transparent; comprehensible.

easily understood, easy to understand, for the million, intelligible to the meanest capacity, popularized.

plain, distinct, explicit, clear-cut; positive; definite &c. (*precise*) 494.

graphic, vivid, telling; expressive &c. (*meaning*) 516; illustrative &c. (*explanatory*) 522.

un-ambiguous, -equivocal, -mistakable &c. (*manifest*) 525, -confused; legible, recognizable; obvious &c. 525.

Adv. in plain -terms, – words, – English.

Phr. he that runs may read &c. (*manifest*) 525.

---

519. Unintelligibility.—N. unintelligibility, incomprehensibility, imperspicuity; inconceivableness, vagueness &c. *adj.*; obscurity; ambiguity &c. 520; doubtful meaning; uncertainty &c. 475; perplexity &c. (*confusion*) 59; spinosity; *obscurum per obscurius*; mystification &c. (*concealment*) 528; latency &c. 526; transcendentalism.

paradox; enigma, riddle &c. (*secret*) 533; *dignus vindice nodus*; sealed book; steganography, Freemasonry.

pons asinorum, asses' bridge; double –, high- Dutch, Greek, Hebrew; jargon &c. (*unmeaning*) 517.

obscurantist.

V. be -unintelligible &c. *adj.*; require -explanation &c. 522; have a doubtful meaning, pass comprehension.

render -unintelligible &c. *adj.*; conceal &c. 528; darken &c. 421; confuse &c. (*derange*) 61; perplex &c. (*bewilder*) 475.

not -understand &c. 518; lose, – the clue; miss; not know what to make of, be able to make nothing of, give it up; not be able to -account for, – make either head or tail of; be at sea &c. (*uncertain*) 475; wonder &c. 870; see through a glass darkly &c. (*ignorance*) 491.

not understand one another; play at cross purposes &c. (*misinterpret*) 523.

Adj. un-intelligible, -accountable, -decipherable, -discoverable, -knowable, -fathomable; in-cognizable, -explicable, -scrutable; inap-, incomprehensible; insol-vable, -uble; impenetrable.

illegible, indecipherable, as Greek to one, unexplained, paradoxical; enigmatic, -al; puzzling, baffling.

obscure, dark, muddy, clear as mud, seen through a mist, dim, nebulous, shrouded in mystery; undiscernible &c. (*invisible*) 447; misty &c. (*opaque*) 426; hidden &c. 528; latent &c. 526.

indefinite &c. (*indistinct*) 447; perplexed &c. (*confused*) 59; undetermined, vague, loose, ambiguous; mysterious; mystic, -al; transcendental; occult, recondite, esoteric, abstruse, crabbed.

incon-ceivable, -ceptible; searchless; above –, beyond –, past- comprehension; beyond one's depth; unconceived.

inexpressible, undefinable, incommunicable, unutterable, ineffable, unpronounceable.

520. [Having a double sense.] **Equivocalness.—N.** equivocalness &c. *adj.*; double -meaning &c. 516; ambiguity, *double entendre*, pun, paragram, *calembour*, quibble, *équivoque*, anagram; conundrum &c. (*riddle*) 533; word-play &c. (*wit*) 842; homonym, -y; amphibo-ly, -logy; ambiloquy.

Sphinx, Delphic oracle.

equivocation &c. (*duplicity*) 544; white lie, mental reservation &c. (*concealment*) 528.

V. be -equivocal &c. *adj.*; have two -meanings &c. 516; equivocate &c. (*palter*) 544.

Adj. equivocal, ambiguous, amphibolous, homonymous; double-tongued &c. (*lying*) 544.

521. Metaphor.—N. figure of speech; *façon de parler*, way of speaking, colloquialism.

phrase &c. 566; figure, trope, metaphor, tralatition, metonymy, enallage, *catachresis*, *synecdoche*, *antonomasia*; irony, satire, figurativeness &c. *adj.*; image, -ry; *metalepsis*, type, anagoge, simile, personification, *prosopopæia*, allegory, apologue, parable, fable; allusion, adumbration; application; euphemism; euphuism.

V. employ -metaphor &c. *n.*; personify, allegorize, adumbrate, shadow forth, apply, allude –, refer- to.

Adj. metaphorical &c. *n.*; figurative, catachrestical, typical, tralatitious, parabolic, allegorical, allusive, anagogical; ironical; colloquial.

Adv. so to -speak, – say, – express oneself; as it were.

Phr. *mutato nomine de te fabula narratur.*

522. Interpretation.—N. interpretation, definition; explan-, explic-ation; solution, answer; rationale; plain –, simple –, strict- interpretation; meaning &c. 516.

translation; rend-ering, -ition; reddition; literal –, free- translation; key, crib; secret; clew &c. (*indication*) 550; Rosetta stone.

exegesis; ex-pounding, -position; Hermeneutics; comment, -ary; inference &c. (*deduction*) 480; illustration, exemplification; gloss, annotation, *scholium*, note; e-, di-lucidation, enucleation; *éclaircissement*, *mot de l'énigme*.

symptomat-, semei-ology; metoposcopy, physiognomy; diagnosis, prog-

523. Misinterpretation. — N. misinterpretation, -apprehension, -understanding, -acceptation, -construction, -application; *catachresis*; cross -reading, – purposes; mistake &c. 495.

misrepresentation, perversion, exaggeration &c. 549; false -colouring, – construction; abuse of terms; parody, travesty; falsification &c. (*lying*) 544.

V. mis-interpret, -apprehend, -understand, -conceive, -judge, -doubt, -spell, -translate, -construe, -apply; mistake &c. 495.

misrepresent, pervert; garble &c. (*falsify*) 544; distort, detort; travesty, play upon words; stretch –, strain –, wrest- the -sense, – meaning; explain

nosis; paleography &c. (*philology*) 560.

accept-ion, -ation, -ance; light, reading, lection, construction, version.

equivalent, – meaning &c. 516; synonym; para-, meta-phrase; convertible terms, apposition; dictionary &c. 562; polyglot.

V. interpret, explain, define, construe, translate, render; do –, turn- into; transfuse the sense of.

find out &c. 480*a*- -the meaning &c. 516- of; read; spell –, figure –, make- out; decipher, decode, unravel, disentangle, puzzle out; find the key of, enucleate, resolve, solve; read between the lines.

account for; find –, tell- the cause &c. 153- of; throw –, shed- -light, – new light, – a fresh light- upon; clear up, elucidate.

illustrate, exemplify; unfold, expound, comment upon, annotate; popularize &c. (*render intelligible*) 518.

take –, understand –, receive –, accept- in a particular sense; understand by, put a construction on, be given to understand.

Adj. explanatory, expository; explica-tive, -tory; exegetical; hermeneutic, interpretive, illustrative, elucidative, annotative, scholiastic.

polyglot; literal; para-, meta-phrastic; cosignificative, synonymous; equivalent &c. 27.

Adv. in -explanation &c. *n.*; that is to say, *id est*, *videlicet*, to wit, namely, in other words.

literally, strictly speaking; in -plain, – plainer- -terms, – words, – English, more simply.

524. Interpreter.—**N.** interpreter, translator, ex-positor, -pounder, -ponent, -plainer; demonstrator.

scholiast, commentator, annotator; meta-, para-phrast.

spokesman, speaker, mouthpiece, prolocutor; diplomat &c. 758.

guide, courier, dragoman, *valet de place*, *cicerone*, showman; oneirocritic; Œdipus; oracle &c. 513.

away; put a -bad, – false- construction on; give a false colouring, look through -rose coloured –, – dark – spectacles.

be –, play- at cross purposes.

Adj. misinterpreted &c. *v.*; untranslat-ed, -able.

Adv. at cross purposes.

Section II. Modes of Communication

525. Manifestation.—**N.** manifestation; unfolding; plainness &c. *adj.*; plain speaking; expression; showing &c. *v.*; exposition, demonstration, *séance*; exhibition, production; display, showing off &c. 882, premonstration. [Thing shown] exhibit, show.

indication &c. (*calling attention to*) 457; publicity &c. 531; disclosure &c. 529; openness &c. (*honesty*) 543, (*artlessness*) 703; *épanchement*, prominence.

V. make –, render- -manifest &c. *adj.*; bring -forth, – forward, – to the front, – into view; give notice; express; represent, set forth, exhibit; show, – up; expose; produce; hold up –, expose- to view; set –, place –, lay-

526. Latency.—**N.** latency, inexpression; hidden –, occult- meaning; occultness, occultism, mysticism, mystery, cabala, symbolism, anagoge; silence &c. (*taciturnity*) 585; concealment &c. 528; more than meets the -eye, – ear; Delphic oracle; *le dessous des cartes*, undercurrent.

allusion, insinuation, implication; innuendo &c. 527; adumbration; 'something rotten in the state of Denmark.'

snake in the grass &c. (*pitfall*) 667; secret &c. 533.

darkness, invisibility, imperceptibility.

latent influence, power behind the throne; friend at court, wire puller.

before -one, – one's eyes; tell to one's face; trot out, put through one's paces, unfold, show off, show forth, unveil, bring to light, display, demonstrate, unroll; lay open; draw –, bring- out; bring out in strong relief; call –, bring- into notice; hold up the mirror; wear one's heart upon his sleeve; show one's -face, – colours; mainfest oneself; speak out; make no -mystery, – secret- of; unfurl the flag; proclaim &c. (*publish*) 531.

indicate &c. (*direct attention to*) 457; disclose &c. 529; elicit &c. 480*a*; interpret &c. 522.

be -manifest &c. *adj.*; appear &c. (*be visible*) 446; transpire &c. (*be disclosed*) 529; speak for itself, stand to reason; stare one in the face; loom large, appear on the horizon, rear its head; give -token, – sign, – indication of; tell its own tale &c. (*intelligible*) 518; go without saying.

Adj. manifest, apparent; salient, striking, demonstrative, prominent, in the foreground, notable, pronounced.

flagrant; notorious &c. (*public*) 531; arrant; stark staring;unshaded, glaring.

defin-ed, -ite; distinct, conspicuous &c. (*visible*) 446; obvious, evident, incontestable, unmistakable, not to be mistaken, plain, clear, palpable, self-evident, autoptical; intelligible &c. 518; clear as -day, – daylight, – noonday; plain as -a pikestaff, – the sun at noonday, – the nose on one's face, – the way to the parish church.

ostensible; open, – as day; overt, patent, express, explicit; naked, bare, literal, downright, undisguised, exoteric.

V. be -latent &c. *adj.*; lurk, smoulder, underlie, make no sign; escape -observation, – detection, – recognition; lie hid &c. 528.

laugh in one's sleeve; keep back &c. (*conceal*) 528.

involve, imply, implicate, connote, import, understand, allude to, infer, leave an inference; symbolize; whisper &c. (*conceal*) 528.

Adj. latent; lurking &c. *v.*; secret &c. 528; occult, symbolic, mystic; implied &c. *v.*; dormant.

un-apparent, -known, -seen &c. 441; in the background; invisible &c. 447; indiscoverable, dark; impenetrable &c. (*unintelligible*) 519; un-spied, -suspected.

un-said, -written, -published, -breathed, -talked of, -told &c. 527, -sung, -exposed, -proclaimed, -disclosed &c. 529, -pronounced, -mentioned, -expressed; not expressed, tacit.

un-developed, -solved, -explained, -traced, -discovered &c. 480*a*, -tracked, -explored, -invented.

indirect, crooked, inferential; by -inference, – implication; implicit; constructive; allusive, covert, muffled; steganographic; under-stood, -hand, -ground; concealed &c. 528; delitescent.

Adv. by a side wind; *sub silentio*; in the background; behind -the scenes, – one's back, – the veil; below the surface; on the tip of one's tongue; secretly &c. 528; between the lines; by a mutual understanding.

Phr. 'thereby hangs a tale,' 'that is another story.'

unreserved; frank, plain spoken &c. (*artless*) 703; barefaced, brazen, bold, shameless, daring, flaunting, loud.

manifested &c. *v.*; disclosed &c. 529; expressible, capable of being shown, producible; in-, un-concealable.

Adv. manifestly, openly &c. *adj.*; before one's eyes, under one's nose, to one's face, face to face, above board, *cartes sur table*, on the stage, in plain sight, in open court, in the open, – streets; at the cross roads; in market overt; in the face of -day, – heaven; in -broad –, open- daylight; without reserve; at first blush, *primâ facie*, on the face of; in set terms.

Phr. *cela saute aux yeux*; he that runs may read; you can see it with half an eye; it needs no ghost to tell us; the meaning lies on the surface; *cela va sans dire*; *res ipsa loquitur*.

527. Information.—N. information, enlightenment, acquaintance, knowledge &c. 490; publicity &c. 531.

communication, intimation; not-ice, -ification; e, -an-nunciation; announcement; representation, round robin, presentment.

case, estimate, specification, report, advice, monition; news &c. 532; return &c. (*record*) 551; account &c. (*description*) 594; statement &c. (*affirmation*) 535.

mention; acquainting &c. *v.*; instruction &c. (*teaching*) 537; outpouring; intercommunication, communicativeness.

informant, authority, teller, announcer, annunicator, harbinger, herald, intelligencer, commentator, columnist, reporter, exponent, mouthpiece; informer, keek, eavesdropper, delator, detective, sleuth; *mouchard*, spy, stool pigeon, newsmonger; messenger &c. 534; *amicus curiæ*.

valet de place, *cicerone*, pilot, guide; guide-, hand-book; *vade mecum*; manual; map, plan, chart, gazetteer; itinerary &c. (*journey*) 266.

hint, suggestion, wrinkle, innuendo, inkling, whisper, passing word, word in the ear, subaudition, cue, by-play; gesture &c. (*indication*) 550; gentle – broad- hint; *verbum sapienti*; word to the wise; insinuation &c. (*latency*) 526.

V. tell; inform, – of; acquaint, – with; impart, – to; make acquainted with, bring to the ears of, apprise, advise, enlighten, awaken.

let fall, mention, express, intimate, represent, communicate, make known; publish &c. 531; notify, signify, specify, convey the knowledge of.

let one –, have one to- know; serve notice, give one to understand; give notice; set –, lay –, put- before; point out, put into one's head; put one in possession of; instruct &c. (*teach*) 537; direct the attention to &c. 457.

an-nounce, -nunciate; report, – progress; bring –, send –, leave –, write- word; tele-graph, -phone; ring –, call- up; wire; retail, render an account; give an account &c. (*describe*) 594; state &c. (*affirm*) 535.

528. Concealment.—N. concealment; hiding &c. *v.*; occultation, mystification.

seal of secrecy; screen &c. 530; disguise &c. 530; masquerade; masked battery; hiding place &c. 530; cipher, code, crypt-, stegan-ography; invisible –, sympathetic- ink; palimpsest; Freemasonry.

stealth, -iness; obreption; slyness &c. (*cunning*) 702.

latit-ancy, -ation; seclusion &c. 893; privacy, secrecy, secretness; *incognita*.

reticence; reserve; mental –, reservation, aside; *arrière pensée*, suppression, evasion, white lie, misprision; silence &c. (*taciturnity*) 585; suppression of truth &c. 544; underhand dealing; close-, secretive-ness &c. *adj.*; mystery.

latency &c. 526; snake in the grass; secret &c. 533.

V. conceal, hide, secrete, stow away, put out of sight; lock –, seal –, bottle- up.

cover, screen, cloak, veil, shroud; screen from -sight, – observation; draw the veil; draw –, close- the curtain; curtain, shade, eclipse, throw a veil over; be-cloud, -fog, -mask; mask, disguise; ensconce, muffle, smother; whisper.

keep -from, – back, – to oneself; keep -snug, – close, – secret, – dark, bury; sink, suppress; keep -from, – out of- -view, – sight; keep in –, throw into- the -shade, – background; cover up one's tracks; stifle, hush up, withhold, reserve; fence with a question; ignore &c. 460.

code, codify, use a cipher.

keep -a secret, – one's own counsel; hold one's tongue &c. (*silence*) 585; make no sign, not let it go further; not breathe a -word, – syllable- about; not let the right hand know what the left is doing; hide one's light under a bushel, bury one's talent in a napkin.

keep –, leave- in -the dark, – ignorance; blind, – the eyes; blindfold,, hoodwink, mystify; puzzle &c. (*render uncertain*) 475; bamboozle &c. (*deceive*) 545.

be -concealed &c. *v.*;suffer an eclipse;

disclose &c. 529; show cause; explain &c. (*interpret*) 522.

hint; give an inkling of; give –, drop –, throw out- a hint; insinuate; allude –, make allusion- to; glance at; tip off, tip the wink &c. (*indicate*) 550; suggest, prompt, give the cue, breathe; whisper, – in the ear.

give a bit of one's mind; tell one plainly, – once for all; speak volumes.

un-deceive, -beguile; set right, correct, open the eyes of, disabuse.

be -informed of &c.; know &c. 490; learn &c. 539; get scent of, gather from; awaken –, open one's eyes- to; become -alive, – awake- to; keep posted; hear, overhear, understand.

come to one's -ears, – knowledge; reach one's ears.

Adj. informed &c. *v.*; *communiqué*; reported &c. *v.*; published &c. 531; advisory.

expressive &c. 516; explicit &c. (*open*) 525, (*clear*) 518; plain-spoken &c. (*artless*) 703.

declara-, nuncupa-, exposi-tory; declarative, enunciative, communicat-ive, -ory; oral.

Adv. from information received; according to -rumour, – report; in the air; from what one can gather.

Phr. a little bird told me.

---

retire from sight, couch; hide oneself; lie -hid, – in ambush, – low, – *perdu*, – snug, – close; seclude oneself &c. 893; lurk, sneak, skulk, slink, pussyfoot, prowl; steal -into, – out of, – by, – along; play at -bopeep, – hide and seek; hide in holes and corners.

Adj. concealed &c. *v.*; hidden; veiled, secret, recondite, mystic, cabalistic, occult, dark; cryptic, -al; private, privy, *in petto*, auricular, clandestine, close, inviolate.

behind a -screen &c. 530; under -cover, – an eclipse; in -ambush, – hiding, – disguise; in a -cloud, – fog, – mist, – haze, – dark corner; in the -shade, – dark; clouded, wrapt in clouds; invisible &c. 447; buried, underground, *perdu*; incommunicado; secluded &c. 893.

un-disclosed &c. 529, -told &c. 527; covert &c. (*latent*) 526; mysterious &c. (*unintelligible*) 519.

irrevealable, inviolable; confidential; esoteric; not to be spoken of.

obreptitious, furtive, stealthy, feline; skulking &c. *v.*; surreptitious, underhand, hole and corner; sly &c. (*cunning*) 702; secretive, evasive, non-committal, reserved, reticent, uncommunicative, buttoned up; close, – as wax; taciturn &c. 585.

Adv. secretly &c. *adj.*; in -secret, – private, – one's sleeve, – holes and corners; in the dark &c. *adj.*

januis clausis, with closed doors, *à huis clos*; hugger-mugger, *à la dérobée*; under the -cloak of, – rose, – table; *sub rosâ, en tapinois*, in the background, aside, on the sly, with bated breath, *sotto voce*, in a whisper, without beat of drum, *à la sourdine*.

in –, strict- confidence; confidentially &c. *adj.*; between -ourselves, – you and me; *entre nous, inter nos*, under the seal of secrecy; in -code, – cipher.

underhand, by stealth, like a thief in the night; stealthily &c. *adj.*; behind -the scenes, – the curtain, – one's back, – a screen &c. 530; *incognito*; *in camerâ*.

Phr. it -must, – will- go no further; 'tell it not in Gath,' nobody the wiser.

529. Disclosure.—**N.** disclosure; retection; unveiling &c. *v.*; deterration, revealment, revelation; divulgence, expos-ition, -ure; *exposé*; whole truth; tell-tale &c. (*news*) 532.

acknowledgment, avowal; confession, -al; shrift.

530. Ambush. [Means of concealment.]—**N.** hiding-place; secret -place, – drawer; recess, hole, funk hole, holes and corners; closet, crypt, *adytum*, abditory, *oubliette*, safe, – deposit; cache.

am-bush, -buscade; stalking horse; lurking-hole, -place; secret path,

bursting of a bubble; *dénouement*.

V. dis-close, -cover, -mask; draw –, draw aside –, lift –, raise –, lift up –, remove –, tear- the -veil, – curtain; un-mask, -veil, -fold, -cover, -seal, -kennel; take off –, break- the seal; lay -open, – bare; expose; open, – up; bare, bring to light; evidence; make - clear, – evident, – manifest; evince.

divulge, reveal, break; let into the secret; reveal the secrets of the prison-house; tell &c. (*inform*) 527; breathe, utter, blab, peach; let -out, – fall, – drop, – the cat out of the bag; betray; tell tales, – out of school; come out with; give -vent, – utterance- to; open the lips, blurt out, vent, whisper about; speak out &c. (*make manifest*) 525; make public &c. 531; unriddle &c. (*find out*) 480*a*; split; blow the gaff; break the news.

acknowledge, allow, concede, grant, admit, own, confess, avow, throw off all disguise, turn inside out, make a clean breast; show one's -hand, – cards; unburden –, disburden- one's -mind, – conscience, – heart; open –, lay bare –, tell a piece of- one's mind; unbosom oneself, own to the soft impeachment; say –, speak- the truth; turn -King's, –Queen's, –State's- evidence.

raise –, drop –, lift –, remove –, throw off- the mask; expose; debunk; lay open; un-deceive, -beguile; disabuse, set right, correct, open the eyes of; *désillusionner*.

be -disclosed &c.; transpire, come to light; come in sight &c. (*be visible*) 446; become known, escape the lips; come –, ooze –, creep –, leak –, peep –, crop- out; show its -face, – colours; discover &c. itself; break through the clouds, flash on the mind.

Adj. disclosed &c. *v.*

Int. out with it!

Phr. the murder is out; a light breaks in upon one; the scales fall from one's eyes; the eyes are opened.

backstairs; retreat &c. (*refuge*) 666.

screen, cover, shade, blinker; veil, curtain, blind, *purdah*, cloak, cloud.

mask, vizor, visor, disguise, masquerade dress, domino; *camouflage*.

pitfall &c. (*source of danger*) 667; trap &c. (*snare*) 545.

V. ambush, ambuscade, lie in ambush &c. (*hide oneself*) 528; lie in wait for; set a trap for &c. (*deceive*) 545.

Adv. *aux aguets*.

---

531. Publication.—N. publication; public -announcement &c. 527; promulgation, propagation, proclamation, pronouncement, encylical, *pronunciamento*; circulation, indiction, edition, imprint, impression, printing; hue and cry.

publicity, notoriety, currency, flagrancy, cry, *bruit*; *vox populi*; report &c. (*news*) 532.

the Press, fourth estate, public press, newspaper, periodical, journal, gazette; house organ, trade publication, tabloid; daily, weekly, monthly, quarterly, annual, magazine, monograph, book; review; news sheet, special edition, supplement, feature, rotogravure, comic strips; leaflet, pamphlet; telegraphy; publisher &c. *v.*

circular, – letter; manifesto, advertisement, puff, placard, bill, *affiche*, broadside, poster; notice &c. 527; programme.

V. publish; make -public, – known &c. (*information*) 527; speak –, talk- of; broach, utter; put forward; circulate, propagate, promulgate; spread –, abroad; rumour, diffuse, disseminate, evulgate; put –, give –, send- forth; emit, edit, get out; issue; cover, report; bring –, lay –, drag- before the public; give -out, – to the world; put –, bandy –, hawk –, buzz –, whisper –, bruit –, blaze- about; drag into the -open day, – limelight; voice.

proclaim, herald, blazon; blaze –, noise- abroad; sound a trumpet; trumpet –, thunder- forth; give tongue; announce with -beat of drum, – flourish of trumpets; proclaim -from the housetops, – at Charing Cross, at the cross roads; declare, declaim.

advertise, placard; post, – up; *afficher*, publisher in the Gazette, send round the crier.

raise a -cry, – hue and cry, – report; set news afloat.

telegraph, cable, wireless, broadcast.

be -published &c.; be –, become- public &c. *adj.*; come out; go–, fly –, buzz –, blow- about; get -about, – abroad, – afloat, – wind: find vent; see the light; go forth, take air, acquire currency, pass current; go -the rounds, – the round of the newspapers, – through the length and breadth of the land; *virum volitare per ora*; pass from mouth to mouth; spread; run –, spread- like wildfire.

Adj. published &c. *v.*; current &c. (*news*) 532; in circulation, public; notorious; flagrant, arrant; open &c. 525; trumpet-tongued; encyclical, promulgatory; exoteric.

Adv. publicly &c. *adj.*; in open court, with open doors; in the limelight.

Int. *Oyez*! O yes! notice!

Phr. notice is hereby given; this is –, these are- to give notice.

532. News.—N. news; information &c. 527; piece –, budget- of -news, – information; report, story, yarn, copy, filler, intelligence, tidings; stop press news.

word, advice, *aviso*, message; dis-, des-patch; radio, telegram, cablegram, wireless telegram, radiogram, marconigram, communication, errand, embassy; *bulletin*, *petit bleu*.

rumour, hearsay, *on dit*, flying rumour, news stirring, cry, buzz, *bruit*, fame; talk, *ouï-dire*, scandal, eavesdropping; town –, table- talk; tittle-tattle; *canard*, topic of the day, idea afloat.

fresh –, stirring –, old –, stale- news; glad tidings; old –, stale- story.

narrator &c. (*describe*) 594; news-, scandal-monger; tale-bearer; tell-tale, gossip, tattler, busy-body, chatterer, informer.

V. transpire &c. (*be disclosed*) 529; rumour &c. (*publish*) 531;

Adj. many-tongued; rumoured; publicly –, currently- -rumoured, – reported; rife, current, floating, afloat, going about, in circulation, in everyone's mouth, all over the town.

Adv. as the story -goes, – runs; as they say, it is said.

533. Secret.—N. secret; dead –, profound- secret; *arcanum*, mystery; latency &c. 526; Asian mystery; sealed book, secrets of the prison-house; *le dessous des cartes*.

enigma, riddle, puzzle, nut to crack, conundrum, charade, rebus, logogriph; mono-, ana-gram; acrostic, cross-word puzzle; Sphnix; *crux criticorum*.

maze, labyrinth, Hyrcynian wood.

problem &c. (*question*) 461; paradox &c. (*difficulty*) 704; unintelligibility &c. 519; *terra incognita* &c. (*ignorance*) 491.

Adj. secret &c. (*concealed*) 528.

---

534. Messenger.—N. messenger, envoy, emissary, legate; nuncio, internuncio; intermediary; ambassador &c. (*diplomatist*) 758.

marshal, flag-bearer, herald, crier, trumpeter, bellman, pursuivant, *parlementaire*, *apparitor*.

courier, runner, dawk, *estafette*; Hermes, Mercury, Iris, Ariel.

postman, letter carrier, telegraph boy, messenger boy, district messenger; despatch rider, commissionaire, errand-boy.

mail; post, -office; letter-bag; mail -boat, – train, – coach, – van, air mail; tele-graph, -phone; cable, wire; carrier-pigeon; wireless tele-graph, -phone; radiotele-graph, -phone.

journalist, newspaperman, reporter; gentleman –, representative- of the press; sob sister; penny-a-liner; special –, war –, own- correspondent; spy, scout; informer &c. 527.

535. Affirmation.—**N.** affirm-ance, -ation; statement, allegation, assertion, predication, declaration, word, averment.

asseveration, adjuration, swearing; oath, affidavit; deposition &c. (*record*) 551; avouchment, assurance; protest, -ation; profession; acknowledgement &c. (*assent*) 488; pledge.

vote, voice, suffrage, ballot.

remark, observation; position &c. (*proposition*) 514; saying, *dictum*, sentence, *ipse dixit*.

emphasis, positiveness, peremptoriness; dogmatism &c. (*certainty*) 474; dogmatist &c. 887.

V. assert; make -an assertion &c. *n.*; have one's say; say, affirm, predicate, declare, state, represent; protest, profess.

put -forth, – forward; advance allege, propose, propound, enunciate, enounce, broach, set forth, hold out, maintain, contend, pronounce, pretend.

depose, depone, aver, avow, avouch, asseverate, swear; make –, take one's oath; make –, swear –, put in- an affidavit; take one's Bible oath, kiss the book, vow, *vitam impendere vero*; swear till -one is black in the face, – all's blue; be sworn, call Heaven to witness; vouch, warrant, certify, assure, swear by bell, book and candle.

swear by &c. (*believe*) 484; insist –, take one's stand- upon; emphasize, lay stress on; assert -roundly, – positively; lay down, – the law; raise one's voice, dogmatize, have the last word; rap out; repeat; re-assert, -affirm.

announce &c. (*infornation*) 527; acknowledge &c. (*assent*) 488; attest &c. (*evidence*) 467; adjure &c. (*put to one's oath*) 768.

Adj. asserting &c. *v.*; declaratory, predicatory, pronunciative, affirmative, *soi-disant*; positive; certain &c. 474; express, explicit &c. (*patent*) 525; absolute, emphatic, flat, broad, round, pointed, marked, distinct, decided, confident, assertive, insistent, trenchant, dogmatic, definitive, formal, solemn, categorical, peremptory; unretracted; predicable, affirmable.

536. Negation.—**N.** ne-, abne-gation; denial; dis-avowal, -claimer; abjuration; contra-diction, -vention; recusation, protest; rebuttal; recusancy &c. (*dissent*) 489; flat –, emphatic- -contradiction, – denial; *démenti*.

qualification &c. 469; repudiation &c 610; retractation &c. 607; confutation &c. 479; refusal &c. 764; prohibition &c. 761.

V. deny; contra-dict, -vene; controvert, give denial to, gainsay, negative, shale the head.

dis-own, -affirm, -claim, -avow; recant &c. 607; revoke &c. (*abrogate*) 756.

dispute, impugn, traverse, rebut, join issue upon; bring –, call- in question &c. (*doubt*) 485.

deny -flatly, – peremptorily, – emphatically, – absolutely, – wholly, – entirely; give the lie to, belie.

repudiate &c. 610; set aside, ignore &c. 460; rebut &c. (*confute*) 479; qualify &c. 469; refuse &c. 764.

Adj. denying &c. *v.*; denied &c. *v.*; contradictory; negat-ive, -ory; revocatory; recusant &c. (*dissenting*) 489; at issue upon.

Adv. no, nay, not, nowise; not a -bit, – whit, – jot; not -at all, – in the least, – so; no such thing; nothing of the -kind, – sort; quite the contrary, *tout au contraire*, far from it; *tant s'en faut*; on no account, in no respect; by -no, – no manner of- means; negatively.

Phr. there never was a greater mistake; I know better; *non hæc in fœdera*.

Adv. affirmatively &c. *adj.*; in the affirmative.

with emphasis, *ex cathedrâ*, without fear of contradiction.

I must say, indeed, i' faith, let me tell you, why, give me leave to say, marry, you may be sure, I'd have you to know; upon my -word, - honour; by my troth, egad, I assure you; by -jingo, - Jove, - George, - &c.; troth, seriously, sadly; in -, in sober- -sadness, - truth, - earnest; of a truth, truly, pardi, perdy; in all conscience, upon oath; be assured &c. (*belief*) 484; yes &c. (*assent*) 488; I'll -warrant, - warrant you, - engage, - answer for it, - be bound, - venture to say, - take my oath; in fact, as a matter of fact, forsooth, joking apart; so help me God; not to mince the matter.

Phr. quoth he; *dixi*.

537. Teaching.—**N.** teaching &c. *v.*; instruction; edification; education; pedagogy; tuition; tutor-, tutel-age; direction, guidance.

qualification, preparation; train-, school-ing &c. *v.*; discipline; exer-cise, -citation; drill, practice.

persuasion, proselytism, propagandism, *propaganda*; in-doctrination, -culcation, -oculation.

explanation &c. (*interpretation*) 522; lesson, lecture, sermon, homily; apologue, parable; discourse, prelection, preachment, disquisition.

exercise, task; *curriculum*; course, - of study; grammar, three R's, initiation, A. B. C. &c. (*beginning*) 66.

elementary -, primary -, secondary -, grammar school -, high school -, college -, university -, technical -, liberal -, classical -, religious -, denominational -, moral -, secular- education; technical -, vocational- training; university extension lectures; propædeutics, moral tuition; evening classes, correspondence course.

physical education, gymnastics, calisthenics, eurythmics; *sloyd*.

V. teach, instruct, edify, school, tutor; cram, prime, coach; enlighten &c. (*inform*) 527.

in-culcate, -doctrinate, -oculate, -fuse, -stil, -fix, -graft, -filtrate; imbue, -pregnate, -plant; graft, sow the seeds of, disseminate, propagandize.

give an idea of; put -up to, - in the way of; set right.

sharpen the wits, enlarge the mind; give new ideas, open the eyes, bring forward, 'teach the young idea how to shoot'; improve &c. 658.

538. Misteaching.—**N.** mis-teaching, -information, -intelligence, -guidance, -direction, -persuasion, -instruction, -leading &c. *v.*; perversion, false teaching; sophistry &c. 477; college of Laputa; the blind leading the blind.

V. mis-inform, -teach, -direct, -guide, -instruct, -correct; pervert; put on a false -, throw off the- scent; deceive &c. 545; mislead &c. (*error*) 495; misrepresent; lie &c. 544; *spargere voces in vulgum ambiguas*, preach to the wise, teach one's grandmother to suck eggs.

render unintelligible &c. 519; bewilder &c. (*uncertainty*) 475; mystify &c. (*conceal*) 528; unteach.

Adj. misteaching &c. *v.*; unedifying.

Phr. *piscem natare doces*.

539. Learning.—**N.** learning; acquisition of -knowledge &c. 490, - skill &c. 698; acquirement, attainment; edification, scholarship, erudition; lore; information; self-instruction; study, reading, perusal; inquiry &c. 461.

ap-, prenticeship; pupil-age, -arity; tutelage, novitiate, matriculation.

docility &c. (*willingness*) 602; aptitude &c. 698.

V. learn; acquire -, gain -, receive -, take in -, drink in -, imbibe -, pick up -, gather -, get -, obtain -, collect -, glean- -knowledge, - information, - learning.

acquaint oneself with, master; make oneself -master of, - acquainted with; grind, cram; get -, coach- up; learn by -heart, - rote.

read, spell, peruse; con -, pore -, thumb- over; wade through; dip into;

expound &c. (*interpret*) 522; lecture; prelect; read –, give- a -lesson, – lecture, – sermon, – discourse; hold forth, preach; sermon-, moral-ize; point a moral.

train, discipline; bring up, – to; educate, form, ground, prepare, qualify, drill, exercise, practice, habituate, familiarize with, nurture, dry-nurse, breed, rear, take in hand; break, – in; tame; pre-instruct; initiate; inure &c. (*habituate*) 613.

put to nurse, send to school.

direct, guide; direct attention to &c. (*attention*) 457; impress upon the -mind, – memory; beat into, – the head; convince &c. (*belief*) 484.

Adj. teaching &c. *v.*; taught &c. *v.*; educational; scholastic, academic, doctrinal; disciplinal; instructive, didactic, hortative, pedagogic, tutorial.

Phr. the schoolmaster abroad.

run the eye -over, – through; turn over the leaves.

study; be -studious &c. *adj.*; consume the midnight oil, mind one's book.

go to -school, – college, – the university; serve -an (*or* one's) apprenticeship, – one's time; learn one's trade; be -informed &c. 527; be -taught &c. 537.

Adj. studious; schol-astic, -arly; teachable; docile &c. (*willing*) 602; apt &c. 698, industrious &c. 682; learned, erudite.

Adv. at one's books; *in statu pupillari* &c. (*learner*) 541.

---

540. Teacher.—**N.** teacher, trainer, instructor, institutor, master, tutor, don, director, Corypheus, dry nurse, coach, grinder, crammer; governor, bear-leader; governess, duenna; disciplinarian.

professor, lecturer, reader, prelector, prolocutor, preacher; Boanerges; pastor &c. (*clergy*) 996; schoolmaster, dominie, usher, pedagogue, abecedarian; schoolmistress, dame, monitor, proctor, pupil-teacher.

expositor &c. 524; preceptor, guide; mentor &c. (*adviser*) 695; pioneer, apostle, missionary, propagandist, moonshee; example &c. (*model for imitation*) 22.

professorship &c. (*school*) 542.

tutelage &c. (*teaching*) 537.

Adj. professorial, tutorial &c. 537.

541. Learner.—**N.** learner, scholar, student, *alumnus*, *élève*, pupil; apprentice; articled clerk; school-boy, -girl, beginner, tyro, abecedarian, alphabetarian.

recruit, novice, neophyte, tenderfoot, inceptor, *débutant*, catechumen, probationer; undergraduate; freshman, frosh; sophomore, junior, senior; junior –, senior- soph; sophister, questionist, fellow-, commoner, pensioner, exhibitioner, sizar, scholar, fellow, advanced –, post graduate –, research- student.

class, form, grade, standard, remove; pupilage &c. (*learning*) 539.

disciple, follower, apostle, proselyte; fellow student, school-mate, -fellow, class mate, condisciple.

Adj. *in statu pupillari*, in leading strings, sophomoric.

542. School.—**N.** school, academy, university, *alma mater*, college, seminary, Lyceum; instit-ute, -ution, *conservatoire*; *palæstra*, *gymnasium*.

day –, boarding –, public –, preparatory –, elementary –, primary –, infant –, dame's –, grammar –, middle class –, Board –, County –, Council –, parochial –, denominational –, Sunday –, National –, British and Foreign –, collegiate –, secondary –, continuation –, night –, correspondence –, secretarial –, military –, law –, medical –, business –, technical- school; technical –, training- college; Polytechnic; training ship; *Kindergarten*, nursery, *crèche*, reformatory.

pulpit, desk, reading desk, ambo, class-, lecture-room, theatre, amphitheatre, forum, stage, rostrum, platform, hustings, tribune.

school –, horn –, text- book; grammar, primer, abecedary, rudiments, manual, *vade mecum*, Lindley Murray, Cocker.

professor-, lecture-, reader-ship; chair; schoolmaster &c. 540.

School Board, Council of Education; *propaganda*.

Adj. scholastic, academic, collegiate; educational.

Adv. *ex cathedrâ*.

543. Veracity.—N. veracity; truthfulness, frankness &c. *adj.*; truth, sooth, sincerity, candour, honesty, fidelity; plain dealing, *bona fides*; love of truth; probity &c. 939; ingenuousness &c. (*artlessness*) 703.

the truth the whole truth and nothing but the truth; honest –, sober- truth &c. (*fact*) 494; unvarnished tale; light of truth.

V. speak –, tell- the truth; speak by the card; paint in its –, show oneself in one's-true colours; make a clean breast &c. (*disclose*) 529; speak one's mind &c. (*be blunt*) 703; not -lie &c. 544, – deceive &c. 545.

Adj. truthful, true; ver-acious, -edical; scrupulous &c. (*honourable*) 939; sincere, candid, frank, open, straightforward, unreserved; open-, true-, simple- hearted; honest, trustworthy; undissembling &c. (dissemble &c. 544); guileless, pure; unperjured, true blue, as good as one's word; unaffected, unfeigned, *bonâ fide*; outspoken, ingenuous &c. (*artless*) 703; undisguised &c. (*real*) 494.

Adv. truly &c. (*really*) 494; on oath; in plain words &c. 703; in –, with –, of a –, in good –, very- truth; as the -dial to the sun, – needle to the pole; honour bright; troth; in good -sooth, – earnest; unfeignedly, with no nonsense, in sooth, sooth to say, *bonâ fide*, *in foro conscientiæ*; without equivocation; *cartes sur table*, from the bottom of one's heart, by my troth &c. (*affirmation*) 535.

544. Falsehood. — N. false-hood, -ness; fals-ity, -ification; misrepresentation; deception &c. 545; untruth &c. 546; guile; bad faith; lying &c. *v.*; misrepresentation; mendacity, perjury, false swearing; forgery, invention, fabrication; subreption; covin.

perversion –, suppression- of truth; *suppressio veri*; perversion, distortion, false colouring; exaggeration &c. 549; prevarication, equivocation, shuffling, fencing, evasion, fraud; *suggestio falsi* &c. (*lie*) 546; mystification &c. (*concealment*) 528; simulation &c. (*imitation*) 19; dis-simulation, -sembling; deceit.

sham; pretence, pretending, malingering.

lip-homage, – service; mouth honour; hollowness; mere -show, – outside, eye-wash, window dressing; duplicity, double dealing, insincerity, hypocrisy, cant, humbug, casuistry; jesuit-ism, -ry; pharisaism; Machiavellism, 'organized hypocrisy'; crocodile tears, mealy-mouthedness, quackery; charlatan-ism, -ry; gammon; bun-kum, -come; flam, bam, flim-flam, cajolery, flattery; Judas kiss; perfidy &c. (*bad faith*) 940; *il volto sciolto i pensieri stretti*.

unfairness &c. (*dishonesty*) 940; artfulness &c. (*cunning*) 702; misstatement &c. (*error*) 495.

V. be -false &c. *adj.*, – a liar &c. 548; speak -falsely &c. *adv.*; tell -a lie &c. 546; lie, fib; lie like a trooper; swear falsely, forswear, perjure oneself, bear false witness.

mis-state, -quote, -cite, -report, -represent; belie, falsify, pervert, distort; put a false construction upon &c. (*misinterpret*) 523.

prevaricate, equivocate, quibble; palter, – to the understanding; *répondre en Normand*; trim, shuffle, fence, mince the truth, beat about the bush, blow hot and cold, play fast and loose.

garble, gloss over, disguise, give a colour to; give –, put- a -gloss, – false colouring- upon; colour, varnish, cook, dress up, embroider; varnish right and puzzle wrong, exaggerate &c. 549.

invent, fabricate; trump –, get- up; forge, hatch, concoct; romance &c. (*imagine*) 515; cry 'wolf!'

dis-semble, -simulate; feign, assume, put on, pretend, make believe; play -false, – a double game; coquet; act –, play- a part; affect &c. 855; simulate, pass off for; counterfeit, fake, sham, make a show of; malinger; swing the lead; say the grapes are sour.

cant, play the hypocrite, sham Abraham, *faire pattes de velours*, put on the mask, clean the outside of the platter, lie like a conjuror; hang out –, hold out –, sail under- false colours; 'commend the poisoned chalice to the lips'; *spargere voces in vulgum ambiguas*; deceive &c. 545.

Adj. false, deceitful, mendacious, unveracious, fraudulent, untruthful, dishonest; faith-, truth-, troth-less; un-fair, -candid; evasive; un-, dis-ingenuous; hollow, insincere, *Parthis mendacior*; forsworn.

canting; hypocrit-, jesuit-, pharisa-ical; tartuffish; Machiavelian; double-tongued, -faced, -handed, -minded, -hearted, -dealing; two-faced, bare-faced; Janus-faced; smooth-faced, -spoken, -tongued; plausible; mealy-mouthed; affected &c. 855.

collus-ive, -ory; artful &c. (*cunning*) 702; perfidious &c. 940, spurious &c. (*deceptive*) 545; untrue &c. 546; falsified &c. *v.*; covinous.

Adv. falsely &c. *adj.*; *à la Tartufe*, with a double tongue; out of whole cloth; slily &c. (*cunning*) 702.

545. Deception.—N. deception; falseness &c. 544; untruth &c. 546; impos-ition, -ture; fraud, deceit, guile; fraudulen-ce, -cy; covin; knavery &c. (*cunning*) 702; misrepresentation &c. (*falsehood*) 544.

delusion, gullery, bluff, spoof, *blague*; juggl-ing, -ery; sleight of hand, legerdemain; presti-giation, -digitation; magic &c. 992; conjur-ing, -ation; hocus-pocus, jockeyship; trickery, coggery, hanky-panky, chicanery, pettifogging, sharp practice; *supercherie*, cozenage, circumvention, ingannation, collusion; treachery &c. 940; practical joke.

trick, cheat, wile, ruse, blind, feint, plant, bubble, fetch, catch, chicane, juggle, reach, hocus, bite; thimble-rig, card-sharping, artful dodge, machination, swindle, hoax; tricks upon travellers; confidence trick; stratagem &c. (*artifice*) 702; theft &c. 791.

snare, trap, pitfall, decoy, gin; sprin-ge, -gle; noose, hook; bait, decoy-duck, tub to the whale, baited trap, *guet-à-pens*; cobweb, net, meshes, toils, mouse-trap, bird-lime; ambush &c. 530; trap-door, sliding panel, false bottom; spring-net, -gun; mask, -ed battery; mine; booby trap.

Cornish hug; wolf in sheep's clothing &c. (*deceiver*) 548; disguise, -ment; false colours, masquerade, mummery, borrowed plumes; *pattes de velours*.

mockery &c. (*imitation*) 19; copy &c. 21; counterfeit, sham, Brummagem, make-believe, forgery, fraud, fake; lie &c. 546; 'a mockery, a delusion, and a snare,' hollow mockery.

whited –, painted- sepulchre; tinsel, paste, false jewellery, scagliola, ormolu, German silver, Britannia metal, paint; jerry building; man of straw.

illusion &c. (*error*) 495; *ignis fatuus* &c. 423; *mirage* &c. 443.

V. deceive, take in; defraud, cheat, jockey, do, cozen, diddle, nab, gyp, chouse, double cross, play one false, bilk, cully, jilt, bite, pluck, swindle, victimize; abuse; mystify; blind one's eyes; blindfold, hoodwink, spoof, bluff; throw dust into the eyes, 'keep the word of promise to the ear and break it to the hope,' 'draw a herring across the trail.'

impose –, practise –, play –, put –, palm –, foist- upon; snatch a verdict.

circumvent, overreach; out-reach, -wit, -manœuvre; steal a march upon, give the go-by to, leave in the lurch.

set –, lay- a -trap, – snare- for; bait the hook, forelay, spread the toils, lime; decoy, waylay, lure, beguile, delude, inveigle; tra-, tre-pan; kidnap; let-, hook-in; trick; en-, in-trap, -snare, entoil, benet; nick, springe; catch, – in a trap; sniggle, entangle, illaqueate, hocus, practise on one's credulity, dupe, gull, hoax, fool, befool, bamboozle; hum, -bug; gammon, stuff up, dope, sell; play a -trick, – practical joke- upon one; balk, trip up, throw a tub to a whale; fool to the top of one's bent, send on -a wild goose chase, – a fool's errand; make -game, – a fool, – an April fool, – an ass- of; trifle with, cajole, flatter; come over &c. (*influence*) 615; gild the pill, make things pleasant, divert, put a good face upon; dissemble &c. 544.

cog, – the dice, play with marked cards; live by one's wits, play at hide and seek; obtain money under false pretences &c. (*steal*) 791; conjure, juggle, practise chicanery; gerrymander.

play –, palm –, foist –, fob- off.

lie &c. 544; misinform &c. 538; mislead &c. (*error*) 495; betray &c. 940; be -deceived &c. 547.

Adj. deceived &c. *v.*; deceiving &c. *v.*; cunning &c. 702; prestigi-ous, -atory; decept-ive, -ious; deceitful, covinous; delus-ive, -ory; illus-ive, -ory; elusive, insidious, *ad captandum vulgus.*

untrue &c. 546; mock, sham, make-believe, counterfeit, faked, pseudo, spurious, so-called, pretended, feigned, trumped up, bogus, scamped, fraudulent, tricky, factitious, artificial, bastard; surreptitious, illegitimate, contraband, adulterated, sophisticated; unsound, rotten at the core; colourable; disguised; meretricious; tinsel, pinchbeck, plated; catch-penny; Brummagem; simulated &c. 544.

Adv. under -false colours, – the garb of, – cover of; over the left.

Phr. *fronti nulla fides.*

546. Untruth.—N. untruth, falsehood, lie, story, thing that is not, fib, bounce, crammer, taradiddle, whopper.

forgery, fabrication, invention; mis-statement, -representation; perversion, falsification, gloss, *suggestio falsi*; exaggeration &c. 549.

fiction; fable, nursery tale; romance &c. (*imagination*) 515; untrue –, false –, trumped up- -story, – statement; thing devised by the enemy; *canard*; shave, sell, hum, yarn, traveller's tale, Canterbury tale, cock and bull story, fairy tale, clap-trap.

myth, moonshine, bosh, all my eye, -and Betty Martin, mare's nest, farce.

irony; half truth, white lie, pious fraud; mental reservation &c. (*concealment*) 528.

pretence, pretext; false -plea &c. 617; subterfuge, evasion, shift, shuffle, make-believe; sham &c. (*deception*) 545.

profession, empty words; Judas kiss &c. (*hypocrisy*) 544; disguise &c. (*mask*) 530.

V. have a false meaning; not ring true.

pretend, sham, feign, counterfeit, make believe.

Adj. untrue, false, trumped up; void of –, without- foundation; far from the truth, false as dicer's oaths; unfounded, *ben trovato*, invented, fabulous, fabricated, forged; fict-, fact-, supposit-, surrept-itious; e-, il-lusory; ironical; satirical; evasive; *soi-disant* &c. (*misnamed*) 565.

Phr. *se non è vero è ben trovato*.

547. Dupe.—**N.** dupe, gull, gudgeon, *gobemouche*, cull, cully, victim, sucker, pigeon, April fool; laughing stock &c. 857; Cyclops, simple Simon, flat, mug, greenhorn; fool &c. 501; puppet, cat's paw.

V. be -deceived &c. 545, – the dupe of; fall into a trap; swallow –, nibble at- the bait; bite; catch a Tartar.

Adj. credulous &c. 486; mistaken &c. (*error*) 495.

548. Deceiver.—**N.** deceiver &c. (deceive &c. 545); dissembler, hypocrite; sophist, Pharisee, Jesuit, Mawworm, Pecksniff, Joseph Surface, Tartufe, Janus; serpent, snake in the grass, cockatrice, Judas, wolf in sheep's clothing; Molly Maguire; jilt; shuffler.

liar &c. (lie &c. 544); story-teller, perjurer, false-witness, *menteur*, *-à triple étage*, *-à payer patente*; Scapin.

impostor, pretender, capper, decoy, fraud, *soi-disant*, humbug; adventurer; Cagliostro, Fernam Mendez Pinto; ass in lion's skin &c. (*bungler*) 701; actor &c. (*stage player*) 599.

quack, *charlatan*, mountebank, saltimbanco, *saltimbanque*, empiric, quacksalver, medicaster.

conjuror, juggler, magician, necromancer, trickster, prestidigitator, medium, jockey; crimp; decoy-duck, stool pigeon; rogue, knave, cheat; swindler &c. (*thief*) 792; jobber.

549. Exaggeration.—**N.** exaggeration; expansion &c. 194; hyperbole, stretch, strain, colouring; high colouring, caricature, *caricatura*; extravagance &c. (*nonsense*) 497; Baron Munchausen; men in buckram, yarn, fringe, embroidery, traveller's tale; Ossa upon Pelion.

storm in a teacup; much ado about nothing &c. (*over-estimation*) 482; puffery &c. (*boasting*) 884; rant &c. (*turgescence*) 577.

figure of speech, *façon de parler*; stretch of -fancy, – the imagination; flight of fancy &c. (*imagination*) 515.

false colouring &c. (*falsehood*) 544; aggravation &c. 835.

V. exaggerate, magnify, pile up, aggravate; amplify &c. (*expand*) 194; overestimate &c. 482; hyperbolize; over-charge, -state, -draw, -lay, -shoot the mark, -praise; make -much, – the most- of; strain, – a point; stretch, – a point; go great lengths; spin a long yarn; draw –, shoot with- a long-bow; deal in the marvellous.

out-Herod Herod, run riot, talk at random.

heighten, overcolour; colour -highly, – too highly; embroider, *broder*; flourish; colour &c. (*misrepresent*) 544; puff &c. (*boast*) 884.

Adj. exaggerated &c. *v.*; overwrought; bombastic &c. (*magniloquent*) 577; hyperbolical, on stilts; fabulous, extravagant, preposterous, egregious, *outré*, high-flying.

Adv. hyperbolically &c. *adj.*

Section III. Means of Communicating Ideas

1.° *Natural Means*

550. Indication.—**N.** indication; symbol-ism, -ization; semeio-logy, -tics; sign of the times.

lineament, feature, *trait*, characteristic, trick, diagnostic; divining-rod; cloven hoof; footfall; means of recognition; earmark.

sign, symbol; ind-ex, -ice, -icator; point, -er; marker; exponent, note, token, symptom.

type, figure, emblem, cipher, device; representation &c. 554; epigraph, motto, posy.

gest-ure, -iculation; pantomime; wink, glance, leer; nod, shrug, beck; touch, nudge; grip; dactylo-logy, -nomy; Freemasonry, telegraphy, chirology, by-play, dumb-show; cue; hint &c. 527; clue, clew, key, scent, track &c. 551.

signal, -post; rocket, blue light; watch-fire, -tower; telegraph, semaphore, flag-staff; cresset, fiery cross; calumet; heliograph, signal-, flash-lamp.

mark, line, stroke, dash, score, stripe, streak, scratch, tick, dot, point, notch, nick, blaze; asterisk, red letter, italics, heavy type, inverted commas, quotation marks, sublineation, underlining, jotting; print; impr-int, -ess, -ession; note, annotation, mark of exclamation.

[For identification] badge, criterion; counter-check, -mark, -sign, -foil; duplicate, tally; label, tab, ticket, stub, billet, letter, counter, *tessera*, card, bill, check; witness, voucher; stamp; *cachet*; trade –, hall- mark; broad arrow; signature; address –, visiting- card; *carte de visite*; credentials &c. (*evidence*) 467; passport, indentity book, *carte d' identité*; attestation; hand, – writing, sign-manual; cipher; monogram, – mark, seal, sigil, signet; autograph, -y; paraph, brand; superscription; in-, en-dorsement; title, heading, rubric, docket; *mot-de passe, – du guet*; *passe-parole*; shibboleth; watch-, catch-, pass-word; *open sesame!*

insignia; banner, -et, -ol; bandrol; flag, colours, streamer, standard, eagle, labarum, oriflamb, *oriflamme*; figure-head; ensign; pen-non, -nant, -dant; burgee, blue Peter, jack, ancient, gonfalon, Union jack; tricolour, stars and stripes; bunting, Jolly Roger, *drapeau*, *pavillon*.

heraldry, crest; coat of –, arms; armorial bearings, hatchment; e-, scutcheon; shield, supporters; livery, uniform; cockade, *epaulette*, brassard, chevron; garland, chaplet, love-knot, fillet, favour.

[Of locality] beacon, cairn, post, staff, flagstaff, hand, pointer, vane, cock, weathercock; guide-, hand-, finger-, directing-, sign-post; pillars of Hercules, pharos, signal fire; bench-, land-, sea-mark; lighthouse, balize; pole-, load-, lode-star; cynosure, guide; address, direction, name; sign, -board.

[Of the future] warning &c. 668; omen &c. 512; prefigurement &c. 511. [Of the past] trace record &c. 551. [Of danger] warning &c. 668; alarm &c. 669. [Of authority] sceptre &c. 747. [Of triumph] trophy &c. 733. [Of quantity] gauge &c. 466. [Of distance] mile-stone, -post. [Of disgrace] brand, fool's cap, stigma, mark of Cain. [For detection] check, tell-tale; test &c. (*experiment*) 463.

notification &c. (*information*) 527; advertisement &c. (*publication*) 531.

word of command, call; bugle-, trumpet-call; reveille, taps; bell, alarum, cry; battle –, rallying- cry.

church, bell, angelus, sacring bell; muezzin.

exposition &c. (*explanation*) 522; proof &c. (*evidence*) 467; pattern &c. (*prototype*) 22.

V. indicate; be the -sign &c. *n.*- of; denote, betoken; argue, testify &c. (*evidence*) 467; bear the -impress &c. *n.*- of; con-note, -notate.

represent, stand for; typify &c. (*prefigure*) 511; symbolize.

put -an indication, – a mark, – &c. *n.*; note, mark, tick, blaze, stamp, earmark; set one's seal upon; label, ticket, docket; dot, spot, score, dash, trace, chalk; print; im-print, -press, surprint; engrave, stereotype, electrotype.

make a -sign &c. *n.*; signalize; give –, hang out- a signal; beck, -on; gesture; nod; wink, glance, leer, nudge, shrug, tip the wink; gesticulate; raise –, hold up- the -finger, – hand; saw the air, suit the action to the word.

wave –, unfurl –, hoist –, hang out- a banner &c. *n.*; wave -the hand, – a kerchief; give the cue &c. (*inform*) 527; show one's colours; give –, sound- an alarm; beat the drum, sound the trumpets, raise a cry.

sign, seal, attest &c. (*evidence*) 467; underline &c. (*give importance to*) 642; call attention to &c. (*attention*) 457; give notice &c. (*inform*) 527.

Adj. indicat-ing &c. *v.*, -ive, -ory; de-, con-notative; diacritical, representative, typical, symbolic, pantomimic, pathognomonic, symptomatic, ominous, characteristic, demonstrative, diagnostic, exponential, emblematic, armorial; individual &c. (*special*) 79.

known –, recognizable- by; indicated &c. *v.*; pointed, marked.

[Capable of being denoted] denotable; indelible.

Adv. in token of; symbolically &c. *adj.*; in dumb show.

Phr. *ecce signum*; *ex ungue leonem*, *ex pede Herculem*.

551. Record.—N. trace, vestige, relic, remains; scar, *cicatrix*; foot-step, -mark, -print; track, mark, wake, trail, spoor, scent, *piste*.

monument, hatchment, escutcheon, slab, tablet, trophy, achievement; obelisk, pillar, column, monolith, cromlech, dolmen; memorial; *memento* &c. (*memory*) 505; testimonial, medal, ribbon, order; commemoration &c. (*celebration*) 883.

record, note, minute; *dossier*; register, -try; census, roll &c. (*list*) 86; cartulary, diptych, Domesday book; entry, memorandum, indorsement, inscription, copy, duplicate, docket; notch &c. (*mark*) 550; muniment, deed &c. (*security*) 771; document; deposition, *procès-verbal*; affidavit; certificate &c. (*evidence*) 467.

note-, memorandum-, pocket-, commonplace-book; portfolio; scoring-board, -sheet; bulletin board; card index, file; pigeon-holes, *excerpta*, *adversaria*, jottings, dottings.

gazette, -er; newspaper, magazine &c. 531; alman-ac, -ack; calendar, ephemeris, noctuary, diary, log, journal, account-, cash-, day-book, ledger.

archive, scroll, state-paper, Congressional Record, return, blue-book; statistics &c. 86; *compte rendu*; Acts –, Transactions –, Proceedings- of; Hansard's Debates; chronicle, annals; legend; history, biography &c. 594.

registration; en-, in-rolment; tabulation; entry, booking; signature &c. (*identification*) 550; recorder &c. 553; journalism.

drawing, photograph &c. 554; phonograph –, gramophone-record; music roll.

552. [Suppression of sign.] **Obliteration.—N.** obliteration; erasure, rasure; effacement; cancel, -lation; cassation; circumduction; deletion, blot; *tabula rasa*.

V. efface, obliterate, erase, rase, expunge, cancel; blot –, take –, rub –, scratch –, strike –, wipe –, wash –, sponge- out; wipe –, rub- off; wipe away; deface, render illegible; draw the pen through, apply the sponge.

be -effaced &c.; leave no -trace &c. 449; 'leave not a rack behind.'

Adj. obliterated &c. *v.*; out of print; printless; leaving no trace; intestate; un-recorded, -registered, -written.

Int. *dele*; out with it!

V. record; put –, place- upon record; go on record; chronicle, calendar, hand down to posterity; keep up the memory of &c. (*remember*) 505; commemorate &c. (*celebrate*) 883; report &c. (*inform*) 527; commit to –, reduce to- writing; put –, set down- -in writing, – in black and white; put –, jot –, take –, write –, note –, set- down; note, minute, put on paper; take –, make- a -note, – minute, – memorandum; make a return.

mark &c. (*indicate*) 550; sign &c. (*attest*) 467.

enter, book; post, – up; insert, make an entry of; mark –, tick-off; register, list, docket, enroll, inscroll; file &c. (*store*) 636.

Adv. on record.

553. Recorder.—N. recorder, notary, clerk; regis-trar, -trary, -ter; prothonotary; amanuensis, secretary, scribe, stenographer, remembrancer, book-keeper, *custos rotulorum*, Master of the Rolls.

annalist; histori-an, -ographer; chronicler, journalist, reporter, columnist; biographer &c. (*narrator*) 594; antiquary &c. (*antiquity*) 122; memorialist.

draughtsman &c. 559; engraver 558; photographer, cinematographer, camera man.

Recording instrument, recorder, camera, phonograph, gramophone, dictaphone, telegraphone, telautograph, printing telegraph, tape machine, ticker, time recorder, cash register, turnstile, speedometer, voting machine, seismograph, photostat.

554. Representation.—N. representation, -ment; imitation &c. 19; illustration, delineation, depictment, portrayal; imagery, portraiture, iconography; design, -ing; art, fine arts; painting &c. 556; sculpture &c. 557; engraving &c. 558; photography, radiography, skiagraphy.

person-ation, -ification; impersonation; drama &c. 599.

picture, drawing, sketch, draught, draft; tracing; copy &c. 21; photo-, helio-graph; daguerreo-, talbo-, calo-, helio-type; cabinet, *carte-de-visite*, snapshot; X-ray photograph; radio-gram, -graph, skia-graph, -gram.

image, likeness, icon, portrait; striking –, speaking- likeness; very image; effigy, fac-simile.

figure, – head; puppet, doll, *figurine*, aglet, manikin, lay-figure, model, *marionnette*, *fantoccini*, bust; waxwork, statue, -tte, automaton, Robot.

hieroglyphic, anaglyph; dia-, mono-gram, -graph.

map, plan, chart; ground plan, projection, elevation; ichno-, carto-graphy; atlas; outline, scheme; view &c. (*painting*) 556.

artist, draughtsman &c. 559.

V. represent, delineate; depict, -ure; portray; picture; take –, catch- a likeness &c. *n.*; hit off, photograph, daguerreotype; figure; shadow -forth, – out; adumbrate; body forth; describe &c. 594; trace, copy; mould.

dress up; illustrate, symbolize.

paint &c. 556; carve &c. 557; engrave &c. 558.

person-ate, -ify; impersonate; assume a character; pose as; act;

555. Misrepresentation.—N. misrepresentation, distortion, exaggeration; daubing &c. *v.*; bad likeness, daub, sign-painting; scratch, caricature; *anamorphosis*.

V. misrepresent, distort, overdraw, travesty, parody, burlesque, exaggerate, caricature, daub.

Adj. misrepresented &c. *v.*

play &c. (*drama*) 599; mimic &c. (*imitate*) 19; hold the mirror up to nature.

Adj. represent-ing &c. *v.*, -ative; illustrative; represented &c. *v.*; imitative, figurative.

like &c. 17; graphic &c. (*descriptive*) 594.

556. Painting.—**N.** painting; depicting; drawing &c. *v.*; design; perspective, skiagraphy; *chiaroscuro* &c. (*light*) 420; composition; treatment, values, atmosphere, tone, technique.

historical –, portrait –, miniature –, battle -, *genre* -, landscape –, marine –, fruit and flower –, scene- painting; scenography.

school, style; the grand style, high art, *genre*, portraiture; ornamental art &c. 847.

mono-, poly-chrome; *grisaille.*

pallet, palette; easel; brush, pencil, stump; blacklead, charcoal, crayons, chalk, pastel; paint &c. (*colouring matter*) 428; water-, body-, oil-colour; oils, oil-paint; varnish &c. 356*a*; *gouache*, tempera, distemper, fresco; enamel; encaustic painting; *graffito*, *gesso*; mosaic; tapestry.

picture, painting, piece, *tableau*, canvas; oil &c.- painting; cartoon; easel –, cabinet- picture; drawing, draught, draft; pencil &c. –, water-colour- drawing; sketch, outline; study.

portrait &c. (*representation*) 554; whole –, full –, half- length; kitcat, head; miniature; shade, *silhouette*; profile.

landscape, sea-piece, -scape; view, scene, prospect; interior; bird's-eye view; pan-, di-orama; still life.

picture –, art- gallery; studio, *atelier*.

V. paint, design, limn, draw, sketch, pencil, scratch, shade, stipple, hatch, dash off, chalk out, square up; colour, dead-colour, wash, varnish; draw in -pencil &c. *n.*; paint in -oils &c. *n.*; stencil; depict &c. (*represent*) 554.

Adj. painted &c. *v.*; pictorial, graphic, picturesque, decorative; classical, romantic, pre-Raphaelite, modern, cubist, futurist, vorticist, post-, impressionist.

pencil, oil &c. *n.*

Adv. in -pencil &c. *n.*

Phr. *fecit, delineavit, pinxit.*

557. Sculpture.—**N.** sculpture, insculpture; carving &c. *v.*; statuary, ceramics, plastic arts.

high –, low –, bas- relief; relievo; *basso-*, *alto-*, *mezzo-rilievo*; *intaglio*, anaglyph; medal, -lion; *cameo*.

marble, bronze, terracotta; ceramic ware, pottery, porcelain, china, earthenware, faïence, enamel, *cloisonné*.

statue &c. (*image*) 554; cast &c. (*copy*) 21; glyptotheca.

V. sculpture, carve, cut, chisel, model, mould; cast.

Adj. sculptured &c. *v.*; in relief, anaglyptic, ceroplastic, ceramic; parian; marble &c. *n.* **Phr.** *sculpsit.*

558. Engraving.—**N.** engraving, chalcography; line –, mezzotint –, stipple –, chalk- engraving; dry-point, bur; etching, aquatinta; plate –, copper-plate –, steel –, wood-, process-, photo-engraving; xylo-, ligno-, glypto-, cero-, litho-, chromolitho-, photolitho-, zinco-, glypho- -graphy, -graph.

impression, print, engraving, plate; steel-, copper-plate; etching; mezzo-, aqua-, litho-tint; cut, woodcut, block; stereo-, grapho-, auto-, helio-type; half-tone; *photogravure, rotogravure*.

graver, *burin*, etching-point, style; plate, stone, wood-block, negative; die, punch, stamp.

printing; plate –, copper-plate –, intaglio –, anastatic –, lithographic –, colour –, three or four colour- printing; type-printing &c. 591.

illustr-, illumin-ation; *vignette*, initial letter, *cul de lampe*, tail-piece.

V. engrave, grave, stipple, scrape, etch; bite, – in; lithograph &c. *n.*; print.

Adj. insculptured; engraved &c. *v.*

Phr. *fecit*, *sculpsit*, *imprimit*, *incisit*.

559. Artist.—N. artist; painter, limner, drawer, sketcher, delineator; cartoon-, caricatur-ist, designer, engraver; draughtsman; copyist; enamel-ler, -list.

historical –, landscape –, battle-, *genre* –, marine –, fruit and flower –, portrait –, miniature –, scene –, sign- painter; engraver; Apelles; sculptor, carver, chaser, modeller, lapidary, *figuriste*, statuary; Phidias, Praxiteles; Royal Academician.

photographer, retoucher.

2°. *Conventional Means*

1. *Language generally*

560. Language.—N. language; phraseology &c. 569; speech &c. 582; tongue, lingo, vernacular, slang; mother –, vulgar –, native- tongue; household words; King's *or* Queen's English; idiom; dialect &c. 563.

Volapuk, Esperanto, Ido, occidental, Ro.

confusion of tongues, Babel, *pasigraphie*; pantomime &c. (*signs*) 550; *onomatopœia*.

phil-, gloss-, glott-ology; linguistics, chrestomathy; paleo-logy; -graphy; comparative grammar.

literature, letters, polite literature, *belles lettres*, muses, humanities, *literæ humaniores*, republic of letters, dead languages, classics; genius of a language; scholarship &c. (*knowledge*) 490.

linguist &c. (*scholar*) 492.

V. speak, say, express by words &c. 566.

Adj. lingu-al, -istic; dialectic; vernacular, current, colloquial, slangy; bilingual, polyglot; literary.

561. Letter.—N. letter; character; hieroglyphic &c. (*writing*) 590; type &c. (*printing*) 591; capitals; majus-, minus-cule; alphabet, ABC, abecedary, Christ-cross-row.

consonant, vowel, diphthong; mute, surd; sonant, liquid, labial, dental, palatal, guttural.

syllable; mono-, dis-, poly-syllable; affix, prefix, suffix.

spelling, orthography; phon-ography, -etic spelling; ana-, meta-grammatism.

cipher, monogram, anagram; double –, acrostic.

V. spell.

Adj. literal; alphabetical, abecedarian; syllabic; uncial &c. (*writing*) 590; phonetic, voiced, mute &c. *n.*

562. Word.—N. word, term, vocable; name &c. 564; phrase &c. 566; root, etymon; derivative; part of speech &c. (*grammar*) 567.

dictionary, vocabulary, word book,

563. Neology.—N. neolo-gy, -gism; new-fangled expression; barbarism; caconym; archaism, black letter, monkish Latin; corruption; missaying, antiphrasis.

lexicon, index, glossary, thesaurus, *gradus*, *delectus*, concordance.

etymology, lexicology, derivation; phonology, orthoepy; gloss-, termin-, orism-ology; paleology &c. (*philology*) 560; comparative philology.

lexicograph-er, -y; glossographer &c. (*scholar*) 492; etymologist; logolept.

verbosity, verbiage, loquacity &c. 584.

Adj. verbal, literal; titular, nominal. [Similarly derived] conjugate, paronymous; derivative.

Adv. verbally &c. *adj.*; *verbatim* &c. (*exactly*) 494.

---

paronomasia, play upon words; word-play &c. (*wit*) 842; pun; *double-entendre* &c. (*ambiguity*) 520; palindrome, paragram, clinch; abuse of -language, - terms.

dialect, brogue, *patois*, provincialism, broken English, *lingua franca*; Brit-, Gall-, Scott-, Hibern-icism; Americanism; Gipsy lingo, Romany, pidgin English.

dog Latin, macaronics, gibberish, confusion of tongues, Babel; jargon.

colloquialism &c. (*figure of speech*) 521; by-word; technicality, lingo, slang, cant, *argot*, St. Giles's Greek, thieves' Latin, peddler's French, flash tongue, Billingsgate, Wall Street slang.

pseudonym &c. (*misnomer*) 565; Mr. So-and-so; what d'ye call 'em, what's his name; N. N.; *Monsieur Un Tel*; thingum-my, -bob; gadget, dooflicker, do-funny, *oo-ja-ka-pi-vi*; *je ne sais quoi*.

neologist, coiner of words.

V. coin words.

Adj. neologic, -al; rare; archaic; obsolete &c. (*old*) 124; colloquial, dialectic, slang, cant.

Phr. *Il a passé par Marseille*.

564. Nomenclature. — N. nomenclature; naming &c. *v.*; nuncupation, nomination, baptism; orismology; *onomatopœia*; antonomasia.

name; appella-tion, -tive; designation; title; head, -ing, caption; denomination; by-name, epithet.

style, proper name; præ-, ag-, cognomen; patronymic, surname; cognomination; compellation, description; empty -title, - name; handle to one's name; namesake, eponym.

synonym, antonym.

term, expression, noun; by-word; convertible terms &c. 522; technical term; cant &c. 563.

V. name, call, term, denominate, designate, style, entitle, intitule, clepe, dub, christen, baptize, nickname, characterize, specify, define, distinguish by the name of; label &c. (*mark*) 550.

be -called &c. *v.*; take -, bear -, go (*or* be known) by -, go (*or* pass) under -, rejoice in- the name of.

Adj. named &c. *v.*; hight, yclept, known as; what one may -well, - fairly, - properly, - fitly- call.

nuncupa-tory, -tive; cognominal, titular, nominal; orismological.

565. Misnomer.—N. misnomer; *lucus a non lucendo*; Mrs. Malaprop; what d'ye call 'em &c. (*neologism*) 563.

nickname, *sobriquet*, by-name, handle, moniker; assumed -name, - title; *alias*; *nom de -guerre, - plume, - théâtre*; pseudonym, pen name, stage name.

V. mis-name, -call, -term; nickname; assume -a name, - an alias.

Adj. misnamed &c. *v.*; pseudonymous; *soi-disant*; self-called, -styled, -christened; so-called.

nameless, anonymous; without a -, having no- name; innominate, unnamed.

Adv. in no sense.

---

566. Phrase.—N. phrase, expression, set phrase; sentence, paragraph; figure of speech &c. 521; idi-om, -otism; turn of expression.

paraphrase &c. (*synonym*) 522; periphrase &c. (*circumlocution*) 573; motto &c. (*proverb*) 496; phraseology &c. 569.

V. express, phrase; word, – it; give -words, – expression- to; voice; arrange in –, clothe in –, put into –, express by- words; couch in terms; find words to express; speak by the card.

Adj. expressed &c. *v.*; idiomatic.

Adv. in -round, – set, – good, set- terms; in set phrases.

567. Grammar.—**N.** grammar, accidence, syntax, *praxis*, analysis, paradigm, punctuation; parts of speech; inflexion, case, declension, conjugation; *jus et norma loquendi*; Lindley Murray &c. (*school-book*) 542; correct style; philology &c. (*language*) 560.

V. parse, analyze; decline, conjugate; punctuate.

Adj. grammatical; syntactic; inflexional.

568. Solecism.—**N.** solecism; bad –, false –, faulty- grammar; slip, error; slip of the -pen, – tongue; *lapsus calami-*, – *linguæ*; *faux pas*; slip-slop; bull.

V. use -bad, – faulty- grammar; solecize, commit a solecism; murder the -King's, – Queen's- English; break Priscian's head.

Adj. ungrammatical; in-correct, -accurate; faulty, improper, incongruous. abnormal.

---

569. Style.—**N.** style, diction, phraseology, wording; manner, strain; composition; mode of expression, choice of words, literary power, ready pen, pen of a ready writer; command of language &c. (*eloquence*) 582; authorship; *la morgue littéraire*.

V. express by words &c. 566; write.

Various Qualities of Style

570. Perspicuity.—**N.** perspicuity &c. (*intelligibility*) 518; plain speaking &c. (*manifestation*) 525; defin-iteness, -ition; exactness &c. 494; perspicuousness, logical acuteness.

Adj. lucid &c. (*intelligible*) 518; explicit &c. (*manifest*) 525; exact &c. 494.

571. Obscurity.—**N.** obscurity &c. (*unintelligibility*) 519; involution; hard words; ambiguity &c. 520; vagueness &c. 475, inexactness &c. 495; what d'ye call 'em &c. (*neologism*) 563; cloudiness, confusion.

Adj. obscure &c. *n.*; crabbed, involved, confused.

572. Conciseness.—**N.** conciseness &c. *adj.*; brevity, 'the soul of wit,' laconism; Tacitus; ellipsis; syncope; abridgment &c. (*shortening*) 201; compression &c. 195; epitome &c. 596; monostitch; portmanteau word, telescope word, protogram.

V. be -concise &c. *adj.*; condense &c. 195; abridge &c. 201; abstract &c. 596; come to the point.

Adj. concise, brief, short, terse, close; to the point, exact; neat, compact, condensed, pointed; laconic, curt, pithy, trenchant, summary; pregnant; compendious &c. (*compendium*) 596; succinct; elliptical, epigrammatic, crisp, sententious.

Adv. concisely &c. *adj.*; briefly,

573. Diffuseness.—**N.** diffuseness &c. *adj.*; amplification &c. *v.*; dilating &c. *v.*; verbosity, verbiage, wordiness, cloud of words, *copia verborum*; flow of words &c. (*loquacity*) 584.

poly-, tauto-, batto-, perisso-logy; pleonasm, exuberance, redundance; thrice-told tale; prolixity; circumlocution, *ambages*; periphra-se, -sis; roundabout phrases; episode; expletive; penny-a-lining; padding, drivel, twaddle, rigmarole; richness &c. 577.

V. be -diffuse &c. *adj.*; run out on, descant, expatiate, enlarge, dilate, amplify, expand, inflate, pad; launch –, branch- out; rant.

maunder, prose; harp upon &c. (*repeat*) 104; dwell on, insist upon.

summarily; in -brief, – short, – a word, – few words, – a nutshell; for shortness sake; to -come to the point, – make a long story short, – cut the matter short, – be brief; it comes to this, the long and the short of it is.

---

digress, ramble, *battre la campagne*, beat about the bush, perorate, spin a long yarn, protract; spin –, swell –, draw- out, drivel.

Adj. dif-, pro-fuse; wordy, verbose, largiloquent, copious, exuberant, effusive, pleonastic, lengthy; long, -some, -winded, -spun, -drawn out; diffusive, spun out, protracted, prolix, prosing, maundering; circumlocutory, periphrastic, ambagious, roundabout; digressive; dis-, ex-cursive; rambling, episodic; flatulent, frothy.

Adv. diffusely &c. *adj.*; at large, *in extenso*; about it and about it.

574. Vigour.—**N.** vigour, power, force; boldness, raciness &c. *adj.*; spirit, point, antithesis, piquancy; *verve*, glow, fire, warmth, ardour, enthusiasm; 'thoughts that breathe and words that burn'; strong language; punch; gravity, sententiousness; elevation, loftiness, sublimity.

eloquence; command of -words, – language.

Adj. vigorous, nervous, powerful, forcible, trenchant, mordant, biting, incisive, impressive; sensational.

spirited, lively, glowing, sparkling, racy, bold, slashing; pungent, *piquant*, full of point, pointed, pithy, antithetical; sententious.

lofty, elevated, sublime, grand, weighty, ponderous; eloquent; vehement, petulant, impassioned; poetic.

Adv. in -glowing, – good set, – no measured- terms.

575. Feebleness.—**N.** feebleness &c. *adj.*

Adj. feeble, bald, tame, meagre, insipid, nerveless, jejune, vapid, trashy, cold, frigid, poor, dull, dry, languid; pros-ing, -y, -aic; unvaried, monotonous, weak, frail, washy, wishy-washy, sloppy; sketchy, slight; careless, slovenly, loose, lax; slip-shod, -slop; inexact; dis-jointed, -connected; puerile, childish; flatulent; rambling &c. (*diffuse*) 573.

---

576. Plainness.—**N.** plainness &c. *adj.*; simplicity, severity; plain -terms, – English; Saxon English; household words.

V. speak plainly; call a spade 'a spade'; plunge *in medias res*; come to the point.

Adj. plain, simple; un-ornamented, -adorned, -varnished; home-ly, -spun; neat; severe, chaste, pure, Saxon; commonplace, matter of fact, natural, prosaic, sober, unimaginative.

dry, unvaried, monotonous &c. 575.

Adv. in plain -terms, – words, – English, – common parlance; point blank.

---

577. Ornament. — **N.** ornament; floridness &c. *adj.*; turg-idity, -escence; altiloquence &c. *adj.*; orotundity; declamation, teratology; well-rounded periods; elegance &c. 578.

inversion, antithesis, alliteration, *paronomasia*; figurativeness &c. (*metaphor*) 521.

flourish; flowers of -speech, – rhetoric; euph-uism, -emism.

big-, high-sounding words; macrology, *sesquipedalia verba*, sesquipedalianism; Alexandrine; inflation, pretension; rant, bombast, fustian, bunkum, balderdash, prose run mad; fine writing; Minerva press.

phrasemonger; euph-uist, -emist.

V. ornament, overlay with ornament, overcharge; smell of the lamp.

Adj. ornamented &c. *v.*; beautified &c. 847; ornate, florid, rich, flowery; euph-uistic, -emistic; sonorous; high-, big-sounding; inflated, swelling, tumid; turg-id, -escent; pedantic, pompous, stilted;

high-flown, -flowing; sententious, rhetorical, declamatory; grandiose; grand-, magn-, alt-iloquent; sesquipedal, -ian; Johnsonian, mouthy; bombastic; fustian; frothy, flashy, flaming, flamboyant.

antithetical, alliterative; figurative &c. 521; artificial &c. (*inelegant*) 579.

Adv. *ore rotundo*; with rounded phrase.

578. Elegance.—N. elegance, purity, grace, ease, felicity, distinction, gracefulness, refinement, readiness &c. *adj.*; concinnity, euphony, numerosity, balance, rhythm, symmetry, proportion; restraint; good taste, propriety.

well rounded –, well turned –, flowing- periods; the right word in the right place; antithesis &c. 577.

purist, stylist.

V. point an antithesis, round a period.

Adj. elegant, polished, classical, Attic, correct, Ciceronian, artistic; chaste, pure, Saxon, academical.

graceful, easy, readable, fluent, flowing, tripping; unaffected, natural, unlaboured; mellifluous; euph-onious, -emistic; rhythmical, balanced, symmetrical.

felicitous, happy, neat; well –, neatly- -put, – expressed.

579. Inelegance. — N. inelegance; vulgarity, bad taste; stiffness &c. *adj.*; unlettered Muse; barbarism; slang &c. 563; solecism &c. 568; mannerism &c. (*affectation*) 855; euphuism; fustian &c. 577; cacophony; want of balance; words that -break the teeth, – dislocate the jaw.

V. be -inelegant &c. *adj.*

Adj. inelegant, graceless, ungraceful, unpolished; harsh, abrupt; dry, stiff, cramped, formal, *guindé*; forced, laboured, awkward; artificial, mannered, ponderous; turgid &c. 577; affected, euphuistic; barbarous, uncouth, grotesque, rude, crude, halting; vulgar, offensive to ears polite.

---

2. *Spoken Language*

580. Voice.—N. voice; vocality; organ, lungs, bellows; good –, fine –, powerful &c. (*loud*) 404 –, musical &c. 413- voice; intonation; tone &c. (*sound*) 402- of voice.

vocalization; cry &c. 411; strain, utterance, prolation; exclam-, ejacul-, vocifer-ation; enunci-, articul-ation; articulate sound, distinctness; clearness, – of articulation; stage whisper; delivery; attack.

accent, -uation; emphasis, stress; broad –, strong –, pure –, native –, foreign- accent; pronunciation.

[Word similarly pronounced] homonym.

orthoepy; euphony &c. (*melody*) 413.

gastri-, ventri-loquism; ventriloquist; polyphon-ism, -ist.

[Science of voice] phonology &c. (*sound*) 402.

V. sing, speak, utter, breathe, voice; give -utterance, – tongue; cry &c.

581. Aphony.—N. aphony, *aphonia*; dumbness &c. *adj.*; obmutescence; absence –, want- of voice; dysphony; silence &c. (*taciturnity*) 585; raucity; harsh &c. 410 –, unmusical &c. 414- voice; *falsetto*, 'childish treble'; mute, dummy, deaf mute.

V. keep silence &c. 585; speak -low, – softly; whisper &c. (*faintness*) 405.

silence; render -mute, – silent &c. 403; muzzle, muffle, suppress, smother, gag, strike dumb, dumb-found, -founder; drown the voice, put to silence, stop one's mouth, cut one short. stick in the throat.

Adj. aphon-ous, -ic, dumb, mute; deaf-mute, – and dumb; mum; tongue-tied; breath-, tongue-, voice-, speech-, word-less; mute as a -fish, – stockfish, – mackerel; silent &c. (*taciturn*) 585; muzzled; in-articulate, -audible.

croaking, raucous, hoarse, husky,

(*shout*) 411; ejaculate, rap out; vocalize, prolate, articulate, enunciate, enounce, pronounce, accentuate, aspirate, deliver, mouth; emit, murmur, whisper, – in the ear, croon, yodel.

Adj. vocal, phonetic, oral; ejaculatory, articulate, distinct, stertorous; enunciative; accentuated, aspirated; euphonious &c. (*melodious*) 413.

dry, hollow, sepulchral, hoarse as a raven.

Adv. with -bated breath, – the finger on the lips; *sotto voce*; in a -low tone, – cracked voice, – broken voice; in an aside.

Phr. *vox faucibus hæsit.*

---

582. Speech.—N. speech, faculty of speech; locution, talk, parlance, verbal intercourse, prolation, oral communication, word of mouth, *parole*, palaver, prattle; effusion.

oration, recitation, delivery, say, address, speech, lecture, harangue, sermon, *tirade*, screed, formal speech, salutatory, peroration; prelection; speechifying; soliloquy &c. 589; allocution &c. 586; interlocution &c. 588.

oratory; elo-cution, -quence; rhetoric, declamation; grandi-, multiloquence; burst of eloquence; facundity; talkativeness; flow –, command- of -words, – language; *copia verborum*; power of speech, gift of the gab; *usus loquendi*.

speaker &c. *v.*; spokesman; pro-, inter-locutor; mouthpiece, Hermes; ora-tor, -trix, -tress; Demosthenes, Cicero; rhetorician; stump –, platform-orator, tub-thumper; elocutionist; speech-maker, patterer, *improvisatore*.

V. speak, – of; say, utter, pronounce, deliver, give utterance to; utter –, pour- forth; breathe, let fall, come out with; rap –, blurt- out; have on one's lips; have at the -end, – tip- of one's tongue.

break silence; open one's -lips, – mouth; lift –, raise- one's voice; give –, wag the- tongue; talk, outspeak; put in a word or two.

hold forth; make –, deliver- -a speech &c. *n.*; speechify, harangue, declaim, stump, flourish, spout, rant, recite, lecture, preach, sermonize, discourse, be on one's legs; have –, say- one's say; expatiate &c. (*speak at length*) 573; speak one's mind.

soliloquize &c. 589; tell &c. (*inform*) 527; speak to &c. 586; talk together &c. 588.

be -eloquent &c. *adj.*; have -a tongue in one's head, – the gift of the gab &c. *n.*

pass –, escape- one's lips; fall from the -lips, – mouth.

Adj. speaking &c., spoken &c. *v.*; oral, lingual, phonetic, not written, unwritten, outspoken; elo-quent, -cutionary; orat-, rhetorical; declamatory; grandiloquent &c. 577; talkative &c. 584.

583. [Imperfect Speech.] **Stammering.—N.** inarticulateness; stammering &c. *v.*; hesitation &c. *v.*; impediment in one's speech; aphasia, titubancy, traulism; whisper &c. (*faint sound*) 405; lisp, drawl, tardiloquence; nasal -tone, – accent; twang; *falsetto* &c. (*want of voice*) 581; broken -voice, – accents, – sentences.

brogue &c. 563; slip of the tongue, *lapsus linguæ*.

V. stammer, stutter, hesitate, falter, hammer; balbu-tiate, -cinate; haw, hum and haw, be unable to put two words together.

mumble, mutter; maund, -er; whisper &c. 405; mince, lisp; jabber, gabble, gibber; sp-, spl-utter; muffle, mump; drawl, mouth; croak; speak -thick, – through the nose; snuffle, clip one's words; murder the -language, – King's (*or* Queen's) English; mis-pronounce, -say.

Adj. stammering &c. *v.*; inarticulate, guttural, nasal; tremulous.

Adv. *sotto voce* &c. (*faintly*) 405.

Adv. orally &c. *adj.*; by word of mouth, *vivâ voce*, from the lips of.

Phr. quoth –, said- he &c.

584. Loquacity. — N. loquac-ity, -iousness; talkativeness &c. *adj.*; garrulity; multiloquence, much speaking, effusion, wordiness.

jaw; gab, -ble; jabber, chatter; prate, prattle, cackle, clack; twaddle, twattle, rattle; *caquet*, *-terie*; blabber, *bavardage*, bibble-babble, gibble-gabble; small talk &c. (*converse*) 588.

fluency, flippancy, volubility, flowing tongue; flow, – of words; *flux de -bouche*, *– mots*, *– paroles*; *copia verborum*, *cacoëthes loquendi*; verbosity &c. (*diffuseness*) 573; gift of the gab &c. (*eloquence*) 582.

talker; chatter-er, -box; babbler &c. *v.*; rattle; ranter; sermonizer, proser, driveller; windbag; gossip &c. (*converse*) 588; magpie, jay, parrot, poll, Babel; *moulin à paroles*.

V. be -loquacious &c. *adj.*; talk glibly, pour forth, patter; prate, palaver, prose, chatter, prattle, clack, jabber, jaw; rattle, – on; twaddle, twattle; babble, gabble; out-talk; talk oneself -out of breath, – hoarse; maunder, gush, blather; talk a donkey's hind leg off; expatiate &c. (*speak at length*) 573; gossip &c. (*converse*) 588; din in the ears &c. (*repeat*) 104; talk -at random, – nonsense &c. 497; be hoarse with talking.

Adj. loquacious, talkative, conversational, garrulous, linguacious, multiloquous; chattering &c. *v.*; chatty &c. (*sociable*) 892; declamatory &c. 582; open-mouthed.

fluent, voluble, glib, flippant; long-tongued, -winded &c. (*diffuse*) 573.

Adv. trippingly on the tongue; glibly &c. *adj.*

Phr. the tongue running -fast, – loose, – on wheels.

585. Taciturnity.—N. silence, muteness, obmutescence; taciturnity, pauciloquy, costiveness, curtness; reserve, reticence &c. (*concealment*) 528; *aposiopesis*.

man of few words.

V. be -silent &c. *adj.*; keep silence; hold one's -tongue, – peace, – jaw; not speak &c. 582; say nothing; seal –, close –, put a padlock on- the -lips, – mouth; put a bridle on one's tongue; keep one's tongue between one's teeth; make no sign, not let a word escape one; keep a secret &c. 528; not have a word to say; lay –, place- the finger on the lips; render mute &c. 581.

stick in one's throat.

Adj. silent, mute, mum; silent as -a post, – a stone, – the grave &c. (*still*) 403; dumb &c. 581.

taciturn, sparing of words; close, – mouthed, – tongued; laconic, costive, inconversable, curt; reserved; reticent &c. (*concealing*) 528.

Int. tush! silence! mum! hush! *chut!* hist! tut! &c. 403.

586. Allocution. — N. allocution, alloquy, address; speech &c. 582; apostrophe, interpellation, appeal, invocation, salutation; word in the ear.

[Feigned dialogue] dialogism.

platform &c. 542; audience &c. (*interview*) 588.

V. speak to, address, accost, make up to, apostrophize, appeal to, invoke; hail, salute; call to, halloo.

take -aside, – by the button, button-hole; talk to in private.

lecture &c. (*make a speech*) 582.

Int. soho! halloo! hey! hist! hi!

587. Response &c., *see* Answer 462.

588. Interlocution.—**N.** interlocution; collocution, colloquy, converse, conversation, confabulation, talk, discourse, verbal intercourse; communion, oral communication, commerce; dia-, duo-, tria-logue.

causerie, chat, chit-chat; small –, table –, tea-table –, town –, village –, idle- talk; tattle, gossip, tittle-tattle; babble, -ment; *tripotage*, cackle, prittle-prattle, *on dit*; talk of the -town, - village.

conference, parley, interview, audience, *pourparler*; *tête-à-tête*; reception, *conversazione*; congress &c. (*council*) 696; pow-wow.

hall of audience, *durbar*, coliseum, assembly hall, auditorium.

palaver, debate, logomachy, war of words, controversy.

talker, gossip, tattler; Paul Pry; tabby; chatterer &c. (*loquacity*) 584; interlocutor &c. (*spokesman*) 582; conversation-ist, -alist; dialogist.

'the feast of reason and the flow of soul'; *mollia tempora fandi*.

V. talk together, converse, confabulate; hold –, carry on –, join in –, engage in- a conversation; put in a word; shine in conversation; bandy words; parley; palaver; chat, gossip, tattle; prate &c. (*loquacity*) 584.

discourse –, confer –, commune –, commerce- with; hold -converse, – conference, – intercourse; talk it over; be closeted with; talk with one -in private, – *tête-à-tête*.

Adj. conversing &c. *v.*; interlocutory; convers-ational, -able; discursive, -coursive; chatty &c. (*sociable*) 892; colloquial, *tête-à-tête*, confabulatory.

589. Soliloquy.—**N.** soliloquy, monologue, apostrophe.

solilo-quist, -quizer, monologist.

V. soliloquize; say –, talk- to oneself; say aside, think aloud, apostrophize.

Adj. soliloquizing &c. *v.*

Adv. aside.

3. *Written Language*

590. Writing.—**N.** writing &c. *v.*; chiro-, stelo-, cero-graphy, graphology; stylography; pen-craft, -script, -manship; quill-driving; typewriting.

writing, manuscript, MS., *literæ scriptæ*; these presents.

stroke –, dash- of the pen; *coup de plume*; line; pen and ink.

letter &c. 561; uncial writing, cuneiform character, arrow-head, Ogham, Runes, futhorc; hieroglyphic, hieratic, demotic; script; contraction.

short-hand; steno-, brachy-, tachygraphy; secret writing, writing in cipher; crypt-, stegan-ography; phono-, pasi-, poly-, logo-graphy.

copy; tran-, re-script; draft, rough –, fair- copy; handwriting; signature, sign-manual; auto-, mono-, holo-graph; hand, fist; mark.

calligraphy; good –, running –,

591. Printing.—**N.** printing; block –, type- printing, lino-, mono-type; plate printing &c. (*engraving*) 558; the press &c. (*publication*) 531; composition.

print, letterpress, text, matter, standing type; context, note, page, column; over-running; head-, foot-line, title.

typography; stereo-, electro-, aprotype; type, black letter, heavy type, font, fount; pi, pie; capitals &c. (*letters*) 561; diamond, pearl, nonpareil, minion, brevier, bourgeois, long primer, small pica, pica, english, great primer.

folio &c. (*book*) 593; copy, impression, pull, proof, galley –, author's –, page- proof, revise.

printer, compositor, reader; printer's devil.

V. print; compose; put –, go- to press; pass –, see- through the press;

flowing –, cursive –, legible –, copper-plate –, round –, bold- hand.

cacography, *griffonage, barbouillage*; bad –, cramped –, crabbed –, illegible- hand; scribble &c. *v.*; *pattes de mouche*; ill-formed letters; pot-hooks and hangers.

stationery; pen, quill, goose-quill, reed; stylographic-, fountain-pen; pencil, style, stylus; paper, foolscap, parchment, vellum, papyrus, pad, tablet, block, note-book, slate, marble, pillar, table, black board.

ink-bottle, -pot, -stand, -well, -horn; typewriter.

transcription &c. (*copy*) 21; inscription &c. (*record*) 551; superscription &c. (*indication*) 550.

composition, authorship; *cacoëthes scribendi.*

writer, scribe, amanuensis, scrivener, secretary, clerk, penman, copyist, transcriber, quill-driver; writer for the press &c. (*author*) 593.

shorthand writer, stenographer; typewriter, typist.

V. write, pen; copy, engross; write out, – fair; transcribe; scribble, scrawl, scrabble, scratch; interline; stain paper; write down &c. (*record*) 551; sign &c. (*attest*) 467; take down, – in shorthand; typewrite, type.

compose, indite, draw up, redact, draft, formulate; dictate; inscribe, throw on paper, dash off; concoct.

take -up the pen, – pen in hand; shed –, spill –, dip one's pen in- ink.

Adj. writing &c. *v.*; written &c. *v.*; in -writing, – black and white; under one's hand.

uncial, Runic, cuneiform, hieroglyphical &c. *n.*

Adv. *currente calamo*; pen in hand.

592. Correspondence. — N. correspondence, letter, epistle, note, *billet*, post-, letter-card, missive, circular, form letter; favour, *billet-doux*; des-, dis-patch; *bulletin*, communication &c. 532; these presents; rescript, -ion; post &c. (*messenger*) 534; letter writer, correspondent.

V. correspond, – with; write –, send a letter- to; keep up a correspondence; drop a line to; despatch; communicate with; circularize.

Adj. epistolary.

publish &c. 531; bring out; appear in –, rush into- print.

Adj. printed &c. *v.*; in type; typographical &c. *n.*

593. Book.—N. book, -let; writing, work, volume, tome, opuscule; tract, -ate; *livret*; *brochure, libretto*, handbook, treatise, text-book, codex, manual, pamphlet, monograph, enchiridion, circular, publication; book of poems; novel; chap-book.

part, issue, number, *livraison*; album, portfolio; periodical, serial, magazine, ephemeris, annual, journal.

paper, bill, sheet, broadsheet, screed; leaf, -let; fly-leaf, page; quire, ream.

chapter, section, head, article, paragraph, passage, clause, supplement, appendix; *feuilleton*.

folio, quarto, octavo; duo-, sexto-, octo-decimo.

en-, cyclopædia, dictionary, lexicon, thesaurus, concordance, anthology, bibliography; compilation, compendium, catalogue &c. 86; library, bibliotheca; the press &c. (*publication*) 531.

writer, author, *littérateur, homme de lettres*, essayist, journalist, publicist; scribe, penman, war –, special –, correspondent; pen, scribbler, the scribbling race; ghost, hack, literary hack, Grub-street writer; writer for –, gentleman of –, representative of- the press; reporter, penny-a-liner; editor, sub-editor; literary agent; playwright &c. 599; poet &c. 597.

bookseller, publisher; biblio-pole, -polist, -grapher; librarian; book -collector, – worm.

book -shop, – club, circulating –, lending –, public- library; publishing house.

knowledge of books, bibliography; book-learning &c. (*knowledge*) 490.

594. Description.—N. description, account, statement, report; *exposé* &c. (*disclosure*) 529; specification, particulars, scenario, plot; state –, summary- of facts; brief &c. (*abstract*) 596; return &c. (*record*) 551; *catalogue raisonné* &c. (*list*) 86; guide-book &c. (*information*) 527.

delineation &c. (*representation*) 554; sketch, vignette; monograph; minute –, detailed –, particular –, circumstantial –, graphic- account; narration, recital, rehearsal, relation.

histori-, chron-ography; historic Muse, Clio; history; bi-, autobi-ography; necrology, obituary.

narrative, history; memoir, memorials; annals &c. (*chronicle*) 551; tradition, legend, saga, epic, epos, story, tale, historiette; personal narrative, journal, letters, life, adventures, fortunes, experiences, confessions; anecdote, ana, *trait.*

work of fiction, short story, novelette, novel, romance, penny dreadful, shilling shocker, Minerva press; fairy –, nursery- tale; fable, allegory, parable, apologue.

relator &c. *v.*; *raconteur*; historian &c. (*recorder*) 553; biographer, fabulist, novelist, story teller, romancer, teller of tales, spinner of yarns, anecdotist.

V. describe; set forth &c. (*state*) 535; draw a picture, picture; portray &c. (*represent*) 554; characterize, particularize; narrate, relate, recite, recount, sum up, run over, recapitulate, rehearse, fight one's battles over again.

unfold &c. (*disclose*) 529- a tale; tell; give –, render- an account of; report, make a report, draw up a statement.

detail; enter into –, descend to- -particulars, – details.

Adj. descriptive, graphic, narrative, epic, suggestive, well-drawn; historic; auto-, biographical, realistic, expository, tradition-al, -ary; legendary; fabulous, mythical; anecdotic, storied; described &c. *v.*

595. Dissertation.—N. dissertation, treatise, essay; *thesis*, theme; tract, -ate, -ation, excursus; discourse, memoir, disquisition, lecture, sermon, homily, pandect.

commentary, review, *critique*, criticism, article; lead-er, -ing article, editorial; argument, running commentary.

investigation &c. (*inquiry*) 461; study &c. (*consideration*) 451; discussion &c. (*reasoning*) 476; exposition &c. (*explanation*) 522.

commentator, critic, essayist, pamphleteer; publicist, reviewer, leader writer, editor, annotator.

V. dissert –, descant –, write –, touch- upon a subject; dissertate; treat of –, take up –, ventilate –, discuss –, deal with –, go into –, canvass –, handle –, do justice to- a subject; comment, criticize, interpret &c. 522; argue.

Adj. dis-cursive, -coursive; disquisitional, disquisitionary; expository, critical.

596. Compendium.—N. compend, -ium; abstract, *précis*, epitome, *multum in parvo*, analysis, pandect, digest, sum and substance, brief, abridgment, summary, *aperçu*, draft, minute, note; synopsis, text-book, *conspectus*, outlines, syllabus, contents, heads, prospectus.

album; scrap –, note –, memorandum –, commonplace- book; extracts, *excerpta*, cuttings; fugitive -pieces, – writings; *spicilegium*, flowers, anthology, miscellany, *collectanea*, *analecta*; compilation.

recapitulation, *résumé*, review.

abbrevia-tion, -ture; contraction; shortening &c. 201; compression &c. 195.

V. abridge, abstract, epitomize, summarize; make –, prepare –, draw –, compile- an abstract &c. *n.*

recapitulate, review, skim, run over, sum up.

abbreviate &c. (*shorten*) 201; condense &c. (*compress*) 195; compile &c. (*collect*) 72; edit, blue pencil.

Adj. compendious, synoptic, analectic, analytical; abridged &c. *v.*

Adv. in -short, – epitome, – substance, – few words.

Phr. it lies in a nutshell.

597. Poetry.—N. poetry, poetics, poesy, Muse, Calliope, tuneful Nine, Parnassus, Helicon, Pierides, Pierian spring, afflatus, inspiration.

versification, rhyming, making verses; prosody, scansion, orthometry.

poem; epic, – poem; epopee, *epopæa*, ode, epode, idyl, lyric, eclogue, pastoral, bucolic, georgic, dithyramb, anacreontic, sonnet, roundelay, *rondel*, *rondoletto*, *rondeau*, *rondo*, triolet; madrigal, canzonet, *cento*, monody, elegy, palinode; rhapsody.

dramatic –, lyric- poetry; opera; posy, anthology.

song, ballad, lay; love –, drinking –, war –, folk –, sea- song; lullaby; music &c. 415; nursery rhymes.

[Bad poetry] doggerel, Hudibrastic verse, prose run mad; macaronics; macaronic –, leonine- verse; runes.

canto, stanza, distich, verse, line, couplet, triplet, quatrain, sestet; *strophe*, *antistrophe*, refrain, chorus, burden.

verse, rhyme, assonance, crambo, metre, measure, foot, numbers, strain, rhythm; accentuation &c. (*voice*) 580; iambus, dactyl, spondee, trochee, anapæst &c.; hex-, pent-ameter; Alexandrine; blank verse, alliteration.

elegiacs &c. *adj.*; elegiac &c. *adj.* -verse, – metre, – poetry.

poet, – laureate; laureate; minor poet, bard, lyrist, scald, troubadour, *trouvère*; minstrel; minne-, meister-singer; *improvisatore*; versifier, sonneteer; ballad monger; rhym-er, -ist, -ester; poetaster.

V. poetize, sing, versify, make verses, rhyme, scan.

Adj. poetic, -al; lyric, -al; tuneful; epic; dithyrambic &c. *n.*; metrical; a-, catalectic; elegiac, iambic, trochaic, spondaic, dactylic, anapæstic; Ionic, Sapphic, Alcaic, Pindaric.

598. Prose.—N. prose, – writer, pros-aism, -aist, -er.

V. prose, write prose.

write -prose, – in prose.

Adj. pros-y, -aic; unpoetical.

rhymeless, unrhymed, in prose, not in verse.

599. The Drama.—N. the -drama, – stage, – theatre, – play; theatricals, dramaturgy, histrionic art, buskin, sock, *cothurnus*, Melpomene and Thalia, Thespis.

play, drama, stage-play, piece, five-act play, tragedy, comedy, opera, comic opera, *vaudeville*, *comedietta*, *lever de rideau*, curtain raiser, interlude, afterpiece, exode, farce, *divertissement*, *extravaganza*, burletta, harlequinade, pantomime, mimodrama, burlesque, *opéra bouffe*, musical comedy, review, revue, intimate revue, variety, cabaret entertainment, *ballet*, *spectacle*, masque, *drame*, *comédie drame*; melo-drama, -drame; *comédie larmoyante*, emotional drama, sensation drama, tragi-, farcical-comedy; mono-drame, -logue; duologue; trilogy; charade, *proverbe*; mystery, miracle –, morality- play.

act, scene, *tableau*; in-, intro-duction; pro-, epi-logue, curtain; *libretto*, book, script.

performance, representation, show, *mise en scène*, stagery, *jeu de théâtre*, stage-craft; acting; gesture &c. 550; impersonation &c. 554; stage business, gag, patter, buffoonery.

theatre; play-, opera-house; house; music hall; *cabaret*; amphitheatre, circus, hippodrome; puppet-show, *fantoccini*; *marionnettes*, Punch and Judy.

cinema, -tograph-, picture –, theatre, the pictures, the movies, the talkies.

auditory, *auditorium*, front of the house, stalls, boxes, balcony, dress –, upper- -circle, – boxes, amphitheatre, pit, gallery; *foyer*; green-room; dressing rooms, *coulisses*.

flat; drop, – scene; wing, screen, side-scene; transformation scene, curtain, act-drop, safety –, fire- curtain; *proscenium*, forestage.

stage, revolving stage, scene, the boards; star –, grave –, trap, mezzanine floor; flies; gridiron, floats, battens, footlights; lime –, spot –, flood –, bunch-lights; scenery, set, *décor*; orchestra.

theatrical -costume, – properties, props.

part, *rôle*, character, cast, *dramatis personæ*; *répertoire*.

actor, player; stage –, strolling- player; old –, stager, performer; mime, -r; *artiste*; com-, trag-edian, straight man; *tragédienne*, Thespian, Roscius, star.

pantomimist, clown, harlequin, *buffo*, buffoon, *farceur*, *grimacier*, pantaloon, columbine; *Pierrot*, *Pierrette*; punch, -inello; *pulcinell-o*, *-a*; mute, *figurante*, general utility; super, -numerary, extra.

mummer, guiser, guisard, gysart, masque.

mountebank, Jack Pudding; tumbler, posture-master, acrobat, equilibrist, juggler, contortionist; *danseuse*, *ballerina*, ballet -dancer, – girl, *coryphée*; *bayadère*, *geisha*; chorus -singer, – girl.

company; first tragedian, *prima donna*, lead, leading lady, protagonist; *jeune premier*; juvenile lead, *débutant*, *-e*; light –, genteel –, low- -comedy, – comedian; *soubrette*, walking gentleman, *amoroso*, heavy, heavy father, *ingénue*, *jeune veuve*, *commère*, *compère*.

property man, *costumier*, machinist, stage hand, electrician, prompter, call-boy; director, manager; stage –, acting –, business- manager; *entrepreneur*, *impresario*, producer, press agent.

dramatic -author, – writer; play-writer, -wright; dramatist, mimographer; dramatic critic.

V. act, play, perform; stage, produce, put on the stage; personate &c. 554; mimic &c. (*imitate*) 19; enact; play –, act –, go through –, perform- a part; rehearse, spout, gag, rant; 'strut and fret one's hour upon a stage'; tread the -stage, – boards; come out; star.

Adj. dramatic; theatric, -al; scenic, histrionic, comic, tragic, buskined, farcical, tragi-comic, melodramatic, operatic; stagey, spectacular; stagestruck.

Adv. on the -stage, – boards; before -the floats, – an audience; in the limelight, behind the footlights; behind the scenes.

CLASS V

Words relating to THE VOLUNTARY POWERS*

Division (I.) INDIVIDUAL VOLITION

Section I. Volition in General

1°. *Acts of Volition*

600. Will.—N. will, volition, conation†, velleity; will and pleasure, free-will; freedom &c. 748; discretion; choice, inclination, intent, purpose, option &c. (*choice*) 609; voluntariness; spontane-ity, -ousness; originality.

pleasure, wish, desire, mind; frame of mind &c. (*inclination*) 602; intention &c. 620; predetermination &c. 611; self-control &c. determination &c. (*resolution*) 604; will-power.

V. will, list; see –, think- fit; determine &c. (*resolve*) 604; settle &c. (*choose*) 609; volunteer.

have a will of one's own; do what one chooses &c. (*freedom*) 748; have it all one's own way; have one's -will, – own way.

use –, exercise- one's discretion; take -upon oneself, – one's own course, – the law into one's own hands; do -of one's own accord, – upon one's own -responsibility, – authority; take the bit between one's teeth; take responsibility; originate &c. (*cause*) 153.

Adj. voluntary, volitive, volitional, wilful; free &c. 748; optional; discretion-al, -ary; volitient; dictatorial.

minded &c. (*willing*) 602; prepense &c. (*predetermined*) 611; intended &c. 620; autocratic; unbidden &c. (bid &c. 741); spontaneous; original &c. (*causal*) 153.

Adv. voluntarily &c. *adj.*; at -will, – pleasure; *à -volonté*, – *discrétion*; *al piacere*; *ad -libitum*, – *arbitrium*; as -one thinks proper, – it seems good to.

601. Necessity.—N. involuntariness; instinct, blind –, natural- impulse; inborn –, innate- proclivity; the force of circumstances.

necessi-ty, -tation, necessarianism; obligation; compulsion &c. 744; subjection &c. 749; stern –, hard –, dire –, imperious –, inexorable –, iron –, adverse- -necessity, – fate; what must be.

desti-ny, -nation; fatality, fate, *kismet*, doom, foredoom, election, predestination; pre-, fore-ordination; lot, fortune; fatalism, determinism; inevitableness &c. *adj.*; spell &c. 993.

star, -s; planet, -s; astral influence; sky, Fates, Norns, *Parcæ*, Sisters three, Clotho, Lachesis, Atropos; book of fate; God's will, will of Heaven; wheel of Fortune, Ides of March, Hobson's choice.

last -shift, – resort; *dernier ressort*; *pis aller* &c. (*substitute*) 147; necessaries &c. (*requirement*) 630.

necess-arian, -itarian; fatalist, determinist; automaton.

V. lie under a necessity; be -fated, – doomed, – destined &c., – in for, – under the necessity of; have no -choice, – alternative; be- obliged –, forced –, driven –, one's -fate &c. *n.*- to; be -pushed to the wall, – driven into a corner, – unable to help, – drawn irresistibly.

destine, doom, foredoom, devote; pre-destine, -ordain; cast a spell &c. 992; necessitate; compel &c. 744.

* Conative powers or faculties (Hamilton). †Hamilton.

of one's own -accord, – free will; *proprio* –, *suo* –, *ex mero- motu*; out of one's own head; by choice &c. 609; purposely &c. (*intentionally*) 620; deliberately &c. 611.

Phr. *stet pro ratione voluntas*; *sic volo sic jubeo.*

Adj. necessary; needful &c. (*requisite*) 630.

fated; destined &c. *v.*; fateful; elect; spell-bound.

compulsory &c. (*compel*) 744; uncontrollable, inevitable, unavoidable, irresistible, irrevocable, inexorable, binding; avoid-, resist-less; written in the book of fate.

involuntary, instinctive, automatic, blind, mechanical; un-conscious, -witting, -thinking; unintentional &c. (*undesigned*) 621; impulsive &c. 612.

Adv. necessarily &c. *adv.*; of -necessity, – course; *ex necessitate rei*; needs must; perforce &c. 744; *nolens volens*; will he nil he, willy nilly, *bon gré mal gré*, willing or unwilling, *coûte que coûte*, forcefully; *faute de mieux*; by stress of; if need be.

Phr. it cannot be helped; there is no- help for, – helping- it; it -will, – must, – must needs- be, – be so, – have its way; the die is cast; *jacta est alea*; *che sarà sarà*; 'it is written'; one's- days are numbered, – fate is sealed; *Fata obstant*; *dis aliter visum.*

602. Willingness.—N. willingness, voluntariness &c. *adj.*; willing mind, heart.

disposition, inclination, leaning, *animus*; frame of mind, humour, mood, vein; bent &c. (*turn of mind*) 820; *penchant* &c. (*desire*) 865; aptitude &c. 698.

doc-ility, -ibleness, tractability; persuasi-bleness, -bility; pliability &c. (*softness*) 324.

geniality, cordiality; goodwill; alacrity, readiness, earnestness, forwardness, enthusiasm; zeal, eagerness &c. (*desire*) 865.

assent &c. 488; compliance &c. 762; pleasure &c. (*will*) 600.

labour of love, self-appointed task; volunteer, -ing, gratuitous service; unpaid worker, amateur.

V. be -willing &c. *adj.*; incline, lean to, mind, propend; had as lief; lend –, give –, turn- a willing ear; have -a, – half a, – a great- mind to; hold –, cling- to; desire &c. 865.

see –, think- -good, – fit, – proper; acquiescence &c. (*assent*) 488; comply with &c. 762.

swallow –, nibble at- the bait; gorge the hook; swallow hook, line and sinker; have –, make- no scruple of; make no bones of; jump –, catch- at; meet half way; volunteer, offer oneself &c. 763.

603. Unwillingness.—N. unwillingness &c. *adj.*; indispos-ition, -edness; disinclination, aversation, aversion; nolleity, nolition; renitence; reluctance; indifference &c. 866; backwardness &c. *adj.*; slowness &c. 275; want of -alacrity, – readiness; indocility &c. (*obstinacy*) 606.

scrupul-ousness, -osity; qualms of conscience, delicacy, demur, scruple, qualm, shrinking, recoil; hesitation &c. (*irresolution*) 605; fastidiousness &c. 868.

averseness &c. (*dislike*) 867; dissent &c. 489; refusal &c. 764.

slacker, scrimshanker, *embusqué*, unwilling worker, forced labour.

V. be -unwilling &c. *adj.*; nill; dislike &c. 867; grudge, begrudge; not be able to find it in one's heart to, not have the stomach to.

demur, stick at, scruple, stickle; hang fire, run rusty, slack, shirk, scamp, give up, fight shy of, not pull fair; recoil, shrink, swerve; hesitate &c. 605; avoid &c. 623.

oppose &c. 708; dissent &c. 489; refuse &c. 764.

Adj. unwilling; not in the vein, loth, shy of, disinclined, indisposed, averse, reluctant, not content; adverse &c. (*opposed*) 708; laggard, backward, remiss, slack, slow to; renitent; indifferent &c. 866; scrupulous; squeamish

Adj. willing, minded, fain, disposed, inclined, favourable; favourably-minded, -inclined, -disposed; nothing loth; in the -vein, – mood, – humour, – mind.

ready, forward, enthusiastic, earnest, eager; bent upon &c. (*desirous*) 865; predisposed, propense.

docile; persua-dable, -sible; suasible, easily persuaded, facile, easy-going; amenable; tractable &c. (*pliant*) 324; genial, gracious, cordial, hearty; content &c. (*assenting*) 488.

voluntary, gratuitous, spontaneous; unasked &c. (ask &c. 765); unforced &c. (*free*) 748.

Adv. willingly &c. *adj.*; fain, freely, as lief, heart and soul; with -pleasure, – all one's heart, – open arms; with -good, – right good- will; *de bonne volonté, ex animo*; *con amore*, heart in hand, nothing loth, without reluctance, of one's own accord, graciously, with a good grace, without demur.

à la bonne heure; by all -means, – manner of means; to one's heart's content; yes &c. (*assent*) 488.

Int. sure, -ly! of course!

&c. (*fastidious*) 868; repugnant &c. (*dislike*) 867; rest-iff, -ive; demurring &c. *v.*; unconsenting &c. (*refusing*) 764; involuntary &c. 601; grudging, irreconcilable.

Adv. unwillingly &c. *adj.*; grudgingly, with a heavy heart; with -a bad, – an ill- grace; against –, sore against- -one's wishes, – one's will, – the grain; *invitâ Minervâ*; *à contre cœur*; *malgré soi*; in spite of -one's teeth, – oneself; *nolens volens* &c. (*necessity*) 601; perforce &c. 744; under protest; no &c. 536; not for the world, far be it from me; not if I can help it; if I must I must.

---

604. Resolution.—N. determination, will; iron –, unconquerable- will; will of one's own, decision, resolution, backbone, grit; strength of -mind, – will; resolve &c. (*intent*) 620; *intransigeance*; firmness &c. (*stability*) 150; energy, manliness, vigour; game, pluck; resoluteness &c. (*courage*) 861; zeal &c. 682; *aplomb*; desperation; devot-ion, -edness.

mastery over self; self-control, -command, -mastery, -possession, -reliance, -government, -restraint, -conquest, -denial; moral -courage, – strength, – fibre; perseverance &c. 604*a*; tenacity; obstinacy &c. 606; bull-dog; British lion.

V. have -determination &c. *n.*; know one's own mind; be -resolved &c. *adj.*; make up one's mind, will, resolve, determine; decide &c. (*judgment*) 480; form –, come to- a -determination, – resolution, – resolve; conclude, fix, seal, determine once for all, bring to a crisis, drive matters to an extremity; take a decisive step &c. (*choice*) 609; take upon oneself &c. (*undertake*) 676.

devote oneself –, give oneself up- to; throw away the scabbard, kick down

605. Irresolution.—N. irresolution, infirmity of purpose, indecision; in-, un-determination, loss of will power; unsettlement; uncertainty &c. 475; demur, suspense; hesi-tating &c. *v.*, -tation, -tancy; vacillation; ambivalence; changeableness &c. 149; fluctuation; alternation &c. (*oscillation*) 314; caprice &c. 608; lukewarmness.

fickleness, levity, *légèreté*; pliancy &c. (*softness*) 324; weakness; timidity &c. 860; cowardice &c. 862; half measures.

waverer, ass between two bundles of hay; shuttlecock, butterfly; time-server, opportunist, turn coat.

V. be -irresolute &c. *adj.*; hang –, keep- in suspense; leave '*ad referendum*'; think twice about, pause; dawdle &c. (*inactivity*) 683; remain neuter; dilly-dally, hesitate, boggle, hover, wobble, shilly-shally, hum and haw, demur, not know one's own mind; debate, balance; dally –, coquet- with; will and will not, *chasser-balancer*; go half-way, compromise, make a compromise; be thrown off one's balance, stagger like a drunken man; be afraid &c. 860; let 'I dare not' wait upon 'I would'; falter, waver.

the ladder, nail one's colours to the mast, set one's back against the wall, set one's teeth, put one's foot down, burn one's bridges, take one's stand; stand firm &c. (*stability*) 150; steel oneself; stand no nonsense, not listen to the voice of the charmer.

buckle to; put –, lay –, set- one's shoulder to the wheel; put one's heart into; run the gauntlet, make a dash at, take the bull by the horns; beard the lion in his den; rush –, plunge- *in medias res*; go in for; insist upon, make a point of; set one's heart, – mind- upon.

stick at nothing; make short work of &c. (*activity*) 682; not stick at trifles; go -all lengths, – the whole hog; persist &c. (*persevere*) 604*a*; go down with colours flying, die game; go through fire and water, ride in the whirlwind and direct the storm.

Adj. resolved &c. *v.*; determined; strong-willed, -minded; resolute &c. (*brave*) 861; self-possessed, plucky, tenacious; decided, definitive, peremptory; un-hesitating, -flinching, -shrinking; firm, cast iron, indomitable, game to the backbone; inexorable, relentless, not to be -shaken, – put down; *tenax propositi*; inflexible &c. (*hard*) 323; obstinate &c. 606; steady &c. (*persevering*) 604*a*; unbending, unyielding, irrevocable; firm as a rock; grim.

earnest, serious; set –, bent –, intent- upon.

steeled –, proof- against; *in utrumque paratus*.

Adv. resolutely &c. *adj.*; in –, in good- earnest; seriously, joking apart, earnestly, heart and soul; on one's metal; manfully, like a man, with a high hand; with a strong hand &c. (*exertion*) 686.

at any -rate, – risk, – hazard, – price, – cost, – sacrifice; at all -hazards, – risks, – events; cost what it may; *coûte que coûte*; *à tort et à travers*; once for all; neck or nothing; rain or shine; with colours nailed to the mast.

Phr. *spes sibi quisque*.

vacillate &c. 149; change &c. 140; retract &c. 607; fluctuate; alternate &c. (*oscillate*) 314; keep off and on, play fast and loose; blow hot and cold &c. (*caprice*) 608.

shuffle, palter, blink; trim.

Adj. irresolute, infirm of purpose, double-minded, half-hearted; undecided, -resolved, -determined; drifting; shilly-shally; fidgety, tremulous; wobbly; hesitating &c. *v.*; off one's balance; at a loss &c. (*uncertain*) 475.

vacillating &c. *v.*; unsteady &c. (*changeable*) 149; unsteadfast, fickle, unreliable, irresponsible, unstable, without ballast; capricious &c. 608; volatile, frothy; light, -some, -minded; giddy; fast and loose.

weak, feeble-minded, frail; timid &c. 860; cowardly &c. 862; facile; pliant &c. (*soft*) 324; unable to say 'no,' easy-going.

revocable, reversible.

Adv. irresolutely &c. *adj.*; irresolvedly; in faltering accents; off and on; from pillar to post; see-saw &c. 314.

Int. 'how happy could I be with either!'

604a. Perseverance.—**N.** perseverance; continuance &c. (*inaction*) 143; permanence &c. (*absence of change*) 141; firmness &c. (*stability*) 150.

constancy, steadiness; singleness –, tenacity- of purpose; persistence, plodding, patience; sedulity &c. (*industry*) 682; pertina-cy, -city, -ciousness; iteration &c. 104.

bottom, game, pluck, stamina, backbone, grit; indefatiga-bility, -bleness; bulldog courage.

V. persevere, persist; hold -on, – out; die in the last ditch, be in at the death; stick –, cling –, adhere- to; stick to one's text, keep on; keep to –, maintain- one's -course, – ground; bear –, keep –, hold-up; plod; stick to work &c. (*work*) 686; continue &c. 143; follow up; die -in harness, – at one's post.

Adj. persevering, constant; stead-y, -fast; un-deviating, -wavering, -faltering, -swerving, -flinching, -sleeping, -flagging, -drooping; steady as time; uninter-, un-remitting; plodding; industrious &c. 682; strenuous &c. 686; pertinacious; persist-ing, -ent.

solid, sturdy, staunch, stanch, true to oneself; unchangeable &c. 150; unconquerable &c. (*strong*) 159; indomitable, game to the last, indefatigable, untiring, unwearied, never tiring.

Adv. through -evil report and good report, – thick and thin, – fire and water; *per fas et nefas*; without fail, sink or swim, at any price, *vogue la galère*; in sickness and in health.

Phr. never say die; *vestigia nulla retrorsum*.

606. Obstinacy.—N. obstinateness &c. *adj.*; obstinacy, tenacity; perseverance &c. 604*a*; immovability; old school; inflexibility &c. (*hardness*) 323; obdur-acy, -ation; dogged resolution; resolution &c. 604; ruling passion; blind side.

self-will, contumacy, perversity; pervica-cy, -city; indocility.

bigotry, intolerance, dogmatism; opinia-try, -tiveness; fixed idea &c.; intractability, incorrigibility; (*prejudgment*) 481; fanaticism, zealotry, infatuation, monomania, opinionativeness.

mule; opin-ionist, -ionatist, -iator, -ator; stickler, dogmatist, die-hard, bitter-ender; bigot; zealot, enthusiast, fanatic.

V. be -obstinate &c. *adj.*; stickle, take no denial, fly in the face of facts; opinionate, be wedded to an opinion, hug a belief; have one's own way &c. (*will*) 600; persist &c. (*persevere*) 604*a*; have –, insist on having- the last word.

die -hard, – fighting, fight -against destiny, – to the last ditch; not yield an inch, stand out.

Adj. obstinate, tenacious, stubborn, obdurate, case-hardened; inflexible &c. (*hard*) 323; immovable, not to be moved; inert &c. 172; unchangeable &c. 150; inexorable &c. (*determined*) 604; mulish, obstinate as a mule, pig-headed.

dogged; sullen, sulky; un-moved, -influenced, -affected.

wilful, self-willed, perverse; res-ty, -tive, -tiff; pervicacious, wayward, refractory, unruly; head-y, -strong; *entêté*; contumacious; cross-grained.

607. Tergiversation.—N. change of -mind, – intention, – purpose; afterthought.

tergiversation, recantation; palinode, -ody; renunciation; abjur-ation, -ement; defection &c. (*relinquishment*) 624; going over &c. *v.*; apostasy; retract-ion, -ation; withdrawal, disavowal &c. (*negation*) 536; revo-cation, -kement; reversal; repentance &c. 950; *redintegratio amoris*.

coquetry, flirtation; vacillation &c. 605; back-sliding, recidivation.

turn-coat, -tippet; rat, apostate, renegade, mugwump; con-, per-vert; proselyte, deserter; backslider, recidivist; black leg.

time-server, -pleaser; timist, Vicar of Bray, trimmer, ambidexter; weathercock &c. (*changeable*) 149; Janus.

V. change one's -mind, – intention, – purpose, – note; abjure, renounce; withdraw from &c. (*relinquish*) 624; wheel –, turn –, veer- round; turn a *pirouette*; go over –, pass –, change –, skip- from one side to another; go to the right about; box the compass, shift one's ground, go upon another tack; back down, crawl, crawfish.

apostatize, change sides, go over, rat; recant, retract; revoke; rescind &c. (*abrogate*) 756; recall, forswear, abjure, unsay; come -over, – round- to an opinion.

draw in one's horns, eat one's words; eat –, swallow- the leek; swerve, flinch, back out of, retrace one's steps, think better of it; come back –, return- to one's first love; turn over a new leaf &c. (*repent*) 950.

arbitrary, dogmatic, opinionated, positive, bigoted; prejudiced &c. 481; prepossessed, infatuated; stiff-backed, -necked, -hearted; hard-mouthed, hidebound; unyielding; im-pervious, -practicable, -persuasible; unpersuadable; in-, un-tractable; incorrigible, deaf to advice, impervious to reason; crotchety &c. 608.

Adv. obstinately &c. *adj.*

Phr. *non possumus*; no surrender.

trim, shuffle, play fast and loose, blow hot and cold, coquet, flirt, hold with the hare but run with the hounds; straddle; *nager entre deux eaux*; wait to see how the -cat jumps, – wind blows.

Adj. changeful &c. 149; irresolute &c. 605; ductile, slippery as an eel, trimming, ambidextrous, timeserving; coquetting &c. *v.*

revocatory, reactionary.

Phr. 'a change came o'er the spirit of my dream.'

---

608. Caprice.—N. caprice, fancy, humour; whim, -sey, -wham; crotchet, *capriccio*, quirk, freak, maggot, fad, vagary, prank, fit, flim-flam, *escapade, boutade*, wild-goose chase; capriciousness &c. *adj.*; kink.

V. be -capricious &c. *adj.*; have a maggot in the brain; take it into one's head, strain at a gnat and swallow a camel; blow hot and cold; play -fast and loose, – fantastic tricks.

Adj. capricious; erratic, eccentric, fitful, hysterical; full of -whims &c. *n.*; maggoty; inconsistent, fanciful, fantastic, whimsical, crotchety, particular, humoursome, freakish, skittish, wanton, wayward; contrary; captious; arbitrary; unrestrained, undisciplined; not amenable to reason; uncomfortable &c. 83; penny wise and pound foolish; fickle &c. (*irresolute*) 605; frivolous, sleeveless, giddy, volatile.

Adv. by fits and starts, without rhyme or reason, at one's own sweet will.

Phr. *nil fuit unquam sic impar sibi*; the deuce is in him.

609. Choice.—N. choice, option; discretion &c. (*volition*) 600; preoption; alternative; dilemma; *embarras de choix*; adoption, co-optation; novation; decision &c. (*judgment*) 480.

election, poll, ballot, vote, voice, suffrage, plumper, cumulative vote; *plebiscitum, plébiscite, vox populi*; *referendum*, electioneering; voting &c. *v.*; franchise; ballot box; slate, ticket.

selection, excerption, gleaning, eclecticism; *excerpta*, gleanings, cuttings, scissors and paste; pick &c. (*best*) 650.

preference, prelation; predilection &c. (*desire*) 865.

V. offer for one's choice, set before; hold out –, present –, offer- the alternative; put to the vote.

use –, exercise –, one's- -discretion, – option; adopt, take up, embrace, espouse; choose, elect, co-opt; take –, make- one's choice; make choice of, fix upon.

vote, poll, hold up one's hand; divide.

settle; decide &c. (*adjudge*) 480; list

609a. Absence of Choice.—N. no –, Hobson's- choice; first come, first served; necessity &c. 601; not a pin to choose &c. (*equality*) 27; any, the first that comes.

neutrality, indifference; indecision &c. (*irresolution*) 605.

V. be -neutral &c. *adj.*; have no choice; waive, not vote; abstain –, refrain- from voting; leave undecided; make a virtue of necessity.

Adj. neu-tral, -ter; indifferent; undecided &c. (*irresolute*) 605.

Adv. either &c. (*choice*) 609.

610. Rejection.—N. rejection, repudiation, exclusion; declination; refusal &c. 764.

V. reject; set –, lay- aside; give up; decline &c. (*refuse*) 764; exclude, except, eliminate; pluck, spin; cast.

repudiate, scout, set at naught; fling –, cast –, thrown –, toss- -to the winds, – to the dogs, – overboard, – away; send to the right about; dis-

&c. (*will*) 600; make up one's mind &c. (*resolve*) 604.

select; pick, – and choose; pick –, single- out, excerpt; cull, glean, winnow; sift –, separate –, winnow- the chaff from the wheat; pick up, pitch upon; pick one's way; indulge one's fancy.

set apart, reserve, mark out for; mark &c. 550.

prefer; have -rather, – as lief; fancy &c. (desire) 865; be persuaded &c. 615.

take a -decided, – decisive- step; commit oneself to a course; pass –, cross- the Rubicon; cast in one's lot with; take for better or for worse.

Adj. optional; co-optative; discretional &c. (*voluntary*) 600; on approval.

eclectic; choosing &c. *v.*; preferential; chosen &c. *v.*; choice &c. (*good*) 648.

Adv. optionally &c. *adj.*; at pleasure &c. (*will*) 600; either, – the one or the other; or; at the option of; whether or not; once for all; for one's money.

by -choice, – preference; in preference; rather, before.

claim &c. (*deny*) 536; discard &c. (*eject*) 297, (*have done with*) 678.

Adj. rejected &c. *v.*; reject-aneous, -itious; not -chosen &c. 609, – to be thought of; out of the question.

Adv. neither, – the one nor the other; no &c. 536.

Phr. *non hæc in fœdera.*

---

611. Predetermination. — **N.** pre-meditation, -deliberation, -determination, -destination; foreordination; foregone conclusion; *parti pris*; resolve, propendency; intention &c. 620; project &c. 626.

V. pre-determine, -destine, -meditate, -resolve, -concert; foreordain; resolve beforehand.

Adj. pre-pense, -meditated &c. *v.*, -designed; advised, studied, designed, calculated; aforethought; intended &c. 620; foregone.

well-laid, -devised, -weighed; maturely considered; cut and dried; cunning.

Adv. advisedly &c. *adj.*; with premeditation, deliberately, all things considered, with eyes open, in cold blood; intentionally &c. 620.

612. Impulse.—**N.** impulse, sudden thought; *impromptu*, improvisation; inspiration, hunch, flash, spurt.

improvisatore, *improvisatrice*, improviser, extemporizer; creature of impulse.

V. flash on the mind.

say what comes uppermost; improvise, extemporize; rise to the occasion; spurt.

Adj. extemporaneous, impulsive, indeliberate; improvis-ed, -ate, -atory; un-, unpre-meditated; *improvisé*; unprompted, -guided; natural, unguarded; spontaneous &c. (*voluntary*) 600; instinctive &c. 601.

Adv. extem-pore, -poraneously; offhand, *impromptu*, *à l'improviste*; improviso; on the spur of the -moment, – occasion.

613. Habit.—**N.** habit, -ude; assuetude, -faction; wont; run, way.

common –, general –, natural –, ordinary –, habitual- -course, – run, – state- of things; matter of course; beaten -path, – track, – ground.

prescription, custom, use, usage, immemorial usage, practice; tradition; prevalence, observance; conventional-

614. Desuetude.—**N.** desuetude, disusage; disuse &c. 678; want of -habit, – practice; inusitation; newness to; new brooms.

infraction of usage &c. (*unconformity*) 83; non-prevalence; 'a custom more honoured in the breach than the observance.'

V. be -unaccustomed &c. *adj.*; leave

ism, -ity; mode, fashion, vogue; *étiquette* &c. (*gentility*) 852; order of the day, cry; conformity &c. 82.

habitué, addict.

one's old way, old school, consuetude, *veteris vestigia flammæ*; *laudator temporis acti.*

rule, standing order, precedent, routine; red-tape, -tapism; pipe-clay; rut, groove.

cacoëthes; bad –, confirmed –, inveterate –, intrinsic &c. 5- habit; addiction, trick.

training &c. (*education*) 537; seasoning, hardening, inurement; radication; second nature, acclimatization; knack &c. (*skill*) 698.

V. be -wont &c. *adj.*

fall into a custom &c. (*conform to*) 82; tread –, follow- the beaten -track, – path; *stare super antiquas vias*; move in a rut, run on in a groove, go round like a horse in a mill, go on in the old jog-trot way.

habituate, inure, harden, season, caseharden; accustom, familiarize; naturalize, acclimatize; keep one's hand in; train &c. (*educate*) 537.

get into the -way, – knack- of; learn &c. 539; cling –, adhere- to; repeat &c. 104; acquire –, contract –, fall into- a -habit, – trick; addict oneself –, take- to; accustom oneself to.

be -habitual &c. *adj.*; prevail; come into use, become a habit, take root; gain –, grow- upon one.

Adj. habitual; ac-, customary; prescriptive; accustomed &c. *v.*; traditional; of -daily, – every-day- occurrence; wonted, usual, general, ordinary, common, frequent, every-day, household, jog-trot; well-trodden, -known; familiar, vernacular, trite, commonplace, banal, bromidic, conventional, regular, set, stock, officinal, established, stereotyped; pre-vailing, -valent; current, received, acknowledged, recognized, accredited; of course, admitted, understood.

conformable &c. 82; according to -use, – custom, – routine; in -vogue, – fashion; fashionable &c. (*genteel*) 852.

wont; used – given – addicted –, attuned –, habituated &c. *v.*- to; in the habit of; *habitué*; at home in &c. (*skilful*) 698; seasoned; permeated –, imbued- with; devoted –, wedded- to; never free from.

hackneyed, fixed, rooted, deep-rooted, ingrafted, permanent, inveterate, besetting; naturalized; ingrained &c. (*intrinsic*) 5.

Adv. habitually &c. *adj.*; always &c. (*uniformly*) 16.

as -usual, – is one's wont, – things go, – the world goes, – the sparks fly upwards; *more -suo, – solito.*

as a rule, for the most part; generally &c. *adj.*; most often, – frequently.

Phr. *cela s'entend.*

off –, cast off –, break off –, wean oneself of –, violate –, break through –, infringe- -a habit, – a custom, – a usage; break one's fetters; disuse &c. 678; wear off.

Adj. un-accustomed, -used, -wonted, -seasoned, -inured, -habituated, -trained; new; green &c. (*unskilled*) 699; fresh, original, unhackneyed.

unusual &c. (*unconformable*) 83; unconventional, non-observant; disused &c. 678.

Adv. just for once.

2°. *Causes of Volition*

615. Motive.—N. motive, springs of action.

reason, ground, call, principle; main-

615a. Absence of Motive.—N. absence of motive; caprice &c. 608; chance &c. (*absence of design*) 621.

spring, *primum mobile,* key-stone; the why and the wherefore; *pro* and *con,* reason why; secret –, ulterior- motive, *arrière-pensée;* intention &c. 620.

inducement, consideration; attraction &c. 288; loadstone; magnet, -ism, -ic force; allect-ation, -ive; temptation, enticement, *agacerie,* allurement, witchery; bewitch-ment, -ery; charm; spell &c. 993; fascination, blandishment, cajolery; seduc-tion, -ement; honeyed words, voice of the tempter, song of the Sirens; forbidden fruit, golden apple.

persuasi-bility, -bleness; attractability; impress-, suscept-ibility; softness; persuas-, attract-iveness; tantalization.

influence, prompting, dictate, instance; impuls-e, -ion; incit-ement, -ation; press, instigation; provocation &c. (*excitation of feeling*) 824; inspiration; per-, suasion; encouragement, advocacy; exhortation, advice &c. 695; solicitation &c. (*request*) 765; lobbying.

incentive, stimulus, spur, fillip, whip, goad, rowel, provocative, whet, dram.

bribe, lure; decoy, – duck; bait, trail of a red herring; bribery and corruption; sop, – for Cerberus.

prompter, tempter; seduc-er, -tor; suggester, coaxer, wheedler; instigator, firebrand, incendiary; Siren, Circe; *agent provocateur;* lobbyist.

V. induce, move; draw, – on; bring in its train, give an -impulse &c. *n.*- to; inspire; put up to, prompt, call up; attract, beckon.

stimulate &c. (*excite*) 824; spirit up, inspirit; a-, rouse; ecphorize; animate, incite, provoke, instigate, set on, actuate; act –, work –, operate- upon; encourage; pat –, clap- on the -back, – shoulder.

influence, weigh with, bias, sway, incline, dispose, predispose, turn the scale, inoculate; lead, – by the nose; have –, exercise- influence- -with, – over, – upon; go –, come- round one; turn the head, magnetize.

persuade; prevail -with, – upon; overcome, carry; bring -round, – to one's senses; draw –, win –, gain –, come –, talk- over; procure, enlist, engage; invite, court.

tempt, seduce, overpersuade, entice, allure, captivate, fascinate, intrigue, bewitch, carry away, charm, conciliate, wheedle, coax, lure, suggest; inveigle; tantalize; cajole &c. (*deceive*) 545.

tamper with, bribe, suborn, grease the palm, bait with a silver hook, gild the pill, make things pleasant, put a sop into the pan, throw a sop to, bait the hook.

V. have no motive; scruple &c. (*be unwilling*) 603.

Adj. without rhyme or reason; aimless &c. (*chance*) 621.

Adv. capriciously; out of mere caprice.

616. Dissuasion.—**N.** dissuasion, dehortation, expostulation, remonstrance; deprecation &c. 766.

discouragement, damper, wet blanket; warning.

cohibition &c. (*restraint*) 751; curb &c. (*means of restraint*) 752; check &c. (*hindrance*) 706.

reluctance &c. (*unwillingness*) 603; contraindication.

V. dissuade, dehort, cry out against, remonstrate, expostulate, warn, contraindicate.

disincline, indispose, shake, stagger; dispirit; dis-courage, -hearten, -enchant; deter; hold –, keep- back &c. (*restrain*) 751; render -averse &c. 603; repel; turn aside &c. (*deviation*) 279; wean from; act as a drag &c. (*hinder*) 706; throw cold water on, damp, cool, chill, blunt, calm, quiet, quench; deprecate &c. 766.

Adj. dissuading &c. *v.*; dissuasive; dehortatory, expostulatory; monit-ive, -ory.

dissuaded &c. *v.*; uninduced &c. (induce &c. 615); unpersuadable &c. (*obstinate*) 606; averse &c. (*unwilling*) 603; repugnant &c. (*dislike*) 867.

enforce, force; impel &c. (*push*) 276; propel &c. 284; whip, lash, goad, spur, prick, urge; egg –, hound –, hurry- on; drag &c. 285; exhort; advise &c. 695; call upon &c., press &c. (*request*) 765; advocate.

set -an example, – the fashion; keep in countenance; back up.

be -persuaded &c.; yield to temptation, come round; concede &c. (*consent*) 762; obey a call; follow -advice, – the bent, – the dictates of; act on principle.

Adj. impulsive, motive; suas-, persuas-, hortat-ive, -ory; protreptical; inviting, tempting &c. *v.*; seductive, attractive, irresistible; fascinating &c. (*pleasing*) 829; provocative &c. (*exciting*) 824.

induced &c. *v.*; disposed; persuadable &c. (*docile*) 602; spellbound; instinct –, smitten- with; inspired &c. *v.*- by.

Adv. because, therefore &c. (*cause*) 155; from -this, – that- motive; for -this, – that- reason; for; by reason –, for the sake –, on the score –, on account- of; out of, from, as, forasmuch as.

for all the world; on principle.

617. [Ostensible motive, ground, or reason assigned.] **Plea.—N.** plea, pretext; allegation, advocation; ostensible -motive, – ground, – reason; excuse &c. (*vindication*) 937; colour; gloss, guise.

loop-, starting-hole; how to creep out of, salvo, come off.

handle, peg to hang on, room, *locus standi*; stalking-horse, *cheval de bataille*, cue.

pretence &c. (*untruth*) 546; put off, subterfuge, dust thrown in the eyes; blind; moonshine; mere –, shallow- pretext; lame -excuse, – apology; tub to a whale; false plea, sour grapes; makeshift, shift, white lie; special pleading &c. (*sophistry*) 477; soft sawder &c. (*flattery*) 933.

V. plead, allege; shelter oneself under the plea of; excuse &c. (*vindicate*) 937; gloss over; lend a colour to; furnish a -handle &c. *n.*; make a -pretext, – handle- of; use as a plea &c. *n.*; take one's stand upon, make capital out of; pretend &c. (*lie*) 544.

Adj. ostensible &c. (*manifest*) 525; excusing; alleged, apologetic; pretended &c. 545.

Adv. ostensibly; under -colour, – the plea, – the pretence- of.

3°. *Objects of Volition*

618. Good.—N. good, benefit, advantage; improvement &c. 658; interest, service, behoof, behalf; weal; main chance, *summum bonum*, common weal; 'consummation devoutly to be wished'; gain, boot; profit, harvest.

boon &c. (*gift*) 784; good turn; blessing, benison; world of good; piece of good -luck, – fortune; nuts, prize, windfall, godsend, waif, treasure trove.

good fortune &c. (*prosperity*) 734; happiness &c. 827.

[Source of good] goodness &c. 648; utility &c. 644; remedy &c. 662; pleasure-giving &c. 829.

Adj. commendable &c. 931; useful &c. 644; good &c., beneficial &c. 648.

619. Evil.—N. evil, ill, harm, hurt, mischief, nuisance; machinations of the devil, Pandora's box, ills that flesh is heir to.

blow, buffet, stroke, scratch, bruise, wound, gash, mutilation; mortal -blow, – wound; *immedicabile vulnus*; damage, loss &c. (*deterioration*) 659.

disadvantage, prejudice, drawback.

disaster, accident, casualty; mishap &c. (*misfortune*) 735; bad job, devil to pay; calamity, bale, woe, catastrophe, tragedy; ruin &c. (*destruction*) 162; adversity &c. 735.

mental suffering &c. 828. [Evil spirit] demon &c. 980. [Cause of evil] bane &c. 663. [Production of evil]

V. benefit, profit, advantage, serve, help, avail; do good to, gain, prosper, flourish.

Adv. well, aright, satisfactorily, favourably, not amiss; all for the best; to one's -advantage &c. *n.*; in one's -favour, – interest &c. *n.*

Phr. so far so good.

badness &c. 649; painfulness &c. 830; evil doer &c. 913.

outrage, wrong, injury, foul play; bad –, ill- turn; disservice; spoliation &c. 791; grievance, crying evil.

V. be in trouble &c. (*adversity*) 735; harm, injure, hurt, do disservice to.

Adj. disastrous, bad &c. 649; awry, out of joint; disadvantageous, injurious, harmful.

Adv. amiss, wrong, ill, to one's cost.

Section II. Prospective Volition*

1°. *Conceptional Volition*

620. Intention.—N. intent, -ion, -ionality; purpose; *quo animo*; project &c. 626; undertaking &c. 676; predetermination &c. 611; design, ambition.

contemplation, mind, *animus*, view, purview, proposal; study; look out.

final cause; *raison d'être*; *cui bono*; object, aim, end; 'the be all and the end all'; drift &c. (*meaning*) 516; tendency &c. 176; destination, mark, point, butt, goal, target, bull's-eye, quintain; prey, quarry, game.

decision, determination, resolve; set –, settled- purpose; *ultimatum*; resolution &c. 604; wish &c. 865; *arrière-pensée*; motive &c. 615.

[Study of final causes] teleology.

V. intend, purpose, design, mean; have to; propose to oneself; harbour a design; have in -view, – contemplation, – one's eye, – *petto*; have an eye to.

bid –, labour- for; be –, aspire –, endeavour- after; be –, aim –, drive –, point–, level - at; take aim; set before oneself; study to.

take upon oneself &c. (*undertake*) 676; take into one's head; meditate, contemplate; think –, dream –, talk- of; premeditate &c. 611; compass, calculate; dest-ine, -inate; propose.

project &c. (*plan*) 626; have a mind to &c. (*be willing*) 602; desire &c. 865; pursue &c. 622.

Adj. intended &c. *v.*; intentional, advised, express, determinate; prepense &c. 611; bound for; intending &c. *v.*; minded, disposed, inclined;

621. [Absence of purpose in the succession of events.] **Chance.†—N.** chance &c. 156; lot, fate &c. (*necessity*) 601; luck; good luck &c. (*good*) 618; bad luck &c. 735; wheel of fortune; mascot; swastika.

speculation, venture, stake, flutter, flier, gamble, game of chance; mere –, random- shot; blind bargain, leap in the dark; pig in a poke &c. (*uncertainty*) 475; fluke, pot-luck.

drawing lots; sorti-legy, -tion; *sortes*, – *Virgilianæ*, *-biblicæ*; *rouge et noir*, hazard, *roulette*, pitch and toss, chuck-farthing, cup-tossing, heads or tails, cross and pile, wager; bet, -ting; risk, stake, plunge; gambling; the turf.

stock exchange, bourse, board of trade (U.S.A.), curb exchange.

gaming-, gambling-, betting-house; hell; betting ring, totalisator; dice, – box; dicer; gam-bler, -ester, plunger, stock operator, manipulator, punter; man of the turf; adventurer, speculator; bookmaker, layer, backer.

V. chance &c. (*hap*) 156; stand a chance &c. (*be possible*) 470.

toss up; cast –, draw- lots; leave –, trust- -to chance, – to the chapter of accidents; tempt fortune; chance it, take one's chance; run –, incur –, encounter- the -risk, – chance; stand the hazard of the die.

speculate, try one's luck, set on a cast, raffle, put into a lottery, buy a pig in a poke, shuffle the cards.

risk, venture, hazard, stake; lay, – a wager; make a bet, wager, bet, gamble,

* That is, volition having reference to a future object.

† See note on 156.

bent upon &c. (*earnest*) 604; at stake, on the -anvil, – *tapis*; in -view; – prospect, – the breast of; *in petto*; teleological.

Adv. intentionally &c. *adj.*; advisedly, wittingly, knowingly, designedly, purposely, on purpose, by design, studiously, pointedly; with -intent &c. *n.*; deliberately &c. (*with premeditation*) 611; with one's eyes open, in cold blood.

for; with -a view, – an eye- to; in order -to, – that; to the end –, with the intent- that; for the purpose –, with the view –, in contemplation –, on account- of.

in pursuance of, pursuant to; *quo animo*; to all intents and purposes.

game, play for; play at chuck-farthing.

Adj. fortuitous &c. 156; unintentional, -ded; accidental; not meant; un-designed, -purposed; unpremeditated &c. 612; never thought of.

indiscriminate, promiscuous; undirected, random; aim-, drift-, design-, purpose-, cause-less; without purpose.

possible &c. 470.

Adv. casually &c. 156; unintentionally &c. *adj.*; unwittingly.

en passant, by the way, incidentally; as it may happen; at -random, – a venture, – haphazard; as luck would have it, by -chance, – good fortune; un-, -luckily.

---

622. [Purpose in action.] **Pursuit.**—**N.** pursuit; pursuing &c. *v.*; prosecution; pursuance; enterprise &c. (*undertaking*) 676; business &c. 625; adventure &c. (*essay*) 675; quest &c. (*search*) 461; scramble, hue and cry, game; hobby.

chase, hunt, *battue*, race, steeple-chase, hunting, coursing; ven-ation, -ery; fox-chase; sport, -ing; shooting, angling, fishing, hawking.

pursuer; hunt-er, -sman; sportsman, Nimrod, the field; hound &c. 366.

V. pursue, prosecute, follow; run –, make –, be –, hunt –, prowl- after; shadow; carry on &c. (*do*) 680; engage in &c. (*undertake*) 676; set about &c. (*begin*) 66; endeavour &c. 675; court &c. (*request*) 765; seek &c. (*search*) 461; aim at &c. (*intention*) 620; follow the trail &c. (*trace*) 461; fish for &c. (*experiment*) 463; press on &c. (*haste*) 684; run a race &c. (*velocity*) 274.

chase, give chase, course, dog, hunt, hound, stalk; tread –, follow- on the heels of &c. (*sequence*) 281.

rush upon; rush headlong &c. (*violence*) 173; ride –, run- full tilt at; make a leap –, jump –, snatch- at; run down; start game.

tread a path; take –, hold- a course; shape –, direct –, bend- one's -steps, – course; play a game; fight –, elbow- one's way; follow up; take -to, – up; go in for; ride one's hobby.

Adj. pursuing &c. *v.*; in quest of &c.

623. [Absence of pursuit.] **Avoidance.**—**N.** abst-ention, -inence; forbearance; refraining &c. *v.*; inaction &c. 681; neutrality.

avoidance, evasion, elusion; seclusion &c. 893.

avolation, flight; escape &c. 671; retreat &c. 287; recoil &c. 277; departure &c. 293; rejection &c. 610.

shirker &c. *v.*; slacker; truant; fugitive, refugee; runa-way, -gate; renegade; deserter.

V. abstain, refrain, spare, not attempt; not do &c. 681; maintain the even tenor of one's way.

eschew, keep from, let alone, have nothing to do with; keep –, stand –, hold- -aloof, – off; take no part in, have no hand in.

avoid, shun; steer –, keep- clear of; fight shy of; keep -one's, – at a respectful- distance; keep –, get- out of the way; evade, elude, turn away from; set one's face against &c. (*oppose*) 708; deny oneself.

shrink; hang –, hold –, draw- back; recoil &c. 277; retire &c. (*recede*) 287; flinch, blink, blench, shy, shirk, dodge, parry, make way for, give place to.

beat a retreat; turn -tail, – one's back; take to one's heels; run, -away, – for one's life; cut and run; be off, – like a shot; fly, flee; fly –, flee –, run away- from; take –, take to- flight; desert, elope; make –, scamper –, sneak –, shuffle –, sheer- off; break –,

(*inquiry*) 461; in -pursuit, - full cry, - hot pursuit; on the scent.

Adv. in pursuance of &c. (*intention*) 620; after.

Int. tally-ho! yoicks! so-ho!

---

burst -, tear oneself -, slip -, slink -, steal- -away, - away from; slip cable, part company, turn on one's heel; sneak out of, play truant, give one the go by, give leg bail, take French leave, slope, decamp, flit, bolt, abscond, levant, skedaddle, absquatulate, cut one's stick, walk one's chalks, show a light pair of heels, make oneself scarce; escape &c. 671; go away &c. (*depart*) 293; abandon &c. 624; reject &c. 610.

lead one a -dance, - a merry chase, - pretty dance; throw off the scent, play at hide and seek.

Adj. unsought, unattempted; avoiding &c. *v.*; neutral; shy of &c. (*unwilling*) 603; elusive, evasive, distant; fugitive, runaway; shy, wild.

Adj. lest, in order to avoid.

Int. forbear! keep -, hands- off! *sauve qui peut!* devil take the hindmost!

624. Relinquishment.—**N.** relinquish-, abandon-ment; desertion, defection, secession, withdrawal; cave of Adullam; *nolle prosequi.*

discontinuance &c. (*cessation*) 142; renunciation &c. (*recantation*) 607; abrogation &c. 756; resignation &c. (*retirement*) 757; desuetude &c. 614; cession &c. (*of property*) 782.

V. relinquish, give up, abandon, desert, forsake, leave in the lurch; depart -, secede -, withdraw- from; back - out of, - down from, leave, go back on one's word, quit, take leave of, bid a long farewell; vacate &c. (*resign*) 757.

renounce &c. (*abjure*) 607; forego, have done with, drop; write off; disuse &c. 678; discard &c. 782; wash one's hands of; drop all idea of; *nolle-pros.*; lose interest in.

break -, leave- off; desist; stop &c. (*cease*) 142; hold -, stay- one's hand; quit one's hold; give over, shut up shop.

throw up the -game, - cards; give up the -point, - argument; pass to the order of the day, move the previous question, table the motion.

Adj. unpursued; relinquished &c. *v.*; relinquishing &c. *v.*

Int. avast &c.! (*stop*) 142.

625. Business.—**N.** business, occupation, employment; pursuit &c. 622; what one is doing-, - about; affair, concern, matter, case, undertaking.

matter in hand, irons in the fire; thing to do, *agendum*, task, work, job, chore, errand, transaction, commission, mission, charge, care; duty &c. 926.

part, *rôle*, cue; province, function, look-out, department, capacity, sphere, orb, field, line; walk, - of life; beat, round, routine; race, career.

office, place, post, incumbency, living; situation, appointment, billet, berth, employ; service &c. (*servitude*) 749; engagement; undertaking &c. 676.

vocation, calling, profession, *métier*, cloth, faculty; industry, art; industrial arts; craft, mystery, handicraft; trade &c. (*commerce*) 794.

exercise; work &c. (*action*) 680; avocation; press of business &c. (*activity*) 682.

V. pass -, employ -, spend- one's time in; employ oneself -in, - upon;

occupy –, concern- oneself with; make it one's -business &c. *n.*; undertake &c. 676; enter a profession; betake oneself to, turn one's hand to; have to do with &c. (*do*) 680.

drive a trade; carry on –, do –, transact- -business, – a trade &c. *n.*; keep a shop; ply one's task, – trade; labour in one's vocation; pursue the even tenor of one's way; attend to -business, – one's work.

officiate, serve, act; act –, play- one's part; do duty; serve –, discharge –, perform- the -office, – duties, – functions- of; hold –, fill- -an office, – a place, – a situation; hold a portfolio.

be -about, – doing, – engaged in, – employed in, – occupied with, – at work on; have one's hands in, have in hand; have on one's -hands, – shoulders; bear the burden; have one's hands full &c. (*activity*) 682.

be -in the hands of, – on the stocks, – on the anvil; pass through one's hands.

Adj. business-like; work-a-day; professional; official, functional; busy &c. (*actively employed*) 682; on –, in- -hand, – one's hands; afoot; on -foot, – the anvil; going on; acting.

Adv. in the course of business, all in a day's work; professionally &c. *adj.*

626. Plan.—**N.** plan, scheme, design, project; propos-al, -ition; suggestion; resolution, motion; precaution &c. (*provision*) 673; deep-laid &c. (*premeditated*) 611- plan &c.; racket.

system &c. (order) 58; organization &c. (*arrangement*) 60; germ &c. (*cause*) 153; Five Year Plan.

sketch, skeleton, outline, draught, draft, *ébauche*, *brouillon*; rough -cast, – draft, – draught, – copy; copy; proof, revise.

forecast, *programme*, prospectus, scenario; *carte du pays*; card; bill, protocol; order of the day, list of agenda, *memorandum*; bill of fare &c. (*food*) 298; base of operations; platform, plank.

rôle; policy &c. (*line of conduct*) 692.

contrivance, invention, expedient, receipt, nostrum, artifice, device, gadget; stratagem &c. (*cunning*) 702; trick &c. (*deception*) 545; alternative, loophole, shift &c. (*substitute*) 147; last shift &c. (*necessity*) 601.

measure, step; stroke, – of policy; master stroke; trump-, court-card; *cheval de bataille*, great gun; *coup*, – *d'état*; clever –, bold –, good- -move, – hit, – stroke; bright -thought, – idea, great idea.

intrigue, cabal, plot, frame-up, conspiracy, complot, machination; under-, counter-plot.

schem-ist, -atist; strategist, machinator, schemer; projector, author, builder, artist, promoter, designer &c. *v.*; conspirator; *intrigant* &c. (*cunning*) 702.

V. plan, scheme, design, frame, contrive, project, forecast, sketch; conceive, devise, invent &c. (*imagine*) 515; set one's wits to work &c. 515; spring a project; fall –, hit- upon; strike –, chalk –, cut –, lay –, map-out; lay down a plan; shape –, mark- out a course; predetermine &c. 611; concert, preconcert, preestablish; prepare &c. 673; hatch, – a plot; concoct; take -steps, – measures.

cast, recast, systematize, organize; arrange &c. 60; digest, mature.

plot; counter-plot, -mine; dig a mine; lay a train; intrigue &c. (*cunning*) 702.

Adj. planned &c. *v.*; strategic, -al; planning &c. *v.*; in course of preparation &c. 673; under consideration; on the -*tapis*, – carpet, – table.

627. Method. [Path.]—**N.** method, way, manner, wise, gait, form, mode, fashion, tone, guise; *modus operandi*; procedure &c. (*line of conduct*) 692.

path, road, route, course; line of -way, – road; trajectory, orbit, track, beat, tack.

steps; stair, -case; flight of stairs, ladder, stile.

bridge, viaduct, gauntry, pontoon, stepping stone, plank, gangway, catwalk, drawbridge; pass, ford, ferry, tunnel, subway, elevated; pipe &c. 260.

door; gateway &c. (*opening*) 260; channel, passage, avenue, means of access, approach, perron, adit, entrance; artery, lane, alley, aisle, lobby, corridor, cloister; back- door, -stairs; secret passage; covert-way.

road-, path-, stair-way; thoroughfare; highway, pike, turnpike, trail, parkway, *boulevard*; turnpike –, royal –, coach- road; broad –, King's –, Queen's- highway; beaten -track, – path; horse –, bridle- road, – track, – path; pathway; walk, *trottoir*, foot-path, pavement, flags, side-walk; by –, cross- -road, – path, – way; cut; short -cut &c. (*mid-course*) 628; *carrefour*; private –, occupation- road; highways and byways; rail-, tram-road, -way; funicular, ropeway, causeway; defile, cutting; canal &c. (*conduit*) 350; street &c. (*abode*) 189.

Adv. how; in what -way, – manner; by what mode; so, in this way, after this fashion, on these lines.

one way or another, anyhow; somehow or other &c. (*instrumentality*) 631; by way of; *viâ*; *in transitu* &c. 270; on the high road to.

Phr. *hæ tibi erunt artes.*

628. Mid-course.—N. middle-, mid-course; moderation, mean &c. 29; middle &c. 68; *juste milieu*, *mezzo termine*, golden mean, *aurea mediocritas*.

straight &c. (*direct*) 278 -course, – path; short –, cross- cut; short-circuit; great circle sailing.

neutrality; half –, half and half-measures; compromise.

V. keep in –, steer –, preserve- -a middle, – an even- course; go straight &c. (*direct*) 278.

go half way, compromise, make a compromise.

Adj. neutral, average, even, impartial, moderate, straight &c. (*direct*) 278.

629. Circuit.—N. circuit, roundabout way, digression, divagation, *détour*, circum-ambience, -ambulation, -bendibus, *ambages*, loop; winding &c. (*circuition*) 311; zigzag &c. (*deviation*) 279.

V. perform –, make- a circuit; go -round about, – out of one's way; make a *détour*; meander &c. (*deviate*) 279; circumambulate.

lead a pretty dance; beat about, – the bush; make two bites of a cherry.

Adj. circuitous, indirect, roundabout; zig-zag &c. (*deviating*) 279; circum-ambient, -ambulatory.

Adv. by -a side wind, – an indirect course; in a roundabout way; from pillar to post.

630. Requirement.—N. requirement, need, wants, necessities; necessaries, – of life; stress, exigency, pinch, *sine quâ non*, matter of necessity; case of -need, – life or death.

needfulness, essentiality, necessity, indispensability, urgency, prerequisite.

requisition &c. (*request*) 765, (*exaction*) 741; run upon; demand –, call- for.

desideratum &c. (*desire*) 865; want &c. (*deficiency*) 640.

charge, claim, command, injunction, requisition, mandate, order, *ultimatum*.

V. require, need, want, have occasion for, entail; not be able to -do without, - dispense with; prerequire.

render necessary, necessitate, create a necessity for, call for, put in requisition; make a requisition &c. (*ask for*) 765, (*demand*) 741.

stand in need of; lack &c. 640; desiderate; desire &c. 865; be -necessary &c. *adj.*

Adj. required &c. *v.*; requisite, needful, necessary, imperative, essential, indispensable, prerequisite; called for; in -demand, - request.

urgent, exigent, pressing, instant, crying, absorbing.

in want of; destitute of &c. 640.

Adv. *ex necessitate rei* &c. (*necessarily*) 601; of -, out of stern- necessity; at a pinch.

Phr. there is no time to lose; it cannot be -spared, - dispensed with.

2° *Subservience to Ends*

1. *Actual Subservience*

631. Instrumentality.—N. instrumentality; aid &c. 707; subservien-ce, -cy; mediation, inter-vention, -mediacy, medium, inter-medium, -mediary, vehicle, hand; agency &c. 170.

minister, handmaid, servant, slave, maid, valet; midwife, *accoucheur*, obstetrician; go-between; cat's paw; stepping-stone.

key; master -, pass -, latch- key; 'open sesame'; passport, *passe-partout*, safe-conduct; influence.

instrument &c. 633; expedient &c. (*plan*) 626; means &c. 632.

V. subserve, minister, tend, mediate, intervene; come -, go- between, interpose; pull the strings; be -instrumental &c. *adj.*; pander to.

Adj. instrumental; useful &c. 644; ministerial, subservient, mediatorial; inter-mediate, -vening; conducive.

Adv. through, by, *per*; where-, there-, here-by; by the -agency &c. 170- of; by dint of; by -, in- virtue of; through the -medium &c. *n.*- of; along with; on the shoulders of; by means of &c. 632; by -, with- -the aid &c. (*assistance*) 707- of.

per fas et nefas, by fair means or foul; somehow, - or other; by hook or by crook.

632. Means.—N. means, resources, revenue, wherewithal, ways and means, income; capital &c. (*money*) 800; stock in trade &c. 636; provision &c. 637; a shot in the locker; appliances &c. (*machinery*) 633; means and appliances; conveniences; cards to play; expedients &c. (*measures*) 626; two strings to one's bow; sheet anchor &c. (*safety*) 666; aid &c. 707; medium &c. 631.

V. find -, have -, possess- means &c. *n.*; provide the wherewithal.

Adj. instrumental &c. 631; mechanical &c. 633.

Adv. by means of, with; by -what, - all, - any, - some- means; where-, here-, there-with; wherewithal.

how &c. (*in what manner*) 627; through &c. (*by the instrumentality of*) 631; with -, by- the aid &c. (*assistance*) 707- of; by the -agency &c. 170- of.

633. Instrument.—N. machinery, mechanism, engineering.

instrument, organ, tool, implement, utensil, contrivance, machine, motor, engine, lathe, gin, mill, pump.

gear; tack-le, -ling, trice, rigging, gear, apparatus, appliances; plant, *matériel*; harness, trappings, fittings, accoutrements; equip-ment, -age;

appointments, furniture, upholstery; chattels; paraphernalia &c. (*belongings*) 780; *impedimenta.*

mechanical powers; lever, -age; mechanical advantage; crow, -bar; handspike, gavelock, jemmy, arm, limb, wing; oar, paddle; pulley, sheave; parbuckle; wheel and axle; wheel-, clock-work; wheels within wheels; pinion, gear wheel, spur –, bevel- gearing, chains, belting, crank, winch, capstan, windlass, crane, derrick, hoist, lift &c. 307; cam; pedal; wheel &c. (*rotation*) 312; inclined plane; wedge; screw; jack; spring, mainspring.

handle, hilt, haft, shaft, heft, shank, blade, trigger, tiller, helm, treadle, key; turnscrew, screwdriver, spanner, wrench.

hammer &c. (*impulse*) 276; edge tool &c. (*cut*) 253; borer &c. 262; vice, teeth &c. (*hold*) 781; nail, rope &c. (*join*) 45; peg &c. (*hang*) 214; support &c. 215; spoon &c. (*vehicle*) 272; arms &c. 727; oar &c. (*navigation*) 267.

Adj. instrumental &c. 631; mechanical, machinal, automatic, self-acting; brachial.

634. Substitute.—N. substitute &c. 147; deputy &c. 759; proxy, alternative, understudy.

635. Materials.—N. material, raw material, stuff, stock, staple; building materials, bricks and mortar; metal; stone; clay, brick; crockery &c. 384; compo, -sition; reinforced –, ferro-, concrete; cement; wood, ore, timber; gravel, cobbles, macadam, asphalt, tarmac.

materials; supplies, munition, fuel, grist, household stuff; *pabulum* &c. (*food*) 298; ammunition &c. (*arms*) 727; contingents; relay, reinforcement; baggage &c. (*personal property*) 780; means &c. 632.

Adj. raw &c. (*unprepared*) 674; wooden &c. *n.*

636. Store.—N. stock, fund, mine, vein, lode, quarry; spring; fount, -ain; well, -spring; milch cow.

stock in trade, supply; heap &c. (*collection*) 72; treasure; reserve, *corps de réserve*, reserve fund, nest-egg, savings, *bonne bouche.*

crop, harvest, mow, vintage; yield, product, gleanings.

store, accumulation, hoard, rick, stack; lumber; relay &c. (*provision*) 637.

store-house, -room, -closet; depository, depot, *cache*, safe deposit, vault, pantechnicon, re-pository, -servatory, -pertory; *repertorium*; promptuary, warehouse, *entrepôt*, magazine, dump, buttery, larder, pantry, panary, lanary, still-room, spence; crib, garner, granary, silo, barn; bunker; thesaurus; bank &c. (*treasury*) 802; armoury; arsenal; dock; gallery, museum, library, conservatory, hot-house; menag-ery, -erie, aquarium, zoological gardens.

reservoir, cistern, tank, sump, pond, mill-pond; gasometer.

budget, quiver, bandolier, portfolio; coffer &c. (*receptacle*) 191;

conservation; storing &c. *v.*; storage.

dictionary &c. 562; list &c. 86.

V. store; put –, lay –, set- by; stow away; set –, lay- apart; store –, hoard –, treasure –, lay –, heap –, put –, garner –, save- up; *cacher*; accumulate, amass, hoard, fund, garner, save, bank.

conserve, reserve; keep –, hold- back; husband, – one's resources;

deposit; stow, stack, load, dump; harvest; heap, collect &c. 72; lay -in, – down, – by, store &c. *adj.*; keep, file [papers]; lay in &c. (*provide*) 637; preserve &c. 670; put by for a rainy day.

Adj. stored &c. *v.*; in -store, - reserve, - ordinary; spare, supernumerary.

637. Provision.—**N.** provision, supply; grist, - to the mill; subvention &c. (*aid*) 707; resources &c. (*means*) 632.

providing &c. *v.*; purveyance; reinforcement; commissary, commissariat.

rations; iron –, emergency- rations; provender &c. (*food*) 298; *viaticum*; ensilage.

caterer, purveyor, commissary, quartermaster, steward, housekeeper, manciple, feeder, batman, victualler, storekeeper, provision merchant, green-, grocer, *comprador*, *restaurateur*; sutler &c. (*merchant*) 797; innkeeper, publican, confectioner, baker, butcher, wine merchant, vintner.

V. provide; make -provision, - due provision for; lay in, - a stock, - a store.

sup-ply, -peditate; furnish; find, - one in; arm.

cater, victual, provision, purvey, forage; beat up for; stock, - with; make good, replenish; fill, - up; recruit, feed, ration.

have in -store, - reserve; keep, - by one, - on foot; have to fall back upon; store &c. 636; provide against a rainy day &c. (*economy*) 817.

638. Waste.—**N.** consumption, expenditure, exhaustion; dispersion &c. 73; ebb; leakage &c. (*exudation*) 295; loss &c. 776; wear and tear; waste; prodigality &c. 818; misuse &c. 679; wasting &c. *v.*; rubbish &c. (*useless*) 645.

mountain in labour.

V. spend, expend, use, consume, swallow up, exhaust, deplete; impoverish; spill, drain, empty; disperse &c. 73.

cast –, throw –, fling –, fritter- away; burn the candle at both ends, waste; squander &c. 818.

'waste its sweetness on the desert air'; cast -one's bread upon the waters, - pearls before swine; employ a steam hammer to crack a nut, waste powder and shot, break a butterfly on a wheel; labour in vain &c. (*useless*) 645; cut a whetstone with a razor, pour water into a sieve; tilt at windmills.

leak &c. (*run out*) 295; run to waste; ebb; melt away, run dry, dry up.

Adj. wasted &c. *v.*; at a low ebb.

wasteful &c. (*prodigal*) 818; penny wise and pound foolish.

Phr. *magno conatu magnas nugas*; *le jeu n'en vaut pas la chandelle.*

639. Sufficiency.—**N.** sufficiency, adequacy, enough, withal, *quantum sufficit*, satisfaction, competence; no less.

mediocrity &c. (*average*) 29.

fill; fulness &c. (*completeness*) 52; plen-itude, -ty; abundance; copiousness &c. *adj.*; amplitude, galore, lots, profusion; full measure; 'good measure pressed down, shaken together and running over.'

luxuriance &c. (*fertility*) 168; affluence &c. (*wealth*) 803; fat of the land; 'a land flowing with milk and honey'; cornucopia; horn of -plenty, - Amalthæa; mine &c. (*stock*) 636.

outpouring; flood &c. (*great quantity*) 31; tide &c. (*river*) 348; repletion &c. (*redundance*) 641; satiety &c. 869; rich man &c. 803.

640. Insufficiency.—**N.** insufficiency; inadequa-cy, -teness; incompetence &c. (*impotence*) 158; deficiency &c. (*incompleteness*) 53; imperfection &c. 651; shortcoming &c. 304; paucity; stint; scantiness &c. (*smallness*) 32; none to spare; bare subsistence.

scarcity, dearth; want, need, lack, poverty, exigency; inanition, starvation, famine, drought.

dole, pittance, mite; short -allowance, - commons; half-rations; banyan –, fast- day, Lent.

emptiness, poorness &c. *adj.*; depletion, vacancy, flaccidity; ebb-tide; low water; 'a beggarly account of empty boxes'; indigence &c. (*poverty*) 804; insolvency &c. (*non-payment*) 808; poor man &c. 804; bankrupt &c. 808.

V. be -insufficient &c. *adj.*; not -suf-

V. be -sufficient &c. *adj.*; suffice, do, just do, satisfy, pass muster; have -enough &c. *n.*; eat –, drink –, have-one's fill; roll –, swim- in; wallow in &c. (*superabundance*) 641.

abound, exuberate, teem, flow, stream, rain, shower down; pour, – in; swarm; bristle with.

render -sufficient &c. *adj.*; replenish &c. (*fill*) 52.

Adj. sufficient, enough, adequate, up to the mark, commensurate, competent, satisfactory, valid, tangible.

measured; moderate &c. (*temperate*) 953.

full &c. (*complete*) 52; ample; plen-ty, -tiful, -teous; plenty as blackberries; copious, abundant; abounding &c. *v.*; replete, enough and to spare, flush; choke-full; well-stocked, -provided; liberal; unstint-ed, -ing; stintless; without stint; un-sparing, -measured; lavish &c. 641; wholesale.

rich; luxuriant &c. (*fertile*) 168; affluent &c. (*wealthy*) 803; wantless; big with &c. (*pregnant*) 161.

un-exhausted, -wasted; exhaustless, inexhaustible.

Adv. sufficiently, amply &c. *adj.*; full; in -abundance &c. *n.*; with no sparing hand; to one's heart's content, *ad libitum*, without stint.

Phr. cut and come again.

---

fice &c. 639; come short of &c. 304; run dry.

want, lack, need, require; *caret*; be in want &c. (*poor*) 804; live from hand to mouth.

render- insufficient &c. *adj.*; drain of resources; impoverish &c. (*waste*) 638; stint &c. (*begrudge*) 819; put on short -commons, – allowance.

do -insufficiently &c. *adv.*; scotch the snake.

Adj. insufficient, inadequate; too -little &c. 32; not -enough &c. 639; unequal to; incompetent &c. (*impotent*) 158; 'weighed in the balance and found wanting'; perfunctory &c. (*neglect*) 460; deficient &c. (*incomplete*) 53; wanting &c. *v.*; imperfect &c. 651; ill-furnished, -provided, -stored, -off.

slack, at a low ebb; empty, vacant, bare; short –, out –, destitute –, devoid –, bereft &c. 776 –, denuded- of; dry, drained.

un -provided, -supplied, -furnished; un-replenished, -fed; un-stored, -treasured; empty-handed.

meagre, poor, thin, scrimp, sparing, spare, stinted, stunted; skimpy; starv-ed, -eling; half-starved, emaciated, famine-stricken, famished, underfed, undernourished; jejune.

scant &c. (*small*) 32; scarce; not to be had, – for love or money, – at any price; scurvy; stingy &c. 819; at the end of one's tether; without -resources &c. 632; in want &c. (*poor*) 804; in debt &c. 806.

Adv. insufficiently &c. *adj.*; in default –, for want- of; failing.

641. Redundance.—N. redundance; too -much, – many; superabundance, -fluity, -fluence, -saturation; nimiety, transcendency, exuberance, profuseness; profusion &c. (*plenty*) 639; repletion, enough in all conscience, *satis superque*, lion's share; more than -enough &c. 639; plethora, engorgement, congestion, load, surfeit, sickener; turgescence &c. (*expansion*) 194; over-dose, -measure, -supply, -flow; inundation &c. (*water*) 348; *avalanche*.

accumulation &c. (*store*) 636; heap &c. 72; drug, – in the market; glut; crowd; burden.

excess; sur-, over-plus, epact; margin; remainder &c. 40; duplicate; surplusage, expletive; work of –, supererogation; *bonus*, *bonanza*.

luxury; intemperance &c. 954; extravagance &c. (*prodigality*) 818; exorbitance, lavishment.

pleonasm &c. (*diffuseness*) 573; too many irons in the fire; embarrassment of riches; money to burn.

V. super-, over-abound; know no bounds, swarm; meet one at every turn; creep –, bristle- with; overflow; run –, flow –, well –, brim-over; run riot; over-run, -stock, -lay, -charge, -dose, -feed, -burden, -load, -do, -whelm, -shoot the mark &c. (*go beyond*) 303; surcharge, supersaturate, gorge, glut, load, drench, whelm, inundate, deluge, flood; drug, – the market.

choke, cloy, accloy, suffocate; pile up, lay it on, – with a trowel, lay on thick; impregnate with; lavish &c. (*squander*) 818.

send –, carry- coals to Newcastle, – owls to Athens; teach one's grandmother to suck eggs; *pisces natare docere*; kill the slain, 'gild refined gold,' 'paint the lily'; butter one's bread on both sides, put butter upon bacon; employ a steam-hammer to crack a nut &c. (*waste*) 638.

exaggerate &c. 549; wallow in; roll in &c. (*plenty*) 639; remain on one's hands, hang heavy on hand, go a begging.

Adj. redundant; too -much, – many; exuberant, inordinate, superabundant, excessive, overmuch, replete, profuse, lavish; prodigal &c. 818; exorbitant; overweening; extravagant; overcharged &c. *v.*; supersaturated, drenched, overflowing; running -over, – to waste, – down.

crammed –, filled- to overflowing; gorged, stuffed, ready to burst; dropsical, turgid, plethoric, full-blooded; obese &c. 194; voluminous.

superfluous, unnecessary, needless, supervacaneous, uncalled for, to spare, in excess; over and above &c. (*remainder*) 40; *de trop*; adscititious &c. (*additional*) 37; supernumerary &c. (*reserve*) 636; on one's hands, spare, duplicate, supererogatory, expletive; *un peu fort*.

Adv. over, too, over and above; over –, too- much; too far; without –, beyond –, out of- measure; with : : : to spare; over head and ears; up to one's -eyes, – ears; *extra*; beyond the mark &c. (*transcursion*) 303; over one's head.

Phr. it never rains but it pours.

2. *Degree of Subservience*

642. Importance.—N. importance, consequence, moment, prominence, consideration, mark, materialness.

import, significance, concern; emphasis, interest.

greatness &c. 31; superiority &c. 33; notability &c. (*repute*) 873; weight &c. (*influence*) 175; value &c. (*goodness*) 648; usefulness &c. 644.

gravity, seriousness, solemnity; no -joke, – laughing matter; pressure, urgency, stress; matter of life and death.

memorabilia, *notabilia*, great doings; red-letter day.

great -thing, – point; main chance, 'the be all and end all,' cardinal point, outstanding feature; substance, gist &c. (*essence*) 5; sum and substance, *gravamen*, head and front; important –, principal –, prominent –, essential- part; half the battle; *sine quâ non*; breath of one's nostrils &c. (*life*) 359; cream, salt, core, kernel, heart, nucleus;

643. Unimportance.—N. unimportance, insignificance, nothingness, immateriality.

triviality, trivia, fribble, levity, frivolity; paltriness &c. *adj.*; poverty; smallness &c. 32; vanity &c. (*uselessness*) 645; matter of -indifference &c. 866; no object; side issue.

nothing, – to signify, – worth speaking of, – particular, – to boast of, – to speak of; small –, no great –, trifling &c. *adj.* -matter; mere -joke, – nothing; hardly –, scarcely- anything; nonentity, cipher, figurehead; no great shakes, *peu de chose*; child's play; small beer.

toy, plaything, popgun, paper pellet, gimcrack, gewgaw, bauble, trinket, *bagatelle*, kickshaw, knicknack, whim-wham, trifle, 'trifles light as air.'

trumpery, trash, rubbish, stuff, *fatras*, frippery; 'leather or prunello'; chaff, drug, froth, bubble, smoke, cob-

key, -note, -stone; corner stone; trump-card &c. (*device*) 626; salient points.

top-sawyer, first fiddle, *prima donna*, chief, big-wig; triton among the minnows.

V. be -important &c. *adj.*, – somebody, – something; import, signify, matter, be an object; carry weight &c. (*influence*) 175; make a figure &c. (*repute*) 873; be in the ascendant, come to the front, lead the way, take the lead, play first fiddle, throw all else into the shade; lie at the root of; deserve –, merit –, be worthy- -of notice, – regard, – consideration.

attach –, ascribe –, give- importance &c. *n.*- to; value, care for; set store -upon, – by; mark &c. 550; mark with a white stone, underline; write –, put –, print- in -italics, – capitals, – large letters, – large type, – letters of gold; accentuate, emphasize, lay stress on.

make -a fuss, – a stir, – a piece of work, – much ado- about; make -of, – much of.

Adj. important; of -importance &c. *n.*; momentous, material; to the point; not to be -overlooked, – despised, – sneezed at; egregious; weighty &c. (*influential*) 175; of note &c. (*repute*) 873; notable, prominent, salient, signal; memorable, remarkable; worthy of -remark, – notice; never to be forgotten; stirring, eventful.

grave, serious, earnest, noble, grand, solemn, impressive, commanding, imposing.

urgent, pressing, critical, instant.

paramount, essential, vital, all-absorbing, radical, cardinal, chief, main, prime, primary, principal, leading, capital, foremost, overruling; of vital &c. importance.

in the front rank, first-rate, A1; superior &c. 33; considerable &c. (*great*) 31; marked &c. *v.*; rare &c. 137.

significant, telling, trenchant, emphatic, pregnant; *tanti.*

Adv. materially &c. *adj.*; in the main; above all, *par excellence*, to crown all.

---

web; weed; refuse &c. (*inutility*) 645; scum &c. (*dirt*) 653.

joke, jest, snap of the fingers; fudge &c. (*unmeaning*) 517; fiddlestick, - end; pack of nonsense, mere farce.

straw, pin, fig, continental, button, rush; bulrush, feather, halfpenny, farthing, brass farthing, doit, peppercorn, jot, rap, pinch of snuff, old song.

minutiæ, details, minor details, small fry; dust in the balance, feather in the scale, drop in the ocean, flea-bite, molehill; fingle-fangle.

nine days' wonder, *ridiculus mus*; flash in the pan &c. (*impotence*) 158; much ado about nothing &c. (*overestimation*) 482; storm in a teacup.

V. be -unimportant &c. *adj.*; not -matter &c. 642; go for –, matter –, signify- -little, – nothing, – little or nothing; not matter a -straw &c. *n.*

make light of &c. (*underestimate*) 483; catch at straws &c. (*overestimate*) 482.

Adj. unimportant; of -little, – small, – no- -account, – importance &c. 642; immaterial; un-, non-essential; not vital; irrelevant, incidental, indifferent.

subordinate &c. (*inferior*) 34; *médiocre* &c. (*average*) 29; passable, fair, respectable, tolerable, commonplace; uneventful, mere, common; ordinary &c. (*habitual*) 613; inconsiderable, so-so, insignificant, inappreciable, nugatory.

trifling, trivial; slight, slender, light, flimsy, frothy, idle; puerile &c. (*foolish*) 499; airy, shallow; weak &c. 160; powerless &c. 158; frivolous, petty, niggling; pid-, ped-dling; fribble, inane, ridiculous, farcical; fini-cal, -kin; fiddle-faddle, namby-pamby, wishy-washy, milk and water.

poor, paltry, pitiful; contemptible &c. (*contempt*) 930; sorry, mean, meagre, shabby, miserable, wretched, vile, scrubby, scrannel, weedy, niggardly, scurvy, putid, beggarly, worthless, twopenny-halfpenny, cheap, trashy, catchpenny, gimcrack, trumpery, one-horse; toy.

not worth -the pains, – while, – mentioning, – speaking of, – a thought, – a curse, – a straw, – rap &c. *n.*; beneath –, unworthy of- -notice, – regard, – consideration, – contempt; *de landâ caprinâ*; vain &c. (*useless*) 645.

Adv. slightly &c. *adj.*; rather, somewhat, pretty well, fairly well, tolerably.

for aught one cares.

Int. no matter! pish! tush! tut! pshaw! pugh! pooh, -pooh! fudge! bosh! humbug! fiddle-stick, – end! fiddlededee! never mind! *n'importe!* what -signifies, – matter, – boots it, – of that, –'s the odds! a fig for! stuff! nonsense! stuff and nonsense!

Phr. *magno conatu magnas nugas*; *le jeu n'en vaut pas la chandelle*; it -matters not, – does not signify; it is of no -consequence, – importance.

644. Utility.—N. utility; usefulness &c. *adj.*; efficacy, efficiency, adequacy; service, use, stead, avail; help &c. (*aid*) 707; applicability &c. *adj.*; subservience &c. (*instrumentality*) 631; function &c. (*business*) 625; value; worth &c. (*goodness*) 648; money's worth; productiveness &c. 168; *cui bono* &c. (*intention*) 620; utilization &c. (*use*) 677; step in the right direction.

common weal, public good; utilitarianism &c. (*philanthropy*) 910.

V. be -useful &c. *adj.*; avail, serve; subserve &c. (*be instrumental to*) 631; conduce &c. (*tend*) 176; answer –, serve- -one's turn, – a purpose.

act a part &c. (*action*) 680; perform –, discharge- -a function &c. 625; do –, render- -a service, – good service, – yeoman's service; bestead, stand one in good stead; be the making of; help &c. 707.

bear fruit &c. (*produce*) 161; bring grist to the mill; profit, remunerate; benefit &c. (*do good*) 648.

find one's -account, – advantage- in; reap the benefit of &c. (*be better for*) 658.

render useful &c. (*use*) 677.

Adj. useful; of -use &c. *n.*; serviceable, usable, proficuous, good for; subservient &c. (*instrumental*) 631; conducive &c. (*tending*) 176; subsidiary &c. (*helping*) 707.

advantageous &c. (*beneficial*) 648; profitable, gainful, remunerative, worth one's salt; in-, valuable; prolific &c. (*productive*) 168.

adequate; ef-ficient, -ficacious; ef-fect-ive, -ual; practicable, expedient &c. 646.

645. Inutility.—N. inutility; uselessness &c. *adj.*; inefficacy, futility; inep-, inap-titude; unsubservience; inadequacy &c. (*insufficiency*) 640; inefficiency &c. (*incompetence*) 158; unskilfulness &c. 699; disservice; unfruitfulness &c. (*unproductiveness*) 169; labour -in vain, – lost, – of Sisyphus; lost -trouble, – labour; work of Penelope; sleeveless errand, wild goose chase, mere farce.

tautology &c. (*repetition*) 104; supererogation &c. (*redundance*) 641.

vanitas vanitatum, vanity, inanity, worthlessness, nugacity; triviality &c. (*unimportance*) 643.

caput mortuum, waste paper, dead letter; blunt tool.

litter, rubbish, lumber, odds and ends, cast-off clothes; button-top; shoddy; rags, orts, trash, refuse, sweepings, scourings, off-scourings, dross, slag, waste, rubble, dottle, drast, *débris*; stubble, leavings; broken meat; dregs &c. (*dirt*) 653; weeds, tares; rubbish heap, dust hole; *rudera*, deads.

fruges consumere natus &c. (*drone*) 683.

V. be -useless &c. *adj.*; go a begging &c. (*redundant*) 641; fail &c. 732.

seek –, strive- after impossibilities; use vain efforts, labour in vain, roll the stone of Sisyphus, beat the air, lash the waves, *battre l'eau avec un bâton, donner un coup d'épée dans l'eau*, fish in the air, milk the ram, drop a bucket into an empty well, sow the sand; bay the moon; preach –, speak- to the winds; whistle jigs to a milestone; kick against the pricks, *se battre contre des moulins*; lock the stable door

applicable, available, ready, handy, at hand, tangible; commodious, adaptable; of all work.

Adv. usefully &c. *adj.*; *pro bono publico.*

---

when the steed is stolen &c. (*too late*) 135; hold a farthing candle to the sun; cast pearls before swine &c. (*waste*) 638; carry coals to Newcastle &c. (*redundance*) 641; wash a blackamoor white &c. (*impossible*) 471.

render -useless &c. *adj.*; dis-mantle, -mast, -mount, -qualify, -able; unrig; cripple, lame &c. (*injure*) 659; spike guns, clip the wings; put out of gear.

Adj. useless, inutile, inefficacious, futile, unavailing, bootless; inoperative &c. 158; inadequate &c. (*insufficient*) 640; in-, unsub-servient; inept, inefficient &c. (*impotent*) 158; of no -avail &c. (*use*) 644; ineffectual &c. (*failure*) 732; incompetent &c. (*unskilful*) 699; 'stale, flat and unprofitable'; superfluous &c. (*redundant*) 641; dispensable; thrown away &c. (*wasted*) 638; abortive &c. (*immature*) 674.

worth-, value-less; unsaleable; not worth a straw &c. (*trifling*) 643; dear at any price.

vain, empty, inane; gain-, profit-, fruit-less; un-serviceable, -profitable; ill-spent; unproductive &c. 169; *hors de combat*; barren, sterile, impotent, unproductive; effete, past work &c. (*impaired*) 659; obsolete &c. (*old*) 124; fit for the -dust-hole, – wastepaper basket; good for nothing; of no earthly use; not worth -having, – powder and shot; leading to no end, uncalled for; un-necessary, -needed, superfluous.

Adv. uselessly &c. *adj.*; to -little, – no, – little or no- purpose.

Int. *cui bono?* what's the good!

646. [Specific subservience.] **Expedience.—N.** expedien-ce, -cy; desirableness, -bility &c. *adj.*; fitness &c. (*agreement*) 23; utility &c. 644; propriety; advantage; opportunism, pragmatism.

high time &c. (*occasion*) 134.

V. be -expedient &c. *adj.*; suit &c. (*agree*) 23; befit; suit –, befit- the -time, – season, – occasion.

conform &c. 82.

Adj. expedient; desir-, advis-, acceptable; convenient; worth while, meet; fit, -ting; due, proper, eligible, seemly, becoming; befitting &c. *v.*; opportune &c. (*in season*) 134; *in loco*; suitable &c. (*accordant*) 23; applicable &c. (*useful*) 644; practical, effective, pragmatical; suitable, handy; appropriate.

Adv. in the right place; conveniently &c. *adj.*; in the nick of time.

Phr. *operæ pretium est.*

---

647. Inexpedience.—N. inexpedien-ce, -cy; undesira-bleness, -bility &c. *adj.*; discommodity, impropriety; unfitness &c. (*disagreement*) 24; inutility &c. 645; inconvenience, inadvisability; disadvantage.

V. be -inexpedient &c. *adj.*; come amiss &c. (*disagree*) 24; embarrass &c. (*hinder*) 706; put to inconvenience; pay too dear for one's whistle.

Adj. inexpedient, undesirable; un-, in-advisable; objectionable; troublesome, in-apt, -eligible, -admissible, -convenient; in-, dis-commodious; disadvantageous; inappropriate, unsuitable, unfit &c. (*inconsonant*) 24.

ill-contrived, -advised; unsatisfactory; unprofitable &c., unsubservient &c. (*useless*) 645; inopportune &c. (*unseasonable*) 135; out of –, in the wrong- place; improper, unseemly.

clumsy, awkward; cum-brous, -bersome; lumbering, unwieldy, hulky; unmanageable &c. (*impracticable*) 704; impedient &c. (*in the way*) 706.

unnecessary &c. (*redundant*) 641.

Phr. it will never do.

648. [Capability of producing good. Good qualities.] **Goodness.—N.** goodness &c. *adj.*; excellence, merit; virtue &c. 944; value, worth, price.

super-excellence, -eminence; superiority &c. 33; perfection &c. 650; *coup de maître*; master-piece, *chef d'œuvre*, prime, flower, cream, *élite*, pick, A1, none such, *nonpareil*, *crême de la crême*, flower of the flock, cock of the roost, salt of the earth; champion.

tid-bit; gem, – of the first water; *bijou*, precious stone, jewel, pearl, diamond, ruby, brilliant, treasure; good thing; *rara avis*, one in a thousand.

beneficence &c. 906; good man &c. 948.

V. be -beneficial &c. *adj.*; produce –, do- -good &c. 618; profit &c. (*be of use*) 644; benefit; confer a -benefit &c. 618.

be the making of, do a world of good, make a man of.

produce a good effect; do a good turn, confer an obligation; improve &c. 658.

do no harm, break no bones.

be -good &c. *adj.*; excel, transcend &c. (*be superior*) 33; bear away the bell.

stand the -proof, – test; pass -muster, – an examination.

challenge comparison, vie, emulate, rival.

Adj. harm-, hurt-less; unobnoxious; in-nocuous, -nocent, -offensive.

beneficial, valuable, of value; serviceable &c. (*useful*) 644; advantageous, profitable, edifying; salutary &c. (*healthful*) 656.

favourable; propitious &c. (*hope-giving*) 858; fair.

good, – as gold; excellent; better; superior &c. 33; above par; nice, fine; genuine &c. (*true*) 494.

best, choice, select, picked, elect, eximious, *recherché*, rare, priceless; unpara-goned, -lleled &c. (*supreme*) 33; superlatively &c. 33; good; superfine, -excellent; bonzer; of the first water; first-rate, -class; high-wrought; exquisite, very best, crack, prime, tip-top, gilt-edged, capital, cardinal; standard &c. (*perfect*) 650; inimitable.

admirable, estimable; praiseworthy &c. (*approve*) 931; pleasing &c. 829; *couleur de rose*, precious, of great price;

649. [Capability of producing evil. Bad qualities.] **Badness.—N.** hurtfulness &c. *adj.*; virulence.

evil doer &c. 913; bane &c. 663; plague-spot &c. (*insalubrity*) 657; evil star, ill wind; snake in the grass, skeleton in the closet; *amari aliquid*, thorn in the side; Jonah, jinx, hoodoo.

malignity; malevolence &c. 907; tender mercies [ironically].

ill-treatment, annoyance, molestation, abuse, oppression, persecution, outrage; misusage &c. 679; injury &c. (*damage*) 659.

badness &c. *adj.*; peccancy, abomination; painfulness &c. 830; pestilence &c. (*disease*) 655; guilt &c. 947; depravity &c. 945.

V. be -hurtful &c. *adj.*; cause –, produce –, inflict –, work –, do- evil &c. 619; damnify, endamage, hurt, harm, scathe; injure &c. (*damage*) 659; pain &c. 830.

wrong, aggrieve, oppress, persecute; trample –, tread –, bear hard –, put- upon; overburden; weigh -down, – heavy on; victimize; run down; molest &c. 830.

maltreat, abuse; ill-use, -treat; thwart, buffet, bruise, scratch, maul; smite &c. (*scourge*) 972; do -violence, – harm, – a mischief; stab, pierce, outrage.

do –, make- mischief; bring –, get- into trouble.

destroy &c. 162.

Adj. hurt-, harm-, scath-, bane-, baleful; injurious, deleterious, detrimental, noxious, pernicious, mischievous, full of mischief, mischief-making, malefic, malignant, nocuous, noisome; prejudicial; dis-serviceable, -advantageous; wide-wasting.

unlucky, sinister; obnoxious, untoward, disastrous.

oppressive, burdensome, onerous; malign &c. (*malevolent*) 907.

corrupting &c. (corrupt &c. 659); virulent, venomous, envenomed, corrosive; poisonous &c. (*morbific*) 657; deadly &c. (*killing*) 361; destructive &c. (*destroying*) 162; inauspicious &c. 859.

bad, ill, arrant, as bad as bad can be, dreadful; hor-rid, -rible; dire; rank,

costly &c. (*dear*) 814; worth -its weight in gold, - a Jew's eye, - a king's ransom; matchless, peerless, invaluable, inestimable, precious as the apple of the eye.

tolerable &c. (*not very good*) 651; up to the mark, un-exceptionable, -objectionable; satisfactory, tidy.

in -good, - fair- condition; fresh; unspoiled; sound &c. (*perfect*) 650.

Adv. beneficially &c. *adj.*; well &c. 618.

peccant, foul, fulsome; rotten, - at the core.

vile, base, villainous; mean &c. (*paltry*) 643; injured &c., deteriorated &c. 659; unsatisfactory, exception, -able, indifferent; below par &c. (*imperfect*) 651; ill-contrived, -conditioned; wretched, sad, grievous, deplorable, lamentable; piti-ful, -able, woeful &c. (*painful*) 830.

evil, wrong; depraved &c. 945; shocking; reprehensible &c. (*disapprove*) 932.

hateful, - as a toad; abominable, detestable, execrable, cursed, accursed, confounded; damn-ed, -able; infernal; diabolic &c. (*malevolent*) 907.

inadvisable &c. (*inexpedient*) 647; unprofitable &c. (*useless*) 645; incompetent &c. (*unskilful*) 699; irremediable &c. (*hopeless*) 859.

Adv. badly &c. *adj.*; wrong, ill; to one's cost; where the shoe pinches.

Phr. bad is the best; the worst come to the worst.

650. Perfection. — **N.** perfection; perfectness &c. *adj.*; indefectibility; impecc-ancy, -ability.

pink, *beau idéal*, phœnix, paragon; pink -, acme- of perfection; *ne plus ultra*; summit &c. 210.

cygne noir; philosopher's stone; chrysolite, Koh-i-noor, black tulip.

model, standard, pattern, mirror, admirable Crichton; trump; very prince of.

master-piece, -stroke, super-excellence &c. (*goodness*) 648; transcendence &c. (*superiority*) 33.

V. be -perfect &c. *adj.*; transcend &c. (*be supreme*) 33.

bring to perfection, perfect, ripen, mature; consummate, complete &c. 729; put in trim &c. (*prepare*) 673; put the finishing touch to.

Adj. perfect, faultless, ideal; indefective, -ficient, -fectible; immaculate, spotless, impeccable; free from -imperfection &c. 651; un-blemished, -injured &c. 659; sound, - as a roach; in perfect condition; scathless, intact, harmless; seaworthy &c. (*safe*) 644; right as a trivet; *in seipso totus teres atque rotundus*; consummate &c. (*complete*) 52; finished &c. 729; complete in itself.

best &c. (*good*) 648; model, standard; inimitable, unparagoned, unparalleled &c. (*supreme*) 33; superhuman, divine;

651. Imperfection.—**N.** imperfection; imperfectness &c. *adj.*; deficiency; inadequacy &c. (*insufficiency*) 640; peccancy &c. (*badness*) 649; immaturity &c. 674.

fault, defect, weak point; screw loose; rift within the lute; fly in the ointment; flaw &c. (*break*) 70; gap &c. 198; twist &c. 243; taint, attainder; bar sinister, hole in one's coat; blemish &c. 848; weakness &c. 160; half-blood, touch of the tar brush; shortcoming &c. 304; drawback; seamy side.

mediocrity; no great -shakes, - catch; not much to boast of.

V. be -imperfect &c. *adj.*; have a -defect &c. *n.*; lie under a disadvantage; spring a leak.

not -, barely- pass muster; fall short &c. 304.

Adj. imperfect; not -perfect &c. 650; de-ficient, -fective; faulty, unsound, mutilated, tainted; out of -order, - tune; cracked, leaky; sprung; warped &c. (*distort*) 243; lame; injured &c. (*deteriorated*) 659; peccant &c. (*bad*) 649; frail &c. (*weak*) 160; inadequate &c. (*insufficient*) 640; crude &c. (*unprepared*) 674; incomplete &c. 53; found wanting; below par; short-handed; below -, under- its full -strength, - complement.

indifferent, middling, ordinary, medi-

beyond all praise &c. (*approbation*) 931; *sans peur et sans reproche*.

Adv. to perfection, to the limit; perfectly &c. *adj.*; *ad unguem*; clean, – as a whistle.

ocre; average &c. 29; so-so; *così-così*, milk and water; tolerable, fair, passable; pretty -well, – good; rather –, moderately- good; good –, well- enough; decent; not -bad, – amiss; unobjectionable, admissible, bearable, only better than nothing.

secondary, inferior; second-rate, -best, one-horse.

Adv. almost &c.; to a limited extent, rather &c. 32; pretty, moderately; only; considering, all things considered, enough.

Phr. *surgit amari aliquid*.

652. Cleanness.—N. cleanness &c. *adj.*; purity; cleaning &c. *v.*; purification, defecation &c. *v.*; purgation, lustration; de-, abs-tersion; epuration, mundation, ablution, lavation, colature; disinfection &c. *v.*; drain-, sewerage.

lavatory, bath, -room; swimming pool, natatorium; public baths; hot –, cold –, Turkish –, Swedish –, Russian –, vapour- bath; *hammam*, laundry, washhouse; washerwoman, laundress, laundryman; scavenger, cleaner, sweeper, goody; crossing sweeper, white wings, dustman, sweep.

brush; broom, besom, carpet-sweeper, vacuum-cleaner, mop, squilgee, rake, shovel, sieve, riddle, screen, filter; scraper, strigil.

napkin, *serviette*, cloth, table-, carving-cloth, table-linen, napery, maukin, handkerchief, towel, sudary; doyley, doily, duster, sponge, mop, swab.

cover, drugget, mat, doormat.

soap, wash, lotion, detergent, cathartic, purgative; purifier &c. *v.*; dentifrice, tooth-powder, -paste; mouth wash; disinfectant.

V. be –, render- clean &c. *adj.*

clean, -se; mundify, rinse, wring, flush, full, wipe, mop, sponge, scour, swab, scrub, holystone, brush up.

wash, shampoo, lave, launder, buck; abs-, de-terge; clear, purify; de-purate, -spumate, -fecate; purge, expurgate; Bowdlerize; elutriate, lixiviate, edulcorate, clarify, refine, rack; fil-ter, -trate; drain, strain.

disinfect, sterilize, pasteurize, fumigate, ventilate, deodorize; whitewash.

sift, winnow, screen, riddle, pick, weed, comb, rake, brush, sweep.

653. Uncleanness.—N. uncleanness &c. *adj.*; impurity; immundi-ty, -city; impurity &c. [of mind] 961.

defilement, contamination &c. *v.*; defœdation; soil-ure, -iness; abomination; leaven; taint, -ure; fetor &c. 401.

decay; putre-scence, -faction; corruption; mould, must, mildew, dry-rot, *mucor*, rubigo, caries.

slovenry; slovenliness &c. *adj.*; squalor.

dowdy, drab, slut, malkin, slattern, sloven, slammerkin, scrub, draggletail, mudlark, dustman, sweep; beast.

dirt, filth, soil, slop; dust, cobweb, flue; smoke, soot, smudge, smut, grime, raff.

sordes, dregs, grounds, lees; sedi-, settle-ment; heel-tap; dross, -iness; mother, precipitate, *scoriæ*, ashes, cinders, recrement, slag; scum, froth.

hog-wash, swill, ditch-, dish-, bilge-water; rinsings, cheese-parings; sweepings &c. (*useless refuse*) 645; off-, out-scourings; off-scum; *caput mortuum*, *residuum*, sprue, feculence, clinker, draff; scurf, -iness; *exuviæ*, morphew; fur, -fur; dandruff; tartar.

riffraff; vermin, louse, cootie, flea, bug.

mud, mire, quagmire, *alluvium*, silt, sludge, slime, slush, slosh.

spawn, offal, garbage, carrion; *excreta* &c. 299; slough, peccant humour, pus, matter, suppuration, *lienteria*; *fæces*, excrement, ordure, dung; sew-, sewer-age; muck, coprolite; guano, manure, compost.

dunghill, *colluvies*, mixen, midden, bog, laystall, sink, w.c., water-, earth-closet, latrine, privy, jakes, John's; cess, -pool; sump, sough, *cloaca*, drain,

rout –, clear –, sweep &c.- out; make a clean sweep of.

Adj. clean, -ly; pure; immaculate; spot-, stain-, taint-less; without a stain, un-stained, -spotted, -soiled, -sullied, -tainted, -infected, -adulterated; aseptic; sweet, – as a nut.

neat, spruce, tidy, trim, gimp, clean as a new penny, like a cat in pattens; cleaned &c. *v.*; kempt.

Adv. neatly &c. *adj.*; clean as a whistle.

---

sewer, common sewer; Cloacina; dust-hole.

sty, pig-sty, lair, den, Augean stable, sink of corruption; slum, rookery.

V. be –, become- unclean &c. *adj.*; rot, putrefy, fester, rankle, reek; stink &c. 401; mould, -er; go -bad &c. *adj.*

render -unclean &c. *adj.*; dirt, -y; soil, smoke, tarnish, slaver, spot, smear, daub, blot, blur, smudge, smutch, smirch; d-, dr-abble, -aggle; spatter, slubber; be-smear &c., -mire, -slime, -grime, -foul; splash, stain, distain, maculate, sully, pollute, defile, debase, contaminate, taint, leaven; corrupt &c. (*injure*) 659; cover with -dust &c. *n.*; drabble in the mud.

wallow in the mire; slob-, slab-ber.

Adj. unclean, dirty, filthy, grimy; soiled &c. *v.*; not to be handled with kid gloves; dusty, snuffy, smutty, sooty, smoky; thick, turbid, dreggy; slimy.

uncleanly, slovenly, untidy, sluttish, dowdy, slatternly, draggle-tailed; un-combed, -kempt, -scoured, -swept, -wiped, -washed, -strained, -purified; squalid.

nasty, coarse, foul, impure, offensive, abominable, beastly, reeky, reechy; fetid &c. 401.

mouldy, lentiginous, musty, mildewed, rusty, moth-eaten, mucid, rancid, bad, gone bad, touched, fusty, reasty, rotten, corrupt, tainted, high, fly-blown, maggoty; putr-id, -escent, -efied; purulent, carious, peccant, fec-al, -ulent; stercoraceous, excrementitious; scurfy, impetiginous; gory, bloody; rotting &c. *v.*; rotten as -a pear, – cheese.

crapulous &c. (*intemperate*) 954; gross &c. (*impure in mind*) 961.

654. Health.—**N.** health, sanity; soundness &c. *adj.*; vigour; good –, perfect –, excellent –, rude –, robust- health; bloom, *mens sana in corpore sano*; Hygeia; incorrupti-on, -bility; good state –, clean bill- of health, eupepsia.

V. be in health &c. *adj.*; bloom, flourish.

keep -body and soul together, – on one's legs; enjoy -good, – a good state of- health; have a clean bill of health.

return to health; recover &c. 660; get better &c. (*improve*) 658; take a -new, – fresh- lease of life; convalesce, be convalescent, recruit; restore to health; cure &c. (*restore*) 660.

Adj. health-y, -ful; in -health &c. *n.*; well, sound, strong, fit, hearty, hale, fresh, blooming, green, whole; florid, flush, hardy, stanch, staunch,

655. Disease.*—**N.** disease; illness, sickness &c. *adj.*; ailing &c. *v.*; 'the ills that flesh is heir to'; morb-idity, -osity; infirmity, ailment, indisposition; complaint, disorder, malady; distemper, -ature.

visitation, attack, seizure, stroke, fit, epilepsy, apoplexy, shock, shell-shock.

delicacy, loss of health, valetudinarianism, invalidism, cachexy; *cachexia*, atrophy, *marasmus*; indigestion, *dyspepsia*; decay &c. (*deterioration*) 659; malnutrition, decline, consumption, palsy, paralysis, prostration; occupational diseases.

taint, pollution, infection, contagion, septicity, septicæmia, blood poisoning, pyæmia, epi-, en-demic; murrain, plague, pestilence, virus, pox.

sore, ulcer, abscess, fester, boil; pimple &c. (*swelling*) 250; carbuncle,

* Extended lists of different diseases are beyond the scope of this work.

brave, robust, vigorous, weather-proof; convalescent.

un-scathed, -injured, -maimed, -marred, -tainted; sound of wind and limb, safe and sound; without a scratch.

on one's legs; sound as a -roach, – bell; fresh as -a daisy, – a rose, – April; picture of health; bursting with health; fit as a fiddle; hearty as a buck; in -fine, – high- feather; in -good case, – full bloom; in fine fettle; pretty bobbish, tolerably well, as well as can be expected.

sanitary &c. (*health-giving*) **656**; sanatory &c. (*remedial*) 662.

gathering, whitlow, imposthume, peccant humour, issue; rot, canker, cancer, *carcinoma*, *caries*, mortification, corruption, gangrene, *sphacelus*, leprosy, eruption, rash, breaking out, venereal disease.

fever, calenture; inflammation.

fatal &c. (*hopeless*) 859- -disease &c.; dangerous illness, galloping consumption, churchyard cough; general breaking up, break up of the system.

[Disease of mind] neurasthenia; idiocy &c. 499; insanity &c. 503.

martyr to disease; cripple; 'the halt, the lame and the blind'; valetudinar-y, -ian; invalid, patient, case; sick-room, -chamber, hospital &c. 662.

[Science of disease] path-, eti-, nos-ology, therapeutics, diagnosis, prognosis.

V. be -ill &c. *adj.*; ail, suffer, labour under, be affected with, complain of; droop, flag, languish, halt; sicken, peak, pine, waste away, fail, lose strength; gasp.

keep one's bed; feign sickness &c. (*falsehood*) 544, malinger.

lay -by, – up; take –, catch- -a disease &c. *n.*, – an infection; be stricken by; break out.

Adj. diseased; ailing &c. *v.*; ill, – of; taken ill, seized with; indisposed, unwell, sick, squeamish, poorly, seedy; affected –, afflicted- with illness; laid up, confined, bed-ridden, invalided, in hospital, on the sick list; out of -health, – sorts; valetudinary.

un-sound, -healthy; sickly, morbose, healthless, infirm, chlorotic, unbraced, drooping, flagging, lame, halt, crippled, halting.

morbid, tainted, vitiated, peccant, contaminated, poisoned, septic, tabid, mangy, leprous, cankered; rotten, – to, – at- the core; withered, palsied, paralytic, tuberculous; dyspeptic.

touched in the wind, broken-winded, spavined, gasping; *hors de combat* &c. (*useless*) 645.

weak-ly, -ened &c. (*weak*) 160; decrepit; decayed &c. (*deteriorated*) 659; incurable &c. (*hopeless*) 859; in declining health; cranky; in a bad way, in danger, prostrate; moribund &c. (*death*) 360.

morbific, epidemic &c. 657.

656. Salubrity.—N. salubrity, salubriousness; healthiness &c. *adj.*

fine -air, – climate; eudiometer.

[Preservation of health] *hygiène*; valetudinarian, -ism, preventorium, sanitarian; *sanitarium, sanitorium*, immunity.

V. be -salubrious &c. *adj.*; agree with, be good for; assimilate &c. 23.

Adj. salu-brious, -tary, -tiferous, wholesome; health-y, -ful; sanitary, prophylactic, benign, bracing, tonic,

657. Insalubrity.—N. insalubrity; unhealthiness &c. *adj.*; non-naturals; plague spot; malaria &c. (*poison*) 663; death in the pot, contagion.

Adj. insalubrious; un-healthy, -wholesome; noxious, noisome, foul; morbi-fic, -ferous; mephitic, septic, azotic, deleterious; pesti-lent, -ferous, -lential; virulent, venomous, envenomed, poisonous, toxic, narcotic.

contagious, infectious, catching, taking, communicable, epidemic, zymotic;

invigorating, good for, nutritious, hyg-eian, -ienic.

in-noxious, -nocuous, -nocent; harmless, uninjurious, uninfectious; immune.

sanative &c. (*remedial*) 662; restorative &c. (*reinstate*) 660; useful &c. 644.

658. Improvement.—N. improvement; a-, melioration; betterment; mend, amendment, emendation; mending &c. *v.*; advancement; advance &c. (*progress*) 282; ascent &c. 305; promotion, preferment; elevation &c. 307; increase &c. 35.

cultiv-, civiliz-ation; menticulture, culture, march of intellect; eugenics, euthenics, meliorism, telesis.

reform, -ation; revision, radical reform; second thoughts, correction, *limæ labor*, refinement, elaboration; purification &c. 652; repair &c. (*restoration*) 660; recovery &c. 660.

revise; revised –, new- edition.

reformer, radical, progressive.

V. improve; be –, become –, get-better; mend, amend.

advance &c. (*progress*) 282; ascend &c. 305; increase &c. 35; fructify, ripen, mature; pick up, come about, rally, take a favourable turn; turn -over a new leaf, – the corner; raise one's head, sow one's wild oats; recover &c. 660.

be -better &c. *adj.*, – improved by; turn to -right, – good, – best- account; profit by, reap the benefit of; make -good use of, – capital out of; place to good account; take advantage of.

render better, improve, emend, make over, better; a-, meliorate; correct.

improve –, refine- upon; rectify; enrich, mellow, elaborate, fatten.

promote, cultivate, advance, forward, enhance; bring -forward, – on; foster &c. 707; invigorate &c. (*strengthen*) 159.

touch –, rub –, brush –, furbish –, bolster –, vamp –, brighten –, warm-up; polish, cook, make the most of, set off to advantage; prune; repair &c. (*restore*) 660; put in order &c. (*arrange*) 60.

review, revise, edit, redact; make -corrections, – improvements &c. *n.*; doctor &c. (*remedy*) 662; purify &c. 652.

sporadic, endemic, pandemic, epizoötic.

innutritious, indigestible, ungenial; uncongenial &c. (*disagreeing*) 24.

deadly &c. (*killing*) 361.

---

659. Deterioration.—N. deterioration, debasement; want, ebb; recession &c. 287; retrogradation &c. 283; decrease &c. 36.

degenera-cy, -tion, -teness; degradation; deprav-ation, -ement; depravity &c. 945; demoralization, retrogression.

impairment, inquination, injury, damage, loss, detriment, delaceration, outrage, havoc, inroad, ravage, scath; perversion, prostitution, vitiation, discoloration, oxidation, pollution, defœdation, poisoning, venenation, leaven, contamination, canker, corruption, adulteration, alloy.

decl-ine, -ension, -ination; decadence, -cy; falling off &c. *v.*; caducity, decreptitude, senility.

decay, dilapidation, ravages of time, wear and tear; cor-, e-rosion; mouldi-, rotten-ness; moth and rust, dry-rot, blight, marasmus, atrophy, collapse; disorganization; *délabrement* &c. (*destruction*) 162.

wreck, mere wreck, honeycomb, *magni nominis umbra.*

V. be –, become- -worse, – deteriorated &c. *adj.*; have seen better days, deteriorate, degenerate, fall off; wane &c. (*decrease*) 36; ebb; retrograde &c. 283; decline, droop; go down &c. (*sink*) 306; go -downhill, – on from bad to worse, – farther and fare worse; jump out of the frying pan into the fire.

run to -seed, – waste; swale, sweal; lapse, be the worse for; break, – down; spring a leak, crack, start; shrivel &c. (*contract*) 195; fade, go off, wither, moulder, rot, rankle, decay, go bad; go to –, fall into- decay; 'fall into the sear and yellow leaf,' rust, crumble, shake; totter, – to its fall; perish &c. 162; die &c. 360.

[Render less good] deteriorate; weaken &c. 160; put back; taint, infect, contaminate, poison, empoison,

relieve, refresh, revive, infuse new blood into, recruit, re-invigorate, renew, revivify, freshen, build -afresh, – anew; uplift, inspire.

re-form, -model, -organise; new model, civilize.

view in a new light, think better of, appeal from Philip drunk to Philip sober.

palliate, mitigate; lessen &c. 36- an evil.

Adj. improving &c. *v.*; progressive, improved &c. *v.*; better, – off, – for; all the better for; better advised.

reform-, emend-atory; reparatory &c. (*restorative*) 660; remedial &c. 662.

corrigible, improvable, curable, accultural.

Adv. on -consideration, – reconsideration, – second thoughts, – better advice; *ad melius inquirendum*; on the -mend, – up grade.

---

envenom, canker, corrupt, exulcerate, pollute, vitiate, inquinate; de-, embase; denaturalize, leaven; de-flower, -bauch, -file, -prave, -grade; stain &c. (*dirt*) 653; discolour; alloy, adulterate, sophisticate, tamper with, prejudice.

pervert, prostitute, demoralize, brutalize; render vicious &c. 945; compromise.

embitter, ex-, acerbate, aggravate.

injure, impair, labefy, damage, harm, hurt, shend, scathe, spoil, mar, despoil, dilapidate, waste; overrun; ravage; pillage &c. 791.

wound, stab, pierce, maim, lame, surbate, cripple, hough, hamstring, hit between wind and water, scotch, mangle, mutilate, disfigure, blemish, deface, warp.

blight, rot; cor-, e-rode, eat away; wear -away, – out; gnaw, – at the root of; sap, mine, undermine, shake, sap the foundations of, break up; dis-organize, -mantle, -mast; destroy &c. 162.

damnify &c. (*aggrieve*) 649; do one's worst; knock down; deal a blow to; play -havoc, – sad havoc, – the mischief, – the deuce, – the very devil- -with, – among; decimate.

Adj. unimproved &c. (improve &c. 658); deteriorated &c. *v.*; altered, – for the worse; injured &c. *v.*; sprung; withering, spoiling, &c. *v.*; on the -wane, – decline; tabid; degenerate; worse; the –, all the- worse for; out of -repair, – tune; imperfect &c. 651; the worse for wear; battered; weather-ed, -beaten; stale, *passé*, shaken, dilapidated, frayed, faded, wilted, shabby, second-hand, second-rate, threadbare; worn, – to- -a thread, – a shadow, – the stump, rags; reduced, – to a skeleton, skeletonized; far gone.

decayed &c. *v.*; moth-, worm-eaten; mildewed, rusty, mouldy, spotted, seedy, time-worn, moss-grown; discoloured; effete, wasted, crumbling, mouldering, rotten, cankered, blighted, tainted; depraved &c. (*vicious*) 945; decrep-id, -it; broken down; done, – for, – up; worn out, used up; fit for the -dust-hole, – wastepaper basket; past work &c. (*useless*) 645.

at a low ebb, in a bad way, on one's last legs, washed -up, – out; undermined, deciduous; nodding to its fall &c. (*destruction*) 162; tottering &c. (*dangerous*) 665; past cure &c. (*hopeless*) 859; fatigued &c. 688; backward, retrograde &c. (*retrogressive*) 283; deleterious &c. 649; behind the times.

Adv. on the down grade; beyond hope.

Phr. out of the frying pan into the fire; *ægrescit medendo.*

660. Restoration.—N. restor-ation, -al; re-instatement, -placement, -habilitation, -establishment, -construction; reproduction &c. 163; re-novation, -newal; reviv-al, -escence; refreshment

661. Relapse.—N. relapse, lapse; falling back &c. *v.*; retrogradation &c. (*retrogression*) 283; deterioration &c. 659.

[Return to, or recurrence of a bad

&c. 689; re-suscitation, -animation, -vivification, -viction; Phœnix; reorganization.

renaissance, renascence, rebirth, second youth, rejuvenation, rejuvenescence, new birth; regenera-tion, -cy, -teness; palingenesis, reconversion, resurgence, resurrection.

redress, retrieval, reclamation, recovery; convalescence; resumption, *résumption.*

recurrence &c. (*repetition*) 104; *réchauffé, rifacimento.*

cure, recure, sanation; healing &c. *v.*; redintegration; rectification, instauration.

repair, reparation, mending; recruiting &c. *v.*; cicatrization; disinfection; tinkering.

reaction; redemption &c. (*deliverance*) 672; restitution &c. 790; relief &c. 834.

mender, repairer, renewer; tinker, cobbler; doctor &c. 662; *vis medicatrix* &c. (*remedy*) 662.

curableness.

V. return to the original state; recover, rally, revive; come -to, – round, – to oneself; pull through, weather the storm, be oneself again; get -well, – round, – the better of, – over, – about; rise from -one's ashes, – the grave; resurge, resurrect; survive &c. (*outlive*) 110; resume, reappear; come to, – life again; live –, rise- again; relive.

heal, skin over, cicatrize; right itself.

restore, put back, place *in statu quo*; re-instate, -place, -seat, -habilitate, -establish, -estate, -install.

re-construct, -build, -organize, -constitute; reconvert; re-new, -novate; recondition; regenerate; rejuvenate.

re-deem, -claim, -cover, -trieve; rescue &c. (*deliver*) 672.

redress, recure; cure, heal, remedy, doctor, physic, medicate; break of; bring round, set on one's legs.

re-suscitate, -vive, -animate, -vivify, -call to life; reproduce &c. 163; warm up; reinvigorate, refresh &c. 689.

redintegrate, make whole; recoup &c. 790; make -good, – all square; rectify; put –, set- -right, – to rights, – straight; set up, correct; put in order &c. (*arrange*) 60; refit, recruit; fill up, – the ranks; reinforce.

repair, mend; put in -repair, – thorough repair, – complete repair; retouch, botch, vamp, tinker, doctor, cobble; do –, patch –, plaster –, vamp- up; darn, fine-draw, heel-piece; stop a gap, stanch, staunch, caulk, calk, careen, splice, bind up wounds.

Adj. restored &c. *v.*; *redivivus*, convalescent; in a fair way; none the worse; rejuvenated, renascent.

restoring &c. *v.*; restorative, recuperative; sana-, repara-tive, -tory; curative, remedial.

restor-, recover-, san-, remedi-, retriev-, cur-able.

Adv. *in statu quo*; as you were.

Phr. *revenons à nos moutons.*

state] backsliding, recidivation, recrudescence.

V. relapse, lapse; fall –, slide –, sink-back; have a relapse; return; retrograde &c. 283; recidivate; fall off &c. 659- again.

---

662. Remedy.—N. remedy, help, redress; antidote, anti-toxin, anti-,

663. Bane.—N. bane, curse, thorn in the -side, -flesh, bugbear, *bête noire*;

counter-poison, prophylactic, antiseptic, germicide, bactericide, corrective, restorative, stimulant, pick-me-up, tonic; sedative &c. 174; palliative; febrifuge; alter-ant, -ative; specific; emetic, carminative; narcotic &c. *adj.*; Nepenthe, Mithridate.

cure; radical –, perfect –, certain- cure; sovereign remedy.

physic, medicine, patent medicine, Galenicals, simples, drug, potion, draught, dose, pill, bolus, lozenge, tablet, tabloid, capsule; electuary; linct-us, -ure; medicament.

nostrum, receipt, recipe, prescription; catholicon, panacea, elixir, *elixir vitæ*, philosopher's stone; balm, balsam, cordial, theriac, ptisan.

salve, ointment, cerate, oil, lenitive, lotion, cosmetic; plaster; epithem, embrocation, liniment, cataplasm, sinapism, arquebusade, traumatic, vulnerary, pepastic, poultice, collyrium, depilatory.

compress, pledget; bandage &c. (*support*) 215.

treatment, medical treatment, regimen; diet-ary, -etics; *vis medicatrix, naturæ*; *médicine expectante*; seton, blood-letting, bleeding, venesection, phlebotomy, cupping, leeches; operation, surgical operation; tonsillectomy, appendectomy; injection, electrolysis, massage.

pharma-cy, -cology, -ceutics; acology; materia medica, pharmacopœia, therapeutics, therapy, posology, pathology &c. 655; homœ-, heter-, all-, hydr-opathy; cold water –, open air- cure; dietetics; sur-, chirur-gery, osteopathy; healing art, leechcraft, practice of medicine; ortho-pædy, -praxy; dentistry, midwifery, obstetrics, gynæcology.

faith -cure, – healing; psycho-therapy, -analysis, psychiatry.

hospital, infirmary, clinic; pest-, lazar-house; lazaretto, lazaret; lock hospital; *maison de santé*; *ambulance*; dispensary; *sanatorium, sanitarium*, spa, baths, pump-room, well; *hospice*; Red Cross; nursing home; asylum.

doctor, physician, surgeon; medical –, general- practitioner, consultant, specialist; medical attendant; medical student, medico; chemist, apothecary, pharmacopolist, druggist; leech; Æsculapius, Hippocrates, Galen; *accoucheur*, gynæcologist, midwife, oculist, aurist, dentist; operator; osteopath, bonesetter; nurse, monthly nurse, sister; dresser; *masseur*, *masseuse*.

V. apply a -remedy &c. *n.*; doctor, dose, physic, nurse, minister to, attend, dress the wounds, plaster, bandage, poultice; heal, cure, work a cure, kill or cure, remedy, stay (disease), snatch from the jaws of death; prevent &c. 706; relieve &c. 834; palliate &c. 658;

evil &c. 619; hurtfulness &c. (*badness*) 649; painfulness &c. (*cause of pain*) 830; scourge &c. (*punishment*) 975; *damnosa hereditas*; white elephant.

sting, fang, thorn, tang, bramble, brier, nettle.

poison, leaven, virus, venom; intoxicant; arsenic, Prussic acid, antimony, tartar emetic, strychnine, nicotine, cyanide of potassium, corrosive sublimate; curare; hyoscine &c.; poison-, mustard-, tear-gas; carbon di-, monoxide; ptomaine poisoning, botulism; miasm, mephitis, malaria, azote, sewer gas; pest, stench &c. 401.

rust, worm, moth, moth and rust, fungus, mildew; dry-rot; canker, -worm; cancer; torpedo; viper &c. (*evil-doer*) 913; demon &c. 980.

hemlock, hellebore, nightshade, *belladonna*, henbane, aconite; Upas tree.

drugs, dope, opium, morphia, morphine, cocaine, heroin, hashish, bhang.

[Science of poisons] Toxicology.

Adj. baneful &c. (*bad*) 649; poisonous &c. (*unwholesome*) 657.

restore &c. 660; drench with physic; consult, operate, extract, deliver; bleed, cup, let blood, transfuse; electrolyse; psycho-analyse.

Adj. remedial; restorative &c. 660; corrective, palliative, healing; sana-tory, -tive; prophylactic; salutiferous &c. (*salutary*) 656; medic-al, -inal; therapeutic, surgical, chirurgical, orthopedic, epulotic, paregoric, tonic, corroborant, analeptic, balsamic, anodyne, hypnotic, neurotic, narcotic, sedative, lenitive, demulcent, emollient; depuratory; deter-sive, -gent; abstersive, disinfectant, febrifugal, alternative; traumatic, vulnerary.

dietetic, alimentary; nutrit-ious, -ive; peptic; alexi-pharmic, -teric; remedi-, cur-able.

3. *Contingent Subservience*

664. Safety.—N. safety, security, impregnability; invulnera-bility, -bleness &c. *adj.*; danger -past, – over; storm blown over; coast clear; escape &c. 671; means of escape, safety-valve; safeguard, palladium, sheet anchor, rock, tower of strength.

guardian-, ward-, warden-ship; tutelage, custody, safe keeping; preservation &c. 670; protection, auspices.

safe-conduct, escort, convoy; guard, shield &c. (*defence*) 717; guardian angel, tutelary -god, – deity, – saint; *genius loci.*

protector, guardian; ward-en, -er; preserver, custodian, *duenna*, *chaperon*, third person.

watch-, ban-dog; Cerberus; watch-, patrol-, police-man, constable, peeler, bobby, copper, cop, bull, flat-foot, detective, armed guard; sentinel, sentry, scout &c. (*warning*) 668; garrison; guard-ship.

[Means of safety] refuge &c., anchor &c. 666; precaution &c. (*preparation*) 673; quarantine, *cordon sanitaire.* [Sense of security] confidence &c. 858.

V. be -safe &c. *adj.*; keep one's head above water, tide over, save one's bacon; ride out –, weather- the storm; light upon one's feet; bear a charmed life; escape &c. 671; possess nine lives.

make –, render- -safe &c. *adj.*; protect, watch over; take care of &c. (*care*) 459; preserve &c. 670; cover, screen, shelter, shroud, flank, ward; guard &c. (*defend*) 717; secure &c. (*restrain*) 751; intrench, fence round &c. (*circumscribe*) 229; house, nestle, ensconce; take charge of.

665. Danger.—N. danger, peril, insecurity, jeopardy, risk, hazard, venture, precariousness, slipperiness; instability &c. 149; defencelessness &c. *adj.*

exposure &c. (*liability*) 177; vulnerability; vulnerable point, heel of Achilles; forlorn hope &c. (*hopelessness*) 859.

[Dangerous course] leap in the dark &c. (*rashness*) 863; road to ruin, *facilis descensus Averni*, hair-breadth escape.

cause for alarm; source of danger &c. 667. [Approach of danger] rock –, breakers- ahead; storm brewing; clouds -in the horizon, – gathering; warning &c. 668; alarm &c. 669. [Sense of danger] apprehension &c. 860.

V. be -in danger &c. *adj.*; be exposed to –, run into –, incur –, encounter- -danger &c. *n.*; run a risk; lay oneself open to &c. (*liability*) 177; lean on –, trust to- a broken reed; feel the ground sliding from under one, have to run for it; have the -chances, – odds- against one.

hang by a thread, totter; tremble on the -verge, – brink; sleep –, stand -on a volcano; sit on a barrel of gunpowder, live in a glass house.

bring –, place –, put- in -danger &c. *n.*; endanger, expose to danger, imperil; jeopard, -ize, compromise; sail too near the wind &c. (*rash*) 863; put one's head in the lion's mouth.

adventure, risk, hazard, venture, stake, set at hazard; run the gauntlet &c. (*dare*) 861; engage in a forlorn hope.

threaten &c. 909- danger; run one

escort, convoy; garrison; watch, mount guard, patrol, scout, spy.

make assurance double sure &c. (*caution*) 864; take up a loose thread; take precautions &c. (*prepare for*) 673; take in a reef; double reef topsails.

seek safety; take –, find- shelter &c. 666; run into port.

Adj. safe, secure, sure; in -safety, – security; have an anchor to windward; on the safe side; under the -shield of, – shade of, – wing of, – shadow of one's wing; under -cover, – lock and key; out of -danger, – the meshes, – harm's way; in -harbour, – port; on sure ground, at anchor, high and dry, above water, on *terra firma*; unthreatened, -molested; protected &c. *v.*; *cavendo tutus*; panoplied &c. (*defended*) 717.

snug, sea-, air-worthy; weather-, water-, fire-, bomb-proof.

defensible, tenable, proof against, invulnerable; un-assailable, -attackable; im-pregnable, -perdible; founded on a rock; inexpugnable.

safe and sound &c. (*preserved*) 670; harmless; scathless &c. (*perfect*) 650; unhazarded; not -dangerous &c. 665.

protecting &c. *v.*; guardian, tutelary; preservative &c. 670; trustworthy &c. 939.

Adv. *ex abundanti cautelâ*; with impunity.

Phr. all's well; all clear; *salva res est*; *suave mari magno*; safety first.

hard; lay a trap for &c. (*deceive*) 545.

Adj. in -danger &c. *n.*; endangered &c. *v.*; fraught with danger; danger-, hazard-, peril-, parl-, pericul-ous; unsafe, unprotected &c. (safe, protect &c. 664); insecure, untrustworthy, unreliable; built upon sand, on a sandy basis.

defence-, fence-, guard-, harbourless; unshielded; vulnerable, expugnable, unsheltered, exposed; open to &c. (*liable*) 177.

aux abois, at bay; on -the wrong side of the wall, – a lee shore, – the rocks.

at stake, in question; precarious, aleatory, critical, ticklish; slip-pery, -py; hanging by a thread &c. *v.*; with a halter round one's neck; between -the hammer and the anvil, – Scylla and Charybdis, – two fires; on the -edge, – brink, – verge of a- -precipice, – volcano; in the lion's den, on slippery ground, under fire; not out of the wood.

un-warned, -admonished, -advised; unprepared &c. 674; off one's guard &c. (*inexpectant*) 508.

tottering; un-stable, -steady; shaky, top-heavy, tumble-down, ramshackle, crumbling, waterlogged; help-, guideless; in a bad way; reduced to –, at- the last extremity; trembling in the balance; nodding to its fall &c. (*destruction*) 162.

threatening &c. 909; ominous, ill-omened; alarming &c. (*fear*) 860; explosive; poisonous &c. 657.

adventurous &c. (*rash*) 863, (*bold*) 861.

Int. stop! look out! beware! take care!

Phr. *incidit in Scyllam qui vult vitare Charybdim*; *nam tua res agitur paries dum proximus ardet.*

666. [Means of safety.] **Refuge.—N.** refuge, sanctuary, retreat, fastness; stronghold, keep, last resort; ward; prison &c. 752; asylum, ark, home, almshouse, refuge for the destitute; hiding-place &c. (*ambush*) 530; *sanctum sanctorum* &c. (*privacy*) 893; cache.

roadstead, anchorage; breakwater, mole, port, haven; harbour, – of refuge; sea-port; pier, jetty, embankment, quay.

667. [Source of danger.] **Pitfall.—N.** rocks, reefs, coral reef, sunken rocks, snags; sands, quicksands, Goodwin sands, sandy foundation; slippery ground; breakers, shoals, shallows, bank, shelf, flat, lee shore, iron-bound coast; rock –, breakers- ahead; derelict.

precipice; abyss, chasm, pit, crevasse; maelstrom, whirlpool, eddy, vortex, rapids, current, bore, tidal wave; storm, squall, hurricane, whirl-

covert, shelter, abri, screen, lee-wall, wing, shield, umbrella; splash-, dash-board, mudguard.

wall &c. (*inclosure*) 232; fort &c. (*defence*) 717.

anchor, kedge; grap-nel, -pling iron; sheet-, mushroom-anchor, main-stay; support &c. 215; check &c. 706; ballast.

jury-mast; vent-peg; safety -valve, – lamp; lightning conductor.

means of escape &c. (*escape*) 671; life-boat, swimming belt, cork jacket; life preserver, breeches buoy; parachute, plank, stepping-stone.

safeguard &c. (*protection*) 664.

V. seek –, take –, find- refuge &c. *n.*; seek –, find- safety &c. 664; throw oneself into the arms of; claim sanctuary; take to the -hills, – woods; make port, reach shelter, bar –, bolt –, lock -the door, – gate; let the portcullis down; raise the drawbridge.

wind; volcano; ambush &c. 530; pit-fall, trap-door; trap &c. (*snare*) 545.

sword of Damocles; wolf at the door, snake in the grass, viper in one's bosom, death in the pot; latency &c. 526.

ugly customer, dangerous person, *le chat qui dort*; firebrand, hornet's nest.

Phr. *latet anguis in herbâ*; *proximus ardet Ucalegon.*

---

668. Warning.—N. warning, caution, *caveat*; notice &c. (*information*) 527; premoni-tion, -shment; prediction &c. 511; contraindication; symptom; lesson, dehortation; admonition, monition; alarm &c. 669.

handwriting on the wall, *tekel upharsin*, yellow flag; fog-signal, -horn; siren; monitor, warning voice, Cassandra, signs of the times, Mother Carey's chickens, stormy petrel, bird of ill omen, gathering clouds, clouds in the horizon, cloud no bigger than a man's hand, death-watch.

watch-tower, beacon, signal-post; light-house &c. (*indication of locality*) 550.

sent-inel, -ry; watch, -man; watch and ward; watch-, ban-, house-dog; patrol, vedette, picket, bivouac, scout, spy, spial; advanced –, rear-guard, lookout, flagman.

cautiousness &c. 864.

V. warn, caution; fore-, pre-warn; ad-, pre-monish; give -notice, – warning; menace &c. (*threaten*) 909; put on one's guard; sound the alarm &c. 669; croak.

beware, ware; take -warning, – heed at one's peril; watch out for; keep watch and ward &c. (*care*) 459.

Adj. warning &c. *v.*; premonitory, monitory, cautionary; admonitory, -tive; ominous, threatening, lowering, minatory, symptomatic.

warned &c. *v.*; on one's guard &c. (*careful*) 459, (*cautious*) 864.

Adv. *in terrorem* &c. (*threat*) 909.

Int. beware! ware! take care! mind –, take care-what you are about; mind! look out!

Phr. *ne reveillez pas le chat qui dort*; *fœnum habet in cornu.*

669. [Indication of danger.] **Alarm.**—N. alarm; alarum, larum, alarm bell, tocsin, *alerte*, beat of drum, sound of trumpet, note of alarm, hue and cry, signal of distress, S.O.S.; blue-lights; war-cry, -whoop; warning &c. 668; fog-signal, -horn; siren; yellow flag; danger signal; red -light, – flag; fire -bell, – alarm; burglar alarm, police whistle, watchman's rattle.

false alarm, cry of wolf; bugbear, -aboo.

V. give –, raise –, sound –, beat- the *or* an -alarm &c. *n.*; alarm; warn &c. 668; ring the tocsin; *battre la générale*; cry wolf.

Adj. alarming &c. *v.*

Int. *sauve qui peut! qui vive?* who goes there?

670. Preservation.—N. preservation; safe keeping; **conservation &c.** (*storage*) 636; maintenance, upkeep, support, sustentation, conservatism; *vis conservatrix*; salvation &c. (*deliverance*) 672; drying &c. *v.*

[Means of preservation] prophylaxis; preserv-er, -ative; canned goods; cold pack; hygi-astics, -antics; cover, drugget; *cordon sanitaire.*

[Superstitious remedies] charm &c. 993.

V. preserve, maintain, keep, sustain, support; keep -up, – alive; not willingly let die; shore –, bank- up; nurse; save, rescue; be –, make- -safe &c. 664; take care of &c. (*care*) 459; guard &c. (*defend*) 717.

stare super antiquas vias; hold one's own; hold –, stand- -one's ground &c. (*resist*) 719.

embalm, dry, cure, smoke, salt, pickle, season, kyanize, bottle, pot, tin, can; husband &c. (*store*) 636.

Adj. preserving &c. *v.*; conservative; prophylactic; preserva-tory, -tive; hygienic.

preserved &c. *v.*; un-impaired, -broken, -injured, -hurt, -singed, -marred; safe, – and sound; intact, with a whole skin, without a scratch.

Phr. *nolumus leges Angliæ mutari.*

671. Escape.—N. escape, scape; avolation, elopement, flight, get-away; evasion &c. (*avoidance*) 623; retreat; narrow –, hairbreadth- escape; close –, near- shave; come off, impunity.

[Means of escape] loophole &c. (*opening*) 260; path &c. 627; secret -door, – passage; refuge &c. 666; vent, – peg; safety-valve; draw-bridge, fire-escape.

reprieve &c. (*deliverance*) 672; liberation &c. 750.

refugee &c. (*fugitive*) 623.

V. escape, scape; make –, effect –, make good- one's escape, make a get-away; get -off, – clear off, – well out of; *échapper belle*, save one's bacon; weather the storm &c. (*safe*) 664; escape scot-free.

elude &c., make off &c. (*avoid*) 623; march off &c. (*go away*) 293; give one the slip; slip through the -hands, – fingers; slip the collar, wriggle out of; break -loose, – from prison; break –, slip –, get- away; find -vent, – a hole to creep out of.

Adj. escap-ing, -ed &c. *v.*; stolen away, fled.

Phr. the bird has flown.

672. Deliverance.—N. deliverance, extrication, rescue; repriev-e, -al; respite; ransom; liberation &c. 750; truce, armistice; redemption, salvation; riddance; gaol delivery; exemption, day of grace; redeemableness.

V. deliver, extricate, rescue, save, redeem, ransom, free, liberate, release, set free, redeem, emancipate; bring -off, – through; *tirer d'affaire*, get the wheel out of the rut; snatch from the jaws of death, come to the rescue; rid; retrieve &c. (*restore*) 660; be –, get- rid of.

Adj. saved &c. *v.*; extric-, redeem-, rescu-able.

Phr. to the rescue!

3°. *Precursory Measures*

673. Preparation.—N. preparation; providing &c. *v.*; provi-sion, -dence; anticipation &c. (*foresight*) 510; pre-caution, -concertation, -disposition;

674. Non-Preparation.—N. non-, absence of –, want of- preparation; un-preparedness; inculture, inconcoction, improvidence.

forecast &c. (*plan*) 626; rehearsal, note of preparation.

[Putting in order] arrangement &c. 60; clearance; adjustment &c. 23; tuning; equipment, outfit, accoutrement, armament, array.

ripening &c. *v.*; maturation, evolution; elaboration, concoction, digestion; gestation, hatching, incubation, sitting.

groundwork, datum, first stone, cradle, stepping-stone; foundation, scaffold &c. (*support*) 215; scaffolding, *échafaudage*.

[Preparation -of men] training &c. (*education*) 537; inurement &c. (*habit*) 613; novitiate; [– of food] cook-ing, -ery; brewing, culinary art; [– of the soil] till-, plough-, sow-ing; semination, cultivation.

[State of being prepared] prepared-, readi-, ripe-, mellow-ness; maturity; *un impromptu fait à loisir*.

[Preparer] preparer, teacher, coach, trainer, pioneer; *avant-courrier*, *-coureur*; sappers and miners, paviour, navvy; packer, stevedore; warming-pan; precursor &c. 64.

V. prepare; get –, make- ready; make preparations, settle preliminaries, get up, sound the note of preparation; address oneself to.

set –, put- in order &c. (*arrange*) 60; forecast &c. (*plan*) 626; prepare –, plough –, dress- the ground; till –, cultivate- the soil; predispose, sow the seed, lay a train, dig a mine; lay –, fix- the -foundations, – basis, -groundwork; dig the foundations, erect the scaffolding; lay the first stone &c. (*begin*) 66.

rough-hew; cut out work; block –, hammer- out; lick into shape &c. (*form*) 240.

elaborate, mature, ripen, mellow, season, bring to maturity; nurture &c. (*aid*) 707; hatch, cook, brew; temper; anneal, smelt; dry, cure &c. 670.

immaturity, crudity; rawness &c. *adj.*; abortion; disqualification.

[Absence of art] nature, state of nature; virgin soil, unweeded garden; rough diamond, neglect &c. 460.

rough copy &c. (*plan*) 626; germ &c. 153; raw material &c. 635.

improvisation &c. (*impulse*) 612.

V. be -unprepared &c. *adj.*; want –, lack- preparation; lie fallow; *s'embarquer sans biscuits*; live from hand to mouth.

[Render unprepared] dismantle &c. (*render useless*) 645; undress &c. 226.

extemporize, improvise.

surprise, pay a surprise visit, take by surprise, drop in upon, take unawares; take pot-luck.

Adj. un-prepared &c. [prepare &c. 673]; without -preparation &c. 673; incomplete &c. 53; rudimental, embryonic, abortive; immature, unripe, raw, green, crude; coarse; rough, -cast, -hewn; in the rough; un-hewn, -formed, -fashioned, -wrought, -laboured, -blown, -cooked, -boiled, -concocted, -cut, -polished.

callow, un-hatched, -fledged, -nurtured, -licked, -taught, -educated, -cultivated, -trained, -tutored, -drilled, -exercised; precocious, premature; un-, in-digested; un-mellowed, -seasoned, -leavened.

fallow; un-sown, -tilled; natural, in a state of nature; undressed; in dishabille, *en déshabillé*, *en négligé*.

un-, dis-qualified; unfitted; ill-digested; un-begun, -ready, -arranged, -organized, -furnished, -provided, -equipped, -trimmed; out of -gear, – order; dismantled &c. *v.*

shiftless, improvident, unthrifty, thoughtless, unguarded; happy-go-lucky; caught napping &c. (*inexpectant*) 508; unpremeditated &c. 612.

Adv. extempore &c. 612.

---

equip, arm, man; fit-out, -up; furnish, rig, dress, garnish, betrim, accoutre, array, fettle, fledge; dress –, furbish –, brush –, vamp- up; refurbish; sharpen one's tools, trim one's foils, set, prime, attune; whet the -knife, – sword; wind –, screw- up; adjust &c. (*fit*) 27; put in -trim, – train, – gear, – working order, – tune, – a groove for, – harness; pack, stow away, store.

train &c. (*teach*) 537; inure &c. (*habituate*) 613; breed; prepare &c.- for; rehearse; make provision for; take -steps, – measures, – precautions; provide, – against; beat up for recruits; open the door to &c. (*facilitate*) 705.

set one's house in order, make all snug; clear -decks, – for action; close one's ranks; shuffle the cards.

prepare oneself; serve an apprenticeship &c. (*learn*) 539; lay oneself out for, get into harness, gird up one's loins, buckle on one's armour, *reculer pour mieux sauter*, prime and load, shoulder arms, get the steam up, put the horses to.

guard –, make sure- against; forearm, make sure, prepare for the evil day, have a rod in pickle, provide against a rainy day, feather one's nest; lay in provisions &c. 637; make investments; keep on foot.

be -prepared, – ready &c. *adj.*; hold oneself in readiness, watch and pray, keep one's powder dry; lie in wait for &c. (*expect*) 507; anticipate &c. (*foresee*) 510; *principiis obstare*; *veniente occurrere morbo*.

Adj. preparing &c. *v.*; in -preparation, – course of preparation, – agitation, – embryo, – hand, – train; afoot, afloat; on -foot, – the stocks, – the anvil; under consideration &c. (*plan*) 626; brewing, hatching, forthcoming, brooding; in -store for, – reserve.

precautionary, provident; prepara-tive, -tory; provisional, inchoate, under revision; preliminary &c. (*precedent*) 62.

prepared &c. *v.*; in readiness; ready, – to one's hand, – made, cut and dried; ready for use, reach me down; made to one's hand, handy, on the table, made to order; in gear; in working -order, – gear; snug; in practice.

ripe, mature, mellow; practised &c. (*skilled*) 698; laboured, elaborate, highly-wrought, smelling of the lamp, worked up.

in -full feather, – best bib and tucker; in –, at- harness; in – the saddle, – arms, – battle array, – war paint; up in arms; armed -at all points, – to the teeth, – *cap-à-pie*; sword in hand; booted and spurred.

in utrumque –, *semper- paratus*; on the alert &c. (*vigilant*) 459; at one's post.

Adv. in -preparation, – anticipation of; afoot, astir, abroad; abroach.

675. Essay.—N. essay, trial, endeavour, aim, attempt; venture, adventure, speculation, *coup d'essai, début*; probation &c. (*experiment*) 463.

V. try, essay; experiment &c. 463; endeavour, strive; tempt, tackle, take on, attempt, make an attempt; venture, adventure, speculate, take one's chance, tempt fortune; try one's -fortune, – luck, – hand; use one's endeavour; feel –, grope –, pick- one's way.

try hard, push, make a bold push, use one's best endeavour; do one's best &c. (*exertion*) 686.

Adj. essaying &c. *v.*; experimental &c. 463; tentative, empirical, probationary.

Adv. experimentally &c. *adj.*; on trial, at a venture; by rule of thumb. if one may be so bold.

676. Undertaking.—N. undertaking; compact &c. 769; engagement &c. (*promise*) 768; enter-, em-prise; venture &c. 675; pilgrimage; matter in hand &c. (*business*) 625; move; first move &c. (*beginning*) 66.

V. undertake; engage –, embark- in; launch –, plunge- into; volunteer; apprentice oneself to; engage &c. (*promise*) 768; contract &c. 769; take upon -oneself, – one's shoulders; devote oneself to &c. (*determination*) 604.

take -up, – in hand; tackle; set –, go- about; set –, fall- -to, – to work; launch forth; set up shop; put in -hand, – execution; set forward; break the neck of a business, be in for; put one's hand to; betake oneself to, turn one's hand to, go to do; begin &c. 66; broach, institute, &c. (*originate*) 153; put –, lay- one's -hand to the plough, – shoulder to the wheel.

have in hand &c. (*business*) 625; have many irons in the fire &c. (*activity*) 682.

Adj. undertaking &c. *v.*; on the anvil &c. 625; adventurous, venturesome.

Int. here goes!

677. Use.—N. use; employ, -ment; exer-cise, -citation; appli-cation, -ance; adhibition, disposal; consumption; agency &c. (*physical*) 170; usufruct; usefulness &c. 644; recourse, resort, avail, pragmatism.

[Conversion to use] utilization, service, wear.

[Way of using] usage.

V. use, make use of, employ, put to use; apply, put in -action, – operation, – practice; set -in motion, – to work.

ply, work, wield, handle, manipulate; play, – off; exert, exercise, practise, avail oneself of, profit by; resort –, have recourse –, recur –, take –, betake oneself- to; take -up with, – advantage of; lay one's hands on, try.

render useful &c. 644; mould; turn to -account, – use; convert to use, utilize, administer; work up; call –, bring- into play; put into requisition; call –, draw- forth; press –, enlist- into the service; bring to bear upon, devote, dedicate, consecrate, apply, adhibit, dispose of; make a -handle, – cat's paw- of.

fall back upon, make a shift with; make the -most, – best- of.

use –, swallow- up; consume, absorb, expend; tax, task, wear, put to task.

Adj. in use; used &c. *v.*; well-worn, -trodden.

useful &c. 644; subservient &c. (*instrumental*) 631; utilitarian; pragmatical.

---

678. Disuse.—N. forbearance, abstinence; disuse; relinquishment &c. 782; desuetude &c. (*want of habit*) 614.

V. not use; do without, dispense with, let alone, not touch, forbear, abstain, spare, waive, neglect; keep back, reserve.

lay -up, – by, – on the shelf, – up in a napkin; shelve; set –, put –, lay- aside; disuse, leave off, have done with; supersede; discard &c. (*eject*) 297; dismiss, give warning.

throw aside &c. (*relinquish*) 782; make away with &c. (*destroy*) 162; cast –, heave –, throw- overboard; cast to the -dogs, – winds; dismantle &c. (*render useless*) 645.

lie –, remain- unemployed &c. *adj.*

Adj. not used &c. *v.*; un-employed, -applied, -disposed of, -spent, -exercised, -touched, -trodden, -essayed, -gathered, -culled; uncalled for, not required.

disused &c. *v.*; done with; run down, used up, cast off.

679. Misuse.—N. mis-use, -usage, -employment, -application, -appropriation.

abuse, profanation, prostitution, desecration; waste &c. 638.

V. mis-use, -employ, -apply, -appropriate.

desecrate, abuse, profane, prostitute; waste &c. 638; over-task, -tax, -work; squander &c. 818.

cut a whetstone with a razor, employ a steam-engine to crack a nut; catch at a straw.

Adj. misused &c. *v.*

Section III. Voluntary Action

1°. *Simple Voluntary Action*

680. Action.—N. action, performance; doing &c. *v.*; perpetration; exercise, -citation; movement, operation, evolution, work; labour &c. (*exertion*) 686; *praxis*, execution; procedure &c. (*conduct*) 692; handicraft; business &c. 625; agency &c. (*power at work*) 170.

deed, act, overt act, stitch, touch, gest; transaction, job, doings, dealings, proceeding, measure, step, manœuvre, bout, passage, move, stroke, blow; *coup*, – *de main*, – *d'état*; *tour de force* &c. (*display*) 882; feat, exploit, stunt; achievement &c. (*completion*) 729; handiwork, workmanship. craftsmanship; manufacture; stroke of policy &c. (*plan*) 626.

actor &c. (*doer*) 690.

V. do, perform, execute; achieve &c. (*complete*) 729; transact, enact; commit, perpetrate, inflict; exercise, prosecute, carry on, work, practise, play.

employ oneself, ply one's task; officiate, have in hand &c. (*business*) 625; labour &c. 686; be at work; pursue a course; shape one's course &c. (*conduct*) 692.

act, operate; take -action, – steps; strike a blow, lift a finger, stretch forth one's hand; take in hand &c. (*undertake*) 676; put oneself in motion; put in practice; carry into execution &c. (*complete*) 729; act upon.

be -an actor &c. 690; take –, act –, play –, perform- a part in; participate in; have a -hand in, – finger in the pie; have to do with; be a -party to, – participator in; bear –, lend- a hand; pull an oar, run in a race; mix oneself up with &c. (*meddle*) 682.

be in action; come into operation &c. (*power at work*) 170.

Adj. doing &c. *v.*; acting; in action; in harness; on duty; at work; in operation &c. 170; up to one's ears in work, in the midst of things.

Adv. in the -act, – midst of, – thick of; red-handed, *in flagrante delicto*; while one's hand is in.

681. Inaction.—N. inaction, passiveness, abstinence from action; non-interference; Fabian –, conservative- policy; neglect &c. 460; stagnation, vegetation; loafing.

inactivity &c. 683; rest &c. (*repose*) 687; quiescence &c. 265; want of –, in- occupation; unemployment; idle hours, time hanging on one's hands, *dolce far niente*; sinecure.

V. not -do, – act, – attempt; be -inactive &c. 683; abstain from doing, do nothing, hold, spare; not -stir, – move, – lift- a -finger, – foot, – peg; fold one's -arms, – hands; leave –, let- alone; let -be, – pass, – things take their course, – it have its way, – well alone; *quieta non movere*; *stare super antiquas vias*; rest and be thankful, live and let live; lie –, rest- upon one's oars; *laisser -aller*, – *faire*; stand aloof; refrain &c. (*avoid*) 623; keep oneself from doing; remit –, relax- one's efforts; desist &c. (*relinquish*) 624; stop &c. (*cease*) 142; pause &c. (*be quiet*) 265.

wait, lie in wait, bide one's time, take time, tide it over.

cool –, kick- one's heels; loaf, while away the -time, – tedious hours; pass –, fill up –, beguile- the time; talk against time; waste time &c. (*inactive*) 683.

lie -by, – on the shelf, – in ordinary, – idle, – to, – fallow; keep quiet, slug; have nothing to do, whistle for want of thought; twiddle one's thumbs.

undo, do away with; take -down, – to pieces; destroy &c. 162.

Adj. not doing &c. *v.*; not done &c. *v.*; undone; passive; un-occupied, -employed; out of -employ, – work, – a job; fallow; *désœuvré*.

Adv. *re infectâ*, at a stand, *les bras croisés*, with folded arms; with the hands -in the pockets, – behind one's back; *pour passer le temps*.

Int. so let it be! stop! &c. 142; hands off!

Phr. nothing doing; *cunctando restituit rem.*

682. Activity.—N. activity; briskness, liveliness &c. *adj.*; animation, life, vivacity, spirit, verve, dash, energy, go.

nimbleness, agility; smartness, quickness &c. *adj.*; velocity &c. 274; alacrity, promptitude; des-, dis-patch; expedition; haste &c. 684; punctuality &c. (*early*) 132.

eagerness, zeal, ardour, *perfervidum ingenium*, *empressement*, earnestness, intentness; *abandon*; vigour &c. (*physical energy*) 171; devotion &c. (*resolution*) 604; exertion &c. 686.

industry, assiduity; assiduousness &c. *adj.*; sedulity; laboriousness; drudgery &c. (*labour*) 686; painstaking, diligence; perseverance &c. 604*a*; indefatigation; habits of business.

vigilance &c. 459; wakefulness; sleep-, rest-lessness; *pervigilium*, *insomnia*; racketing.

movement, bustle, hustle, stir, fuss, ado, bother, pottering; fidgets, -iness; flurry &c. (*haste*) 684.

officiousness; dabbling, meddling; inter-ference, -position, -meddling, butting in, intrusiveness; tampering with, intrigue.

press of business, no sinecure, plenty to do, many irons in the fire, great doings, busy hum of men, battle of life, thick of -things, – the action; the madding crowd.

housewife, busy bee; new brooms; sharp fellow, blade; hustler, devotee, enthusiast, fan, zealot, fanatic; meddler, intermeddler, intriguer, busybody, kibitzer, pickthank.

V. be -active &c. *adj.*; busy oneself in; stir, -about, – one's stumps; bestir –, rouse- oneself; speed, hasten, peg away, lay about one, bustle, fuss; raise –, kick up- a dust; push; make a -push, – fuss, – stir; go ahead, push forward; fight –, elbow- one's way; make progress &c. 282; toil &c. (*labour*) 686; drudge, plod, persist &c. (*persevere*) 604*a*; keep -up the ball, – the pot boiling.

look sharp; have all one's eyes about one &c. (*vigilance*) 459; rise, arouse oneself, get up early, hustle, push; be about, keep moving, steal a march, kill two birds with one stone; seize the opportunity &c. 134; lose no time, not

683. Inactivity.—N. inactivity; inaction &c. 681; inertness, inertia &c. 172; obstinacy &c. 606.

lull &c. (*cessation*) 142; quiescence &c. 265; rust, -iness.

idle-, remiss-ness &c. *adj.*; sloth, indolence, indiligence; otiosity, dawdling &c. *v.*

dullness &c. *adj.*; languor; segni-ty, -tude; lentor; sluggishness &c. (*slowness*) 275; procrastination &c. (*delay*) 133; torp-or, -idity, -escence; stupor &c. (*insensibility*) 823; somnolence; drowsiness &c. *adj.*; nodding &c. *v.*; oscit-ation, -ancy; pandiculation, hypnotism, lethargy; heaviness, heavy eye-lids, sand in the eyes.

sleep, slumber; sound –, heavy –, balmy- sleep; Morpheus, dreamland; coma, trance, catalepsy, hypnosis, *ecstasis*, dream, hibernation, nap, doze, snooze, *siesta*, wink of sleep, forty winks, snore; Hypnology.

dull work; pottering; relaxation &c. (*loosening*) 47; Castle of Indolence.

[Cause of inactivity] lullaby, *berceuse*; anæsthetic, sedative &c. 174; torpedo.

idler, drone, droil, dawdle, mopus; do-little, *fainéant*, dummy, sleeping partner; afternoon farmer; truant &c. (*runaway*) 623; lounger, *lazzarone*, floater, loafer, tramp, beggar, cadger; lub-ber, -bard; slow-coach &c. (*slow*) 275; opium –, lotus- eater; slug; lag-, slug-gard, lie-abed; slumberer, dormouse, marmot; waiter on Providence, *fruges consumere natus*.

V. be -inactive &c. *adj.*; do nothing &c. 681; move slowly &c. 275; let the grass grow under one's feet; take one's time, dawdle, poke, drawl, droil, lag, hang back, slouch; loll, -op; lounge, loaf, loiter; go to sleep over; sleep at one's post, *ne battre que d'une aile*.

take -it easy, – things as they come; lead an easy life, vegetate, swim with the stream, eat the bread of idleness; loll in the lap of -luxury, – indolence; waste –, consume –, kill –, lose- time; burn daylight, waste the precious hours.

idle –, trifle –, fritter –, fool- away time; spend –, take- time in; ped-, pid-dle; potter, putter, dabble, faddle,

lose a moment, make the most of one's time, not suffer the grass to grow under one's feet, improve the shining hour, make short work of; dash off; make haste &c. 684; do one's best, take pains &c. (*exert oneself*) 686; do –, work- wonders.

have -many irons in the fire, – one's hands full, – much on one's hands; have other -things to do, – fish to fry; be busy; not have a moment -to spare, – that one can call one's own.

have one's fling, run the round of; go all lengths, stick at nothing, run riot.

outdo; over-do, -act, -lay, -shoot the mark; make a toil of a pleasure.

have a hand in &c. (*act in*) 680; take an active part, put in one's oar, have a finger in the pie, mix oneself up with, trouble one's head about, intrigue; agitate.

tamper with, meddle, moil; intermeddle, -fere, -pose; obtrude; poke –, thrust- one's nose in, butt in.

Adj. active; brisk, – as a lark, – as a bee; lively, animated, vivacious; alive, – and kicking; frisky, spirited, stirring.

nimble, – as a squirrel; agile; light-, nimble-footed; featly, tripping.

quick, prompt, yare, instant, ready, alert, spry, sharp, smart, slick, go-ahead; fast &c. (*swift*) 274; quick as a lamplighter, expeditious; awake, broad awake; wide awake &c. (*intelligent*) 498.

forward, eager, ardent, strenuous, zealous, enterprising, pushing, in earnest; resolute &c. 604.

industrious, assiduous, diligent, sedulous, notable, painstaking; intent &c. (*attention*) 457; indefatigable &c. (*persevering*) 604*a*; unwearied; unsleeping, sleepless, never tired; plodding, hard-working &c. 686; business-like, workaday.

bustling; restless, – as a hyæna; fussy, fidgety, pottering; busy, – as a hen with one chicken.

working, labouring, at work, on duty, in harness; up in arms; on one's legs, at call; up and -doing, – stirring.

busy, occupied; hard at -work, – it; up to one's ears in, full of business, busy as a bee.

meddling &c. *v.*; meddlesome, pushing, officious, overofficious, *intrigant*.

astir, stirring; a-going, -foot; on foot; in full swing; eventful; on the alert &c. (*vigilant*) 459.

fribble, fiddle-faddle; dally, dilly-dally.

sleep, slumber, be asleep; hibernate; oversleep; sleep like a -top, – log, – dormouse; sleep -soundly, – heavily; doze, drowze, snooze, nap; take a -nap &c. *n.*; dream; snore; settle –, go –, go off- to sleep; drop off; fall –, drop- asleep; close –, seal up- -the -eyes, – eyelids; weigh down the eyelids; get sleepy, nod, yawn; go to bed, turn in.

languish, expend itself, flag, hang fire; relax.

render -idle &c. *adj.*; sluggardize; mitigate &c. 174.

Adj. inactive; motionless &c. 265; unoccupied &c. (*doing nothing*) 681.

indolent, lazy, slothful, idle, otiose, lusk, remiss, slack, inert, torpid, sluggish, languid, supine, heavy, dull, leaden, lumpish; exanimate, soulless; listless; dron-y, -ish; lazy as Ludlam's dog.

dilatory, laggard; lagging &c. *v.*; slow &c. 275; rusty, flagging; lackadaisical, maudlin, fiddle-faddle; pottering &c. *v.*; shilly-shally &c. (*irresolute*) 605.

sleeping &c. *v.*; asleep; fast –, dead –, sound- asleep; in a sound sleep; sound as a top, dormant, comatose; in the -arms, – lap- of Morpheus.

sleep-y, -ful; dozy, drowsy, somnolent, torpescent; lethargic, -al; heavy, – with sleep; napping; somni-fic, -ferous; sopor-ous, -ific, -iferous; hypnotic; balmy, dreamy; un-, una-wakened.

sedative &c. 174.

Adv. inactively &c. *adj.*; at leisure &c. 685.

Phr. the eyes begin to draw straws.

Adv. actively &c. *adj.*; with -life and spirit, – might and main &c. 686, – haste &c. 684, – wings; full tilt, *in mediis rebus.*

Int. be –, look- -alive, – sharp! move –, push- on! keep moving! go ahead! stir your stumps! *age quod agis!*

Phr. *carpe diem* &c. (*opportunity*) 134; *nulla dies sine lineâ*; *nec mora nec requies*; no sooner said than done &c. (*early*) 132; catch a weasel asleep.

684. Haste.—**N.** haste, urgency; des-, dis-patch; acceleration, spurt, spirt, forced march, rush, dash; velocity &c. 274; precipit-ancy, -ation, -ousness &c. *adj.*; impetuosity; *brusquerie*; hurry, scurry, scuttle, drive, scramble, push, hustle, bustle, fuss, fidgets, flurry, flutter, splutter.

V. haste, hasten; make -haste, – a dash &c. *n.*; hurry –, dash –, whip –, push –, press- -on, – forward; hurry, skurry, scuttle along, bundle on, dart to and fro, bustle, flutter, scramble; plunge, – headlong; run, race, speed; dash off; rush &c. (*violence*) 173.

bestir oneself &c. (*be active*) 682; lose -no time, – not a moment, – not an instant; make short work of; make the best of one's -time, – way.

be -precipitate &c. *adj.*; jump at; be in -haste, – a hurry &c. *n.*; have -no time, – not a moment- -to lose, – to spare; work -under pressure, – against time.

quicken &c. 274; accelerate, expedite, put on, precipitate, urge, whip, spur, flog, goad.

Adj. hasty, hurried, *brusque*; scrambling, cursory, precipitate, headlong, furious, boisterous, impetuous, hot-headed; feverish, fussy; pushing.

in -haste, – a hurry &c. *n.*; in -hot, – all- haste; breathless, pressed for time, hard pressed, urgent.

Adv. with -haste, – all haste, – breathless speed; in haste &c. *adj.*; apace &c. (*swiftly*) 274; amain; all at once &c. (*instantaneously*) 113; at short notice &c., immediately &c. (*early*) 132; posthaste; by -express, – telegraph, – wire, – wireless, – air mail.

hastily, precipitately &c. *adj.*; helter-skelter, hurry-skurry, holus-bolus; slap-dash, -bang; full-tilt, -drive; heels over head, head and shoulders, headlong, *à corps perdu.*

by -fits and starts, – spurts; hop, skip and jump.

Phr. *sauve qui peut*, devil take the hindmost, no time to be lost; no sooner said than done &c. (*early*) 132; a word and a blow.

Int. hurry up! look alive! get a move on! buck up! double march! rush! urgent!

685. Leisure.—**N.** leisure; spare -time, – hours, – moments; vacant hour; time, – to spare, – on one's hands; holiday &c. (*rest*) 687; *otium cum dignitate*, ease.

V. have -leisure &c. *n.*; take one's -time, – leisure, – ease; repose &c. 687; move slowly &c. 275; while away the time &c. (*inaction*) 681; be -master of one's time, – an idle man; *desipere in loco.*

Adj. leisurely; slow &c. 275; deliberate, quiet, calm, undisturbed; at -leisure, – one's ease, – a loose end.

Phr. time hanging heavy on one's hands.

---

686. Exertion.—**N.** exertion, effort, strain, tug, pull, stress, force, pressure, throw, stretch, struggle, spell, spurt, spirt; stroke –, stitch- of work.

687. Repose.—**N.** repose, rest, silken repose; sleep &c. 683.

relaxation, breathing time; halt, pause &c. (*cessation*) 142; respite.

'a strong pull, a long pull and a pull all together'; dead lift; heft; gymnastics, sports; exer-cise, -citation; wear and tear; ado; toil and trouble; uphill –, hard –, warm- work; harvest time.

labour, work, toil, travail, manual labour, sweat of one's brow, swink, operoseness, drudgery, slavery, fagging, hammering; *limæ labor*.

trouble, pains, duty; resolution &c. 604; energy &c. (*physical*) 171.

V. exert oneself; exert –, tax- one's energies; use exertion.

labour, work, toil, moil, sweat, fag, drudge, slave, drag a lengthened chain, wade through, strive, strain; make –, stretch- a long arm; pull, tug, ply; ply –, tug at- the oar; do the work; take the labouring oar.

bestir oneself (*be active*) 682; take trouble, trouble oneself.

work hard; rough it; put forth -one's strength, – a strong arm; fall to work, bend the bow; buckle to, set one's shoulder to the wheel &c. (*resolution*) 604; work like a -Briton, – horse, – carthorse, – galley-slave, – coalheaver; labour –, work- day and night; redouble one's efforts; do double duty; work double -hours, – tides; sit up, burn the -midnight oil, – candle at both ends; stick to &c. (*persevere*) 604*a*; work –, fight- one's way; lay about one, hammer at.

take pains; do one's -best, – level best, – utmost; do -the best one can, – all one can, – all in one's power, – as much as in one lies, – what lies in one's power; use one's -best, – utmost- endeavour; try one's -best, – utmost; play one's best card; put one's -best, – right- leg foremost; have one's whole soul in one's work, put all one's strength into, strain every nerve; spare no -efforts, – pains; go all lengths; go through fire and water &c. (*resolution*) 604; move heaven and earth, leave no stone unturned.

Adj. labouring &c. *v.*

laborious, operose, elaborate; strained; toil-, trouble-, burden-, weari-some; uphill; herculean, gymnastic, athletic, palestric.

hardworking, painstaking, strenuous, energetic.

hard at work, on the stretch.

Adv. laboriously &c. *adj.*; lustily; with -might and main, – all one's might, – a strong hand, – sledge-hammer, – much ado; to the best of one's abilities, *totis viribus, vi et armis, manibus pedibusque*, tooth and nail, *unguibus et rostro*, hammer and tongs, heart and soul; through thick and thin &c. (*perseverance*) 604*a*.

by the sweat of one's brow, *suo Marte*.

day of rest, *dies non*, Sabbath, Lord's day, holiday, red-letter day, vacation, recess.

V. repose; rest, – and be thankful; take -rest, – one's ease.

relax, unbend, slacken; take breath &c. (*refresh*) 689; rest upon one's oars; pause &c. (*cease*) 142; stay one's hand.

lie down; recline, – on a bed of down, – on an easy chair; go to -rest, – bed, – sleep &c. 683.

take a holiday, shut up shop; lie fallow &c. (*inaction*) 681.

Adj. reposing &c. *v.*; unstrained.

Adv. at rest.

---

688. Fatigue.—**N.** fatigue; weariness &c. 841; yawning, drowsiness &c. 683; lassitude, tiredness, fatigation, exhaustion; sweat.

anhelation, shortness of breath, panting; faintness; collapse, prostration,

689. Refreshment.—**N.** bracing &c. *v.*; recovery of -strength &c. 159; restoration, revival &c. 660; repair, refection, refocillation, refreshment, regalement, bait; relief &c. 834.

V. brace &c. (*strengthen*) 159; rein-

swoon, fainting, *deliquium*, syncope, lipothymy.

V. be -fatigued &c. *adj.*; yawn &c. (*get sleepy*) 683; droop, sink, flag; lose -breath, – wind; gasp, pant, puff, blow, drop, swoon, faint, succumb.

fatigue, tire, weary, bore, irk, fag, jade, harass, exhaust, knock up, wear out, prostrate.

tax, task, strain; over-task, -work, -burden, -tax, -strain.

Adj. fatigued &c. *v.*; weary &c. 841; drowsy &c. 683; drooping &c. *v.*; haggard; toil-, way-worn; footsore, surbated, weatherbeaten; faint; done –, used –, knocked- up; exhausted, prostrate, spent; over-tired, -spent, -fatigued; forspent; unre-freshed, -stored.

worn, – out; battered, shattered, pulled down, seedy, altered.

breath-, wind-less; short of –, out of -breath, – wind; blown, puffing and blowing; short-breathed; anhelous; broken-, short-winded.

ready to drop, more dead than alive, dog -tired, – weary, walked off one's legs, tired to death, on one's last legs, played out, *hors de combat*.

fatiguing &c. *v.*; tire-, irk-, weari-some; weary; trying.

vigorate; air, freshen up, refresh, recruit; repair &c. (*restore*) 660; fan, refocillate.

breathe, respire; draw –, take –, gather –, take a long –, regain –, re-cover- breath; get better, raise one's head; recover –, regain –, renew- one's strength &c. 159; perk up.

come to oneself &c. (*revive*) 660; feel like a giant refreshed.

Adj. refreshing &c. *v.*; recuperative &c. 660.

refreshed &c. *v.*; un-tired, -wearied.

---

690. Agent.—N. doer, actor, agent, performer, perpetrator, operator; execu-tor, -trix; practitioner, worker, stager.

bee, ant, working bee, labouring oar, shaft horse, servant –, maid- of all work, general servant, factotum.

workman, artisan; crafts-, handicrafts-man; mechanic, operative; working –, labouring- man; hewers of wood and drawers of water, labourer, navvy; hand, man, day labourer, journeyman, hack; mere -tool &c. 633; porter, docker, stevedore, beast of burden, drudge, fag.

maker, artificer, artist, wright, manufacturer, architect, contractor, builder, mason, bricklayer, smith, forger, Vulcan; black-, tin-smith; carpenter; ganger, platelayer.

machinist, mechanician, engineer, electrician, plumber, gasfitter &c.

semp-, sem-, seam-stress; needle-, char-, work-woman; tailor, cord-wainer.

minister &c. (*instrument*) 631; servant &c. 746; representative &c. (*commissioner*) 758, (*deputy*) 759.

co-worker, fellow-worker, party to, participator in, co-operator, col-league, associate, collaborator, *particeps criminis*, *dramatis personæ*; *personnel*.

Phr. '*quorum pars magna fui*.'

691. Workshop.—N. work-shop, -house; laboratory; manufactory, mill, factory, armoury, arsenal, mint, forge, loom; cabinet, studio, *bureau*, *atelier*; hive, – of industry; nursery; hot-house, -bed; kitchen, kitchenette; dock, -yard; slip, yard, wharf; found-ry, -ery; furnace; vineyard, orchard, farm, kitchen garden.

melting pot, crucible, alembic, caldron, mortar, *matrix*.

2°. *Complex Voluntary Action*

692. Conduct.—N. dealing, transaction &c. (*action*) 680; business &c. 625.

tactics, game, policy, polity; general-, statesman-, seaman-ship; strate-gy, -gics; plan &c. 626.

husbandry; house-keeping, -wifery; stewardship; *ménage*; regimen, *régime*; econom-y, -ics; political economy; management; government &c. (*direction*) 693.

execution, manipulation, treatment, campaign, career, life, course, walk, race.

conduct; behaviour; de-, com-portment; carriage, *maintien*, demeanour, guise, bearing, manner, mien, air, observance.

course –, line- of -conduct, – action, – proceeding; *rôle*; process, ways, practice, procedure, *modus operandi*; method &c., path &c. 627.

V. transact, execute; des-, dis-patch; proceed with, discharge; carry -on, – through, – out, – into effect; work out; go –, get- through; enact; put into practice; officiate &c. 625.

behave –, comport –, demean –, carry –, bear –, conduct –, acquit- oneself.

run a race, lead a life, play a game; take –, adopt- a course; steer –, shape- one's course; play one's- -part, – cards; shift for oneself; paddle one's own canoe.

conduct; manage &c. (*direct*) 693.

deal –, have to do- with; treat, handle a case; take -steps, – measures.

Adj. conducting &c. *v.*; strategical, business-like, practical, economic, executive.

693. Direction.—N. direction; manage-ment, -ry; government, gubernation, conduct, legislation, regulation, guidance; steer-, pilot-age; reins, – of government; helm, rudder, controls, joy stick, needle, compass, binnacle; guiding –, load –, lode –, pole- star; cynosure.

super-vision, -intendence; *surveillance*, oversight; eye of the master; control, charge, auspices; board of control &c. (*council*) 696; command &c. (*authority*) 737.

premier-, senator-ship; director &c. 694; chair, seat, portfolio.

statesmanship; state-, king-craft.

minis-try, -tration; administration; steward-, proctor-ship; agency.

V. direct, manage, govern, conduct; order, prescribe, cut out work for; head, lead; lead –, show- the way; take the lead, lead on; regulate, guide, steer, pilot; take –, be at- the helm; have –, handle –, hold –, take- the reins, handle the ribbons; drive, tool; tackle.

super-intend, -vise; overlook, control, keep in order, look after, see to, oversee, legislate for; administer, ministrate; patronize; have the -care, – charge- of; have –, take- the direction; pull the -strings, – wires; rule &c. (*command*) 737; have –, hold- -office, – the portfolio; preside, – at the board; take –, occupy –, be in- the chair; pull the stroke oar.

Adj. directing &c. *v.*; executive, supervisory, hegemonic.

Adv. at the -helm, – head of, in charge of; under the auspices of.

694. Director.—N. director, manager, governor, rector, comptroller; super-intendent, -visor; intendant; over-seer, -looker; foreman, boss, straw boss; supercargo, husband, inspector, visitor, ranger, surveyor, ædile, moderator, monitor, taskmaster; master &c. 745; leader, ringleader, demagogue, corypheus, conductor, fugleman, precentor, bellwether, agitator.

guiding star &c. (*guidance*) 693; adviser &c. 695; guide &c. (*information*) 527; pilot; helmsman; steers-man, -mate; man at the wheel; wire-puller.

driver, whip, Jehu, charioteer; coach-, car-, cab-man, jarvey; postilion, *vetturino*, muleteer, teamster; whipper in; engineer, engine driver, motorman, *chauffeur*.

head, – man; principal, president, speaker; chair, -man; captain &c. (*master*) 745; superior; dean; mayor &c. (*civil authority*) 745; vice-president, prime minister, premier, vizier, grand vizier; dictator.

officer, functionary, minister, official, red-tapist, bureaucrat; man –, Jack- in office; office-bearer; person in authority &c. 745.

statesman, strategist, legislator, lawgiver, politician, administrator, statist, statemonger; Minos, Draco; arbiter &c. (*judge*) 967; king maker, power behind the throne.

board &c. (*council*) 696.

secretary, – of state; Reis Effendi; vicar &c. (*deputy*) 759; steward, factor; agent &c. 758; bailiff, middleman; ganger, clerk of works; landreeve; factotum, major-domo, seneschal, housekeeper, shepherd, *croupier*; proctor, procurator, curator, librarian.

Adv. *ex officio*.

695. Advice.—N. advice, counsel, adhortation; word to the wise; suggestion, submonition, recommendation, advocacy, consultation.

exhortation &c. (*persuasion*) 615; expostulation &c. (*dissuasion*) 616; admonition &c. (*warning*) 668; guidance &c. (*direction*) 693.

instruction, charge, injunction.

adviser, prompter; counsel, -lor; monitor, mentor, Nestor, *magnus Apollo*, senator; teacher &c. 540.

guide, manual, chart &c. (*information*) 527.

physician, leech, archiater; arbiter &c. (*judge*) 967.

refer-ence, -ment; consultation, conference, parley, *pourparler* &c. 696.

V. advise, counsel; give -advice, – counsel, – a piece of advice; suggest, prompt, submonish, recommend, prescribe, advocate; exhort &c. (*persuade*) 615.

enjoin, enforce, charge, instruct, call; call upon &c. (*request*) 765; dictate.

expostulate &c. (*dissuade*) 616; admonish &c. (*warn*) 668.

advise with; lay heads –, consult- together; compare notes; hold a council, deliberate, be closeted with.

confer, consult, refer to, call in; take –, follow- advice; follow implicitly; be advised by, have at one's elbow, take one's cue from.

Adj. recommendatory; hortative &c. (*persuasive*) 615; dehortatory &c. (*dissuasive*) 616; admonitory &c. (*warning*) 668; consultative.

Int. go to!

696. Council.—N. council, committee, subcommittee, *comitia*, court, chamber, cabinet, board, bench, staff; consultation.

senate, *senatus*, parliament, House, – of Lords, – Peers, – Commons, legislature, legislative assembly, federal council, chamber of deputies, directory, *Reichsrath*, *rigsdag*, *cortes*, storthing, witenagemote, *junta*, divan, *musnud*, *sanhedrim*, Amphictyonic council; *duma*, *zemstvo*, *soviet*, *cheka*, *ogpu*; *Dail Eireann*; caput, consistory, chapter, syndicate; court of appeal &c. (*tribunal*) 966; board of -control, – works; vestry; county –, borough –, district –, parish –, town- council, local board.

cabinet –, privy- council, royal commission; cockpit, convocation, synod, congress, congregation, convention, diet, states-general, aulic council.

League of Nations, assembly, *caucus*, conclave, *clique*, conventicle; meeting, sitting, *séance*, conference, session, hearing, palaver, *pourparler*, *durbar*, pow-wow, house; *quorum*.

senator; member, – of parliament; councillor, M.P., representative of the people.

Adj. senatorial, curule, parliamentary.

697. Precept.—N. precept, direction, instruction, charge; prescript, -ion; *recipe*, receipt; golden rule; maxim &c. 496.

commandment, rule, ruling, canon, law, code, *corpus juris*, *lex scripta*, common –, unwritten –, canon-law; the Ten Commandments; act, statute, convention, rubric, stage direction, regulation; form, -ula, -ulary; technicality; nice point.

order &c. (*command*) 741.

698. Skill.—N. skill, skilfulness, address; dexter-ity, -ousness; adroitness, expertness &c. *adj.*; proficiency, competence, craft, callidity, facility, knack, trick, sleight; master-y, -ship; excellence, panurgy; ambidext-erity, -rousness; sleight of hand &c. (*deception*) 545.

sea-, air-, marks-, horse-manship; tight-, rope-dancing.

accomplish-, acquire-, attain-ment; art, science; techn-icality, -ology, -ique; practical –, technical- knowledge; technocracy; finish, technic.

knowledge of the world, world wisdom, *savoir-faire*; tact; mother wit &c. (*sagacity*) 498; discretion &c. (*caution*) 864; *finesse*; craftiness &c. (*cunning*) 702; management &c. (*conduct*) 692; *ars celare artem*; self-help.

cleverness, talent, ability, ingenuity, capacity, parts, talents, faculty, endowment, *forte*, turn, gift, genius, flair, feeling; intelligence &c. 498; sharpness, readiness &c. (*activity*) 682; invention &c. 515; apt-ness, -itude; turn –, capacity –, genius- for; felicity, capability, *curiosa felicitas*, qualification, habilitation.

proficient &c. 700.

masterpiece, *coup de maître*, *chef-d'œuvre*, *tour de force*; good stroke &c. (*plan*) 626.

V. be -skilful &c. *adj.*; excel in, be master of; have -a turn for &c. *n.*

know -what's what, – a hawk from a handsaw, – what one is about, – on

699. Unskilfulness.—N. unskilfulness &c. *adj.*; want of -skill &c. 698; incompeten-ce, -cy; in-ability, -felicity, -dexterity, -experience; clumsiness; disqualification, unproficiency; quackery.

folly, stupidity &c. 499; indiscretion &c. (*rashness*) 863; thoughtlessness &c. (*inattention*) 458, (*neglect*) 460.

mis-management, -conduct; impolicy; maladministration; mis-rule, -government, -application, -direction, -feasance.

absence of rule, rule of thumb; bungling &c. *v.*; failure &c. 732; screw loose; too many cooks.

blunder &c. (*mistake*) 495; *étourderie*, *gaucherie*, act of folly, *balourdise*; botch, -ery; bad job, sad work.

sprat sent out to catch a whale, much ado about nothing, wildgoose chase.

bungler &c. 701; fool &c. 501.

layman, amateur.

V. be -unskilful &c. *adj.*; not see an inch beyond one's nose; blunder, bungle, boggle, fumble, muff, botch, bitch, flounder, loppet, stumble, trip; hobble &c. 275; put one's foot in it; make a -mess, – hash, – sad work- of; overshoot the mark.

play -tricks with, – Puck; mismanage, -conduct, -direct, -apply, -send.

stultify –, make a fool of –, commit- oneself; act foolishly; play the fool; put oneself out of court; lose one's -head, – cunning.

begin at the wrong end; do things

which side one's bread is buttered, – what's o'clock, – a thing or two; have cut one's -eye, – wisdom- teeth.

see -one's way, – where the wind lies, – which way the wind blows; have -all one's wits about one, – one's hand in; *savoir-vivre*; *scire quid valeant humeri quid ferre recusent*.

look after the main chance; cut one's coat according to one's cloth; live by one's wits; exercise one's discretion, feather the oar, sail near the wind; stoop to conquer &c. (*cunning*) 702; play one's -cards well, – best card; hit the right nail on the head, put the saddle on the right horse.

take advantage of, make the most of; profit by &c. (*use*) 677; make a hit &c. (*succeed*) 731; make a virtue of necessity; make hay while the sun shines &c. (*occasion*) 134.

Adj. skilful, dexterous, adroit, expert, apt, slick, handy, quick, deft, ready, resourceful, gain; smart &c. (*active*) 682; proficient, good at, up to, at home in, master of, a good hand at, *au fait*, thoroughbred, masterly, crack, accomplished; conversant &c. (*knowing*) 490.

experienced, practised, skilled; up –, well up- in; in -practice, – proper cue; competent, efficient, qualified, capable, fitted, fit for, up to the mark, trained, initiated, prepared, primed, finished.

clever, able, ingenious, felicitous, gifted, talented, endowed, cute, inventive &c. 515; shrewd, sharp &c. (*intelligent*) 498; cunning &c. 702; alive to, up to snuff, not to be caught with chaff; discreet.

neat-handed, fine-fingered, ambidextrous, sure-footed; cut out –, fitted- for.

technical, artistic, scientific, dædalian, shipshape; workman-, business-, statesman-like.

Adv. skillfully &c. *adj.*; well &c. 618; artistically; with -skill, – consummate skill; *secundum artem*, *suo Marte*; to the best of one's abilities &c. (*exertion*) 686; like a machine.

---

by halves &c. (*not complete*) 730; make two bites of a cherry; play at cross purposes; strain at a gnat and swallow a camel &c. (*caprice*) 608; put the cart before the horse; lock the stable door when the horse is stolen &c. (*too late*) 135.

not know -what one is about, – one's own interest, – on which side one's bread is buttered; stand in one's own light, quarrel with one's bread and butter, throw a stone in one's own garden, kill the goose which lays the golden eggs, pay dear for one's whistle, cut one's own throat, burn one's fingers; knock –, run- one's head against a stone wall; fall into a trap, catch a Tartar, bring the house about one's ears; have too many -eggs in one basket (*imprudent*) 863, – irons in the fire.

mistake &c. 495; take the shadow for the substance &c. (*credulity*) 486; be in the wrong box, aim at a pigeon and kill a crow; take –, get- the wrong sow by the ear, – the dirty end of the stick; put -the saddle on the wrong horse, – a square peg into a round hole, – new wine into old bottles.

cut a whetstone with a razor; hold a farthing candle to the sun &c. (*useless*) 645; fight with –, grasp at- a shadow; catch at straws, lean on a broken reed, reckon without one's host, pursue a wildgoose chase; go on a fool's –, sleeveless- errand; go further and fare worse; loose –, miss- one's way; fail &c. 732.

Adj. un-skilful &c. 698; unskilled, inexpert; bungling &c. *v.*; awkward, clumsy, unhandy, lubberly, *gauche*, *maladroit*; left-, heavy-handed; slovenly, slatternly; gawky.

adrift, at fault.

in-, un-apt; inhabile; un-tractable, -teachable; giddy &c. (*inattentive*) 458; inconsiderate &c. (*neglectful*) 460; stupid &c. 499; inactive &c. 683; incompetent; un-, dis-, ill-qualified; unfit; quackish; raw, green, inexperienced, rusty, out of practice.

un-accustomed, -used, -trained &c. 537, -initiated, -conversant &c. (*ignorant*) 491; shiftless; unbusinesslike, unpractical; unstatesmanlike.

un-, ill-, mis-advised; ill-devised, -imagined, -judged, -contrived, -conducted; un-, mis-guided; misconducted, foolish, wild; infelicitous; penny wise and pound foolish &c. (*inconsistent*) 608.

Phr. one's fingers being all thumbs; the right hand forgets its cunning.

il se noyerait dans une goutte d'eau.

incidit in Scyllam qui vult vitare Charybdim; out of the frying pan into the fire.

700. Proficient.—N. proficient, expert, adept, dab; *connoisseur* &c. (*scholar*) 492; master, -hand; top-sawyer, *prima donna*, first fiddle, *cordon bleu*; protagonist; past master; profess-or, -ional, specialist.

picked man; medallist, prizeman.

veteran; old -stager, – campaigner, – soldier, – file, – hand; man of -business, – the world.

nice –, good –, clean- hand; practised –, experienced- -eye, – hand; marksman; good –, dead –, crack- shot; rope-dancer, funambulist, acrobat, contortionist; cunning man; conjuror &c. (*deceiver*) 548; wizard &c. 994.

genius; master-mind, – head, – spirit; cunning –, sharp -blade, – fellow; jobber; cracksman &c. (*thief*) 792; politician, tactician, diplomat, -ist, strategist.

pantologist, admirable Crichton, Jack of all trades; prodigy of learning; walking encyclopædia; mine of information.

701. Bungler.—N. bungler; blunderer, -head; marplot, fumbler, lubber, lout, oaf, duffer, stick, clown; bad –, poor- -hand, – shot; butter-fingers.

no conjuror, flat, muff, slow coach, looby, lubber, swab; clod, yokel, hick, awkward squad, novice, greenhorn, jaywalker, *blanc-bec.*

land lubber; fresh water –, fair weather- sailor; horse-marine; fish out of water, ass in lion's skin, jackdaw in peacock's feathers; quack &c. (*deceiver*) 548; Lord of Misrule.

sloven, slattern, trapes.

Phr. *il n'a pas inventé la poudre*; he will never set the Thames on fire.

---

702. Cunning.—N. cunning, craft; cunningness, craftiness &c. *adj.*; subtlety, artificiality; manœuvring &c. *v.*; temporization; circumvention.

chicane, -ry; sharp practice, knavery, jugglery; concealment &c. 528; nigger in the woodpile; guile, duplicity &c. (*falsehood*) 544; foul play.

diplomacy, politics; Machiavellism; jobbery, back-stairs influence, gerrymandering.

art, -ifice; device, machination; plot &c. (*plan*) 626; manœuvre, stratagem, dodge, artful dodge, wile; trick, -ery &c. (*deception*) 545; *ruse*, – *de guerre*; *finesse*, side-blow, thin end of the wedge, shift, go by, subterfuge, evasion; white lie &c. (*untruth*) 546; juggle, *tour de force*; tricks -of the trade, – upon travellers; imposture, deception; *espièglerie*; net, trap &c. 545.

Ulysses, Machiavel, sly boots, fox,

703. Artlessness.—N. artlessness &c. *adj.*; nature, simplicity; innocence &c. 946; *bonhomie*, *naïveté*, *abandon*, candour, sincerity; singleness of -purpose, – heart; honesty &c. 939; plain speaking; *épanchement.*

rough diamond, matter of fact man; *le palais de vérité*; *enfant terrible.*

V. be -artless &c. *adj.*; look one in the face; wear one's heart upon his sleeve for daws to peck at; think aloud; speak -out, – one's mind; be free with one, call a spade a spade.

Adj. artless, natural, pure, native, simple, plain, inartificial, untutored, unsophisticated, *ingénue*, unaffected, *naïve*; sincere, frank; open, – as day; candid, ingenuous, guileless, unsuspicious, childlike; honest &c. 939; innocent &c. 946; Arcadian; undesigning, straightforward, unreserved, unvarnished, above-board; simple-, single-

reynard; Scotch-, Yorkshire-man; Jew, Greek, Yankee; intriguer, *intrigant*, schemer, trickster.

V. be -cunning &c. *adj.*; have cut one's eye-teeth; contrive &c. (*plan*) 626; live by one's wits; manœuvre; intrigue, gerrymander, *finesse*, double, temporize, stoop to conquer, *reculer pour mieux sauter*, circumvent, steal a march upon; overreach &c. 545; throw off one's guard; surprise &c. 508; outdo, get the better of, snatch from under one's nose; snatch a verdict; waylay, undermine, introduce the thin end of the wedge; play -a deep game, – tricks with; have an axe to grind; *spargere voces in vulgum ambiguas*; flatter, make things pleasant.

Adj. cunning, crafty, artful; skilful &c. 698; subtle, feline, vulpine; cunning as a -fox, – serpent; deep, – laid; profound; designing, contriving; intriguing &c. *v.*; strategic, diplomatic, politic, Machiavellian, time-serving; artificial; trick-y, -sy; wily, sly, slim, insidious, stealthy, foxy; underhand &c. (*hidden*) 528; subdolous; deceitful &c. 545; double-tongued, -faced; shifty; crooked; arch, pawky, shrewd, acute; sharp, – as a needle; canny, astute, leery, knowing, up to snuff, too clever by half, not to be caught with chaff.

Adv. cunningly &c. *adj.*; slily, on the sly, by a side wind.

Phr. diamond cut diamond.

minded; frank-, open-, single-, simple-hearted; open and above-board.

free-, plain-, out-spoken; blunt, downright, direct, matter of fact, unpoetical; unflattering.

Adv. in plain -words, – English; without mincing the matter; not to mince the matter &c. (*affirmation*) 535.

Phr. *Davus sum non Œdipus*; *liberavi animam meam.*

Section IV. Antagonism

1°. *Conditional Antagonism*

704. Difficulty.—N. difficulty; hardness &c. *adj.*; impracticability &c. (*impossibility*) 471; tough –, hard –, uphill- work; hard –, Herculean –, Augean- task; task of Sisyphus, Sisyphean labour, tough job, teaser, rasper, dead lift.

dilemma, embarrassment; perplexity &c. (*uncertainty*) 475; involvement; intricacy; entanglement &c. 59; cross fire; awkwardness, delicacy, ticklish card to play, deadlock, knot, Gordian knot, *dignus vindice nodus*, net, meshes, maze; coil &c. (*convolution*) 248; crooked path.

nice –, delicate –, subtle –, knotty- point; vexed question, *vexata quæstio*, poser; puzzle &c. (*riddle*) 533; paradox; hard –, nut to crack; bone to pick, *crux*, *pons asinorum*, where the shoe pinches.

nonplus, quandary, strait, pass, pinch, pretty pass, stress, brunt; criti-

705. Facility. — N. facility, ease; easiness &c. *adj.*; capability; feasibility &c. (*practicability*) 470; flexibility, pliancy &c. 324; smoothness &c. 255; convenience.

plain –, smooth –, straight- sailing; mere child's play, holiday task.

smooth water, fair wind; smooth – royal- road; clear -coast, – stage; *tabula rasa*; full play &c. (*freedom*) 748.

disen-cumbrance, -tanglement; deoppilation; permission &c. 760.

V. be -easy &c. *adj.*; go on –, run- smoothly; have -full play &c. *n.*; go –, run- on all fours; obey the helm, work well.

flow –, swim –, drift –, go- with the- -stream, – tide; see one's way; have -it all one's own way, – the game in one's own hands; walk over the course, win -at a canter, – hands down; make -light of, – nothing of; be at home in &c. (*skilful*) 698.

cal situation, crisis; trial, rub, emergency, exigency, scramble.

scrape, hobble, slough, quagmire, hot water, hornet's nest; sea –, peck- of troubles; pretty kettle of fish; pickle, stew, *imbroglio*, mess, muddle, botch, fuss, bustle, ado; false position; set fast, stand; dead -lock, – set; fix, horns of a dilemma, *cul de sac*; hitch; stumbling block &c. (*hindrance*) 706.

V. be -difficult &c. *adj.*; run one hard, go against the grain, try one's patience, put one out; put to one's -shifts, – wit's end; go hard with –, try- one; pose, perplex &c. (*uncertain*) 475; bother, nonplus, gravel, bring to a dead lock; be -impossible &c. 471; be in the way of &c. (*hinder*) 706.

meet with –, labour under –, get into –, plunge into –, struggle with –, contend with –, grapple with- difficulties; labour under a disadvantage; be -in difficulty &c. *adj.*

fish in troubled waters, buffet the waves, swim against the stream, scud under bare poles.

have -much ado with, – a hard time of it; come to the -push, – pinch; bear the brunt.

grope in the dark, lose one's way, weave a tangled web, walk among eggs.

get into a -scrape &c. *n.*; bring a hornet's nest about one's ears; be put to one's shifts; flounder, boggle, struggle; not know which way to turn &c. (*uncertain*) 475; get -tangled up, – wound up; *perdre son latin*; stick - at, – in the mud, – fast; come to a -stand, – dead lock; hold the wolf by the ears.

render -difficult &c. *adj.*; encumber, embarrass, ravel, entangle; put a spoke in the wheel &c. (*hinder*) 706; lead a pretty dance.

Adj. difficult, not easy, hard, tough; trouble-, toil-, irk-some; operose, laborious, onerous, arduous, Herculean, formidable; sooner –, more easily- said than done; difficult –, hard- to deal with; ill-conditioned, crabbed; not -to be handled with kid gloves, – made with rosewater.

awkward, unwieldy, unmanageable; intractable, stubborn &c. (*obstinate*) 606; perverse, refractory, plaguy, trying, thorny, rugged; knot-ted, -ty; invious; path-, track-less; labyrinthine &c. (*convoluted*) 248; intricate, complicated &c. (*tangled*) 59; impracticable &c. (*impossible*) 471; not -feasible &c. 470; desperate &c. (*hopeless*) 859.

embarrassing, perplexing &c. (*uncertain*) 475; delicate, ticklish,

render -easy &c. *adj.*; facilitate, smooth, ease; popularize; lighten, – the labour; free, clear; dis-encumber, -embarrass, -entangle, -engage; deobstruct, unclog, extricate, unravel; untie –, cut- the knot; disburden, unload, exonerate, emancipate, free from, deoppilate; humour &c. (*aid*) 707; lubricate &c. 332; relieve &c. 834.

leave -a hole to creep out of, – a loophole, – the matter open; give -the reins to, – full play, – full swing; make way for; open the -door to, – way; prepare –, smooth –, clear- the -ground, – way, – path, – road; pave the way, bridge over; permit &c. 760.

Adj. easy, facile; feasible &c. (*practicable*) 470; easily -managed, – accomplished; within reach, accessible, easy of access, for the million, open to.

manageable, wieldy; towardly, tractable; submissive; yielding, ductile; pliant &c. (*soft*) 324; glib, slippery; smooth &c. 255; on -friction wheels, – velvet; convenient.

un-, dis-burdened, -encumbered, -embarrassed; exonerated; un-loaded, -obstructed, -trammelled, - impeded, -restrained &c. (*free*) 748; at ease, light.

at –, quite at- home; in -one's element, – smooth water.

Adv. easily &c. *adj.*; readily, smoothly, swimmingly, *ad lib.*, on easy terms, single-handed.

Phr. touch and go.

Int. all clear!

---

critical; beset with –, full of –, surrounded by –, entangled by –, encompassed with- difficulties.

under a difficulty; in -difficulty, – hot water, – the suds, – a cleft stick, – a fix, – the wrong box, – a scrape &c. *n.*, – deep water, – a fine pickle; *in extremis*; between -two stools, – Scylla and Charybdis; surrounded by -shoals, – breakers, – quicksands; at cross purposes; not out of the wood.

reduced to straits; hard –, sorely- pressed; run hard; pinched, put to it, straitened; hard -up, – put to it, – set; put to one's shifts; puzzled, at a loss &c. (*uncertain*) 475; at -the end of one's tether, – one's wit's end, – a nonplus, – a standstill; gravelled, nonplussed, stranded, aground; stuck –, set- fast; up a tree, at bay, *aux abois*, driven -into a corner, – from post to pillar, – to extremity, – to one's wit's end, – to the wall; *au bout de son latin*; out of one's -depth, – reckoning; put –, thrown -out.

accomplished with difficulty; hard-fought, -earned.

Adv. with -difficulty, – much ado; hardly &c. *adj.*; uphill; against the -stream, – grain; *à rebours*; *invitâ Minervâ*; in the teeth of; at –, upon- a pinch; at long odds.

Phr. ay there's the rub; *hic labor hoc opus*; things are come to a pretty pass.

2°. *Active Antagonism*

706. Hindrance. — N. prevention, preclusion, obstruction, stoppage; prohibition; inter-ruption, -ception, -clusion; hindrance, impedition; retardment, -ation; constriction; embarrassment, oppilation; coarctation, stricture, restriction; anchor &c. 666; restraint &c. 751 & 752; inhibition &c. 761; blockade &c. (*closure*) 261; picketing.

inter-ference, -position; obtrusion; dis-couragement, -countenance, -approval, -approbation; opposition &c. 708.

impediment, let, obstacle, obstruction, knot, knag; check, hitch, *contretemps*, *impasse*, screw loose, grit in the oil.

bar, stile, barrier; turn-stile, -pike; gate, portcullis; bulwark, parapet, barricade &c. (*defence*) 717; wall, dead wall, breakwater, groyne; bulkhead, block, buffer; stopper &c. 263; boom, dam, weir, burrock.

drawback, objection; stumbling-block, -stone; lion in the path; snag; snags and sawyers.

en-, in-cumbrance; clog, skid, shoe, spoke; brake, drag, – chain, – weight; stay, stop; preventive, prophylactic; contraception; load, burden, fardel,

707. Aid.—N. aid, -ance; assistance, help, opitulation, succour; support, lift, advance, furtherance, promotion; coadjuvancy &c. (*co-operation*) 709.

patronage, championship, countenance, favour, interest, advocacy, auspices.

sustentation, subvention, subsidy, bounty, alimentation, nutrition, nourishment, maintenance; manna in the wilderness; food &c. 298; means &c. 632.

ministr-y, -ation; subministration; accommodation.

relief, rescue; help at a dead lift; supernatural aid; *deus ex machinâ*.

supplies, reinforcements, succours, contingents, recruits; support &c. (*physical*) 215; adjunct, ally &c. (*helper*) 711.

V. aid, assist, help, succour, lend one's aid; come to the aid &c. *n.*- of; contribute, subscribe to; bring –, give –, furnish –, afford –, supply- -aid &c. *n.*; render assistance; give –, stretch –, lend –, bear –, hold out- a -hand, – helping hand; give one a -lift, – cast, – turn; take -by the hand, – in tow; help a lame dog over a stile, lend wings to.

onus, millstone round one's neck, *impedimenta*; dead weight; lumber, pack; nightmare, Ephialtes, incubus, old man of the sea; remora.

difficulty &c. 704; insuperable &c. 471- obstacle; estoppel; ill wind; head wind &c. (*opposition*) 708; trammel, tether &c. (*means of restraint*) 752; hold back, counterpoise; damper, wet blanket, hinderer, marplot, kill-joy, dog in the manger, interloper; trail of a red herring; opponent &c. 710.

V. hinder, impede, impedite, embarrass.

keep –, stave –, ward- off; picket; obviate; a-, ante-vert; turn aside, draw off, prevent, forefend, nip in the bud; retard, slacken, check, let; counter-act, -check; preclude, debar, foreclose, estop; inhibit &c. 761; shackle &c. (*restrain*) 751; restrict, restrain, cohibit.

obstruct, filibuster, stop, stay, bar, bolt, lock; block, – up; belay, barricade; block –, stop- the way; dam up &c. (*close*) 261; put on the -brake &c. *n.*; scotch –, lock –, put a spoke in- the wheel; put a stop to &c. 142; traverse, contravene; inter-rupt, -cept; oppose &c. 708; hedge -in, – round; cut off; interclude.

inter-pose, -fere, -meddle &c. 682.

cramp, hamper; clog, – the wheels; cumber; en-, in-cumber; handicap; choke; saddle –, load- with; over-load, -lay; lumber, trammel, tie one's hands, put to inconvenience; in-, discommode; discompose; hustle, drive into a corner; choke off.

run –, fall- foul of; cross the path of, break in upon.

thwart, frustrate, disconcert, balk, foil, baffle, snub, override, circumvent; defeat &c. 731; spike guns &c. (*render useless*) 645; spoil, mar, clip the wings of; cripple &c. (*injure*) 659; put an extinguisher on; damp; dishearten &c. (*dissuade*) 616; discountenance, throw cold water on, spoil sport; lay –, throw- a wet blanket on; cut the ground from under one, take the wind out of one's sails, undermine; be –, stand- in the way of; act as a drag; hang like a millstone round one's neck.

relieve, rescue; set -up, – agoing, – on one's legs; bear –, pull- through; give new life to, be the making of; reinforce, recruit; set –, put –, push- forward; give -a lift, – a shove, – an impulse- to; promote, further, forward, advance; speed, expedite, quicken, hasten.

support, sustain, uphold, prop, hold up, bolster.

cradle, nourish; nurture, nurse, dry nurse, suckle, put out to nurse; manure, cultivate, force; foster, cherish, foment; feed –, fan- the flame.

serve; do service to, tender to, pander to; ad-, sub-, minister to; tend, attend, wait on; take care of &c. 459; entertain; smooth the bed of death.

oblige, accommodate, consult the wishes of; humour, cheer, encourage.

second, stand by; back, – up; pay the piper, abet; work –, make interest –, stick up –, take up the cudgels- for; take up –, espouse –, adopt- the cause of; advocate, beat up for recruits, press into the service; squire, give moral support to, keep in countenance, countenance, patronize; lend -oneself, – one's countenance- to; smile –, shine- upon; favour, befriend, take up, take in hand, enlist under the banners of; side with &c. (*co-operate*) 709.

be of use to; subserve &c. (*instrument*) 631; benefit &c. 648; render a service &c. (*utility*) 644; conduce &c. (*tend*) 176.

Adj. aiding &c. *v.*; auxiliary, adjuvant, helpful; coadjuvant &c. 709; subservient, ministrant, ancillary, accessory, subsidiary.

at one's beck; friendly, amicable, favourable, propitious, well-disposed; neighbourly; obliging &c. (*benevolent*) 906.

Adv. with –, by- -the aid &c. *n.*- of; on –, in- behalf of; in -aid, – the service, – the name, – favour, – furtherance- of; on account of; for the sake of, on the part of; *non obstante*.

Int. help! save us! to the rescue! SOS! *à moi!*

Adj. hindering &c. *v.*; obstr-uctive, -uent; impedi-tive, -ent; intercipient; prophylactic &c. (*remedial*) 662.

in the way of, unfavourable; onerous, burdensome; cumb-rous, -ersome; obtrusive.

hindered &c. *v.*; wind-bound, water-logged, heavy laden; hard pressed.

unassisted &c. (*see* assist &c. 707); single-handed, alone; deserted &c. 624.

708. Opposition.—**N.** opposition, antagonism; oppug-nancy, -nation; impugnation; contravention; counteraction &c. 179; counterplot, obstacle.

cross-fire, under-current, head-wind.

clashing, collision, conflict, lack of harmony, contest.

competition, two of a trade, rivalry, emulation, race; war to the knife.

absence of -aid &c. 707; resistance &c. 719; restraint &c. 751; hindrance &c. 706.

V. oppose, counteract, run counter to; withstand &c. (*resist*) 719; control &c. (*restrain*) 751; hinder &c. 706; antagonize, oppugn, fly in the face of, go dead against, kick against, fall foul of; set –, pit- against; face, confront, cope with; make a -stand, – dead set- against; set -oneself, one's face- against; protest –, vote –, raise one's voice- against; disfavour, turn one's back upon; set at naught, slap in the face, slam the door in one's face.

be –, play- at cross purposes; counter-work, -mine; thwart, overthwart.

stem, breast, encounter; stem –, breast- the -tide, – current, – flood; buffet the waves; beat up –, make head- against; grapple with; kick against the pricks &c. (*resist*) 719; contend &c. 720 –, do battle &c. (*warfare*) 722- -with, – against.

contra-dict, -vene; belie; go –, run –, beat –, militate- against; come in conflict with.

emulate &c. (*compete*) 720; rival, spoil one's trade.

Adj. oppos-ing, -ed &c. *v.*; adverse, antagonistic; ambivalent; contrary &c. 14; at variance &c. 24; at issue, at war with; in opposition; 'agin the Government.'

un-favourable, -friendly; hostile, inimical, cross, unpropitious.

709. Co-operation.—**N.** co-operation; coadju-vancy, -tancy; coagency, co-efficiency; concert, concurrence, complicity, participation; union &c. 43; amalgamation, combination &c. 48; collusion.

association, alliance, colleagueship, jointstock, copartnership, trust, cartel, pool, ring, combine, interlocking directorate; confederation &c. (*party*) 712; federation, coalition, fusion; a long pull, a strong pull and a pull all together; log-rolling, Freemasonry.

unanimity &c. (*assent*) 488; *esprit de corps*, party spirit; clan-, partisan-ship; reciprocity, concord &c. 714.

V. co-operate, co-adjute, concur; conduce &c. 178; combine, cartelize, unite one's efforts; keep –, draw –, pull –, club –, hang –, hold –, league –, band –, be banded- together; stand –, put- shoulder to shoulder; act in concert, join forces, fraternize, cling to one another, conspire, concert, lay one's heads together; confederate, be in league with; collude, understand one another, play into the hands of, hunt in couples.

side –, take side –, go along –, go hand in hand –, join hands –, make common cause –, strike in –, unite –, join –, mix oneself up –, take part –, play along –, cast in one's lot- with; join –, enter into- partnership with; rally round, follow the lead of; come to, pass over to, come into the views of; be –, row –, sail- in the same boat; sail on the same tack.

be a party to, lend oneself to; participate; have a -hand in, – finger in the pie; take –, bear- part in; second &c. (*aid*) 707; take the part of, play the game of; espouse a -cause, – quarrel.

Adj. co-operating &c. *v.*; in -co-operation &c. *n.*, – league &c. (*party*) 712;

in hostile array, front to front, with crossed bayonets, at daggers drawn; up in arms; resistant &c. 719.

competitive, emulous.

Adv. against, *versus*, counter to, in conflict with, at cross purposes.

against the -grain, - current, - stream, - wind, - tide; with a head-wind; with the wind -ahead, - in one's teeth.

in spite, in despite, in defiance; in the -way, - teeth, - face- of; across; a-, over-thwart; where the shoe pinches.

though &c. 30; even; *quand même*; *per contra*.

Phr. *nitor in adversum*.

coadju-vant, -tant; hand and glove with.

favourable &c. 707- to; un-opposed &c. 708.

Adv. as one man &c. (*unanimously*) 488; shoulder to shoulder; in co-operation with.

---

710. Opponent.—N. opponent, antagonist, adversary; adverse party, opposition; enemy &c. 891; assailant.

oppositionist, obstructive; obscurantist; brawler, wrangler, brangler, disputant, extremist, irreconcilable, die-hard, bitter-ender.

malcontent; Jacobin, Fenian &c. 742; demagogue, reactionist.

passive resister, conscientious objector.

rival, competitor, contestant.

---

711. Auxiliary.—N. auxiliary; recruit; assistant; adju-vant, -tant; adjunct; help, -er, -mate, -ing hand; midwife; colleague, partner, mate, *confrère*, co-operator; coadju-tor, -trix; collaborator.

ally; friend &c. 890, confidant, *fidus Achates*, pal, chum, buddy, *alter ego*.

confederate; ac-, complice; accessory, - after the fact; *particeps criminis*.

aide-de-camp, secretary, clerk, associate, marshal; right-hand; candle-, bottle-holder; hand-maid; servant &c. 746; puppet, cat's-paw, stooge, dependent, creature, jackal; tool, *âme damnée*; satellite, adherent, parasite.

votary, disciple; secta-rian, -ry; seconder, backer, upholder, supporter, abettor, advocate, partisan, champion, patron, friend at court, mediator.

friend in need, Jack at a pinch, *deus ex machinâ*, guardian angel, fairy godmother; special providence, tutelary genius.

712. Party.—N. party, faction, side, denomination, class, communion, set, crowd, crew, band, horde, posse, phalanx; regiment &c. 726; family, clan &c. 166.

Tories, Conservatives, Unionists, Whigs, Liberals, Radicals, Labour party, Socialists, Communists &c.; Republicans, Democrats, Farmer-Labor; *Fascisti*, Revolutionaries &c. 742.

community, body, fellowship, sodality, solidarity; con-, fraternity; sorority; brother-, sister-hood.

Freemasons, Knights Templars, Odd Fellows, Ku Klux Klan &c.

knot, gang, *clique*, ring, circle; *coterie*, club, *casino*.

corporation, corporate body, guild; establishment, company; co-partnership; firm, house; joint concern, joint-stock company, trust, investment trust, combine &c. 709.

society, association; instit-ute, -ution; union; trade-union; league, syndicate, alliance, *Verein*, *Bund*, *Zollverein*, combination; league -, alliance- offensive and defensive; coalition; federation; confedera -tion, -cy; junto, cabal, *camarilla*, *Camorra*, *brigue*; Freemasonry; party spirit &c. (*co-operation*) 709.

staff; cast, *dramatis personæ*.

V. unite, join; club together &c. (*co-operate*) 709; cement –, form- a party &c. *n.*; associate &c. (*assemble*) 72.

Adj. in -league, – partnership, – alliance &c. *n.*

bonded –, banded –, linked &c. (*joined*) 43- together; embattled; confederated, federative, joint, corporate, leagued, fraternal, Masonic, cliquish.

Adv. hand in hand, side by side, shoulder to shoulder, *en masse*, in the same boat.

713. Discord.—N. disagreement &c. 24; dis-cord, -accord, -sidence, -sonance; jar, clash, shock; jarring, jostling &c. *v.*; screw loose.

variance, difference, dissension, misunderstanding, cross purposes, odds, *brouillerie*; division, split, rupture, disruption, division in the camp, house divided against itself, rift within the lute; disunion, breach; schism &c. (*dissent*) 489; feud, faction.

quarrel, dispute, rippet, spat, tiff, *tracasserie*, squabble, altercation, words, high words; wrangling &c. *v.*; jangle, brabble, cross questions and crooked answers, snip-snap; family jars.

polemics; litigation; strife &c. (*contention*) 720; warfare &c. 722; outbreak, open rupture; breaking off of negotiations, recall of ambassadors; declaration of war.

broil, brawl, row, racket, hubbub, rixation; embroilment, embranglement, *imbroglio*, *fracas*, breach of the peace, piece of work, scrimmage, rumpus; breeze, squall; riot, disturbance &c. (*disorder*) 59; commotion &c. (*agitation*) 315; bear garden, Donnybrook Fair.

subject of dispute, ground of quarrel, battle ground, disputed point; bone -of contention, – to pick; apple of discord, *casus belli*; question at issue &c. (*subject of inquiry*) 461; vexed question, *vexata quæstio*, brand of discord.

troublous times; cat-and-dog life; contentiousness &c. *adj.*; enmity &c. 889; hate &c. 898; Kilkenny cats; disputant &c. 710; strange bedfellows.

V. be -discordant &c. *adj.*; disagree, come amiss &c. 24; clash, jar, jostle, pull different ways, conflict, have no measures with, misunderstand one another; live like cat and dog; differ; dissent &c. 489; have a -bone to pick, – crow to pluck- with.

fall out, quarrel, dispute; litigate; controvert &c. (*deny*) 536;

714. Concord.—N. concord, accord, harmony, symphony, homology; agreement &c. 23; sympathy &c. (*love*) 897; response; union, unison, unity; bonds of harmony; peace &c. 721; unanimity &c. (*assent*) 488; league &c. 712; happy family.

rapprochement; *réunion*; amity &c. (*friendship*) 888; reciprocity; alliance, *entente cordiale*, good understanding, conciliation, arbitration, peacemaker &c. 724.

V. agree &c. 23; accord, harmonize with; fraternize; be -concordant &c. *adj.*; go hand in hand; blend –, tone in- with; run parallel &c. (*concur*) 178; understand one another; pull together &c. (*co-operate*) 709; put up one's horses together, sing in chorus.

side –, sympathize –, go –, chime in –, fall in- with; come round; be pacified &c. 723; assent &c. 488; enter into the -ideas, – feelings- of; reciprocate.

hurler avec les loups; go –, swim- with the stream.

pour oil on troubled waters, keep in good humour, render accordant, put in tune; come to an understanding, meet half-way; keep the –, remain at- peace.

Adj. concordant, congenial; agreeing &c. *v.*; in- accord &c. *n.*; harmonious, united, cemented; banded together &c. 712; allied; friendly &c. 888; fraternal; conciliatory; at one with; of one mind &c. (*assent*) 488.

at peace, in still water; tranquil &c. (*pacific*) 721.

Adv. with one voice &c. (*assent*) 488; in concert with, hand in hand; on one's side, unanimously.

squabble, wrangle, jangle, brangle, bicker, nag; spar &c. (*contend*) 720; have -words &c. *n.* with; fall foul of.

split; break –, break squares –, part company- with; declare war, try conclusions; join –, put in- issue; pick a quarrel, fasten a quarrel on; sow –, stir up- -dissension &c. *n.*; embroil, estrange, entangle, disunite, widen the breach; set -at odds, – together by the ears; set –, pit- against; rub up the wrong way.

get into hot water, fish in troubled waters, brawl; kick up a -row, – dust; turn the house out of window.

Adj. discordant; disagreeing &c. *v.*; out of tune, dissonant, inharmonious, harsh, grating, jangling, ajar, on bad terms; dissentient &c. 489; inconsistent, contradictory, incongruous, discrepant; un- -reconciled, -pacified.

quarrelsome, unpacific; gladiatorial, controversial, polemic, disputatious; factious; liti-gious, -gant; pettifogging.

at odds, at loggerheads, at daggers drawn, at variance, at issue, at cross purposes, at sixes and sevens, at feud, at high words; up in arms, together by the ears, in hot water, embroiled.

torn, disunited.

Phr. *quot homines tot sententiæ*; no love lost between them, *non nostrum tantas componere lites*.

715. Defiance.—N. defiance; daring &c. *v.*; dare, challenge, *cartel*; threat &c. 909; war-cry, -whoop.

V. defy, dare, beard; brave &c. (*courage*) 861; bid defiance to; set at -defiance, – naught; hurl defiance at; dance the war dance; snap the fingers at, laugh to scorn; disobey &c. 742.

show -fight, – one's teeth, – a bold front; bluster, look big, stand akimbo; double –, shake- the fist; threaten &c. 909.

challenge, call out; throw –, fling- down the -gauntlet, – gage, – glove.

Adj. defiant; defying &c. *v.*; with arms akimbo; rebellious, insolent; reckless, greatly daring.

Adv. in -defiance, – the teeth- of; under one's very nose.

Int. do your worst! come if you dare! come on! marry come up! hoity toity!

Phr. *noli me tangere*; *nemo me impune lacessit*.

716. Attack.—N. attack; assault, – and battery; onset, onslaught, charge.

aggression, drive, offence; incursion, inroad, invasion; irruption; outbreak; *estrapade*, *ruade*; *coup de main*, sally, *sortie*, *camisade*, raid, foray; run -at, – against; dead set at.

storm, -ing; boarding, *escalade*; siege, investment, obsession, bombardment, cannonade; air raid.

fire, volley; platoon –, file –, rapid-fire; *fusillade*; sharp-shooting, sniping; broadside; raking –, cross –, machine gun- fire; volley of grapeshot, *feu d'enfer*; salvo.

cut, thrust, lunge, pass, *passado*, *carte* and *tierce*, home thrust; *coup de pied*; kick, punch &c. (*impulse*) 276.

717. Defence.—N. defence, protection, guard, ward; shielding &c. *v.*; propugnation; preservation &c. 670; guardianship.

self-defence, -preservation; resistance &c. 719.

safeguard &c. (*safety*) 664; screen &c. (*shelter*) 666, (*concealment*) 530; barrage; fortification; muni-tion, -ment; bulwark, fosse, moat, ditch, intrenchment, trench, dugout, gas mask; dike, dyke; parapet, parados, sunk fence, embankment, mound, mole, bank; earth- field-work, gabions; fence, wall, dead wall, contravallation; paling &c. (*inclosure*) 232; palisade, ha-ha, stockade, *stoccado*, *laager*, *sangar*; barri-er, -cade; boom; portcullis, *chevaux de*

battue, razzia, Jacquerie, dragonnade; devastation &c. 162.

assailant, aggressor, invader.

base of operations, point of attack.

V. attack, assault, assail; set –, fall- upon; charge, impugn, break a lance with, enter the lists.

assume –, take- the offensive; be –, become- the aggressor; strike the first blow, fire the first shot, throw the first stone at; lift a hand –, draw the sword- against; take up the cudgels; advance –, march- against; march upon, invade, harry; come on, show fight.

strike at, poke at, thrust at; aim –, deal- a blow at; give –, fetch- one a -blow, – kick; have a -cut, – shot, – fling, – shy- at; be down –, pounce- upon; fall foul of, pitch into, launch out against; bait, slap on the face; make a -thrust, – pass, – set, – dead set- at; dunt; bear down upon.

close with, come to close quarters, bring to bay.

ride full tilt against; let fly at, dash at, run a tilt at, rush at, tilt at, run at, fly at, hawk at, have at, let out at; make a -dash, – rush at; attack tooth and nail; strike home; drive –, press- one hard; be hard upon, run down, strike at the root of.

lay about one, run amuck.

fire -upon, – at, – a shot at; shoot at, pop at, level at, let off a gun at; open fire, pepper, bombard, shell, pour a broadside into; fire -a volley, – red-hot shot; spring a mine.

throw -a stone, – stones- at; stone, lapidate, pelt; hurl -at, – against, – at the head of.

beset, besiege, beleaguer; lay siege to, invest, open the trenches, plant a battery, sap, mine; storm, board, scale the walls.

cut and thrust, bayonet, butt; kick, strike &c. (*impulse*) 276; whip &c. (*punish*) 972.

Adj. attacking &c. *v.*; aggressive, offensive, obsidional.

up in arms; on the warpath; over the top.

Adv. on the offensive.

Int. 'up and at them!'

---

frise; aba-, abat-, abba-tis; *vallum*, circumvallation, battlement, rampart, scarp; e-, counter-scarp; glacis, casemate, obstacle.

mine, countermine.

buttress, abutment; shore &c. (*support*) 215.

breastwork, *banquette*, curtain, mantlet, bastion, demilune, redan, ravelin; advanced –, horn –, out- work, lunette; barb-acan, -ican; redoubt; fort-elage, -alice; lines; coast defence.

loop-hole, machicolation; sally-port, postern gate.

hold, stronghold, fastness; asylum &c. (*refuge*) 666; keep, donjon, fortress, citadel; capitol, castle; tower, – of strength; fort, barracoon, pah, sconce, martello tower, peel-house, block-house, rath; wooden walls; turret, barbette.

buffer, corner-stone, fender, apron, mask, gauntlet, thimble, carapace, armour, shield, buckler; target, targe, ægis, breastplate, cuirass, plastron, habergeon, mail, coat of mail, brigandine, hauberk, lorication, helmet, helm, basinet, sallet, salade, heaume, morion, murrion, armet, cabaset, vizor, casquetel, siege-cap, head-piece, casque, steel helmet, tin hat; *Pickelhaube*, csako; shako &c. (*dress*) 225; bearskin; panoply; truncheon &c. (*weapon*) 727.

garrison, picket, piquet; defender, protector; guardian &c. (*safety*) 664; trabant, body guard, champion; knight-errant, Paladin; propugner.

V. defend, forfend, fend; shield, screen, shroud; fence round &c. (*circumscribe*) 229; fence, intrench; guard &c. (*keep safe*) 664; guard against; take care of &c. (*vigilance*) 459; bear harmless; keep –, ward –, beat- off; hinder &c. 706.

parry, repel, propugn, put to flight; give a warm reception to [*ironical*]; hold –, keep- at -bay, – arm's length.

stand –, act- on the defensive; show fight; maintain –, stand- one's ground; stand by; hold one's own; bear –, stand- the brunt; fall back upon, hold, stand in the gap.

Adj. defending &c. *v.*; defensive; mural; armed, – at all points, – *cap-à-pie*, – to the teeth; panoplied, accoutred, harnessed; iron-plated, -clad; loop-holed, castellated, machicolated, casemated; defended &c. *v.*; proof against, bomb-, bullet-proof; protective.

Adv. defensively; on the -defence, – defensive; in defence; at bay, *pro aris et focis.*

Int. no surrender! *ils ne passeront pas!*

Phr. defence not defiance.

718. Retaliation. — N. retaliation, reprisal, retort; counter-stroke, -blast, -plot, -project; retribution, *lex talionis*; reciprocation &c. (*reciprocity*) 12.

requital, desert, tit for tat, give and take, blow for blow, *quid pro quo*, a Roland for an Oliver, measure for measure, an eye for an eye, diamond cut diamond, the biter bit, a game at which two can play; boomerang.

recrimination &c. (*accusation*) 938; revenge &c. 919; compensation &c. 30; reaction &c. (*recoil*) 277.

V. retaliate, retort, turn upon; pay -off, – back; pay in -one's own, – the same- coin; cap; reciprocate &c. 148; turn the tables upon, return the compliment; give -a *quid pro quo* &c. *n.*, – as much as one takes; give and take, exchange -blows, – fisticuffs; be -quits, – even- with; pay off old scores.

serve one right, be hoist on one's own petard, throw a stone in one's own garden, catch a Tartar.

Adj. retaliating &c. *v.*; retalia-tory, -tive; retributive, recriminatory, reciprocal.

Adv. in retaliation; *en revanche.*

Phr. *mutato nomine de te fabula narratur*; *par pari refero*; *tu quoque*; you're another; *suo sibi gladio hunc jugulo.*

719. Resistance. — N. resistance, stand, front, oppugnation; opposition &c. 708; renitence, reluctation, recalcitration, recalcitrance; repugnance; kicking &c. *v.*

repulse, rebuff.

insurrection &c. (*disobedience*) 742; strike; turn –, lock –, barring- out; *levée en masse, Jacquerie*; riot &c. (*disorder*) 59.

V. resist; not -submit &c. 725; repugn, reluctate, withstand; stand up –, strive –, bear up –, be proof –, make head- against; stand, – firm, – one's ground, – the brunt of, – out; hold -one's ground, – one's own, – out.

breast the -wave, – current; stem the -tide, – torrent; face, confront, grapple with; show a bold front &c. (*courage*) 861; present a front; make a –, take one's- stand.

kick, – against; recalcitrate, kick against the pricks; oppose &c. 708; fly in the face of; lift the hand against &c. (*attack*) 716; rise up in arms &c. (*war*) 722; strike, turn out; draw up a round robin &c. (*remonstrate*) 932; revolt &c. (*disobey*) 742; make a riot.

prendre le mors aux dents; take the bit between the teeth; sell one's life dearly, die hard, keep at bay; repel, repulse.

Adj. resisting &c. *v.*; resist-ive, -ant; refractory &c. (*disobedient*) 742; recalcitrant, re-nitent, -pulsive, -pellant; up in arms.

proof against; unconquerable &c. (*strong*) 159; stubborn, unconquered; indomitable &c. (*persevering*) 604*a*; unyielding &c. (*obstinate*) 606.

Int. hands off! keep off!

720. Contention. — N. contention, strife; contest, -ation; struggle; belligerency; opposition &c. 708.

controversy, polemics; debate &c. (*discussion*) 476; war of words, logomachy, litigation; paper war, ink slinging; high words &c. (*quarrel*) 713; sparring &c. *v.*

721. Peace.—N. peace; amity &c. (*friendship*) 888; harmony &c. (*concord*) 714; tranquillity &c. (*quiescence*) 265; truce &c. (*pacification*) 723; pacificism; pipe –, calumet- of peace.

piping time of peace, quiet life; neutrality.

V. be at peace; keep the peace &c.

competition, rivalry; corrival-ry, -ship; agonism, *concours*, match, race, horse-racing, heat, steeple chase, point-to-point race, handicap; boat race, regatta; field-day; sham fight, Derby day; turf, sporting, bull-fight, tauromachy, *gymkhana*, rodeo, Olympiad.

wrestling, *ju-jitsu*, pugilism, boxing, fisticuffs, spar, mill, set-to, scrap, round, bout, event; prize-fighting; quarter-staff, single stick; gladiatorship, gymnastics; athletic-s, – sports; games of skill &c. 840.

shindy; *fracas* &c. (*discord*) 713; clash of arms; tussle, scuffle, broil, fray; affray, -ment; velitation; col-, luctation; brabble, *brigue*, scramble, *mêlée*, scrimmage, stramash, bush-fighting.

free –, stand up –, hand to hand –, running- fight.

conflict, skirmish; ren-, en-counter; *rencontre*, collision, affair, brush, fight; battle, – royal; combat, action, engagement, joust, tournament; tilt, -ing; tourney, list; pitched battle, guerilla warfare.

death-struggle, struggle for life or death, Armageddon; hard knocks, sharp contest, tug of war.

naval -engagement, – battle; *naumachia*, sea-fight.

duel, -lo; single combat, monomachy, satisfaction, *passage d'armes*, passage of arms, affair of honour; triangular duel; hostile meeting, digladiation; appeal to arms &c. (*warfare*) 722.

deeds –, feats- of arms; pugnacity; combativeness &c. *adj.*; bone of contention &c. 713.

V. contend; contest, strive, struggle, scramble, wrestle; spar, square; exchange -blows, – fisticuffs; scrap, mix with, fib, justle, tussle, tilt, box, stave, fence; skirmish; fight &c. (*war*) 722; wrangle &c. (*quarrel*) 713.

contend &c. –, grapple –, engage –, close –, buckle –, bandy –, try conclusions –, have a brush &c. *n.* –, tilt- with; encounter, fall foul of, pitch into, clapperclaw, run a tilt at; oppose &c. 708; reluct.

join issue, come to blows, be at loggerheads, set-to, come to the scratch, exchange shots, measure swords, meet hand to hand; take up the -cudgels, – glove, – gauntlet; enter the lists; couch one's lance; give satisfaction; appeal to arms &c. (*warfare*) 722.

lay about one; break the peace.

compete –, cope –, vie –, race- with; outvie, emulate, rival; run a race; contend &c. –, stipulate –, stickle- for; insist upon, make a point of.

Adj. contending &c. *v.*; together by the ears, at loggerheads, at war, at issue.

competitive, rival; belligerent; contentious, combative, bellicose, unpeaceful; warlike &c. 722; quarrelsome &c. 901; pugnacious; pugilistic, gladiatorial; palestric, -al; irenic.

Phr. *a verbis ad verbera*; a word and a blow

(*concord*) 714; make peace &c. 723.

Adj. pacific; peace-able, -ful; calm, tranquil, untroubled, halcyon; bloodless; neutral.

Phr. the storm blown over; the lion lies down with the lamb.

---

722. Warfare.—N. warfare; fighting &c. *v.*; hostilities; war, arms, the sword; Mars, Bellona, grim visaged war, *horrida bella*, Armageddon.

appeal to -arms, – the sword; ordeal

723. Pacification.—N. pacification, conciliation; reconcil-iation, -ement; shaking of hands, accommodation, arrangement, adjustment; terms, compromise; amnesty, deed of release.

–, wager- of battle; *ultima ratio regum*, arbitrament of the sword.

battle array, campaign, crusade, expedition; mobilization; state of siege; battle-field &c. (*arena*) 728; warpath.

art of war, tactics, strategy, castrametation; general-, soldier-ship; aerial –, submarine –, naval –, chemical- warfare; military evolutions, ballistics, gunnery; chivalry; poison gas; gunpowder, shot, – and shell.

battle, tug of war &c. (*contention*) 720; service, campaigning, active service, tented field; fiery cross, trumpet, clarion, bugle, pibroch, slogan; war-cry, -whoop; battle cry, beat of drum, rappel, tom-tom; word of command; pass-, watch-word.

war to the -death, – knife; *guerre à -mort, – outrance*; open –, internecine –, civil- war.

V. arm; raise –, mobilize- troops; rise up in arms; take up the cudgels &c. 720; take up –, fly to –, appeal to- -arms, – the sword; draw –, unsheathe- the sword; dig up the hatchet; go to –, declare –, wage –, let slip the dogs of- war; cry havoc; kindle –, light- the torch of war; raise one's banner, send round the fiery cross; hoist the black flag; throw –, fling- away the scabbard; enrol, enlist, join up; take the field; take the law into one's own hands; do –, give –, join –, engage in –, go to- battle; flesh one's sword; set to, fall to, engage, measure swords with, draw the trigger, cross swords; come to -blows, – close quarters; fight; combat; contend &c. 720; battle –, break a lance- with.

serve; see –, be on- -service, – active service; campaign; wield the sword, shoulder a musket, smell powder, be under the fire; spill –, imbrue the hands in- blood; be on the warpath.

carry on -war, – hostilities; keep the field; fight the good fight; go over the top; cut one's way through; fight -it out, – like devils, – one's way, – hand to hand; sell one's life dearly.

Adj. conten-ding, -tious &c. 720; armed, – to the teeth, – cap-à-pie; sword in hand; in –, under –, up in- arms; at war with; bristling with arms; in -battle array, – open arms, – the field; embattled.

unpacific, unpeaceful; belligerent, combative, armigerous, bellicose, martial, warlike; mili-tary, -tant; soldier-like, -ly; chivalrous; strategical, internecine.

Adv. *flagrante bello*, in the -thick of the fray, – cannon's mouth; at the -sword's point, – point of the bayonet.

Int. *væ victis!* to arms! to your tents O Israel!

Phr. the battle rages.

peace-offering; olive-branch; overtures; pipe –, calumet –, preliminaries- of peace.

truce, armistice; suspension of -arms, – hostilities; breathing-time; convention; *modus vivendi*; flag of truce, white flag, *parlementaire, cartel.*

hollow truce, *pax in bello*; drawn battle.

V. pacify, tranquillize, compose; allay &c. (*moderate*) 174; reconcile, propitiate, placate, conciliate, meet half-way, hold out the olive-branch, heal the breach, make peace, restore harmony, bring to terms.

settle –, arrange –, accommodate- -matters, – differences; set straight; make up a quarrel, *tantas componere lites*; come to -an understanding, – terms; bridge over, hush up; make -it, – matters- up; shake hands.

raise a siege; put up –, sheathe- the sword; bury the hatchet, lay down one's arms, turn swords into ploughshares; smoke the calumet of peace, close the temple of Janus; keep the peace &c. (*concord*) 714; be -pacified &c.; come round.

Adj. conciliatory, pacificatory; composing &c. *v.*; pacified &c. *v.*

Phr. *requiescat in pace.*

---

724. Mediation.—**N.** media-tion, -torship, -tization; inter-vention, -position, -ference, -meddling, -cession; parley, negotiation, arbitration; flag of truce &c. 723; good offices, peace-offering; diploma-tics, -cy; compromise &c. 774.

mediator, intercessor, peacemaker, make-peace, negotiator, go-between; diplomatist &c. (*consignee*) 758; moderator, propitiator, umpire, arbitrator.

V. media-te, -tize; inter-cede, -pose, -fere, -vene; step in, negotiate; meet half-way; arbitrate; *magnas componere lites.*

Adj. mediatory, propitiatory, diplomatic.

725. Submission.—**N.** submission, yielding, acquiescence, compliance; non-resistance; obedience &c. 743; submissiveness, deference.

surrender, cession, capitulation, resignation.

obeisance, homage, kneeling, genuflexion, courtesy, curtsy, *salaam, kowtow,* prostration.

V. succumb, submit, yield, bend, resign, defer to, accede.

lay down –, deliver up- one's arms; hand over one's sword; lower –, haul down –, strike- one's flag, – colours; deliver the keys of the city;

surrender, – at discretion; cede, capitulate, come to terms, retreat, beat a retreat; draw in one's horns &c. (*humility*) 879; give -way, – ground, – in, – up; cave in; suffer judgment by default; bend, – to one's yoke, – before the storm; reel back; bend –, knuckle- -down, – to, – under; knock under.

humble oneself; eat -dirt, – the leek, – humble pie; bite –, lick- the dust; be –, fall- at one's feet; craven; crouch before, throw oneself at the feet of; swallow the -leek, – pill; kiss the rod; turn the other cheek; *avaler des couleuvres,* gulp down.

obey &c. 743; kneel to, bow to, pay homage to, cringe to, truckle to; bend the -neck, – knee; kneel, fall on one's knees, bow submission, courtesy, curtsy, *kowtow;* make obeisance.

pocket the affront; make -the best of, – a virtue of necessity; grin and abide, shrug the shoulders, resign oneself; submit with a good grace &c. (*bear with*) 826.

Adj. surrendering &c. *v.*; submissive, resigned, crouching; down-trodden; down on one's marrow bones; on one's bended knee; weak-kneed, un-, non-resisting; pliant &c. (*soft*) 324; undefended.

untenable, indefensible; humble &c. 879.

Phr. have it your own way; it can't be helped; amen &c. (*assent*) 488.

726. Combatant.—**N.** combatant; disputant, controversialist, polemic, litigant, belligerent; competitor, rival, corrival; fighter, assailant, aggressor; champion, Paladin; moss-trooper, swashbuckler, fire-eater, duellist, bully, bludgeon-man, rough, fighter, fighting-man, prize-fighter, pugilist, pug, boxer, bruiser, the fancy, gladiator, athlete, wrestler; fighting-, game-cock; swordsman, *sabreur.*

warrior, soldier, Amazon, man-at-arms, armigerent; campaigner, veteran; red-coat, military man, *rajpoot,* brave.

armed force, troops, soldiery, military, forces, sabaoth, the army, standing army, regulars, the line, troops of the line, militia, territorials, yeomanry, volunteers, trainband, fencible; auxiliary –, reserve- forces; reserves, *posse comitatus,* national guard, *gendarme,* beefeater; guards, -man; yeoman of the guard, life guards, household troops.

janissary; myrmidon; Mama-, Mame-luke; spahee, *spahi,* Cossack,

Croat, Pandour; irregular, free lance, *franc-tireur*, *bashi-bazouk*, *guerilla*, *condottiere*; mercenary.

levy, draught, commando; *Land-wehr*, *-sturm*; conscript, recruit, rookie, cadet, raw levies.

private, – soldier; Tommy Atkins, rank and file, peon, trooper, doughboy, sepoy, *askari*, *légionnaire*, legionary, food for powder, cannon fodder; officer &c. (*commander*) 745; subaltern, ensign, shave-tail, standard bearer, non-com; spear-, pike-man; halberdier, lancer; musketeer, carabineer, rifleman, sharpshooter, yager, skirmisher; grenadier, fusileer; archer, bowman.

horse and foot; horse –, foot- soldier; cavalry, horse, artillery, horse –, field –, heavy –, mountain- artillery, infantry, light horse, *voltigeur*, *Uhlan*, mounted rifles, dragoon, hussar, trooper; light –, heavy-dragoon; heavy; *cuirassier*; gunner, cannoneer, bombardier, artilleryman, matross; sapper, – and miner; engineer; light infantry, rifles, *chasseur*, *zouave*; military train, supply and transport, coolie.

army, – corps, *corps d'armée*, host, division, column, wing, detachment, *escadrille*, garrison, flying column, brigade, regiment, *corps*, battalion, squadron, company, platoon, battery, subdivision, section, squad; piquet, picket, guard, rank, file; legion, phalanx, cohort; cloud of skirmishers; impi.

war-horse, charger, *destrier*.

armoured -train, – car; tank.

marine, man of war's man &c. (*sailor*) 269; navy, first line of defence, wooden walls; naval forces, fleet, flotilla, armada, squadron.

man-of-war, warship; H.M.S., U.S.S.; capital ship; line-of-battle ship, battle ship; super-, dreadnought, battle –, armoured –, protected – light- cruiser; scout, flotilla leader; destroyer, torpedo boat; submarine, submersible, U-boat; submarine chaser, eagle boat, mystery ship, Q-boat; mine-layer, -sweeper; ship of the line, iron-clad, turret-ship, ram, Monitor, floating battery; first-rate, frigate, sloop of war, corvette, gunboat, bomb-vessel, fire-boat; flag ship, guard ship, cruiser; aircraft carrier; privateer; tender; depot –, parent- ship; store –, troop- ship; transport, catamaran.

aircraft &c. 273, air force, scout, fighter, bomber, troop carrier, aerial patrol, seaplane, flying boat, torpedo plane; airship, Zeppelin; rigid –, semi-rigid –, non-rigid- airship; dirigible –, free –, captive –, kite –, observation- balloon.

anti-aircraft guns, searchlights, sound locators; catapult.

727. Arms.—N. arm, -s; weapon, deadly weapon; arma-ment, -ture; panoply, stand of arms; armour &c. (*defence*) 717; armoury &c. (*store*) 636.

ammunition; powder, – and shot; explosive; propellant; gun-powder, -cotton; dynam-, melin-, cord-, lydd-ite; trinitrotoluene, T.N.T., ammonal; cartridge; ball cartridge, *cartouche*, fire-ball; dud, black Maria; 'villainous saltpetre'; poison –, mustard –, lachrymatory –, tear- gas.

sword, sabre, broadsword, cutlass, falchion, scimitar, cimeter, brand, whinyard, bilbo, glaive, glave, rapier, skean, Toledo, Ferrara, tuck, claymore, creese, kris, *kukri*, dagger, dirk, hanger, poniard, stiletto, stylet, dudgeon, bayonet; sword-bayonet, -stick; side arms, foil, blade, steel; axe, bill; pole-, battle-axe; gisarm, halberd, partisan, tomahawk, bowie-knife; at-, att-, yat-aghan; yatachan; good –, trusty –, naked-sword; cold –, naked- steel.

club, mace, truncheon, staff, bludgeon, cudgel, life-preserver, shillelagh, sprig; hand-, quarter-staff; bat, cane, stick, knuckle-duster, sand bag.

gun, piece; fire-arms; artillery, ordnance; siege –, battering-train; park, battery; cannon, gun of position, heavy –, siege –, field –, mountain –, anti-aircraft –, breech loading –, quick firing- gun; field piece, mortar, trench mortar, mine thrower, howitzer, carronade, culverin, basilisk; falconet, jingal, swivel, *pederero*, *bouche à feu*; smooth bore, rifled cannon; Armstrong –, Lancaster –, Paixhan –, Whitworth –, Parrott –, Krupp –, Gatling –, Maxim –, Vickers –, Hotchkiss –, Lewis –, machine- gun; tommy gun, Thompson submachine gun; *mitrailleu-r*, *-se*; pom-pom; blow pipe.

small arms; musket, -ry, firelock, flintlock, fowling-piece, shot gun, rifle, *fusil*, caliver, carbine, blunderbuss, musketoon, Brown Bess, matchlock, harquebuss, *arquebuse*, haguebut; petronel; smallbore; breech-, muzzle-loader; Minié –, Enfield –, Westley Richards –, Snider –, Springfield –, Martini-Henry –, Lee-Metford –, Lee-Enfield –, Mauser –, Männlicher –, magazine –, repeating- rifle; needle-gun, *chassepot*; pistol, -et; revolver, automatic pistol, automatic; wind-, air-gun; flame –, gas-projector.

bow, cross-bow, arbalest, balister, catapult, sling; battering-ram &c. (*impulse*) 276; gunnery; ballistics &c. (*propulsion*) 284.

missile, bolt, projectile, shot, pellet, ball; grape; grape –, canister –, bar –, cannon –, langrel –, langrage –, round –, chain- shot; explosive; incendiary –, expanding –, soft-nosed –, dum-dum- bullet; slug, stone, brickbat; hand –, rifle- grenade; high explosive –, incendiary –, star –, gas- shell; depth –, gas –, incendiary –, stink- bomb; petard, torpedo, carcass, rocket; congreve, – rocket; shrapnel, *mitraille*; thunderbolt; mine, land mine, infernal machine.

pike, lance, spear, spontoon, javelin, assagai, throwing stick, dart, djerrid, arrow, reed, shaft, bolt, boomerang, harpoon, gaff.

728. Arena.—N. arena, field, platform; scene of action, theatre; walk, course; hustings; stage, boards &c. (*playhouse*) 599; amphitheatre; Coli-, Colos-seum; Flavian amphitheatre, hippodrome, circus, race-course, track, *stadium*, *corso*, turf, cockpit, bear-garden, playground, playing fields, *gymnasium*, *palæstra*, ring, lists; tilt-yard, -ing ground; *Campus Martius*, *Champ de Mars*; aerodrome, airport, air base, flying field.

theatre –, seat- of war; battle-field, -ground; field of -battle, – slaughter; no man's land; Aceldama, camp; the enemy's camp; trysting-place &c. (*place of meeting*) 74.

Section V. Results of Voluntary Action

729. Completion.—N. completion; accomplish-, achieve-, fulfil-ment; performance, execution; des-, dis-patch; consummation, culmination, climax; finish, conclusion, effectuation; close &c. (*end*) 67; terminus &c. (*arrival*) 292; winding up; *finale*, *dénouement*, catastrophe, issue, upshot, result; final –, last –, crowning –, finishing- -touch, – stroke; last finish, *coup de grâce*;

730. Non-Completion.—N. non-completion, -fulfilment; shortcoming &c. 304; incompleteness &c. 53; drawn -battle, – game; work of Penelope, task of Sisyphus.

non-performance, inexecution; neglect &c. 460.

V. not -complete &c. 729; leave -unfinished &c. *adj.*, – undone; neglect &c. 460; let -alone, – slip; lose sight of.

crowning of the edifice; coping-, keystone; missing link &c. 53; superstructure, *ne plus ultra*, work done, *fait accompli*.

elaboration; finality; completeness &c. 52.

V. effect, -uate; accomplish, achieve, compass, consummate, hammer out; bring to -maturity, - perfection; perfect, complete; elaborate.

do, execute, make; go –, get- through; work out, enact; bring -about, – to bear, – to pass, – through, – to a head.

des-, dis-patch; knock –, finish –, polish- off; make short work of; dispose of, set at rest; perform, discharge, fulfil, realize; put in -practice, – force; carry -out, – into effect, – into execution; make good; be as good as one's word.

do thoroughly, not do by halves, go the whole hog; drive home; be in at the death &c. (*persevere*) 604*a*; carry through, play out, exhaust, deliver the goods, fill the bill.

finish, bring to a close &c. (*end*) 67; wind up, stamp, clinch, seal, set the seal on, put the seal to; give the -final touch &c. *n.* to; put the -last, – finishing- hand to; crown, – all; cap.

ripen, culminate; come to a -head, – crisis; come to its end; die -a natural death, – of old age; run -its course, – one's race; touch –, reach –, attain- the goal; reach &c. (*arrive*) 292; get in the harvest.

Adj. completing, final; conclu-ding, -sive; crowning &c. *v.*; exhaustive, complete, mature, perfect, consummate.

done, completed &c. *v.*; done for, sped, wrought out; highly wrought &c. (*preparation*) 673; thorough &c. 52; ripe &c. (*ready*) 673.

Adv. completely &c. (*thoroughly*) 52; to crown all, out of hand.

Phr. the race is run; *actum est*; *finis coronat opus*; *consummatum est*; *c'en est fait*; it is all over; the game is played out, the bubble has burst.

fall short of &c. 304; do things by halves; scotch the snake, not kill it; hang fire; be slow to; collapse &c. 304.

Adj. not completed &c. *v.*; incomplete &c. 53; uncompleted, unfinished, unaccomplished, unperformed, unexecuted; sketchy, addle.

in progress, in hand; going on, proceeding; on one's hands; on the fire; on the stocks; in preparation; lacking the finishing touch.

Adv. *re infectâ*.

---

731. Success.—N. success, -fulness; speed; advance &c. (*progress*) 282.

trump card; hit, stroke; lucky –, fortunate –, good- -hit, – stroke; bold –, master- stroke; *coup de maître*, checkmate; half the battle, prize; profit &c. (*acquisition*) 775; best seller.

continued success; good fortune &c. (*prosperity*) 734; time well spent.

advantage over; edge; upper-, whiphand; ascendancy, mastery; expugnation, conquest, victory, subdual; subjugation &c. (*subjection*) 749.

triumph &c. (*exultation*) 884; proficiency &c. (*skill*) 698; conqueror, victor, winner, champion; master of the -situation, – position.

V. succeed; be -successful &c. *adj.*;

732. Failure. — N. failure; nonsuccess, -fulfilment; dead failure, successlessness; abortion, miscarriage; *brutum fulmen* &c. 158; labour in vain &c. (*inutility*) 645; no go; inefficacy; inefficaciousness &c. *adj.*; vain –, ineffectual –, abortive- -attempt, – efforts; flash in the pan, 'lame and impotent conclusion'; frustration; slip 'twixt cup and lip &c. (*disappointment*) 509.

blunder &c. (*mistake*) 495; fault, omission, miss, oversight, slip, trip, stumble, claudication, footfall; false –, wrong- step; *faux pas*, titubation, *bévue*, *faute*, lurch; botchery &c. (*want of skill*) 699; scrape, jam, mess, muddle, foozle, *fiasco*, breakdown.

mishap &c. (*misfortune*) 735; split,

gain one's -end, – ends; crown with success.

gain –, attain –, carry –, secure –, win- -a point, – an object; put over; make a go of; manage to, contrive to; accomplish &c. (*effect, complete*) 729; do –, work- wonders.

come off -well, – successfully, – with flying colours; make short work of; take –, carry- by storm; bear away the bell; win -one's spurs, – the battle; win –, carry –, gain- the -day, – prize, – palm; climb on the bandwagon; have -the best of it, – it all one's own way, – the game in one's own hands, – the ball at one's feet, – one on the hip; walk over the course; carry all before one, remain in possession of the field; score a success, win hands down.

speed; make progress &c. (*advance*) 282; win –, make –, work –, find- one's way; strive to some purpose; prosper &c. 734; drive a roaring trade; make profit &c. (*acquire*) 775; reap –, gather- the -fruits, – benefit of, – harvest; make one's fortune, get in the harvest, turn to good account; turn to account &c. (*use*) 677.

triumph, be triumphant; gain –, obtain- -a victory, – an advantage; chain victory to one's car.

surmount –, overcome –, get over- -a difficulty, – an obstacle &c. 706; *se tirer d'affaire*; make head against; stem the -torrent, – tide, – current; weather -the storm, – a point; turn a corner, keep one's head above water, tide over; master; get –, have –, gain- the -better of, – best of, – upper hand, – ascendancy, – whip hand, – start of; distance; surpass &c. (*superiority*) 33.

defeat, conquer, vanquish, discomfit; over-come, -throw, -power, -master, -match, -set, -ride, -reach; out-wit, -do, -flank, -manœuvre, -general, -vote; take the wind out of one's adversary's sails; beat, – hollow; rout, lick, drub, floor, worst; put -down, – to flight, – to the rout, – *hors de combat*, – out of court.

silence, quell, nonsuit, checkmate, upset, confound, nonplus, trump; baffle &c. (*hinder*) 706; circumvent, elude; trip up, – the heels of; drive collapse, smash, blow, explosion.

repulse, rebuff, defeat, rout, overthrow, discomfiture; beating, drubbing; *quietus*, nonsuit, subjugation; check-, fool's-mate.

fall, downfall, ruin, perdition; wreck &c. (*destruction*) 162; death-blow; bankruptcy &c. (*non-payment*) 808.

losing game, *affaire flambée*.

victim, prey; bankrupt.

V. fail; be -unsuccessful &c. *adj.*; not -succeed &c. 731; make -vain efforts &c. *n.*; do –, labour –, toil- in vain; lose one's labour, take nothing by one's motion; bring to naught, make nothing of; wash a blackamoor white &c. (*impossible*) 471; roll the stone of Sisyphus &c. (*useless*) 645; do by halves &c. (*not complete*) 730; lose ground &c. (*recede*) 283; flunk; fall short of &c. 304.

miss, – one's aim, – the mark, – one's footing, – stays; slip, trip, stumble; make a -slip &c. *n.*, – blunder &c. 495, – mess of, – botch of; bitch it, miscarry, abort, go up like a rocket and come down like the stick, reckon without one's host; get the wrong sow by the ear &c. (*blunder, mismanage*) 600.

limp, halt, hobble, titubate; fall, tumble; lose one's balance; fall -to the ground, – between two stools; flounder, falter, stick in the mud, run aground, split upon a rock; run –, knock –, dash- one's head against a stone wall; break one's back; break down, sink, drown, founder, have the ground cut from under one; get into -trouble, – a mess, – a scrape; come to grief &c. (*adversity*) 735; go to -the wall, – the dogs, – pot; lick –, bite- the dust; be -defeated &c. 731; have the worst of it, lose the day, come off second best, lose; fall a prey to; succumb &c. (*submit*) 725; not have a leg to stand on.

come to nothing, end in smoke; fall -to the ground, – through, – dead, – still-born, – flat; slip through one's fingers; hang –, miss- fire; flash in the pan, collapse; topple down &c. (*descent*) 305; go to wrack and ruin &c. (*destruction*) 162.

go amiss, go wrong, go cross, go hard with, go on a wrong tack; go on –,

-into a corner, – to the wall; run hard, put one's nose out of joint.

settle, do for; break the -neck of, – back of; capsize, sink, shipwreck, drown, swamp; subdue; subjugate &c. (*subject*) 749; reduce; make the enemy bite the dust; victimize, roll in the dust, trample under foot, put an extinguisher upon.

answer, – the purpose; avail, prevail, take effect, do, turn out well, work well, take, tell, bear fruit; hit -it, – the mark, – the right nail on the head; nick it; turn up trumps, make a hit; find one's account in.

Adj. succeeding &c. *v.*; successful; prosperous &c. 734; triumphant; flushed –, crowned- with success; victorious; set up; in the ascendant; unbeaten &c. (*see* beat &c. *v.*); well-spent; felicitous, effective, in full swing.

Adv. successfully &c. *adj.*; with flying colours, in triumph, swimmingly; *à merveille*, beyond all hope; to some –, good- purpose; to one's heart's content.

Phr. *veni vidi vici*, the day being one's own, one's star in the ascendant; *omne tulit punctum.*

---

come off –, turn out –, work- ill; take -a wrong, – an ugly- turn; gang agley.

be all -over with, – up with; explode; dash one's hopes &c. (*disappoint*) 509; defeat the purpose; upset the apple cart; sow the wind and reap the whirlwind, jump out of the frying pan into the fire.

Adj. unsuccessful, successless; failing, tripping &c. *v.*; at fault; unfortunate &c. 735.

abortive, addle, still-born; fruitless, sterile, bootless; ineffect-ual, -ive; inefficient &c. (*impotent*) 158; inefficacious; lame, hobbling, *décousu*; insufficient &c. 640; unavailing &c. (*useless*) 645; of no effect.

aground, grounded, swamped, stranded, cast away, wrecked, foundered, capsized, shipwrecked, nonsuited; foiled; defeated &c. 731; struck –, borne –, broken- down; down-trodden; over-borne, -whelmed; all up with; beaten to a frazzle.

lost, undone, ruined, broken; bankrupt &c. (*not paying*) 808; played out; done -up, – for; dead beat, ruined root and branch, *flambé*, knocked on the head; destroyed &c. 162.

frustrated, thwarted, crossed, unhinged, disconcerted, dashed; thrown -off one's balance, – on one's back, – on one's beam ends; unhorsed, in a sorry plight; hard hit.

stultified, befooled, dished, hoist on one's own petard; victimized, sacrificed.

wide of the mark &c. (*error*) 495; out of one's reckoning &c. (*inexpectation*) 508; left in the lurch; thrown away &c. (*wasted*) 638; unattained; uncompleted &c. 730.

Adv. unsuccessfully &c. *adj.*; to little or no purpose, in vain, *re infectâ.*

Phr. the bubble has burst, the game is up, all is lost; the devil to pay; *parturiunt montes* &c. (*disappointment*) 509.

733. Trophy.—**N.** trophy; medal, prize, palm; ribbon, blue ribbon, *cordon bleu*; citation; cup; laurel, -s; bays, crown, chaplet, wreath, civic crown; Victoria Cross, V.C., *Croix de Guerre*, Iron Cross; Distinguished Service Cross, Medal of Honor, Congressional Medal; insignia &c. 550; feather in one's cap &c. (*honour*) 873; decoration &c. 877; garland, triumphal arch.

triumph &c. (*celebration*) 883; flying colours &c. (*show*) 882.

monumentum ære perennius.

734. Prosperity.—**N.** prosperity, welfare, well-being; affluence &c. (*wealth*) 803; success &c. 731; thrift, roaring

735. Adversity.—**N.** adversity, evil &c. 619; failure &c. 732; bad –, ill –, evil –, adverse –, hard- -fortune, – hap,

trade; chicken in every pot, the full dinner pail; good –, smiles of- fortune; blessings, godsend.

luck; good –, run of- luck; sunshine; fair -weather, – wind; palmy –, bright –, halcyon- days; piping times, tide, flood, high tide.

Saturnia regna, Saturnian age; golden -time, – age; bed of roses; fat of the land, milk and honey, loaves and fishes, fleshpots of Egypt.

made man, lucky dog, *enfant gâté*, spoiled child of fortune.

upstart, *parvenu*, *nouveau riche*, profiteer, skipjack, mushroom.

V. prosper, thrive, flourish; be -prosperous &c. *adj.*; drive a roaring trade; go on -well, – smoothly, – swimmingly; sail before the wind, swim with the tide; run -smooth, – smoothly, – on all fours.

rise –, get on- in the world; work –, make- one's way; look up; lift –, raise- one's head, make one's -fortune, – pile, feather one's nest.

flower, blow, blossom, bloom, fructify, bear fruit, fatten, batten.

keep oneself afloat; keep –, hold- one's head above water; light –, fall- on one's -legs, – feet; drop into a good thing; bear a charmed life; bask in the sunshine; have a good, – fine- time of it; have a run, – of luck; have the -good fortune &c. *n.* to; take a favourable turn; live -on the fat of the land, – in clover.

Adj. prosperous; thriving &c. *v.*; in a fair way, buoyant; well -off, – to do, – to do in the world; set up, at one's ease; rich &c. 803; in good case; in -full, – high- feather; fortunate, lucky, in luck; born -with a silver spoon in one's mouth, – under a lucky star; on the sunny side of the hedge.

auspicious, propitious, providential.

palmy, halcyon; agreeable &c. 829; *couleur de rose.*

Adv. prosperously &c. *adj.*; swimmingly; as good luck would have it; beyond all -expectation, – hope, – one's wildest dreams.

Phr. one's star in the ascendant, all for the best, one's course runs smooth.

– luck, – lot; frowns of fortune; evil -dispensation, – star, – genius; ups and downs of life, broken fortunes; hard -case, – lines, – life; sea –, peck- of troubles; hell upon earth; slough of despond; jinx.

trouble, humiliation, hardship, curse, blight, blast, load, pressure, plight.

pressure of the times, iron age, evil day, time out of joint; hard –, bad –, sad- times; rainy day, cloud, dark cloud, gathering clouds, ill wind; visitation, infliction; affliction &c. (*painfulness*) 830; bitter -pill, – cup; care, trial; the sport of fortune.

mis-hap, -chance, -adventure, -fortune; disaster, calamity, catastrophe; accident, casualty, cross, reverse, check, *contretemps*, rub, pinch, setback.

losing game; falling &c. *v.*; fall, down-fall, come-down; ruin-ation, -ousness; undoing; extremity; ruin &c. (*destruction*) 162.

V. be -ill off &c. *adj.*; go hard with; fall on evil, – days; go on ill; not -prosper &c. 734.

go -downhill, – to rack and ruin &c. (*destruction*) 162, – to the dogs; fall, – from one's high estate; decay, sink, decline, go down in the world; have seen better days; bring down one's grey hairs with sorrow to the grave; come to grief; be all -over, – up- with; bring a -wasp's, – hornet's- nest about one's ears.

Adj. unfortunate, unblest, unhappy, unlucky; im-, un-prosperous; luck-, hap-less; out of luck; in trouble, in a bad way, in an evil plight; under a cloud; clouded; ill –, badly- off; in adverse circumstances; poor &c. 804; behindhand, down in the world, decayed, undone; on the road to ruin, on its last legs, on the wane; in one's utmost need.

planet-struck, devoted; born -under an evil star, – with a wooden ladle in one's mouth; ill-fated, -starred, -omened; inconspicuous, ominous, doomed, unpropitious.

adverse, untoward; disastrous, calamitous, ruinous, dire, deplorable.

Adv. if the worst come to the worst, as ill luck would have it, from bad to worse, out of the frying pan into the fire.

Phr. one's star is on the wane; one's luck -turns, – fails; the game is up, one's doom is sealed, the ground crumbles under one's feet, *sic transit gloria mundi, tant va la cruche à l'eau qu'à la fin elle se casse.*

736. Mediocrity.—N. moderate –, average- circumstances; respectability; middle classes, *bourgeoisie*; mediocrity; golden mean &c. (*mid-course*) 628, (*moderation*) 174.

V. jog on; go –, get on- -fairly, – quietly, – peaceably, – tolerably, – respectably; steer a middle course &c. 628.

Adj. middling, so-so, fair, medium, moderate, mediocre, second-, third- &c. -rate.

Division (II). INTERSOCIAL VOLITION*

Section I. General Intersocial Volition

737. Authority.—N. authority; influence, patronage, power, preponderance, credit, *prestige*, prerogative, jurisdiction; right &c. (*title*) 924.

divine right, dynastic rights, authoritativeness; absolut-eness, -ism; despotism, tyranny; *jus nocendi.*

command, empire, sway, rule; domin-ion, -ation; sovereignty, supremacy, suzerainty; lord-, head-ship; chiefdom; seignior-y, -ity, hegemony, patriarchate, patriarchy; master-y, -ship, -dom; government &c. (*direction*) 693; dictation, control.

hold, grasp; grip, -e; reach; iron sway &c. (*severity*) 739; fangs, clutches, talons; rod of empire &c. (*sceptre*) 747.

reign, regnancy, *régime*, dynasty; director-, dictator-ship; protector-ate, -ship; caliphate, pashalic, electorate; presiden-cy, -tship; administration; pro-, consulship; prefecture; seneschalship; magistra-ture, -cy; raj.

empire; monarchy; king-hood, -ship; royalty, regality, autocracy, monocracy, arist-archy, -ocracy; oligarchy, democracy, demogogy; republic, -anism, federalism; socialism, collectivism; communism, bolshevism, syndicalism; mob law, mobocracy, ochlocracy, ergatocracy; *vox populi, imperium in imperio*; bureaucracy; beadle-, bumble-dom; stratocracy; martial law, military -power, – government; feodality, feudal system, feudalism.

Thearchy, dinarchy, diarchy; du-, tri-, heter-archy; du-, tri-umvirate; auto-cracy, -nomy; limited monarchy; constitutional -government, – monarchy; home rule, self-government, -determination; representative government; Soviet government.

738. [Absence of authority.] **Laxity.—N.** laxity; lax-, loose-, slack-ness; toleration &c. (*lenity*) 740; freedom &c. 748.

anarchy, interregnum; relaxation; loosening &c. *v.*; remission; dead letter, *brutum fulmen*, misrule; licence, licentiousness; insubordination &c. (*disobedience*) 742; lynch law &c. (*illegality*) 964; nihilism.

[Deprivation of power] dethronement, deposition, usurpation, abdication.

V. be -lax &c. *adj.*; *laisser -faire, – aller*; hold a loose rein; give -the reins to, – rope enough, – a loose to; tolerate; relax; misrule.

go beyond the length of one's tether; have one's -swing, – fling; act without -instructions, – authority; act on one's own responsibility, usurp authority.

dethrone, depose; abdicate.

Adj. lax, loose; slack; remiss &c. (*careless*) 460; weak.

relaxed; licensed; reinless, unbridled; anarchical; unauthorized &c. (*unwarranted*) 925.

*Implying the action of the will of one mind over the will of another.

gyn-archy, -ocracy, -æocracy; petticoat government, matriarchate, matriarchy.

[Vicarious authority] commission &c. 755; deputy &c. 759; permission &c. 760.

country, state, realm, commonwealth, canton, constituency, toparchy, municipality, polity, body politic, *posse comitatus.*

person in authority &c. (*master*) 745; judicature &c. 965; cabinet &c. (*council*) 696; usurper; seat of -government, - authority; headquarters.

[Acquisition of authority] accession; installation &c. 755; usurpation.

V. authorize &c. (*permit*) 760; warrant &c. (*right*) 924; dictate &c. (*order*) 741; have –, hold –, possess –, exercise –, exert –, wield- -authority &c. *n.*

be -at the head of &c. *adj.*; hold –, be in –, fill an- office; hold –, occupy- a post; be -master &c. 745.

rule, sway, command, control, administer; govern &c. (*direct*) 693; lead, preside over, reign; possess –, be seated on –, occupy- the throne; sway –, wield- the sceptre; wear the crown.

have –, get- the -upper, – whip- hand; gain a hold upon, preponderate, dominate, boss, rule the roost; over-ride, -rule, -awe; lord it over, hold in hand, keep under, make a puppet of, lead by the nose, hold in the hollow of one's hand, turn round one's little finger, bend to one's will, hold one's own, wear the breeches; have -the ball at one's feet, – it all one's own way, – the game in one's own hand, – on the hip, – under one's thumb; be master of the situation; take the lead, play first fiddle, set the fashion; give the law to; carry with a high hand; lay down the law; 'ride in the whirlwind and direct the storm'; rule with a rod of iron &c. (*severity*) 739.

ascend –, mount- the throne, take the reins, – into one's hand; assume -authority &c. *n.*, – the reins of government; take –, assume the- command.

be -governed by, – in the power of; be under -the rule of, – the domination of.

Adj. ruling &c. *v.*; regnant, at the head, dominant, paramount, supreme, predominant, preponderant, in the ascendant, influential; gubernatorial; imperious; authoritative, executive, administrative, clothed with authority, official, *ex officio*, ministerial, bureaucratic, departmental, imperative, peremptory, overruling, absolute; hegemonic, -al; arbitrary; compulsory &c. 744; stringent.

regal, sovereign; royal, -ist; monarchical, kingly; imperial, -istic; princely; feudal; aristo-, auto-cratic; oligarchic &c. *n.*; democratic, republican, dynastic.

at one's command; in one's -power, – grasp; under control; authorized &c. (*due*) 924.

Adv. in the name of, by the authority of, *de par le Roi*, in virtue of; under the auspices of, in the hands of.

at one's pleasure; by a -dash, – stroke- of the pen; *ex mero motu*; *ex cathedrâ.*

Phr. the grey mare the better horse; 'every inch a king.'

739. Severity.—N. severity; strictness, formalism, harshness &c. *adj.*; rigour, stringency, austerity; inclem-

740. Lenity. — N. leni-ty, -ence, -ency; moderation &c. 174; toler-ance, -ation; mildness, gentleness; favour;

ency &c. (*pitilessness*) 914*a*; arrogance &c. 885.

arbitrary power; absolut-, despotism; dictatorship, autocracy, tyranny, domineering, oppression; assumption, usurpation; inquisition, reign of terror, martial law; iron -heel, – rule, – hand, – sway; tight grasp; brute -force, – strength; coercion &c. 744; strong –, tight- hand.

hard -lines, – measure; tender mercies [ironical]; sharp practice; bureaucracy, red tape; pipe-clay, officialism.

tyrant, disciplinarian, martinet, stickler, formalist, bashaw, despot, hard master, Draco, oppressor, inquisitor, extortioner, harpy, vulture, bird of prey.

V. be -severe &c. *adj.*

assume, usurp, arrogate, take liberties; domineer, bully &c. 885; tyrannize, inflict, wreak, stretch a point, put on the screw; be hard upon; bear –, lay- a heavy hand on; be –, come- down upon; ill-treat; deal -hardly with, – hard measure to; rule with a rod of iron, chastise with scorpions; dye with blood; oppress, override; trample –, tread- -down, – upon, – under foot; crush under an iron heel, ride roughshod over; rivet the yoke; hold –, keep- a tight hand; force down the throat; coerce &c. 744; give no quarter &c. (*pitiless*) 914*a*.

Adj. severe; strict, hard, harsh, dour, rigid, stiff, stern, rigorous, uncompromising, exacting, exigent, *exigeant*, inexorable, inflexible, obdurate, austere, relentless, Spartan, Draconian, stringent, strait-laced, puritanical, prudish, searching, unsparing, ironhanded, hard-headed, peremptory, absolute, positive, arbitrary, imperative; coercive &c. 744; tyrannical, despotic, masterful, extortionate, grinding, withering, oppressive, inquisitorial; inclement &c. (*ruthless*) 914*a*; cruel &c. (*malevolent*) 907; haughty, arrogant &c. 885.

Adv. severely &c. *adj.*; with a -high, – strong, – tight, – heavy-hand.

at the point of the -sword, – bayonet.

Phr. *Delirant reges plectuntur Achivi.*

indulgen-ce, -cy; clemency, mercy, forbearance, quarter; compassion &c. 914.

V. be -lenient &c. *adj.*; tolerate, bear with; *parcere subjectis*, give quarter.

indulge, allow one to have his own way, spoil.

Adj. lenient; mild, – as milk; gentle, soft; tolerant, indulgent, easy-going; clement &c. (*compassionate*) 914; forbearing; complaisant, long-suffering.

---

741. Command.—N. command, order, ordinance, act, *fiat*, bidding, *dictum*, hest, behest, call, beck, nod.

des-, dis-patch; message, direction, injunction, charge, instructions; appointment, fixture.

demand, exaction, imposition, requisition, claim, reclamation, revendication; *ultimatum* &c. (*terms*) 770; request &c. 765; requirement.

dictation; dict-, mand-ate; *caveat*, decree, decree -nisi, – absolute, *senatus consultum*; precept; pre-, re-script; writ, ordination, bull, edict, decretal, dispensation, prescription, brevet, placet, ukase, *firman*, hatti-sheriff, warrant, passport, *mittimus*, *mandamus*, summons; subpœna, –*duces tecum*, *nisi prius*, interpellation, citation; word, – of command; *mot d'ordre*; bugle –, trumpet- call; beat of drum, tattoo; order of the day; enactment &c. (*law*) 963; *plébiscite* &c. (*choice*) 609.

V. command, order, decree, enact, ordain, dictate, direct, give orders.

prescribe, set, appoint, mark out; set –, prescribe –, impose- a task; set to work, put in requisition &c. 926.

bid, enjoin, charge, call upon, instruct; require, – at the hands of; exact, impose, tax, task; demand; insist on &c. (*compel*) 744.

claim, lay claim to, revendicate, reclaim.

cite, summon; call –, send- for; subpœna; beckon.

issue a command; make –, issue –, promulgate- -a requisition, – a decree, – an order &c. *n.*; give the -word of command, – word, – signal; call to order; give –, lay down- the law; assume the command &c. (*authority*) 737; remand.

be -ordered &c.; receive an order &c. *n.*

Adj. commanding &c. *v.*; authoritative &c. 737; decret-ory, -ive, -al; imperative, jussive, decisive, final.

Adv. in a commanding tone; by a -stroke, – dash- of the pen; by order, at beat of drum, on the first summons; at the word of command.

Phr. the decree is gone forth; *sic volo sic jubeo*; *le Roi le veut.*

742. Disobedience.—N. disobedience, insubordination, contumacy; infraction, -fringement; violation, noncompliance; non-observance &c. 773.

revolt, rebellion, mutiny, outbreak, rising, uprising, putsch, insurrection, *émeute*; riot, tumult &c. (*disorder*) 59; strike &c. (*resistance*) 719; barring out; defiance &c. 715.

mutinousness &c. *adj.*; mutineering; sedition, treason; high –, petty –, misprision of- treason; *premunire*; *lèse-majesté*; violation of law &c. 964; defection, secession, revolution, *sabotage*, bolshevism, *Sinn Fein.*

insurgent, mutineer, rebel, revolter, rioter, traitor, *carbonaro*, *sansculottes*, red republican, communist, Fenian, chartist, *frondeur*; seceder, runagate, brawler, anarchist, demagogue; suffragette; Spartacus, Masaniello, Wat Tyler, Jack Cade; bolshevist, bolshevik, maximalist, ringleader.

V. disobey, violate, infringe; shirk; set at defiance &c. (*defy*) 715; set authority at naught, run riot, fly in the face of, bolt, take the law into one's own hands; kick over the traces.

turn –, run- restive; champ the bit; strike &c. (*resist*) 719; rise, – in arms; secede; mutiny, rebel.

Adj. disobedient; uncompl-ying, -iant; unsubmissive, unruly, ungovernable; insubordinate, impatient of control; rest-iff, -ive; refractory, contumacious; recusant &c. (refuse) 764; recalcitrant; resisting &c. 719; lawless, mutinous, seditious, insurgent, riotous, revolutionary.

disobeyed, unobeyed; unbidden.

743. Obedience.—N. obedience; observance &c. 772; compliance; submission &c. 725; subjection &c. 749; non-resistance; passiveness, passivity, resignation.

allegiance, loyalty, fealty, homage, deference, devotion, fidelity, constancy.

submiss-ness, -iveness; ductility &c. (*softness*) 324; obsequiousness &c. (*servility*) 886.

V. be -obedient &c. *adj.*; obey, bear obedience to; submit &c. 725; comply, answer the helm, come at one's call; do -one's bidding, – what one is told, – suit and service; attend to orders, serve -devotedly, – loyally, – faithfully.

follow, – the lead of, – to the world's end; serve &c. 746; play second fiddle.

Adj. obedient; compl-ying, -iant; law-abiding, loyal, faithful, leal, devoted; at one's -call, – command, – orders, – beck and call; under -beck and call, – control.

restrainable; resigned, passive; submissive &c. 725; henpecked; pliant &c. (*soft*) 324.

unresist-ed, -ing.

Adv. obediently &c. *adj.*; in compliance with, in obedience to.

Phr. to hear is to obey; as –, if- you please; at your service.

---

744. Compulsion.—**N.** compulsion, coercion, coaction, constraint, eminent domain, duress, enforcement, press, conscription.

force; brute –, main –, physical- force; the sword, *ultima ratio*; club –, mob –, lynch- law; *argumentum ad baculum, le droit du plus fort*, martial law.

restraint &c. 751; necessity &c. 601; *force majeure*; Hobson's choice; the spur of necessity.

V. compel, force, make, drive, coerce, constrain, enforce, necessitate, oblige.

force upon, press; cram –, thrust –, force- down the throat; say it must be done, make a point of, insist upon, take no denial; put down, dragoon.

extort, wring from; put –, turn- on the screw; drag into; bind, – over; pin –, tie- down; require, tax, put in force; commandeer; restrain &c. 751.

Adj. compelling &c. *v.*; coercive, coactive; inexorable &c. 739; compuls-ory, -atory; obligatory, stringent, peremptory, binding.

forcible, not to be trifled with; irresistible &c. 601; compelled &c. *v.*; fain to.

Adv. by -force &c. *n.*, – force of arms; on compulsion, perforce; *vi et armis*, under the lash; at the point of the -sword, – bayonet; forcibly; by a strong arm.

under protest, in spite of one's teeth; against one's will &c. 603; *nolens volens* &c. (*of necessity*) 601; by stress of -circumstances, – weather; under press of; *de rigueur*.

745. Master.—**N.** master, *padrone*; lord, – paramount; command-er, -ant; captain; chief, -tain; *sahib*, sirdar, sachem, sheik, head, senior, governor, *duce*, ruler, dictator; leader &c. (*director*) 694.

lord of the ascendant; cock of the -walk, – roost; grey mare; mistress.

potentate; liege, – lord; suzerain, sovereign, monarch, autocrat, despot, tyrant, oligarch, overlord.

crowned head, emperor, king, anointed king, majesty, *imperator*, protector, president, stadtholder, judge.

cæsar, kaiser, czar, sultan, grand Turk, caliph, imaum, shah, padishah, sophi, mogul, great mogul, khan, cham; lama, tycoon, mikado, inca, cazique; domn; vaivode; wai-, way-wode; landamman; seyyid, cacique.

prince, duke &c. (*nobility*) 875; archduke, doge, elector; seignior; mar-, land-grave; rajah, emir, nizam, nawab, negus.

empress, queen, sultana, czarina, princess, infanta, duchess, margravine, begum, maharani.

regent, viceroy, exarch, palatine,

746. Servant.—**N.** subject, liegeman; servant, retainer, follower, henchman, servitor, domestic, menial, help, lady help, *employé, attaché*; official.

retinue, suite, *cortège*, staff, court.

attendant, squire, usher, page, buttons, donzel, footboy; dog robber; train-, cup-bearer; waiter, busboy, tapster, butler, livery servant, lackey, footman, flunkey, valet, *valet de chambre*; boots; scout, gyp; equerry, groom; jockey, hostler, ostler, tiger, orderly, messenger, cad, gillie, caddie; *wallah*; journeyman, herdsman, swineherd.

bailiff, castellan, seneschal, chamberlain, *major-domo*, groom of the chambers.

secretary; under –, assistant- secretary; clerk; clerical staff, stenographer, subsidiary; agent &c. 758; subaltern; under-ling, -strapper; man.

maid, -servant, waitress; handmaid; *confidente*, lady's maid, abigail, *soubrette*; nurse, *bonne, ayah*; nurse-, nursery-, house-, parlour-, waiting-, chamber-, kitchen-, scullery-, between –, laundry –, dairy-maid; *femme –, fille-de chambre*; *camarista*; *chef de cuisine*,

khedive, hospodar, beglerbeg, three-tailed bashaw, pasha, pashaw, bashaw, bey, beg, dey, scherif, tetrarch, satrap, mandarin, subahdar, Nabob, maharajah; burgrave; laird &c. (*proprietor*) 779; High Commissioner.

the -authorities, – powers that be, – government; staff, *état major*, aga, official, man in office, person in authority.

[Naval authorities] admiral, -ty, – of the fleet; rear-, vice-, port-admiral; senior-, naval officer, S.N.O., commodore, captain, commander, lieutenant-commander, lieutenant, sub-lieutenant, midshipman, warrant –, petty- officer, leading seaman; skipper, mate, master.

[Military authorities] marshal, field-marshal, *maréchal*; general, -issimo; commander-in-chief, *seraskier*, *hetman*; lieutenant-, major-general; commandant; colonel, lieutenant-colonel, major, captain, centurion, skipper, lieutenant, second-lieutenant, officer, staff-officer, *aide-de-camp*, brigadier, brigade-major, adjutant, *jemidar*, ensign, cornet, cadet, subaltern, warrant officer, quartermaster, noncommissioned officer, N.C.O.; sergeant, -major; top-sergeant, troop-sergeant, colour sergeant; corporal, -major; lance-, acting-corporal; drum major; shavetail.

[Air authorities] air -marshal, – commodore; group captain, squadron leader, wing commander, flight lieutenant, flying –, pilot-officer.

[Civil authorities] judge &c. 967; mayor, -alty; prefect, chancellor, archon, provost, magistrate, syndic; alcalde, alcaid; burgomaster, *corregidor*, seneschal, alderman, warden, constable, portreeve; lord mayor, sheriff; officer &c. (*executive*) 965.

cordon bleu, cook, scullion, Cinderella; maid –, servant- of all work, tweeny, general servant, girl, slavey; laundress, bed-maker, goody, char-woman &c. (*worker*) 690.

serf, vassal, slave, negro, helot; bondsman, -woman; bondslave; *âme damnée*, *odalisque*, ryot, *adscriptus glebæ*; vill-ain, -ein; bead-, bede-sman; sizar; pension-er, -ary; client; dependant, -ent; hanger on, stooge, satellite; parasite &c. (*servility*) 886; led captain; *protégé*, ward, hireling, mercenary, puppet, creature.

badge of slavery; bonds &c. 752.

V. serve; minister to, wait –, attend –, dance attendance –, pin oneself-upon; squire, tend, hang on the sleeve of, char, do for; fag; valet.

Adj. in the train of; in one's -pay, – employ; at one's call &c. (*obedient*) 743; in bonds.

747. [Insignia of authority.] **Sceptre.—N.** sceptre, regalia, rod of empire, sword of state, mace, *fasces*, wand; staff, – of office; *bâton*, truncheon; flag &c. (*insignia*) 550; ensign –, emblem –, badge –, insignia- of authority, rank marks, brassard, badge, sash; cocked –, brass- hat.

epaulette, *aiguillette*, crown, star, eagle, bar, double bar, pip, stripe, chevron, curl, ring, anchor, shoulder-strap, tab.

throne, chair, musnud, divan, dais, woolsack.

toga, pall, mantle, robes of state, ermine, purple.

crown, coronet, diadem, tiara, triple crown, mitre, crozier, cardinal's hat &c.; cap of maintenance; decoration; title &c. 877; portfolio.

key, signet, seals, talisman; helm; reins &c. (*means of restraint*) 752.

748. Freedom.—N. freedom, liberty, independence; licence &c. (*permission*) 760; facility &c. 705.

scope, range, latitude, play; free –, full- -play, – scope; free stage and no

749. Subjection. — N. subjection; depend-ence, -ance, -ency; subordination; thrall, thraldom, enthralment, subjugation, bondage, serfdom; feudal-ism, -ity; vassalage, villenage; slavery,

favour; swing, full swing, elbow-room, margin, rope, wide berth; Liberty Hall.

franchise, denization; free –, freed-, livery- man; denizen.

autonomy, self-government, home-rule, self-determination, liberalism, free trade; non-interference &c. 706.

immunity, exemption; emancipation &c. (*liberation*) 750; en-, af-franchisement; rights, privileges.

free land, freehold; allodium; frank-almoigne, mortmain.

independent, free-lance, -thinker, -trader.

V. be -free &c. *adj.*; have -scope &c. *n.*, – the run of, – one's own way, – a will of one's own, – one's fling; do what one -likes, – wishes, – pleases, – chooses; go at large, feel at home, paddle one's own canoe; stand on one's -legs, – rights; shift for oneself.

take a liberty; make -free with, – oneself quite at home; use a freedom; take -leave, – French leave.

set free &c. (*liberate*) 750; give the reins to &c. (*permit*) 760; allow –, give- scope &c. *n.* to; give a horse his head.

make free of; give the -freedom of, – franchise; en-, af-franchise.

laisser -faire, – aller; live and let live; leave to oneself; leave –, let- alone; mind one's own business.

Adj. free, – as air; out of harness, independent, at large, loose, scot free; left -alone, – to oneself.

in full swing; uncaught, unconstrained, unbuttoned, unconfined, unrestrained, unchecked, unprevented, unhindered, unobstructed, unbound, uncontrolled, untrammelled.

unsubject, ungoverned, unenslaved, unenthralled, unchained, unshackled, unfettered, unreined, unbridled, uncurbed, unmuzzled, unimpeded.

unrestricted, unlimited, unconditional; absolute; discretionary &c. (*optional*) 600.

unassailed, unforced, uncompelled.

unbiassed, unprejudiced, uninfluenced, spontaneous.

free and easy; at –, at one's- ease; *dégagé*, quite at home; wanton, rampant, irrepressible, unvanquished.

exempt; freed &c. 750; freeborn; autonomous, freehold, allodial; *gratis* &c. 815.

unclaimed, going a begging.

Adv. freely &c. *adj.*; *ad libitum* &c. (*at will*) 600.

enslavement, involuntary servitude.

service; servi-tude, -torship; tendence, employ, tutelage, clientship; liability &c. 177; constraint &c. 751; oppression &c. (*severity*) 739; yoke &c. (*means of restraint*) 752; submission &c. 725; obedience &c. 743.

V. be -subject &c. *adj.*; be –, lie- at the mercy of; depend –, lean –, hang- upon; fall -a prey to, – under; play second fiddle.

be a -mere machine, – puppet, – football; not dare to say one's soul is his own; drag a chain.

serve &c. 746; obey &c. 743; submit &c. 725.

break in, tame; subject, subjugate; master &c. 731; tread -down, – under foot; weigh down; drag at one's chariot wheels; reduce to -subjection, – slavery; en-, in-, be-thral; enslave, lead captive; take into custody &c. (*restrain*) 751; rule &c. 737; drive into a corner, hold at the sword's point; keep under; hold in -bondage, – leading strings, – swaddling clothes.

Adj. subject, dependent, subordinate; feud-al, -atory; in subjection to, under control; in -leading strings, – harness; subjected, enslaved &c. *v.*; constrained &c. 751; subservient, servile, fawning, slavish, obsequious, cringing; down-trodden; over-borne, -whelmed; under the lash, on the hip, led by the nose, henpecked; the -puppet, – sport, – plaything- of; under one's -orders, – command, – thumb; like dirt under one's feet; a slave to; at the mercy of; in the -power, – hands, – clutches- of; at the feet of; at one's beck and call &c. (*obedient*) 743; liable &c. 177; parasitical; stipendiary.

Adv. under.

750. Liberation.—N. liberation, disengagement, release, disenthrallment, enlargement, emancipation; af-, enfranchisement; manumission; discharge, dismissal.

deliverance &c. 672; redemption, extrication, acquittance, absolution; acquittal &c. 970; escape &c. 671.

V. liberate, free; set -free, – clear, – at liberty; render free, emancipate, release; en-, af-franchise; manumit; enlarge; dis-band, -charge, -miss, -enthral; let -go, – loose, – out, – slip; cast –, turn- adrift; deliver &c. 672; absolve &c. (*acquit*) 970; reprieve.

unfetter &c. 751; untie &c. 44; loose &c. (*disjoin*) 44; loosen, relax; un-bolt, -bar, -close, -cork, -clog, -hand, -bind, -latch, -chain, -harness; dis-engage, -entangle; clear, extricate, unloose.

gain –, obtain –, acquire- one's -liberty &c. 748; get -rid, – clear- of; deliver oneself from; shake off the yoke, slip the collar; break -loose, – prison; tear asunder one's bonds, cast off trammels; escape &c. 671.

Adj. at -liberty, – large, free, liberated &c. *v.*; out of harness &c. 748; adrift.

Int. unhand me! let me go!

---

751. Restraint.—N. restraint; hindrance &c. 706; coercion &c. (*compulsion*) 744; cohibition, constraint, repression; discipline, control, self-restraint &c. 604.

confinement; durance, duress; im-, prisonment; incarceration, coarctation, entombment, mancipation, durance vile, thrall, -dom, limbo, captivity; blockade; quarantine; detention.

arrest, -ation; custody, keep, care, charge, ward, restringency.

curb &c. (*means of restraint*) 752; *lettre de cachet.*

limitation, restriction, protection, monopoly; prohibition &c. 761; economic pressure.

prisoner &c. 754.

V. restrain, check; put –, lay- under restraint; en-, in-, be-thral; restrict; debar &c. (*hinder*) 706; constrain; coerce &c. (*compel*) 744; curb, control; hold –, keep- -back, – from, – in, – in check, – within bounds; hold in -leash, – leading strings; withhold.

keep under; repress, suppress; smother; pull in, rein in; hold, – fast; keep a tight hand on; prohibit &c. 761; in-, co-hibit.

enchain; fasten &c. (*join*) 43; fetter, shackle; en-, trammel; bridle, muzzle, gag, pinion, manacle, handcuff, tie one's hands, hobble, bind hand and foot; swathe, swaddle; pin –, peg- down; tether, picket; tie, – up, – down; secure; forge fetters; belay.

confine; shut –, clap –, lock –, box –, mew –, bottle –, cork –, seal –, button- up; shut –, hem –, bolt –, wall –, rail- in; impound, pen, coop; enclose &c. (*circumscribe*) 229; cage; in-, en-cage; close the door upon, cloister; imprison, immure; incarcerate, entomb; clap –, lay- under hatches; put in -irons, – a strait waistcoat; throw –, cast- into prison; put into bilboes.

arrest; take -up, – charge of, – into custody; take –, make- -prisoner, – captive; captivate; lead -captive, – into captivity; send –, commit- to prison; commit; give in -charge, – custody; subjugate &c. 749.

Adj. re-, con-strained; imprisoned &c. *v.*; pent up; jammed in, wedged in; under -restraint, – lock and key, – hatches; serving –, doing- time; in swaddling clothes; on *parole*; in custody &c. (*prisoner*) 754; cohibitive; coactive &c. (*compulsory*) 744.

stiff, restringent, straitlaced, hide-bound.

ice-, wind-, weather-bound; 'cabined, cribbed, confined'; in Lob's pound, laid by the heels.

Adv. in captivity, under arrest, behind the bars, in -prison, – jail, – durance vile.

752. [Means of restraint.] **Prison.—N.** prison, -house; jail, gaol, cage, coop, den, death house, condemned –, cell; stronghold, fortress, keep, donjon, dungeon, *Bastille, oubliette*, bridewell, house of correction, hulks, toll-booth, panopticon, penitentiary, guard-room, clink, can, stir, tronk, jug, lock-up, hold; round –, watch –, station –, sponging-house; station; house of detention, black hole, pen, fold, pound; enclosure &c. 232; penal settlement; chain gang; debtors' prison; reformatory; federal penitentiary, state prison; criminal lunatic asylum; bilboes, stocks, limbo, quod.

Dartmoor, Newgate, Fleet, Marshalsea; King's (*or* Queen's) Bench; Sing Sing, Dannemora.

bond; strap, bandage, splint, tourniquet; irons, pinion, gyve, fetter, shackle, trammel, manacle, handcuff, bracelets, darbies, strait waistcoat, strait-jacket.

yoke, collar, halter, harness; muzzle, gag, bit, brake, curb, snaffle, bridle; rein, -s; ribbons, lines, bearing-rein; martingale, leading string; tether, picket, band, guy, chain; cord &c. (*fastening*) 45.

bolt, bar, lock, padlock, rail, wall; paling, palisade; fence; barrier, barricade.

brake, drag &c. (*hindrance*) 706.

753. Keeper.—N. keeper, custodian, *custos*, ranger, warder, jailer, gaoler, turnkey, castellan, guard; watch, -dog, -man; Charley; sen-try, -tinel; watch and ward; *concierge*, coast-guard, *guarda costa*, gamekeeper.

escort, body guard, convoy.

protector, governor, duenna; guardian; governess &c. (*teacher*) 540; nurse, *bonne, ayah, amah.*

754. Prisoner.—N. prisoner, captive, *détenu*, close prisoner.

jail-bird, ticket-of-leave man.

V. stand committed; be -imprisoned &c. 751.

Adj. imprisoned &c. 751; in -prison, – quod, – durance vile, – limbo, – custody, – charge, – chains; under -lock and key, – hatches; on *parole*; detained at his Majesty's pleasure.

755. [Vicarious authority.] **Commission.—N.** commission, delegation; con-, as-signment; procuration; deputation, legation, mission, embassy; agency, agentship; power of attorney, proxy; clerkship.

errand, charge, *brevet*, diploma, *exequatur*, permit &c. (*permission*) 760.

appointment, nomination, return; charter; ordination; installation, inauguration, investiture; accession, coronation, enthronement.

vicegerency; regency, regentship.

viceroy &c. 745; consignee &c. 758; deputy &c. 759.

V. commission, delegate, depute; consign, assign; charge; in-, en-trust; turn over to; commit, – to the hands of; authorize &c. (*permit*) 760.

put in commission, accredit, engage, hire, bespeak, appoint, name, nominate, return, ordain; install, induct,

756. Abrogation.—N. abrogation, annulment, nullification; cancelling &c. *v.*; cancel; revo-cation, -kement; repeal, rescission, defeasance.

dismissal, *congé*, demission; depos-al, -ition; sack, dethronement; disestablish-, disendow-ment; deconsecration.

aboli-tion, -shment; dissolution.

counter-order, -mand; repudiation, retractation; recantation &c. (*tergiversation*) 607.

V. abrogate, annul, cancel; destroy &c. 162; abolish; revoke, repeal, rescind, reverse, retract, recall; over-rule, -ride; set aside; disannul, dissolve, quash, nullify, declare null and void; dis-establish, -endow; deconsecrate.

disclaim &c. (*deny*) 536; ignore, repudiate; recant &c. 607; divest oneself, break off.

counter-mand, -order; do away with; sweep –, brush- away; throw -over-

inaugurate, invest, crown; en-roll, -list.

employ, empower; give power of attorney to; set –, place- over; send out.

be commissioned, be accredited; represent, stand for; stand in the -stead, – place, – shoes- of.

Adj. commissioned &c. *v.*

Adv. *per procuratione.*

---

board, – to the dogs; scatter to the winds, cast behind.

dismiss, discard; cast –, turn- -off, – out, – adrift, – out of doors, – aside, – away; send -off, – away, – about one's business; discharge, get rid of, fire out, fire &c. (*eject*) 297; jilt.

cashier; break; oust; set down, unseat, -saddle; un-, de-, disen-throne; depose, uncrown; unfrock, strike off the roll; dis-bar, -bench.

be -abrogated &c.; receive its quietus.

Adj. abrogated &c. *v.*; *functus officio.*

Int. get along with you! begone! go about your business! away with!

757. Resignation.—N. resignation, retirement, abdication, renunciation, abjuration, disclaimer, abandonment, relinquishment.

V. resign; give –, throw- up; lay down, throw up the cards, wash one's hands of, abjure, renounce, forego, disclaim, abandon, relinquish, retract, demit; deny &c. 536.

abrogate &c. 756; desert &c. (*relinquish*) 624; get rid of &c. 782.

abdicate; vacate, – one's seat; apply for –, accept- the stewardship of the Chiltern Hundreds; retire; tender –, send in –, hand in- one's resignation.

Adj. abdicant, renunciatory &c. *v.* **Phr.** 'Othello's occupation's gone.'

758. Consignee.—N. consignee, trustee, nominee, committee.

delegate; commiss-ary, -ioner; emissary, envoy, commissionaire; messenger &c. 534.

diplomatist, diplomat, *corps diplomatique*, embassy; am-, em-bassador; representative, resident, consul, legate, nuncio, internuncio, *chargé d'affaires*, *attaché*.

vicegerent &c. (*deputy*) 759; plenipotentiary.

functionary, placeman, curator; treasurer &c. 801; agent, factor, bailiff, steward, clerk, secretary, attorney, solicitor, proctor, broker, underwriter, commission agent, auctioneer, one's man of business; factotum &c. (*director*) 694; caretaker.

negotiator, go between; middleman; under agent, *employé*; servant &c. 746.

salesman; commercial, – traveller; bagman, *commis-voyageur*, touter.

newspaper –, own –, war –, special- correspondent; reporter.

759. Deputy.—N. deputy, substitute, vice, proxy, *locum tenens*, delegate, representative, next friend, surrogate, secondary.

regent, vicegerent, vizier, minister, vicar; premier &c. (*director*) 694; chancellor, prefect, provost, warden, lieutenant, archon, consul, proconsul; viceroy &c. (*governor*) 745; commissioner &c. 758; plenipotentiary, *alter ego.*

team, eight, eleven; champion.

V. be -deputy &c. *n.*; stand –, appear –, hold a brief –, answer- for; represent; stand –, walk- in the shoes of; stand in the stead of.

substitute, ablegate, accredit; commission, empower, delegate &c. 755.

Adj. acting; vice, -regal; accredited to.

Adv. in behalf of, by proxy.

Section II. Special Intersocial Volition

760. Permission.—N. permission, leave; allow-, suffer-ance; toler-ance, -ation; liberty, law, licence, concession, grace; indulgence &c. (*lenity*) 740; favour, dispensation, exemption, release; connivance; vouchsafement.

authorization, warranty, accordance, admission.

permit, warrant, *brevet*, precept, sanction, authority, *firman*; pass, -port; furlough, licence, *carte blanche*, ticket of leave; grant, charter, patent.

V. permit; give -permission &c. *n.*, - power; let, allow, admit; suffer, bear with, tolerate, recognize; concede &c. 762; accord, vouchsafe, favour, humour, gratify, indulge, stretch a point; wink at, connive at; shut one's eyes to.

grant, empower, charter, enfranchise, privilege, confer a privilege, license, authorize, warrant; sanction; entrust &c. (*commission*) 755.

give -*carte blanche*, - the reins to, - scope to &c. (*freedom*) 748; leave -alone, - it to one, - the door open; open the -door to, - floodgates; give a loose to.

let off; absolve &c. (*acquit*) 970; release, exonerate, dispense with.

ask -, beg -, request- -leave, - permission.

Adj. permitting &c. *v.*; permissive, indulgent; permitted &c. *v.*; patent, chartered, permissible, allowable, lawful, legitimate, legal; legalized &c. (*law*) 963; licit; unforbid, -den; unconditional.

Adv. permissibly; by -, with -, on- -leave &c. *n.*; *speciali gratiâ*; under favour of; *pace*; *ad libitum* &c. (*freely*) 748, (*at will*) 600; by all means &c. (*willingly*) 602; yes &c. (*assent*) 488.

761. Prohibition.—N. pro-, in-hibition; *veto*, disallowance; interdict, -ion; injunction; embargo, ban, *verboten*, taboo, proscription; *index expurgatorius*; restriction &c. (*restraint*) 751; hindrance &c. 706; forbidden fruit.

V. pro-, in-hibit; forbid, put one's *veto* upon, disallow; bar; debar &c. (*hinder*) 706, forefend.

keep -in, - within bounds; restrain &c. 751; cohibit, withhold, limit, circumscribe, clip the wings of, restrict, narrow; interdict, taboo; put -, place- under -an interdiction, - the ban; proscribe, censor; exclude, shut out; shut -, bolt -, show- the door; warn off; dash the cup from one's lips; forbid the banns.

Adj. prohibit-ive, -ory; interdictive; proscriptive; restrictive, exclusive; forbidding &c. *v.*

prohibited &c. *v.*; not -permitted &c. 760; unlicensed, contraband, under the ban of; illegal &c. 964; unauthorized, not to be thought of.

Adv. on no account &c. (*no*) 536.

Int. forbid it heaven! &c. (*deprecation*) 766.

hands -, keep- off! hold! stop! avast!

Phr. that will never do.

---

762. Consent.—N. consent; assent &c. 488; acquiescence; approval &c. 931; compliance, agreement, concession; yield-ance, -ingness; accession, acknowledgment, acceptance, agnition.

settlement, ratification, confirmation, adjustment.

permit &c. (*permission*) 760; promise &c. 768.

V. consent; assent &c. 488; yield assent, admit, allow, concede, grant, yield; come -over, - round; give in to, acknowledge, agnize, give consent, comply with, acquiesce, agree to, fall in with, accede, accept, embrace an offer, close with, take at one's word, have no objection.

satisfy, meet one's wishes, settle, come to terms &c. 488; not -refuse &c. 764; turn a willing ear &c. (*willingness*) 602; jump at; deign, vouchsafe; promise &c. 768.

Adj. consenting &c. *v.*; agreeable, compliant; agreed &c. (*assent*) 488; unconditional.

Adv. yes &c. (*assent*) 488; by all means &c. (*willingly*) 602; if –, as- you please; be it so, so be it, well and good, of course.

763. Offer.—N. offer, proffer, presentation, tender, bid, overture; propos-al, -ition; motion, invitation; candidature; offering &c. (*gift*) 784.

V. offer, proffer, present, tender; bid; propose, move; make -a motion, – advances; start; invite, hold out, place- at one's disposal, – in one's way, put forward.

hawk about; offer for sale &c. 796; press &c. (*request*) 765; lay at one's feet.

offer –, present- oneself; volunteer, come forward, be a candidate; stand –, bid- for; seek; be at one's service; go a begging; bribe &c. (*give*) 784.

Adj. offer-ing, -ed &c. *v.*; in the market, for sale, to let, disengaged, on hire.

---

764. Refusal.—N. refusal, rejection; non-, in-compliance; denial; declining &c. *v.*; declension; peremptory –, flat –, point blank- refusal; repulse, rebuff; discountenance.

recusancy, renunciation, abnegation, negation, protest, disclaimer; dissent &c. 489; revocation &c. 756.

V. refuse, reject, deny, decline; nill, negative; refuse –, withhold- one's assent; shake the head; close the -hand, – purse; grudge, begrudge, be slow to, hang fire.

be deaf to; turn -a deaf ear to, – one's back upon; set one's face against, discountenance, not hear of, have nothing to do with, wash one's hands of, stand aloof, forswear, set aside, cast behind one; not yield an inch &c. (*obstinacy*) 606.

resist, cross; not -grant &c. 762; repel, repulse; shut –, slam- the door in one's face; rebuff; send -back, – to the right about, – away with a flea in the ear; deny oneself, not be at home to; discard &c. (*repudiate*) 610; rescind &c. (*revoke*) 756; disclaim, protest; dissent &c. 489.

Adj. refusing &c. *v.*; rest-ive, -iff; recusant; uncomplying, noncompliant, unconsenting, uncomplaisant, protestant; not willing to hear of, deaf to.

refused &c. *v.*; ungranted, out of the question, not to be thought of, impossible.

Adv. no &c. 536; on no account, not for the world; no thank you.

Phr. *non possumus*; [ironically] your humble servant; *bien obligé*.

765. Request.—N. requ-est, -isition; claim &c. (*demand*) 741; petition, suit, prayer; begging letter, round-robin.

motion, overture, application, canvass, address, appeal, apostrophe; imprecation; rogation; proposal, proposition.

orison &c. (*worship*) 990; incantation &c. (*spell*) 993.

mendicancy; asking, panhandling, begging &c. *v.*; postulation, solicitation, invitation, entreaty, importunity, supplication, instance, impetration, imploration, obsecration, obtestation, invocation, interpellation.

V. request, ask; beg, crave, sue, pray, petition, solicit, invite, pop the question, make bold to ask; beg -leave, – a boon; apply to, call to, put to; call -upon, – for; make –, address –, prefer –, put up- a -request, – prayer, – petition;

766. [Negative request.] **Deprecation.—N.** deprecation, expostulation; remonstrance; intercession, mediation.

V. deprecate, protest, expostulate, enter a protest, intercede for.

Adj. deprecatory, expostulatory, intercessory, mediatorial.

deprecated, protested.

un-, unbe-sought; unasked &c. (*see* ask &c. 765).

Int. cry you mercy! God forbid! forbid it Heaven! Heaven -forefend, – forbid! far be it from! hands off! &c. (*prohibition*) 761.

---

make -application, – a requisition; ask –, trouble- one for; claim &c. (*demand*) 741; offer up prayers &c. (*worship*) 990; whistle for.

beg hard, entreat, beseech, plead, supplicate, implore, apostrophize; conjure, adjure; obtest; cry to, kneel to, appeal to; invoke, evoke; impetrate, imprecate, ply, press, urge, beset, importune, dun, tax, clamour for; cry -aloud, – for help; fall on one's knees; throw oneself at the feet of; come down on one's marrow-bones.

beg from door to door, send the hat round, go a begging; mendicate, mump, cadge, panhandle, beg one's bread.

dance attendance on, besiege, knock at the door.

bespeak, canvass, tout, make interest, court; seek, bid for &c. (*offer*) 763; publish the banns.

Adj. requesting &c. *v.*; precatory; suppli-ant, -cant, -catory; invoc-, imprec-, rog-atory; postulant, mendicant.

importunate, clamorous, urgent; solicitous; cap in hand; on one's -knees, – bended knees, – marrow-bones.

Adv. prithee, do, please, pray; be so good as, be good enough; have the goodness, vouchsafe, will you, I pray thee, if you please.

Int. for -God's, – heaven's, – goodness', – mercy's- sake.

767. Petitioner.—**N.** petitioner, solicitor, applicant; suppli-ant, -cant; suitor, candidate, claimant, postulant, aspirant, competitor, bidder; place –, pot –, mug- hunter; prizer.

beggar, mendicant, mumper, sturdy beggar, cadger, panhandler.

canvasser, barker, touter &c. 758.

sycophant, parasite &c. 886.

Section III. Conditional Intersocial Volition

768. Promise.—**N.** promise, undertaking, word, troth, plight, pledge, *parole*, word of honour, vow; oath &c. (*affirmation*) 535; profession, assurance, warranty, guarantee, insurance, obligation; contract &c. 769.

engagement, pre-engagement: affiance; betroth, -al, -ment; marriage -compact, – vow.

V. promise; give a -promise &c. *n.*; undertake, engage; make –, form- an engagement; enter -into, – on- an engagement; bind –, tie –, pledge –, commit –, take upon- oneself; vow; swear &c. (*affirm*) 535, give –, pass –, pledge –, plight- one's -word, – honour, – credit, – troth; betroth, plight faith; take the vows.

assure, warrant, guarantee, vouch for, avouch, covenant &c. 769; attest &c. (*bear witness*) 467.

hold out an expectation; contract an obligation; become -bound to, – sponsor for; answer –, be answerable- for; secure; give security &c. 771; underwrite.

adjure, administer an oath, put to one's oath, swear a witness.

Adj. promising &c. *v.*; promissory; votive; under hand and seal; upon -oath, – affirmation.

promised &c. *v.*; affianced, pledged, bound; committed, compromised; in for it.

Adv. as one's head shall answer for; upon my honour.

Phr. in for a penny, in for a pound.

768a. Release from engagement.—**N.** release &c. (*liberation*) 750.

Adj. absolute; unconditional &c. (*free*) 748.

769. Compact.—**N.** compact, contract, agreement, bargain, deal, transaction; affidation; pact, -ion; bond, covenant, indenture.

stipulation, settlement, convention; compromise, *cartel*.

protocol, treaty, *concordat*, *Zollverein*, *Sonderbund*, charter, *Magna Charta*, Pragmatic Sanction.

negotiation &c. (*bargaining*) 794; diplomacy &c. (*mediation*) 724; negotiator &c. (*agent*) 758.

ratification, completion, signature, seal, sigil, signet.

V. contract, covenant, agree for, engage &c. (*promise*) 768.

treat, negotiate, stipulate, make terms; bargain &c. (*barter*) 794.

make –, strike- a bargain; come to -terms, – an understanding; compromise &c. 774; set at rest; close, – with; conclude, complete, settle; confirm, ratify, clench, subscribe, underwrite; en-, in-dorse; put the seal to; sign, seal &c. (*attest*) 467; indent.

take one at one's word, bargain by inch of candle.

Adj. contractual, agreed &c. *v.*; conventional; under hand and seal; signed, sealed and delivered.

Phr. *caveat emptor*.

770. Conditions.—**N.** conditions, terms; articles, – of agreement.

clauses, provisions; proviso &c. (*qualification*) 469; covenant, stipulation, obligation, *ultimatum*, *sine quâ non*; *casus fœderis*.

V. make –, come to- -terms &c. (*contract*) 769; make it a condition, stipulate, insist upon, make a point of; bind, tie up.

Adj. conditional, provisional, guarded, fenced, hedged in.

Adv. conditionally &c. (*with qualification*) 469; provisionally, *pro re natâ*; on condition; with a reservation.

771. Security.—**N.** security; guaran-ty, -tee; gage, warranty, bond, tie, pledge, plight, mortgage, debenture, hypothecation, bill of sale, lien, pignus, pawn, pignoration; real security; bottomry; collateral, vadium.

stake, deposit, earnest, handsel, caution.

promissory note; bill, – of exchange; I.O.U.; personal security, covenant, specialty; *parole* &c. (*promise*) 768.

acceptance, indorsement, signature, execution, stamp, seal.

spon-sor, -sion, -sorship; surety, bail; mainpernor, hostage.

recognizance; deed –, covenant- of indemnity.

authentication, verification, warrant, certificate, voucher, docket, doquet; record &c. 551; probate, attested copy.

receipt; ac-, quittance; discharge, release.

muniment, title-deed, instrument; deed, – poll; assurance, insurance, indenture; charter &c. (*compact*) 769; charter-poll; paper, parchment, settlement, will, testament, last will and testament, codicil.

V. give -security, – bail, – substantial bail; go bail; pawn, impawn, hock, spout, mortgage, hypothecate, impignorate.

guarantee, warrant, assure; accept, indorse, underwrite, insure.

execute, stamp; sign, seal &c. (*evidence*) 467.

let, sett; grant –, take –, hold- a lease; hold in pledge; lend on security &c. 787.

Adj. secure, -ed; pledged &c. *v.*; in pawn, on deposit.

772. Observance.—**N.** observance, performance, compliance; obedience

773. Non-observance. — **N.** non-observance &c. 772; evasion, inob-

&c. 743; fulfilment, satisfaction, discharge; acquit-tance, -tal.

adhesion, acknowledgment; fidelity &c. (*probity*) 939; exact &c. 494- observance.

V. observe, comply with, respect, acknowledge, abide by; cling to, adhere to, be faithful to, act up to; meet, fulfil; carry -out, - into execution; execute, perform, keep, satisfy, discharge; do one's office.

perform -, fulfill -, discharge -, acquit oneself of- an obligation; make good; make good -, keep- one's -word, - promise; redeem one's pledge; keep faith with, stand to one's engagement.

Adj. observant, faithful, true, loyal; honourable &c. 939; true as the -dial to the sun, - needle to the pole; punct-ual, -ilious; meticulous; literal &c. (*exact*) 494; as good as one's word.

Adv. faithfully &c. *adj*.

servance, failure, omission, neglect, laches, laxity, informality.

infringement, infraction; violation, transgression.

retractation, repudiation, nullification; protest; forfeiture.

lawlessness; disobedience &c. 742; bad faith &c. 940.

V. fail, neglect, omit, elude, evade, give the go by to, cut, set aside, ignore; shut -, close- one's eyes to, avoid.

infringe, transgress, pirate, violate, break, trample under foot, do violence to, drive a coach and six through.

discard, protest, repudiate, fling to the winds, set at naught, nullify, declare null and void; cancel &c. (*wipe off*) 552.

retract, go back from, be off, forfeit, go from one's word, palter; stretch -, strain- a point.

Adj. violating &c. *v.*; lawless, transgressive; elusive, evasive; lax, casual; non-observant.

unfulfilled &c. (*see* fulfil &c. 772).

---

774. Compromise.—N. com-promise, -mutation, -position; middle term, *mezzo termine*; compensation &c. 30; adjustment, mutual concession.

V. com-promise, -mute, -pound; take the mean; split the difference, meet one half way, give and take; come to terms &c. (*contract*) 769; submit to -, abide by- arbitration; patch up, bridge over, fix up, arrange; adjust, - differences; agree; make -the best of, - a virtue of necessity; take the will for the deed.

Section IV. Possessive Relations*

1°. *Property in general*

775. Acquisition.—N. acquisition; gaining &c. *v.*; obtainment; procuration, -ement; purchase, descent, inheritance; gift &c. 784.

recovery, retrieval, revendication, replevin; redemption, salvage, trover; find, *trouvaille*, foundling.

gain, thrift; money-making, -grubbing; lucre, filthy lucre, loaves and fishes, the main chance, pelf; emolument &c. 973; wealth &c. 803.

profit, earnings, winnings, innings, clean-up, pickings, perquisite, net profit; income &c. (*receipt*) 810; proceeds, -duce, -duct; out-come, -put;

776. Loss.—N. loss; de-, perdition; forfeiture, lapse.

privation, bereavement; deprivation &c. (*dispossession*) 789; riddance.

V. lose; incur -, experience -, meet with- a loss; miss; mislay, let slip, allow to slip through the fingers, squander; be without &c. (*exempt*) 777*a*; forfeit.

get rid of &c. 782; waste &c. 638.

be lost, lapse.

Adj. losing &c. *v.*; not having &c. 777*a*.

shorn of, deprived of; denuded, bereaved, bereft, *minus*, cut off; dispos-

* That is, relations which concern property.

return, fruit, crop, harvest, tilth; second crop, aftermath; benefit &c. (*good*) 618.

sweepstakes, trick, prize, pool.

[Fraudulent acquisition] subreption; theft, stealing &c. 791.

V. acquire, get, gain, win, earn, obtain, procure, gather, annex; collect &c. 72; pick, – up; glean, take &c. 789.

find; come –, pitch –, light- upon; scrape -up, – together; get in, reap and carry, net, bag, sack, bring home, secure, come across, derive, draw, get in the harvest.

profit; make –, draw- profit; turn to -profit, – account; make -capital out of, – money by; obtain a return, reap the fruits of; reap –, gain- an advantage; turn -a penny, – an honest penny; make the pot boil, bring grist to the mill; make –, coin –, raise- money; raise -funds, – the wind; fill one's pocket &c. (*wealth*) 803.

treasure up &c. (*store*) 636; realize, clear; produce &c. 161; take &c. 789.

get back, recover, regain, retrieve, revendicate, replevy, redeem, come by one's own.

come -by, – in for; receive &c. 785; inherit; step into, – a fortune, – the shoes of; succeed to.

get -hold of, – between one's finger and thumb, – into one's hand, – at; take –, come into –, enter into- possession.

be -profitable &c. *adj.*; pay, answer.

accrue &c. (*be received*) 785.

Adj. acquir-ing, -ed &c. *v.*; acquisitive; productive, profitable, advantageous, gainful, remunerative, paying, lucrative.

sessed &c. 789; rid of, quit of; out of pocket.

lost &c. *v.*; long lost; irretrievable &c. (*hopeless*) 859; irredentist; off one's hands.

Int. farewell to! adieu to! good riddance!

---

777. Possession.—N. possession, seisin; ownership &c. 780; occupancy; hold, -ing; tenure, tenancy, feodality, dependency; villenage; socage, chivalry, knight service.

exclusive possession, impropriation, monopoly, corner; retention &c. 781; pre-possession, -occupancy; nine points of the law.

future possession, heritage, inheritance, heirship, reversion, fee, seigniority, feud, fief.

bird in hand, *uti possidetis*, *chose* in possession.

V. possess, have, hold, occupy, enjoy; be -possessed of &c. *adj.*; have -in hand &c. *adj.*; own &c. 780; command.

inherit; come -to, – in for.

engross, monopolize, forestall, regrate, impropriate, have all to oneself, corner; have a firm hold of &c. (*retain*) 781; get into one's hand &c. (*acquire*) 775.

belong to, appertain to, pertain to; be -in one's possession &c. *adj.*; vest in.

Adj. possessing &c. *v.*; worth; possessed of, seized of, master of, in possession of; endowed –, blest –, instinct –, fraught –, laden –, charged –, instilled –, with.

possessed &c. *v.*; on hand, by one; in hand, in store, in stock; in one's -hands, – grasp, – possession; at one's -command, – disposal; one's own &c. (*property*) 780.

unsold; unshared.

777a. Exemption.—N. exemption; exception, immunity, privilege, release &c. 927*a*; absence &c. 187.

V. not -have &c. 777; be -without &c. *adj.*

Adj. exempt from, devoid of, without, unpossessed of, unblest with, immune from.

not -having &c. 777; unpossessed; untenanted &c. (*vacant*) 187; without an owner.

unobtained, unacquired.

778. [Joint possession.] **Participation.—N.** participation; co-, joint-tenancy; possession –, tenancy- in common; joint –, common- stock; co-, partnership; communion; community of -possessions, – goods; communalism, communism, socialism, collectivism; co-operation &c. 709; profit sharing.

snacks, co-portion, picnic, hotchpotch; co-heirship, -parceny, -parcenary; gavelkind.

participator, sharer; co-, partner; shareholder; co-, joint-tenant; tenants in common; co-heir, -parcener.

communist, socialist.

V. par-ticipate, -take; share, – in; come in for a share; go -shares, – snacks, – halves; share and share alike.

have –, possess –, be seized- -in common, – as joint tenants &c. *n.*; join in; have a hand in &c. (*co-operate*) 709.

Adj. partaking &c. *v.*; communistic, socialistic, co-operative, profit sharing.

Adv. share and share alike.

779. Possessor.—N. possessor, holder; occup-ant, -ier; tenant; person –, man- -in possession &c. 777; renter, lodger, lessee, under-lessee; zemindar, ryot; tenant -on sufferance, – at will, – from year to year, – for years, – for life.

owner; propriet-or, -ress, -ary; impropriator, master, mistress, lord.

land-holder, -owner, -lord, -lady; lord -of the manor, – paramount; heritor, laird, vavasour, landed gentry, mesne lord.

cestui-que-trust, beneficiary, mortgagor.

grantee, feoffee, relessee, devisee; legat-ee, -ary.

trustee; holder &c.- of the legal estate; mortgagee.

right –, rightful- owner.

[Future possessor] heir, – apparent; – presumptive; heiress; inherit-or, -ress, -rix; reversioner, remainder-man.

780. Property.—N. property, possession, *suum cuique, meum et tuum.*

owner-, proprietor-, lord-ship; seignority; empire &c. (*dominion*) 737.

interest, stake, estate, right, title, claim, demand, holding; tenure &c. (*possession*) 777; vested –, contingent –, beneficial –, equitable- interest; use, trust, benefit; legal –, equitable- estate; seisin.

absolute interest, paramount estate, freehold; fee, – simple, – tail; estate -in fee, – in tail, – tail; estate in tail -male, – female, – general.

limitation, term, lease, settlement, strict settlement, particular estate; estate -for life, – for years, – *pur autre vie*; remainder, reversion, expectancy, possibility.

dower, dowry, *dot*, jointure, marriage portion, appanage, inheritance, heritage, patrimony, alimony; legacy &c. (*gift*) 784.

assets, belongings, means, resources, circumstances; wealth &c. 803; money &c. 800; what one -is worth, – will cut up for; estate and effects.

landed –, real- -estate, – property; realty; land, -s; subdivision; plot, site; tenements; hereditaments; corporeal –, incorporeal- hereditaments; acres; ground &c. (*earth*) 342; acquest; messuage.

territory, state, kingdom, principality, realm, empire, protectorate, margravate, dependancy, colony, sphere of influence, mandate.

manor, honour, domain, demesne; farm, ranch, plantation, *hacienda*; allodium &c. (*free*) 748; fief, feoff, feud, zemindary, dependency.

free-, copy-, lease-holds; chattels real; fixtures, plant, heirloom . easement; folkland; right of -common, – user.

personal -property, – estate, – effects; personalty, chattels, goods, effects, movables; stock, – in trade; things, traps, rattle-traps, paraphernalia; equipage &c. 633.

parcels, appurtenances.

impedimenta; lug-, bag-gage; bag and baggage; pelf; cargo, lading.

rent-roll; income &c. (*receipts*) 810.

patent, copyright; *chose* in action; credit &c. 805; debt &c. 806.

V. possess &c. 777; be the -possessor &c. 779- of· own; have for one's own, – very own; come in for, inherit; enfeoff.

savour of the realty.

be one's -property &c. *n.*; belong to; ap-, pertain to.

Adj. one's own; landed, predial, manorial, allodial, seigniorial; free-, copy-, lease-hold; feu-, feo-dal; hereditary, entailed, personal.

Adv. to one's -credit, – account; to the good.

to one and -his heirs for ever, – the heirs of his body, – his heirs and assigns, – his executors, administrators and assigns.

781. Retention.—N. retention; retaining &c. *v.*; keep, detention, custody; tenacity, firm hold, grasp, gripe, grip, iron grip.

fangs, teeth, claws, talons, nail, hook, tentacle, *tenaculum*; bond &c. (*vinculum*) 45.

clutches, tongs, forceps, pincers, nippers, pliers, tweezers, vice.

paw, hand, finger, wrist, fist, neaf, neif.

bird in hand; captive &c. 754.

V. retain, keep; hold, – fast, – tight, – one's own, – one's ground; clinch, clench, clutch, grasp, gripe, hug, have a firm hold of.

secure, withold, detain; hold –, keep- back; keep close; husband &c. (*store*) 636; reserve; have –, keep- in stock &c. (*possess*) 777; entail, tie up, settle.

Adj. retaining &c. *v.*; retentive, tenacious.

unforfeited, undeprived, undisposed, uncommunicated.

incommunicable, inalienable; in mortmain; in strict settlement.

Phr. *uti possidetis.*

782. Relinquishment. — N. relinquishment, abandonment &c. (*of a course*) 624; renunciation, expropriation, dereliction; cession, surrender, dispensation; resignation &c. 757; riddance.

derelict &c. *adj.*; jetsam; waif, foundling, orphan.

V. relinquish, give up, surrender, yield, cede; let -go, – slip; spare, drop, resign, forego, renounce, abjure, abandon, expropriate, give away, dispose of, part with; lay -aside, – apart, – down, – on the shelf &c. (*disuse*) 678; set –, put- aside; make away with, cast behind; discard, cast off, dismiss; maroon.

give -notice to quit, – warning; supersede; be –, get- -rid of, – quit of; eject &c. 297.

rid –, disburden –, divest –, dispossess- oneself of; wash one's hands of; divorce, desert; disinherit, cut off.

cast –, throw –, pitch –, fling- -away, – aside, – overboard, – to the dogs; cast –, throw –, sweep- to the winds; put –, turn –, sweep- away; jettison. quit one's hold.

Adj. relinquished &c. *v.*; cast off, derelict; unowned, unappropriated, unculled; left &c. (*residuary*) 40; divorced; disinherited.

Int. away with!

2°. *Transfer of Property*

783. Transfer.—N. transfer, conveyance, assignment, alienation, abalienation; demise, limitation; conveyancing; transmission &c. (*transference*) 270; enfeoffment, bargain and sale, lease and release; exchange &c. (*interchange*) 148; barter &c. 794; substitution &c. 147.

succession, reversion; shifting -use, – trust; devolution.

V. transfer, convey; alien, -ate; assign; grant &c. (*confer*) 784; consign; make –, hand- over; pass, hand, transmit, negotiate; hand down; exchange &c. (*interchange*) 148.

change -hands, – from one to another; devolve, succeed; come into possession &c. (*acquire*) 775; take over.

abalienate; disinherit; dispossess &c. 789; substitute &c. 147.

Adj. alienable, negotiable, transferable, reversional.

Phr. estate coming into possession.

784. Giving.—N. giving &c. *v.*; bestowal, donation; present-ation, -ment; accordance; con-, cession; delivery, consignment, dispensation, communication, endowment; invest-ment, -iture; award.

almsgiving, charity, liberality, generosity; philanthropy &c. 910.

[Thing given] gift, donation, present, *cadeau*; fairing; free gift, boon, favour, benefaction, grant, offering, oblation, sacrifice, immolation.

grace, act of grace, *bonus*, *bonanza*.

allowance, contribution, subscription, subsidy, tribute, subvention.

bequest, legacy, devise, will, dotation, appanage; dowry; voluntary -settlement, – conveyance &c. 783; amortization.

alms, largess, bounty, dole, sportule, donative, help, oblation, offertory, Peter's pence, *honorarium*, gratuity, Maundy money, Christmas box, Easter offering, vail, tip, *douceur*, drink money, *pourboire*, *Trinkgeld*, *backsheesh*; fee &c. (*recompense*) 973; consideration.

bribe, bait, ground-bait; peace-offering, handsel.

giver, grantor &c. *v.*; donor, feoffer, settlor; almoner; testator; investor, subscriber, contributor; fairy godmother; Santa Claus, benefactor &c. 816.

V. deliver, hand, pass, put into the hands of; hand –, make –, deliver –, pass –, turn- over.

present, give away, dispense, dispose of; give –, deal –, dole –, mete –, fork –, shell –, squeeze- out.

pay &c. 807; render, impart, communicate.

785. Receiving.—N. receiving &c. *v.*, acquisition &c. 775; reception &c. (*introduction*) 296; suscipiency, acceptance, admission.

re-, ac-cipient; assignee, devisee; lega-tee, -tary; grantee, feoffee, donee, relessee, lessee.

sportulary, stipendiary; beneficiary; pension-er, -ary; almsman.

income &c. (*receipt*) 810.

V. receive; take &c. 789; acquire &c. 775; admit.

take in, catch, touch; pocket; put into one's -pocket, – purse; accept; take off one's hands.

be received; come -in, – to hand; pass –, fall- into one's hand; go into one's pocket; fall to one's -lot, – share; come –, fall- to one; accrue; have -given &c. 784 to one.

Adj. receiving &c. *v.*; re-, suscipient.

received &c. *v.*; given &c. 784; second-hand.

not given, unbestowed &c. (*see* give, bestow &c. 784).

concede, cede, yield, part with, shed cast; spend &c. 809.
give, bestow, confer, grant, accord, award, assign.
entrust, consign, vest in.
make a present; allow, contribute, subscribe, donate, furnish its quota.
invest, endow, settle upon; bequeath, leave, devise.
furnish, supply, help; ad-, minister to; afford, spare; accommodate –, indulge –, favour- with; shower down upon; lavish, pour on, thrust upon; tip, bribe; tickle –, grease- the palm; offer &c. 763; sacrifice, immolate.
Adj. giving &c. *v.*; given &c. *v.*; allow-ed, -able; concessional; communicable; charitable, eleemosynary, sportulary, tributary; *gratis* &c. 815.

786. Apportionment.—N. apportion-, allot-, consign-, assign-, appointment; appropriation; dis-pensation, -tribution; allocation, division, deal; repartition; administration.
dividend, portion, contingent, share, allotment, lot, cut, split, measure, dose; dole, meed, pittance; *quantum*, ration; ratio, proportion, quota, *modicum*, mess, allowance.
V. apportion, divide; cut, split, divvy; distribute, administer, dispense; billet, allot, detail, cast, share, mete; portion –, parcel –, dole- out; deal, carve.
partition, assign, appropriate, appoint.
come in for one's share &c. (*participate*) 778.
Adj. apportioning &c. *v.*; respective.
Adv. respectively, each to each.

787. Lending.—N. lending &c. *v.*; loan, advance, accommodation, feneration; mortgage &c. (*security*) 771; investment.
mont-de-piété, pawnshop, hock shop, spout, my uncle's.
lender, pawnbroker, money-lender, usurer, Jew, Shylock.
V. lend, advance, loan, accommodate with; lend on security; pawn &c. (*security*) 771.
intrust, invest; place –, put- out to interest; sink, risk.
let, demise, lease, sett, under-, sub-let.
Adj. lending &c. *v.*; lent &c. *v.*; unborrowed &c. (*see* borrowed &c. 788).
Adv. in advance; on -loan, – security.

788. Borrowing. — N. borrowing pledging, pawning.
borrowed plumes; plagiarism &c. (*thieving*) 791.
replevin.
V. borrow, desume; pawn.
hire, rent, farm; take a -lease, – demise; take –, hire- by the -hour, – mile, – year &c.
raise –, take up- money; float bonds; raise the wind; fly a kite, borrow of Peter to pay Paul; run into debt &c. (*debt*) 806.
make use of, plagiarize, pirate.
replevy.

789. Taking.—N. taking &c. *v.*; reception &c. (*taking in*) 296; deglutition &c. (*taking food*) 298; appropriation, prehension, prensation; capture, caption; ap-, de-prehension; abreption, seizure; ab-duction, -lation; subtraction &c. (*subduction*) 38; abstraction, ademption.

790. Restitution.—N. restitution, return; ren-, red-dition; reinstatement, restoration; reinvestment, recuperation; repatriation; rehabilitation &c. (*reconstruction*) 660; reparation, atonement, indemnity, compensation, recompense.
release, replevin, redemption; recov-

dispossession; depriv-ation, -ement; bereavement; divestment; disherison; distraint, distress; sequestration, confiscation, attachment, execution; eviction &c. 297.

rapacity, extortion, vampirism, predacity, blood-sucking; theft &c. 791.

resumption; repris-e, -al; recovery &c. 775.

clutch, swoop, wrench; grip &c. (*retention*) 781; haul, take, catch; scramble.

taker, captor, capturer; vampire; extortioner.

V. take, catch, hook, nab, bag, sack, pocket, put into one's pocket, scrounge; receive; accept.

reap, crop, cull, pluck; gather &c. (*get*) 775; draw.

ap-, im-propriate; assume, possess oneself of; take possession of; commandeer; lay –, clap- one's hands on; help oneself to; make free with, dip one's hands into, lay under contribution; intercept; scramble for; deprive of.

take –, carry –, bear- -away, – off; abstract; hurry off –, run away- with; abduct; steal &c. 791; ravish; seize; pounce –, spring- upon; swoop -to, – down upon; take by -storm, – assault; snatch, reave.

snap up, nip up, whip up, catch up; kidnap, crimp, capture, lay violent hands on.

get –, lay –, take –, catch –, lay fast –, take firm- hold of; lay by the heels, take prisoner; fasten upon, grip, grapple, embrace, gripe, clasp, grab, clutch, collar, throttle, take by the throat, claw, clinch, clench, make sure of; apprehend.

catch at, jump at, make a grab at, snap at, snatch at; reach, make a long arm, stretch forth one's hand.

take -from, – away from; deduct &c. 38; retrench &c. (*curtail*) 201; dispossess, ease one of, snatch from one's grasp; tear –, tear away –, wrench –, wrest –, wring- from; extort; deprive of, bereave; disinherit, cut off with a shilling.

oust &c. (*eject*) 297; divest; levy, distrain, confiscate; sequest-er, -rate, accroach; usurp; despoil, strip, fleece, shear, displume, impoverish, eat out of house and home; drain, – to the dregs; gut, dry, exhaust, swallow up; absorb &c. (*suck in*) 296; draw off; suck, – like a leech, – the blood of.

retake, resume; recover &c. 775.

Adj. taking &c. *v.*; privative, prehensile; pred-aceous, -al, -atory, -atorial; rap-acious, -torial; ravenous: parasitic; all-devouring, -engulfing.

bereft &c. 776.

Adv. at one fell swoop.

Phr. give an inch and take an ell.

ery &c. (*getting back*) 775; remitter, reversion.

V. return, restore; recondition; give –, carry –, bring- back; render, – up; give up; let go, unclutch; dis-, re-gorge; regurgitate; recoup, reimburse, repay, indemnify, reinvest, remit, rehabilitate; repair &c. (*make good*) 660.

redeem, recover &c. (*get back*) 775; take back again; revest, revert.

Adj. restoring &c. *v.*; recuperative &c. 660; in full restitution, to compensate for.

Phr. *suum cuique*.

---

791. Stealing.—N. stealing &c. *v.*; theft, thievery, robbery, latrociny, direption; abstraction, appropriation; plagiar-y, -ism; rape, kidnapping, depredation; raid, hold up.

spoliation, plunder, pillage; sack, -age; rapine, *brigandage*, highway robbery, foray, *razzia*; black-mail; piracy, privateering, buccaneering; filibuster-ing, -ism; burglary; house-breaking; cattle-stealing, -rustling, -lifting.

peculation, embezzlement; fraud &c. 545; larceny, petty larceny, pilfering, shop-lifting.

thievishness, rapacity, kleptomania, Alsatia; den of -Cacus, – thieves.

licence to plunder, letters of marque.

V. steal, thieve, rob, purloin, pilfer, filch, lift, prig, bag, nim, crib, cabbage, palm; abstract; appropriate, plagiarize.

convey away, carry off, abduct, kidnap, shanghai, impress, crimp; make –, walk –, run- off with; run away with; spirit away; seize &c. (*lay violent hands on*) 789.

plunder, pillage, rifle, sack, loot, ransack, spoil, spoliate, despoil, strip, sweep, gut, forage, levy black-mail, pirate, pickeer, maraud, lift cattle, rustle, poach, smuggle, run.

stick –, hold- up.

swindle, peculate, embezzle; sponge, mulct, rook, bilk, pluck, pigeon, skin, fleece, diddle; defraud &c. 545; obtain under false pretences; live by one's wits.

rob –, borrow of- Peter to pay Paul; set a thief to catch a thief.

disregard the distinction between *meum* and *tuum*.

Adj. thieving &c. *v.*; thievish, light-fingered; fur-acious, -tive; piratical; pred-aceous, -al, -atory, -atorial; raptorial &c. (*rapacious*) 789.

stolen &c. *v.*

Phr. *sic vos non vobis*.

792. Thief.—N. thief, robber, ***homo trium literarum***, pilferer, rifler, filcher, plagiarist.

spoiler, depredator, pillager, marauder; harpy, shark, land-shark, falcon, moss-trooper, bushranger, Bedouin, brigand, freebooter, bandit, thug, dacoit, pirate, corsair, viking, Paul Jones; buccan-eer, -ier; piqu-, pick-eerer; rover, ranger, privateer, filibuster; rapparee, wrecker, picaroon; smuggler, poacher, plunderer; racketeer.

highwayman, Dick Turpin, Claude Duval, Macheath, knight of the road, footpad, sturdy beggar; abductor, kidnapper.

cut-, pick-purse; pick-pocket, light-fingered gentry; sharper; card-, skittle-sharper; crook; thimble-rigger; rook, Greek, blackleg, leg, welsher, defaulter; Autolycus, Cacus, Barabbas, Jeremy Diddler, Robert Macaire, artful dodger, trickster; swell mob, *chevalier d'industrie*; shop-lifter.

swindler, peculator; forger, coiner, counterfeiter, shoful; fence, receiver of stolen goods, duffer; smasher.

burglar, housebreaker; cracks-, mags-man; Bill Sikes, Jack Sheppard, Jonathan Wild, Raffles, cat burglar.

793. Booty.—N. booty, spoil, plunder, prize, loot, graft, swag, pickings, boodle; *spolia opima*, prey; blackmail; stolen goods.

Adj. looting &c. *n.*; manubial, spoliative.

3°. *Interchange of Property*

794. Barter.—N. barter, exchange, scorse, truck system; interchange &c. 148.

a Roland for an Oliver; *quid pro quo*; com-mutation, -position.

trade, commerce, mercature, buying and selling, bargain and sale; traffic, business, nundination, custom, shopping; commercial enterprise, speculation, jobbing, stock-jobbing, *agiotage*, brokery, arbitrage.

dealing, transaction, negotiation, bargain.

free trade.

V. barter, exchange, truck, scorse, swop; interchange &c. 148; commutate &c. (*substitute*) 147; compound for.

trade, traffic, buy and sell, give and take, nundinate; carry on –, ply –, drive- a trade; be in -business, – the city; keep a shop, deal in, employ one's capital in.

trade –, deal –, have dealings- with; transact –, do- business with; open –, keep- an account with.

bargain; drive –, make- a bargain; negotiate, bid for; dicker, haggle, higgle; chaffer, huckster, cheapen, beat down; stickle, – for; out-, under-bid; ask, charge; strike a bargain &c. (*contract*) 769.

speculate, give a sprat to catch a herring; buy in the cheapest and sell in the dearest market; rig the market.

Adj. commercial, mercantile, trading; interchangeable, marketable, staple, in the market, for sale.

wholesale, retail.

Adv. across the counter; on 'change.

795. Purchase.—**N.** purchase, emption; buying, purchasing, shopping; pre-emption, refusal.

coemption, bribery; slave trade.

buyer, purchaser, *emptor*, vendee; patron, employer, client, customer, *clientèle*.

V. buy, purchase, invest in, procure; rent &c. (*hire*) 788; repurchase, buy in.

keep in one's pay, bribe, suborn; pay &c. 807; spend &c. 809.

make –, complete- a purchase; buy over the counter; pay cash for.

shop, market, go a shopping.

Adj. purchased &c. *v.*

Phr. *caveat emptor*.

796. Sale.—**N.** sale, vent, disposal; auction, roup, Dutch auction; custom &c. (*traffic*) 794.

vendi-bility, -bleness.

seller, salesman; peddler, smous; vender, vendor, consignor; merchant &c. 797; auctioneer.

V. sell, vend, dispose of, effect a sale; sell -over the counter, – by auction &c. *n.*; dispense, retail; deal in &c. 794; sell -off, – out; turn into money; realize; bring -to, – under- the hammer; put up to auction; auction, offer –, put up- for sale; hawk, peddle, bring to market; offer &c. 763; undersell; dump, unload.

let; mortgage &c. (*security*) 771.

Adj. under the hammer, in the market, for sale.

saleable, marketable, vendible, in demand, having a ready sale; unsaleable &c., unpurchased, unbought; on one's hands.

797. Merchant.—**N.** merchant, trader, dealer, monger, chandler, salesman; changer; regrater; shop-keeper, -man; trades-man, -people, -folk.

retailer; chapman, hawker, huckster, higgler; peddler, smous, pedlar, *colporteur*, cadger, Autolycus; sutler, *vivandière*; coster-man, -monger; market woman; cheap jack; caterer &c. 637; tallyman.

money-broker, -changer, -lender; stock-broker, -jobber; cambist, usurer, moneyer, banker.

jobber; broker &c. (*agent*) 758; buyer &c. 795; seller &c. 796.

concern; firm &c. (*partnership*) 712.

798. Merchandise. — **N.** merchandise, ware, commodity, effects, goods, article, stock, produce, staple commodity; stock in trade &c. (*store*) 636; cargo &c. (*contents*) 190.

799. Mart.—**N.** mart; market, -place, *forum*; fair, bazaar, staple; stock –, exchange; 'change, *bourse*, Wall Street, Rialto, hall, guildhall; toll-booth, custom-house; Tattersalls.

shop, stall, booth; wharf; office, chambers, counting-house, *bureau*; coun-, comp-ter.

ware-house, -room; depot, interposit, *entrepôt*, *emporium*, establishment; store &c. 636.

open market, market-overt.

4°. *Monetary Relations*

800. Money.—**N.** money -matters, – market; finance; accounts &c. 811; funds, treasure; capital, stock; assets &c. (*property*) 780; wealth &c. 803; supplies, ways and means, wherewithal, sinews of war, almighty dollar, needful, cash.

sum, amount; balance, -sheet; sum total; proceeds &c. (*receipts*) 810.

currency, circulating medium, specie; coin, – of the realm; piece, hard cash, dollar, sterling coin; pounds shillings and pence; £ s. d., guineas; pocket, breeches pocket, purse; money in hand; the best, ready, – money; filthy lucre, shekels, roll, jack, rhino, blunt, dust, bawbees, brass, dibs, dough, mopus, tin, salt, chink, oof, spondulics, pile, wads.

precious metals, gold, silver, copper, nickel; bullion, bar, ingot, nugget.

petty cash; pocket-, pin-money; small –, change; small coin, loose cash; doit, stiver, rap, mite, farthing, *sou*, penny, shilling, bob, tanner, tester, groat, guinea, ducat; *rouleau*; *wampum*; good –, round –, lump-sum; power –, mint –, tons- of money; plum, lac of rupees, millions, money-bags, miser's hoard, stocking, mine of wealth &c. 803.

[Science of coins] numismatics, chrysology.

paper-money; money –, postal –, Post Office- order; note, – of hand; bank –, treasury- note; Bradbury; promissory note; I O U., bond; bill, – of exchange; draft, cheque, order, warrant, coupon, debenture, exchequer bill, *assignat*, greenback, gold –, silver- certificate.

copper, nickel, dime, quarter, two bits, half a dollar, dollar, buck, simoleon, fiver, tenner, a twenty, a sawbuck, a century, a grand; eagle, double eagle.

gold standard, bimetallism, fiat money; rate of –, exchange; in-, de-flation.

remittance &c. (*payment*) 807; credit &c. 805; liability &c. 806; solvency &c. 803.

draw-er, -ee; oblig-or, -ee; moneyer, coiner, counterfeiter, forger.

false –, bad- money; base –, counterfeit- coin, flash note, slip, kite; Bank of Elegance.

argumentum ad crumenam.

V. amount to, come to, mount up to; touch the pocket; draw, – upon; endorse &c. (*security*) 771; issue, utter, circulate; discount &c. 813.

forge, counterfeit, coin, circulate –, pass- bad money.

Adj. monetary, pecuniary, crumenal, fiscal, financial, sumptuary, numismatical; sterling; solvent &c. 803.

801. Treasurer.—N. treasurer; bursar, -y; purser, purse-bearer; cash-keeper, banker; depositary; questor, receiver, steward, trustee, chartered –, accountant; Accountant-General, almoner, liquidator, paymaster, cashier, teller; cambist; money-changer &c. (*merchant*) 797.

financier, Chancellor of the Exchequer, minister of finance; Secretary of the Treasury, Director of the Budget, Controller of Currency.

802. Treasury.—N. treasury, thesaurus, bank, exchequer, almonry, fisc, hanaper, bursary; safe; strong-box, -hold, -room; coffer; chest &c. (*receptacle*) 191; depository &c. 636; till, -er; cash-box, -register, purse, pocket-book, wallet; money-bag, -belt, -box; *porte-monnaie*.

purse-strings; pocket, breeches pocket.

sinking fund; stocks; government –, public –, parliamentary- -stocks, – funds, – securities, bonds; gilt-edged securities; Consols, Liberty bonds, government bonds, *crédit mobilier*.

803. Wealth.—N. wealth, riches, fortune, handsome fortune, opulence, affluence; good –, easy- circumstances; independence; competence &c. (*sufficiency*) 639; solvency, soundness, solidity.

provision, livelihood, maintenance; alimony, dowry; means, resources, substance; property &c. 780; command of money.

income &c. 810; capital, money; round sum &c. (*treasure*) 800; mint of money, mine of wealth, *El Dorado*, Pactolus, Golconda, Potosi, *bonanza*; philosopher's stone.

long –, full –, well lined –, heavy- purse; purse of Fortunatus.

pelf, Mammon, lucre, filthy lucre; loaves and fishes; fleshpots of Egypt.

rich –, moneyed –, warm- man; man of substance; capitalist, millionaire, Nabob, Crœsus, Midas, Plutus, Dives, Timon of Athens; Timo-, Pluto-cracy; Danaë.

V. be -rich &c. *adj.*; roll –, wallow- in -wealth, – riches; have money to burn.

afford, well afford; command -money, – a sum; make both ends meet, hold one's head above water.

become -rich &c. *adj.*; fill one's -pocket &c. (*treasury*) 802; feather one's nest, clean up –, make- a fortune; make money &c. (*acquire*) 775.

enrich, imburse.

worship -Mammon, – the golden calf.

Adj. wealthy, rich, affluent, opulent, moneyed, monied, worth -a great deal,

804. Poverty.—N. poverty, indigence, penury, pauperism, destitution, want; need, -iness; lack, necessity, privation, distress, difficulties, wolf at the door.

bad –, poor –, needy –, embarrassed –, reduced –, straitened- circumstances; slender –, narrow- means; straits; hand to mouth existence, *res angusta domi*, low water, impecuniosity.

beggary; mendi-cancy, -city; broken –, loss of- fortune; insolvency &c. (*non-payment*) 808.

empty -purse, – pocket; light purse; beggarly account of empty boxes.

poor man, pauper, mendicant, mumper, beggar, starveling; *pauvre diable*.

V. be -poor &c. *adj.*; want, lack, starve, live from hand to mouth, have seen better days, go down in the world, be on one's uppers, come upon the parish; go to -the dogs, – wrack and ruin; not have a -penny &c. (*money*) 800, – shot in one's locker; beg one's bread; *tirer le diable par la queue*; run into debt &c. (*debt*) 806.

render -poor &c. *adj.*; impoverish; reduce, – to poverty; pauperize, fleece, ruin, bring to the parish.

Adj. poor, indigent; poverty-stricken; badly –, poorly –, ill- off; poor as -a rat, – a church mouse, – Job's turkey, – Job; fortune-, dower-, money-, penni-less; unportioned, unmoneyed; impecunious; broke, flat; out –, short- of -money, – cash; without –, not worth- a rap &c. (*money*) 800; *qui n'a pas le sou*, out of pocket, hard up; out at

– much; well -to do, – off; warm; well –, provided for.

made of money; rich as Crœsus; rolling in -riches, – wealth.

flush, – of -cash, – money, – tin; in -funds, – cash, – full feather; solvent, solid, sound, pecunious, out of debt, all straight; able to pay 20s in the £.

Phr. one's ship coming in.

elbows, down at heels; seedy, bare-foot; beggar-ly, -ed; destitute; fleeced, strapped, stripped; bereft, bereaved; reduced.

in -want &c. *n.*; needy, necessitous, distressed, pinched, straitened; put to one's -shifts, – last shifts; unable to -keep the wolf from the door, – make both ends meet; embarrassed, under hatches; involved &c. (*in debt*) 806; insolvent &c. (*not paying*) 808.

Adv. *in formâ pauperis.*

Phr. *zonam perdidit.*

---

805. Credit.—**N.** credit, trust, tick, score, tally, account.

letter of credit, circular note; duplicate; mortgage, lien, debenture, paper credit, floating capital; draft; securities.

creditor, lender, lessor, mortgagee; dun; usurer.

V. keep –, run up- an account with; entrust, credit, accredit.

place to one's -credit, – account; give –, take- credit; fly a kite.

Adj. credit-ing, -ed; accredited.

Adv. on -credit &c. *n.*; to the -account, – credit- of.

---

806. Debt.—**N.** debt, obligation, liability, indebtment, debit, score.

arrears, deferred payment, deficit, default; insolvency &c. (*non-payment*) 808; bad debt.

interest; usance, usury; premium; floating -debt, – capital.

debtor, debitor; mortgagor; defaulter &c. 808; borrower.

V. be -in debt &c. *adj.*; owe; incur –, contract- a debt &c. *n.*; run up -a bill, – a score, – an account; go on tick, put on the cuff; borrow &c. 788; run –, get- into debt; outrun the constable.

answer –, go bail- for; back one's note.

Adj. indebted; liable, chargeable, answerable for.

in -debt, – embarrassed circumstances, – difficulties; incumbered, involved; involved –, plunged –, deep –, over head and ears- in debt; deeply involved; fast tied up; insolvent &c. (*not paying*) 808; *minus*, out of pocket.

unpaid; unrequited, unrewarded; owing, due, in arrear, outstanding.

807. Payment.—**N.** pay-, defrayment; discharge; ac-, quittance; settlement, clearance, liquidation, satisfaction, reckoning, arrangement.

acknowledgment, release; receipt, – in full, – in full of all demands; voucher.

repayment, reimbursement, retribution; pay &c. (*reward*) 973; money paid &c. (*expenditure*) 809.

ready money &c. (*cash*) 800; stake, remittance, instalment.

payer, liquidator &c. 801.

V. pay, defray, make payment; pay -down, – on the nail, – ready money, – at sight, – in advance; cash, honour a bill, acknowledge; redeem; pay in kind.

808. Non-payment.—**N.** non-payment; default, defalcation; protest, repudiation; application of the sponge; whitewashing.

insolvency, bankruptcy, failure; overdraft, overdrawn account; insufficiency &c. 640; run upon a bank.

waste paper bonds; dishonoured –, protested- bills; bogus cheque.

bankrupt, insolvent debtor, lame duck, man of straw, welsher, stag, defaulter, absconder, levanter.

V. not -pay &c. 807; fail, break, stop payment; become -insolvent, – bankrupt; be gazetted; abscond.

protest, dishonour, repudiate, nullify.

pay under protest; button up one's

pay one's -way, – shot, – footing; pay -the piper, – sauce for all, – costs; do the needful; come across; shell –, fork- out; come down with, – the dust; tickle –, grease- the palm; expend &c. 809; put –, lay- down.

discharge, settle, quit, acquit oneself of; account –, reckon –, settle –, be even –, be quits- with; strike a balance; settle –, balance –, square- accounts with; quit scores; foot the bill; wipe –, clear- off old scores; satisfy; pay in full; satisfy –, pay in full of- all demands; clear, liquidate; pay -up, – old debts.

disgorge, make repayment; repay, refund, reimburse, retribute; make compensation &c. 30.

Adj. paying &c., paid &c. *v.*; owing nothing, out of debt, all straight, clear of -debt, – encumbrance; unowed, never indebted.

Adv. to the tune of; on the nail; money –, cash- down; cash on delivery.

pockets, draw the purse strings; apply the sponge; pay over the left shoulder, get whitewashed; swindle &c. 791; run up bills, fly kites.

Adj. not paying; in debt &c. 806; behindhand, in arrear; beggared &c. (*poor*) 804; unable to make both ends meet; *minus*; worse than nothing.

insolvent, bankrupt, in the gazette, gazetted, ruined.

unpaid &c. (*outstanding*) 806; *gratis* &c. 815; unremunerated.

---

809. Expenditure.—N. expenditure, money going out; out-goings, -lay; expenses, disbursement; prime cost &c. (*price*) 812; circulation; run upon a bank.

[Money paid] payment &c. 807; pay &c. (*remuneration*) 973; bribe &c. 973; fee, footing, garnish; subsidy; tribute, Peter's pence; contingent, quota; donation &c. 784.

pay in advance, earnest, handsel, deposit, instalment.

investment; purchase &c. 795.

V. expend, spend; run –, get- through; pay, disburse; open –, loose –, untie- the purse strings; lay –, shell –, fork- out; bleed; make up a sum, invest, sink money.

fee &c. (*reward*) 973; pay one's way &c. (*pay*) 807; subscribe &c. (*give*) 784; subsidize, bribe.

Adj. expend-ing, -ed &c. *v.*; sumptuary, liberal &c. 816; open-handed, lavish &c. 818; expensive &c. 814.

810. Receipt.—N. receipt, accountable –, conditional –, binding –, return- receipt; value received, money coming in; income, incomings, innings, revenue, return, proceeds; gross receipts, net profit; earnings &c. (*gain*) 775.

rent, – roll; rent-al, -age; rack-rent.

premium, *bonus*; sweepstakes, tontine, prize, drawing.

pension, annuity; jointure &c. (*property*) 780; alimony, pittance; emolument &c. (*remuneration*) 973.

V. receive &c. 785; take money; draw –, derive- from; get, be in receipt of, acquire &c. 775; take &c. 789.

bring in, yield, afford, pay, return; accrue &c. (*be received from*) 785.

Adj. receiv-ing, -ed &c. *v.*; profitable &c. (*gainful*) 775.

---

811. Accounts.—N. accounts, accompts; commercial –, monetary- arithmetic; statistics &c. (*numeration*) 85; money matters, finance, budget, bill, score, reckoning, account.

books, account book, ledger; day –, cash –, pass- book; journal; debtor and creditor –, cash –, petty cash –, running- account; account- current; balance, – sheet; *compte rendu*, account settled.

book-keeping, audit; double –, single- entry; reckoning &c. 85.

chartered –, certified public –, accountant; auditor, actuary, book-keeper; financier &c. 801; accounting party.

V. keep accounts, enter, post, book, credit, debit, carry over; take stock; balance –, make up –, square –, settle –, wind up –, cast up –, add up –, tot up- accounts; make accounts square.

bring to book, audit, tax, surcharge and falsify.

falsify –, garble –, cook –, doctor- an account.

Adj. monetary &c. 800; account-able, -ing; statistical.

812. Price.—**N.** price, amount, cost, expense, prime cost, charge, figure, demand, damage, fare, hire; wages &c. (*remuneration*) 973.

dues, duty, toll, tax, impost, cess, sess, tallage, levy, capitation-, poll-, income-, sur-, sales-, super-tax; gabel, *gabelle*; gavel, *octroi*, custom, tariff, excise, assessment, taxation, benevolence, tithe, tenths, exactment, ransom, salvage; broker-, wharf-, lighter-, ton-, freight-age.

worth, rate, value, valuation, appraisement, money's worth, par value; penny &c. -worth; price current, market price, quotation; what it will -fetch &c. *v.*

bill &c. (*account*) 811; shot.

V. bear –, set –, fix- a price; appraise, assess, price, charge, demand, ask, require, exact, run up; distrain; run up a bill &c. (*debt*) 806; have one's price; liquidate.

amount to, come to, mount up to; stand one in.

fetch, sell for, cost, bring in, yield, afford.

Adj. priced &c. *v.*; to the tune of, *ad valorem*; mercenary, venal.

Phr. no penny, no paternoster; *point d'argent, point de Suisse*; no longer pipe, no longer dance; no song, no supper.

one may have it for.

813. Discount.—**N.** discount, abatement, concession, reduction, depreciation, allowance, qualification, set off, drawback, poundage, *agio*, percentage; rebate, -ment; backwardation, contango; salvage; tare and tret.

V. discount, bate; a-, re-bate; deduct, reduce, mark down, take off, allow, give, make allowance; tax, depreciate.

Adj. discounting &c. *v.*

Adv. at a discount, below par.

814. Dearness. — **N.** dearness &c. *adj.*; high –, famine –, fancy- price; overcharge; extravagance; exorbitance, extortion; heavy pull upon the purse; Pyrrhic victory.

V. be -dear &c. *adj.*; cost -much, – a pretty penny; rise in price, look up.

overcharge, bleed, fleece, skin, extort.

pay -too much, – through the nose, – too dear for one's whistle.

Adj. dear; high, -priced; of great price, expensive, costly, precious, worth a Jew's eye, dear bought; unreasonable, extravagant, exorbitant, extortionate.

at a premium; not to be had, – for love or money; beyond –, above- price; priceless, of priceless value.

Adv. dear, -ly; at great –, heavy-cost; *à grands frais*.

Phr. prices looking up; *le jeu n'en vaut pas la chandelle*.

815. Cheapness.—**N.** cheapness, low price; depreciation; bargain; good penny &c.- worth, *bon marché*.

[Absence of charge] gratuity; free -quarters, – seats, – admission, – warren; pass, Annie Oakley; run of one's teeth; nominal price, peppercorn rent; labour of love.

drug in the market.

V. be -cheap &c. *adj.*; cost little; come down –, fall- in price.

buy for -a mere nothing, – an old song; have one's money's worth; cheapen, beat down.

Adj. cheap; low, – priced; moderate, reasonable; in-, un-expensive; well –, worth the money; *magnifique et pas cher*; good –, cheap- at the price; dirt –, dog- cheap; cheap, -as dirt, – and nasty; catchpenny.

reduced, marked down, half-price, depreciated, unsaleable.

gratuitous, *gratis*, free, for love,

– nothing; cost-, expense-less; without charge, not charged, untaxed; scot –, shot –, rent- free; free of -cost, – expense; honorary, unbought, unpaid, complimentary.

Adv. for a mere song; at -cost price, – prime cost, – a reduction, – a bargain; on the cheap.

816. Liberality.—**N.** liberality, generosity, munificence; bount-y, -eousness, -ifulness; hospitality; charity &c. (*beneficence*) 906.

benefactor, free giver, Lady Bountiful.

V. be -liberal &c. *adj.*; spend –, bleed- freely; shower down upon; open one's purse strings &c. (*disburse*) 809; spare no expense, give -with both hands, – *carte blanche.*

Adj. liberal, free, generous; charitable &c. (*beneficent*) 906; hospitable; bount-iful, -eous; handsome; unsparing, ungrudging; open-, free-, full-handed; open-, large-, free-hearted; munificent, princely, unstinting.

overpaid.

Adv. liberally, ungrudgingly, with open hand.

817. Economy.—**N.** economy, frugality; thrift, -iness; prudence, care, husbandry, good housewifery, savingness, retrenchment.

savings; prevention of waste, save-all; cheese parings and candle ends; parsimony &c. 819.

V. be -economical &c. *adj.*; economize, save; retrench; cut- down expenses, – one's coat according to one's cloth, make both ends meet, keep within compass, meet one's expenses, pay one's way; keep one's head above water; husband &c. (*lay by*) 636; save –, invest- money; put out to interest; provide –, save- -for, – against- a rainy day; feather one's nest; look after the main chance.

Adj. economical, frugal, careful, thrifty, saving, chary, spare, sparing; parsimonious &c. 819.

underpaid.

Adv. sparingly &c. *adj.*; *ne quid nimis.*

---

818. Prodigality.—**N.** prodi-gality, -gence; unthriftiness, waste, -fulness; profus-ion, -eness; extravagance; squandering &c. *v.*; lavishness; malversation.

prodigal; spend-, waste-thrift; losel, play-boy, spender, squanderer, locust.

V. be -prodigal &c. *adj.*; squander, lavish, sow broadcast; pour forth like water; pay through the nose &c. (*dear*) 814; spill, waste, dissipate, exhaust, drain, eat out of house and home, overdraw, outrun the constable; run -out, – through; misspend; throw -good money after bad, – the helve after the hatchet; burn the candle at both ends; make ducks and drakes of one's money; squander one's substance, spend money like water; fool –, potter –, muddle –, fritter –, throw- away one's money; pour water into a sieve, kill the goose that lays the golden eggs; *manger son blé en herbe.*

Adj. prodigal, profuse, thriftless, unthrifty, improvident, wasteful, losel,

819. Parsimony. — **N.** parsimony, parcity; parsimoniousness, stinginess &c. *adj.*; stint; illiberality, avarice, tenacity, avidity, rapacity, extortion, venality, cupidity; selfishness &c. 943; *auri sacra fames.*

miser, niggard, churl, screw, tightwad, skinflint, crib, codger, muckworm, money-grubber, pinchfist, scrimp, lickpenny, hunks, curmudgeon, *Harpagon*, Silas Marner, harpy, extortioner, Jew, usurer.

V. be -parsimonious &c. *adj.*; grudge, begrudge, stint, skimp, pinch, gripe, screw, dole out, hold back, withhold, starve, famish, live upon nothing, skin a flint.

drive a -bargain, – hard bargain; cheapen, beat down; stop one hole in a sieve; have an itching palm, grasp, grab.

Adj. parsimonious, penurious, stingy, miserly, mean, shabby, peddling, scrubby, pennywise, near, niggardly,

extravagant, lavish, dissipated, over liberal; full-handed &c. (*liberal*) 816.

penny wise and pound foolish.

Adv. with an unsparing hand; money burning one's pocket; recklessly profuse.

Int. hang the expense!

---

frugal to excess; close; fast-, close-, strait-handed; close-, hard-, tight-fisted; tight, sparing; chary; grudging, griping &c. *v.*; illiberal, ungenerous, churlish, hidebound, sordid, mercenary, venal, covetous, usurious, avaricious, greedy, extortionate, rapacious.

Adv. with a sparing hand.

CLASS VI

WORDS RELATING TO THE SENTIENT AND MORAL POWERS.

SECTION I. AFFECTIONS IN GENERAL

820. Affections.—N. affections, character, qualities, disposition, nature, spirit, tone; temper, -ament; *diathesis*, idiosyncrasy; cast –, habit –, frame- of -mind, – soul; predilection, turn; natural –, turn of mind; bent, bias, predisposition, proneness, proclivity; propen-sity, -sedness, -sion, -dency; vein, humour, mood, grain, mettle; sympathy &c. (*love*) 897.

soul, heart, breast, bosom, inner man; heart's -core, – strings, – blood; heart of hearts, *penetralia mentis*; secret and inmost recesses of the –, cockles of one's- heart; inmost -heart, – soul; back-bone.

passion, pervading spirit; ruling –, master- passion; *furore*; fulness of the heart, heyday of the blood, flesh and blood, flow of soul, force of character.

V. have –, possess- -affections &c. *n.*; be of a -character &c. *n.*; be -affected &c. *adj.*; breathe.

Adj. affected, characterized, formed, moulded, cast; at-, tempered; framed; pre-, disposed; prone, inclined; having a -bias &c. *n.*; tinctured –, imbued –, penetrated –, eaten up- with.

inborn, inbred, ingrained, in the grain, congenital, inherent, bred in the bone; deep-rooted, ineffaceable, inveterate; pathoscopic.

Adv. in one's -heart &c. *n.*; at heart; heart and soul &c. 821; in the -vein, – mood.

821. Feeling.—N. feeling; suffering &c. *v.*; endurance, tolerance, sufferance, supportance, experience, response; sympathy &c. (*love*) 897; impression, inspiration, affection, sensation, emotion, pathos, deep sense.

fire, warmth, glow, unction, *gusto*, vehemence; ferv-our, -ency; heartiness, cordiality; earnestness, eagerness; *empressement*, ardour, zeal, passion, enthusiasm, *verve*, *furore*, fanaticism; excitation of feeling &c. 824; fulness of the heart &c. (*disposition*) 820; passion &c. (*state of excitability*) 825; ecstasy &c. (*pleasure*) 827.

blush, suffusion, flush; hectic; tingling, thrill, kick, turn, shock; agitation &c. (*irregular motion*) 315; quiver, heaving, flutter, flurry, fluster, twitter, tremor; throb, -bing; pulsation, palpitation, panting; trepid-, perturb-ation; ruffle, hurry of spirits, pother, stew, ferment.

V. feel; receive an -impression &c. *n.*; be -impressed with &c. *adj.*; entertain –, harbour –, cherish- -feeling &c. *n.*

respond; catch the -flame, – infection; enter the spirit of.

bear, suffer, support, sustain, endure, brook, thole, aby; abide &c.

(*be composed*) 826; experience &c. (*meet with*) 151; taste, prove; labour –, smart- under; bear the brunt of, brave, stand.

swell, glow, warm, flush, blush, change colour, mantle; turn -colour, – pale, – red, – black in the face; blench, crimson, whiten, pale, tingle, thrill, heave, pant, throb, palpitate, go pit-a-pat, tremble, quiver, flutter, twitter; stagger, reel; shake &c. 315; be -agitated, – excited &c. 824; look -blue, – black; wince, draw a deep breath.

impress &c. (*excite the feelings*) 824.

Adj. feeling &c. *v.*; sentient; sensuous; sensor-ial, -y; emo-tive, -tional; of –, with- feeling &c. *n.*

warm, quick, lively, smart, strong, sharp, acute, cutting, piercing, incisive; keen, – as a razor; trenchant, pungent, racy, *piquant*, poignant, caustic.

impressive, deep, profound, indelible; deep-, home-, heart-felt; swelling, soul-stirring, deep-mouthed, heart-expanding, electric, thrilling, rapturous, ecstatic.

earnest, wistful, eager, breathless; fer-vent, -vid; gushing, passionate, warmhearted, hearty, cordial, sincere, zealous, enthusiastic, glowing, ardent, burning, red-hot, fiery, flaming; boiling, – over.

pervading, penetrating, absorbing; rabid, raving, feverish, fanatical, hysterical; impetuous &c. (*excitable*) 825; overmastering.

impressed –, moved –, touched –, affected –, penetrated –, seized –, imbued &c. 820- with; devoured by; wrought up &c. (*excited*) 824; struck all of a heap; rapt; in a -quiver &c. *n.*; enraptured &c. 829.

Adv. heart and soul, from the bottom of one's heart, *ab imo pectore*, *de profundis*, at heart, *con amore*, heartily, devoutly, over head and ears.

Phr. the heart -big, – full, – swelling, – beating, – pulsating, – throbbing, – thumping, – beating high, – melting, – overflowing, – bursting, – breaking.

822. Sensibility. — **N.** sensi-bility, -bleness, -tiveness; moral sensibility; impress-, affect-ibility; suscepti-bleness, -bility, -vity; mobility; viva-city, -ciousness; tender-, soft-ness; sentimental-ity, -ism.

excitability &c. 825; fastidiousness &c. 868; physical sensibility &c. 375.

sore -point, – place; where the shoe pinches.

V. be -sensible &c. *adj.*; have a -tender, – warm, – sensitive- heart.

take to –, treasure up in the- heart; shrink.

'die of a rose in aromatic pain'; touch to the quick.

Adj. sensi-ble, -tive; impressi-ble, -onable; suscepti-ve, -ble; alive to, impassion-able, -ed; gushing; warm-, tender-, soft-hearted; tender –, as a chicken; soft, sentimental, romantic; enthusiastic, highflying, spirited, mettlesome, vivacious, lively, expressive, mobile, tremblingly alive; excitable

823. Insensibility.—**N.** insensi-bility, -bleness; moral insensibility; inertness, *inertia*, *vis inertiæ*; impassi-bility, -bleness; inappetency, apathy, phlegm, dulness, hebetude, supineness, lukewarmness, insusceptibility, unimpressibility.

cold -fit, – blood, – heart; cold-, cool-ness; frigidity, *sang-froid*; stoicism, imperturbation &c. (*inexcitability*) 826; *nonchalance*, unconcern, dry eyes; *insouciance* &c. (*indifference*) 866; recklessness &c. 863; callousness; heart of stone, stock and stone, marble, deadness.

torp-or, -idity; obstupefaction, lethargy, coma, trance; sleep &c. 683; suspended animation; stup-or, -efaction; paralysis, palsy; numbness &c. (*physical insensibility*) 376.

neutrality; quietism, vegetation.

V. be -insensible &c. *adj.*; have a rhinoceros hide; show -insensibility &c. *n.*; not -mind, – care, – be affected

&c. 825; over-sensitive, without skin, thin-skinned; fastidious &c. 868.

Adv. sensibly &c. *adj.*; to the -quick, - inmost core.

---

by; have no desire for &c. 866; have –, feel –, take- no interest in; *nil admirari*; not care a -straw &c. (*unimportance*) 643 for; disregard &c. (*neglect*) 460; set at naught &c. (*make light of*) 483; turn a deaf ear to &c. (*inattention*) 458; vegetate.

render -insensible, – callous; blunt, obtund, numb, benumb, paralyze, chloroform, deaden, hebetate, stun, stupefy; brut-ify, -alize.

inure; harden, – the heart; steel, case-harden, sear.

Adj. insensible, unconscious; impassi-ve, -ble; blind to, deaf to, dead to; un-, in-susceptible; unimpress-ionable, -ible; passion-, spirit-, heart-, soul-less; unfeeling, unmoral.

apathetic; leuco-, phlegmatic; dull, frigid; cold, -blooded, -hearted; unemotional; cold as charity; flat, obtuse, inert, supine, sluggish, torpid; sleepy &c. (*inactive*) 683; languid, half-hearted, tame; numb, -ed; comatose; anæsthetic &c. 376; stupefied, chloroformed, palsy-stricken.

indifferent, lukewarm; Laodicean; careless, mindless, regardless; inattentive &c. 458; neglectful &c. 460; disregarding.

unconcerned, *nonchalant*, *pococurante*, *insouciant*, *sans souci*; unambitious &c. 866.

un-affected, -ruffled, -impressed, -inspired, -excited, -moved, -stirred, -touched, -shocked, -struck; unblushing &c. (*shameless*) 885; unanimated; vegetative.

callous, thick-skinned, pachydermatous, impervious; hard, -ened; inured, case-hardened; steeled –, proof- against; imperturbable &c. (*inexcitable*) 826; unfelt.

Adv. insensibly &c. *adj.*; *æquo animo*; without being -moved, – touched, – impressed; in cold blood; with -dry eyes, – withers unwrung.

Phr. never mind; it is of no consequence &c. (*unimportant*) 643; it cannot be helped; nothing coming amiss; it is all -the same, – one- to.

824. Excitation.—N. excitation of feeling; mental –, excitement; suscitation, galvanism, stimulation, piquancy, provocation, inspiration, calling forth, infection; interest, animation, agitation, perturbation; subjugation, fascination, intoxication; en-, ravishment; entrancement, high pressure.

unction, impressiveness &c. *adj.*; emotional appeal; melodrama; psychological moment, crisis; sensationalism.

trial of temper, *casus belli*; irritation &c. (*anger*) 900; passion &c. (*state of excitability*) 825; thrill &c. (*feeling*) 821; repression of feeling &c. 826.

V. excite, affect, touch, move, impress, strike, interest, intrigue, animate, inspire, impassion, smite, infect; stir –, fire –, warm- the blood; set astir; a-, wake; a-, waken; call forth; e-, pro-voke; raise up, summon up, call up, wake up, blow up, get up, light up; raise; get up steam, rouse, arouse, stir, fire, kindle, enkindle, apply the torch, set on fire, inflame, illuminate.

stimulate; ex-, suscitate; inspirit; spirit up, stir up, work up; infuse life into, give new life to; bring –, introduce- new blood; quicken;

sharpen, whet; work upon &c. (*incite*) 615; hurry on, give a fillip, put on one's mettle.

fan the -fire, - flame; blow the coals, stir the embers; fan, - into a flame; foster, heat, warm, foment, raise to a fever heat; keep -up, - the pot boiling; revive, rekindle; rake up, rip up.

stir -, play on -, come home to- the feelings; touch -a string, - a chord, - the soul, - the heart; go to one's heart, penetrate, pierce, go through one, touch to the quick, open the wound; possess -, pervade -, penetrate -, imbrue -, absorb -, affect -, disturb- the soul.

absorb, rivet the attention; sink into the -mind, - heart; prey on the mind; intoxicate; over-whelm, -power; *bouleverser*, upset, turn one's head.

fascinate; enrapture &c. (*give pleasure*) 829.

agitate, perturb, ruffle, fluster, flutter, shake, disturb, faze, startle, shock, stagger; give one a -shock, - turn; strike -dumb, - all of a heap; stun, astound, electrify, galvanize, petrify.

irritate, sting; cut, - to the -heart, - quick; try one's temper; fool to the top of one's bent, pique; infuriate, madden, make one's blood boil; lash into fury &c. (*wrath*) 900.

be -excited &c. *adj.*; flash up, flare up; catch the infection; thrill &c. (*feel*) 821; mantle; work oneself up; seethe, boil, simmer, foam, fume, flame, rage, rave; run mad &c. (*passion*) 825.

Adj. excited &c. *v.*; wrought up, on the *qui vive*, astir, sparkling; in a -quiver &c. 821, - fever, - ferment, - blaze, - state of excitement; in hysterics; black in the face, over-wrought; hot, red-hot, flushed, feverish; all -of a twitter, - of a flutter, - of a dither, - in a pucker; with -quivering lips, - tears in one's eyes.

flaming; boiling, - over; ebullient, seething; foaming, - at the mouth; fuming, raging, carried away by passion, wild, raving, frantic, mad, distracted, distraught, beside oneself, out of one's wits, amuck, ready to burst, *bouleversé*, demoniacal.

lost, *éperdu*, tempest-tossed; haggard; ready to sink.

stung to the quick, up, on one's high ropes.

exciting &c. *v.*; impressive, warm, glowing, fervid, swelling, imposing, spirit-stirring, thrilling; high-wrought; soul-stirring, -subduing; heart-swelling, -thrilling; agonizing &c. (*painful*) 830; telling, sensational, melodramatic, hysterical; over-powering, -whelming; more than flesh and blood can bear.

piquant &c. (*pungent*) 392; spicy, appetizing, provocative, *provoquant*, tantalizing.

Adv. till one is black in the face.

Phr. the heart -beating high, - going pit-a-pat, - leaping into one's mouth; the blood -being up, - boiling in one's veins; the eye -glistening, - 'in a fine frenzy rolling'; the head turned.

825. [Excess of sensitiveness.] **Excitability.—N.** excitability, impetuosity, vehemence; boisterousness &c. *adj.*; turbulence; impatience, intolerance, non-endurance; irritability &c. (*irascibility*) 901; itching &c. (*desire*) 865; wincing; disquiet, -ude; restlessness; fidgets, fidgetiness; agitation &c. (*irregular motion*) 315.

826. [Absence of excitability, or of excitement.] **Inexcitability.—N.** inexcit-, imperturb-, inirrit-ability; even temper, tranquil mind, dispassion; tolerance, toleration, patience.

passiveness &c. (*physical inertness*) 172; hebet-ude, -ation; impassibility &c. (*insensibility*) 823; stupefaction.

coolness, calmness &c. *adj.*; compo-

trepidation, perturbation, ruffle, hurry, -skurry, fuss, flurry; fluster, flutter; pother, stew, ferment; whirl; thrill &c. (*feeling*) 821; state –, fever- of excitement; transport.

passion, excitement, flush, heat; fever, -heat; fire, flame, fume, blood boiling; tumult; effervescence, ebullition; boiling, – over; whiff, gust, storm, tempest; scene, breaking out, burst, fit, paroxysm, explosion; out-break, -burst; agony.

violence &c. 173; fierceness &c. *adj.*; rage, fury, *furor, furore*, desperation, madness, distraction, raving, delirium, brain storm; frenzy, hysterics; intoxication; tearing –, raging- passion, towering rage; anger &c. 900.

fascination, infatuation, fanaticism; Quixot-ism, -ry; *tête montée*.

V. be -impatient &c. *adj.*; not be able to -bear &c. 826; bear ill, wince, chafe, champ the bit; be in a -stew &c. *n.*; be out of all patience, fidget, fuss, not have a wink of sleep; toss, – on one's pillow.

lose one's temper &c. 900; break –, burst –, fly- out; go –, fly- -off, – off the handle, – off at a tangent; explode; flare up, flame up, fire up, burst into a flame, take fire, fire, burn; boil, – over; foam, fume, rage, rave, rant, tear; go –, run- -wild, – mad; go into hysterics; run -riot, – amuck; *battre la campagne, faire le diable à quatre*, play the deuce; raise -Cain, – the devil.

Adj. excitable, easily excited, in an excitable state; highly strung; irritable &c. (*irascible*) 901; impatient, intolerant.

feverish, febrile, hysterical; delirious, mad, moody, maggoty-headed.

unquiet, mercurial, electric, galvanic, hasty, hurried, restless, fidgety, fussy; chafing &c. *v.*

startlish, mettlesome, high mettled, skittish.

vehement, demonstrative, violent, wild, furious, fierce, fiery, hot-headed, mad-cap.

over-zealous, enthusiastic, impassioned, fanatical; rabid &c. (*eager*) 865.

rampant, clamorous, uproarious, turbulent; tempestuous, boisterous; ...

sure, placidity, indisturbance, imperturbation, *sang-froid*, tranquillity, serenity; quiet, -ude; peace of mind, mental calmness.

staidness &c. *adj.*; gravity, sobriety, Quakerism; philosophy, equanimity, stoicism, command of temper; self-possession, -control, -command, -restraint; presence of mind.

submission &c. 725; resignation; suffer-, support-, endur-, long-suffer-, forbear-ance; longanimity; fortitude; patience -of Job, – 'on a monument,' – 'sovereign o'er transmuted ill'; moderation; repression –, subjugation- of feeling; restraint &c. 751.

tranquillization &c. (*moderation*) 174.

V. be -composed &c. *adj.*

laisser -faire, – aller; take things -easily, – as they come; take it easy, run on, live and let live; take -easily, – coolly, – in good part; *æquam servare mentem*.

bear, – well, – the brunt; go through, support, endure, brave, disregard.

tolerate, suffer, stand, bide; abide, aby; bear –, put up –, abide- with; acquiesce; submit &c. (*yield*) 725; submit with a good grace; resign –, reconcile- oneself to; brook, digest, eat, swallow, pocket, stomach; make -light of, – the best of, – a virtue of necessity; put a good face on, keep one's countenance; carry -on, – through; check &c. 751- oneself.

compose, appease &c. (*moderate*) 174; propitiate; repress &c. (*restrain*) 751; render insensible &c. 823; overcome –, allay –, repress- one's -excitability &c. 825; master one's feelings.

make -oneself, – one's mind- easy; set one's mind at -ease, – rest.

calm –, cool- down; thaw, grow cool.

be -borne, – endured; go down.

Adj. in-, un-excitable; imperturbable; unsusceptible &c. (*insensible*) 823; un-, dis-passionate; cold-blooded, inirritable; enduring &c. *v.*; stoical, Platonic, philosophic, staid, stayed; sober, – minded; grave; sober –, grave- as a judge; sedate, demure, cool-, level-headed; steady.

easy-going, peaceful, placid, calm; quiet, – as a mouse; tranquil, serene;

bulent, tempestuous, tumultuary, boisterous.

impulsive, impetuous, passionate; uncontroll-ed, -able; ungovernable, irrepressible, stanchless, inextinguishable, burning, simmering, volcanic, ready to burst forth.

excit-ed, -ing &c. 824.

Int. pish! pshaw!

Phr. *noli me tangere.*

---

cool, – as -a cucumber, – custard; undemonstrative.

temperate &c. (*moderate*) 174; composed, collected; un-excited, -stirred, -ruffled, -disturbed, -perturbed, -impassioned; unoffended; unresisting.

meek, tolerant; patient, – as Job; submissive &c. 725; tame; content, resigned, chastened, subdued, lamblike; gentle, – as a lamb; *suaviter in modo*; mild, – as mother's milk; soft as peppermint; armed with patience, bearing with, clement, forbearant, long-suffering.

Adv. 'like patience on a monument smiling at grief'; *æquo animo*, in cold blood &c. 823; more in sorrow than in anger.

Int. patience! and shuffle the cards.

SECTION II. PERSONAL AFFECTIONS*

1°. PASSIVE AFFECTIONS

827. Pleasure.—N. pleasure, gratification, enjoyment, fruition; ob-, delectation; relish, zest; *gusto* &c. (*physical pleasure*) 377; satisfaction &c. (*content*) 831; complacency.

well-being; good &c. 618; snugness, comfort, ease; cushion &c. 215; *sans souci*, mind at ease.

joy, gladness, delight, glee, cheer, sunshine; cheerfulness &c. 836.

treat, refreshment; frolic, fun, lark, gambol, merry-making; amusement &c. 840; luxury &c. 377; hedonism.

mens sana in corpore sano.

happiness, felicity, bliss; beati-tude, -fication; enchantment, transport, rapture, ravishment, ecstasy; *summum bonum*; paradise, elysium &c. (*heaven*) 981; third –, seventh- heaven; unalloyed -happiness &c.

honeymoon; palmy –, halcyon- days; golden -age, – time; *Saturnia regna*, Eden, Arcadia, happy valley, Agapemone; Cockaigne.

V. be pleased &c. 829; feel –, experience- pleasure &c. *n.*; joy; enjoy –, hug- oneself; be in -clover &c. 377, – elysium &c. 981; tread on enchanted ground; fall –, go- into raptures.

feel at home, breathe freely, bask in the sunshine.

be -pleased &c. 829- with; receive –, derive- pleasure &c. *n.*- from; take -pleasure &c. *n.*- in; delight in, rejoice

828. Pain. — N. mental suffering, pain, dolour; suffer-ing, -ance; ache, smart &c. (*physical pain*) 378; passion.

displeasure, dissatisfaction, discomfort, discomposure, disquiet; *malaise*; inquietude, uneasiness, vexation of spirit; taking; discontent &c. 832.

dejection &c. 837; weariness &c. 841.

annoyance, irritation, worry, infliction, visitation; plague, bore; bother, -ation; stew, vexation, mortification, chagrin, *esclandre*; *mauvais quart d'heure.*

care, anxiety, solicitude, trouble, trial, ordeal, fiery ordeal, shock, blow, cark, dole, fret, burden, load.

concern, grief, sorrow, distress, affliction, woe, bitterness, gloom, heartache; heavy –, aching –, bleeding –, broken- heart; heavy affliction, gnawing grief. unhappiness, infelicity, misery, tribulation, wretchedness, desolation; despair &c. 859; extremity, prostration, depth of misery.

nightmare, *ephialtes*, incubus.

anguish, agony; throe, tor-ture, -ment; crucifixion, martyrdom; pang, twinge, stab; the rack, the stake; purgatory &c. (*hell*) 982.

hell upon earth; iron age, reign of terror; slough of despond &c. (*adversity*) 735; peck –, sea- of troubles; ills that flesh is heir to &c. (*evil*) 619;

* Or those which concern one's own state of feeling.

in, indulge in, luxuriate in; gloat over &c. (*physical pleasure*) 377; enjoy, relish, like; love &c. 897; take -to, – a fancy to; have a liking for; enter into the spirit of.

take in good part.

treat oneself to, solace oneself with.

Adj. pleased &c. 829; not sorry; glad, -some; pleased as Punch.

happy, blest, blessed, blissful, beatified; happy as -a king, – the day is long; thrice happy, *ter quaterque beatus*; enjoying &c. *v.*; joyful &c. (*in spirits*) 836; hedonic.

in -a blissful state, – paradise &c. 981, – raptures, – ecstasies, – a transport of delight; rapturous.

comfortable &c. (*physical pleasure*) 377; at ease; content &c. 831; *sans souci*, in clover.

overjoyed, entranced, enchanted; enraptured; en-, ravished; transported; fascinated, captivated.

with -a joyful face, – sparkling eyes.

pleasing &c. 829; ecstatic, beat-ic, -ific; painless, unalloyed, without alloy, cloudless.

Adv. happily &c. *adj.*; with pleasure &c. (*willingly*) 602; with -glee &c. *n.*

Phr. one's heart leaping with joy.

---

miseries of human life; unkindest cut of all.

sufferer, victim, prey, martyr, object of compassion, wretch, shorn lamb.

V. feel –, suffer –, experience –, undergo –, bear –, endure- pain &c. *n.*; smart, ache &c. (*physical pain*) 378; suffer, bleed, ail; be the victim of; bear –, take up- the cross.

labour under afflictions; quaff the bitter cup, have a bad time of it; fall on evil days &c. (*adversity*) 735; go hard with, come to grief, fall a sacrifice to, drain the cup of misery to the dregs, sup full of horrors.

sit on thorns, be on pins and needles, wince, fret, chafe, worry oneself, be in a taking, fret and fume, take -on, – to heart.

grieve; mourn &c. (*lament*) 839; yearn, repine, pine, droop, languish, sink; give way; despair &c. 859; break one's heart; weigh upon the heart &c. (*inflict pain*) 830.

Adj. in –, in a state of –, full of- pain &c. *n.*; suffering &c. *v.*; pained, afflicted, worried, displeased &c. 830; aching, griped, sore &c. (*physical pain*) 378; on the rack, in limbo; between hawk and buzzard.

un-comfortable, -easy; ill at ease; in a -taking, – way; disturbed; discontented &c. 832; out of humour &c. 901*a*; weary &c. 841.

heavy laden, stricken, crushed, a prey to, victimized, ill-used.

unfortunate &c. (*hapless*) 735; to be pitied, doomed, devoted, accursed, undone, lost, stranded.

unhappy, infelicitous, poor, wretched, miserable, woe-begone; cheerless &c. (*dejected*) 837; careworn.

concerned, sorry; sorrow-ing, -ful; cut up, chagrined, horrified, horror-stricken; in –, plunged in –, a prey to- grief &c. *n.*; in tears &c. (*lamenting*) 839; steeped to the lips in misery; heart-stricken, -broken, -scalded; broken-hearted; in despair &c. 859.

Phr. 'the iron entered into the soul'; '*hæret lateri lethalis arundo*'; one's heart bleeding.

829. [Capability of giving pleasure; cause or source of pleasure.] Pleasurableness.—**N.** pleasurable-, pleasant-, agreeable-ness &c. *adj.*; pleasure giving, jocundity, delectability; amusement &c. 840.

attraction &c. (*motive*) 615; attractiveness, -ability; invitingness &c. *adj.*; charm, fascination, captivation, en-

830. [Capability of giving pain; cause or source of pain.] Painfulness. —**N.** painfulness &c. *adj.*; trouble, care &c. (*pain*) 828; trial; af-, in-fliction; cross, blow, stroke, burden, load, curse; bitter -pill, – draught, – cup; waters of bitterness.

annoyance, grievance, nuisance, vexation, mortification, sickener; bore,

chantment, witchery, seduction, winsomeness, winning ways, amenity, amiability, sweetness.

loveliness &c. (*beauty*) 845; sunny –, bright- side; sweets &c. (*sugar*) 396; goodness &c. 648; manna in the wilderness, land flowing with milk and honey.

treat; regale &c. (*physical pleasure*) 377; dainty; tit-, tid-bit; nuts, *sauce piquante*.

V. cause –, produce –, create –, give –, afford –, procure –, offer –, present –, yield- pleasure &c. 827.

please, charm, delight; gladden &c. (*make cheerful*) 836; take, captivate, fascinate; enchant, entrance, enrapture, transport, bewitch; en-, ravish.

bless, beatify; satisfy; gratify, – desire &c. 865; slake, satiate, quench; indulge, humour, flatter, tickle; tickle the palate &c. (*savoury*) 394; regale, refresh; enliven; treat; amuse &c. 840; take –, tickle –, hit- one's fancy; meet one's wishes; win –, gladden –, rejoice –, warm the cockles of- the heart; do one's heart good.

attract, allure &c. (*move*) 615; stimulate &c. (*excite*) 824; interest, intrigue.

make things pleasant, popularize, gild the pill, sweeten.

Adj. causing pleasure &c. *v.*; pleasure-giving; pleas-ing, -ant, -urable; agreeable, cushy; grat-eful, -ifying; leef, lief, acceptable; welcome, – as the roses in May; welcomed; favourite; to one's -taste, – mind, – liking, – heart's content; satisfactory &c. (*good*) 648.

refreshing; comfortable; cordial; genial; glad, -some; sweet, delectable, nice, dainty; delic-ate, -ious; dulcet; luscious &c. 396; palatable &c. 394; luxurious, voluptuous; sensual &c. 377.

attractive &c. 615; inviting, prepossessing, engaging; win-ning, -some; taking, fascinating, captivating, killing; seduc-ing, -tive; alluring, enticing; appetizing &c. (*exciting*) 824; cheering &c. 836; bewitching; interesting, absorbing, enchanting, entrancing, enravishing.

charming; delightful, felicitous, exquisite; lovely &c. (*beautiful*) 845; bother, pother, hot water, sea of troubles, hornet's nest, plague, pest.

cancer, ulcer, sting, thorn; canker &c. (*bane*) 663; scorpion &c. (*evil-doer*) 913; dagger &c. (*arms*) 727; scourge &c. (*instrument of punishment*) 975; carking –, canker worm of- care.

mishap, misfortune &c. (*adversity*) 735; *désagrément*, *esclandre*, rub.

source of -irritation, – annoyance; wound, sore subject, skeleton in the closet; thorn in -the flesh, – one's side; where the shoe pinches, gall and wormwood.

sorry sight, heavy news, provocation; affront &c. 929; head and front of one's offending.

infestation, molestation; malignity &c. (*malevolence*) 907; acrimony.

V. cause –, occasion –, give –, bring –, induce –, produce –, create –, inflict- pain &c. 828; pain, hurt, wound.

pinch, prick, gripe &c. (*physical pain*) 378; pierce, lancinate, cut.

hurt –, wound –, grate upon –, jar upon- the feelings; wring –, pierce –, lacerate –, break –, rend- the heart; make the heart bleed; tear –, rend- the heart-strings; draw tears from the eyes.

sadden; make -unhappy &c. 828; plunge into sorrow, grieve, fash, afflict, distress; cut -up, – to the heart.

displease, annoy, incommode, discommode, discompose, trouble, disquiet, disturb, thwart, cross, perplex, molest, tease, rag, tire, irk, vex, mortify, wherret, worry, plague, bother, pester, bore, pother, harass, harry, badger, heckle, bait, beset, infest, persecute, importune, be troublesome.

wring, harrow, torment, torture; put to the -rack, – question; break on the wheel, rack, scarify; cruci-ate, -fy; convulse, agonize; barb the dart; plant a -dagger in the breast, – thorn in one's side.

irritate, provoke, sting, nettle, try the patience, pique, fret, rile, tweak the nose, chafe, gall; sting –, wound –, cut- to the quick; aggrieve, affront, enchafe, enrage, ruffle, sour the temper; give offence &c. (*resentment*) 900.

ravishing, rapturous; heartfelt, thrilling, ecstatic; beat-ic, -ific; seraphic; empyrean; elysian &c. (*heavenly*) 981.

palmy, halcyon, Saturnian.

Phr. *decies repetita placebit.*

---

maltreat, bite, snap at, assail, bully; smite &c. (*punish*) 972.

sicken, disgust, revolt, nauseate, disenchant, repel, offend, shock, stink in the nostrils; go against –, turn- the stomach; make one sick, set the teeth on edge, go against the grain, grate on the ear; stick in one's -throat, – gizzard; rankle, gnaw, corrode, horrify, appal, freeze the blood; chill the spine; make the -flesh creep, – hair stand on end; make the blood -curdle, – run cold; make one shudder.

haunt, – the memory; weigh –, prey- on the -heart, – mind, – spirits; bring one's grey hairs with sorrow to the grave; add a nail to one's coffin.

Adj. causing pain, hurting &c. *v.*; hurtful &c. (*bad*) 649; painful; dolor-ific, -ous; unpleasant; un-, dis-pleasing; disagreeable, unpalatable, bitter, distasteful; uninviting; unwelcome; undesir-able, -ed; obnoxious; unacceptable, unpopular, thankless.

unsatisfactory, untoward, unlucky, uncomfortable.

distressing; afflict-ing, -ive; joy-, cheer-, comfort-less; dismal, disheartening; depress-ing, -ive; dreary, melancholy, grievous, piteous; woeful, rueful, mournful, deplorable, pitiable, lamentable; sad, affecting, touching, pathetic.

irritating, provoking, stinging, annoying, aggravating, mortifying, galling; unaccommodating, invidious, vexatious; trouble-, tire-, irk-, weari-some; plagu-ing, -y; awkward.

importunate; teas-, pester-, bother-, harass-, worry-, torment-, cark-ing.

in-toler-, -suffer-, -support-able; un-bear-, -endur-able; past bearing; not to be -borne, – endured; more than flesh and blood can bear; enough to -drive one mad, – provoke a saint, – make a parson swear, – try the patience of Job.

shocking, terrific, grim, appalling, crushing; dreadful, fearful, frightful; thrilling, tremendous, dire; heart-breaking, -rending, -wounding, -corroding, -sickening; harrowing, rending.

odious, hateful, execrable, repulsive, repellent, abhorrent; horri-d, -ble, -fic, -fying; offensive; nause-ous, -ating; disgust-, sicken-, revolt-ing; nasty; loath-some, -ful; fulsome; vile &c. (*bad*) 649; hideous &c. 846.

sharp, acute, sore, severe, grave, hard, harsh, cruel, biting, acrimonious, caustic; cutting, corroding, consuming, racking, excruciating, searching, searing, grinding, grating, agonizing; envenomed.

ruinous, disastrous, calamitous, tragical; desolating, withering; burdensome, onerous, oppressive; cumb-rous, -ersome.

Adv. painfully &c. *adj.*; with -pain &c. 828; deuced.

Int. *hinc illæ lachrymæ!* woe is me!

Phr. *surgit amari aliquid*; the place being too hot to hold one; the iron entering into the soul.

831. Content.—**N.** content, -ment, -edness; complacency, satisfaction, entire satisfaction, ease, heart's ease, peace of mind; serenity &c. 826; cheer-

832. Discontent. — **N.** discontent, -ment; dissatisfaction; dissent &c. 489; labour unrest.

disappointment, mortification; cold

fulness &c. 836; ray of comfort; comfort &c. (*well-being*) 827.

re-, conciliation; resignation &c. (*patience*) 826.

waiter on Providence.

V. be -content &c. *adj.*; rest -satisfied, - and be thankful; take the good the gods provide, let well alone, feel oneself at home, hug oneself, lay the flattering unction to one's soul.

take -up with, - in good part; assent &c. 488; be reconciled to, make one's peace with; get over it; take -heart, - comfort; put up with &c. (*bear*) 826.

render -content &c. *adj.*; set at ease, comfort; set one's -heart, - mind- at -ease, - rest; speak peace; conciliate, reconcile, win over, propitiate, disarm, beguile; content, satisfy; gratify &c. 829.

be -tolerated &c. 826; go down, - with; do.

Adj. content, -ed; satisfied &c. *v.*; at -ease, - one's ease, - home; with the mind at ease, *sans souci, sine curâ*, easy-going, not particular; conciliatory; unrepining, of good comfort; resigned &c. (*patient*) 826; cheerful &c. 836.

un-afflicted, -vexed, -molested, -plagued; serene &c. 826; at rest; snug, comfortable; in one's element.

satisfactory, satisfying, ample, sufficient, adequate, tolerable.

Adv. to one's heart's content; *à la bonne heure*; all for the best.

Int. amen &c. (*assent*) 488; very well, so much the better, well and good; it -, that- will do; it cannot be helped.

Phr. nothing comes amiss.

comfort; regret &c. 833; repining, taking on &c. *v.*; inquietude, vexation of spirit, soreness; heart-burning, -grief; querulousness &c. (*lamentation*) 839; hypercriticism.

malcontent, grumbler, growler, croaker, *laudator temporis acti*; censurer, complainer, faultfinder, murmurer, Adullamite, Diehard, Bitter-ender.

the Opposition, cave of Adullam, indignation meeting, 'winter of our discontent.'

V. be -discontented &c. *adj.*; quarrel with one's bread and butter; repine; regret &c. 833; wish one at the bottom of the Red Sea; take -on, - to heart; shrug the shoulders; make a wry -, pull a long- face; knit one's brows; look -blue, - black, - black as thunder, - blank, - glum.

take -in bad part, - ill; fret, chafe, make a piece of work; grumble, croak, grouse; lament &c. 839.

cause -discontent &c. *n.*; dissatisfy, disappoint, mortify, put out, disconcert; cut up; dishearten.

Adj. discontented; dissatisfied &c. *v.*; unsatisfied, ungratified; dissident; dissentient &c. 489; malcontent, exigent, exacting, hypercritical.

repining &c. *v.*; regretful &c. 833; down in the mouth &c. (*dejected*) 837.

in -high dudgeon, - a fume, - the sulks, - the dumps, - bad humour; glum, sulky; sour, - as a crab; soured, sore; out of -humour, - temper.

disappointing &c. *v.*; unsatisfactory;

Int. so much the worse!

Phr. that -, it- will never do.

833. Regret.—**N.** regret, repining; home sickness, nostalgia; *mal -, maladie-du pays*; lamentation &c. 839, contrition, compunction, penitence &c. 950.

bitterness, heart-burning.

laudator temporis acti &c. (*discontent*) 832.

V. regret, deplore; bewail &c. (*lament*) 839; repine, cast a longing lingering look behind; rue, - the day; repent &c. 950; *infandum renovare dolorem*.

prey -, weigh -, have a weight- on the mind; leave an aching void.

Adj. regretting &c. *v.*; regretful; home-sick.

regretted &c. *v.*; much to be regretted, regrettable; lamentable &c. (*bad*) 649.

Int. what a pity! hang it!
Phr. 'tis -pity, – too true.

834. Relief.—N. relief; deliverance; refreshment &c. 689; easement, softening, alleviation, mitigation, palliation &c. 174; soothing, lullaby; cradle song, *berceuse.*

solace, consolation, comfort, encouragement.

lenitive, restorative &c. (*remedy*) 662; poultice &c. *v.*; cushion &c. 215; crumb of comfort, balm in Gilead; aspirin.

V. relieve, ease, alleviate, mitigate, palliate, soothe, addulce; salve; soften, – down; foment, stupe, poultice; assuage, allay.

cheer, comfort, console; encourage, bear up, pat on the back, give comfort, set at ease; enliven, gladden –, cheer- the heart.

remedy; cure &c. (*restore*) 660; refresh; pour -balm into, – oil on.

smooth the ruffled brow of care, temper the wind to the shorn lamb, lay the flattering unction to one's soul.

disburden &c. (*free*) 705; take off a load of care.

be relieved; breathe more freely, draw a long breath; take comfort; dry –, wipe- the -tears, – eyes.

Adj. relieving &c. *v.*; consolatory, soothing; assua-ging, -sive; bal-my, -samic; lenitive, palliative; anodyne &c. (*remedial*) 662; curative &c. 660.

835. Aggravation.—N. aggravation, heightening; exacerbation; exasperation; overestimation &c. 482; exaggeration &c. 549.

V. aggravate, render worse, heighten, embitter, sour; ex-, acerbate; exasperate, envenom; tease, provoke, enrage.

add fuel to the -fire, – flame; fan the flame &c. (*excite*) 824; go from bad to worse &c. (*deteriorate*) 659.

Adj. aggravated &c. *v.*; worse, unrelieved; aggravable; aggravating &c. *v.*

Adv. out of the frying pan into the fire, from bad to worse, worse and worse.

Int. so much the worse!

---

836. Cheerfulness.—N. cheerfulness &c. *adj.*; geniality, gaiety, *l'allegro*, cheer, good humour, spirits; high –, animal –, flow of- spirits; glee, high glee, light heart; sunshine of the -mind, – breast; *gaieté de cœur, bon naturel.*

liveliness &c. *adj.*; life, alacrity, vivacity, animation, *allégresse*; jocundity, joviality, jollity; levity; jocularity &c. (*wit*) 842.

mirth, merriment, hilarity, exhilaration; laughter &c. 838; merry-making &c. (*amusement*) 840; heyday, rejoicing &c. 838; marriage bells.

nepenthe, Euphrosyne.

optimism &c. (*hopefulness*) 858; self-complacency.

V. be -cheerful &c. *adj.*; have the mind at ease, smile, put a good face upon, keep up one's spirits; view -the bright side of the picture, – things *en couleur de rose*; *ridentem dicere verum,*

837. Dejection.—N. dejection; dejectedness &c. *adj.*; depression, prosternation; lowness –, depression- of spirits; weight –, oppression –, damp- on the spirits; low –, bad –, drooping –, depressed- spirits; heart sinking; heaviness –, failure- of heart.

heaviness &c. *adj.*; infestivity, gloom; weariness &c. 841; *tædium vitæ*, disgust of life; *mal du pays* &c. (*regret*) 833.

melancholy; sadness &c. *adj.*; *il penseroso, melancholia*, dismals, mumps, mopes, lachrymals, dumps, blues, blue devils, doldrums, vapours, megrims, spleen, horrors, hypochondriasis, pessimism; despondency, slough of Despond; disconsolateness &c. *adj.*; hope deferred, blank despondency.

prostration, – of soul; broken heart; despair &c. 859; cave of -despair, – Trophonius.

cheer up, brighten up, light up, bear up; chirp, take heart, cast away care, drive dull care away, perk up.

rejoice &c. 838; carol, chirrup, lilt; frisk, rollick, give a loose to mirth.

cheer, enliven, elate, exhilarate, gladden, inspirit, animate, raise the spirits, inspire; put in good humour; cheer –, rejoice- the heart; delight &c. (*give pleasure*) 829.

Adj. cheerful; happy &c. 827; cheer-y, -ly; of good cheer, smiling; blithe; in –, in good- spirits; in high -spirits, – feather; happy as -the day is long, – a king; gay, – as a lark; *allegro*; light, -some, -hearted; buoyant, *débonnaire*, bright, free and easy, airy; janty, jaunty, canty; spright-ly, -ful; spry; spirit-ed, -ful; lively; animated, breezy, vivacious; brisk, – as a bee; sparkling; sportive; full of -play, – spirit; all alive.

sunny, palmy; hopeful &c. 858.

merry, – as a -cricket, – grig, – marriage bell; joyful, joyous, jocund, jovial; jolly, – as a thrush, – as a sandboy; blithesome; glee-ful, -some; hilarious, rattling.

winsome, bonny, hearty, buxom.

play-ful, -some; *folâtre*, playful as a kitten, tricksy, frisky, frolicsome; gamesome; jocose, jocular, waggish; mirth-, laughter-loving; mirthful, rollicking.

elate, -d; exulting, jubilant, flushed; rejoicing &c. 838; cock-a-hoop.

cheering, inspiriting, exhilarating; cardiac, -al; pleasing &c. 829; flourishing, halcyon.

Adv. cheerfully &c. *adj.*

Int. never say die! come! cheer up! hurrah! &c. 838; 'hence loathed melancholy!' begone dull care! away with melancholy!

---

demureness &c. *adj.*; gravity, solemnity; long –, grave- face.

hypochondriac, seek-sorrow, self-tormentor, *heautontimorumenos*, *malade imaginaire*, *médecin tant pis*; croaker, pessimist; mope, mopus.

[Cause of dejection] affliction &c. 830; sorry sight; *memento mori*; damper, wet blanket, Job's comforter; death's head, skeleton at the feast.

V. be -dejected &c. *adj.*; grieve; mourn &c. (*lament*) 839; take on, give way, lose heart, despond, droop, sink.

lower, look downcast, frown, pout; hang down the head; pull –, make- a long face; laugh on the wrong side of the mouth; grin a ghastly smile; look -blue, – like a drowned man; lay –, take- to heart.

mope, brood over; fret; sulk; pine, – away; yearn; repine &c. (*regret*) 833; despair &c. 859.

refrain from laughter, keep one's countenance; be –, look- grave &c. *adj.*; repress a smile, keep a straight face.

depress; dis-courage, -hearten; dispirit; damp, dull, deject, lower, sink, dash, knock down, unman, prostrate, break one's heart; frown upon; cast a -gloom, – shade- on; sadden; damp –, dash –, wither- one's hopes; weigh –, lie heavy –, prey- on the -mind, – spirits; damp –, depress- the spirits.

Adj. cheer-, joy-, spirit-less; uncheerful, -y; unlively; unhappy &c. 828; melancholy, dismal, sombre, dark, gloomy, adust, *triste*, clouded, murky, lowering, frowning, lugubrious, Acherontic, funereal, mournful, lamentable, dreadful.

dreary, flat; dull, – as -a beetle, – ditchwater; depressing &c. *v.*

'melancholy as a gib cat'; oppressed with –, a prey to- melancholy; downcast, -hearted; down -in the mouth, – on one's luck; heavy-hearted; in the -dumps, – suds, – sulks, – doldrums; in doleful dumps, in bad humour; sullen; mumpish, dumpish; mopish, moping; moody, glum; sulky &c. (*discontented*) 832; out of -sorts, – humour, – heart, – spirits; ill at ease, low-spirited, in low spirits, a cup too low; weary &c. 841; dis-couraged, -heartened; desponding; chop-, jaw-, crest-fallen.

sad, pensive, *penseroso*, tristful; dole-some, -ful; woebegone, lachrymose, in tears, melancholic, hipped, hypochondriacal, bilious, jaundiced, atrabilious, saturnine, splenetic; lackadaisical.

serious, sedate, staid, stayed; grave, – as -a judge, – an undertaker, – a mustard pot; sober, solemn, demure; grim; grim-faced, -visaged; rueful, wan, long-faced.

disconsolate; un-, in-consolable; forlorn, comfortless, desolate, *désolé*, sick at heart; soul-, heart-sick; *au désespoir*; in despair &c. 859; lost.

overcome; broken-, borne-, bowed-down; heart-stricken &c. (*mental suffering*) 828; cut up, dashed, sunk; unnerved, unmanned; down-fallen, -trodden; broken-hearted; care-worn.

Adv. with -a long face, – tears in one's eyes; sadly &c. *adj.*

Phr. the countenance falling; the heart -failing, – sinking within-one.

838. [Expression of pleasure.] **Rejoicing.**—**N.** rejoicing, exultation, triumph, jubilation, heyday, flush, revelling; merry-making &c. (*amusement*) 840; jubilee &c. (*celebration*) 883; pæan, *Te Deum* &c. (*thanksgiving*) 990; congratulation &c. 896; applause &c. 931.

smile, simper, smirk, grin; broad –, sardonic- grin.

laughter, giggle, titter, crow, cheer, chuckle, snicker, snigger, shout; Homeric laughter, horse –, hearty- laugh; guffaw; burst –, fit –, shout –, roar –, peal- of laughter; cachinnation.

risibility; derision &c. 856.

Momus; Democritus the Abderite; rollicker; Laughter holding both his sides.

V. rejoice; thank –, bless- one's stars; congratulate –, hug- oneself; rub –, clap- one's hands; smack the lips, fling up one's cap; dance, skip, caleer; sing, carol, chirrup, chirp; hurrah; cry for –, leap with- joy; exult &c. (*boast*) 884; triumph; hold jubilee &c. (*celebrate*) 883; make merry &c. (*sport*) 840; sing a pæan of joy.

smile, simper, smirk; grin, – like a Cheshire cat; mock, laugh in one's sleeve; laugh, – outright; giggle, titter, snigger, crow, smicker, chuckle, snicker, cackle; burst -out, – into a fit of laughter; shout, split, roar.

shake –, split –, hold both- one's sides; roar –, die- with laughter.

raise laughter &c. (*amuse*) 840.

Adj. rejoicing &c. *v.*; jubilant, exultant, triumphant; flushed, elated; laughing &c. *v.*; risible; ready to -burst, – split, – die with laughter; convulsed with laughter.

839. [Expression of pain.] **Lamentation.**—**N.** lament, -ation; wail, complaint, plaint, murmur, mutter, grumble, groan, moan, whine, whimper, sob, sigh, suspiration, heaving, deep sigh.

cry &c. (*vociferation*) 411; scream, howl; outcry, wail of woe, frown, scowl.

tear; weeping &c. *v.*; flood of tears, fit of crying, lachrymation, melting mood, weeping and gnashing of teeth.

plaintiveness &c. *adj.*; languishment; condolence &c. 915.

mourning, weeds, willow, cypress, crêpe, crape, deep mourning; sackcloth and ashes; knell &c. 363; dump, death-song, dirge, coronach, keen, *nenia*, requiem, elegy, *epicedium*; threne; mon-, thren-ody; jeremiad; ululation.

mourner, professional mourner, keener; grumbler &c. (*discontent*) 832; Niobe; Heraclitus.

V. lament, mourn, deplore, grieve, weep over; be-wail, -moan; keen; condole with &c. 915; fret &c. (*suffer*) 828; wear –, go into –, put on- mourning; wear -the willow, – sackcloth and ashes; *infandum renovare dolorem* &c. (*regret*) 833; give sorrow words.

sigh; give –, heave –, fetch- a sigh; 'waft a sigh from Indus to the pole'; sigh 'like furnace'; wail.

cry, weep, sob, greet, blubber, pipe, snivel, bibber, whimper, pule; pipe one's eye; drop –, shed- -tears, – a tear; melt –, burst- into tears; *fondre en larmes*; cry -oneself blind, – one's eyes out.

scream &c. (*cry out*) 411; mew &c. (*animal sounds*) 412; groan, moan,

laughable &c. (*ludicrous*) 853.

Int. hip, hip, -hurrah! huzza! aha! hail! tolderolloll! tra-la la! Heaven be praised! *io triumphe! tant mieux!* so much the better.

Phr. the heart leaping with joy.

---

whine, yammer; roar; roar –, bellow- like a bull; cry out lustily, rend the air, yell.

frown, scowl, make a wry face, grimace, gnash one's teeth, wring one's hands, tear one's hair, beat one's breast, roll on the ground, burst with grief.

complain, murmur, mutter, grumble, growl, clamour, make a fuss about, croak, grunt, maunder; deprecate &c. (*disapprove*) 932.

cry out before one is hurt, complain without cause.

Adj. lamenting &c. *v.*; in mourning, in sackcloth and ashes; crying, sorrowing, -ful &c. (*unhappy*) 828; mourn-, tear-ful; lachrymose; plaint-ive, -ful, quer-ulous, -imonious; in the melting mood.

in tears, with tears in one's eyes; with -moistened, – watery- eyes; bathed –, dissolved- in tears; 'like Niobe all tears.'

elagiac, epicedial, threnetic.

Adv. *de profundis*; *les larmes aux yeux.*

Int. heigh-ho! alas! alack! O dear! ah –, woe is- me! lackadaisy! well –, lack –, alack- a day! well-a-way! alas the day! *O tempora! O mores!* what a pity! *miserabile dictu!* O lud lud! too true!

Phr. tears -standing in, – starting from- the eyes; eyes -suffused, – swimming, – brimming –, overflowing- with tears.

840. Amusement.—N. amuse-, entertain-ment; diver-sion, -tissement; recreation, relaxation, solace; pastime, *passetemps*, sport; labour of love; pleasure &c. 827.

fun, frolic, merriment, whoopee, jollity; jovial-ity, -ness; heyday; laughter &c. 838; jocos-ity, -eness; droll-, buffoon-, tomfool-ery; mummery, masquing, pleasantry; wit &c. 842; quip, quirk.

play; game, – at romps; gambol, romp, prank, antic, rig, lark, spree, skylarking, vagary, trick, monkey trick, *gambade, fredaine, escapade, échappée*, bout, *espièglerie*; practical joke &c. (*ridicule*) 856.

dance; round –, square –, solo –, step –, tap –, clog –, skirt –, sand –, folk –, morris- dance, *pas seul*, step, turn, *chassé*, cut, shuffle, double shuffle; hop, reel, rigadoon, saraband, hornpipe, bolero, fandango, pavan, tarantella, minuet, waltz, polka; galop, -ade; schottische, *pas de quatre*, Boston, one-, two-step, rumba, tango, maxixe, fox-, turkey-trot, shimmy, ragtime, cakewalk, jazz, blues, Charleston; jig, breakdown, fling, strathspey; *alle-*

841. Weariness.—N. weariness, defatigation, boredom, *ennui*; lassitude &c. (*fatigue*) 688; drowsiness &c. 683.

disgust, nausea, loathing, sickness; satiety &c. 869; *tædium vitæ* &c. (*dejection*) 837.

wearisome-, tedious-ness &c. *adj.*; dull work, tedium, monotony, twice told tale.

bore, button-holer, proser, wet blanket; heavy hours, 'the enemy' [time].

V. weary; tire &c. (*fatigue*) 688; bore; bore –, weary –, tire- -to death, – out of one's life, – out of all patience; set –, send- to sleep; buttonhole.

pall, sicken, nauseate, disgust.

harp on the same string; drag its -slow, – weary- length along.

never hear the last of; be -tired &c. *adj.* -of, – with; yawn; die with *ennui.*

Adj. wearying &c. *v.*; wearing; weari-, tire-, irk-some; uninteresting, stupid, bald, devoid of interest, dry, monotonous, dull, arid, tedious, humdrum, mortal, flat; pros-y, -ing; slow; soporific, somniferous, dormitive.

disgusting &c. *v.*; unenjoyed.

weary; tired &c. *v.*; drowsy &c. (*sleepy*) 683; uninterested, flagging,

mande; gavot, -te; mazurka, morisco; quadrille, lancers, country dance, *cotillon*, polonaise, Sir Roger de Coverley, Swedish dance; *ballet* &c. (*drama*) 599; ball; *bal, – masqué, – costumé*; masquerade, fancy dress ball; *thé dansant*; Terpsichore, choreography, Russian ballet, classical dancing; eurythmics; nautch dance, *danse du ventre*, cancan.

festivity, merry-making; party &c. (*social gathering*) 892; *fête*, festival, gala, *ridotto*; revel-s, -ry, -ling; carnival, brawl, saturnalia, high jinks; feast, banquet &c. (*food*) 298; regale, *symposium*, wassail; carous-e, -al; jollification, junket, wake, picnic, *fête champêtre*, garden party, gymkhana, regatta, track meet, field-day, jamboree, treat.

round of pleasures, dissipation, a short life and a merry one, racketing, holiday making, high jinks.

rejoicing &c. 838; jubilee &c. (*celebration*) 883.

bonfire, fireworks, *feu-de-joie*, rocket, Catherine wheel, roman candle &c.

holiday; gala –, red letter –, play- day; high days and holidays; high –, Bank- holiday; May –, Derby- day; Saint –, Easter –, Whit- Monday; King's birthday, Empire Day; *mi-carême*; *Bairam*; wayzgoose, beanfeast, beano.

place of amusement, theatre &c. 599; concert-, ball-, assembly-room; music-hall, cinema, movies, talkies, vaudeville; hippodrome, circus, rodeo; *casino, kursaal*; winter garden; park, pleasance, arbour; garden &c. 371; pleasure-, play-, cricket-, football-, polo-, croquet-, archery-, hunting-ground; golf links, race course, stadium, gridiron, bowl, speedway, racing track, ring; gymnasium, swimming pool; shooting gallery; tennis-, racket-court; bowling-green, -alley; croquet-lawn, rink, skating rink; roller-coaster, roundabout, carousel, merry-go-round; swing; *montagne russe*; switchback, scenic railway &c.

game, – of -chance, – skill; athletic sports, gymnastics; fencing; archery, rifle-shooting; tournament, pugilism &c. (*contention*) 720; sporting &c. 622; horse-racing, the turf; aquatics &c. 267; skating, roller skating; ski-running, -joring, -jumping, bobsleighing, luging, tobogganing, winter sports; sliding; cricket, tennis, lawn –, table –, deck- tennis, rackets, fives, squash, ping-pong, trap bat and ball, battledore and shuttlecock, badminton, *la grâce*; pall mall, tip-cat, croquet, golf, curling, hockey, basketball, soccer, football, Rugby, Association, *pallone*, polo; tent-pegging, tilting at the ring, quintain, greasy pole; quoits, *discus*; throwing the hammer, putting the -weight, – shot, tossing the caber; knurr and spell; leap-frog, hop, skip and jump; French and English, tug of war; blind man's buff, hunt the slipper, hide-and-seek, kiss in the ring; snapdragon; cross questions and crooked answers; jig-saw puzzle; rounders, base-ball, lacrosse &c.; angling; swimming, diving, water-polo.

billiards, pool, pyramids, snooker, bagatelle; bowls, skittles, ninepins, kail, American bowls.

cards; bridge, auction, contract, whist, rubber; round game, coon-can, loo, cribbage, *bésique*, pinocle, euchre, drole, *écarté*, skat, picquet, all-fours, quadrille, ombre, reverse, Pope Joan, commit;

used up, worn out, *blasé*, life-weary, weary of life; sick of.

Adv. wearily &c. *adj.*; *usque ad nauseam*.

Phr. time hanging heavily on one's hands; *toujours perdrix*; *crambe repetita*.

---

bo-, boa-ston; *vingt-et-un*; *quinze*, thirty-one, put-and-take, speculation, connections, brag, cassino, lottery, commerce, snip-snap-snorem, lift smoke, blind hookey, Polish bank, poker, banker; faro; Earl of Coventry, Napoleon, nap, patience, pairs; old maid, fright, beggar-my-neighbour; *baccarat, chemin de fer, monte;* craps.

chess, draughts, backgammon, dominoes, checkers, mah jong, merelles, nine men's morris, go-bang, solitaire; game of –, fox and-geese; lotto; &c.*

morra; gambling &c. (*chance*) 621; roulette.

toy, plaything, bauble; doll &c. (*puppet*) 554; teetotum; knick-knack &c. (*trifle*) 643; magic lantern &c. (*show*) 448; peep-, puppet-, raree-, gallanty-show; marionnettes, Punch and Judy; toy-shop; 'quips and cranks and wanton wiles, nods and becks and wreathèd smiles.'

sportsman, gamester, gambler &c. 621; reveller, master of the -ceremonies, – revels; *arbiter elegantiarum.*

V. amuse, entertain, divert, enliven; tickle, – the fancy; titillate, raise a smile, put in good humour; cause –, create –, occasion –, raise –, excite –, produce –, convulse with- laughter; set the table in a roar, be the death of one.

recreate, solace, cheer, rejoice; please &c. 829; interest; treat, regale.

amuse oneself; game; play, – a game, – pranks, – tricks; sport, disport, toy, wanton, revel, junket, feast, carouse, banquet, make merry; drown care; drive dull care away; frolic, gambol, frisk, romp; caper; dance &c. (*leap*) 309; keep up the ball; run a rig, sow one's wild oats, have one's fling, paint the town red, take one's pleasure; see life; *desipere in loco*, play the fool.

make –, keep- holiday; go a Maying.

while away –, beguile- the time; kill time, dally.

Adj. amusing, entertaining, diverting &c. *v.*; recreative, lusory; pleasant &c. (*pleasing*) 829; laughable &c. (*ludicrous*) 853; witty &c. 842; fest-ive, -al; jovial, jolly, jocund, roguish, rompish; sporting; playful, – as a kitten; sportive, ludibrious.

amused &c. *v.*; 'pleased with a feather, tickled with a straw.'

Adv. 'on the light fantastic toe,' at play, in sport.

Int. *vive la bagatelle! vogue la galère!*

Phr. *Deus nobis hæc otia fecit*; *dum vivimus vivamus.*

842. Wit.—N. wit, -tiness; attic -wit, – salt; atticism; salt, *esprit*, point, fancy, whim, humour, drollery, pleasantry.

farce, buffoonery, fooling, tomfoolery; harlequinade &c. 599; broad -farce, – humour; fun, *espièglerie*; *vis comica.*

jocularity; jocos-ity, -eness; facetiousness; wagg-ery, -ishness; whimsicality; comicality &c. 853.

smartness, ready wit, banter, *badi-*

843. Dulness.—N. dulness, heaviness, flatness; infestivity &c. 837; stupidity &c. 499; want of originality, dearth of ideas.

prose, matter of fact; heavy book, *conte à dormir debout*; platitude.

V. be -dull &c. *adj.*; prose, platitudinize, take *au sérieux*, be caught napping.

render -dull &c. *adj.*; damp, depress, throw cold water on, lay a wet blanket on; fall flat upon the ear; hang fire.

* A curious list of games is given in Sir Thomas Urquhart's translation of Rabelais' *Life of Gargantua*, book i. chapter 22.

nage, *persiflage*, retort, repartee, *quid pro quo*; ridicule &c. 856.

facetiæ, quips and cranks; jest, joke, capital joke; standing -jest, - joke; conceit, quip, quirk, crank, quiddity, *concetto*, *plaisanterie*, brilliant idea; merry –, bright –, happy- thought; sally; flash, - of wit, - of merriment; scintillation; *mot*, - *pour rire*; witticism, smart saying, *bon mot*, *jeu d'esprit*, epigram; jest book; dry joke, *quodlibet*, cream of the jest.

word-play, *jeu de mots*; play -of, - upon- words; pun, -ning; *double entendre* &c. (*ambiguity*) 520; quibble, verbal quibble; conundrum &c. (*riddle*) 533; anagram, acrostic, double acrostic, *nugæ canoræ*, trifling, idle conceit, *turlupinade*.

old joke, Joe Miller, chestnut, hoary-headed jest.

V. joke, jest, cut jokes; crack a joke; perpetrate a -joke, - pun; make -fun of, - merry with; set the table in a roar &c. (*amuse*) 840; scintillate.

retort, flash back; banter &c. (*ridicule*) 856; *ridentem dicere verum*; joke at one's expense.

Adj. witty, attic, salty; quick-, nimble-witted; keen, clever, smart, brilliant, pungent, jocular, jocose, funny, waggish, facetious, whimsical, humorous, Gilbertian; playful &c. 840; merry and wise; pleasant, sprightly, *spirituel*, sparkling, epigrammatic, full of point, *ben trovato*; comic &c. 853.

Adv. in joke, in jest, in sport, in play.

Adj. dull, - as ditch water; dry, insipid, jejune; unentertaining, uninteresting, unlively, unimaginative; heavisome, heavy-gaited; insulse; dry as dust; pros-y, -ing, -aic; matter of fact, commonplace, banal, pointless; 'weary, flat, stale and unprofitable.'

stupid, slow, flat, sluggish, ponderous, humdrum, monotonous; melancholic &c. 837; stolid &c. 499; plodding.

Phr. *Davus sum non Œdipus.*

---

844. Humorist.—N. humorist, wag, wit, reparteeist, epigrammatist, gag-man, punster; *bel esprit*, life of the party; wit-snapper, -cracker, -worm; joker, jester, jokesmith, Joe Miller, *drôle de corps*, *gaillard*, spark, *persifleur*, banterer.

buffoon, *farceur*, merry-andrew, mime, tumbler, acrobat, mountebank, charlatan, posturemaster, harlequin, punch, *pulcinella*, scaramouch, clown; wearer of the -cap and bells, - motley; motley fool; pantaloon, gipsy; jack -pudding, - in the green, - a dandy; zany; mad-cap, pickle-herring, witling, caricaturist, *grimacier*.

2°. Discriminate Affections

845. Beauty.—N. beauty, the beautiful, *le beau idéal*, loveliness.

[Science of the perception of beauty] Callæsthetics.*

form, elegance, grace, beauty unadorned; symmetry &c. 242; comeliness, fairness &c. *adj.*; pulchritude, polish, gloss; good -effect, - looks; *belle tournure*; bloom, brilliancy, radiance, splendour, gorgeousness, magnificence; sublimi-ty, -fication.

846. Ugliness.—N. ugliness &c. *adj.*; deformity, inelegance; disfigurement &c. (*blemish*) 848; want of symmetry, inconcinnity; distortion &c. 243; squalor &c. (*uncleanness*) 653.

forbidding countenance, vinegar aspect, hanging look, wry face, '*spretæ injuria formæ*.'

eyesore, object, figure, sight, fright, spectre, scarecrow, hag, harridan, satyr, witch, toad, baboon, monster,

* Whewell, 'Philosophy of the Inductive Sciences.'

concinnity, delicacy, refinement; charm, *je ne sais quoi*, style, *chic*, swank.

Venus, – of Milo; Aphrodite, Hebe, the Graces, Peri, Houri, Cupid, Apollo, Hyperion, Adonis, Antinous, Narcissus; Helen of Troy.

peacock, butterfly; flower, flow'ret gay, rose, lily, asphodel; garden; flower of, pink of; *bijou*; jewel &c. (*ornament*) 847; work of art.

pleasurableness &c. 829.

beautifying; landscape gardening; decoration &c. 847; calisthenics.

V. be -beautiful &c. *adj.*; shine, beam, bloom; become one &c. (*accord*) 23; set off, grace, flatter one.

render -beautiful &c. *adj.*; beautify; polish, burnish; gild &c. (*decorate*) 847; set out.

'snatch a grace beyond the reach of art.'

Adj. beaut-iful, -eous; handsome; pretty; lovely, graceful, elegant; delicate, dainty, refined, exquisite; fair, personable, comely, seemly; bonny; good-looking; well-favoured, -made, -formed, -proportioned; proper, shapely; symmetrical &c. (*regular*) 242; harmonious &c. (*colour*) 428; sightly.

fit to be seen, passable, not amiss.

goodly, dapper, tight, jimp; gimp; janty, jaunty; natty, quaint, trim, tidy, neat, spruce, smart, tricksy.

bright, -eyed; rosy-, cherry-cheeked; rosy, ruddy; blooming, in full bloom.

brilliant, shining; beam-y, -ing; sparkling, swanky, splendid, resplendent, dazzling, glowing; glossy, sleek.

showy, specious; rich, gorgeous, superb, magnificent, grand, fine, sublime, imposing; majestic 873.

artistic, -al; æsthetic; pict-uresque, -orial; *fait à peindre*, paintable; well-composed, -grouped, -varied; curious.

Caliban, Æsop, '*monstrum horrendum informe ingens cui lumen ademptum.*'

V. be -ugly &c. *adj.*; look ill, grin horribly a ghastly smile, make faces.

render -ugly &c. *adj.*; deface; dis-, de-figure; deform, spoil, distort &c. 243; blemish &c. (*injure*) 659; soil &c. (*render unclean*) 653.

Adj. ugly, – as -sin, – a toad, – a scarecrow, – a dead monkey; plain, bald &c. 226; homely &c. (*unadorned*) 849; ordinary, unornamental, inartistic; unsightly, unseemly, uncomely. unshapely, unlovely; sightless, seemless; not fit to be seen; unbeaut-eous, -iful; beautiless; shapeless &c. (*amorphous*) 241; course; garish, over-decorated &c. 882.

mis-shapen, -proportioned; monstrous; gaunt &c. (*thin*) 203; dumpy &c. (*short*) 201; curtailed of its fair proportions; ill-made, -shaped, -proportioned; crooked &c. (*distorted*) 243; hard-featured, -visaged; ill-, hard-, evil-favoured; ill-looking; unprepossessing.

graceless, inelegant; ungraceful, ungainly, uncouth; stiff; rugged, rough, gross, rude, awkward, clumsy, slouching, rickety; gawky; lump-ing, -ish; lumbering; hulk-y, -ing; unwieldy.

squalid, haggard; grim, -faced, -visaged; grisly, ghastly, ghost-, deathlike; cadaverous, gruesome.

frightful, hideous, odious, uncanny, forbidding, repellant repulsive; horri-d, -ble; shocking &c. (*painful*) 830.

foul &c. (*dirty*) 653; dingy &c. (*colourless*) 429; gaudy &c. (*colour*) 428; disfigured &c. *v.*; discoloured (*blemished*) &c. 848.

enchanting &c. (*pleasure-giving*) 829; attractive &c. (*inviting*) 615; becoming &c. (*accordant*) 23; ornamental &c. 847.

undeformed, undefaced, unspotted; spotless &c. (*perfect*) 650.

847. Ornament. — N. ornament, -ation, -al art; ornat-ure, -eness; adorn-ment, decoration, embellishment; architecture.

garnish, polish, varnish, French pol-

848. Blemish.—N. blemish, disfigurement, deformity; defect &c. (*imperfection*) 651; flaw; injury &c. (*deterioration*) 659; spots on the sun; eyesore.

ish, gilding, japanning, lacquer, ormolu, enamel.

cosmetics, rouge, powder, lipstick, lip salve, mascara; manicure, nail polish; permanent –, Marcel –, finger-wave.

pattern, diaper, powdering, panelling, graining, pargeting, inlay, detail; texture &c. 329; richness; tracery, moulding, beading, reeding, fillet, listel, strapwork, *coquillage*, flourish, *fleur-de-lis*, arabesque, fret, *anthemion*; egg and -tongue, – dart; *astragal*, zigzag, *acanthus*, *cartouche*; pilaster &c. (*projection*) 250; cyma, ogee.

em-, broidery, needlework; knitting, crochet, tatting, brocade, *brocatelle*, beads, bugles; galloon, lace, gimp, *guipure*, fringe, trapping, border, edging, insertion, *motif*, trimming; *passementerie*; drapery, hanging, tapestry, arras; millinery, ermine.

wreath, festoon, garland, lei, chaplet, flower, nosegay, *bouquet*, posy, 'daisies pied and violets blue.'

tassel, knot; shoulder-knot, *épaulette*, epaulet, aigulet, *aiguillette*, frog; star, rosette, bow; feather, plume, *panache*, *aigrette*.

jewel, -ry, -lery; bijoutry; *bijou*, *-terie*; diadem, tiara; pendant, trinket, locket, necklace, armilla, bracelet, bangle, armlet, anklet, ear-, nose- ring, carcanet, chain, *châtelaine*, albert, brooch, torque.

gem, precious stone; diamond, brilliant, beryl, aquamarine, alexandrite, cat's eye, emerald, calcedony, chrysoprase, cornelian, jasper, bloodstone, agate, heliotrope; girasol, -e; onyx, plasma; sard, -onyx; garnet, lapis-lazuli, opal, peridot, chrysolite, sapphire, ruby; spinel, -le; balais; oriental –, topaz; turquois, -e; zircon, jacinth, hyacinth, carbuncle, amethyst; moonstone; pearl, coral.

finery, frippery, gewgaw, gimcrack, knick-knack, tinsel, spangle, sequin, *clinquant*, pinch-beck, paste; excess of ornament &c. (*vulgarity*) 851; gaud, pride, ostentation; frills and furbelows.

illustration, illumination, *vignette*; *fleuron*; head-, tail-piece; *cul-de-lampe*; flowers of rhetoric &c. 577; work of art, article of vertu, *bric-à-brac*, curio, *bibelot*.

V. ornament, embellish, enrich, decorate, adorn, beautify, adonize.

smarten, furbish, polish, gild, varnish, whitewash, enamel, japan, lacquer, paint, grain.

garnish, trim, dizen, bedizen, prink, prank; trick –, fig- out; deck, bedeck, dight, bedight, array; dress, – up, preen, spruce up,

stain, blot, slur; spot, -tiness; speck, -le; blur, freckle, mole, *macula*, patch, blotch, birthmark, blain, maculation, tarnish, smudge, smear; dirt &c. 653; bruise, black eye, scar, wem; pustule; excrescence, pimple &c. (*protuberance*) 250.

V. disfigure &c. (*injure*) 659; speckle; render ugly &c. 846.

Adj. pitted, freckled, discoloured, bloodshot, bruised, disfigured; stained &c. *n.*; imperfect &c. 651; injured &c. (*deteriorated*) 659.

849. Simplicity. — N. simplicity; plain-, homeli-ness; undress, nudity, nakedness, beauty unadorned, chastity, chasteness.

V. be -simple &c. *adj.*

render -simple &c. *adj.*; simplify, chasten, strip of ornament.

Adj. simple, plain; home-ly, -spun; ordinary, household.

natural, unaffected; free from -affectation, – ornament; *simplex munditiis*; *sans façon*, *en déshabillé*, nude, naked.

chaste, inornate, severe.

un-adorned, -ornamented, -decked, -garnished, -arranged, -trimmed, -varnished.

bald, flat, dull, blank.

---

titivate; spangle, bespangle, powder; embroider, work; chase, tool, emboss, fret; emblazon, blazon, illuminate; illustrate.

become &c. (*accord with*) 23.

Adj. ornamented, beautified &c. *v.*; ornate, rich, gilt, begilt, tesselated, enamelled, inlaid; festooned; topiary.

smart, gay, tricksy, flowery, glittering; new-gilt, -spangled; fine, – as -a Mayday queen, – fivepence, – a carrot fresh scraped; pranked out, bedight, well-groomed.

in full dress &c. (*fashion*) 852; *en grande -tenue, – toilette*; in best bib and tucker, in Sunday best, *endimanché*; dressed to advantage.

showy, flashy; gaudy &c. (*vulgar*) 851; garish; gorgeous.

ornamental, decorative; becoming &c. (*accordant*) 23.

850. [Good taste.] **Taste.—N.** taste; good –, refined –, cultivated- taste; delicacy, refinement, fine feeling, gust, *gusto*, tact, *finesse*; nicety &c. (*discrimination*) 465; polish, elegance, grace.

virtu; dilettanteism, virtuosity; fine art; cul-ture, -ivation.

[Science of taste] æsthetics.

man of -taste &c.; *connoisseur*, judge, critic, *conoscente, virtuoso, amateur, dilettante*, Aristarchus, Corinthian, *arbiter elegantiarum*, stagirite, euphemist.

'caviare to the general.'

V. appreciate, judge, criticize, discriminate &c. 465.

Adj. in good taste; tasteful, tasty; unaffected, pure, chaste, classical, attic; cultivated, refined; dainty; æsthetic, artistic; elegant &c. 578; euphemistic.

to one's -taste, – mind; after one's fancy; *comme il faut*; *tiré à quatre épingles*.

Adv. elegantly &c. *adj.*

Phr. *nihil tetigit quod non ornavit.*

852. Fashion.—N. fashion, style, *ton, bon ton*, society; good –, polite- society; drawing room, civilized life, civilization, town, *beau monde*, high life, court; world; fashionable –, gay- world; Vanity Fair; show &c. (*ostentation*) 822.

manners, breeding &c. (*politeness*) 894; air, demeanour &c. (*appearance*) 448; *savoir-faire*; gentlemanliness, gentility, decorum, propriety, *bienséance*; conventions –, dictates- of society; Mrs. Grundy; convention, -ality; punctilio; form, -ality; etiquette, point of

851. [Bad taste.] **Vulgarity.—N.** vulgar-ity, -ism; barbar-, Vandal-, Gothic-ism; *mauvais goût*, bad taste; Babbittry; *gaucherie*, awkwardness, want of tact; ill-breeding &c. (*discourtesy*) 895; ungentlemanly behaviour.

coarseness &c. *adj.*; indecorum, misbehaviour.

low-, homeli-ness; low life, *mauvais ton*, rusticity; boorishness &c. *adj.*; brutality; rowdy-, ruffian-, blackguard-ism; ribaldry; slang &c. (*neology*) 563.

bad joke, *mauvaise plaisanterie*.

[Excess of ornament] gaudi-, tawdriness; false ornament; finery, frippery, trickery, tinsel, gewgaw, *clinquant*.

rough diamond, tomboy, hoyden, cub, unlicked cub; clown &c. (*commonalty*) 876; Hun, Goth, Vandal, Bœotian; vulgarian; snob, cad, bounder, gent; *parvenu* &c. 876; frump, dowdy; slattern &c. 653.

V. be -vulgar &c. *adj.*; misbehave; talk –, smell of the- shop.

Adj. in bad taste, vulgar, unrefined, gutter.

coarse, indecorous, ribald, gross; unseemly, unbeseeming, unpresentable; *contra bonos mores*; ungraceful &c. (*ugly*) 846.

dowdy; slovenly &c. (*dirty*) 653; ungenteel, shabby genteel; low &c. (*plebeian*) 876; uncourtly; uncivil &c. (*discourteous*) 895; ill-bred, -mannered; underbred; ungentleman-ly, -like; unladylike, unfeminine; wild, – as an unbacked colt.

unkempt, uncombed, untamed, unlicked, unpolished, uncouth, plebeian;

etiquette; custom &c. 613; mode, vogue, style, go; rage &c. (*desire*) 865; prevailing taste, *dernier cri*, dress &c. 225.

man –, woman- of -fashion, – the world; height –, pink –, star –, glass –, leader- of fashion; *arbiter elegantiarum* &c. (*taste*) 850; upper ten thousand &c. (*nobility*) 875; *élite* &c. (*distinction*) 873.

V. be -fashionable &c. *adj.*, – the rage &c. *n.*; have a run, pass current.

follow –, conform to –, fall in with- the fashion &c. *n.*; go with the stream &c. (*conform*) 82; *savoir -vivre, – faire*; keep up appearances, behave oneself.

set the –, bring into- fashion; give a tone to –, cut a figure in- society, rub shoulders with nobility, keep one's carriage.

Adj. fashionable; in -fashion &c. *n.*; *à la mode, comme il faut*; admitted –, admissible- in -society &c. *n.*; presentable, decorous, punctilious, conventional &c. (*customary*) 613; genteel; well-bred, -mannered, -behaved, -spoken; gentleman-like, -ly; ladylike; civil, polite &c. (*courteous*) 894.

polished, refined, thoroughbred, courtly; *distingué*, aristocratic, unembarrassed, poised, *dégagé*; ja-, jau-nty; dashing, fast, showy, high toned, toney.

modish, stylish, in the latest style, *recherché*; new-fangled &c. (*unfamiliar*) 83.

in -court, – full, – evening- dress; *en grande tenue* &c. (*ornament*) 847.

Adv. fashionably &c. *adj.*; for fashion's sake.

incondite; heavy, rude, awkward; home-ly, -spun, -bred; provincial, hick, countrified, rustic, uncultivated, fresh-water; boorish, clownish; savage, brutish, blackguard, rowdy, snobbish; barbar-ous, -ic; Gothic, unclassical, doggerel, heathenish, tramontane, outlandish; Bohemian.

obsolete &c. (*antiquated*) 124; unfashionable, old-fashioned, out of date; new-fangled &c. (*unfamiliar*) 83; fantastic, odd &c. (*ridiculous*) 853.

particular; affected &c. 855; meretricious; extravagant, monstrous, horrid; shocking &c. (*painful*) 830.

gaudy, tawdry, bedizened, tricked out, gingerbread; obtrusive, flaunting, loud, flashy, garish, showy.

---

853. Ridiculousness.—N. ridiculousness &c. *adj.*; comical-, odd-ity &c. *adj.*; extravagance, drollery.

farce, comedy; burlesque &c. (*ridicule*) 856; buffoonery &c. (*fun*) 840; frippery; doggerel verses; Irish bull, Hibernianism, Hibernicism; Spoonerism; absurdity &c. 497; bombast &c. (*unmeaning*) 517; anti-climax, bathos; monstrosity &c. (*unconformity*) 83; laughing stock &c. 857.

V. be -ridiculous &c. *adj.*; pass from the sublime to the ridiculous; make one laugh; play the fool, make a fool of oneself, commit an absurdity.

play a joke on, make a -fool of, – sucker of, – monkey of.

Adj. ridiculous, ludicrous; comic, -al; droll, funny, laughable, *pour rire*, grotesque, farcical, odd; whimsical, – as a dancing bear; fanciful, fantastic, queer, rum, quizzical, waggish, quaint, *bizarre*; eccentric &c. (*unconformable*) 83; strange, outlandish, out of the way, *baroque*, *rocaille*, rococo; awkward &c. (*ugly*) 846.

absurd, extravagant, *outré*, monstrous, preposterous, bombastic, inflated, stilted, burlesque, mock heroic.

drollish; serio-, tragic-comic; gimcrack, contemptible &c. (*unimportant*) 643; doggerel; ironical &c. (*derisive*) 856; risible.

Phr. *'risum teneatis amici?' rideret Heraclitus.*

854. Fop.—**N.** fop, fine gentleman; swell; dand-y, -iprat; exquisite, coxcomb, toff, beau, macaroni, blade, blood, buck, man about town, fast man; fribble, jemmy, spark, popinjay, puppy, prig, *petit maître*; jacka-napes, -dandy; man milliner; Jemmy Jessamy, carpet-knight, masher, Dundreary, Johnnie, dude.

belle, fine lady, *coquette*, flirt.

855. Affectation.—**N.** affectation; affectedness &c. *adj.*; acting a part &c. *v.*; pretence &c. (*falsehood*) 544, (*ostentation*) 882; boasting &c. 884;

charlatanism, quackery, shallow profundity, humbug, pretension, airs, pedantry, purism, precisianism, euphuism, prunes and prisms; teratology &c. (*altiloquence*) 577.

mannerism, *simagrée*, grimace.

conceit, foppery, dandyism, man millinery, coxcombry, puppyism.

stiffness, formality, buckram; prudery, demureness, coquetry, mock modesty, *minauderie*, sentimentalism; *mauvaise honte*, false shame.

affector, performer, actor; pedant, pedagogue, *doctrinaire*, purist, euphuist, mannerist; shoneen; *grimacier*; lump of affectation, *précieuse ridicule*, *bas bleu*, blue stocking, poetaster; prig, hypocrite; charlatan &c. (*deceiver*) 548; *petit maître* &c. (*fop*) 854; flatterer &c. 935; *coquette*, prude, puritan; precisian, formalist.

V. affect, act a part, put on; give oneself airs &c. (*arrogance*) 885; boast &c. 884; coquet; simper, mince, attitudinize, strike a pose, pose; flirt a fan; over-act, -play, -do.

Adj. affected, full of affectation, pretentious, pedantic, stilted, stagey, theatrical, big-sounding, *ad captandum*, canting, insincere.

not natural, unnatural; self-conscious; *maniéré*; artificial; overwrought, -done, -acted; euphuistic &c. 577.

stiff, starch, formal, prim, smug, demure, *tiré à quatre épingles*, quakerish, puritanical, prudish, pragmatical, priggish, conceited, coxcomical, foppish, dandified; fini-cal, -kin, -cky, mincing, simpering, namby-pamby, sentimental, languishing.

856. Ridicule.—**N.** ridicule, derision; sardonic -smile, - grin; irrision; snigger; scoffing &c. (*disrespect*) 929; mockery, quiz, banter, irony, *persiflage*, raillery, chaff, *badinage*; quizzing &c. *v.*

squib, satire, skit, quip, quib, grin.

parody, burlesque, travesty; farce &c. (*drama*) 599; caricature, take-off.

buffoonery &c. (*fun*) 840; practical joke, horseplay.

V. ridicule, deride; laugh at, grin at, smile at; snigger; laugh in one's sleeve; banter, rally, chaff, joke, twit, quiz, poke fun at, jolly, roast, rag; fleer; play -, play tricks- upon; fool, - to the top of one's bent; show up.

satirize, parody, caricature, burlesque, travesty.

turn into ridicule; make merry with; make -fun, - game, - a fool, - an April fool- of; rally; scoff &c. (*disrespect*) 929.

raise a laugh &c. (*amuse*) 840; play the fool, make a fool of oneself.

be ridiculous &c. 853.

Adj. deris-ory, -ive; mock; sarcastic, ironical, quizzical, burlesque, Hudibrastic; scurrilous &c. (*disrespectful*) 929.

Adv. in -ridicule &c. *n.*

857. [Object and cause of ridicule.] **Laughing-stock.—N.** laughing-, jesting-, gazing-stock; butt, game, fair game; April fool &c. (*dupe*) 547.

original, oddity; queer –, odd- fish; quiz, square-toes; old –, fogey *or* fogy.

monkey; buffoon &c. (*jester*) 844; pantomimist &c. (*actor*) 599.

jest &c. (*wit*) 842.

3°. Prospective Affections

858. Hope.—N. hope, -s; desire &c. 865; fervent hope, sanguine expectation, trust, confidence, reliance; faith &c. (*belief*) 484; affiance, assurance; secur-eness, -ity; reassurance.

good -omen, – auspices; promise, well-grounded hopes; good –, bright- prospect; clear sky.

as-, pre-sumption; anticipation &c. (*expectation*) 507.

hopefulness, buoyancy, optimism, enthusiasm, heart of grace, aspiration; optimist, utop-ian, -ist; Pollyanna.

castles in the air, *châteaux en Espagne*, hope chest, *le pot au lait*, Utopia, millennium; day –, golden- dream; dream of Alnaschar; airy hopes, fool's paradise; *mirage* &c. (*fallacies of vision*) 443; fond hope.

beam –, ray –, gleam –, glimmer –, dawn –, flash –, star- of hope; cheer; bit of blue sky, silver lining of the cloud, bottom of Pandora's box, balm in Gilead.

anchor, sheet-anchor, main-stay; staff &c. (*support*) 215; heaven &c. 981.

V. hope, trust, confide, rely on, put one's trust in, lean upon; pin one's -hope, – faith- upon &c. (*believe*) 484.

feel –, entertain –, harbour –, indulge –, cherish –, feed –, foster –, nourish –, encourage –, cling to –, live in- hope &c. *n.*; see land; feel –, rest- -assured, – confident &c. *adj.*

presume; promise oneself; expect &c. (*look forward to*) 507.

hope for &c. (*desire*) 865; anticipate.

be -hopeful &c. *adj.*; look on the bright side of, view on the sunny side, make the best of it, hope for the best; put -a good, – a bold, – the best- face upon; keep one's spirits up; take heart, – of grace; be of good -heart, – cheer; flatter oneself, lay the flattering unction to one's soul.

859. [Absence, want, or loss of hope.] **Hopelessness.—N.** hopelessness &c. *adj.*; despair, desperation; despondency &c. (*dejection*) 837; pessimism.

hope deferred, dashed hopes; vain expectation &c. (*disappointment*) 509.

airy hopes &c. 858; forlorn hope; bad -job, – business; *enfant perdu*; gloomy –, black spots in the- horizon; slough of Despond, cave of Despair.

Job's comforter; bird of -bad, – ill- omen.

V. despair; lose –, give up –, abandon –, relinquish- -all hope, – the hope of; give -up, – over; yield to despair; falter; despond &c. (*be dejected*) 837; *jeter le manche après la cognée.*

inspire –, drive to- despair &c. *n.*; disconcert; dash –, crush –, shatter –, destroy- one's hopes; hope against hope.

Adj. hopeless, desperate, despairing, in despair, *au désespoir*, forlorn; inconsolable &c. (*dejected*) 837; broken-hearted.

out of the question, not to be thought of; impracticable &c. 471; past -hope, – cure, – mending, – recall; at one's last gasp &c. (*death*) 360; given -up, – over.

incurable, cureless, immedicable, remediless, beyond remedy; incorrigible; irre-parable, -mediable, -coverable, -versible, -trievable, -claimable, -deemable, -vocable; ruined, undone; immitigable.

unpromising, unpropitious; inauspicious, ill-omened, threatening, clouded over, lowering, ominous.

Phr. *'lasciate ogni speranza voi ch' entrate'*; its days are numbered; the worst come to the worst.

860. Fear.—N. fear, timidity, diffidence, want of confidence; apprehensive-, fearful-ness &c. *adj.*; solicitude,

catch at a straw, hope against hope, count one's chickens before they are hatched.

give –, inspire –, raise –, hold out- hope &c. *n.*; raise expectations; encourage, hearten, cheer, assure, reassure, buoy up, embolden; promise, bid fair, augur well, be in a fair way, look up, flatter, tell a flattering tale.

Adj. hoping &c. *v.*; in -hopes &c. *n.*; hopeful, confident; secure &c. (*certain*) 484; sanguine, in good heart, buoyed up, buoyant, elated, flushed, exultant, enthusiastic; utopian.

unsus-pecting, -picious; fearless, free –, exempt from- -fear, – suspicion, – distrust, – despair; undespairing, self-reliant.

probable, on the high road to; within sight of -shore, – land; promising, propitious; of –, full of- promise; of good omen; auspicious, *de bon augure*; reassuring; encouraging, cheering, inspiriting, looking up, bright, roseate, *couleur de rose*, rose-coloured.

Adv. hopefully &c. *adj.*

Int. God speed! good luck!

Phr. *nil desperandum*; never say die, *dum spiro spero, latet scintillula forsan*, all is for the best, *spero meliora*; the wish being father to the thought; 'hope told a flattering tale'; *rusticus expectat dum defluat amnis.*

---

anxiety, care, apprehension, misgiving; mistrust &c. (*doubt*) 485; suspicion, qualm; hesitation &c. (*irresolution*) 605.

nervous-, restless-ness &c. *adj.*; in-, dis-quietude; flutter, trepidation, fear and trembling, perturbation, tremor, quivering, shaking, trembling, throbbing heart, palpitation, ague fit, cold sweat; abject fear &c. (*cowardice*) 862; mortal funk, heart-sinking, despondency; despair &c. 859.

fright; affright, -ment; alarm, pavor, dread, awe, terror, horror, dismay, consternation, panic, scare, stampede [of horses].

intimidation, terrorism, reign of terror.

[Object of fear] bug-bear, -aboo; scarecrow; hobgoblin &c. (*demon*) 980; daymare, nightmare, Gorgon, Medusa, mormo, ogre, Hurlothrumbo, raw head and bloody bones, fee faw fum, *bête noire, enfant terrible.*

alarmist &c. (*coward*) 862.

V. fear, stand in awe of; be -afraid &c. *adj.*; have -qualms &c. *n.*; apprehend, sit upon thorns, eye askance; distrust &c. (*disbelieve*) 485.

hesitate &c. (*be irresolute*) 605; falter, funk, cower, crouch; skulk &c. (*cowardice*) 862; let 'I dare not' wait upon 'I would'; take -fright, – alarm; start, wince, flinch, shy, shrink; fly &c. (*avoid*) 623.

tremble, shake; shiver, – in one's shoes; shudder, flutter; shake –, tremble- -like an aspen leaf, – all over; quake, quaver, quiver, quail; get the wind up.

grow –, turn- pale; blench, stand aghast; not dare to say one's soul is one's own.

inspire –, excite- -fear, – awe; raise apprehensions; give –, raise –, sound- an alarm; alarm, startle, scare, cry 'wolf,' disquiet, dismay; fright, -en; affright, terrify; astound; frighten from one's propriety; frighten out of one's -wits, – senses, – seven senses; awe; strike -all of a heap, – an awe into, – terror; harrow up the soul, appal, unman, petrify, horrify.

make one's -flesh creep, – hair stand on end, – blood run cold, – teeth chatter; chill one's spine; take away –, stop- one's breath; make one -tremble &c.

haunt, obsess, beset; prey –, weigh- on the mind.

put in -fear, – bodily fear; terrorize, intimidate, cow, daunt, overawe, abash, deter, discourage; browbeat, bully; threaten &c. 909.

Adj. fearing &c. *v.*; frightened &c. *v.*; in -fear, – a fright &c. *n.*; haunted with the -fear &c. *n.*- of.

afraid, fearful; tim-id, -orous; nervous, diffident, coy, faint-hearted, tremulous, shaky, afraid of one's shadow, apprehensive, restless, fidgety; more frightened than hurt.

aghast; awe-, horror-, terror-, panic- -struck, -stricken; frightened to death, white as a sheet; pale, – as -death, – ashes, – a ghost; breathless, in hysterics.

inspiring fear &c. *v.*; alarming; formidable, redoubtable; perilous &c. (*danger*) 665; portentous; fear-ful, -some; dread, -ful; fell; dire, -ful; shocking; terri-ble, -fic; tremendous; horri-d, -ble, -fic; ghastly; awful, awe-inspiring, eerie, weird; revolting &c. (*painful*) 830.

Adv. *in terrorem.*

Int. 'angels and ministers of grace defend us!'

Phr. *ante tubam trepidat*; *horresco referens*, one's heart failing one, *obstupui steteruntque comæ et vox faucibus hæsit.*

861. [Absence of fear.] **Courage.—N.** courage, bravery, valour; resolute-, bold-ness &c. *adj.*; spirit, daring, gallantry, intrepidity; contempt –, defiance- of danger; derring-do; audacity; rashness &c. 863; dash; defiance &c. 715; confidence, self-reliance.

man-liness, -hood; nerve, pluck, mettle, game; heart, – of grace; spunk, gameness, grit, face, virtue, hardihood, fortitude; firmness &c. (*stability*) 150; heart of oak; bottom, backbone &c. (*perseverance*) 604*a*.

resolution &c. (*determination*) 604; tenacity, bull-dog courage.

prowess, heroism, chivalry.

exploit, feat, achievement; heroic -deed, – act; bold stroke.

man, – of mettle; hero, demigod, paladin, heroine, Amazon, Hector, Joan of Arc; lion, tiger, panther, bull-dog; game-, fighting-cock; bully, fire-eater &c. 863; dare-devil.

V. be -courageous &c. *adj.*; dare, venture, make bold; face –, front –, affront –, confront –, brave –, defy –, despise –, mock- danger; look in the face; look -full, – boldly, – danger- in the face; face; meet, – in front; brave, beard; defy &c. 715.

take –, muster –, summon up –, pluck up- courage; nerve oneself, take heart; take –, pluck up- heart of grace; hold up one's head, screw one's courage to the sticking place; come -to, – up to- the scratch; stand, – to one's guns, – fire, – against; bear up, – against; hold out &c. (*persevere*) 604*a*.

put a bold face upon; show –,

862. [Excess of fear.] **Cowardice.—N.** cowardice, pusillanimity; cowardliness &c. *adj.*; timidity, effeminacy.

poltroonery, baseness; dastard-ness, -y; abject fear, funk; Dutch courage; fear &c. 860; white feather, faint heart.

coward, poltroon, dastard, sneak, recreant; shy –, dunghill- cock; coistril, milksop, white-liver, nidget, cur, craven, one that cannot say 'Bo' to a goose; Bob Acres, Jerry Sneak.

alarm-, terror-, pessim-ist; runagate &c. (*fugitive*) 623; shirker.

V. quail &c. (*fear*) 860; be -cowardly &c. *adj.*, – a coward &c. *n.*; funk; cower, skulk, sneak; flinch, shy, fight shy, slink, turn tail; run away &c. (*avoid*) 623; show the white feather, have cold feet, show a yellow streak.

Adj. coward, -ly; fearful, shy; tim-id, -orous; skittish; poor-spirited, spiritless, soft, effeminate.

weak-minded; infirm of purpose &c. 605; weak-, faint-, chicken-, lily-, pigeon-hearted; yellow; white-, lily-, milk-livered; milksop, smock-faced; unable to say 'Bo' to a goose.

dastard, -ly; base, craven, sneaking, dunghill, recreant; unwar-, unsoldier-like.

'in face a lion but in heart a deer.'

unmanned; frightened &c. 860.

Int. *sauve qui peut!* devil take the hindmost!

Adv. in fear and trembling, in fear of one's life, in a blue funk.

Phr. *ante tubam trepidat*, one's courage oozing out.

present- a bold front, face the music; envisage; show fight.

bell the cat, take the bull by the horns, beard the lion in his den, march up to the cannon's mouth, go through fire and water, run the gauntlet, go over the top.

give –, infuse –, inspire- courage; reassure, encourage, embolden, inspirit, cheer, hearten, nerve, put upon one's mettle, rally, raise a rallying cry; pat on the back, make a man of, keep in countenance.

Adj. courageous, brave; val-iant, -orous; gallant, intrepid; spirit-ed, -ful; high-spirited, -mettled; mettlesome, game, plucky; man-ly, -ful; resolute; stout, -hearted; iron-, lion-hearted; heart of oak; Penthesilean.

bold, – spirited; daring, audacious; fear-, daunt-, dread-, awe-less; un-daunted, -appalled, -dismayed, -awed, -blenched, -abashed, -alarmed, -flinching, -shrinking, -blenching, -apprehensive; confident, self-reliant; bold as -a lion, – brass.

enterprising, adventurous; ventur-ous, -esome; dashing, chivalrous; soldierly &c. (*warlike*) 722; heroic.

fierce, savage; pugnacious &c. (*bellicose*) 720.

strong-minded, hardy, doughty; firm &c. (*stable*) 150; determined &c. (*resolved*) 604; dogged, indomitable &c. (*persevering*) 604*a*.

up to, – the scratch; upon one's mettle; reassured &c. *v.*; unfeared, undreaded.

Phr. one's blood being up.

863. Rashness.—N. rashness &c. *adj.*; temerity, want of caution, imprudence, indiscretion; over-confidence, presumption, audacity.

precipit-ancy, -ation; impetuosity; levity; foolhardi-hood, -ness; heed-, thought-lessness &c. (*inattention*) 458; carelessness &c. (*neglect*) 460; desperation; Quixotism, knight-errantry; fire-eating.

gam-ing, -bling; blind bargain, leap in the dark, fool's paradise; too many eggs in one basket.

desperado, rashling, mad-cap, dare-devil, Hotspur, fire-eater, bully, *bravo*, Hector, scapegrace, *enfant perdu*; Don Quixote, knight-errant, Icarus; adventurer; gam-bler, -ester; dynamitard.

V. be -rash &c. *adj.*; stick at nothing, play a desperate game; run into danger &c. 665; play with -fire, – edge tools.

carry too much sail, sail too near the wind, ride at single anchor, go out of one's depth.

take a leap in the dark, buy a pig in a poke.

donner tête baissée; knock one's head against a wall &c. (*be unskilful*) 699; rush on destruction; kick against the

864. Caution.—N. caution; cautiousness &c. *adj.*; discretion, prudence, cautel, heed, circumspection, calculation, deliberation; safety first.

foresight &c. 510; vigilance &c. 459; warning &c. 668.

coolness &c. *adj.*; self-possession, -command; presence of mind, *sang-froid*; well-regulated mind; worldly wisdom, Fabian policy.

V. be -cautious &c. *adj.*; take -care, – heed, – good care; have a care; mind, – what one is about; be on one's guard &c. (*keep watch*) 459; make assurance double sure; ca' canny.

bespeak &c. (*be early*) 132.

think twice, look before one leaps, keep one's weather eye open, count the cost, look to the main chance, cut one's coat according to one's cloth; feel one's -ground, – way; see how the land lies &c. (*foresight*) 510; wait to see how the cat jumps; bridle one's tongue; *reculer pour mieux sauter* &c. (*prepare*) 673; let well alone, let sleeping dogs lie, *ne pas réveiller le chat qui dort*.

keep out of -harm's way, – troubled waters; keep at a respectful distance, stand aloof; keep –, be- on the safe side

pricks, tempt Providence, go on a forlorn hope.

count one's chickens before they are hatched; reckon without one's host; catch at straws; trust to –, lean on- a broken reed.

Adj. rash, incautious, indiscreet, injudicious; imprudent, improvident, temerarious; uncalculating; heedless; careless &c. (*neglectful*) 460; without ballast, heels over head; giddy &c. (*inattentive*) 458; wanton, reckless, wild, madcap; desperate, devil-may-care.

hot-blooded, -headed, -brained; head-long, -strong; break-neck; foolhardy; hare-brained; precipitate, impulsive.

over-confident, -weening; ventur-esome, -ous; adventurous, Quixotic; fire-eating, cavalier; free-and-easy.

off one's guard &c. (*inexpectant*) 508.

Adv. post haste, *à corps perdu*, hand over head, *tête baissée*, headforemost; happen what may.

Phr. neck or nothing, the devil being in one.

husband one's resources &c. 636. caution &c. (*warn*) 668.

Adj. cautious, wary, guarded; on one's guard &c. (*watchful*) 459; *cavendo tutus*; *in medio tutissimus*.

care-, heed-ful; cautelous, stealthy, chary, shy of, circumspect, prudent, canny, safe, non-committal, discreet, politic; sure-footed &c. (*skilful*) 698.

unenterprising, unadventurous, cool, steady, self-possessed; over-cautious.

suspicious, leery, vigilant.

Adv. cautiously, gingerly &c. *adj.*

Int. have a care! look out! *cave canem!*

Phr. *timeo Danaos*; *festina lente*.

---

865. Desire.—N. desire, wish, fancy, fantasy; want, need, exigency.

mind, inclination, leaning, bent, *animus*, partiality, *penchant*, predilection; propensity &c. 820; willingness &c. 602; liking, love, fondness, relish.

longing, hankering; solicitude, anxiety; yearning, coveting; aspiration, ambition, vaulting ambition; eagerness, zeal, ardour, *empressement*, breathless impatience, over-anxiety; solicitude, impetuosity &c. 825.

appet-ite, -ition, -ence, -ency; sharp appetite, keenness, hunger, stomach, twist; thirst, -iness; drouth, mouthwatering; itch, -ing; prurience, *cacoëthes*, cupidity, lust, concupiscence.

edge of -appetite, – hunger; torment of Tantalus; sweet –, lickerish- tooth; itching palm; longing –, wistful –, sheep's- eye.

avidity; greed, -iness; covetous-, ravenous-ness &c. *adj.*; grasping, craving, canine appetite, rapacity; voracity &c. (*gluttony*) 957.

passion, rage, *furore*, mania, *manie*; inextinguishable desire; dips-, klept-, mon-omania.

[Person desiring] desirer, lover, *ama-*

866. Indifference.—N. indifference, neutrality; coldness &c. *adj.*; unconcern, *insouciance*, *nonchalance*; want of -interest, – earnestness; anorexy, inappetency; apathy &c. (*insensibility*) 823; supineness &c. (*inactivity*) 683; disdain &c. 930; recklessness &c. 863; inattention &c. 458.

V. be -indifferent &c. *adj.*; stand neuter; take no interest in &c. (*insensibility*) 823; have no -desire &c. 865, – taste, – relish- for; not care for; care nothing -for, – about; not care a -straw &c. (*unimportance*) 643 -about, – for; not mind.

set at naught &c. (*make light of*) 483; spurn &c. (*disdain*) 930.

Adj. indifferent, cold, frigid, lukewarm; cool, – as a cucumber; unconcerned, *insouciant*, phlegmatic, *pococurante*, easy-going, devil-may-care, careless, listless, lackadaisical, feckless; half-hearted; un-ambitious, -aspiring, -desirous, -solicitous, -attracted.

un-attractive, -alluring, -desired, -desirable, -cared for, -wished, -valued, all one to.

insipid &c. 391; vain.

Adv. for aught one cares.

teur, votary, devotee, aspirant, solicitant, candidate; cormorant &c. 957; sycophant.

[Object of desire] *desideratum*; want &c. (*requirement*) 630; 'consummation devoutly to be wished'; attraction, magnet, allurement, fancy, temptation, seduction, lure, fascination, *prestige*, height of one's ambition, idol; whim, -sey; maggot; hobby, -horse.

Fortunatus's cap, wishing cap, love potion.

V. desire; wish, – for; be -desirous &c. *adj*.; have a -longing &c. *n*.; hope &c. 858.

care for, affect, like, list; take to, cling to, take a fancy to; fancy; prefer &c. (*choose*) 609.

have -an eye, – a mind- to; find it in one's heart &c. (*be willing*) 602; have a fancy for, set one's eyes upon; cast a sheep's eye –, look sweet- upon; take into one's head, have at heart, be bent upon; set one's -cap at, – heart upon, – mind upon; covet.

want, miss, need, lack, desiderate, feel the want of; would fain -have, – do; would be glad of.

be -hungry &c. *adj*.; have a good appetite, play a good knife and fork; hunger –, thirst –, crave –, lust –, itch –, hanker –, run mad- after; raven –, die- for; burn to.

desiderate; sigh –, cry –, gape –, gasp –, pine –, pant –, languish –, yearn –, long –, be on thorns –, hope- for; aspire after; catch at, grasp at, jump at.

woo, court, solicit; fish –, spell –, whistle –, put up- for; ogle.

cause –, create –, raise –, excite –, provoke- desire; whet the appetite; appetize, titillate, allure, attract, take one's fancy, tempt; hold out -temptation, – allurement; tantalize, make one's mouth water, *faire venir l'eau à la bouche*.

gratify desire &c. (*give pleasure*) 829.

Adj. desirous; desiring &c. *v*.; orectic, appetitive; inclined &c. (*willing*) 602; partial to; fain, wishful, optative; anxious, wistful, curious; at a loss for, sedulous, solicitous.

craving, hungry, sharp-set, peckish,

Int. never mind.

867. Dislike.—N. dis-like, -taste, -relish, -inclination, -placency.

reluctance; backwardness &c. (*unwillingness*) 603.

repugnance, disgust, queasiness, turn, nausea, loathing; avers-eness, -ation, -ion; abomination, antipathy, abhorrence, horror; mortal –, rooted- -antipathy, – horror; hatred, detestation; hate &c. 898; animosity &c. 900; hydrophobia.

sickener; gall and wormwood &c. (*unsavoury*) 395; shuddering, cold sweat.

V. dis-, mis-like, -relish; mind, object to; have rather not, not care for; have –, conceive –, entertain –, take- -a dislike, – an aversion- to; have no -taste, – stomach- for.

shun, avoid &c. 623; eschew; withdraw –, shrink –, recoil- from; not be able to -bear, – abide, – endure; shrug the shoulders at, shudder at, turn up the nose at, look askance at; make a -mouth, – wry face, – grimace; make faces.

loathe, nauseate, abominate, detest, abhor; hate &c. 898; take amiss &c. 900; have enough of &c. (*be satiated*) 869.

cause –, excite- dislike; disincline, repel, sicken; make –, render- sick; turn one's stomach, nauseate, wamble, disgust, shock, stink in the nostrils; go against the -grain, – stomach; stick in the throat; make one's blood run cold &c. (*give pain*) 830; pall.

Adj. disliking &c. *v*.; averse to, loth, adverse; shy of, sick of, out of conceit with; disinclined; heart-, dog-sick; queasy.

disliked &c. *v*.; uncared for, unpopular; out of favour; repulsive, repugnant, repellent; abhorrent, insufferable, fulsome, nauseous; loath-some, -ful; offensive; disgusting &c. *v*.; disagreeable &c. (*painful*) 830; unsavoury &c. 395.

Adv. *usque ad nauseam*.

Int. faugh! foh! ugh!

868. Fastidiousness.—N. fastidiousness &c. *adj*.; nicety, meticulosity,

ravening, with an empty stomach, esurient, lickerish, thirsty, athirst, parched with thirst, pinched with hunger, famished, dry, drouthy; hungry as a -hunter, - hawk, - horse, - church mouse.

greedy, - as a hog; over-eager, voracious; ravenous, - as a wolf; open-mouthed, covetous, rapacious, grasping, extortionate, exacting, sordid, *alieni appetens*; insati-able, -ate; unquenchable, quenchless; omnivorous.

unsatisfied, unsated, unslaked.

eager, avid, keen; burning, fervent, ardent; agog; all agog; breathless; impatient &c. (*impetuous*) 825; bent -, intent -, set- -on, - upon; mad after, *enragé*, rabid, dying for, devoured by desire.

aspiring, ambitious, vaulting, sky-aspiring.

desirable; popular; desired &c. *v.*; in demand; pleasing &c. (*giving pleasure*) 829; appeti-zing, -ble; tantalizing.

Adv. wistfully &c. *adj.*; fain.

Int. would -that, - it were! O for! *esto perpetua!* if only!

Phr. the wish being father to the thought; *sua cuique voluptas*; *hoc erat in votis*, the mouth watering, the fingers itching; *aut Cæsar aut nullus*.

---

hypercriticism, difficulty in being pleased, *friandise*, epicurism, *omnia suspendens naso*.

discrimination, discernment, good taste, perspicacity.

epicure, gourmet.

[Excess of delicacy] prudery, prudishness, primness.

V. be -fastidious &c. *adj.*; split hairs, discriminate, have a sweet tooth.

mince the matter; turn up one's nose at &c. (*disdain*) 930; look a gift horse in the mouth, see spots on the sun.

Adj. fastidious, meticulous, exacting, nice, delicate, *délicat*, finical, finicky, difficult, dainty, lickerish, squeamish, thin-skinned; s-, queasy; hard -, difficult- to please; querulous, particular, over-particular, straitlaced, prudish, prim, scrupulous; censorious &c. 932; hypercritical, discriminating, discerning, perspicacious.

Phr. *noli me tangere.*

869. Satiety.—N. satiety, satisfaction, saturation, repletion, glut, surfeit; weariness &c. 841.

spoiled child; *enfant gâté*; too much of a good thing, *toujours perdrix*; *crambe repetita*.

V. sate, satiate, satisfy, saturate; cloy, quench, slake, pall, glut, gorge, surfeit; bore &c. (*weary*) 841; tire &c. (*fatigue*) 688; spoil.

have -enough of, - quite enough of, - one's fill, - too much of; be -satiated &c. *adj.*

Adj. satiated &c. *v.*; overgorged; *blasé*, used up, sick of, heart-sick.

Int. enough! hold! *eheu jam satis!*

4°. Contemplative Affections

870. Wonder.—N. wonder, marvel; astonish-, amaze-, wonder-, bewilder-ment; amazedness &c. *adj.*; admiration, awe; stup-or, -efaction; stound, fascination; sensation; surprise &c. (*inexpectation*) 508; cynosure.

note of admiration; thaumaturgy &c. (*sorcery*) 992.

V. wonder, marvel, admire; be -surprised &c. *adj.*; start; stare; open -, rub -, turn up- one's eyes; gloar; gape, open one's mouth, hold one's breath;

871. [Absence of wonder.] **Expectance.—N.** expectan-ce, -cy &c. (*expectation*) 507; calmness, composure, tranquillity, serenity, coolness, imperturbability &c. 826.

nine days' wonder.

V. expect &c. 507; not -be surprised, - wonder &c. 870; *nil admirari*, make nothing of.

Adj. expecting &c. *v.*; unamazed, astonished at nothing; *blasé* &c. (*weary*) 841; unimaginative, calm, serene, im-

look –, stand- -aghast, – agog; look blank &c. (*disappointment*) 509; *tomber des nues*; not believe one's -eyes, – ears, – senses.

not be able to account for &c. (*unintelligible*) 519; not know whether one stands on one's head or one's heels.

surprise, astonish, amaze, astound; dumbfound, -er; startle, dazzle; strike, – with -wonder, – awe; electrify; stun, stupefy, petrify, confound, bewilder, flabbergast; stagger, throw on one's beam ends, fascinate, turn the head, take away one's breath, strike dumb; make one's -hair stand on end, – tongue cleave to the roof of one's mouth; make one stare.

take by surprise &c. (*be unexpected*) 508.

be -wonderful &c. *adj.*; beggar –, baffle- description; stagger belief.

Adj. surprised &c. *v.*; aghast, all agog, breathless, agape; open-mouthed; awe-, thunder-, moon-, planet-struck; spell-bound; lost in -amazement, – wonder, – astonishment; struck all of a heap, unable to believe one's senses, like a duck in thunder.

wonderful, wondrous; surprising &c. *v.*; unexpected &c. 508; unheard of; mysterious &c. (*inexplicable*) 519; miraculous; *foudroyant.*

in-describable, -expressible, -effable; un-utterable, -speakable.

monstrous, prodigious, stupendous, marvellous; in-conceivable, -credible; in-, un-imaginable; strange &c. (*uncommon*) 83; passing strange.

striking &c. *v.*; over-whelming; wonder-working.

Adv. wonderfully &c. *adj.*; fearfully; for a –, in the name of- wonder; strange to say; *mirabile -dictu, – visu*; to one's great surprise.

with -wonder &c. *n.*, – gaping mouth, – open eyes, – upturned eyes; eyes starting out of one's head.

Int. lo, – and behold! O! hey-day! halloo! what! indeed! really! surely! humph! hem! good -lack, – heavens, – gracious! – lord! by jove! gad so! well a day! dear me! only think! lack-a-daisy! my -stars, – goodness! gracious goodness! goodness gracious! mercy on us! heavens and earth! God bless me! bless -us, – my heart! odzookens! *O gemini!* adzooks! hoity-toity! strong! Heaven save –, bless- the mark! can such things be! zounds! 'sdeath! what -on earth, – in the world! who would have thought it! &c. (*inexpectation*) 508; fancy! did you ever? you don't say so! what do you say to that! how now! where am I? well I'm blowed! &c.

Phr. *vox faucibus hæsit*; one's hair standing on end.

perturbable &c. 826; expected &c. *v.*; foreseen.

common, ordinary &c. (*habitual*) 613.

Int. no wonder; of course; why not?

---

872. Prodigy.—N. prodigy, phenomenon; wonder, -ment; genius, marvel, miracle; freak, monster &c. (*unconformity*) 83; curiosity, lion, infant prodigy, sight, spectacle; *jeu –, coup- de théâtre*; gazing-stock; sign; portent &c. 512.

bursting of a -shell, – bomb; volcanic eruption, peal of thunder; thunder-clap, -bolt.

what no words can paint; wonders of the world; *annus mirabilis*; *dignus vindice nodus.*

5°. Intrinsic Affections*

873. Repute.—N. distinction, mark, name, figure; repute, reputation, char-

874. Disrepute.—N. disrepute, discredit; ill-, bad- -repute, -name, -odour,

* Or personal affections derived from the opinions or feelings of others.

acter; good –, high- repute; note, notability, notoriety, *éclat*, 'the bubble reputation,' vogue, celebrity; fame, famousness; renown; popularity, *aura popularis*; esteem, approval, approbation &c. 931; credit, *succès d'estime*, *prestige*, talk of the town; name to conjure with.

glory, honour; lustre &c. (*light*) 420; illustriousness &c. *adj*.

account, regard, respect; reputableness &c. *adj*.; respectability &c. (*probity*) 939; good -name, – report; fair name.

dignity; stateliness &c. *adj*.; solemnity, grandeur, splendour, nobility, majesty, sublimity.

rank, standing, brevet rank, precedence, *pas*, station, place, *status*; position, – in society; order, degree, *locus standi*, caste, condition.

greatness &c. *adj*.; eminence; height &c. 206; importance &c. 642; pre-, super-eminence; high mightiness, primacy; top of the -ladder, – tree.

elevation; ascent &c. 305; super-, ex-altation; dignification, aggrandizement.

dedication, consecration, enthronement, canonization, apotheosis, deification, celebration, enshrinement, glorification.

hero, man of mark, great card, celebrity, champion, worthy, lion, *rara avis*, notability, somebody; man of rank &c. (*nobleman*) 875; pillar of the -state, – society, – church.

chief &c. (*master*) 745; first fiddle &c. (*proficient*) 700; scholar &c. 492; cynosure, mirror; flower, pink, pearl; paragon &c. (*perfection*) 650; choice and master spirits of the age; *élite*; star, sun, constellation, galaxy.

ornament, honour, feather in one's cap, halo, aureole, nimbus; halo –, blaze- of glory; blushing honours; laurels &c. (*trophy*) 733.

memory, posthumous fame, niche in the temple of fame; immor-tality, -tal name; *magni nominis umbra*.

V. be conscious of glory; be proud of &c. (*pride*) 878; exult &c. (*boast*) 884; be vain of &c. (*vanity*) 880.

be -distinguished &c. *adj*.; shine &c. -favour; disapprobation &c. 932; ingloriousness, derogation; a-, de-basement; abjectness &c. *adj*.; degradation, dedecoration; 'a long farewell to all one's greatness'; odium, obloquy, opprobrium, ignominy.

dishonour, disgrace; shame, humiliation; scandal, baseness, vileness; perfidy, turpitude &c. (*improbity*) 940; infamy.

tarnish, taint, defilement, pollution.

stain, blot, spot, blur, stigma, brand, reproach, imputation, slur.

crying –, burning- shame; *scandalum magnatum*, badge of infamy, blot in one's escutcheon; bend –, bar- sinister; champain, point champain; by-word of reproach; Ichabod.

argumentum ad verecundiam; sense of shame &c. 879.

V. be -inglorious &c. *adj*.; incur -disgrace &c. *n*.; have –, earn- a bad name; put –, wear- a halter round one's neck; disgrace –, expose- oneself.

play second fiddle; lose caste; pale one's ineffectual fire; recede into the shade; fall from one's high estate; keep in the background &c. (*modesty*) 881; be conscious of disgrace &c. (*humility*) 879; look -blue, – foolish, – like a fool; cut a -poor, – sorry- figure; laugh on the wrong side of the mouth; make a sorry face, go away with a flea in one's ear, slink away.

cause -shame &c. *n*.; shame, disgrace, put to shame, dishonour; throw –, cast –, fling –, reflect- dishonour &c. *n*. upon; be a -reproach &c. *n*. to; derogate from.

tarnish, stain, blot, sully, taint; discredit; degrade, debase, defile; beggar; expel &c. (*punish*) 972.

impute shame to, brand, post, stigmatize, vilify, defame, slur, cast a slur upon, hold up to shame, send to Coventry; tread –, trample- under foot; show up, drag through the mire, heap dirt upon; reprehend &c. 932.

bring low, put down, snub; take down a peg, – lower, – or two.

obscure, eclipse, outshine, take the shine out of; throw –, cast- into the shade; overshadow; leave –, put- in the background; push into a corner,

(*light*) 420; shine forth, figure; make –, cut- a -figure, – dash, – splash.

rival, surpass; out-shine, -rival, -vie, -jump; emulate, vie with, eclipse; throw –, cast- into the shade; overshadow.

live, flourish, glitter, scintillate, flaunt; gain –, acquire- honour &c. *n.*; play first fiddle &c. (*be of importance*) 642; bear the -palm, – bell; lead the way; take -precedence, – the wall of; gain –, win- -laurels, – spurs, – golden opinions &c. (*approbation*) 931; graduate, take one's degree, pass one's examination, win a -scholarship, – fellowship.

make -a, – some- -noise, – noise in the world; leave one's mark, exalt one's horn, star, have a run, be run after; enjoy popularity, come -into vogue, – to the front; raise one's head.

enthrone, signalize, immortalize, deify, exalt to the skies; hand one's name down to posterity.

consecrate; dedicate to, devote to; enshrine, inscribe, blazon, lionize, blow the trumpet, crown with laurel.

confer –, reflect- honour &c. *n.* on; shed a lustre on; redound to one's honour, ennoble.

give –, do –, pay –, render- honour to; honour, accredit, pay regard to, dignify, glorify; sing praises to &c. (*approve*) 931; look up to; exalt, aggrandize, elevate, nobilitate.

Adj. distinguished, *distingué*, noted; of -note &c. *n.*; honoured &c. *v.*; popular; fashionable &c. 852.

in good odour; in –, in high- favour; reput-, respect-, credit-able.

remarkable &c. (*important*) 642; notable, notorious; celebrated, renowned, in every one's mouth, talked of; fam-ous, -ed; far-famed; conspicuous, to the front; foremost; in the -front rank, – ascendant.

imperishable, deathless, immortal, never fading, *ære perennius*; time-honoured.

illustrious, glorious, splendid, brilliant, radiant; bright &c. 420; full-blown; honorific.

eminent, prominent; high &c. 206; in the zenith; at the -head of, – top of the tree; peerless, of the first water; superior &c. 33; super-, pre-eminent.

great, dignified, proud, noble, honourable, worshipful, lordly, grand, stately, august, princely, imposing, solemn, transcendent, majestic, sacred, sublime, heaven-born, heroic, *sans peur et sans reproche*; sacrosanct.

Int. hail! all hail! *ave! viva! vive!* long life to! glory –, honour- be to!

put one's nose out of joint; put out, – of countenance.

upset, throw off one's centre; discompose, disconcert; put to the blush &c. (*humble*) 879.

Adj. disgraced &c. *v.*; blown upon; shorn of -its beams, – one's glory; overcome, down-trodden; loaded with -shame &c. *n.*; in -bad repute &c. *n.*; out of -repute, – favour, – fashion, – countenance; at a discount; under -a cloud, – an eclipse; unable to show one's face; in the -shade, – background; out at elbows, down in the world, down and out.

inglorious; nameless, renownless, obscure, unknown to fame; un-noticed, -noted, -honoured, -glorified.

shameful; dis-graceful, -creditable, -reputable; despicable; questionable; unbecoming, unworthy; derogatory; degrading, humiliating, *infra dignitatem*, dedecorous; scandalous, infamous, too bad, unmentionable; ribald, opprobrious; arrant, shocking, outrageous, notorious, shady.

ignominious, scrubby, dirty, abject, vile, beggarly, pitiful, low, mean, shabby; base &c. (*dishonourable*) 940.

Adv. to one's shame be it spoken.

Int. fie! shame! for shame! *pro pudor! O tempora! O mores!* ough! *sic transit gloria mundi!*

Phr. one's name -being in every mouth, – living for ever; *sic itur ad astra, fama volat, aut Cæsar aut nullus*; not to know him argues oneself unknown; none but himself could be his parallel, *palmam qui meruit ferat.*

875. Nobility.—**N.** nobility, rank, condition, distinction, optimacy, blood, *pur sang*, birth, high descent, order; quality, gentility; blue blood of Castile; *ancien régime.*

high life, *haut monde*; upper -classes, – ten thousand; *élite*, aristocracy, great folks; fashionable world &c. (*fashion*) 852; salariat.

peer, -age; House of -Lords, – peers; lords, – temporal and spiritual; *noblesse*; baronage, knightage; noble, -man; lord, -ling; grandee, *magnifico, hidalgo*; don, -ship; aristocrat, swell, three-tailed bashaw; gentleman, squire, squireen, patrician, laureate.

gentry, gentlefolk; squirarchy, better sort, *magnates, primates, optimates.*

king &c. (*master*) 745; prince, crown prince, *Dauphin*; duke; marquis, -ate; earl, viscount, baron, thane, banneret; baronet, -cy; knight, -hood; count, armiger, laird; sig-, seig-nior; esquire, boyar, margrave, vavasour, sheik, emir, ameer, scherif, *pasha*, effendi, sahib.

queen &c. 745; princess, begum, duchess, marchioness; countess &c.; lady, dame.

personage –, man- of -distinction, – mark, – rank; nota-bles, -bilities; celebrity, big-wig, magnate, great man, star; *magni nominis umbra*; 'every inch a king'; grand Panjandrum.

V. be -noble &c. *adj.*

Adj. noble, exalted; of -rank &c. *n.*; princely, titled, patrician, aristocratic; high-, well-born; of gentle blood; genteel, *comme il faut*, gentlemanlike, courtly &c. (*fashionable*) 852; highly respectable.

Adv. in high quarters.

877. Title.—**N.** title, honour; knighthood &c. (*nobility*) 875.

royal –, serene- highness, excellency, grace; lordship, worship, Rt. Hon., rever-ence, -end; esquire, sir; madam, *madame*; master, mistress, Mr., Mrs., *signor, señor, Mein Herr, mynheer*;

876. Commonalty.—**N.** commonalty, democracy; obscurity; low -condition, – life, – society, – company; *bourgeoisie*; mass of -the people, – society; Brown, Jones, and Robinson; Tom, Dick, and Harry; lower –, humbler- -classes, – orders; vulgar –, common- herd; rank and file, *hoc genus omne*; the -many, – general, – crowd, – people, – populace, – multitude, – million, – masses, – mobility, – peasantry; king Mob; proletariat, *fruges consumere nati*, great unwashed; man in the street.

mob; rabble, – rout; chaff, rout, horde, *canaille*; scum –, *residuum* –, dregs- of -the people, – society; swinish multitude, *fæx populi*; *profanum* –, *ignobile- vulgus*; vermin, riff-raff, tag-rag and bobtail; small fry.

commoner, one of the people, democrat, plebeian, republican, proletary, *prolétaire, roturier*, Mr. Snooks, *bourgeois, épicier*, Philistine, cockney; *grisette, demi-mondaine.*

peasant, countryman, boor, carle, churl; vill-ain, -ein; serf, kern, tyke, tike, chuff, ryot, fellah; long-shoreman; swain, clown, hind; clod, -hopper; hobnail, yokel, hick, rube, cider squeezer, bog-trotter, bumpkin; ploughman, -boy; rustic, chawbacon, tiller of the soil; hewers of wood and drawers of water, groundling; gaffer, loon, put, cub, Tony Lumpkin, looby, lout, underling; *gamin*, guttersnipe, street arab, mudlark; rough, rowdy, ruffian, roughneck; pot-wallopper, slubberdegullion; vulgar –, low- fellow; cad, curmudgeon.

upstart, *parvenu, nouveau-riche*, skipjack; nobody, – one knows; *hesterni quirites, pessoribus orti*; *bourgeois gentilhomme, novus homo*, snob, gent, mushroom, no one knows who, adventurer; man of straw.

beggar, panhandler, gaberlunzie, muckworm, mudlark, *sans-culotte*, raff, tatterdemalion, caitiff, ragamuffin, Pariah, outcast of society, tramp, weary Willie, bum, vagabond, *chiffon-*

your –, his- honour; handle to one's name.

decoration, laurel, palm, wreath, garland, bays, medal, ribbon, riband, blue ribbon, *cordon*, cross, crown, coronet, star, garter; feather, – in one's cap; chevron, epaulet, *épaulette*, colours, cockade; livery; order, arms, armorial bearings, shield, scutcheon, crest, reward &c. 973.

---

nier, rag-picker, Cinderella, cinder-wench, scrub, jade; boots, gossoon.

Goth, Vandal, Hottentot, savage, barbarian, Yahoo; unlicked cub, rough diamond.

barbar-ousness, -ism; Bœotia.

V. be -ignoble &c. *adj.*, – nobody &c. *n.*

Adj. ignoble, common, mean, low, base, vile, sorry, scrubby, beggarly, below par; no great shakes &c. (*unimportant*) 643; home-ly, -spun; vulgar, low-minded; snobbish, *parvenu*.

plebeian, proletarian; of -low, – mean- -parentage, – origin, extraction; low-, base-, earth-born, low bred; mushroom, dunghill, risen from the ranks; unknown to fame, obscure, untitled.

rustic, uncivilized; lout-, boor-, clown-, churl-, brut-, raff-ish; rude, unlicked, unpolished.

barbar-ous, -ian, -ic, -esque; cockney, born within sound of Bow bells.

underling, menial, servile, subaltern.

Adv. below the salt.

878. Pride.—**N.** dignity, self-respect, *mens sibi conscia recti*.

pride; haughtiness &c. *adj.*; high notions, *hauteur*; vainglory, crest; arrogance &c. (*assumption*) 885; pomposity &c. 882.

proud man, highflier; fine -gentleman, – lady; *grande dame*.

V. be -proud &c. *adj.*; put a good face on; look one in the face; stalk abroad, perk oneself up; presume, swagger, strut; rear –, lift up –, hold up- one's head; hold one's head high, look big, take the wall, 'bear like the Turk no rival near the throne,' carry with a high hand; ride the –, mount on one's- high horse; set one's back up, bridle, toss the head; give oneself airs &c. (*assume*) 885; boast &c. 884.

pride oneself on; glory in, take a pride in; pique –, plume –, hug- oneself; stand upon, be proud of; put a good face on; not -hide one's light under a bushel, – put one's talent in a napkin; not think small beer of oneself &c. (*vanity*) 880.

Adj. dignified; stately; proud, -crested; lordly, baronial; lofty-minded; high-souled, -minded, -mettled, -handed, -plumed, -flown, -toned.

879. Humility.—**N.** hum-ility, -bleness; meek-, low-ness; lowli-ness, -hood; abasement, self-abasement, -effacement; submission &c. 725; resignation.

condescension; affability &c. (*courtesy*) 894.

modesty &c. 881; verecundity, blush, suffusion, confusion; sense of -shame, – disgrace; humiliation, mortification; let –, set- down.

V. be -humble &c. *adj.*; deign, vouchsafe, condescend; humble –, demean- oneself; stoop, – to conquer; carry coals; submit &c. 725; submit with a good grace &c. (*brook*) 826; yield the palm.

lower one's -tone, – note; sing small, draw in one's horns, sober down; hide one's -face, – diminished head; not dare to show one's face, take shame to oneself, not have a word to say for oneself; feel –, be conscious of- -shame, – disgrace; drink the cup of humiliation to the dregs; eat -humble pie, – one's words, – dirt; be humiliated, receive a snub.

blush -for, – up to the eyes; redden, change colour; colour up; hang one's head, look foolish, feel small.

render humble; humble, humiliate;

haughty, paughty, insolent, lofty, high, mighty, swollen, puffed up, flushed, blown; vain-glorious; purse-proud, fine; proud as -a peacock, Lucifer; bloated with pride.

supercilious, disdainful, bumptious, magisterial, imperious; high -handed, - and mighty; overweening, consequential; arrogant &c. 885; unblushing &c. 880.

stiff, -necked; starch; perked -, stuck- up; in buckram, straitlaced; prim &c. (*affected*) 855.

on one's -high horses, - tight ropes, - high ropes; on stilts; *en grand seigneur*.

Adv. with head erect, with one's nose in the air.

Phr. *odi profanum vulgus et arceo.*

---

let -, set -, take -, tread -, frown-down; snub, abash, abase, make one sing small, strike dumb; teach one -his distance, - his place; take down a peg, - lower; throw -, cast- into the shade &c. 874; stare -, put- out of countenance; put to the blush; confuse, ashame, mortify, disgrace, crush; send away with a flea in one's ear.

get a set down.

Adj. humble, lowly, meek; modest &c. 881; humble-, sober-minded; unoffended; submissive &c. 725; servile &c. 886.

condescending; affable &c. (*courteous*) 894.

humbled &c. *v.*; bowed down, resigned; abashed, ashamed, dashed; out of countenance; down in the mouth; down on one's -knees, - marrow-bones; humbled in the dust, brow-beaten; chap-, crest-fallen; dumbfoundered, flabbergasted, struck all of a heap.

shorn of one's glory &c. (*disrepute*) 874.

Adv. with -downcast eyes, - bated breath, - bended knee; on all fours, on one's feet.

under correction, with due deference.

Phr. I am your -obedient, - very humble- servant; my service to you.

880. Vanity.—**N.** vanity; conceit, -edness; self-conceit, -complacency, -confidence, -sufficiency, -esteem, -love, -approbation, -praise, -glorification, -laudation, -gratulation, -applause, -admiration; *amour-propre*; selfishness &c. 943.

airs, pretensions, mannerism; egotism; prigg-ism, -ishness; coxcombry, gaudery, vainglory, elation; pride &c. 878; ostentation &c. 882; assurance &c. 885.

vox et præterea nihil; *cheval de bataille*.

ego-ist, -tist; peacock, coxcomb &c. 854; Sir Oracle &c. 887.

V. be -vain &c. *adj.*, - vain of; pique oneself &c. (*pride*) 878; lay the flattering unction to one's soul.

have -too high, - an overweening-opinion of -oneself, - one's talents; blind oneself as to one's own merit; not think -small beer, - *vin ordinaire*- of oneself; put oneself forward; fish

881. Modesty.—**N.** modesty; humility &c. 879; diffidence, timidity; retiring disposition, unobtrusiveness, bashfulness &c. *adj.*; *mauvaise honte*; blush, -ing; verecundity; self-knowledge.

reserve, constraint; demureness &c. *adj.*; blushing honours.

V. be -modest &c. *adj.*; retire, reserve oneself; give way to; draw in one's horns &c. 879; hide one's face.

keep -private, - in the background, - one's distance; pursue the noiseless tenor of one's way, 'do good by stealth and blush to find it fame,' hide one's light under a bushel, cast a sheep's eye.

Adj. modest, diffident; humble &c. 879; timid, timorous, bashful; shy, nervous, skittish, coy, sheepish, shame-faced, blushing, over-modest.

unpreten-ding, -tious; un-obtrusive, -assuming, -ostentatious, -boastful, -aspiring; poor in spirit.

for compliments; give oneself airs &c. (*assume*) 885; boast &c. 884.

render -vain &c. *adj.*; inspire with -vanity &c. *n.*; inflate, puff up, turn up, turn one's head.

Adj. vain, – as a peacock; conceited, assured, overweening, pert, forward, perky; vain-glorious, high-flown; ostentatious &c. 882; puffed up, inflated, flushed.

out of countenance &c. (*humbled*) 879.

reserved, constrained, demure.

Adv. humbly &c. *adj.*; quietly, privately; without -ceremony, – beat of drum; *sans façon*.

---

self-satisfied, -confident, -sufficient, -flattering, -admiring, -applauding, -glorious, -opinionated; *entêté* &c. (*wrong-headed*) 481; wise in one's own conceit, pragmatical, overwise, pretentious, priggish; egotistic, -al; *soi-disant* &c. (*boastful*) 884; arrogant &c. 885.

un-abashed, -blushing; un-constrained, -ceremonious; free and easy.

Adv. vainly &c. *adj.*

Phr. how we apples swim!

882. Ostentation.—N. ostentation, display, show, flourish, parade, *étalage*, pomp, array, state, solemnity; dash, splash, glitter, strut, swank, side, swagger, pomposity; preten-se, -sions; showing off; fuss.

magnificence, splendour; *coup d'œil*; grand doings.

coup de théâtre; stage -effect, – trick; clap-trap; *mise en scène*; *tour de force*; *chic*.

demonstration, flying colours; tomfoolery; flourish of trumpets &c. (*celebration*) 883; pageant, -ry; spectacle, exhibition, procession; turn –, set- out; grand function; *fête*, gala, field-day, review, march past, promenade, insubstantial pageant.

dress; court –, full –, evening –, ball –, fancy- dress; tailoring, millinery, man-millinery, frippery; foppery, equipage.

ceremon-y, -ial; ritual; form, -ality; etiquette; punct-o, -ilio, -iliousness; starched-, stateli-ness.

mummery, solemn mockery, mouth honour.

attitudinarian; fop &c. 854.

V. be -ostentatious &c. *adj.*; come –, put oneself- forward; attract attention, star it.

make –, cut- a -figure, – dash, – splash; strut, blow one's own trumpet; figure, – away; make a show, – display; glitter.

show -off, – one's paces; parade, march past; display, exhibit, put forward, hold up; trot –, hang- out; sport, brandish, blazon forth; dangle, – before the eyes.

cry up &c. (*praise*) 931; *prôner*, flaunt, emblazon, prink, set off, mount, have framed and glazed.

put a good, – smiling- face upon; clean the outside of the platter &c. (*disguise*) 544.

Adj. ostentatious, showy, dashing, pretentious; ja-, jau-nty; grand, pompous, palatial; high-sounding; turgid &c. (*big-sounding*) 577; garish, gorgeous; gaudy, – as a -peacock, – butterfly, – tulip; flaunting, flashing, flaming, glittering; gay &c. (*ornate*) 847; colourful.

splendid, magnificent, sumptuous.

theatrical, dramatic, spectacular, scenic, ceremonial, ritual, -istic.

solemn, stately, majestic, formal, stiff, ceremonious, punctilious, starch-ed, -y.

en grande tenue, in best bib and tucker, in Sunday best, *endimanché*.

Adv. with -flourish of trumpet, – beat of drum, – flying colours, – a brass band.

ad captandum vulgus.

883. Celebration.—N. celebration, solemnization, jubilee, diamond jubilee, commemoration, ovation, pæan, triumph, jubilation.

triumphal arch, bonfire, salute; salvo, – of artillery; *feu de joie*, flourish of trumpets, *fanfare*, colours flying, illuminations, fireworks.

inauguration, installation, presentation; *début*, coming out, birthday anniversary, bi-, ter-, centenary; silver –, golden –, diamond-wedding, -day; coronation; Lord Mayor's show; harvest home, red letter day, festival; trophy &c. 733; *Te Deum* &c. (*thanksgiving*) 990; fête &c. 882; holiday &c. 840.

V. celebrate, keep, signalize, do honour to, commemorate, solemnize, hallow, mark with a red letter, hold high festival, maffick.

pledge, drink to, toast, hob and nob.

inaugurate, install, instate, induct, chair.

rejoice &c. 838; kill the fatted calf, hold jubilee, roast an ox, fire a salute.

Adj. celebrating &c. *v.*; commemorative, celebrated, immortal.

Adv. in -honour, – commemoration, – celebration of.

Int. hail! all hail! *io -pæan*, – *triumphe!* 'see the conquering hero comes!'

884. Boasting.—N. boasting &c. *v.*; boast, vaunt, crake; preten-ce, -sions; puff, -ery; flourish, *fanfaronnade*; gasconade; bluff, swank, brag, -gardism; bravado, bunkum, Buncombe; highfalutin; jact-itation, -ancy; bounce, rant, bluster; venditation, vapouring, rodomontade, bombast, fine talking, tall talk, magniloquence, teratology, heroics; jingoism, Chauvinism; exaggeration &c. 549; gas, hot air.

vanity &c. 880; *vox et præterea nihil*; much cry and little wool, *brutum fulmen*.

exultation; glorification; flourish of trumpets; triumph &c. 883.

boaster; bragg-art, -adocio; hot air merchant; Gascon, *fanfaron*, pretender, fourflusher, *soi-disant*; windbag, blowhard, bluffer; chauvinist; blusterer &c. 887; charlatan, jack-pudding, trumpeter; puppy &c. (*fop*) 854.

V. boast, make a boast of, brag, vaunt, puff, show off, flourish, crake, crack, trumpet, strut, swagger, vapour, bluff; draw the long bow.

exult, crow over, neigh, chuckle, triumph; glory, gloat, jubilate; throw up one's cap; talk big, *se faire valoir, faire claquer son fouet*, take merit to oneself, make a merit of, sing *Io triumphe*, holloa before one is out of the wood.

Adj. boasting &c. *v.*; magniloquent, flaming, Thrasonic, stilted, gasconading, braggart, boastful, pretentious, *soi-disant*; vain-glorious &c. (*conceited*) 880.

elate, -d; jubilant, triumphant, exultant; in high feather; flushed, – with victory; cock-a-hoop; on stilts.

vaunted &c. *v.*

Adv. vauntingly &c. *adj.*; with a brass band.

Phr. 'let the galled jade wince.'

885. [Undue assumption of superiority.] **Insolence.—N.** insolence; haughtiness &c. *adj.*; arrogance, airs; overbearance, brashness, bumptiousness, contumely, disdain; domineering &c. *v.*; tyranny &c. 739.

impertinence; cheek, nerve, sauce; sauciness &c. *adj.*; flippancy, dicacity, petulance, procacity, bluster; swagger, -ing &c. *v.*; bounce; terrorism; jingoism, chauvinism.

as-, pre-sumption; beggar on horseback; usurpation.

impudence, assurance, audacity, self-assertion, hardihood, front, face, brass; shamelessness &c. *adj.*; effrontery, hardened front, face of brass.

assumption of infallibility.

malapert, saucebox &c. (*blusterer*) 887.

V. be -insolent &c. *adj.*; bluster, vapour, swagger, swell, give oneself airs, snap one's fingers, kick up a dust; swear &c. (*affirm*) 535; rap out oaths; roister.

arrogate; as-, pre-sume; make -bold, – free; take a liberty, give an inch and take an ell.

domineer, bully, dictate, hector; lord it over, bulldoze; *traiter de haut, regarder de haut en bas*; exact; snub, huff, beard, fly in the face of; put to the blush; bear –, beat- down; browbeat, intimidate; trample –, tread- -down, – under foot; dragoon, ride roughshod over, terrorize.

out-face, -look, -stare, -brazen, -brave; stare out of countenance; brazen out; lay down the law; teach one's grandmother to suck eggs; assume a lofty bearing; talk –, look- big; put on big looks, act the *grand seigneur*; mount –, ride- the high horse; toss the head, carry with a high hand.

tempt Providence, want snuffing.

Adj. insolent, haughty, arrogant, imperious, magisterial, dictatorial, arbitrary; high-handed, high and mighty; contumelious, supercilious, overbearing, intolerant, domineering; overweening, high-flown.

flippant, pert, cavalier, saucy, forward, impertinent, fresh, malapert.

precocious, assuming, would-be, bumptious.

bluff; brazen-, -browed, -faced, shameless, aweless, unblushing, unabashed; bold-, bare-faced; dead –, lost- to shame.

886. Servility.—N. servility; slavery &c. (*subjection*) 749; obsequiousness &c. *adj.*; subserviency; abasement; pros-tration, -ternation; genuflexion &c. (*worship*) 990; fawning &c. *v.*; tuft-hunting, time-serving, flunkeyism; sycophancy &c. (*flattery*) 933; humility &c. 879.

sycophant, parasite, yes-man; toad, -y, -eater; tuft-hunter; snob, flunkey, lap-dog, spaniel, lickspittle, smell-feast, *Græculus esuriens*, hanger on, stooge, *cavaliere servente*, led captain, carpet knight; time-server, fortune-hunter, Vicar of Bray, Sir Pertinax Mac Sycophant, pick-thank; flatterer &c. 935; doer of dirty work; *âme damnée*, tool; reptile; slave &c. (*servant*) 746; courtier; sponge, jackal; truckler.

V. cringe, bow, stoop, kneel, bend the knee; fall on one's knees, prostrate oneself; worship &c. 990.

sneak, crawl, crouch, cower, truckle to, grovel, fawn, toady, lick the feet of, kiss the hem of one's garment.

pay court to; feed –, fatten –, batten- on; dance attendance on, pin oneself upon, hang on the sleeve of, *avaler des couleuvres*, keep time to, fetch and carry, do the dirty work of.

go with the stream, follow the crowd, worship the rising sun, hold with the hare and run with the hounds.

Adj. servile, obsequious; supple, – as a glove; soapy, oily, pliant, cringing, fawning, slavish, grovelling, snivelling, mealy-mouthed; beggarly, sycophantic, parasitical; abased, abject, prostrate, down on one's marrow-bones; base, mean, sneaking; crouching &c. *v.*

Adv. hat –, cap- in hand.

impudent, audacious, presumptuous, free and easy, devil-may-care, rollicking; janty, jaunty; roistering, blustering, hectoring, swaggering, vapouring; thrasonic, fire-eating, 'full of sound and fury.'

Adv. insolently, with a high hand; *ex cathedrâ*.

Phr. one's bark being worse than his bite.

887. Blusterer.—N. bluster-, swagger-, vapour-, roister-, brawl-er; brazen-face; *fanfaron*; braggart &c. (*boaster*) 884; bully, terrorist, rough, rough-neck; hooligan, hoodlum, larrikin, ruffian; Mo-hock, -hawk; drawcansir, swashbuckler, Captain Boabdil, Sir Lucius O'Trigger, Thraso, Pistol, Parolles, Bombastes Furioso, Hector, Chrononhotonthologos; jingo; desperado, dare-devil, fire-eater; fury &c. (*violent person*) 173; rowdy.

puppy &c. (*fop*) 854; prig; Sir Oracle, dogmatist, *doctrinaire*, stump orator, jack-in-office; saucebox, malapert, jackanapes, minx; bantam-cock.

SECTION III. SYMPATHETIC AFFECTIONS

1°. SOCIAL AFFECTIONS

888. Friendship. — N. friendship, amity; friendliness &c. *adj.*; brotherhood, fraternity, sodality, confraternity, sorosis, sisterhood; harmony &c. (*concord*) 714; peace &c. 721.

firm –, staunch –, intimate –, familiar –, bosom –, cordial –, tried –, devoted –, lasting –, fast –, sincere –, warm –, ardent- friendship.

cordiality, fraternization, *entente cordiale*, good understanding, *rapprochement*, sympathy, fellow-feeling, response, welcomeness; *camaraderie*.

affection &c. (*love*) 897; favouritism; goodwill &c. (*benevolence*) 906; partiality.

acquaintance, familiarity, intimacy, intercourse, fellowship, knowledge of; introduction.

V. be -friendly &c. *adj.*, – friends &c. 890, – acquainted with &c. *adj.*; know; have the ear of; keep company with &c. (*sociality*) 892; hold communication –, have dealings –, sympathize- with; have a leaning to; bear good will &c. (*benevolence*) 906; love &c. 897; make much of; befriend &c. (*aid*) 707; introduce to.

set one's horses together; hold out –, extend- the right hand of -friendship, – fellowship; become -friendly &c. *adj.*; make -friends &c. 892 with; break the ice, be introduced to; make –, pick –, scrape- acquaintance with; get into favour, gain the friendship of.

shake hands with, fraternize, embrace; receive with open arms, throw oneself into the arms of; meet half way, take in good part.

Adj. friendly; amic-able, -al; well affected, unhostile, neighbourly, brotherly, fraternal, sisterly, sympathetic, harmonious, hearty, cordial, warm-hearted, devoted.

889. Enmity.—N. enmity, hostility, unfriendliness &c. *adj.*; discord &c. 713.

alienation, estrangement; dislike &c. 867; hate &c. 898; antagonism.

heartburning; animosity &c. 900; malevolence &c. 907.

V. be -inimical &c. *adj.*; keep –, hold- at arm's length; be at loggerheads; bear malice &c. 907; fall out; take umbrage &c. 900; harden the heart, alienate, estrange.

Adj. inimical, unfriendly, hostile; at -enmity, – variance, – swords points, – daggers drawn, – open war with; up in arms against; in bad odour with.

on bad –, not on speaking- terms; cool; cold, -hearted; estranged, alienated, disaffected, irreconcilable.

friends –, well –, at home –, hand in hand- with; on -good, – friendly, – amicable, – cordial, – familiar, – intimate- -terms, – footing; on -speaking, – visiting- terms; in one's good -graces, – books.

acquainted, familiar, intimate, thick, hand and glove, hail fellow well met, free and easy; welcome.

Adv. amicably &c. *adj.*; with open arms; *sans cérémonie*; arm in arm.

890. Friend.—N. friend, – of one's bosom, intimate acquaintance, neighbour, well-wisher; *alter ego*; best –, bosom –, fast- friend; *amicus usque ad aras*; *fidus Achates*; *persona grata.*

favourer, *fautor*, patron, backer, Mæcenas; tutelary saint, good genius, advocate, partisan, sympathiser; ally; friend in need &c. (*auxiliary*) 711.

associate, compeer, comrade, mate, companion, *confrère, camarade, confidante,* colleague; old –, crony; side-kick; chum, buddy, bunkie, roommate, pal; play-fellow, -mate; classmate, schoolfellow; bedfellow, -mate; maid of honour.

compatriot; fellow –, countryman, – townsman.

shop-, ship-, mess-mate; fellow –, boon –, pot- companion; copartner.

Arcades ambo, Pylades and Orestes, Castor and Pollux, Nisus and Euryalus, Damon and Pythias, *par nobile fratrum.*

host, Amphitryon, Boniface; guest, visitor, frequenter, *habitué*; *protégé.*

891. Enemy.—N. enemy; antagonist, foeman; open –, bitter- enemy; opponent &c. 710; back friend.

public enemy, enemy to society, traitor, anarchist &c. 742; *persona non grata.*

Phr. every hand being against one.

---

892. Sociality.—N. soci-ality, -ability, -ableness &c. *adj.*; social intercourse; consociation; inter-course, -community; consort-, companion-, fellow-, comrade-ship; clubbism; *esprit de corps.*

conviviality; good -fellowship, – company, *camaraderie*; joviality, jollity, *savoir-vivre,* festivity, festive board, merry-making; loving cup; hospitality, heartiness; cheer.

welcome, -ness; greeting; hearty –, warm –, welcome- reception; urbanity &c. (*courtesy*) 894; intimacy, familiarity.

good –, jolly- fellow, good mixer, Rotarian; *bon enfant.*

social –, family- circle; circle of acquaintance, *coterie,* society, company.

social -gathering, – *réunion*; assembly &c. (*assemblage*) 72; party, entertainment, reception, *levée,* at home, *conversazione, soirée, matinée,* evening –, morning –, afternoon –, garden –, dinner –, tea –, cocktail- party; symposium, sing-song; kettle-, drum; *partie carrée,* dish of tea, *ridotto,* rout, house-

893. Seclusion. Exclusion.—N. seclusion, privacy; retirement; concealment; reclusion, recess; snugness &c. *adj.*; delitescence; rustication, *rus in urbe*; solitude; solitariness &c. (*singleness*) 87; isolation; loneliness &c. *adj.*; estrangement from the world, anchoritism, voluntary exile; aloofness.

cell, hermitage; convent &c. 1000; *sanctum sanctorum*; study, library, den; hide-out.

depopulation, desertion, desolation; wilderness &c. (*unproductive*) 169; howling wilderness; rotten borough, Old Sarum.

exclusion, excommunication, banishment, exile, ostracism, proscription; cut, – direct; dead cut.

inhospit-ality, -ableness &c. *adj.*; un-, dis-sociability; domesticity, Darby and Joan.

recluse, hermit, eremite, cenobite; anchor-et, -ite; Simon Stylites; Troglodyte, Timon of Athens, Santon, *solitaire,* ruralist, disciple of Zimmermann, closet cynic, Diogenes; outcast, pariah,

warming; ball, prom, hop, dance, *thé dansant*; festival &c. (*amusement*) 840; wedding breakfast; 'the feast of reason and the flow of soul.'

visit, -ing; round of visits; call, morning call; interview &c. (*interlocution*) 588; assignation; tryst, -ing place; appointment.

club &c. (*association*) 712.

V. be -sociable &c. *adj.*; know; be -acquainted &c. *adj.*; associate –, sort –, keep company –, walk hand in hand -with; eat off the same trencher, club together, consort, bear one company, join; make acquaintance with &c. (*friendship*) 888; make advances, fraternize, embrace; intercommunicate.

be –, feel –, make oneself- at home with; make free with; crack a bottle with; take pot luck with, receive hospitality, live at free quarters.

visit, pay a visit; interchange -visits, – cards; call -at, – upon; leave a card; drop in, look in; look one up, beat up one's quarters.

entertain; give a -party &c. *n.*; be at home, see one's friends, hang out, keep open house, do the honours; receive, – with open arms; welcome; give a warm reception &c. *n.* to; kill the fatted calf.

Adj. sociable, companionable, clubbable, clubby, conversable, cosy, cosey, chatty, conversational; homiletical.

convivial; fest-ive, -al; jovial, jolly, hospitable.

welcome, – as the roses in May; *fêté*, entertained.

free and easy, hail fellow well met, familiar, on visiting terms, acquainted.

social, neighbourly; international, cosmopolitan, gregarious.

Adv. *en famille*, in the family circle; *sans -façon*, – *cérémonie*, arm in arm.

894. Courtesy.—N. courtesy; respect &c. 928; good -manners, – behaviour, – breeding; manners; politeness &c. *adj.*; *bienséance*, urbanity, comity, gentility; gentle –, breeding; polish, presence, cultivation, culture; civili-ty, -zation; amenity, suavity; good -temper, – humour; amiability, easy temper, complacency, soft tongue,

castaway, outsider, pilgarlic; wastrel, foundling, orphan.

V. be –, live- secluded &c. *adj.*; keep –, stand –, hold oneself- -aloof, – in the background; keep snug; shut oneself up; deny –, seclude- oneself; creep into a corner, rusticate, *aller planter ses choux*; retire, – from the world; hermetize, take the veil; abandon &c. 624.

cut, – dead; refuse to -associate with, – acknowledge; look cool –, turn one's back –, shut the door- upon; repel, blackball, excommunicate, exclude, exile, expatriate; banish, outlaw, maroon, ostracize, proscribe, cut off from, send to Coventry, keep at arm's length, draw a cordon round; boycott, blockade, lay an embargo on, isolate.

depopulate; dis-, un-people.

Adj. secluded, sequestered, retired, delitescent, private, bye; out of the -world, -way; in a backwater; 'the world forgetting by the world forgot.'

snug, domestic, stay-at-home.

unsociable; un-, dis-social; inhospitable, cynical, inconversable, unclubbable, *sauvage*, eremetic.

solitary; lone-ly, -some; isolated, single.

excluded, estranged; unfrequented; uninhabit-able, -ed; tenantless; un-tenanted, -occupied; abandoned; deserted, – in one's utmost need; unfriended; kith-, friend-, home-less; lorn, forlorn, desolate.

un-visited, -introduced, -invited, -welcome; under a cloud, left to shift for oneself, derelict, outcast, outside the gates.

banished &c. *v.*; under an embargo.

Phr. *noli me tangere.*

---

895. Discourtesy.—N. discourtesy; ill-breeding; ill –, bad –, ungainly- manners; insuavity; grouchiness; uncourteousness &c. *adj.*, tactlessness; rusticity, inurbanity; illiberality, incivility, displacency.

disrespect &c. 929; procacity, impudence; barbar-ism, -ity; misbehaviour, brutality, blackguardism, conduct un-

mansuetude; condescension &c. (*humility*) 879; affability, complaisance, *prévenance*, amiability, gallantry, chivalry; pink of -politeness, - courtesy.

compliment; fair -, soft -, sweet- words; honeyed phrases, flattering remarks, ceremonial; salutation, reception, presentation, introduction, *accueil*, greeting, recognition; welcome, *abord*, respects, *devoir*, regards, remembrances; kind -regards, - remembrances; love, best love, duty; deference.

obeisance &c. (*reverence*) 928; bow, courtesy, curtsy, scrape, *salaam*, *kowtow*, bowing and scraping; kneeling; genuflexion &c. (*worship*) 990; obsequiousness &c. 886; capping, shaking hands &c. *v.*; grip of the hand, embrace, hug, squeeze, *accolade*, loving cup, *vin d'honneur*, pledge; love token &c. (*endearment*) 902; kiss, buss, salute.

mark of recognition, nod; 'nods and becks and wreathed smiles'; valediction &c. 293; condolence &c. 915.

V. be -courteous &c. *adj.*; show -courtesy &c. *n.*

mind one's P's and Q's, behave oneself, be all things to all men, conciliate, speak one fair, take in good part; make -, do- the amiable; look as if butter would not melt in one's mouth; mend one's manners.

receive, do the honours, usher, greet, hail, bid welcome; welcome, - with open arms; shake hands; hold out -, press -, squeeze- the hand; bid God speed; speed the parting guest; cheer, serenade.

salute; embrace &c. (*endearment*) 902; kiss, - hands; drink to, pledge, hob and nob; move to, nod to; smile upon.

uncover, cap; touch -, take off- the hat; doff the cap; pull the forelock; present arms; make way for; bow; make one's bow; scrape, curtsy, courtesy; bob a -curtsy, - courtesy; kneel; bow -, bend- the knee; salaam, *kowtow*.

visit, wait upon, present oneself, pay one's respects, pay a visit &c. (*sociability*) 892; dance attendance on &c. (*servility*) 886; pay attentions to; do homage to &c. (*respect*) 928.

becoming a gentleman, *grossièreté*, *brusquerie*; vulgarity &c. 851.

churlishness &c. *adj.*; spinosity, perversity; moroseness &c. (*sullenness*) 901*a*.

bad-, ill-temper; sternness &c. *adj.*; austerity; moodishness, captiousness &c. 901; cynicism; tartness &c. *adj.*; acrimony, acerbity, virulence, asperity.

scowl, black looks, frown; short answer, rebuff; hard words, contumely; unparliamentary language, personality.

bear, bruin, brute, grouch, blackguard, beast; unlicked cub; frump, cross-patch; saucebox &c. 887.

V. be -rude &c. *adj.*; insult &c. 929; treat with discourtesy; take a name in vain; make -bold, - free- with; take a liberty; stare out of countenance, ogle, point at, put to the blush.

cut; turn -one's back upon, - on one's heel; give the cold shoulder; keep at -a distance, - arm's length; look -cool, - coldly, - black- upon; show the door to, send away with a flea in the ear.

lose one's temper &c. (*resentment*) 900; sulk &c. 901*a*; frown, scowl, glower, pout; snap, snarl, growl.

render -rude &c. *adj.*; brut-alize, -ify.

Adj. dis-, un-courteous; uncourtly; ill-bred, -mannered, -behaved, -conditioned; unbred; unmanner-ly, ed; im-, un-polite; un-polished, -civilized, -genteel; ungentleman-like, -ly; unladylike; blackguard; vulgar &c. 851; dedecorous; foul-mouthed, -spoken; abusive.

un-civil, -gracious, -ceremonious; cool; pert, forward, obtrusive, impudent, rude, saucy, precocious; insolent &c. 885.

repulsive; un-complaisant, -accommodating, -neighbourly, -gallant; inaffable; un-gentle, -gainly; rough, rugged, bluff, blunt, gruff; churl-, boor-, bear-ish; brutal, *brusque*; stern, harsh, austere; cavalier.

tart, sour, crabbed, sharp, short, trenchant, sarcastic, crusty, biting, caustic, virulent, bitter, acrimonious, venomous, contumelious; snarling &c, *v.*; surly, - as a bear; perverse; grim,

prostrate oneself &c. (*worship*) 990.
give –, send- one's duty &c. *n.* to.
render -polite &c. *adj.*; polish, civilize, humanize.

sullen &c. 901*a*; peevish &c. (*irascible*) 901.
Adv. discourteously &c. *adj.*; with -discourtesy &c. *n.*, – a bad grace.

Adj. courteous, polite, civil, mannerly, urbane; well-behaved, -mannered, -bred, -brought up, gently bred, of gentle -breeding, – manners, good-mannered, polished, civilized, cultivated; refined &c. (*taste*) 850; gentlemanlike &c. (*fashion*) 852; gallant, chivalrous, on one's good behaviour.

fine –, fair –, soft- spoken; honey-mouthed, -tongued; oily, unctuous, bland, suave; obliging, conciliatory, complaisant, complacent; obsequious &c. 886.

ingratiating, winning; gentle, mild; good-humoured, cordial, gracious, amiable, tactful, addressful, affable, genial, friendly, familiar; neighbourly.

Adv. courteously &c. *adj.*; with a good grace; with -open, – outstretched- arms; *à bras ouverts*; *suaviter in modo*, in good humour.

Int. hail! welcome! well met! *ave!* all hail! good -day, – morning &c., – morrow! God speed! *pax vobiscum!* may your shadow never be less! *chin-chin!*

896. Congratulations.—N. con-, gratulation; felicitation; salute &c. 894; condolence &c. 915; compliments of the season; good –, best- wishes.

V. con-, gratulate; felicitate, compliment; give –, wish one- joy; tender –, offer- one's congratulations; wish -many happy returns of the day, – a merry Christmas and a happy new year.

congratulate oneself &c. (*rejoice*) 838.

Adj. con-, gratulatory.

897. Love.—N. love; fondness &c. *adj.*; liking; inclination &c. (*desire*) 865; regard, dilection, admiration, fancy.

affection, sympathy, fellow-feeling; tenderness &c. *adj.*; heart, brotherly love; benevolence &c. 906; attachment.

yearning, tender passion, *affaire de cœur*, *amour*, gallantry, passion, flame, devotion, fervour, enthusiasm, transport of love, rapture, enchantment, infatuation, adoration, idolatry.

narcissism, Œdipus complex, Electra complex.

Cupid, Venus, Eros; myrtle; true lover's knot; love -token, – suit, – affair, – tale, – story; the old story, plighted love; courtship &c. 902; *amourette*.

maternal love.

attractiveness, charm; popularity; favourite &c. 899.

lover, suitor, follower, admirer, adorer, wooer, amoret, beau, sweet-

898. Hate.—N. hate, hatred, vials of hate; Hymn of Hate.

dis-affection, -favour; alienation, estrangement, coolness; enmity &c. 889; animosity &c. 900.

umbrage, pique, grudge; dudgeon, spleen; bitterness, – of feeling; ill –, bad- blood; acrimony; malice &c. 907; implacability &c. (*revenge*) 919.

repugnance &c. (*dislike*) 867; odium, unpopularity; loathing, detestation, antipathy; object of -hatred, – execration; abomination, aversion, *bête noire*; enemy &c. 891; bitter pill; source of annoyance &c. 830.

V. hate, detest, abominate, abhor, loathe; recoil –, shudder- at; shrink from, view with horror, hold in abomination, revolt against, execrate; scowl &c. 895; disrelish &c. (*dislike*) 867.

owe a grudge; bear -spleen, – a grudge, – malice &c. (*malevolence*) 907; conceive an aversion to.

heart, inamorato, swain, young man, flame, love, truelove; leman, Lothario, gallant, paramour, *amoroso*, *cavaliere servente*, captive, *cicisbeo*; *caro sposo*, Don Juan, sheik, ladies' man, squire of dames, Knave of Hearts.

inamorata, lady-love, idol, darling, duck, Dulcinea, angel, goddess, *cara sposa*; mistress.

betrothed, affianced, *fiancée*.

flirt, *coquette*; amorette; pair of turtle doves; abode of love, *agapemone*.

V. love, like, affect, fancy, care for, take an interest in, be partial to, sympathize with; be -in love &c. *adj.*- with; have –, entertain –, harbour –, cherish- a -love &c. *n.* for; regard, revere; take to, bear love to, be wedded to; set one's affections on; make much of, feast one's eyes on; hold dear, prize, treasure; hug, cling to, cherish, pet, caress &c. 902.

burn; adore, idolize, love to distraction, *aimer éperdument*; dote -on, – upon:

take a fancy to, fall for, be stuck on, look sweet upon; become -enamoured &c. *adj.*; fall in love with, lose one's heart; desire &c. 865.

excite love; win –, gain –, secure –, engage- the -love, – affections, – heart; take the fancy of; have a place in –, wind round- the heart; attract, attach, endear, charm, fascinate, captivate, bewitch, seduce, enamour, enrapture, turn the head.

get into favour; ingratiate –, insinuate –, worm- oneself; propitiate, curry favour with, pay one's court to, make a date with, *faire l'aimable*, set one's cap at, flirt, coquet.

Adj. loving &c. *v.*; fond of; taken –, struck- with; smitten, bitten; attached to, wedded to; enamoured; charmed &c. *v.*; in love; lovesick; over head and ears in love.

affectionate, tender, sweet upon, sympathetic, loving, fond, amorous, amatory; erotic, uxurious, ardent, passionate, rapturous, devoted, motherly.

loved &c. *v.*; beloved; well –, dearly- beloved; dear, precious, darling, pet, little; favourite, popular.

congenial; to –, after- one's -mind, – taste, – fancy, – own heart:

in one's good -graces &c. (*friendly*) 888; dear as the apple of one's eye, nearest to one's heart.

lovable, adorable; lovely, sweet; attractive, seductive, winning; charming, engaging, interesting, enchanting, captivating, fascinating, intriguing, bewitching; amiable, like an angel, angelic, seraphic.

excite –, provoke- hatred &c. *n.*; be -hateful &c. *adj.*; stink in the nostrils; estrange, alienate, repel, set against, sow dissension, set by the ears, envenom, incense, irritate, rile, ruffle, vex; horrify &c. 830.

Adj. hating &c. *v.*; abhorrent; averse from &c. (*disliking*) 867; set against.

bitter &c. (*acrimonious*) 895; implacable &c. (*revengeful*) 919.

un-loved, -beloved, -lamented, -deplored, -mourned, -cared for, -endured, -valued; disliked &c. 867.

crossed in love, forsaken, rejected, love-lorn, jilted.

obnoxious, hateful, odious, abominable, repulsive, offensive, shocking; disgusting &c. (*disagreeable*) 830.

invidious, spiteful; malicious &c. 907.

insulting, irritating, provoking.

[Mutual hate] at -daggers drawn, – swords points; not on speaking terms &c. (*enmity*) 889.

Phr. no love lost between.

---

899. Favourite.—N. favourite, pet, cosset, minion, idol, jewel, spoiled child, *enfant gâté*; led captain; crony; fondling; apple of one's eye, man after one's own heart; *persona grata*.

love, dear, darling, duck, honey, jewel; mopsey, moppet; sweetheart &c. (*love*) 897.

general –, universal- favourite; idol of the people; matinée idol, movie –, radio- star.

900. Resentment.—**N.** resentment, displeasure, animosity, anger, wrath, indignation; vexation, exasperation, bitter resentment, wrathful indignation.

pique, umbrage, huff, miff, soreness, dudgeon, acerbity, virulence, bitterness, acrimony, asperity, spleen, gall; heart-burning, -swelling; rankling.

ill –, bad- -humour, – temper; irascibility &c. 901; ill blood &c. (*hate*) 898; revenge &c. 919.

excitement, irritation; warmth, bile, choler, ire, fume, pucker, dander, ferment, ebullition; towering -passion, – rage, *acharnement*, angry mood, taking, pet, tiff, passion, fit, tantrums.

burst, explosion, paroxysm, storm, rage, fury, desperation; violence &c. 173; fire and fury; vials of wrath; gnashing of teeth, hot blood, high words.

scowl &c. 895; sulks &c. 901*a*.

[Cause of umbrage] affront, provocation, offence; indignity &c. (*insult*) 929; grudge, crow to pluck, sore subject; red rag to a bull; *casus belli*.

Furies, Erinys, Eumenides, Alecto, Megæra, Tisiphone.

buffet, slap in the face, box on the ear, rap on the knuckles.

V. resent; take -amiss, – ill, – to heart, – offence, – umbrage, – huff, – exception; take in -ill part, – bad part, – dudgeon; *ne pas entendre raillerie*; breathe revenge, cut up rough.

fly –, fall –, get- into a -rage, – passion; bridle –, bristle –, froth –, fire –, flare- up; open –, pour out- the vials of one's wrath.

pout, knit the brow, frown, scowl, lower, snarl, growl, gnarl, gnash, snap; redden, colour; look -black, – black as thunder, – daggers; bite one's thumb; show –, grind- one's teeth; champ the bit.

chafe, mantle, fume, kindle, fly out, take fire; boil, – over; boil with -indignation, – rage; rage, storm, foam; vent one's -rage, – spleen; lose one's temper, stand on one's hind legs, stamp the foot, kick up a row, fly off the handle, cut up rough; stamp –, quiver –, swell –, foam- with rage; burst with anger; raise Cain, breathe fire and fury.

have a fling at; bear malice &c. (*revenge*) 919.

cause –, raise- anger; affront, offend; give -offence, – umbrage; anger; hurt the feelings; insult, discompose, fret, ruffle, nettle, heckle, huff, pique; excite &c. 824; irritate, stir the blood, stir up bile; sting, – to the quick; rile, provoke, chafe, wound, incense, inflame, enrage, aggravate, add fuel to the flame, fan into a flame, widen the breach, envenom, embitter, exasperate, infuriate, kindle wrath; stick in one's gizzard; rankle &c. 919.

put out of humour; put one's -monkey, – back- up; set –, get- one's back up; raise one's -gorge, – dander, – choler; work up into a passion; make -one's blood boil, – the ears tingle; throw into a ferment, madden, drive one mad; lash into -fury, – madness; fool to the top of one's bent; set by the ears.

bring a hornet's nest about one's ears.

Adj. angry, wrath, irate; ire-, wrath-ful; cross &c. (*irascible*) 901; sulky &c. 901*a*; bitter, virulent; acrimonious &c. (*discourteous*) &c. 895; violent &c. 173.

warm, burning; boiling, – over; fuming, raging; foaming, – at the mouth; convulsed with rage.

offended &c. *v.*; waxy, *acharné*; wrought, worked up; indignant, hurt, sore, peeved; set against.

fierce, wild, rageful, furious, mad with rage, fiery, infuriate, rabid, savage; relentless &c. 919.

flushed with -anger, – rage; in a -huff, – stew, – fume, – pucker, – passion, – rage, – fury; on one's high ropes, up in arms; in high dudgeon.

Adv. angrily &c. *adj.*; in the height of passion; in the heat of -passion, – the moment.

Int. *tantæne animis cœlestibus iræ!* marry come up! zounds! 'sdeath!

Phr. one's -blood, – back, – monkey- being up; *fervens difficili bile jecur*; the gorge rising, eyes flashing fire; the blood -rising, – boiling; *hæret lateri lethalis arundo.*

901. Irascibility.—N. irascibility, temper; crossness &c. *adj.*; susceptibility, procacity, petulance, irritability, tartness, acerbity, protervity; pugnacity &c. (*contentiousness*) 720.

excitability &c. 825; bad –, fiery –, crooked –, irritable &c. *adj.*- temper; *genus irritabile*, hot blood.

ill humour &c. (*sullenness*) 901*a*; asperity &c., churlishness &c. (*discourtesy*) 895.

huff &c. (resentment) 900; a word and a blow.

Sir Fretful Plagiary; brabbler, Tartar; shrew, vixen, virago, termagant, dragon, scold, Xanthippe; porcupine; spit-fire; fire-eater &c. (*blusterer*) 887; fury &c. (*violent person*) 173.

V. be -irascible &c. *adj.*; have a -temper &c. *n.*, – devil in one; fire up &c. (*be angry*) 900.

Adj. irascible; bad-, ill-tempered; irritable, susceptible; excitable &c. 825; thin-skinned &c. (*sensitive*) 822; fretful, fidgety; on the fret.

hasty, over-hasty, quick, warm, hot, testy, touchy, techy, tetchy; like -touchwood, – tinder; huffy; pet-tish, -ulant; waspish, snapp-y, -ish, peppery, fiery, passionate, choleric, shrewish, 'sudden and quick in quarrel.'

querulous, captious, mood-y, -ish; quarrelsome, contentious, disputatious; pugnacious &c. (*bellicose*) 720; cantankerous, exceptious; restive &c. (*perverse*) 901*a*; churlish &c. (*discourteous*) 895.

cross, – as -crabs, – two sticks, – a cat, – a dog, – the tongs; like a bear with a sore head; fractious, peevish, *acariâtre.*

in a bad temper; sulky &c. 901*a*; angry &c. 900.

resent-ful, -ive; vindictive &c. 919.

Int. pish!

901a. Sullenness.—N. sullenness &c. *adj.*; morosity, spleen; churlishness &c. (*discourtesy*) 895; irascibility &c. 901.

moodiness &c. *adj.*; perversity; obstinacy &c. 606; torvity, spinosity; crabbedness &c. *adj.*

ill –, bad- -temper, – humour; sulks, dudgeon, mumps, doleful dumps, doldrums, fit of the sulks, *bouderie*, black looks, scowl; huff &c. (*resentment*) 900.

V. be -sullen &c. *adj.*; sulk; frown, scowl, lower, glower, grouse, grouch, crab, gloam, pout, have a hang-dog look, glout.

Adj. sullen, sulky; ill-tempered, -humoured, -affected, -disposed; in -an ill, – a bad, – a shocking- -temper, – humour; out of -temper, –

humour; knaggy, **torvous**, crusty, crabbed; sore as a boil; surly &c. (*discourteous*) 895.

moody; spleen-ish, -ly; splenetic, cankered.

cross, -grained; perverse, wayward, humoursome; restive; cantankerous, refractory, intractable, exceptious, sinistrous, deaf to reason, unaccommodating, rusty, crusty, froward.

dogged &c. (*stubborn*) 606.

grumpy, glum, grim, grum, morose, frumpish; in the -sulks &c. *n.*; out of sorts; scowl-, glower-, growl-ing.

peevish &c. (*irascible*) 901.

902. [Expression of affection or love.] **Endearment.—N.** endearment, caress; blandish-, blandi-ment; *épanchement*, fondling, billing and cooing, dalliance.

embrace, salute, kiss, buss, smack, osculation, deosculation; amorous glances; ogle, side glance, sheep's eyes.

courtship, wooing, suit, addresses, the soft impeachment; love-making; an affair; serenading; caterwauling.

flirting &c. *v.*; flirtation, gallantry; coquetry, spooning.

true lover's knot, plighted love, engagement, betrothal; love -tale, – token, – letter; *billet-doux*, valentine.

honeymoon; Strephon and Chloe, 'Arry and 'Arriet.

V. caress, fondle, pet, dandle, nurse; pat, – on the -head, – cheek; chuck under the chin, smile upon, coax, wheedle, cosset, coddle, cocker; make -of, – much of, pamper; cherish, foster, kill with kindness.

clasp, hug, cuddle; fold –, strain- in one's arms; nestle, nuzzle, neck, embrace, kiss, buss, smack, blow a kiss; salute &c. (*courtesy*) 894.

bill and coo, spoon, toy, dally, flirt, coquet; galli-, gala-vant; philander; make love; pay one's -court, – addresses, – attentions- to; serenade; court, woo; set one's cap at; be –, look- sweet upon; ogle, cast sheep's eyes upon; *faire les yeux doux.*

fall in love with, win the affections &c. (*love*) 897; die for.

propose; make –, have- an offer; pop the question; plight one's -troth, – faith; become -engaged, – betrothed.

Adj. caressing &c. *v.*; 'sighing like furnace'; love-sick, spoony.

caressed &c. *v.*

903. Marriage.—N. marriage, matrimony, wedlock, union, intermarriage, *vinculum matrimonii*, nuptial tie, knot.

married state, coverture, bed, cohabitation.

match; betrothment &c. (*promise*) 768; wedding, nuptials, Hymen, bridal; e-, spousals; leading to the altar &c. *v.*; nuptial benediction, *epithalamium.*

torch –, temple- of Hymen; hymeneal altar; honeymoon.

bride, bridegroom; brides-maid, -man.

best –, grooms-man, page, usher.

married -man, – woman, – couple; neogamist, Benedick, partner, spouse, mate, yokemate; husband, man, con-

904. Celibacy.—N. celibacy, singleness, single blessedness; bachelor-hood, -ship; miso-gamy, -gyny.

virginity, *pucelage*; maiden-hood, -head.

unmarried man, bachelor, Cœlebs, agamist, old bachelor; miso-gamist, -gynist; celibate.

unmarried woman, spinster; maid, -en; virgin, *femme sole*, old maid; bachelor girl; nun &c.

V. live single; keep bachelor hall.

Adj. un-married, -wedded; wife-, spouse-less; single, virgin, celibate.

905. Divorce.—N. divorce, -ment; separation; judicial separation, separ-

sort, baron; old -, good- man; wife of one's bosom; help-meet, -mate, rib, better half, grey mare, old woman, good wife; *femme couverte*; squaw, lady; matron, -age, -hood; man and wife; wedded pair, Darby and Joan.

affinity, soul-mate.

mono-, bi-, di-, deutero-, tri-, polygamy; mormonism; poly-andry; Turk, Bluebeard.

unlawful -, left-handed -, companionate -, morganatic -, ill-assorted- marriage; *mésalliance*; *mariage de convenance*; an affair.

match-maker, marriage broker, matrimonial agent.

V. marry, wive, take to oneself a wife; be -married, - spliced; go -, pair- off; wed, espouse, lead to the hymeneal altar, take 'for better, for worse,' give one's hand to, bestow one's hand upon; remarry; intermarry.

marry, join, handfast; couple &c. (*unite*) 43; tie the nuptial knot; give -away, - in marriage; affy, affiance; betroth &c. (*promise*) 768; publish -, bid- the banns; be asked in church.

Adj. married &c. *v.*; one, - bone and one flesh.

marriageable, nubile.

engaged, betrothed, affianced.

matrimonial, marital, conjugal, connubial, wedded; nuptial, hymeneal, spousal, bridal.

Phr. the grey mare the better horse.

ate maintenance; *separatio a -mensâ et thoro, - vinculo matrimonii.*

widowhood, viduage, viduity, weeds.

widow, -er; relict; dowager; *divorcée*; cuckold.

V. live -separately, - apart; separate, divorce, disespouse, put away; wear the horns.

2°. Diffusive Sympathetic Affections

906. Benevolence.—N. benevolence, Christian charity; God's -love, - grace; good-will; philanthropy &c. 910; unselfishness &c. 942.

good -nature, - feeling, - wishes; kind-, kindli-ness &c. *adj.*; lovingkindness, benignity, brotherly love, charity, humanity, fellow-feeling, sympathy; goodness -, warmth- of heart; *bonhomie*; kind-heartedness; amiability, milk of human kindness, tenderness; love &c. 897; friendship &c. 888.

toleration, consideration, generosity; mercy &c. (*pity*) 914.

charitableness &c. *adj.*; bounty, alms-giving; good works, beneficence, the luxury of doing good.

acts of kindness, a good turn; good -, kind- -offices, - treatment.

good Samaritan, sympathizer, well-wisher, philanthropist, *bon enfant*; altruist.

V. be -benevolent &c. *adj.*; have one's heart in the right place, bear good will; wish -well, - God speed;

907. Malevolence.—N. malevolence; bad intent, -ion; un-, dis-kindness; ill -nature, - will, - blood; acrimony; bad blood; enmity &c. 889; hate &c. 898; malignity; malice, - aforethought, - prepense; maliciousness &c. *adj.*; spite, despite; resentment &c. 900.

uncharitableness &c. *adj.*; incompassionateness &c. 914*a*; gall, venom, rancour, rankling, virulence, mordacity, acerbity; churlishness &c. (*discourtesy*) 895.

hardness of heart, heart of stone, obduracy; cruelty; cruelness &c. *adj.*; brutality, savagery; fer-ity, -ocity; barbarity, inhumanity, immanity, truculence, ruffianism; evil eye, cloven -foot, - hoof; inquisition; torture.

ill -, bad- turn; affront &c. (*disrespect*) 929; outrage, atrocity; ill usage; intolerance, bigotry, persecution; tender mercies [ironical]; 'unkindest cut of all.'

V. be -malevolent &c. *adj.*; bear -, harbour- -spleen, - a grudge, - mal-

view –, regard- with an eye of favour; take in good part; take –, feel- an interest in; be –, feel- interested- in; sympathize with, feel for; fraternize &c. (*be friendly*) 888.

enter into the feelings of others, do as you would be done by, meet halfway.

treat well; give comfort, smooth the bed of death; do -good, – a good turn; benefit &c. (*goodness*) 648; render a service, be of use; aid &c. 707.

Adj. benevolent; kind, -ly; well-meaning, amiable; obliging, accommodating, indulgent, considerate, gracious, complacent, good-humoured.

warm-, soft-, kind-, tender-, large-, broad-hearted; merciful &c. 914; philanthropic &c. 910; charitable, beneficent, humane, benign, benignant; bount-eous, -iful &c. 816.

good-, well-natured; spleenless; sympath-izing, -etic; complaisant &c. (*courteous*) 894; kindly, well-meant, -intentioned.

fatherly, motherly, brotherly, sisterly; pat-, mat-, frat-ernal; friendly &c. 888.

Adv. with -a good intention, – the best intentions.

Int. God speed! much good may it do!

---

ice; betray –, show- the cloven foot.

hurt &c. (*physical pain*) 378; annoy &c. 830; injure, harm, wrong; do -harm, – an ill office- to; outrage; disoblige, malign, plant a thorn in the breast.

molest, worry, harass, haunt, harry, bait, tease, throw stones at; play the devil with; hunt down, dragoon, hound; persecute, oppress, grind; maltreat; ill-treat, -use.

wreak one's malice on, do one's worst, break a butterfly on the wheel; dip –, imbrue- one's hands in blood; have no mercy &c. 914*a*.

Adj. male-, unbene-volent; unbenign; ill-disposed, -intentioned, -natured, -conditioned, -contrived; evil-minded, -disposed.

malicious; malign, -ant; rancorous; de-, spiteful; mordacious, caustic, bitter, envenomed, acrimonious, virulent; un-amiable, -charitable; maleficent, venomous, grinding, galling.

harsh, disobliging; un-kind, -friendly, -gracious; treacherous; inofficious; invidious; uncandid; churlish &c. (*uncourteous*) 895; surly, sullen &c. 901*a*.

cold, -blooded, -hearted; hard-, flint-, marble-, stony-hearted; hard of heart, unnatural; ruthless &c. (*unmerciful*) 914*a*; relentless &c. (*revengeful*) 919.

cruel; brut-al, -ish; savage, – as a -bear, – tiger; ferine, feral, ferocious; inhuman; barbarous, fell, untamed, tameless, truculent, incendiary; bloodthirsty &c. (*murderous*) 361; atrocious.

fiend-ish, -like; demoniacal; diabolic, -al; devilish, infernal, hellish, Satanic.

Adv. malevolently &c. *adj.*; with -bad intent &c. *n.*

908. Malediction.—N. malediction, malison, curse, imprecation, denunciation, execration, anathema, ban, proscription, excommunication, commination, thunders of the Vatican, fulmination, aspersion, vilification, vituperation, scurrility.

abuse; foul –, bad –, strong –, unparliamentary- language, Limehouse; Billingsgate, sauce, evil speaking; cursing &c. *v.*; profane swearing, oath.

threat &c. 909; more bark than bite; invective &c. (*disapprobation*) 932.

V. curse, accurse, imprecate, damn, swear at; slang; curse with bell, book and candle; invoke –, call down- curses on the head of; devote to destruction.

execrate, beshrew, scold; anathematize &c. (*censure*) 932; hold up to execration, denounce, proscribe, excommunicate, fulminate, thunder against; threaten &c. 909; curse up hill and down dale.

curse and swear; swear, – like a trooper; fall a cursing, rap out an oath, damn, cuss.

Adj. curs-ing, -ed &c. *v.*; maledictory.

Int. woe to! beshrew! *ruat cœlum!* ill –, woe- betide! confusion seize! damn! confound! blast! curse! devil take! hang! out with! a plague –, out- upon! aroynt! *honi soit!*

Phr. *delenda est Carthago.*

909. Threat.—N. threat, menace; defiance &c. 715; abuse, minacity, intimidation; fulmination; commination &c. (*curse*) 908; gathering clouds &c. (*warning*) 668.

V. threat, -en; menace; snarl, growl, gnarl, mutter, bark, bully. defy &c. 715; intimidate &c. 860; keep –, hold up –, hold out- *in terrorem*; shake –, double –, clinch- the fist at; thunder, talk big, fulminate, use big words, bluster, look daggers.

Adj. threatening, menacing; mina-tory, -cious; comminatory, abusive; *in terrorem*; ominous &c. (*predicting*) 511; defiant &c. 715; under the ban.

Int. *væ victis!* at your peril! do your worst!

910. Philanthropy. — N. philanthropy; altruism, humanit-y, -arianism; universal benevolence; *deliciæ humani generis*; cosmopolitanism, utilitarianism, the greatest happiness of the greatest number, social science, sociology.

common weal, public welfare, socialism, communism.

patriotism, civism, nationality, love of country, *amor patriæ*, public spirit.

chivalry, knight errantry; generosity &c. 942.

philanthropist, altruist &c. 906; utilitarian, Benthamite, socialist, communist, cosmopolite, citizen of the world, *amicus humani generis*; knight errant; patriot.

Adj. philanthropic, altruistic, humanitarian, utilitarian, cosmopolitan; public-spirited, patriotic; humane, large-hearted &c. (*benevolent*) 906; chival-ric, -rous, generous &c. 942.

Adv. *pro -bono publico, – aris et focis.*

Phr. '*humani nihil a me alienum puto.*'

911. Misanthropy.—N. misanthropy, incivism; egotism &c. (*selfishness*) 943; moroseness &c. 901*a*; cynicism; defeatism.

misanthrope, misanthropist, egotist, cynic, man-hater, Timon, Diogenes.

woman-hater, misogynist.

Adj. misanthropic, antisocial, unpatriotic; egotistical &c. (*selfish*) 943; morose &c. 901*a*.

912. Benefactor. — N. benefactor, saviour, good genius, tutelary saint, patron, guardian angel, fairy godmother, good Samaritan; *pater patriæ*; salt of the earth &c. (*good man*) 948; auxiliary &c. 711.

913. [Maleficent being.] **Evil-doer. —N.** evil- -doer, – worker; wrong doer &c. 949; mischief maker, marplot; oppressor, tyrant; firebrand, incendiary, pyromaniac, anarchist, destroyer, Hun, *Boche*, Vandal, iconoclast; communist; terrorist, *apache*, gunman, gangster, racketeer.

savage, brute, ruffian, barbarian, semi-barbarian, caitiff, desperado; Mo-hock, -hawk; bludgeon man, bully, rough, hooligan, larrikin, dangerous classes, ugly customer; thief &c. 792.

cockatrice, scorpion, hornet; viper, adder; snake, – in the grass;

serpent, cobra, asp, rattlesnake, anaconda; canker-, wire-worm; locust, Colorado beetle; torpedo; bane &c. 663.

cannibal; Anthropophag-us, -ist; bloodsucker, vampire, ogre, ghoul, gorilla; vulture; gyr-, ger-falcon.

wild beast, tiger, hyæna, butcher, hangman; cut-throat &c. (*killer*) 361; blood-, sleuth-, hell-hound.

hag, hellhag, beldam, Jezebel.

monster; fiend &c. (*demon*) 980; homicidal maniac, devil incarnate, demon in human shape; Frankenstein's monster.

harpy, siren, vampire; Furies, Eumenides &c. 900.

Attila, scourge of the human race.

Phr. *fœnum habet in cornu.*

3°. Special Sympathetic Affections

914. Pity.—N. pity, compassion, commiseration; bowels, - of compassion; condolence &c. 915; sympathy, fellow-feeling, tenderness, yearning, forbearance, humanity, mercy, clemency, exorability; leniency &c. (*lenity*) 740; charity, ruth, long-suffering.

melting mood; *argumentum ad misericordiam*; quarter, grace, *locus pœnitentiæ*.

sympathizer, champion, partisan.

V. pity; have –, show –, take- pity &c. *n.*; commiserate, compassionate; condole &c. 915; sympathize; feel –, be sorry –, yearn- for; weep, melt, thaw, enter into the feelings of.

forbear, relent, relax, give quarter, wipe the tears, *parcere subjectis*, give a *coup de grâce*, put out of one's misery; be cruel to be kind.

raise –, excite- pity &c. *n.*; touch, soften; melt, - the heart; appeal to one's better feelings; propitiate, disarm.

ask for -mercy &c. *n.*; supplicate &c. (*request*) 765; cry for quarter, beg one's life, kneel; deprecate.

Adj. pitying &c. *v.*; pitiful, compassionate, sympathetic, touched.

merciful, clement, ruthful; humane; humanitarian &c. (*philanthropic*) 910; tender, - hearted, - as a chicken; soft, - hearted; unhardened; lenient &c. 740; exorable, forbearing; melting &c. *v.*; weak.

Int. for pity's sake! mercy! have –, cry you- mercy! God help you! poor -thing, - dear, - fellow! woe betide! *quis talia fando temperet a lachrymis!*

Phr. one's heart bleeding for; *haud ignara mali miseris succurrere disco.*

914a. Pitilessness.—N. pitilessness &c. *adj.*; inclemency; inexorability, hardness of heart; inflexibility; severity &c. 739; malevolence &c. 907.

V. have no –, shut the gates of- mercy &c. 914; give no quarter.

Adj. piti-, merci-, ruth-, bowel-less; unpitying, unmerciful, inclement; in-, un-compassionate; inexorable, inflexible; harsh &c. 739; cruel &c. 907; unrelenting &c. 919.

---

915. Condolence.—N. condolence; lamentation &c. 839; sympathy, consolation.

V. condole with, console, sympathize &c. 914, share one's misery; feel for; express –, testify- pity; afford –, supply- consolation; lament &c. 839- with; send one's condolences.

4°. Retrospective Sympathetic Affections

916. Gratitude. — N. gratitude, thankfulness, gratefulness, feeling of obligation.

acknowledgment, recognition thanksgiving, giving thanks.

thanks, praise, benediction; pæan; *Te Deum* &c. (*worship*) 990; grace, – before, – after- meat; thank-offering.

requital.

V. be -grateful &c. *adj.*; thank; give –, render –, return –, offer –, tender- thanks &c. *n.*; acknowledge, requite.

feel –, be –, lie- under an obligation; *savoir gré*; not look a gift horse in the mouth; never forget, overflow with gratitude; thank –, bless- one's stars; fall on one's knees.

Adj. grateful, thankful, obliged, beholden, indebted to, under obligation.

Int. thanks! many thanks! gramercy! much obliged! thank you! thank Heaven! Heaven be praised!

917. Ingratitude.—N. ingratitude, thanklessness, oblivion of benefits; unthankfulness.

'benefits forgot'; thankless -task, – office.

V. be -ungrateful &c. *adj.*; forget benefits; look a gift horse in the mouth.

Adj. un-grateful, -mindful, -thankful; thankless, ingrate, wanting in gratitude, insensible of benefits.

forgotten; un-acknowledged, -thanked, -requited, -rewarded; ill-requited.

Int. thank you for nothing! '*et tu Brute!*'

---

918. Forgiveness.—N. forgiveness, pardon, condonation, grace, remission, absolution, amnesty, oblivion; indulgence; reprieve.

conciliation; reconciliation &c. (*pacification*) 723; propitiation.

excuse, exoneration, quittance, release, indemnity; bill –, act –, covenant –, deed- of indemnity; exculpation &c. (*acquittal*) 970.

longanimity, placability, forbearance; *amantium iræ*; *locus pænitentiæ*.

V. forgive, – and forget; pardon, condone, think no more of, let bygones be bygones, shake hands; forget an injury, bury the hatchet; clean the slate.

excuse, pass over, overlook; wink at &c. (*neglect*) 460; bear with; allow –, make allowances- for; let one down easily, not be too hard upon, pocket the affront; blot out one's transgression.

let off, remit, absolve, give absolution, reprieve; acquit &c. 970.

beg –, ask –, implore- pardon &c. *n.*; conciliate, propitiate, placate; make up a quarrel &c. (*pacify*) 723; let the wound heal.

919. Revenge.—N. revenge, -ment; vengeance; avenge-ment, -ance; sweet revenge, *vendetta*, death-feud, eye for an eye, blood for blood, a Roland for an Oliver; retaliation &c. 718; day of reckoning.

rancour, vindictiveness, implacability; malevolence &c. 907; ruthlessness &c. 914*a*.

avenger, vindicator, Nemesis, Eumenides.

V. re-, a-venge; take –, have one's- revenge; breathe -revenge, – vengeance; wreak one's -vengeance, – anger; give no quarter.

have -accounts to settle, – a crow to pluck, – a rod in pickle; pay off old scores.

keep the wound green; harbour -revenge, – vindictive feeling; bear malice; rankle, – in the breast; have at one's mercy.

Adj. revenge-, venge-ful; vindictive, rancorous; pitiless &c. 914*a*; ruthless, rigorous, avenging, retaliative.

unforgiving, unrelenting; inexorable, stony-hearted, implacable; relent-, remorse-less.

æternum servans sub pectore vulnus; rankling, immitigable.

Adj. forgiving, placable, conciliatory.
forgiven &c. *v.*; un-resented, -avenged, -revenged.

Adv. cry you mercy.

Phr. *manet -cicatrix, – altâ mente repostum.*
revenge is sweet.

Phr. *veniam petimusque damusque vicissim*; more in sorrow than in anger.

920. Jealousy.—N. jealous-y, -ness; jaundiced eye, heartburning; green-eyed monster; yellows; Juno.

V. be -jealous &c. *adj.*; view with -jealousy, – a jealous eye.

Adj. jealous, – as a Barbary pigeon; jaundiced, yellow-eyed, horn-mad.

921. Envy.—N. envy; enviousness &c. *adj.*; rivalry; *jalousie de métier.*

V. envy, covet, lust after, crave, burst with envy, regard with envious eyes.

Adj. envious, invidious, covetous; *alieni appetens.*

Section IV. MORAL AFFECTIONS

1°. Moral Obligations

922. Right.—N. right; what -ought to, – should- be; fitness &c. *adj.*; *summum jus.*

justice, equity; equitableness &c. *adj.*; propriety; fair play, impartiality, measure for measure, give and take, *lex talionis*, square deal.

Astræa, Nemesis, Themis.

scales of justice, even-handed justice, retributive justice, *suum cuique*; clear stage –, fair field- and no favour; Queensberry rules.

morals &c. (*duty*) 926; law &c. 963; honour &c. (*probity*) 939; virtue &c. 944.

V. be -right &c. *adj.*; stand to reason.

see -justice done, – one righted, – fair play; do justice to; recompense &c. (*reward*) 973; hold the scales even, give and take; serve one right, put the saddle on the right horse; give -every one, – the devil- his due; *audire alteram partem.*

deserve &c. (*be entitled to*) 924.

Adj. right, good; just, reasonable; fit &c. 924; equ-al, -able, -itable; even-handed, fair, – and square.

legitimate, justifiable, rightful; as it -should, – ought to- be; lawful &c. (*permitted*) 760, (*legal*) 963.

deserved &c. 924.

Adv. rightly &c. *adj.*; in -justice, – equity, – reason.

without -distinction of, – regard to, – respect to- persons; upon even terms.

Int. all right!

923. Wrong. — N. wrong; what -ought not to, – should not- be; *malum in se*; unreasonableness, grievance; shame.

injustice; unfairness &c. *adj.*; iniquity, foul play, partiality, leaning; favour, -itism; nepotism, party spirit, partisanship; undueness &c. 925; unlawfulness &c. 964.

robbing Peter to pay Paul &c. *v.*; the wolf and the lamb; vice &c. 945.

a custom more honoured in the breach than the observance.

V. be -wrong &c. *adj.*; cry to heaven for vengeance.

do -wrong &c. *n.*; be -inequitable &c. *adj.*; favour, lean towards; encroach; impose upon; reap where one has not sown; give an inch and take an ell; rob Peter to pay Paul.

Adj. wrong, -ful; bad, too bad; unjust, -fair; in-, un-equitable; unequal, partial, one-sided.

objectionable; un-reasonable, -allowable, -warrantable, -justifiable; not cricket, not playing the game; improper, unfit; unjustified &c. 925; illegal &c. 964; iniquitous, criminal; immoral &c. 945; injurious &c. 649.

in the wrong, – box.

Adv. wrongly &c. *adj.*

Phr. it will not do; this is too bad.

---

924. Dueness.—N. due, -ness; right, privilege, prerogative, prescription, title, claim, pretension, demand, birthright.

immunity, licence, liberty, franchise; vested -interest, - right; licitness.

sanction, authority, warranty, charter; warrant &c. (*permission*) 760; constitution &c. (*law*) 963; tenure; bond &c. (*security*) 771.

deserts, merits, dues.

claimant, appellant; plaintiff &c. 938.

V. be -due &c. *adj.* to, - the due &c. *n.* of; have -right, - title, - claim- to; be entitled to; have a claim upon; belong to &c. (*property*) 780.

deserve, merit, be worthy of, richly deserve.

demand, claim; call upon -, come upon -, appeal to- for; re-vendicate, -claim; exact; insist -on, - upon; challenge; take one's stand, make a point of, require, lay claim to, assert, assume, arrogate, make good; substantiate; vindicate a -claim, - right; make out a case.

give -, confer- a right; sanction, entitle; authorize &c. 760; sanctify, legalize, ordain, prescribe, allot.

give every one his due &c. 922; pay one's dues; have one's -due, - rights; stand upon one's rights.

use a right, assert, enforce, put in force, lay under contribution.

Adj. having a right to &c. *v.*; entitled to; claiming; deserving, meriting, worthy of.

privileged, allowed, sanctioned, warranted, authorized; ordained, prescribed, constitutional, chartered, enfranchised.

prescriptive, presumptive; absolute, indefeasible; un-, in-alienable; imprescriptible, inviolable, unimpeachable, unchallenged; sacrosanct.

due to, merited, deserved, condign, richly deserved, *emeritus*.

allowable &c. (*permitted*) 760; lawful, licit, legitimate, legal; legalized &c. (*law*) 963.

square, unexceptionable, right; equitable &c. 922; due, *en règle*; fit, -ting; correct, proper, meet, befitting, becoming, seemly; decorous; creditable, up to the mark, right as a trivet; just -, quite- the thing; *selon les règles*.

Adv. duly, *ex officio*, *de jure*; by -right, - divine right; as is -fitting, - proper, - fitting and proper; *jure divino*, *Dei gratiâ*, in the name of.

Phr. *civis Romanus sum.*

925. [Absence of right.] **Undueness —N.** undueness &c. *adj.*; *malum prohibitum*; impropriety; illegality &c. 964.

falseness &c. *adj.*; emptiness -, invalidity- of title; illegitimacy.

loss of right, disfranchisement, forfeiture.

usurpation, assumption, tort, violation, breach, encroachment, presumption, seizure, stretch, exaction, imposition, lion's share.

usurper, pretender, Carlist; impostor.

V. be -undue &c. *adj.*; not be -due &c. 924.

infringe, encroach, trench on, exact; arrogate, - to oneself; give an inch and take an ell; stretch -, strain- a point; usurp, violate, do violence to; sail under false colours.

dis-franchise, -entitle, -qualify; invalidate.

relax &c. (*be lax*) 738; misbehave &c. (*vice*) 945; misbecome.

Adj. undue; unlawful &c. (*illegal*) 964; unconstitutional, *ultra vires*; illicit; un-authorized, -warranted, -allowed, -sanctioned, -justified; un-, dis-entitled, -qualified; un-privileged, -chartered.

illegitimate, bastard, spurious, false; usurped, tortious.

un-deserved, -merited, -earned; unfulfilled.

forfeited, disfranchised.

improper; un-meet, -fit, -befitting, -seemly; un-, mis-becoming; seemless; *contra bonos mores*; not the thing, out of the question, not to be thought of; preposterous, pretentious, would- be.

926. Duty.—**N.** duty, what ought to be done, moral obligation, accountableness, liability, *onus*, responsibility; bounden –, imperative- duty; call, – of duty.

allegiance, fealty, tie; engagement &c. (*promise*) 768; part; function, calling &c. (*business*) 625.

morality, morals, decalogue; case of conscience; conscientiousness &c. (*probity*) 939; conscience, inward monitor, still small voice within, sense of duty, tender conscience.

dueness &c. 924; propriety, fitness, seemliness, amenableness, decorum; the -thing, – proper thing; the -right, – proper- thing to do.

[Science of morals] eth-ics, -ology; deon-, are-tology; moral –, ethical- philosophy; casuistry, polity.

observance, fulfilment, discharge, performance, acquittal, satisfaction, redemption; good behaviour.

V. be -the duty of, – incumbent &c. *adj.* on, – responsible &c. *adj.*; behoove, become, befit, beseem; belong –, pertain- to; fall to one's lot; devolve on; lie -upon, – on one's head, – at one's door; rest -with, – on the shoulders of.

take upon oneself &c. (*promise*) 768; be –, become- -bound to, – sponsor for; be responsible for; incur a -responsibility &c. *n.*; be –, stand –, lie- under an obligation; have to answer for, owe it to oneself.

impose a -duty &c. *n.*; enjoin, require, exact; bind, – over; saddle with, prescribe, assign, call upon, look to, oblige.

enter upon –, perform –, observe –, fulfil –, discharge –, adhere to –, acquit oneself of –, satisfy- -a duty, – an obligation; act one's part, redeem one's pledge, do justice to, be at one's post; do duty; do one's duty &c. (*be virtuous*) 944.

be on one's good behaviour, mind one's P's and Q's.

Adj. obligatory, binding; imperative, peremptory; stringent &c. (*severe*) 739; behooving &c. *v.*; incumbent –, chargeable- on; under obligation; obliged –, bound –, tied- by; saddled with.

due –, beholden –, bound –, indebted- to; tied down; compromised &c. (*promised*) 768; in duty bound.

amenable, liable, accountable, responsible, answerable.

right, meet &c. (*due*) 924; moral, ethical, casuistical, conscientious, ethological.

Adv. with a safe conscience, as in duty bound, on one's own re-

927. Dereliction of Duty.—**N.** dereliction of duty; fault &c. (*guilt*) 947- sin &c. (*vice*) 945; non-observance, -performance, -co-operation; neglect, carelessness, laziness, incompetence, eye-service, relaxation, infraction, violation, transgression, failure, evasion, indolence; dead letter.

slacker, loafer, striker, non-cooperator.

V. violate; break, – through; infringe; set -aside, – at naught; trample -on, – under foot; slight, neglect, evade, renounce, forswear, repudiate; wash one's hands of; escape, transgress, fail.

call to account &c. (*disapprobation*) 932.

927a. Exemption.—**N.** exemption, freedom, irresponsibility, immunity, liberty, licence, release, exoneration, excuse, dispensation, absolution, franchise, renunciation, discharge; exculpation &c. 970; *ægrotat*.

V. be -exempt &c. *adj.*

exempt, release, acquit, discharge, quit-claim, remise, remit; free, set at liberty, let off, pass over, spare, excuse, dispense with, give dispensation, license; stretch a point; absolve &c. (*forgive*) 918; exonerate &c. (*exculpate*) 970; save the necessity.

Adj. exempt, free, immune, at liberty, scot free; released &c. *v.*; unbound, unencumbered; irresponsible, unaccountable, not answerable; excusable.

sponsibility, at one's own risk, *suo periculo*; *in foro conscientiæ*; *quamdiu se bene gesserit*; at one's post, on duty.

Phr. *dura lex sed lex.*

2°. Moral Sentiments

928. Respect.—N. respect, regard, consideration; courtesy &c. 894; attention, deference, reverence, honour, esteem, estimation, veneration, admiration; approbation &c. 931.

homage, fealty, obeisance, genuflexion, kneeling, prostration; obsequiousness &c. 886; salaam, *kowtow*, bow, presenting arms, salute.

respects, regards, duty, *devoirs*, *égards*.

devotion &c. (*piety*) 987.

V. respect, regard; revere, -nce; hold in reverence, honour, venerate, hallow; esteem &c. (*approve of*) 931; think much of; entertain –, bear- respect for; have a high opinion of; look up to, defer to; pay -attention, – respect &c. *n.*- to; do –, render- honour to; do the honours, hail; show courtesy &c. 894; salute, present arms; do –, pay- homage to; pay tribute to, kneel to, bow to, bend the knee to; fall down before, prostrate oneself, kiss the hem of one's garment; worship &c. 990.

keep one's distance, make room, observe due decorum, stand upon ceremony.

command –, inspire- respect; awe, impose, overawe, dazzle.

Adj. respecting &c. *v.*; respectful, deferential, decorous, reverential, obsequious, ceremonious, bare-headed, cap in hand, on one's knees; prostrate &c. (*servile*) 886.

respected &c. *v.*; in high -esteem, – estimation; time-honoured, venerable, *emeritus*.

Adv. in deference to; with -all, – due, – the highest- respect; with submission.

saving your -grace, – presence; *salva sit reverentia*; *pace tanti nominis*.

Int. hail! all hail! *esto perpetua!* may your shadow never be less!

---

929. Disrespect. — N. dis-respect, -esteem, -estimation, -favour, -repute; low estimation; disparagement &c. (*dispraise*) 932, (*detraction*) 934.

irreverence; slight, neglect; *spretæ injuria formæ*; superciliousness &c. (*contempt*) 930.

vilipendency, contumely, affront, dishonour, insult, indignity, outrage, discourtesy &c. 895; practical joking; scurrility, scoffing, sibilation; ir-, derision; mockery; irony &c. (*ridicule*) 856; sarcasm.

hiss, hoot, gibe, flout, jeer, scoff, gleek, taunt, sneer, quip, fling, wipe, slap in the face.

V. hold in disrespect &c. (*despise*) 930; misprize, disregard, slight, undervalue, depreciate, trifle with, set at naught, pass by, push aside, overlook, turn one's back upon, laugh in one's sleeve; be -disrespectful &c. *adj.*, – discourteous &c. 895; treat with -disrespect &c. *n.*; set down, browbeat.

dishonour, desecrate; insult, affront, outrage.

speak slightingly of; disparage &c. (*dispraise*) 932; vilipend, call names; throw –, fling- dirt; drag through the mud, point at, indulge in personalities; make -mouths, – faces; bite the thumb; take –, pluck- by the beard; toss in a blanket, tar and feather.

have –, hold- in derision; deride, scoff, sneer, laugh at, snigger, ridicule, gibe, mock, jeer, taunt, twit, niggle, gleek, gird, flout, fleer; roast, turn into ridicule; guy, burlesque &c. 856; laugh to scorn &c. (*contempt*) 930; smoke; fool; make -game, – a fool, – an April fool- of; play a practical joke; rag; lead one a dance, run the rig upon, have a fling at, scout, hiss, hoot, mob.

Adj. disrespectful; aweless, irreverent; disparaging &c. 934; insulting &c. *v.*; supercilious &c. (*scornful*) 930; rude, derisive, contemptuous, sarcastic; scurri-le, -lous; contumelious.

un-respected, -worshipped, -envied, -saluted; un-, dis-regarded.

Adv. disrespectfully &c. *adj.*

930. Contempt.—N. contempt, disdain, scorn, sovereign contempt; despi-sal, -ciency; vilipendency, contumely; slight, sneer, spurn, by-word.

contemptuousness &c. *adj.*; scornful eye; smile of contempt; derision &c. (*disrespect*) 929.

[State of being despised] despisedness.

V. despise, contemn, scorn, disdain, feel contempt for, view with a scornful eye, disregard, slight, not mind; pass by &c. (*neglect*) 460.

look down upon; hold -cheap, – in contempt, – in disrespect; think -nothing, – small beer- of; make light of; underestimate &c. 483; esteem -slightly, – of small or no account; take no account of, care nothing for; set no store by; not care a -straw &c. (*unimportance*) 643; set at naught, laugh in one's sleeve, snap one's fingers at, shrug one's shoulders, turn up one's nose at, pooh-pooh, damn with faint praise; sneeze –, whistle –, sneer- at; curl up one's lip, toss the head, *traiter de haut*; laugh at &c. (*be disrespectful*) 929.

point the finger of –, hold up to –, laugh to- scorn; scout, hoot, flout, hiss, scoff at.

turn -one's back, – a cold shoulder- upon; tread –, trample- -upon, – under foot; spurn, kick; fling to the winds &c. (*repudiate*) 610; send away with a flea in the ear.

Adj. contemptuous; disdain-, scorn-ful; withering, contumelious, supercilious, cynical, haughty, bumptious, cavalier; derisive.

contemptible, despicable; pitiable; pitiful &c. (*unimportant*) 643; despised &c. *v.*; down-trodden; unenvied.

Adv. contemptuously &c. *adj.*

Int. a fig for &c. (*unimportant*) 643; bah! never mind! away with! hang it! fiddle-de-dee!

931. Approbation.—N. approbation; approv-al, -ement; sanction, advocacy; nod of approbation; esteem, estimation, good opinion, golden opinions, admiration; love &c. 897; appreciation, regard, account, popularity, *kudos*, credit; repute &c. 873.

commendation, praise; laud, -ation; good word; meed –, tribute- of praise; encomium; eulog-y, -ium; *éloge*, panegyric; homage, hero worship; benediction, blessing, benison.

applause, plaudit, clap; clapping, – of hands; accl-aim, -amation; cheer; pæan, hosannah; shout –, peal –, chorus –, thunders- of -applause &c.; Kentish fire; Prytaneum; blurb.

V. approve; think -good, – much of, – well of, – highly of; esteem, value, prize; set great store -by, – on.

do justice to, appreciate; honour, hold in esteem, look up to, admire; like &c. 897; be in favour of, wish God speed; hail, – with satisfaction.

stand –, stick- up for; uphold, hold

932. Disapprobation.—N. disapprobation, -val; improbation; dis-esteem, -valuation, -placency; odium; dislike &c. 867; dissent &c. 489.

dis-praise, -commendation; blame, censure, obloquy; detraction &c. 934; disparagement, depreciation; denunciation; condemnation &c. 971; ostracism; boycott; black-list, -ball; *index -expurgatorius, – librorum prohibitorum.*

animadversion, reflection, stricture, objection, exception, criticism; sardonic -grin, – laugh; sarcasm, insinuation, innuendo; bad –, poor –, left-handed- compliment.

satire; sneer &c. (*contempt*) 930; taunt &c. (*disrespect*) 929; cavil, carping, censoriousness; hypercriticism &c. (*fastidiousness*) 868.

reprehension, remonstrance, expostulation, reproof, reprobation, admonition, increpation, reproach; rebuke, reprimand, castigation, jobation, lecture, curtain lecture, blow up, wigging, dressing, – down; rating, scolding, trim-

up, countenance, sanction; clap –, pat- on the back; keep in countenance, endorse, give credit, recommend; mark with a white -mark, – stone.

commend, praise; be-, laud; compliment, pay a tribute, bepraise; clap, – the hands; applaud, cheer, acclaim, acclamate, encore; panegyrize, eulogize, cry up, *prôner*, puff; extol, – to the skies; magnify, glorify, exalt, boost, swell, make much of; flatter &c. 933; bless, give a blessing to; have –, say- a good word for; speak -well, – highly, – in high terms- of; sing –, sound –, chaunt –, resound- the praises of; sing praises to; cheer –, applaud- to the -echo, – very echo.

redound to the -honour, – praise, – credit- of; do credit to; deserve -praise &c. *n.*; recommend itself; pass muster.

be -praised &c.; receive honourable mention; be in -favour, – high favour- with; ring with the praises of, win golden opinions, gain credit, find favour with, stand well in the opinion of; *laudari a laudato viro*.

Adj. approving &c. *v.*; in favour of; lost in admiration.

commendatory, complimentary, benedictory, laudatory, panegyrical, eulogistic, encomiastic, acclamatory, lavish of praise, uncritical.

approved, praised &c. *v.*; un-censured, -impeached; popular, in good odour; in high esteem &c. (*respected*) 928; in –, in high- favour.

deserving –, worthy of- praise &c. *n.*; praiseworthy, commendable, of estimation; good &c. 648; meritorious, estimable, creditable, plausible, unimpeachable; beyond all praise.

Adv. commendably, with credit, to admiration; well &c. 618; with three times three.

Int. hear, hear! well done! *brav-o! -a! -i! bravissimo! euge! macte virtute!* so far so good, that's right, quite right; *optime!* one cheer more; may your shadow never be less! *esto perpetua!* long life to! *viva! evviva!* God speed! *valete et plaudite! encore! bis!*

Phr. *probatum est.*

---

ming; correction, set down, rap on the knuckles, *coup de bec*, rebuff; slap, – on the face; home thrust, hit; frown, scowl, black look.

diatribe; jeremiad *tirade*, philippic.

clamour, outcry, hue and cry; hiss, -ing; sibilation, cat-call; execration &c. 908.

chiding, upbraiding &c. *v.*; exprobration, abuse, vituperation, invective, objurgation, contumely, personal remarks; hard –, cutting –, bitter- words.

evil-speaking; bad language &c. 908; personality.

V. disapprove; dislike &c. 867; lament &c. 839; object to, take exception to; be scandalized at, think ill of; view with -disfavour, – dark eyes, – jaundiced eyes; *nil admirari*, disvalue, improbate.

frown upon, look grave; bend –, knit- the brows; shake the head at, shrug the shoulders; turn up the nose &c. (*contempt*) 930; look -askance, – black upon; look with an evil eye; make a wry -face, – mouth- at; set one's face against.

dis-praise, -commend, -parage; deprecate, speak ill of, not speak well of, slate, condemn &c. (*find guilty*) 971; blame; lay –, cast- blame upon; censure, *fronder*, reproach, pass censure on, reprobate, impugn.

remonstrate, expostulate, recriminate.

reprehend, chide, admonish; bring –, call- -to account, – over the coals, – to order; take to task, reprove, lecture, bring to book; read a -lesson, – lecture- to; rebuke, correct.

reprimand, chastise, castigate, lash, blow up, trounce, trim, *laver la tete*, overhaul; give it one, – finely; gibbet.

accuse &c. 938; impeach, denounce; hold up to -reprobation, – execration; expose, brand, gibbet, stigmatize; show –, pull –, take- up; cry 'shame' upon; be outspoken; raise a hue and cry against.

execrate &c. 908; exprobrate, speak daggers, vituperate; abuse, – like a pickpocket; scold, rate, objurgate, upbraid, fall foul of; jaw; rail, – at, – in good set terms; bark at; anathematize, call names; call by -hard, – ugly- names; a-, re-vile; vili-fy, -pend; bespatter; backbite; clapperclaw; rave –, thunder –, fulminate- against; load with reproaches; lash with the tongue.

exclaim –, protest –, inveigh –, declaim –, cry out –, raise one's voice- against.

decry; cry –, run –, frown- down; clamour, hiss, hoot, mob, ostracize; draw up –, sign- a round robin; black-ball, -list.

animadvert –, reflect- upon; glance at; cast -reflection, – reproach, – a slur- upon; insinuate, damn with faint praise; 'hint a fault and hesitate dislike'; not to be able to say much for.

scoff at, point at; twit, taunt &c. (*disrespect*) 929; sneer at &c. (*despise*) 930; satirize, lampoon; defame &c. (*detract*) 934; depreciate, find fault with, criticize, cut up; pull –, pick- to pieces; take exception; cavil; peck –, nibble –, carp- at; be -censorious &c. *adj.*; pick -holes, – a hole, – a hole in one's coat; make a fuss about.

take –, set- down; snub, snap one up, give a rap on the knuckles; throw a stone -at, – in one's garden; have a -fling, – snap- at; have words with, pluck a crow with; give one a -wipe, – lick with the rough side of the tongue.

incur blame, excite disapprobation, scandalize, shock, revolt; get a bad name, forfeit one's good opinion, be under a cloud, come under the ferule, bring a hornet's nest about one's ears.

take blame, stand corrected; have to answer for.

Adj. disapproving &c. *v.*; scandalized.

disparaging, condemnatory, damnatory, denunciatory, reproachful, abusive, objurgatory, clamorous, vituperative; defamatory &c. 934.

satirical, sarcastic, sardonic, cynical, dry, sharp, cutting, biting, severe, virulent, withering, trenchant, hard upon; censorious, critical, captious, carping, hypercritical; fastidious &c. 868; sparing of –, grudging- praise.

disapproved, chid &c. *v.*; in bad odour, blown upon, unapproved; unblest; at a discount, exploded; weighed in the balance and found wanting.

blameworthy, reprehensible &c. (*guilt*) 947; to –, worthy of- blame, answerable, uncommendable, exceptionable, not to be thought of, bad &c. 649; vicious &c. 945.

un-lamented, -bewailed, -pitied.

Adv. with a wry face; reproachfully &c. *adj.*

Int. it is too bad! it -won't, – will never- do! marry come up! Oh! come! 'sdeath!

forbid it Heaven! God –, Heaven- forbid! out –, fie- upon it! away with! tut! *O tempora! O mores!* shame! fie, – for shame! out on you!

tell it not in Gath!

933. Flattery.—N. flattery, adulation, gloze; bland-ishment, -iloquence; cajolery; fawning, wheedling &c. *v.*; captation, coquetry, sycophancy, obsequiousness, flunkeyism, toad-eating, tuft-hunting; snobbishness.

incense, honeyed words, flummery; bun-kum, -combe; blarney, *placebo*, but-

934. Detraction.—N. detraction, disparagement, depreciation, vilification, obloquy, scurrility, scandal, defamation, aspersion, traducement, slander, calumny, obtrectation, evil-speaking, backbiting, *scandalum magnatum.*

personality, libel, squib, lampoon, skit, pasquinade; *chronique scandaleuse*,

ter; soft -soap, – sawder; rose water.

voice of the charmer, mouth honour; lip-homage; euphemism; unctuousness &c. *adj*.

V. flatter, praise to the skies, puff; wheedle, cajole, glaver, coax; fawn, – upon; humour, gloze, soothe, pet, coquet, slaver, butter; be-spatter, -slubber, -plaster, -slaver; lay it on thick, overpraise; earwig, cog, collogue; truckle –, pander *or* pandar –, pay court- to; court; creep into the good graces of; curry favour with, hang on the sleeve of; fool to the top of one's bent; lick the dust.

lay the flattering unction to one's soul, gild the pill, make things pleasant.

overestimate &c. 482; exaggerate &c. 549.

Adj. flattering &c. *v.*; adulatory; mealy-, honey-mouthed; honeyed; smooth, – tongued; soapy, oily, unctuous, blandiloquent, specious; fine-, fair-spoken; plausible, servile, sycophantic, fulsome; courtier-ly, -like.

Adv. *ad captandum*.

---

935. Flatterer.—N. flatterer, adulator; eu-logist, -phemist; optimist, encomiast, *laudator*, whitewasher, booster.

toad-y, -eater; sycophant, courtier, pickthank, Sir Pertinax MacSycophant; *flâneur*, *prôneur*; puffer, touter, *claqueur*; claw-back, ear-wig, doer of dirty work; parasite, hanger on &c. (*servility*) 886.

---

937. Vindication.—N. vindication, justification, warrant; exoneration, exculpation; acquittal &c. 970; whitewashing.

extenuation; pallia-tion, -tive; softening, mitigation.

reply, defence; recrimination &c. 938.

apology, gloss, varnish; plea &c. 617; salvo; excuse, extenuating circumstances; allowance, – to be made; *locus pœnitentiæ*.

apologist, vindicator, justifier; defendant &c. 938.

justifiable charge, true bill.

sarcasm, cynicism; criticism (*disapprobation*) 932; invective &c. 932; envenomed tongue; *spretæ injuria formæ*.

detractor &c. 936.

V. detract, derogate, decry, depreciate, disparage; run –, cry- down; minimize, make light of; belittle, sneer at &c. (*contemn*) 930; criticize, pull to pieces, pick a hole in one's coat, asperse, cast aspersions, blow upon, bespatter, blacken; vili-fy, -pend; avile; give a dog a bad name, brand, malign, backbite, libel, lampoon, traduce, slander, defame, calumniate, bear false witness against; speak ill of behind one's back.

'damn with faint praise, assent with civil leer; and without sneering, others teach to sneer.'

fling dirt &c. (*disrespect*) 929; anathematize &c. 932; dip the pen in gall, view in a bad light.

Adj. detracting &c. *v.*; defamatory, detractory, derogatory; disparaging, libellous; scurril-e, -ous; abusive; foulspoken, -tongued, -mouthed; slanderous; calumni-ous, -atory; sar-castic, -donic; satirical, cynical.

936. Detractor.—N. detractor, reprover; cens-or, -urer; cynic, critic, caviller, carper, wordcatcher.

defamer, backbiter, slanderer, knocker, Sir Benjamin Backbite, lampooner, satirist, traducer, libeller, calumniator, dearest foe, dawplucker, Thersites; Zoilus; good-natured –, candid- friend [satirically]; reviler, vituperator, castigator; shrew &c. 901.

disapprover, *laudator temporis acti*.

938. Accusation. — N. accusation, charge, imputation, slur, inculpation, exprobration, delation; crimination; in-, ac-, re-crimination; *tu quoque* argument; invective &c. 932.

de-nunciation, -nouncement; libel, challenge, citation, arraignment; im-, ap-peachment; indictment, bill of indictment, true bill; lawsuit &c. 969; condemnation &c. 971.

gravamen of a charge, head and front of one's offending, *argumentum ad hominem*; scandal &c. (*detraction*) 934; *scandalum magnatum*.

V. justify, warrant; be an -excuse &c. *n.*- for; lend a colour, furnish a handle; vindicate; ex-, dis-culpate; acquit &c. 970; clear, set right, exonerate, whitewash.

extenuate, palliate, excuse, soften, apologize, varnish, slur, gloze; put a -gloss, – good face- upon; mince; gloss over, bolster up, help a lame dog over a stile.

advocate, defend, plead one's cause; stand –, stick –, speak- up for; contend –, speak- for; bear out, keep in countenance, support; plead &c. 617; say in defence; plead ignorance; confess and avoid, propugn, put in a good word for.

take the will for the deed, make allowance for, do justice to; give -one, – the Devil- his due.

make good; prove -the truth of, – one's case; be justified by the event.

Adj. vindicat-ed, -ing &c. *v.*; vindicat-ive, -ory; palliative; exculpatory; apologetic.

excusable, defensible, pardonable; veni-al, -able; specious, plausible, justifiable.

Phr. '*honi soit qui mal y pense.*'

---

accuser, prosecutor, plaintiff, complainant, petitioner; relator, informer; appellant.

accused, defendant, prisoner, panel, co-, respondent; litigant.

V. accuse, charge, tax, impute, twit, taunt with, reproach.

brand with reproach; stigmatize, slur; cast a -stone at, – slur on; incriminate; inculpate, implicate; call to account &c. (*censure*) 932; take to -blame, – task; put in the black book.

inform against, indict, denounce, arraign; im-, ap-peach; have up, show up, pull up; challenge, cite, lodge a complaint; prosecute, bring an action against &c. 969.

charge –, saddle- with; lay to one's -door, – charge; lay the blame on, bring home to; cast –, throw- in one's teeth; cast the first stone at.

have –, keep- a rod in pickle for; have a crow to pluck with.

trump up a charge.

Adj. accusing &c. *v.*; accusat-ory, -ive; imputative, denunciatory; re-, criminatory.

accused &c. *v.*; suspected; under -suspicion, – a cloud, – *surveillance*; in -custody, – detention; in the -lock up, – watch house, – house of detention.

accusable, imputable; in-defensible, -excusable; un-pardonable, -justifiable; vicious &c. 945.

Int. look at home; *tu quoque* &c. (*retaliation*) 718.

3°. Moral Conditions

939. Probity.—N. probity, integrity, rectitude; uprightness &c. *adj.*; honesty, faith; honour; good faith, *bona fides*; purity, clean hands.

fairness &c. *adj.*; fair play, justice, equity, impartiality, principle; grace.

constancy; faithfulness &c. *adj.*; fidelity, loyalty; incorrupt-ion, -ibility.

trustworthiness &c. *adj.*; truth, candour, singleness of heart; veracity &c. 543; tender conscience &c. (*sense of duty*) 926.

punctil-iousness, -io; delicacy, nicety; scrupul-osity, -ousness &c. *adj.*; scruple; point, – of honour; punctuality.

dignity &c. (*repute*) 873; respectability, -bleness &c. *adj.*; gentleman; man of -honour, – his word; *fidus*

940. Improbity. N. improbity; dishon-esty, -our; deviation from rectitude; disgrace &c. (*disrepute*) 874; fraud &c. (*deception*) 545; lying &c. 544; bad –, Punic- faith; *mala* –, *Punica- fides*; infidelity; faithlessness &c. *adj.*; Judas kiss, betrayal; scrap of paper.

breach of -promise, – trust, – faith; prodition, disloyalty, divided allegiance, treason, high treason; apostasy &c. (*tergiversation*) 607; non-observance &c. 773.

shabbiness &c. *adj.*; villainy; baseness &c. *adj.*; abjection, debasement, turpitude, moral turpitude, laxity, trimming, shuffling.

perfidy; perfidiousness &c. *adj.*;

Achates, *preux chevalier*, *galantuomo*; truepenny, trump, brick; true Briton, white man, sportsman.

court of honour, a fair field and no favour; *argumentum ad verecundiam*.

V. be -honourable &c. *adj.*; deal -honourably, – squarely, – impartially, – fairly; speak the truth &c. (*veracity*) 543; tell the truth and shame the devil, *vitam impendere vero*; show a proper spirit, make a point of; do one's duty &c. 944; play the game.

redeem one's pledge &c. 926; keep –, be as good as- one's -promise, – word; keep faith with, not fail.

give and take, *audire alteram partem*, give the devil his due, put the saddle on the right horse.

redound to one's honour.

Adj. upright; honest, – as daylight; veracious &c. 543; virtuous &c. 944; honourable; fair, right, just, equitable, impartial, even-handed, square; fair –, open- and aboveboard.

constant, – as the northern star; faithful, loyal, staunch; true, – blue, – to one's colours, – to the core, – as the needle to the pole; true-hearted, trust-y, -worthy; as good as one's word, to be depended on, incorruptible.

manly, straightforward &c. (*ingenuous*) 703; frank, candid, open-hearted.

conscientious, tender - conscienced, right-minded; high-principled, -minded; scrupulous, religious, strict; nice, punctilious, correct, punctual; respect-, reput-able; gentlemanlike.

inviol - able, - ate; un - violated, -broken, -betrayed; un-bought, -bribed.

innocent &c. 946; pure; stainless; un-stained, -tarnished, -sullied, -tainted, -perjured; uncorrupt, -ed; unde-filed, -praved, -bauched; *integer vitæ scelerisque purus*; *justus et tenax propositi*.

chivalrous, jealous of honour, *sans peur et sans reproche*; high-spirited.

supra-mundane, unworldly, overscrupulous.

Adv. honourably &c. *adj.*; *bona fide*; on the square, in good faith, honour bright, *foro conscientiæ*, with clean hands; by fair means.

treachery, double-dealing; unfairness &c. *adj.*; knavery, roguery, rascality, foul-play; jobb-ing, -ery; Tammany, graft; venality, nepotism; corruption, job, shuffle, fishy transaction, barratry; sharp practice, heads I win, tails you lose; mouth-honour &c. (*flattery*) 933.

V. be -dishonest &c. *adj.*; play false; break one's -word, – faith, – promise; jilt, betray, forswear; shuffle &c. (*lie*) 544; live by one's wits, sail near the wind; play with marked cards.

disgrace –, dishonour –, demean –, degrade- oneself; derogate, stoop, grovel, sneak, lose caste; sell oneself, go over to the enemy; seal one's infamy.

Adj. dishon-est, -ourable; un-conscientious, -scrupulous; fraudulent &c. 545; knavish; disgraceful &c. (*disreputable*) 874; wicked &c. 945.

false-hearted, disingenuous; unfair, one-sided; double, -tongued, -faced; time-serving, crooked, tortuous, insidious, Machiavellian, dark, slippery; questionable; fishy; perfidious, treacherous, perjured.

infamous, arrant, foul, base, vile, low, ignominious, blackguard.

contemptible, abject, mean, shabby, little, paltry, dirty, scurvy, scabby, sneaking, grovelling, scrubby, rascally, pettifogging; beneath one; not cricket.

low-minded, -thoughted; baseminded.

undignified, indign; unbe-coming, -seeming, -fitting; de-rogatory, -grading; *infra dignitatem*; ungentleman-ly, -like; un-knightly, -chivalric, -manly, -handsome; recreant, inglorious.

corrupt, venal; debased, mongrel.

faithless, of bad faith, false, unfaithful, disloyal; untrustworthy; trust-, troth-less; lost to shame, dead to honour.

Adv. dishonestly &c. *adj.*; *malâ fide*, like a thief in the night, by crooked paths; by foul means.

Int. *O tempora! O mores!*

---

941. Knave.—**N.** knave, rogue, villain; Scapin, rascal; Lazarillo de Tormes: bad man &c. 949; blackguard &c. 949.

traitor, betrayer, arch-traitor, conspirator, stool pigeon, Judas, Catiline; reptile, serpent, snake in the grass, wolf in sheep's clothing, sneak, Jerry Sneak, tell-tale, squealer, mischief-maker, trimmer; renegade &c. (*tergiversation*) 607; truant, recreant; sycophant &c. (*servility*) 886.

942. Disinterestedness.—N. disinterestedness &c. *adj.*; generosity; liberal-ity, -ism; altruism; benevolence &c. 906; elevation, loftiness of purpose, exaltation, magnanimity; chival-ry, -rous spirit; heroism, sublimity.

self-denial, -abnegation, -effacement, -sacrifice, -immolation, -control &c. (*resolution*) 604; stoicism, devotion, martyrdom, *suttee*.

labour of love.

V. be -disinterested &c. *adj.*; make a sacrifice, lay one's head on the block; put oneself in the place of others, do as one would be done by, do unto others as we would men should do unto us.

Adj. disinterested; unselfish; self-denying, -sacrificing, -devoted; generous.

handsome, liberal, noble; noble-, high-minded; princely, great, high, elevated, lofty, exalted, spirited, stoical, magnanimous; great-, large-hearted, chivalrous, heroic, sublime.

un-bought, -bribed; uncorrupted &c. (*upright*) 939.

943. Selfishness.—N. selfishness &c. *adj.*; self-love, -indulgence, -worship, -interest; ego-tism, -ism; egocentrism, narcissism; *amour propre* &c. (*vanity*) 880; nepotism.

worldliness &c. *adj.*; world wisdom.

illiberality; meanness &c. *adj.*

time-server; tuft-, fortune-hunter; self-seeker; jobber, worldling; egotist, egoist, monopolist, nepotist, profiteer; temporizer, trimmer; dog in the manger, charity that begins at home.

V. be -selfish &c. *adj.*; please –, indulge –, coddle- oneself; consult one's own -wishes, – pleasure; look after one's own interest; feather one's nest; take care of number one, have an eye to the main chance, know on which side one's bread is buttered; give an inch and take an ell; wangle.

Adj. selfish; self-seeking, -indulgent, -interested; wrapped up –, centred- in self; egotistic, -al; egoistical; egocentric.

illiberal, mean, ungenerous, narrow-minded; mercenary, venal; covetous &c. 819.

unspiritual; earthly, -minded; mundane; worldly, -minded, -wise; time-serving.

interested; *alieni appetens sui profusus*.

Adv. ungenerously &c. *adj.*; to gain some private ends; from selfish –, interested- motives.

Phr. *après nous le déluge*.

944. Virtue.—N. virtue; virtuousness &c. *adj.*; morality; moral rectitude; integrity &c. (*probity*) 939; nobleness &c. 873.

morals; ethics &c. (*duty*) 926; cardinal virtues.

merit, worth, desert, excellence, credit; self-control &c. (*resolution*) 604; self-denial &c. (*temperance*) 953.

well-doing; good -actions, – behaviour; discharge –, fulfilment –, performance- of duty; well-spent life; innocence &c. 946.

V. be -virtuous &c. *adj.*; practise -virtue &c. *n.*; do –, fulfil –, perform –,

945. Vice.—N. vice; evil -doing, – courses; wrong doing; wickedness, viciousness &c. *adj.*; iniquity, peccability, demerit; sin, Adam; old –, offending- Adam.

immorality, impropriety, indecorum, scandal, laxity, looseness of morals; want of -principle, – ballast; obliquity, backsliding, infamy, demoralization, pravity, depravity, pollution; hardness of heart; brutality &c. (*malevolence*) 907; corruption &c. (*debasement*) 659; knavery &c. (*improbity*) 940; profligacy; lust &c. 961; flagrancy, atrocity; cannibalism.

discharge- one's duty; redeem one's pledge &c. 926; act well, – one's part; fight the good fight; acquit oneself well; command –, master- one's passions; keep -straight, – in the right path.

set -an, – a good- example; be on one's -good, – best- behaviour.

Adj. virtuous, good; innocent &c. 946; meritorious, deserving, worthy, desertful, correct; dut-iful, -eous; moral; right, -eous, -minded; well-intentioned, creditable, laudable, commendable, praiseworthy; above –, beyond- all praise; excellent, admirable; sterling, pure, noble.

exemplary; match-, peer-less; saintly, -like; heaven-born, angelic, seraphic, godlike.

Adv. virtuously &c. *adj.*; *e merito.*

infirmity; weakness &c. *adj.*; weakness of the flesh, frailty, imperfection; error; weak side; foible; fail-ing, -ure; crying –, besetting- sin; defect, deficiency, shortcoming; cloven foot.

lowest dregs of vice, sink of iniquity, Alsatian den; *gusto picaresco.*

fault, crime; criminality &c. (*guilt*) 947.

sinner &c. 949.

V. be -vicious &c. *adj.*; sin, commit sin, do amiss, err, transgress; misdemean –, forget –, misconduct- oneself; mis-do, -behave; fall, lapse, slip, trip, offend, trespass; deviate from the -line of duty, – path of virtue &c. 944; take a wrong course, go astray; hug a -sin, – fault; sow one's wild oats.

render -vicious &c. *adj.*; demoralize, brutalize; corrupt &c. (*degrade*) 659.

Adj.* vicious; sinful; sinning &c. *v.*; wicked, iniquitous, bad, immoral, unrighteous, wrong, criminal; naughty, incorrect; undut-eous, -iful.

unprincipled, lawless, disorderly, *contra bonos mores*, indecorous, unseemly, improper; dissolute, profligate, scampish; unworthy; worth-, desert-less; disgraceful, recreant; reprehensible, blameworthy, uncommendable; dis-creditable, -reputable.

base, sinister, scurvy, foul, gross, vile, black, grave, facinorous, felonious, nefarious, shameful, scandalous, infamous, villainous, of a deep dye, heinous; flag-rant, -itious; atrocious, incarnate, accursed.

Mephistophelian, satanic, diabolic, hellish, infernal, stygian, fiend-ish, -like, hell-born, demoniacal, devilish.

mis-created, -begotten; demoralized, corrupt, depraved.

evil-minded, -disposed; ill-conditioned; malevolent &c. 907; heart-, grace-, shame-, virtue-less; abandoned, lost to virtue; unconscionable; sunk –, lost –, deep –, steeped- in iniquity.

incorrigible, irreclaimable, obdurate, reprobate, past praying for; culpable, reprehensible &c. (*guilty*) 947.

unjustifiable; in-defensible, -excusable; inexpiable, unpardonable, irremissible.

weak, frail, lax, infirm, imperfect, indiscreet; demoralizing, degrading.

Adv. wrong; sinfully &c. *adj.*; without excuse.

Int. *O tempora! O mores!*

946. Innocence. — **N.** innocence; guiltlessness &c. *adj.*; incorruption, impeccability.

clean hands, clear conscience, *mens sibi conscia recti.*

innocent, new born babe, lamb, dove.

V. be -innocent &c. *adj.*; *nil conscire sibi nullâ pallescere culpâ.*

947. Guilt.—**N.** guilt, -iness; culpability; crimin-ality, -ousness; deviation from rectitude &c. (*improbity*) 940; sinfulness &c. (*vice*) 945; peccability.

mis-conduct, -behaviour, -doing, -deed; malpractice, fault, sin, error, transgression; dereliction, delinquency; indiscretion, lapse, slip, trip, *faux pas,*

* Most of these adjectives are applicable both to the act and to the agent.

acquit &c. 970; exculpate &c. (*vindicate*) 937.

Adj. innocent, not guilty; unguilty; guilt-, fault-, sin-, stain-, blood-, spotless; clear, immaculate; *rectus in curiâ*; un-spotted, -blemished, -erring; undefiled &c. 939; unhardened, Saturnian; Arcadian &c. (*artless*) 703.

in-, un-culpable; unblam-ed, -able; blameless, inerrable, above suspicion; irrepr-oachable, -ovable, -ehensible; un-exceptionable, -objectionable, -impeachable; salvable; venial &c. 937.

harmless; in-offensive, -noxious, -nocuous; dove-, lamb-like; pure, harmless as doves; innocent as -a lamb, – the babe unborn; more sinned against than sinning.

virtuous &c. 944; un-reproved, -impeached, -reproached.

Adv. innocently &c. *adj.*; with clean hands; with a -clear, – safe- conscience.

948. Good Man. — **N.** good man, worthy.

good woman, goddess, *madonna*, virgin.

model, paragon &c. (*perfection*) 650; good example; hero, demigod, seraph, angel; innocent &c. 946; saint &c. (*piety*) 987; benefactor &c. 912; philanthropist &c. 910; Aristides.

brick, trump, rough diamond, ugly duckling.

salt of the earth; one in ten thousand; one of the best.

Phr. *si sic omnes!*

---

peccadillo; flaw, blot, omission; fail-ing, -ure.

offence, trespass; mis-demeanour, -feasance, -prision; tort; mal-efaction, -feasance, -versation; crime, felony.

enormity, atrocity, outrage; deadly –, mortal –, unpardonable- sin; died without a name.

corpus delicti.

Adj. guilty, to blame, culpable, peccable, in fault, censurable, reprehensible, blameworthy, uncommendable, illaudable; weighed in the balance and found wanting; exceptionable, objectionable.

Adv. *in flagrante delicto*; red-handed, in the very act.

---

949. Bad Man.—**N.** bad man, wrongdoer, worker of iniquity; evil-doer &c. 913; sinner; the -wicked &c. 945; bad example.

rascal, scoundrel, villain, miscreant, caitiff; wretch, reptile, viper, serpent, cockatrice, basilisk, urchin; tiger, monster; devil &c. (*demon*) 980; devil incarnate; demon in human shape, Nana Sahib; hell-hound, -cat; rake-hell.

bad woman, jade, Jezebel, adultress, &c. 962.

scamp, scapegrace, rip, runagate, ne'er-do-well, reprobate, *roué*, rake; limb; one who has sold himself to the devil, fallen angel, *âme damnée*, *vaurien*, *mauvais sujet*, loose fish, sad dog; lost –, black- sheep; castaway, recreant, defaulter; prodigal &c. 818; libertine &c. 962.

rough, rowdy, ugly customer, ruffian, hoodlum, bully; Jonathan Wild; hangman; incendiary; thief &c. 792; murderer &c. 361.

culprit, delinquent, criminal, malefactor, misdemeanant; felon; convict, jail-bird, ticket-of-leave man; outlaw.

blackguard, *polisson*, loafer, sneak; raps-, ras-callion; cullion, mean wretch, varlet, kern, *âme-de-boue*, *drôle*; cur, dog, hound, whelp, mongrel; lown, loon, runnion, outcast, vagabond; rogue &c. (*knave*) 941; scum of the earth, riff-raff; *Arcades ambo*.

Int. sirrah!

950. Penitence.—**N.** penitence, contrition, compunction, repentance, remorse; regret &c. 833.

self-reproach, -reproof, -accusation,

951. Impenitence.—**N.** impenitence, irrepentance, recusance.

hardness of heart, seared conscience, induration, obduracy.

-condemnation, -humiliation; stings –, pangs –, qualms –, prickings –, twinge –, twitch –, touch –, voice- of conscience; compunctious visitings of nature.

acknowledgment, confession &c. (*disclosure*) 529; apology &c. 952; recantation &c. 607; penance &c. 952; resipiscence.

awakened conscience, deathbed repentance, *locus pœnitentiæ*, stool of repentance, cutty stool.

penitent, Magdalen, prodigal son, returned prodigal, a sadder and a wiser man.

V. repent, be sorry for; be -penitent &c. *adj.*; rue; regret &c. 833; think better of; recant &c. 607; knock under &c. (*submit*) 725; plead guilty; sing -*miserere*, – *de profundis*; cry *peccavi*; own oneself in the wrong; acknowledge, confess &c. (*disclose*) 529; humble oneself; beg pardon &c. (*apologize*) 952; turn over a new leaf, put on the new man, turn from sin; reclaim; repent in sackcloth and ashes &c. (*do penance*) 952; learn by experience.

Adj. penitent; repenting &c. *v.*; repentant, contrite; conscience-smitten, -stricken; self-accusing, -convicted.

penitenti-al, -ary; chastened, reclaimed; not hardened; unhardened.

Adv. *meâ culpâ*.

Phr. *peccavi*; *erubuit*; *salva res est*; *vous l'avez voulu, Georges Dandin*.

V. be -impenitent &c. *adj.*; steel –, harden- the heart; die -game, – and make no sign.

Adj. impenitent, uncontrite, obdurate; hard, -ened; seared, recusant; unrepentant; relent-, remorse-, grace-, shrift-less.

lost, incorrigible, irreclaimable.

unre-claimed, -formed; unrepented, unatoned.

---

952. Atonement.—N. atonement, reparation; compromise, composition; compensation &c. 30; quittance, quits; indemni-ty, -fication; expiation, redemption, reclamation, conciliation, propitiation.

amends, apology, *amende honorable*, satisfaction; peace –, sin –, burnt- offering; scapegoat, sacrifice.

penance, fasting, maceration, sackcloth and ashes, white sheet, shrift, flagellation, lustration; purga-tion, -tory.

V. atone, – for; expiate; propitiate; make -amends, – good; reclaim, redeem, repair, ransom, absolve, purge, shrive, do penance, stand in a white sheet, repent in sackcloth and ashes.

set one's house in order, wipe off old scores, make matters up; pay the -forfeit, – penalty.

apologize, beg pardon, express regret, *faire amende honorable*, give satisfaction; come –, fall- down on one's -knees, – marrow bones.

Adj. propitiatory, expiatory; sacrific, -ial, -atory; piacul-ar, -ous.

4°. Moral Practice

953. Temperance.—N. temperance moderation, sobriety, soberness.

forbearance, abnegation; self-denial, -restraint, -control &c. (*resolution*) 604.

frugality; vegetarianism, teetotalism, total abstinence, prohibition; abst-inence, -emiousness, asceticism &c. 955; system of -Pythagoras, – Cornaro; Pythagorism, Stoicism.

954. Intemperance.—N. intemperance; sensuality, animalism, carnality; pleasure; effeminacy, silkiness; luxur-y, -iousness; lap of -pleasure, – luxury.

indulgence; high-, free- living, inabstinence, self-indulgence; voluptuousness &c. *adj.*; epicur-ism, -eanism; sybaritism.

vegetarian; Pythagorean, gymnosophist; teetotaler &c. 958; abstainer.

V. be -temperate &c. *adj.*; abstain, forbear, refrain, deny oneself, spare; know when one has had enough; take the pledge; look not upon the wine when it is red.

Adj. temperate, moderate, sober, frugal, sparing; abst-emious, -inent; within compass; measured &c. (*sufficient*) 639.

Pythagorean; vegetarian; teetotal, pussy-foot.

---

dissipation; licentiousness &c. *adj.*, debauchery; crapulence.

revel-s, -ry; debauch, carousal, jollification, drinking bout, wassail, Saturnalia, orgies; excess, too much; intoxication &c. 959.

Circean cup; drug habit &c. 663.

V. be -intemperate &c. *adj.*; indulge, exceed; live -well, – high, – on the fat of the land; give a loose to -indulgence &c. *n.*; dine not wisely but too well; wallow in -voluptuousness &c. *n.*; plunge into dissipation.

revel, rake, live hard, run riot, sow one's wild oats; slake one's -appetite, – thirst; swill; pamper.

Adj. intemperate, inabstinent, intoxicated &c. 959; sensual, self-indulgent; voluptuous, luxurious, licentious, wild, dissolute, rakish, fast, debauched.

brutish, crapulous, swinish, piggish, porcine, hoggish, bestial.

Paphian, Epicurean, Sybaritical; bred –, nursed- in the lap of luxury; indulged, pampered, full-fed.

954a. Sensualist.—N. Sybarite, voluptuary, Sardanapalus, man of pleasure, carpet knight; epicure, -an; *gourm-et, -and*; gormandizer, gutling, glutton, pig, hog; votary –, swine- of Epicurus; sensualist; Heliogabalus; free –, hard- liver; libertine &c. 962; hedonist.

955. Asceticism.—N. asceticism, puritanism, sabbatarianism; cynicism, austerity; total abstinence.

mortification, maceration, sackcloth and ashes, flagellation; penance &c. 952; fasting &c. 956; martyrdom.

ascetic; anchor-et, -ite; martyr; *Heautontimorumenos*; hermit &c. (*recluse*) 893; puritan, sabbatarian, cynic.

Adj. ascetic, austere, puritanical; cynical; over-religious.

956. Fasting. — N. fasting; xerophagy; famishment, starvation; banting.

fast, *jour maigre*; fast –, banyan-day; Lent, quadragesima; Rama-dan, -zan; spare –, meagre- diet; lenten -diet, – entertainment; *soupe maigre*, short -rations, – commons; Barmecide feast; hunger strike.

V. fast, starve, clem, famish, perish with hunger; dine with Duke Humphrey; make two bites of a cherry.

Adj. lenten, quadragesimal; unfed; starved &c. *v.*; half-starved; fasting &c. *v.*; hungry &c. 865.

---

957. Gluttony.—N. gluttony; greed; greediness &c. *adj.*; voracity.

epicurism; good –, high- living; edacity, gulosity, crapulence; gutt-, guzz-ling; over-indulgence.

good cheer, blow out; feast &c. (*food*) 298; gastronomy.

epicure, *bon vivant*, *gourmand*; glutton, cormorant, hog, belly-god, Apicius, gastronome, gormandizer.

V. gormandize, gorge; over-gorge, -eat- oneself; engorge, eat one's fill, cram, stuff, stodge, glut, satiate; gutt-le, guzz-le; bolt, devour, gobble up; gulp &c. (*swallow food*) 298; raven, eat out of house and home.

have the stomach of an ostrich; play a good knife and fork &c. (*appetite*) 865.

pamper, indulge.

Adj. gluttonous, greedy; gormandizing &c. *v.*; edacious, omnivorous, crapulent, swinish, voracious, devouring.

pampered; over-fed, -gorged.

958. Sobriety.—N. sobriety; teetotalism, temperance &c. 953.

water-drinker; teetotal-er, -ist; abstainer, Good Templar, Rechabite, band of hope; prohibitionist, pussyfoot.

V. take the pledge.

Adj. sober, – as a judge; dry, on the water wagon.

959. Drunkenness.—N. drunkenness &c. *adj.*; intemperance; drinking &c. *v.*; inebri-ety, -ation; ebri-ety, -osity; befuddlement; insobriety; intoxication; temulency, bibacity, wine-bibbing; com-, potation; deep potations, bacchanals, *bacchanalia*, libations.

oino-, dipso-mania; *delirium tremens*, d.t.; alcohol, -ism.

drink; alcoholic drinks, alcohol, booze; gin, blue ruin, grog, brandy, port wine; punch, -bowl; cup, rosy wine, flowing bowl; drop, – too much; dram; beer, wine, spirits &c. (*beverage*) 298; cocktail, nip, peg; stirrup cup.

drunkard, sot, toper, tippler, bibber, wine-bibber; hard –, gin –, dram- drinker; soak, soaker, sponge, tun; love-, toss-pot; thirsty soul, reveller, carouser; Bacchanal, -ian; Bacch-al, -ante; devotee to Bacchus, dipsomaniac.

V. get –, be- drunk &c. *adj.*; see double; take a -drop, – glass- too much; drink, tipple, tope, booze, bouse, guzzle, swill, soak, sot, lush, bib, swig, carouse; sacrifice at the shrine of Bacchus; take to drinking; drink -hard, – deep, – like a fish; have one's swill, drain the cup, splice the main brace, take a hair of the dog that bit you.

liquor, – up; wet one's whistle, take a whet; lift one's elbow; crack a –, pass the- bottle; toss off &c. (*drink up*) 298; go to the -ale, – public-house.

make one -drunk &c. *adj.*; inebriate, fuddle, fuzzle, get into one's head.

Adj. drunk, tipsy; intoxicated; inebri-ous, -ate, -ated; in one's cups; in a state of -intoxication &c. *n.*; temulent, -ive; fuddled, mellow, cut, boosy, fou, fresh, merry, elevated, squiffy; plastered, befuddled, sozzled; flush, -ed; flustered, disguised, groggy, beery; topheavy; pot-valiant, glorious; potulent; over-come, -taken; whittled, screwed, tight, primed, oiled, corned, raddled, sewed up, lushy, nappy, muddled, muzzy, bosky, obfuscated, maudlin; crapulous, dead –, blind- drunk.

inter pocula; in –, the worse for- liquor, having had a drop too much, half seas over, three sheets in the wind; under the table, blind to the world, one over the eight.

drunk as -a piper, – a fiddler, – a lord, – Chloe, – an owl, – David's sow, – a wheelbarrow.

drunken, bibacious, bibulous, sottish; given –, addicted- to -drink, – the bottle; toping &c. *v.*; wet.

Phr. *nunc est bibendum.*

960. Purity.—N. purity; decency, decorum, delicacy; continence, chastity, honesty, virtue, modesty, shame; pudicity, *pucelage*, virginity.

vestal, virgin, Joseph, Hippolytus; Lucretia, Diana; prude.

961. Impurity.—N. impurity; uncleanness &c. (*filth*) 653; immodesty; grossness &c. *adj.*; indelicacy, indecency; impudicity; obscenity, ribaldry, smut, bawdry, *double entendre*, *équivoque*; Aretinism; pornography.

Adj. pure, undefiled, modest, delicate, decent, decorous; *virginibus puerisque*; chaste, continent, virtuous, honest, Platonic.

---

concupiscence, lust, carnality, flesh, salacity; pruriency, lechery, lascivi-ency, lubricity, lewdness.

incontinence, intrigue, *faux pas*; *amour*, *-ette*; gallantry; debauchery, libertinism, *libertinage*, fornication; *liaison*; wenching, venery, dissipation.

seduction; defloration, defilement, abuse, violation, rape; incest.

social evil, harlotry, stupration, whoredom, concubinage, cuckoldom, adultery, advoutry, *crim. con.*; free love.

seraglio, harem, zenana; brothel, bagnio, stew, bawdy-house, *lupanar*, house of ill fame, *bordel*, kip.

V. be -impure &c. *adj.*; intrigue; debauch, defile, assault, attack, seduce; prostitute; abuse, violate, deflower; commit -adultery &c. *n.*

Adj. impure; unclean &c. (*dirty*) 653; not to be mentioned to ears polite; immodest, shameless; in-decorous, -delicate, -decent; loose, suggestive, *risqué*, coarse, gross, broad, free, equivocal, smutty, fulsome, ribald, obscene, bawdy, pornographic.

concupiscent, prurient, lickerish, rampant, lustful; carnal, -minded; lewd, lascivious, lecherous, libidinous, erotic, ruttish, salacious; Paphian; voluptuous; incestuous.

unchaste, light, wanton, licentious, adulterous, debauched, dissolute; of -loose character, - easy virtue; frail, gay, riggish, incontinent, meretricious, rakish, gallant, dissipated; no better than she should be; on the -town, - streets, - *pavé*, - loose.

adulterous, incestuous, bestial.

962. Libertine.—N. libertine; voluptuary &c. 954*a*; rake, debauchee, loose fish, rip, rake-hell, fast man; *intrigant*, gallant, seducer, fornicator, lecher, satyr, goat, whoremonger, *paillard*, adulterer, gay deceiver, Lothario, Don Juan, Bluebeard.

adulteress, advoutress, courtesan, prostitute, strumpet, tart, hustler, chippy, broad, harlot, whore, punk, *fille de joie*; woman, - of the town; street-walker, Cyprian, miss, piece; frail sisterhood, fallen woman; demirep, wench, trollop, trull, baggage, hussy, drab, bitch, jade, skit, rig, quean, mopsy, slut, minx, harridan; woman -of easy virtue &c. (*unchaste*) 961; wanton, fornicatress; Jezebel, Messalina, Delilah, Thaïs, Phryne, Aspasia, Lais, *lorette, cocotte, petite dame, grisette*; *demi-mondaine*; white slave.

concubine, mistress, fancy woman, kept woman, doxy, *chère amie*, *bona roba*.

pimp; pand-er, -ar; bawd, *conciliatrix*, procuress, mackerel; wittol.

5°. Institutions

963. Legality.—N. legality; legitimacy, -teness, legitimization.

legislature; law, code, *corpus juris*, constitution, pandect, charter, act, enactment, statute, rule; canon &c. (*precept*) 697; ordinance, institution, regulation; by-, bye-law, rescript; decree &c. (*order*) 741; *ordonnance*;

964. [Absence or violation of law.] **Illegality.**—N. lawlessness; breach -, violation- of law; disobedience &c. 742; unconformity &c. 83.

arbitrariness &c. *adj.*; antinomy, violence, brute force, despotism, outlawry.

mob -, lynch -, club -, Lydford -,

standing order; *plébiscite* &c. (*choice*) 609.

legal process; form, -ula, -ality; rite; arm of the law; *habeas corpus*.

[Science of law] jurisprudence, nomology; legislation, codification.

equity, common law; *lex* –, *lex non-scripta*, unwritten law; law of nations, international law, *jus gentium*; *jus civile*; civil –, criminal –, canon –, statute –, ecclesiastical- law; *lex mercatoria*.

constitutional-ism, -ity; justice &c. 922.

V. legalize, legitimize; enact, ordain; decree &c. (*order*) 741; pass a law; legislate; codify, formulate; authorize.

Adj. legal, legitimate; according to law; vested, constitutional, chartered, legalized; lawful &c. (*permitted*) 760; statut-able, -ory; legislat-orial, -ive.

Adv. legally &c. *adj.*; in the eye of the law; *de jure*.

martial –, drumhead- law; *coup d'état*; *le droit du plus fort*; *argumentum ad baculum*.

illegality, informality, unlawfulness, illegitimacy, bar sinister.

trover and conversion; smuggling, boot-legging, rum-running, poaching; simony.

speakeasy, speakie, blind pig.

V. offend against –, violate- the law; set the law at defiance, ride rough-shod over, drive a coach and six through a statute; make the law a dead letter, take the law into one's own hands.

smuggle, run, poach.

Adj. illegal; prohibited &c. 761; not allowed, unlawful, illegitimate, illicit, contraband, actionable.

unchartered, unconstitutional; unwarrant-ed, -able; unauthorized; informal, unofficial; in-, extra-judicial.

lawless, arbitrary; despotic, -al; summary, irresponsible; un-answerable, -accountable.

null and void; a dead letter.

Adv. illegally &c. *adj.*; with a high hand, in violation of law.

965. Jurisdiction. [Executive.]—**N.** jurisdiction, judicature, administration of justice, soc; executive, commission of the peace; magistracy &c. (*authority*) 737.

judge &c. 967; tribunal &c. 966; municipality, corporation, bailiwick, shrievalty; lord lieutenant; lord –, mayor, city manager, alderman &c. 745; sheriff, bailie, shrieve, chief –, constable; police, – force; constabulary, bumbledom.

officer; proctor, high –, commissioner; bailiff, tipstaff, bum-bailiff, catchpoll, beadle; police-man, -constable, -sergeant; *sbirro*, *alguazil*, *gendarme*, kavass, *lictor*, macebearer, *huissier*, bedel.

press-gang; exciseman, gauger, custom-house officer, *douanier*.

coroner, edile, ædile, portreeve, paritor; *posse comitatus*.

V. judge, sit in judgment.

Adj. executive, administrative, municipal; inquisitorial, causidical; judic-atory, -iary, -ial; juridical.

Adv. *coram judice*.

966. Tribunal.—**N.** tribunal, court, board, bench, judicatory, curia; court of -justice, – law, – arbitration; inquisition; guild.

justice –, judgement –, mercy- seat; woolsack; bar, – of justice; dock; forum, hustings, *bureau*, drum-head; jury-, witness-box.

senate-house, town-hall, theatre; House of -Lords, – Commons.

assize, eyre; ward-, burgh-mote; superior courts of Westminster; court of -record, – oyer and terminer, – assize, – appeal, – error; High court of -Judicature, – Appeal; Judicial Committee of the Privy Council; Star-Chamber; Court of -Chancery, – King's *or* Queen's Bench, – Exchequer, – Common Pleas, – Probate, – Arches, – Admiralty, – Criminal Appeal; Lords Justices' –, Rolls –, Vice-Chancellor's –,

Stannary –, Divorce –, Palatine –, ecclesiastical –, county –, police-court; sessions; quarter –, petty- sessions; court -leet, – baron, – of pie poudre, – of common council; board of green cloth.

court-martial; drum-head court-martial; *durbar*, divan; Areopagus; *rota*.

Adj. judicial &c. 965; appellate; curial.

967. Judge.—N. judge; justi-ce, -ciar, -ciary; chancellor; justice –, judge- of assize; recorder, common serjeant; puisne –, assistant –, county court- judge; conservator –, justice- of the peace, J.P.; court &c. (*tribunal*) 966; grand –, petty –, coroner's- jury; panel, juror, juryman; twelve men in a box; magistrate, police magistrate, stipendiary, the great unpaid, beak; his -worship, – honour, – lordship; deemster, moderator.

Lord -Chancellor, – Justice; Master of the Rolls, Vice-Chancellor; Lord Chief -Justice, – Baron; Mr. Justice; Baron, – of the Exchequer.

jurat, assessor; arbi-ter, -trator; umpire; refer-ee, -endary; revising barrister; domesman; censor &c. (*critic*) 480; official –, receiver.

archon, tribune, prætor, *ephor*, syndic, *podestà*, mullah, ulema, mufti, cadi, kadi; Rhadamanthus.

litigant &c. (*accusation*) 938.

V. adjudge &c. (*determine*) 480; try a -case, – prisoner.

Adj. judicial &c. 965. **Phr.** 'a Daniel come to judgment.'

968. Lawyer.—N. lawyer, jurist, legist, civilian, pundit, publicist, jurisconsult, legal adviser, advocate; barrister, – at law; counsel, -lor; King's *or* Queen's counsel; K.C.; Q.C.; silk gown, leader; junior, – counsel; stuff gown, serjeant-at-law, bencher; tubman; judge &c. 967.

bar, legal profession, gentleman of the long robe; junior –, outer –, inner- bar; Inns of Court; equity draftsman, conveyancer, pleader, special pleader.

solicitor, attorney, proctor; notary, – public; scrivener, cursitor; writer, – to the signet; S.S.C.; limb of the law; pettifogger.

V. practise -at, – within- the bar; plead; call –, be called- -to, – within- the bar; take silk.

Adj. learned in the law; at the bar; forensic.

969. Lawsuit.—N. lawsuit, suit, action, cause, petition; litigation; dispute &c. 713.

citation, arraignment, prosecution, impeachment; accusation &c. 938; presentment, true bill, indictment.

apprehension, arrest; committal; imprisonment &c. (*restraint*) 751.

writ, summons, subpœna, -*duces tecum*, *latitat*, *nisi prius*; *habeas corpus*.

pleadings; declaration, bill, claim; *procès-verbal*, bill of right, information, *corpus delicti*; affidavit, state of facts; answer, replication, plea, demurrer, rebutter, rejoinder; surre-butter, -joinder.

suitor, party to a suit; litigant &c. 938; libellant.

hearing, trial; verdict &c. (*judgment*) 480; appeal, – motion; writ of error; *certiorari*.

case, decision, precedent, ruling; decided case, reports.

V. go to –, appeal to the- law; bring to -justice, – trial, – the bar; put on trial, pull up; accuse &c. 938; prefer –, file- a claim &c. *n.*; take the law of, inform against.

serve with a writ, cite, apprehend, arraign, sue, prosecute, bring an action against, indict, impeach, attach, distrain, commit; arrest; summon, -s; give in charge &c. (*restrain*) 751.

empanel a jury, implead, join issue; close the pleadings; set down for hearing.

try, hear a cause; sit in judgment; adjudicate &c. 480.

Adj. litigious &c. (*quarrelsome*) 713; *qui tam*; *coram –, sub- judice*.

Adv. *pendente lite*.

Phr. *adhuc sub judice lis est*.

970. Acquittal. — N. acquit-tal, -ment; clearance, exculpation, exoneration; discharge &c. (*release*) 750; *quietus*, absolution, compurgation, reprieve, respite; pardon &c. (*forgiveness*) 918.

[Exemption from punishment] impunity, immunity.

V. acquit, exculpate, exonerate, clear; absolve, whitewash, assoil, discharge, release; liberate &c. 750.

reprieve, respite; pardon &c. (*forgive*) 918; let off, – scot free.

Adj. acquitted &c. *v.*; un-condemned, -punished, -chastised; recommended to mercy.

971. Condemnation.—N. condemnation, conviction, proscription, damnation; death warrant; penalty &c. 974.

attain-der, -ture, -tment.

V. condemn, convict, cast, bring home to, find guilty, damn, doom, sign the death warrant, sentence, pass sentence on, attaint, confiscate, proscribe, sequestrate; non-suit.

disapprove &c. 932; accuse &c. 938.

stand condemned.

Adj. condem-, dam-natory; condemned &c. *v.*; non-suited &c. (*failure*) 732; self-convicted.

Phr. *mutato nomine de te fabula narratur*.

972. Punishment. — N. punishment, punition; chast-isement, -ening; correction, castigation.

discipline, infliction, trial; judgement; penalty &c. 974; retribution; thunderbolt, Nemesis; requital &c. (*reward*) 973; penology; retributive justice.

lash, scaffold &c. (*instrument of punishment*) 975; imprisonment &c. (*restraint*) 751; chain gang; transportation, banishment, expulsion, deportation, exile, involuntary exile, ostracism; penal servitude, hard labour; galleys &c. 975; beating &c. *v.*; flagellation, fustigation, ga-ntlet, *strappado, estrapade, bastinado, argumentum ad baculum*, stick law, rap on the knuckles, box on the ear; blow &c. (*impulse*) 276; stripe, cuff, kick, buffet, pummel; slap, – in the face; wipe, douse; *coup de grâce*; torture, rack; picket, -ing; *dragonnade*; capital punishment, extreme penalty; execution; hanging &c. *v.*; de-capitation, -collation; *garrotte*; electrocution, lethal chamber; crucifixion, impalement; martyrdom, *auto-da-fé*; *noyade*; *hara-kiri*, happy despatch.

V. punish; chast-ise, -en; castigate, correct, inflict punishment, administer correction, deal retributive justice.

visit upon, pay; pay –, serve- out; settle with, get even with, get one's own back; do for; make short work of, give a lesson to, strafe, serve one right, make an example of; have a rod in pickle for; give it one.

strike &c. 276; deal a blow to, administer the lash, smite; slap, – the face; smack, cuff, box the ears, spank, thwack, thump, beat, lay on, swinge, buffet; thresh, thrash, pummel, drub, leather, trounce, baste, belabour; lace, – one's jacket; dress, give a -dressing, – down; trim, warm, wipe, tund, cob, bang, strap, comb, lash, lick, larrup, whallop, whop, flog, scourge, whip, birch, cane, give the stick, switch, flagellate, horsewhip, *bastinado*, towel, rub down with an oaken towel, rib roast, dust one's jacket, fustigate, pitch into, lay about one, beat black and blue; beat to a -mummy, – jelly; give a black eye; hit on the head; sandbag.

tar and feather; pelt, stone, lapidate; mast-head, keelhaul.

execute; bring to the -block, – gallows; behead; de-capitate, -collate; guillotine; hang, turn off, gibbet, bowstring, hang, draw and quarter; shoot; decimate; burn; electrocute; break on the wheel, crucify; em-, im-pale; flay; lynch; put to death.

torture; put -on, – to- the rack; picket.

banish, exile; trans-, de-port; expel, ostracize; rusticate; drum out; dismiss, -bar, -bench; strike off the roll, unfrock; post.

suffer, – for, – punishment; be -flogged, – hanged &c.; come to the gallows, dance upon nothing, die in one's shoes; be rightly served.

Adj. punishing &c. *v.*; penal; puni-tory, -tive; inflictive, castigatory; punished &c. *v.*

Int. *à la lanterne!*

973. Reward.—N. reward, recompense, remuneration, prize, meed, guerdon, reguerdon; indemni-ty, -fication, price; quittance; compensation; reparation, *ersatz*, assythment, redress; retribution, reckoning, acknowledgment, requital, amends, sop; atonement; consideration, return, *quid pro quo*; salvage, perquisite; vail &c. (*donation*) 784; *douceur*, bribe, bait, baksheesh, tip; hush-, smart-money; blackmail; carcelage; *solatium*.

allowance, salary, stipend, wages; pay, -ment; emolument; tribute; batta, shot, scot; premium, fee, *honorarium*; hire.

crown &c. (*decoration of honour*) 877.

V. re-ward, -compense, -pay, -quite; re-, munerate; compensate; fee, tip, bribe; pay one's footing &c. (*pay*) 807; make amends, indemnify, atone; satisfy, acknowledge.

get for one's pains, reap the fruits of.

Adj. remunerat-ive, -ory; munerary, compensatory, retributive, reparatory.

974. Penalty.—N. penalty; retribution &c. (*punishment*) 972; pain, pains and penalties; *peine forte et dure*; penance &c. (*atonement*) 952; the devil to pay.

fine, mulct, amercement; forfeit, -ure; escheat, damages, deodand, sequestration, confiscation, *premunire*.

V. penalize, fine, mulct, amerce, sconce, confiscate; sequest-rate, -er; escheat; estreat, forfeit.

975. [Instrument of punishment.] **Scourge.—N.** scourge, rod, cane, stick; ra-, rat-tan; birch, – rod; rod in pickle; switch, ferule, cudgel, truncheon; rubber hose.

whip, lash, strap, thong, cowhide, knout; cat, – o'-nine-tails, *sjambok*, quirt; rope's end.

pillory, stocks, whipping-post; cuck-, duck-ing stool; brank; triangle, wooden horse, maiden, thumbscrew, boot, rack, wheel, iron heel; treadmill, crank, galleys.

scaffold; block, axe, *guillotine*; stake; cross; gallows, gibbet, Tyburn tree; drop, noose, rope, halter, bowstring; electric chair, lethal chamber.

house of correction &c. (*prison*) 752.

gaol-, jail-er; executioner; hang-, heads-man; Jack Ketch; lyncher.

Section V. RELIGIOUS AFFECTIONS

1°. Superhuman Beings and Regions

976. Deity.—N. Deity, Divinity; God-head, -ship; Omnipotence, Providence.

[Quality of being divine] divin-eness, -ity.

God, Lord, Jehovah, *Deus*; The -Almighty, – Supreme Being, – First Cause; *Ens Entium*; Author –, Creator- of all things; Author of our being; The -Infinite, – Eternal; The All-powerful, -wise, -merciful, -holy; The Omni-potent, -scient.

[Attributes and perfections] infinite -power, – wisdom, – goodness, – justice, – truth, – love, – mercy; omni-potence, -science, -presence; unity, immutability, holiness, glory, majesty, sovereignty, infinity, eternity.

The -Trinity, – Holy Trinity, – Trinity in Unity, – Triune God; Three in One and One in Three.

God the Father; The -Maker, – Creator, – Preserver.

[Functions] creation, preservation, divine government; The-ocracy, -archy; providence; ways –, dealings –, dispensations –, visitations- of Providence.

God the Son, Jesus, Christ; The -Messiah, – Anointed, – Saviour, – Redeemer, – Mediator, – Intercessor, – Advocate, – Judge; The Son of -God, – Man, – David; The Only Begotten; The Lamb of God, The Word; Em-, Im-manuel; The -King of Kings and Lord of Lords, – King of Glory, – Prince of Peace, – Good Shepherd, – Way, – Truth, – Life, – Bread of Life, – Light of the World; The -Lord our, – Sun of- Righteousness.

The -Incarnation, – Hypostatic Union, – Word made Flesh.

[Functions] salvation, redemption, atonement, propitiation, mediation, intercession, judgment.

God the Holy Ghost, The Holy Spirit, Paraclete; The -Comforter, – Consoler, – Spirit of Truth, – Dove.

[Functions] inspiration, unction, regeneration, sanctification, consolation.

eon, æon, special providence, *Deus ex machinâ*; *Avatar*.

V. create, uphold, preserve, govern &c.

atone, redeem, save, propitiate, mediate &c.

predestinate, elect, call, ordain, bless, justify, sanctify, glorify &c.

Adj. almighty, holy, hallowed, sacred, divine, heavenly, celestial; messianic; sacrosanct; all-powerful, -wise, -seeing, -knowing; omnipotent, omniscient; supreme.

super-human, -natural; ghostly, spiritual, hyperphysical, unearthly; the-istic, -ocratic, deistic; anointed.

Adv. *jure divino*, by divine right; *Deo volente*, D.V.

977. [Beneficent spirits.] **Angel.—N.** angel, archangel; heavenly host, choir invisible, host of heaven, sons of God; Michael, Gabriel &c.; seraph, -im; cherub, -im; ministering spirit, morn-

978. [Maleficent spirits.] **Satan.—N.** Satan, the Devil, Lucifer, Ahrimanes, Belial; Sammael, Zamiel, Beelzebub, the Prince of the Devils; Mephistopheles, his satanic majesty.*

* The slang expressions 'the -deuce, – dickens, – old Gentleman; old -Nick, – Scratch, – Horny, – Harry, – Gooseberry,' have not been inserted in the text.

ing star; saint, *Madonna*; Our Lady, the Blessed Virgin, the Virgin Mary.

Adj. angelic, seraphic, cherubic.

---

the tempter; the evil -one, – spirit; the -author of evil, – wicked one, – old Serpent; the Prince of -darkness, – this world, – the power of the air; the -foul, – arch- fiend; the devil incarnate; the -common enemy, – angel of the bottomless pit; Abaddon, Apollyon, Mammon.

fallen angels, unclean spirits, devils; the -rulers, – powers- of darkness; inhabitants of Pandemonium; demon &c. 980.

diabolism; devil-ism, -ship, -dom, -ry, -worship; *diablerie*; satanism, manicheism; the cloven foot; black magic &c. 992.

Adj. satanic, diabolic, devilish, infernal, hell-born.

*Heathen, Mythological and other fabulous Deities and Powers**

979. Jupiter.—N. god, -dess; heathen gods and goddesses; Pantheon; Jupiter, Jove, Zeus, Apollo, Mars, Mercury, Neptune, Vulcan, Bacchus, Pluto, Saturn, Cupid, Eros, Pan; Juno, Ceres, Proserpina, Diana, Minerva, Pallas Athene, Venus, Aphrodite, Vesta; The Fates &c. 601.

Allah, Brahma, Vishnu, Siva, Shiva, Krishna, Juggernaut, Buddha; Ra, Isis, Osiris; Belus, Bel, Baal, Asteroth &c.; Thor, Odin; Mumbo Jumbo; good –, tutelary- genius; demiurge, familiar, – spirit; Sibyl; fairy, fay; sylph, -id; Ariel, peri, nymph, nereid, dryad, oread, sea-maid, Banshee, Benshie, Ormuzd; Oberon, Titania, Mab, hamadryad, naiad, mermaid, kelpie, Ondine, nix, nixie, sprite; denizens of the air; pixy &c. (*bad spirit*) 980.

mythology; heathen –, fairy- mythology; Lemprière, folklore.

Adj. fairy-, sylph-like; sylphic.

---

980. Demon.—N. demon, -ry, -ism, -ology; evil genius, fiend, familiar, – spirit, devil; bad –, unclean- spirit; cacodemon, incubus, Frankenstein's monster, succubus and succuba, Titan, Shedim, Mephistopheles, Asmodeus, Moloch, Belial, Ahriman, fury, The Furies &c. 900; harpy; Friar Rush.

vampire, ghoul; af-, ef-freet; afrite; ogre, -ss; gnome, gin, djinn, imp, deev, *lamia*; bo-gie, -gle; nis, kobold, flibbertigibbet, fairy, brownie, pixy, elf, dwarf, urchin, Puck, Robin Goodfellow; lepre-, cluri-chaune; troll, dwerger, sprite, oaf, changeling, bad fairy, nixe, pigwidgeon, Will-o'-the-wisp; Erl King.

[Supernatural appearance] ghost, spectre, apparition, genie, spirit, shade, shadow, vision, phantom &c. 443; materialization (*spiritualism*) 992; hob-, goblin; wraith, spook, werwolf, boggart, banshee, *loup-garou*, *lemures*; evil eye.

nisse, necks; mer-man, -maid, -folk; siren, Lorelei; satyr, faun.

Adj. supernatural, weird, uncanny, unearthly, spectral; ghost-ly, -like; elf-in, -like; fiend-ish, -like; impish, demoniacal; haunted.

981. Heaven.—N. heaven; kingdom of -heaven, – God; heavenly kingdom; throne –, presence- of God; inheritance of the saints in light.

Paradise, Eden, abode of the blessed; Holy City, New Jerusalem; celestial bliss, glory.

[Mythological -heaven] Olympus; [– paradise] Elysium, Elysian fields, Arcadia, bowers of bliss, garden of the Hesperides, Islands of the Blessed;

982. Hell.—N. hell, bottomless pit, place of torment; habitation of fallen angels; Pandemonium, Abaddon, Domdaniel.

hell fire; everlasting -fire, – torment; lake of fire and brimstone; fire that is never quenched, worm that never dies.

purgatory, limbo, gehenna, abyss.

[Mythological hell] Tartarus, Hades, Avernus, Styx, Stygian creek, pit of Acheron, Cocytus, Phlegethon, Lethe;

* Only a selection of those best known to literature is included.

happy hunting-ground; third –, seventh- heaven; Valhalla (Scandinavian); Nirvana (Buddhist).

future state, eternity, eternal life, life after death, eternal home, resurrection, translation; resuscitation &c. 660; apotheosis, deification.

Adj. heavenly, celestial, supernal, unearthly, from on high, paradisiacal, beatific, elysian, Olympian, Arcadian.

infernal regions, *inferno*, shades below, realms of Pluto.

Pluto, Rhadamanthus, Erebus, Charon, Cerberus; Tophet.

Adj. hellish, infernal, stygian.

2°. Religious Doctrines

983. [Religious Knowledge.] **Theology.**—**N.** Theology (natural and revealed); Theo-gony, -sophy; Divinity; Hagio-logy, -graphy; Caucasian mystery; monotheism; religion; religious -persuasion, – sect, – denomination; cult; creed &c. (*belief*) 484; articles –, declaration –, profession –, confession- of faith.

theolog-ue, -ian; divine, schoolman, canonist, monotheist.

Adj. theological, religious; canonical; denominational; sectarian &c. 984.

983a. Orthodoxy.—**N.** orthodoxy; strictness, soundness, religious truth, true faith; truth &c. 494.

Christian-ity, -ism; Catholic-ism, -ity; 'the faith once delivered to the saints'; hyperorthodoxy &c. 984; iconoclasm.

the Holy –, the Orthodox- Church; Catholic –, Universal –, Apostolic –, Established- Church; temple of the Holy Ghost; Church –, body –, members –, disciples –, followers- of Christ; Christian, – community; true believer; canonist &c. (*theologian*) 983; Christendom, collective body of Christians, the Church Militant.

canons &c. (*belief*) 484; thirty-nine articles; Apostles' –, Nicene –, Athanasian- Creed; Church Catechism; textuary.

Adj. orthodox, sound, literal, strict, faithful, catholic, schismless, Christian, evangelical, scriptural, divine, monotheistic; true &c. 494.

High –, Low –, Broad –, Free- Church; ultramontanism; monasticism; pap-ism, -istry; papacy; Anglican-, Catholic-, Roman-ism; popery, Scarlet Lady, Church of Rome, Greek Church; Christian Science, The Church of Christ Scientist.

---

984. Heterodoxy. [Sectarianism.]—**N.** heterodoxy; error &c. 495; false doctrine, heresy, schism; schismatic-ism, -alness; recusancy, backsliding, apostasy; atheism &c. (*irreligion*) 989.

bigotry &c. (*obstinacy*) 606; fanaticism, iconoclasm; hyperorthodoxy, precisianism, bibliolatry, hagiolatry, sabbatarianism, puritanism; idolatry &c. 991; superstition &c. (*credulity*) 486; dissent &c. 489.

sectar-ism, -ianism; nonconformity; secularism; syncretism, religious sects; the clash of creeds.

protestant-, advent-, Arian-, Erastian-, Calvin-, quaker-, method-, anabapt-, Pusey-, tractarian-, ritual-, Origen-, Sabellian-, Socinian-, De-, The-, mon-, material-, positiv-, latitudinarian-ism &c.

pagan-, heathen-, ethic-ism; mythology; animism; poly-, di-, tri-, pantheism; dualism; heathendom.

Juda-, Gentil-, Mahometan-, Islam-, Turc-, Brahmin-, Hindoo-, Buddh-, Lama-, Confucian-, Shinto-, Sabian-, Gnostic-, Soofee-, Hylothe-, Mormonism.

Theosophy; Spiritualism, Occultism.

heretic, antichrist; pagan, heathen; pai-, pay-nim; *giaour*; gentile; pan-, poly-theist; idolator; misbeliever, apostate, backslider.

bigot &c. (*obstinacy*) 606; fanatic, dervish, abdal, iconoclast.

latitudinarian, limitarian, Deist, Theist, Unitarian; positivist, materialist; agnostic, skeptic &c. 989.

schismatic; sectar-y, -ian, -ist; seceder, separatist, recusant, dissenter; non-conformist, -juror; Huguenot, Protestant; orthodox dissenter, Congregationalist, Independent; Episcopalian, Presbyterian; Lutheran, Calvinist, Quaker, Methodist, Wesleyan; Ana-, Baptist; Dunker; Mormon, Latter-day Saint, Irvingite, Sandemanian, Glassite, Erastian; Sub-, Supra-lapsarian; Gentoo, Antinomian, Swedenborgian, Adventist, Plymouth Brother; Theosophist &c.

Catholic, Roman Catholic, Romanist, papist, ultramontane; Old Catholic, tractarian, Anglican, Puseyite, ritualist; Puritan.

Jew, Hebrew, Rabbist; Mahometan, Mohammedan, Mussulman, Moslem, Islamite, Osmanli; Brahm-in, -an; Parsee, Sofi, Soofee; Buddhist; Zoroastrian, Magi, Gymnosophist, fire-worshipper, Sabian, Gnostic, Sadducee, Rosicrucian &c.

Adj. heterodox, heretical; un-orthodox, -scriptural, -canonical; antiscriptural, apocryphal; un-, anti-christian; schismatic, recusant, iconoclastic; sectarian; dis-senting, -sident; secular &c. (*lay*) 997.

pagan; heathen, -ish; ethnic, -al; gentile, painim; pan-, polytheistic; agnostic, skeptic.

Judaical, Mohammedan, Moslem, Brahminical, Buddhist &c. *n.*; Romish, Protestant &c. *n.*

bigoted &c. (*prejudiced*) 481, (*obstinate*) 606; superstitious &c. (*credulous*) 486; fanatical; idolatrous &c. 991; visionary &c. (*imaginative*) 515.

985. Revelation.—N. revelation, inspiration, *afflatus*.

Word, – of God; Scripture; the -Scriptures, – Bible, – Book of Books; Holy -Writ, – Scriptures; inspired writings, Gospel.

Old Testament, Septuagint, Vulgate, Pentateuch; Octateuch; the -Law, – Jewish Law, – Prophets; major –, minor- Prophets; Hagio-grapha, -logy; Hierographa; Apocrypha.

New Testament; Gospels, Evangelists, Acts, Epistles, Apocalypse, Revelations.

Talmud; Mishna, Masorah.

prophet &c. (*seer*) 513; evangelist, apostle, disciple, saint; the –, the Apostolical- fathers; Holy Men of old, inspired -writers, – penmen.

Adj. scriptural, biblical, sacred, prophetic; evangel-ical, -istic; apostolic, -al; inspired, theopneustic, apocalyptic, ecclesiastical, canonical, textuary.

986. Pseudo-Revelation.*—N. the -Koran, – Alcoran; Ly-king, Shaster, Vedas, Zendavesta, Vedidad, Purana, Edda; Go-, Gau-tama; Book of Mormon.

[False prophets and religious founders] Buddha, Zoroaster, Zerdhusht, Confucius, Mahomet.

[Idols] golden calf &c. 991; Baal, Moloch, Dagon.

* See note on page 378.

3°. Religious Sentiments

987. Piety.—N. piety, religion, theism, faith; religiousness, holiness &c. *adj.*; saintship; religionism; sanctimony &c. (*assumed piety*) 988; reverence &c. (*respect*) 928; humility, veneration, devotion; prostration &c. (*worship*) 990; grace, unction, edification; sancti-ty, -tude; consecration.

spiritual existence, odour of sanctity, beauty of holiness.

theopathy, beatification, adoption, regeneration, conversion, justification, sanctification, salvation, inspiration, bread of life; Body and Blood of Christ.

believer, convert, theist, Christian, devotee, pietist; the -good, – righteous, – just, – believing, – elect; Saint, *Madonna*.

the children of -God, – the kingdom, – light.

V. be -pious &c. *adj.*; have -faith &c. *n.*; believe, receive Christ; revere &c. 928; worship &c. 990; be -converted &c.

convert, edify, sanctify, hallow, keep holy, beatify, regenerate, inspire, consecrate, enshrine.

Adj. pious, religious, devout, devoted, reverent, godly, heavenly minded, humble; pure, – in heart; holy, spiritual, pietistic; saint-ly, -like; seraphic, sacred, solemn.

believing, faithful, Christian, Catholic.

elected, adopted, justified, sanctified, regenerated, inspired, consecrated, converted, unearthly, not of the earth.

988. Impiety.—N. impiety; sin &c. 945; irreverence; profan-eness &c. *adj.*, -ity, -ation; blasphemy, desecration, sacrilege; scoffing &c. *v.*

[Assumed piety] hypocrisy &c. (*falsehood*) 544; pietism, cant, pious fraud; lip-devotion, -service, -reverence; misdevotion, formalism, austerity; sanctimon-y, -iousness &c. *adj.*; pharisaism, precisianism; sabbat-ism, -arianism; *odium theologicum*, sacerdotalism; bigotry &c. (*obstinacy*) 606, (*prejudice*) 481.

hardening, backsliding, declension, perversion, reprobation, apostasy, recusancy.

sinner &c. 949; scoffer, blasphemer; sacrilegist; worldling; hypocrite &c. (*dissembler*) 548; Scribes and Pharisees; Tartufe, Maw-worm.

bigot; saint [ironically]; Pharisee, sabbatarian, formalist, methodist, puritan, pietist, precisian, religionist, devotee, ranter, fanatic, wowser.

the -wicked, – evil, – unjust, – reprobate; son of -men, – Belial, – the wicked one; children of darkness.

V. be -impious &c. *adj.*; profane, desecrate, blaspheme, revile, scoff; swear &c. (*malediction*) 908; commit sacrilege.

snuffle; turn up the whites of the eyes; idolize.

Adj. impious; irreligious &c. 989; desecrating &c. *v.*; profane, irreverent, sacrilegious, blasphemous.

un-hallowed, -sanctified, -regenerate; hardened, perverted, reprobate.

hypocritical &c. (*false*) 544; canting, pietistical, sanctimonious, unctuous, pharisaical, over-righteous, righteous over much.

bigoted, fanatical &c. 481 & 606; priest-ridden.

Adv. under the -mask, cloak, – pretence, – form, – guise- of religion.

989. Irreligion.—N. irreligion, indevotion; ungodliness &c. *adj.*; laxity, quietism, apathy, indifference, passivity.

scepticism, doubt; un-, dis-belief; incredul-ity, -ousness &c. *adj.*; want of -faith, – belief; pyrrhonism; doubt &c. 485; agnosticism.

atheism, deism; hylotheism; materialism; positivism; nihilism.

infidelity, freethinking, antichristianity, rationalism.

atheist, anti-christian, sceptic, unbeliever, deist, infidel, pyrrhonist; *giaour*, heathen, alien, gentile, Nazarene; *esprit fort*, freethinker, latitudinarian, rationalist; materialist, positivist, nihilist, agnostic.

V. be -irreligious &c. *adj.*; disbelieve, lack faith; doubt, question &c. 485.

dechristianize; serve Mammon, love darkness better than light.

Adj. irreligious; in-, un-devout; devout-, god-, grace-less; ungodly, -holy, -sanctified, -hallowed; atheistic, without God.

sceptical, free-thinking; un-believing, -converted; incredulous, faithless, lacking faith; deistical; un-, anti-christian.

worldly, mundane, earthly, carnal, unspiritual; worldly &c.-minded.

Adv. irreligiously &c. *adj.*

4°. Acts of Religion

990. Worship.—N. worship, adoration, devotion, aspiration, latria, homage, service, humiliation; kneeling, genuflexion, prostration.

prayer, invocation, supplication, rogation, intercession, orison, holy breathing; petition &c. (*request*) 765; collect, litany, Lord's prayer, paternoster, *Ave Maria*, rosary; bead-roll; latria, dulia, hyperdulia, vigils; revival; cult.

thanksgiving; giving –, returning- thanks; grace, praise, glorification, benediction, doxology, hosanna; h-, allelujah; *Te Deum*, *non nobis Domine*, *nunc dimittis*; pæan.

psalm, -ody; hymn, plainsong, chant, chaunt, response, anthem, motet; antiphon, -y.

oblation, sacrifice, incense, libation; burnt –, votive –, thank-offering; offertory, collection.

discipline; self-discipline, -examination, -denial; fasting.

divine service, office, duty; morning prayer; mass, matins, evensong, vespers, compline; holy day &c. (*rites*) 998.

worshipper, congregation, communicant, celebrant.

V. worship, lift up the heart, aspire; revere &c. 928; adore, do service, pay homage; humble oneself, kneel; bow –, bend- the knee; fall -down, – on one's knees; prostrate oneself, bow down and worship, recite the rosary.

pray, invoke, supplicate; put –, offer- up -prayers, – petitions; beseech &c. (*ask*) 765; say one's prayers, tell one's beads.

return –, give- thanks; say grace, bless, praise, laud, glorify, magnify, sing praises; give benediction, lead the choir, intone, chant, sing.

propitiate, offer sacrifice, fast, deny oneself; vow, offer vows, give alms.

work out one's salvation; go to church; attend -service, – mass; communicate &c. (*rite*) 998.

Adj. worshipping &c. *v.*; devout, devotional, reverent, pure, solemn; fervid &c. (*heartfelt*) 821.

Int. h-, allelujah! hosanna! glory be to God! O Lord! pray God that! God -grant, – bless, – save, – forbid! *sursum corda.*

991. Idolatry.—N. idol-atry, -ism; demon-ism, -olatry; idol –, demon –, devil –, fire- worship; zoolatry, fetishism, Mari-, Bibli-, ecclesi-, heli-olatry.

deification, apotheosis, canonization; hero worship.

sacrifices, hecatomb, holocaust; human sacrifices, immolation, mactation, infanticide, self-immolation, *suttee*.

idol, golden calf, graven image, fetish, *avatar*, Juggernaut, joss, *lares et penates*; Baal &c. 986.

idolater &c. *n.*

V. worship -idols, – pictures, – relics; put on a pedestal, bow down to, prostrate oneself before, make sacrifice to; deify, canonize, idolize.

Adj. idolatrous.

992. Sorcery.—N. sorcery; superstition; occult -art, – sciences; black –, magic; the black art, necromancy, theurgy, thaumaturgy; demon-ology, -omy, -ship; *diablerie*, bedevilment; witch-craft, -ery; glamour; fetis-hism, -ism; ghost dance; hoodoo, voodoo; Shamanism [Esquimaux], vampirism; conjuration; bewitchery, exorcism, enchantment, incantation, obsession, possession, mysticism, second sight, mesmerism, animal magnetism; od –, odylic- force; electro-biology, *clairvoyance*; spiritualism, spirit-rapping, table-turning; thought reading, telepathy, thought transference, automatic writing, *planchette*, ouija board; crystal gazing; spirit manifestation, materialization, astral body, ectoplasm &c.

divination &c. (*prediction*) 511; sortilege, ordeal, *sortes Virgilianæ*, *-biblicæ*, hocus-pocus &c. (*deception*) 545; oracle &c. 513.

V. practice -sorcery &c. *n.*; cast a -horoscope, – nativity; conjure, exorcise, charm, enchant; be-witch, -devil; overlook, look on with the evil eye; entrance, mesmerize, magnetize; fascinate &c. (*influence*) 615; taboo; wave a wand; rub the -ring, – lamp; cast a spell; call up spirits, – from the vasty deep; raise spirits from the dead; raise –, lay- ghosts; command genii.

Adj. magic, -al; mystic, weird, cabalistic, talismanic, phylacteric, incantatory; charmed &c. *v.*

993. Spell.—N. spell, charm, incantation, exorcism, weird, cabala, exsufflation, cantrap, runes, abracadabra, hocus-pocus, open *sesame*, counter-charm, Ephesian letters, bell, book and candle, Mumbo Jumbo, evil-eye, fee-faw-fum.

talisman, amulet, periapt, telesm, phylactery, philtre, wish-bone, merry-thought, mascot, scarab, swastika; fetish; *agnus Dei*.

wand, caduceus, rod, divining rod, lamp of Aladdin, magic carpet, seven-league boots; magic ring; wishing –, Fortunatus's- cap.

994. Sorcerer.—N. sorcerer, magician; thaumat-, the-urgist; conjuror, necromancer, seer, wizard, witch; fairy &c. 980; *lamia*, hag, warlock, charmer, exorcist, voodoo, mage, diviner, dowser; cunning –, medicine- man, witch doctor; Shaman, figure-flinger, ecstatica, medium, *clairvoyant*, mesmerist, hypnotist; *deus ex machinâ*; astrologer; soothsayer &c. 513.

Katerfelto, Cagliostro, Merlin, Comus, Mesmer, Rosicrucian; Hecate, Circe, Lilith, siren, weird sisters; witch of Endor.

5°. Religious Institutions

995. Churchdom.—N. church, -dom; ministry, apostleship, priesthood, prelacy, hierarchy, church government, christendom, pale of the church.

clerical-, sacerdotal-, episcopalian-, ultramontan-ism; Theocracy; ecclesiolog-y, -ist; priestcraft, *odium theologicum*.

monach-ism, -y; monasticism, monkhood.

[Ecclesiastical offices and dignities] pontificate, primacy, archbishopric, archiepiscopacy; prelacy; bishop-ric, -dom; episcop-ate, -acy; see, diocese; deanery, stall; canon-ry, -icate; prebend, -aryship; benefice, incumbency, glebe, advowson, living, cure, – of souls; rectorship; vicar-iate, -ship; pastor-ate, -ship; deacon-ry, -ship; -curacy; chaplain, -cy, -ship; cardinal-ate, -ship; abbacy, presbytery.

holy orders, ordination, institution, consecration, induction, reading in, preferment, translation, presentation.

popedom, papacy; the -Vatican, – apostolic see, – see of Rome; religious sects &c. 984.

council &c. 696; conclave, college of cardinals, convocation, synod, consistory, chapter, vestry, presbytery; sanhedrim, *congé d'élire*; ecclesiastical courts, consistorial court, court of Arches.

V. call, ordain, induct, prefer, translate, consecrate, present, elect, bestow.

take -orders, – the veil, – vows.

Adj. ecclesi-astical, -ological; clerical, sacerdotal, priestly, prelatical, pastoral, ministerial, capitular, theocratic; hierarchical, archiepiscopal; episcopal, -ian; canonical; mon-astic, -achal; monkish; abbati-al, -cal; pontifical, papal, apostolic; ultramontane, priest-ridden.

996. Clergy.—N. clergy, clericals, ministry, priesthood, presbytery, the cloth, the pulpit.

clergyman, divine, ecclesiastic, churchman, priest, presbyter, hierophant, pastor, shepherd, minister, clerk in holy orders; father, – in Christ; *padre, abbé, curé*; patriarch; reverend; black coat; confessor; sky pilot.

dignitaries of the church; ecclesi-, hier-arch; eminence, reverence, elder, primate, metropolitan, archimandrite, archbishop, bishop, prelate, diocesan, suffragan, dean, subdean, archdeacon, prebendary, canon, rural dean, rector, parson, vicar, perpetual curate, residentiary, beneficiary, incumbent, chaplain, curate, – in charge; deacon, -ess; preacher; lay reader, lecturer; capitular; missionary, propagandist, Jesuit, revivalist, field preacher.

churchwarden, sidesman; clerk, precentor, choir; almoner, *suisse*, verger, beadle, sexton, sacristan; acol-yth, -othyst, -yte; thurifer; chorister, choir boy.

[Roman Catholic priesthood] Pope, *Papa*, Holy Father, pontiff, high priest, cardinal; ancient –, flamen; confessor, penitentiary; spiritual director.

cenobite, conventual, abbot, prior, monk, friar, lay brother, beadsman, mendicant, pilgrim, palmer; canon-regular, -secular; Jesuit, Franciscan, Friars minor, Minorites; Observant, Capuchin, Dominican, Carmelite; Augustinian; Gilbertine; Austin-, Black-, White-, Grey-, Crossed-, Crutched-Friars; Bonhomme, Carthusian, Benedictine, Cistercian, Trappist, Cluniac, Premonstratensian, Maturine; Templar, Hospitaller.

997. Laity.—N. laity, flock, fold, congregation, assembly, brethren, people.

temporality, secularization.

layman, civilian; parishioner, catechumen; secularist.

V. secularize.

Adj. secular, lay, laical, civil, temporal, profane.

abb-, prior-, canon-ess; mother superior; *religieuse*, nun, sister, *béguine*, novice, postulant.

[Under the Jewish dispensation] prophet, priest, high priest, Levite; Rabbi, -n; scribe.

[Mohammedan &c.] mullah, ulema, imaum, sheik; so-fi, -phi; mufti, hadji, muezzin, dervish; fa-kir, -quir; brahmin, gooroo, druid, bonze, santon, abdal, Lama, talapoin, caloyer &c.

V. take orders &c. 995.

Adj. the –, the very –, the Right- Reverend; ordained, in orders, called to the ministry.

998. Rite.—N. rite; ceremon-y, -ial; ordinance, observance, function, duty; form, -ulary; solemnity, sacrament; incantation &c. (*spell*) 993; service, psalmody &c. (*worship*) 990; liturgies.

ministration; preach-ing, -ment; predication, sermon, homily, exhortation, lecture, discourse, pastoral.

baptism, christening, chrism, immersion; baptismal regeneration; font; circumcision.

confirmation; imposition –, laying on- of hands; churching, purification, ordination &c. (*churchdom*) 995; excommunication.

Eucharist, Lord's supper, communion; the –, the holy- sacrament; celebration, high celebration; *missa cantata*; offertory; introit; consecration; con-, tran-substantiation; real presence; elements, bread and wine; mass; high –, low –, dry- mass.

matrimony &c. 903; burial &c. 363; visitation of the sick.

seven sacraments, impanation, extreme unction, last rites, *viaticum*, invocation of saints, canonization, transfiguration, auricular confession; fasting; maceration, flagellation, sackcloth and ashes; penance &c. (*atonement*) 952; absolution; telling of beads, reciting the rosary, processional; thurification, incense, holy water, aspersion.

relics, rosary, beads, reliquary, host, cross, rood, crucifix, pax, pix, pyx, *agnus Dei*, censer, thurible, patera, urceole; chalice, patten, Holy Grail, sangrail; seven-branch candle stick, monstrance, sacring bell.

ritual, rubric, canon, ordinal; liturgy, prayer-book, book of common prayer, pietas, euchology, litany, lectionary; missal, breviary, massbook, bead-roll.

psalter; psalm –, hymn- book; hymn-al, -ology; psalmody.

ritual-, ceremonial-ism; sabbat-ism, -arianism; ritualist, sabbatarian.

holyday, feast, fast; Sabbath, Passover, Pentecost; Advent, Christmas, Noël, Epiphany, Lent, Shrove Tuesday, Ash Wednesday, Maundy Thursday; Passion –, Holy- week; Good Friday, Easter, Ascension Day, Whitsuntide; Trinity Sunday, Corpus Christi; All-Saints' –, – Souls'- Day; Candle-, Lam-, Martin-, Michael-mas; hogmanay; Rama-dan, -zan; Bairam &c. &c.

V. perform service, do duty, minister, officiate, baptize, dip, sprinkle; confirm, lay hands on; give –, administer –, take –, receive –, attend –, partake of- the -sacrament, – communion; communicate; celebrate mass; administer –, receive- extreme unction; anele, shrive, absolve, confess; do penance; genuflect; cross oneself, make the sign of the cross.

excommunicate, ban with bell, book and candle.

preach, sermonize, predicate, lecture.

Adj. ritual, -istic; ceremonial, liturgic; baptismal, eucharistical; paschal.

999. Canonicals.—N. canonicals, vestments; robe, gown, Geneva gown, frock, pallium, surplice, cassock, dalmatic, scapulary, cope. scarf, tunicle, chasuble, alb, *alba*, stole; fan-on, -nel; tonsure, cowl, hood; calo-te, -tte; bands; capouch, amice, orarium, ephod; apron, lawn sleeves, pontificals, pall; mitre, tiara, triple crown; shovel –, cardinal's-hat; biretta; crosier; pastoral staff; costume &c. 225.

1000. Temple.—N. place of worship; house of -God, – prayer.

temple, cathedral, minster, church, kirk, chapel, meeting-house, bethel, tabernacle, conventicle, *basilica*, fane, holy place, chantry, oratory.

synagogue; mosque; marabout; pantheon; pagoda; joss-house; dagobah, tope; kiosk.

parsonage, rectory, vicarage, manse, deanery, glebe, church house; Vatican; bishop's palace; Lambeth.

altar, shrine, sanctuary, Holy of Holies, *sanctum sanctorum*, sacrarium, -isty; communion –, holy –, Lord's- table; table of the Lord; pyx; baptistery, font; piscina, stoup; aumbry; sedile; reredos; rood-loft, – screen; jube.

chancel, quire, choir, nave, aisle, transept, lady chapel, vestry, crypt, cloisters, porch; triforum, clerestory, churchyard, *golgotha*, calvary, Easter sepulchre; stall, pew, sitting; pulpit, ambo, lectern, reading-desk, confessional, prothesis, credence, baldachin, *baldacchino*; jesse, apse, belfry; chapter-house; presbytery.

monastery, priory, abbey, friary, convent, nunnery, cloister.

Adj. claustral, cloistered; monast-ic, -erial; conventual.

INDEX

N.B.: The numbers refer to the headings under which the words or phrases occur. When the same word or phrase may be used in various senses, the several headings under which it, or its synonyms, will be found, according to those meanings, are indicated by the words printed in Italics. These words in Italics are not intended to explain the meaning of the word or phrase to which they are annexed, but only to assist in the required reference.

When the word given in the Index is itself the title or heading of a category, the number of reference is printed in blacker type, thus: abode **189.**

A

A 1 642, 648
a – fortiori 33
– se 10
à – fond 52
– outrance, 52
plomb 212
– propos *relative* 9
apt 23
occasion 134
– propos de bottes 10
A.B. 269
ab – extra 220
– initio 66
– intra 221
– ovo 66
– ovo usque ad mala 52
– uno disce omnes 16
abacist 85
aback 235
take – 508
abacus 85
Abaddon 978, 982
abaft 235
abalienate 783
abandon
depart from 293
- *a purpose* 624
relinquish 757
- *property* 782
- *hope* 859
- *society* 893
abandon
lively 682
artless 703
abandoned
neglected 460
forsaken 893
vicious 945
abase 308, 879
abased 886
abasement 874, 886
abash *daunt* 860
humiliate 879
abate *lessen* 36
– *a price* 813
abatjour 260
abattis 717
abattoir 361
abba 166
abbacy 995
abbatial 995
abbatis 717
abbess 996
abbey 1000
abbot 996
abbreviation 201, 596
A B C *beginning* 66
teaching 537
letters 561
abdal *fanatic* 984
clergy 996
abdicate
- *a throne* 738
resign 757
abditory 530
abdomen 191, 221
abducent 289
abduct *take* 789
steal 791
repel 289
abeam 236
abecedarian 540, 541
abecedary
school 542
letter 561
aberrant
exceptional 83
deviating 279
divergent 291
erroneous 495
aberration [*see* aberrant]
variation 20*a*
mental - 503
abet 707
abettor 711
abeyance
extinction 2
suspense 142
expectation 507
in – 172
abhor 867, 898
abhorrent 830
abide *endure* 106
remain 110
continue 141, 143
dwell 186
quiet 265
expect 507
not – 867
– by 488, 772
– with 826
abigail 746
abilities, to the best of one's – 686
ability 157, 698
abiogenesis 161
abject
vile 874, 940
servile 886
– fear 862
abjure 607, 757, 780
ablation 38, 789
ablaze 382, 420
able 157, 698
– seaman 269
able-bodied 159
ablegate 185, 759
ablepsy 442
ablude 15
ablution 652
abnegation
denial 536
refusal 764
forbearance 953
self – 942
abnormal 83, 568
– mind 503
abnormis sapiens 498
aboard *present* 186
ship 273
go – 293
abode **189**
presage 511
take up one's – 150, 184
abodement 511
abois, aux –
dying 360
danger 665
difficulty 704
abolish 162, 756
abominable
bad 649
foul 653
hateful 898
abominate 867, 898
abord 894
aboriginal 66, 153
aborigines 188
aborticide 361
abortion 674, 732
abound 639
about *relative to* 9
nearly 32
near 197
around 227
be – *busy with* 625
active 682
beat – 629

come – 658
get – *public* 531
recover 660
go – *turn* 311
going – *news* 532
not know what one is – 699
put –
turn round 283
round – 311
send – one's business 756
set – 676
turn – *invert* 218
what it is – 454
what one is – 625
– it and about it 573
– to 121
– to be 152
above 206
– all 33, 642
– board
manifest 525
artless 703
fair 939
– comprehension 519
– ground 359
– the mark 33
– par 31, 648
– praise 944
– price 814
– stairs 206
– suspicion 946
– water *safe* 664
above-mentioned
preceding 62
repeated 104
prior 116
abracadabra 993
Abraham,
sham – 544
abrasion
paring 38
filing 330, 331
abreast 216, 236
abreption 789
abri 666
– tente d' – 223
abridge *lessen* 36
shorten 201
- *in writing* 572, 596
abridgment
compendium 596
abroach 673
abroad
extraneous 57
distant 196
uncertain 475
get – *public* 531
abrogation 756
abrupt *sudden* 113
violent 173
steep 217
unexpected 508
style 579
abruption 44
abscess 655
abscissa 466
abscission
retrenchment 38
division 44
abscond
escape 623
not pay 808
absence 187
– of choice 609*a*
– of influence 175*a*
– of intellect 450*a*
– of mind 458
– of motive 615*a*
absentee 187
absinthe 298
absolute
not relative 1
great 31
complete 52
certain 474
affirmative 535
authoritative 737
severe 739
free 748
unalienable 924
make – 467, 480
– interest 780
absolution 998
absolutism 737
absolve
liberate 750
forgive 918
exempt 927*a*
shrive 952
acquit 970
absonant 414, 477
absorb *combine* 48
take in 296
consume 677
– the mind 457, 458
– the soul 824
– ed in thought 451
absorbing 630, 821, 829
absquatulate 623
abstain 623
disuse 678
temperance 953
– from action 681
– from voting 609*a*
abstainer 953, 958
abstemious 953
absterge 652
abstersive 662
abstinence [*see* abstain]
total – 953, 955
abstract
separate 44
abridge 596
take 789
steal 791
in the – *apart* 44
alone 87
– idea 453
– oneself
inattention 458
– thought 451
attention 457
abstracted
inattentive 458
abstruse 519
absurdity
impossible 471
nonsense 497
ridiculous 853
abundant *great* 31, 52
enough 639
abundanti cautelâ, ex – 664
abuse *deceive* 545
ill-treat 649
misuse 679
malediction 908
threat 909
upbraid 932
violate 961
– of language 563
– of terms 523
abusive 895, 934
abut *near* 197 *touch* 199, 215
abutment 717
aby *remain* 141
endure 821, 826
abysmal *deep* 208
abyss *space* 180
depth 208
interval 198
danger 667
hell 982
A.C. 106
academic
teaching 537, 542
theory 514
academical
style 578
academicals
robes 225
academician 492
Royal – 559
academy 542
acanthus 847
a capite ad calcem 52
acariâtre 901
acarpous 169
acatalectic 597
acaudal 38
accede 488, 725, 762
accelerate
early 132
stimulate 173
velocity 274
hasten 684
accension 384
accent *sound* 402
tone of voice 580
rhythm 597
accentuate 642
accentuated 580
accept *assent* 488
consent 762
receive 785
take 789
acceptable 646, 829
acceptance 771
acceptation 522
acception 522
access 286
easy of – 705
means of – 627
accessible 470, 705
accession
adjunct 39
increase 35
addition 37
- *to office* 737, 755
consent 762
accessory
extrinsic 6
additive 37
adjunct 39
accompanying 88
aid 707
auxiliary 711
acciaccatura 413
accidence 567
accident *event* 151
chance 156
disaster 619
misfortune 735
fatal – 361
accidental
extrinsic 6
fortuitous 156
undesigned 621
accidents,
trust to the chapter of – 621

accipient 785
acclamation
assent 488
approbation 931
acclimatize 370, 613
acclivity 217
accloy 641
accolade 894
accommodate
suit 23
adjust 27
aid 707
reconcile 723
give 784
lend 787
– oneself to 82
accommodation
space 180
accommodating
kind 906
accompaniment
adjunct 39
coexistence **88**
musical 415
accompany
add 37
coexist 88
concur 120
music 416
accompli, fait – 729
accomplice 711
accomplish
execute 161
complete 729
succeed 731
accomplishment
490, 698
accompts 811
accord
uniform 16
agree 23
music 413
assent 488
concord 714
grant 760
give 784
of one's own – 602
according
– as *qualification* 469
– to *evidence* 467
– to circumstances 8
– to law 963
– to rule
conformably 82
– rumour 527
accordingly
logically 476
accordion 417
accost 586
accoucheur 631, 662
accouchement 161
account *list* 86
adjudge 480
description 594
credit 805
money - 811
fame 873
approbation 931
call to – 932
find one's – in
useful 644
success 731
make no – of 483, 930
not – for 519
on – of *motive* 615
behalf 707
on no – 536
send to one's – 361
take into – 457, 469
small – 643
to one's – 780
turn to –
improve 658
use 677
success 731
gain 775
– as *deem* 484
– book 551
– for 155, 522
– with 794, 807
accountable
liable 177
debit 811
duty 926
accountant 801, 811
certified public – 811
accounts **811**
accouple 43
accoutred
armed 717
accoutrement
dress 225
appliance 633
equipment 673
accoy 174
accredit
commission 755, 759
money 805
honour 873
accredited 484, 613
– to 755, 759
accretion 35, 46
accrimination 938
accroach 789
accrue *add* 37
result 154
acquire 775
be received 785, 810
accubation 213
accueil 894
accultural 658
accumbent 213
accumulate
collect 72
store 636
redundance 641
accurate 494
– knowledge 490
accurse 908
accursed
disastrous 649
undone 828
vicious 945
accusation **938**
accuse
disapprove 932
charge 938
lawsuit 969
accustom 613
ace *small* 32
unit 87
within an – 197
aceldama *kill* 361
arena 728
acephalous 59
acerbate 659, 835
acerbity
acrimony 395
sourness 397
rudeness 895
spleen 900, 901
malevolence 907
acervate 72
acetous 397
acetylene 388
acharné 900
Achates, fidus – 890, 939
ache *physical* 378
mental 828
Acheron
pit of – 982
Acherontic
moribund 360
gloomy 837
achievable 470
achieve *end* 67
produce 161
do 680
accomplish 729
achievement 551, 861
Achilles, heel of –
vulnerable 665
achromatism **429**
acicular 253
acid 397
acid test 463
acknowledge
answer 462
assent 488
disclose 529
avow 535
consent 762
observe 772
pay 807
thank 916
repent 950
reward 973
acknowledged
custom 613
acme 210
– of perfection 650
Acology 662
acolyte 996
acomous 226
aconite 663
acoustic 418
– organs 418
acoustics 402
acquaint
– oneself with 539
– with 527
acquaintance
knowledge 490
information 527
friend 890
make – with 888
acquiesce
assent 488
willing 488
consent 762
tolerate 826
acquire
develop 161
get 775
receive 785
– a habit 613
– learning 539
acquirement
knowledge 490
learning 539
talent 698
receipt 810
acquisition
knowledge 490
gain 775
acquit
liberate 750
exempt 927*a*
vindicate 937
innocent 946
absolve 970
acquit oneself
behave 692
– of a debt 807
– of a duty 926

- of an obligation 772
acquittal 506, 970
acquittance 771
acres *space* 180
land 342
property 780
Acres, Bob 862
acrid 392, 395
acridity 171
acrimony
physical 171
caustic 830
discourtesy 895
hatred 898
anger 900
malevolence 907
acroamatics 490
acrobat
strength 159
actor 599
proficient 700
mountebank 844
Acropolis 210
across 219, 708
acrostic 533, 561, 842
act *imitate* 19
physical 170
- *of a play* 599
personate 599
voluntary 680
statute 697
in the – 680, 947
– a part *feign* 544
– one's part 625, 926
– upon
physical 170
mental 615
take steps 680
– up to 772
– well one's part 944
– without authority 738
acting *deputy* 759
actinic 420
actinometer 445
action *physical* 170
voluntary 680
battle 720
law 969
line of – 692
put in – 677
suit the – to the word 550
thick of the – 682
activate 171
actionable 964
active *physical* 171
voluntary 682
– service 722
– thought 457
activity 682
actor
impostor 548
player 599
agent 690
affectation 855
Acts *record* 551
Apostolic 985
actual *existing* 1
present 118
real 494
actuary 85, 811
actuate 175, 615
actum est 729
acu tetigisti, rem 465, 494
acuity 253
aculeate 253
acumen 498
acuminate 253
acupuncture 260
acustics 402
acute *energetic* 171
physically violent 173
pointed 253
physically sensible 375
musical tone 410
perspicacious 498
cunning 702
strong feeling 821
morally painful 830
– angle 244
– ear 418
– note 410
acutely 31
acuteness 465
ad
– eundem 27
– hominem 79
– infinitum 105
– instar 82
– interim 106
– lib 705
– rem 23
A.D. 106
adage 496
adagio *music* 415
slow 275
Adam *sin* 945
–'s apple 250
adamant 159, 323
adapt 23, 27
– oneself to 82
adaptable
conformable 82
useful 644
add *increase* 35
join 37
numerically 85
– up 811
addendum 39
adder 913
addict *habit* 613
adding machine 85
additament 39
addition
extrinsical 6
increase 35
adjunction **37**
thing added 39
arithmetical 85
addle *barren* 169
incomplete 730
abortive 732
– the wits, 475, 503
addlehead 501
addleheaded 499
address
residence 189
direction 550
speech 582
speak to 586
skill 698
request 765
– oneself to 673
addresses
courtship 902
addressful 894
adduce
bring to 288
evidence 467
addulce 834
ademption 789
adenoid 250
adenology 329
adept 700
adequate *power* 157
sufficient 639
for a purpose 644
adhere *stick* 46
– to 604*a*, 613
– to an obligation 772
– to a duty 926
adherent
follower 711
adhesive, 46, 327, 352
adhibit 677
adhortation 695
adieu *departure* 293
loss 776
adipocere 356
adipose 355
adit *orifice* 260
conduit 350
passage 627
adjacent 197
adjection 37
adjective 39
adjoin 197, 199
adjourn 133
adjudge 480
adjudicate 480
adjunct
thing added **39**
accompaniment 88
aid 707
auxiliary 711
adjuration 535
adjure 765, 768
adjust *adapt* 23
equalize 27
order 58
prepare 673
settle 723, 762
– differences 774
adjutage 260, 350
adjutant
auxiliary **711**
military 745
adjuvant *helping* 707
auxiliary 711
admeasurement 466
adminicle 467
administer
utilize 677
conduct 693
exercise authority 737
distribute 786
– correction 972
– oath 768
– sacrament 998
– to *aid* 707
give 784
administration of justice 965
administrative 737, 965
administrator 694
admirable 648, 944
admiral 745
Admiralty, court of – 966
admirari, nil – 871, 932
admiration
wonder 870
love 897
respect 928
approval 931
admired disorder 59
admirer 897
admissible

relevant 23
receivable 296
tolerable 651
– in society 852
admit
composition 54
include 76
let in 296
assent 488
acknowledge 529
permit 760
concede 762
accept 785
– exceptions 469
– of 470
admitted
customary 613
– maxim &c. 496
admixture 41
admonish
warn 668
advise 695
reprove 932
ado *activity* 682
exertion 686
difficulty 704
make much – about 642
much – about nothing
overestimate 482
unimportant 643
unskilful 699
adolescence 131
Adonis 845
adonize 847
adopt
naturalize 184
choose 609
– a cause *aid* 707
– a course 692
– an opinion 484
adoption
religious 987
adore 897, 990
adorn 847
adown 207
adrift *unrelated* 10
disjoined 44
dispersed 73
uncertain 475
unapt 699
free 750
go – *deviate* 279
turn – *disperse* 73
liberate 750
dismiss 756
adroit 698
adscititious
extrinsic 6
added 37
redundant 641
adscriptus glebæ 746
adulation 933
adulator 935
Adullam, cave of – 624, 832
Adullamite 832
adult 131
adulterate *mix* 41
deteriorate 659
adulterated 545
adulterer 962
adultery 961
adumbrate
darkness 421
allegorize 521
represent 554
adumbration
semblance 21
allusion 526
aduncity 244, 245
adust
colour 433
gloomy 837
adustion 384
advance *increase* 35
course 109
progress 282
assert 535
improve 658
aid 707
succeed 731
lend 787
in – *precedence* 62
front 234
precession 280
in – of 33
in – of one's age 498
– against 716
– of learning &c. 490
advanced 282
– in life 128
– guard 234
– student 541
– work 717
advances, make –
offer 763
social 892
advantage
superiority 33
influence 175
good 618
expedience 646
mechanical – 633
dressed to – 847
find one's – in 644
gain an – 775
set off to – 658
take – of 677, 698
– over *success* 731
advantageous
beneficial 648
profitable 775
advene 37
advent
futurity 121
event 151
approach 286
arrival 292
Advent 998
adventism 984
adventitious 6, 156
adventive 156
adventure *event* 151
chance 156
pursuit 622
danger 665
trial 675
the great – 360
adventurer
traveller 268
deceiver 548
experimenter 463
gambler 621
rash 863
ignoble 876
adventures 594
adventurous
undertaking 676
bold 861
rash 863
adversaria 551
adversary 710
adverse
contrary 14
opposed 708
unprosperous 735
disliking 867
– party 710
adversity 735
advert 457
advertise 531
advice *notice* 527
news 532
counsel 695
advisable 646
advise *predict* 511
inform 527
counsel 695
– with one's pillow 451
advised *predetermined* 611
intended 620
better – 658
adviser 540, 695
advocacy 931
advocate
prompt 615
recommend 695
aid 707
auxiliary 711
friend 890
vindicate 937
counsellor 968
Advocate, the – 976
advocation 617
advoutress 962
advoutry 961
advowson 995
adynamic 160
adytum *room* 191
prediction 511
secret place 530
adze 253
adzooks 870
ædile 965
ægis 717
ægrescit medendo 659
ægrotat 927*a*
æolian 349
– harp 417
æon 976
æquam servare mentem 826
æquo animo 823, 826
aerate 334, 353
ære perennius 873
aerial 273
elevated 206
flying 267
gas 334
air 338
– navigation 267
– navigator 269
– mail 534
– patrol 726
– perspective 428
– warfare 722
aerie 189
aerify 334
aerodonetics 267
aerodrome 728
aerodynamics 267, 334, 349
aerolite 318
aerology 338
aeromancy 511
aeromechanics 267
aerometer 338
aeronaut 269
aeronautical 273
aeronautics 267, 338
aeroplane 273
aerostat *balloon* 273
aerostatics 267, 334
aerostation 338

aery 317
Æsculapius 662
Æsop 846
æsthetic
sensibility 375
beauty 845
taste 850
æstival 125
æternum servans sub pectore vulnus 919
ætiology [*see* etiology]
afar 196
affable 879, 894
affair *event* 151
topic 454
business 625
battle 720
love 902, 903
– of honour 720
affaires, chargé d' – 758
affaire de cœur 897
affect *relate to* 9
tend to 176
qualify 469
feign 544
touch 824
desire 865
love 897
affectation 855
affected with
feeling 821
disease 655
affectibility 822
affecting 830
affection 821, 897
affections 820
affettuoso 415
affiance 768, 858
affianced 897, 903
affiche 531
affidation 769
affidavit
affirmation 535
record 551
lawsuit 969
affiliation
relation 9
kindred 11
attribution 155
affine 11
affinitive 9
affinity 9, 17
mate 903
affirmation 535, 488
affix *add* 37
sequel 39
fasten 43
letter 561
afflation 349
afflatus 349, 597, 985
afflict 830
– with illness 655
affliction *pain* 828
infliction 830
adversity 735
affluence
sufficiency 639
prosperity 734
wealth 803
affluent *river* 348
afflux 286
afford *supply* 784
wealth 803
yield 810
sell for 812
– aid &c. 707
afforestation 371
affranchise
make free of 748
liberate 750
affray 720
affreet 980
affriction 331
affright 860
affront *molest* 830
provocation 900
insult 929
– danger 861
affuse 337
afield 186
afire 382
afloat *extant* 1
unstable 149
going on 151
ship 273
navigation 267
ocean 341
news 532
preparing 673
keep oneself – 734
set – *publish* 531
afoot *on hand* 625
preparing 673
astir 682
afore 116
aforementioned 116
aforesaid
preceding 62
repeated 104
prior 116
aforethought 611
aforetime 116
afraid 860
be – *irresolute* 605
– to say *uncertain* 475
afresh 104, 123
Afric heat 382
Afrikander 57
afrite 980
aft 235
after *in order* 63
in time 117
too late 135
rear 235
pursuit 622
be – *intention* 620
pursuit 622
go – *follow* 281
– all *for all that* 30
qualification 469
on the whole 476
– time 133
after acceptation 516
after-age 124
after-clap 509
after-crop 65, 168
after-dinner 117
after-glow 40, 65, 420
after-growth 65
after-life 152
aftermath
sequel 65
fertile 168
profit 775
aftermost 235
afternoon 126
– farmer 683
after-part 65, 235
after-piece 599
after-taste 65, 390
after-thought
thought 451
memory 505
change of mind 607
after-time 121
afterwards 117
aga 745
agacerie 615
again 90, 104
– and again 136
come – *periodic* 138
fall off – 661
live – 660
against
counteraction 179
anteposition 237
provision 673
voluntary opposition 708
chances – 473
declaim – 932
false witness – 934
go – 708
set – *actively* 898
set one's face – 764, 932
stand up – *resist* 719
raise &c. one's voice – 489
– one's will 744
– one's expectation 508
– the grain *difficult* 704
painful 830
dislike 867
– the stream 704
– the time when 510
– one's will 744
– one's wishes 603
agamist 904
agape *open* 260
curious 455
expectant 507
wonder 870
Agapemone 827, 897
agate 847
age *time* 106
period 108
long time 110
era 114
present time 118
oldness 124
advanced life 128
of – 131
from age to – 112
age quod agis! 682
agency
physical 170
instrumentality 631
means 632
employment 677
voluntary action 680
direction 693
commission 755
agenda 625, 626
agent *physical* 153
intermediary 228
voluntary 690
consignee 758
– provocateur 615
agentship 755
ages: for – 110
– ago 122
agglomerate 46, 72
agglutinate 46
aggrandize
in degree 35
in bulk 194
honour 873
aggravate

increase 35
vehemence 173
exaggerate 549
render worse 659
distress 835
exasperate 900
aggravating 830
aggravation **835**
aggregate 50, 72, 84
aggregation 46
aggression 716
aggressor 726
aggrieve 649, 830
aggroup 72
aghast
disappointed 509
fear 860
wonder 870
agile 274, 682
agio 813
agiotage 794
agitate *move* 315
inquire 461
activity 682
excite the feelings 824
– a question 476
agitation [*see* agitate]
changeableness 149
energy 171
motion **315**
in – *preparing* 673
agitator *leader* 694
aglet 554
agley, gang – 732
aglow 382, 420
agnate 11
agnition 762
agnomen 564
agnostic 487
agnosticism 984, 989
agnus Dei 993, 998
ago 122
not long – 123
agog *expectant* **507**
desire 865
wonder 870
agoing 682
set – 707
agonism 720
agonizing 824, 830
agony 378, 828
– of death 360
– of excitement 825
agrarian 371
agree *accord* 23
concur **178**
assent 488
concord 714
consent 762
compact 769
compromise 774
– in opinion 488
– with *salubrity* 656
agreeable
comfortable 82
physically 377
mentally 829
agreeably to 82
agreement **23** [*see* agree]
compact 769
agrestic 371
agriculture **371**
agronomy 371
aground *fixed* 150
in difficulty 704
failure 732
ague-fit 860
aguets, aux –
expectation 507
ambush 530
aguish *cold* 383
ah me! 839
aha! *rejoicing* 838
ahead 234, 280
go – *progression* 282
shoot – *transcursion* 303
activity 682
rock – 665, 667
Ahrimanes 978, 980
aid **707,** 906
by the – of 631, 632
aide-de-camp **711,** 745
aidless 160
aigrette 847
aiguille 253
aiguillette 747, 847
aigulet 847
ail 655, 828
aileron 267, 273
ailment 655
aim 278, 620, 675
– a blow at 716
aimable 894
faire l' – 897
aimer éperdument 897
aimless *without motive* 615a
chance 621
air *unsubstantial* 4
broach 66
lightness 320
gas 334
atmospheric **338**
wind 349
tune 415
appearance 448
refresh 689
demeanour 692
fashionable 852
beat the – 645
fill the – 404
fine – *salubrity* 656
fish in the – 645
fowls of the – 366
in the – 527
rend the – 404
take – 531
air-balloon 273
air base 728
air-commodore 745
aircraft 273, 726
air-drawn 515
airdrome 273
air-force 726
air-gun 727
airing 266
air-mail 273
airman 269
airmanship 698
air-marshal 745
air-passage 351
air-pipe **351**
airport 273, 292, 728
air-pump 349
air-raid 716
airs *affectation* 855
pride 878
vanity 880
arrogance 885
air-shaft 351
air service 267
airship 273, 726
air-tight 261
airways 267
airworthy 273, 664
airy [*see* air]
windy 349
unimportant 643
gay 836
– hopes 858, 859
give to – nothing a local habitation &c. 515
aisle *passage* 260
way 627
in a church 1000
ait 346
ajar *open* 260
discordant **713**
ajee **217**
ajutage 260, 350
akimbo *angular* 244
stand – 715
akin *related* 9
consanguineous 11
similar 17
al fresco 220
alabaster *white* 430
alack! 839
alacrity *willing* 602
active 682
cheerful 836
Aladdin's lamp 993
alar 267
alarm *warning* 668
notice of danger **669**
fear 860
cause for – 665
give an – *indicate* 550
alarmist 862
alarum 114, 550, 669
alas! 839
alate 267
alb 999
albeit 30
albert
chain 847
albification 430
albinescence 430
albinism 430
albino 430
album 593, 596
albumen
semi-liquid 352
protein 357
Alcaic 597
alcaid 745
alcalde 745
alcazar 189
alchemy 144
alcohol 959
Alcoran 986
alcove 191, 252
Aldebaran 423
alderman 745
ale 298
alea, jacta est – 601
aleatory 665
Alecto 173
alectryomancy 511
alehouse 189
go to the – 959
alembic
conversion 144
vessel 191
furnace 386
laboratory 691
alentours 197
alert *watchful* 457,

459
active 682
alerte 669
aleuromancy 511
Alexandrine
ornate style 577
verse 597
alexandrite 847
alexipharmic 662
alexiteric 662
algebra 85
algid 383
algology 369
algorithm 85
alguazil 965
alias
otherwise 18
pseudonym 565
alibi 187
alien *irrelevant* 10
foreign 57
transfer 783
gentile 989
alienable 783
alienate
transfer 783
estrange 44, 889
set against 898
alienation
mental – 503
alieni appetens
grasping 865
envious 921
selfish 943
alienism 57
alight *stop* 265
arrive 292
descend 306
on fire 382
align 278
alike 17
share and share – 778
aliment *food* 298
alimentary 662
– canal 350
alimentation
aid 707
alimony
property 780
provision 803
income 810
aliquot 51, 84
aliter visum, dis – 601
alive
living 359
intelligent 498
active 682
cheerful 836
be – with 102
keep – *continue* 143
keep the memory – 505
look – 684
– to *attention* 457
cognizant 490
informed 527
able 698
sensible 822
alkahest 335
all *whole* 50
complete 52
generality 78
– absorbing 642
in – ages 112
– abroad 495
– agog 865
– in all 50
– along 106
– along of 154
– but 32
– colours 440
– considered 451, 480
– day long 110
– devouring 789
in – directions 278
– engulfing 789
at – events *compensation* 30
qualification 469
true 494
resolve 604
– fours *easy* 705
cards 840
– in good time 152
– hail! *welcome* 292
honour to 873
celebration 883
courtesy 894
– hands *everybody* 78
on – hands 488
– of a dither 824
– of a heap 72
– knowing 976
– manner of *difference* 15
multiform 81
with – one's might 686
– at once 113
– one 27, 866
– out 52
– over *end* 67
universal 78
destruction 162
space 180
at – points 52
– in one's power 686
– powerful
mighty 159
God 976
in – quarters 180
with – respect 928
in – respects 52, 494
– right! 922
– Saints' day 998
– searching 461
– seeing 976
on – sides 227
– sorts *diverse* 16a
mixed 41
multiform 81
– talk 4
– things to all men 894
– the time 106
at – times 136
– together 50
– ways 243, 279
– wise 976
– the world and his wife 78
of – work
useful 644
maid - 746
Allah 979
allay
moderate 174
pacify 723
relieve 834
– excitability 826
allective 615
allege *evidence* 467
assert 535
plea 617
allegiance 743, 926
allegory 464, 521, 594
allegro *music* 415
cheerful 836
allelujah 990
allemande 840
all-embracing 76
alleviate 174, 834
alley *court* 189
passage 260
way 627
alliance *relation* 9
kindred 11
physical co-operation 178
voluntary co-operation 709
party 712
union 714
allied to *like* 17
alligation 43
allign 278
alliteration
similarity 17
style in writing 577
poetry 597
allocation 60, 786
allocution 586
allodium *free* 748
property 780
allopathy 662
alloquy 586
allot *arrange* 60
distribute 786
due 924
allow *assent* 488
admit 529
permit 760
consent 762
give 784
– to have one's own way 740
allowable 760, 924
allowance
qualification 469
gift 784
allotment 786
discount 813
salary 973
with grains of – 485
make – for *forgive* 918
vindicate 937
alloy *mixture* 41
combination 48
debase 659
allude *hint* 514
mean 516
refer to 521
latent 526
inform 527
allure *move* 615
create desire 865
alluring 829
allusive
relative 9
alluvial *level* 213
land 342
plain 344
alluvium
deposit 40
land 342
soil 653
ally *combine* 48
auxiliary 711
friend 890
alma mater 542
almanac
list 86
chronometry 114

record 551
almighty 157
Almighty, the – 976
almoner
treasurer 801
giver 784
church officer 996
almonry 802
almost *nearly* 32
not quite 651
– all 50
– immediately 132
alms *gift* 784
benevolence 906
worship 990
almshouse 189, 666
almsman 785
Alnaschar's dream 515, 858
aloes 395
aloft 206
alogy 497
alone *single* 87
unaided 706
let – *not use* 678
not restrain 748
along 200
get – *progress* 282
go – *depart* 293
go – with *concur* 178
assent 488
co-operate 709
– of *caused by* 154
– with *added* 37
together 88
by means of 631
alongside *near* 197
parallel 216
laterally 236
aloof *distant* 196
high 206
secluded 893
stand – *inaction* 681
refuse 764
cautious 864
alopecia 226
aloud 404
think – 589
naïveté 703
Alp 206
alpenstock 215
Alpha 66
– and Omega 50
alphabet
beginning 66
letters 561
alphabetarian 541
alphabeticize 60
Alphitomancy 511
alpine *high* 206
Alpine Club 268, 305
already
antecedently 116
even now 118
past time 122
Alsatia 791, 945
also 37
altar 903, 1000
alter 140
– the case 468
– one's course 279
alter ego *similar* 17
auxiliary 711
deputy 759
friend 890
alterable 149
alteram partem, audire – 468, 922
alterative
substitute 634
remedy 662
altercation 713
altered *worn* 688
– for the worse 659
alternate
reciprocal 12
sequence 63
discontinuous 70
periodic 138
changeable 149
oscillate 314
alternative
substitute 147
choice 609
plan 626
although
compensation 30
counteraction 179
unless 469
altiloquence 577
altimetry
height 206
angle 244
measurement 466
altitude *height* 206
– and azimuth 466
alto 410, 416
– part 415
alto-rilievo 250, 557
altogether 50, 52
nude 226
altruism 910, 942
altruist 906
alum 397
alumnus 541
alveolus 252
always
uniformly 16
generally 78
during 106
perpetually 112
habitually 613
a.m. 114, 125
amah 753
amain 173, 684
amalgam, -ate 41, 48
amalgamation 709
Amalthæa's horn 639
amantium iræ 918
amanuensis 553, 590
amaranthine 112
amari aliquid
bad 649
imperfect 651
painful 830
amaritude 395
amass *whole* 50
collect 72
store 636
amateur *volunteer* 602
layman 699
taste 850
votary 865
amatory 897
amaurosis 442
amaze 870
amazingly 31
Amazon
woman 374
warrior 726
courage 861
ambages
convolutions 248
circumlocution 573
circuit 629
ambagious 573
ambassador
messenger 534
representative 758
recall of –s 713
amber 356*a*
– colour 436
ambidexter
right and left 238
fickle 607
clever 698
ambient 227
ambigu 41
ambiguas spargere voces
uncertain 475
misteach 538
false 544
cunning 702
ambiguous
uncertain 475
unintelligible 519
equivocal 520
obscure 571
ambiloquy 520
ambit 230
ambition 620, 865
ambivalence 605, 708
amble 266
ambo *school* 542
pulpit 1000
ambo, Arcades –
alike 17
friends 890
bad men 949
ambrosia 298
ambrosial 394, 490
ambulance
vehicle 272
hospital 662
ambulation 266
ambuscade 530
ambush 530, 667
lie in – 528
âme – de boue 949
– damnée
catspaw 711
servant 746
servile 886
bad man 949
– qui vive 101, 187
ameer 875
ameliorate 658
amen *assent* 488
submission 725
content 831
amenable 177, 602, 926
not – to reason 608
amend 658
amendatory 20
amende honorable 952
amends
compensation 50
atonement 952
reward 973
amenity 829, 894
amentia 503
amerce 974
American organ 417
Americanism 563
amethyst
purple 437
jewel 847
amiable
courteous 894
loving 897
kind 906
amiability 829, 894
amicable 707, 888

amice 999
amicus – curiæ 527
– humani generis 910
– usque ad aras 890
amidships 68
amidst 41, 228
amiss 619
come – *disagree* 24
mistime 135
inexpedient 647
do – 945
nothing comes – 823
take – 867, 900
amity *concord* 714
peace 721
friendship 888
ammunition 635, 727
amnesia 506
amnesty 506, 723, 918
amnis, rusticus expectat dum defluat – *hope* 858
amœbæan 63
amok 503
among 41, 228
amor patriæ 910
amore, con – 602, 821
amoroso 599
amorous 897
– glances 902
amorphous 83, 241
amorphism **241**
amortization 784
amotion 270
amount
quantity 25
degree 26
sum of money 800
price 812
gross – 50
– to 27, 85
amour 897, 961
– propre 880
ampere 466
amphibian 366
amphibious 83
amphibology 520
Amphictyonic council 696
amphigouri 497
amphitheatre
prospect 441
school 542
theatre 599
arena 728
Amphitryon 890
amphora 191
ample *much* 31
spacious 180
large 192
broad 202
copious 639
amplify
expand 194
exaggerate 549
diffuse style 573
amplitude
quantity 25
degree 26
size 192
breadth 202
enough 639
ampoule 191
ampulla 191
amputate 38
amuck 173, 361, 503, 716, 825
amulet 247, 993
amusare la bocca, per – 394
amuse 829, 840
amusement **840**
place of – 840
amussim, ad – 494
amylaceous 352
an *if* 514
ana 594
Anabaptist 984
anabasis 35
anachronism
false time **115**
inopportune 135
error 495
anacoluthon 70
anaconda 913
anacreontic 597
anæmia 160
anæsthesia 376, 381, 683
anaglyph 554, 557
anagoge 521, 526
anagram
double sense 520
secret 533
letter 561
wit 842
analecta 596
analeptic 662
analgesia 376
analogy 9, 17
analogous 12
analysis
decomposition 49
arrangement 60
algebra 85
inquiry 461
experiment 463
reasoning 476
grammar 567
compendium 596
analyst 461, 463
anamorphosis
distortion 243
optical 443
misrepresentation 555
anapæst 597
anaphylaxis 375
anarchist
destroyer 165
disobedient 742
evil-doer 913
anarchy 59, 738
anastatic printing 558
anastomosis 43, 219
anastrophe 218
anathema 908
anathematize 908
censure 932
detract 934
anatomize *dissect* 44
investigate 461
anatomy
dissection 44
leanness 203
texture 329
science 357
comparative – 368
anatriptic 331
ancestral
bygone 122
old 124
aged 128
ancestry 166
anchor
connection 45
stop 265
safeguard 666
badge 747
hope 858
at – *fixed* 150
stationed 184
safe 664
cast – *settle* 184
arrive 292
have an – to windward 664
sheet – *means* 632
anchorage
location 184
roadstead 189
refuge 666
anchored 150
anchorite 893, 955
ancien régime 875
ancient *old* 124
flag 550
– times 122
ancientness 122
ancillary 707
and 37, 88
andante 415
andiron 386
androgynous 83
anecdote 594
anele 998
anemography 349
anemometer
wind 349
measure 466
anent 9
aneroid 338
anew *again* 104
newly 123
anfractuosity 248
angel
object of love 897
good person 948
supernatural being **977**
fallen –
bad man 949
devil 978
guardian –
safety 664
auxiliary 711
benefactor 912
– of Death 360
– 's visits 137
angelic 944
angels and ministers of grace defend us! 860
angelus 550
anger 900
more in sorrow than in – 826, 918
angiology 329
angle 244
try 463
at an – 217
Anglicanism 984
angling 622, 840
anguille au genou, rompre l' – 158, 471
anguilliform 205, 248
anguis in herbâ 667
anguish
physical 378
moral 828

angular 244
 – velocity 264
angularity 244
angusta domi, res – 804
angustation 203
anhelation 688
anhydrate 340
anhydrous 340
aniline dyes 437
anility 128, 499
animadvert
 consider 451
 attend to 457
 reprehend 932
animal 366
 female – 374
 – cries 412
 – economy 359
 – gratification 377
 – life 364
 – physiology 368
 – spirits 836
 – and vegetable kingdom 357
animalcule 193, 366
animalism
 sensuality 954
animality 364
animate
 induce 615
 excite 824
 enliven 836
animation
 life 359
 animality 364
 activity 682
 vivacity 836
 suspended – 823
animism 984
animo, ex – 602
 quo – 620
animosity
 dislike 867
 enmity 889
 hatred 898
 anger 900
animus
 willingness 602
 intention 620
 desire 865
ankle 244
 – deep 208, 209
anklet 847
ankylosis 150
annalist 114, 553
annals
 chronology 114
 record 551
 account 594
anneal 673
annex
 addition 37
 adjunct 39
 junction 43
 acquire 775
Annie Oakley 815
annihilate 2, 162
anniversary 138
anno 106
Anno Domini
 era 106
 old age 124
annotation 522, 550
annotator 524
 scholar 492
 interpreter 524
 editor 595
annotto 434
announce
 predict 511
 inform 527
 publish 531
 assert 535
announcer 527
annoy
 molest 649, 907
 disquiet 830
annoyance 828
 source of – 830
annual *periodic* 138
 plant 367
 book 593
annuity 810
annul 162, 756
annular 247
annunciate 527
annus magnus 108
anodyne
 lenitive 174
 remedial 662
 relief 834
anoint *coat* 223
 lubricate 332
 oil 355
anointed
 deity 976
 king 745
anomaly
 disorder 59
 irregularity 83
anon 132
anonymous 565
anopsia 442
anorexy 866
another
 different 15
 repetition 104
 – story 468, 526
 go upon – tack 607
 – time 119
answer
 to an inquiry 462
 confute 479
 solution 522
 succeed 731
 pecuniary profit 775
 pleadings 969
 require an – 461
 – for *deputy* 759
 promise 768
 go bail 806
 I'll – for it 535
 – the helm 743
 – the purpose 731
 – to *correspond* 9
 – one's turn 644
answerable
 agreement 23
 liable 177
 bail 806
 duty 926
 censurable 932
ant 690
Antæus 159, 192
antagonism
 difference 14
 physical 179
 voluntary 708
 enmity 889
antagonist 710, 891
antagonistic 24
antarctic 237
antecedence 62, 116
antecedent 64
antechamber 191
ante Christum 106
antedate 115
antediluvian 124
antelope 274
antemundane 124
antenna 379
anteposition 62
anterior
 in order 62
 in time 116
 in place 234
 – to reason 477
anteroom 191
antevert 706
anthem 990
anthemion 847
anthology
 book 593
 collection 596
 poem 597
anthracite 388
anthropoid 372
anthropology
 zoology 368
 mankind 372
anthropomancy 511
anthropophagi 913
anthroposcopy 511
anthroposophy 372
anti-aircraft gun 564, 727
antic 840
antichambre, faire – 133
antichristian 984, 989
antichronism 115
anticipate
 anachronism 115
 priority 116
 future 121
 early 132
 expect 507
 foresee 510
 prepare 673
 hope 858
 in – 116
anticlimax
 decrease 36
 bathos 497, 853
anticlinal 217
anticyclone 265
antidote 662
antigropelos 225
antilogarithm 84
antilogy 477
antimony 663
Antinomian 984
antinomy 964
Antinous 845
antiparallel 217
antipathy 867, 898
antiphon *music* 415
 answer 462
 worship 990
antiphrasis 563
antipodes
 difference 14
 distance 196
 contraposition 237
antipoison 662
antiquary
 past times 122
 scholar 492
 historian 553
antiquas vias, stare super – 613, 670
antiquated 128
antique 124
antiquity 122
antiscriptural 984
antiseptic 652, 662
antisocial 911
antistrophe 597

antithesis
contrast 14
difference 15
opposite 237
style 574, 577
antitoxin 662
antitype 22
antler 253
antonomasia
metaphor 521
nomenclature 564
antonym 14
antrum 252
anvil *support* 215
on the –
intended 620
in hand 625
preparing 673
anxiety *pain* 828
fear 860
desire 865
anxious expectation 507
any *some* 25
part 51
no choice 609*a*
at – price 604*a*
at – rate
certain 474
true 494
at all hazards 604
anybody 78
anyhow 460, 627
anything one knows, for – 491
aorist 109, 119
aorta 350
apace *early* 132
swift 274
apache 913
apart 44, 87
set – 636
wide – 196
apartment 191
–s 189
–s to let
imbecile 499
apathetic 275
apathy
indifference 456
insensibility 823
irreligion 989
ape *imitate* 19
Apelles 559
aperçu 596
aperture 260
apex 210
aphasia 583
aphelion 196
aphonic 403
aphony 581
aphorism 496
Aphrodite 845, 979
apiary 370
apiculture 370
Apicius 957
apiece 79
apish 19, 499
aplanatic 429
aplomb
stability 150
self-possession 498
resolution 604
Apocalypse 985
Apocrypha 985
apocryphal
uncertain 475
erroneous 495
heterodox 984
apodictic 478
apodosis 67
apogee 210
apograph 21
Apollo *sun* 318
music 416
luminary 423
beauty 845
god 979
magnus – 500, 695
Apollyon 978
apologue
metaphor 521
teaching 537
description 594
apology *excuse* 617
vindication 937
penitence 950
atonement 952
apophthegm 496
apophysis 250
apoplexy 158, 655
aporetic 487
aposiopesis 585
apostasy
recantation 607
dishonour 940
heterodoxy 984
apostate
convert 144
turncoat 607
impiety 988
apostle *teacher* 540
disciple 541
inspired 985
–'s creed 983*a*
apostolic 985
– church 983*a*
– see 995
apostrophe
address 586
soliloquy 589
appeal 765
apothecary 662
–'s weight 319
apothegm 496
apotheosis
resuscitation 163
canonization 873
heaven 981
hero worship 991
apozem 335, 384
appal 830, 860
appanage
property 780
gift 784
apparatus 633
apparel 225
apparent
visible 446
appearing 448
probable 472
manifest 525
heir – 779
apparition
fallacy of vision 443
spirit 980
apparitor 534
appeach 938
appeal 586, 765
court of – 966
– to arms 722
– motion 969
– from Philip drunk to Philip sober 658
– to *call to witness* 467
– to for (*claim*) 924
appear 446, 525
– for 759
– in print 591
appearance 448
make one's – 292
to all – 448
probable 472
appearances
keep up – 852
appease 174
appellant 924, 938
appellate 966
appellation 564
append *add* 37
sequence 63
hang 214
appendage 39
appendectomy 662
appendix
adjunct 39
sequel 65
end 67
book 593
appertain
related to 9
component 56
belong 777
property 780
appetite 865
tickle the –
savoury 394
appetizing 865
exciting 824
applaud 931
apple – of discord 713
golden –
allurement 615
– of one's eye *good* 648
love 897
favorite 899
– off another tree 15
how we –s swim! 880
apple-green 435
apple-pie order 58
appliance *use* 677
–s *means* 632
machinery 633
applicable *relevant* 23
useful 644
expedient 646
applicability 9
applicant 767
application *study* 457
metaphor 521
use 677
request 765
apply, *use* 677
– a match 384
– the match to a train 66
– the mind 457
– a remedy 662
appoggiatura 413
appointment
employment 625
order 741
charge 755
assignment 786
interview 892
appointments
gear 633
apportion *arrange* 60
disperse 73
allot 786
apportionment 786
appositeness 9
apposition

relation 9
relevancy 23
closeness 199
paraphrase 522
appraise 466, 812
appreciate
realize 450, 451
measure 466
judge 480
know 490
taste 850
approve 931
apprehend
believe 484
know 490
fear 860
seize 789
apprehension
idea 453
taking 789
apprentice 541
– oneself 676
apprenticeship 539, 673
apprise 527
apprised of 490
approach
of time 121
impend 152
nearness 197
move 286
path 627
approaching 9
approbation **931**
appropinquation 286
appropriate *fit* 23
peculiar 79
expedient 646
assign 786
take 789
steal 791
approval 488, 931
on – 609
approximate
related to 9
resemble 17
in mathematics 85
nearness 197
approach 286
appulse *meeting* 199
collision 276
approach 286
convergence 290
appurtenance
part 51
component 56
belongings 780
accompaniment 88
appurtenant 9

après nous le déluge 943
apricot *colour* 439
April
– fool 547, 857
make an – fool of 545
– showers 149
apron *extension* 39
clothing 225
defence 717
canonicals 999
àpropos [*see* à]
aprotype 591
apse 1000
apt *consonant* 23
tendency 176, 177
docile 539
willing 602
clever 698
aqua-fortis 335
aquamarine 435
aquarium 370
Aquarius 348, 636
aquatic *water* 337
aquatics 267
aquatinta 558
aqueduct 350
aqueous 337
aquiline 244
A.R. 106
Arab *wanderer* 268
horse 271
street – 876
araba 272
arabesque 847
Arabian
– perfumes 400
– nights 515
arable 371
arbalest 727
arbiter *critic* 480
director 694
adviser 695
judge 967
– elegantiarum
revels 840
taste 850
fashion 852
arbitrage 794
arbitrament
judgment 480
– of the sword 722
arbitrary
without relation 10
irregular 83
wilful 606
capricious 608
authoritative 737
severe 739

insolent 885
lawless 964
– power 739
arbitrate
adjudicate 480
mediate 724
arbitration
court of – 966
submit to – 774
arbitrium, ad – 600
arbor 215, 312
arborescent
ramifying 242
rough 256
trees 367
arboriculture 371
arbour *abode* 189
summer-house 191
plaisance 840
arc 245
heat 382
arcade *street* 189
curve 245
gateway 260
Arcades ambo
alike 17
friends 890
bad men 949
Arcadia 827, 981
Arcadian 703, 946
arcanum 533
arch *great* 31
support 215
curve 245
convex 250
concave 252
clever 498
cunning 702
triumphal – 733, 883
archæologist
pastimes 122
scholar 492
archæology 122
archaic *old* 124
archaism 122, 563
archangel 977
archbishop 996
archbishopric 995
archdeacon 996
archduchy 181
archduke 745
archegenesis 161
archer 726
archery 840
Arches, court of – 966, 995
archetype 22
archetypal 20
Archeus 359

archfiend 978
archiater 695
archiepiscopal 995
archimandrite 996
archipelago 346
architect 164, 390
architectonic 161
architecture
arrangement 60
construction 161
fabric 329
ornament 847
architrave 210
archive 551
archlute 417
archon *ruler* 745
deputy 759
judge 967
archtraitor 941
arctic *northern* 237
cold 383
arctics 225
arcuation 245
ardent *fiery* 382
eager 682
feeling 821
loving 897
– expectation 507
– imagination 515
ardet, proximus – 665, 667
ardour *vigour* 574
activity 821
feeling 821
desire 865
arduous 704
area 181, 182
arefaction 340
arena *space* 180
region 181
field of view 441
field of battle **728**
arenaceous 330
areola 247
areolar 219
areometer 321
Areopagus 966
arête 253
aretinism 961
aretology 926
Argand lamp 423
argent 430
argillaceous 324
argosy 273
argot 563
argonaut 269
argue *evidence* 467
reason 476
indicate 550
dissertation 595
argument *disagree-*

ment 24
topic 454
discussion 476
meaning 516
have the best of an – 478
argumentum
– ad baculum
compel 744
lawless 964
punish 972
– ad crumenam 800
– ad hominem
reasoning 476
accuse 938
– ad verecundiam 939
Argus-eyed 441, 459
argute 498
aria 415
arianism 984
arid 340
unproductive 169
uninteresting 841
Ariel *courier* 268
swift 274
messenger 534
spirit 979
arietation 276
arietta 415
aright *well* 618
Ariman [*see* Ahrimanes]
ariolation 511
arioso 415
aris et focis, pro –
defence 717
philanthropy 910
arise *exist* 1
begin 66
happen 151
mount 305
appear 446
– from 154
Aristarchus 850
Aristides
good man 948
aristocracy
power 737
fashion 852
nobility 875
Arithmancy 511
arithmetic 85
ark *abode* 189
asylum 666
arm *part* 51
power 157
instrument 633
provide 637
prepare 673
war 722
weapon 727
make a long – 200
– chair 215
– in arm
together 88
friends 888
sociable 892
– of the law 963
– of the sea 343
armada 726
Armageddon 720, 722
armament 673, 727
armed 717
– at all points 673
– force 726
– guard 664
armet 717
armful 25
armiger 875
armigerent 726
armigerous 722
armilla 247, 847
armillary sphere 466
armipotent 157
armistice
cessation 142
respite 672
pacification 723
armless 158
armlet *ring* 247
gulf 343
ornament 847
armorial bearings 550, 877
armour *cover* 223
defence 717
arms 727
buckle on one's – 673
– plated 223
armoured
– car 726
– cruiser 726
– train 726
armoury *store* 636
workshop 691
arm's length
at – 196
keep at –
repel 289
defence 717
enmity 889
seclusion 893
discourtesy 895
arms **727** [*see* arm]
heraldry 550
war 722
honours 877
clash of – 720
deeds of – 720
with folded – 681
in – *infant* 129
throw oneself into the – of 666, 888
under – 722
up in – *active* 682
discord 713
resistance 719
resentment 900
enmity 889
Armstrong gun **727**
army *collection* 72
multitude 102
troops 726
aroma 400
around 227
lie – 220
arouse *move* 615
excite 824
– oneself 682
aroynt *begone* 297
malediction 908
arquebusade 662
arquebuse 727
arraign 938, 969
arrange
set in order 60
plan 626
compromise 774
– with creditors 807
– itself 58
arrange – matters
pacify 723
– music 413, 416
– in a series 69
– under 76
arrangement 23, **60**
[*see* arrange]
order 58
temporary – 111
arrant *identical* 31
manifest 525
notorious 531
bad 649
disreputable 874
base 940
arras 847
array *order* 58, 60
series 69
assemblage 72
multitude 102
dress 225
prepare 673
adorn 847
ostentation 882
battle – 722
arrear, in – 53, 808
arrears *debt* 806
arrectis auribus
hear 418
expect 507
arrest *stop* 142
restrain 751
in law 969
– the attention **457**
arrière-pensée
after-thought 65
mental reservation 528
motive 615
set purpose 620
arrival **292**
arrive *happen* 151
reach 292
complete 729
– at a conclusion 480
– at the truth 480*a*
arrogant *severe* 739
proud 878
insolent 885
arrogate 885, 924
– to oneself
undue 925
arrondissement 181
arrosion 331
arrow *swift* 274
missile 284
arms 727
broad – 550
arrow-head
form 253
writing 590
'Arry and 'Arriet 902
ars celare artem 698
arsenal *store* 636
workshop 691
arsenic 663
arson 384
art *representation* 554
business 625
skill 698
cunning 702
fine – 850
work of – 845, 847
– gallery 556
artery 350, 627
artes, hæ tibi erunt – 627
artesian well 343
artful 544, 702
– dodge 545, 702
article *thing* 3
part 51
matter 316

chapter 593
review 595
goods 798
articled clerk 541
articles
thirty-nine – 983*a*
– of agreement 770
– of faith 484, 983
articulate 366
articulation
junction 43
speech 580
articulo, in –
transient **111**
dying 360
artifice 626, **702**
artificer 690
artificial
fictitious 545
cunning 702
affected 855
– language 579
artillery
explosion 404
arms 727
artilleryman 726
artisan 690
artist *painter* &c. **559**
contriver 626
agent 690
artiste *music* 416
drama 599
artistic *skilful* 698
beautiful 845
taste 850
– language 578
artlessness **703**
arundo, hæret lateri lethalis – 828
aruspex 513
aruspicy 511
as *motive* 615
– broad as long 27
– can be 52
– good as 27
– if *similar* 17
suppose 514
– little as may be 32
– it may be
circumstance 8
event 151
chance 156
– much again 90
– soon as 120
– they say 496, 532
– things are 7
– things go 151, 613
– to 9
– usual 82
– it were 17, 521
– you were 141, 283
– well as 37
– the world wags 151
ascend *be great* 31
increase 35
rise 305
improve 658
ascendancy
power 157
influence 175
success 731
ascendant
lord of the – 745
in the –
influence 175
important 642
success 731
authority 737
repute 873
one's star in the –
prosperity 734
ascension
[*see* ascend]
calefaction 384
– Day 998
ascent
[*see* ascend]
gradient 217
rise **305**
glory 873
ascertain *fix* 150
determine 480
ascertained 474, 490
ascertainment 480*a*
asceticism **955**
ascititious
intrinsic 6
additional 37
supplementary 52
ascribe 155
aseptic 652
ash 384
– coloured 432
– blond 430
Ash Wednesday 998
ashamed 879
ashen 429
ashes *corpse* 362
dirt 653
lay in – 162
pale as – 429, 860
rise from one's – 660
ashore 342
go – *arrive* 292
ashy 429
Asian mystery 533
aside *laterally* 236
whisper 405
private 528
say – 589
set &c. – *displace* 185
neglect 460
negative 536
reject 610
disuse 678
abrogate 756
discard 782
step – 279
asinine *ass* 271
fool 499
ask *inquire* 461
request 765
for sale 794
price 812
– leave 760
askance 217
eye – *fear* 860
look – *vision* 441, 443
dissent 489
dislike 867
disapproval 932
askari 726
asked in church 903
askew 217, 243
aslant 217
asleep 683
aslope 217
Asmodeus 980
asomatous 317
asp *animal* 366
evil-doer 913
Aspasia 962
aspect *feature* 5
state 7
situation 183
appearance 448
aspen leaf
shake like an – 315, 860
asperity
roughness 256
discourtesy 895
anger 900
irascibility 901
asperse 934
aspersion
malediction 908
rite 998
asphalt
smooth 255
resin 356*a*
material 635
asphodel 845
asphyxia 360
asphyxiate 361
aspic 352
aspirant 767, **865**
aspirate 580
aspirator 349
aspire *rise* 305
hope 858
desire 865
worship 990
aspirin 834
asportation 270
asquint 217
ass *beast of burden* 271
fool 501
make an – of
delude 545
– between two bundles of hay 605
–'s bridge 519
– in lion's skin
cheat 548
bungler 701
assafœtida 401
assagai 727
assail 716, 830
assailant 710, 726
assassin, -ate 361
assault 716, 961
take by – 789
assay 463
asseguay 727
assemblage **72**
assembly
council 696
society 892
religious 997
assembly hall 588
assembly room 189
assent *belief* 484
agree **488**
willing 602
consent 762
content 831
assert 535, 924
assess *measure* 466
determine 480
tax 812
assessor
judge 967
assets 780, 800
asseverate 535
assiduity 110
assiduous 682
assign
commission 755
transfer 270, 783

give 784
allot 786
– as cause 155
– a duty 926
– places 60
assignat 800
assignation 892
place of – 74
assignee *donee* 785
assimilate
uniform 16
resemble 17
imitate 19
agree 23
transmute 144
assist 707
– at 186
assistant 711
assister *be present* 186
assize *measure* 466
tribunal 966
justice of – 967
associate *mix* 41
unite 43
collect 72
accompany 88
colleague 690
auxiliary 711
friend 890
– with 892
association
[*see* associate]
relation 9
combination 48
co-operation 709
partnership 712
– of ideas
intellect 450
thought 451
intuition 477
hint 514
– football 840
assoil *acquit* 970
assonance
music 413
poetry 597
assort *arrange* 60
assortment 72, 75
assuage 174, 834
assuetude 613
assume *believe* 484
suppose 514
falsehood 544
take 789
insolent 885
right 924
– authority 737
– a character 554
– command 741
– a form 144
– the offensive 716
assumed name 565
assumption
[*see* assume]
severity 739
hope 858
usurpation 925
assurance
speculation 156
certainty 474
belief 484
assertion 535
promise 768
security 771
hope 858
vanity 880
insolence 885
make – double sure *safe* 664
caution 864
assuredly
assent 488
assythment 973
astatic 320
asterisk 550
astern 235
put the engines – 275
fall – 283
asteroid 318
Asteroth 979
asthenia 160
astigmatism 443
astir 682
set – 824
astonish 870
astonished
– at nothing 871
astonishing
great 31
astound *excite* 824
fear 860
surprise 870
astra, sic itur ad – 360, 873
Astræa 922
astraddle 215
astragal 847
astral 318
– body 317, 992
– influence 601
– plane 317
astray 475, 495
go – *deviate* 279
sin 945
astriction 43
astride 215
astringent 195
astrolabe 466
astrologer 994
astrology 511
astromancy 511
astronomy 318
astute 498, 702
asunder 44, 196
as poles – 237
asylum *hospital* 663
retreat 666
defence 717
asymptote 290
at, be – 620
up and – them! 716
ataghan 727
atavism 145, 163
ataxia 158
atelier 556, 691
athanasia 112
Athanasian creed 983*a*
athanor 386
atheism 989
atheist 487
Athenae 979
Athens, owls to – 641
athirst 865
athlete *strong* 159
gladiator 726
athletic *strong* 159
strenuous 686
– sports
contest 720
games 840
athwart
oblique 217
crossing 219
opposing 708
Atkins, Tommy 726
Atlantis 515
Atlas *arrangement* 60
list 86
strength 159
support 215
maps 554
atmosphere
circumambience 227
air 338
painting 556
atmospheric blue 438
atoll 346
atom *small* 32, 193
atomic energy 157
atomizer 336
atoms
crush to – 162
atomy 193
atonement
restitution 790
expiation 952
amends 973
religious 976
atony 160
atrabilious 837
atramentous 431
atrium 191
atrocity
malevolence 907
vice 945
guilt 947
atrophy
shrinking 195
disease 655
decay 659
Atropos 601
attach *join* 43
love 897
legal 969
– importance to 642
attaché
employé 746
diplomatic 758
– case 191
attack *singing* 580
disease 655
assault 716
debauch 961
attaghan 727
attain *arrive* 292
succeed 731
– majority 131
attainable 470
attainder
taint 651
at law 971
attainment
knowledge 490
learning 539
skill 698
attar 400
attemper 41, 174
attempered 820
attempt 675
vain – 732
– impossibilities 471
attend
accompany 88
be present 186
follow 281
apply the mind 457
medically 662
aid 707
serve 746
– to business 625
– to orders 743

attendance on
dance – 886
attendant
[see attend]
attention 457
care 459
respect 928
attract – 882
call to – 457
call – to 550
give – 418
pay –s to 894
pay one's –s to 902
attenuate
decrease 36
weaken 158
reduce 195
rarefy 322
attenuated 203
attest
bear testimony 467
affirm 535
adjure 768
attested copy 771
attic *simple* 42
garret 191
summit 210
style 578
wit 842
taste 850
Attila 913
attire 225
attitude
circumstance 8
situation 183
posture 240
attitudinarian 882
attitudinize 855
attollent 307
attorney
consignee 758
at law 968
power of – 755
attract
bring towards 288
induce 615
allure 865
excite love 897
– the attention 457
visible 446
attraction
[see attract]
natural power 157
bring towards 288
attractive
[see attract]
pleasing 829
beautiful 845
attrahent 288
attribute
speciality 79
accompaniment 88
power 157
–s of the Deity 976
– to 155
attribution 155
attrite 330
attrition 330, 331
attroupement 72
attune *music* 415
prepare 673
attuned to
habit 613
attunement 23
auburn 433
A.U.C. 106
auction 796, 840
auctioneer 758, 796
auctorial 599
audacity
courage 861
rashness 863
insolence 885
audible 402
become – 418
scarcely – 405
audience
hearing 418
conversation 588
before an – 599
audire alteram partem
counter-evidence 468
right 922
justice 939
audit
numeration 85
examination 461
accounts 811
auditive 418
auditor
hearer 418
accountant 811
auditorium 189, 588
auditory
sound 402
hearing 418
theatre 599
– apparatus 418
au fait 698
au fond 5
auf Wiedersehen 293
Augean
– stable 653
– task 704
auger 262
aught 51
for – one cares
unimportant 643
indifferent 866
for – one knows
ignorance 491
conjecture 514
augment
increase 35
thing added 39
expand 194
augur 513
– well 858
augurate 511
augury 512
august 873
Augustinian 996
auk 366
auld lang syne 122
aulic council 696
aumbry 1000
aunt 11
aura *wind* 349
sensation 380
aurea mediocritas 628
aureate 436
aureola 420
aureole 420, 873
aureolin 436
auribus, arrectis – 418
auricular *hearing* 418
clandestine 528
– confession 998
auri sacra fames 819
aurist 662
aurora
dawn 125
light 420, 423
twilight 422
– australis 423
– borealis 423
Auroral 236
ausculation 418
auspice *omen* 512
auspices
influence 175
prediction 511
protection 664
direction 693
aid 707
under the – of 693, 737
auspicious
opportune 134
prosperous 734
hopeful 858
austerity
harsh taste 395
severe 739
discourteous 895
ascetic 955
pietism 988
austral 237
austromancy 511
authentic 467
certain 474
true 494
authentication
evidence 467
security 771
author 164, 593
projector 626
dramatic – 599
– of our being 976
– of evil 978
– 's proof 591
authoritative 474, 741
authority
testimony 467
sage 500
informant 527
power **737**
permission 760
right 924
ensign of – 747
person in – 745
do upon one's own – 600
authorized *due* 924
legalized 963
authorship
production 161
style 569
writing 590
autobiography 594
autocar 272
autochthonous 188
autocracy 737, 739
autocrat 745
autocratic 600, 737
auto-da-fé 384, 972
autograph 550, 590
Autolycus *thief* 792
pedlar 797
automaniac 504
automatic 601, 633
- pistol 727
- writing 992
automaton 554, 601
automobile 272
automobilist 268
automotive 266
autonomasia 521
autonomy 737, 748
autopsy
post-mortem 363
vision 441

autoptical 446, 525
autotype 558
autumn 126
auxiliary **711**
additional 37
helpful 707
– forces 726
avail *benefit* 618
useful 644
succeed 731
of no – 645
– oneself of 677
avalanche *fall* 306
snow 383
redundance 641
avaler des couleuvres 725, 886
avant-coureur 64, 673
avant-propos 64
avarice 819
avast! *stop* 142, 265
desist 624
forbid 761
avatar *change* 140
deity 976
idol 991
avaunt! 297, 449
ave! *honour* 873
courtesy 894
Ave maria 990
avenge 919
avenue
plantation 371
way 627
aver 535
average *mean* 29, 628
médiocre 651
– circumstances 736
take an – 466
Averni, facilis descensus – 217, 665
Avernus 982
averruncate 297, 301
aversion *unwillingness* 603
dislike 867
hate 898
avert 706
– the eyes 442
aviary 370
aviation 267
aviator 269
avidity *avarice* 819
desire 865
aviette 273
avile 932, 934
avion 273
aviso 532
avocation 625
avoidance **623**
avoidless 474, 601
avoirdupois 319
avolation 623, 671
avouch 535, 768
avow *assent* 488
disclose 529
assert 535
avulsion 44, 301
avuncular 11
await *future* 121
be kept waiting 133
impend 152
expect 507
awake *attentive* 457
careful 459
intelligent 498
active 682
– to life immortal 360
awaken *inform* 527
excite 824
– the attention **457**
– the memory 505
award *adjudge* 480
give 784
aware 490
away 187, 196
break – 623
fly – 293
move – 287
take – from 789
get &c. – 671
throw &c. –
eject 297
reject 610
waste 638
relinquish 782
– from *unrelated* 10
– with! 930, 932
do – with *undo* 681
abrogate 756
awe *fear* 860
wonder 870
respect 928
aweless *fearless* 861
insolent 885
disrespectful 929
awful 31, 860
– silence 403
awhile 111
awkward
inelegant 579
inexpedient 647
unskilful 699
difficult 704
painful 830
ugly 846
vulgar 851
ridiculous 853
– squad 701
awl 262
awn 253
awning 223, 424
awry *oblique* 217
distorted 243
evil 619
axe *edge tool* 253
impulse 276
weapon 727
for beheading 975
have an – to grind 702
Axinomancy 511
axiom 496
axiomatic 474
axis *support* 215
centre 222
rotation 312
axle 312
wheel and – 633
axle load 466
axletree 215
ay 488
ayah 746, 753
aye *ever* 112
yes 488
azimuth
horizontal 213
direction 278
measurement 466
– circle 212
azoic 358
azote 663
azotic 657
azure 438
azygous *single* **87**

B

Baal 979, 986
Babbittry 851
babble *rivulet* 348
faint sound 405
unmeaning 517
talk 584, 588
babbler 501
babbling
foolish 499
babe 129
innocent as the – unborn 946
Babel *confusion* 59
discord 414
tongues 560
jargon 563
loquacity 584
baboon 846
baby *infant* 129
fool 501
– linen 225
babyhood 127
babyish 499
baccarat 840
bacchanals 959
Bacchus 979
drink 959
bachelor 904
– of arts 492
– girl 374
bacillus 193
back *rear* 235
shoulder 250
aid 707
behind one's –
latent 526
hidden 528
come – 292
give – 790
fall – *relapse* 661
go – 283
go – from *retract* 773
have at one's – 215
hold – *avoid* 623
keep – *reserve* 636
look – 505
on one's – *impotent* 158
horizontal 213
failure 732
pat on the –
incite 615
encourage 861
approve 931
pay – *retaliate* 718
put – *deteriorate* 659
restore 660
send – 764
take – again 790
carry one's thoughts – 505
some time – 122
spring – 277
trace – 505
turn – 283
turn one's – 283
turn one's – upon
repel 289
inattention 458
avoid 623
oppose 708
seclusion 893
discourtesy 895
disrespect 929
contempt 930
set one's – against

the wall 604
– to back 235
– down 283
– one's note 806
– out *retire* 283
change sides 607
relinquish 624
– pedal 275
– up *support* 215
influence 615
aid 707
put one's – up
anger 900
set one's – up
pride 878
backbite 932, 934
backbiter 936
backbone
intrinsic 5
energy 171
frame 215
centre 222
resolution 604
persevere 604*a*
soul 820
game to the – 604
back door 627
back down 607
backer 711
back-fire 406
back friend 891
backgammon 840
background
distance 196
rear 235
in the –
latent 526
ignoble 874
keep in the –
hide 528
modest 881
seclusion 893
put one in the – 874
throw into the – 460
backsheesh 784, 973
backside 235
backslider 607
backsliding
regression 283
tergiversation 607
relapse 661
vice 945
heterodox 984
impiety 988
backstairs
ambush 530
way 627
– influence 702

backward
tardy 133
regression 283
unwilling 603
deteriorate 659
backwardation 813
backwards 283
bend – 235
– and forwards
interchange 148
oscillation 314
backwater 275, 283
in a – 893
backwoodsman
inhabitant 188
agriculture 371
bacon
butter upon – 641
save one's – 664, 671
Baconian method 461
bacteria 193
bactericide 662
baculinum, argumentum –
compel 744
lawless 964
punish 972
bad 649
unclean 653
wrong 923
– blood 898, 907
go – 653, 659
– business 859
– case 477
– chance 473
put a – construction on 523
– debt 806
– fairy 980
– faith 940
– grace 895
– habit 613
– hand 701
– humour
discontent 832
dejection 837
anger 900
sullen 901*a*
not a – idea 498
– intent 907
– job *evil* 619
botch 699
hopeless 859
– joke 851
– language 908
view in a – light 934
– luck &c. 735

– man 949
– money 800
– name 932, 934
in – odour 889
take in – part 832, 900
– repute 874
– smell 401
– spirit 980
– spirits 837
– taste 579, 851
– temper 900, 901, 901*a*
on – terms 713, 889
– time of it 828
– turn 619, 907
in a – way
disease 655
worse 659
danger 665
adversity 735
– woman 949
from – to worse
aggravation 835
badaud 501
badge 550
– of authority 747
– of infamy 874
– of slavery 746
badger 830
– dog 366
badinage 842, 856
badly off
adversity 735
poor 804
badminton 840
badness 649
Baedeker 266
baffle *hinder* 706
defeat 731
– description
unconformable 83
wonder 870
baffling
puzzling 519
bag *put up* 184
receptacle 191
protrude 250
acquire 775
take 789
steal 791
– and baggage 780
bagatelle
trivial 643
pastime 840
baggage 270
minx 129
materials 635
property 780

hussy 962
baggy 47
bagman 758
bagnio 961
bagpipes 417
bah! 930
bail 771
go – 806
leg – 623
bailie 965
bailiff
director 694
servant 746
factor 758
officer 965
bailiwick
region 181
jurisdiction 965
Bairam
holiday 840
rite 998
bairn 129
bait *attraction* 288
food 298
trap 545
lure 615
refresh 689
attack 716
bribe 784
harass 830
swallow the – 547
bake 384
bakehouse 386
baker 637
baker's dozen 98
baking heat 382
bal 840
Balaclava helmet 225
balais 847
balance *equal* 27
mean 29
compensate 30
remainder 40
numeration 85
weigh 319
compare 464
style 578
hesitate 605
money 800
accounts 811
in the – 475
the mind losing its – 503
off one's –
irresolute 605
fail 732
want of – 579
– accounts with
pay 807

balanced 150, 242
balbucinate 583
balbutiate 583
balcony 250
theatre 599
bald *bare* 226
style 575
uninteresting 841
ugly 846
plain 849
baldachin 223, 1000
balderdash 517, 577
baldric 230, 247
bale *bundle* 72
load 190
ladle 270
evil 619
– out 297
baleful 649
balister 727
balize 550
balk *disappoint* 509
deceive 545
hinder 706
Balkanize 713
ball *globe* 249
missile 284
shot 727
dance 840
party 892
– at one's feet 731, 737
keep up the – 143, 682
ballad 415, 597
– monger 597
ballast
compensation 30
weight 319
wisdom 498
safety 666
without – *rash* 863
vicious 945
ballerina 599
ballet 599, 840
ballet-dancer 599
ballistics
projectiles 284
war 722
arms 727
ballon d'essai 463
balloon 273, 726
balloonist 269
balloonry 267
ballot 535, 609
ball-room 840
balm *moderate* 174
fragrance 400
remedy 662
relief 834
Balmoral *boot* 225

balmy
sleep 683
balneal 337
balourdise 699
balsam 662
balsamic
salubrious 834
balustrade
support 215
inclosure 232
bam 544
bambino 129
bamboozle 545
ban *exclude* 55
prohibit 761
denounce 908
under the – 909
– with bell, book, and candle 998
banal 613, 843
band *ligature* 45
assemblage 72
filament 205
belt 230
ring 247
music 415, 416, 417
party 712
shackle 752
– of hope 958
– together 709
– with 720
bandage 43, 45
support 215
cover 223
remedy 662
restraint 752
the eyes -d 442
bandana 225
bandbox 191
banded together 178, 713
bandit 792
bandog 664, 668
bandolier 636
bandore 417
bandrol 550
bands 999
bandurria 417
bandy
exchange 148
agitate 315
– about 531
– legged 243
– words 476, 588
bane 619, 663
baneful 649
bang *impel* 276
sound 406
beat 972
bangle 847

banish *eject* 297
seclude 893
punish 972
banister 215
banjo 417
bank *acclivity* 217
side of lake 342
store 636
sand 667
fence 717
money 802
sea – 342
– of elegance 800
– holiday 840
– up 670
banker 797, 801
game 840
bank-note 800
bankruptcy 732, 808
banlieue 197, 227
banner 550
enlist under the -s of 707
raise one's – 722
banneret 875
banns
forbid the – 761
publish the –
ask 765
marriage 903
banquet 298, 840
banquette 717
banshee 979, 980
bantam cock 887
banter 842, 856
banterer 844
banting 956
bantling 129, 167
banyan *stint* 640
fast 956
baptism *name* 564
rite 998
Baptist 984
baptistery 1000
bar *except* 38
exclude 55
hotel 189
line 200
support 215
inclosure 232
close 261
music 413
hindrance 706
insignia 747
prison 752
prohibit 761
ingot 800
tribunal 966
legal profession 968
– sinister *flaw* 651

disrepute 874
illegal 964
crossing the – 360
Barabbas 792
baragouin 517
barb *spike* 253
nag 271
– the dart *pain* 830
barbacan 717
barbarian
uncivilized 876
evil-doer 913
barbaric 851, 876
barbarism
neology 563
bad style 579
vulgarity 851
discourtesy 895
barbarous
unformed 241
plebeian 876
maleficent 907
barbette 717
barbican 717
barbouillage 590
barcarolle 415
bard 416, 597
bare *mere* 32
nude 226
manifest 525
disclose 529
scanty 640
– back 226
– bone 203
– faced *deceitful* 544, *insolent* 885
– foot 226, 804
- headed 928
scud under - poles 704
- possibility 473
- supposition 514
bargain
compact 769
barter 794
cheap 815
into the - 37
- for 507
- and sale *transfer of property* 783
barge 273
bargee 269
baritone 408
bark *rind* 223
strip 226
ship 273
yelp 412
- at *threaten* 909
censure 932
more - than bite 908

- worse than bite 885
barker 767
barleycorn
little 193
Barleycorn, Sir John - 298
barm leaven 320
bubbles 353
Barmecide feast 956
barmy 320, 503
barn 189
barnacles 445
barndoor fowl 366
barograph 206, 338
barometer air 338
measure 466
consult the - 463
baron peer 875
husband 903
court - 966
- of the Exchequer 967
baronet 875
baronial 878
baroque 853
baroscope 338
barouche 272
barque 273
barrack 189
barracoon 717
barrage 407, 717
barratry 940
barred 219, 440
barrel 191, 249
- organ 417
barren 169, 645
barricade fence 232
obstacle 706
defence 717
prison 752
barrier [see barricade]
barring save 38
excluding 55
except 83
- out resist 719
disobey 742
barrister 968
revising - 967
barrow
mound 206
vehicle 272
grave 363
barter
reciprocate 12
interchange 148
commerce 794
barytone 408
basal 215
bas-bleu
scholar 492
affectation 855
base
site 183
lowest part **211**
support 215
bad 649
cowardly 862
shameful 874
servile 886
dishonourable 940
vicious 945
- ball 840
- born 876
- coin 800
- note 408
- of operations
plan 626
attack 716
- viol 417
baseball diamond 213
baseboard 211
based on ground of belief 467
baseless 2, 4
basement cellar 191
lowest part 207, 211
bash 276
bashaw 739, 745
bashful 881
bashi bazouk 726
basilica 1000
basilisk sight 441
cannon 727
serpent 949
basin dock 189
vessel 191
hollow 252
plain 344
basinet 717
basis
lowest part 211
support 215
preparation 673
bask physical enjoyment 377
warmth 382
prosperity 734
moral enjoyment 827
basket 191
- of 190
bas-relief 250, 557
bass music 415
- note 408
- viol 417
basset horn 417
bassinet 191, 215
bassoon 417
basso-profondo 408
basso-rilievo 250, 557
bastard 545, 925
baste beat 276
punish 972
Bastille 752
bastinado 972
bastion 717
bat 276, 727
batch 25, 72
bate diminish 36
subtract 38
reduce price 813
bated breath
with - faint sound 405
expecting 507
hiding 528
whisper 581
humble 879
bath 337, 652
public -s 652
warm - 386
- room 191, 652
Bath chair 272
bathe immerse 300
plunge 310
water 337
bathos 497
bathysphere 208
batik 440
batman 637
bâton support 215
sceptre 747
batrachian 366
batta 973
battalion 726
batten
feed 298
stage lighting 599
- down the hatches 261
- on 886
batter destroy 162
beat 276
battered 659, 688
battering-ram 276
battering-train 727
battery electric 153
artillery 726
guns 727
floating - 726
plant a - 716
battle 720, 722
half the - 642
win the - 731
- array order 60
prepare 673
war 722
- axe 727
- cruiser 726
- cry 550, 722
- field arena 728
- ground discord 713
- ship 726
- with oppose 708
battledore and shuttlecock
interchange 148
game 840
battlement 257, 717
battre
- la campagne
nonsense 497
diffuse style 573
excitable 825
- l'eau avec un bâton 645
- le fer sur l'enclume 134
- la générale 669
se - contre des moulins 645
ne - que d'une aile 683
battology
repeat 104
diffuse style 573
battue pursuit 622
attack 716
kill 361
bauble 643, 840
bavardage 517, 584
bawd 962
bawdy, - house 961
bawl 411
bawn 189
bay concave 252
gulf 343
cry 412
brown 433
at - danger 665
difficulty 704
defence 717, 719
bring to - 716
- the moon 645
- window 260
bayadère 599
bayard 271
bayonet kill 361
attack 716
weapon 727
crossed -s 708
at the point of the - war 722
severity 739
coercion 744
bays trophy 733
crown 877

bazaar 799
B.C. 106
be 1
– all and end all
whole 50
intention 620
importance 642
– off *depart* 293
eject 297
retract 773
– it so 488
– that as it may 30
beach 231, 342
beach comber 268
beacon 550, 663
bead 249
beadle *janitor* 263
law officer 965
church 996
beadledom 737
beadroll *list* 86
prayers 990
ritual 998
beads
ornament 847
tell one's – 990, 998
beadsman
servant 746
clergy 996
beagle 366
beak *face* 234
nose 250
magistrate 967
beaker 191
beam *support* 215
side 236
weigh 319
light 420
on – ends
powerless 158
horizontal 213
side 236
fail 732
wonder 870
beaming
beautiful 845
bean 276
beanfeast 840
bear *produce* 161
sustain 215
carry 270
admit of 470
suffer 821
endure 826
bring to – 677
more than flesh and blood can – 824
unable to –
excited 825
dislike 867
– away 789
– away the bell 648, 731
– the brunt 704, 717
– the burden 625
– the cross 828
– company 88
– down 173, 885
– down upon 716
– false witness 544
– fruit *produce* 161
useful 644
success 731
prosper 734
– a hand 680
– hard upon 649
– harmless 717
– ill 825
– off *deviate* 279
– on 215
– oneself 692
– out *evidence* 467
vindicate 937
– pain 828
– the palm 33
– a sense 516
– through 707
– up *approach* 286
persevere 604a
relieve 834
cheerful 836
– up against 719, 861
– upon
relevant 9, 23
influence 175
– with
tolerate 740
permit 760
take coolly 826
forgive 918
bear
savage 907
surly 895
had it been a – it would have bitten you 458
– garden
disorder 59
discord 713
arena 728
– leader 540
– pit 370
– skin *cap* 225
helmet 717
– with a sore back 901
bearable 651
beard *hair* 205
prickles 253
rough 256
defy 715
brave 861
insolence 885
pluck by the –
disrespect 929
– the lion 604
beardless 127, 226
bearer 271, 363
bearing *relation* 9
support 215
direction 278
meaning 516
demeanour 692
– rein 706, 752
bearings
circumstances 8
situation 183
armorial – 550
beast *animal* 366
unclean 653
discourteous 895
– of burden 271, 690
beat *be superior* 33
periodic 138
region 181
impulse 276
surpass 303
oscillate 314
agitation 315
crush 330
sound 407
line of pursuit 625
path 627
overcome 731
strike 972
– about
circuit 629
– the air 645
– against 708
– one's breast 839
– about the bush
try for 463
evade the point 477
prevaricate 544
diffuse style 573
– down *destroy* 162
cheapen 794, 819
insolent 885
– of drum
music 416
publish 531
alarm 669
war 722
command 741
pomp 882
without – of drum 528
– into *teach* 537
– off 717
– a retreat
retire 283
avoid 623
submit 725
– time *clock* 114
music 416
– up *churn* 352
– up against
oppose 708
– up for *cater* 637
– up one's quarters
seek 461
visit 892
– up for recruits
prepare 673
aid 707
beaten track
habit 613
way 627
leave the – 83
tread the – 82
beatic 827
beatific 829, 981
beatification 827, 987
beating high
the heart – 824
beatitude 827
beau *man* 373
fop 854
admirer 897
– idéal 650, 845
– monde 852
beautify 845, 847
beautiless 846
beauty 845
beaver *hat* 225
becalm 265
because *cause* 153
attribution 155
answer 462
reasoning 476
motive 615
bechance 151
beck *rill* 348
sign 550
mandate 741
at one's – *aid* 707
obey 743
beckon *sign* 550
motive 615
call 741
becloud *dark* 421
hide 528
become
accord with 23
change to 144
behove 926
– of 151
becoming

accordant 23
proper 646
beautiful 845, 847
due 924
becripple 158
bed *lodgment* 191
layer 204
support 215
garden 371
marriage 903
brought to – 161
death – 360
smooth the – of death 707
go to – 265, 683
keep one's – 655
– of down 687
– gown 255
– maker 746
– out 371
– ridden 655
– room 191
– of roses 377, 734
put to – with a shovel 363
– time 126
bedarken 421
bedaub 223
bedazzle 420
bedding 215
bedeck 847
bedel 965
bedesman
[*see* beadsman]
bedevil *derange* 61
sorcery 992
bedew 339
bedight 847
bedim 421, 422
bedizen *clothe* 225
ornament 847
vulgar 851
Bedlam
– broke loose 59
candidate for – 504
be-dog 281
Bedouin 792
bedraggled 59
bedwarf 195
bee 690
busy – 682
swarm like –s 102
– in one's bonnet 503
– in a bottle 407
– line 246, 278
–'s wax 352
beef-eater 726
beef-headed 499
beehive 250
Beelzebub 978
beer 298
beery 959
beetle *overhang* 206, 214
project 250
blind as a – 442
Colorado – 913
– head 501
befall 151
befit *agree* 23
expedient 646
due 924, 926
befog 353, 528
befool *mad* 503
deceive 545
befooled
victimized 732
before *in order* 62
in time 116
presence 186
in space 234
precession 280
preference 609
set – one 525
– Christ 106
– long 132
– mentioned 62, 116
– now 122
– one's eyes 446, 525
– one's time 132
– you could –turn round, – say Jack Robinson 113
beforehand
prior 116
early 132
foresight 510
resolve – 611
befoul 653
befriend 707, 888
befuddlement 959
beg *Turk* 745
ask 765
– one's bread 765
poor 804
– leave 760
– one's life 914
– pardon 952
– the question 477
beget 161
begetter 166
beggar *idler* 683
petitioner 767
poor 804
degrade 874
low person 876
sturdy – 792
– description 83, 870
– my neighbour 840
– on horseback 885
beggared
bankrupt 808
beggarly *mean* 643
vile 874
vulgar 876
servile 886
– account of empty boxes 640, 804
begging
go a –
too much 641
useless 645
offered 763
free 748
– letter 765
begilt 847
begin 66
– again 104
beginner 541
beginning 66
begird 227, 229
beglerbeg 745
begone
depart 293
ejection 297
abrogate 756
– dull care 836
Begotten, the only – 976
begrime 653
begrudge
unwilling 603
refuse 764
stingy 819
beguile *mislead* 495
deceive 545
reconcile 831
– the time
inaction 681
amusement 840
béguine 996
begum 745, 875
behalf 618, 707
in – of 759
behave oneself
conduct 692
fashion 852
courtesy 894
behaviour 692
on one's good – 894, 944
behead 361, 972
behemoth 192
behest 741
behind
in order 63
in space 235
sequence 281
– the age 124, 491
– one's back 187
speak ill of – one's back 934
– the bars 751
– the scenes
cause 153
unseen 447
cognizant 490
latent 526
hidden 528
playhouse 599
– time 133
behindhand
late 133
shortcoming 304
adversity 735
insolvent 808
behold 441, 457
beholden 916, 926
beholder 444
behoof 618
behoove 926
being 1, 3
created – 366
human – 372
time – 106
Bel 979
belabour 276, 972
belated *late* 133
ignorant 491
belaud 931
belay *join* 43
restrain 706
belch 297
beldam 130, 913
beldame 173
beleaguer 716
bel esprit 844
belfry 206, 1000
Belial 978, 980
son of – 988
belie *deny* 536
falsify 544
contradict 708
belief 484, 488
easy of – 472
hug a – 606
believe
[*see* belief]
suppose 514
reason to – 472
– who may 485
not – one's senses 870
believer
religious 987
true – 983*a*

belike 472
belittle
decrease 36
underestimate 482
disparage 934
bell 417, 550
alarm – 669
bear away the –
goodness 648
success 731
repute 873
church – 550
cracked – 408*a*
passing – 363
– book and candle
swear 535
curse 908
spell 993
rite 998
– the cat 861
– shape 249, 252
belladonna 663
belle 374, 854
a la – étoile 220, 338
belles-lettres 560
belli, casus – 824
bellicose 720, 722
bellied 250
belligerent
contentious 720
warlike 722
combatant 726
belling 412
bellman 534
bello, flagrante – 722
Bellona 722
bellow *loud* 404
cry 411
animal cry 412
wail 839
bellows 349, 580
bells, peal of – 407
bellwether 64, 694
belly *receptacle* 191
inside 221
convex 250
–ful 52
– god 957
– timber 298
belomancy 511
belong to *related* 9
component 56
included 76
attribute 157
property 777, 780
duty 926
beloved 897
below 207
here – 318
– the mark 32
– par 34, 207
bad 649
indifferent 651
discount 813
ignoble 876
– its full strength 651
– stairs 207
belt *outline* 230
ring 247
strait 343
swimming – 666
belting 633
Belus 979
belvedere 441
bemask 528
bemingle 41
bemire 653
bemoan 839
bemused 458
bench *support* 215
council 696
tribunal 966
Bench, King's – 752
bencher 968
bend *oblique* 217
angle 244
curve 245
incline 278
deviate 279
depression 308
circuit 311
give 324
submit 725
– backwards 235
– the bow 686
– the brows 932
– one's course 27
– the knee
bow down 308
submit 725
humble 879
servile 886
courtesy 894
respect 928
worship 990
– one's looks upon 441
– the mind 457
– over 250
– to rules &c. 82
– sinister 874
– one's steps 622
– to *tend* 176
– towards 278
– to one's will 737
beneath 207
– one 940
– notice 643
Benedick 903
Benedictine 996
benediction
gratitude 916
approval 931
worship 990
nuptial – 903
benefaction 784
benefactor 816, 912
benefice 995
beneficent 906
beneficial 648
– interest 780
beneficiary
possessor 779
receive 785
clergy 996
benefit *good* 618
use 644
do good 648
aid 707
acquisition 775
property 780
benevolence 906
reap the – of 658
benefits forgot 917
bene gesserit, quamdiu se – 926
benet 545
benevolence
tax 812
love 897
kindness **906**
universal – 910
Bengal heat 382
benighted
dark 421
ignorant 491
benign 656, 906
benignant 906
benison 618, 931
Benjamin's mess 33, 50
Benshie 979
bent *tendency* 176
angle 244
turn of mind 820
desire 865
fool to the top of one's – 856
– on *willing* 602
resolved 604
intention 620
desirous 865
Benthamite 910
ben trovato
likely 472
imagination 515
untruth 546
wit 842
benumb
insensible 376
cold 385
deaden affections 823
beplaster 933
bepraise 931
bequest 270
gift 784
bereavement
death 360
loss 776
take away 789
bereft *poor* 804
– of life 360
– of reason 503
béret 225
berg, ice – 383
bergamot 400
berlin 272
berserk 173, 503
berth *lodging* 189
bed 215
office 625
beryl *green* 435
jewel 847
beseech 765, 990
beseem 926
beset *surround* 227
follow 281
attack 716
entreat 765
annoy 830
haunt 860
– with difficulties 704
besetting 78, 613
– sin 945
beshrew 908
beside *except* 83
near 197
alongside 236
– the mark 10, 495
– oneself 503, 824
besides 37
besiege
surround 227
attack 716
solicit 765
bésique 840
beslaver 933
beslime 653
beslubber 933
besmear 223, 653
besom 652
besotted 481
bespangle 847
bespatter *dirt* 653
disapprove 932
flatter 933
detract 934

bespeak *early* 132
evidence 467
indicate 516
engage 755
ask for 765
bespeckle 440
bespot 440
besprinkle 41, 440
best 648, 650
all for the –
good 618
prosper 734
content 831
hope 858
bad is the – 649
do one's –
care 459
try 675
activity 682
exertion 686
have the – of it 731
make the – of it
over-estimate 482
use 677
submit 725
compromise 774
take easily 826
hope 858
the – 800
to the – of one's belief 484
– bib and tucker
prepared 673
ornament 847
ostentation 882
– friends 890
– intentions 906
– man 903
– part 31, 50
– seller 731
make the – of one's time 684
bestead 644
bestial 954, 961
bestir oneself
activity 682
haste 684
exertion 686
bestow 784
– one's hand 903
– thought 451
bestraddle 215
bestrew 73
bestride 206, 215
bet 621
betake oneself to
journey 266
business 625
use 677
bête, pas si – 498
bête noire *bane* 663
fear 860
hate 898
bethel 1000
bethink 451, 505
bethral 749, 751
betide 151
betimes 132
betoken
evidence 467
predict 511
indicate 550
betray *disclose* 529
deceive 545
dishonour 940
– itself *visible* 446
betrayer 941
betrim 673
betroth 768, 903
betrothed 897
better *good* 648
improve 658
appeal to one's – feelings 914
get – *health* 654
improve 658
refreshment 689
restoration 660
get the – of, 479, 702, 731
think – of 658, 950
seen – days
deteriorate 659
adversity 735
poor 804
– half 903
only – than nothing 651
– sort 875
for – for worse
choice 609
marriage 903
between 228
– cup and lip 111
far – 198
lie – 228
– the lines 526
vibrate – two extremes 149
– ourselves 528
– two fires 665
– maid 746
betwixt 228
bevel 217
– gearing 633
bever 298
beverage 298
bévue 732
bevy 72, 102
bewail *regret* 833
lament 839
beware 665, 668
bewilder
put out 458
uncertainty 475
astonish 870
bewitch
fascinate 615
please 829
excite love 897
exorcise 992
bey 745
beyond *superior* 33
distance 196
go – 303
– compare 31, 33
– control 471
– one's depth 208, 519
– expression 31
– one's grasp 471
– hope 731, 534
– the mark 303, 641
– measure 641
– possibility 471
– praise
perfect 650
approbation 931
virtue 944
– price 814
– question 474, 494
– reason 471
– remedy 859
– seas 57
bezel 217
bhang 663
bias *influence* 175
tendency 176
slope 217
prepossession 481
disposition 820
bib *pinafore* 225
drink 959
bibber *weep* 839
toper 959
bibble-babble 584
bibelot 847
bibendum, nunc est – 959
Bible 985
– oath 535
biblioclasm 162
bibliography 593
bibliolatry
learning 490
heterodoxy 984
idolatry 991
bibliomancy 511
bibliomania 490
bibliomaniac 492
bibliophile 492
bibliopole 593
bibliotheca 593
bibulous 298, 959
bicameral 90
bicapital 90
bice 435, 438
bicentenary 98, 138, 883
bicker *flutter* 315
quarrel 713
bicolour 440
biconjugate 91
bicuspid 91
bicycle 272
bid *order* 741
offer 763
– the banns 903
– defiance 715
– fair *tend* 176
probable 472
promise 511
hope 858
– a long farewell 624
– for *intend* 620
offer 763
request 765
bargain 794
bidder 767
bide *wait* 133
remain 141
take coolly 826
– one's time 133
watch 507
inactive 681
bidet 271
biennial
periodic 138
plant 367
bienséance 852, 894
bier 363
bifacial 90
bifarious 90
bifid 91
bifold 90
biform 90
bifurcate 91, 244
big *in degree* 31
in size 192
wide 194
look – *defy* 715
proud 878
insolent 885
talk – 885, 909
– sounding
loud 404
words 577
affected 855
– swollen 194
– with 161
– with the fate of 511

bigamy 903
biggin 191
bight 343
bigot *positive* 474
prejudice 481
obstinate 606
heterodox 984
impious 988
bigotry 907
bigwig *scholar* 492
sage 500
nobility 875
bijou *goodness* 648
beauty 845
ornament 847
bilander 273
bilateral 90, 236
bilbo 727
bilboes 752
put into – 751
bile 900
bilge *base* 211
convex 250
yawn 260
– water 653
bilingual 560
bilious 837
bilk
disappoint 509
cheat 545
steal 791
bill *list* 86
hatchet 253
placard 531
ticket 550
paper 593
plan 626
weapon 727
money order 800
money account 811
charge 812
in law 969
true – 969
– and coo 902
– of exchange 771
– of fare *food* 298
plan 626
– of indictment 938
–s of mortality 360
– of sale 771
billet *locate* 184
ticket 550
apportion 786
billet *epistle* 592
– doux 902
billfold 191
billhook 253
billiard – ball 249
– room 191

– table *flat* 213
billiards 840
Billingsgate 563, 908
billion 98
billow *sea* 348
river 341
billy-cock 225
billy-goat 373
bimetallism 800
bin 191
binary 89
bind *connect* 43
cover 223
compel 744
condition 770
obligation 926
– hand and foot 751
– oneself 768
– over 744
– up wounds 660
binding 744
bine 367
binnacle 693
binocular 445
binomial 89
biogenesis 161
biograph 448
biography 594
biology 357, 359
bioscope 448
biota 357
biparous 89
bipartite 44, 91
biplane 273
biplicity 89
biquadrate 96
birch *flog* 972
– rod 975
bird 366
kill two –s with one stone 682
–'s eye view 441, 448
–s of a feather 17
the – has flown 187, 671
– in hand 777, 781
– of ill omen
omen 512
warning 668
hopeless 859
– of passage 268
– of prey 739
a little – told me 527
birdcage 370
birdlime *glue* 45
trap 545
biretta 999

birth *beginning* 66
production 161
paternity 166
nobility 875
– place 153
– right 924
birthday 138, 883
– suit 226
birthmark 848
bis *repeat* 104
approval 931
biscuits, s'embarquer sans – 674
bise 349
bisection 68, **91**
bishop *punch* 298
clergy 996
–'s palace 1000
–'s purple 437
bishopric 995
bisque 33
bissextile 138
bistoury 253
bistre 433
bisulcate 259
bit
small quantity 32
part 51
interval 106
curb 752
just a – 26
– by bit
by degrees 26
by instalments 51
in detail 79
slowly 275
– between the teeth 600, 719
bitch *animal* 366
female 374
clumsy 699
fail 732
impure 962
bite *eat* 298
physical pain 378
cold 385
cheat 545
dupe 547
etch 558
mental pain 830
– the dust 725
– in 259
– the thumb 900, 929
– the tongue 392
biter bit 718
biting *pain* 378
cold 383
pungent 392
painful 830
discourteous 895

censorious 932
bitten 897
bitter *beer* 298
cold 383
taste 392, 395
painful 830
acrimonious 895
hate 898
angry 900
malevolent 907
– end 67
– ender 606, 710, 832
– pill 735
– words 932
bitterly *greatly* 31
bitterness
[*see* bitter]
pain 828
regret 833
bitumen 356*a*
bituminous coal 388
bivouac
encamp 184
camp 189
repose 265
watch 668
bi-weekly 138
bizarre 83, 853
blab 529
blabber 584
black *colour* 431
crime 945
look – *feeling* 821
discontent 832
angry 900
– art 992
– and blue
beat 972
– board 590
– book 938
– eye 848, 972
– in the face
swear 535
excitement 821, 824
– flag 722
– hole *crowd* 72
prison 752
– lead 556
– letter *old* 124
barbarism 563
print 591
– list 932
– looks
discourteous 895
sullen 901*a*
disapprove 932
magic 992
– mail *theft* 791

booty 793
bribe 973
– sheep 949
– spots in the horizon 859
– swan 83
– and white
chiaroscuro 420
colourless 429
record 551
writing 590
prove that – is white 477
blackamoor 431
wash a – white 471
blackball 55, 893, 932
blackcoat 996
blacken [*see* black]
defame 934
blackguard
vulgar 851
rude 895
base 940
vagabond 949
blackleg 792
black Maria 727
blackness 431
blacksmith 690
bladder 191
blade *edge tool* 253
man 373
instrument 633
sharp fellow 682
proficient 700
sword 727
fop 854
blague 545
blain 250, 848
blame 155, 932
lay – on 938
take – 932
blameless 946
blameworthy
disapprove 932
vice 945
guilt 947
blanc-bec 701
blanch 429, 430
blancmange 298
bland 174, 894
blandiloquence 933
blandishment
inducement 615
endearment 902
flattery 933
blank 2, 4
empty 187
simple 849
look –
disappointed 509
discontent 832
wonder 870
point – 576
– cartridge 158
– verse 597
blanket 223, 384
wet – 174
toss in a – 929
blare 404, 412
blarney 933
blasé 841, 869
blasphemy 988
blast
destroy 162
explosion 173
wind 349
sound 404
adversity 735
curse 908
– furnace 386
blatant *loud* 404
cry 412
silly 499
blather 584
blatter 412
blaze *heat* 382
light 420
mark 550
excitement 824
– abroad 531
blazer 225
blazing
luminary 423
blazon *publish* 531
repute 873
ornament 847
ostentation 882
blé: manger son – en herbe 818
bleach 429, 430
bleak 383
blear-eyed 443
bleary 422
bleat 412
bleed
physical pain 378
remedy 662
spend money 809
extort money 814
moral pain 828
make the heart – 830
– freely *liberal* 816
bleeding
hemorrhage 299
remedy 662
– heart 828
blemish
imperfection 651
injure 659
ugly 846
defect 848
blench *avoid* 623
whiten 821
fear 860
blend 41, 48
– with 714
bless
give pleasure 829
approve 931
divine function 976
worship 990
– my heart 870
– one's stars 838, 916
blessed 827
abode of the – 981
blessedness
single – 904
blessing *good* 618
approval 931
blessings 734
blest 827
– with 177
bletonism 511
blight
deteriorate 659
adversity 735
– hope 509
blighty 189
blimp 273
blind 223
shade 424
cecity 442
inattentive 458
ignorant 491
conceal 528
screen 530
deception 545
instinctive 601
pretext 617
insensible 823
drunk 959
– alley 261
– bargain
uncertain 475
purposeless 621
rash 863
– the eyes *hide* 528
deceive 545
– hookey 840
– lead the blind 538
– man's buff 840
– man's holiday
evening 126
dark 421, 422
– to one's own merit 880
– to the world 959
– of one eye 443
– reasoning 486
– side *prejudice* 481
credulity 486
obstinacy 606
blinders 424, 443
blindness 442
blind pig 964
blink *wink* 443
neglect 460
falter 605
avoid 623
– at *blind to* 442, 458
blinkard 443
blinker 424, 530
bliss 827
celestial 981
blister 250
blithe 836
blizzard 349
bloat 194
bloated
expanded 194
misshapen 243
convex 250
– with pride 878
blob 250
block *mass* 192
support 215
dense 321
hard 323
fool 501
engraving 558
writing 590
hinder 706
execution 975
bring to the – 972
wood – 558
– of buildings 189
– out 230, 240, 673
– printing 591
– up 261, 706
blockade
surround 227
close 261
restrain 751
exclude 893
blockhead 501
blockhouse 717
blockish 499
blond 429, 430
blood
consanguinity 11
fluid 333
kill 361
fop 854
nobility 875
dye with –

severe 739
hands in – *cruel* 907
in the – 5
life – 359
new – 658, 824
spill – *war* 722
– for blood 919
– boil *excite* 824, 825
anger 900
– run cold 830, 860
– heat 382
– horse 271
– hound 913
– letting 297, 662
– poisoning 655
– red 434
– stained 361
– sucker 789, 913
– thirsty
murderous 361
cruel 907
– up *excited* 824
angry 900
bloodless 160
peace 721
virtue 946
bloody [*see* blood]
red 434
unclean 653
cruel 907
bloom *youth* 127
flower 367
blue 438
health 654
prosperity 734
bloomer 495
bloomers 225
blooming 654, 845
blossom
flower 154, 161, 367
prosperity 734
blot *blacken* 431
error 495
obliterate 552
dirty 653
blemish 848
disgrace 874
guilt 947
– out *destroy* 162
forgive 918
blotch 848
blouse 225
blow *expand* 194
knock 276
wind 349
unexpected 508
disappointment 509
evil 619
action 680
get wind 688
failure 732
prosper 734
pain 828, 830
come to –s 720, 722
deal a – at 716
deal a – to 972
death – 360, 361
– for blow 718
– one's brains out 361
– the coals 824
– down 162
– the fire 384
– the gaff 529
– hole 351
– the horn 416
– hot and cold
lie 544
irresolute 605
tergiversation 607
caprice 608
– a kiss 902
– off *disperse* 73
– out *food* 298
darken 421
gorge 957
– over *past* 122
– pipe 349, 727
– the trumpet 873
– one's own trumpet 882
– up *destroy* 162
eruption 173
inflate 194
wind 349
excite 824
objurgate 932, 934
blower 349
blowhard 884
blown [*see* blow]
fatigued 688
proud 878
storm – over 664, 721
– upon 874, 932
blow-out 406
blowzy *swollen* 194
red 434
blubber *fat* 356
cry 839
Blücher boot 225
bludgeon 727
– man 726, 913
blue *sky* 338
colour 438
learned 490
bit of – hope 858
look –
disappointed 509
feeling 821
discontent 832
disrepute 874
out of the – 508
swear till all's – 535
true – 543, 939
– book 86, 551
– blood 875
– devils 837
– jacket 269
– light 550, 669
– pencil 174, 596
– moon 110
– Peter 293, 550
– and red 437
– ribbon 733, 877
– ruin 959
– stocking
scholar 492
affectation 855
– and yellow 435
Bluebeard
marriage 903
libertine 962
blueness 438
blues 837, 840
bluff *violent* 173
high cliff 206
blunt 254
deceive 545
boasting 884
insolent 885
discourteous 895
blunder *error* 495
absurdity 497
awkward 699
failure 732
– upon 156
blunderbuss 727
blunderhead 701
blunderheaded 499
blunt *weaken* 160
inert 172
moderate v. 174
obtuse 254
benumb 376
damp v. 616
plain-spoken 703
cash 800
deaden 823
discourteous 895
– tool 645
– witted 499
bluntness 254
blur
imperfect vision 443
dirt 653
blemish 848
stigma 874
blurb 931
blurred
invisible 447
blurt out 529, 582
blush *flush* 382
redden 434
feel 821
humbled 879
modest 881
at first – *see* 441
appear 448
manifest 525
put to the –
humble 897
browbeat 885
discourtesy 895
blushing honours 873, 881
bluster *violent* 173
defiant 715
boasting 884
insolent 885
threaten 909
blusterer 887
blustering [*see* bluster]
windy 349
Bo to a goose, not say – 862
boa 225
Boanerges 540
boar 366, 373
board *layer* 204
support 215
food 298
hard 323
council 696
attack 716
tribunal 966
festive – 892
go by the – 158, 162
go on – 293
on – 186, 273
preside at the – 693
– of trade 621
– school 542
boarder 188
boarding-house 189
boards 599, 728
boast 884
not much to – of 651
boasting 884
boaston 840
boat 273

in the same – 88
– race 720
boating 267
boatman 269
boatswain 269
bob *depress* 308
leap 309
oscillate 314
agitate 315
money 800
– a curtsy 894
– for *fish* 463
Bobadil, Captain – 887
bobbed
hair 53
bobbin 312
bobbing *fuel* 388
bobbish 654
bobby *police* 664
bobsleigh 272
bobsleighing 840
bobtailed 53
bocage 367
bocca, per amusare la – 394
Boche 913
boddice 225
bode 511
bodega 189
bodily
substantially 3
wholly 50
material 316
– enjoyment 377
– fear 860
– pain 378
bodkin
go between 228
perforator 262
body *substance* 3
whole 50
assemblage 72
frame 215
matter 316
party 712
in a – *together* 88
– and blood of Christ 987
– clothes 225
– colour 556
– of doctrine 490
– forth 554
– guard 717, 753
– of knowledge 490
– politic
mankind 372
authority 737
keep – and soul together 654
– of water 438
Bœotian *rustic* 371
stupid 499
fool 501
vulgar 851
ignoble 876
Boer 371
bog 345, 653
– trotter 876
boggart 980
boggle *hesitate* 605
awkward 699
difficulty 704
bogie 980
truck 272
bogle 980
bogus 545
Bohemian
unconventional 83
nomad 268
ungenteel 851
boil *violence* 173
effervesce 315
bubble 353
heat 382, 384
ulceration 655
excitement 824, 825
anger 900
– down 195
boiler 386
boisterous
violent 173
hasty 684
excitable 825
bold *prominent* 250
unreserved 525
vigorous 574
brave 861
make – with 895
show a – front 715, 861
– faced 885
– push *essay* 675
– relief *visible* 446
– stroke *plan* 626
success 731
bole 50
bolero 840
bollard 45
bolshevik 146, 742
bolshevist 737, 742
bolster *support* 215
repair 658
aid 707
– up *vindicate* 937
bolt *sift* 42
fasten 43
fastening 45
close 261
move rapidly 274
propel 284
run away 623
escape 671
hindrance 706
shaft 727
disobey 742
shackle 752
thunder – 872
– the door 761
– food 298, 957
– in 751
– upright 212
bolthead 191
bolus *mouthful* 298
remedy 662
bomb 404, 727
– proof 664, 717
– vessel 726
bombard 716
bombardier 726
bombardon 417
bombast
unmeaning 517
magniloquence 577
ridiculous 853
boasting 884
exaggeration 549
Bombastes Furioso 887
bomber
aeroplane 726
bombilation 404
bon – de augure 858
– enfant *social* 892
kindly 906
– gré mal gré 601
– marché 815
– mot 842
– naturel 836
– ton 852
– vivant 957
– voyage 293
bona – fides
veracity 543
probity 939
– roba 962
bonanza 641, 784
wealth 803
bonbon 396
bond *relation* 9
tie 45
compact 769
security 771
money 800
right 924
– of union 9, 45
government – 802
Liberty – 802
bondage 749
bonded together 712
bonds [*see* **bond**]
fetters 752
funds 802
in – *service* 746
tear asunder one's – 750
– of harmony 714
bondsman 746
bone *strength* 159
dense 321
hard 323
bred in the – 5
feel it in one's – 510
– of contention 713, 720
one – and one flesh 903
– to pick *difficulty* 704
discord 713
– setter 662
bonehouse 363
boner 495
bones [*see* **bone**]
corpse 362
music 417
break no – 648
make no – 602, 705
boneyard 363
bonfire 382
festivity 840
celebration 883
make a – of 384
bonhomie 703, 906
bonhomme 996
Boniface 890
bonne 746, 753
– bouche *end* 67
pleasant 377
savoury 394
saving 636
à la – heure 602, 831
de – volonté 602
bonnet 225
bonny 836, 845
bono: cui –
intention 620
utility 644
inutility 645
pro – publico 644, 910
bonus *extra* 641
gift 784
money 810
bony 323
bonze 996

bonzer 648
booby 501
- trap 545
boodle 793
book *register* 86
publication 531
record 551
volume **593**
script 599
enter accounts 811
at one's -s 539
bring to -
evidence 467
account 811
reprove 932
mind one's - 539
school - 542
without -
by heart 505
- of Books 985
- club 593
- of fate 601
- learning 490
- shop 593
book-case 191
booked *dying* 360
bookish 490
bookkeeper 553
bookkeeping 811
bookless
unlearned 493
bookmaking 156
bookseller 593
bookworm 492, 593
boom
support 215
sail 267
rush 274
impulse 276
sound 404
obstacle 706
defence 717
boomerang
recoil 277
retribution 718
weapon 727
boon 784
beg a - 765
- companion 890
boor *clown* 876
boorish 851, 895
boost 276, 482, 931
booster 935
boot *box* 191
dress 225
advantage 618
punishment 975
to - *added* 37
- legging 964
booted and spurred 673

booth 189, 799
bootless 645, 732
boots *dress* 225
servant 746
low person 876
what - it? 643
booty **793**
booze 959
bo-peep 441, 528
bordel 961
border *edge* 231
limit 233
flower bed 371
ornament 847
- upon 197, 199
bore *diameter* 202
hole 260
tide 348, 667
fatigue 688
trouble 828
plague 830
weary 841
bored 456
boreal
Northern **237**
cold 383
Boreas 349
boredom 841
borer 262
born 359
- so 5
- under an evil star 735
- under a lucky star **734**
borne 826
- down *failure* 732
defection 837
borné 499
borough 181, **189**
rotten - 893
- council 696
borrow 19, 788
- of Peter &c. 147
borrowed plumes
deception 545
borrower 806
borrowing 788
bosh *absurdity* 497
unmeaning 517
untrue 546
trifling 643
bosky 959
bosom *breast* 221
mind 450
affections 820
in the - of 229
- of one's family 221
- friend **890**

boss 250, 694, **737**
straw - 694
Boston 840
botanic garden 369, 371
Botanomancy 511
Botany 367, **369**
botch *bungle* 59
mend 660
unskilful 699
difficulty 704
fail 732
both 89
listen with - ears 418
burn the candle at - ends 638
butter one's bread on - sides 641
bother
uncertainty 475
bustle 682
difficulty 704
trouble 828
harass 830
bothy 189
bottle
receptacle 191
preserve 670
bee in a - 407
crack a - 298
pass the - 959
smelling - 400
- green 435
- holder
auxiliary 711
mediator 724
- up *remember* 505
hide 528
restrain 751
bottom
lowest part 211
support 215
posterior 235
combe 252
ship 273
pluck 604*a*
courage 861
at - 5
at the - of
cause 153
go to the - 310
probe to the - 461
from the - of one's heart *veracity* 543
feeling 821
- upwards 218
- land 180, 207
bottomless 208
- pit 982

angel of the - pit 978
bottomry 771
botulism 663
bouche:
bonne - *end* **67**
savoury 394
saving 636
pleasant 829
- à feu 727
bouderie 901*a*
boudoir 191
bouffe, opera **599**
bouge 250
bough *part* **51**
curve 245
tree 367
bought *flexure* **245**
bougie 423
boulder 249
boulevards 227
bouleversement
revolution 146
destruction 162
excite 824
bouillabaisse 298
bouillon 298
bounce *violence* 173
jump 309
lie 546
boast 884
insolence 885
- upon 292, 508
bouncing *large* 192
bound
circumscribe 229
swift 274
leap 309
certain 474
I'll be - 535
- back *recoil* **277**
- by 926
- for *direction* 278
destination 620
- to *promise* 768
responsible 926
boundary 233
bounden duty 926
bounder 851
boundless 105, 180
bounds 230, 235
keep within -
moderation 174
shortcoming 304
restrain 751
prohibit 761
- of possibility 470
bountiful 816, 906
Lady - 816
bounty *gift* 784
bouquet

fragrant 400
beauty 847
bourdon 215
bourgeois
middle class 29
type 591
commoner 876
bourgeon 194
bourn 233
bourse 621, 799
bouse 959
bout *turn* 138
job 680
fight 720
prank 840
drinking – 954
bout
au – du compte 476
au – de son latin
sophistry 477
ignorance 491
difficulty 704
boutade 497, 608
boutonnière 400
bovine 366, 499
bow *be inferior* 34
fore part 234
curve 245
projection 250
stoop 308
fiddlestick 417
weapon 727
ornament 847
servility 886
reverence 894
respect 928
bend the – 686
draw the long – 884
– down *worship* 990, 991
– out 297
– submission 725
– window 260
Bow bells
born within sound of – 876
Bowdlerize 652
bowed down 837, 879
bowelless 914a
bowels *inside* 221
– of compassion 914
– of the earth 208
bower 189, 191
–s of bliss 981
bowery 424
bowie knife 727
bowl *vessel* 191
rotate 312
stadium 840
flowing – 959
– along *walk* 266
swift 274
bowlder 249
bowline 45
bowler *hat* 225
bow-legged 243
bowling-green 213, 840
bowls 840
bowman 726
bowshot 197
bowsprit 234
bowstring *execution* 972, 975
box *house* 189
chest 191
seat 215
theatre 599
fight 720
horse – 272
musical – 417
wrong – *error* 495
unskilful 699
dilemma 704
– the compass
direction 278
rotation 312
change of mind 607
– the ear 900, 972
– up 751
boxer 726
boy 129
– scout 534
boyar 875
boycott 55, 297, 893
boyhood 127
brabble 713, 720
brabbler 901
brace *tie* 43
fasten 45
two 89
strengthen 159
support 215
music 413
refresh 689
bracelet *circle* 247
handcuff 752
ornament 847
bracer 392
braces 45
brachial 633
Brachygraphy 590
bracing 656
bracken 367
bracket *tie* 43, 45
couple 89
support 215
brackish 392
brad 45
bradawl 262
Bradbury 800
Bradshaw 266
brae 206
brag *cards* 840
boast 884
Braggadocio 884
braggart 884
Brahma 979
Brahmin 984, 996
braid *tie* 43
ligature 45
net 219
variegate 440
brain *kill* 361
intellect 450
skill 498
blow one's –s out 361
coinage of the – 515
suck one's –s 461
rack one's –s 451, 515
brainless 499
brainpan 450
brainsick 458
brain-storm 503, 825
brainwork 451
brainy 498
brake *carriage* 272
copse 367
hindrance 706
curb 752
apply the – 275
brakeman 268
bramble *thorn* 253
bane 663
bran 330
brancard 272
branch *member* 51
class 75
posterity 167
fork 244
tree 367
– off 91, 291
– out *ramify* 91
diffuse style 573
branching
symmetry 242
brand *burn* 384
fuel 388
torch 423
mark 550
sword 727
disrepute 874
censure 932
stigmatize 934
– of discord 713
– new 123
– with reproach 938
brandish
oscillate 314
flourish 315
display 882
brandy 959
brangle 713
brangler 710
brank 975
bras
les – croisés 681
à – ouverts 894
brashness 885
brasier 386
brass *alloy* 41
money 800
insolence 885
bold as – 861
– band 417, 884
with a – 884
– coloured 439
– hat 747
– farthing 643
brassard 550, 747
brat 129
brattice 224, 228
bravado 884
brave *confront* 234
healthy 654
defy 715
warrior 726
bear 821, 826
courage 861
– a thousand years 110
bravo
assassin 361
desperado 863
applause 931
bravura 415
brawl *cry* 411
discord 713
revel 840
brawler
disputant 710
rioter 742
blusterer 887
brawny 159, 192
bray *grind* 330
cry 412
Bray, Vicar of – 607, 886
braze 43
brazen 525, 885
– browed 885
– faced 885
brazier
[*see* brasier]

breach *crack* 44
gap 198
quarrel 713
violation 925
custom honoured in the – 614
– of faith 940
– of law 83, 964
– of the peace 713
bread 298
beg – 765
selfish 943
quarrel with – and butter 699
– of idleness 683
– of life *Christ* 976
piety 987
– upon the waters 638
– and wine 998
breadbasket 191
breadth 202
chiaroscuro 420
break
fracture 44
discontinuity 70
change 140
gap 198
carriage 272
crumble 328
disclose 529
cashier 756
violate 773, 927
bankrupt 808
– away 623
– bread 298
– bulk 297
– camp 293
– of day *morning* 125
twilight 422
– down *destroy* 162
fall short 304
decay 659
fail 732
dance 840
– one's fetters 614
– forth 295
– ground 66
– a habit 614
– the heart *pain* 828, 830
dejection 837
– the ice 888
– in *ingress* 294
domesticate 370
teach 537
tame 749
– in upon *derange* 61
inopportune 135
hinder 706
– a lance 716, 722
– a law 83
– loose 671, 750
– one's neck
powerless 158
die 360
– the neck of
task 676
success 731
– the news 529
– no bones 648
– of 660
– off *cease* 142
relinquish 624
abrogate 756
– out *begin* 66
violent 173
disease 655
excited 825
– the peace 173, 720
– Priscian's head 568
– prison 750
– the ranks 61
– short 328
– silence 582
– the teeth 579
– the thread 70
– through the clouds *visible* 446
disclose 529
– through a custom 614
– up *disjoin* 44
decompose 49
end 67
revolution 146
destroy 162
– up of the system, 360, 655
– on the wheel
physical pain 378
mental pain 830
punishment 972
– with 713
– with the past 146
– word *deceive* 545
improbity 940
breaker
of horses 268
reef 346
wave 348
breakers 348, 667
surrounded by – 704
– ahead 665
breakfast 298
breakneck
precipice 217
rash 863
breakwater
refuge 666
obstruction 706
breast *interior* 221
confront 234
convex 250
mind 450
oppose 708
soul 820
at the – 129
in the – of 620
– the current 719
– high 206
breastplate 717
breastwork 717
breath *instant* 113
breeze 349
life 359
animality 364
faint sound 405
with bated – 581
hold – *quiet* 265
expect 507
wonder 870
not a – of air 265, 382
out of – 688
in the same – 120
shortness of – 688
take – 265, 689
take away one's –
unexpected 508
fear 860
wonder 870
breathe *exist* 1
blow 349
live 359
faint sound 405
evince 467
mean 516
inform 527
disclose 529
utter 580
speak 582
refresh 689
– freely 827, 834
– one's last 360
not – a word 528
breathing time 687, 723
breathless
voiceless 581
out of breath 688
feeling 821
fear 860
eager 865
wonder 870
– attention 457
– expectation 507
– impatience 865
– speed 684
bred in the bone 820
breech 235
– loader 727
breeches 225
wear the – 737
– buoy 666
– maker 225
– pocket
money 800, 802
breed *kind* 75
multiply 161
progeny 167
animals 370
rear 537
breeding 161, 852, 894
breeze *wind* 349
discord 713
breezy 836
brethren 997
breve 413
brevet
warrant 741
commission 755
permit 760
– rank 873
breviary 998
brevier 591
brevity 201, 572
brew 41, 673
brewing
impending 152
storm – 665
bribe *equivalent* 30
tempt 615
offer 763
gift 784
buy 795
expenditure 809
reward 973
bric-à-brac 847
brick *hard* 323
pottery 384
material 635
trump 939, 948
make -s without straw 471
– colour 434
brickbat 727
bricklayer 690
bride 903
bridewell 752
bridge 45, 627
– over *join* 43
facilitate 705
make peace 723
compromise 774

cards 840
bridle *restrain* 751
rein 752
– road 627
– one's tongue 585, 864
– up 900
brief *time* 111
space 201
concise 572
compendium 596
hold a – for 759
– case 191
briefly *anon* 132
brier
sharp 253
pipe 392
bane 663
brig 273
brigade 726
brigadier 745
brigand 792
brigandage 791
brigandine 717
brigantine 273
bright *shine* 420
colour 428
intelligent 498
cheery 836
beauty 845
glory 873
– days 734
– eyed 845
– prospect 858
– side 829
look at the – side 836, 858
– thought
sharp 498
good stroke 626
wit 842
brighten up
furbish 658
brigue 712, 720
brilliant
shining 420
good 648
wit 842
beautiful 845
gem 847
glorious 873
– idea 842
brilliantine 356
brim 231
– over 641
brimful 52
brimstone 388
brindled 440
brine 341, 392
bring 270
– about 153, 729
– back 790
– back to the memory 505
– to bear upon
relation 9
action 170
– into being 161
– to a crisis 604
– forth 161
– forward
evidence 467
manifest 525
teach 537
improve 658
– grey hairs to the grave 735, 830
– grist to the mill 644
– home 775
– home to 155
– in *receive* 296
income 810
price 812
– to life 359
– to light 480*a*
– low 874
– to maturity 673, 729
– to mind 505
– under one's notice 457
– off 672
– out
discover 480*a*
manifest 525
publish 591
– over
persuade 484
– to perfection 650, 729
– into play 677
– to a point 74
– in question 461
– up the rear 235
– round
persuade 615
restore 660
– to terms 723
– to *convert* 144
halt 265
– together 72
– in its train 88
– to trial 969
– up *develop* 161
vomit 297
educate 537
– in a verdict 480
– word 527
brink 231
on the –
almost 32
coming 121
near 197
– of the grave 360
briny 392
– ocean 341
brio *music* 415
active 682
brisk *prompt* 111
energetic 171
active 682
cheery 836
bristle 253
– up *stick up* 250
angry 900
– with 639, 641
– with arms 722
bristly 256
Britannia metal 545
Briticism 563
British 188
– lion 604
Briton, true – 939
work like a – 686
brittleness 328
britzska 272
broach *begin* 66
found 153
reamer 262
tap 297
publish 531
assert 535
broad *general* 78
space 202
lake 343
emphatic 535
indelicate 961, 962
– accent 580
– awake 459, 682
– daylight 420, 525
– farce 842
– grin 838
– highway 627
– hint 527
– meaning 516
– minded 498
broadcast
disperse 73
spread 78
publish 531
sow – 818
broadcloth 219
broadhearted 906
broadsheet 593
broad-shouldered 159
broadside 236
publication 531
cannonade 716
broadsword 727
Brobdingnagian 192
brocade 847
brochure 593
Brocken, spectre of the 443
broder 549
brogue *boot* 225
dialect 563
broidery 847
broil *heat* 382
fry 384
fray 713, 720
broke *poor* 804
broken
discontinuous 70
weak 160
– colour 428
– down
decrepit 659
failing 732
dejected 837
– English 563
– fortune 735, 804
– heart 828, 837
hopeless 859
– reed 160, 665
– meat 645
– voice 581, 583
– winded
disease 655
fatigue 688
broker 758, 797
brokerage *pay* 812
brokery 794
bromidic 613
bronchia 351
bronze *alloy* 41
brown 433
sculpture 557
brooch 847
brood 102, 167
– over 451, 847
brooding
preparing 673
brook *stream* 348
bear 821, 826
broom 652
broth 298
brothel 961
brother *kin* 11
similar 17
equal 27
brotherhood 712
brotherly
friendship 888
love 897
benevolence 906
brougham 272
brought to bed 161

brouillerie 713
brouillon 626
brow *top* 210
edge 231
front 234
browbeat
intimidate 860
swagger 885
disrespect 929
–en *humbled* 879
brown 433
– Bess 727
– study 451, 458
Brown, Jones and Robinson 876
brownie 980
browse 298
bruin 895
bruise *powder* 330
hurt 619
injure 649
blemish 848
bruiser 726
bruit
report 531, 532
brumal 126, 383
Brummagem 545
brumous 353
brunette 433
brunt *beginning* 66
impulse 276
bear the –
difficulty 704
defence 717
endure 821, 826
brush *rough* 256
rapid motion 274
graze 379
clean 652
fight 720
paint – 556
– away *reject* 297
abrogate 756
– up *clean* 652
furbish 658
prepare 673
brushwood 367
brusque *violent* 173
haste 684
discourtesy 895
brutal *vulgar* 851
rude 895
savage 907
brutalize
[*see* brutal]
corrupt 659
deaden 823
vice 945
brute *animal* 366
rude 895
maleficent 913
– force
strength 159
violence 173
animal 450*a*
severe 739
compulsion 744
lawless 964
– matter 316, 358
Brute, et tu 917
brutish [*see* brute]
vulgar 851
ignoble 876
intemperate 954
brutum fulmen
impotent 158
failure 732
lax 738
boast 884
bubble
unsubstantial 4
transient 111
little 193
convexity 250
light 320
water 348
air 353
error 495
deceit 545
trifle 643
– burst
fall short 304
disappoint 509
fail 732
– reputation 873
– and squeak 298
– up *agitation* 315
buccaneer 791, 792
bucentaur 273
Bucephalus 271
buck *stag* 366
male 373
wash 652
money 800
fop 854
– basket 191
– jump 309
– up 684
bucket 191
kick the – 360
drop – in empty well 645
like –s in well 314
buckle *tie* 43
fastening 45
distort 243
curl 248
– on one's armour 673
– to 604, 686
– with *grapple* 720
buckler 717
buckram 855, 878
men in – 549
bucolic
pastoral 370
poem 597
bud 367
beginning 66
germ 153
expand 194
graft 300
– from 154
Buddha 979, 986
Buddhism 984
budding *young* 127
buddy 711, 890
budge 264
budget *heap* 72
bag 191
store 636
finance 811
– of news 532
buff 436
blind man's – 840
native – 226
buffer
hindrance 706
defence 717
buffet 191
strike 276
agitate 315
evil 619
bad 649
affront 900
smite 972
– the waves 704, 708
bar 189
buffo 599
buffoon *actor* 599
humorist 844
butt 857
buffoonery 840, 842
bug 653
bugaboo 669, 860
bugbear
imaginary 515
bane 663
alarm 669
fear 860
buggy 272
bugle
instrument 417
war-cry 722
ornament 847
– call 550, 741
build *construct* 161
form 240
– anew 658
– upon a rock 150
– up *compose* 54
– upon *belief* 484
builder 626, 690
building material 635
buildings 189
built on *basis* 211
bulb 249, 250
bulge 250
bulk 50, 192
– large 31
bulkhead 228, 706
bull *animal* 366
male 373
error 495
absurdity 497
solecism 568
police 664
ordinance 741
– in a china shop 59
like a – at a gate 173
take the – by the horns 604, 861
Bull, John – 188
bullcalf 501
bulldog *animal* 366
pluck 604, 604*a*
courage 861
bulldoze 885
bullet *ball* 249
arms 727
missile 284
bulletin 532, 592
– board 551
bullfight 720
bullhead 501
bullion 800
bullseye *centre* 222
lantern 423
aim 620
bully *fighter* 726
maltreat 830
frighten 860
courage 861
rashness 863
bluster 885
blusterer 887
threaten 909
evil doer 913
bad man 949
bulrush
worthless 643
bulwark 706, 717
bum 876
bumbailiff 965
bumbledom 737, 965
bumboat 273
bump 250, 276
– off 361
bumper 52

bumpkin 876
bumptious
proud 878
insolent 885
contemptuous 930
bun 298
bunch *collection* 72
protuberance 250
– light 599
bunchbacked 243
Buncombe
[*see* bunkum]
Bund 712
bundle *packet* 72
go 266
– on 275, 684
– out 297
bung 263
– up 261
bungalow 189
bungle 59, 699
bungler 701
bunion 259
bunk 186, 215
bunker 191
bunkie 890
bunkum *lie* 544
style 577
boast 884
flattery 933
bunting 550
buoy *raise* 307
float 320
hope 858
buoyant
floating 305
light 320
elastic 325
prosperous 734
cheerful 836
hopeful 858
bur *clinging* 46
sharp 253
rough 256
in engraving 558
burden *lading* 190
weight 319
melody 413
poetry 597
too much 641
clog 706
oppress 828
care 830
– the memory 505
– of a song
repetition 104
burdensome
[*see* burden]
hurtful 649
labouring 686
bureau *chest* 191
office 691
shop 799
tribunal 966
bureaucracy 737
bureaucrat 694
burgee 550
burgeon
[*see* bourgeon]
burgess 188
burgh 189
burgher 188
burghmote 966
burglar 792
– alarm 669
burglary 791
burgomaster 745
burgrave 745
burial 363
buried *deep* 208
imbedded 229
hidden 528
– in a napkin 460
– in oblivion 506
burin 558
burke 361
burlesque
imitation 19
travesty 21
absurdity 497
misrepresent 555
drama 599
comic 853
ridicule 856
burletta 599
burly 192
burn *near* 197
rivulet 348
hot 382
consume 384
near the truth 480a
excited 825
love 897
punish 972
– the candle at both ends
waste 638
exertion 686
prodigal 818
– daylight 683
– one's bridges 604
– one's fingers 699
– in 384
– out 385
– to 865
burner 423
burning [*see* burn]
passion 821
angry 900
– glass 445
– with curiosity 455
– pain 378
– shame 874
burnish *polish* 255
shine 420
beautify 845
burnous 225
burnt [*see* burn]
red 434
– offering 952, 990
burr 410
burrock 706
burrow *lodge* 184
excavate 252
bursar 801
bursary 802
burst *disjoin* 44
instantaneous 113
explosion 173
brittle 328
sound 406
paroxysm 825
bubble –
disclosure 529
all over 729
ready to –
replete 641
excited 824
– of anger 900
– away 623
– of eloquence 582
– of envy 921
– into a flame 825
– forth *begin* 66
expand 194
be seen 446
–ing with health 654
– with grief 839
– in 294
– of laughter 838
– out 295
– upon *arrive* 292
unexpected 508
– into tears 839
burthen
[*see* burden]
bury *enclose* 229
inter 363
conceal 528
– the hatchet 918
– one's talent 528
busboy 746
busby 225
bush *branch* 51
jungle 344
shrub 367
beat about the – 629
bushel *much* 31
multitude 102
receptacle 191
size 192
hid under a – 460
not hide light under a – 878
bush-fighting 720
bushing 224
bushranger 792
bushy 256
business *event* 151
topic 454
occupation 625
commerce 794
full of – 682
man of –
proficient 700
consignee 758
mind one's –
incurious 456
attentive 457
careful 459
let alone 748
send about one's – 297
stage – 599
business-like
orderly 58
business 625
active 682
practical 692
skilful 698
buskin *dress* 225
drama 599
buss *boat* 273
courtesy 894
endearment 902
bust 554
bustle *energy* 171
dress 225
agitation 315
activity 682
haste 684
difficulty 704
bustling
[*see* bustle]
eventful 151
busy 682
busybody 532, 682
but
on the other hand 30
except 83
limit 233
qualifying 469
– now 118
butcher *kill* 361
provisions 637
evil-doer 913
butler 746
butt *cask* 191
push 276

aim 620
attack 716
laughing-stock 857
– in 294, 682
– end 67
butte 206
butter 356
flattery 933
– bread on both sides 641
– not melt in mouth 894
buttered *side*
know – *skill* 698
selfish 943
not know – 699
butter-fingers 701
butterfly
variegated 440
fickle 605
beauty 845
gaudy 882
break – on wheel
waste 638
spite 907
butter-scotch 396
buttery 636
buttock 235
button *fasten* 43
fastening 45
little 193
hanging 214
knob 250
trifle 643
ake by the – 586
– hole 586
– up *close* 261
restrain 751
– up one's pockets 808
buttoned-up
reserved 528
buttonholer 841
buttons *page* 746
button-top
useless 645
buttress
strengthen 159
support 215
defence 717
butyraceous 355
buxom 836
buy 795
– a pig in a poke 621
– and sell 794
buzz *hiss* 409
insect cry 412
publish 531
news 532
buzzard *fool* 501
blind as a – 442
between hawk and –
agitation 315
worry 828
by *alongside* 236
instrumental 631
go – *pass* 303
– air mail 684
– and by 121, 132
– the card 82
– the hour &c.
hire 788
– itself 87
– means of 632
– no means 32
have – one 637, 777
– my troth &c. 535
– the way
à propos 9
beside the purpose 10
parenthetical 134
– wire 684
– wireless 684
bye *departure* 293
sequestered 893
bygone 122, 506
let –s be bygones 918
by-law 963
by-name 565
by-path 279
by-play 527, 550
byre 189
byssus 256
bystander 197, 444
byway 627
by-word
maxim 496
cant term 563
reproach 574
contempt 930

C

C 3 160
cab 272
cabal *plan* 626
confederacy 712
cabala 526, 993
cabalistic 528, 992
cabaret 599
cabasset 717
cabbage 791
caber, tossing the – 840
cabin 189, 191
cabined, cribbed, confined 751
cabinet
photograph 554
receptacle 191
workshop 691
council 696
– picture 556
cable 45, 205
news 531, 532
slip – 623
telegraphic – 534
cabman 268, 694
caboose 386
cabriolet 272
cacation 299
cache 189, 530, 636, 666
cachet 550
lettre de – 751
cachexy 160, 655
cachinnation 838
cacique 745
cackle *of geese* 412
chatter 584
talk 588
laugh 838
cacodemon 980
cacoëthes 613, 865
– loquendi 584
– scribendi 590
cacography 590
caconym 563
cacophony
stridor 410
discord 414
style 579
Cacus 792
den of – 791
cad *servant* 746
vulgar 851
plebeian 876
cadastre 86, 466
cadaverous
corpse 362
pale 429
hideous 846
caddie 746
caddy 191
cadeau 784
cadence *pace* 264
fall 306
sound 402
music 415
cadenza 415
cadet *junior* 129
soldier 726
officer 745
cadge 765
cadger *idler* 683
beggar 767
huckster 797
cadi 967
cadit quæstio 479
cadmium 439
cadre 726
caduceus 993
caducity
fugacity 111
age 128
impotence 158
decay 659
cæcum 261
Cæsar 745
aut – aut nullus
ambition 865
fame 873
cæsura
disjunction 44
discontinuity 70
cessation 142
interval 198
cætera desunt 53
cæteris paribus 27
café 189
cafeteria 189
caftan 225
cage *receptacle* 191
restrain 751
prison 752
Cagliostro 548, 994
cahotage 59, 315
Cain 361
mark of – 550
raise – 825
caique 273
cairn 363, 550
caisse
grand – 417
caisson 191
caitiff *churl* 876
ruffian 913
villain 949
cajolery
imposition 544, 545
persuasion 615
flattery 933
cake *stick* 46
food 298
consolidate 321
sweet 396
– walk 840
calabash 191
calamity *evil* 619
adversity 735
suffering 830
calamo, currente – 590
calash *cap* 225
vehicle 272
calcedony 847

calcine 384
calcitrate 276
calculate
reckon 85
investigate 461
expect 507
intend 620
– upon 484
calculated
tending 176
premeditated 611
calculation
[*see* calculate]
caution 864
calculating [*ditto*]
prudent 498
– machine 85
calculus 85
caldron
convert 144
vessel 191
heat 386
laboratory 691
calèche 272
caleer 838
calefaction 384
calembour 520
calendar *list* 86
chronicle 114
record 551
calender 255
calenture 503, 655
calf *young* 129
give birth 161
leather 223
animals 366
fool 501
golden– 986, 991
Caliban 846
calibrate 26
calibre *degree* 26
size 192
breadth 202
opening 260
intellectual
capacity 498
calidarium 386
calidity 382
caliginous 421
caliph 745
caliphate 737
calisthenics
training 537
beauty 845
caliver 727
calk 660
call *cry* 412
signal 550
name 564
motive 615
visit 892
sanctify 976
ordain 995
at one's – 682, 743
within – 197
– to account 932
– attention to 457
– to the bar 968
– into being 161
– of duty 926
– for *require* 630
order 741
ask 765
– forth
resort to 677
excite 824
– in *advice* 695
– to mind 505
– to the ministry 996
– names 929, 932
– into notice 525
– off the attention 458
– to order 741
– out *cry* 411
challenge 715
– over *number* 85
– into play 677
– in question 485
– the roll 85
– up 527
– up spirits 992
– to 586
– up *recollect* 505
motive 615
excite 824
– upon
demand 741
request 765
visit 892
duty 924, 926
– to witness 467
callæsthetics 845
callant 129
call-boy
theatre 599
called, so – 545
callidity 698
calligraphy 590
calling
business 625
Calliope 417, 597
callipers 466
callosity 323
callous 376, 823
callow *young* 127
infant 129
bare 226
unprepared 674
calm *physical* 174
quiet 265
dissuade 616
leisure 685
peace 721
moral 826
unamazed 871
– belief &c. 484
– before a storm 145
calmative 174
caloric 382
calorimeter 389
calote 999
calotype 554
caloyer 996
calumet *token* 550
– of peace 721, 723
calumniator 936
calumny 934
calvary 1000
Calvinism 984
calyx 191
cam 633
camarade 890
camaraderie 888, 892
camarilla 712
camarista 746
camber 250
cambist 797, 801
camboose 386
camel 271
swallow a – 608, 699
cameo *convex* 250
sculpture 557
camera 445, 553
in – 528
– lucida 445
– obscura 445
camerated 191
Camilla 274
camisade 716
camisole 225
camorra 712
camouflage 530
camp *locate* 184
abode 189
military 728
– bed 215
– stool 215
campagna 180, 344
campaign 692, 722
campaigner 726
campaigning 266
campaniform 249, 252
campanile 206
campestrian 344
Campus Martius 728
can *power* 157
mug 191
preserve 670
jail 752
best one – 686
– it be! 870
canaille 876
canal *opening* 260
conduit 350
way 627
– boat 273
canard 532, 546
canary 366
cancan
dance 840
cancel
compensate 30
neutralize 179
obliterate 552
abrogate 756
repudiate 773
cancellated 219
cancelli 191
cancer *disease* 655
bane 663
painful 830
candelabrum 423
candent 382
candid *white* 430
sincere 543
ingenuous 703
honourable 939
candidate 767, 865
candidature 763
candle 423
bargain by inch of – 769
burn – at both ends 686
not fit to hold a – to 34
– ends 40, 817
– holder 711
– light 126, 422
– power 466
– stick 423, 998
hold – to sun 645
Candlemas 998
candour
veracity 543
artlessness 703
honour 939
candy *dense* 321
sweet 396
cane *weapon* 727
punish 972
scourge 975
canescent 430
Canicula 423
canicular 382
caniculated 259
canine 366

- appetite 865
canister 191
canker *disease* 655
deterioration 659
bane 663
pain 830
canned goods 670
cannel coal 388
cankered
sullen 901*a*
cankerworm 663
evil-doer 913
care 830
cannibal 913
cannibalism 945
cannon
collision 276
loud 404
arms 727
- fodder 726
-'s mouth *war* 722
courage 861
cannonade 716
cannonball 249, 274
cannoneer 726
cannot 471
cannular 260
canny 498, 702
ca' - 864
canoe 273
paddle one's own - 748
canon *rule* 80
ravine 198
music 415
belief 484
precept 697
priest 996
rite 998
- law 697
canonical
regular 82
inspired 985
ecclesiastical 995
canonicals 999
canonist 983
canonization
repute 873
deification 991
rite 998
canonry 995
canopy 223
- of heaven 318
canorous 413
cant *oblique* 217
jerk 276
hypocrisy 544
neology 563
impiety 988
cantabile 415
cantankerous 901, 901*a*
cantata 415
missa - 998
cantatrice 416
canteen 189, 191
canter 266, 274
win at a - 705
canterbury
receptacle 191
Canterbury tale 546
cantharides 171
canticle 415
cantilever 215
canting 855
cantle 51
cantlet 32, 51
canto 597
canton 181, 737
cantonment 184, 189
cantrap 993
canty 836
canvas *sail* 267
picture 556
under press of - 274
canvass
investigate 461
discuss 476
dissert 595
solicit 765
canvasser 767
canyon 350
canzonet 415, 597
caoutchouc 325
cap *be superior* 33
height 206
summit 210
cover 223
hat 225
retaliate 718
complete 729
salute 894
fling up one's - 838
Fortunatus's - 993
set one's - at 897, 902
- and bells 844
- fits 23
- in hand
request 765
servile 886
respect 928
- of maintenance 747
capability
endowment 5
power 157
skill 698
facility 705
capacious *space* 180
- memory 505
capacity
endowment 5
power 157
space 180
size 192
intellect 450
wisdom 498
office 625
talent 698
cap-à-pie
complete 52
armed -
prepared 673
defence 717
war 722
caparison 225
cape *height* 206
cloak 225
projection 250
capella, alla - 415
caper *leap* 309
dance 840
capful *quantity* 25
small 32
- of wind 349
capillament 205
capillary
hairlike 205
thin 203
capital *city* 189
top 210
letter 561
important 642
excellent 648
money 800
wealth 803
make - out of
pretext 617
acquire 775
print in -s 642
- messuage 189
- punishment 972
ship 726
capitalist 803
capitation 85
- tax 812
capitol 189, 717
capitular 995, 996
capitulate 725
capnomancy 511
capon 373
caponize 38, 158
capote 225
capouch 999
capper 548
capriccio *music* 415
whim 608
caprice 608
out of - 615*a*
capricious
irregular 139
changeable 149
irresolute 605
whimsical 608
capriole 309
capsize 218, 731
capsized 732
capstan 307, 633
capstone 210
capsular 252
capsule *vessel* 191
tunicle 223
medicine 662
captain 269, 745
captandum, ad -
sophistry 477
deception 545
affectation 855
ostentation 882
flattery 933
captation 933
captious
capricious 608
irascible 901
censorious 932
caption
taking 789
beginning 66
heading 564
captivate
induce 615
restrain 751
please 829
captivated 827
captivating 829, 897
captive
prisoner 754
adorer 897
lead - 749
make - 751
- balloon 273
captivity 751
capture 789
Capuchin 996
caput 696
- mortuum 645, 653
caquet 584
car 272
carabineer 726
carack 273
caracole 309
caracoler 266
carafe 191
caramel 396
carambole 276
carapace 717
cara sposa 897
carat 319

caravan 266, 272
caravansary 189
caravel 273
carbine 727
carbohydrates 298
carbon 388
– dioxide 663
– monoxide 663
carbonaro 742
carbonization 384
carboy 191
carbuncle *red* 434
abscess 655
jewel 847
carcanet 847
carcass
structure 329
corpse 362
bomb 727
carcelage 973
carcinoma 655
card *unravel* 60
ticket 550
plan 626
address – 550
by the – 82
great – 873
house of –s 328
leave a – 892
on the –s 152, 177, 470
play one's – 692
play one's best – 686
play one's –s well 698
playing –s 840
shuffle the –s
begin again 66
change 140
chance 621
prepare 673
speak by the –
care 459
veracity 543
phrase 566
throw up the –s 757
ticklish – 704
trump – 626
– index 60, 86, 551
–s to play 632
cardcase 191
cardiac 836
cardigan 225
cardinal *intrinsic* 5
dress 225
red 434
important 642
excellent 648
priest 995, 996
–'s hat 747
– points 278
– virtues 944
cardioid 245
card-sharper 792
card-sharping 545
care *attention* **459**
business 625
adversity 735
custody 751
economy 817
pain 828
fear 860
for aught one –s 643, 866
begone dull – 836
drive – away 840
have the – of 693
take – 665, 864
take – of 459
– for *important* 642
desire 865
love 897
careen *slope* 217
repair 660
career 625, 692
careless
inattentive 458
neglectful 460, 927
feeble 575
insensible 823
indifferent 866
caress 897, 902
caret *incomplete* 53
want 640
careworn 828, 837
cargo 270
large quantity 31
contents 190
property 780
goods 798
– boat 273
caricature
likeness 19
copy 21
exaggerate 549
misrepresent 555
ridicule 856
caricaturist 844
caries 49, 653, 655
carillon 417
cariole 272
carious 563
carking 828
– care 830
carle 876
Carlist 925
car-load 31
carman 694
Carmelite 996
carminative 662
carmine 434
carnage 361
carnal 364
intemperate 954
impure 961
irreligious 989
carnation 434
carnival 840
carnivorous 298
carol
music 415, 416
cheerful 836
rejoice 838
caro sposo 897
carouse *feast* 298
festivity 840
intemperance 954
drinking 959
carousel 840
carp at 932
carpe diem 134
carpenter 690
carper 936
carpet 211
on the –
topic 454
project 626
– bag 191
– knight *fop* 854
servile 886
sybarite 954a
– sweeper 652
carrefour 627
carriage *gait* 264
transference 270
vehicle 272
aspect 448
conduct 692
keep one's – 852
carried
– by acclamation &c. 488
– away by passion 824
carrier **271**
– pigeon 534
carrion 362, 653
carronade 727
carroty 434
carry
conduce to 176
support 215
transfer 270
induce 615
reap and – 775
– all before one 731
– coals 879
– conviction 484
– into execution 729, 772
– with a high hand
authority 737
pride 878
insolence 885
– in the mind **505**
– off *take* 789
steal 791
– on [*see below*]
– oneself 692
– out *conduct* 692
complete 729
– over
transfer 270
accounts 811
– a point 731
– by storm 731
– through 692, 729
– weight
influence 175
evidence 467
importance 642
carry on
continue 143
pursue 622
do 680
conduct 692
undertake 326
– an argument 476
– business 625
– an enquiry 461
– a trade 794
– war 722
cart 272
– away 185
– before the horse
disorder 59
inversion 218
bungling 699
– horse 271
work like a – horse 686
– load 31, 190
cartage 270
carte *list* 86
à la – 298
– blanche 760, 816
– du pays 626
– and tierce 716
– de visite 550
photograph 554
cartel
combination 709
defiance 715
truce 723
compact 769
cartelize 709
carter 268

cartes sur table 525, 543
Carthago, delenda est – 908
Carthusian 996
cartilage
dense 321
hard 323
tough 327
cartography 466, 554
cartoon 21, 556
cartoonist 559
cartouche
ammunition 727
ornament 847
cartridge 727
cartulary 86, 551
caruncle 250
carve *cut* 44
make 161
form 240
sculpture 557
apportion 786
– one's way 282
carvel 273
carver 559
caryatides 215
Cary's chickens, Mother – 668
cascade 348
case *state* 7
box 191
sheath 223
topic 454
argument 476
specification 527
grammar 567
affair 625
patient 655
law-suit 969
be the – 1, 494
in good – 654, 734
in –
circumstance 8
event 151
supposition 514
make out a – 467, 924
– in point 23, 82
caseation 321
caseharden
strengthen 159
habituate 613
case-hardened
callous 376, 823
obstinate 606
casemate 189, 717
casement 260
casern 189
cash *money* 800
pay 807
in – 803
pay – for 795
– account 811
– book 551
– box 802
– down 807
– register 85, 553, 802
cashier *dismiss* 756
treasurer 801
casing 223
casino 712; 840
cask 191
casket 191
casque 717
Cassandra 513, 668
cassation 552
casserole 191
Cassiopeia's chair 318
cassock 999
cast *mould* 21
small quantity 32
spread 73
tendency 176
form 240
throw 284
tinge 428
aspect 448
drama 599
reject 610
plan 626
company 712
give 784
allot 786
condemn 971
give one a – 707
set on a – 621
– about for 463
– accounts 811
– adrift *disperse* 73
eject 297
liberate 750
dismiss 756
– anchor 265, 292
– aside 460
– aspersions 934
– away 610, 638
lost 732
– behind one
forget 506
refuse 764
relinquish 782
– away care 836
– off clothes 645
– of countenance 448
– of the dice 156
– in a different mould 18
– dishonour &c. upon 874
– to the dogs 162
– down 308, 837
– in the eye 443
– the eyes back 122
– eyes on 441
– the eyes over 457
– a gloom 837
– off a habit 614
– iron 323
resolute 604
– in one's lot with 609
– lots 621
– lustre upon 420
– of mind 820
– a nativity 511, 992
– one's net 463
– off *divest* 226
disused 678
dismiss 756
relinquish 782
– over-board 678
– the parts 60
– reflection upon 932
– in the same mould 17
– a shade 421
– the skin 226
– a slur 874
accuse 938
– a spell 992
– off trammels 750
– up *add* 85
happen 151
eject 297
castanet 417
castaway *exile* 893
reprobate 949
caste 75, 873
lose – 940
castellan 746, 753
castellated 717
caster *cruet* 191
wheel 312
castigate 932, 972
castigator 936
casting 21
casting – vote 480
– weight 28, 30
castle *at chess* 148
abode 189
defence 717
– in the air
impossible 471
imagination 515
hope 858
Castle of Indolence 683
castor *hat* 225
Castor and Pollux 89, 890
castrametation 189, 722
castrate *subduct* 38
impotent 158
casual *extrinsic* 6
chance 156
uncertain 475
lax 773
casualty *event* 151
killed 361
evil 619
misfortune 735
casuist 476
casuistry
sophistry 477
falsehood 544
duty 926
casus belli
quarrel 713
irritation 824, 900
casus fœderis 770
cat *nine lives* 359
animal 366
keen sight 441
fall on one's feet 734
cross 901
gib –, tom – *male* 373
rain –s and dogs 348
let – out of bag 529
– boat 273
– burglar 792
– call *whistle* 417
disapproval 932
–'s cradle 219
– and dog life 713
as the – jumps
event 151
see how the – jumps 510
fickleness 607
caution 864
– o' nine tails 975
– in pattens 652
–'s paw *dupe* 547
instrumental 631
use 677
auxiliary 711
catabasis 36
catachresis 521, 523

cataclysm
convulsion 146
destruction 162
deluge 348
catacomb 363
catacoustics 402
catadupe 348
catafalque 363
catalectic 597
catalepsy 265, 376, 683
catalogue 60, 86
catalysis 49, 140
catamaran 273, 726
catamenial 138, 299
cataphonics 402
cataplasm 662
catapult 284, 726, 727
cataract
waterfall 348
blindness 442, 443
catarrh 299
catastrophe
disaster 619
finish 729
misfortune 735
end 67
catch *imitate* 19
fastening 45
song 415
detect 480*a*
joke 497
gather the meaning 518
cheat 545
receive 785
take 789
by –es 70
no great – 651
– at *willing* 602
desire 865
– the attention 457
– one's death 360
– a disease 655
– the ear 418
– the eye 446
– fire 384
– a glimpse of 441
– an idea 498
– the infection
excitation 824
– a likeness 554
– a sound 418
– at straws
overrate 482
credulous 486
unskilful 699
rash 863
– by surprise 508
– a Tartar *dupe* 547
retaliate 718
– in a trap 545
– tripping 480*a*
– up 789
catching
infectious 657
catchpenny
deceiving 545
trumpery 643
cheap 815
catchpoll 965
catchword 550
catechism 461, 484
church – 983*a*
catechize 461
catechumen 541, 997
categorical
positive 474
demonstrative 478
affirmative 535
categorically true 494
category 7, 75
in the same – **9**
catena 69
catenary 245
catenation 69
cater 298, 637
caterpillar tractor 271
caterwaul
cat-cry 412
discord 414
courting 902
cates 298
catgut 417
– scraper 416
cathartic 652
cathedrâ, ex –
affirm 535
school 542
authority 737
audacity 885
cathedral 1000
Catherine wheel 840
catholic
universal 78
religious 987
– church 983*a*
Roman – 984
catholicon 662
Catiline 941
catopsis 441
catoptrics 420
catoptromancy 511
cattle 271, 366
– truck 272
catwalk 273, 627
Caucasian mystery 983
caucus 696
caudal 67, 235
caudate 214
caudex 215
Caudine forks 162
cauf 370
caught tripping 491
caulk 660
cause *source* **153**
law-suit 969
final – 620
take up the – of 707
tell the – of 522
–d by 154
causeless
casual 156
aimless 621
causerie 588
causeway 627
causidical 965
caustic
energetic 171
feeling 821
painful 830
gruff 895
malevolent 907
– curve 245
cautel 864
cautelâ, ex abundanti – 664
cautery 384
caution *warn* 668
prudence 864
security 771
want of – 863
cavalcade 69, 266
cavalier
horseman 268
rash 863
insolent 885
discourteous 895
contemptuous 930
cavaliere servente
servile 886
lover 897
cavalry 726
cavatina 415
cave *dwelling* 189
cell 191
cavity 252
– canem 864
– of Adullam 624, 832
– in *hollow* 252
submit 725
caveat
warning 668
command 741
– emptor 769
cavendo tutus 664, 864
cavern [*see* cave]
cavernous 252
caviare 392, 393
– to the general 850
cavil *sophistry* 477
dissent 489
censure 932
caviller 936
cavity 252
caw 412
cayak 273
cayenne 392, 393
cazique 745
cease 142
– to breathe 360
– to exist 2
ceaseless 112
cecity 442
cede *submit* 725
relinquish 782
give 784
ceiling 206, 210, 223
celare artem, ars – 698
cela va sans dire
conformity 82
consequence 154
celebrant 990
celebration 883, 998
celebrity 873, 875
celerity 274
celeste 417
celestial
physical 318
religious 976
heaven 981
celibacy 904
cell *abode* 189
receptacle 191
cavity 221, 252
prison 752
hermitage 893
cellar 191
cellaret 191
cello 417
cellular 191, 252
cement
medium 45
unite 43, 46, 48
covering 223
hard 323
material 635
– a party 712
cemented
concord 714

cemetery 363
cenobite 893, 996
cenotaph 363
censer 998
censor
moderate **174**
critic 480
ban 761
detractor 936
censorious 480, 932
censurable 947
censure 932
censurer 936
census 85, 86
record 551
centaur 83, 366
centenarian 130
centenary
hundred 98
period 138
celebration 883
centesimal 99
cento 597
centrality 222
centralize
combine 48
centre 68, 222
– round 72, 290
centrifugal 291
centripetal 290
centroidal 222
centuple 98
centurion 745
century
hundred 98
period 108
long time 110
money 800
ceramic
bake 384
– ware **557**
cerate 662
Cerberus
janitor 263
custodian 664
hades 932
sop for – 615
cereal 298
cerebration 451
cerebrum 450
cere-cloth 363
cerement
covering 223
wax 356
burial 363
ceremonious 928
ceremony
parade 882
courtesy 894
rite 998
Ceres 979
cerise 434
cerography 558, 590
Ceromancy 511
ceroplastic 557
certain *special* 79
indefinite number 100
sure 474
belief 484
true 494
make – of 480*a*
of a – age 128
to a – degree 32
certainly *yes* 488
certainness 474
certainty **474**
certes 474, 488
certificate
evidence 467
record 551
security 771
certify 467, 535
certiorari 969
certitude 474
cerulean 438
cess *tax* 812
sewer 653
cessation **142**
cession
surrender 725
of property 782
gift 784
cesspool 653
cestui-que trust 779
cestus 45, 247
chafe
physical pain 378
warm 384
irritate 825
mental pain 828, 830
discontent 832
incense 900
chaff *trash* 643
ridicule 856
vulgar 876
not to be caught with – 698, 702
winnow – from wheat 609
chaffer 794
chafing-dish 386
chagrin 828
chain *fasten* 43
vinculum 45
series 69
measure 200
interlinking 219
measure 466
gearing 633
imprison 752
ornament 847
drag a – 749
drag a lengthened – 686
in –s 754
chain gang 752, 972
chain-shot 727
chair *support* 215
vehicle 272
professorship 542
throne 747
celebration 883
president 694
in the – 693
chairman 694
chaise 272
chalcography 558
chalet 189
chalice 191, 998
chalk *earth* 342
white 430
mark 550
drawing 556
– from cheese 14, 491
– out *plan* 626
challenge
question 461
doubt 485
claim 924
defy 715
accuse 938
– comparison 648
cham 745
chamber *room* 191
council 696
mart 799
sick – 655
chamberlain 746
chambermaid 746
chameleon 149, 440
chamfer 259
chamois 309
champ 298
– the bit *disobedient* 742
chafe 825
angry 900
champagne 298
champaign 344
Champ de Mars 728
champêtre, fête – 840
champion
best 648
auxiliary 711
defence 717
combatant 726
representative 759
sympathizer 914
championship 707
chance **156**, **621**
be one's – 151
game of – 840
great – 472
small – 473
stand a – 177, 470
take one's – 675
–s against one 665
whirligig of – 156
as – would have it 152
chancel 1000
chancellor
president **745**
deputy 759
judge 967
– of the exchequer 801
chancery
court of – 966
– suit *delay* 133
chandelier 214, 423
chandelle, le jeu n'en vaut pas la – 638, 643
dear 814
chandler 797
change
alteration **140**
mart 799
small coin 800
inter– 148
radical – 146
sudden – 146
– about 149
– colour 821
– for 147
– hands 783
– of mind 607
– of opinion **485**
– of place 264
changeableness **149**, **605**
changeful
fickle 607
changeling
substitute 147
fool 501
changeless 16
changer 797
channel
furrow 259
opening 260
conduit 350
way 627
chant *song* 415
sing 416
worship 990

chant du cygne 360
chanter 416
chanticleer 366
chantry 1000
chaomancy 511
chaos 59
chap *crack* 198
jaw 231
fellow 373
– book 593
chapel 1000
chaperon
accompany 88
watch 459
protect 664
chapfallen 878
chaplain 995, 996
chaplet *circle* 247
garland 550
trophy 733
ornament 847
chapman 797
chapter *part* 51
topic 454
book 593
council 696
church 995
– of accidents 156, 621
– house 1000
– and verse 467, 494
char *burn* 384
serve 746
char-à-banc 272
character
nature 5
state 7
class 75
oddity 83
letter 561
drama 599
disposition 820
reputation 873
characteristic
intrinsic 5
special 79
tendency 176
mark 550
characterize 564, 594
characterized 820
charade 533, 599
charcoal *fuel* 384, 388
black 431
drawing 556
charge *fill* 52
contents 190
business 625
requisition 630
direction 693
advice 695
precept 697
attack 716
order 741
custody 751
commission 755
bargain for 794
price 812
accusation 938
in – prisoner 754
justifiable – 937
take – of 664
take in – 751
– on *attribute* 155
– with 155, 777
chargé d'affaires 758
chargeable *debt* 806
– on *duty* 926
charger
carrier 271
fighter 726
Charing Cross, proclaim at – 531
chariot 272
drag at one's – wheels 749
charioteer 268, 694
charity *give* 784
liberal 816
beneficent 906
pity 914
Christian – 906
cold as – 823
– that begins at home 943
charivari 404, 407
charlatan
ignoramus 493
impostor 548
mountebank 844
boaster 884
charlatanism
ignorance 491
falsehood 544
affectation 855
Charles's wain 318
Charleston 840
Charley 753
charm *motive* 615
please 829
beauty 845
love 897
conjure 992
spell 993
bear a –ed life 664, 734
charmer 994
voice of the – 933
not listen to voice of – 604
charnel-house 363
Charon 982
chart 527, 554
charter
commission 755
permit 760
compact 769
security 771
privilege 924
chartered
legal 963
– accountant 801, 811
– libertine 962
Chartist 742
charwoman 690, 746
chary
economical 817
stingy 819
cautious 864
Charybdis 312, 665
chase *emboss* 250
furrow 259
drive away 289
killing 361
forest 367
pursue 622
ornament 847
wild goose – 645
chaser 559
chasm *interval* 198
opening 260
chassé 840
chassemarée 273
chassepot 727
chasser 297
– balancer 605
chasseur 726
chassis 215
chaste
shapely 242
language 576, 578
simple 849
good taste 850
pure 960
chasten
moderate 174
punish 972
chastened
subdued spirit 826
penitent 950
chastise 932, 972
– with scorpions 739
chasuble 999
chat 588
chat qui dort 667, 668
château 189
– en Espagne 858
chatelaine 847
chatoyant 440
chattels 633, 780
chatter 314, 584
chatterbox 584
chattering of teeth
cold 383
chatty 584, 892
chauffeur 268
chaunt
song 415
sing 416
worship 990
chaussé 225
chauvinism 884, 885
chawbacon 876
cheap 643, 815
hold – 930
– jack 797
cheapen *haggle* 794
begrudge 819
cheapness 815
cheat 545, 548
check
numerical 85
stop 142
moderate 174
counteract 179
slacken 275
plaid 440
experiment 463
measure 466
evidence 468
ticket 550
dissuade 616
hinder 706
misfortune 735
restrain 751
money order 800
– the growth 201
– oneself 826
checkered 149
checkers 440, 840
checkmate
stop 142
success 731
failure 732
check-roll 86
check-string
pull the – 142
cheek *side* 236
impertinence 885
– by jowl *with* 88
near 197
cheeks *dual* 89
cheep 412
cheer *repast* 298

cry 411
aid 707
pleasure 827
relief 834
mirth 836
rejoicing 838
amusement 840
courage 861
sociality 892
welcome 894
applaud 931
good – *hope* 858
high living 957
cheerfulness 836
cheerless 830, 837
cheeseparings
remains 40
dirt 653
economy 817
chef de cuisine
servant 746
chef-d'œuvre 648, 698
cheka 696
chemin
– de fer
game 840
– faisant 270
chemise 225
chemist 662
Chemistry 144
organic – 357
cheque 800
chequer 440
– roll 86
cherchez la femme 155
chère amie 962
cherish *aid* 707
love 897
endearment 902
– a belief 484
– feelings &c. 821
– an idea &c. 451
cheroot 392
cherry
– red 434
two bites of a –
overrate 482
roundabout 629
clumsy 699
cherry-cheeked 845
cherry-coloured 434
cherub 977
Cheshire cat 838
chess 840
chessboard 440
chest 191, 802
chestnut-colour 433
cheval-de-bataille
plea 617
plan 626
vanity 880
cheval-glass 445
chevalier 875
– d'industrie 792
chevaux de frise 253, 717
chevron
angle 217
indication 550
badge 747
decoration 877
chew 298
– the cud 451
– tobacco 392
chiaroscuro
light 420
grey 432
painting 556
chiasma 43
chic 845, 882
chicane
sophistry 477
deceit 545
cunning 702
chicken 129, 366
– in every pot 733
count –s before hatched 858, 863
tender as a – *soft* 324
sensitive 822
compassionate 914
chickenhearted 862
chide 932
chief *principal* 642
master 745
evidence in – 467
– constable 765
– part 31
Chief Justice 967
chiefdom 737
chieftain 745
chiffonnier 876
chiffonnière 191
chignon 225
chilblain 383
child
infant 129
offspring 167
fool 501
– of God 987
–'s play 643, 705
with – 161
childbirth 161
childhood 127
childish
credulous 486
foolish 499
feeble 575
– treble 581
childlike 703
chiliad 98
chill *cold* 383
render cold 385
indispose 616
– the spine 830, 860
chillies 393
Chiltern Hundreds 757
chime
repetition 104
roll 407
resonance 408
melody 413
– in with *agree* 23
conform 82
assent 488
concord 714
chimera 83, 515
chimney 260, 351
– corner 189
– pot 249
china 384, 557
China to Peru 180
chine 235
chinese white 430
chink *gap* 198
sound 408
money 800
chip *small* 32
detach 44
bit 51
reduce 195
– of the old block
similar 17
copy 21
offspring 167
chippy 962
Chirography 590
Chirology 550
Chiromancy 511
chirp
bird-note 412
sing 416
cheerful 836
rejoice 838
chirrup [*see* chirp]
chirurgery 662
chisel
fabricate 161
form 240
sharp 253
sculpture 557
chit 129, 193
chit-chat 588
chitterlings 221
chivalry *war* 722
tenure 777
courage 861
courtesy 894
philanthropy 910
honour 939
generosity 942
chlamys 225
chloroform 376, 823
chlorophyl 435
chlorotic 655
chock full 52
chocolate
food 298
colour 433
choice *will* 600
election 609
excellent 648
absence of – **609a**
by – 600
– spirits 873
– of words 569
choir *sing* 416
church music 996
church 1000
– boy 996
– invisible 360, 977
choke *close* 261
stifle 361
redundant 641
hinder 706
–full *complete* 52
replete 639
–off 706
choler 900
choleric 901
choose 609
do what one –s 748
chop *disjoin* 44
change 140
– logic 476
– up 201
chopfallen 837
chopper 330
chopping
large 192
– sea 348
chops *mouth* 66
jaws 231
food 298
chorale 415
chord 413
chore 625
choreography 840
chorister 416, 996
chorography 183
chorus
shout 411
song 415
singers 416

unanimity 488
poetry 597
opera 599
concord 714
– girl 599
chose
– in action 780
– in possession 777
chouse 545
choux gras, faire ses – 377
chrestomathy 560
chrism 998
Christ 976
Church of – 893*a*
receive – 987
Christ-cross-row 561
christen 564, 998
Christendom 983*a*, 995
Christian 983*a*, 987
– charity 906
– science 662, 984
Christmas 138, 998
Christmas-box 784
chromatic
colour 428
– scale *music* 413
chromato-pseudo-blepsis 443
chromatrope 445
chrome 436
chromolithograph 558
chromosphere 318
chronic 110
chronicle
measure time 114
annals 551
chronicler 553
chronography
measure time 114
description 594
chronology 114
chronometry 114
Chrononhotonthologos 887
chrysalis 129
chrysoprase 847
chrysolite 847
perfection 650
chrysology 800
chubby 192
chuck *throw* 284
animal cry 412
– it 142
– under chin 902
chuck-farthing 621
chuckle
animal cry 412
laugh 838
exult 884
chuff 876
chum 711, 890
chunk 51
Church
infallible 474
orthodox 983*a*
Christendom 995
temple 1000
dignitaries of – 996
go to – 990
High –, Low – &c. 984
– of Christ 983*a*
– bell 550
– house 1000
churchdom **995**
churching 998
churchman 996
churchwarden 996
pipe 392
churchyard 363, 1000
– cough 655
churl *boor* 876
churlish
niggard 819
rude 895
sulky 901*a*
malevolent 907
churn 315, 352
chut! *silent* 403
taciturn 585
chute 348
chutney 393
chypre 400
cibarious 298
cicatrix 551
manet – 919
cicatrize 660
Cicero 582
cicerone 524, 527
ciceronian 578
cicisbeo 897
cicuration **370**
cider 298
cider squeezer 876
ci-devant 122
cigar 392
ci-gît 363
cilia 205, 256
cimeter 727
Cimmerian 421
cinch 45
cincture 247
cinder
combustion 384
dirt 653
Cinderella
servant 746
commonalty 876
cinema 448, 599, 840
cinematograph 448
cinematographer 553
cinerary 363
cineration 384
cinereous 432
cingle 230
cinnabar 434
cinnamon 393, 433
cinque 98
cipher
unsubstantial 4
number 84
compute 85
zero 101
concealment 528
mark 550
letter 561
unimportant 643
writing in – 590
Circe 615, 994
–an cup 377, 954
circination 312
circle *region* 181
embrace 227
form 247
party 712
describe a – 311
great – sailing 628
– of acquaintance 892
– of the sciences 490
circlet 247
circling 248
circuit *region* 181
outline 230
winding 248
tour 266
indirect path 311
indirect course **629**
circuition **311**
circuitous 279, 311
– method 629
circular *round* 247
publication 531
letter 592
pamphlet 593
– note 805
circularity **247**
circularize 592
circulate
circuit 311
rotate 312
publish 531
circulating medium 800
circulation
[*see* circulate]
in – *news* 532
– of money 809
circumambient 227, 229, 311, 629
circumambulate
travel 266
go round 311, 629
circumaviate 311
circumbendibus 248, 629
circumcision 44, 998
circumduction 552
circumference 230
circumferential 227
circumflex 311
circumfluent
lie round 227
move round 311
circumforaneous
travelling 266
circuition 311
circumfuse 73
circumgyration 312
circumjacence **227**
circumlocution 573
circumnavigate
navigation 267
circuition 311
circumrotation 312
circumscribe
surround 229
limit 233, 761
circumscription **229**
circumspection
attention 457
care 459
caution **459**
circumstance
phase 8
event **151**
circumstances
property 780
bad – 804
depend on – 475
good – 803
under the – 8
circumstantial 8
– account 594
– evidence 467
probability 472
circumstantiality 459
circumstantiate 467
circumvallation
enclosure 229, 232

defence 717
line of – 233
circumvent
environ 227
move round 311
cheat 545
cunning 702
hinder 706
defeat 731
circumvest 225
circumvolution
winding 248
rotation 312
circus
buildings 189
drama 599
arena 728
amusement 840
cirrus 353
cistern
receptacle 191
store 636
Cistercian 996
cit 188
citadel 717
citation 467, 733
cite
quote as example 82
as evidence 467
summon 741
accuse 938
arraign 969
cithern 417
citizen 188
– of the world 910
citriculture 371
citrine 436
city 189
in the – 794
city manager 965
civet 400
civic 372
civil *courteous* 894
laity 997
– authorities 745
– crown 733
– law 963
– war 722
civilian *lawyer* 968
layman 997
civilization
improvement 658
fashion 852
courtesy 894
civilized life 852
civism 910
clack *clatter* 407
animal cry 412
talkative 584
clad 225
claim *requisition* 630
demand 741
property 780
right 924
lawsuit 969
– the attention 457
claimant
petitioner 767
right 924
clair-obscur 420
clairvoyance 992
clairvoyant 513, 994
clamant 411
clamber 305
clammy 352
clamorous
[*see* clamour]
loud 404
excitable 825
clamour *cry* 411
wail 839
– against 932
– for 765
clamp *fasten* 43
fastening 45
clan *race* 11
class 75
family 166
party 712
clandestine 528
clangor 404
clank 410
clannishness 481
clanship 709
clap *explosion* 406
applaud 931
thunder –
prodigy 872
– the hands
rejoice 838
– on 37
– on the shoulder 615
– together 43
– up *imprison* 751
clapperclaw
contention 720
censure 932
claptrap
pretence 546
display 882
claquer 935
faire – son fouet 884
clarence 272
claret colour 434
clarify 652
clarinet 417
clarion *music* 417
war 722
clarity 518
clash *disagree* 24
cross 179
concussion 276
sound 406
oppose 708
discord 713
– of arms 720
clasp *fasten* 43
fastening 45
stick 46
come close 197
belt 230
embrace 902
class *arrange* 60
category 75
learners 541
party 712
– prejudice 481
– room 542
classic *old* 124
symmetry 242
classical
elegant writing 578
taste 850
– art 556
– dancing 840
– education 537
– music 415
classicist 492
classics 560
classify 60
classmate 890
clatter 404, 407
claudication
slowness 275
failure 732
clause *part* 51
passage 593
condition 770
clausis, janius – 528
claustral 110
clavate 250
clavichord 417
clavier 417
claw *hook* 781
grasp 789
– back 935
clay *soft* 324
earth 342
corpse 362
material 635
– pipe 392
clay-cold 383
claymore 727
clean
entirely 52
perfect 650
unstained 652
– bill of health 654
– breast
disclose 529
– forgotten 506
– hand
proficient 700
with – hands
honesty 939
innocence 946
– out *empty* 297
– shaven 226
– sweep
revolution 146
destruction 162
clean-up 775
clear *simple* 42
sound 413
light 420
transparent 425
visible 446
certain 474
intelligible 518
manifest 525
easy 705
liberate 750
profit 775
vindicate 937
innocent 946
acquit 975
all – 664, 705
coast – 664
get – off 671
keep – of 623
make – 529
– for action
prepare 673
– articulation 580
– conscience 946
– the course 302
– cut 518
– the ground
facilitate 705
– of *distant* 196
– off *pay* 807
– out *empty* 297
clean 652
– sighted
vision 441
shrewd 498
– sky *hope* 858
– stage
occasion 134
easy 705
right 922
– thinking 498
– the throat 297
– up *light* 420
intelligible 518
interpret 522
clearheaded 498

clear-obscure 420
cleat 45
cleavage
cutting 44
structure 329
cleave *sunder* 44
adhere 46
bisect 91
cleaver 253
cledge 342
clef 413
cleft *divided* 44
bisected 91
chink 198
in a – stick
difficulty 704
clem 956
clement
lenient 740
long-suffering 826
compassionate 914
clench *compact* 769
retain 781
take 789
clepe 564
clepsydra 114
clerestory 191, 1000
clergy 996
clerical 995, 996
– error 495
– staff 746
clerk *scholar* 492
recorder 553
writer 590
helper 711
servant 746
agent 758
clergy 996
articled – 541
– in holy orders 995
– of works 694
clerkship
commission 755
cleromancy 511
clever
intelligent 498
skilful 698
smart 842
too – by half 702
clew *ball* 249
interpretation 522
indication 550
seek a – 461
click 406
client
dependant 746
customer 795
clientship
subjection 749
cliff *height* 206
vertical 212
steep 217
land 342
climacteric 128
climate *region* 181
weather 338
fine – 656
climatology 338
climax
supremacy 33
summit 210
culmination 729
climb 305
– on the band-wagon 731
clime 181
clinal 217
clinch *fasten* 43
close 261
certify 474
pun 563
complete 729
clutch 781
snatch 789
– an argument 47
– the fist at 909
clincher 479
cling *adhere* 46
– to *near* 197
willing 602
persevere 604a
habit 613
observe 772
desire 865
love 897
– to hope 858
– to one another 709
clinic 662
clink
resonance 408
stridor 410
prison 752
clinker *brick* 384
dirt 653
clinometer
oblique 217
angle 244
clinquant
ornament 847
vulgar 851
Clio 594
clip *shorten* 201
– the wings
powerless 158
speed 264
slow 275
useless 645
hinder 706
prohibit 761
– one's words 583
clipper 273
clipping
small piece 51
clique *conclave* 696
party 712
cloaca *conduit* 350
foul 653
Cloacina 653
cloak *dress* 225
conceal 528
disguise 530
cloaked 223
cloche 371
clock 114
clockwork 633
by – *uniform* 16
order 58
regular 80
clod *lump* 192
earth 342
fool 501
bungler 701
clodhopper 876
clodpated
stupid 499
clog *shoe* 225
hinder 706
– dance 840
cloison 228
cloisonné 557
cloister *arcade* 189
way 627
restraint 751
convent 1000
close *similar* 17
tight 43
end 67
field 181
court 189
near 197
narrow 203
shut 261
dense 321
warm 382
hidden 528
concise 572
taciturn 585
complete 729
stingy 819
examine –ly 457
keep – *hide* 528
retain 781
tread – upon 281
– the door upon
restrain 751
– the ears 419
– the eyes
die 360
not see 442
– one's eyes to
not attend 458
set at naught 773
– at hand
to-morrow 121
imminent 152
near 197
– the hand
refuse 764
– in upon 290
– inquiry 461
–ly packed 72
– prisoner 754
– quarters 197
approach 286
attack 716
battle 722
– one's ranks 673
– study
thought 451
attention 457
– up 197, 290
– with *cohere* 46
assent 488
attack 716
contend 720
consent 762
compact 769
close-mouthed 585
closet
receptacle 191
ambush 530
closeted with
conference 588
advice 695
close-up 197
closure 142, **261**
clot *solidify* 321
earth 342
cloth *vocation* 625
napkin 652
clergy 996
clothes 225
grave – 363
– basket 191
clothier 225
Clotho 601
clotpoll 501
clotted 352
cloud
assemblage 72
multitude 102
mist 353
shade 424
screen 530
break through the –s 446
drop from the –s 508
in a – 475, 528
in the –s

lofty 206
inattentive 458
dreaming 515
under a –
insane 503
adversity 735
disrepute 874
secluded 893
censured 932
accused 938
– burst 348
–capt 206
– of dust 330, 353
–s gathering
dark 421
danger 665
warning 668
– no bigger than a man's hand 668
– of skirmishers 726
– of smoke 353
– of words 573
clouded
variegated 440
dejected 837
hopeless 859
– perception 499
cloudiness 571
cloudland 515
cloudless
light 420
happy 827
cloudy *dim* 422, 426
clough 206
clout 276
cloven 91
cloven foot
mark 550
malevolence 907
vice 945
Satan 978
see the – 480*a*
show the – 907
clover
luxury 377
prosperity 734
comfort 827
clown
pantomime 599
bungler 702
buffoon 844
vulgar 851
rustic 876
cloy 641, 869
club
place of meeting 74
house 189
association 712
weapon 727
sociality 892
– law
compulsion 744
lawless 964
– together
co-operate 709
clubby 892
club car 272
clubfooted 243
cluck 412
clue 550
seek a – 461
clump
assemblage 72
projecting mass 250
– of trees 367
clumsy
unfit 647
awkward 699
ugly 846
Cluniac 996
clurichaune 980
cluster 72
clutch *retain* 781
seize 789
clutches 737
in the – of 749
clutter 407
coacervation 72
coach
carriage 272
teach 537
tutor 540, 673
– painter 540
– road 627
drive a – and six through 964
– up 539
coachhouse 191
coachman 268, 694
coaction 744
coadjutant 709
coadjutor 711
coadjuvancy 709
coagency 178, 709
coagmentation 72
coagulate
cohere 46
density 321
semi-liquid 352
coal 388
call over the –s 932
carry –s 879
– black 431
carry –s to Newcastle 641
coalesce
identity 13
combine 48
coalheaver
work like a – 686
coalition 43, 709, 712
coaming 232
coaptation 23
coarctation
decrease 36
contraction 195
narrow 203
impede 706
restraint 751
coarse *harsh* 410
dirty 653
unpolished 674
garish 846
vulgar 851
impure 961
– grain 329
coast *border* 231
slide 266
navigate 267
land 342
– defence 717
– line 230
coaster 273
coastguard 753
coat *layer* 204
paint 223
habit 225
cut – according to cloth 698
– of arms 550
– of mail 717
coating, inner – 224
coax *persuade* 615
endearment 902
flatter 933
cob *horse* 271
punish 972
cobalt 438
cobble *mend* 660
cobbler 225
cobbles 635
coble 273
cobra 913
cobweb *light* 320
fiction 545
flimsy 643
dirt 653
–s of antiquity 124
–s of sophistry 477
cocaine 376, 381, 663
cochineal 434
cock *bird* 366
male 373
game – 861
– boat 273
– and bull story 546
– the eye 441
– of the roost
best 648
master 745
– up *vertical* 212
convex 250
cockade *badge* 550
title 877
cock-a-hoop
gay 836
exulting 884
Cockaigne 827
cockatrice
monster 83
piercing eye 548
evil-doer 913
miscreant 949
cockcrow 125
cocked hat 225, 745
cocker *fold* 258
caress 902
Cocker
school book 542
according to – 82
cockle *fold* 258
– of one's heart 820
cockleshell 273
cockloft 191
cockney
Londoner 188
plebeian 876
cockpit *hold* 191
council 696
arena 728
cockshut
morning 125
evening 126
dusk 422
cock-sparrow 193
cocksure 484
cockswain 269
cocktail 298, 959
– party 892
cocoa 298
cocotte 962
coction 384
Cocytus 982
cod *shell* 223
coddle 902
– oneself 943
code *conceal* 528
precept 697
law 963
codex 593
codger 819
codicil *sequel* 65

testament 771
codify 60, 963
codlin 129
cœcum 261
coefficient
factor 84
accompany 88
co-operate 709
Cœlebs 904
coemption 795
coequal 27
coerce *compel* 744
restrain 751
coetaneous 120
coeternal
perpetual 112
synchronous 120
cœur, à contre – 603
coeval 120
– with birth 5
coexist *exist* 1
accompany 88
synchronism 120
contiguity 199
coextension
equality 27
parallelism 216
symmetry 242
coffee 298
coffee-house 189
coffee-pot 191
coffer *chest* 191
store 636
money chest 802
cofferdam 55
coffin 363
add a nail to one's – 830
cog *tooth* 253
boat 273
deceive 545
flatter 933
cogent
powerful 157
– reasoning 476
cogitate 451
cogitative faculties 450
cognate
consanguineous 11
related 9
similar 17
cognition 490
cognitive faculties 450
cognizance 490
take – of
intellect 490
attention 457
cognomen 564
cognoscence 490
cog-wheel 312
cohabitation
location 184
marriage 903
coheir 778
coherence *unite* **46**
dense 321
cohesive 46
cohibit
restrict 706
restrain 751
prohibit 761
cohobation 336
cohort 726
cohue 72
coif 225
coiffure 225
coign of vantage 33
coil *disorder* 59
curve 245
convolution 248
circuition 311
shuffle off this mortal – 360
coin *fabricate* 161
imagine 515
money 800
– money 775
– words 563
coincidence
identity 13
in time 120
chance 156
concurrence 178
in place 199
in opinion 488
coiner *thief* 792
coistril 862
coition 43
coke 388
colander 260
colature 652
cold *frigid* **383**
colour 429, 438
style 575
insensible 823
indifferent 866
in – blood
premeditated 611
purposely 620
unfeeling 823
dispassionate 826
– comfort 832
– shoulder
discourtesy 895
contempt 930
– steel 727
– storage 387
– sweat *fear* 860
dislike 867
– water cure 662
throw – water on
dissuade 616
hinder 706
dull 843
cold feet 862
coldhearted
unfeeling 823
hostile 889
malevolent 907
cold pack 670
Coliseum 189, 588, 728
collaboration 178
collaborator 690, 711
collapse
prostration 158
contract 195
shortcoming 304
deteriorate 659
fatigue 688
failure 732
collar *dress* 225
circlet 247
shackle 752
seize 789
slip the – 750
collate 464
collateral
relation 9, 11
parallel 216
lateral 236
security 771
– evidence 467
collation
repast 298
comparison 464
colleague
accompany 88
co-worker 690
co-operation 709
auxiliary 711
friend 890
collect
assemble 72
opine 480
understand 518
acquire 775
prayer 990
– evidence 467
– knowledge 539
– one's thoughts 451
collectanea
assemblage 72
compendium 596
collected *calm* 826
collection
assemblage 72
offertory 998
collectively
whole 50
generality 78
together 88
collectivism 737, 778
college 542
go to – 539
– of cardinals 996
– education 537
colleen 129
collie 366
collide 276
collier 273
colligate 72
collimation 216, 278
colliquate 335
collision *disagreement* 24
clash 179
percussion 276
opposition 708
encounter 720
collocate
arrange 60
assemble 72
place 184
collocution 588
collogue 933
colloid 352
collop 51, 298
colloquial
figure of speech 521
neology 563
conversation 588
– meaning 516
colluctation 720
collusion *deceit* 545
conspiring 709
collusive 544
colluvies 653
collyrium 662
Cologne
eau de – 400
colon 142
colonel 745
colonist 188
colonize 184, 294, 295
colonnade
series 69
houses 189
colony 184, 188, 780
colophon 65
colophony 356*a*
Colorado beetle 913
coloration 428
coloratura 415, 416

Colosseum 728
colossus 192, 206
colour *hue* 428
tone 431
appearance 448
probability 472
disguise 544
paint 556
plea 617
be angry 900
all –s 440
change –
shame 879
give a – to
change 140
qualify 469
probable 472
falsehood 544
lend a – to
plea 617
vindicate 937
man of – 431
show in true –s 543
– blindness 443
– printing 558
– sergeant 745
–ed spectacles 424
– too highly 549
– up *redden* 434
blush 879
colourable
ostensible 472
deceptive 545
colourful 882
colouring
[see colour]
meaning 516
false – 523
– matter 428
colourless
weak 160
pale 429
colours
ensign 550
decoration 877
with – flying
resolution 604
false – 544, 545
flying –
display 882
celebration 883
lower one's – 735
nail one's – to the mast 604
show one's –
manifest 525
disclose 529
true to one's – 939
colporteur 797
colstaff 215
colt *young* 129
horse 271
fool 501
columbine 599
columella 215
column *series* 69
height 206
support 215
cylinder 249
caravan 266
monument 551
printing 591
troop 726
columnist 527, 553
colures 318
coma *inactive* 683
insensible 376, 823
comb *teeth* 253
clean 652
punish 972
combat 720, 722
combat, hors de –
useless 645
tired 688
combatant 726
combe 252
comber 348
combination 48
arithmetical 84
party 712
combine *unite* 48
co-operate 709
combustible 388
combustion 384
come *happen* 151
approach 286
arrive 292
cheer up! 836
out upon! 932
to – *future* 121
destiny 152
– about 658
– across
discover 480*a*
acquire 775
pay up 807
– after
sequence 63
posterior 117
– between 631
cut and – again 639
– of age 131
– amiss
disagreeable 24
ill-timed 135
– back 283
– before 116
– by 775
– at one's call 743
– to a determination 604
– down with 807
– into existence
be 1
begin 66
– first *superior* 33
precede 62
– forth
egress 295
appear 446
– forward 763
– from 154
– to the front 303
– and go 314
– to hand 785
– to a head
climax 33
complete 52
– in *ingress* 294
receipt 785
– in for
property 778, 780
– to one's knowledge 527
– to life 359
– what may 474
– near 286
– to nothing
unproductive 169
fail 732
– of 154
– off *event* 151
disjoin 44
loop-hole 617
escape 671
– on *future* 121
destiny 152
I defy you 715
attack 716
– to oneself 660
– into operation 170
– out
disclosure 529
publication 531
on the stage 599
– out of *effect* 154
egress 295
– out with
disclose 529
speak 582
– over
influence 615
consent 762
– to pass *state* 7
event 151
– to pieces 44
– to the point
speciality 79
attention 457
concise 572
– to the rescue 672
– round
period 138
conversion 144
belief 484
assent 488
change of mind 607
influence 615
restoration 660
be pacified 723
consent 762
– to the same thing 27
– short of
inferior 34
fall short 304
– to one's senses 502
– to a stand 142
– to terms
assent 488
contract 769
it –s to this
concisely 572
– to *equal* 27
whole 50
arithmetic 85
become 144
effect 154
inherit 777
money 800
price 812
– together
assemble 72
converge 290
– under 76
– upon
unexpected 508
acquire 775
claim 924
– into use 613
– into view 446
– into the views of
co-operate 709
– off well 731
– into the world 359
come-down 306, 735
comedy
drama 599
comic 853
comely 845
comestible 298
comet
wanderer 268
star 318
cometary 111

comfit 396
comfort
pleasure **377**
delight 827
content 831
relief 834
give – 906
comfortable
pleasing 829
comforter
covering 223
Comforter 976
comfortless
painful 830
dejected 837
comic *wit* 842
ridiculous 853
– opera 599
– strips 531
coming [*see* come]
impending 152
– events
prediction 511
– out 883
– time 121
comitia 696
comity 894
comma 142
inverted –s 550
command *high* 206
requisition 630
authority 737
order **741**
possess **777**
at one's –
obedient 743
– belief 484
– of language
writing 574
speaking 582
– of money 803
– one's passions 944
– respect 928
– one's temper 826
– a view of 441
commandant 745
commandeer 744, 789
commander 269
commanding
[*see* command]
important 642
commando 726
commandment 697
comme deux gouttes d'eau 17
comme il faut
taste 850
fashion 852
genteel 875
commemorate 883
commence 66
commencement de la fin *end* 67
destruction 162
commend 931
– the poisoned chalice 544
commendable 944
commensurate
accordant 23
numeral 85
adequate 639
comment
reason 476
judgment 480
interpretation 522
criticize 595
commentary 595
commentator 492, 524, 527
commerce
conversation 588
barter 794
cards 840
commercial 811
– arithmetic 811
– traveller 758
commère 599
commination 908, 909
commingle 41
comminute 330
commiserate 914
commissariat 637
commissary
provisions 637
consignee 758
commission
task 625
delegate **755,** 759
Royal – 696
– of the peace 965
commissioner 758
commissionaire
doorkeeper 263
messenger 534
consignee 758
commissure 43
commis-voyageur 758
commit *do* 680
delegate 755
cards 840
arrest 969
– an absurdity 853
– oneself to a course 609
– to the flames 384
– to memory 505
– oneself
clumsy 699
promise 768
– to prison 751
– sin 945
– to writing 551
committee
council 696
consignee 758
(*director* 694)
commix 41
commode 191
commodious 644
commodity 798
commodore 745
common
general 78
ordinary 82
plain 344
habitual 613
trifling 643
base 876
in – *related* 9
participate 778
right of – 780
short –s 640
tenant in – 778
make – cause 709
– consent 488
– council 966
– course 613
– herd 876
– law *old* 124
law 697, 963
– measure 84
– origin 153
– parlance 576
– place 82
– place book
record 551
compendium 596
– saying 496
– sense 498
– sewer 653
– stock 778
– weal
mankind 372
good 618
utility 644
philanthropy 910
Common Pleas
Court of – 966
commonalty **876**
commoner 876
commonplace
usual 82
known 490
plain 576
habit 613
unimportant 643
dull 843
commons 298
commonwealth
territory 181
community 372
authority 737
commorant 188
commotion 315
communalism 778
commune
township 181
commune with 588
– oneself 451
communibus annis 29
communicant 990
communicate
join 43
tell 527
correspond 592
give 784
sacrament 998
communication
news 532
of disease 657
oral – 582, 588
communion
discourse 588
society 712
participation 778
sacrament 998
hold – with 888
– table 1000
communiqué 527
communism 737
communist
party 712
rebel 742
participation 778
philanthropy 910
evil doer 913
community
party 712
– at large 372
– of goods 778
commutation
compensation 30
substitution 147
interchange 148
compromise 774
barter 794
commutual 12
compact
joined 43
united 87
receptacle 191
small 193
compressed 195
compendious 201
dense 321
bargain **769**

compages
whole 50
structure 329
compagination 43
companion *match* 17
accompaniment 88
ladder 305
friend 890
companionable 892
companionship 892
companionway 305
company
assembly 72
actors 599
party, partnership 712
troop 726
sociality 892
bear – 88
in – with 88
comparable 9
comparative 464
degree 26
– anatomy 368
comparatively 32
compare 464
– notes 695
comparison **464**
compartition 44
compartment
part 51
region 181
place 182
cell 191
carriage 272
compass
degree 26
space 180
surround 227
measure 466
intend 620
guidance 693
achieve 729
box the –
direction 278
rotation 312
keep within –
moderation 174
fall short 304
economy 817
points of the – 236
in a small – 193
– about 229
– of thought 498
compassion 914
object of – 828
compatible
consentaneous 23
possible 470
compatriot
inhabitant 188
friend 890
compeer *equal* 27
friend 890
compel 744
compellation 564
compendency 43
compendious 201
compendium **596**
book 593
compensate
make up for 30
requite 973
compensation **30**
compère 599
competence
power 157
sufficiency 639
skill 698
wealth 803
competition
opposition 708
contention 720
competitor
opponent 710
combatant 726
candidate 767
compilation
collect 72
book 593
compendium 596
compile 54
complacent
pleased 827
content 831
courteous 894
kind 906
complain 839
complainant 938
complaint
illness 655
murmur 839
lodge a – 938
– without cause 839
complaisant
lenient 740
courteous 894
kind 906
complement
adjunct 39
remainder 40
part 52
arithmetic 84
complementary
correlation 12
colour 428
complete
entire 52
accomplish 729
compact 769
– answer 479
– circle 311
in a – degree 31
completeness **52**
completion **729**
complex 59
complexion
state 7
colour 428
appearance 448
compliance
conformity 82
obedience 743
consent 762
observance **772**
complicate
derange 61
complicated
disorder 59
convolution 248
complice 711
complicity 709
compliment
courtesy 894, 896
praise 931
poor – 932
–s of season 896
complimentary
free 815
complot 626
comply [*see* compliance]
compo *coating* 223
material 635
component **56**
componere lites 723, 724
comport
– oneself 692
– with 23
compos mentis 502
compose
make up 54, 56
produce 161
moderate 174
music 416
write 590
printing 591
pacify 723
assuage 826
composed
self-possessed 826
composer
music 413
composite 41
composition **54**
[*see* compose]
combination 48
piece of music 415
picture 556
style 569
writing 590
building material 635
compromise 774
barter 794
atonement 952
compositor
printer 591
compost 653
composure 826, 871
compotation 959
compote 298
compound
mix 41
combination 48
limited space 182
enclosure 232
compromise 774
– arithmetic 466
– for *substitute* 147
barter 794
comprador 637
comprehend
compose 54
include 76
know 490
understand 518
comprehension [*see* comprehend]
intelligence 498
comprehensive 76
complete 50
general 78
wide 192
– argument 476
compress
contract 195
curtail 201
condense 321
remedy 662
compressible 322
comprise 76
comprobation
evidence 467
demonstration 478
compromise
dally with 605
mid-course 628
taint 659
danger 665
pacify 723
compact 769
compound **774**
atone 952
compromised
promised 768
compter 799
compte rendu
record 551
accounts 811

comptroller 694
compulsion **744**
compunction 833, 950
compurgation
evidence 467
acquittal 970
compute 85
comrade 890
comradeship 892
con *think* 451
get by heart 505
learn 539
conation 600
conatu magnas nugas, magno –
waste 638
unimportance 643
conatus 176
concamerate 245
concatenation
junction 43
continuity 69
concavity **252**
conceal
invisible 447
hide 528
cunning 702
concealment **528**, 893
concede
assent 488
admit 529
permit 760
consent 762
give 784
conceit *idea* 453
folly 499
supposition 514
imagination 515
wit 842
affectation 855
vanity 880
conceited
dogmatic 481
conceivable 470
conceive *begin* 66
beget 161
teem 168
believe 484
understand 490
imagine 515
plan 626
concent 413
concentrate
assemble 72
centrality 222
converge 290
concentric 216, 222
conception
[*see* conceive]
intellect 450
idea 453
concern
relation 9
event 151
business 625
importance 642
firm 797
grief 828
– oneself with 625
concert
agreement 23
synchronism 120
music 415
act in – 709
in – *musical* 413
concord 714
– measures 626
concertina 417
concerto 415
concert-room 840
concession
permission 760
consent 762
compromise 774
giving 784
discount 813
concesso, ex –
reasoning 476
assent 488
concetto 842
conchoid 245
conchology 223
concierge 263, 753
conciliate
talk over 615
pacify 723
satisfy 831
courtesy 894
atonement 952
conciliatory [*see* conciliate]
concord 714
forgiving 918
conciliatrix 962
concinnity
agreement 23
style 578
beauty 845
conciseness **572**
concision 201
conclave
assembly 72
council 696
church 995
conclude
end 67
infer 480
resolve 604
complete 729
compact 769
conclusion
[*see* conclude]
sequel 65
germination 161
judgment 480
try –s 476
forgone – 611
hasty – 481
conclusive
[*see* conclude]
answer 462
evidence 467
certain 474
proof 478
– reasoning 476
concoct *lie* 544
write 590
plan 626
prepare 673
concomitant
accompany 88
same time 120
concurrent 178
concord *agree* 23
music **413**
assent 488
harmony **714**
concordance 562
book 593
concordant 173
concordat 769
concordia discors 24, 59
concours 720
concourse
assemblage 72
convergence 290
concremation 384
concrete *existent* 3
mass 46
definite 79
density 321
hardness 323
materials 635
concubinage 961
concubine 926
concupiscence 865, 961
concur
co-exist 120
causation 178
converge 290
assent 488
concert 709
concurrence **178**, 216
concussion 276
condemnation 932, **971**
condemned cell 752
condense
compress 195
dense 321
condensed
concise 572
condescend 879
condign 924
condiment **393**
condisciple 541
condition *state* **7**
modification 469
supposition 514
term 770
repute 873
rank 875
in – *plump* 192
in good – 648
on – 770
in perfect – 650
physical – 316
conditional 8
conditions **770**
condolence 914, **915**
condone 918
condottiere
traveller 268
fighter 726
conduce
contribute **153**
tend 176
concur 178
avail 644
conducive 631
conduct
transfer 270
music 416
procedure **692**
lead 693
safe –
passport 631
safety 664
– a funeral 363
– an inquiry 461
– to 278
conduction 264
conductor 268
conveyer 271
director 694
lightning – 666
conduit **350**
conduplicate 89
condyle 250
cone *round* 249
pointed 253
confabulation 588
confection 396
confectionery 396
confectioner 637
confederacy
co-operation **709**
party 712
confederate **711**

confer *advise* 695
give 784
– benefit 648
– power 157
– privilege 760
– right 924
– with 588
conference [*see* confer]
council 696
confess *assent* 488
avow 529
penitence 950, 998
– and avoid 937
confession [*see* confess]
auricular – 998
– of faith 983
confessional 1000
confessions
biography 594
confessor 996
confidant 711
confidante
servant 746
friend 890
confidence
trust 484
hope 858
courage 861
in – 528
– trick 545
confident 535
configuration 240
confine
region 182
circumscribe 229
limit 231, 233
imprison 751
confined
narrow judgment 481
ill 655
confinement
childbed 161
confines of
on the – 197
confirm
corroborate 467
assent 488
consent 762
compact 769
rite 998
confirmed 150
– habit 613
confiscate *take* 789
condemn 971
penalty 974
confiture 396
conflagration 382, 384
conflexure 245
conflict
opposition 708
discord 713
contention 720
conflicting
contrary 14
counteracting 179
– evidence 468
confluence
junction 43
convergence 290
river 348
conflux
assemblage 72
convergence 290
conform *assent* 488
– to rule 494
conformable 23, 178
conformation 54, 240
conformity **82,** 178
confound
disorder 61
destroy 162
not discriminate 465a
perplex 475
defeat 731
astonish 870
curse 908
confounded
great 31
bad 649
confraternity
party 712
friendship 888
confrère
colleague 711
friend 890
confrication 331
confront *face* 234
compare 464
oppose 708
resist 719
– danger 861
– witnesses 467
confucianism 984
Confucius 986
confuse *derange* 61
perplex 458
obscure 519
not discriminate 465a
abash 879
confused *disorder* 59
invisible 447
uncertain 475
style 571
confusion
[*see* confuse]
– seize 908
– of tongues 560, 563
– of vision 443
– worse-confounded 59
confutation **479**
congé 293, 756
– d'élire 995
congeal *dense* 321
cold 385
congeneric
similar 17
included 76
congenial
related 9
agreeing 23
concord 714
love 897
congenital 5, 820
congeries 72
congestion 641
conglaciation 385
conglobation 72
conglomerate
cohere 46
assemblage 72
council 696
dense 321
conglutinate 46
congratulate 896
– oneself 838
congratulation **896**
congregation
assemblage 72
worshippers 990
laity 997
Congregationalist 984
congress
assembly 72
convergence 290
conference 588
council 696
Congressional Medal 733
Congressional Record 551
congreve *fuel* 388
– rocket 727
congruous
agreeing 23
(*expedient* 646)
conical *round* 249
pointed 253
conjecture 475, 514
conjoin 43
conjoint 48
conjointly **37**
conjugal 903
conjugate
words 562
grammar 567
– in all its tenses &c. 104
conjugation
junction 43
pair 89
phase 144
grammar 567
conjunction 43
in – with 37
conjuncture
contingency 8
occasion 134
conjure *deceive* 545
entreat 765
sorcery 992
name to – with 873
– up *recall* 505
– up a vision 505
conjuror
deceiver 548
sorcerer 994
connaître le dessous des cartes 490
connate
intrinsic 5
kindred 11
cause 153
connatural
uniform 16
similar 17
connect *relate* 9
link 43
connection
[*see* connect]
kin 11
in – with 9
connections
cards 840
connective 45
conned, well – 490
connive
overlook 460
co-operate 709
allow 760
connoisseur
critic 480
scholar 492
taste 850
connotate 550
connote 516, 550
imply 526
connubial 903
connuted 9
conoscente **850**

conquer 731
conquered
(*failure* 732)
conquering hero comes 883
conqueror 731
consanguinity 11
consciarecti, mens–
pride 878
innocence 946
conscience
knowledge 490
moral sense 926
in all – *great* 31
affirmation 535
awakened – 950
qualms of – 603
clear – 946
stricken – 950
tender – 926
honour 939
conscientious 926
scrupulous 939
– objector 489
conscious
intuitive 450
knowledge 490
– of disgrace 874
– of glory 873
conscript 726
conscription 744
consecrate *use* 677
dedicate 873
sanctify 987
holy orders 995
consecration
rite 998
consectary 478
– reasoning 476
consecution 63
consecutive
following 63
continuous 69
– fifth 414
consecutively
slowly 275
consensus 488
– of opinion 23
consent *assent* 488
compliance 762
with one – 178
consentaneous
agreeing 23
(*expedient* 646)
consequence
event 151
effect 154
importance 642
in – 478
of no – 643
take the –s 154
consequent 63
consequential
deducible 478
arrogant 878
consequently
reasoning 476
effect 154
conservation
permanence 141
storage 636
preservation 670
conservatism 141, 670
conservative 141, 712
– policy 681
conservatoire 542
conservator
of the peace 967
conservatory
receptacle 191
floriculture 371
furnace 386
store 636
conserve 396, 636
consider *think* 451
attend to 457
examine 461
adjudge 480
believe 484
considerable
in degree 31
in size 192
important 642
considerate
careful 459
judicious 498
benevolent 906
consideration
purchase money 147
thought 451
idea 453
attention 457
qualification 469
inducement 615
importance 642
gift 784
benevolence 906
respect 928
requital 973
deserve – 642
in – of
compensation 30
reasoning 476
on – 658
take into –
thought 451
attention 457
under –
topic 454
inquiry 461
plan 626
considered, all things –
collectively 50
judgment 480
premeditation 611
imperfection 651
consign
transfer 270
commission 755
property 783
give 784
– to the flames 384
– to oblivion 506
– to the tomb 363
consignee 758
consignor 796
consignment
commission 755
gift 784
apportionment 786
consilience 178
consist
– in 1
– of 54
consistence
density 321
consistency
uniformity 16
agreement 23
consistently with 82
consistory
council 696
church 995
consolation
relief 834
condole 915
religious 976
console
table 215
Consoler
the – 976
consolidate
unite 46, 48
condense 321
consols 802
consommé 298
consonant
agreeing 23
musical 413
letter 561
consort
accompany 88
associate 892
spouse 903
– with 23
consortium 23
consortship 892
conspection 441
conspectus 596
conspicuous
visible 446
famous 873
conspiracy 626
conspirator 626
traitor 941
conspire
concur 178
co-operate 709
constable
policeman 664
governor 745
officer 965
constant
fixed 5
uniform 16
continuous 69
regular 80
continual 112
frequent 136
regular 138
immutable 150
exact 494
persevering 604a
obey 743
faithful 939
– flow 69
constellation
stars 318
luminary 423
glory 873
consternation 860
constipation
closure 261
density 321
constituency 181, 737
constituent 51, 56
constitute
compose 54, 56
produce 161
constitution
nature 5
state 7
composition 54
structure 329
charter 924
law 963
constitutional
walk 266
– government 737
constrain
compel 744
restrain 751
abash 881
constraint 195
constrict 195, 706
constringe 195
construct 161

construction 161
form 240
structure 329
meaning 522
put a false – upon 523
constructive
latent 526
– evidence 467
constructor 164
construe 522
consubstantiation 998
consuetude 613
consul 758, 759
consulship 737
consult 695
– one's pillow 133
– one's own wishes 943
– the wishes of 707
consultant 662
consultation 695, 696
consume
destroy 162
waste 638
use 677
– away 36
– time
time 106
inactivity 683
consumere natus, fruges – 683
consuming 830
consummate
great 31
complete 52
completed 729
– skill 698
consummation
end 67
completion 729
– devoutly to be wished
good 618
desire 865
consumption [*see* consume]
decrease 36
shrinking 195
disease 655
contact 199
come in –
arrive 292
contagion
transfer 270
disease 655
unhealthy 657
contain
be composed of 54
include 76
container 191
contaminate
soil 653
spoil 659
contaminated
diseased 655
contango 133, 813
contemn 930
contemper 174
contemplate
view 441
think 451
expect 507
purpose 620
contemporary 120
contemporation 174
contempt **930**
– of danger 861
contemptible
unimportant 643
dishonourable 940
contend
reason 476
assert 535
fight 720
– with difficulties 704
– for
vindicate 937
content
assenting 488
willing 602
calm 826
satisfied **831**
to one's heart's –
sufficient 639
success 731
contention **720**
contentious 901
contents
ingredients 56
list 86
components **190**
synopsis 596
conterminate
end 67
limit 233
conterminous 199
contesseration 72
contest 708, 720
contestant 710
context 591
from the – 516
contexture 329
contiguity **199**
continence 960
continent
land 342
continental 643
contingency
event 151
uncertainty 475
expectation 507
contingent
conditional 8
casual 156
liable 177
possible 470
uncertain 475
supply 635
aid 707
allotted 786
donation 809
unforeseen 508
– duration **108a**
– interest 780
continual
perpetual 112
frequent 136
continuance **143**
continuation
adjunct 39
sequence 63
sequel 65
– school 542
continue
endure 106, 110
persist 143
continued 69
– success 731
continuity **69**
uniformity 16
contortion
distortion 243
convolution 248
contortionist 599, 700
contour
outline 230
appearance 448
contra 14
per – 708
– bonos mores
vulgar 851
improper 925
vice 945
contraband
deceitful 545
prohibited 761
illicit 964
contrabasso 417
contraception 706
contract
shrink 195
narrow 203
promise 768
bargain 769
bridge 840
– a debt 806
– a habit 613
– an obligation 768
contractility 195
contraction **195**
short-hand 590
compendium 596
contractor 690
contradict
contrary 14
answer 462
dissent 489
deny 536
oppose 708
contradictory
disagreement 24
evidence 468
discord 713
contradistinction **15**
contraindicate
dissuade 616
warning 668
contraire, tout au – 536
contralto 408, 416
contraposition
inversion 218
reversion **237**
contrapuntist 413
contrariety **14**
contrary
opposite 14
antagonistic 179
captious 608
opposing 708
quite the – 536
– to expectation
improbable 473
unexpected 508
– to reason 471
contrast
contrariety 14
difference 15
comparison 464
contravallation **717**
contravene
contrary 14
counterevidence 468
deny 536
hinder 706
oppose 708
contre cœur, à – 603
contre-coup 277
contretemps
ill-timed 135
hindrance 706
misfortune 735
contribute
cause 153
tend 176
concur 178

aid 707
give 784
contribution 784
lay under – 789, 924
contrition
abrasion 331
regret 833
penitence 950
contrivance 633
contrive
produce 161
plan 626
– to *succeed in* 731
contriving
cunning 702
control
power 157
influence 175
regulate 693
authority 737
restrain 751
board of – 696
under –
obedience 743
subjection 749
controller of currency 801
controls 273, 693
controversial
discussion 476
discordant 713
controversialist 476, 726
controversy
disagreement 24
discussion 476
debate 588
contention 720
controvert
deny 536
controvertible
uncertain 475
debatable 476
untrue 495
contumacy
obstinacy 606
disobedience 742
contumely
arrogance 885
rudeness 895
disrespect 929
scorn 930
reproach 932
contund 330
contuse 330
conundrum *pun* 520
riddle 533
wit 842
convalescence 654, 660
convection 270
convenance
mariage de – 903
convene 72
conveniences 632
convenient 646, 705
convent 1000
conventicle
assembly 72
council 696
chapel 1000
convention
agreement 23
assembly 72
rule 80
council 696
precept 697
treaty of peace 723
compact 769
–s of society 852
conventional 82, 613
conventual 996, 1000
convergence 290
convergent 286
conversable
talk 588
sociable 892
conversant
know 490
skilful 698
conversation 588
conversational
loquacious 584
interlocution 588
sociable 892
conversazione 588, 892
converse
reverse 14
talk 588
conversely 468
conversion 144
trover and – 964
convert
change to 140, 144
opinion 484
tergiversation 607
religion 987
– to use 677
convertible 13, 27
– terms 522
convexity 250
convey
transfer 270
mean 516
assign 783
– away 791
– the knowledge of 527
conveyance
[*see* convey]
vehicle 272
conveyancer 968
conveyancing 783
convict
convince 484
condemned 949
condemn 971
convicted, self – 950
conviction
confutation 479
belief 484
prove guilty 971
convince
belief 484
confute 479
teach 537
convivial 892
convocate 72
convocation
council 696
church 995
convoke 72
convolution
coil 248
rotation 312
convoy
accompany 88
transfer 270
guard 664
escort 753
convulse
derange 61
violent 173
agitate 315
bodily pain 378
mental pain 830
convulsed with
– laughter 838
– rage 900
convulsion
[*see* convulse]
disorder 59
revolution 146
in –s 315
coo 412
cook *heat* 384
falsify 544
improve 658
prepare 673
servant 746
too many –s 699
– accounts 811
cool *moderate* 174
cold 383
refrigerate 385
grey 432
dissuade 616
cautious 864
indifferent 866
unamazed 871
unfriendly 889
discourteous 895
look – upon
unsocial 893
take –ly 826
– down 826
– one's heels
kept waiting 133
inaction 681
cooler 387
coolheaded
judicious 498
unexcitable 826
coolie
bearer 271
military 726
coolness
insensibility 823
estrangement 898
coon-can 840
coop *abode* 189
restrain 751
prison 752
co-operation
physical 178
voluntary 709
participation 778
co-operator 690, 711
co-optation 609
co-ordinate
equal 27
arrange 60
measure 466
cootie 653
cop 664
copal 356a
coparcener 778
copartner
accompanying 88
participator 778
associate 890
copartnership
co-operation 709
party 712
cope *equal* 27
oppose 708
contend 720
canonicals 999
copia verborum
diffuse 573
loquacious 584
coping stone
top 210
completion 729
copious
diffuse style 573
abundant 639

coportion 778
copper *money* 800
policeman 664
copper-coloured 433, 439
copper-plate
engraving 558
writing 590
coppice 367
coprolite 653
copse 367
copula 45
copulation **43**
copy
imitate 19
facsimile **21**
prototype 22
news 532
record 551
represent 554
write 590
for the press 591
plan 626
– book 22
copyhold 780
copyist
imitator 19
artist 559
writer 590
copyright 780
coquet *lie* 544
change the mind 607
affected 855
endearment 902
flattery 933
– with
irresolute 605
coquette
affected 854, 855
flirt 897
coquillage 847
coracle 273
coral 847
– reef 667
coram judice
jurisdiction 965
lawsuit 969
cor Anglais 417
corbeille 191
corbel 215
cord *tie* 45
filament 205
cordage 45
cordated 245
cordial
pleasure 377
dram 392
willing 602
remedy 662
feeling 821
grateful 829
friendly 888
courteous 894
cordiform 245
cordite 727
cordon
inclosure 232
circularity 247
decoration 877
– bleu 733, 746
– sanitaire
safety 664
preservation 670
corduroy 259
cordwainer
shoemaker 225
artificer 690
core *gist* 5
source 153
centre 222
gist 642
true to the – 939
coriaceous 327
Corinthian 850
co-rival
[*see* corrival]
cork *plug* 263
lightness 320
– jacket 666
– up *close* 261
restrain 751
corking pin 45
corkscrew
spiral 248
perforator 262
circuition 311
cormorant
desire 865
gluttony 957
corn
projection 250
Cornaro 953
cornea 441
corned 959
cornelian 847
corneous 323
corner *place* 182
receptacle 191
angle 244
monopoly 777
– creep into a – 893
in a dark – 528
drive into a – 706
push into a – 874
rub off –s 82
– turn a – 311
turn the – 658
– stone
support 215
importance 642
defence 717
cornet *music* 417
officer 745
cornice 210
corniculate 253
cornification 323
Cornish hug 545
corno 417
cornopean 417
cornucopia 639
cornute
projecting 250
sharp 253
corollary
adjunct 39
deduction 480
corona 247
coronach 839
coronation
enthronement 755
celebration 883
coroner 363, 965
–'s jury 967
coronet *hoop* 247
insignia 747
title 877
corporal
corporeal 316
officer 745
corporate 43
– body 712
corporation
bulk 192
convex 250
association 712
jurisdiction 965
corporeal 3, 316, 364
– hereditaments 780
corporeity 316
corps *assemblage* 72
troops 726
à – perdu
haste 684
rash 863
– de reserve 636
corpse **362**
corpulence 192
corpus 316
– Christi 998
– delicti
guilt 947
lawsuit 969
– juris
precept **697**
law 963
corpuscle
small 32
little 193
corradiation
focus 74
convergence 290
corral 232, 370
correct
orderly 58
true 494
inform **527**
disclose 529
improve 658
repair 660
due 924
censure 932
honourable 939
virtuous 944
punish 972
– ear 416, 418
– memory 505
– reasoning 476
– style
grammatical 567
elegant 578
correction
[*see* correct]
house of – 752
under – 879
corrective 662
corregidor 745
correlation
relation 9
reciprocity **12**
correspondence
correlation 12
similarity 17
agreement 23
writing **592**
– course 537
correspondent
messenger 534
journalist 593
consignee 758
corresponding
similar 17
agreeing 23
corridor *region* 181
place 191
passage 627
– train 272
corrigendum 495
corrigible 658
corrival 726
corrivalry 720
corrivation 348
corroborant 662
corroboration
evidence 467
assent 488
corrode *burn* 384
erode 659
afflict 830
corrosive
[*see* corrode]

acrid 171
destructive 649
– sublimate 663
corrugate
derange 61
constrict 195
roughen 256
rumple 258
furrow 259
corruption
decomposition 49
neology 563
foulness 653
disease 655
deterioration 659
improbity 940
vice 945
corrupting
noxious 649
corsage 225
corsair 273, 792
corse 362
corselet 225
corset 225
corso 728
cortège
adjunct 39
continuity 69
accompaniment 88
journey 266
suite 746
cortes 696
cortex
cortical 223
coruscate 420
corvette 273, 726
corybantic 503
coryphée 599
Corypheus
teacher 540
director 694
coscinomancy 511
cosey 892
cosignificative 522
cosine 217
cosmetic
remedy 662
ornament 847
cosmic 318
cosmogony &c. 318
cosmopolitan
abode 189
mankind 372
philanthropic 910
sociality 892
cosmorama 448
cosmos 60, 318
Cossack 726
cosset
darling 899

caress 902
cost 812
pay –s 807
to one's –
evil 619
badness 649
– what it may 604
– price 815
costermonger 797
costless 815
costly 814
costive
taciturn 585
costume 225
theatrical – 599
costumé 225
bal – 840
costumier 225
theatrical 599
cosy *snug* 377
sociable 892
cot *abode* 189
bed 215
cote 189
cotenancy 778
coterie *class* 75
junto 712
society 892
coterminous 120
cothurnus 599
cotillon 840
cottage 189
– piano 417
cottager 188
cotter 188
cotton 205
– seed oil 356
couch *lie* 213
bed 215
stoop 308
lurk 528
– one's lance 720
– in terms 566
couchant 213
couci-couci 651
cough 349
churchyard – 655
couleur de rose
good 648
prosperity 734
view en – 836
coulisses 599
coulter 253
council
senate **696**
church 995
hold a – 695
– of education 542
– school 542
councillor 696
counsel

advice 695
lawyer 968
keep one's own – 528
take – *think* 451
inquire 461
be advised 695
count *clause* 51
item 79
compute 85
estimate 480
lord 875
– one's chickens before they are hatched 858, 863
– the cost 864
– upon
believe 484
expect 507
to be –ed on one's fingers 103
countenance
face 234
appearance 448
favour 707
approve 931
keep in –
conform 82
induce 615
encourage 861
vindicate 937
keep one's –
brook 826
not laugh 837
out of –
abashed 879
put out of – 874
stare out of – 885
– falling
disappointment 509
dejection 837
counter *contrary* 14
number 84
table 215
stern 235
token 550
shop-board 799
over the –
barter 794
buy 795
sell 796
run – 179
– to 708
counteract
compensate 30
physically 179
hinder 706
voluntarily 708
counteraction 14,

179
counterbalance 30
counterblast
counteract 179
retaliate 718
countercharge 462
counterchange
correlation 12
interchange 148
countercharm 993
countercheck
mark 550
hindrance 706
counterclaim 30
counter-evidence 468
counterfeit
imitate 19
copy 21
simulate 544
sham 545
coinage 792
counterfoil 550
countermand 756
countermarch 266, 283
countermark 550
countermine
plan 626
oppose 708
countermotion 283
counterorder 756
counterpane 223
counterpart
match 17
copy 21
reverse 237
counterplot
plan 626
oppose 708
retaliate 718
counterpoint 415
counterpoise
compensate 30
weight 319
hinder 706
counter-poison 662
counterpole 14
counter-project 718
counter-protest 468
counter-revolution 146
counterscarp 717
countersign
evidence 467
assent 488
mark 550
counterstroke 718
countervail
outweigh 28
compensate 30

evidence 468
counterwork 708
countess 875
counting-house 799
countless 105
countrified 189
vulgar 851
country
region 181
abode 189
rural 371
authority 737
love of – 910
country-dance 840
countryman
commonalty 876
friend 890
county 181
– seat 189
– town 189
– school 542
– council 696
– court 966
coup
instantaneous 113
action 680
– de bec
attack 716
censure 932
– d'épée dans l'eau 645
– d'essai 675
– d'état
revolution 146
plan 626
action 680
lawless 964
– de grâce
end 67
death-blow 361
completion 729
punishment 972
– de main
violence 173
action 680
attack 716
– de maître
excellent 648
skilful 698
success 731
– d'œil
sight 441
appearance 448
display 882
– de plume 590
– de soleil
hot 384
mad 503
à – sûr 474
– de théâtre
appearance 448
display 882
coupé 272
couple
unite 43
two 89
–d with
added 37
accompanied 88
coupler 45
couplet 89, **597**
coupling 45
coupon 800
courage **861**
moral – 604
– oozing out 862
courant, au – 490
coureur, avant – 673
courier
traveller 268
guide 524
messenger 534
course *order* 58
continuity 69
time 106, **109**
layer 204
motion 264
locomotion 266, 267
direction 278
dinner 298
river 348
pursuit 622
way 627
conduct 692
arena 728
bend one's – 266
in due – 134
hold a – 278
in the – of
during 106
keep one's –
progress 282
persevere 604*a*
let things take their –
continue 143
inaction 681
follow as of – 478
mark out a – 626
of –
conformity 82
effect 154
certain 474
assent 488
necessity 601
willingly 602
custom 613
consent 762
expect 871
race – 840
run its –
end 67
complete 729
take a – 622
take its – 151
– of action 692
– of business 625
– of events 151
– of inquiry 461
– of preparation 673
– runs smooth 734
– of study 537
– of things 151
– of time 121
courser
horse 271
swift 274
coursing
kill 361
pursue 622
court *close* 181, 182
house 189
hall 191
flatness 213
invite 615
pursue 622
council 696
retinue 746
solicit 765
gentility 852
wish 865
woo 902
flatter 933
tribunal 966
bring into – 467
friend at – 526, 711
pay – to
servile 886
love 897, 902
flatter 933
put out of – 731
– card 626
– of honour 939
courteous 894
courtesan 962
courtesy
stoop 308, 314
submit 725
politeness **894**
show –
respect 928
courtier
servile 886
flatterer 935
–like 933
courtly 852
courtship 902
courtyard 182
cousin 11
coûte-que-coûte
certainly 474
necessary 601
resolution 604
cove *cell* 191
hollow 252
bay 343
covenant
compact 769
condition 770
security 771
covenanter 488
Coventry
Earl of –
cards 840
send to –
eject 297
disrepute 874
seclusion 893
cover
compensate 30
include 76
superpose, lid 223
dress 225
stopper 263
meal 298
conceal 528
retreat 530
report 531
keep clean 652
keep safe 664
preserve 670
under –
hidden 528
pretence 545
safe 664
with dust 653
covercle 223
covering **223**
coverlet 223
Coverley, Sir Roger de – 840
covert *abode* 189
invisible 447
latent 526
refuge 666
feme –e 903
– way 627
coverture 903
covet *desire* 865
envy 921
covetous
miserly 819
covey
assemblage 72
multitude 102
cow
animal 366
female 374
intimidate 860
coward 862

cowardice 862
cowboy 370
cower *stoop* 308
fear 860
cowardice 862
servile 886
cowherd 370
cowhide 223, 975
cowhouse 189
cowkeeper 370
cowl *sacerdotal* 999
dress 225
cowled 223
cowl-staff 215
co-worker 690
coxcomb 854
coxcombry
affectation 855
vanity 880
coxswain 269
coy *timid* 860
modest 881
cozen 545
crab *sourness* 397
–like motion
deviation 279
regression 283
grouch 901*a*
crabbed *sour* 397
unintelligible 519
obscure style 571
difficult 704
uncivil 895
sulky 901*a*
crack *split* 44
discontinuity 70
instantaneous 113
fissure 198
furrow 259
brittle 328
sound 406
excellent 648
injure 659
skilful 698
boast 884
– a bottle
food 298
social 892
drunken 959
– of doom
end 67
future 121
destruction 162
– one's invention 515
– a joke 842
– shot 700
crackbrained 503
cracked
unmusical 410
fanatical 481
mad 503
faulty 651
– bell 408*a*
– voice 581
cracker 406
crackle 406
cracksman 792
crack-up 162
cradle
beginning 66
infancy 127
origin 153
placing 184
bed 215
training 673
aid 707
in the – 129
– song 415
craft *shipping* 273
business 625
skill 698
cunning 702
craftiness 498
craftsman 690
craftsmanship 680
crag *pointed* 253
hard 323
land 342
craggy
rough 256
craig *height* 206
crake 884
cram *crowd* 72
stuff 194
choke 261
teach 537
learn 539
gorge 957
– down the throat
induce belief 484
compel 744
crambe repetita
weariness 841
satiety 869
crambo 597
crammed 52
– to overflowing 641
crammer *lie* 546
teacher 537
cramp
fastening 45
paralyze 158
weaken 160
little 193
compress 195
spasm 378
hinder 706
cramped *style* 579
cran 191
cranch
[*see* craunch]
crane *angle* 244
elevate 307
instrument 633
– neck 245
craniology &c. 450
cranium 450
crank
fanatic 504
instrument 633
wit 842
treadmill 975
crankle *fold* 258
crankling
rough 256
cranky *weak* 160
ill health 655
cranny 198
crape
crinkle 248
mourning 839
crapulence
intemperance 954
gluttony 957
drunken 959
crash
destruction 162
collision 276
gain entrance 294
sound 406
crasis *nature* 5
coherence 48
composition 54
crass 31
– ignorance 491
crassitude
breadth 202
thickness 352
crate
receptacle 191
vehicle 272
crater *deep* 208
hollow 252
craunch
shatter 44
chew 298
pulverize 330
cravat 225
crave *ask* 765
desire 865
envy 921
craven *submit* 725
cowardly 862
craw 191
crawfish 607
crawl *time* 109
creep 275
back down 283, 606
servile 886
– with 102
crawling 102
crayons 556
craze 481
crazy *weak* 160
mad 503
creachy 160
creak 410
cream
emulsion 352
oil 356
important part 642
best 648
– colour
white 430
yellow 436
– of the jest 842
creamy 352
crease 258
create *cause* 153
produce 161
imagine 515
created being 366
creation
[*see* create]
effect 154
world 318
Creator 976
creator 164
creature *thing* 3
effect 154
animal 366
man 372
parasite 711
slave 746
– comforts
food 298
pleasure 377
crèche 542
credat Judæus Apella
unbelief 485
absurdity 497
credence *belief* 484
church 1000
credenda 484
credential 467
credible
possible 470
probable 472
belief 484
credit *belief* 484
influence 737
pecuniary 805
account 811
repute 873
approbation 931
desert 944
to one's –
property 780
crédit mobilier 802

creditable *right* 924
creditor 805
credo quia impossibile 486
credulity 486
credulous person
dupe 547
creed *belief* 484
theology 983
Apostles' – 983*a*
creek *interval* 198
water 343
creel 191
creep *crawl* 275
tingle 380
(*inactivity* 683)
– in 294
– into a corner 893
– into the good graces of 933
– out 529
– upon one 508
– with
multitude 102
redundance 641
creeper 367
creeping
sensation 380
– thing 366
creese 727
cremation
of corpses 363
burning 384
crematorium 363, 386
crematory 386
crême de la crême 648
Cremona 417
crenate 257
crenelle 257
crenulate 257
creole 57
crêpe 248, 839
crepidam, ultra – 471
crepitation 406
crepuscule
dawn 125
dusk 422
crescendo
increase 35
musical 415
crescent
growing 35
street 189
curve 245
cresset 423, 550
crest *supremacy* 33
summit 210
pointed 253
tuft 256
sign 550
armorial 877
pride 878
on the – 33
crest-fallen
dejected 837
humble 879
crevasse 198, 667
crevice 198
crew *assemblage* 72
inhabitants 188
mariners 269
party 712
crib *bed* 215
key 522
granary 636
steal 791
parsimony 819
cribbage 840
cribbed, confined, cabined – 751
cribble 260
cribriform 260
Crichton, Admirable –
scholar 492
perfect 650
proficient 700
crick *pain* 378
cricket *game* 840
not – 940
– ground 213
crier 534
send round the – 531
crim. con. 961
crime 945, 947
criminal 923, 945
culprit 949
– law 963
court of – appeal 966
criminality 947
criminate 938
crimp *crinkle* 248
notch 257
brittle 328
deceiver 548
take 789
steal 791
crimple 258
crimson 434, 821
cringe *submit* 725
subject 749
servility 886
crinite 256
crinkle *angle* 244
convolution 248
roughen 256
fold 258
crinoline 225
cripple *disable* 158
weaken 160
injure 659
crippled
disease 655
crisis
conjuncture 8
present time 118
opportunity 134
event 151
strait 704
excitement 824
bring to a – 604
come to a – 729
crisp *rumpled* 248
rough 256
brittle 328
style 572
Crispin 225
criss-cross 219
cristallomantia 511
criterion *test* 463
evidence 467
indication 550
crithomancy 511
critic *judge* 480
taste 850
detractor 936
critical
contingent 8
opportune 134
discriminating 465
important 642
dangerous 665
difficult 704
censorious 932
criticism
judgment 480
dissertation 595
disapprobation 932
detraction 934
critique
[*see* criticism]
croak *cry* 412
hoarseness 581
stammer 583
warning 668
discontent 832
lament 839
croaker 832, 837
Croat 726
crochet 847
crock 191
crockery 384
crocodile tears 544
crocus *yellow* 436
Crœsus 803
croft 189, 232
Croix de Guerre 733
cromlech 363, 551
crone *veteran* 130
fool 501
crony *friend* 890
favourite 899
crook *curve* 245
deviation 279
thief 792
crooked
sloping 217
distorted 243
angular 244
latent 526
crafty 702
ugly 846
dishonourable 940
– path 704
– temper 901
– ways 279
croon 580
crop
stomach 191
harvest 154
shorten 201
eat 298
vegetable 367
store 636
gather 775
take 789
second – 167, 775
– out *visible* 446
disclose 529
– up *begin* 66
take place 151
reproduction 163
cropper *fall* 306
croquet *game* 840
– ground *level* 213
croquette 298
crosier 747, 999
cross *mix* 41
across 219
pass 302
grave 363
oppose 708
failure 732
disaster 735
refuse 764
pain 830
decoration 877
fretful 901
punishment 975
rites 998
fiery – 722
proclaim at the – roads 531
red – 662
–ed bayonets 708
– breed 83
– cut 628

– fire *interchange* 148
difficulty 704
opposition 708
attack 716
–ed in love 898
– the mind 451
– the path of 706
– and pile 621
– purposes 14
disorder 59
error 495
misinterpret 523
unskilful 699
difficulty 704
opposition 708
discord 713
– oneself 998
– questions
inquiry 461
discord 713
game 840
– road 627
– the Rubicon 609
– sea 348
– swords 722
crossbow 727
cross-examine 461
cross-grained 256
obstinate 606
sulky 901*a*
crossing 219
– sweeper 652
crosspatch 895
crossroads 8
cross-word puzzle 533
crotch 244
crotchet
eccentric 83
music 413
misjudgment 481
obstinacy 606
caprice 608
crouch *lower* 207
stoop 308
fear 860
servile 886
– before 725
croup 235
croupier 694
crow *cry* 412
black 431
rejoice 838
boast 884
pluck a – with 932
as the – flies 278
–'s foot (*age*) 128
–'s nest 210
– to pluck
discord 713
anger 900
accuse 938
crowbar 633
crowd 72
multitude 102
close 197
redundance 641
party 712
vulgar 876
in the – *mixed* 41
madding – 682
crown *top* 210
circle 247
complete 729
trophy 733
sceptre 747
install 755
decoration 877
reward 973
to – all 33, 642
–ed head 745
– with laurel 873
– with success 731
crowning
[*see* crown]
superior 33
end 67
– point 210
cruche à l'eau &c. tant va la – 735
crucial
crossing 219
proof 478
– test 463
cruciate
physical pain 378
mental pain 830
crucible
dish 191
conversion 144
furnace 386
experiment 463
laboratory 691
put into the – 163
crucifix 219, 998
crucifixion 828
cruciform 219
crucify
physical torture 378
mental agony 830
execution 972
crucis, experimentum – 463
crude *colour* 428
- *style* 579
unprepared 674
cruel
painful 830
inhuman 907
– to be kind 914
cruelly *much* 31
cruet 191
cruise
vessel 191
navigation 267
cruiser 726
cruising 267
crumb *small* 32
powder 330
– of comfort 834
crumble
decrease 36
weak 160
destruction 162
brittle 328
pulverize 330
spoil 659
– into dust
decompose 49
– under one's feet 735
crumbling
[*see* crumble]
dangerous 665
crumenal 800
crump
distorted 243
curved 245
crumple
ruffle 256
fold 258
– up *destroy* 162
crush 195
crunch
shatter 44
chew 298
pulverize 330
crupper 235
crusade 722
crush *crowd* 72
destroy 162
compress 195
pulverize 330
humble 879
– under an iron heel 739
– one's hopes
disappoint 509
hopeless 859
crushed 828
crushing 830
crust 223
crustacean 366
crusty 895, 901*a*
crutch
support 215
angle 244
–ed Friars 996
crux 219, 704
– criticorum 533
cry *human* 411
animal 412
publish 531, 532
call 550
voice 580
vogue 613
weep 839
far – to 196
full – *loud* 404
raise a – 550
– aloud
implore 765
– out against
dissuade 616
censure 932
– down 932, 934
– for 865
– before hurt 839
– for joy 838
– you mercy
deprecate 766
pity 914
forgive 918
– shame 932
– to *beseech* 765
– up 931
– for vengeance 923
– wolf *false* 544
alarm 669
– and little wool
overrate 482
boast 884
disappoint 509
crying [*see* cry]
urgent 630
weary 841
– evil 619
– shame 874
– sin 945
crypt *cell* 191
grave 363
ambush 530
altar 1000
cryptic 475, 528
cryptography
hidden 528
writing 590
crystal *hard* 323
transparent 425
snow – 383
– gazer 513
– gazing 511, 992
– oil 356
clear as – 518
crystalline
dense 321
hard 323
transparent 425
crystallization 321, 323
csako 225, 717

cub *young* 129
vulgar 851
clown 876
unlicked – 241
cubby-hole 191
cube
three dimensions 92, 93
form 244
cubicle 191
cubist 556
cubit 200
cucking stool 975
cuckold 905
cuckoldom 961
cuckoo
imitation 19
repetition 104
sound 407
cry 412
cuddle 197, 902
cudgel *beat* 276
weapon 727
punish 975
take up the –s
aid 707
attack 716
contention 720
– one's brains
think 451
imagine 515
cue *hint* 527
watchword 550
plea 617
rôle 625
take one's – from 695
in proper – 698
cuff *sleeve* 225
blow 276
punishment 972
cui bono 644, 645
cuique voluptas sui – 865
cuirass 717
cuirassier 726
cuisine 298
batterie de – 957
culbute
inversion 218
fall 306
cul-de-lampe
engraving 558
ornament 847
cul-de-sac
concave 252
closed 261
difficulty 704
culinary 298
– art 673
cull *dupe* 547
choose 609
take 789
cullender 260
cullibility 486
cullion 949
cully *deceive* 545, 547
culm 388
culminate
maximum 33
height 206
top 210
complete 729
culpability *vice* 945
guilt 947
culprit 949
cult 983
cultivate *till* 365, 371
sharpen 375
improve 658
prepare 673
aid 707
cultivated
courteous 894
– taste 850
cultivator 371
culture
knowledge 490
improvement 658
taste 850
politeness 894
culverin 727
culvert 350
cum multis aliis 37, 102
cumber *load* 319
obstruct 706
cumbersome
incommodious 647
disagreeable 830
cummerbund 225
cumulative 72
increasing 35
assembled 72
– evidence 467
– vote 609
cumulus 353
cunctando restituit rem 681
cunctation 133
cuneiform 244
– character 590
cunning
prepense 611
sagacious 698
artful 702
– fellow 700
– man 994
cup *vessel* 191
hollow 252
beverage 298
remedy 662
trophy 733
tipple 959
between – and lip 111
in one's –s 959
– that cheers &c. 298
– of humiliation 879
dash the – from one's lips 509
– too low 837
cupbearer 746
cupboard 191
cupellation 384
Cupid *beauty* 845
love 897
gods 979
cupidity
avarice 819
desire 865
cupola *height* 206
roof 223
dome 250
cup-tossing 621
cur *dog* 366
coward 862
sneak 949
curable 658, 660, 662
curacy 995
curare 663
curate 996
curative 660
curator 694, 758
curb *moderate* 174
slacken 275
dissuade 616
restrain 751
shackle 752
curb exchange 621
curbstone 233
curd *density* 321
pulp 354
(*cohere* 46)
curdle *condense* 321
(*cohere* 46)
make the blood – 830
curdled 352
cure *reinstate* 660
remedy 662
preserve 670
benefice 995
curé 996
cureless 859
curfew 126
curia 966
curio 847
curiosa felicitas 698
curiosity
unconformity 83
inquiring 455
phenomenon 872
curious
exceptional 83
inquisitive 455
true 494
beautiful 845
desirous 865
curiously *very* 31
curl *bend* 245
convolution 248
hair 256
cockle up 258
badge 747
– up one's lip 930
curling *game* 840
curmudgeon
miser 819
plebeian 876
currency
publicity 531
money 800
current *existing* 1
usual 78
present 118
happening 151
flow 264
of water 348
of air 349
rife 531, 532
language 560
habit 613
danger 667
account – 811
against the – 708
go with the – 82
pass –
believed 484
fashion 852
stem the – 708
– belief 488
– of events 151
– of ideas 451
– of time 109
currente calamo 590
curricle 272
curriculum 537
curry *food* 298
rub 331
condiment 392, 393
– favour with
love 897
flatter 933
curry-comb 370
curse *bane* 663

adversity 735
painful 830
malediction 908
cursed *bad* 649
cursitor 968
cursive 590
cursory
transient 111
inattentive 458
hasty 684
take a – view of 457
neglect 460
curst 901*a*
curt *short* 201
concise 572
taciturn 585
curtail *retrench* 38
shorten 201
–ed of its fair proportions
distorted 243
ugly 846
curtain 223
shade 424
hide 528, 530
theatre 599
fortification 717
behind the –
invisible 447
inquiry 461
knowledge 490
close the – 528
raise the – 529
rising of the – 448
– lecture 932
– raiser 66, 599
curtsy
stoop 308, 314
submit 725
polite 894
curule 696
curvature 245
curvet *leap* 309
turn 311
oscillate 314
agitate 315
curvilinear 245
– motion 311
cushion *pillow* 215
soft 324
relief 834
cushy 829
cusp *angle* 244
sharp 253
cuspidor 191
cuss 908
custard 298
custodes? quis custodiet – 459
custodian 753
custody *safe* 664
captive 751
retention 781
in – *prisoner* 754
accused 938
take into – 751
custom *old* 124
habit 613
barter 794
sale 796
tax 812
fashion 852
– honoured in breach 614
customary
[see custom]
regular 80
customer 795
custom-house 799
– officer 965
custos 753
– rotulorum 553
cut *divide* 44
bit 51
discontinuity 70
interval 198
curtail 201
layer 204
form 240
notch 257
blow 276
eject 297
reap 371
physical pain 378
cold 385
neglect 460
carve 557
engraving 558
road 627
attack 716
portion 786
affect 824
mental pain 830
dance step 840
decline acquaintance 893
discourtesy 895
tipsy 959
– short 628
unkindest – of all
pain 828
malevolence 907
– across 302
– adrift 44
– along 274
have a – at 716
– away 274
– a whetstone with a razor
sophistry 477
waste 638
misuse 679
– both ways 468
– capers 309
– according to cloth
economy 817
caution 864
– and come again
repeat 104
enough 639
– dead 893
– direct 893
– down *destroy* 162
shorten 201
fell 308
kill 361
– down expenses 817
– and dried
arranged 60
prepared 673
– a figure
appearance 448
fashion 852
repute 873
display 882
– the first turf 66
– the ground from under one
confute 479
hinder 706
– to the heart 824, 830
– ice with
influence 175
– of one's jib 448
– jokes 842
– the knot 705
– off *subduct* 38
disjoin 44
kill 361
impede 706
bereft 776
secluded 893
– off with a shilling 789
– open 260
– out *surpass* 33
stop 142
substitute 147
plan 626
– out for 698
– out work
prepare 673
direct 693
– to pieces
destroy 162
kill 361
– a poor figure 874
– to the quick 830
– up root and branch 162
– up rough 900
– and run 274
depart 293
escape 623
– short *stop* 142
destroy 162
shorten 201
silence 581
– one's stick
depart 283
avoid 623
– one's own throat 699
– and thrust 716
– in two 91
– up *divide* 44
destroy 162
pained 828
give pain 830
discontented 832
dejected 837
censure 932
what one will – up for 780
– one's way through 302
cutaneous 223
cute 698
cuticle 223
cutlass 727
cutlery 253
cut-purse 792
cutter 273
cut-throat
killer 361
evil-doer 913
cutting *sharp* 253
cold 383
path 627
affecting 821
painful 830
reproachful 932
cuttings
excerpta 596
selections 609
cutty stool 950
cwt. 98, 319
cyanogen 438
cyanide of potassium *poison* 663
cycle *time* 106
period 138
circle 247
ride 266
vehicle 272
– car 272
cyclist 268
cycloid 247
cyclometer 200
cyclone

rotation 312
wind 349
cyclopædia
knowledge 490
book 593
Cyclopean
strong 159
huge 192
Cyclops
monster 83
mighty 159
huge 192
dupe 547
cygne
chant du – 360
– noir 650
cylindric 249
cyma 847
cymbal 417
cymbalo 417
cymophanous 440
cynic
misanthrope 911
detractor 936
ascetic 955
closet – 893
cynical
contemptuous 930
censorious 932
detracting 934
cynicism
discourtesy 895
contempt 930
cynosure *sign* 550
direction 693
wonder 870
repute 873
Cynthia of the minute 149
cypher [*see* cipher]
cypress
interment 363
mourning 839
Cyprian 962
cyst 191
czar 745

D

da capo 104
dab *small* 32
paint 223
slap 276
clever 700
dabble *water* 337
dirty 653
meddle 682
fribble 683
dabbled *wet* 339
dabbler 493
dachshund 366
dacoit 792
dactyl 597
dactylogram 467
dactyliomancy 511
dactylonomy
numeration 85
symbol 550
dad 166
daddy 166
dado 211
dædal
variegated 440
dædalian
convoluted 248
artistic 698
daft 503
dagger 727
look –s *anger* 900
threat 909
air drawn – 515
plant – in breast
give pain 830
speak –s 932
at –s drawn
opposed 708
discord 713
enmity 889
hate 898
daggle *hang* 214
dirty 653
dagobah 1000
Dagon 986
daguerreotype
represent 554
paint 556
dahabeah 273
Dail Eireann 696
daily
frequent 136
periodic 138
– occurrence
normal 82
habitual 613
– paper 531
dainty *food* 298
savoury 394
pleasing 829
delicate 845
tasty 850
fastidious 868
dairy 191, 370
– maid 746
dais *support* 215
throne 747
daisy
fresh as a – 654
– pied 847
dale 252
dally *delay* 133
irresolute 605
inactive 683
amuse 840
fondle 902
dalmatic 999
Daltonism 443
dam *parent* 166
close 261
pond 343
obstruct 706
damage *evil* 619
injure, spoil 659
price 812
damages 974
damascene 440
damask 434
dame
woman 374
teacher 540
lady 875
damn
malediction 908
condemn 971
– with faint praise 932, 934
damnable 649
damnatory
disapprove 932
condemn 971
damnify
damage 649
spoil 659
damnosa hereditas 663
Damocles
sword of – 667
Damon and Pythias 890
damozel 129
damp
moderate 174
moist 339
cold 385
sound 405
dissuade 616
hinder 706
depress 837
dull 843
– the sound 408*a*
damper 387
damsel
youth 129
female 374
Dan to Beersheba 52, 180
Danaë 803
Danaos, timeo –
doubt 485
caution 864
dance
jump 309
oscillate 314
agitate 315
rejoice 838
sport 840
sociality 892
lead the – 175
lead one a –
run away 623
circuit 629
difficult 704
practical joke 929
St. Vitus' – 315
– attendance
waiting 133
follow 281
servant 746
petition 765
servility 886
– the back step 283
– upon nothing 972
– the war dance 715
dance-band 417
dance-music 415
dander 900
Dandie Dinmont 366
dandiprat 193
dandle 902
dandruff 653
dandy
ship 273
fop 854
dandyism 855
danger 665
in – *liable* 177
source of – 667
– past 664
– signal 669
dangerous
[*see* danger]
– classes 913
– illness 655
– person 667
dangle *hang* 214
swing 314
display 882
dangler 281
Daniel *sage* 500
judge 967
dank 339
Dannemora 752
danseuse 599
dapper
little 193
elegant 845
dapple 433
dappled 440
darbies
handcuffs 752

Darby and Joan
secluded 893
married 903
dare *defy* 715
face danger 861
– not 860
– say *probable* 472
believe 484
suppose 514
dare-devil
courage 861
rash 863
bluster 887
daring 861
unreserved 525
– imagination 515
dark
obscure 421
dim 422
black 431
blind 442
invisible 447
unintelligible 519
latent 526
joyless 837
insidious 940
in the –
ignorant 491
leap in the –
experiment 463
chance 621
rash 863
keep – *hide* 528
– ages 491
– cloud 735
view with – eyes 932
– lantern 423
darkly
see through a glass – 443
darkness [*see* dark] 421
children of – 988
love – better than light 989
powers of – 978
darky 431
darling *beloved* 897
favourite 899
darn 660
dart *swift* 274
propel 284
missile 727
– to and fro 684
Dartmoor 752
Darwinism 357
dash
small quantity 32
mix 41
swift 276
fling 284
mark 550
courage 861
cut a – *repute* 873
display 882
– at *resolution* 604
attack 716
– board 666
– cup from lips 761
– down 308
– hopes
disappoint 509
fail 732
dejected 837
despair 859
– on 274
– off *paint* 556
write 590
active 682
haste 684
– of the pen 590
dashed [*see* dash]
humbled 879
dashing
fashionable 852
brave 861
ostentatious 882
dastard 862
data *evidence* 467
reasoning 476
supposition 514
date *time* 106
chronology 114
datum 673
daub *cover* 223
paint 428
misrepresent 555
dirt 653
daughter 167
daunt 860
dauntless 861
Dauphin 875
davenport 191, 215
davit 214
Davus sum non Œdipus
unintelligent 499
artless 703
dull 843
Davy Jones' locker 310
dawdle *tardy* 133
slow 275
inactive 683
dawk 534
dawn
precursor 64
begin 66
priority 116
morning 125
light 420
dim 422
glimpse 490
dawplucker 936
day
period 108
present time 118
light 420
all – 110
clear as –
certain 474
intelligible 518
manifest 525
close of – 126
decline of – 126
denizens of the – 366
good old –'s 122
have had its – 124
one fine – 119
open as – 703
order of the – 613
red letter – 642
see the light of – 446
– after day
diuturnal 110
frequent 136
– by day
repeatedly 104
time 106
periodic 138
– after the fair 135
–s gone by 122
– of judgment 121
happy as the – is long 827, 836
– and night
frequent 136
labour – and night 686
–s numbered
transient 111
death 360
– one's own 731
– of rest 687
– star 423
– after to-morrow 121
– before yesterday 122
–s of week 138
all in –'s work 625
daybed 215
daybook *record* 551
accounts 811
daybreak
morning 125
dim 422
day-dream
fancy 515
hope 858
day-labourer 690
daylight 125, 420
see – *intelligible* 518
– saving 114
daymare 859
daze 420
dazed 376
dazzle
light 420
blind 422, 443
put out 458
astonish 870
awe 928
dazzling
[*see* dazzle]
beautiful 845
de: – die in diem
time 106
periodic 138
– facto 1
– fond en comble 52
– novo 104
– omnibus rebus 81
– profundis 821
deacon 996
deaconry 995
dead *complete* 52
inert 172
colourless 429
lifeless 360
insensible 376
– against
contrary 14
oppose 708
more – than alive 688
– asleep 683
– beat
powerless 158
– certainty 474
– colour 556
– cut 893
– drunk 959
– failure 732
– flat 213
– heat 27
– languages 560
– letter
impotent 158
unmeaning 517
useless 645
laxity 738
exempt 927
illegal 964
– level 16
– lift *exertion* 686
difficulty 704, 706

– lock *cease* 142
stoppage 265
– march 363, 415
– of night
midnight 126
dark 421
– reckoning
numeration 85
measurement 466
– secret 533
– set against 708
– set at
attack 716
– shot 700
– silence 403
– sound 408*a*
– stop 142
– to 823
– wall
hindrance 706
defence 717
– weight 706
– water 343
deaden
weaken 158
moderate 174
sound 405
mute 408*a*
benumb 823
dead-house 363
deadlock 142, 704
deadly *killing* 361
pernicious 649
unhealthy 657
– sin 947
– weapon 727
deads 645
deaf 419
inattentive 458
– to advice 606
– and dumb 581
turn – ear to
neglect 460
unbelief 487
refuse 764
– to reason 901*a*
– to *insensible* 823
deafen *loud* 404
deafness 419
deal *much* 31
arrange 60
bargain 768
allot 786
– a blow
injure 659
attack 716
punish 972
– board 323
– in 794
– out *scatter* 73
give 784
– with
treat of 595
handle 692
barter 794
dealer 797
dealings *action* 680
have – with
trade 794
friendly 888
dean 128, 694, 996
deanery *office* 995
house 1000
dear
high-priced 814
loved 897
favourite 899
O – ! *lament* 839
– at any price 646
– me *wonder* 870
pay – for whistle 647
dearest foe 936
dearness 814
dearth 640
– of ideas 843
death 360
house of – 363
in at the –
arrive 292
kill 361
persevere 604*a*
pale as –
colourless 429
fear 860
put to – 361, 972
still as – 265
violent – 361
be the – of one
amuse 480
–'s head 837
– in the pot
unhealthy 657
hidden danger 667
deathbed repentance 950
death-blow
end 67
killing 361
failure 732
death-house 752
deathless
perpetual 112
fame 873
deathlike
silent 403
hideous 846
death-song 839
death-struggle 720
death-warrant 971
death-watch 668
débâcle 146
destruction 162
downfall 306
torrent 348
debar *hinder* 706
restrain 751
prohibit 761
debark 292
debase *depress* 308
foul 653
deteriorate 659
degrade 874
debased
lowered 207
dishonoured 940
debate *reason* 476
talk 588
hesitate 605
dispute 720
debatable 475
debauch
spoil 659
intemperance 954
impurity 961
debauchee 962
debenture
security 771
money 800
credit 805
debility 160
debit *debt* 806
accounts 811
debitor 806
débonnaire 836
debouch 293, 295
débris
fragments 51
crumbled 330
useless 645
debt 806
out of – 803
get out of – 807
– of nature 360
debtor 806
– and creditor 811
debunk 529
début *beginning* 66
essay 675
celebration 883
débutant
learner 541
drama 599
decade *ten* 98
period 108
decadence 659
decagon 244
decalescence 382
decalogue 926
decamp
go away 293
run away 623
decant 270
decanter 191
decapitate *kill* 361
punish 972
decay *decrease* 36
decompose 49
shrivel 195
unclean 653
disease 655
spoil 659
adversity 735
natural – 360
– of memory 506
decayed
[*see* decay]
old 124
rotten 160
decease 360
deceit
falsehood 544
deception 545
cunning 702
deceived
in error 495
duped 547
deceiver 548
gay – 962
decelerate 275
decennium 108
decent
mediocre 651
pure 960
decentralize 49
deceptio visûs 443
deception 545
deceptive reasoning 477
decession 293
dechristianize 989
decide
turn the scale 153
judge 480
choose 609
decided *great* 31
ended 67
certain 474
resolved 604
take a – step 609
deciduous
transitory 111
falling 306
spoiled 659
decies repetita placebit 829
decimal 84, 98, 99
decimate
subtract 38
tenth 99
few 103
weaken 160

kill 361
play havoc 659
punish 972
decipher 522
decision
judgment 480
resolution 604
intention 620
law case 969
decisive
certain 474
proof 478
commanding 741
take a – step 609
deck *floor* 211
beautify 847
declaim 531, 582
– against 932
declamatory
style 577
speech 582
declaration
affirmation 535
law pleadings 969
– of faith
belief 484
theology 983
– of war 713
declaratory
meaning 516
inform 527
declare
publish 531
declension
[*see* decline]
grammar 567
backsliding 988
declensions 5
declination
[*see* decline]
deviation 279
measurement 466
rejection 610
decline *decrease* 36
old 124
weaken 160
descent 306
grammar 567
be unwilling 603
reject 610
disease 655
become worse 659
adversity 735
refuse 764
– of day 126
– of life 128
declivity *slope* 217
descent 306
decoction 335, 384
decode 522
decollate 972
décolleté 226
decoloration 429
decomposition 49
deconsecrate 756
decontrol 158
décor 448, 599
decoration
insignia 747
ornament 847
title 877
decorative 556
decorous
[*see* decorum]
fashionable 862
proper 924
respectful 928
decorticate 226
decorum
fashion 852
duty 926
purity 960
décousu
discontinuous 70
failure 732
decoy *attract* 288
deceive 545
deceiver 548
entice 615
decrease 36, 195
decree
judgment 480
order 741
law 963, 969
decrement
decrease 36
thing deducted 40a
contraction 195
decrepit *old* 128
weak 158, 160
disease 655
decayed 659
decrepitate 406
decrescendo 36
decretal 741
decry *underrate* 483
censure 932
detract 934
decumbent 213
decuple 98
decursive 306
decurtation 201
decussation 219
dedecorous
disreputable 874
discourteous 895
dedicate *use* 677
inscribe 873
deduce *deduct* 38
infer 480
deducible
evidence 467
proof 478
deduct *retrench* 38
deprive 789
subtract 813
deduction
[*see* deduce]
decrement 40a
reasoning 476
deed *evidence* 467
record 551
act 680
security 771
–s of arms 720
– without a name 947
deem 484
deemster 967
deep *great* 31
profound 208
sea 341
sonorous 404
cunning 702
plough the – 267
– colour 428
– in debt 806
– game 702
– knowledge 490
– mourning 839
– note 408
– potations 959
– reflection 451
– sense 821
– sigh 839
– study 457
in – water 704
deepen 35
deep-dyed
intense 171
black 431
vicious 945
deep-felt 821
deep-laid *plan* 626
deep-mouthed
resonant 408
bark 412
thrilling 821
deep-musing 458
deep-read 490
deep-rooted
stable 150
strong 159
belief 484
habit 613
affections 820
deep-sea 208
deep-seated 208, 221
deer 366
in heart a – 862
deev 980
deface
destroy form 241
obliterate 552
injure 659
render ugly 846
defalcation
incomplete 53
contraction 195
shortcoming 304
non-payment 808
defame *shame* 874
censure 932
detract 934
defamer 936
defatigation 841
default
incomplete 53
shortcoming 304
neglect 460
insufficiency 640
debt 806
non-payment 808
in – of 187
judgment by – 725
defaulter *thief* 792
non-payer 808
rogue 949
defeasance 756
defeat
confute 479
succeed 731
failure 732
– one's hope 509
defeatism 911
defecate 652
defecation 299
defect
decrement 40a
incomplete 53
imperfect 651
failing 945
defection
relinquishment 624
disobedience 742
defective
incomplete 53
insufficient 640
imperfect 651
defence
plea 462
resist 717
vindication 937
first line of – 726
defenceless
impotent 158
weak 160
exposed 665
defendant 938
defensible *safe* 664
excusable 937
defensive alliance

712
defer 133
– to *assent* 488
submit 725
respect 928
deference
obedience 743
humility 879
courtesy 894
respect 928
defiance **715**, 909
threat 909
in – *opposition* 708
set at – *disobey* 742
– of danger 861
deficiency
[*see* deficient]
vice 945
deficient
inferior 34
incomplete 53
shortcoming 304
insufficient 640
imperfect 651
deficit
incompleteness 53
debt 806
defigure 846
defile
interval 198
march 266
dirt 653
spoil 659
shame 874
impure 961
define
specify 79
limit 233
explain 522
name 564
definite
[*see* define]
visible 446
certain 474
exact 494
intelligible 518
manifest 525
perspicuous 570
definition
interpretation 522
definitive *final* 67
affirmative 535
decided 604
deflagration 384
deflate 195
deflation
currency 800
deflect
curve 245
deviate 279
deflower
spoil 659
violate 961
defluxion
egress 295
flowing 348
defœdation 653, 659
deform 241
deformity
distortion 243
ugliness 846
blemish 848
defraud *cheat* 545
swindle 791
defray 807
deft *suitable* 23
clever 698
defunct 360, 362
defy 715
disobey 742
threaten 909
– danger 861
dégagé *free* 748
fashion 852
degenerate 659
deglutition 298
degradation
deterioration 659
shame 874
dishonour 940
degree **26**
term 71
honour **873**
by –s 26
by slow –s 275
degustation 390
dehiscence 260
dehort
dissuade 616
advise 695
dehydrate 340
Dei gratiâ 924
deification 873, 981
deify
honour 873
idolatry 991
deign
condescend 762
consent 879
Deism
heterodoxy 984
irreligion 989
Deity **976**
tutelary – 664
dejection
excretion 299
melancholy **837**
déjeuner 298
délabrement 162
delaceration 659
delation 938
delator 527
delay 133
dele 552
delectable
savoury 394
agreeable 829
delectation 827
delectus 562
delegate
transfer 270
commission 755
consignee 758
deputy 759
delenda est Carthago
destroy 162
curse 908
delete 162
deleterious
pernicious 649
unwholesome 657
deletion 552
deletory
destructive 162
deliberate
slow 275
think 451
attentive **457**
leisure 685
advise 695
cautious 864
deliberately
[*see* deliberate]
late 133
with premeditation 611
delicacy *weak* 160
slender 203
dainty 298
brittleness 328
texture 329
savoury 394
colour 428
exact 494
scruple 603
ill health 655
difficult 704
pleasing 829
beauty 845
taste 850
fastidious 868
honour 939
pure 960
delicate ear 418
délice 377
delicious *taste* 394
pleasing 829
delicti, corpus –
guilt 947
lawsuit 969
delicto, in flagrante – 947
delight
pleasure 827
pleasing 829
Delilah 962
delimit 233
delineate
outline 230
represent 554
describe 594
delineator 559
delineavit 556
delinquency 304, 947
delinquent 949
deliquation 335
deliquesce 36
deliquescence 335
deliquium
paralysis 158
fatigue 688
delirant reges plectuntur Achivi 739
delirium
raving 503
passion 825
– tremens **503**, 959
delitescence
invisible 447
latency 526
seclusion **893**
deliver
transfer 270
utter 580, **582**
birth 662
rescue 672
liberate 750
give 784
relieve 834
– as one's act and deed 467
– the goods 729
– judgment 480
– a speech 582
deliverance **672**
delivery
[*see* deliver]
bring forth 161
cash on – 807
dell 252
Delphic oracle
prophetic 513
equivocal 520
latent 526
delta 342
delude *error* 495
deceive 545
deluge *crowd* 72
water **337**

flood 348
redundance 641
delusion
[*see* delude]
insane 503
self – *credulous* 486
delve *dig* 252
till 371
– into *inquire* 461
demagogue
director 694
malcontent 710
rebel 742
demagogy 737
demand
inquire 461
order 741
ask 765
price 812
claim 924
in – *require* 630
desire 865
saleable 796
demarcation 233
dematerialize 317
demean oneself
conduct 692
humble 879
dishonour 940
demeanour
aid 448
conduct 692
fashion 852
demency 503
démenti 536
dementia 503
demerit 945
demesne
abode 189
property 780
demi- 91
demigod *hero* 861
angel 948
demigration 266
demijohn 191
demi-jour 422
demi-lune 717
demi-mondaine
plebeian 876
licentious 962
demirep 962
demise *death* 360
transfer 783
lease 787
demisemiquaver 413
demission 756
demit 757
demiurge
deity **979**
demivolt 309
demobilize 73
democracy *rule* 737
commonalty 876
Democrats
party 712
Democritus 838
demoiselle 129
demolish 479
demon *violent* 173
bane 663
devil **980**
– in human shape 913, 949
– worship 991
demoniacal
malevolent 907
furious 824
wicked 945
demonology
demons 980
sorcery 992
demonstration
number 85
proof **478**
manifest 525
ostentation 882
ocular – 441, 446
demonstrative
manifest 525
indicative 550
vehement 825
demonstrator 524
demoralize
unnerve 158
spoil 659
vicious 945
Demosthenes 582
demotic 590
demulcent
mild 174
soothing 662
demur
disbelieve 485
dissent 489
unwilling 603
hesitate 605
without – 602
demure
grave 826
sad 837
affected 855
modest 881
demurrage 133
demurrer 969
den *abode* 189
study 191, 893
sty 653
prison 752
– of thieves **791**
denary 98
denaturalize
corrupt 659
denaturalized
abnormal 83
dendriform 242, 367
dendrology 369
denial
negation 536
refusal 764
self– 953
denigrate 431
denization 748
denizen
inhabitant 188
freeman 748
–s of the air 979
–s of the day 366
Denmark, rotten in the state of – 526
denomination
class 75
name 564
sect 712
religious – 983
denominational
dissent 489
theological 983
– education 537
denominator 84
denote
specify 79
mean 516
indicate 550
dénouement
end 67
result 154
disclosure 529
completion 729
denounce
curse 908
disapprove 932
accuse 938
dense
crowded 72
ignorant 493
density **321**
dent 252, 257
dental 561
denticulated 253, 257
dentifrice 652
dentistry 662
denude 226
denuded *loss* 776
– of
insufficient 640
denunciation
[*see* denounce]
deny *dissent* 489
negative 556
refuse 764
– oneself
avoid 623
seclude 893
temperate 953
ascetic 990
Deo volente 470, 976
deobstruct 705
deodand 974
deodorize 399
clean 652
deontology 926
deoppilation 705
deorganization 61
deosculation 902
depart 293
– from
deviate 15, 279
relinquish 624
– this life 360
departed
non-existent 2
department
class 75
region 181
business 625
departure 293
new – 66
point of – 293
depend *hang* 214
contingent 475
– upon
be the effect of 154
evidence 467
trust 484
– on circumstances 475
depended on, to be –
certain 474
reliable 484
honourable 939
dependency 777, 780
dependent
effect 154
liable 177
hanging **214**
puppet 711
servant 746
subject 749
deperdition 776
dephlegmation 340
depict 554, 556
describe 594
depilation 226
depilatory 662
depletion 638, 640
deplorable *bad* 649

disastrous **735**
painful 830
deplore *regret* 833
complain 839
remorse 950
deploy 194
depone 535
deponent 467
depopulate
eject 297
desert 893
deportation
removal 270
emigration 297
expulsion 972
deportment 692
depose
evidence 467
declare 535
dethrone 738, 756
deposit *place* 184
precipitate 321
store 636
security 771
payment 809
depositary 801
deposition
[*see* depose, deposit]
record 551
depository 636
depot *terminal* 292
store 636
shop 799
– ship 726
deprave *spoil* 659
depraved *bad* 649
vicious 945
deprecation **766**
pity 914
disapprove 932
depreciation
decrease 36
underestimate 483
discount 813
cheap 815
disrespect 929
censure 932
detraction 934
accusation 938
depredation 791
depredator 792
deprehension 789
depression
lowness 207
depth 208
concavity 252
lowering **308**
dejection 837
dulness 843
depressing
painful 830
deprive *subduct* 38
take 789
– of life 361
– of power 158
– of property 789
– of strength 160
deprived of 776
depth *physical* **208**
mental 498
out of one's – 304, 310
– bomb **727**
– of misery 828
– of thought 451
– of winter 383
depurate *clean* 652
improve 658
depuratory 662
deputation 755
depute 755
deputies, chamber of – 696
deputy **759**
dequantitate 36
derangement **61**
mental – 503
Derby day 720
derelict *land* 342
danger 667
relinquish 782
outcast 893
dereliction
relinquishment 624, 782
guilt 947
– of duty **927**
deride
ridicule 856
disrespect 929
contempt 930
derivation
origin 153, 154, 155
verbal 562
derive
attribute 155
deduce 480
acquire 775
income 810
dermal 223
dermatology 223
dernier
– cri 850
– ressort 601
dérobée, à la – 528
derogate
underrate 483
disparage 934
dishonour 940
– from 874
derogatory
shame 874
dishonour 940
derrick 307, 633
derring-do 861
dervish 996
désagrément 830
descant *music* 415
diffuseness 573
loquacity 584
dissert 595
descend *slope* 217
go down 306
– to particulars
special 79
describe 594
descendant 167
descensus Averni, facilis – 665
descent *lineage* 166
fall **306**
inheritance 775
description
kind 75
name 564
narration **594**
descriptive music 415
descry 441
desecrate
misuse 679
disrespect 929
profane 988
desert
unproductive 169
empty 187
plain 344
run away 623
relinquish 624, 782
merit 944
waste sweetness on – air 638
deserted
outcast 893
deserter 144, 607, 623
desertless 945
deserts 924
deserve
be entitled to 924
merit 944
– notice 642
– belief 484
désespoir, au –
dejected 837
hopeless 859
déshabillé, en –
not dressed 226
unprepared 674
simplicity 849
desiccate 340
desiccator 340
desiderate *need* 630
desire 865
desideratum
inquiry 461
requirement 630
desire 865
design
prototype 22
form 240
delineation 554
painting 556
intention 620
plan 626
designate
specify **79**
call 564
designation **75**
designed
aforethought 611
designer 164, 559
designing
cunning 702
designless 621
désillusioner 529
desinence *end* 67
discontinuance 142
desipience 499
desipere in loco 840
desirable 646
desire **865**
will 600
have no – for 866
desist
discontinue 142
relinquish 624
inaction 681
desk *box* 191
support 215
school 542
pulpit 1000
désobligeant 272
désœuvré 681
desolate *alone* 87
ravage 162
afflicted 828
dejected 837
secluded 893
desolating
painful 830
désorienté 475
despair *grief* 828, 859
despatch *eject* 297
kill 361
news 532
epistle 592
expedition 682
haste 684

conduct 692
complete 729
command 741
happy – 972
– case 191
– food 298
– rider 534
desperado
rash 863
blusterer 887
evil-doer 913
desperate *great* 31
violent 173
impossible 471
resolved 604
difficult 704
excitable 825
hopeless 859
rash 863
anger 900
despicable
trifling 643
shameful 874
contemptible 930
despise 930
– danger 861
despite 30, 907
in – 708
despoil *injure* 659
take 789
rob 791
despond 837, 860
despot 745
despotism
authority 737
severity 739
arbitrary 964
despumate 652
desquamation 226
dessert 298
dessous des cartes
cause 153
latent 526
secret 533
connaître le – 490
dessus dessous
sens – 218
destination *end* 67
arrival 292
intention 620
destiny *chance* **152**
fate 601
fight against – 606
destitute
insufficient 640
poor 804
refuge for – 666
destrier 726
destroy
demolish 162
injure 659
– hopes 859
– life 361
destroyed
[*see* destroy]
inexistent 2
failure 732
destroyer **165**
warship 726
evil-doer 913
destructive
bad 649
destructor 383
desuetude **614**
disuse 678
desultory
disordered **59**
fitful 70
multiform 81
irregular in time 139
changeable 149
deviating 279
agitated 315
desume 788
detach 44
detached
irrelated **10**
loose 47
detachment
part 51
army 726
detail *describe* 594
special portions 79
allot 786
ornament 847
attention to – 457, 459
in – 51
details
minutiæ 32
unimportant 643
detain 781
detect 480*a*
detective 527, 664
detention 133, 751, 781
house of – 752
in house of – 938
détenu 754
deter *dissuade* 616
alarm 860
deterge *clean* 652
detergent
remedy 662
deterioration **659**
determinate
special 79
exact 474
conclusive 480
intended 620
determine *end* 67
define 79
cause 153
direction 278
satisfy 462
make sure 474
judge 480
discover 480*a*
resolve 604
determined
resolute 604
determinism 601
deterration 529
detersion 652
detersive 662
detest *dislike* 867
hate 898
detestable 649
dethronement
anarchy 738
abrogation 756
detonate
explode 173
sound 406
detortion *form* 243
meaning 523
détour *curve* 245
circuit 629
detract *subduct* 38
underrate 483
defame 934
slander 938
detraction 934
detractor 936
detrain 292
detriment
evil 619
deterioration 659
detrimental 649
detrition 330
detritus
fragments 51
deposit 270
powder 330
detrude
cast out 297
cut down 308
detruncate 38
deuce *two* 89
devil 978
play the – 825
– is in him 608
deuced *great* 31
painful 830
deus 976
– ex machinâ
aid 707
auxiliary 711
deity 976
sorcerer 994
deuterogamy 903
devastate
destroy **162**
havoc 659
develop
increase 35
produce 161
expand 194
evolve 313
development **144**, **154**
devexity
bending 217
curvature 245
deviate *vary* 20*a*
change 140
turn 279
diverge 291
circuit 629
– from 15
– from rectitude 940
– from virtue 945
deviation **279**
device *motto* 550
expedient 626
artifice 702
devil
seasoned food 392
evil-doer 913
bad man 949
Satan 978
demon 980
fight like –s **722**
have a – 503
machinations of the – 619
play the – with
injure 659
malevolent 907
printer's – 591
raise the – 825
– may care
rash 863
indifferent 866
insolent 885
give the – his due
right 922
vindicate 937
fair 939
– in one
headstrong **863**
temper 901
– to pay
disorder 59
violence **173**
evil 619
failure 732
penalty 974
– take 908
– take the hindmost

run away 623
haste 684
cowardice 862
–'s tattoo 407
devilish *great* 31
bad 649
malevolent 907
devious *curved* 245
deviating 279
circuitous 311
devisable 270
devise *imagine* 515
plan 626
bequeath 784
devised by the enemy 546
devisee *possess* 779
receive 785
deviser 164
devitalize 158
devoid *absent* 187
empty 640
not having 777a
devoir *courtesy* 894
respect 928
devolve 783
– on 926
devote *destine* 601
employ 677
consecrate 873
– to destruction 908
– the mind to 457
– oneself to 604
devoted
habit 613
ill-fated 735
obedient 743
undone 828
friendship 888
love 897
devotee
zealot 682
aspirant 865
pious 987
fanatic 988
devotion [*see* devotee, devoted]
love 897
piety 987
worship 990
self – 942
devour
destroy 162
eat 298
gluttony 957
devoured by
feeling 821
devouring element 382
devout 987, 990
devoutless 989
devoutly 821
dew 339
shake as –drops from lion's mane 483
dewy eve 126
dexterous 238, 698
dextrality **238**
dey 745
dhow 273
diable:
avoir le – au corps 503
– à quatre
disorder 59
violence 173
loud 404
excitement 825
tirer le – par la queue 804
diablerie 978, 992
diabolic
bad 649
malevolent 907
wicked 945
Satanic 978
Diacoustics 402
diacritical 550
diadem 747, 847
diaeresis 49
diagnosis 465, 655
diagnostic
special 79
experiment 463
indication 550
(*intrinsic* 5)
diagonal 217
diagram 554
dial 114
as the – to the sun
veracious 543
faithful 772
dialect 563
dialectic
argument 476
language 560
dialogism 586
dialogue 588
diameter 202
diametrically opposite
contrariety 14
contraposition 237
diamond
lozenge 244
type 591
goodness 648
ornament 847
rough – 703
– cut diamond
cunning 702
retaliation 718
– jubilee 883
– wedding 883
Diana *moon* 318
chaste 960
goddess 979
diapason 413
diaper 847
diaphanous 425
diaphonics 402
diaphoresis 299
diaphragm 68, 228
diaporesis 475
diarchy 737
diarrhœa 299
diary 114, 551
diastole 194
diatessaron 413
diathermancy 384
diathesis
nature 5
state 7
temperament 820
diatonic 413
diatribe 932
dibble
perforator 262
till 371
dibs *money* 800
dicacity 885
dice 156, 621
on the – 470
dicer 621
false as –'s oaths 546
dichotomy
bisect 91
angle 244
dichroism 440
dichromatic 443
dickens 978
dicker 794
dicky 215, 225
dictaphone 553
dictate
write 590
enjoin 615
advise 695
authority 737
command 741
–s of society 852
dictator 694, 745
dictatorial
dogmatic 481
wilful 600
insolent 885
dictatorship 737, 739
diction 569
dictionary
list 86
words 562
book 593
dictum
judgment 480
maxim 496
affirmation 535
command 741
didactic 537
didder 383
diddle 545, 791
Diddler, Jeremy – 792
diduction 44
die *mould* 22
expire 360
engraving 558
hazard of the – 621
never say – 604a
not willingly let – 670
– away
vanish 4
decrease 36
cease 142
the – is cast 601
– with ennui 841
– for *desire* 865
endearment 902
– game 951
– hard
obstinate 606
resist 719
– in harness 143, 604a
– in the last ditch 604a
– with laughter 838
– from the memory 536
– and make **no** sign 951
– out 2, 4
– of a rose in aromatic pain 822
– in one's shoes 972
– a violent death 361
– hard 710, 832
dies non *never* 107
rest 687
diet *food* 298
council 696
spare – 956
dietetics 662
differ 15
discord **713**

agree to – 489
beg to – 489
– in opinion 489
– toto cœlo
contrary 14
dissimilar 18
dissent 489
difference 15
[*see* differ]
numerical 84
perception of – 465
split the – 774
– engine 85
different 15
multiform 81
– time **119**
differentia 15
differential 15, 84
– calculus 85
differentiate 79, 465
differentiation
calculation 85
discrimination 465
difficult 704
– to please 868
difficulties
poverty 804
in – 806
difficulty 704
question 461
diffide 485
diffident 860, 881
diffluent 348
diffraction 420
– grating 445
diffuse *mix* 41
disperse 73
publish 531
style 573
diffuseness 104, 573
dig *deepen* 208
excavate 252
till 371
– out 461
– the foundations 673
– up 455, 480*a*
digamy 903
digest *arrange* 60
boil 384
think 451
compendium 596
plan 626
prepare 673
brook 826
diggings 189
dight *dress* 225
ornament 847
digit 84
digitate 44
digitated 253
digladiation 720
dignify 873
dignitary
clergy 996
dignity
glory 873
pride 878
honour 939
dignus vindice nodus
unintelligible 519
difficulty 704
prodigy 872
digress
deviate 279
style 573
digression
circuit 629
dihedral 89
– angle 244
dijudication 480
dike *gap* 198
fence 232
furrow 259
gulf 343
conduit 350
defence 717
dilaceration 44
dilapidation 659
dilate
increase 35
swell 194
widen 202
rarefy 322
expatiate 573
dilatory
slow 275
inactive 683
dilection 897
dilemma
uncertain 475
logic 476
choice 609
difficulty 704
dilettante 492, 850
dilettantism
knowledge 490
diligence
coach 272
diligent
active 682
– thought 457
dilly-dally
irresolution 605
inactivity 683
dilucidation 522
diluent 335
dilute *weaken* 160
water 337
diluvian 124
dim *dark* 421
faint 422
invisible 447
unintelligible 519
dime 800
dimension 192
dimidiate 91
diminish
lessen 36
contract 195
– the number 103
diminutive 32, 193
diminuendo
decreasingly 36
music 415
dimness 422
dimple 252, 257
dimsightedness 443
unwise 499
din 404
– in the ear
repeat 104
drum 407
loquacity 584
dine 298
– with Duke Humphrey 87
ding 408
ding-dong
repeat 104
chime 407
dining-car 272
dining-room 191
dingle 252
dingy *boat* 273
dark 421, 422
colourless 429
black 431
gray 432
dinner 298
– jacket 225
– party 892
dint *power* 157
concavity 252
blow 276
by – of
instrumentality 631
dio, sub – 220, 338
diocesan 996
diocese 181, 995
Diogenes
recluse 893
cynic 911
lantern of –
inquiry 461
dioptrics 420
diorama *view* 448
painting 556
diorism 465
dip *slope* 217
concavity 252
ladle 270
direction 278
insert 300
descent 306
plunge 310
water 337
candle 423
baptize 998
– one's hands into
take 789
– into
glance at **457**
inquire 461
learn 539
diphthong 561
diploma
evidence 467
commission 755
diplomacy
artfulness 702
mediation 724
negotiation 769
diplomatist
messenger 534
expert 700
consignee 758
dipper 191
dipsomania
insanity 503
desire 865
drunkenness 959
dipsomaniac 504
diptych 86, 551
dire *hateful* 649
disastrous 735
grievous 830
fearful 860
direct
straight 246
teach 537
artless 703
command 741
– attention to **457**
– one's course
motion 278
pursuit 622
– the eyes to 441
direction
[*see* direct]
tendency **278**
indication 550
management **693**
precept 697
directly *soon* 132
director
teacher 540
theatre 599
manager **694**
master **745**

– of the budget 801
directorship 737
directory *list* 86
council 696
diremption 44
direption 791
dirge
funeral 363
song 415
lament 839
dirigible balloon 273, 726
dirk 727
dirt 653
throw –
defame 874
disrespect 929
– cheap 815
like – under one's feet 749
dirty *dim* 422
opaque 426
unclean 653
disreputable 874
dishonourable 940
– end of stick 699
– sky 353
– weather 349
do – work
servile 886
flatterer 935
diruption 162
dis aliter visum
disappointment 509
necessity 601
disability
impotence **158**
disable 158
weaken 160
disabuse 527, 529
disaccord 713
disadvantage
evil 619
inexpedience 647
at a – 34
lie under a – 651
disadvantageous 647, 649
disaffection
dissent 489
enmity 889
hate 898
disaffirm 536
disagreeable 830, 867
disagreement
difference 15
incongruity **24**
dissent 489
discord 713
disallow 761
disannul 756
disappearance **449**
disappointment
balk **509**
fail 732
discontent 832
disapprobation 706, **932**
disapprover 936
disarm *disable* 158
weaken 160
reconcile 831
propitiate 914
disarrange 61
disarray
disorder 59
undress 226
disaster *evil* 619
failure 732
adversity 735
calamity 830
disastrous *bad* 649
disavow 536
disband
separate 44
disperse 73
liberate 750
disbar
abrogate 756
punish 972
disbarment 55
disbelief 485, 487
religious 989
disbench 756, 972
disbowel 297
disbranch 44
disburden
facilitate 705
– one's mind 529
– oneself of 782
disburse 809
disc 220, 234
discard *eject* 297
relinquish 624
disuse 678
abrogate 756
refuse 764
repudiate 773
surrender 782
– from one's thoughts 458
discarded 495
disceptation 476
discern *see* 441
know 490
discernible 446
discernment 498, 868
discerption **44**
discharge
violence 173
propel 284
emit 297
excrete 299
sound 406
acquit oneself 692
complete 729
liberate 750
abrogate 756
pay 807
exempt 927*a*
acquit 970
– a duty 926, 944
– a function
business 625
utility 644
– itself *egress* 295
river 348
– from the memory 506
– from the mind 458
– an obligation 772
discind 44
disciple *pupil* 541
votary 711
Christian 985
disciplinarian
master 540
martinet 739
discipline
order 58
teaching 537
training 673
restraint 751
punishment 972
religious 990
disclaim *deny* 536
repudiate 756
abjure 757
refuse 764
disclosure 480*a*, **529**
discoid *layer* 204
frontal 220
flat 251
discoloration 429
discoloured
shabby 659
ugly 846
blemish 848
discomfit 731
discomfiture 732
discomfort
physical 378
mental 828
discommend 932
discommode
hinder 706
annoy 830
discommodious 645, 647
discompose
derange 61
put out 458
hinder 706
pain 830
disconcert 874
anger 900
discomposure 828
disconcert
derange 61
distract 458
disappoint 509
hinder 706
discontent 832
confuse 879
disconcerted
hopeless 859
disconformity 83
discongruity 24
disconnected
style 575
disconnection
irrelation 10
disjunction 44
discontinuity 70
disconsolate 837
discontent **832**
discontinuance
cessation 142
relinquishment 624
discontinuity **70**
discord
difference 15
disagreement 24
of sound **414**
of colour 428
dissension **713**
discount
decrease 36
decrement 40*a*
money **813**
at a –
disrepute 874
disapproved 932
discountenance
disfavour 706
refuse 764
discourage
dissuade 616
sadden 837
frighten 860
discourse
teach 537
speech 582
talk 588
dissert 595
sermon 998
discourtesy **895**

discous 202
discover
perceive 441
solve 462
find 480*a*
disclose 529
– itself
be seen 446
discovery 480*a*
discredit
disbelief 485
dishonour 874
discreditable
vicious 945
discreet *careful* 459
cautious 864
discrepancy 15
discrepant 24, 713
discrete
separate 44, 70
single 87
discretion *will* 600
choice 609
skill 698
caution 864
surrender at – 725
use – 609
years of – 131
discrétion à – 600
discrimination
difference 15
nice perception 465
wisdom 498
taste 850
fastidiousness 868
disculpate 937
discumbency 213
discursion 266
discursive
moving 264
migratory 266
wandering 279
argumentative 476
diffuse style 573
conversable 588
disserting 595
discus 840
discuss *eat* 298
reflect 451
inquire 461
reason 476
dissert 595
discussion
[see discuss]
open to – 475
under – 461
disdain
indifference 866
fastidious 868
arrogance 885
pride 878
contempt 930
disease **655**
occupational – 655
–d mind 503
disembark 292
disembarrass 705
disembody
decompose 49
disperse 73
spiritualize 317
disembogue
emit 295
eject 297
flow out 348
disembowel 297, 301
disembroil 60
disenable 158
disenchant
discover 480*a*
dissuade 616
displease 830
disencumber 705
disendow 756
disengage
detach 44
facilitate 705
liberate 750
disengaged
to let 763
disentangle
separate 44
arrange 60
unroll 313
decipher 522
facilitate 705
liberate 750
disenthral 750
disenthrone 756
disentitle 925
disespouse 905
disestablish
displace 185
abrogate 756
disesteem 929, 932
disfavour
oppose 708
hate 898
disrespect 929
view with – 932
disfigure
deface 241
injure 659
deform 846
blemish 848
disfranchise 925
disgorge *emit* 297
flow out 348
restore 790
pay 807
disgrace
shame 874
dishonour 940
sense of – 879
disgraceful
vice 945
disgruntle 509
disguise
unlikeness 18
conceal 528
mask 530
falsify 544
untruth 546
disguised in drink 959
disgust *taste* 395
offensive 830
weary 841
dislike 867
hatred 898
– of life 837
dish *destroy* 162
plate 191
food 298
– of tea 892
dishabille
undress 226
unprepared 674
dishearten
dissuade 616
pain 830
discontent 832
deject 837
dished 252, 732
disherison 789
dishevel
loose 47
untidy 59
disorder 61
disperse 73
intermix 219
dishonest *false* 544
base 940
dishonour
disrepute 874
disrespect 929
baseness 940
– bills 808
dish-water 653
disillusion 509
disincline
dissuade 616
dislike 867
disinclined 603
disinfect
purify 652
restore 660
disinfectant 662
disingenuous
false 544
dishonourable 940
disinherit
relinquish 782
transfer 783
deprive 789
disintegrate
separate 44
decompose 49
pulverize 330
disinter *exhume* 363
discover 480*a*
disinterested **942**
disjecta membra
separate 44
disorder 59
dispersed 73
– poetæ 597
disjoin 44
disjointed
disorder 59
powerless 158
style 575
disjunction **44**
disjunctive 70
diskindness 907
dislike **867**
reluctance 603
hate 898
dislocate
separate 44
put out of joint 61
dislocated
disorder 59
dislodge
displace 185
eject 297
disloyal 940
dismal
depressing 830
dejected 837
dismantle
destroy 162
divest 226
render useless 645
injure 659
disuse 678
dismask 529
dismast
render useless 645
injure 659
disuse 678
dismay 860
dismember
separate 44
disperse 73
dismiss
send away 289
discharge 297
discard 678
liberate 750
abrogate 756
relinquish 782

punish 972
– from the mind 452, 458
dismount
arrive 292
descend 306
render useless 645
disnest 185
disobedience **742**
non-observance 773
disoblige 907
disorder
confusion **59**
derange 61
turbulent 173
disease 655
–ed intellect 503
disorderly
unprincipled 945
disorganize
derange 61
destroy 162
spoil 659
disorganized 59
disown 536
dispair 44
disparage
underrate 483
disrespect 929
dispraise 932
detract 934
disparity
different 15
dissimilar 18
disagreeing 24
unequal 28
isolated 44
dispart 44
dispassionate 826
– opinion 484
dispatch
[*see* despatch]
dispel *scatter* 73
destroy 162
displace 185
repel 289
dispensable
useless 645
dispensary 662
dispensation
[*see* dispense]
command 741
licence 760
relinquishment 782
exemption 927*a*
–s of Providence 976
dispense
disperse **73**
give 784
apportion 786
retail 796
– with
disuse 678
permit 760
exempt 927*a*
cannot be –d with 630
dispeople
eject 297
expatriate 893
disperse
separate 44
scatter 73
diverge 291
waste 638
dispersion **73**
– of light 420
chromatic – 428
dispirit
discourage 616
sadden 837
displacement
derange 61
remove **185**
transfer 270
displacency
dislike 867
incivility 895
disapprobation 932
displant 185
display *appear* 448
show 525
parade 882
displease 830
displeasure 828
anger 900
displosion 173
displume 789
disport 840
disposal
[*see* dispose]
at one's – **763**, **777**
dispose
arrange 60
tend 176
induce 615
– of *use* 677
complete 729
relinquish 782
give 784
sell 796
disposed 620
disposition
nature **5**
order 58
arrangement 60
inclination 602
mind 820
dispossess
transfer 783
take away 789
– oneself of 782
dispraise 932
dispread 73
disprize 483
disproof
counter-evidence 468
confutation 479
disproportion
irrelation 10
disagreement 24
disprove 479
disputable 475, 485
disputant 710, 726
disputatious 901
dispute
discuss **476**
doubt 485
deny 536
discord 713
in – 461
disqualification
incapacitate 158
useless 645
unprepared 674
unskilful 699
disentitle 925
disquiet
changeable 149
agitation 315
excitement 825
uneasiness 828
give pain 830
disquietude
apprehension 860
disquisition 539, 595
disregard
overlook 458
neglect 460
make light of 483
insensible to 823, 826
disrespect **929**
contempt 930
– of time 115
disrelish 867, 898
disreputable 874
vicious 945
disrepute **874**, 929
disrespect **929**
despise 930
disrobe 226
disruption
disjunction 44
destruction 162
discord 713
dissatisfaction
disappointment 509
sorrow 828
discontent 832
dissect
anatomize 44, 49
investigate 461
dissemblance 18
dissemble 544
dissembler 548
disseminate
scatter 73
pervade 186
publish 531
teach 537
dissension 713
sow – 898
dissent
disagree **489**
refuse 764
heterodoxy 984
dissentient 15
dissentious 24
dissertation **595**
disservice
disadvantage 619
useless 645
disserviceable 649
dissever 44
dissidence
disagreement 24
dissent 489
discord 713
discontent 832
heterodoxy 984
dissilience 173
dissimilarity **18**
dissimulate 544
dissipate *scatter* **73**
destroy 162
pleasure 377
prodigality 818
amusement 840
intemperance **954**
dissolute 961
dissocial 893
dissociate 44
dissociation
irrelation 10
separation 44
dissolute 961
profligate 945
intemperate 954
dissolution
[*see* dissolve]
decomposition 49
destruction 162
death 360
dissolve *vanish* **2, 4**
liquefy 335
disappear 449

abrogate 756
dissolving views 448, 449
dissonance
disagreement 24
unmusical 414
discord 713
dissuasion **616**
dissyllable 561
distaff
– side 374
distain *dirty* 653
ugly 846
distal 196
distance **196**
overtake 282
go beyond 303
defeat 731
angular – 244
keep at a –
discourtesy 895
keep one's –
avoid 623
modest 881
respect 928
teach one his – 879
– of time
long time 110
past 122
distaste 867
distasteful 830
distemper 299, 428
colour 428
painting 556
disease 655
distend 194
distended 192
distich 89, 597
distil *come out* 295
extract 301
evaporate 336
drop 348
distinct
disjoined 44
audible 402
visible 446
intelligible 518
manifest 525
express 535
articulate 580
distinction
difference 15
discrimination 465
style 578
fame 873
rank 875
– without a difference 27
distinctive 15
– feature 79
distinctness 15
distingué 852, 873
distinguish
perceive 441
discriminate 465
– by the name of 564
distinguishable 15
distinguished
superior 33
repute 873
Distinguished Service Cross 733
distortion
obliquity 217
twist **243**
of vision 443
misinterpret 523
falsehood 544
misrepresent 555
ugly 846
distract 458
distracted
confused 475
insane 503
excited 824
distraction
passion 825
love to – 897
distrain *take* 789
appraise 812
attach 969
distrait 458
distraught 824
distress
distraint 789
poverty 804
affliction 828
cause pain 830
signal of – 669
distressingly
excessively 31
distribute
arrange 60
disperse 44, 73
allot 786
district 181
– council 696
distrust
disbelief 485
fear 860
distrustful 487
disturb
derange 61
change 140
agitate 315
excite 824
distress 828, 830
disturbance 59
disunion
discord 24
separation 44
disorder 59
discord 713
disuse
desuetude 614
relinquish 624
unemploy **678**
disused
old 124
disvalue 932
ditch
inclosure 232
trench 259
water 343
conduit 350
defence 717
to the last – 606
ditch-water 653
ditheism 984
dither 315
dithyramb
music 415
poetry 597
dithyrambic 503
ditto 13, 104
say – to 488
ditty 415
– box 191
diurnal 138
diuturnity **110**
diva 416
divagate 279, 629
divan *sofa* 215
council 696
throne 747
tribunal 966
divaricate *differ* 15
bifurcate 91
diverge 291
dive *swim* 267
fly 267
plunge 306, 310
– into *inquire* 461
divellicate 44
diver 208
divergence
difference 15
variation 20a
disagreement 24
deviation 279
separation **291**
divers *different* 15
multiform 81
many 102
– coloured 440
diverse 15
diversify
very 20a
change 140
diversion
change 140
deviation 279
pleasure 377
amusement 840
diversity
difference 15
irregular 16a
dissimilar 18
multiform 81
– of opinion 489
divert *turn* 279
deceive 545
amuse 840
– the mind 452, 458
divertissement
diversion 377
drama 599
amusement 840
Dives 803
divest *denude* 226
take 789
– oneself of
abrogate 756
relinquish 782
divestment **226**
divide *differ* 15
separate 44
part 51
arrange 60
arithmetic 85
bisect 91
vote 609
apportion 786
dividend *part* 51
number 84
portion 786
divina particula auræ 450
divination
prediction 511
sorcery 992
divine *predict* 511
guess 514
perfect 650
of God 976, 983, 983a
clergyman 996
divine afflatus 515
– right
authority 737
due 924
– service 990
diving 840
diving-bell 208
divining-rod 550, 993
Divinity *God* 976
theology 983
divisible
number 84

division
[*see* divide]
part 51
class 75
arithmetic 85
discord 713
military 726
divisor 84
divorce
separation 44
relinquish 782
matrimonial **905**
Divorce Court 966
divulge 529
divulsion 44
divvy 786
dixi 535
dizen 847
dizzard 501
dizzy
dimsighted 443
confused 458
vertigo 503
– height 206
– round 312
djerrid 727
djinn 980
do *fare* 7
suit 23
produce 161
cheat 545
act 680
complete 729
succeed 731
I beg 765
all one can – 686
plenty to – 682
thing to – 625
– away with
destroy 162
eject 297
abrogate 756
– battle 722
– one's bidding 743
– business 625
– to death 361
– as done by 906, 942
– for *destroy* 162
kill 361
conquer 731
serve 746
punish 972
– good 906
– harm 907
– honour 873
– into
translate 522
– justice to 595
– like 19
– little 683
– no harm 648
– nothing 681
– nothing but 136
– one's office 772
– as others do 82
– over 223
– as one pleases 748
– a service
useful 644
aid 707
– up 660
have to – with 680, 692
– without 678
– the work 686
– wrong 923
docere, pisces natare – 641
docile *domesticated* 370
learning 539
willing 602
docimastic 463
dock *diminish* 36
cut off 38
port 189
shorten 201
edge 231
store 636
tribunal 966
docked
incomplete 53
docker 690
docket
list 86
evidence 467
note 550
record 551
security 771
dockyard 691
doctor
learned man 492
restore 660
remedy 662
after death the – 135
– accounts 811
when –s disagree 475
doctrinaire
positive 474
pedant 492
affectation 855
blusterer 887
doctrinal 537
doctrinarian 514
doctrine *tenet* 484
knowledge 490
document 551
documentary evidence 467
dodder 315
doddering 128
dodecahedron 244
dodge *change* 140
shift 264
deviate 279
oscillate 314
pursue 461
avoid 623
stratagem 702
dodger, artful – 792
dodo 366
extinct as the – 122
Doe, John 4
doe *swift* 274
deer 366
female 374
doer
originator 164
agent 690
doff 226
– the cap 894
dog *follow* 281
animal 366
male 373
pursue 622
wretch 949
cast to the –s
reject 610
disuse 678
abrogate 756
relinquish 782
fire – 386
go to the –s
destruction 162
fail 732
adversity 735
poverty 804
sea – 269
watch –
safety 664
warning 668
keeper 753
hair of – that bit you 959
let sleeping –s lie 141
– in manger 706, 943
–tired 688
–s of war 722
dog-cart 272
dog-cheap 815
dog-days 382
doge 745
dogged
obstinate 606
valour 861
sullen 901*a*
dogger 273
doggerel
verse 597
ridiculous 851, 853
dog-hole 189
dog Latin 563
dogma *tenet* 484
theology 983
dogmatic
certain 474
positive 481
assertion 535
obstinate 606
dogmatist 887
dog's ear 258
dog robber 746
dog-sick 867
dog-star 423
dog-trot 275
dog-weary 688
doily 652
doing
up and – 682
what one is – 625
doings
events 151
actions 680
conduct 692
doit *trifle* 643
coin 800
dolce far niente 681
doldrums
dejection 837
sulks 901*a*
dole
small quantity 32
scant 640
give 784
allot 786
parsimony 819
grief 828
doleful 837
– dumps 901*a*
doll *small* 193
image 554
dollar 800
dolman 225
dolmen 363, 551
dolorem, infandum renovare – 833
dolorous 830
dolour
physical 378
moral 828
dolphin 341
dolt 501
doltish 499
domain
class 75

region 181
property 780
Domdaniel 982
dome *high* 206
roof 223
curvature 245
convex 250
Domesday book
list 86
record 551
domesman 967
domestic
inhabitant 188
home 189
interior 221
servant 746
secluded 893
– animals 366
domesticate
locate 184
acclimatize 613
– animals 370
domicile 189
domiciled 186
domiciliary 188
– visit 461
dominant 175
note in music 413
domination 737
dominical 998
domineer
tyrannize 739
insolence 885
Domini, anno – 106
Dominican 996
Dominie 540
dominion 181, 737
domino *dress* 225
mask 530
game 840
domn 745
don *put on* 225
scholar 492
teacher 540
noble 875
Don Juan 897
donation 784
done *finished* 729
work – 729
– for *spoilt* 659
failure 732
– up
impotent 158
tired 688
have – with
cease 142
relinquish 624
disuse 678
donee 785
donjon 717, 752
donkey *ass* 271
fool 501
talk a –'s hind leg off 584
donna 374
Donnybrook Fair
disorder 59
discord 713
donor 784
donzel 746
doodle 501
doom *end* 67
fate 152
destruction 162
death 360
judgment 480
necessity 601
sentence 971
– sealed
death 360
adversity 735
doomed 735, 828
doomsday
end 67
future 121
till – 112
door *entrance* 66
cover 223
brink 231
barrier 232
opening 260
passage 627
at one's – 197
beg from door to – 765
bolt the – 666
close the – upon 751
death's – 360
keep within –s 265
lie at one's – 926
lock the – 666
open a – to
liable 177
open the – to
receive 296
facilitate 705
permit 760
show the – to
eject 297
discourtesy 895
– mat 652
doorkeeper 263
doorway 260
dope 376, 545, 663
doquet
security 771
Dorado, El – 803
Doric mode 413
dormant
inert 172
latent 526
asleep 683
dormer 260
dormeuse 272
dormir debout,
conte à – 843
dormitive 841
dormitory 191
dormouse 683
dorp 189
dorsal 235
dorser 191
dorsum 235, 250
dory 273
dose *quantity* 25
part 51
medicine 662
apportion 786
dosser 191
dossier *bundle* 72
record 551
dossil 223, 263
dot *small* 32
place 182
little 193
variegate 440
mark 550
dowry 780
on the – 113
dotage 128, 499
dotard 130, 501
dotation 784
dottle 40, 645
dote *drivel* 499, 503
– upon 897
douanier 965
double
similar 17
increase 35
duplex 90
substitute 147
fold 258
turn 283
finesse 702
march at the – 274
see –
dim sight 443
drunk 959
– acrostic
letters 561
wit 842
– dutch 519
– entry 811
– the fist 909
– march 684
– meaning 520
– a point 311
in – quick time 274
– reef topsails 664
– sure 474
work – tides 686
– up
render powerless 158
double bar 747
double-bass 417
doublecross 545
double-dealing
lie 544
cunning 940
double-distilled 171
double-dyed 428
double-eagle 800
double-edged 90, 171
double entendre
ambiguity 520
impure 961
double-faced
lie 544
cunning 702, 940
double-headed 90
double-minded 605
double-shotted 171
doublet 225
double-tongued
lie 544
cunning 702, 940
doubt
uncertain 475
disbelieve 485
sceptic 989
doubtful 475
more than – 473
– meaning
unintelligible 519
doubtless
certain 474
belief 484
assent 488
douceur 784, 973
douche 337
dough 324, 354, 800
doughty 861
dour 739
douse
immerse 310
splash 337
blow 972
Dove
Holy Ghost 976
dove
innocent 946
roar like sucking – 174
dovecote 189
dovetail
agree 23
join 43
intersect 219
intervene 228
angle 244

insert 300
dowager 374, 905
dowdy 653, 851
dower 780, 803, 810
dowerless 804
down
below 207
light 320
bear – upon 716
bed of –
pleasure 377
repose 687
come – 306
get – 306
go –
sink 306
calm 826
keep – 36
money – 807
take –
lower 308
rebuff 874
humble 879
– on one's marrow-bones 886
– in the mouth 837
– and out 874
– in price 815
go – like a stone 310
be – upon
attack 716
severe 739
downcast 306, 837
– eyes 879
downfall
destruction 162
fall 306
failure 732
misfortune 735
downhill 217, 306
go –
adversity 735
downpour 348
downright
absolute 31
manifest 525
sincere 703
downs 206, 344
down-trodden
submission 725
vanquished 732
subject 749
dejected 837
disrepute 874
contempt 930
downwards 306
downy
smooth 255
plumose 256
soft 324
dowry 780, 784
dowse 276
dowser 994
doxology 990
doxy 962
doyen 128
doyley 652
doze 683
dozen 98
drab *colour* 432
slut 653
hussy 962
drabble 653
drachm 319
Draco 694, 739
draff 653
draft [*see also* draught]
multitude 102
drawing 554, 556
write 590
abstract 596
plan 626
cheque 800
credit 805
– off *displace* 185
transfer 270
draft-horse 271
drag *carriage* 272
crawl 275
traction 285
impediment 706
put on the – 275
– a chain
tedious 109, 110
exertion 686
subjection 749
– into
implicate 54
compel 744
– through mire
disrepute 874
disrespect 929
– on *tedious* 110
– into open day 531
– towards
attract 288
– slow length
long 200
weary 841
draggle 285, 653
– tail 59
drag-net
all sorts 78
dragoman 524
dragon *monster* 83
violent 173
animal 366
irascible 901
dragonnade ,
attack 716
punish 972
dragoon
soldier 726
compel 744
insolent 885
worry 907
drain
flow out 295
empty 297
dry 340
conduit 350
waste 638
clean 652
unclean 653
exhaust 789
dissipate 818
– the cup
drink 298
drunken 959
– the cup of misery 828
– into 348
– pipe 249
– of resources 640
drake *male* 373
fire – 423
dram *drink* 298
pungent 392
stimulus 615
– drinking 959
drama 599
dramatic 599
ostentation 882
– author 599
– critic 599
– poetry 597
dramatis personæ
mankind 372
play 599
agents 690
party 712
drapery 225, 847
drast 645
drastic 171
draught
[*see also* draft]
depth 208
traction 285
drink 298
stream of air 349
delineation 554, 556
plan 626
physic 662
troops 726
– off 73
draughts
game 840
draughtsman
artist 559
draw *equality* 27
compose 54
pull 285
delineate 554, 556
– aside 279
– off the attention 458
– back
deduction 40a
regret 283
avoid 623
– breath
refresh 689
feeling 821
relief 834
– a cheque 800
– a curtain 424
– down 153
– forth 677
– from 810
– on futurity 132
– in one's horns
tergiversation 607
humility 879
– in 195
– an inference 480
– the line 465
– lots 621
– near *time* 121
approach 286
– off *eject* 297
hinder 706
take 789
– on *time* 121
event 151
induce 615
– out
protract 110
late 133
prolong 200
extract 301
discover 480a
exhibit 525
diffuse style 573
– over *induce* 615
– a parallel 9
– the pen through 552
– a picture 594
– profit 775
– and quarter 972
– the sword
attack 716
war 722
– the teeth of 158
– together
assemble 72
co-operate 709
– towards 288
– up *order* 58
stop 265

write 590
– up a statement 594
– upon *money* 800
– the veil 528
drawback *evil* 619
imperfection 651
hindrance 706
discount 813
drawbar 45
drawbridge
way 627
escape 671
raise the – 666
drawcansir 887
drawee 800
drawer
receptacle 191
artist 559
– of water 690
drawers
dress 225
drawhead 45
drawing
delineation 554, 556
prize 810
drawing-room
assembly 72
room 191
fashion 852
drawl *prolong* 200
creep 275
in speech 583
sluggish 683
drawn *equated* 27
– battle
– irresistibly 601
pacification 723
incomplete 730
dray 272
– horse 271
drayman 268
dread 860
dreadful *great* 31
bad 649
dire 830
depressing 837
fearful 860
dreadless 861
dreadnought
warship 726
dream
unsubstantial 4
error 495
fancy 515
sleep 683
golden – 858
– of *think* 451
intend 620
– on other things 458
dreamer
madman 504
imaginative 515
dreamy
unsubstantial 4
inattentive 458
sleepy 683
dreary
monotonous 16
solitary 87
melancholy 830, 837
dredge *collect* 72
extract 301
raise 307
dregs
remainder 40
refuse 645
dirt 653
– of the people 876
– of vice 945
drench *drink* 298
water 337
redundance 641
– with physic 662
drencher 248
drenching rain 348
dress
uniformity 16
agree 23
equalize 27
clothes 225
prepare 673
ornament 847
ostentation 882
full – 852
– circle 599
– the ground 371
– up *falsehood* 544
represent 554
– wounds 662
– to advantage 847
dress-coat 225
dresser
sideboard 215
surgeon 662
dressing 932, 972
– room 191, 599
dressing-gown 225
dressmaker 225
dribble 295, 348
driblet 25, 32
drift
accumulate 72
distance 196
motion 264
flying 267
float 267
transfer 270
direction 278
deviation 279
approach 286
wind 349
meaning 516
intention 620
snow – 383
drifter 273
drifting 605
driftless 621
drill *fabric* 219
bore 260
auger 262
teach 537
prepare 673
– hall 191
drink
swallow 296
liquor 298
tipple 959
– one's fill
enough 639
– in *imbibe* 296, 298
– in learning 539
– to *celebrate* 883
courtesy 894
drinking-bout 954
drink-money 784
drip 295, 348
dripping *wet* 339
fat 356
drive *airing* 266
impel 276
propel 284
break in 370
urge 615
haste 684
direct 693
attack 716
compel 744
– at *mean* 516
intend 620
– a bargain
barter 794
parsimony 819
– care away 836
– a coach and six through 83
– into a corner
difficult 704
hinder 706
defeat 731
subjection 749
– to despair 859
– matters to an extremity 604
– from *repel* 289
– one hard 716
– home 729
– in 300
– to the last 133
– out 297
– trade
business 625
barter 794
drivel *slobber* 297
imbecile 499
mad 503
rubbish 517
driveller 501, 584
driver 268
director 694
driving rain 348
drizzle 348
droil 683
droit du plus fort 744
drôle *cards* 840
drôle 949
– de corps 844
drollery
amusement 840
wit 842
ridiculous 853
dromedary 271
drone *slow* 275
sound 407, 412, 413
inactive 683
drool 297
droop
weak 160
hang 214
sink 306
disease 655
decline 659
flag 688
sorrow 828
dejection 837
drop *small quantity* 32
discontinue 142
powerless 158
bring forth 161
spherule 249
emerge 295
fall 306
trickle 348
relinquish 624
discard 782
gallows 975
let – 308
ready to –
fatigue 688
– asleep 683
– astern 283
– from the clouds 508
– dead 360
– by drop
by degrees 26

in parts 51
– in the bucket 32
– in upon 674
– into a good thing 734
– into the grave 360
– a hint 527
– all idea of 624
– in *arrive* 292
immerse 300
sociality 892
– the mask 529
– off *decrease* 36
die 360
sleep 683
– in the ocean
trifling 643
– the subject 458
– too much 959
dropping fire 70
drop-scene 599
dropsical 194, 641
droshki 272
dross
remainder 40
slag 384
trash 643, 645
dirt 653
drought
dryness 340
insufficiency 640
drouth *desire* 865
drove
assemblage 72
multitude 102
drover 370
drown
affusion 337
kill 361
ruin 731, 732
– care 840
– the voice 581
drowsy *slow* 275
sleepy 683
weary 841
drub
defeat 731, 732
punish 972
drudge *labour* 686
worker 682, 690
drug
render insensible 376
superfluity 641
trash 643
remedy 662
bane 663
– in the market 815
drugget
cover 223
clean 652
preserve 670
druggist 662
druid 996
drum
repeat 104
cylinder 249
sound 407
music 417
party 892
beat of –
signal 550
alarm 669
war 722
command 741
parade 882
ear – 418
muffled –
funeral 363
non-resonance 408*a*
– and fife band 417
– fire 407
– out 972
drum-head 964, 966
drum-major 745
drummer 416
drunken 959
reel like a – man 315
drunkenness 959
dry *arid* 340
style 575, 576, 579
hoarse 581
scanty 640
preserve 670
exhaust 789
tedious 841
dull 842
thirsty 865
cynical 932
teetotal 958
run – 640
with – eyes 823
– dock 189
– joke 842
– land 342
– the tears 834
– up 340, 638
dryad 979
dry-as-dust
antiquarian 122
dull 843
dryness 340
dry-nurse
teach 537
teacher 540
aid 707
dry-point 558
dry-rot
dirt 653
decay 659
bane 663
dualism 984
duality 89
duarchy 737
dub 564
dubious 475
ducat 800
duce 745
duchess 745, 875
duchy 181
duck *stoop* 308
plunge 310
water 337
darling 897, 899
play –s and drakes
recoil 277
prodigality 818
–'s egg
zero 101
– in thunder 870
ducking-stool 975
duckling 129
duck-pond 370
duct 350
ductile
elastic 325
flexible 324
trimming 607
easy 705
docile 743
dud 158, 727
dude 854
duds 225
dudgeon
dagger 727
discontent 832
churlishness 895
hate 898
anger 900
sullenness 901*a*
due
expedient 646
owing 806
proper 924, 926
give his – to
right 922
vindication 937
fair 939
in – course 109
occasion 134
– respect 928
– sense of 498
– time
soon 132
– to
cause and effect 154, 155
give – weight 465
duel 720
duellist 726
dueness 924
duenna
teacher 540
guardian 664
keeper 753
dues 812
duet 415
duff 298
duffer
bungler 701
smuggler 792
dug 250
dug-out
old man 130
boat 273
defence 717
duke *ruler* 745
noble 875
dulce domum 189
dulcet
sweet 396
sound 405
melodious 413
agreeable 829
dulcify 174, 396
dulcimer 417
Dulcinea 897
dulcorate 396
dulia 990
dull *weak* 160
inert 172
moderate 174
blunt 254
insensible 376, 381
sound 405
dim 422
colourless 429
ignorant 493
stolid 499
style 575
inactive 683
unapt 699
callous 823
dejected 837
weary 841
prosing 843
simple 849
– of hearing 419
– sight 443
dullard 501
dullness 843
duly 924
duma 696
dumb 581
– animal 366
– show 550
– waiter 307

strike –
ignorant 493
astonish 870
humble 879
dumbfounder
disappoint 509
silence 581
astonish 870
humble 879
dummy
substitute 147
impotent 158
speechless 581
inactive 683
dump *music* 415
store 636
lament 839
undersell 796
dumpling 298
dumps
discontent 832
dejection 837
sulk 901*a*
dumpy *little* 193
short 201
thick 202
dun *dim* 422
colourless 429
grey 432
importune 765
creditor 805
dunce
ignoramus 493
fool 501
dunderhead 501
dune 206
dung 653
dungeon 752
dunghill
dirt 653
cowardly 862
baseborn 876
– cock 366
Dunker 984
dunt 716
duo 415
duodecimal 99
duodecimo
little 193
book 593
duodenary 98
duologue
interlocution 588
drama 599
dupe
credulous 486
deceive 545
deceived **547**
duplex 90, 189
duplicate
imitate 19
copy 21
double 90
tally 550
record 551
redundant 641
pawn 805
duplication
imitation 19
doubling **90**
repetition 104
duplicature
fold 258
duplicity
duality 89
falsehood 544
dura lex sed lex 926
durable
long time 110
stable 150
durance 141, 751
in – 754
duration 106
contingent – **108a**
infinite – 112
durbar
conference 588
council 696
tribunal 966
duress
compulsion 744
restraint 751
during 106
– pleasure &c. 108*a*
durity 323
dusk
evening 126
half-light 422
dusky
dark 421
black 431
dust *levity* 320
powder 330
corpse 362
trash 643
dirt 653
money 800
come to –
die 360
come down with the – 807
humbled in the – 879
kick up a – 885
level with the – 162
lick the –
submit 725
fail 732
make to bite the – 731
turn to –
deorganized 358
die 360
– in the balance 643
throw – in the eyes
blind 442
deceive 545
plead 617
– one's jacket 972
duster 652
dust-bin, dust-hole 191, 645
fit for the –
useless 645
dirty 653
spoilt 659
dustman 653
cleaner 652
dust-storm 330
dusty
powder 330
dirt 653
Dutch
double – 519
high – 519
– auction 796
– courage 862
Dutchman, flying 515
dutiful 944
duty
business 625
work 686
tax 812
courtesy 894
obligation **926**
respect 928
worship 990
rite 998
do one's –
virtue 944
on – 680, 682
duumvirate 737
Duval, Claude – 792
D.V. 470, 976
dwarf
lessen 36
small 193
elf 980
dwell
reside 186
abide 265
– upon
descant 573
dweller 188
dwelling 184, 189
dwindle *lessen* 36
shrink 195
dyad 89
dye 428
dying 360
dyke [*see* dike]
dynamic energy 157
dynamics 276
dynamitard 863
dynamite 727
dynamo 153
dynasty 737
dysentery 299
dyspepsia 655
dysphony 581

E

each 79
– to each 786
– other 12
– in his turn 148
eager
willing 602
active 682
ardent 821
desirous 865
– expectation 507
eagle
standard 550
money 800
– boat 726
– eye *sight* 441
intelligence 498
– winged *swift* 274
insignia 747
eagre 348
ean 161
ear 418
corn 154
come to one's –s 527
din in the –
loud 404
drum 407
all – 418
have the – of
belief 484
friendship 888
lend an –
hear 418
attend 457
meet the – 418
nice – 418
no – 419
offend the – 410
pick up the –s
attention 457
expectation 507
put about one's –s 308

quick – 418
reach one's –s 527
ring in the – 408
set by the –s
discord 713
hate 898
resentment 900
split the –s 404
together by the –s
discord 713
contention 720
up to one's –s
redundance 641
active 680, 682
willing – 602
word in the – 586
– for music 416, 418
in at one – out at the other
inattention 458
forget 506
not for –s polite 961
make the –s tingle
anger 900
– ache 378
ear-drum 418
earl 875
earless 419
earliness **132**
early 132
get up – 682
earmark 550
earn 775
earnest *willing* 602
determined 604
emphatic 642
pledge 771
pay in advance 809
eager 821
in –
affirmation 535
veracious 543
strenuous 682
ear-piercing 410
ear-ring 847
ear-shot 197
out of – 405
ear-splitting 404
earth *ground* 211
world 318
land 342
corpse 362
what on –
inquiry 461
wonder 870
– closet 653
earthenware
baked 384
sculpture 557
earthling 372
earthly 318
end of one's – career 360
of no – use 645
earthly-minded 943, 989
earthquake 146, 173
earthwork 717
earwig *flatter* 933, 935
ear-witness 467
ease *bodily* 377
style 578
leisure 685
facility 705
mental 827
content 831
at one's –
prosperous 734
mind at –
cheerful 836
set at – *relief* 834
take one's – 687
– off *deviate* 297
– one of *take* 789
easel *support* 215
painting 556
– picture 556
easement
property 780
relief 834
easily
[*see* easy]
let one down – 918
– accomplished 705
– deceived 486
– persuaded 602
East 236, 278
Easter *period* 138
rite 998
– Monday
holiday 840
– offering
gift 784
– sepulchre 1000
easy *gentle* 275
style 578
facile 705
make oneself – about 484
take it –
inactive 683
inexcitable 826
– ascent 217
– of belief 472
– chair
support 215
repose 687
– circumstances 803
– going
willing 602
irresolute 605
lenient 740
inexcitable 826
contented 831
indifferent 866
– sail
moderate 174
slow 275
– temper 894
– terms 705
– to understand 518
– virtue 961
eat *food* 298
tolerate 826
– dirt 725, 879
– one's fill
enough 639
gorge 957
– heartily 298
– one's words 879
– out of house and home *take* 789
prodigal 818
gluttony 957
– of the same trencher 892
– one's words 607
eatables 298
eaten up with 820
eau, battre l' – 645
faire venir l' – à la bouche 865
mettre de l' – dans son vin 174
eaves 250
eavesdropper 455, 527
eavesdropping 418, 532
ébauche 626
ebb *decrease* 36
contract 195
regress 283
recede 287
waste 638
spoil 659
low – 36
low 207
depression 308
insufficient 640
– and flow 314
– of life 360
ebb-tide *low* 207
dry 340
ebony 431
ebriety 959
ebullient
violent 173
hot 382
excited 824
ebullition
energy 171
violence 173
agitation 315
heating 384
excitation 825
anger 900
écarté 840
ecce
– iterum Crispinus 104
– signum 550
eccentric 220
irregular 83
foolish 499
crazed 503, 504
capricious 608
ecchymosis 299
ecclesiastic
church 995
clergy 996
ecclesiastical
canonical 985
– court 966
– law 963
ecclesiolatry 991
écervelé 458
échafaudage 673
échappée 840
échapper belle 671
échelon 279
echo *imitate* 19
copy 21
repeat 104
reflection 277
resonance 408
answer 462
assent 488
applaud to the – 931
awake –es 404
éclaircissement 522
éclat 873
eclectic 609
eclipse *surpass* 33
disappearance 449
hide 528
outshine 873, 874
partial – *dim* 422
total – *dark* 421
under an –
invisible 447
out of repute 874
ecliptic 318
eclogue 597

economic pressure 751
economy
order 58
conduct 692
frugality **817**
animal – 359
écorcher les oreilles 410
ecphorize 615
écru 433
ecstasis 683
ecstasy
frenzy 515
transport 821
rapture 827
ecstatic 829
ecstatica 994
ectoplasm 992
ectype 21
ecumenical 78
edacity 957
Edda 986
eddy
whirlpool 348
current 312
danger 667
Eden 827
edge *energy* 171
height 206
brink **231**
sidle 279
advantage 731
cutting – 253
on – 256, 507
take the – off 174
– of hunger 865
– in 228
– one's way 282
edge-tools 253
play with – 863
edgewise 217
edging
obliquity 217
border 231
ornament 847
edible 298
edict 741
edification
building 161
teaching 537
learning 539
piety 987
edifice 161
edifying *good* 648
edile 965
edit
publication 531
condense 596
revise 658
edition, new – 658
editor 593
educate 537
educated 490
self – 490
education
teaching 537
knowledge 490
man of – 492
higher – 490
educational 537, 542
educe *extract* 301
discover 480*a*
educt 40
eduction 40*a*
edulcorate 396, 652
eel 248
wriggle like an – 315
eerie 860
efface
delete 162
disappear 449
obliterate 552
– from the memory 506
effect
consequence **154**
product 161
impression 375
complete 729
carry into – 692
with crushing – 162
in – 5
take – **731**
to that – **516**
effective
capable 157
useful 644
effectuation 729
expedient 646
effects 780, 798
effectual 731
effectually 52
effectuate 729
effeminate
weak 160
womenlike 374
timorous 862
sensual 954
effeminize 158
effendi 875
effervesce
energy 171
violence 173
agitate 315
bubble 353
excited 825
effervescent 338
effete *old* 128
weak 160
useless 645
spoiled 659
efficacious
[*see* efficient]
efficient
power 157
agency 170
utility 644
skill 698
effigy 21, 554
effleurer *skim* 267, 460
efflorescence 330
effluxion of time 109
effluence *egress* 295
flow 348
effluvium 334, 398
efflux 295
efformation 240
effort 686
effreet 980
effrontery 885
effulgence 420
effuse
pour out 295, 297
excrete 299
speech 582
loquacity 584
effusion of blood 361
effusive 573
eft 366
eftsoons 117
egad 535
égards 928
egesta 299
egestion 297
egg *beginning* 66
cause 153
food 298
walk among –s 704
too many –s in one basket
unskilful 699
(*imprudent* 863)
– and dart
ornament 847
– on 615
egg-shaped 247, 249
ego *intrinsic* 5
speciality 79
immaterial 317
non – 6
egocentrism 943
egotism
vanity 880
cynicism 911
selfishness **943**
egregious
exceptional 83
absurd 497
exaggerated 549
important 642
egregiously 31, 33
egress **295**
Egyptian darkness 421
eheu! fugaces labuntur anni 111
eiderdown 223
eidouranion 318
Eiffel tower 206
eight *number* 98
boat 273
representative 759
eisteddfod 72, 416
eighty 98
either *choice* 609
happy with – 605
ejaculate
propel 284
utter 580
ejection 185, **297**
ejecta 299
ejector 349
eke *also* 37
– out *complete* 52
spin out 110
ekka 272
El Dorado 803
elaborate
improve 658
prepare 673
laborious 686
work out 729
elaine 356
élan 276
elapse 109, 122
elastic fluid 334
elasticity
power 157
strength 159
energy 171
spring **325**
elate *cheer* 836
rejoice 838
hope 858
vain 880
boast 884
elbow *angle* 244
projection 250
push 276
at one's –
near 197
advice 695
lift one's –

drink 959
out at –s
undress 226
poor 804
disrepute 874
– one's way
progress 282
pursuit 622
active 682
elbow-chair 215
elbow-grease 331
elbow-room 180, 748
elder *older* 124
aged 128
veteran 130
clergy 996
elect *choose* 609
good 648
predestinate 976
pious 987
clergy 996
election
numerical 84
necessity 601
electioneering 609
elector 745
electorate 737
Electra complex 897
electric
swift 274
sensation 821
excitable 825
car 272
– blue 438
– chair 974
– light 423
– piano 417
electrician 599, 690
electricity 157, 388
electrify
unexpected 508
excite 824
astonish 870
electro-biology 992
electrocution 972
electrolier 214, 423
electrolyze 49
electro-magnetism 157
electromobile 272
electron 32
electroplate 223
electrotype 21, 591
electuary 662
eleemosynary 784
elegance
in style 578
beauty 845
taste 850

Bank of – 800
elegy *interment* 363
poetry 597
lament 839
element
component 56
beginning 66
cause 153
matter 316
in one's –
facility 705
content 831
devouring – 382
out of its – 195
elementary 42
– education 537
– school 542
elements
Eucharist 998
elench 477
elephant
large 192
carrier 271
white – *bane* 663
elevated
tipsy 959
elevation
height 206
vertical 212
raising 307
plan 554
– of style 574
improvement 658
glory 873
– of mind 942
angular – 244
élève 541
eleven 98
representative 759
eleventh hour
evening 126
late 133
opportune 134
elf *infant* 129
little 193
imp 980
elicit *cause* 153
draw out 301
discover 480a
manifest 525
eligible 646
Elijah's mantle 63
eliminant 299
eliminate
subduct 38
simplify 42
exclude 55
weed 103
extract 301
reject 610
elision 44, 201

élite *best* 648
distinguished 873
aristocratic 875
elixation 384
elixir 662
– of life 471
elk 223
ell 200
take an –
take 789
insolence 885
wrong 923
undue 925
selfish 943
ellipse 247
ellipsis *shorten* 201
style 572
ellipsoid 247, 249
elocation 185, 270
elocution 582
éloge 931
elongation 196, 200
elopement 623, 671
eloquence 574, 582
else 37
elsewhere 187
elucidate 522
elude
sophistry 477
avoid 623
escape 671
succeed 731
palter 773
elusive 545
elusory 546
elutriate 652
elysian 829, 981
Elysium 827, 981
elytron 223
Elzevir edition 193
emaciation 195, 203, 640
emanate 151
go out of 295
excrete 299
– from 544
emanation 398
emancipate
facilitate 705
free 748, 750
emasculate
impotent 158
embalm
interment 363
perfume 400
preserve 670
– in the memory 505
embankment
esplanade 189
refuge 666

fence 717
embar 229
embargo
stoppage 265
prohibition 761
exclusion 893
embark
transfer 270
depart 293
– in *begin* 66
engage in 676
embarquer sans biscuits, s' – 674
embarras de – choix 609
embarrass 641, 704, 706
embarrassed 804, 806
embarrassing 475
embase 659
embassy
errand 532
commission 755
consignee 758
embattled
arranged 60
leagued 712
war array 722
embed
locate 184
base 215
enclose 221
insert 300
embellish 847
embers 384
embezzle 791
embitter
deteriorate 659
aggravate 835
acerbate 900
emblazon
colour 428
ornament 847
display 882
emblem 550, 747
embody
join 43
combine 48
form a whole 50
compose 54
embolden
hope 858
encourage 861
embolism 228, 261, 300
embonpoint 192
embosomed
lodged 184
interjacent 228
circumscribed 229

emboss *convex* 250
ornament 847
embouchure 260
embowel 297
embrace
cohere 46
compose 54
include 76
enclose 227
choose 609
take 789
friendship 888
sociality 892
courtesy 894
endearment 902
– an offer 762
embrangle 61
embranglement 713
embrasure 257, 260
embrocation 662
embroider
variegate 440
lie 544
ornament 847
embroidery
adjunct 39
exaggeration 549
embroil *derange* 61
discord 713
embroilment 59
embrown 433
embryo
beginning 66
cause 153
in – *destined* 152
preparing 673
embryology 357
embryonic 193, 674
embus 293
embusqué 603
emendation 658
emerald *green* 435
jewel 847
emerge 295, 446
emergency
circumstance 8
event 151
difficulty 704
emeritus 500, 928
emersion 295, 446
emery
sharpener 253
– paper
smooth 255
emetic *remedy* 662
émeute 742
emication 420
emigrant 57, 268
emigrate 266, 295
emigré 268, 295
eminence
height 206
fame 873
church dignitary 996
eminent domain 744
eminently 33
emir 745, 875
emissary
messenger 534
consignee 758
emission 297
emit *eject* 297
publish 531
voice 580
– vapour 336
Emmanuel 976
emmet 193
emollient 662
emolument
acquisition 775
receipt 810
remuneration 973
emotion 821
–al appeal 824
–al drama 599
empale 260, 972
empanel 86, 969
empathy 515
emperor 745
emphasis 580
emphatic 535, 642
emphatically 31
empierce
perforate 260
insert 300
empire 737, 789
– day 840
empiric 548
empirical 463, 675
empiricism 463
emplane 293
employ
business 625
use 677
servitude 749
commission 755
in one's – 746
– one's capital in 794
– oneself 680
– one's time in 625
employé
servant 746
agent 758
employer 795
empoison 659
emporium 799
empower
power 157
commission 755
accredit 759
permit 760
empress 745
empressement
activity 682
emotion 821
desire 865
emprise 676
emption 795
emptor 795
caveat – 769
empty *clear* 185
vacant 187
deflate 195
drain 297
ignorant 491
waste 638
deficient 640
useless 645
beggarly account of – boxes
poverty 804
– one's glass 298
– purse 804
– sound 517
– stomach 865
– title *name* 564
undue 925
– words 546
empty-handed 640
empty-headed 491
empurple 437
empyrean *sky* 318
blissful 829
empyreuma 41
empyrosis 384
emulate *imitate* 19
goodness 648
rival 708
compete 720
glory 873
emulsion 352
emunctory 350
en – bloc 50
– masse 50
– passant
parenthetical 10
transient 111
à propos 134
– rapport 9
– règle *order* 58
conformity 82
– route
journey 266
progress 282
enable 157
enact *drama* 599
action 680
conduct 692
complete 729
order 741
law 963
enallage 521
enamel *coating* 223
painting 556
ornament 847
enameller 559
enamour 897
encage 751
encamp 184, 189
encampment 184
encaustic 556
enceinte
with child 161
region 181
inclosure 232
enchafe 830
enchain 751
enchant *please* 829
enchanted 827
enchanting 845, 897
enchantment
sorcery 992
enchase 43, 259
enchiridion 593
enchorial 188
encincture 229
encircle 76, 227, 311
enclave *close* 181
boundary 233
enclose 227, 229
enclosure
region 181
envelope 232
fence 752
encomiast 935
encomium 931
encompass 227, 233
–ed with difficulties 704
encore 104, 931
encounter
undergo 151
clash 276
meet 292
withstand 708
contest 720
– danger 665
– risk 621
encourage
animate 615
aid 707
comfort 834
hope 858
embolden 861
encroach
transcursion 303
do wrong 923

infringe 925
encumber 704, 706
encumbrance
clear of – 807
encyclical 531
encyclopædia 490, 593
walking – 700
encyclopædical
general 78
– knowledge 490
encysted 229
end
termination 67
effect 154
object 620
at an – 142
come to its – 729
one's journey's – 292
on – 212
put an – to
destroy 162
kill 361
begin at the wrong – 699
– one's days 360
–s of the earth 196
– to end *space* 180
touching 199
length 200
– of life 360
– in smoke 732
– of one's tether
sophistry 477
ignorant 491
insufficient 640
difficult 704
endamage 649
endanger 665
endear 897
endearment 902
endeavour
pursuit 622
attempt 675
use one's best – 686
– after 620
endemic
special 79
interior 221
disease 657
endimanché 847, 882
endless
multitudinous 102
infinite 105
perpetual 112
endlessly 16
endlong 200
endocrine 221
endogenous 367
endorse
evidence 467
assent 488
compact 769
- *a bill* 800
approve 931
endorsement 550
endosmose 302
endow
confer power 157
endowed with
possessed of 777
endowment
intrinsic 5
power 157
talent 698
gift 784
endrogynous 83
endue 157
endure *time* 106
last 110
persist 143
continue 141
undergo 151
feel 821
submit to 826
unable to – 867
– for ever 112
– pain 828
enduring
indelible 505
endwise 212
enemy *time* 841
foe 891
the common – 978
thing devised by the – 546
– to society 891
energumen 504
energy *power* 157
strength 159
physical 171
resolution 604
activity 682
enervate 158, 160
enfant, bon – 906
– gâté
prosperity 734
satiety 869
favourite 899
– perdu
hopeless 859
reckless 863
– terrible
curiosity 455
artless 703
object of fear 860
enfeeble 160
enfeoff 780, 783
Enfield rifle 727
enfilade
lengthwise 200
pierce 260
pass through 302
enfold 229
enforce *urge* 615
advise 695
compel 744
require 924
enfranchise
free 748
liberate 750
permit 760
enfranchised 924
engage
bespeak 132
induce 615
undertake 676
do battle 722
commission 755
promise 768
compact 769
I'll –
affirmation 535
– the attention 457
– with 720
engaged
marriage 903
be – 135
– in *attention* 457
engagement
business 625
battle 720
betrothal 902
engaging
pleasing 829
amiable 897
engender 161
engine 153, 633
engine-driver 268
engineer 690, 694, 726
engineering 633
engird 227
English 188
broken – 563
king's – 560
murder the king's – 568
plain –
intelligible 518
interpreted 522
style 576
– horn 417
engorge
swallow 296
gluttony 957
engorgement
too much 641
engrail 256
engrave
furrow 259
mark 550
– in the memory 505
engraver 559
engraving 21, 22, 558
engross *write* 590
possess 777
– the thoughts
thought 451
attention 457
engrossed in thought 451
engulf
destroy 162
plunge 310
swallow up 296
enhance
increase 35
improve 658
enharmonic 413
enigma
question 461
secret 533
enigmatic
uncertain 475
unintelligible 517
obscure 519
énigme, mot d' – 522
enjoin *advise* 695
command 741
prescribe 926
enjoy
physically 377
possess 777
morally 827
– health 654
– popularity 873
– a state 7
enkindle *heat* 384
excite 824
enlarge
increase 35
swell 194
in writing 573
liberate 750
– the mind 537
enlarged views 498
enlighten
illumine 420
inform 527
teach 537
enlightened
knowledge 490
enlist *engage* 615
war 722
commission 755

under the banners of 707
– into the service 677
enliven
delight 829
cheer 836
amuse 840
enmity 889
ennoble 873
ennui 841
enormity
crime 947
enormous *great* 31
big 192
– number 102
enough *much* 31
no more! 142
sufficient 639
moderately 651
satiety 869
know when one has had – 953
– in all conscience 641
– to drive one mad 830
– and to spare 639
enounce 535, 580
enrage 830, 900
enragé 865
enrapture
excite 824
beatify 829
love 897
enraptured 827
enravish 829
enravished 827
enravishment 824
enrich
improve 658
wealth 803
ornament 847
enrobe 225
enroll *list* 86
record 551
– troops 722
commission 755
ens *essence* 1
Ens Entium 976
ensample 22
ensanguined 361
ensconce
conceal 528
safety 664
ensconced
located 184
ensemble 50
enshrine
circumscribe 229
repute 873
sanctify 987
– in the memory 505
ensiform 253
ensign
standard 550
officer 726
master 745
– of authority 747
ensilage 637
enslave 749
ensnare 545
ensue *follow* 63, 117
happen 151
ensure 474
entablature 210
entail *cause* 153
tie up property 781
entangle
interlink 43
derange 61
ravel 219
entrap 545
embroil 713
entangled
disorder 59
– by difficulties 704
entend, cela s' – 613
entente
agreement 23
alliance 714
friendship 888
enter *go in* 294
appear 446
note 551
accounts 811
– into the composition of 56
– into details
special 79
describe 594
– into an engagement 768
– into the feelings of 914
– into the ideas of
understand 518
concord 714
– in *converge* 290
– the lists
attack 716
contention 720
– the mind 451
– a profession 625
– into the spirit of
feel 821
delight 827
– upon 66
– into one's views
488
enterprise
pursuit 622
undertaking 676
commercial – 794
enterprising
active 171, 682
courageous 861
entertain
bear in mind 457
support 707
amuse 840
sociality 892
– doubts 485
– feeling 821
– an idea 451
– an opinion 484
entertainment 840
pleasure 377
repast 298
entêté 481, 606
enthral
subjection 749
restraint 751
enthrone 873
enthronement 755
enthusiasm
language 574
willingness 602
feeling 821
hope 858
love 897
enthusiast
madman 504
obstinate 606
active 682
enthusiastic
imaginative 515
sensitive 822
excitable 825
sanguine 858
enthymeme 476
entice 615
enticing 829
entire *whole* 50
complete 52
continuous 69
– horse 373
entirely *much* 31
entitle *name* 564
give a right 924
entity 1
entoil 545
entomb *inter* 363
imprison 751
Entomology 368
entourage 88, 183, 227
entozoon 193
entrails 221
entrain 293
entrammel 751
entrance
beginning 66
ingress 294
way 627
enrapture 827, 829
magic 992
give – to 296
entranced 515
entrancement 824
entrap 545
entre nous 528
entreat 765
entrée
reception 296
dish 298
give the – 296
have the – 294
– dish 191
entremet 298
entrepôt 636, 799
entrepreneur 599
entresol 191
entrust
commission 755
give 784
credit 805
entry *beginning* 66
ingress 294
record 551
entwine *join* 43
intersect 219
convolve 248
enucleate 522
enumerate 85
– among 76
enumeration 86
enunciate
inform 527
affirm 535
voice 580
envelop 225
envelope 223, 232
envenom
deprave 659
exasperate 835
hate 898
anger 900
envenomed
bad 649
insalubrious 657
painful 830
malevolent 907
– tongue 934
environ 227
environment 183
environs 197
in such and such – 183
envisage 515, 861

envoy
messenger 534
consignee 758
envy **921**
enwrap 225
enzyme 320
Eolian harp 417
Eolus 349
eon 976
épanchement
manifest 525
artless 703
endearment 902
epact 641
épaulette
badge 550, 747
ornament 847
decoration 877
éperdu 824
épergne 191
ephemeral 111
ephemeris
calendar 114
record 551
book 593
Ephesian letters 993
ephialtes
physical pain 378
hindrance 706
mental pain 828
ephod 999
ephor 967
epic 594, 597
epicedium 839
epicene 81, 83
épicier 876
epicure
fastidious 868
sybarite 954a
glutton 957
epicurean 954
Epicurus, system of – 954
epicy-cle, -cloid 247
epidemic
general 78
disease 655
insalubrity 657
epidermis 223
epigenesis 161
epigram 496, 842
epigrammatic 572
epigrammatist 844
epigraph 550
epilepsy 315, 655
epilogue
sequel 65
end 67
drama 599

êpingles, tiré à quatre – 855
Epiphany 998
episcopal 995
Episcopalian 984
episcopate 995
episode
adjunct 39
discontinuity 70
interjacence 228
episodic
irrelative **10**
style 573
epistle 592
Epistles 985
epistrophe 104
epistyle 210
epitaph 363
epithalamium 903
epithem 662
epithet 564
epitome
miniature 193
short 201
concise 572
epizoötic 657
epoch *time* 106
instant 113
date 114
present time **118**
epode 597
eponym 564
epopœa 597
epos 594
epulation 298
epulotic 662
epuration 652
equable 16, 922
equal *even* 27
equitable 922
– chance 156
– times 120
– to *power* 157
equality 13, **27**
equalize 213
equanimity 826
equate 27, 30
equations 85
equator 68, 318
equatorial 68, 236
equerry 746
equestrian 268
equibalanced 27
equidistant 68
equilibration 27
equilibrist 599
equilibrium 27
equine *carrier* 271
horse 366
equinox 125, 126
equip 225, 673

equipage
vehicle 272
instruments 633
display 882
equiparent 27
equipment 633
equipoise &c. 27, 30
equiponderate 30
equitable *wise* 498
just 922
due 924
honourable 939
– interest 780
equitation 266
equity *right* 922
honour 939
law 963
in – 922
– draftsman 968
equivalent
identical 13
equal 27
compensation 30
substitute 147
translation 522
equivocalness
dubious 475
double meaning **520**
impure 961
equivocate
sophistry 477
palter 520
lie 544
equivocation
[see equivocate]
without – 543
équivoque
double meaning 520
impure 961
era *time* 106, 108
date 114
eradicate
destroy 162
extract 301
erase *destroy* 162
obliterate 331, 552
Erastian 984
erasure 552
Erato 416
ere 116
– long 132
– now 116
past 122
Erebus *dark* 421
hell 982
erect *build* 161
vertical 212
raise 307
with head – 878

– the scaffolding 673
erewhile 116, 122
ergatocracy 737
ergo 476
ergotism 480
ergotize 485
eriometer 445
Erinys 900
Erl King 980
ermine
badge of authority 747
ornament 847
erode 36, 659
Eros 897, 979
erosion 36
erotic 897, 961
err – *in opinion* 495
– *morally* 945
errand
message 532
business 625
commission 755
errand-boy 534
errant 279
erratic
irregular 139
changeable 149
wandering 279
capricious 608
erratum 495
erroneous 495
error *fallacy* **495**
vice 945
guilt 947
court of – 966
writ of – 969
ersatz 973
erst 122
erubescence 434
erubuit salva res est 95
eruct 297
eructate 297
erudition 490, 539
eruption
upheaval 146
violence 173
egress 295, 297
disease 655
volcanic – 872
escadrille 726
escalade
mounting 305
attack 716
escalator 307
escalop 248
escapade
absurdity 497
freak 608

prank 840
escape 671
liberate 750
evade 927
means of – 664, 666
– the lips
disclosure 529
speech 582
– the memory 506
– notice &c.
invisible 447
inattention 458
latent 526
escarp 717
escarpment
stratum 204
height 206
oblique 217
escharotic
caustic 171
pungent 392
eschatology 67
escheat 145, 974
eschew
avoid 623
dislike 867
esclandre 828, 830
escort
accompany 88
safeguard 664
keeper 753
escritoire 191
esculent 298
escutcheon 550
esoteric
private 79
concealed 528
Espagne, château en – *fancy* 515
hope 858
espalier 232
especial 79
especially 33
Esperanto 560
espial 441
espièglerie
cunning 702
fun 840
wit 842
espionnage 441, 461
esplanade
houses 189
flat 213
espouse
choose 609
marriage 903
– a cause *aid* 707
co-operate 709
esprit
shrewdness 498
wit 842
bel – 844
– de corps
bias 481
co-operation 709
sociality 892
(*party* 712)
– fort
thinker 500
irreligious 989
espy 441
esquire 875, 877
essay
experiment 463
dissertation 595
endeavour 675
essayist 593, 595
esse 1
essence
nature 5
scent 398
essential
intrinsic 5
great 31
required 630
important 642
essentially
intrinsically 5
substantially 3
essential stuff 5
establish
settle 150
create 161
place 184
evidence 467
demonstrate 478
– equilibrium 27
established
permanent 141
habit 613
– church 983*a*
establishment
party 712
shop 799
estafette 534
estaminet 189
estate *condition* 7
property 780
come to man's – 131
esteem
believe 484
repute 873
approve 931
in high – 928
estimable 648
estimate
measure 466
adjudge 480
information 527
– too highly 482
estimation
[*see* esteem, estimate]
estime
succès d' – 873
estival 382
esto perpetua!
perpetuity 112
permanence 141
desire 865
estop 706
estrade 213
estrange
alienate 44, 889
discord 713
hate 898
estranged
secluded 893
estrapade
attack 716
punishment 972
estreat 974
estuary 343
estuation 384
esurient 865
et – cætera
add 37
include 76
plural 100
– hoc genus omne
similar 17
include 76
multiform 81
étalage 882
état major 745
etch *furrow* 259
engraving 558
eternal 112
– home 981
Eternal, the – 976
eterne 112
eternify 112
eternity 112
an – 110
launch into – 360, 361
ether
lightness 320
rarity 322
vapour 334
anæsthetic 376
ethereal 4
ethicism 984
ethics 926
Ethiopian 431
–'s skin 150
Ethiopian's skin
unchangeable 150
ethnology 372
ethnic 984
ethology 926
ethos 5
etiolate 429, 430
etiology *causes* 155, 359
knowledge 490
disease 655
etiquette
custom 613
fashion 852
ceremony 882
étoile, à la belle –
out of doors 220
in the air 338
Eton jacket 225
étourderie
inattention 458
unskilfulness 699
etymological 560
etymology 562
etymon *origin* 153
verbal 562
Eucharist 998
euchology 998
euchre 840
eudiometer
air 338
salubrity 656
euge! 931
eugenics 658
eulogist 935
eulogize 482
eulogy 931
Eumenides *fury* 900
evil-doers 913
revenge 919
eunuch 158
eupepsia 654
euphemism
metaphor 521
style 577, 578
flattery 933
euphemist
man of taste 850
flatterer 935
euphony 413, 578
Euphrosyne 836
euphuism
metaphor 521
elegant style 577
affected style 579
affectation 855
Eurasian 41
eureka! 462, 480*a*
Euripus 343
Eurus 349
eurythmics 537, 840
eurythmy 242
Euterpe 416

euthanasia 360
euthenics 658
evacuate
 quit 293
 excrete 295
 emit 297
evacuation 299
evade *sophistry* 477
 avoid 623
 not observe 773
 exempt 927
evagation 279
evanescent
 small 32
 transient 111
 little 193
 disappearing 449
evangelical 983*a*, 985
Evangelists 985
evanid 160
evaporable 334
evaporate
 unsubstantial 4
 transient 111
 vaporize 336
evaporation 340
evasion
 sophistry 477
 concealment 528
 falsehood 544
 untruth 546
 avoidance 623
 escape 671
 cunning 702
 non-observance 773
 dereliction 927
eve 126
 on the – of
 transient 111
 prior 116
 future 121
evection 61
even
 uniform 16
 equal 27
 still more 33
 regular 138
 level 213
 straight 246
 flat 251
 smooth 255
 although 469
 in spite of 708
 – course 628
 – now 118
 – so
 for all that 30
 yes 488
 – temper 826
 – terms 922
 – tenor
 uniform 16
 order 58
 continuity 58
 pursue the – tenor
 continue 143
 avoid 623
 business 625
 be – with
 retaliate 718
 pay 807
 get – with 972
even-handed 922, 939
evening **126**
 shades of – 422
 – classes 537
 – star 423
evenness 16
evensong 126, 990
event 151
 bout 720
 in the – of
 circumstance 8
 expectation 507
 supposition 514
 justified by the – 937
eventful 151
 remarkable 642
 stirring 682
eventide 126
eventual 121
eventuality **151**
eventually
 effect 154
ever 16, 112
 did you – ? 870
 – and anon 136
 – changing 149
 – recurring 104
ever so 31
 – little 32
 – long 110
 – many 102
evergreen
 continuous 69
 lasting 110
 always 112
 fresh 123
everlasting 112
 – life 152
 – fire 982
evermore 112
eversion 218
evert 140
every 78
 – hand against one 891
 – day
 conformity 82
 frequent 136
 habit 613
 – description 81
 – inch 50
 in – mouth
 assent 488
 news 532
 repute 873
 – other 138
 in – quarter 180
 in – respect 494
 on – side 227
 at – turn 186
 – whit 52
everybody 78
everyone 78
 – his due 922
 – in his turn 148
everywhere 180, 186
evict 297
evidence **467**
 disclose 529
 ocular – 446
évidence, en – 446
evident
 concrete 3
 visible 446
 certain 474
 manifest 525
evidently 516
evil *harm* **619**
 badness 649
 impious 988
 – day
 prepare for – 673
 adversity 735
 – eye *vision* 441
 malevolence 907
 disapprobation 932
 demon 980
 sorcery 992
 spell 993
 – favoured 846
 – fortune 735
 – genius 980
 – hour 135
 – one 978
 – plight 735
 through – report &c. 604*a*
 – star 649
evil-doer **913**
evil-doing 945
evil-minded 907, 945
evil-speaking
 malediction 908
 censure 932
 detraction **934**
evince *show* **467**
 prove 478
 disclose 529
eviscerate 297, 301
eviscerated 4
evoke *cause* 153
 call upon 765
 excite 824
evolution
 numerical 85
 production 161
 motion 264
 extraction 301
 circuition 311
 turning out **313**
 organization 357
 training 673
 action 680
 military –s 722
evolve
 discover 480*a*
evolved from 154
 [*and see* evolution]
evulgate 531
evulsion 301
evivva! 931
ewe 366, 374
 – lamb 366
ewer 191
ex
 – animo 602
 – cathedra 542
 – officio 494, 924
 – parte 467
 – pede Herculem 82
 – post facto 122, 133
 – tempore
 instant 113
 occasion **134**
exacerbate
 increase 35
 exasperate **173**
 aggravate 659, 835
exact *similar* **17**
 special **79**
 true 494
 style 572
 require **741**
 tax 812
 insolence 885
 claim 924, 926
 – meaning 516
 – memory 505
 – observance **772**
 – truth 494

exacting
severe 739
discontented 832
grasping 865
fastidious 868
exaction
[*see* exact]
undue 925
exactly
just so 488
exaggeration
increase 35
expand 194
overestimate 482
magnify **549**
misrepresent 555
exalt
increase 35
elevate 307
extol 931
– one's horn 873
exalté 504
tête –e 503
exalted *high* 206
repute 873
noble 875
magnanimous 942
examination
[*see* examine]
evidence 467
undergo – 461
examine 457, 461
example
pattern 22
instance 82
bad – 949
good – 948
make an – of 972
set a good – 944
exanimate
dead 360
supine 683
exarch 745
exasperate
exacerbate 173
aggravate 835
enrage 900
excavate 252
excecation 442
exceed *surpass* 33
remain 40
transgress 303
intemperance 954
excel *surpass* 33
– in *skilful* 698
excellence 648, 944
excellence, par – 642
excellency 877
excelsior 305
except *subduct* 38
exclude 55
reject 610
exception
unconformity 83
qualification 469
exemption 777*a*
disapproval 932
take –
qualify 469
resent 900
exceptionable
bad 649
guilty 947
exceptional
original 20
extraneous 57
unconformable 83
in an – degree 31
exceptious 901, 901*a*
exceptis excipiendis 469
excern 297
excerpt 609
excerpta *parts* 51
compendium 596
selections 609
excerption 609
excess
remainder 40
redundance 641
intemperance 954
excessive 31
exchange
reciprocity 12
interchange 148
transfer 783
barter 794
mart 799
bill of – 771
rate of – 800
– blows &c.
retaliation 718
battle 720
Exchequer 802
Baron of – 967
Court of – 966
– bill 800
excise 812
exciseman 965
excision 38
excitability **825**, 901
excitation **824**
excite *energy* 171
violence 173
- *morally* 824
– attention 457
– desire 865
– hope 811
– an impression 375
– love 897
excited fancy 515
excitement 824, 825
anger 900
exclaim 411
– against 932
exclamation 580
mark of – 550
exclude
leave out 42, 55
reject 610
prohibit 761
banish 893
exclusion **55, 57**
exclusive
simple 42
omitting 55
special 79
irregular 83
forbidding 761
– of 38
– possession 777
– thought 457
excogitate 451, 515
excommunicate
banish 893
curse 908
rite 998
excoriate 226
excrement
excretion 299
dirt 653
excrescence
projection 250
blemish 848
excreta
excretion 299
dirt 653
excretion 297, **299**
excruciating 378, 830
exculpate
forgive 918
vindicate 937
acquit 970
excursion 266, 311
excursionist 268
excursive
deviating 279
- *style* 573
excursus 595
excuse *plea* 617
forgive 918
exempt 927*a*
vindicate 937
execrable 649, 830
execrate 898, 908
execution
music 416
action 680
conduct 692
signing 771
observance 772
punishment 972
carry into –
complete 729
put in –
undertaking 676
executioner 975
executive
conduct 692
direction 693
authority 737
judicature 965
executor 690
to one and his –s
&c., *property* 780
exegetical 522
exemplar 22
exemplary 944
exemplify
quote 82
illustrate 522
exempt *free* 748
dispensation 927*a*
– from *absent* 187
unpossessed 777*a*
exemption
exception 83
qualification 469
deliverance 672
permission 760
non-possession **777*a***
non-liability **927*a***
exenterate 297
exequatur 755
exequies 363
exercise
operation **170**
teach 537
task 625
use 677
act 680
exert 686
– authority 737
– discretion 609
– the intellect 451
– power 157
exergue 231
exert *use* 677
– authority 737
– oneself 686
exertion 171, **686**
exfoliate 226
exhalation
ejection 297
excretion 299
vapour 336

breath 349
odour 398
exhaust
paralyze 158
empty 195
waste 638
fatigue 688
complete 729
drain 789
squander 818
exhausted
inexistent 2
exhauster 349
exhaustive
complete 52
– inquiry 461
exhaustless
infinite 105
enough 639
exhibit *evidence* 467
show 525
display 882
exhilarate 836
exhort
persuade 615
advise 695
exhortation 998
exhume
past times 122
disinter 363
exigeant 739
exigency *crisis* 8
requirement 630
dearth 640
difficulty 704
need 865
exigent
exacting 739
discontented 832
exiguous 103, 193
exile
transport 185
banish 893
punish 972
voluntary – 893
exility 203
eximious 648
existence *being* 1
thing 3
- *in time* 118
- *in space* 186
come into – 151
exit
departure 293
egress 295
disappear 449
give – to 297
ἐξοχήν, κατ' –
supreme 33
important 642
exode 599
exodus 293
exogenous 367
exonerate
disburden 705
release 760
forgive 918
exempt 927a
vindicate 937
acquit 970
exorable 914
exorbitant
enormous 31
redundant 641
dear 814
exorcise 297
exorcism 992, 993
exorcist 994
exordium 64, 66
exosmose 302
exostosis 250
exoteric 525, 531
exotic *alien* 10
exceptional 83
plant 367
expand *increase* 35
swell 194
- *in breadth* 202
rarefy 322
- *in writing* 573
expanse 180, 192
expansion 194
expatiate
range 266
- *in writing* &c. 573
- *in discourse* 584
expatriate 295, 893
expect
look forward to 507
hope 858
not wonder 871
future 121
reason to – 472
expectance 871
expectancy 780
expectante, médecine –
wait 133
remedy 662
expectation 507
beyond – 508
hold out an – 768
expected
as well as can be – 654
expectorate 297
expedience 646
expedient
plan 626
means 632
useful 646
temporary – 147
expedite *early* 132
quickening 274
hasten 684
aid 707
expedition
[*see* expedite]
march 266
activity 682
war 722
expel *push* 284
eject 297
punish 972
expend *waste* 638
use 677
pay 809
– itself 683
expenditure 809
expense *price* 812
joke at one's – 842
spare no – 816
expenseless 815
expenses 809
expensive 814
experience
meet with 151
knowledge 490
undergo 821
learn by – 950
experienced 698
– eye &c. 700
experiences
narrative 594
experiment 463, 675
Experimental Philosophy 316
experimentum crucis *test* 463
proof 478
expert 698, 700
expiate 952
expire *end* 67
run its course 109
die 360
expired *past* 122
explain 462, 522
– away 523
explainer 524
expletive 573, 641
explication 522
explicit *clear* 518
patent 525
explode *burst* 173
confute 479
failure 732
passion 825
exploded *past* 122
antiquated 124
error 495
blown upon 932
exploit 680, 861
exploitation 461
explore 461, 463
explorer 268
explosion
[*see* explode]
revolution 146
violence 173
sound 406
anger 900
explosive
dangerous 665
ammunition 727
exponent
numerical 84
interpreter 524
informant 527
index 550
export 295
expose *denude* 226
confute 479
disclose 529
censure 932
– to danger 665
– oneself
disreputable 874
– to view
visible 446
manifest 525
exposé
disclosure 529
description 594
exposed to
liable 177
exposition [*see* expose]
explanation 522
expositor 524, 540
expository
explaining 522
informing 527
describing 594
disserting 595
expostulate
dissuade 616
advise 695
deprecate 766
reprehend 932
exposure [*see* expose]
appearance 448
– to weather 338
expound
interpret 522
teach 537
expounder 524
express
rapid 274
squeeze out 301

mean 516
declare 525
inform 527
journal 531
intentional 620
by – *haste* 684
– train 272
– by words 566
expressed, well – 578
expressible 525
expression [*see* express]
musical 416
aspect 448
nomenclature 564
phrase 566
mode of – 569
new fangled – 563
expressive
meaning 516
sensibility 822
exprobation 932, 938
expropriation 782
expugnable 665
expugnation 731
expulsion 55 [*see* expel]
expunge 162, 552
expurgate 38, 652
expurgatorius, index – 761
exquisite
savoury 394
excellent 648
pleasurable 829
beautiful 845
fop 854
exquisitely 31
exsiccate 340
exsudation 299
exsufflation 993
exsuscitate 824
extant 1
extasy [*see* ecstasy]
extemporaneous [*see* extempore]
transient 111
extempore
instant 113
early 132
occasion 134
off-hand 612
unprepared 674
extend
expand 194
prolong 200
– to 196
extended 202
extensibility 324
extensile 324
extension [*see* extend] 35, 142, 180
– of time 110
extensive 31, 180
– knowledge 490
extenso, in –
whole 50
diffuse 573
extent 26, 180, 200, 202
extenuate
decrease 36
weaken 160
excuse 937
extenuated 203
extenuating circumstances 469, 937
extenuatory 469
exteriority 220
exterminate 162
extermination 301
external 57, 220
– evidence 467
– senses 375
extinct
inexistent 2
past 122
destroyed 162
darkness 421
become – 4
extincteur 385
extinction of life 360
extinguish
destroy 162
blow out 385
darken 421
extinguisher 385
put an – upon
hinder 706
extirpate 301
extispicious 511
extol
over-estimate 482
praise 931
extort *extract* 301
compel 744
despoil 789
extorted
dissent 489
extortion 814, 819
extortionate 739, 865
extra 37, 599, 641
ab – 220
extract
draw off 297
take out 301
quotation 596
remedy 662
extraction 301
paternity 166
– of roots 85
extractor 301
extradition 270, 297
extrajudicial 964
extramundane 317
extramural 220
extraneous
extrinsic 6
not related 10
foreign 57
outside 220
extraneousness 57
extraordinary
great 31
exceptional 83
extraregarding 220
extravagant
inordinate 31
violent 173
absurd 497
foolish 499
fanciful 515
exaggerated 549
excessive 641
high-priced 814
prodigal 818
vulgar 851
ridiculous 853
extravaganza
fanciful 515
drama 599
extravagation 303
extravasate 295, 297
extreme
inordinate 31
end 67
– unction 998
extremis, in –
dying 360
difficulty 704
extremist 710
extremity *end* 67
adversity 735
tribulation 828
drive matters to an – 604
at the last – 665
extricate
take out 301
deliver 672
facilitate 705
liberate 750
extrinsicality 6
extrinsic evidence 467
extrusion 297, 299
exuberant
– *style* 573
redundant 639
exudation 295, 299
exulcerate 659
exult 838, 884
exultant 858
exulting 836
exunge 356
exuviæ 653
eye *circle* 247
opening 260
organ of sight 441
all my – and Betty Martin 546
appear to one's – 446
before one's –s
front 234
visible 446
manifest 525
cast the –s on
see 441
cast the –s over
attend to 457
catch the – 457
close the –s
blind 442
death 360
sleep 683
dry –s 823
fix the –s on 457
have an – to
attention 457
intention 620
desire 865
in one's –
visible 446
expectant 507
in the –s of
appearance 448
belief 484
keep an – upon 459
look with one's own –s 459
make –'s at 441
mind's – 515
with moistened –s 839
open the –s to 480*a*
with open –s 870
set one's –s upon 865
shut one's –s to
inattention 458
permit 760
to the –s 448
under the –s of

186
up to one's –s
641
have one's –s
about one 459
– askance 860
–s draw straws 683
an – for an – 718,
919
– glistening 824
in the – of the law
963
– of the master
693
– of a needle 260
–s open
attention 457
care 459
intention 620
–s opened
disclosure 529
–s out 442
eye-ball 441
eyebrows 256
eyeglass 445
eyelashes 256
eyeless 442
eyelet 260
eyelid 223
eye-shade 443
eye-sight 441
eyesore 846, 848
eye-teeth
have cut one's –
adolescence 131
skill 698
cunning 702
eye-wash 544
eye-witness
spectator 444
evidence 467
eyot 346
eyre 966
eyry 189

F

Fabian policy
delay 133
inaction 681
caution 864
fable *error* 495
metaphor 521
fiction 546
description 594
fabric *state* 7
effect 154
texture 329
fabricate
composition 54
make 161
invent 515
falsify 544
fabrication *lie* 546
fabula narratur, de
te – *retaliate* 718
condemn 971
fabulist 594
fabulous
enormous 31
imaginary 515
untrue 546
exaggerated 549
faburden 413
façade 234
face *exterior* 220
covering 223
front 234
aspect 448
oppose 708
resist 719
brave 861
impudence 885
change the – of
146
fly in the – of
disobey 742
put a good – upon
sham 545
calm 826
cheerful 836
hope 858
pride 878
display 882
vindicate 93
in the – of
presence 186
opposite 708
look in the –
see 441
proud 878
make –s
distort 243
ugly 846
disrespect 929
on the – of
manifest 525
show –
present 186
visible 446
not show –
disreputable 874
bashful 879
to one's – 525
wry – 378
– about 279
set one's – against
708
– of the country
344
on the – of the
earth
space 180
world 318
– to face *front* 234
contraposition
237
manifest 525
– of the thing
appearance 448
facet 220
facetiæ 842
facetious 842
facia 234
facile *willing* 602
irresolute 605
easy 705
facile princeps 33
facilis descensus
Averni
sloping 217
danger 665
facilitate 705
facility *skill* 698
easy 705
facing *covering* 223
facinorous 945
façon de parler 521,
549
fac-simile 21, 554
fact *existence* 1
event 151
certainty 474
truth 494
in – 535
faction 712, 713
factious 24
factitious 545, 546
factor
numerical 84
director 694
consignee 758
factory 691
factotum
agent 690
manager 694
employé 758
facts *evidence* 467
summary of – 594
at variance with –
471
facula 420
faculties 450
in possession of
one's – 502
faculty
power 157
profession 625
skill 698
facundity 582
fad 481, 608
faddle 683
fade *vanish* 4
transient 111
become old 124
droop 160
grow dim 422
lose colour 429
disappear 449
spoil 659
– from the
memory 506
fade 391
fadge 23
fæces 299, 653
fæx populi 876
fag *cigarette* 392
labour 686
fatigue 688
drudge 690, 746
– end
remainder 40
end 67
faggot 72, 388
fagots et fagots 15,
465
faïence 557
fail *droop* 160
shortcoming 304
be confuted 479
illness 655
not succeed 732
not observe 773
not pay 808
dereliction 927
failing [see fail]
incomplete 53
insufficient 640
vice 945
guilt 947
– heart 837
– luck 735
– memory 506
– sight 443
– strength 160
failure 732
heart – 360
fain *willing* 602
compulsive 744
wish 865
fainéant 683
faint 32
impotent 158
weak 160
sound 405
dim 422
colour 429
swoon 688
– heart *fear* 860
cowardice 862
damn with –
praise 930, 932,
934

faintness 405
fair *in degree* 31
pale 429
white 430
wise 498
important 643
good 648
moderate 651
mart 799
beautiful 845
just 922
honourable 939
– chance 472
– copy *copy* 21
writing 590
– field
occasion 134
– game 857
by – means 631, 939
– name 873
– play 922, 923
– question 461
– sex 374
in a – way
tending 176
probable 472
convalescent 660
prosperous 734
hopeful 858
– weather 734
– weather sailor 701
– wind 705
– words 894
fairing 784
fairly
intrinsically 5
get on – 736
– well 643
fair-spoken
courtesy 894
flattery 933
fairy *fanciful* 515
fay 979
imp 980
– godmother 711, 784, 912
– tale 546, 594
fairy-land 515
fait: au –
knowledge 490
skilful 698
– accompli
certain 474
complete 729
faith *belief* 484
hope 858
honour 939
piety 987
declaration of – 983
bad – 544
i' – 535
keep – with
observe 772
plight –
promise 768
love 902
true –
orthodox 983a
want of –
incredulity 487
irreligious 989
– healing 662
faithful [*see* faith]
like 17
copy 21
exact 494
obedient 743
– memory 505
– to 772
faithless *false* 544
dishonourable 940
sceptical 989
fake 544, 545
fakir 996
falcate 244, 245
falchion 727
falciform
[*see* falcate]
falcon 792
falconet 727
faldstool 215
fall *autumn* 126
happen 151
perish 162
slope 217
regression 283
descend 306
die 360
fail 732
adversity 735
vice 945
let – *lower* 308
inform 527
water– 348
– asleep 683
– astern 235, 283
– away 105
– back *return* 283
recede 287
relapse 661
– back upon 677, 717
have to – back upon 637
– a cursing 908
– of the curtain 67
– into a custom 82
– of day 125
– dead 360
– into decay 659
– down 990
– down before 928
– upon the ear 418
– flat on the ear 843
– at one's feet 725
– foul of *blow* 276
hinder 706
oppose 708
discord 713
attack 716
contention 720
censure 932
– for 897
– to the ground
be confuted 479
fail 732
– into a habit 613
– from one's high estate
adversity 735
disrepute 874
– in *order* 58
continuity 69
event 151
– into
conversion 144
river 348
– in with *agree* 23
conform 82
converge 2
discover 480a
concord 714
consent 762
– on one's knees
submit 725
servile 886
gratitude 916
worship 990
– of the leaf 126
– from the lips 582
– in love with 897
– to one's lot
event 151
chance 156
receive 785
duty 926
– under one's notice 457
– into oblivion 506
– off *decrease* 36
deteriorate 659
– off again 661
– out *happen* 151
quarrel 713
enmity 889
– into a passion 900
– to pieces
disjunction 44
destruction 162
brittle 328
– a prey to 732, 749
– in price 815
– into raptures 827
– short *inferior* 32
contract 195
shortcoming 304
– of snow 383
– through 304
– to *eat* 298
take in hand 676
do battle 722
– into a trap 547
– under
inclusion 76
subjection 749
– upon
discover 480a
unexpected 508
devise 626
attack 716
– in the way of 186
– to work 686
fallacy *sophistry* 477
error 495
show the – of 479
fallen angel 949, 978
fallible 475, 477
falling-out 24
falling star 318, 423
fallow
unproductive 169
yellow 436
unready 674
inactive 681
false *imitation* 19
sophistry 477
error 495
untrue 544, 546
spurious 925
dishonourable 940
– alarm 669
– colouring
misinterpretation 523
falsehood 544
– construction 523, 544
– doctrine 984
– expectation 509
– hearted 940
– impression 495
– light *vision* 443
– money 800
– ornament 851

- plea *untruth* 546
plea 617
- position 704
- pretences 791
- prophet
disappoint 509
pseudo-revelation 986
- reasoning 477
- scent 495, 538
- shame 855
- statement 546
- step 732
- teaching 538
- witness
deceiver 548
detraction 934
falsehood 544, 546
falsetto *squeak* 410
want of voice 581
falsify *error* 495
falsehood 544, 546
- accounts 811
- one's hope 509
falter *slow* 275
stammer 583
hesitate 605
slip 732
hopeless 859
fear 860
faltering accents 605
fame *greatness* 31
news 532
renown 873
familiar
known 490
habitual 613
sociable 892
affable 894
- *spirit* 979, 980
on - terms 888
familiarize
teach 537
habit 613
famille, en - 892
family
kin 11
class 75
ancestors 166
posterity 167
party 712
in the bosom of one's - 221
happy - 714
- circle 892
- jars 713
- likeness 17
- tie 11
in the - way 161
famine 640
- price 814
famine-stricken 640
famish
stingy 819
fasting 956
famished
insufficient 640
hungry 865
famous 873
famously 31
fan *blow* 349
cool 385
refresh 689
stimulate 824
flirt a - 855
- the embers 505
- the flame
violence 173
heat 384
aid 707
excite 824
- into a flame
anger 900
-shaped 194
fanatic
madman 504
imaginative 515
zealot 682
religious - 988
fanatical
misjudging 481
insane 503
emotional 821
excitable 825
heterodox 984
over-righteous 988
fanaticism 606
fanciful
imaginative 515
capricious 608
ridiculous 853
fancy *think* 451
idea 453
believe 484
suppose 514
imagine 515
caprice 608
choice 609
pugilism 726
wit 842
desire 865
wonder 870
love 897
after one's - 850
indulge one's - 609
take a - to
delight in 827
desire 865
take one's -
please 829
- dog 366
- dress 840
- price 814
- woman 962
fandango 840
fandi, mollia tempora - 588
fane 1000
fanfare *loudness* 404
celebration 883
fanfaron 887
fanfaronnade 884
fangs *venom* 663
rule 737
retention 781
fan-light 260
fan-like 202
fannel 999
fanon 999
fantasia 415
fantastic *odd* 83
absurd 497
imaginative 515
capricious 608
unfashionable 851
ridiculous 853
fantasy
imagination 515
desire 865
fantoccini 554, 599
faquir 996
far - away 196
- be it from
unwilling 603
deprecation 766
- between
disjunction 44
few 103
interval 198
- from it
unlike 18
shortcoming 304
no 536
- from the truth 546
- and near 180
- off 196
- and wide 31, 180, 196
farce
absurdity 497
untruth 546
drama 599
wit 842
ridiculous 853
mere -
unimportant 643
useless 645
farceur
actor 599
humorist 844
fardel
bundle 72
hindrance 706
fare *state* 7
food 298
price 812
bill of -
list 86
farewell
departure 293
relinquishment 624
loss 776
- to greatness 874
far-famed 873
far-fetched 10
far-flung 73
far-gone
much 31
insane 503
spoiled 654
farinaceous 330
farm *till* 371
property 780
rent 788
farmer 188, 342, 371
afternoon - 683
farm-house 189
Farmer-Labor 712
faro 840
farrago 59
farrier 370
farrow
produce 161
litter 167
multitude 102
far-sighted 442, 510
farther 196
[*and see* further]
farthing
quarter 97
worthless 643
coin 800
- candle 422
farthingale 225
fasces 747
fascia 205, 247
fascicule 51
fasciculated 72
fascinate
influence 615
excite 824
please 829
astonish 870
love 897
conjure 992
fascinated

pleased 827
fascination [*see* fascinate]
infatuation 825
desire 870
fascine 72
Fascisti 712
fas et nefas, per – 604*a*, 631
fash 830
fashion
state 7
form 240
custom 613
method 627
ton 852
after a –
middling 32
after this – 627
follow the – 82
be in the – 488
man of – 852
set the –
influence 175
authority 737
for –'s sake 852
fast *joined* 43
steadfast 150
rapid 274
fashionable 852
intemperate 954
not eat 956
worship 990
rite 998
stick – 704
– asleep 683
– by 197
– day 956
– friend 890
– and loose
sophistry 477
falsehood 544
irresolute 605
tergiversation 607
caprice 608
– man *fop* 854
libertine 962
fasten *join* 43
hang 214
restrain 751
– on the mind 451
– a quarrel upon 713
– upon 789
fastening 45
fast-handed 819
fastidious
censorious 932
fastidiousness 868
fasting
insufficiency 640
worship 990
penance 952
abstinence 956
fastness
asylum 666
defence 717
fat *corpulent* 192
expansion 194
unctuous 355
oleaginous 356
kill the -ted calf
celebration 883
sociality 892
– in the fire
disorder 59
violence 173
– of the land
pleasure 377
enough 639
prosperity 734
intemperance 95
fata – Morgana
occasion 134
ignis fatuus 423
– obstant 601
fatal 361
– disease 655
fatalism 601
fatality 601
fate *end* 67
necessity 601
chance 621
be one's – 156
sure as – 474
Fates 601, 979
fat-head 501
father *eldest* 128
paternity 166
priest 996
Apostolical -s 985
gathered to one's -s 360
heavy – 599
– upon 155
Father, God the – 976
fatherland 189
fatherless 158
fatherly 906
fathom
length 200
investigate 461
solve 462
measure 466
discover 480*a*
knowledge 490
fathomless 208
fatidical 511
fatigation 688
fatigue 688
fatras 643
fatten
expand 194
improve 658
prosperous 734
– on *parasite* 886
– upon
feed 298
fatuity 4, 499
fatuous 517
fat-witted 499
faubourg 227
fauces 231
faucet 252
faugh! 867
fault
break 70
error 495
imperfection 651
failure 732
vice 945
guilt 947
at –
uncertain 475
ignorant 491
unskilful 699
find – with 932
faultless 650, 946
faulty 495, 651
faun 980
fauna 366
faut: comme il –
taste 850
fashion 852
il s'en – bien 489
tant s'en – 536
faute 732
– de mieux
substitution 147
necessity 601
fauteuil 215
fautor 890
faux pas
error 568
failure 732
misconduct 947
intrigue 961
favour
resemble 17
badge 550
letter 592
aid 707
indulgence 740
permit 760
gift 784
partiality 923
appearances in – of 472
get into –
friendship 888
love 897
in – *repute* 873
approbation 931
in – of
approve 931
under – of 760
view with – 906
– with 784
favourable
occasion 134
willing 602
good 648
aid 707
– prospect 472
– to 709
take a – turn
improve 658
prosperity 734
favourably
well 618
favourer 890
favourite
pleasing 829
beloved 897, 899
favouritism
friendship 888
wrong 923
fawn *colour* 433
cringe 749, 886
flatter 933
fay 979
fealty
obedience 743
duty 926
respect 928
fear 860
fearful
painful 830
timid 862
fearfully 31, 870
fearless *hope* 858
courage 861
fearsome 860
feasible 470, 705
feast *period* 138
repast 298
pleasure 377
revel 840
rite 998
– one's eyes 897
feast of reason
conversation 588
– and flow of soul
sociality 892
feat *action* 680
courage 861
– of arms 720
– of strength 159
feather
class 75
tuft 256
light 320
trifle 643

ornament 847
decoration 877
in full –
prepared 673
prosperous 734
rich 803
hear a – drop 403
in high –
health 654
cheerful 884
pleased with a – 840
– in one's cap
honour 873
decoration 877
– one's nest
prepare 673
prosperity 734
wealth 803
economy 817
selfish 943
– the oar 698
– in the scale 643
feather-bed 324
feathered tribes 366
feathery 256
featly 682
feature
character 5
component 56
form 240
appearance 448
press 531
lineament 550
– in 56
features
face 234
febrifuge 662
febrile 382, 825
fecal 653
fecit 556
feckless 866
feculence 653
fecund 168
fecundate 161
federal council 696
– penitentiary 752
federalism 737
federation 48, 709, 712
fee *possession* 777
property 780
pay 809
reward 973
feeble *weak* 160
illogical 477
feeble-minded 497, 605
feebleness
style 575
feed *eat* 298
supply 637
– the flame 707
fee-faw-fum
bugbear 860
spell 993
feel *sense* 375
touch 379
emotion 821
– for *try* 463
benevolence 906
pity 914
condole with 915
– the pulse 461
– the want of 865
– one's way
essay 675
caution 864
feeler 379
inquiry 461
experiment 463
feeling 698, 821
feet *low* 207
walkers 266
at one's –
near 197
subjection 749
humility 879
fall at one's –
submit 725
fall on one's –
prosper 734
lick the – of
servile 886
light upon one's –
safe 664
spring to one's – 307
throw oneself at the – of
entreat 765
feign 544, 546
feigned 545
feint 545
felicitas, curiosa – 698
felicitate 896
felicitous
agreeing 23
- *style* 578
skilful 698
successful 731
pleasant 829
felicity 827
feline *cat* 366
stealthy 528
cunning 702
fell *destroy* 162
mountain 206
lay flat 21
skin 223
lay low 308
moor 344
dire 860
malevolent 907
fellah 876
felloe 231
fellow *similar* 17
equal 27
companion 88
dual 89
man 373
scholar 492, 541
fellow-commoner 541
fellow-companion 890
fellow-countryman 890
fellow-creature 372
fellow-feeling
friendship 888
love 897
benevolence 906
pity 914
fellowship
partnership 712
distinction 873
friendship 888
companionship 890
good – 892
fellow-student 541
fellow-worker 690
felly 231
felo-de-se 361
felon 949
felonious 945
felony 947
felt *texture* 219
heart– 821
felucca 273
female 374
feme coverte 903
feme sole 904
feminality
weakness 160
woman 374
feminine 374
feminism 374
femme de chambre 746
fen 345
fence *enclose* 232
evade 544
defence 717
fight 720
prison 752
thief 792
– round 229
– with a question 528
fenced 770
fenceless 665
fencible 726
fencing 840
feneration 787
fend 717
fender 717
Fenian 710, 742
fenum habet in cornu 668, 913
feodal 780
feodality 737, 777
feoff *property* 780
feoffee 779, 785
feoffer 784
feræ naturæ 366
feral 907
ferine 907
ferment
disorder 59
energy 171
violence 173
agitation 315
lightness 320
effervesce 353
emotion 821
excitement 824, 825
anger 900
fermentation, acetous – 397
fern 367
ferocity 173, 907
Ferrara
sword 727
ferret out 461, 480a
ferro-concrete 635
ferrule 223
ferry 270, 627
ferry-boat 273
ferry-man 269
fertile 161, 168
– imagination 515
ferule 975
come under the – 932
fervent *hot* 382
desirous 865
– hope 858
fervid *hot* 382
heartfelt 821
excited 824
fervour *heat* 382
animation 821
love 897
festal *eating* 298
social 892
fester 653, 655
festina lente 864
festival
music 416

celebration 883
festivity 840, 892
festoon 245, 847
fetch *bring* 270
arrive 292
evasion 545
sell for 812
– one a blow
strike 276
attack 716
– and carry
servile 886
– a sigh 839
fête 840, 882
fêté 892
fetishism 992
fetid 401
fetish 991, 993
fetter 751, 752
fettle 673
state 5
prepare 673
in fine – 159, 654
feu
– d'enfer 716
– de joie
amusement 840
celebration 883
feud *discord* 713
possess 777
property 780
death – 919
feudal 737, 780
feudatory 749
feuilleton 593
fever *heat* 382
disease 655
excitement 825
feverish *hurry* 684
animated 821
excited 824
few
a – 100
– and far between 70
– words
concise 572
taciturn 585
compendium 596
fewness 103
fey 360
fez 225
fiancée 897
fiasco 732
fiat 741
– money 800
fib *falsehood* 544, 546
thump 720
fibre *link* 45
filament 205
moral – 60
fickle 149, 605
fictile 240
fiction *untruth* 546
work of – 594
fictitious 515, 546
fiddle 416, 417
fiddle-de-dee
absurd 497
unimportant 643
contempt 930
fiddlefaddle
unmeaning 517
trifle 643
dawdle 683
fiddler 416
fiddlestick 417
– end 643
fidelity
veracity 543
obedience 743
observance 772
honour 939
fidgets *changes* 149
activity 682
hurry 684
excitability 825
fidgety
irresolute 605
fearful 860
irascible 901
fiducial 156
fiduciary 484
fidus Achates
auxiliary 711
associate 743
friend 890
fie *disreputable* 874
– upon it
censure 932
fief 777
field *opportunity* 134
scope 180
region 181
plain 344
agriculture 371
business 625
arena 728
property 780
the – *hunting* 622
beasts of the – 366
playing –s 728
the potter's – 361
take the – 722
– artillery 726
the – of blood 361
– of inquiry
topic 454
inquiry 461
– of view
vista 441
idea 453
field-day
contention 720
amusement 840
display 882
field-glass 445
field-marshal 745
field-piece 727
field-preacher 996
field-work 717
fiend 913, 980
fiend-like
malevolent 907
wicked 945
fiend 980
fierce *violent* 173
passion 825
daring 861
angry 900
fiery *violent* 173
hot 382
strong feeling 821
excitable 825
angry 900
irascible 901
– cross 550, 722
– furnace 386
– imagination 515
– ordeal 828
fife 417
fifer 416
fifth 98, 99
fifty 98
fig
unimportance 643
in the name of the prophet –s! 497
– out 847
fight
contention 720
warfare 722
show –
defence 717
courage 861
– one's battles again 594
– against destiny 606
– the good fight 944
– it out 722
– shy *avoid* 603, 623
coward 862
– one's way
pursue 622
active 682
exertion 686
fighter 726
fighting-cock 726, 861
fighting-man 726
figment 515
figurante 599
figurate number 84
figuration 240
figurative
metaphorical 521
representing 554
– *style* 577
figure
number 84
form 240
appearance 448
metaphor 521
indicate 550
represent 554
price 812
ugly 846
cut a –
repute 873
display 882
poor – 874
– to oneself 515
– of speech 521
– out 522
exaggeration 549
figure-flinger 994
figure-head 4, 550, 554, 643
figurine 554
figuriste 559
filaceous 205
filament 205
filamentous 256
filch 791
filcher 762
file *subduct* 38
arrange 60
row 69
assemblage 72
list 86
reduce 195
smooth 255
pulverize 330
record 551
store 636
soldiers 726
– a claim &c. 969
– off *march* 266
diverge 291
file-fire 716
filial 167
filiation
consanguinity 11
attribution 155
posterity 167
filibuster 133, 706, 792
filibustering 791
filiform 205

filigree 219
filings 330
fill *complete* 52
occupy 186
contents 190
stuff 224
provision 637
eat one's – 957
have one's –
enough 639
satiety 869
– the bill 229
– an office
business 625
government 737
– out
expand 194
–ed to overflowing 641
– one's pocket 803
– time 106
– up *compensate* 30
compose 54
close 261
restore 660
– up the time
inaction 681
fille
– de chambre 746
– de joie 962
filled
– to overflowing 641
filler 532
fillet *band* 45
filament 205
circle 247
insignia 550
ornament 847
fillibeg 225
filling 224
fillip
impulse 276
propulsion 284
stimulus 615
excite 824
filly 271
film *layer* 204
opaque 426
semitransparent 427
– over the eyes
dim sight 443
cinema 448
ignorant 491
filmy *texture* 329
filter *percolate* 295
clean 652
filth 653
–y lucre 800
filtrate 652
fimbriated 256
fin 267
final *ending* 67
conclusive 474
completing 729
court of – appeal 474
– cause 620
– stroke 729
– touch 729
finale *end* 67
completion 729
finality 67, 729
finally
for good 141
on the whole 476
finance 800, 811
minister of – 801
financier 801
finch 366
find
eventuality 151
adjudge 480
discover 480a
acquire 775
– one's account in 644
– the cause of 522
– a clue to 480a
– to one's cost 509
– credence 484
– it in one's heart 602
– in *provide* 637
– the key of 522
– the meaning 522
– means 632
– oneself *be* 1
present 186
– out 480a
– vent 671
– one's way 731
– one's way into 294
finding
judgment 480
fine *small* 32
large 192
thin 203
rare 322
not raining 340
exact 494
good 648
beautiful 845
adorned 847
proud 878
mulct 974
in – *end* 67
after all 476
– air 656
– arts 554
– feather 159, 654
– feeling 850
– frenzy 515
– gentleman
fop 854
proud 878
– grain 329
– lady 854, 878
one – morning 106
some – morning 119
– powder 330
– talking
overrate 482
boast 884
– writing 577
– time of it 734
– voice 580
fine-draw 660
fine-fingered 698
fine-spoken 894, 933
fine-spun *thin* 203
sophistry 477
fine-toned 413
finem, respicere – 510
finery 847, 851
finesse *tact* 698
artifice 702
taste 850
finger *touch* 379
hold 781
lay the – on
point out 457
discover 480a
lift a – 680
not lift a – 681
point the – at 457
turn round one's little – 737
–'s breadth 203
at one's –s' end
near 197
know 490
remember 505
– on the lips
aphony 581
taciturnity 585
– in the pie
cause 153
interfere 228
act 680
active 682
co-operate 709
fingerling 193
finger-post 550
finger-print 467
finger-stall 223
fingle-fangle 643
finical
trifling 643
affected 855
fastidious 868
finicky 855, 868
finikin 643
finis 67
– coronat opus 729
finish *lend* 67
symmetry 242
complete 729
skill 698
finished
absolute 31
perfect 650
skilled 698
finishing
– stroke 361
– touch 729
finite 32
fiord 343
fire *energy* 171
heat 382
make hot 384
stoke 388
vigour 574
discharge 756
enthusiasm 821
excite 824, 825
catch – 384
hell – 982
on – 382
open – *begin* 66
play with – 863
signal – 550
take –
excitable 825
angry 900
between two –s 665
under – 665, 722
– at 716
– the blood 824
– and fury 900
– the first shot 716
– of genius 498
– off 284
– a salute 883
– and sword 162
– up *excite* 825
anger 900
– a volley 716
go through – and water
resolution 604
perseverance 604a
courage 861
fire-alarm 669
fire-annihilator 385
fire-arms 727

fire-ball *fuel* 388
arms 727
fire-balloon 273
fire-barrel 388
fire-bell 669
fire-boat 726
fire-brand
fuel 388
instigator 615
dangerous man 667
incendiary 913
fire-brigade 385
fire-curtain 599
fire-drake 423
fire-eater
fighter 726
blusterer 887
fire-eating
rashness 863
insolence 885
fire-engine 348
fire-escape 671
fire-extinguisher 385
fire-fly 423
fireless cooker 386
fire-light 422
firelock 727
fireman *stoker* 268
extinguisher 385
fire-place 386
fire-proof 385
fireside 189
firewood 388
firework
fire 382
luminary 423
celebration 883
amusement 840
fire-worship 991
fire-worshipper 984
firing *fuel* 388
explosion 406
firkin 191
firm
junction 43
stable 150
hard 323
resolute 604
partnership 712
merchant 797
brave 861
stand – 719
– as a rock 604
– belief 484
– hold 781
firmament 318
firman 741, 760
first 66
– blush
morning 125
leading 280
vision 441
appearance 448
manifest 525
– blow 716
– cause 976
– that comes 609*a*
– fiddle
importance 642
proficient 700
authority 737
– come first served 609*a*
– and foremost 66
– impression 66
– and last 87
– line 234
come back to – love 607
– move 66
– opportunity 132
at – sight 448
– stage 66
– stone
preparation 673
attack 716
on the – summons 741
of the – water
best 648
repute 873
first-born 124, 128
first-fruits 154
first-hand 20, 467
firstlings 128, 154
first-rate
important 642
excellent 648
man-of-war 726
firth 343
fisc 802
fiscal 800
fish *food* 298
sport 361, 622
animal 366
food for –es 362
other – to fry
ill-timed 135
busy 682
queer – 857
– in the air 645
– for compliments 880
– for *seek* 4
experiment 463
desire 865
– hatchery 370
– out *inquire* 461
discover 480*a*
– in troubled waters
difficult 704
discord 713
– up *raise* 307
find 480*a*
– out of water
disagree 24
unconformable 83
displaced 185
bungler 701
fisherman 361
fishery 370
fishing *kill* 361
pursue 622
fishing-boat 273
fishpond 343, 370
fish-tail 267
fishy transaction 940
fisk 266, 274
fissile 328
fission 44
fissure 44
chink 198
fist
handwriting 590
grip 781
shake the –
defy 715
threat 909
fisticuffs 720
fistula 260
fit *state* 7
agreeing 23
equal 27
paroxysm 173
agitation 315
caprice 608
expedient 646
healthy 654
disease 655
excitement 825
anger 900
right 922
due 924
duty 926
in –s 315
think – 600
– of abstraction 458
– of crying 839
– for 698
– out *dress* 225
prepare 673
– to be seen 845
by –s and starts
irregular 59
discontinuous 70
agitated 315
capricious 608
haste 684
fitful
irregular 139
changeable 149
capricious 608
fittings 633
five 98
division by – 99
– act play 599
– and twenty 98
Five Year Plan 626
fiver 800
fives *game* 840
fix *join* 43
arrange 60
establish 150
place 184
immovable 265
solidify 321
resolve 604
difficulty 704
– the eyes upon 441
– the foundations 673
– the memory 505
– the time 114
– the thoughts 457
– up 774
– upon *discover* 480*a*
choose 609
fixed *intrinsic* 5
permanent 141
stable 150
quiescent 265
habitual 613
– idea 481
– opinion 484
– periods 138
fixity 141
fixity of purpose 141
fixture
appointment 741
property 780
fizgig 423
fizz 409
fizzle 353
– out 304
flabelliform 194
flabbergast 870, 879
flabby 324
flabbiness 324
flaccid *weak* 160
soft 324
empty 640
flag *weak* 160
flat stone 204
floor 211

smoothness 255
slow 275
leaf 367
sign 550
path 627
infirm 655
inactive 683
tired 688
weary 841
lower one's – 725
red – *alarm* 669
yellow –
warning 668
alarm 669
– man 668
– ship 726
– of truce 723
flag-bearer 534
flagellation
penance 952
asceticism 955
flogging 972
rite 998
flagelliform 205
flageolet 417
flagitious 945
flagon 191
flagrant
great 31
manifest 525
notorious 531
atrocious 945
flagrante
– bello 722
– delicto
sure enough 474
act 680
guilt 947
flagration 384
flagstaff *tall* 206
signal 550
flail 276
flair 450, 698
flake 204
snow – 383
– white 430
flam 544
flambé 732
flambeau 423
flamboyant 577
flame *fire* 382
light 420
luminary 423
passion 824, 825
love 897
catch the –
emotion 821
consign to the –s 384
add fuel to the – 173
in –s 382
– up 825
–coloured
red 434
orange 439
flame-projector 727
flamen 996
flaming *violent* 173
feeling 821
excited 824
ostentatious 882
boasting 884
flâneur 935
flange *support* 215
rim 231
projection 250
flank *side* 236
protect 664
flannel 384
flap *adjunct* 39
hanging 214
move to and fro 315
– the memory 505
flapdoodle 517
flapper *girl* 129
flapping *loose* 47
flare *violent* 173
glare 420
light 423
– up
excited 824, 825
angry 900
flaring *colour* 428
flash *instant* 113
violent 173
fire 382
light 420
eyes – fire 900
– lamp 550
– light 423
– across the memory 505
– on the mind
thought 451
disclose 529
impulse 612
– note 800
– in the pan
unsubstantial 4
transientness 111
impotent 158
unproductive 169
failure 732
– tongue 563
– up *excited* 824
– upon
unexpected 508
– of wit 842
flashing
ostentatious 882
flashy
gaudy colour 428
style 577
ornament 847
vulgar 851
flask 191
flat *inert* 172
abode 189
story 191
low 207
horizontal 213
vapid 391
low tone 408
musical note 413
positive 535
dupe 547
back-scene 599
shoal 667
bungler 701
poor 804
insensible 823
dejected 837
weary 841
dull 843
simple 849
fall – 732
– contradiction 536
– iron 255
– refusal 764
flatfoot 664
flatness **251**
flatter *deceive* 545
cunning 702
please 829
grace 845
encourage 858
approbation 931
adulation 933
– oneself
probable 472
hope 858
– the palate 394
flatterer **935**
flattering
– remarks 894
– tale
hope 858
– unction to one's soul
content 831
vain 880
flattery 933
flattery 544, **933**
flatulent
gaseous 334
air 338
wind 349
– *style* 573, 575
flatus 334, 349
flaunt 873, 882
flaunting *vulgar* 851
gaudy 428
unreserved 525
flautist 416
Flavian amphitheatre 728
flavour 390
flavouring 393
flavous 436
flaw *break* 70
crack 198
error 495
imperfection 651
blemish 848
fault 947
– in an argument 477
flaxen 436
flay *divest* 226
punish 972
flea *jumper* 309
dirt 653
– in one's ear
repel 289
eject 297
refuse 764
disrepute 874
abashed 879
discourteous 895
contempt 930
flea-bite 643
flea-bitten 440
fleck 32
flecked 440
flection 279
fled *escaped* 671
fledge 673
fledgling 123
flee *avoid* 623
fleece *tegument* 223
strip 789
rob 791
impoverish 804
surcharge 814
fleet *ridicule* 856
insult 929
fleet *ships* 273
swift 274
navy 726
Fleet *prison* 752
fleeting 4, 111
flesh *bulk* 192
animal 364
mankind 372
carnal 961
gain – 194
ills that – is heir to *evil* 619
disease 655
in the – 359
one – 903

way of all – 360
weakness of the – 945
– and blood
substance 3
materiality 316
animality 364
affections 820
make the – creep
pain 830
fear 860
flesh-colour 434
flesh-pots 298
– of Egypt 734, 803
fleshly 316
fleur-de-lis 847
fleuron 847
flexible 324, 705
flexion
curvature 245
fold 258
deviation 279
flexuous 248
flexure 245, 258
flibbertigibbet 980
flicker
changing 149
waver 314
flutter 315
light 420
dim 422
flickering 139
flier 621
flies *theatre* 599
flight *flock* 102
volitation 267
swiftness 274
departure 293
avoidance 623
escape 671
– lieutenant 745
put to –
propel 284
repel 717
vanquish 731
– of fancy 515
– of stairs 305, 627
– of time 109
flighty *inattentive* 458
mad 503
fanciful 515
flim-flam 544, 608
flimsy *unsubstantial* 4
weak 160
rarity 322
soft 324
sophistical 477
trifling 643
flinch *swerve* 607
avoid 623
fear 860
cowardice 862
fling *propel* 284
jig 840
jeer 929
have one's –
active 682
laxity 738
freedom 748
amusement 840
– aside 782
have a – at
attack 716
resent 900
disrespect 929
censure 932
– away *reject* 610
waste 638
relinquish 782
– down 308
– to the winds
destroy 162
not observe 773
flint *hard* 323
flint-hearted 907
flintlock 727
flip *beverage* 298
flippant *fluent* 584
pert 885
flipper *paddle* 267
flirt *propel* 284
coquet 607, 854
love 897
endearment 902
– a fan 855
flit *elapse* 109
changeable 149
move 264
travel 266
swift 274
depart 293
run away 623
flitter
small part 32
changeable 149
flutter 315
flitting 111
float *establish* 150
navigate 267
boat 273
buoy up 305
lightness 320
before the –s
on the stage 599
– on the air 405
– before the eyes 446
– bonds 788
– in the mind
thought 451
imagination 515
floater 683
floating
[*see* float]
rumoured 532
– battery 726
– capital 805
– debt 806
– dock 189
flocculent
woolly 256
soft 324
pulverulent 330
flock
assemblage 72
multitude 102
laity 997
–s and herds 366
– together 72
floe *ice* 383
flog 972
hasten 684
flood *much* 31
crowd 72
river 348
abundance 639
redundance 641
prosperity 734
stem the – 708
– of light 420
– of tears 839
flood-gate
limit 233
egress 295
conduit 350
open the –s
eject 297
permit 760
flood-light 423, 599
flood-mark 466
flood-tide
increase 35
complete 52
height 206
advance 282
water 337
floor *level* 204
base 211
horizontal 213
support 215
overthrow 731
ground – 191
flop 315
Flora 369
floral 367
florescence 154
floriculture 371
florid *colour* 428
red 434
– *style* 577
health 654
florist 371
floss 256
flotilla 273, 726
flotsam and jetsam 73
flounce
trimming 231
jump 309
agitation 315
flounder
change 149
toss 315
uncertain 475
bungle 699
difficulty 704
fail 732
flour 330
flourish
brandish 314, 315
exaggerate 549
language 577
speech 582
prosper 618
healthy 654
prosperous 734
ornament 847
repute 873
display 882
boast 884
– of trumpets
loud 404
cheerfulness 836
publish 531
ostentation 882
celebrate 883
boast 884
flout 929, 936
flow *course* 109
hang 214
motion 264
stream 348
murmur 405
abundance 639
– from
result 154
– of ideas 451
– in 294
– into *river* 348
– out 295
– over 641
– of soul
conversation 588
affections 820
cheerful 836
social 892
– with the tide 705
– of time 109

- of words 582, 584
flower *essence* 5
produce 161
vegetable 367
prosper 734
beauty 845
ornament 847
repute 873
- of age 131
- of flock 648
- of life 127
- painting 556, 559
flowering plant 367
flowers
anthology 596
- of rhetoric 577
flowing
[*see* flow]
- periods 578
fluctuate
change 149
oscillate 314
irresolute 605
flue *opening* 260
air-pipe 351
down 320
dust 653
fluent
differential 84
fluid 333
stream 348
- language 578
speech 584
fluff 256
little bit of - 374
fluid 333
- in motion 347
fluidity 333
fluke *hook* 244
chance 621
flummery
unmeaning 517
flattery 933
flunk 732
flunkey
servant 746
servile 886
flunkeyism 933
flurry *hurry* 684
agitation 821
excitability 825
flush *flat* 251
flood 348
heat 382
light 420
colour 428
red 434
abundant 639
wash 652
health 654
feeling 821
passion 825
rejoicing 838
in liquor 959
- of cash 803
flushed
[*see* flush]
excited 824
cheerful 836
hopeful 858
proud 878
vain 880
- with rage 900
- with success 731
- with victory 884
fluster
distract 458
move 821
excite 824, 825
flustered *tipsy* 959
flute
furrow 259
music 417
flutter
variable 149
agitation 315
gamble 621
hurry 684
emotion 821
excite 824, 825
fear 860
fluvial 348
flux
conversion 144
motion 264
liquefaction 335
flow 348
- and reflux 314
- of time 109
flux de paroles 584
fluxion 84
fluxions 85
fly *vanish* 4
time 109
transient 111
burst 173
minute 193
wings 267
vehicle 272
swift 274
depart 293
break 328
lose colour 429
shun 623
- to arms 722
- at 716
- back 277
- in the face of
oppose 708
resist 719
disobey 742
insolence 885
- in the face of facts 481, 606
- from 623
- kites
borrow 788
credit 805
not pay 808
- off 291
- in the ointment 651
- open 260
- out *violent* 173
excitable 825
angry 900
fly-blown 653
fly-boat 273
flyer 269
flying [*see* fly]
- colours
success 731
display 882
celebrate 883
- boat 273, 726
- column 726
- field 728
- fish 83
- machine 273
- officer 745
- rumour 532
fly-leaf
interjacent 228
book 593
fly-wheel 312
foal 129, 271
foam *violent* 173
boil 315
spray 353
excitement 824, 825
- with rage 900
fob 191
- off 545
focal 222
focis, pro aris et - 717
focus 74
centre 222
furnace 386
bring into a -
collect 72
convergence 290
in - *visible* 446
out of - *dim* 447
- the thoughts 457
fodder 298
foe 891
fœderis, casus - 770
föhn 349
fœnum habet in cornu 668, 913
fœtor 401
fœtus 129, 153
fog 353, 475
in a - 528
London - 436
fogey 501, 857
foggy
opaque 426
fog-signal 668, 669
foh! 867
foible 945
foil *contrast* 14
lamina 204
baffle 706
weapon 727
defeat 731
foiled 732
foin 276
foist *ship* 273
- in 228
- upon 545
folâtre 836
fold *fold* 39
bisect 91
inclosure 232
plait 258
prison 752
congregation 997
- one's arms 681
- in one's arms 902
- up 225
foliaceous 204
foliage 367
foliate 85
foliated 204
folio 593
folk 372
folk-dance 840
folk-lore 124, 979
folk-song 597
follicle *cyst* 191
hollow 252
follicular 260
follow
- in order 63
conform to 82
- in time 117
- in motion 281
understand 518
pursue 622
obey 743
- advice 695
- the dictates of 615
- the example of 19
- from
result from 154
be proved by 478

– implicitly 486, 695
– the lead of
co-operate 709
– suit *imitate* 19
– the trail 461
– up
continue 143
persevere 604*a*
follower
[*see* follow]
successor 65
learn 541
servant 746
lover 897
folly
building 189
irrationality 499
act of –
mismanagement 699
foment
stimulate 173
warm 384
promote 707
excite 824
relieve 834
fond 897
– hope 858
fondle 902
fondling 899, 902
fondness
desire 865
fondre en larmes 839
fons et origo 153
font *origin* 153
type 591
rite 998
altar 1000
food 298
preparation of – 673
– for the mind 454
– for powder 726
fool 501
pudding 354
deceive 545
ridicule 856
disrespect 929
make a – of oneself
bungle 699
motley – 844
play the –
folly 499
amusement 840
–'s errand
deceived 545
unskilful 699
–'s mate 732
–'s paradise
unsubstantial 4
misjudgment 481
disappoint 509
hope 858
rash 863
– to the top of one's bent
excite 824
anger 900
flatter 933
– away money 818
– away time 683
foolhardy 863
fooling 842
foolish 499
act –ly 699
look –
disrepute 874
shame 879
foolscap 550, 559
foot
length 200
stand 211
metre 597
at the – of 207
keep on –
continue 143
support 251
provide 637
prepare 673
not stir a – 681
on – *existing* 1
during 106
journey 266
topic 454
business 625
preparing 673
active 682
put one's – down
resolved 604
put one's – in
undertake 676
bungle 699
set – on land 342
trample under – 930
– the bill 807
– by foot 51
one – in the grave
age 128
death 360
it *journey* 266
dance 309
at –'s pace 275
foot-ball
subjection 749
game 840
footboy 746
footfall
motion 264
indication 550
stumble 732
footing
circumstances 8
rank 71
influence 175
situation 183
foundation 211
support 215
payment 809
friendly – 888
get a –
location 184
be on a –
state 7
pay one's – 807
footlights 599
footman 746
footmark 551
footpad 792
foot-passenger 268
footpath 627
foot pound 466
footprint 551
foot-soldier 726
foot-warmer 386
footsore 688
footstep 551
footstool 215
foozle 732
fop 854
foppery 882
foppish 855
for *cause* 155
tendency 176
reason 476
motive 615
intention 620
preparation 673
have –
price 812
– all that
notwithstanding 30
qualification 469
– all the world
like 17
– aught one knows 156
– better for worse 78
– ever 112
– example 82
– form's sake 82
– good
complete 52
diuturnity 110
permanence 141
– the most part
great 31
general 78
special 79
– the nonce 118
– nothing 815
– a season 106
– a time 111
– the time being 106
forage
food 298
provision 637
steal 791
forage-cap 225
foramen 260
foraminous 260
forasmuch as
relating to 9
cause 155
reason 476
motive 615
foray *attack* 716
robbery 791
forbear
avoid 623
spare 678
lenity 740
sufferance 826
pity 914
abstain 953
forbearance 918
forbid 761
God –
dissent 489
deprecation 766
censure 932
prayer 990
forbidden fruit
seduction 615
prohibition 761
forbidding
ugly 846
force *corps* 72
power 157
strength 159
agency 170
energy 171
violence 173
cultivate 371, 707
cascade 348
- *of style* 574
urge 615
exertion 686
compulsion 744
armed – 726
brute – 964
put in – 924
– of argument 476
– of arms 744
– of character 820
– down the throat
severe 739
compel 744

– majeure 744
– open 173
– one's way
progression 282
passage 302
forced *irrelative* 10
- *style* 579
be – to 601
– labor 603
– march 274
forcefully 601
forceps
extraction 301
grip 781
forces 726
forcible [*see* force]
ford 302, 627
fore 234
fore and aft
complete 52
lengthwise 200
– schooner 273
forearm 673
forebears 166
forebode 511
forecast
foresight 510
prediction 511
plan 626
foreclose 706
foredoom 152, 601
forefathers 166
forefend
prohibit 761
forefinger 379
forego
relinquish 624
renounce 757
surrender 782
foregoing 62, 116
foregone
past 122
– conclusion
prejudged 481
predetermined 611
foreground 234
in the –
manifest 525
forehead 234
foreign
alien 10
extraneous 57
– accent 580
– parts 196
foreigner 57
forejudge
prejudge 481
foresight 510
foreknow 510
foreland 206, 254
forelay 545
forelock
pull the – 894
take time by the –
early 132
occasion 134
foreman 694
foremost
superior 33
beginning 66
front 234
in advance 280
important 642
reputed 873
forenoon 125
forensic 968
foreordain 152
foreordination 601, 611
fore part 234
forerun 62, 116, 280
forerunner 64, 512
foresee 507, 510
foreseen 871
foreshadow 152, 511
foreshorten 201
foreshow 511
foresight 116, **510**
caution 864
forest 367
forestage 599
forestall
prior 116
early 132
possession **777**
forestry 371
foretaste 510
foretell 511
forethought 459, 510
foretoken 511
forewarn 511, 668
foreword 64
forfeit *fail* 773
lose 776
penalty 974
– one's good opinion 932
forfeiture
disfranchisement 925
forfend 706, 717
forgather 72
forge *imitate* 19
produce 161
furnace 386
trump up 544
workshop 691
– fetters 751
forged
false 546
forger
maker 690
thief 792
forgery
deception 545
forget 506
hand – cunning 699
– benefits 917
– injury 918
– oneself 945
forgive **918**
forgo
relinquish 624
renounce 757
surrender 782
forgotten
past 122
ingratitude 917
not to be – 505
– by the world 893
fork *bifid* 91
pointed 244
– lightning 423
– out
give 784
pay 807
expenditure 809
forlorn
dejected 837
hopeless 859
deserted 893
– hope
danger 665
rashness 863
form *state* 7
likeness 21
make up 54
order 58
arrange 60
convert 144
produce 161
bench 215
shape **240**
educate 537
pupils 541
manner 627
beauty 845
fashion 852
etiquette 882
law 963
rite 998
– letter 592
– part of 56
– a party 712
– a resolution 604
formal [*see* form]
regular 82
definitive 535
- *style* 579
affected 855
stately 882
– speech 582
formalism 739, 988
formalist 82
formality [*see* formal]
ceremony 852
affectation 855
law 963
formation
composition 54
production 161
shape 240
formative 153
formed [*see* form]
attempered 820
former
in order 62
prior in time 116
past 122
formication 380
formidable 704, 860
formless 241
formula *rule* 80
arithmetic 84
maxim 496
precept 697
law 963
formulary 998
formulate 590
fornication 961
fornicator 962
foro conscientiæ
veracity 543
duty 926
probity 939
forsake 624
forsaken 898
forsooth 535
forspent 688
forswear *lie* 544
tergiversation 607
refuse 764
transgress 927
improbity 940
fort 666, 717
fort
le droit du plus –
compulsion 744
illegality 964
un peu – 641
fortalice 717
forte 415, 698
fortelage 717
forth 282
come –
egress 295
visible 446
go – *depart* 293

the decree has gone – 741
forthcoming 152, 673
forthwith 132
fortification 717
fortify 159
fortiori, a – 467, 476
fortissimo 404
fortiter in re 171
fortitude 826, 861
fortnightly 138
fortress 717, 752
fortuitous
extrinsic 6
chance 156
undesigned 621
– concourse of atoms 59
fortunate
opportune 134
successful 731
prosperous 734
Fortunatus's – cap
wish 865
spell 993
– purse 803
fortune *chance* 156
fate 601
wealth 803
be one's – 151
clean up a – 803
evil – 621, 735
good – 734
make one's –
succeed 731
wealth 803
tempt –
hazard 621
essay 675
trick of – 509
try one's – 675
wheel of – 601, 621
fortune-hunter 886, 943
fortuneless 804
fortune-teller 513
fortune-telling 511
fortunes of
narrative 594
forty 98
– winks 683
forum 799
school 542
tribunal 966
forward *early* 132
transmit 270
advance 282
willing 602
improve 658
active 682
help 707
vain 880
insolent 885
uncourteous 895
bend – 234
come –
in sight 446
offer 763
display 882
look – to 507
move – 282
press – *haste* 684
put – *aid* 507
offer 763
put oneself – 880
set – 676
– in *knowledge* 490
foss 348
fosse
inclosure 232
ditch 259
defence 717
fossil
ancient 124
hard 323
organic 357
dry bones 362
foster *aid* 707
excite 824
caress 902
– a belief 484
fou 959
foudroyant 870
foul
collide 276
bad 649
dirty 653
unhealthy 657
ugly 846
base 940
vicious 945
fall – of
oppose 708
quarrel 713
attack 716
fight 720
censure 932
run – of
impede 706
– fiend 978
– means 940
– language
malediction 908
– odour 401
– play *evil* 619
cunning 702
wrong 923
improbity 940
foul-mouthed 895
foul-spoken 934
found 153, 215
foundation
beginning 66
stability 150
base 211
support 215
lay the –s 673
sandy – 667
shake to its –s 315
founded
well – 472
– on *base* 211
evidence 467
founder
originator 164
sink 310
fail 732
religious –s 986
foundery 691
founding 22
foundling
trover 775
derelict 782
outcast 893
fount *type* 591
fountain
source 153
river 348
store 636
– head 210
– pen 590
four 95
on all –s 13, 23
horizontal 213
easy 705
prosperous 734
humble 879
– in hand 272
– score &c. 98
– square 244
– times 96
from the – winds 278
fourflusher 884
fourfold 96
four-oar 273
four-poster 215
fourth 96, 97
musical 413
– estate 531
four-wheeler 272
fowl 366
fowling-piece 727
fox *animal* 366
cunning 702
– chase 622
fox-trot 840
foxy *colour* 433, 434
cunning 702
foyer 191, 599
fracas
disorder 59
noise 404
discord 713
contention 720
fraction *part* 51
numerical 84
less than one **100a**
fractious 901
fracture
disjunction 44
discontinuity 70
fissure 198
fragile 160, 328
fragment
small 32, 193
part 51, 100*a*
fragrance 400
fragrant weed 392
frail *weak* 160
brittle 328
feeble 575
irresolute 605
imperfect 651
failing 945
impure 961
– sisterhood 962
frais, à grands – 481
frame
condition 7
make 161
support 215
border 231
form 240
substance 316
structure 329
contrive 626
cucumber – 371
have –d and glazed 822
– of mind
inclination 602
disposition 820
frame-up 626
framework
support 215
structure 329
franchise
voting 609
freedom 748
right 924
exemption 927*a*
Franciscan 996
franc-tireur 726
frangible 160, 328
frank *open* 525
sincere 543
artless 703
honourable 939
frankalmoigne 748
Frankenstein 913, 980

frankincense 400
frantic
violent 173
delirious 503
excited 824
fraternal
brother 11
concord 714
friendly 888
fraternity
[*see* fraternal]
party 712
fraternize
co-operate 48, 709
agree 714
sympathize 888
associate 892
fratricide 361
Frau 374
fraud
falsehood 544
deception 545
pretender 548
dishonour 940
pious – 988
fraught *full* 52
pregnant 161
possessing 777
– with danger 665
fray *rub* 331
battle 720
in the thick of the – 722
frayed 659
frazzle
beaten to a – 732
freak 608, 872
– of Nature 83
freckle 848
freckled 440
fredaine 840
free
detached 44
unconditional 52
liberate 672
unobstructed 705
at liberty 748, 750
gratis 815
liberal 816
insolent 885
exempt 927a
impure 961
– balloon 273
– and easy
cheerful 836
adventurous 863
vain 880
insolent 885
friendly 888
sociable 892
– fight 720
– from
simple 42
never – from 613
– gift 784
– from imperfection 650
– lance 726
– land 748
– liver 954a
– love 961
make – of 748
– play 170, 748
– quarters
cheap 815
hospitality 892
– space 180
– stage 748
– trade
commerce 794
– translation 522
– will 600
make – with
frank 703
take 789
sociable 892
uncourteous 895
freebooter 792
freeborn 748
freedman 748
freedom **748**
free-handed 816
freehold 780
freely
willingly 602
freeman 748
freemasonry
unintelligible 519
secret 528
sign 550
co-operation 709
party 712
free-spoken 703
freethinker 989
freeze
benumb 381
cold 385
– the blood 830
freezing 383
– mixture 387
freight *lade* 184
cargo 190
transfer 270
freightage 812
freighter 273
freight train 272
French
peddler's – 563
– and English 840
– horn 417
– leave *avoid* 623
freedom 748
– polish 847
frenetic 503
frenzy
madness 503
imagination 515
excitement 825
frequency **136**
frequent
in number 104
in time 136
in space 186
habitual 613
visit 892
fresco *cold* 383
painting 556
al –
out of doors 220
in the air 338
fresh *additional* 37
new 123
flood 348
cold 383
colour 428
remembered 505
unaccustomed 614
good 648
healthy 654
impertinent 885
tipsy 959
– breeze 349
– colour 434
– news 532
freshen 658, 689
freshet 348
freshman 541
freshwater 851
freshwater sailor 701
fret *suffer* 378
grieve 828
gall 830
discontent 832
sad 837
ornament 847
irritate 900
– and fume 828
fretful 901
fret-work 219
friable 328, 330
friandise 868
friar 996
–'s lantern 423
– Rush 980
Black –*s* 996
friary 1000
fribble
slur over 460
trifle 643
dawdle 683
fop 854
fricassee 298
frication 331
friction *force* **157**
obstacle 179
rubbing **331**
on – wheels 705
friend 711, **890**
candid – 936
next – 759
friendless 893
friendly 714, 894
friends, be – 888
see one's – 892
friendship 9, **888**
frieze 210
frigate 726
fright
cards 840
alarm 860
frightful 31, 830, 846
frightfully 31
frightfulness 860
frigid
cold 383
- style 575
callous 823
indifferent 866
frigidarium 387
frigorific 385
frill 231, 248
frills and furbelows 847
fringe
border 231
lace 256
exaggeration 549
ornament 847
frippery
trifle 643
ornament 847
finery 851
ridiculous 853
ostentation 882
frisk *prance* 266
leap 309
search 461
gay 836
amusement 840
frisky 682, 836
frith *chasm* 198
strait 343
forest 367
fritinancy 412
fritter *small* 32
– away *lessen* 36
waste 638
– away time 683
fritters 298
frivolous
unreasonable 477
foolish 499

capricious 608
trivial 643
frizz *curve* 245, 248
fold 258
frock *dress* 225
canonicals 999
– coat 225
frog *fastening* 45
leaper 309
ornament 847
frolic 827, 840
frolicsome 836
from *motive* 615
– this cause 155
– day to day 106, 138
– end to end 52
– that time 117
– time immemorial 122
– time to time 136
frond 367
fronder
censure 932
frondeur
disobey 742
front *foremost* 66
wig 225
fore part **234**
resist 719
insolence 885
bring to the –
manifest 525
come to the –
surpass 303
important 642
repute 873
in – 280
present a – 719
– danger 861
– to front 708
– of the house 599
– rank 234
in the – rank
important 642
repute 873
frontage 234
frontal 220
fronti nulla fides
doubt 485
deception 545
frontier 199, 233
fronting 237
frontispiece 64
frost 383
frosted 430
– glass 427
frostbite 383
froth
bubble **353**
trifle 643
dirt 653
– up *angry* 900
frothy 320, 353
– *style* 573, 577
irresolute 605
frounce 258
frouzy 401
froward 901*a*
frown *lower* 837
scowl 839
discourteous 895
angry 900
sulky 901*a*
disapprove 932
– down
abash 879
–s of fortune 735
frozen 383, 385
fructify
produce 161
be productive 168
improve 658
prosper 734
frugal 817, 953
– to excess 819
fruges consumere natus *drone* 683
peasant 876
frugivorus 298
fruit *result* 154
produce 161
food 298
profit 775
forbidden – 615
reap the –s
succeed 731
reward 973
– tree 367
fruitful 168
fruition 161, 827
fruitless
unproductive 169
useless 645
failure 732
frump 851, 895
frumpish 901*a*
frustrate 179, 706
frustrated 732
frustum 51
fry *shoal* 102
child 129
heat 384
small –
unimportant 643
commonalty 876
frying-pan 386
out of – into fire
worse 659
clumsy 699
failure 732
misfortune 735
aggravation 835
fuddled 959
fudge 517, 643
fuel **388**, 638
add – to the flame 835
– oil 388
increase 35
heat 384
aggravate 835
anger 900
fugaces labuntur anni 111
fugacious 111
fugitive
transient 111
emigrant 268
avoiding 623
– writings 596
fugleman
pattern 22
director 694
fugue 415
fulciment 215
fulcrum 215
fulfil
complete 729
– a duty 926
– an obligation 772
fulgent 420
fuliginous
dim 422
opaque 426
black 431
full *much* 31
complete 52
large 192
loud 404
abundant 639
cleanse 652
hands –
active 682
receipt in – 807
– blooded 641
– bloom 131
health 654
beauty 845
– blown 131
expanded 194
glorious 873
– of business 682
– coloured 428
– cry *loud* 404
bark 412
pursuit 622
– dinner pail 734
dress 225
ornament 847
fashion 852
show 882
– drive 274
– feather
prepared 673
– force 159
– gallop 274
– heart 820
– of incident 151
– many 102
– of meaning 516
– measure 639
– of people 186
– play
facility 705
freedom 748
– of point 842
– scope 748
– score 415
– size 912
– of sound and fury &c.
unmeaning 517
– speech 274
– stop
cease 142
rest 265
– swing
strong 159
active 682
successful 731
free 748
– as a tick 52
– tide 348
– tilt *active* 682
haste 684
– view 446
– of whims 608
full-fashioned 240
full-fed 954
full-flavoured 392
full-grown 131, 192
full-handed 816, 818
full-length 556
full-mouthed 412
full-toned 413
fully 31
fulminate
violent 173
propel 284
loud 404
malediction 908
threat 909
– against
accuse 932
fulness
[see full]
in the – of time 109
fulsome
nauseous **395**

fetid 401
bad 649
abhorrent 867
adulatory 933
impure 961
fulvid 436
fulvous 436
fumble
derange 61
handle 379
grope 463
awkward 699
fumbler 701
fume
violent 173
exhalation 334, 336
froth 353
heat 382
odour 398
excitement 824, 825
anger 900
in a –
discontented 832
–s of fancy 515
fumid 426
fumigate
vaporize 336
cleanse 652
fumigator 388
fumo, dare pondus – 481
fun 827, 840, 842
make – of 856
funambulist 700
function
algebra 84
office 170
business 625
utility 644
pomp 882
rite 998
duty 926
functionary
director 694
consignee 758
functus officio 756
fund *store* 636
sinking – 802
fundamental
intrinsic 5
base 211
support 215
– bass 413
– note 413
fundamentally 31
funds 800
in – 803
public – 802
funebrial 363
funeral 363
– pace 275
– march 415
funereal
interment 363
dismal 837
fungiform 249
fungology 369
fungosity 250
fungus
projection 250
vegetable 367
fœtor 401
bane 663
funicle 205
funicular 627
funk 860, 862
– hole 530
funnel *opening* 260
conduit 350
air-pipe 351
funnel-shaped 252
funny *odd* 83
boat 273
humorous 842
comic 853
fur *covering* 223
hair 256
warm 384
dirt 653
furacious 791
furbelow 231
furbish
improve 658
prepare 673
adorn 847
furcated 244
furcation 91
furcular 244
furfur 653
furfuraceous 330
Furies *anger* 900
evil-doers 913
demons 980
furious *violent* 173
haste 684
passion 825
anger 900
furiously 31
furl 312
furlong 200
furlough 760
furnace 386
workshop 691
like a – *hot* 382
sighing like –
lament 839
in love 902
furnish
provide 637
prepare 673
give 784
– aid 707
– a handle 617
– its quota 784
furniture 633
– van 272
furor
insanity 503
passion 825
furore
emotion 820, 821
passion 825
desire 865
furrow 259
further
added 37
distant 196
aid 707
go – and fare worse
worse 659
bungle 699
not let it go – 528
furthermore 37
furtive
clandestine 528
stealing 791
furuncle 250
fury *violence* 173
excitation 825
anger 900
demon 980
furze 367
fuscous 433
fuse *join* 43
combine 48
heat 382, 384
torch 388
fuselage 215
fusel oil 356
fusiform 244, 253
fusil 727
fusileer 726
fusillade 361, 716
fusion *union* 48
heat 384
co-operation 709
fuss *agitation* 315
activity 682
haste 684
difficulty 704
excitement 825
ostentation 882
kick up a – 173
make a – about
importance 642
lament 839
disapprove 932
fussy *crotchety* 481
bustling 682
excitable 825
fustian
absurd 497
unmeaning 517
- *style* 577, 579
fustigate 972
fusty 124, 401, 653
futhorc 590
futile 497, 645
future 121
eye to the – 510
– possession 777
– state
destiny 152
heaven 981
futurity 121
fuzzle 959
fuzzy 447

G

gab 584
gift of the – 582
gabardine 225
gabble 517, 583
gabelle 812
gaberlunzie 876
gabion 717
gable *side* 236
– end 67
Gabriel 977
gaby 501
gad
about 266, 268
gadget 626
gad-so 870
gaff 727
gaffer *old* 130
man 373
clown 876
gag
closure 261
render mute 403, 581
dramatic 599
muzzle 751
imprison 752
gage *measure* 466
security 771
throw down the – 715
gaggle 412
gag-man 844
gaieté de cœur 836
gaiety
[see gay] 836
gaillard 844
gain
increase 35
advantage 618
skilful 698

acquisition 775
- the confidence of 484
- credit 931
- one's ends 731
- ground
progress 282
improve 658
- head 175
- laurels 873
- learning 539
- over 615
- a point 731
- private ends 943
- the start
priority 116
early 132
- strength 35
- time
protract 110
early 132
late 133
- upon
approach 286
pass 303
become a habit 613
- a victory 731
gainful *useful* 644
gainless 645
gainsay 536
gait 264, 627
gaiter 225
gala 840, 882
galactic circle 318
galantuomo 939
galavant 902
galaxy
assemblage 72
multitude 102
stars 318
luminary 423
glory 873
gale 349
Galen 662
galenicals 662
galimatias 497
galipot 191
galopade 840
galore 639
gall *hurt* 378
bitter 395
annoy 830
anger 900
malevolence 907
dip the pen in - 934
gallant *brave* 861
courteous 894
love 897
licentious 961, 962
gallantry
dalliance 902
gallanty-show 448, 840
galled jade wince, let the - 884
galleon 273
gallery *room* 191
passage 260
auditory 599
museum 636
picture - 556
galley *ship* 273
punishment 972, 975
work like a - slave 686
- proof 591
galliass 273
Gallicism 563
galligaskin 225
gallimaufry 41
galliot 273
gallipot 191
gallivant 902
galloon 847
gallop
pass away 111
ride 266
scamper 274
galloping consumption 655
galloway 271
gallows 361, 975
come to the - 972
galoche 225
galore 102
galvanic
excitable 825
galvanism 157
galvanize 824
gamache 225
Gamaliel
brought up at the feet of - 492
gambade *leap* 309
prank 840
gambado
gaiter 225
leap 309
gambit 66
gamble 156
gambling
chance 621
rashness 863
gambling-house 621
gamboge 436
gambol 309, 827, 840
game *lame* 160
food 298
animal 366
savoury 394
resolute 604
persevering 604*a*
aim 620
gamble 621
pursuit 622
tactics 692
amusement 840
laughing-stock 857
brave 861
make - of
deceive 545
ridicule 856
disrespect 929
play the - 709, 939
- in one's hands
easy 705
succeed 731
command 737
- to the last 604*a*
- at which two can play 718
- up 732
game-cock 726, 861
game-keeper 370, 753
gameness 861
gamesome 836
gamester
chance 621
play 840
rash 863
gamey 392
gamin 876
gaming-house 621
gammer *old* 130
woman 374
gammon 544, 545
gamut 413
gander 373
gang
assemblage 72
go 264
party 712
- agley 732
ganger 690
gangrene 655
gangster 361, 913
gangway 260, 627
gantlet 972
run the -
resolution 604
dare 861
gaol 752
- delivery 672
gaoler 753, 975
gap 70, 198, 252
stand in the - 717
gape *open* 260
curiosity 455
wonder 870
- for *desire* 865
gaping [*see* gape]
expectant 507
gar 161
garage 191
garb 225
under the - of 545
garbage 653
garble
take from 38
exclude 55
erroneous 495
misinterpret 523
falsify 544
- accounts 811
garbled
incomplete 53
garden *grounds* 189
horticulture 371
beautiful 845
botanic - 371
zoological - 370
- party 840
gardener 371
gardens *street* 189
Gargantua 192
gargle 337
gargoyle 350
garish
light 420
colour 428
ugly 846
ornament 847
vulgar 851
display 882
garland
circle 247
sign 550
trophy 733
ornament 847
decoration 877
garlic
condiment 393
fetid 401
garment 225
garner 636
garnet 847
red 434
garnish
addition 39
prepare 673
fee 809
ornament 847
garniture 225
garran 271
garret 191, 210
garrison

occupant 188
safety 664
defence 717
soldiers 726
garrotte
render powerless 158
kill 361
punishment 972
garrulity 584
garter
fastening 45
decoration 877
– blue 438
garth 181
gas 334
talk 482
fuel 388
boasting 884
– balloon 273
– stove 386
– bomb 727
– fitter 690
– mask 717
– projector 727
gasconade 884
gaseity 334
gaselier 214
gash *cut* 44
interval 198
wound 619
gasification 334, 336
gaskins 225
gas-light 423
gasoline 388
gasometer 636
gasp *blow* 349
droop 655
fatigue 688
at the last – 360
– for *desire* 865
gasper 392
gastriloquism 580
Gastromancy 511
gastronomy 298, 957
gate *beginning* 66
inclosure 232
mouth 260
barrier 706
water – 350
-way *way* 627
– keeper 263
gâté, enfant – 734
Gath, tell it not in –
conceal 528
disapprove 932
gather *collect* 72
expand 194
fold 258
conclude 480
acquire 775
take 789
– breath 689
– flesh 194
– from one
information 527
– fruits 731
gathered
– to one's fathers 360
gathering
assemblage 72
abscess 655
– clouds *dark* 421
shade 424
omen 512
danger 665
warning 668
adversity 735
gathering-place 74
gauche *clumsy* 699
gaucherie 699, 851
gaud 847
gaudery 880
gaudy *colour* 428
vulgar 851
showy 882
gauge 466
rain– 348
wind– 349
gauger 965
gaunt *bulky* 192
lean 203
ugly 846
gauntlet *glove* 225
armour 717
fling down 715
run the – 665, 972
take up the – 720
gauntry 627
Gautama 986
gauze *shade* 424
semitransparent 427
gavel 72, 812
gavelkind 778
gavelock 633
gavot 840
gawky
awkward 699
ugly 846
(*ridiculous* 853)
gay *colour* 428
cheerful 836
adorned 847
showy 882
dissipated 961
– deceiver 962
– world 852
gaze 441
gazebo 441
gazelle *swift* 274
gazette
publication 531
record 551
in the –
bankrupt 808
gazetteer
list 86
information 527
record 551
gazing-stock
ridiculous 857
wondrous 872
géant, à pas de – 274
gear *clothes* 225
harness 633
high – 274
in – 673
low – 275
out of –
disjoin 44
derange 61
useless 645
unprepared 674
– wheel 633
geese are swans, all his – 482
gehenna 982
geisha 599
Geist 498
gel 352
gelatin 352
gelatinify 352
geld 38, 158
gelding 271, 373
gelid 383
Geloscopy 511
gem 648, 847
geminate 90
Gemini *twins* 89
O – ! 870
gemote 72
gendarme 726, 965
gender 75
genealogy 69, 166
general
generic 78
habitual 613
officer 745
the –
commonalty 876
things in – 151
– breaking up 655
– favourite 899
– information 490
– meaning 516
– public 372
– run 613
– servant 690, 746
generalissimo 745
generality
mean 29
universal 78
generalize 476
generally speaking 613
generalship 692, 722
generate 161, 168
generation
consanguinity 11
period 108
production 161
mankind 372
rising – 167
spontaneous – 161
wise in one's – 498
generator 164
generic 78
generosity
giving 784
liberality 816
benevolence 906
disinterestedness 942
genesis
beginning 66
production 161
genet 271
Genethliacs 511
genetic 161
Geneva gown 999
genial
productive 161
sensuous 377
warm 382
willing 602
delightful 829
affable 894
geniality 836
geniculated 244
genie 980
genital 161
genitor 166
geniture 161
genius
intellect 450
talent 498
skill 698
proficient 700
prodigy 872
evil – 980
good –
friend 898
benefactor 912
spirit 979
tutelary – 711
– for 698
– of a language 560

- loci 664
genre 556, 559
gent 851, 876
genteel 852, 875
- comedy 599
gentile 984, 989
gentility
fashion 852
rank 875
politeness 894
gentium, jus - 963
gentle *moderate* 174
slow 275
domesticated 370
faint sound 405
lenient 740
meek 826
courteous 894
- blood 875
- breeding 894
- hint 527
- as a lamb 174
- slope 217
gentlefolk 875
gentleman
male 373
squire 875
man of honour 939
the old - 978
walking - 599
gentlemanly 852
gently bred 894
Gentoo 984
gentry 875
landed - 779
genuflexion
bowing 308
submission 725
servility 886
courtesy 894
respect 928
worship 990, 998
genuine 494, 648
genus 75, 901
- irritabile vatum 597
geodesist 85, 318
geodesy 318, 466
geography 183, 318
geoid 249
geology &c. 358
geomancer 513
geomancy 511
geometry 466
geoponics 371
georama 448
Georgics 371
geotic 318
gerfalcon 913
germ 153
german 11
- band 417
- silver 545
germane 23
germicide 662
germinal 153
germinate 161, 194, 365
- from 154
gerontic 128
gerrymander 545
gesso 556
gest 680
gestation
propagation 161
carriage 270
maturation 673
gesticulate 550
gesture *hint* 527
indication 550
get *become* 144
beget 161
acquire 775
receive 810
- ahead 35
- ahead of 33
- along 282
- along with you
ejection 297
dismissal 756
- at 480*a*
- away 287
- back
retire 283
regain 775
- the best of 731
- better 658
- down
swallow 298
descend 306
- you gone 297
- into harness 673
- by heart 505
- home 292
- in *collect* 72
gather 775
- loose 44
- near 286
- off *depart* 293
escape 671
- on *advance* 282
prosper 734
- out *eject* 297
extract 301
publish 531
- over
recover from 660
succeed 731
be content 831
- over the ground 274
- for one s pains 973
- ready 673
- rid of 672
- a sight of 441, 490
- through
end 67
transact 692
complete 729
expend 809
- to
extend to 196
arrive 292
- together 72
- into trouble 732
- the wind up 860
- up *produce* 161
ascend 305
raise 307
learn 539
fabricate 544
prepare 673
rise early 682
foment 824
- into the way of 613
get-away 671
gewgaw
trifle 643
ornament 847
vulgar 851
geyser 382, 386
ghastly
pale 429
hideous 846
frightful 860
ghaut 203
ghetto 189
ghost *shade* 362
fallacy of vision 443
soul 450
writer 593
apparition 980
give up the - 360
needs no - to tell us 525
pale as a -
colourless 429
fear 860
- dance 992
ghost-like
ugly 846
ghostly
intellectual 450
supernatural 976, 980
Ghost, Holy - 976
ghoul 913, 980
ghyll 348
giant
large 192
tall 206
- refreshed
strong 159
refreshed 689
-'s strides
distance 196
swift 294
giaour 984, 989
gibber 583
gibberish 517, 563
gibbet
brand 932
execute 972
gallows 975
gibble-gabble 584
gibbous 249, 250
gib-cat *male* 373
gibe 929
giblets 298
gibus 225
giddy
inattentive 458
vertiginous 503
irresolute 605
capricious 608
bungling 699
giddy-head 501
giddy-paced 315
gift *power* 157
talent 698
given 784
- of the gab 582
look a - horse in the mouth
fastidious 868
ungrateful 917
gifted 698
gig 272, 273
gigantic
strong 159
large 192
tall 206
giggle 838
giglamps 445
Gilbertian 842
Gilbertine 996
gild *coat* 223
colour 439
ornament 847
- refined gold 641
- the pill
deceive 545
tempt 615
please 829
flatter 933
Gilead, balm in - 834, 858
Giles's Greek, St. - 563

gill 348
gillie 746
gilt 436, 847
 – edged 648
gimbals 312
gimcrack
 weak 160
 brittle 328
 trifling 643
 ornament 847
 ridiculous 853
gimlet 262
gimp
 clean 652
 pretty 845
 decoration 847
gin *trap* 545
 instrument 633
 intoxicating 959
 demon 980
gin mill 189
gin palace 189
gingerbread
 weak 160
 vulgar 851
gingerly 174, 459, 864
gingle 408
gipsy
 wanderer 268
 wag 844
 – lingo 563
giraffe 206
girandole 423
girasol 847
gird *bind* 43
 strengthen 159
 surround 227
 jeer 929
 – up one's loins
 brace 159
 prepare 673
girder 45, 215
girdle *bond* 45
 encircle 227
 circumference 230
 circle 247
 put a – round the earth 311
girl 129, 374
girlhood 127
girt 45
girth
 bond 45
 circumference 230
gisarm 727
gist *essence* 5
 meaning 516
 important 642
gît, ci – 363
gittern 417
give *yield* 324
 melt 382
 bestow 784
 discount 813
 – away 782, 784
 in marriage 903
 – back 790
 – birth to 161
 – with both hands 816
 – in charge
 restrain 751
 – chase 622
 – consent 762
 – one credit for 484
 – in custody 751
 – expression to 566
 – forth 531
 – the go by 623
 – a horse his head 748
 – in *submit* 725
 – into *consent* 762
 – light 420
 – the mind to 457
 – notice
 inform 527
 warn 668
 – it one
 censure 932
 punish 972
 – out *emit* 297
 publish 531
 bestow 784
 – over *cease* 142
 relinquish 624
 lose hope 859
 – place to
 substitute 147
 avoid 623
 – play to the imagination 515
 – points to 27
 – quarter 740
 – rise to 153
 – one the slip 671
 – security 771
 – and take
 reciprocate 12
 compensation 30
 interchange 148
 retaliation 718
 compromise 774
 barter 794
 equity 922
 honour 939
 – tongue 531
 – a turn to 140
 – one to understand 527
 – up
 not understand 519
 unwilling 603
 reject 610
 relinquish 624
 submit 725
 resign 757
 surrender 782
 restore 790
 hopeless 859
 – up the ghost 360
 – way *weak* 160
 brittle 328
 submit 725
 pine 828
 despond 837
 modest 881
given [*see* give]
 circumstances 8
 supposition 514
 received 785
 – over *dying* 360
 – time 134
 – to 613
giving 784
gizzard 191
 stick in one's – 900
glabrous 255
glacial 383
glaciate 385
glacier 383
glacis 217, 717
glad 827, 829
 give the – eye 441
 would be – of 865
 – tidings 532
gladden 834, 836
glade *hollow* 252
 opening 260
 shade 424
gladiator 726
gladiatorial 361, 713, 720
gladsome 827, 829
Gladstone bag 191
glair 352
glaive 727
glamour 992
glance *look* 441
 sign 550
 see at a – 498
 – at
 take notice of 457
 allude to 527
 censure 932
 – off *deviate* 279
 diverge 291
gland 221
glare *light* 420
 stare 441
 imperfect vision 443
 visible 446
glaring
 [*see* glare]
 great 31
 colour 428
 visible 446
 manifest 525
glass *vessel* 191
 smooth 255
 brittle 328
 transparent 425
 lens 445
 musical –es 417
 see through a – darkly 491
 – of fashion 852
 live in a – house
 brittle 328
 visible 446
 danger 665
 – too much 959
glass-coach 272
glasshouse 191, 371
Glassite 984
glassy [*see* glass]
 shining 420
 colourless 429
glaucous 435
glave 727
glaver 933
glaze 255
gleam *small* 32
 light 420
glean 609, 775
gleanings 636
glebe *land* 342
 ecclesiastical 995
 church 1000
glee *music* 415
 satisfaction 827
 merriment 836
gleek 929
glen 252
glengarry 225
glib *voluble* 584
 facile 705
glide *lapse* 109
 move 264
 travel 266
 fly 267
 – into
 conversion 144
glider 273
glimmer
 light 420
 dim 422
 visible 446

slight knowledge 490, 491
glimpse 441, 490
glint 420
glissade 306
glisten 420
glitter
shine 420
appear 446
illustrious 882
glittering
ornament 847
display 882
gloam 901*a*
gloaming 126, 422
gloar *look* 441
wonder 870
gloat 884
- on *look* 441
- over 441
pleasure 377
delight 827
globated 249
globe
sphere 249
world 318
on the face of the - 318
- trotter 268
globule 32, 249
glomeration 72
gloom 421, 837
gloomy horizon 859
glorification 884
glorify
honour 873
approve 931
worship 990
glorious
illustrious 873
tipsy 959
glory
light 420
honour 873
heaven 981
King of - 976
- in 878, 884
- be to God 990
gloss *smooth* 255
sheen 420
interpretation 522
falsehood 546
plea 617
beauty 845
- of novelty 123
- over
neglect 460
sophistry 477
falsehood 544
vindicate 937
glossary 86, 562
glossographer 492
glossologist 492
glossology 560, 562
glossy [*see* gloss]
glottology 560
glout 901*a*
glove 225
take up the - 720
throw down the - 715
glow *warm* 382
shine 420
appear 446
colour 428
style 574
passion 821
glower
glare 443
discourteous 895
sullen 901*a*
glowing
[*see* glow]
orange 439
excited 824
beautiful 845
- terms 574
glow-worm 423
gloze 933, 937
glucose 396
glue *cement* 45
cementing 46
semiliquid 352
glum
discontented 832
dejected 837
sulky 901*a*
glut
redundance 641
satiety 869
gluttony 957
glutinous 352
glutton 954*a*, 957
gluttony 957
glycerine 332, 356
glyphography 558
glyptography 558
glyptotheca 557
gnarl *protuberance* 250
anger 900
threat 909
gnarled 256, 321
gnash one's teeth 839, 900
gnat *little* 193
strain at a - &c.
caprice 608
gnaw *eat* 298
rub 331
injure 659
gnawing
- grief 828, 830
- pain 378
gnome 496, 980
gnomic 496
gnomon 114
Gnostic 984
go
cease to exist 2
energy 171, 682
move 264
recede 287
depart 293
fade 429
disappear 449
fashion 852
come and - 314
as things - 613
- about
turn round 311
published 531
undertake 676
- across 302
- after
in time 117
in motion 281
- ahead
energetic 171
precede 280
advance 282
active 682
- against 708
- astray 495
- away 293
- back 283, 624
- bad 659
- bail 771
- before 280
- between
interjacent 228
instrumental 631
mediate 631, 724
- beyond 303
- by the board 158
- about your business
ejection 297
dismissal 756
- by
conform to 82
elapse 109
past 122
outrun 303
subterfuge 702
give the - by to
neglect 460
deceive 545
avoid 623
not observe 773
- by the name of 564
- deep into 461
- down *sink* 306
decline 659
- down with
believed 484
tolerated 826
content 831
- farther and fare worse 659
- forth *depart* 293
publish 531
- halves 91
- hand in hand
accompany 88
same time 120
- hard 704
- on ill 735
- in 294
- in for
resolution 604
pursuit 622
- into
ingress 294
inquire 461
dissert 595
- all lengths
complete 52
resolve 604
exertion 686
- mad 503
- near 286
- no further
keep secret 528
- for nothing
sophistry 477
unimportant 643
- off *explode* 173
depart 293
die 360
wither 659
marry 903
- on *time* 106
continue 143
advance 282
- on for ever 112
- one better 303
- out
cease 142
egress 295
extinct 385
- out of one's head 506
- over
passage 302
explore 461
apostate 607
faithless 940
- to pieces 162
- on record 551
- round 311
- shares 778

– to sleep 683
– through
meet with 151
pass 302
explore 461
perform 599
conduct 692
complete 729
endure 826
– to *extend* 196
travel 266
direction 278
remonstrance 695
– up 305
– to war 722
– with
assent 488
concord 714
– with the stream
conform 82
servile 886
– from one's word 773
goad 615
hasten 684
goal *end* 67
reach 292
object 620
reach the –
complete 729
goat *substitute* 147
jumper 309
lecher 962
he – *male* 373
play the – 499
gob 269
gobang 840
gobbet
small piece 32
food 298
gobble *cry* 412
gormandize 957
eat 298
gobemouche 501, 547
go-between 758
goblet 191
goblin 980
go-cart 272
GOD 976
house of – 1000
kingdom of – 981
sons of – 977
–'s acre 363
– bless me! 870
– bless you
farewell 293
– forbid 766
–'s grace 906
– grant 990
– knows 491
–'s love 906
for –'s sake 765
–'s will 601
– willing 470
god 979
household –s 189
tutelary – 664
goddess *love* 897
good woman 948
heathen 979
Godhead 976
godlike 944
godly 987
godsend *good* 618
prosperity 734
Godspeed
farewell 293
hope 858
courtesy 894
benevolence 906
approbation 931
goer *horse* 271
goes [*see* go]
as one – 270
here – 676
Gog and Magog 192
goggle 441
– eyes 443
goggles 445
going [*see* go]
general 78
rumour 532
– to happen 152
– on
incomplete 53, 730
current 151
transacting 625
goitre 250
Golconda 803
gold *yellow* 436
orange 439
money 800
write in letters of – 642
worth its weight in – 648
gold certificate 800
golden [*see* gold]
– age
prosperity 734
pleasure 827
– apple 615
– calf
wealth 803
idol 986
idolatry 991
– dream
imagination 515
hope 858
– mean
moderation 174
mid-course 628
– opinions 931
– opportunity 134
– rule
precept 697
– season of life 127
– wedding 883
golf 840
Golgotha 363, 1000
Goliath 159, 192
goloshes 225
gondola 273
gondolier 269
gone [*see* go]
past 122
absent 187
dead 360
– bad 653
– by 122
antiquated 124
– out of one's recollection 506
gonfalon 550
gong 417
goniometer 244, 466
good
complete 52
palatable 394
assent 488
benefit 618
beneficial 648
right 922
virtuous 944
pious 987
as – as 197
be so – as 765
do – 906
for –
diuturnal 110
permanent 141
make –
evidence 467
provide 637
restore 660
complete 729
substantiate 924
vindicate 937
atone for 952
so far so – 931
think – 931
to the – 780
turn to – account 731
what's the – 645
– actions 944
– at 698
– auspices 858
– behaviour
contingent 108a
duty 926
virtue 944
in one's – books 888
– bye 293
in – case 192
– chance 472
– cheer *food* 298
cheerful 826
– circumstances 803
– condition 192
– day
arrival 292
departure 293
courtesy 894
– effect
goodness 648
beauty 845
– enough
not perfect 651
be – enough 765
put a – face upon
cheerful 836
proud 878
– fellow 892
– fight *war* 722
virtue 944
– for
useful 644
salubrious 656
– fortune 734
– Friday 998
– genius
friend 890
benefactor 912
god 979
in one's – graces 888
– hand 700
– humour
concord 714
cheerfulness 836
amuse 840
courtesy 894
kindly 906
– intention 906
– judgment 498
– lack! 870
– living
food 298
gluttony 957
– look-out 459
– looks 845
– luck 734
– man *man* 373
husband 903
worthy 948
– manners 894
much – may it do

906
– morrow 292
– name 873
– nature 906
– night 293
– for nothing
impotence 158
useless 645
in – odour
repute 873
approbation 931
– offices
mediation 724
kind 906
– old time 122
– omen 858
– opinion 931
take in – part
pleased 827
courteous 894
kind 906
– pennyworth 815
– at the price 815
to – purpose 731
– repute 873
– sense 498
– society 852
– taste 578, 850
– temper 894
– thing 648
– time *early* 132
opportune 134
prosperous 734
– turn
kindness 906
– understanding 714
– wife
woman 374
spouse 903
– will
willingness 602
benevolence 906
– word
approval 931
vindication 937
– as one's word
veracity 543
observance 772
probity 939
– works 906
goodie 652, 746
goodly
great 31
large 192
handsome 845
good mixer 892
goodness
[*see* good] **648**
virtue 944
have the –
request 765
– gracious! 870
– of heart 906
goods *effects* 270, 780
merchandise 798
good taste 868
Goodwin sands 667
goody 374, 652, 746
gooroo 996
goose *hiss* 409
game of – 840
giddy as a – 458
tailor's – 255
kill the – with golden eggs 699, 818
a wild – chase 545
gooseberry
old – 978
play – 459
– eyes 441, 443
goosecap 501
goose egg 101
gooseflesh 383
goosequill 590
goose-skin 383
Gordian knot 59, 704
gore *stab* 260
blood 361
gorge *ravine* 198
conduit 350
fill 641
satiety 869
gluttony 957
raise one's – 900
– the hook 602
gorge de pigeon 440
gorgeous
colour 428
beauty 845
ornament 847
ostentation 882
Gorgon 860
gorilla 913
gormandize 298, 954*a*, 957
gorse 367
gory *red* 434
murderous 361
unclean 653
gospel
certainty 474
truth 494
take for – 484
Gospels 985
gossamer
filament 205
light 320
texture 329
gossip *news* 532
babbler 584
conversation 588
gossoon 876
Gotama 986
Goth 851, 876
Gotham, wise men of – 501
gothic
amorphous 241
gouache 556
gouge *concave* 252
perforator 262
goulash 298
gourd 191
gourmand 954*a*, 957
gourmet 868, 954*a*
gout 378
goût, haut – 392
goutte d'eau, il se noyerait dans une – 699
govern 693, 737
governess 540
[*see* govern]
ruling power 745
divine – 976
petticoat – 737
governor
tutor 540
director 694
ruler 745
keeper 753
gowk 501
gown *dress* 225
canonicals 999
gownsman 492
grab *take* 789
miser 819
grabble 379
grace *style* 578
permission 760
concession 784
elegance 845
polish 850
title 877
pity 914
forgiveness 918
honour 939
piety 987
worship 990
act of – 784
God's – 906
with a bad – 603
with a good –
willing 602
courteous 894
in one's good –s 888
heart of – 861
say – 990
submit with a good – 826
– before meat 916
grâce: coup de – 914
la – 840
graceless
inelegant 579
ugly 846
vicious 945
impenitent 951
irreligious 989
Graces 845
gracile 203
gracious
willing 602
courteous 894
kind 906
good – 870
grade *degree* 26
arrange 60
term 71
ascent 217
on the down – 658
on the up – 659
gradatim
gradually 26
in order 58
continuous 69
slow 275
gradation
degree 26
order 58
continuity 69
gradient 217
gradual *degree* 26
continuous 69
slow 275
graduate
adjust 23
calibrate 26
arrange 60
series 69
measure 466
scholar 492, 873
graduated scale 466
gradus 86, 562
Græculus esuriens 886
graft *join* 43
locate 184
insert 300
trees 371
teach 537
booty 794
corruption 940
Grail
holy – 998
grain *essence* 5
small 32

tendency 176
little 193
rough 256
weight 319
texture 329
powder 330
paint 428
temper 820
ornament 847
against the –
rough 256
unwilling 603
opposing 708
in the – 820
–s of allowance
qualification 469
doubt 485
like –s of sand
incoherent 47
gramercy 916
graminivorous 298
grammar
beginning 66
teaching 537
school 542
language **567**
bad – 568
comparative – 560
grammarian 492
gramme 319
gramophone 417, 418, 553
granary 636
grand
great 31
style 574
important 642
money 800
handsome 845
glorious 873
ostentatious 882
– climacteric 128
– doings 882
– duchy 181
– jury 967
en – seigneur
proud 878
insolent 885
en –e tenue
ornament 847
show 882
– piano 417
– style 556
– tour 266
– Turk 745
– vizier 694
grandam 130
grandchildren 167
grandee 875
grande dame 878
grandeur 873
grandfather 130, 166
grandiloquent 577
grandiose 577
grandmother 166
simple 501
teach – 538
grandsire 130, 166
grange 189
granite 323
granivorous 298
grano salis, cum 469, 485
grant *admit* 529
permit 760
consent 762
confer 784
God – 990
– a lease 771
granted 488
take for –
believe 484
suppose 514
grantee
possessor 779
receiver 785
granular 330
granulate 330
granulc 32
grapes, sour –
unattainable 471
falsehood 544
excuse 617
grape-shot
attack 716
arms 727
graph 554
graphic
intelligible 518
painting 556
descriptive 594
graphite 332
graphito 556
graphology 590
graphometer 244
graphotype 558
grapnel 666
grapple
fasten 43
clutch 789
– with
- *a question* 461
- *difficulties* 704
oppose 708
resist 719
contention 720
grappling-iron
fastening 45
safety 666
grasp
comprehend 518
power 737
retain 781
seize 789
in one's – 737
possess 777
tight – *severe* 739
– at 865
– of intellect 498
grasping
miserly 819
covetous 865
grass 344, 367
let the – grow under one's feet
neglect 460
inactive 683
not let the – &c.
active 682
grasshopper 309
grass-plat 371
grate *rub* 330
physical pain **378**
stove 386
– on the ear
harsh sound 410
– on the feelings 830
grated
barred 219
grateful
physically pleasant 377
agreeable 829
thankful 916
grater 260, 330
gratification
animal – 377
moral – 827
gratify 829
permit 760
please 829
grating [*see* grate]
lattice 219
harsh 713
gratis 815
gratitude **916**
gratuitous
inconsequent 477
supposititious 514
voluntary 602
payless 815
gratuity
gift 784
gratis 815
gratulate 896
gravaman 642
– of a charge 938
grave *great* 31
engrave 259, 558
tomb 363
important 642
composed 826
distressing 830
sad 837
heinous 945
beyond the – 360
look –
disapprove 932
rise from the – 660
silent as the – 403
sink into the – 360
on this side of the – 359
– in the memory 505
– note 408
– trap 599
gravel
earth 342
material **635**
puzzle 704
graven image 991
graveolent 398
graver 558
graving dock 189
gravitate
descend 306
weigh 319
– towards 176
gravity *force* **157**
weight **319**
vigour 574
importance 642
sedateness 826
seriousness 837
centre of – 222
specific –
weight 319
density 321
gravy 333
– boat 191
gray **432** [and *see* grey]
graze *touch* 199
browse 298
rub 331
brush 379
grazier 370
gré, savoir – **916**
grease
lubricate 332
oil 356
– the palm
tempt 615
give 784
pay 807
greasy 355
great *much* **31**
big 192
glorious 873
magnanimous

942
(*important* 642)
– bear 318
– circle sailing 628
– coat 225
– doings
importance 642
bustle 682
– folks 875
– gun 626
– hearted 942
– Mogul 745
– number 102
– primer 591
– quantity 31
greater 33
– number 102
– part 31
nearly all 50
greatest 33
greatness **31**
greave 225
greed
desire 865
gluttony 957
greedy
avaricious 819
Greek
unintelligible 519
sharper 792
St. Giles's – 563
– Church 984
– Kalends 107
green
new 123
young 127
lawn 344
grass 367
unripe 397
colour 435
credulous 486
novice 491
unused 614
healthy 654
immature 674
unskilled 699
board of – cloth 966
– memory 505
– old age 128
greenback 800
green-eyed monster 920
greenhorn
novice 493
dupe 547
bungler 701
greenhouse
receptacle 191
horticulture 371
greenness **435**
green-room 599
greensward 344
Greenwich time 114
greenwood 367
greet *weep* 839
hail 894
greeting
sociality 892
–'s! 292
gregarious 892
grenade 727
grenadier
tall 206
soldier 726
grey 432
– beard 130
– friar 996
– hairs 128
bring – hairs to the grave
adversity 735
harass 830
– mare
ruler 737
master 745
wife 903
– matter
brain 498
–hound
swift 274
animal 366
ocean –hound 273
gridelin 437
gridiron
flatness 213
crossing 219
stove 386
stage 599
stadium 840
grief 828
come to – 735
grievance
evil 619
painful 830
wrong 923
grieve *mourn* 828
pain 830
dejected 837
complain 839
grievous 649, 830
grievously 31
griffin 83, 366, 493
griffo 41
griffonage 590
grig *merry* 836
grill 382, 384, 461
– room 189
grille 219
grim
resolved 604
painful 830
doleful 837
ugly 846
discourteous 895
sullen 901*a*
–visaged war 722
grimace 243, 839, 855
grimacier
actor 599
humorist 844
affected 855
grimalkin 366
grime 653
grin *laugh* 838
ridicule 856
– and abide 725
– a ghastly smile
dejected 837
ugly 846
grind
reduce 195
sharpen 253
pulverize 330
pain 378
learn 539
oppress 907
– the organ 416
– one's teeth 900
grinder
teacher 330
noise 404
grinding 739, 830
grindstone 253, 330
grip
indication 550
power 737
retention 781
clutch 789
– of the hand 894
gripe [*see* grip]
pain 378
parsimony 819
grisaille
grey 432
painting 556
grisette
woman 374
commonalty 876
libertine 962
grisly 846
grist
materials 635
provision 637
– to the mill
useful 644
acquire 775
gristle 321, 327
grit
strength 159
powder 330
stamina 604*a*
courage 861
– in the oil
hindrance 706
gritty 323
grizzled
grey 432
variegated 440
groan 411, 839
groat 800
grocer 637
grocery 396
grog 298, 959
groin 244
groom 370, 746
– well
– of the chambers 746
–'s man 903
groove
furrow 259
habit 613
in a – 16
move in a – 82
put in a – for 673
grope
feel 379
experiment 463
try 675
in the dark 442, 704
gross
great 31
whole 50
number 98
ugly 846
vulgar 851
vicious 945
impure 961
– credulity 486
– receipts 810
grosshead 501
grossheaded 499
grossièreté 895
grot [*see* grotto]
grotesque
odd 83
distorted 243
- *style* 579
ridiculous 853
grotto
alcove 191
hollow 252
grouch 895, 901*a*
ground
cause 153
region 181
base 211
lay down 213
support 215
coating 223

land 342
plain 344
evidence 467
teach 537
motive 615
plea 617
above – 359
down to the – 52
dress the – 371
fall to the – 732
get over the – 274
go over the – 302
level with the – 162
maintain one's –
persevere 604*a*
play– 840
prepare the – 673
stand one's –
defend 717
resist 719
– bait 784
– cut from under one 732
– floor
chamber 191
low 207
base 211
– on
attribute 155
– plan 554
– of quarrel 713
– sliding from under one 665
– swell
agitation 315
waves 348
grounded
stranded 732
well– 490
– on *basis* 211
evidence 467
groundless
unsubstantial 4
illogical 477
erroneous 495
groundling 876
grounds
dregs 653
groundwork
precursor 64
cause 153
basis 211
support 215
preparation 673
group
marshal 60
cluster 72
– captain 745
grouping 60
grouse 832, 901*a*

grout 45
grove
street 189
glade 252
wood 367
grovel
below 207
move slowly 275
cringe 886
base 940
grow
increase 35
become 144
expand 194
– from
effect 154
– into 144
– less 195
– taller 206
– together 46
– up 194
– upon one 613
grower 164
growl *cry* 412
complain 839
discourtesy 895
anger 900
threat 909
growler *cab* 272
discontented 832
sulky 901*a*
grown up 131
growth [*see* grow]
development 161
– *in size* 194
tumour 250
vegetation 367
groyne 706
grub
small animal 193
food 298
– up
eradicate 301
discover 480*a*
Grub-street writer 593
grudge
unwilling 603
refuse 764
stingy 819
hate 898
anger 900
bear a – 907
owe a – 898
grudging 603
– praise 932
gruel 298
gruesome 846
gruff
harsh sound 410
discourteous 895

grum
harsh sound 410
morose 901*a*
grumble
cry 411
complain 832, 839
grume 321, 354
grumous 321, 354
grumpy 901*a*
Grundy, Mrs. 852
grunt 412
complain 839
guano 653
guarantee 768, 771
guard
travelling 268
safety 664
defence 717
soldier 726
sentry 753
advanced – 668
mount –
care 459
safety 664
off one's –
inexpectant 508
throw off one's –
cunning 702
on one's –
careful 459
cautious 864
rear – 668
– against
prepare 673
defence 717
– ship 664, 726
guarda costa 753
guarded
conditions 770
guardian
safety 664
defence 717
keeper 753
– angel
helper 711
benefactor 912
guardless 665
guard-room 752
gubernation 693
gubernatorial 737
gudgeon 547
guerdon 973
guernsey 225
guerre:
nom de – 565
– à outrance &c. 722
guerilla 726
– warfare 720
guess 514

guesswork 514
guest 890
paying – 188
guet:
mot de – 550
-à-pens 545
guffaw 838
guggle
gush 348
bubble 353
resound 408
cry 412
guide
pattern 22
courier 524
teach 537
teacher 540
indicate 550
direct 693
director 694
advise 695
guide-book 527
guided by, be – 82
guideless 665
guide-post 550
guiding star 693
guild 712, 966
guildhall 799
guile
deceit 544, 545
cunning 702
guileless 543, 703
guillotine 972, 975
guilt 947
guiltless 946
guilty:
find – 971
plead – 950
guindé 579
guinea 800
guipure 847
guisard 599
guise
state 7
dress 225
appearance 448
plea 617
mode 627
conduct 692
guiser 599
guitar 417
gulch 198
gules 434
gulf
interval 198
deep 208
lake 343
gull 545, 547
gullet *throat* 260
rivulet 348
gullible 486

gully *gorge* 198
hollow 252
opening 260
conduit 350
gulosity 957
gulp *swallow* 296
take food 298
– down
credulity 486
submit 725
gum *fastening* 45
fasten 46
resin 356*a*
– elastic 325
– tree 367
gumbo 298
gummy 352
gumption 498
gun *report* 406
weapon 727
great – 626
blow great –s 349
sure as a – 474
gunboat 726
gunfire 404
gunlayer 284
gunman 361
gunner 726
gunnery
warfare 722
cannon 727
gunpowder
warfare 722
ammunition 727
not invent – 665
sit on barrel of – 501
gunroom 191
gun-shot 197
gunwale 232
gurge 312, 348
gurgle
flow 348
bubble 353
faint sound 405
resonance 408
gurgoyle 350
gush
flow out 295
flood 348
exaggeration 482
talk 584
gushing
emotional 821
impressible 822
gusset 43
gust *wind* 349
physical taste 390
passion 825
moral taste 850
gustation 390
gustful 394
gustless 391
gusto [*see* gust]
physical pleasure 377
emotion 821
gut *destroy* 162
opening 260
strait 343
eviscerate 297
sack 789
steal 791
gutling 954*a*
guts *inside* 221
guttapercha 325
gutter *groove* 259
conduit 350
vulgarity 851
guttersnipe 876
guttle 957
guttural
letter 561
inarticulate 583
guy
fastening 45, 752
fellow 373
disrespect 929
grotesque 853
guzzle
gluttony 957
drunkenness 959
gybe [*see* jibe]
gymkhana 720, 840
gymnasium 189
school 542
arena 728, 840
gymnast 159
gymnastics
training 537
exercise 686
contention 720
sport 840
gymnosophist
abstainer 953
sectarian 984
gynander 83
gynarchy 727
gynecæum 374
gynecology 662
gyniatrics 374
gynics 374
gyp 545, 746
gyre 311
gyrate 312
gyrfalcon 913
gyromancy 511
gyrostat 312
gysart 599
gyve 752

H

habeas corpus 963, 969
haberdasher 225
habergeon 717
habiliment 225
habilitation 698
habit
essence 5
coat 225
custom **613**
want of – 614
–s of business 682
– of mind 820
habitant 188
habitat 189
habitation 189
habit-maker 225
habitual
unvariable **16**
orderly 58
ordinary 82
customary 613
habituate 537, 613
habitude
state **7**
habit 613
habitué 613
hacienda 189, 780
hack *cut* 44
shorten 201
horse 271
writer 593
worker 690
literary – 593
hackle 44
hackney-coach 272
hackneyed
known 490
trite 496
habitual **613**
Hades 982
Hadji
traveller 268
priest 996
hæ tibi erunt artes 627
hæret lateri lethalis arundo
displeasure 828
anger 900
haft 633
hag *age* 130
ugly 846
wretch 913
witch 994
haggard
insane 503
tired 688
wild 824
ugly 846
haggis 298
haggle *cut* 44
chaffer 794
Hagiographa 985
Hagiolatry 984
Hagiology 983, 985
haguebut 727
ha-ha *trench* 198, 717
haik 225
hail *welcome* 292
ice 383
call 586
rejoicing 838
honour to 873
celebration 883
courtesy 894
salute 928
approve 931
–fellow well met
friendship 888
sociality 892
hailstone 383
hair *small* 32
filament 205
roughness 256
to a – 494
–'s breadth
near **197**
narrow **203**
–breadth escape
danger 665
escape 671
–s on the head
multitude 102
make one's – stand on end
distressing 830
fear 860
wonder 870
hairless 226
hairy *rough* 256
halberd 727
halberdier 726
halcyon *calm* 174
peace 721
prosperous 734
joyful 827, 829
hale 654
half 91
– the battle
important 642
success 731
– distance 68
– a dozen *six* 98
several 102
see with – an eye
intelligent 498
intelligible 518
manifest 525

– a gale 349
– and half
equal 27
mixed 41
incomplete 53
– a hundred 98
– light 422
– measures
incomplete 53
vacillating 605
mid-course 628
– moon 245
– price 815
– rations 640
– scholar 493
– seas over 959
– sight 443
– speed
moderate 174
slow 275
– truth 546
half-blind 443
half-blood
mixture 41
unconformity 83
imperfect 651
half-frozen 352
half-hearted
irresolute 605
insensible 823
indifferent 866
half-learned 491
half-melted 352
halfpenny
trifle 643
half-starved
insufficient 640
fasting 956
half-way
small 32
middle 68
between 228
go – *irresolute* 605
mid-course 628
meet –
willing 602
compromise 774
half-witted 499, 501
hall *house* 189
lobby 191
mart 799
music – 599
– of audience 588
– mark 550
hallelujah 990
halliard 45
halloo *cry* 411
look here! 457
call 586
wonder 870
hallow
celebrate 883
respect 928
hallowed 976
hallucination
error 495
insanity 503
halo *light* 420
glory 873
Halomancy 511
halser 45
halt *cease* 142
weak 160
rest 265
go slowly 275
lame 655
fail 732
at the – 265
halter *rope* 45
restraint 752
punishment 975
wear a – 874
with a – round one's neck 665
halting
style 579
– place 292
halve [*see* half]
halves
do by –
neglect 460
not complete 730
not do by – 729
go – 778
ham *house* 189
hamadryad 979
hamlet 189
hammam 386, 652
hammer
repeat 104
knock 276
stammer 583
under the –
auction 796
between the – and the anvil 665
– at *think* 451
work 686
– out *form* 240
prepare 673
complete 729
hammock 215
hamper *basket* 191
obstruct 706
hamstring 158, 659
hanaper 802
hand
measure of length 200
side 236
transfer 270
man 372
organ of touch 379
indicator 550
writing 590
medium 631
agent 690
grasp 781
transfer 783
at – *future* 121
destined 152
near 197
useful 644
bad – 590
bird in – 781
come to – 292, 785
fold one's –s 681
give one's – to
marry 903
good –
writing 590
skill 698
proficiency 700
helping – 707, 711
hold in – 737
hold out the – 894
hold up the –
vote 609
in –
incomplete 53
business 625
preparing 673
not finished 730
possessed 777
money 800
in the –s of
authority 737
subjection 749
lay –s on
discover 480a
use 677
take 789
rite 998
much on one's –s 682
on one's –s
business 625
redundant 641
not finished 730
for sale 796
on the other – 468
no – in 623
poor – 701
put into one's –s 784
put one's – to 676
ready to one's – 673
shake –s 918
stretch forth one's – 680
take by the – 707
take in –
teach 537
undertake 676
time hanging on one's –s
inaction 681
leisure 685
weary 841
try one's – 675
turn one's – 675
turn one's – to 625
under one's –
in writing 590
promise 768
compact 769
– back 683
– cart 272
– of death 360
– down
record 551
transfer 783
have one's –s full 682
– gallop 274
– glass 445
– and glove 709, 888
– in hand
joined 43
accompanying 88
same time 120
concur 178
co-operate 709
party 712
concord 714
friend 888
social 892
– to hand
touching 199
transfer 270
fight 720, 722
– over head
inattention 458
neglect 460
reckless 863
have a – in
cause 153
act 680
co-operate 709
have one's – in
skill 698
keep one's – in 613
live from – to mouth
insufficient 640
unprepared 674
poor 804
–s off! *avoid* 623
leave alone 681
prohibition 761

– over
transfer 783
give 784
win –s down 731
with the –s in the pockets 681
hand-bag 191
hand-barrow 272
handbook
travel 266
information 527
book 593
handcuff 751, 752
handfast 903
handful
quantity 25
small 32
few 103
handicap
equalize 27
inferiority 34
encumber 706
race 720
handicraft 625, 680
handicraftsman 690
effect 154
doing 680
handkerchief
clothes 225
cleaner 652
handle
feel, touch 379
name 565
dissert 595
plea 617
instrument 633
use 677
manage 693
furnish a – 937
make a – of 677
– a case 693
– to one's name
name 564
honour 877
handmaid
instrumentality 631
auxiliary 711
servant 746
handpost 550
handsel
begin 66
security 771
gift 784
pay 809
handsome
liberal 816
beautiful 845
disinterested 942
– fortune 803
handspike 633
handstaff 727
handwriting
signature 550
autograph 590
– on the wall
warning 668
handy
near 197
useful 644, 646
ready 673
dexterous 698
hang
pendency 214
kill 361
curse 908
execute 972
– about 133, 197
– back 133, 623
– in the balance 133
– in doubt 485
– fire *late* 133
cease 142
unproductive 169
inert 172
slow 275
reluctance 603
inactive 683
not finish 730
fail 732
refuse 764
dullness 843
– on hand 641
– down the head 837
– over the head 152
– it! *regret* 833
contempt 930
– out a light 420
– upon the lips of 418
– on
accompany 88
– out
display 882
entertain 892
– over
destiny 152
height 206
project 250
– out a signal 550
– on the sleeve of
servant 746
servility 886
flattery 933
– in suspense 605
– by a thread 665
– together
joined 43
cohere 46
concur 178
co-operate 709
– upon
effect 154
dependency 749
hangar 191, 273
hang-dog look 901*a*
hanged if, I'll be – 489
hanger
weapon 727
suspender 45, 214
pothooks and –s 590
– on
accompaniment 88
servant 746
servile 886
hanging [*see* hang]
elevated 307
ornament 847
– look 846
hangman
evil-doer 913
bad man 949
executioner 975
hank *tie* 45
hanker 865
hanky-panky 545
Hansard 551
hansom 272
hap 156
haphazard
chance 156, 621
hapless
unfortunate 735
(*miserable* 828)
(*hopeless* 859)
haply
possibly 470
(*by chance* 156)
happen 151
– as it may
chance 621
– what may
certain 474
reckless 863
happening 151
happiness
[*see* happy]
the greatest – of the greatest number 910
happy *fit* 23
opportune 134
style 578
glad 827
cheerful 836
– despatch 972
– go lucky 674
– hunting grounds 981
– returns of the day 896
– thought 842
– valley
imagination 515
delight 827
harangue 582
hara-kiri 972
harass
fatigue 688
vex 830
worry 907
harbinger
precursor 64
omen 512
informant 527
harbour
abode 189
haven 292
refuge 666
cherish 821
natural – 343
– a design 620
in – 664
– an idea 451
– revenge 919
harbourless 665
hard *strong* 159
dense 323
physically insensible 376
sour 397
difficult 704
severe 739
morally insensible 823
grievous 830
impenitent 951
blow – 349
go –
difficult 704
failure 732
adversity 735
pain 828
hit – 276
look – at 441
not be too – upon 918
strike –
energy 171
impulse 276
try – 675
work – 686
– at it 682
– bargain 819
– of belief 487
– to believe 485
– by 197
– case 735

- cash 800
- earned 704
- and fast rule 80
- fought 704
- frost 383
- of hearing 419
- heart
malevolent 907
vicious 945
impenitent 951
- hit 732
- knocks 720
- life 735
- lines
adversity 735
severity 739
- liver 954*a*
- lot 735
- master 739
- measure 739
- names 932
- necessity 601
- nut to crack 704
- to please 868
- pressed
haste 684
difficulty 704
hindrance 706
- put to it 704
- set 704
- tack 298
- task 703
- time 704
- up 704, 804
- upon
attack 716
severe 739
censure 932
- winter 383
- words
obscure 571
rude 895
censure 932
- work 686
- at work 682
harden [*see* hard]
strengthen 159
accustom 613
- the heart
insensible 823
enmity 889
impenitence 951
hardened
impious 988
- front
insolent 885
hardening
habit 613
hard-featured 846
hard-fisted 819
hard-headed 498, 739
hardihood 861, 885
hardly
scarcely 32
deal - with 739
- any *few* 103
- anything
small 32
unimportant 643
- ever 137
hard-mouthed 606
hardness 323
- of heart 914*a*
hardship 735
hardy
strong 159
healthy 654
brave 861
hare 274
hold with the - and run with the hounds
fickle 607
servile 886
hare-brained 458, 863
harem 961
hariolation 511
hark 418, 457
- back 283
harl 205
harlequin
changeable 149
nimble 274
motley 440
pantomimic 599
humorist 844
harlequinade 599
harlot 962
harlotry 961
harm
evil 619
badness 649
malevolence 907
harmattan 349
harmless
impotent 158
good 648
perfect 650
salubrious 656
safe 664
innocent 946
bear - 717
harmonica 417
harmonics 413
harmonist 413
harmonium 417
harmonize 178, 416
harmony
agreement 23
order 58
music 413
colour 428
concord 714
peace 721
friendship 888
harness
fasten 43
fastening 45
accoutrement 225
yoke 370
instrument 633
restraint 752
in -
prepared 673
in action 680
active 682
subjection 749
- up 293
harp
repeat 104
musical instrument 417
weary 841
Harpagon 819
harper 416
harpist 416
harpoon 727
harpsichord 417
harpy
relentless 739
thief 792
miser 819
evil-doer 913
demon 980
harquebuss 727
harridan 846, 962
harrier 366
harrow
agriculture 371
- up the soul 860
harrowing 830
harry *pain* 830
attack 716
persecute 907
Harry, old - 978
harsh
acrid 171
sound 410
style 579
discordant 713
severe 739
disagreeable 830
morose 895
malevolent 907
- voice 581
hart 366, 373
hartal 142, 489
harum-scarum 59, 458
haruspice 513
Haruspicy 511
harvest
effect 154
profit 618
store 636
acquisition 775
get in the -
complete 729
succeed 731
- home
celebration 883
- time
autumn 126
exertion 686
has been 122
hash *mix* 41
cut 44
confusion 59
food 298
make a - 699
hashish 663
hasp 43, 45
hassock 215
hastate 253
haste
velocity 274
activity 682
hurry 684
hasten
promote 707
hasty
transient 113
hurried 684
impatient 825
irritable 901
- pudding 298
hat 225
cardinal's - 999
send round the - 765
shovel - 999
- in hand 886
hatch
produce 161
gate 232
opening 260
chickens 370
fabricate 544
shading 556
plan 626
prepare 673
- a plot 626
hatches, under -
restraint 751
prisoner 754
poor 804
hatchet
cutting 253
bury the - 918
dig up the - 722
throw the helve after the - 818

hatchet-faced 203
hatchment
funeral 363
arms 550
record 551
hatchway 260
hate 867, 898
hateful 649, 830
hath been, the time – 122
hatrack 215
hatred [*see* hate]
object of – 898
hatter 225
mad as a – 503
hatti-sheriff 741
hauberk 717
haud passibus æquis 28, 275
haugh 344
haughty
proud 878
insolent 885
contemptuous 930
haul *drag* 285
catch of fish &c. 789
– down one's flag 725
– in 10
haunch 236
haunt *focus* 74
presence 186
abode 189
alarm 860
persecute 907
– the memory
remember 505
trouble 830
haunted 980
haut
traiter de –
insolence 885
contempt 930
hautboy 417
haut-goût 392
haut-monde 875
hauteur 878
have *confute* 479
ken 490
possess 777
– the advantage 28, 33
– at 716
– no choice 609*a*
– done! 142
– to do with 9
– no end 112
– other fish to fry 135
– it
discover 480*a*
believe 484
– one to know 527
– some knowledge of 490
– nothing to do with 10
– for one's own 780
– rather 609
– one's rights 924
– the start 116
– in store 152, 637
– to 620
– up 638
– it your own way
submission 725
haven 292, 666
haversack 191
havoc
destruction 162
cry – *war* 722
play – *spoil* 659
haw 583
hawk *spit* 297
stammer 583
eye of a – 498
– about
publish 531
offer 763
sell 796
– at 716
between – and buzzard 315, 828
know a – from a handsaw 465, 698
hawker 796
hawk-eyed 441
hawking *chase* 622
hawser 45
hay while the sun shines, make – 134
haycock 72
hazard
chance 156, 621
danger 665
at all –s 604
– a conjecture 514
– a proposition 477
haze *mist* 353
uncertainty 475
in a –
hidden 528
hazel 433
hazy *opaque* 426
he 373
head *precedence* 62
beginning 66
class 75
summit 210
coiffure 225
lead 280
froth 353
person 372
intellect 450
topic 454
wisdom 498
picture 556
nomenclature 564
chapter 593
direct 693
director 694
master 745
at the – of
direction 693
authority 737
repute 873
bow the – 308
bring to a – 729
come into one's – 451
come to a – 729
drive into one's – 505
gain – 175
get into one's –
thought 451
learn 505
belief 484
intoxicate 959
give a horse his – 748
hang one's – 879
have in one's – 490
from – to heels 52, 200
hit on the – 912
knock on the – 361
knock one's – against
impulse 276
unskilful 699
fail 732
lie on one's – 926
lift up one's – 878
make – against
oppose 708
resistance 719
success 731
never entered into one's – 458
have no – 506
on one's – 218
off one's – 503
can't get out of one's – 505
over – and ears
deep 641
debt 806
love 897
put into one's –
supposition 514
information 527
put out of one's – 458
run in the – 505
not know whether one stands on – or heels
uncertain 475
wonder 870
take into one's –
thought 451
caprice 608
intention 620
turn the – 824
trouble one's – about 457
as one's – shall answer for 768
with – erect 878
from – to foot 200
– and front
important 642
– and front of one's offending
provocation 830
charge 938
– over heels
inversion 218
rotation 312
– light 423
– line 591
– and shoulders
irrelevant 10
complete 52
haste 684
make neither – nor tail of 519
hold one's – up 307
– above water
safe 664
prosperous 734
wealth 803
with a – on 353
headache 378
head-dress 225
header 310
head-foremost
violent 173
rash 863
head-gear 225
heading *prefix* 64
beginning 66
indication 550
title 564
headland

height 206
projection 250
headlong
hurry 684
rush 863
rush –
violence 173
headman 694
headmost
front 234
precession 280
head-piece
summit 210
intellect 450
helmet 717
ornament 847
headquarters
focus 74
abode 189
authority 737
head-race 350
heads
compendium 596
– or tails 156, 621
lay – together
advice 695
co-operate 709
– I win tails you lose
unfair 940
headship 737
headsman 975
head-stone 363
headstrong
violent 173
obstinate 606
rash 863
headway *space* 180
navigation 267
progression 282
headwind 708
headwork 451
heady 606
heal *restore* 660
remedy 662
let the wound –
forgive 918
– the breach
pacify 723
healing art 662
health 654
picture of – 654
healthiness 655
health resort 189
healthy 656
heap *quantity* 31
collection 72
store 636
too many 641
heaps 102
rubbish – 645
hear
audition 418
be informed 527
not – of (refuse) 764
– a cause
adjudge 480
lawsuit 969
– hear! 931
– and obey 743
– out 457
hearer 418
hearing 418, 696
[*see* hear]
gain a – 175
give a – 418
hard of – 419
out of – 196
within – 197
hearken 457
hearsay 532
– evidence 467
hearse 363
heart
intrinsicality 5
interior 221
centre 222
mind 450
willingness 602
essential 642
affections 820
courage 861
love 897
man after one's own – 899
with all one's – 438, 602
at – 820, 821
from bottom of – 543
beating – 821, 824
break the – 830
by –
memory 505
go to one's – 824
in good – 858
with a heavy – 603
know by – 490
lay to – 837
learn by – 539
lift up the – 990
lose – 837
lose one's – 897
nearest to one's – 897
not find it in one's – 603
have a place in the – 897
put one's – into 604
set one's – upon 604
take –
content 831
hope 858
courage 861
take to –
sensibility 822
discontent 832
dejection 837
anger 900
warm – 822
wind round the – 897
– bleeding for 914
to one's –'s content
willing 602
enough 639
success 731
pleasure 829
–'s core
mind 450
affections 820
– expanding 821
– failing one 837, 860
do one's – good 829
– of grace 858
– in hand 602
– leaping with joy 827, 838
– leaping into one's mouth 824
– of oak
strong 159
hard 323
– in right place 906
– sinking *fear* 860
– and soul
completely 52
willing 602
resolute 604
exertion 686
feeling 821
– of stone 823, 907
– swelling 824
heartache 828
heart-breaking 821, 830
heart-broken 828
heartburning
discontent 832
regret 833
enmity 889
anger 900
jealousy 920
hearten 858, 861
heartfelt 821, 829
hearth
home 189
fireplace 386
heartless 823, 945
heart-rending 830
heartsease 831
heart-shaped 245
heart-sick
dejection 837
dislike 867
satiety 869
heart-stricken 828
heart-strings, tear the – 830
hearty
willing 602
healthy 654
feeling 821
cheerful 836
friendly 888
social 892
– laugh 838
– meal 298
– reception 892
heat *warmth* **382**
make hot 384
contest 720
excitement **824**, 825
dead – 27
– of passion 900
– wave 382
heated imagination 515
heater 386
heath *moor* 344
plant 367
heathen 984, 989
– mythology 979
heathenish 851
heather *moor* 344
plant 367
heaume 717
heautontimorumenos 837, 955
heave *raise* 307
emotion 821
– the lead 208, 466
– a sigh 839
– in sight 446
– to 265
heaven 827, **981**
call – to witness 535
in the face of – 525
light of – 420
move – and earth 686

will of – 601
– forfend! 766
– knows 475, 491
– be praised 838, 916
for –'s sake 765
heaven-born
wise 498
repute 873
virtue 944
heaven-directed 498
heaven-kissing 206
heavenly
celestial 318
rapturous 829
divine 976
of heaven 981
– bodies 318
– host 977
– kingdom 981
heavenly-minded 987
heavens 318
– and earth! 870
Heaviside layer 338
heavisome 843
heavy *great* 31
inert 172
weighty 319
stupid 499
actor 599
sleepy 683
dull 843
brutish 851
– affliction 828
– artillery 726
– cost 814
– dragoon 726
– father 599
– gaited 843
– gun 727
– hand
clumsy 699
severe 739
– on hand 641
– heart *loth* 603
pain 828
dejection 837
– hours 841
– on the mind 837
– news 830
– sea
agitation 315
waves 348
– sleep 683
– type 591
– wet 298
heavy-laden 706, 828

hebdomadal 138
Hebe 845
hebetate 823, 826
hebetude
imbecile 499
insensible 823
inexcitable 826
Hebrew
unintelligible 519
Jew 984
Hecate 994
hecatomb
number 98
sacrifice 991
heckle 830, 900
hectic 382, 821
Hector *brave* 861
rash 863
bully 885, 887
hedge
compensate 30
inclosure 232
– in
circumscribe 229
hinder 706
conditions 770
hedgehog 253
hedonism 377, 827
hedonist 954*a*
heed *attend* 457
care 459
beware 668
caution 864
heedful 457
heedless
inattentive 458
neglectful 460
oblivious 506
rash 863
heel *support* 215
lean 217
deviate 279
go round 311
iron – 975
lay by the –s 162
turn on one's –
go back 283
go round 311
avoid 623
– of Achilles 665
heel-piece
sequel 65
back 235
repair 660
heel-tap
remainder 40
dress 653
heels *lowness* 207
at the – of
near 197
behind 235

cool one's – 681
follow on the – of 281
laid by the – 751
lay by the – 789
show a light pair of – 623
take to one's – 623
tread on the – of
near 197
follow 281
approach 286
– over head
inverted 218
hasty 684
rash 863
heft *handle* 633
exertion 686
hegemony
influence 175
direction 693
authority 737
hegira [*see* hejira]
heifer 366
heigho! 839
height *degree* 26
altitude 206
summit 210
at its –
great 31
supreme 33
draw oneself up to his full – 307
– finder 206
heighten
increase 35
elevate 307
exaggerate 549
aggravate 835
heinous 945
heir *futurity* 121
posterity 167
inheritor 779
heirloom 780
heirship 777
hejira 293
Helen of Troy 845
heliacal 318
helical 248
Helicon 597
helicon-horn 417
helicopter 273
Heliogabalus 954*a*
heliograph
signal 550
picture 554
heliography 550
light 420
painting 556
Helios 423

heliotrope 847
heliotype 558
helix 248
hell *abyss* 208
gaming-house 621
gehenna 982
– upon earth
misfortune 735
pain 828
– broke loose 59
hell-born 945, 978
hellebore 663
hell-hound 913, 949
hellish
malevolent 907
vicious 945
hell 982
helluo librorum 492
helm *handle* 633
sceptre 747
(*authority* 737)
answer the – 743
at the – 693
obey the – 705
take the – 693
helmet 225, 717
helminthology 368
helmsman 269, 694
helot 746
help *benefit* 618
utility 644
remedy 662
aid 707
servant 746
give 784
it can't be –ed
submission 725
never mind 823
content 831
God – you 914
so – me God 535
– oneself to 789
helper 711
helpless 158, 665
helpmate
auxiliary 711
wife 903
helter-skelter 59, 684
helve
throw the – after the hatchet 818
hem *edge* 231
fold 258
indeed! 870
kiss the – of one's garment 886
– in *enclose* 227
restrain 751
hemi- 91
hemisphere 181

hemispheric 250
hemlock 663
hemorrhage 299
hemp 205
hen 366
female 374
– with one chicken
busy 682
henbane 663
hence
arising from 155
departure 293
deduction 476
– loathed melancholy 836
henceforth 121
henchman 746
hencoop 370
hendiadys 91
henna 433
henpecked 743, 749
heptagon 244
heptarchy 98
Heraclitus 839
rideret – 853
herald
precursor 64
precession 280
predict 511
forerunner 512
proclaim 531
messenger 534
heraldry 550
herb 367
herbage 365
herbal 369
herbivorous 298
herborize 369
herculean
strong 159
exertion 686
difficult 704
Herculem, ex pede – 550
Hercules 159, 215
pillars of – 233, 550
herd 72, 102
herdsman 746
here
situation 183
presence 186
arrival 292
come –! 286
– below 318
– goes 676
– and there
dispersed 73
few 103
place 182, 183
– there and everywhere
diversity 16a
space 180
omnipresence 186
– to-day and gone to-morrow 111
hereabouts 183, 197
hereafter 121, 152
hereby 631
hereditament 780
hereditary
intrinsic 5
derivative 154, 167
heredity 167
herein 221
heresy 495, 984
heretic 984
heretofore 122
hereupon 106
herewith 88, 632
heritage
futurity 121
possession 777
property 780
heritor 779
hermaphrodite 83
– brig 273
hermeneutics 522
Hermes 534, 582
hermetically 261
hermit 893, 955
hermitage
house 189
cell 191
seclusion 893
hero *brave* 861
glory 873
good man 948
– worship 931, 991
Herod, out-Herod – 549
heroic [*see* hero]
magnanimous 942
mock – 853
heroics 884
heroin 663
heroine 861
herpetology 368
Herr 373
herring
pungent 392
– pond 341
draw a – across the trail 545
trail of a red – 615, 706
herring-gutted 203
hesitate
uncertain 475
sceptical 485
stammer 583
reluctant 603
irresolute 605
fearful 860
Hesperian 236
Hesperides, garden of the – 981
Hesperus 423
Hessian boot 225
hest 741
hesterni quirites 876
heterarchy 737
heteroclite 83
heterodoxy 489, 984
heterogeneous
unrelated 10
different 15
mixed 41
multiform 81
exceptional 83
heterogeneity 15, 16a
heteromorphism 16a
hetman 745
hew *cut* 44
shorten 201
fashion 240
– down 308
hewers of wood
workers 690
commonalty 876
hexagon 98, 244
hexahedron 244
hexameter 98, 597
hey! 586
heyday
exultation 838
festivity 840
wonder 870
– of the blood 820
– of youth 127
hiation 260
hiatus 198
hibernal 383
hibernate 683
Hibernicism 497, 563
hic:
– jacet 363
– labor hoc opus 704
hick 701, 851, 876
hiccup 349
hid under a bushel 460
hidalgo 875
hidden 528
– meaning 526
hide *skin* 223
conceal 528
– diminished head
inferior 34
decrease 36
humility 879
– one's face
modesty 881
– and seek
deception 545
avoid 623
game 840
hide-bound 751, 819
hideous 846
hide-out 893
hiding-place
abode 189
ambush 530
refuge 666
hie 264, 274
– to 266
hiemal 126
hierarch 996
hierarchy 995
hieratic 590
hieroglyphic
representation 554
letter 561
writing 590
hierographa 985
hieromancy 511
hierophant 996
hieroscopy 511
higgle 794
higgledy piggledy 59
higgler 797
high *much* 31
lofty 206
fetid 401
treble 410
foul 653
noted 873
proud 878
from on – 981
on – 206
think –ly of 931
– art 556
– celebration 998
– colour
colour 428
red 434
exaggerate 549
– commissioner 745
– days and holi-

days 840
in a – degree 31
– descent 875
– and dry
stable 150
safe 664
in – esteem 928
in – feather
strong 159
health 654
cheerful 836
boasting 884
– glee 836
– hand
violent 173
resolved 604
authority 737
severe 739
pride 878
insolence 885
lawless 964
– jinks 840
ride the – horse 878
– hat 225
– life *fashion* 852
rank 875
– living
intemperance 954
gluttony 957
– mass 998
– mightiness 873
– and mighty
pride 878
insolence 885
– note 410
– notions 878
– places 210
– pressure
energy 171
excitation of feeling 824
– price 814
– priest 996
in – quarters 875
– relief 448
– repute 873
–ly respectable 875
on the – road to
way 627
hope 858
on one's – ropes
excitation 824
pride 878
anger 900
– seas 341
in – spirits 836
– tide *wave* 348
prosperity 734
– time *late* 133
occasion 134
– in tone
white 430
– treason
disobedience 742
dishonour 940
– words
quarrel 713
anger 900
high-ball 298
high-born 875
high-brow 492
higher 33
highest 210
highfalutin 884
high-flavoured 392
high-flier
madman 504
proud 878
high-flown
imaginative 515
style 577
proud 878
vain 880
insolent 885
high-flying
inattentive 458
exaggerated 549
ostentatious 822
highlands 206
high-low 225
high-mettled
excitable 825
brave 861
high-minded
honourable 939
magnanimous 942
highness *title* 877
high-pitched 410
high-seasoned 392
high-souled 878
high-sounding
loud 404
words 577
display 882
high-spirited 861, 939
hight 564
high-toned 852
high-water
completeness 52
height 206
water 337
– mark
measure 466
highway 627
–s and byways 627
– robbery 791
highwayman 792
high-wrought
good 648
prepared 673
excited 824
hike 266
hilarity 836
hill *height* 206
convexity 250
ascent 305
descent 306
take to the –s 666
–dwelling 206
hillock 206
hilt 633
hinc illæ lachrymæ 155
hind *back* 235
clown 876
on one's – legs
elevation 307
anger 900
– quarters 235
hinder 706
hindermost 67, 235
Hindooism 984
hindrance 706
hinge *fasten* 43
fastening 45
cause 153
depend upon 154
rotate 312
hinny 271
hint *reminder* 505
suppose 514
inform 527
take a – 498
– a fault &c. 932
hinterland 235
hip 236
have on the –
confute 479
success 731
authority 737
subjection 749
– hip, hurrah! 838
hipped [*see* hypped]
hippocentaur 83
Hippocrates 662
hippocratic 360
hippodrome
drama 599
arena 728
amusement 840
hippogriff 83
Hippolytus 960
hippophagy 298
hippopotamus 192
hirdie-girdie 218
hire
commission 755
borrowing 788
price 812
reward 973
on – 763
hireling 746
hirsute 256
hispid 256
hiss *sound* 409
animal cry 412
disrespect 929
contempt 930
disapprobation 932
hist! 585, 586
histology 329
historian 553
historic 594
historiette 594
historical:
– painter 559
– painting 556
historiographer 553
historiography 594
history *past* 122
record 551
narrative 594
History, Natural – 357
histrionic 599
hit *chance* 156
strike 276
reach 292
succeed 731
censure 932
(*punish* 972)
good – 626
make a – 731
– one's fancy 829
– the mark 731
– off 554
– upon
discover 480*a*
plan 626
hitch
fasten 43
knot 45
stoppage 142
hang 214
jerk 315
harness 370
difficulty 704
hindrance 706
– up 293
hither 278, 292
come – 286
hitherto 122
hive
multitude 102
location 184
abode 189
bees 370
workshop 691

H.M.S. 726
hoar *aged* 128
white 430
– frost 383
hoard 636
hoarse
husky 405
harsh 410
voiceless 581
talk oneself – 584
hoary [*see* hoar]
hoax 545
hob *support* 215
stove 386
– and nob
celebration 883
courtesy 894
hobble
limp 275
awkward 699
difficulty 704
fail 732
shackle 751
– skirt 225
hobbledehoy 129
hobby
crotchet 481
pursuit 622
desire 865
hobby-horse 272
hobgoblin
fearful 860
demon 980
hobo 268
hobnail 876
Hobson's choice
necessity 601
no choice 609*a*
compulsion 744
hoc genus omne 876
hock 771
hock shop 787
hockey 840
hockey rink 213
hocus 545
hocus-pocus
interchange 148
unmeaning 517
cheat 545
conjuration 992
spell 993
hod
receptacle 191
support 215
vehicle 272
hoddy-doddy 501
hodge-podge 41
hoe 272, 371
hog *animal* 366
sensualist 954*a*
glutton 957
greedy as a – 865
go the whole – 604
hog's back 206
hogmanay 998
hogshead 191
hog-wash 653
hoist 307
– the black flag 722
– a flag 550
– on one's own petard
retaliation 718
failure 732
hoity-toity! 815, 870
hold *cohere* 46
contain 54
remain 141
cease 142
go on 143
happen 151
receptacle 191
cellar 207
base 211
support 215
halt 265
believe 484
be passive 681
defend 717
power 737
restrain 751
prison 752
prohibit 761
possess 777
retain 781
enough! 869
have a firm – 781
have a – upon 175
gain a – upon 737
get – of 789
quit one's – 782
take – 175
– aloof
stay away 187
distrust 487
avoid 623
– an argument 476
– authority 737
– back *avoid* 623
store 636
hinder 706
restrain 751
retain 781
miserly 819
– one's breath
wonder 870
– converse 588
– a council 695
– fast 751, 781
– forth *teach* 537
speak 582
– good 478, 494
– one's ground 141
– in hand 737
– one's hand
cease 142
relinquish 624
– hard 265
– up one's head 861
– a lease 771
– a meeting 72
– off 623
– office 693
– on
continue 141, 143
persevere 604*a*
– out [*see below*]
– one's own
preserve 670
defend 717
resist 719
– oneself in readiness 673
– in remembrance 505
– both one's sides 838
– a situation 625
– in solution 335
– to 602
– together 43, 709
– one's tongue 403, 585
– up [*see below*]
– oneself up 307
hold out
endure 106
affirm 535
persevere 604*a*
resist 719
offer 763
brave 861
– expectation
predict 511
promise 768
– temptation 865
hold up
continue 143
support 215
not rain 340
aid 707
rob 791
display 882
extol 931
– one's hand
sign 550
threat 609
– to execration
cures 908
censure 932
– the mirror 525
– to scorn 930
– to shame 874
– to view 525
holder 779
holdfast 45
holding
tenancy 777
property 780
hole *place* 182
hovel 189
receptacle 191
opening 260
ambush 530
– in one's coat 651
– and corner
place 182
peer into – 461
hiding 528, 530
– to creep out of
plea 617
escape 671
facility 705
holiday *leisure* 685
repose 687
amusement 840
– task *easy* 705
holiness *God* 976
piety 987
holloa 411
– before one is out of the wood 884
hollow
unsubstantial 4
completely 52
incomplete 53
depth 208
concavity 252
channel 350
- *sound* 408
specious 477
false 544
voiceless 581
beat – 731
– truce 723
holm 346
holocaust
kill 361
sacrifice 991
(*destruction* 162)
holograph 590
holster 191
holt 367
holus bolus 684
Holy *of God* 976
pious 987
keep – 987
– breathing 990

- Church 983*a*
- City 981
- day 998
- Ghost 976
temple of the -
Ghost 983*a*
- men of old 985
- orders 995
- place 1000
- Scriptures 985
- Spirit 976
- water 998
- week 998
holystone 652
homage
submission 725
fealty 743
reverence 928
approbation 931
worship 990
home *focus* 74
habitation 189
near 197
interior 221
arrival 292
refuge 666
at - *party* 72
present 186
within 221
at ease 705
social gathering 892
be at -
- *to visitors* 892
feel at -
freedom 748
pleasure 827
content 831
look at -
accusation 938
make oneself at -
free 748
sociable 892
not be at - 764
stay at - 265
at - in
knowledge 490
skill 698
at - with
friendship 888
bring - to
evidence 467
belief 484
accuse 938
condemn 971
come - 292
eternal - 981
from - 187
get - 292
go - 283
go from - 293
long - 363
strike -
energy 171
attack 716
- stroke 170
- thrust
attack 716
censure 932
home-bred 851
home-felt 821
home-rule 737, 748
homeless
unhoused 185
banished 893
homely
language 576
unadorned 849
common 851, 876
Homeric
- laughter 838
home-sick 833
home-spun
texture 329
home-stall 189
homestead 189
homeward bound 292
homicidal maniac 913
homicide 361
homiletical 892
homily
teaching 537
advice 595
sermon 998
hominem, argumentum ad - 938
homœopathic
small 32
little 193
Homœopathy 662
homogeneity
relation 9
identity 13
uniformity 16
simplicity 42
homogenesis 161
homologous 23
homology
relation 9
uniformity 16
equality 27
concord 714
homonym
equivocal 520
vocal sound 580
homophony 413
homunculus 193
Hon. 817
hone 253
honest
veracious 543
honourable 939
pure 960
- meaning 516
turn an - penny 775
- truth 494
honey
sweet 396
favourite 899
milk and - 734
honeycomb
concave 252
opening 260
deterioration 659
honeyed
- phrases 894
- words
allurement 615
flattery 933
honeymoon
pleasure 827
endearment 902
marriage 903
honey-mouthed 894, 933
honeysuckle 396
honorarium 784, 973
honorary 815
honour
demesne 780
glory 873
title 877
respect 928
approbation 931
probity 939
affair of - 720
do - to 883
do the -s
sociality 892
courtesy 894
respect 928
his - *judge* 967
in - of 883
man of - 939
upon my - 535, 768
word of - 768
- be to 873
- a bill 807
- in the breach 923
- bright
veracity 543
probity 939
honte, mauvaise - 881
hood 225, 999
hooded 223
hoodlum 887
hoodoo 649
hoodwink
ignore 491
blind 442
hide 528
deceive 545
hoof 211
cloven - 907
hook *fasten* 43
fastening 45
hang 214
curve 245
deceive 545
retain 781
take 789
by - or by crook 631
hookah 392
hooker *ship* 273
hookey, blind - 840
hooks, go off the 360
hooligan 887, 913
hoop *circle* 247
cry 411
hoot *cry* 411, 412
deride 929
contempt 930
censure 932
hop *leap* 309
dance 840, 892
- off 293
- skip and jump
leap 309
agitation 315
haste 684
game 840
- the twig 360
hope 858
band of - 958
beyond - 658, 734
dash one's -s 837
excite - 511
foster - 858
well-grounded - 472
- against hope 859
- for the best 858
- deferred
dejection 837
lamentation 859
- for *expect* 507
desire 865
hope chest 858
hopeful *infant* 129
probable 472
hope 858
hopelessness 471, 859
Hop-o'-my-thumb 193

hopper 191
horary 108
horde
assemblage 72
party 712
commonalty 876
horizon
distance 196
view 441
expectation 507
appear on the – 525
gloomy – 859
horizontality 213
horn
receptacle 191
sharp 253
music 417
draw in one's –s
recant 607
submit 725
humility 879
exalt one's – 873
wear the –s 905
–s of a dilemma
reasoning 476
difficulty 704
– in 294
– mad 920
– of plenty 639
hornbook 542
hornet
evil-doer 913
–'s nest
pitfall 667
difficulty 704
adversity 735
painful 830
resentment 900
censure 932
hornpipe 840
hornwork 717
horny 323
Horny, old – 978
horology 114
horoscope 511, 992
horresco referens 860
horrible *great* 31
noxious 649
dire 830
ugly 846
fearful 860
horrid [*see* horrible]
vulgar 851
horrida bella 722
horrific [*see* horrible]
horrified 828, 860
horrify 830, 860
horripilation 383
horrisonous 410
horror 860, 867
view with – 898
horrors 837
sup full of – 828
horror-stricken 828
hors de combat
impotent 158
useless 645
tired out 688
put – 731
hors-d'œuvre 298
horse *hang on* 214
stand 215
carrier 271
animal 366
male 373
cavalry 726
ride the high – 885
put the –s to 673
put up one's –s at 184
put up one's –s together
concord 714
friendship 888
take – 266
to – 293
war – 726
work like a – 686
– artillery 726
– of another colour 15
– doctor 370
– and foot 726
– laugh 838
– marine 701
like a – in a mill 613
– racing
pastime 840
contention 720
– soldier 726
– track 627
horseback 266
horse-cloth 225
horseman 268
horsemanship
riding 266
skill 698
horseplay 856
horse power 466
horse-shoe 245
horse-whip 972
hortation 615, 695
hortative 537
horticulture 371
hortus siccus 369
hosanna 931, 990
hose
stockings 225
pipe 348, 350
extinguisher 385
hosier 225
hospice 189, 662
hospitable 816, 892
hospital 189, 662
in – 655
hospitality [*see* hospitable]
hospodar 745
host *collection* 72
multitude 102
army 726
friend 890
rite 998
reckon without one's –
error 495
unskilful 699
rash 863
– of heaven 977
– in himself 175
hostage 771
hostel 189
hostelry 189
hostile
disagreeing 24
opposed 708
enmity 889
in – array 708
– meeting 720
hostilities 722
hostility 889
hostler 746
hot *violent* 173
warm 382
pungent 392
red 434
orange 439
excited 824
irascible 901
make – 384
– air 482, 884
– bath 386
– blood *rash* 863
angry 900
irascible 901
blow – and cold
inconsistent 477
falsehood 544
tergiversation 607
caprice 608
in – haste 684
in – pursuit 622
– water
difficulty 704
quarrel 713
painful 830
– water bottle 386
hot air merchant 884
hot-bed *cause* 153
centre 222
workshop 691
Hotchkiss gun 727
hotchpotch
mixture 41
confusion 59
participation 778
hotel 189
hot-headed 684, 825
hothouse
conservatory 371, 636
furnace 386
workshop 691
hot-press 255
Hotspur 863
Hottentot 876
hough 659
hound *animal* 366
hunt 622
persecute 907
wretch 949
hold with the hare but run with the –s 607
– on 615
houppelande 225
hour *period* 108
point of time 113
present time 118
improve the shining – 682
one's – is come
occasion 134
death 360
– after hour 110
hour-glass
chronometer 114
contraction 195
narrow 203
Houri 845
hourly *time* 106
frequent 136
periodical 138
house *family* 166
locate 184
abode 189
theatre 599
make safe 664
council 696
firm 712
before the – 454
keep – 184
eat out of – and home
prodigal 818
gluttony 957
turn out of – and

home 297
– of cards 160
– of correction
prison 752
punishment 975
– of death 363
– of detention 752
– divided against itself 713
bring the – about one's ears 699
– of Commons 696, 966
– of God 1000
– of Lords 696, 875, 966
set one's – in order 952
– of peers 696, 875
– of prayer 1000
– built on sand 160
turn – out of window 713
housebreaker 792
housebreaking 791
house-dog 366
household
inhabitants 188
abode 189
– gods 189
– stuff 635
– troops 726
– words
known 490
language 560
plain 576, 849
householder 188
housekeeper 637, 694
housekeeping 692
houseless 185
housemaid 746
house-organ 531
Houses of Parliament 189, 696
house-top 210
proclaim from – 531
house-room 180
house-warming 892
housewife 682
housewifery 692, 817
housing
lodging 189
covering 223
horse-cloth 225
hovel 189
hoveller 269
hover *high* 206
rove 266
soar 267
ascend 305
irresolute 605
– about
move 264
– over
near 197
how *way* 627
means 632
– comes it?
attribution 155
inquiry 461
– now 870
howbeit 30
however
degree 26
notwithstanding 30
except 83
howitzer 727
howker 273
howl
wind 349
human cry 411
animal cry 412
lamentation 839
howler 495
howling wilderness 169, 893
hoy 273
hoyden *girl* 129
rude 851
hub 222
hubble-bubble 392
hubbub *stir* 315
noise 404
discord 713
huckster 794, 797
huddle
disorder 59
derange 61
collect 72
hug 197
– on 225
Hudibrastic 856
– verse 597
hue 428
– and cry *cry* 411
proclaim 531
pursuit 622
alarm 669
raise a – and cry 932
hueless 429
huff 885, 900
huffy 901
hug *cohere* 46
border on 197
retain 781
courtesy 894
love 897
endearment 902
– a belief 606
– oneself
pleasure 827
content 831
rejoicing 838
pride 878
– the shore
navigation 267
approach 286
– a sin 945
huge 31, 192
hugger-mugger 528
Huguenot 984
huis clos, à – 528
huissier 965
huke 225
hulk *body* 50
ship 273
hulks 752
hulky *big* 192
unwieldy 647
ugly 846
hull 50
hullabaloo 404, 411
hullo! 292
hum
faint sound 405
continued sound 407
animal sound 412
sing 416
deceive 545, 546
– and haw
stammer 583
irresolute 605
busy – of men 682
human 372
– race 372
– sacrifices 991
humane
benevolent 906
philanthropic 910
merciful 914
humanitarian 372, 910
humanities 560
humanize 894
humano capiti cervicem jungere equinam 24
humation 363
humble *meek* 879
modest 881
pious 987
–r classes 876
– oneself
submit 725
meek 879
penitent 950
worship 990
eat – pie 725, 879
your – servant
dissent 489
refusal 764
humbug
falsehood 544
deception 545
deceiver 548
trifle 643
affectation 855
humdrum 841, 843
humectate 337, 339
humid 339
humiliate 308
humiliation
adversity 735
disrepute 874
sense of shame 879
worship 990
self – 950
humility 879, 987
humming-top 417
hummock 206, 250
humorist 844
humorous 842
humour *essence* 5
tendency 176
liquid 333
disposition 602
caprice 608
aid 707
indulge 760
affections 820
please 829
wit 842
flatter 933
(*fun* 840)
in the – 602
out of – 901*a*
peccant –
unclean 853
disease 655
humoursome
capricious 608
sulky 901*a*
hump 250
hump-backed 243
humph! 870
Humphrey, dine with Duke – 956
Humpty-dumpty 193
Hun 165, 851, 913
hunch 250, 612
hunch-backed 243
hundred
number 98
many 102
region 181

the same a – years hence 460
hundredth 99
hundredweight 319
hunger 865
hunger-strike 956
hunks 819
hunt *inquiry* 461
pursuit 622
– after 622
– in couples 709
– down 907
– out *inquiry* 461
discover 480a
– slipper 840
hunter *horse* 271
killer 361
pursuer 622
place &c. – 767
hunting 361, 622
hunting-ground 840
happy – 981
hurdle 272
hurdy-gurdy 417
hurl 284
– against 716
– defiance 715
hurler avec les loups 82, 714
Hurlothrumbo 860
hurly-burly 315
hurrah 411, 836, 838
hurricane 349, 667
– deck 210
hurry *haste* 684
excite 825
– forward 684
– off with 789
– on 615
– of spirits 821
– up 684
hurst 367
hurt
physical pain 378
evil 619
maltreat 649
injure 659
more frightened than – 860
– the feelings
pain 830
anger 900
hurtful 649
hurtle 276
hurtless 648
husband
store 636
director 694
spouse 903
husbandman 371
husbandry
agriculture 371
conduct 692
economy 817
hush *moderate* 174
stop 265
silence 403
taciturn 585
– up
conceal 528
pacify 723
hush-money 30, 973
husk 223, 226
husky *strong* 159
dry 340
faint sound 405
hoarse 581
hussar 726
hussy 962
hustings
school 542
arena 728
tribunal 966
hustle
perturb 61
push 276
agitate 315
activity 682
hinder 706
hustler 682, 962
hut 189
hutch 189
huzza 838
hyacinth
jewel 847
hyæna 913
hyaline 425
hybrid
mixture 41
exception 83
hydra
monster 83, 366
productive 168
– headed 163
hydrant 348, 385
hydraulics 333, 348
hydroplane 273
hydrodynamics 333, 348
hydrography 341
hydrology 333
hydrolysis 49
hydromancy 511
hydromel 396
hydropathy 662
hydrophobia 867
hydrostatics 333
hyemal 383
hyetology 348
hygeian 656
hygiantics 670
hygienic 656, 670
hygre 348
hygrometry 339
hyle 316
hylism 316
hylotheism 984, 989
Hymen 903
hymeneal 903
hymn *song* 415
worship 990
– of hate 898
hymn-book 998
hyoscine 663
hypallage 218
hyperbaton 218
hyperbola 245
hyperbole 549
hyperborean
far 196
cold 383
hypercriticism
misjudgment 481
discontent 832
fastidiousness 868
censure 932
hyperdulia 990
Hyperion 423, 845
– to a satyr 14
hyperorthodoxy 984
hyperphysical 976
hypertrophy 194
hyphen 45
hypnology 683
hypnotic
remedy 662
sleep 683
hypnotize 376
hypocaust 386
hypochondriac
madman 504
low spirits 837
hypochondriasis 837
hypocrisy
falsehood 544
religious – 988
hypocrite 548, 855
play the – 544
hypostasis 1, 3
Hypostatic union 976
hypothecate 771
hypothenuse 217
hypothesis 514
hypothesize 514
hypothetical 475, 514
hypped *insane* 503
dejected 837
hypsometer 206
Hyrcynian wood 533
hysteria
insanity 503
hysteric *violent* 173
hysterical
spasmodic 608
emotional 821
excitable 825
hysterics 173
in – *excited* 824
frightened 860
hysteron proteron 218

I

I 79
iambic 597
ibidem 13
Icarus
navigator 269
rash 863
fate of – 306
ice *cold* 383
refrigerate 385
iceberg 383
ice-bound 383
restraint 751
ice-chest 387
ice-house 387
ice-yacht 273
Ichabod 874
ichnography 554
ichor 333
ichthyology 368
ichthyomancy 511
ichthyophagous 298
icicle 383
icon 554
iconoclasm 983a, 984
iconoclast 165, 913
iconography 554
icosahedron 244
id est 522
idea
small quantity 32
notion 453
give an – of 537
ideal *unreal* 2
completeness 52
erroneous 495
imaginary 515
perfect 650
ideality 450, 515
idée fixe 481

identification
identity 13
comparison 464
discovery 480*a*
identity 13
– book 206
Ideology 450
Ides of March 601
idiocrasy
essence 5
tendency 176
idiocy 499
idiom 560, 566
idiomatic 79
idiosyncrasy
essence 5
speciality 79
unconformity 83
tendency 176
temperament 820
idiot 501
tale told by an – 517
idiotic
foolish 499
idiotism
folly 499
phrase 566
idle *foolish* 499
trivial 643
slothful 683
lie – *inaction* 681
– conceit 842
– hours 681
be an – man
leisure 685
– talk 588
– time away 683
idler 683
Ido 560
idol *desire* 865
favourite 899
fetich 991
– of the people 899
idolater 984
idolatry 897, **991**
idolize *love* 897
impiety 988
idoneous 23
idyl 597
if *circumstance* 8
qualification 469
supposition 514
– you please 765
– possible 470
igloo 189
igneous 382
ignis fatuus
luminary 423
phantom 443
ignite 384
ignoble 876
ignominy 874, 940
ignoramus 493
ignorance 491
keep in – 528
plead – 937
ignoratio elenchi 477
ignore
neglect 460
incredulity 487
not known 491
repudiate 756, 773
ignotum per ignotius 477
ilk 13
ill *evil* 619
badness 649
sick 655
go on – *fail* 732
adversity 735
look – 846
take –
discontent 832
anger 900
– betide 908
– blood *hate* 898
malevolence 907
– at ease *pain* 828
dejection 837
house of – fame 961
–s that flesh is heir to *evil* 619
disease 655
– humour
anger 900
sullenness 901*a*
– luck 735
as – luck would have it 135
– off
insufficient 640
adversity 735
poor 804
do an – office to 907
bird of – omen 668
– repute 874
– turn *evil* 619
spiteful 907
– usage 907
– will 907
wind *bad* 649
hindrance 706
adversity 735
ill-adapted 24
ill-advised
foolish 499
inexpedient 647
unskilful 699
ill-affected 901*a*
illapse
conversion 144
ingress 294
illaqueate 545
ill-assorted 24
illation 480
illaudable 947
ill-balanced 28
ill-bred 851, 895
ill-conditioned
bad 649
difficult 704
discourteous 895
malevolent 907
vicious 945
ill-conducted 699
ill-contrived
inexpedient 647
bad 649
unskilful 699
malevolent 907
ill-defined 447
ill-devised 499, 699
ill-digested 674
ill-disposed 901*a*, 907
illegality 964
illegible 519
render – 552
– hand 590
illegitimate
deceitful 545
undue 925
illegal 964
ill-fated 735
ill-flavoured 395
ill-furnished 640
illiberal
narrow-minded 481
stingy 819
uncourteous 895
selfish 943
illicit 925, 964
ill-imagined 499, 699
illimited 105
ill-intentioned 907
illiterate 491, 493
ill-judged 499, 699
ill-judging 481
ill-made 243, 846
ill-mannered 851, 895
ill-marked 447
ill-matched 24
ill-mated 24
ill-natured 907
illogical 477, 495
ill-omened 605, 859
ill-proportioned 243
ill-provided 640
ill-qualified 699
ill-requited 917
ill-spent 645
ill-tempered 901
ill-timed 135
ill-treat *bad* 649
severe 739
malevolent 907
illuminant 388
illuminate
enlighten 420
colour 428
excite 824
ornament 847
illuminati 492
illumination
[*see* illuminate]
book-illustration 558
celebration 883
ill-use 907
ill-used 828
illusion
fallacy of vision 443
error 495
illusive, illusory
sophistical 477
erroneous 495
deceitful 545, 546
illustrate
exemplify 82
interpret 522
represent 554
engravings 558
ornament 847
illustrious 873
image
likeness **17**
copy 21
appearance **448**
idea 453
metaphor 521
representation 554
graven – *idol* 991
imagery *fancy* 515
metaphor 521
representation 554
imaginable 470
imaginary
non-existing 2
fancied 515
– quantity 84
imagination 515

imaum 745, 996
imbecile 158, 499
imbécile 501
imbecility 499
imbed [*see* embed]
imbedded 229
imbibe 296
– learning 539
imbrangle 61
imbricated 223
imbroglio
disorder 59
difficulty 704
discord 713
imbrue
impregnate 300
moisten 339
– one's hands in blood
killing 361
war 722
– the soul 824
imbue *mix* 41
impregnate 300
moisten 339
tinge 428
teach 537
imbued
affections 820
– with
belief 484
habit 613
feeling 821
imburse 803
imitation
copying 19
copy 21
representation 554
immaculate
perfect 650
clean 652
innocent 946
immanent 5, 132
immanity 907
Immanuel 976
immaterial
unsubstantial 4
immateriality
spiritual 317
trifling 643
immature 123, 674
immeasurable 31, 105
immediate
continuous 69
immediately 113, 132
immedicabile vulnus 619
immedicable 859
immelodious 414
immemorial 124
from time – 122
– usage 613
immense *great* 31
infinite 105
– *size* 192
immerge
immerse
introduce 300
dip 337
immersed in 229
immethodical 59
immigrant
alien 57
entering 294
immigration 266, 294
imminent 152, 286
immiscible 47
immission 296
immitigable
hopeless 859
revenge 919
immix 41
immobility 150, 265
immoderately 31
immodest 961
immolation
killing 361
giving 784
sacrifice 991
immoral 923, 945
immortal
perpetual 112
glorious 873
celebrated 883
immotile 265
immovable
stable 150
quiescent 265
obstinate 606
immundicity 653
immunity
health 656
freedom 748
right 924
exemption 777*a*, 927*a*
immure 751
immutable
stable 150
deity 976
imo pectore, ab – 821
imp 980
impact *contact* 43
impulse 276
insertion 300
impair 659
impale *transfix* 260
execute 972
impalpable
small 193
powder 330
intangible 381
impanation 998
impar sibi 608
imparity 28
impart *inform* 527
give 784
impartial
judicious 498
neutral 628
just 922
honourable 939
– opinion 484
impassable
closed 261
impossible 471
impasse 706
impassible 823
impassion 824
impassionable 822
impassioned
– *language* 574
excited 825
impassive 823
impatient 825
– of control 742
impawn 771
impeach
censure 932
accuse 938
go to law 969
impeachment, soft – 902
impeccability 650, 946
impecunious 804
impede 706
impediment 706
– in speech 583
impedimenta 633, 780
impel *push* 276
induce 615
impend
future 121
imminent 132
destiny 152
overhang 206
impenetrable
closed 261
solid 321
unintelligible 519
latent 526
impenitence 951
imperative
require 630
command 737, 741
severe 739
duty 926
imperator 745
imperceptible
small 32
minute 193
slow 275
invisible 447
latent 526
impercipient 376
imperdible 664
imperfect
incomplete 53
failing 651
vicious 945
imperfection 651
inferiority 34
vice 945
imperfectly 32
imperforate 261
imperial
trunk 191
beard 256
authority 737
imperil 665
imperious
command 737
proud 878
arrogant 885
– necessity 601
imperishable 112
stable 150
glorious 873
imperium in imperio 737
impermanent 111
impermeable
closed 261
dense 321
impersonal
general 78
neuter 316
impersonate 19, 554
impersonator 19
imperspicuity 519
impersuasible 606
impertinent
irrelevant 10
insolent 885
imperturbable 823, 826
impervious
closed 261
impossible 471
insensible 823
– to light 426
– to reason 606
impetiginous 653
impetrate 765
impetuous

boisterous 173
hasty 684
excitable 825
rash 863
eager 865
impetus 276
impi 726
impiety 988
impignorate 771
impinge 276
implacable 848, 919
implant *insert* 300
teach 537
implanted
adventitious 6
implausible 473
implead 969
implement 633
impletion 52
implex 41
implicate *involve* 54, 526
accuse 938
implicated *related* 9
component 56
implication
disorder 59
meaning 516
latency 526
implicit 526
– belief 484
implore 765
imply *evidence* 467
mean 516
involve 526
impolicy 699
impolite 895
imponderable 4, 320
imporous 261, 321
import
put between 228
ingress 294
take in 296
insert 300
mean 516
imply 526
be of consequence 642
importance 642
greatness 31
attach – to 642
attach too much – to 482
of no – 643
importune 765, 830
impose *order* 741
awe 928
– upon
credulity 486
deceive 545
be unjust 923
imposing
important 642
exciting 824
glorious 873
imposition [*see* impose]
undue 925
– of hands 998
impossibile, credo quia – 486
impossibilities, seek after – 645
impossibility 471
impossible 471
refusal 764
– quantity
algebra 84
impost 812
imposthume 655
impostor 548, 925
imposture 545
impotence 158
impotent conclusion 732
impound 751
impoverish
weaken 160
waste 638
despoil 789
render poor 804
impracticable
impossible 471
misjudging 481
obstinate 606
difficult 704
imprecation
prayer 765
curse 908
impregnable 159, 664
impregnate *mix* 41
combine 48
fecundate 161, 168
insert 300
teach 537
– with 641
impresario 599
imprescriptible 924
impress *cause*
sensation 375
mark 550
steal 791
excite feeling 824
– upon the mind
memory 505
teach 537
impressed with
belief 484
feeling 821
impressible
motive 615
sensibility 822
impression
sensation 375
idea 453
belief 484
printing 531
mark 550
engraving 558
print 591
emotion 821
make an –
act 171
thought 451
impressionable 375, 822
impressive
language 574
important 642
feeling 821, 824
imprimis 66
imprimit 558
imprint
publisher 531
indication 550
– in the memory 505
imprison
circumscribe 229
restrain 751
punish 972
improbability 473
improbate 932
improbity 940
impromptu 612
– fait à loisir 673
improper
incongruous 24
foolish 499
solecism 568
inexpedient 647
wrong 923
unmeet 925
vicious 945
– time 135
impropriate 777, 789
impropriator 779
improve 658
– the occasion 134
– the shining hour 682
– upon 658
improvement 658
improvident
careless 460
not preparing 674
prodigal 818
rash 863
improvisation
music 415
improvisatore
speech 582
poetry 597
impulse 612
improvise
imagination 515
impulse 612
unprepared 674
improviste, à l'– 508, 612
improvisatrice 612
imprudent 460, 863
impudent 885, 895
impudicity 961
impugn *deny* 536
attack 716
blame 932
impugnation 708
impuissance 158
impulse *push* 276
sudden thought 612
motive 615
blind – 601
creature of – 612
give an – to
propel 284
aid 707
impulsive [*see* impulse]
intuitive 477
excitable 825
rash 863
impunity *escape* 671
acquittal 970
with – *safely* 664
impurity 653, 961
imputation
ascribe 155
slur 874
accuse 938
in 221
go – 294
– as much as
relation 9
degree 26
– the circumstances 8
– doors 221
– durancevile 751
– for
– force 1
undertake 676
promise 768
– re 9
– and out 314
–s and outs 182
in: – articulo 111
– extenso *whole* 50

diffuse 573
– jail 751
– limine 66
– loco 23
– medias res 68
– prison 751
– propriâ personâ 79
– toto 52
– transitu
transient 111
transfer 270
– statu pupillari 127
– statu quo 141
– vogue 1
inability 158, 699
inabstinent 954
inaccessible 196, 471
inaccurate 495, 568
inaction 172, **681**
inactivity **683**, 172
inadequate
powerless 158
insufficient 640
useless 645
imperfect 651
inadmissible
incongruous 24
excluded 55
extraneous 57
inexpedient 647
inadvertence 458
inadvisable 647
inaffable 895
inalienable
retention 781
right 924
inamorato 897
inane *void* 4
unmeaning 517
unthinking 452
insufficient 640
trivial 643
useless 645
inanimate 360
– matter 358
inanition 158
inanity [*see* inane]
inappetency 823, 866
inapplicable 10, 24
inapposite 10, 24
inappreciable 32, 193
unimportant 643
inapprehensible
stolid 499
unintelligible 519
inappropriate 24, 647
inapt
incongruous 24
impotent 158
useless 645
inexpedient 647
unskilful 699
inarticulate 581, 583
inartificial 703
inartistic 846
inasmuch *whereas* 9
however 26
because 476
inattention **458**
inaudible
silence 403
faint sound 405
deaf 419
voiceless 581
inaugural
precursor 64
inaugurate
begin 66
cause 153
install 755
celebrate 883
inauspicious
untimely 135
untoward 649
hopeless 859
inbeing **5**
inborn, inbred
intrinsic **5**
affections 820
– proclivity 601
inca 745
incage 751
incalculable 31, 105
incalescence 382
incandescence 382
incandescent 423
incantation
invocation 765
sorcery 992
spell 993
incantatory 992
incapable 158
incapacious 203
incapacitate 158
incapacity
impotence 158
ignorance 491
stupidity 499
incarcerate 751
incarnadine 434
incarnate
intrinsic 5
bodily 316
fleshly 364
vicious 945
devil –
bad man 949
Satan 978
Incarnation 976
incase 223, 229
incautious 863
incendiary
destroy 162
burn 384
influence 615
malevolent 907
evil-doer 913
bad man 949
incense *fuel* 388
fragrant 400
hate 898
anger 900
flatter 933
worship 990
rite 998
incension
burning 384
incentive 615
inception 66
inceptive 153
inceptor 541
incertitude 475
incessant
repeated 104
ceaseless 112
frequent 136
incest 961
inch *small* 32
length 200
by –es 275
to an – 494
not yield an – 606
give an – and take an ell 789
– by inch
by degrees 26
in parts 51
slowly 275
not see an – beyond one's nose 699
inchoation 66, 673
incide 44
incidence 278
incident 151
incidental
extrinsic 6
circumstance 8
irrelative 10
occurring 151
casual 156
liable 177
chance 621
trivial 643
– music 415
incinerate 384
incipience 66
incircumspect 460
incision 44, 259
incisive *energy* **171**
vigour 574
feeling 821
incisor 253
incite
exasperate **173**
urge 615
incivility 895
incivism 911
inclasp 229
inclement
violent **173**
cold 383
severe 739
pitiless 914*a*
inclination
[*see* incline]
will 600
affection 820
desire 865
love 897
incline *tendency* **176**
slope 217
direction 278
willing 602
induce 615
– an ear to 457
– the head 308
inclined
disposed 620
– plane 633
inclose
surround 227
inclosure **232**
include
composition 54
– *in a class* 76
inclusion **76**
inclusive
additive 37
component 56
class 76
incogitancy **452**
incognita, terra – 491
incognito 528
incognizable 519
incoherence
physical **47**
mental 503
incombustible 385
income *means* 632
profit 775
property 780
wealth 803
receipt 810
– tax 812
incoming

ingress 294
receipt 810
incommensurable 10
– quantity 84, 85
incommode 706
hinder 706
incommunicable
unmeaning 517
unintelligible 519
retention 781
incommunicado 528
incommutable 150
incomparable 33
incompassionate 914*a*
incompatible 24
incompatibility 15
incompetence
inability 158
incapacity 499
unskilful 699
dereliction 927
incompleteness **53**
non-completion 730
incompliance 764
incomprehensible
infinite 105
unintelligible 519
incomprehension 491
incompressible 321
inconcealable 525
inconceivable
unthinkable 452
impossible 471
improbable 473
incredible 485
unintelligible 519
wonder 870
inconceptible 519
inconcinnity
disagreement 24
ugliness 846
inconclusive 477
inconcoction 674
incondite 851
incongruous
differing 15
disagreeing 24
illogical 477
ungrammatical 568
discordant 713
inconnection 10, 44
inconsequence
irrelation 10
inconsequential 477
inconsiderable 32, 643
inconsiderate
thoughtless 452
inattentive 458
neglectful 460
foolish 699
inconsistent
contrary 14
disagreeing 24
illogical 477
absurd 497
foolish 499
capricious 608
discord 713
inconsolable 837
inconsonant
disagreeing 24
fitful 149
inconspicuous 447
inconstant 149
incontestable 159, 474, 525
incontiguous 196
incontinent 961
incontinently 132
incontrollable 173
incontrovertible 150, 474
inconvenience 647
put to – 706
inconversable 585, 893
inconvertible 143
inconvincible 487
incorporate 48
combine 48
include 76
materialize 316
incorporation 761
incorporeal 317
– hereditaments 780
incorrect
illogical **477**
erroneous 495
solecism 568
vicious 945
incorrigible
obstinate 606
hopeless 859
vicious 945
impenitent 951
incorruption
probity 939
innocence 946
incrassate
increase 194
density 321
- *fluids* 352
increase
- *in degree* **35**
- *in number* 102
- *in size* 194
incredible
great 31
impossible 471
improbable 473
doubtful 485
wonderful 870
incredulity 487, 989
increment
increase 35
addition 37
adjunct 39
expansion 194
increpation 932
incriminate 938
incrust 223, 224
incubate 370
incubation 673
incubus
hindrance 706
pain 828
demon 980
inculcate 6, 537
inculpable 946
inculpate 938
inculture 674
incumbency
business 625
churchdom 995
incumbent
inhabitant 188
high 206
weight 319
duty 926
clergyman 996
incumber 706
incumbered 806
incunabula 66, 127
incur 177
– blame 932
– danger 665
– a debt 806
– disgrace 874
– a loss 776
– the risk 621
incurable
ingrained 5
disease 655
hopeless 859
incuriam, per – 458, 460
incuriosity **456**
incursion 294, 716
incurvation 245
indagation 461
indebted
owing 806
gratitude 916
duty 926
indecent 961
indeciduous 150
indecipherable 519
indecision 475, 605
indecisive 475
indeclinable 150
indecorous
vulgar 851
vicious 945
impure 961
indeed *existing* **1**
very 31
assent 488
truly 494
assertion 535
wonder 870
indefatigable
persevering 604*a*
active 682
indefeasible
stable 150, 474
due 924
indefectible 650
indefensible
powerless 158
submission 725
accusable 938
wrong 945
indeficient 650
indefinite
great 31
unspecified **78**
infinite 105
misty 447
uncertain **475**
inexact 495
vague 519
indeliberate 612
indelible *stable* 150
memory 505
mark 550
feeling 821
indelicate 961
indemnity
compensation 30
restitution 790
forgiveness 918
atonement 952
reward 973
deed of – 771
indenizen 184
indent *scollop* 248
list 86
indentation 252, 257
indenture 769, **771**
independence
irrelation 10
freedom 748
wealth 803
Independent 984
indescribable 31,

870
indesinent 112
indestructible 150
indeterminate
indefinite 78
chance 156
uncertain 475
irresolute 605
indevotion 989
index
arrangement 60
exponent 84
list 86
sign 550
words 62
index expurgatorius 761, 932
indexterity 699
Indian:
- file 69
- rubber 325
- summer 126
- weed 392
indicate
specify 79
direct attention to 457
mean 516
mark 550
indication 550
indicative
evidence 467
indict *accuse* 938
arraign 969
indiction 108, 531
indifference
incuriosity 456
unwillingness 603
no choice 609*a*
insensibility 823
unconcern 866
irreligion 989
matter of – 643
indifferent
[*see* indifference]
unimportant 643
bad 649
indigence
insufficiency 640
poverty 804
indigenous 5, 188
indigested 674
indigestible 657
indigestion 655
indigitate 457
indign 940
indignation 900
– meeting 832
indignity 900, 929
indigo 438
indiligence 683
indirect
oblique 217
devious 279
latent 526
circuitous 629
indiscernible 447
indiscerptible
whole 50
unity 87
dense 321
indiscoverable 526
indiscreet 499, 863, 945
indiscretion
guilt 947
indiscriminate
mixed 41
unarranged 59
multiform 81
casual 621
indiscrimination 465a
indispensable 630
indispose
dissuade 616
indisposed
unwilling 603
sick 655
indisputable 474
indissoluble, indissolvable
joined 43
whole 50
stable 150
dense 321
indistinct 447
indistinction 465*a*
indistinguishable
identical 13
invisible 447
indisturbance 265, 826
indite 590
individual
whole 50
special 79
unity 87
person 372
indivisible *whole* 50
dense 321
indocility 158, 606
indoctrinate 537
indolence 683, 927
indomitable
strong 159
determined 604
persevering 604*a*
resisting 719
courage 861
indoor 221
indorse 769, 771
indorsement 550, 551
indraught 343, 348
indubitable 474
induce *cause* 153
power 157
produce 161
motive 615
induct 883
induction
inquiry 461
reasoning 476
drama 599
appointment 755
- *of a priest* 995
indulge *lenity* 740
allow 760
please 829
intemperance 954
gluttony 957
– one's fancy 609
– in 827
– oneself 943
– in reverie
inattention 458
fancy 515
– with *give* 784
indulgence
[*see* indulge]
absolution 918
indulgent *kind* 906
induration
hardening 323
impenitence 951
Indus to the pole, from – 180
industry 625, 682
hive of – 691
indweller 188
indwelling 5
inebriety 959
inedible 395
ineffable *great* 31
inexpressible 519
wonderful 870
ineffaceable 820
ineffectual
incapable 158
useless 645
failing 732
– attempt 732
pale its – fire 422
inefficacious
incapable 158
useless 645
failing 732
inefficient 158
inelastic *soft* 324
– fluid 333
inelasticity **326**
inelegance 579, 846
ineluctable 474
inept 24, 158, 645
inequality 28
inequitable 923
ineradicable
intrinsic 5
stable 150
inerrable 946
inertia 172
inertness
physical **172**
inactive 683
moral 823
inestimable 648
inevitable 474, 601
inexact
erroneous 495
feeble 575
inexcitability **826**
inexcusable
accusable 938
vicious 945
inexecution 730
inexhaustible 105, 639
inexistence **2**
inexorable
unavoidable 601
resolved 604
stern 739
compelling 744
pitiless 914*a*
revengeful 919
inexpectation 508
inexpedience 647
inexpensive 815
inexperience 491, 699
inexpert 699
inexpiable 945
inexplicable 519
inexpressible
great 31
unmeaning 517
unintelligible 519
wonderful 870
inexpressibles 225
inexpression
latency 526
inexpensive 517
inexpugnable 664
inextension 180a
littleness 193
immateriality 317
inextinguishable
stable 150
strong 159
excitable 825
– desire 865
inextricable
coherent 46

disorder 59
impossible 471
infallibility 474
assumption of – 885
infamy *shame* **874**
dishonour **940**
vice 945
infancy 66, 127
infandum renovare dolorem 505, 833
infant 129
fool 501
– prodigy **872**
Infanta 745
infanticide 361, 991
infantine 129
foolish 499
infantry 726
infarction 261
infatuation
misjudgment 481
credulity 486
folly 499
insanity 503
obstinacy 606
passion 825
love 897
infeasible 471
infect *mix with* 41
contaminate 659
excite 824
infectâ, re –
shortcoming 304
non-completion 730
failure 732
infection
transference 270
disease 655
infectious 270, 657
infecund 169
infelicity
inexpertness 699
misery 828
infelicitous 24
infer 472
inference 476, 480
by – 467
inferential
demonstrative 478
latent 526
inferiority
in degree **34**
in size 195
imperfection 651
personal – 34
infernal *bad* 649
malevolent 907
wicked 945
satanic 978
– machine 727
– regions 982
infertility 169
infest 830
infestivity 837, 843
infibulation 43
infidel 487, 989
infidelity
dishonour 940
irreligion 989
infiltrate *mix* 41
intervene 228
interpenetrate 294
moisten 337, 339
teach 537
infiltration
passage 302
Infinite, the – 976
infinite 105
– goodness 976
infinitely *great* **31**
infinitesimal
small 32
little 193
– calculus 85
infinity 105
infirm *weak* 160
disease 655
vicious 945
– of purpose 605
infirmary 662
infirmity
[*see* infirm]
infix 537
inflame
render violent **173**
burn 384
excite 824
anger 900
inflamed 382
inflammable 384, 388
inflammation
heating 384
disease 655
inflate *increase* **35**
expand 194
blow 349
inflated
overestimation 482
style 573, 577
ridiculous 853
vain 880
inflation
[*see* inflate]
rarefaction 322
currency 800
inflect 245
inflexible *hard* **323**
resolved 604
obstinate 606
stern 739
inexorable **914a**
inflexion
change 140
curvature 245
grammar **567**
inflict *act upon* **680**
severity 739
– evil **649**
– pain
bodily pain **378**
mental pain 830
– punishment 972
infliction
adversity 735
mental pain 828, 830
punishment 972
influence 153
change 140
physical – **175**
inducement 615
instrumentality 631
authority 737
absence of – **175a**
sphere of – 780
make one's – felt 631
influx 294
infold 232
inform 527
– against
accuse 938
go to law 969
informal 83, 964
informality 773
informant 527
information
knowledge 490
communication **527**
learning 539
lawsuit 969
pick up – 539
informer 532
informity 241
infra dignitatem 874, 940
infraction
trespass 303
disobedience 742
non-observance **773**
exemption 927
– of usage &c.
unconformity 83
desuetude 614
infrangible
combined 46
dense 321
infra-red rays 420
infrequency 137
infrigidation 385
infringe
transgress 303
disobey 742
not observe **773**
undueness 925
dereliction 927
– a law &c. 83
infundibular 252, 269
infuriate
violent **173**
excite 824
anger 900
infuscate 431
infuse *mix* **41**
insert 300
teach 537
– courage 861
– life into 824
– new blood 658
infusible 321
infusion [*see* infuse]
liquefaction 335
infusoria 193
ingannation 545
ingathering 72
ingemination 90
ingenerate 5
ingenious 515, 698
ingenite 5
ingenium, perfervidum – 682
ingénu *artless* 703
ingénue *actress* 599
ingenuity 698
ingenuous 703
ingesta 298
ingestion 296
ingle 388
inglorious 874, 940
ingluvies 191
ingot 800
ingraft *add* **37**
join 43
insert 300
teach 537
ingrafted
extrinsic **6**
habit 613
ingrain
insinuate 228
colour 428
ingrained
intrinsic 5
combined **48**
habit 613

character 820
ingrate 917
ingratiate 897
ingratiating 894
ingratitude **917**
ingredient 51, 56
ingress **294**
forcible – 300
ingurgitate 296
ingustible 391
inhabile 699
inhabit 186
inhabitant **188**
inhale *receive* 296
breathe 349
smell 398
inharmonious
discord 713
– colour 428
– sound 414
inhere 1
inherent 5, 820
inherit 775, 777
inheritance 780
– of the saints 981
inherited
intrinsic 5
inheritor 779
inhesion 5
inhibit *hinder* 706
restrain 751
prohibit 761
inhospitable 893
inhuman 907
inhume 363
inimaginable
impossible 471
improbable 473
wonderful 870
inimical 708, 889
inimitable
non-imitation 20
supreme 33
very good 648
perfect 650
iniquity 923, 945
worker of – 949
inirritability 826
initial 66
– letter 558
initiate *begin* 66
admit 296
teach 537
initiated *skilful* 698
initiative 66
inject 300, 337
injection 662
injudicial 964
injudicious 499, 863
injunction
acquirement 630
advice 695
command 741
prohibition 761
injure *evil* 619
damage 659
spite 907
injuria formæ, spretæ – 846, 930
injury *evil* 619
badness 649
damage 659
injustice 923
ink 431
pen and – 590
before the – is dry 132
– slinging **720**
inkle 45
inkling
knowledge 490
supposition 514
information 527
inkstand 590
inland 221
inlay 440, 847
inlet *beginning* 66
interval 198
opening 260
ingress 294
- *of the sea* 343
inly 221
inmate 188
inmost 221
to the – core 822
– soul 820
– thoughts 451
inn 189
– s of Court 968
innate 5, 601
innavigable 471
inner 221
– coating 224
– man *intellect* 450
affections 820
innermost recesses 221
innings *land* 342
acquisition 775
receipt 810
innkeeper 601
innocence **946**
innocent *fool* 501
good 648
healthy 656
artless 703
guiltless 946
innocuous *good* 648
healthy 656
innocent 946
innominate 565
innovation
variation 20a
new 123
change 140
innoxious
salubrious 656
innocent 946
innuendo *hint* 527
censure 932
innumerable 105
innutritious 657
inobservance 773
inoccupation 681
inoculate
insert 300
teach 537
influence 615
inodorous **399**
inoffensive 648, 946
inofficious 907
inoperative
powerless 158
unproductive 169
useless 645
inopportune
untimely 135
inexpedient 647
inordinate 31, 641
inorganization **358**
inornate 849
inosculate *join* 43
intersect 219
convoluted 248
inquest 461
inquietude
changeable 149
uneasy 828
discontent 832
apprehension 860
inquinate 659
inquire 461
– into 595
inquirer 461
inquiring mind 455
inquiry **461**
inquisition
inquiry 461
severity 739
torture 907
tribunal 966
inquisitive 455
inquisitorial
prying 455
inquiry 461
severe 739
jurisdiction 965
inroad *ingress* 294
devastation 659
invasion 716
inrolment **551**
insalubrity **657**
insanity **503**
insatiable 865
inscribe 590, **873**
inscription 551
inscroll 551
inscrutable 519
insculpture 557
insculptured 558
insecable 43, 87
insect *minute* **193**
animal 366
– cry 412
insecure
uncertain **475**
danger 665
insensate
foolish 499
insane 503
insensibility
slow 275
physical **376**
moral **823**
– of benefits **917**
– to the past 506
inseparable 43, 46
insert *locate* 184
interpose 228
enter 294
put in 300
record 551
– itself 300
insertion **300**
adjunct 39
ornament 847
inservient 645
inseverable 43, 87
inside 221
– out 218
turn – out 529
insidious
deceitful 545
cunning 702
dishonourable 940
insight 465, 490
insignia 550
– of authority **747**
insignificant
unmeaning 517
unimportant 643
insincere 544, 855
insinuate
intervene 228
ingress 294
insert 300
latency 526
hint 527
ingratiate **897**
blame 932
insipid
style **575**

dull 840
insipidity
tasteless **391**
indifferent 866
insist *argue* 476
command 741
– upon *affirm* 535
dwell on 573
be determined 604
contend 720
compel 744
conditions 770
due 924
insnare 545
insobriety 959
insolation 382, 384
insolence 878, 885
insoluble *dense* 321
unintelligible 519
insolvable 519
insolvent
poverty 804
debt 806
non-payment 808
insomnia 682
insouciance
thoughtlessness 458
supineness 823
indifference 866
inspan 293
inspect 441, 457
inspector 444
inquisitor 461
judge 480
director 694
inspiration
wisdom 498
imagination 515
poetry 597
impulse 612
motive 615
feeling 821
Deity 976
revelation 985
religious - 987
inspire *improve* 658
prompt 615
animate 824
cheer 836
– courage 861
– hope 858
– respect 928
inspirit *incite* 615
animate 824
encourage 861
inspiriting
hopeful 858
inspissate 321, 352
instability 149
install *locate* 184
commission **755**
celebrate 883
instalment
portion **51**
payment 807, 809
instance
example 82
motive 615
solicitation 765
instant *moment* 113
present 118
destiny 152
required 630
importance 642
active 682
lose not an – 684
on the – 132
instantaneity **113**
instanter 113, 132
instar omnium 17, 82
instate 883
instauration 660
instead 147
instep 245
instigate 615
instil *extrinsic* 6
mix 41
insert 300
teach 537
instinct
intellect 450
intuition 477
impulse 601
– with *motive* 615
possession 777
brute – 450*a*
instinctive
inborn 5
institute *begin* 66
cause 153
produce 161
academy 542
society 712
– an inquiry 461
institution
academy 542
society 712
political - 963
church 995
institutor 540
instruct *teach* 537
advise 695
precept 697
order 741
instructed 490
instructor 540
instrument
implement **633**
security 771
musical – 417
optical – 445
recording – 553
instrumental 631
– music 415
instrumentalist 416
instrumentality **631**
insuavity 895
insubordinate 742
insubstantial 4
– pageant 882
insufferable
painful 830
dislike 867
insufficiency **640**
insufflation 349
insular *unrelated* 10
detached 44
single 87
local 181
island 346
prejudice 481
insulate 44
insulse 499, 843
insult *rudeness* 895
offence 900
disrespect 929
insulting 898
insuperable 471
– obstacle 706
insupportable 830
insuppressible 173
insurance 768, 771
insure
make sure 474
obtain security 771
insurgent 742
insurmountable 471
insurrection 719, 742
insusceptible 823
– of change 150
inswept 195
intact
permanent 141
perfect 650
preserved 670
intaglio *mould* 22
concave 252
sculpture 557
engraving 558
intangible *little* 193
numb 381
integer 50, 84
integer vitæ scelerisque purus 939
integral 50
– calculus 85
– part 56
integrate 50
integrity *whole* 50
probity 939
virtue 944
integument 223
intellect **450**
absence of – **450a**
exercise of the – 451
intellectual 450
intelligence
mind 450
capacity **498**
news 532
intelligencer 527
intelligentsia 492
intelligibility **518**
intemperance **954**
drunkenness 959
intempestivity **135**
intend 620
intendant 694
intended *will* 600
predetermined 611
intense *great* 31
energetic 171
– colour 428
– thought 457
intensification 35
intensify
increase 35
stimulate 171
intensity *degree* 26
greatness 31
energy 171
intensive culture 371
intent *attention* 457
will 600
design 620
active 682.
– upon *desire* 865
resolved 604
intention **620**
bad – 907
good – 906
intently, look – 441
intents and purposes, to all – 27, 52
inter 363
interact 12
inter: – alia 82
– nos 528
interaction 170
interbreeding 41
intercalate 228
intercalation 300
intercede
mediate 724
deprecate 766

intercept
hinder 706
take 789
intercession
[*see* intercede]
worship 990
Intercessor 976
interchange 148
barter 794
– visits &c. 892
interchangeable 12
intercipient 706
interclude 706
intercommunication 527
intercommunity 892
interconnection 9
intercourse
copulation 43
friendship 888
sociality 892
verbal – 582, 588
intercurrence
interchange 148
interjacence 228
passage 302
interdependence 12
interdict 761
interdictive 55
interdigitate 219, 228
interest *concern* 9
influence 175
curiosity 455
advantage 618
importance 642
property 780
debt 806
excite 824
please 829
amuse 840
devoid of – 841
feel an – in 906
not know one's own – 699
make – for 707
place out at –
lend 787
economy 817
take an – in
curiosity 455
love 897
take no – in
insensibility 823
indifference 866
want of – 866
interested
selfish 943
– in 457
interesting
lovable 897
interfere *disagree* 24
counteract 179
intervene 228
activity 682
thwart 706
mediate 724
interference
light 420
interfretted 219
interfusion 41
interim 106, 120
interior 221
painting 556
interjacence 68, 228
interject 228, 300
interlace *join* 43
twine 219
interlacing 41
interlard 41, 228
interleave 228
interline
interpolate 228
write 590
interlineation 39
interlink 43, 219
interlocation 228
interlocking directorate 709
interlocution 588
interlocutor 582
interloper
extraneous 57
intervene 228
obstruct 706
interlude
time 106
dramatic 599
intermarriage 903
intermeddle 682, 706
intermeddling 724
intermediary 534
intermediate
mean 29
middle 68
intervening 228
ministerial 631
– time 106
intermedium
mean 29
link 45
intervention 228
instrument 631
interment 363
insertion 300
intermezzo 415
intermigration 266
interminable
infinite 105
eternal 112
long 200
intermingle 41
intermission 106, 142
intermit
interrupt 70
recur 138
discontinue 142
intermittence
time 106
intermix 41, 48
intermutation 148
intermural 278
intern 221
internal 5, 221
– evidence 467
international
reciprocal 12
sociality 892
– law 963
internecine 361
– war 722
internuncio 534, 758
interpel 142
interpellation
inquiry 461
address 586
summons 741
appeal 765
interpenetration
interjacence 228
ingress 294
passage 302
interpolation
adjunct 39
analytical 85
interpose 228
insertion 300
interpose
intervene 228
act 682
hinder 706
mediate 724
interposit 799
interplanetary 228
interpretation 522
interpreter 524
interrelation 9, 12
interregnum
intermission 106
transient 111
discontinuance 142
interval 198
laxity 738
interrogate 461
interrupt
discontinuity 70
cessation 142
hinder 706
interruption
derangement 61
interval 198
intersect 219
interspace 198, 221
intersperse 73, 228
interstellar 228
interstice 198
interstitial 221, 228
intertexture
intersection 219
tissue 329
inter-twine, -twist
unite 43
cross 219
interval
- *of time* 106
- *of space* 198
- *in music* 413
at –s
discontinuously 70
at regular –s 138
intervene
- *in order* 70
- *in time* 106
- *in space* 228
be instrumental 631
mediate 724
intervert 140, 279
interview 588, 892
intervolved 43
interweave *join* 43
cross 219
interjacence 228
interworking 170
intestate 552
intestine 221
inthral 749, 751
intimacy 9
intimate
personal 79
close 197
inside 221
tell 527
friendly 888, 892
intimately
joined 43
intimidate
frighten 860
insolence 885
threat 909
intitule 564
into: go – 294
put – 300
run – 300
intolerable 830
intolerance

prejudice 481
dissent 489
obstinacy 606
impatience 825
insolence 885
malevolence 907
intomb 363
intonation
sound 402
musical 413
voice 580
intone 416, 990
intort 248
intoxicant 663
intoxication
excitement 824, 825
inebriation 959
intra, ab – 221
intractable
obstinate 606
difficult 704
sullen 901*a*
intramural 221
intransient 110
intransigeance 604
intransitive 110
intransmutable 110, 150
intrap 545
intraregarding 221
intrench 717
– on 303
intrepid 861
intricate
confused 59
convoluted 248
difficult 704
intrigant
meddlesome 682
cunning 702
libertine 962
intrigue *fascinate* 615, 897
plot 626
activity 682
cunning 702
excite 824
interest 829
licentiousness 961
intrinsic 5
– evidence 467
– habit 613
– truth 494
intrinsicality 5
introception 296
introduce *lead* 62
interpose 228
precede 280
insert 300
– new blood 140
– new conditions 469
– to 888
introduction
[*see* introduce]
preface 64
reception 296
drama 599
friendship 888
courtesy 894
introductory
precursor 64
beginning 66
priority 116
introgression 294
introit 998
intromission 228
intromit
discontinue 142
receive 296
introspection 441, 457
introspective 451
introvert 218
intrude
interfere 24
inopportune 135
intervene 228
enter 294
encroach 303
intruder 57
intrusiveness 682
intrust 755, 787
intuition *mind* 450
unreasoning 477
knowledge 490
intumescence 194, 250
intwine 43, 248
inunction 223
inundate
effusion 337
flow 348
redundance 641
inunderstanding 452
inurbanity 895
inure 613, 673
inured
insensible 823
inusitation 614
inutility 645
invade *ingress* 294
encroach 303
attack 716
invalid
powerless 158
illogical 477
diseased 655
undue 925
invalidate
disable 158
weaken 160
confute 479
invaluable 648
invariable
intrinsic 5
uniform 16
conformable 82
stable 150
invasion
ingress 294
attack 716
invective 932
inveigh 932
inveigle 545, 615
invent
discover 480*a*
imagine 515
lie 544
devise 626
invented
untrue 546
invention 480*a*
inventive
skilful 698
inventor 164
inventory 86
inverse 14, 218
inversion
derangement 61
change 140
of position 218
contraposition 237
reversion 145
language 577
invertebrate 158
invest
empower 157
clothe 225
besiege 227, 716
commission 755
give 784
lend 787
expend 809
– in *locate* 184
purchase 795
– money 817
– with *ascribe* 155
investigate 461
investment 225
– trust 712
make –s 673
inveterate *old* 124
established 150
inborn 820
– belief 484
– habit 613
invidious
painful 830
hatred 898
spite 907
envy 921
invigorate
strengthen 159
invigorating
healthy 656
invincible 159
inviolable
secret 528
right 924
honour 939
inviolate
permanent 141
secret 528
honourable 939
invious *closed* 261
pathless 704
invisibility 447
invisible *small* 193
not to be seen 447
concealed 526
– ink 528
become – 4
invitâ Minervâ 603, 704
invite *induce* 615
offer 763
ask 765
– the attention 457
inviting
[*see* invite]
pleasing 829
invoice 86
invoke *address* 586
implore 765
pray 990
– curses 908
– saints 998
involucrum 223
involuntary
necessary 601
unwilling 603
– servitude 749
involution [*see* involve]
algebra 85
involve *include* 54
derange 61
wrap 225
evince 467
mean 516
latency 526
involved
disorder 59
convoluted 248
obscure style 571
in debt 806
involvement 704
invulnerable 664
inward *intrinsic* 5

inside 221
– bound 294
– monitor 926
inweave 219
inwrap 225
inwrought 5
io triumphe! 838, 883
Ionic 597
iota 32
I. O. U. 771, 800
ipse dixit 474, 535
ipsissima verba 494
ipso facto 1
iræ
amantium – 918
tantæne animis cœlestibus – 900
irascibility 901
irate 900
ire 900
iridescent 440
Iris 268, 534
iris 440, 441
Irish Bull 853
Irishism 497
irk 688, 830
irksome
tiresome 688
difficult 704
painful 830
weary 841
iron *strength* 159
smooth 255
hard 323
resolution 604
rule with a rod of – 739
– age *adversity* 735
pain 828
– cross 733
– gray 432
– grip 159
– gripe 781
– heel 739
– necessity 601
– rule 739
– entering into the soul 828, 830
– sway 739
– will 604
iron-bound coast
land 342
danger 667
iron-clad
covering 223
defence 717
man of war 726
iron-handed 739
iron-hearted 861
iron-mould 434
irons 752
fire – 386
put in – 751
– in the fire
business 625
redundance 641
active 682
unskilful 699
irony
figure of speech 521
untruth 546
ridicule 856
irradiate 420
irrational
number 84
illogical 477
silly 499
irreclaimable
hopeless 859
vicious 945
impenitent 951
irreconcilable
unrelated 10
discordant 24
unwilling 603
opponent 710
enmity 889
irrecoverable
past 122
hopeless 859
irredeemable 859
irredentist 776
irreducible
discordant 24
out of order 59
unchangeable 150
irrefragable 478
irrefutable 474, 478
irregular
diverse 16a
out of order 59
multiform 81
against rule 83
- in recurrence 139
distorted 243
combatant 726
irregularity 139
irrelation 10
irrelevant
unrelated 10
unaccordant 24
sophistical 477
unimportant 643
irreligion 989
irremediable
bad 649
hopeless 859
(*spoiled* 659)
irremissible 945
irremovable 150
irreparable
hopeless 859
irrepentance 951
irreprehensible 946
irrepressible
violent 173
free 748
excitable 825
irreproachable 946
irreprovable 946
irresistible
strong 159
demonstration 478
necessary 601
irresoluble 150
irresolution 605
irresolvable 87
irresolvedly 605
irrespective 10
irresponsible
irresolute 605
exempt 927a
arbitrary 964
irretrievable
stable 150
lost 776
hopeless 859
irrevealable 528
irreverence 929, 988
irreversible
stable 150
hopeless 859
irrevocable
stable 150
necessary 601
resolute 604
hopeless 859
irrigate 337
irriguous 339
irrision 856, 929
irritabile, genus – 901
irritable 825, 901
irritate *violent* 173
excite 824
pain 830
provoke 898
incense 900
irritation
[*see* irritate]
pain 828
source of – 830
irritating
[*see* irritate]
stringent 171
irruption 294, 716
Irvingite 984
Ishmael 83
is: that – 118
– to be 152
Isis 979
Islamism 984
island 181, 346
–s of the blessed 981
islander 188
isle 346
isobar 338
isocheimal 383
isochronal 114
isochronous 27, 120
isolate 44, 893
isolated 10, 87
isomorphism 240
isoperimetrical 27
isothermal 382
– layer 338
isotonic 413
issue *distribute* 73
focus 74
event 151
effect 154
posterity 167
depart 293
egress 295
stream 348, 349
inquiry 461
publication 531
book 593
ulcer 655
dénouement 729
money 800
at – *discussion* 476
dissent 489
negation 536
opposition 708
discord 713
contention 720
in – 461
join – *lawsuit* 969
– a command 741
issueless 169
isthmus
connection 45
narrow 203
land 342
italics *mark* 550
put in –
importance 642
itch *titillation* 380
desire 865
itching palm 819
item
addition 37, 39
part 51
speciality 79
unit 87
iteration 104
itinerant 266, 268

itinerary 266, 527
itur ad astra, sic – 360
ivory 430
Ixion 312

J

jab 276
jabber
unmeaning 517
stammer 583
chatter 584
jacent 213
jacet, hic – 363
jacinth 847
jack
rotation 312
ensign 550
instrument 633
money 800
Jack – Cade 742
– Ketch 975
– o' lantern 423
– in office
director 694
bully 887
– at a pinch 711
– Pudding
actor 599
humorist 844
boaster 884
before one can say '– Robinson' 132
– tar 269
– of all trades 700
jack-a-dandy 844, 854
jackal
auxiliary 711
servility 886
jackanapes 854, 887
Jackass 271
jack-boot 225
jackdaw in peacock's feathers 701
jacket 225
cork – 666
Jacobin 710
Jacquerie 716, 719
jacta est alea 601
jactitation
tossing 315
boasting 884
jaculation 284
jade *horse* 271
fatigue 688
low woman 876
scamp 949
drab 962
jag 257
jagged 244
jail 752
– bird
prisoner 754
bad man 949
jailer 753, 975
jakes 653
jalousie de métier 921
jam *squeeze* 43
crowd 72
food 298
pulp 354
sweet 396
scrape 732
– in *interpose* 228
jamb 215
jamboree 840
jammed in 751
jangle
harsh sound 410
quarrel 713
janissary 726
janitor 263
janty *gay* 836
pretty 845
stylish 852
showy 882
insolent 885
January 138
januis clausis 528
Janus *deceiver* 607
tergiversation 607
close the temple of – 723
Janus-faced 544
japan *coat* 223
resin 356a
ornament 847
jar *clash* 24
vessel 191
agitation 315
stridor 410
discord 713
– upon the feelings 830
jardinière 191
jargon
absurdity 497
no meaning 517
unintelligible 519
neology 563
jarvey 694
jasper 847
jaundiced
yellow 436
prejudiced 481
dejected 837
jealous 920
view with – eyes
disapprove 932
jaunt 266
jaunting car 272
jaunty [*see* janty]
javelin 727
jaw *chatter* 584
scold 932
jaw-fallen 837
jaws *mouth* 231
eating 298
– of death 360
jay 584
jaywalker 701
jazz 415, 840
– band 417
jealous of honour 939
jealousy 920
suspicion 485
jecur, difficili bile – 900
jeer 929
Jehovah 976
Jehu 268, 694
jejune *insipid* 391
style 575
scanty 640
dull 843
jell 352
jelly 298, 352
beat to a – 972
jemidar 745
jemmy *lever* 633
dandy 854
je ne sais quoi
exceptional 83
what d'ye call 'em 563
beauty 845
jennet 271
jeopardy 665
jerboa 309
jeremiad
lament 839
invective 932
Jericho, send to – 297
jerk *start* 146
throw 284
pull 285
agitate 315
jerkin 225
jerks, by – 70
Jerry Sneak 862, 941
jersey 225
Jerusalem
the new – 981
Jessamy, Jemmy – 854
jesse 1000
jest *trifle* 643
wit 842
jest-book 842
jester 844
jesting-stock 857
Jesuit *deceiver* 548
priest 996
jesuitical 477, 544
Jesus 976
jet *stream* 348
– black 431
jetsam 73, 782
jettison 782
jetty *protection* 250
harbour 666
jeu
le – n'en vaut pas la chandelle
waste 638
unimportant 643
dear 814
– d'esprit 842
– de mots 842
– de théâtre 599
jeune
– premier 599
– veuve 599
Jew *cunning* 702
lender 787
rich 803
extortioner 819
heretic 984
worth a –'s eye 648, 814
–'s harp 417
jewel *gem* 648
ornament 847
favourite 899
jewellery, false – 545
Jezebel *wicked* 913
wretch 949
courtesan 962
jib *front* 234
regression 283
cut of one's –
form 240
appearance 448
jibe 140
jiffy 113
jig 840
jig-saw puzzle 840
jilt *disappoint* 509
deceive 545
deceiver 548
cast off 756
dishonour 940
jilted 898

jimp 845
jingal 727
jingle 408
jingo 887
jingoism 884
jinks, high – 840
jinriksha 272
jinx 649, 735
Joan of Arc 861
job *business* 625
action 680
unfair 940
tough – 704
Job:
patience of – 826, 830
poor as – 804
–'s comforter
dejection 837
hopeless 859
jobation 932
jobber
deceiver 548
tactician 700
merchant 797
trickster 943
jobbernowl 501
jobbery 702, 940
jobbing *barter* 794
jockey *rider* 268
deceive 545
deceiver 548
servant 746
jocose 836, 842
jocoseness *fun* 840
jocular 836, 842
jocund 836, 840
jocundity 829
Joe Miller 842, 844
jog *push* 276
shake 315
– the memory 505
– on *continue* 143
trudge 266
slow 275
advance 282
mediocrity 736
joggle 315
jog-trot
trudge 266
slow 275
habit 613
John Doe and Richard Roe 4
Johnny 854
John's 653
Johnsonian 577
joie, feu de – 883
join *connect* 43
assemble 72
contiguous 199
arrive 292
party 712
sociality 892
marry 903
– battle 722
– in the chorus 488
– forces, hands, 709
– in 778
– issue *discuss* 476
deny 536
quarrel 713
contend 720
lawsuit 969
– the majority 360
– up
enlist 722
– with 709
joint *junction* 43
part 51
accompanying 88
concurrent 178
meat 298
– concern 721
joint-stock 709, 778
joint-tenancy 778
jointure 780
joist 215
joke *absurdity* 497
trifle 643
wit 842
ridicule 856
in – 842
mere – 643
no – *existing* 1
important 642
practical –
deception 545
ridicule 856
disrespect 929
take a – 498
joker 844
jokesmith 844
joking apart 535, 604
jole 236
jollification
amusement 840
intemperance 954
jollity 840, 892
jolly *plump* 192
marine 269
gay 836
ridicule 856
– boat 273
– fellow 892
jolt 276, 315
jolthead 501
Jonah 649
Jones's
Davy – locker 360
Paul – 792
jorum 191
Joseph 960
–'s coat 440
joss 991
– house 1000
jostle *rush* 276
jog 315
clash 713
jot 32, 643
jotting 550, 551
jounce 315
journal *annals* 114
newspaper 531
record 551
magazine 593
narrative 594
accounts 811
journalist
messenger 534
recorder 553
author 593
journey 266
journeyman
artisan 690
servant 746
joust 720
Jove 979
by – 870
sub –
out of doors 220
air 338
jovial *gay* 836
amusement 840
social 892
jowl 236
joy 827
give one – 896
joyful 836
joyless *painful* 830
sad 837
joy stick 693
J.P. 967
Juan, Don – 962
jube 1000
jubeo, sic volo sic – 741
jubilant *gay* 836
rejoicing 838
boastful 884
jubilee 138, 883
jubilitate 884
Judæus Apella, credat –
disbelief 485
absurdity 497
Judaism 984
Judas *deceiver* 548
knave 941
– kiss
hypocrisy 544
base 940
judge *decide* 480
master 745
taste 850
magistrate **967**
Judge *deity* 976
Judgment
Day of – 67
judgement
intellect 450
discrimination 465
decision **480**
wisdom 498
sentence 972
judgement-seat 966
judicata, res –
certain 474
judgment 480
judication 480
judicatory 965, 966
judicature 965
Judicature, High Court of – 966
judice: coram –
jurisdiction 965
lawsuit 969
me – 484
sub – *inquiry* 461
lawsuit 969
judicial 965
– astrology 511
– murder 361
– separation 905
judicious 498
jug 191, 752
juggernaut
kill 361
god 979
idolatry 991
juggle *deceive* 545
cunning 702
juggler 548, 599
jugulate 361
juice 333
juiceless 340
juicy 339
ju-jitsu 718
jujube 396
julep 396
jumble *mixture* **41**
confusion 59
derange 61
indiscriminate 465a
jument 271
jump
sudden change 146
leap 309
neglect 460

at one – 113
– about 315
– at *willing* 602
pursue 622
hasten 684
consent 762
seize 789
desire 865
– to a conclusion
misjudge 481
credulous 486
– over 460
– up 307, 309
jumper 225
junction 43
juncture
circumstance **8**
junction 43
period 134
jungle *disorder* 59
vegetation 367
junior 127, 541
– counsel 968
junk 273
junket *dish* 298
merry-making 840
Juno 920, 979
junta 696
junto 712
jupe 225
Jupiter 979
jurare in verba magistri 481, 486
jurat 967
jure: de – *due* 924
legal 963
– divino *due* 924
God 976
juridical 965
jurisconsult 968
jurisdiction 965
authority 737
Jurisprudence 963
jurist 480, 968
jury 967
empanel a – 969
– box 966
– mast
substitute 147
refuge 666
jus: summum – 922
– civile 963
– gentium 963
– nocendi 737
– et norma loquendi 567
jussive 741
just *accurate* 494
right 922
equitable 939
pious 987
– as *similar* 17
same time 120
– do 639
– now 118
– out 123
– reasoning 476
– so 488
– then 113
– the thing
agreement 23
exact 494
– in time 134
juste milieu
middle 68
moderation 174
mid-course 628
justice
right 922
honour 939
magistrate 967
administration of – 965
bring to – 969
court of – 966
do – to *eat* 298
duty 926
praise 931
vindicate 937
not do – to 483
retributive – 922, 972
– seat 966
justifiable 922, 937
justification
vindication 937
religious 987
justle *push* 276
contend 720
jut out 250
jute 205
jutty 250
juvenile 127
– lead 599
juxtaposition 199
j'y suis j'y reste 141

K

kadi 967
kail 840
kaiser 745
kaleidoscope 149, 445
kangaroo 309
Katerfelto 994
kavass 965
K.C. 968
keck 297
kedge *navigate* 267
anchor 666
keek 527
keel 211
– upwards 218
keelhaul 972
keen *energetic* 171
sharp 253
sensible 375
cold 383
intelligent 498
poignant 821
lament 839
witty 842
eager 865
– blast 349
keener 839
keen-eyed 441
keep *do often* 136
persist 141
continue 143
food 298
store 636
provision 637
refuge 666
preserve 670
citadel 717
custody 751
prison 752
observe 772
retain 781
celebrate 883
– alive 359, 670
– aloof 196, 623
– accounts 811
– an account with 805
– apart 44
– at it 143
– away 187
– back *late* 133
conceal 528
dissuade 616
not use 678
restrain 751
retain 781
– the ball rolling 143
– one's bed 655
– body and soul together *life* 359
health 654
– within bounds 304
– close 781
– company 88
– one in countenance
conformity 82
induce 615
aid 707
encourage 861
– one's countenance
unexcitable 826
sad 837
– one's course 282
– an eye upon 459
– the field 722
– firm 150
– on foot
continuance 143
support 215
preparation 673
– from *conceal* 528
refrain 623
not do 681
restrain 751
– going
continue 143
move 264
– one's ground 141
– one's hand in 613
– one's head above water 731, 817
– hold 150
– holy 987
– house 184
– in ignorance 528
– in *restrain* 751
prohibit 761
– on one's legs 654
– a good look out for 507
– in mind 505
– moving 682
– off *avoid* 623
hinder 706
defend 717
resist 719
prohibition 761
– on *do often* 136
continue 143
persevere 604a
– to oneself 528
– in order 693
– out
– *of the way* 187
– *of harm's way* 864
– pace with 27, 120
– the peace 714
– posted 527
– the pot boiling 143

– one's promise 772
– quiet 265
– a secret 528
– a shop 625
– in sight 459
– silence 585
– straight 944
– in suspense
uncertainty 475
irresolution 605
– in the thoughts 505
– time
punctual 132
music 416
– to 604*a*
– together 709
– under
authority 737
subjection 749
restraint 751
– up [*see below*]
– in view
attend to 457
remember 505
expect 507
– waiting 133
– watch 459
– one's word 939
keep up
continue 143
preserve 670
stimulate 824
– appearances 852
– the ball 682, 840
– a correspondence 592
– the memory of 505
– one's spirits 836
– with 274
keeper 370, 753
keeping
congruity 23
in – 82
safe – *safety* 664
preservation 670
keepsake 505
keg 191
kelpie 979
kelson 211
kempt 652
ken 441, 490
beyond mortal – 360
kennel
assemblage 72
hovel 189
ditch 259
conduit 350
Kentish fire 931
képi 225
kerb-stone 233
kerchief 225
wave a – 550
kern *quern* 330
low fellow 876
varlet 949
kernel *heart* 5
cause 153
central 222
important 642
kerosene 356
ketch
ship 273
Ketch, Jack – 975
kettle *vessel* 191
caldron 386
– drum *music* 417
tea-party 892
– of fish
disorder 59
difficulty 704
key *cause* 153
opener 260
music 413
colour 428
interpretation 522
indication 550
instrument 631, 633
emblem of authority 747
deliver the –s of the city 725
key-hole 260
key-note *model* 22
rule 80
music 413
key-stone
support 215
motive 615
importance 642
completion 729
khaki 225, 433
khan *inn* 189
governor 745
khedive 745
kibitka 272
kibitzer 682
kick *impulse* 276
recoil 277
assault 716
thrill 821
spurn 930
punish 972
– against
oppose 708
resist 719
– against the pricks
useless 645
rash 863
unequal 28
superior 33
– up a dust
active 682
discord 713
insolent 885
– a row 900
– one's heels
kept waiting 133
nothing to do 681
– off 62
– up a row
violent 173
discord 713
– over the traces 742
kicking, alive and – 359
kickshaw *food* 298
trifle 643
kid *child* 129
progeny 167
leather 223
not to be handled with – gloves
dirty 653
difficult 704
kidnap
deceive 545
take 789
steal 791
kidney *class* 75
kilderkin 191
Kilkenny cats 713
kill 361
– or cure 662
– the fatted calf 883
– the goose with golden eggs 699
– with kindness 902
– the slain 641
– time 106
inactivity 683
amusement 840
– two birds with one stone 682
killing 361
delightful 829
kill-joy 706
kiln 386
kilowatt 466
kilt 225
kimbo 244
kimono 225
kin 75
kind *class* 75
benevolent 906
– regards 894
kinder-garten 542
kindle *cause* 153
produce 161
quicken 171
inflame 173
set fire to 384
excite 824
incense 900
kindling wood 388
kindred 9, 11
kine 366
kinematics 264
kinetic energy 157
king 745
every inch a –
authority 737
rank 875
–maker 694
King –'s **Bench** 752, 966
–'s birthday 268
–'s counsel 968
– Death 360
–'s English 560
–'s evidence 529
–'s highway 627
–'s ransom 648
– of Kings 976
kingcraft 693
kingdom
region 181
property 780
– of heaven 981
kingly 737
king-post 215
kink 248, 378, 608
kiosk 189, 1000
kip 961
kirk 1000
kirtle 225
kismet 601
kiss *touch* 199
courtesy 894
endearment 902
– the book 535
– the hem of one's garment 928
– in the ring 840
– the rod 725
kit *class* 75
equipment 191
fiddle 417
–bag 191
kitcat 556
kitchen 191, 691
– maid 746
– range 386
kitchener 386
kitchenette 691
kite *fly* 273

bill 800
fly a – *credit* 805
insolvency 808
– balloon 273, 726
kith 11
kithless 87
kitten *animal* 366
young 129
bring forth 161
playful as a – 836, 840
kleptomania
insanity 503
stealing 791
desire 865
kleptomaniac 504
knack 698
get into the – 613
knacker 361
knag 706
knaggy 901*a*
knap 206
knapsack 191
knave 548, **941**
– of hearts 897
knavery
deception 545
cunning 702
improbity 940
vice 945
knead *mix* 41
mould 240
soften 324
stroke 379
knee *angle* 244
bend the –
stoop 308
submission 725
down on one's –s
humble 879
on one's –s
beg 765
respect 928
atone 952
on the –s of the gods 121, 152
knee-deep 208, 209
kneel *stoop* 308
submit 725
beg 765
servility 886
courtesy 894
ask mercy 914
respect 928
worship 990
knell 363
strike the death – 361
knickerbockers 225
knicknack 643, 847
knife 253
play a good – and fork *eat* 298
appetite 865
war to the – 708
knight 875
– errant
madman 504
defender 717
rash 863
philanthropist 910
–'s move 279
– service 777
– of the road 792
– Templar 712
knit 43
well – 159
– the brow
discontent 832
anger 900
disapprobation 932
knitting 847
knob *pendency* 214
ball 249
protuberance 250
knock *blow* 276
sound 406
hard –s 720
– at the door
death 360
request 765
– down
destroy 162
lay flat 213
lower 308
injure 659
dishearten 837
– on the head
kill 361
– one's head against 699
– off *complete* 729
– out 162
– over 162
– under 725
– up 688
knock-down argument 479
knocked
– to atoms 162
– on the head
failure 732
knocker 936
knock-kneed 243, 244
knoll 206
knot *ligature* 45
entanglement 59
group 72
intersection 219
round 249
dense 321
difficulty 704
hindrance 706
junto 712
ornament 847
marriage 903
true lover's – *love* 897
endearment 902
tie the nuptial – 903
knotted *rough* 256
knout 975
know *believe* 484
knowledge 490
friendly 888
associate 892
I'd have you to – 457, 535
not that one –s 491
– what one is about 698
– all 474
I – better 536
– no bounds
great 31
infinite 105
redundance 641
– for certain 484
– by heart 505
– one's own mind 604
– one's stuff 465
– one's way about 465
– nothing of 491
– what's what 698
– which is which 465
knowing 702
knowingly 620
knowledge **490**
[*and see* know]
acquire – 539
come to one's – 527
practical – 698
– of the world 698
known:
become – 529
make – *inform* 527
publish 531
well – 490
habitual 613
– as 564
– by 550
knuckle 244
– down 725
knuckle-duster 727
knurl 256
knurr and spell 840
kobold 980
Koh-i-noor 650
kopje 206
Koran 986
kotow *bow* 308
submission 725
courtesy 894
respect 928
kraal 189, 232
kraken 83
kris 727
Krishna 979
kudos 931
Ku klux klan 712
Kursaal 840
kyanize 670
kyles 343

L

laager 717
labarum 550
labefy 659
label 39, 550
labent 306
labial *lip* 231
letter 561
labitur et labetur 112, 143
labor hoc opus, hic – 704
laboratory 691
laborious
active 682
exertion 686
difficult 704
labour
parturition 161
work 680
exertion 686
hard –
punishment 972
mountain in – 638
– for 620
– of love
willing 602
amusement 840
disinterested 942
– party 712
– under *state* 7
disease 655
difficulty 704
feeling 821
affliction 828
– in vain
fall short 304
useless 645
– in one's voca-

tion 625
– unrest 832
laboured - *style* 579
prepared 673
– study 457
labourer 690
labouring
– man 690
– oar 686
labyrinth
disorder 59
convolution 248
secret 533
lac *number* 98
resin 356a
– of rupees 800
lace *stitch* 43
netting 219
ornament 847
– one's jacket 972
lacerable 328
lacerate 44
– the heart 830
laches 460, 773
Lachesis 601
lachrymæ, hinc illæ – 830
lachrymatory gas 727
lachrymis, quis temperet a – 914
lachrymose 837
lack *require* 630
insufficient 640
destitute 804
desire 865
– faith 989
– harmony 708
– preparation 674
– wit 501
lackadaisical
inactive 683
melancholy 837
indifferent 866
lackadaisy! 839, 870
lack-brain 499, 501
lacker [*see* lacquer]
lackey 746
lack-lustre 422, 429
laconic 572
lacquer
covering 223
resin 356a
adorn 847
lacrosse 840
lacteal 352
lacuna 198, 252
lacustrine 343
lad 129
ladder 305, 627

kick down the – 604
lade *load* 184
transfer 185
contents 190
dip 270
– out 297
laden 52
heavy – 828
– with 777
ladies' man 897
lading 190, 780
bill of – *list* 86
ladle *receptacle* 191
transfer 270
vehicle 272
lady *woman* 374
rank 875
wife 903
our – 977
– day 138
– help 746
–'s maid 746
lady chapel 1000
ladylike
womanly 374
fashionable 852
lady-love 897
lag *linger* 275
follow 281
dawdle 683
– behind 133
laggard 603, 683
lager *beer* 298
lagoon 343
laical 997
laid: – on one's back 158
– by the heels 751
– low 160
– up 655
lair 189, 653
laird *master* 745
proprietor 779
nobility 875
Lais 962
laisse manger, cela se – 394
laisser: – aller, – faire
permanence 141
neglect 460
inaction 681
laxity 738
freedom 748
inexcitable 826
laity 997
lake *water* 343
pink 434
– of fire and brimstone 982

Lama 745, 996
Lamaism 984
Lamarkism 357
lamb *infant* 129
animal 366
gentle 826
innocent 946
go out like a – 174
lion lies down with – 721
Lamb of God 976
lambent
touching 379
– flame *heat* 382
light 420
Lambeth 1000
lame *incomplete* 53
impotent 158
weak 160
imperfect 651
disease 655
injury 659
failing 732
– conclusion
illogical 477
failure 732
help a – dog over a stile *aid* 707
vindicate 937
– duck 808
– excuse 617
lamellar 204
lamentable *bad* 649
painful 830
sad 837
lamentably *very* 31
lamentation 839
lamia 980, 994
lamina 51, 204
lamination 204
Lammas 998
lamp 423
rub the – 992
safety – 666
smell of the – *style* 577
prepared 673
lamplighter
quick 682
lampoon 932, 934
lampooner 936
lanâ caprinâ, de – 643
lanary 636
lanate 255, 256
lance *pierce* 260
throw 284
spear 727
break a – with
attack 716
warfare 722

couch one's – 720
– corporal 745
lancer 726
–'s *dance* 840
lancet 253, 262
lancinate 378, 830
land *arrive* 292
ground 342
estate 780
gone to a better – 360
hug the – 286
make the – 286
on – 342
see – 858
– covered with water 343
– flowing with milk and honey 168
how the – lies
circumstances 8
experiment 463
foresight 510
in the – of the living 359
landamman 745
landau 272
landed
– gentry 779
– estate 780
landgrave 745
landholder 779
landing field 273
landing-place 215, 292
landlady 779
land-locked 229, 343
landloper 268
landlord 779
land-lubber 343, 701
landmark
limit 233
indication 550
land-mine 727
landreeve 694
landscape
prospect 448
– gardening
agriculture 371
beauty 845
– painting 556
– painter 559
land-shark 792
land-slip 306
landsman 342
Landsturm 726
land-surveying 466
Landwehr 726

lane 189, 260, 627
langrel 727
lang-syne 122
language 560
command of – 582
strong –
vigour 574
malediction 908
languid *weak* 160
inert 172
slow 275
- *style* 575
inactive 683
torpid 823
languish
decrease 36
ill 655
inactive 683
repine 828
– for 865
languishing
weak 160
affected 855
languishment
lament 839
languor
[*see* languid]
lank 200
lanky 203, 206
lantern
window 260
lamp 423
magic – 448
– of Diogenes 461
– jaws 203
lanterne, à la – 972
lanuginous 256
lanyard 45
Laodicean 822
lap *abode* 189
support 215
interior 221
wrap 225
encompass 227, 229
drink 298
– of luxury
pleasure 377
inactivity 683
voluptuousness 954
lap-dog *animal* 366
servile 886
lapel 39
lapidary 559
lapidate *kill* 361
attack 716
punish 972
lapidescence 323
lapis lazuli
blue 438
jewel 847
lappet 39, 214
lapse *course* 109
past 122
conversion 144
fall 306
degeneracy 659
relapse 661
loss 776
vice 945
guilt 947
– of memory 506
– of time 109
lapsus calami 495
lapsus linguæ
mistake 495
solecism 568
stammering 583
Laputa, college of – 538
larboard 239
larceny 791
lard 356
lardaceous 355
larder 636
contents of the – 298
lares et penates
home 189
idols 991
large
quantity 31
size 192
at – *diffuse* 573
free 748
become – 194
– number 102
– type 642
large-hearted
liberal 816
benevolent 906
disinterested 942
larger 194
largest 784
largest portion 192
larghetto 275, 415
largiloquent 573
largo 275, 415
lariat 45, 247
lark *ascent* 305
pleasure 827
spree 840
with the – 125
larmes:
fondre en – 839
– aux yeux 839
larmoyante,
comédie – 599
larrikin 887, 913
larrup 972
larum 404, 669
larva 129
larynx 351
lascar 269
lasciate ogni speranza 859
lascivious 961
lash *tie together* 43
violence 173
incite 615
censure 932
punish 972
scourge 975
under the – *compelled* 744
subject 749
– into fury 900
– with the tongue 932
– the waves 645
lass *girl* 129
lassitude 688, 841
lasso 45, 247
last *model* 22
- *in order* 67
endure 106
durable 110
- in time 122
continue 141
at – 133
breathe one's – 360
game to the – 604*a*
never hear the – of 104
– but one &c. 67
die in the – ditch 604*a*
– for ever 112
at the – extremity 665
– finish 729
– gasp 360
go to one's – home 360
on – legs *weak* 160
dying 360
spoiled 659
adversity 735
– resort 666
– rites 998
– shift 601
– sleep 360
– stage 67
– straw 153
– stroke 729
– touch 729
– word
affirmation 535
obstinacy 606
– year &c. 122
latch 43, 45
latchet 45
latch-key 631
late *past* 122
new 123
tardy 133
dead 360
too – 135
lately 122, 123
latency 526
lateness **133**
latent 172, 526
– organism 153
later 117
laterality **236**
lateritious 434
latest 118
latet anguis in herbâ 667
lath 205
thin as a – 203
lathe
region 181
machine 633
lather 332, 353
Latin
au bout de son – 704
perdre son – 704
thieves' – 563
latitancy 528
latitat 969
latitude *extent* 180
region 181
breadth 202
measurement 466
freedom 748
– and longitude
situation 183
latitudinarian 984, 989
latration 412
latria 990
latrines 653
latrociny 791
latter *sequent* 63
past 122
Latter-day Saint 984
latterly 123
lattice *crossing* 219
opening 260
laud 931, 990
laudable 944
laudanum 174
laudari a laudato viro 931
laudator 935
– temporis acti
past 122
habit 613

discontent 832
detractor 936
laudatory 931
laugh 838
make one – 853
raise a – 840
– at *ridicule* 856
sneer 929
(*undervalue* 483)
– to scorn *defy* 715
despise 930
– in one's sleeve
latent 526
ridicule 856
disrespect 929
contempt 930
– on the wrong side of one's mouth
disappointed 509
dejected 837
in disrepute 874
laughable 853
laughing:
no – matter 642
– gas 376
laughing-stock 857
laughter-loving 836
launch *begin* 66
boat 273
propel 284
– forth 676
– into 676
– into eternity 360, 361
– out 573
– out against 716
laundress 652, 746
laundry *room* 191
heat 386
clean 652
– maid 746
– man 652
laureate 875
poet – 597
laurel *trophy* 733
glory 873
decoration 877
repose on one's –s 265
lava *excretion* 299
semiliquid 352
lavatory 652
lave *water* 337
clean 652
lavender *colour* 437
laver la tête 932
lavish *profuse* 641
give 784
squander 818
– of praise 931
law *regularity* 80
statue 697
permission 760
legality 963
court of – 966
give the – 737
go to – 969
Jewish – 985
lay down the –
certainty 474
affirm 535
command 741
learned in the – 968
set the – at defiance 964
take the – into one's own hands 722, 742
– of the Medes and Persians 80, 141
take the – of 969
law-abiding 743
lawful
permitted 760
due 924
legal 963
lawgiver 694
lawless 59
irregular 83
mutinous 742
non-observant 773
vicious 945
arbitrary 964
lawn *plain* 344
grass 367
agriculture 371
– sleeves 999
– tennis 840
lawsuit 969
lawyer 968
lax *incoherent* 47
soft 324
error 495
- *style* 575
remiss 738
non-observance 773
dishonourable 940
licentious 945
irreligious 989
laxity 738
lay *moderate* 174
place 184
ley 344
music 415
poetry 597
bet 621
secular 997
– about one
active 682
exertion 686
attack 716
contend 720
punish 972
– one's account for 484
– apart
exclude 55
relinquish 782
– aside
neglect 460
reject 610
disuse 678
give up 782
– on the table 133
– the axe at the root of tree 162
– bare 529
– before 527
– brother 996
– by *store* 636
sickness 655
disuse 678
– to one's charge 938
– claim to 924
– in the dust 162
– eggs 161
– at the door of 155
– down [*see* below]
– at one's feet 763
– figure *nonentity* 4
model 22
representation 554
– one's finger upon 480*a*
– the first stone 66
– the flattering unction to one's soul 831, 834
– the foundations 153, 673
– ghosts 992
– hands on
use 677
take 789
rite 998
– under hatches 751
– one's head on the block 942
– heads together 695, 709
– in *eat* 298
store 636
provide 637
– on 972
open *divest* 226
opening 260
show 525
disclose 529
– oneself open to 177
– out
horizontal 213
corpse 363
plan 626
expend 809
– oneself out for 673
– over 133
– reader 996
– under restraint 751
– in ruins 162
– siege to 716
– stress on 642
– to *attribute* 155
rest 265
– it on thick
cover 223
too much 641
flatter 933
– together 43
– train 626
– up *store* 636
sickness 655
disuse 678
– waste 162
lay down *locate* 184
horizontal 213
assert 535
renounce 757
relinquish 782
pay 807
– one's arms
pacification 723
submission 725
– the law
certain 474
assert 535
command 741
insolence 885
– one's life 360
– a plan 626
layer 204
layette 225
layman 699, 997
laystall 653
lazaret 662
lazar-house 662
lazy 683, 927
lazzarone 683
lb. 319
lea *land* 342
plain 344
leach 335
lead *superiority* 33
in order 62

pioneer 64
influence **175**
tend 176
soundings 208
- *in motion* 280
heavy 319
rôle 599
induce 615
direct 693
authority 737
heave the – 466
red – 434
take the –
influence 175
importance 642
authority 737
white – 430
– to the altar 903
– astray 495
– captive
subject 749
restraint 751
– a merry chase 623
– the choir 990
– a dance
run away 623
circuit 629
difficulty 704
disrespect 929
– the dance 280
– one to expect 511
– a life 692
– on 693
– to no end 645
– by the nose 737
– off 62
– the way
precedence 62
begin 66
precession 280
importance 642
direction 693
repute 873
leaden *dim* 422
colourless 429
grey 432
inactive 683
leader
precursor 64
dissertation 595
director 694
counsel 968
– writer 595
leading
beginning 66
important 642
– article 595
– lady 599
– note *music* 413
– part 175
– question 461
– seaman **745**
– strings
childhood 127
child 129
pupil 541
subject 749
restraint 751, 752
leads 223
leaf *part* 51
layer 204
plant 367
- *of a book* 593
turn over a new – 658
– green 435
leafless 226
leaflet 531
leafy 256
league *length* 200
co-operation 709
party 712
– of Nations 696
leak *crack* 198
dribble 295
waste 638
spring a –
injury 659
– out
disclosure 529
leaky *imperfect* 651
leal 743
lean *thin* 203
oblique 217
– on 215
– to *shed* 191
willing 602
– towards 923
– upon *belief* 484
subjection 749
hope 858
leaning
tendency 176
willingness 602
desire 865
friendship 888
favouritism 923
leap
sudden change 146
ascent 305
jump **309**
–s and bounds 274
make a – at 622
– in the dark
experiment 463
uncertain 475
chance 621
rash 863
– with joy 838
– year 138
leap-frog 840
learn 490, 539
– by experience 950
– by heart 505
learned 490
learner **541**
learning 490, **539**
lease *property* 780
lending 787
grant a – 771
take a new – of life 654
– and release 783
leasehold 780
leash *lie* 43
three 92
hold in – 751
least
– *in quantity* 34
– *in size* 193
at the – 32
leather *skin* 223
tough 327
beat 972
nothing like – 481
– bottle 191
– or prunello 643
leave *remainder* 40
part company 44
relinquish 624
permission 760
bequeathe 784
French – 623
take – *depart* 293
freedom 748
– alone
inaction 681
freedom 748
permit 760
– the beaten track 83
– to chance 621
– an inference 526
– a loophole 705
– in the lurch
pass 303
decisive **545**
– no trace
be no more 2
disappear 449
obliterate 552
– it to one 760
– to oneself 748
– off *cease* 142
desuetude 614
relinquish 624
disuse 678
– out 55
– out of one's calculation 460
– a place 293
– ad referendum 605
give me – to say 535
– undecided 609*a*
– undone 730
– a void *regret* 833
– word 527
leaven
component 56
cause 153
lighten 320
qualify 469
unclean 653
deterioration 659
bane 663
leavings
remainder 40
useless 645
lecher 962
lechery 961
lectern 1000
lection *special* 79
interpretation 522
lectionary 998
lecture *teach* 537
speak 582
dissertation 595
censure 932
sermon 998
– room 542
lecturer
teacher 540
preacher 996
lectureship 542
led – captain
follower 746
servile 886
favourite 899
– by the nose 749
ledge *height* 206
horizontal 213
shelf 215
projection 250
ledger *list* 86
record 551
accounts 811
lee 236
leech 662, 695
leef 829
leek eat the –
recant 607
submit 725
Lee-Metford
rifle 727
leer *stare* 441
dumb-show **550**
leery 702, 864
lees 653

lee-shore 665, 667
leet, court – 966
lee-wall 666
leeward 236
lee-way *space* 180
tardy 133
navigation 267
deviation 279
progression 282
shortcoming 304
left *residuary* 40
sinistral 239
over the – 545
– alone 748
– in the lurch 732
– to shift for oneself 893
pay over the – shoulder 808
left-handed
clumsy 699
– compliment 932
– marriage 903
leg *support* 215
walker 266
thief 792
best – foremost 686
fast as –s will carry 274
have a – to stand on 470
keep on one's –s 654
last –s *spoiled* 659
fatigue 688
light on one's –s 734
make a – 894
not a – to stand on
illogical 477
confuted 479
failure 732
off one's –s
propulsion 284
on one's –s
upright 212
elevation 307
speaking 582
in health 654
active 682
free 748
set on one's –s 660
– bail 623
legacy 270, 780, 784
legal *permitted* 760
legitimate 924
relating to law 963
– adviser 968
– estate 780
legality **963**
legate 534
legatee 779, 785
legation 755
legato 415
legend 551, 594
legendary
imaginary 515
legerdemain 146, 545
légèreté 605
leggings 225
leghorn hat 225
legible 518
– hand 590
legion
multitude 102
army 726
legionary 726
legislation 693, 963
legislative assembly 696
legislator 694
legislature 693, 696
legist 968
legitimate *true* 494
permitted 760
right 922
due 924
legal 963
legume 367
lei 847
leisure **685**
at one's – *late* 133
leisurely 275
leman 897
lemma 476
lemon *colour* 436
Lemprière 979
lemures 980
lend 787
– aid 707
– countenance 707
– a hand 680
– oneself to
assent 488
co-operate 709
– on security 789
– wings to 707
lender *creditor* 805
lending **787**
length **200**
go all –s
resolution 604
activity 682
exertion 686
at – *in time* 133
full – *portrait* 556
go great –s 549
– and breadth of 50
– and breadth of the land
space 180
publication 531
– of time 110
lengthen 35, 200
– out
diuturnity 110
late 133
lengthwise 200
lengthy *long* 200
diffuse 573
lenient
moderate 174
mild 740
compassionate 914
lenify 174
lenitive
moderating 174
remedy 662
relieving 834
lenity **740**
lens 445
Lent 956, 998
lenten 956
lenticular 245, 250
lentor *slowness* 275
spissitude 352
inactivity 683
lentous 352
leonem, ex ungue – 550
leonine verses 597
leopard
variegated 440
–'s spots
unchanging 150
leprechaune 980
leprosy 655
lerret 273
lèse-majesté 742
less *inferior* 34
subduction 38
– than no time 113
lessee
possessor 779
receiver 785
lessen
– in quantity or degree 36
– in size 195
– an evil 658
lesson *teaching* 537
warning 668
give a – to
punish 972
read a – to
censure 932
say one's –
memory 505
lessor 805
lest 623
let *hindrance* 706
permit 760
lease 771
lend 787
sell 796
apartments to –
fool 499
to – 763
– alone *besides* 37
permanence 141
quiescence 265
avoid 623
disuse 678
inaction 681
not complete 730
free 748
– be
permanence 141
continuance 143
inaction 681
– blood 297
– 'I dare not' wait upon 'I would' 605
– down
depress 308
humble 879
– down easily
forgive 918
– fall *drop* 308
inform 527
speak 582
– fly *violence* 173
propel 284
– fly at 716
– go *neglect* 460
liberate 750
relinquish 782
restitution 790
– in *interpose* 228
admit 296
trick 545
– into *inform* 490
disclose 529
– one know 527
– off *violent* 173
propel 284
permit 760
forgive 918
exempt 927*a*
acquit 970
– out *disperse* 73
lengthen 200
eject 297
disclose 529
liberate 750
– out at 716
– pass 460

– slip
miss an opportunity 135
neglect 460
not complete 730
lose 776
relinquish 782
– the matter stand over 133
– things take their course 143
– well alone
content 831
caution 864
lethal 361
– chamber 975
lethalis arundo, hæret lateri – 900
lethargy 683, 823
Lethe 982
waters of – 506
lethiferous 361
letter *mark* 550
character **561**
epistle 592
to the – 494
– card 592
– of credit 805
– of the law 494
– writer 592
letter-bag 534
letter-carrier 534
lettered 490
letterpress 591
letters
knowledge 490
language 560
description 594
in large – 642
man of – 492
– of marque 791
lettres de cachet 751
leucophlegmatic 823
leucorrhea 299
Levant *east* 236
levant *abscond* 623
levanter *wind* 349
defaulter 808
levée *assemblage* 72
sociality 892
– en masse 719
level *uniform* 16
equal 27
destroy 162
horizontal 213
instrument 213, 217
flat 251
smooth 255
lower 308
– at *direct* 278
intend 620
attack 716
– best 686
– headed 826
– off 27
– with the ground 207
lever *cause* 153
instrument 633
– de rideau 599
leverage 175
leviathan 192
levigate 255, 330
levitate 320
Levite 996
levity *lightness* **320**
irresolution 605
trifle 643
jocularity 836
rashness 863
levy *muster* 72
military 726
distrain 789
demand 812
lewd 961
Lewis gun 727
lex – mercatoria 963
– scripta 697
– scripta et non-scripta 963
– talionis
retaliation 718
right 922
lexicography 562
lexicology 562
lexicon 86, 562
ley 344
liability **177**
debt 806
duty 926
liaison 961
liar 548
libation
potation 298
drunkenness 959
worship 990
libel 934, 938
libelant 989
libeller 936
liberal *ample* 639
– party 712
generous 816
disinterested 942
over – 818
– education
knowledge 490
teaching 537
liberalism
freedom **748**
liberality
giving 784
generosity **816**
liberate 672
liberation **750**
liberavi animam meam 703
libertinage 961
libertine **962**
libertinism 961
liberty *freedom* 748
permission 760
right 924
exemption 927*a*
gain one's – 750
set at – *free* 750
exempt 927*a*
take a –
arrogate 739
make free 748
insolence 885
discourtesy 895
libidinous 961
libitum, ad –
at will 600
enough 639
freely 748
librarian 593, 694
library *room* 191, 593
books 593
storehouse 636
librate 314
libretto 593, 599
licence *laxity* 738
permission 760
right 924
exemption 927*a*
– to plunder 791
licentiate 492
licentious *lax* 738
dissolute 954
debauched 961
lichgate 363
lichen 367
licit 760, 924
lick *lap* 298
conquer 731
punish 972
– the dust 933
– into shape 240
lickerish
savoury 394
desirous 865
fastidious 868
licentious 961
lickpenny 819
lickspittle 886
lictor 965
lid 223
lie *situation* **183**
presence 186
recline 213
falsehood 544
untruth 546
give the – to 536
white – 617
– abed 683
– in ambush 528
– by 681
– at one's door 926
– down *flat* **213**
rest 687
– fallow 674
– hid 528
– in *be* 1
give birth 161
– low 528
– under a necessity 601
– in a nutshell 32
– on 215
– over *defer* 133
destiny 152
– in one's power 157
– at the root of 153
– still 265
– to
quiescence 265
inaction 681
– under 177
– in wait for
expect 507
inaction 681
lief *pleasant* 829
as – *willing* 602
choice 609
liege 745
liegeman 746
lien 771, 805
lienteria 653
lieu 182
in – of 147
lieutenant 745, 759
lord – 965
life *essence* 5
events 151
vitality **359**
biography 594
activity 682
conduct 692
cheerful 836
animal – 364
battle of – 682
come to – 660
infuse into
excite 824

put – into 359
recall to – 660
see – 840
support – 359
take away – 361
tenant for – 779
– to come 152
– after death 981
– or death
need 630
important 642
contention 720
– and spirit 682
Life, the 976
life-blood 5, 359
life-boat 273, 666
life-giving 168
lifeguards 726
lifeless 172, 360
lifelike 17
lifelong 110
life-preserver 666, 727
life-size 192
lifetime 108
life-weary 841
lift *raise* 307
aid 707
steal 791
– cattle 791
– up the eyes 441
– a finger 680
– hand against 716
– one's head 734
– up the heart 990
– the mask 529
– the voice
shout 411
speak 582
lift-smoke 840
ligament 45
ligation 43
ligature 45
light *state* 7
small 32
window 260
velocity 274
arrive 292
descend 306
levity 320
kindle 384
match 388
luminosity **420**
luminary 423
- *in colour* 429
white 430
aspect 448
knowledge 490
interpretation 522
unimportant 643
easy 705
gay 836
loose 961
blue – *signal* 550
bring to –
discover 480a
manifest 525
disclose 529
children of – 987
come to – 529
false – 443
foot –s 599
half – 422
make – of
underrate 483
easy 705
inexcitable 826
despise 930
in one's own – 699
obstruct the – 426
side – 490
see the – *life* 359
publication 531
transmit – 425
throw – upon 522
a – breaks in upon one 529
– under a bushel
hide 528
not hide 878
modesty 881
– comedy 599
– cruiser 726
– fantastic toe 309
– upon one's feet 664
– heart 836
– of heel 274
– horse 726
– infantry 726
– purse 804
– and shade 420
– of truth 543
– up *illumine* 420
excite 824
cheer 836
– upon *chance* 156
arrive at 292
discover 480a
acquire 775
Light of the World 976
lighten
make light 320
illume 420
facilitate 705
lighter *boat* 273
lighterage 812
lighterman 269
light-fingered 791, 792
light-footed 274, 682
light-headed 503
lighthouse 550
lightless 421
light-minded 605
lightning
velocity 274
flash 420
spark 423
like greased – **113**
lightsome
luminous 420
irresolute 605
cheerful 836
ligneous 367
lignite 388
lignography 558
ligulate 205
like *similar* 17
relish 394
enjoy 377, 827
wish 865
love 897
do what one –s 748
look – 448
we shall not look upon his – again 33
– master like man 19
– a pin in paper 58
likely 472
think – 507
likeness 21, 554
bad – 555
likewise 37
liking 865, 897
have a – for 827
to one's – 829
lilac *colour* 437
Liliputian 193
Lillith 994
lilt 416, 836
lily *white* 430
beauty 845
paint the – 641
lily-livered 862
limæ labor
improve 658
toil 686
limature 330, 331
limb *member* 51
instrument 633
scamp 949
– of the law 968
limber 272, 324
limbo *prison* 751, 752
pain **828**
purgatory 982
lime *entrap* 545
– light 423, 531, 599
Limehouse 908
limine, in – 66
limit *complete* 52
end 67
circumscribe 229
boundary **233**
qualify 469
restrain 751
prohibit 761
limitarian 984
limitation [*see* limit]
estate 780, 783
limited
- *in quantity* 32
- *in size* 193
to a – extent
imperfect 651
limitless 105
limitrophe 197
limn 556
limner 559
limousine 272
limp *weak* 160
slow 275
supple 324
fail 732
limpid 425
lin 343, 348
lincture 662
line *fastening* 45
continuous 69
ancestors 166
descendants 167
length 200
no breadth 203
string 205
lining 224
outline 230
straight 246
of steamers 273
direction 278
music 413
appearance 448
measure 466
mark 550
writing 590
verse 597
vocation 625
army and navy 726
boundary – 233
draw the – 465
drop a – to 526
in a –
continuous 69
straight 246

in a – with 278
read between the –s 522
sounding – 208
straight – 246
troops of the – 726
– of action 692
– of battle 69
– of battle ship 726
– engraving 558
– of march 278
– of road 627
lineage *kindred* 11
series 69
ancestry 166
posterity 167
lineament
outline 230
feature 240
appearance 448
mark 550
linear
continuity 69
pedigree 166
length 200
linen 225
liner 273
lines
fortification 717
hard –
adversity 735
severity 739
reins 752
linger *protract* 110
delay 133
loiter 275
lingerie 225
lingo 560, 563
lingua franca 563
linguacious 584
lingual 560, 582
linguist 492
linguistics 560
liniment 356, 662
lining 224
link *relation* 9
connect 43
connecting - 45
part 51
term 71
crossing 219
torch 423
golf –s 840
missing – 53, 729
linked together
party 712
linoleum 223
linotype 591
linseed oil 356
linsey-wolsey 41
linstock 388
lint 223
lintel 215
lion
courage 861
prodigy 872
repute 873
come in like a – 173
as dewdrops from the –'s mane 483
in the –'s den 665
– lies down with the lamb 721
put one's head in the –'s mouth 665
– in the path 706
–'s share *more* 33
chief part 50
too much 641
undue 925
lioness 374
lion-hearted 861
lionize 455, 873
lip *beginning* 66
edge 231
side 236
prominence 250
between cup and – 111
finger on the –s
silent 581
speechless 585
hang on the –s of 418
open one's –s
speak 582
seal the –s 585
smack the –
taste 390
savoury 394
– homage
flattery 933
– service
falsehood 544
hypocrisy 988
– wisdom 499
lip salve 847
lipstick 847
lipothymy 688
lippitude 443
liquefaction 335, 384
liquescence 335
liqueur 298, 396
liquid
fluid 333
sound 405
letter 561
liquidate 807, 812
liquidator 801
liquor *potable* 298
fluid 333
in – 959
– up 959
liquorice 396
liquorish [*see* lickerish]
lisp 583
lissom 324
list *catalogue* **86**
strip 205
leaning 217
fringe 231
hear 418
record 551
will 600
choose 609
arena 728
desire 865
enter the –s
attack 716
contend 720
listed 440
listel 847
listen 418
– in 457
– to 457
be –ed to **175**
– to reason 498
listless
inattentive 458
inactive 683
indifferent 866
litany 990, 998
lite, pendente – 969
literæ scriptæ 590
literal
imitated 19
exact 494
manifest 525
letter 561
word 562
orthodox 983a
– meaning 516
– translation 522
literarum
homo multarum – 492
homo trium – 792
literary 560
– hack 593
– man 492
– power 569
literati 492
literatim [*see* literal]
literature 490, 560
lithe 324
lithic 323
lithograph 558
lithology 358
lithomancy 511
lithotint 558
litigant
litigious 713
combatant 726
accusation 938
litigation
quarrel 713
contention 720
lawsuit 969
litigious 713
litter *disorder* 59
derange 61
multitude 102
brood 167
support 215
vehicle 272
useless 645
littéraire, la morgue – 569
littérateur 492, 593
little
- *in degree* 32
- *in size* 193
darling 897
mean 940
cost – 815
do – 683
make – of 483
signify – 643
think – of 458
– did one think 508
– by little
degree 26
slowly 275
– Mary 191
– one 129
to – purpose
useless 645
failure 732
littleness **193**
littoral 342
liturgy 998
live *exist* 1
continue **141**
energetic 171
dwell 186
life 359
repute 873
– apart 905
– to fight again 110
– from hand to mouth 674
– hard 954
– in hope 858
– and let live
inaction 681

freedom 748
inexcitability 826
– in the memory 505
– upon nothing 819
– on 298
– separately 905
– by one's wits 545
livelihood 803
livelong 110
lively *keen* 375
- *style* 574
active 682
acute 821
sensitive 822
sprightly 836
– imagination 515
– pace 274
liver 83; hard – 954*a*
white – 862
liver-coloured 433
livery *suit* 225
colour 428
badge 550
decoration 877
– servant 746
liveryman 748
live wire 171
livid *dark* 431
grey 432
purple 437
living *life* 359
business 625
benefice 995
good – 957
– beings 357
–room 191
– soul 372
– thing 366
livraison 593
livret 593
lixiviate 335, 652
lixivium 335
llama 271
lo! 457, 870
load *quantity* 31
fill 52
lade 184
cargo 190
weight 319
store 636
redundance 641
hindrance 706
adversity 735
anxiety 828
oppress 830
prime and – 673
take off a – of care 834
– the memory 505
– with 706
– with reproaches 932
loads 102
loadstar 288, 350, 693
loadstone 288, 615
loaf *mass* 192
do nothing 681
dawdle 683
loafer
stroller 268
inactive 683
neglect 927
bad man 949
loam 342
loan 787
loathe 867, 898
loathing
[*see* loathe]
weariness 841
hate 898
loathsome
unsavoury 395
painful 830
dislike 867
loaves and fishes
prosperity 734
acquisition 775
wealth 803
Lob's pound, in – 751
lobby 191, 615, 627
lobbying 615
lobe 51
local
– habitation 184, 189
– board 966
locale 183
locality 182, 183
localize 184
location 184
loch 343
loci, genius – 664
lock *fasten* 43
fastening 45
tuft 256
canal 350
hindrance 706
prison 752
dead – 265
in the –up 938
under – and key
safe 664
restraint 751
prisoner 754
– hospital 662
–out 55, 719
– the stable door
too late 135
useless 645
unskilful 699
–, stock and barrel 50
– up *hide* 528
imprison 751
locker 191
locket 847
lock-up *prison* 752
lòco, in –
agreeing 23
situation 183
expedience 646
locofoco 388
locomotion 264
– by air 267
– by land 266
– by water 267
locomotive 266, 271
locular 191
locum tenens
substitute 147
inhabitant 188
deputy 759
locus:
– pœnitentiæ 937
– standi
support 215
plea 617
social rank 873
locust *prodigal* 818
evil-doer 913
swarm like –s 102
locution 582
lode 636
lodestar
attraction 288
indication 550
direction 693
lodestone 288, 615
lodge *place* 184
presence 186
dwelling 189
– a complaint 938
lodgement 184
lodger
inhabitant 188
possessor 779
lodging 189
loft 191, 210
lofty *high* 206
- *style* 574
proud 878
insolent 885
magnanimous 942
log *velocity* 274
fuel 388
record 551
heave the – 466
sleep like a – 683
logarithm 84
loggerhead 501
at –s *discord* 713
contention 720
enmity 889
loggia 191
logic 476
– of facts 467
logician 476
logical acuteness 570
logography 590
logogryph 533
logolept 562
logomachy
discussion 476
words 588
dispute 720
logometer 85
logometric 84
log-rolling 709
loin 235, 236
gird up one's –s
strong 159
prepare 673
– cloth 225
loisir, impromptu fait à – 673
loiter *tardy* 133
slow 275
inactive 683
loll *sprawl* 213
recline 215
inactive 683
lollipop 396
lollop 683
Lombard Street to a China orange 472
lone 87
lonesome 893
long - *in time* 110
- *in space* 200
diffuse 573
go to one's – account 360
– ago 122
make a – arm
exertion 686
seize 789
–boat 273
draw the – bow 549
take a – breath
refreshment 689
relief 834
– clothes 129
– drawn out 573
– duration 110
–expected 507

– face 832, 837
– for 865
–headed *wise* 498
– life to *glory* 873
approval 931
–lived 110
– odds *chance* 156
improbability 473
difficulty 704
– pending 110
– primer 591
– pull and strong pull 285
– range 196
– robe 968
– run *average* 29
whole 50
destiny 152
– sea 348
– and the short
whole 50
concise 572
–sighted
dim-sighted 443
wise 498
foresight 510
– since 122
– spun 573
– standing
diuturnal 110
old 124
–suffering
lenient 740
inexcitable 826
pity 914
– time 110
–winded 573
longanimity
inexcitable 826
forgiving 918
longevity 110, 128
longhead 500
longing 865
– lingering look behind 833
longinquity 196
longitude
situation 183
length 200
measurement 466
longitudinal 200
longo intervallo
discontinuity 70
diuturnity 110
distance 196
interval 198
longshore-man
waterman 269
plebeian 876
longways 217
loo 840
looby *fool* 501
bungler 701
clown 876
look *small degree* 32
see 441
appearance 448
attend to 457
– about 459, 461
– after 459, 693
– ahead 510
– alive 457, 684
– another way 442
– back 122
– beyond 510
– black *or* blue
feeling 821
discontent 832
dejection 837
– down upon 930
– in the face
sincerity 703
courage 861
pride 878
– foolish 874
– for 461, 507
– forwards 121, 510
– here 457
– into 457, 461
– before one leaps 864
– like 17, 448
– on 186
– out *view* 448
attention 457
care 459
seek 461
expect 507
intention 620
business 625
danger 665
warning 668
caution 864
– over *examine* 461
– round *seek* 461
– sharp 682
– to 459, 926
– through 461
– up *prosper* 734
high price 814
hope 858
visit 892
– up to *repute* 873
respect 928
approbation 931
– upon as 480, 484
looker-on 444
looking-glass 445
loom *destiny* 152
dim 422
dim sight 443
come in sight 446
weave 691
– of the land 342
– up 31
loon *fool* 501
clown 876
rascal 949
loop 245, 247, 629
– the loop 245
loop-hole
opening 260
vista 441
plea 617
device 626
escape 671
fortification 717
loose *detach* 44
incoherent 47
pendent 214
desultory 279
illogical 477
vague 519
– *style* 575
lax 738
free 748
liberate 750
debauched 961
give a – to
- *imagination* 515
laxity 738
permit 760
indulgence 954
let – 750
on the – 961
screw – 713
– character 961
at a – end 685
– fish 949, 962
– morals 945
– rein 738
– suggestion 514
– thread 495
leave a - 460
take up a - 664
loosen 47, 750
loot 791, 793
lop 201
– and top 371
lopped
incomplete 53
loppet 699
lop-eared 53
lop-sided 28
loquacity 584
loquendi
cacoëthes – 584
jus et norma – 567
usus – 582
lorcha 273
Lord, lord
ruler 745
nobleman 875
God 976
O – *worship* 990
– Chancellor 967
– of the creation 372
–'s day 687
–s Justices 966, 967
the – knows 491
– lieutenant 965
– of Lords 976
– of the manor 779
– it over 737, 885
–'s prayer 990
–'s supper 998
–'s table 1000
lordling 875
lordly 873, 878
Lord Mayor 745, 965
–'s show 883
lordship
authority 737
property 780
title 877
judge 967
lore 490, 539
Lorelei 980
lorette 962
lorgnette 445
lorication
armour 717
loricated
clothed 223
lorn 893
lorry 272
lose *forget* 506
unintelligible 519
fail 732
loss 776
no time to – 684
– one's balance 732
– breath 688
– caste 874, 940
– the clew 475, 519
– colour 429
– one's cunning 699
– the day 732
– flesh 195
– ground
slow 275
regression 283
shortcoming 304
– one's head
bewildered 475

– heart 837
– one's heart 897
– hope 859
– interest in 624
– labour 732
– one's life 360
– no time 682, 684
– oneself 475
– an opportunity 135
– one's reason 503
– sight of
blind 442
disappear 449
neglect 460
oblivion 506
not complete 730
– one's temper 900
– time 683
– one's way
wander 279
uncertainty 475
unskilful 699
difficulty 704
losel 818
losing game 732, 735
loss *decrement* 40*a*
death 360
evil 619
deterioration 659
privation **776**
at a –
uncertain 475
at a – for
desiring 865
– of fortune 804
– of health 655
– of life 360
– of right 925
– of strength 160
lost *non-existing* 2
absent 187
invisible 449
abstracted 458
uncertain 475
failure 732
loss 776
over-excited 824
pain 828
dejection 837
impenitent 951
– in admiration 931
– in astonishment 870
– in iniquity 945
– labour 645
– to shame
insolent 885
improbity 940
bad man 949
– to sight 449
– in thought 458
– to virtue 945
lot *state* 7
quantity 25
group 72
multitude 102
necessity 601
chance 621
sufficient 639
allotment 786
be one's – 151
cast –s 621
cast in one's – with 609, 709
fall to one's – 156
in –s 51
where one's – is cast 189
loth 603, 867
Lothario 897, 962
lotion *liquid* 337
clean 652
remedy 662
loto 840
lottery 156, 840
put into a – 621
lotus-eater 683
loud 404, 525
vulgar 851
lough 343
lounge 191, 683
– suit 225
loup
hurler avec les –s 714
–garou 980
louse 653
lout 501, 701, 876
louvre 351
lovable 897
love *desire* 865
courtesy 894
affection **897**
favourite 899
abode of – 897
labour of –
willing 602
inexpensive 815
amusement 840
disinterested 942
God's – 906
make – 902
no – lost 713
– affair 897
– of country 910
– lock 256
not for – or money 640, 814
love-knot *token* 550
love-lorn 898
lovely 845, 897
love-making 902
love-pot 959
love-potion 865
lover [*see* love]
love-sick 897, 902
love-story 897, 902
love-token 897, 902
loving-cup 892, 894
loving-kindness 906
low *small* 32
not high 207
- sound 405
moo 412
vulgar 851
disreputable **874**
common 876
base 940
bring – 308
– condition 876
– comedy 599
at a – ebb
small 32
inferior 34
depressed 308
waste 638
deteriorated 659
– fellow 876
– life 851
– note 408
– origin 876
– price 815
– spirits 837
– tide 207
– tone *black* 431
mutter 581
– water *low* 207
dry 340
insufficient 640
poor 804
low-born 876
low-brow 491
low-lands 207
low-minded 876, 940
lower *inferior* 34
decrease 36
overhang 214
depress 308
dark 421
dim 422
predict 511
sad 837
irate 900
sulky 901*a*
– one's flag 725
– one's note 879
– orders 876
lowering 668, 859
lowly 879
lown 501, 949
lowness [*see* low] **207**
humility 879
loy 272
loyal *obedient* 743
observant 772
honourable 939
lozenge 244, 662
L. s. d. 800
lubbard [*see* lubber]
lubber 683, 701
lubberly 192, 699
lubricant 332
lubrication 255, **332**
lubricity
slippery 255
unctuous 355
impure 961
lucent 420
lucid
luminous 420
transparent 425
intelligible 518
- style 570
– interval 502
lucidus ordo 58
lucifer 388
Lucifer 423, 978
lucimeter 445
luck *chance* 156, 621
prosperity 734
good – 858
luckless 735
lucky 134, 734
lucrative 775
lucre 775, 803
Lucretia 960
luctation 720
lucubration 451
luculent 420
lucus a non lucendo 18, 565
lud! O – 839
ludibrious 840
ludicrous 853
luff 267
lug *pull* 285
ear 418
luge 272
luggage 270, **780**
– van 272
lugger 273
lugubrious 837
lukewarm
temperate 382
irresolute 605
torpid 823
indifferent 866
lull *cessation* 142

mitigate 174
silence 403
– to sleep 265
lullaby
moderate 174
song 415
verses 597
inactivity 683
relief 834
lumbago 378
lumbar 235
lumber *disorder* 59
slow 275
store 636
useless 645
hindrance 706
lumbering 647, 846
lumber-room 191
lumbriciform 249
luminary *star* 318
light 423
sage 500
luminescence 420
luminous *light* 420
intelligible 518
– paint 423
lump *whole* 50
chief part 51
amass 72
mass 192
projection 250
weight 319
density 321
in the – 50
– of affectation 855
– sum 800
– together *join* 43
combine 48
assemble 72
lumpish [*see* lump]
inactive 683
ugly 846
Luna 318
lunacy 503
lunar 318
– caustic 384
lunatic 503, 504
luncheon 298
lune avec les dents, prendre la – 158, 471
lunette 717
lunge 276, 716
lungs *wind* 349
loudness 404
shout 411
voice 580
luniform &c. 245
lupanar 961
lurch *incline* 217
sink 306
oscillation 314
failure 732
leave in the –
outstrip 303
deceive 545
relinquish 624
left in the –
defeated 732
lure *attraction* 288, 865
deceive 545
entice 615
lurid *dark* 421
dim 422
red 434
lurk *unseen* 447
latent 526
hidden 528
lurking-place 530
luscious 394, 829
lush *vegetation* 365
drunkenness 959
lushy 959
lusk 683
lusory 840
lust 865, 961
– after 921
lustily 404, 686
cry out – 839
lustless 158
lustration 652, 952
lustre
brightness 420
chandelier 423
glory 873
lustrum 108
lusty 159, 192
lusus naturæ 83
lute *cement* 45, 46
guitar 417
luteous 436
Lutheran 984
luxation 44
luxuriant 168, 639
luxuriate in 377, 827
luxurious
pleasant 377
delightful 829
intemperate 954
luxury
physical - 377
redundance 641
enjoyment 827
sensuality 954
lycanthropy 503
Lyceum 542
Lydford law 964
Lydian measure 415
lyddite 727
lying
decumbent 213
deceptive 544
faithless 986
Ly-king 986
lymph *fluid* 333
water 337
transparent 425
lymphatic 337
lynch 972
– law 964
lyncher 975
lynching 361
lynx-eyed 441, 498
lyre 417
lyric 415
– poetry 597
lyrist 597

M

Mab 979
macadamize 255, 035
Macaire, Robert – 792
macaroni 854
macaronic
absurdity 497
neology 563
verses 597
Macchiavel [*see* Machiavellism]
mace
weapon 727
sceptre 747
mace-bearer 965
maceration
saturation 337
atonement 952
asceticism 955
rite 998
Macheath 792
Machiavellism
falsehood 544
cunning 702
dishonesty 940
machicolation 257, 717
machination
trick 545
plan 626
cunning 702
–s of the devil 619
machinator 626
machine 633
like a – 698
– gun 407, 727
be a mere – 749
machinist
theatrical - 599
workman 690
macilent 203
mackerel
mottled 440
procuress 962
– sky 349, 353
mackintosh 225
macrobiotic 110
macrocosm 318
macrography 441
macrology 577
Mac Sycophant, Sir Pertinax – 886, 935
mactation 991
macte virtute 931
macula 848
maculate
unclean 653
maculation 440, 848
mad *insane* 503
excited 824
drive one – 900
go – 825
– after 865
– with rage 900
madam 374
mad-brained 503
madcap
violent 173
lunatic 504
excitable 825
buffoon 844
rash 863
madder *colour* 434
made
– to one's hand 673
– man 734
– to order 673
madefaction 339
madman 504
Madonna
good 948
angel 977
pious 987
madrigal *music* 415
verses 597
Mæcenas 492, 890
maelstrom
whirl 312
water 348
pitfall 667
maestro 415
maffick 883
magazine
periodical 53
record 551
book 593

store 636
- rifle 727
Magdalen 950, 962
mage 994
magenta 434
maggot *little* 193
fancy 515
caprice 608
desire 865
maggoty
capricious 608
unclean 653
- headed
silly 499
excitable 825
Magi *sage* 500
sect 984
magic 175, 992
- lantern
instrument 445
show 448
magician 548, 994
magilp 356*a*
magisterial 878, 885
magistery 330
magistracy 737, 965
magistrate 745, 967
magistrature 737
magistri, jurare in verba - 481
nullius - 487
magma 41
Magna Charta 769
magna pars fui, quorum - 690
magnanimity 942
magnate 875
magnet *attract* 288
desire 865
magnetism
power 157
influence 175
attraction 288
motive 615
animal - 992
magnetize
influence 175
motive 615
conjure 992
magni nominis umbra
wreck 659
repute 873
rank 875
magnificent
large 192
fine 845
grand 882
magnifico 875
magnifier 445
magnifique et pas cher 815
magnify
increase 35
enlarge 194
over-rate 482
exaggerate 549
approve 931
praise 990
magniloquent 577, 884
magnitude 25, 31, 192
magno conatu magnas nugas 638, 643
Magnus Apollo 500
magpie 584
magsman 792
maharajah 745
maharani 745
mah jong 840
mahl-stick [*see* maulstick]
mahogany
colour 433
Mahomet 986
Mahometan 984
maid *girl* 129
servant 631, 746
spinster 374, 904
- of all work 690
- of honour 890
maiden *first* 66
girl 129
punishment 975
- speech 66
maidenhood 904
maidenly 374
maigre 956
mail *post* 270, 534
armour 717
- coach 272, 534
- steamer 273
- van 272, 534
maim 158, 659
main *tunnel* 260
ocean 341
conduit 350
principal 642
coup de - 680
in the -
intrinsically 5
greatly 31
on the whole 50
principally 642
with might and - 686
plough the - 267
main-chance 156
good 618
important 642
profit 775
look to the -
foresight 510
skill 698
economy 817
caution 864
selfish 943
main-force
strength 159
violence 173
compulsion 744
mainland 342
main-part 31, 50
mainpernor 771
main-spring 153, 633
mainstay
support 215
refuge 666
hope 858
maintain
permanence 141
continue 143
sustain 170
support 215
assert 535
preserve 670
- one's course
persevere 604*a*
- the even tenor of one's way 623
- one's ground 717
maintenance [*see* maintain]
assistance 707
wealth 803
maintien 692
maison de santé 662
maisonette 189
maître: coup de -
goodness 648
skill 698
l'œil de - 459
majesté, lèse- 742
majestic 873, 882
majesty *king* 745
rank 873
deity 976
major *greater* 33
officer 745
-domo
director 694
retainer 746
-general 745
- key 413
- part *great* 31
all 50
majority
superiority 33
multitude 102
age 131
join the - 360
majuscule 561
make
constitute 54, 56
render 144
produce 161
form 240
arrive at 292
complete 729
compel 744
- acquainted with 527, 539
- after 622
- its appearance 446
- away with 162, 361
- believe 544, 545, 546
- the best of 725
- bold to differ 489
- a date with 897
- choice of 609
- fast 43
- a fool of 853
- for 278
- one's fortune 734
- fun of 842, 856
- a fuss 642, 682
- good
compensation 30
complete 52, 729
establish 150
evidence 467
demonstrate 478
provide 637
restore 660
- *one's escape* 671
- *one's word* 772
- a go of 731
- haste 684
- hay while the sun shines 134
- interest 765
- known 527
- the land 292
- light of 483, 705, 934
- oneself master of 539
- money 775
- a monkey of 853
- much of 549, 642
- no doubt 484
- no secret of 525
- no sign 526, 528
- nothing of
unintelligible 519
not wonder 871

– of 902
– off 623, 671
– off with 791
– out *see* 441
evidence 467
demonstrate 478
discover 480a
know 490
intelligible 518
interpret 522
due 924
– over 658, 783, 784
– peace **723**, 724
– a piece of work 832
– things pleasant 702
– a present 784
– public 531
– a push 682
– ready 673
– a requisition 741, 765
– a speech 582
– a sucker of 853
– sure 150, 673
– terms 769
– time 110
– tracks 293
– towards 278
– up [*see below*]
– use of 677
– way 282
– one's way 302, 734
– way for 147, 623
– a wry face 867
make up
complete 52
compose 54
– accounts 811
– for 30
– matters 952
– one's mind
judgment 480
belief 484
resolve 604
– a quarrel 723
– a sum 809
– to *approach* 286
address 586
maker *artificer* 690
Maker, the – 976
makeshift 147, 617
make-weight
inequality 28
compensation 30
completeness 52
making of, be the –
utility 644
goodness 648
aid 707
mal du pays 833
mala fides 940
malachite 435
malacology 368
malade imaginaire 837
maladie du pays 833
maladministration 699
maladroit 699
malady 655
malaise 378, 828
malapert 885, 887
Malaprop, Mrs. – 565
malapropism 495
mal à propos 24, 135
malaria 657, 663
malconformation 243
malcontent 710, 832
male 159, 373
– animal 373
malediction **908**
malefaction 947
malefactor 949
malefic 649
maleficent 907
– being 913
malevolence **907**
malfeasance 647
malformed 241
malformation 243
malgré 179
– soi 603
malice *hate* 898
spite 907
bear – *revenge* 919
– aforethought 907
– prepense 907
malign *bad* 649
malevolent 907
detract 934
malignant 649, 907
malignity
violence 173
malinger 544, 655
malison 908
malkin 653
mall *walk* 189
club 276
malleable 324
mallet 276
malnutrition 655
mal-odour 401
malpractice 947
malt liquor 298
maltreat
injure 649
aggrieve 830
molest 907
malum
– prohibitum 925
– in se 923
malversation 818, 947
Mameluke 726
mamelon 250
mamma 166
mammal 366
mammiform 250
mammilla 250
Mammon 803, 978
serve – 989
mammoth 192
man *adult* 131
mankind 372
male **373**
prepare 673
workman 690
servant 746
courage 861
husband 903
make a – of 648, 861
Son of – 976
straight – 599
to a – 488
–at-arms 726
one's – of business 758
–'s estate 131
– in office 745
– in the street 876
–of-war 273, 726
–of-war's man 269
– at the wheel 694
– and wife 903
manacle 751, 752
manage 693
– to *succeed* 731
manageable 705
management
conduct 692
skill 698
manager
stage - 599
director 694
managery 693
manche après la cognée, jeter le – 859
manciple 637
mancipation 751
mandamus 741
mandarin 745
mandate 630, **741**
mandible 298
mandolin 417
mandragora 174
mandrel 312
manducation 298
mane 256
man-eater 361
manège 266, 370
manes 362
manet: altâ mente repostum 505
– cicatrix 919
manful *strong* 159
resolute 604
brave 861
manger 191
manger:
cela se laisse – 394
– son blé en herbe 818
mangle
separate 44
smooth 255
injure 659
mangled 53
mangy 655
man-hater 911
manhood 131, 861
mania *insanity* 503
desire 865
maniac 504
manibus pedibusque 686
manic 503
manic-depressive 503
manicure 847
manicheism 978
manichord 417
manie 865
maniéré 855
manifest
list 86
visible 446
obvious 525
disclose 529
manifestation **525**
manifesto 531
manifold 81, 102
manikin *dwarf* 193
image 554
maniple 103
manipulate
handle 379
use 677
conduct 692
manipulator 621
mankind **372**
manly
adolescent 131

strong 159
male 373
brave 861
honest 939
manna *food* 396
– in the wilderness
aid 707
pleasing 829
manner *kind* 75
style 569
way 627
conduct 692
in a – 32
by all – of means 602
by no – of means 536
to the – born 5
mannered 579
mannerism
special 79
unconformity 83
affectation 855
vanity 880
mannerly 894
manners 852, 894
manœuvre 680, 702
manor 780
lord of the – 779
– house 189
manorial 780
mansard roof 223
manse 1000
mansion 189
manslaughter 361
mansuetude 894
mantelpiece 215
mantilla 225
mantle *spread* 194
dress 225
foam 353
shade 424
redden 434
robes 747
flush 821, 824
anger 900
mantlet *cloak* 225
defence 717
mantology 511
manual *guide* 527
schoolbook 542
book 593
advice 695
– labour 686
manubial 793
manufactory 691
manufacture 161, 680
manufacturer 690
manumission 750
manure
agriculture 371
dirt 653
aid 707
manuscript 22, 590
many 102
the – 876
for – a day 110
– irons in the fire 682
– men many minds 489
– times
repeated 104
frequent 136
many-coloured 440
many-sided 81, 236
many-tongued 532
map 234, 527, 554
– out 626
mar 659, 706
marabou 83
marabout 1000
maranatha 908
marasmus
shrinking 195
atrophy 655
deterioration 659
maraud 791
marauder 792
marble *ball* 249
hard 323
sculpture 557
tablet 590
insensible 823
marble 440
marble-hearted 907
march *region* 181
journey 266
progression 282
music 415
dead – 363
forced – 684
on the – 264
steal a –
advance 280
go beyond 303
deceive 545
active 682
cunning 702
– against 716
– of events 151
– of intellect
knowledge 490
improvement 658
– off 293
– on a point 278
– past 882
– of time 109
– with 199
March, Ides of – 601
marches 233
marchioness 875
marcid 203
marconigram 532
marcor 203
mare *horse* 271
female 374
–'s nest 497, 546
–'s tail *wind* 349
cloud 353
maréchal 745
margarine 356
margin *space* 180
edge 231
redundance 641
latitude 748
margravate 780
margrave 745, 875
marimba 417
marine *fleet* 273
sailor 269
oceanic 341
soldier 726
tell it to the –s 489, 497
– painter 559
– painting 556
mariner 269
Mariolatry 991
marionnette
representation 554
drama 599
amusement 840
marish 345
marital 903
maritime 267, 341
mark *degree* 26
term 71
take cognizance of 450
attend to 457
indication 550
record 551
writing 590
object 620
importance 642
repute 873
beyond the – 303
leave one's – 873
man of – 873, 875
near the – 197
overshoot the – 699
put a – upon 457
save the – 870
up to the –
enough 639
good 648
skill 698
due 924
wide of the – 196, 495
within the – 304
– down 813
– off 551
– out *choose* 609
plan 626
command 741
– of recognition 894
– with a red letter 883
– time
chronometry 114
halt 265
wait 507
– with a white stone 931
marked [*see* mark]
great 31
affirmed 535
well– 446
in a – degree 31
play with – cards 545
– down 815
marker 550
market *buy* 795
mart 799
bring to – 796
buy in the cheapest &c. – 794
in the –
offered 763
barter 794
sale 796
rig the – 794
– garden 371
– overt
manifest 525
mart 799
– place *street* 189
mart 799
– price 812
– woman 797
marketable 794, 796
marksman 700
marksmanship 698
marl 342
marmalade 396
marmot 683
maroon
colour 433, 434
abandon 782, 893
marplot
bungler 701
obstacle 706
malicious 913
marque, letters of – 791
marquee 223

marquetry 440
marquis 875
marriage **903**
companionate – 903
ill-assorted – 903
– bells 836
– portion 780
marriageable 131, 903
marrow *essence* 5
interior 221
central 222
chill to the – 385
marrow-bones, on one's –
submit 725
beg 765
humble 879
servile 886
atonement 952
marrowless 158
marry *combine* 48
assertion 535
wed 903
– come up
defiance 715
anger 900
censure 932
Mars 722, 979
– orange 439
marsh **345**
marshal
arrange 60
messenger 534
auxiliary 711
officer 745
Marshalsea 752
marsupial 191, 366
mart 799
Marte, suo –
exertion 686
skill 698
martello tower 717
martial 722
court– 966
– law 737, 739
compulsory 744
illegal 964
– music 415
martinet 739
martingale 752
Martinmas 998
martyr
bodily pain 378
mental pain 828
ascetic 955
– to disease 655
martyrdom
killing 361
agony 378, 828
unselfish 942
punishment 972
marvel 870, 872
– whether 514
marvellous 31, 870
deal in the – 549
Masaniello 742
mascaro 847
mascot 993
masculine 159, 373
mash *mix* 41
disorder 59
soft 324
semiliquid 352
pulpify 354
masher 854
mask *dress* 225
shade 424
concealment 528
ambush 530
deceit 545
shield 717
put on the – 544
mason 690
Masorah 985
masque 599
masqué, bal – 840
masquerade
dress 225
concealment 528
disguise 530
frolic 840
mass *quantity* 25
much 31
whole 50
heap 72
size 192
gravity 319
density 321
worship 990
rite 998
attend – 990
in the – 50
– book 998
– of society 876
massacre 361
massage 324, 331, 379
masse, en – 712
masses, the – 876
massive *large* 31
huge 192
heavy 319
dense 321
mast 206
master
boy 129
influence 175
man 373
know 490
understand 518
learn 539
teacher 540
director 694
proficient 698, 700
succeed, conquer 731
ruler **745**
possession 777
possessor 779
title 877
eye of the – 693
hard – 739
past – 700
– of Arts 492
– one's feelings 826
– hand 700
– key *open* 260
instrument 631
– mariner 269
– mind *sage* 500
proficient 700
– passion 820
– one's passions 944
– of the position 731
– of the revels 840
– of the Rolls 553, 967
– of self 604
– of the situation 731, 737
– spirit of the age 500, 873
– of one's time 685
masterdom 737
masterpiece
good 648
perfect 650
skill 698
master-stroke 626, 731
mastery 731, 737
get the – over 175
masthead
punish 972
mastic *viscid* 352
resin 356a
masticate 298
mastiff 366
mat *support* 215
woven 219
misty 427
cover 652
matador 361
match *coincide* 13
similar 17
copy 19
equal 27
fuel 388
contest 720
marriage 903
matchless
supreme 33
excellent 648
virtuous 944
matchlock 727
mate *similar* **17**
equal 27
duplicate 89
mariner 269
auxiliary 711
master 745
friend 890
wife 903
check– **732**
maté 298
mater alma – 542
–familias 166
materia medica 662
material
substance 316
stuff 635
important 642
– for thought 454
– point 32
materialism
matter 316
heterodoxy 984
irreligion 989
materiality **316**
materialize 446
materials **635**
matériel 633
maternal
parental 166
benevolent 906
– love 897
maternity 166
mathematical
precise 494
– point 193
mathematics 25
mathesis 25
matin 125
matinée 892
matins 990
matrass 191
matriarch 11, 166
matriarchate 737
matriculate 86
matriculation 539
matrilinear 11, 166
matrimony
mixture 41
wedlock 903
matrix *mould* 22
workshop 691
matron 374, 903
matronly 128, 131

matross 726
matter *substance* 3
material world 316
topic 454
meaning 516
type 591
business 625
importance 642
pus 653
no – 460
what – 643
what's the – 455, 461
– of course
conformity 82
certain 474
habitual 613
– in dispute 461
– of fact *event* 151
certainty 474
truth 494
language 576
artless 703
dull 843
– in hand 454, 625
– of indifference 866
– nothing 643
mattock 253
mattress 215
mature *old* 124
adolescent 131
conversion 144
scheme 626
perfect 650
improve 658
prepare 673
complete 729
– thought 451
maturely considered 611
maturine 996
maturity [*see* mature]
bring to – 729
matutinal 125
matzoon 298
maudlin
inactive 683
drunk 959
maugre 30
maukin 652
maul *hammer* 276
hurt 649
maulstick 215
maund *basket* 191
mumble 583
maunder
diffuse style 573
mumble 583
talk 584
lament 839
maundy
– money 784
– Thursday 988
Mauser rifle 727
mausoleum 363
mauvais
– goût 851
– quart d'heure 828
– sujet 949
– ton 851
mauvaise:
– honte
affectation 855
modesty 881
– plaisanterie 851
mauve 437
maw 191
mawkish 391
Mawworm
deceiver 548
sham piety 988
maxim 80, **496**
Maxim gun 727
maximal 33
maximalist 742
maximum 33, 210
maxixe 840
may be 470
as it – 156
May-day 138, 840
May-fly 111
mayhap 470
mayonnaise 298
mayor 745, 965
maypole 206
May-queen 847
mazard 298
maze
disorder 59
convolution 248
enigma 533
difficulty 704
in a –
uncertain 475
mazed 503
mazurka 840
me 317
me judice 484
meâ culpâ 950
mead *plain* 344
sweet 396
meadow *plain* 344
grass 367
– land 371
meagre *small* 32
incomplete 53
thin 203
– *style* 575
scanty 640
poor 643
– diet 956
meal *repast* 298
powder 330
mealy-mouthed
falsehood 544
servile 886
flattering 933
mean *average* **29**
small 32
middle 68, 228
signify 516
intend 620
contemptible 643
stingy 819
shabby 874
ignoble 876
sneaking 886
base 940
selfish 943
golden – 174
take the – 774
– nothing 517
– parentage 876
– time 114
– wretch 949
meander
convolution 248
deviate 279
circuition 311
river 348
– around Robin Hood's barn 279
meandering
diffuse 573
meanest capacity 499
intelligible to the – 518
meaning **516**
meaningless 517
means
appliances **632**
property 780
wealth 803
by all – 602
by any – 632
by no – 536
– of access 627
meantime 106
meanwhile 106
measurable 466
within – distance 470
measure *extent* 25
degree 26
moderation 174
music 413
compute 466
verse 597
proceeding 626
action 680
apportion 786
angular – 244
full – 639
out of – 641
without – 641
– of inclination 217
measured
moderate 174
sufficient 639
temperate 953
measureless 105
measurement 25, **466**
measures
have no – with 713
take – *plan* 626
prepare 673
conduct 692
– of length 200
meat 298
broken – 645
one man's – is another man's poison 15
mechanic 690
mechanical 601, 633
– warfare 722
– powers 633
mechanician 690
mechanism 633
medal
record 551
sculpture 557
palm 733
decoration 877
– of Honor 733
medallion 557
medallist 700
meddle 682
médecin tant pis 837
médecine expectante 133, 662
Medes and Persians, law of the – 80, 141
mediæval 124
mediævalism 122
medial 29, 68
median 228
mediant 413
medias res, in – 68
plunge – 300, 576
mediation—*instrumentality* 631
intercession **724**
deprecation 766

Christ 976
mediator 711
Mediator
Saviour 976
medical 662
medicament 662
medicaster 548
medicate
compound 41
heal 660
medicine 662
– man 994
medico 662
mediety 68
mediis rebus, in – 682
medio tutissimus, in – 864
mediocritas, aurea – 628
mediocrity
average 29
smallness 32
imperfect 651
- *of fortune* 736
meditate *think* 451
purpose 620
mediterranean 68, 228
medium *mean* 29
middle 68
atmosphere 227
intermediary 228
colour 428
oracle 513
impostor 548
instrument 631
seer 994
transparent – 425
medley 41, 59
music 415
chance – 156
medullary 324
Medusa 860
meed
apportion 786
reward 973
– of praise 931
meek 826, 879
meerschaum 392
meet *agreement* 23
assemble 72
touch 199
converge 290
arrive 292
expedient 646
fulfil 772
proper 924
make both ends –
wealth 803
economy 817
unable to make both ends –
poverty 804
not pay 808
– with attention 457
– one's death 360
– the ear 418
– one at every turn
present 186
redundant 641
– one's expenses 817
– the eye 446
– in front 861
– half way
willing 602
concord 714
pacification 723
mediation 724
compromise 774
friendship 888
benevolence 906
– hand to hand 720
– one's wishes
consent 762
pleasurable 829
– with *event* 151
find 480*a*
meeting [*see* meet]
junction 43
hostile – 720
place of – 74
meeting-house
hall 189
chapel 1000
megacosm 318
megalomania 482, 504
megaphone 404, 418
megascope 445
megatherium 124
Megæra 173, 900
megrims *fits* 315
melancholy 837
mehari 271
Mein Herr 877
meister-singer 597
melancholia
insanity 503
dejection 837
melancholy 830, 837
away with – 836
mélange 41
mêlée *disorder* 59
contention 720
melinite 727
meliora, spero – 858
meliorate 658
meliorism 658
melius inquirendum, ad – 658
melliferous
sweet 396
mellifluous
music 413
- *language* 578
mellow
old 128
grow into 144
soft 324
sound 413
colour 428
improve 658
prepare 673
tipsy 959
melodeon 417
melodious 413
melodist 416
melodrama 599, 824
melody 413
Melpomene 599
melt *convert* 144
liquefy 335
fuse 384
pity 914
– in the air 405
– away
cease to exist 2
unsubstantial 4
decrease 36
disappear 111, 449
waste 638
– the heart 914
– into one 48
– into tears 839
melting-pot 691
member *part* 51
component 56
councillor 696
membrane 204
même, quand – 708
memento 505
– mori 363, 837
meminisse juvabit 505
memoir 594, 595
memorabilia
reminiscences 505
important 642
memorable 642
memorandum
memory 505
record 551
plan 626
– book 505, 551
compendium 596
memorial
record 551
memorialist 553
memorialize 505
memorials 594
memoriam, in – 363, 505
memory 505
fame 873
failing – 506
short – 506
in the – of man 122
– runneth not to the contrary 124
mem-sahib 374
menace 909
ménage 692
menagerie
collection 72
animals 370
store 636
mend 658, 660
– one's manners 894
mendacity 544
mendicancy 765, 804
mendicant
beggar 767
poor 804
monk 996
menhir 363
menial 746, 876
meniscus 245, 445
mens sana 502
– in corpore sano 827
mens sibi conscia recti 878
mensâ et thoro, separatio a – 905
menses 299
menstrual 138
menstruum 335
mensuration 466
mental 450
– calm 826
– excitement 824
– pabulum 454
– philosophy 450
– reservation 528
– suffering 828
menteur à triple étage 548
menticulture 658
mention 527

above –ed 104
not worth –ing 643
mentis gratissimus error 481
mentor *sage* 500
teacher 540
adviser 695
menu 86, 298
Mephistopheles 980
Mephistophelian 945
mephitic 401, 657
mephitis 663
meracious 392
mercantile 794
mercatoria, lex – 963
mercature 794
mercenary
soldier 726
servant 746
price 812
parsimonious 819
selfish 943
mercer 225
merchandise **798**
merchant **797**
merchantman 273
merciful 914
merciless 914*a*
mercurial
changeable 149
mobile 264
quick 274
excitable 825
Mercury 979
traveller 268
quick 274
messenger 534
mercy *lenity* 740
pity 914
at the – of
liable 177
subject 749
cry you – 766
have at one's – 919
have no – 914*a*
– on us! 870
for –'s sake 765
– seat 966
mere *simple* 32
lake 343
trifling 643
– nothing
small 32
trifle 643
buy for a – nothing 815
– pretext 617
– words 477
– wreck 659
merelles 840
meretricious
false 495
vulgar 851
licentious 961
merfolk 980
merge *combine* 48
include 76
insert 300
plunge 337
– in 56
– into *become* 144
merged 228
meridian
region 181
room 125
summit 210
light 420
– of life 131
merit
goodness 648
due 924
virtue 944
make a – of 884
– notice 642
merito, e – 944
meritorious 931
Merlin 994
mermaid 341
monster 83
mythology 979, 980
merman 341
mero motu, ex – 600
merriment
cheerful 836
amusement 840
merry *cheerful* 836
drunk 959
make – *sport* 840
make – with
wit 842
ridicule 856
wish a – Christmas &c. 896
– and wise 842
merry-andrew 844
merry-go-round 312, 840
merry-making 827, 840, 892
merry-thought 842
mersion 337
meruit ferat, palmam qui – 873
merveille, à – 731
mesa 344
mésalliance 24, 903
meseems 484
mesh 198, 219
meshes *trap* 545
difficulty 704
– of sophistry 477
meshwork 219
mesial
middle 68
mesmerism 992
mesmerist 994
mesne lord 779
mess *mixture* 41
disorder 59
barracks 191
meal 298
difficulty 704
portion 786
make a –
unskilful 699
fail 732
message
intelligence 532
command 741
Messalina 962
messenger 271
envoy **534**
servant 746
– balloon 463
Messiah 976
messianic 976
messmate 890
messuage 189
messy 59
metabolism 140
metacentre 222
metachronism 115
metage 466
metagenesis 140
metagrammatism 561
metal 635
Brittania – 545
metallic *sound* 410
metalepsis 521
metallurgy 358
metamorphosis 140
metaphor
comparison 464
figure **521**
(*analogy* 17)
metaphrase 522
metaphrast 524
metaphrastic 516
metaphysics 450
metastasis, metathesis
change 140
inversion 218
displacement 270
mete *measure* 466
distribute 786
– out *give* 784
metempsychosis 140
meteor 318, 423
meteoric 173, 420
meteorology 338
meteoromancy 511
meter 466
metheglin 396
methinks 484
method *order* 58
way **627**
want of – 59
methodical 60
Methodist 984
methodist
journalist 988
methodize 60
Methuselah 130
old as – 124
since the days of – 124
methylated spirit 388
meticulous 772
métier 625
métis 83
metonymy 521
metoposcopy
front 234
appearance 448
interpret 522
metre
length 200
poetry 597
metrical
measured 466
verse 597
metrology 466
moderation 174
mid-course 628
metropolis 189
metropolitan
archbishop 996
mettle *spirit* 820
courage 861
man of – 861
on one's –
resolved 604
put on one's –
excite 824
encourage 861
mettlesome
energetic 171
sensitive 822
excitable 825
brave 861
mettre de l'eau dans son vin 160
meum et tuum 780

disregard distinction between – 791
mew *moult* 226
cry 412
– up 751
mewed up 229
mewl 412
mews 189
mezzanine floor 191, 599
mezzo rilievo
convex 250
sculpture 557
mezzo termine
middle 68
mid-course 628
compromise 774
Mezzofanti 492
mezzosoprano 416
mezzotint 420, 558
miasm 663
mica 425
micacious 204
mi-carême 840
Micawber 160
Michael 977
Michaelmas 998
Micomicon 515
microbe 193
microcosm 193
micrography 193, 441
micrometer 193
micro-organism 193
microphone 418
microscope 193, 445
microscopic 32, 193
mid 68
Midas 803
mid-course 628
mid-day 125
midden 653
middle - *in degree* 29
- *in order* 68
- *in space* 222, 228
– classes 736
– constriction 203
– course 29, 628
– man *director* 694
agent 758
– point 29
– term 68
compromise 774
middlemost 222
middling 29, 32, 68, 651
middy 225, 269
midge 193
midget 193
midland 342
midnight *night* 126
dark 421
– oil 539, 689
mid-progress 282
midriff 68, 228
midshipman 269, 745
midships 68
midst - *in order* 68
central 222
interjacent 228
in the – of
mixed with 41
doing 680
midsummer 125
– day 138
midway 68
midwife
instrument 631
remedy 662
auxiliary 711
midwifery 161, 662
mien 448, 692
miff 900
might *power* 157
violence 173
energy 686
mightily 31
mighty *much* 31
strong 159
large 192
haughty 878
migraine 378
migrate 266, 295
mikado 745
milch cow
productive 168
animal 366
store 636
mild *moderate* 174
warm 382
insipid 391
lenient 740
calm 826
courteous 894
mildew 653, 663
mildewed
spoiled 659
mile 200
milestone 550
whistle jigs to a – 645
milieu, juste – 174, 628
militant 722
church – 983*a*
military
warfare 722
soldiers 726
– authorities 745
– band 417
– power 737
– time 132
– train 726
militate against 708
militia 726
milk *moderate* 174
semiliquid 352
cows &c. 370
white 430
mild 740
– a he-goat into a sieve 471
flow with – and honey *plenty* 639
prosperity 734
pleasant 829
– of human kindness 906
– the ram 645
– and water
weak 160
insipid 391
unimportant 643
imperfect 651
milk-livered 862
milksop
incapable 158
fool 501
coward 862
milky [*see* milk]
semitransparent 427
whiteness 430
– way 318
mill 330
notch 257
machine 633
workshop 691
fight 720
like a horse in a – 312
millennium
number 98
period 108
futurity 121
utopia 515
hope 858
millesimal 99
millet seed 193
milliard 98
milliner 225
man – 854
millinery *dress* 225
ornament 847
display 882
man – 855
million 98
multitude 102
people 372
populace 876
for the –
intelligible 518
easy 705
–s *money* 800
millionaire 803
mill-pond *level* 213
pond 343
store 636
mime 19, 599, 844
mimeograph 19
mimeotype 19
mimic 19
mimodrama 599
minacity 909
minaret 206
minatory 668
minauderie 855
mince *cut up* 44
slow 275
food 298
stammer 583
affected 855
extenuate 937
– the matter 868
not – the matter
affirm 535
artless 703
– the truth 544
mincemeat of
make – 162
mincing 855
– steps 275
mind *intellect* 450
attend to 457
take care 459
believe 484
remember 505
will 600
willing 602
purpose 620
warning 668
desire 865
dislike 867
bear in – 451, 457
bit of one's – 527
food for the – 454
give the – to 457
have a – 602, 865
in the –
thought 451
topic 454
willing 602
make up one's – 484, 604
never – *neglect* 460
unimportant 643
not – 866
out of – 506

set one's – upon 604
speak one's – 582, 703
to one's – *taste* 850
love 897
willing – 602
– one's book 539
– one's business 456, 457
– at ease 826
make one's – easy 826
–'s eye 515
– what one is about 864
minded 602, 620
mindful 457, 505
mindless
inattentive 458
imbecile 499
forgetful 506
insensible 823
mine
sap 162
hollow 252
open 260
snare 545
store 636
abundance 639
damage 659
attack 716
defence 717
explosive 727
dig a – *plan* 626
prepare 673
spring a –
unexpected 508
attack 716
– of information 700
–layer 726
–sweeper 726
–thrower 727
– of wealth 803
miner 252
sapper and – 726
mineral 358
– oil 356
mineralogy 358
Minerva 979
– invita 603, 704
– press 577, 594
mingle 41
miniature *small* 193
portrait 556
– painter 559
Minié rifle 727
minikin 193
minim *small* 32
music 413
minimize 36, 483, 934
minimum *small* 32
inferior 34
minion 899
type 591
minister *instrumentality* 631
remedy 662
director 694
aid 707
deputy 759
give 784
clergy 996
rites 998
– to 746
ministerial
clerical 995
ministering spirit 977
ministration
direction 693
aid 707
rite 998
ministry
direction 693
aid 707
church 995
clergy 996
miniver 223
minnesinger 597
minnow 193
minor *inferior* 34
infant 129
– key 413
Minorites 996
minority *few* 103
youth 127
Minos 694
minotaur 83
minster 1000
minstrel 416, 597
minstrelsy 415
mint *mould* 22
workshop 691
wealth 803
– of money 800
minuend 38
minuet 415, 840
minus *less* 34
subtracted 38
absent 187
deficient 304
loss 776
in debt 806
non-payment 808
minuscule 561
minute
- *in degree* 32
- *of time* 108
instant 113
- *in size* 193
record 551
compendium 596
to the – 132
– account 594
– attention 457
minuteness
care 459
minutiæ 32, 79, 643
minx 887, 962
mirabile
– dictu &c. 870
mirabilis, annus – 872
miracle 83, 872
– play 599
miraculous 870
mirage 443
mire 653
mirror *imitate* 19
reflector 445
perfection 650
glory 873
hold up the – 525
hold the – up to nature 554
magic – 443
mirth 836
misacceptation 523
misadventure 735
misadvised 699
misanthropy 911
misapply
misinterpret 523
misuse 679
mismanage 699
misapprehend 495, 523
misappropriate 679
misarrange 61
misbecome 925
misbegotten 243, 945
misbehave 851, 945
misbehaviour 895, 947
misbelief 485
misbeliever 487, 984
miscalculate
misjudge 481
err 495
disappoint 509
miscall 565
miscarry 732
miscegenation 41
miscellany
mixture 41
collection 72
generality 78
compendium 596
mischance 619, 735
mischief 619
do – 649
make – 649
mischief-maker 913, 941
miscible 41
miscite 544
miscompute 481, 495
misconceive 495, 523
misconduct 699, 947
– oneself 945
misconjecture 481
misconstrue 523
miscorrect 538
miscount 495
miscreance 485
miscreant 949
miscreated 945
misdate 115
misdeed 947
misdemean 945
misdemeanant 949
misdemeanour 947
misdevotion 988
misdirect 538, 699
misdo 945
misdoing 947
misdoubt 485, 523
mise en scène
appearance 448
drama 599
display 882
misemploy 679
miser 819
–'s hoard 800
miserabile dictu 839
miserable *small* 32
contemptible 643
unhappy 828
miserably 31
miserere 215
sing – 950
misericordiam, argumentum ad – 914
miseries of human life 828
miseris succurrere disco 914
miserly 819
misery 828
put out of one's – 914
misestimate
misjudge 481
misfeasance 699, 947

misfit 24
misfortune
adversity 735
unhappiness 830
misgiving 485, 860
misgovern 699
misguide 495, 538
misguided 699
mishap *evil* 619
failure 732
misfortune 735
painful 830
Mishna 985
misinform 538
misinformed 491
misinstruct 538
misintelligence 538
misinterpretation
523
misjoined 24
misjudgment
sophistry 477
misjudge **481**
misinterpretation
523
mislay *derange* 61
lose 776
mislead *error* 495
misteach 538
deceive 545
mislike 867
mismanage 699
mismatch 15, 24
misname 565
misnomer **565**
misogamist 904
misogynist 911
misogyny 904
mispersuasion 538
misplace
derange **61**
misplaced
intrusive 24
unconformable 83
displaced 185
misprint 495
misprision
concealment 528
guilt **947**
– of treason 742
misprize 483, 929
mispronounce 583
misproportioned
243, 846
misquote 544
misreckon 481, 495
misrelish 867
misreport 495, 544
misrepresent
misinterpret 523
misteach 538
lie 544
misrepresentation
555
untruth 544, 546
misrule
misconduct 699
laxity 738
Lord of – 701
miss *girl* 129
neglect 460
error 495
unintelligible 519
fail 732
lose 776
want 865
courtesan 962
– one's aim 732
– fire 732
– stays 304
– one's way
uncertain 475
unskilful 699
missa cantata 998
missal 998
missay 563, 583
missend 699
misshapen 243, 846
missile 727
missing
non-existent 2
absent 187
disappear 449
– link 53, 83, 729
mission 625, 755
missionary 540, 996
missive 592
misspell 523
misspend 818
misstate 495, 544
misstatement 495,
546
mist 353, 424
in a – 528
seen through a –
519
–s of error 495
– before the eyes
443
mistake *error* 495
misconstrue 523
mismanage 699
failure 732
never was a
greater – 536
misteaching **538**
mister 373
misterm 565
misthink 481
mistime 135
mistral 349
mistranslate 523
mistress *lady* 374
master 745
possessor 779
title 877
love 897
concubine 962
mistrust 485
misty [*see* mist]
semi-transparent
427
misunderstand
misinterpret 523
misunderstanding
495, 713
misuse **679**
mite *bit* 32
small 193
insufficiency 640
money 800
little – 129
Mithridate 662
mitigate *abate* 174
improve 658
relieve 834
mitigation
[*see* mitigate]
extenuation 937
mitraille 727
mitrailleur 727
mitre *junction* 43
angle 244
crown 747, 999
mitten 225
mittimus 741
mix 41
– oneself up with
meddle 682
co-operate 709
– with 720
mixen 653
mixture **41**
mere – 59
mix-up 59
mizzen 235
mizzle 348
mnemonics 505
Mnemosyne 505
moa 366
moan 405
cry 411
lament 839
moat *enclosure* 232
ditch 259
canal 350
defence 717
mob *crowd* 72
multitude 102
vulgar 876
hustle 929
scold 932
king – 876
– cap 225
– law
authority **737**
illegality 964
mobile
inconstant **149**
movable 264
sensitive 822
mobility, the – 876
mobilize
assemblage 72
render movable
264
– troops 722
mobocracy 737
mobster 361
moccasin 225
mock *imitate* **17, 19**
repeat 104
erroneous 495
deceptive 545
chuckle 838
ridicule 856
disrespect 929
– danger 861
– modesty 855
– sun 423
mockery
[*see* mock]
unsubstantial 4
solemn – 882
– delusion and
snare
sophistry 477
deception 545
mocking-bird 19
modal 6, 7, 8
mode *state* 7
music 413
habit 613
method 627
fashion 852
– of expression 569
mode, à la – 852
model *copy* 21
prototype 22
rule 80
form 240
representation
554
sculpture 557
perfection 650
good man 948
new – 658
– after 19
– condition 80
modeller 559
moderate
average 29
small 32
allay **174**

slow 275
sufficient 639
cheap 815
temperate 953
– circumstances
mediocrity 736
moderately
imperfect 651
moderation [*see* moderate] **174**
mid-course 628
inexcitability 826
moderato *music* 415
moderator 174
lamp 423
director 694
mediator 724
judge 967
modern 123
music 415
art 556
modest *small* 32
modesty
humility **881**
purity 960
mock – 855
modicum *little* 32
allotment 786
modification
difference 15
variation 20*a*
change 140
qualification 469
modish 852
modulation
variation 20*a*
change 140
music 413
module 22
modulus 84
modus: – operandi
method 627
conduct 692
– in rebus 174
– vivendi 723
mogul 745
Mohammedan 984
Mohawk
swaggerer 887
evil-doer 913
moider 458, 475
moiety 51, 91
moil *active* 682, 686
exertion 686
moisture *wet* 337
humid **339**
mokes 219
molar 330
molasses 396
mole *mound* 206
prominence 250
colour 432
refuge 666
defence 717
spot 848
molecular 32
molecule 193
molehill *little* 193
low 207
trifling 643
molest *trouble* 830
molestation
damage 649
malevolence 907
mollia tempora 134
– fandi 588
mollify *allay* 174
soften 324
mollusk 366
mollycoddle 158
Molly Maguire 548
Moloch
slaughter 361
demon 980
heathen deity 986
molten 384
moment
- *of time* 113
importance 642
for the – 111
lose not a – 684
not have a – 682
on the spur of the – 612
momentous 152
momentum 276
Momus 838
monachism 995
monad 193
monarch 745
monarchy 737
monastery 1000
monastic 995
monasticism 984
monetary 800
– arithmetic 11
money **800**
wealth 803
bad – 800
command of – 803
for one's – 609
made of – 803
make – 775
raise – 788
save – 817
throw away one's – 818
– to burn 641, 803
– burning one's pocket 818
– coming in 810
– down 807
– going out 809
– market 800
– matters 811
– paid 809
–'s worth
useful 644
price 812
cheap 815
money-bag 800, 802
money-belt 802
money-broker 797
money-changer 797, 801
moneyed 803
moneyer 797
money-grubbing 775
moneyless 804
monger 797
mongrel
mixture 41
anomalous 83
dog 366
base 949
moniker 565
moniliform 249
monism 984
monition 527, 668
information 527
warning 668
monitor *hear* 418
oracle 513
pupil-teacher 540
director 694
adviser 695
war-ship 726
inward – 926
monitory
prediction 511
dissuasion 616
warning 668
monk 996
monkey
imitative 19
support 215
catapult 276
ridiculous 857
play the – 499
–jacket 225
– trick
absurdity 497
sport 840
– up 900
monkhood 995
monkish Latin 563
monochord 417
monochrome 429, 556
monocracy 737
monoculous 443
monode 445
monodrame 599
monody 597, 839
monogamist 904
monogamy 903
monogram
sign 550
cipher 533
diagram 554
letter 561
monograph
publication 531
writing 590
book 593
description 594
monolith 551
monolithic 983*a*
monologue
soliloquy 589
drama 599
monomachy 720
monomania 503
obstinacy 606
fanaticism 825
monomaniac 504
monomark 550
monoplane 273
monopolist 943
monopoly
restraint 751
possession 777
monostich 572
monosyllable 561
monotheism 983
monotonous
uniform 16
equal 27
repetition 104
permanent 141
- *style* 575
weary 841
dull 843
monotype 591
monsoon 349
monsieur 373
monster
exception 83
large 192
ugly 846
prodigy 872
evil-doer 913
ruffian 949
monstrance 998
monstrosity [*see* monster]
distortion 243
monstrous
excessive 31
exceptional 83
huge 192

ugly 846
vulgar 851
ridiculous 853
wonderful 870
mont-de-piété 787
montagne russe
slope 217
sport 840
monte *cards* 840
Montgolfier 273
month 108
monthly 138
magazine 531
– nurse 662
monticle 206
monument *tall* 206
tomb 363
record 551
monumentum ære perennius 733
moo 412
mood *nature* 5
state 7
change 140
tendency 176
willingness 602
temper 820
moodish 895, 901
moods and tenses 15, 20*a*
moody *furious* 825
sad 837
sullen 901*a*
moon *changes* 149
world 318
luminary 423
bay the – 645
jump over the – 309
man in the – 515
– of green cheese
credulity 486
moonbeam 420, 422
mooncalf 501
moon-eyed 443
moonshee 492, 540
moonshine
unsubstantial 4
dim 422
absurdity 497
unmeaning 517
untrue 546
excuse 617
moonstone 847
moonstruck 503, 870
moor *fasten* 43
open space 180
locate 184
highland 206
plain 344
Moore, Old – 513
moored *firm* 150
mooring mast 184
moorings 45, 184
moorish 345
moorland 180, 206
moot *inquire* 461
argue 476
– point *topic* 454
question 461
discuss 514
mooted 514
mop 243, 652
mope 837
mope-eyed 443
moppet 899
mopsy 962
mopus *dreamer* 515
drone 683
money 800
sad 837
mora nec requies, nec – 682
moral *judgment* 480
maxim 496
right 922
duty 926
virtuous 944
point a – 537
– certainty 474
– courage 604
– education 537
– obligation 926
– support 707
– tuition 537
– turpitude 940
moral philosophy
mind 450
duty 926
morality play 599
moralize 476
morals *duty* 926
virtue 944
morass 345
moratorium 133
morbid 655
morbific 657
mordacity 907
mordant *keen* 171
pungent 392
colour 428
language 574
more *superior* 33
added 37
– than enough 641
– than flesh and blood can bear 830
– last words 65
– or less
quantity 25
small 32
inexact 495
– than a match for 33, 159
– than meets the eye 526
– than one 100
more:
– majorum 82
– solito
conformable 82
habitual 613
– suo 613
moreover 37
mores, O – 932
Morgana, Fata – 423
morganatic marriage 903
morgue 363
– littéraire 569
mori, memento – 363
moribund 369, 655
dying 360
sick 655
morient 360
morion 717
morisco 840
mormo 860
Mormon 986
Mormonism 903, 984
morning 125
– coat 225
– dress 225
– noon and night
repetition 104
diuturnal 110
frequent 136
– star 423, 977
morocco 223
moron 493, 501
moronic 499
morose 895, 901*a*
morosis 503
Morpheus 683
morphew 653
morphia 381, 663
morphology
form 240
zoology 368
morra 840
morris
nine men's – 840
morris-dance 840
morrow 121
morse 45
morsel *small* 32
portion 51
food 298
mors aux dents, prendre le – 719
mort, guerre à – 722
mortal
transient 111
fatal 361
man 372
wearisome 841
– antipathy 867
– blow 619
– coil 362
– funk 860
– remains 362
– sin 947
mortality
evanescence 111
death 360
mankind 372
bills of – 360
mortar *cement* 45
pulverizer 330
cannon 727
mortem, post – 360, 363
mortgage
security 771
lend 787
sale 796
credit 805
mortgagee 779, 805
mortgagor 779, 806
mortician 363
mortiferous 361
mortification
disease 655
pain 828
vexation 830
discontent 832
humiliation 879
asceticism 955
mortise *unite* 43
intersect 219
interjacence 228
mortmain 748
in – 781
Morton's fork 475
mortuary 360, 363
mosaic *mixture* 41
multiform 81
variegation 440
painting 556
Moslem 984
mosque 1000
moss *tuft* 256
marsh 345
vegetation 367
moss-grown 659
moss-trooper 726, 792
most 31

at – 32
make the – of
over-estimate 482
exaggerate 549
improve 658
use 677
skill 698
the – 33
– often 136
for the – part 78, 613
make the – of one's time 682
mot 496
– de l'énigme 522
– du guet 550
– à mot 19
– d'ordre 741
– de passe 550
– pour rire 842
mote *small* 32
light 320
– in the eye
dim-sighted 443
misjudging 481
motet 990
moth *bane* 663
moth-eaten 124, 653, 659
mother *parent* 166
mould 653
– country 189
– of-pearl 440
– superior 996
– tongue 560
– wit 498
motherly *love* 897
kind 906
motif 415, 847
motile 264
motion
change of place **264**
topic 454
plan 626
proposal 763
request 765
make a – 763
put in – 284
put oneself in – 680
set in – 677
– downwards 306
– from
recession 287
repulsion 289
– into *ingress* 294
reception 296
– out of 295
– through 302
– towards
approach 286
attraction 288
– upwards 305
motionless 265
motive **615**
absence of – **615a**
– power 264
motivity 264
motley 81, 440
wearer of the – 844
motor 153, 266
vehicle 271, 272
instrument 633
–boat 273
–car &c. 272
–driver 268
–man 694
motorist 268
motory 264
mottled 440
motto *maxim* 496
device 550
phrase 566
motu: ex mero – 737
suo – 600
mouchard 527
mould *condition* 7
matrix 22
convert 144
form 240
structure 329
earth 342
vegetation 367
model 554
carve 557
decay 653
turn to account 677
moulded 820
– on 19
moulder 653, 659
moulding 847
mouldy 653, 659
moulin:
se battre contre des –s 645
– à paroles 584
moult 226
mound *large* 192
hill 206
defence 717
mount *increase* 35
hill 206
horse 271
ascend 305
raise 307
display 882
– guard *care* 459
safety 664
– up to *money* 800
price 812
mountain *large* 192
hill 206
weight 319
– artillery 726
– in labour
waste 638
make –s of mole-hills 482
– brought forth mouse
disappoint 509
mountaineer 268
mountainous 206
mountebank
quack 548
drama 599
buffoon 844
mounted rifles 726
mourn 828, 839
mourner 363
mournful
afflicting 830
sad 837
lamentable 839
mourning *dress* 225
in – *black* 431
lament 839
mouse *little* 193
search 461
mountain brought forth – 509
not a – stirring 265
mouse-coloured 432
mousehole 260
mouser 366
mousetrap 545
mousseux 353
moustache 256
mouth *entrance* 66
receptacle 191
brink 231
opening 260
eat 298
estuary 343
enunciate 580
drawl 583
deep –ed
resonant 408
bark 412
down in the – 879
make –s 929
open one's – 582
stop one's – 581
word of – 582
– honour
falsehood 544
show 882
flattery 933
pass from – to mouth 531
– wash 652
– watering 865
mouthful
quantity 25
small 32
food 298
mouthpiece
speaker 524
information 527
speech 582
mouthy *style* 577
moutonné 250
moutons, revenons à nos – 660
movable 264, 270
movables 780
move *begin* 66
motion 264
propose 514
induce 615
undertake 676
act 680
offer 763
excite 824
get a – on 684
good – 626
on the – 293
– forward 282
– from 287
– in a groove 82
– heaven and earth 686
– off 293
– on *progress* 282
activity 682
– out of 295
– quickly 274
– slowly 275
– to 894
moveless 265
movement
motion 264
music 415
action 680
activity 682
moved with 821
mover 164
movies 448, 599, 840
movie star 899
moving
keep – 682
self – 266
– pictures 448
mow *shorten* 201
smooth 255
agriculture 371
store 636
– down

destroy 162
moxa 384
M.P. 696
Mr. 373, 877
Mrs. 374
MS. 22, 590
much 31
make – of
importance 642
friends 888
love 897
endearment 902
approval 931
not say – for 932
think – of 928, 931
– ado *exertion* 686
difficulty 704
– ado about nothing
over-estimate 482
exaggerate 549
unimportant 643
unskilful 699
– cry and little wool 884
– the same
identity 13
similarity 17
equality 27
– speaking 584
mucid 352, 653
mucilage 352
muck 653
run a – *kill* 361
attack 716
excitement 825
muckle 31
muckworm 819, 876
mucor 653
mucosity 352
mucronate 253
muculent 352
mud *marsh* 345
semiliquid 352
dirt 653
clear as – 519
stick in the – 704
– guard 666
muddle *disorder* 59
derange 61
inattention 458
absurd 497
difficulty 704
failure 732
– one's brains 475
muddled 959
muddle-headed 499
muddy *moist* 339
dim 422
opaque 426
colour 429
stupid 499
mudlark *dirty* 653
commonalty 876
muezzin 550, 996
muff *incapable* 158
dress 225
bungle 699
bungler 701
muffettee 225
muffle *wrap* 225
silent 403
deaden 408*a*
conceal 528
voiceless 581
stammer 583
muffled *faint* 405
latent 526
– drums
funeral 363
non-resonance 408*a*
muffler 225, 384
mufti *undress* 225
judge 967
priest 996
mug *cup* 191
face 234, 448
pottery 384
dupe 547
muggy *moist* 339
dim 422
opaque 426
mug-house 189
mugient 412
mugwump 607
mulatto
mixture 41
exception 83
mulct *steal* 791
fine 974
mule *mongrel* 83
beast of burden 271
obstinate 606
muleteer 694
muliebrity 374
mull
prominence 250
sweeten 396
mullah 967, 996
muller 330
mullion 215
mullioned 219
multifarious
irrelevant 10
diverse 16*a*
multiform 81
multiferous 102
multifid
divided 51
multifold 81
multiformity 81
multigenerous 81
multilateral 236, 244
multilocular 191
multiloquence 582, 584
multinomial 102
multiparous 168
multipartite 44
multiple 84, 102
multiplex 81
multiplicand 84
multiplicate 81
multiplication
increase 35
arithmetic 85
multitude 102
reproduction 163
productiveness 168
multiplicator 84
multiplicity 102
multiplier 84
multiply 35
multipotent 157
multisonous 404
multitude 72, 102
the – 876
multum in parvo 596
multure 330
mum 581, 585
–'s the word 403
mumble *chew* 298
mutter 583
Mumbo Jumbo 979, 993
mummer 599
mummery
absurdity 497
imposture 545
masquerade 840
parade 882
mummify 363
mummy *dry* 340
corpse 362
beat to a – 972
mump *mutter* 583
beg 765
mumper 767, 804
mumpish *sad* 837
mumps 837, 901*a*
munch 298
Munchausen 549
mundane
world 318
selfish 943
irreligious 989
mundation 652
mundivagant 266
munerary 973
munerate 973
municipal 965
municipality 737
munificent 816
muniment
evidence 467
record 551
defence 717
security 771
munition
materials 635
defence 717
mural 717
murder 361
– the King's English
solecism 568
stammering 583
the – is out 529
murderer 361
muricated 253
murky *dark* 421
opaque 426
black 431
gloomy 837
murmur *purl* 348
sound 405
voice 580
complain 839
murmurer 832
murrain 655
Murray *travel* 266
Lindley – 542
murrey 434
murrion 717
mus, nascitur ridiculus – 509, 643
muscadine 400
muscle 159
muscular 159
muse 451
[*and see* musing]
Muse *poetry* 597
historic – 594
unlettered – 579
musette 417
Muses, the – 416
museum
collection 72
store 636
mush 354
mushroom
new 123
fungus 367
upstart 734
low-born 876
spring up like –s 163
– anchor 666

music 415
face the – 861
set to – 416
– of the spheres
order 58
universe 318
musical 413, 415, 416
– comedy 599
– ear
musician 416
hearing 418
– instruments **417**
– note 413
– voice 580
music-hall 599, 840
musician 416
musing 451
– on other things 458
musk 400
musket 727
shoulder a – 722
musketeer 726
musketry 727
muslin
semi-transparent 427
musnud
support 215
council 696
sceptre 747
muss 59
Mussulman 984
must *necessity* 601
mucor 653
compulsion 744
it – follow 478
I – say 535
mustachio 256
mustard 392, 393
after meat – 135
– gas 663, 727
mustard-seed 193
muster 72, 85
pass – 639
not pass – 651
– courage 861
muster-roll 86
musty 401, 653
mutable 149
mutation 140
mutatis mutandis
correlation 12
change 140
interchange 148
mutato nomine de te &c.
parable 521
retaliation 718
mute *funeral* 363
silent 403
sordine 405, 408*a*, 417
letter 561
speechless 581
taciturn 585
dramatis persona 599
deaf – 419
render – 581
mutilate
retrench 38
deform 241
injure 659
mutilated 53
mutilation 619
mutineer 742
mutiny 742
mutt 366
mutter
faint sound 405
mumble 583
grumble 839
threaten 909
mutton-chop
whiskers 256
mutual 12, 148
mutualize 12
mutual understanding 23
muzzle
powerless 158
edge 231
opening 260
silence 403
render speechless 581
restrain 751
gag 752
muzzle-loader 727
muzzy 458
in liquor 959
my: all – eye 546
– stars! 870
mycology 369
mynheer 877
myology 329
myomancy 511
myopia 443
myriad 98, 102
myrmidon 726
myrrh 400
myrtle 897
myself *I* 79
immateriality 317
mysterious
invisible 447
uncertain 475
obscure 519
concealed 528
mystery
[*see* mysterious]
latency 526
secret 533
play 599
craft 625
– ship 726
mystic
uncertain **475**
obscure 519
latent 526
concealed 528
sorcery 992
puzzle 475
mystify *falsify* 477
hide 528
misteach 538
deceive 545
myth 515, 546
mythology 979, 984

N

nab *deceive* 545
seize 789
Nabob 745, 803
nacelle 273
nacre 440
nadir 211
nag *horse* 271
quarrel 713
nager entre deux eaux 607
Naiad 341, 979
nail *fasten* 43
fastening 45
measure of length 200
peg 214
sharp 253
hard 323
retain 781
on the –
present 118
pay 807
hit the right – on the head
discover 480*a*
skill 698
– polish 847
naïveté 703
naked *denuded* 226
manifest 525
simplicity 849
– eye 441
– fact 151
– steel 727
– sword 727
– truth 494
namby-pamby 643, 855
name
indication 550
appellation 564
appoint 755
celebrity 873
assume a – 565
call –s
disrespect 929
disapprobation 932
fair – 873
good – 873
in the – of
aid 707
authority **737**
due 924
– to conjure with 873
nameless 565, 874
namely 79, 522
namesake 564
Nana Sahib 949
Nanny-goat 374
nap *down* 256
texture 329
sleep 683
cards 840
nape *back* 235
napery 652
Napier's bones 85
napkin 652
buried in a – 460
lay up in a – 678
napless 226
Napoleon *food* 298
cards 840
napping
inattentive 458
inexpectant 508
dull 843
nappy *frothy* 353
tipsy 959
narcissism 897, 943
Narcissus 845
narcosis 376
narcotic 657, 662
nard 356
narration 594
narrow
contract 195
thin 203
intolerant 481
restrict 761
– down 42
– end of the wedge 66
– escape 671
– house 363
– means 804
– search **461**

narrow-minded 481, 943
narrowness 203
narrows 343
nasal accent 583
nascent 66
nascitur: – ridiculus mus 509
– a sociis 82
naso, omnia suspendens – 868
nasty
unsavoury 395
foul 653
offensive 830
cheap and – 815
natâ, pro re – 770
natal *birth* 66
indigenous 188
natation 267
natatorium 652
nathless 30
nation 372
national 188, 372
– guard 726
nationality 372, 910
nations, law of 963
native
inhabitant 188
artless 703
– accent 580
– land 189
– soil 189
– tongue 560
nativity *birth* 66
cast a –
predict 511
sorcery 992
natty 845
natura il fece e poi roppe la stampa 87
naturæ, vis medicatrix – 662
natural *intrinsic* 5
musical note 413
true 494
fool 501
- *style* 576, 578
spontaneous 612
not prepared 674
artless 703
simple 849
– course of things 613
– death *death* 360
completion 729
– impulse 601
– meaning 516
– order of things 82
– state 80
– turn 820
Natural – History 357
– Philosophy 316
– Theology 983
naturalist 357
naturalization
conformity 82
conversion 144
location 184
naturalize
habit 613
naturalized
inhabitant 188
naturally 154
nature *essence* 5
rule 80
tendency 176
world 318
reality 494
artlessness 703
affections 820
animated – 357
organized – 357
second – 613
state of –
naked 226
raw 674
in –'s garb 226
naught *nothing* 4
zero 101
bring to – 732
set at –
make light of 483
opposition 708
disobey 742
not observe 773
disrespect 929
contempt 930
naughty 945
naumachia 720
nausea 841, 867
nauseate 395, 830
nauseous
unsavoury 395
unpleasant 830
disgusting 867
nautch dancer 840
nautical 267
naval 267
– authorities 745
– engagement 720
– forces 726
nave *middle* 68
centre 222
church 1000
navel 68, 222
navigation 267
navigator 269
navvy 673, 690
navy 273, 726
– blue 438
nay 536
– rather 14
Nazarene 989
naze 250
N.C.O. 745
ne plus ultra
supreme 33
complete 52
distance 196
summit 210
limit 233
perfection 650
completion 729
neaf 781
neap 195, 207
– tide 36, 340
near *like* 17
- *in space* 197
- *in time* 121
soon 132
impending 152
approach 286
stingy 819
bring – 17
draw – 197
come – 286
– one's end 360
– at hand 132
– the mark 32
– run 32
– side 239
– sight 443
– the truth 480*a*
– upon 3
sail – the wind
skilful 698
rash 863
nearly 32
nearness 197
neat *simple* 42
order 58
in writing 572, 576, 578
clean 652
spruce 845
–'s foot oil 356
– as a pin 58
neat-handed 698
neatherd 370
neb 250
nebula *stars* 318
mist 353
nebular *dim* 422
nebulous *misty* 353
obscure 519
necessarian 601
necessaries 630
necessarily 154
necessitate 630
necessity *fate* **601**
requirement 630
compulsion 744
indigence 804
make a virtue of – 698
neck
contraction 195
narrow 203
make love 902
break one's – 360
– and crop
completely 52
turn out - 297
– of land 342
– and neck 27
– or nothing
resolute 604
rash 863
neckcloth 225
necklace 247, 847
necks 980
necrology 360, 594
necromancer 548, 994
necromancy 992
necropsy 363
necroscopic 363
necrosis 49
nectar 394, 396
need *necessity* 601
requirement 630
insufficiency 640
indigence 804
desire 865
friend in – 711
in one's utmost – 735
needful
necessary 601
requisite 630
money 800
do the – *pay* 807
needle *sharp* 253
perforator 262
compass 693
as the – to the pole
veracity 543
observance 772
honour 939
– in a bottle of hay 475
needle-gun 727
needle-shaped 253
needless 641
needle-witted 498
needlewoman 690
needlework 847
ne'er-do-well 949
nefarious 945

negation 536, 764
negative
inexisting 2
contrary 14
prototype 22
quantity 84
confute 479
deny 536
photograph 558
refuse 764
prove a – 468
neglect 460
disuse 678
leave undone 730
omit 773
evade 927
disrespect 929
– of time 115
négligé 225, 674
negligence 460
negotiable 270
negotiate
mediate 724
bargain 769
transfer 783
traffic 794
negotiations
breaking off – 713
negotiator 724, 758
negro 431, 746
negus
drink 298
king 745
neif 781
neigh *cry* 412
boast 884
neighbour 197, 890
neighbourhood 183, 197, 227
neighbourly
aid 707
friendly 888
social 892
courteous 894
neither 610
– here nor there
irrelevant 10
absent 187
– more nor less
equal 27
true 494
– one thing nor another 83
nem. con. 488
Nemesis
vengeance 919
justice 922
punishment 972
nemine contradicente 488
nemo me impune lacessit 715
nenia 839
neogamist 903
neologism 123
neology 563
neophyte 144, 541
neoteric 123
nepenthe 662, 836
nephelogy 353
nephew 11
nepotism
nephew 11
wrong 923
dishonest 940
selfish 943
Neptune 341
Nereid 341, 979
nerve 159, 861, 885
exposed – 378
nerveless 158
nervous *weak* 160
style 574
timid 860
modest 881
nescience 491
nest
multitude 102
cradle 153
lodging 189
– of boxes 204
nest-egg 636
nestle *lodge* 186
safety 664
endearment 902
nestling 129
Nestor *veteran* 130
sage 500
advice 695
net *remainder* 40
receptacle 191
intersection 219
inclosure 232
snare 545
difficulty 704
gain 775
– profit *gain* 775
receipt 810
nether 207
nethermost 211
netting 219
nettle *bane* 663
sting 830
incense 900
network
disorder 59
crossing 219
neuralgia 378
neurasthenia 655
neuritis 378
neurology 329
neurotic 662
neuter *matter* 316
no choice 609a
remain –
irresolute 605
stand –
indifferent 866
neutral *mean* 29
no choice 609a
avoidance 623
– tint
colourless 429
grey 432
peace 721
neutrality
mid-course 628
peace 721
insensibility 823
indifference 866
neutralize
compensate 30
counteract 179
névé 383
never 107
– say die
persevere 604a
cheerful 836
hope 858
it will – do
inexpedient 647
prohibit 761
discontent 832
disapprobation 932
–dying 112
–ending 112
–fading
perpetual 112
glory 873
– forget 916
– to be forgotten 642
– indebted 807
– hear the last of 841
– mind
neglect 460
unimportant 643
insensible 823
indifferent 866
contempt 930
– more 107
– a one 4
– otherwise 16
– to return 122
– was seen the like 83
– so 31
– tell me 489
– thought of 621
– tired *active* 682
– tiring *persevering* 604a
neverness 107
nevertheless 30
new *different* 18
additional 37
novel 123
unaccustomed 614
– birth 660
– blood *change* 140
improve 658
excite 824
– brooms 614, 682
– comer 57
– conditions 469
– departure 66
– edition
repetition 104
reproduction 163
improvement 658
– ideas 537
turn over a – leaf
change 140
repent 950
give – life to 707, 824
view in a – light 658
put on the – man 950
New Year's Day 138
new-born 123, 129
Newcastle, carry coals to – 641
new-fangled
unfamiliar 83
change 140
neology 563
new-fashioned 123
new-fledged 129
Newfoundland dog 366
Newgate 752
new-gilt 847
new-model
convert 144
revolutionize 146
improve 658
newness 123
news 532
– sheet 531
newsmonger
curious 455
informant 527
news 532
newspaper 531, 551
– correspondent 758
newspaperman 534
newt 366

next
following 63
later 117
future 121
near 197
– friend 759
– of kin 11
– to nothing 32
– world 152
nexus 45
Niagara 348
niais 501
niaiserie 517
nib *cut* 44
end 67
summit 210
point 253
nibble *eat* 298
– at *censure* 932
– at the bait
dupe 547
willing 602
nice
savoury 394
discriminative 465
exact 494
good 648
pleasing 829
fastidious 868
honourable 939
– ear 418
– hand 700
– perception 465
– point 704
nicely
completely 52
Nicene Creed 983*a*
nicety 465
niche *recess* 182
receptacle 191
angle 244
– in the temple of fame 873
nicher, se – 184
nick *notch* 257
deceive 545
mark 550
– it 731
– of time 134
Nick, Old – 978
nickel
money 800
nicknack 643
nickname 565
nicotine 392, 663
nictitate 443
nidget 862
nidification 189
nidor 398
nidorous 401
nidus 153, 189
niece 11
niggard 819
nigger 431
– in the woodpile 702
niggle *mock* 929
niggling 643
nigh 197
night 421
labour day and – 686
orb of – 318
– and day 136
– school 542
night-cap 225
nightfall 126
nightingale 416
night-gown 225
nightmare
bodily pain 378
dream 515
incubus 706
mental pain 828
alarm 860
nightshade 663
nigrescent 431
nigrification 431
nihil – ad rem 10
– tetigit quod non ornavit 850
nihilism 989
nihilist 165
nihility 2, 4
nil 2, 4
– admirari
insensible 823
no wonder 871
disapproval 932
– conscire sibi nullâ pallescere culpâ 946
– desperandum 858
nill *unwilling* 603
refuse 764
nim 791
nimble 274, 682
nimble-witted 498, 842
nimbus
cloud 353
halo 420
glory 873
nimiety 641
nimis, ne quid – 817
nimium ne crede colori 485
n'importe 643
Nimrod 361, 622
nincompoop 501
nine 98
tuneful –
music 416
poetry 597
– days' wonder
transient 111
unimportant 643
no wonder 871
– lives 359
– men's morris 840
– points of the law 777
ninefold 98
ninepins 840
ninety 98
ninny 501
Niobe 839
nip *cut* 44
destroy 162
shorten 201
dram 298
freeze 385
pungent 392
drink 959
– in the bud
check 201
kill 361
hinder 706
– up 789
nipperkin 191
nippers 781
nipple 250
Nirvana 981
nis 980
nisi prius 741, 969
Nisus and Euryalus 890
nisus formativus 161
nitid 420
nitor in adversum 708
nitre 392
nitrous oxide 376
nit-wit 499, 501
niveous *cold* 383
white 430
nixe *demon* 980
nixie *fairy* 979
nizam 745
nizy 501
N or M 78
no
dissent 489
negation 536
refusal 764
unable to say – 605
on – account 761
have – business there 83
– chicken 128, 131
– choice 601, 609*a*
– conjuror 501, 701
– consequence 643
in – degree 32
at – great distance 197
– doubt 474, 488
have – end 112
– end of *great* 31
multitude 102
length 200
– fear 473
– go 304, 732
at – hand 32
matter of – import 4
with – interval 199
– one knows who 876
– less 639
– longer 122
– love lost between them 898
– man's land 187
– matter
neglect 460
unimportant 643
and – mistake 474
– more
inexistent 2
past 122
dead 360
– more than 32
have – notion of 489
– object 643
– one 4, 187
– other 13, 87
to – purpose
shortcoming 304
useless 645
failure 732
give – quarter 361
– scholar 493
make – scruple of 602
– great shakes
small 32
trifling 643
imperfect 651
– sooner said than done 113, 132
– stranger to 490
– such thing
non-existent 2
unsubstantial 4

contrary 14
dissimilar 18
– surrender 606, 717
– thank you 764
at – time 107
– wonder 871
Noah's ark 41, 72
nob 210
nobilitate 873
nobility **875**
noble *great* 31
important 642
rank 873
peer 875
disinterested 942
virtuous 944
noblesse 875
nobody
unsubstantial 4
zero 101
absence 187
low-born 876
– knows
ignorance 491
– knows where
distance 196
– present 187
– would think 508
noctambulation 266
noctivagant
travel 266
dark 421
noctograph 421
noctuary 421, 551
nocturnal
night 126
dark 421
black 431
nocturne 415
nocuous 649
nod *wag* 314
assent 488
signal 550
sleep 683
command 741
bow 894
– of approbation 931
– of assent 488
nodding to its fall 162, 306
noddle 210, 450
noddy 501
node 250
nodosity 250, 256
nods and becks and wreathed smiles 894
nodule 250
nodular 256
nodus, dignus vindice – 704
Noel 998
noggin 191
noise 402, 404
– abroad 531
make a – in the world 873
noiseless 403
noisome
fetid 401
bad 649
unhealthy **657**
nolens volens 601
noli me tangere
defiance 715
excitable 825
fastidious 868
nolition 603
nolle prosequi 624
nolumus leges Angliæ mutari
permanence 141
continuance 143
preservation 670
nom de: – guerre 565
– plume 565
nomad 268
nomadic 266
Nomancy 511
nomenclature **564**
nominal
unsubstantial 4
word 562
name 564
– price 815
nomination 564, 755
nominee 758
nominis umbra 4
Nomology 963
non:
– compos mentis 503
– constat 477
– deficit alter 100
– est inventus 187
– hæc in fœdera 536, 610
– nobis Domine 990
– obstante 707
– placet 489
– possumus
impossible 471
obstinate 606
refusal 764
– nostrum tantas componere lites 471, 713
lex – scripta 963
– semper erit æstas 111
– sequitur 70, 477, 495
– sum qualis eram 140, 160
non-addition 38
non-admission 55
nonage 127
nonagenarian 98
non-appearance 447
non-assemblage **73**
non-attendance 187
nonce 118
for the – 118, 134
nonchalance
neglect 460
insensibility 823
indifference 866
non-coincidence 14
non-cohesive 47
non-com. 726
non-commissioned officer 745
non-committal 528, 864
non-completion **730**
non-compliance 742, 764
nonconformity
difference 15
exception 83
dissent 489
sectarianism 984
non-content 489
non-cooperation 489, 927
nondescript 83
none 101
– else 87
– to spare 640
– such
superior 33
exceptional 83
very good 648
– in the world 4
– the worse 660
non-endurance 825
nonentity
inexistence 2
unsubstantial 4
unimportant 643
non-essential 6, 643
non-existence 2
non-expectance 508
non-extension 180*a*
non-fulfilment 730, 732
– of one's hopes 509
non-imitation **20**
non-interference
inaction 681
freedom 748
nonius 466
non-juror 489, 984
non-naturals 657
nonny 501
non-observance
inattention 458
desuetude 614
infraction **773**
dereliction 927
nonpareil 648
type 591
non-payment **808**
non-performance
non-completion 730
dereliction 927
non-plus
uncertain 475
difficulty 704
conquer 731
non-preparation **674**
non-prevalence 614
non-residence 187
non-resistance 725, 743
non-resonance **408a**
nonsense
absurdity 497
unmeaning 517
trash 643
talk – *folly* 499
non-subsistence 2
non-success 732
nonsuch [*see* none]
nonsuit *defeat* 731
fail 732
condemn 971
nonum prematur in annum 133
non-uniformity 16*a*
noodle 501
nook *place* 182
receptacle 191
corner 244
noology 450
noon *mid-day* 125
noon-day *light* 420
clear as –
intelligible 518
manifest 525
nooscopic 450
noose *ligature* **45**
loop 247

snare 545
gallows 975
norma loquendi 567
normal
intrinsic 5
mean 29
regular 82
perpendicular 212
– condition
rule 80
normality 80, 502
Normand, répondre en – 544
Norns 601
North 278
– and South 237
Northern 237
– light 423
– star 939
North-west passage 311
noscitur a sociis 82
nose *prominence* 250
smell 398
with one's – in the air 878
lead by the – 615, 737
led by the – 749
not see beyond one's –
misjudge 481
folly 499
unskilful 699
speak through the – 583
thrust one's – in
interjacence 228
busy 682
under one's –
present 186
near 197
manifest 525
defy 715
put one's – out of joint *defeat* 731
disrepute 874
– ring 847
nose-dive 306
nosegay 400, 847
nosey 455
nosology 655
nostalgia 833
nostril 351
breath of one's –s 359
stink in the –s 401
nostrum 626, 662
not *negation* 536
what is – 546
what ought – 923
– at all 32
– allowed 964
– amiss 618, 651, 845
– any 101
– bad 651
– bargain for 508
– a bit 536
– to be borne 830
– a Chinaman's chance 471
– come up to 34
– cricket 923
– to be despised 642
it will – do 923
– of the earth 987
– expect 508
– fail 939
– far from 197
– a few 102
– fit to be seen 846
– following 477
– grant 764
– guilty 946
– to be had 471, 640
– having 187, 777*a*
– hardened 950
– hear of 764
– included 55
– know what to make of 519
– a leg to stand on 158
– likely 473
– a little 31
– matter 643
– to mention 37
– mind 823, 930
– often 137
– on your life 489
– one 101
– a particle 4
– particular 831
– pay 808
– a pin to choose 27
– playing the game 923
– within previous experience 137
– to be put down 604
– quite 32
– reach 304
– right 503
– sorry 827
– a soul 101
– on speaking terms 889
– the thing 925
– to be thought of
incogitancy 452
impossible 471
refusal 764
hopeless 859
undue 925
disapprobation 932
– trouble oneself about 460
– understand 519
– vote 609*a*
– wonder 871
– for the world 603, 764
– worth
trifling 643
useless 645
nota bene 457
notabilia 642
notabilities 875
notable
manifest 525
important 642
active 682
distinguished 873
notables 875
notably 31
notary 553, 968
notation 85
notch 198, 257, 550
note *cry* 412
music 413
take cognizance 450
remark 457
explanation 522
sign 550
record 551
printing 591
epistle 592
minute 596
money 800
fame 873
change one's – 607
make a – of 551
of – 873
take – of 457
– of admiration 870
– of alarm 669
– of preparation 673
note-book
memorandum 505
record 551
compendium 569
writing 590
noted 490, 873
noteworthy
great 31
exceptional 83
important 642
nothing *nihility* 4
zero 101
trifle 643
come to – 304, 732
do – 681
for – 815
go for – 643
good for – 646
make – of
under-estimate 483
fail 732
take – by 732
think of – 930
worse than – 808
– comes amiss 831
– to do 681
– to do with 764
– doing 681
– to go upon 471
– in it 4
– of the kind 18, 536
– loth 602
– on 226
– more to be said 478
– to signify 643
nothingness 2
notice *intellect* 450
observe 457
review 480
information 527
warning 668
bring into – 525
deserve – 642
give –
manifest 525
inform 527
indicate 550
short – 111
take – of 450
this is to give – 457
worthy of – 642
– is hereby given
publication 531
– to quit 782
noticeable 31
notification 527
notion *idea* 453
notional 515
notoriety 531, 873
notorious
known 490
public 531
famous 873

infamous 874
notturno 415
notwithstanding 30
nought [*see* naught]
noun 564
nourish 707
nourishment
food 298
nous 498
nous avons changé tout cela 140
nouveau riche 123, 734, 876
Nova Zembla 383
novation 609
novel
dissimilar 18
new 123
unknown 491
tale 594
novelette 594
novelist 594
novice
ignoramus 493
learner 541
bungler 701
religious 996
novitiate 539, 673
novocaine 376, 381
novus homo 57, 876
now 118
– and then 136
– or never 134
noways 32
nowhere 187
nowise 32, 536
noxious 649, 657
noyade 361, 972
noyerait dans une goutte d'eau, il se – 699
nozzle
projection 250
opening 260
air-pipe 351
nuance 15, 465
nubibus, in – 2, 515
nubiferous 353, 426
nubile 131, 903
nucleus *middle* 68
cause 153
centre 222
kernel 642
nuda veritas 494
nude 226, 849
nudge 550
nudity 226
nugacity 499, 645
nugæ canoræ 517, 842
nugas, magno conatu magnas – 643
nugatory 158
unimportant 643
nuggar 273
nugget *mass* 192
money 800
nuisance 619, 830
null 4
– and void
inexistence 2
powerless 158
unproductive 169
illegal 964
declare – and void
abrogation 756
non-observance 773
nulla dies sine lineâ 682
nullâ pallescere culpâ, nil conscire sibi – 946
nullah 198
nulli secundus 33
nullibiety 187
nullify *inexistence* 2
compensate 30
destroy 162
abrogate 756
not observe 773
not pay 808
nullity 2, 4
nullius jurare in verba magistri 487
numb
physically insensible 376, 381
morally insensible 823
–skull 493
number
part 51
abstract **84**
count 85
plural 100
– *of a magazine &c.* 593
– among 76
take care of – one 943
– of times 104
numbered: days –
kill 360
necessity 601
hopeless 859
– with the dead 360
numberless 105
numbers *many* 102
verse 597
numbness 375, 381
numerable 85
numeral 84, 85
numeration 85
numerator 84
numerical 85
numerose
many 102
numerous 102
numismatics 800
numps 501
numskull 501
nun 996
nunc dimittis 990
nuncio 534, 758
nuncupation
naming 564
nuncupatory
informing 527
nundination 794
nunnery 1000
nuptials 903
nurse *remedy* 662
preserve 670
help 707
servant 746
custodian 753
fondle 902
put to – 537
nurseling 129
nursery *infancy* 127
nest 153
room 191
garden 371
school 542
workshop 691
– rhymes 597
– tale 546, 594
nursing home 493
nurture *feed* 298
educate 537
prepare 673
aid 707
– a belief 484
– an idea 451
nut
– to crack
fanatic 504
riddle 533
difficulty 704
– oil 365
nut-brown 433
nutmeg 393
nutmeg-grater 330
nuts 618, 829
nutshell *small* 32
lie in a – 572
little 193
compendium 596
nutation 314
nutriment 298
nutrition 707
nutritious *food* 298
healthy 656
remedy 662
nutty 499
nuzzle 902
nyctalopy 443
nymph *girl* 129
woman 374
mythology 979
sea – 341
nystagmus 443

O

O! *wonder* 870
discontent 932
– for *desire* 865
oaf *fool* 501
bungler 701
changeling 980
oak *strong* 159
heart of –
hard 323
brave 861
oakum 205
oar *paddle* 267
oarsman 269
instrument 633
labouring – 686
lie upon one's –s 681
ply the –
navigate 267
exert 686
pull an – 680
put in an – 228, 682
rest on one's –
cease 142
quiescence 265
repose 687
stroke – 693
oarsman 269
oasis *separate* 44
exceptional 83
land 342
oast-house 386
oath
assertion 535
bad language 908
on – 543
rap out –s 885
upon – 768
oatmeal 298
obbligato 88, 415
obduction 223

obdurate
obstinate 606
severe 739
malevolent 907
graceless 945
impenitent 951
obedience 743
obeisance *bow* 308
submission 725
courtesy 894
reverence 928
obelisk 206, 551
Oberon 979
obese 194
obesity 192
obey 743
be subject to 749
– a call 615
– the helm 705
– rules 82
obfuscate 421, 426
obfuscated
drunk 959
obit 360, 363
post – 360, 363
obiter dictum
irrelevant 10
occasion 134
interjacent 228
obituary 360, 594
object *thing* 3
matter 316
take exception 469
intention 620
ugly 846
disapprove 932
be an –
important 642
– to *dislike* 867
– lesson 82
objection 706, 932
no – 762
objectionable
inexpedient 647
wrong 923, 947
objective
extrinsic 6
material 316
objector
conscientious –
710
objurgate 932
oblate 201
– spheroid 249
oblation *gift* 784
religious - 990
oblectation 827
obligation
necessity 601
promise 768
conditions 770
debt 806
confer an – 648
feeling of – 916
under an – 916, 926
oblige *benefit* 707
compel 744
duty 926
obligé, bien –
refusal 764
obliged
necessity 601
grateful 916
duty 926
obligee 800
obliging
helping 707
courteous 894
kind 906
obliquation 279
obliquity
slope **217**
vice 945
– of judgment 481
– of vision 443
obliteration 552
– of the past 506
oblivion 506
nothingness 2
pardon 506
forgiveness 918
redeem from – 505
– of benefits 917
– of time 115
oblivious 506
oblong 200
– spheroid 249
obloquy
disrepute 874
disapprobation 932
detraction 934
obmutescence 581, 585
obnoxious
pernicious 649
unpleasing 830
hateful 898
– to *liable* 177
obnubilated 422
oboe 417
obreption 528
obscene 653, 961
obscurantist 421, 519, 710
obscure *dark* 421
dim 422
unseen 447
uncertain 475
unintelligible 519
eclipse 874
ignoble 876
obscurity *style* **571**
obscurum per obscurius 519
obsecration 765
obsequies 363
obsequious
subject 749
servile 886
courteous 894
respectful 928
flattery 932
observance *rule* 82
attention 457
habit 613
practice 692
fulfilment **772**
duty 926
rite 998
observant
friar 996
observation
intellect 450
idea 453
attention 457
assertion 535
– car 272
observatory 318
observe [*see* observance, observation]
remark 457
– a duty 926
– rules 82
observer 444
obsess 860, 992
obsession 716
obsidional 716
obsolete *old* 124
words 563
effete 645
obstacle 179, 706
obstant, Fata – 601
obstetrician 631
obstetrics 161, 662
obstinacy 606
prejudice 481
obstipation 261
obstreperous 173, 404
obstruct *close* 261
hinder 706
– the passage of light 426
– the view 424
obstructive
opponent 710
obstruent 706
obstupefaction 823
obstupui steteruntque comæ 860
obtain *exist* **1**
prevail 78
get 775
– under false pretences **791**
obtainable 470
obtenebration 421
obtestation 765
obtrectation 934
obtrude
interfere 228
insert 300
meddle 682
obtruncate 201
obtrusion 228, 706
obtrusive
interfering 228
vulgar 851
rude 895
obtund *mitigate* **174**
blunt 254
deaden 376
paralyze 823
obturate 261
obturator 263
obtuse *blunt* 254
insensible 376
imbecile 499
dull 823
– angle 244
obtuseness 456*a*
obumbrate 421
obverse 234
obviate 706
obvious *visible* 446
evident 474
clear 518
manifest 525
ocarina 417
occasion
juncture 8
opportunity **134**
cause 153
befit the – 646
have – for 630
on the present – 118
on the spur of – 612
occasional 475
occasionally 136
occidental 236, 560
occiput 235
occision 361
occlusion 261
unintelligible 919
latent 526
hidden 528
– art 992
occultism 984
occultation 449, 528

occupancy 186, 777
occupant 188, 779
occupation
business 625
in the – of 188
– road 627
occupied 682
– by 188
– with 457, 625
occupier 188, 779
occupy 186, 777
– the chair 693
– oneself with 457, 625
– the mind 451, 457
– a post 737
– time 106
occur 1, 151
– to the mind 451
– in a place 186
occurrence 151
of daily – 613
occursion 276
ocean 341
plough the – 267
oceanography 341
ochlocracy 737
ochre 433, 439
yellow – 436
o'clock 114
know what's – 698
octagon 244
octahedron 244
Octateuch 985
octave
eight 98
music 413
period 108
octavo 593
octet 98
octifid 99
octodecimo 593
octogenarian 98, 130
octoroon 41
octroi 812
octuple 98
ocular 441
– demonstration
see 441
visible 446
– inspection 441
oculis subjecta fidelibus 446
oculist 662
od force 992
odalisque 746
odd *remaining* 40
exception 83
single 87
insane 503
vulgar 851
ridiculous 853
– fellows 712
– fish 857
oddity 857
oddments 51
odds *inequality* 28
superiority 33
chance 156
discord 713
at – 24, 713
long – 704
what's the – 643
– against one 665
the – are 472
– and ends
remainder 40
mixture 41
part 51
useless 645
ode 597
odi profanum vulgus 878
Odin 979
odious
disagreeable 830
ugly 846
hateful 898
odium *disgrace* 874
hatred 898
blame 932
odium theologicum 481, 988
church 995
odograph 200
odometer 200
odontoid 250, 253
odour 398
in bad – 932
– of sanctity 897
odylic force 992
odzookens 870
œcumenical 78
œdematous 194, 324
Œdipus 462, 524
– complex 897
Davus sum non – 703
œil de maître 459
o'er [*see* over]
œsophagus 260
œuvre 161
of: – all things 33
– course 82, 154
– late 123
– one mind 23
– no effect 169
– old 122
– a piece
uniform 16
similar 17
agreeing 23
off 196
be – 623
keep – 623
make – with 791
move – 287
sheer – 287
stand – 287
start – 293
– one's balance 605
throw – one's centre 874
– one's guard 260, 508
– one's hands 776
take – one's hands 785
– one's head 503
– one's legs 284, 309
– one's mind 452
– and on
periodical 138
changeable 149
irresolute 605
throw – the scent
uncertain 475
avoid 623
– side 238
– with you 297
offal 653
offence *attack* 716
anger 900
guilt 947
offend 830, 945
– against the law 964
offensive
unsavoury 395
fetid 401
foul 653
aggressive 716
displeasing 830
distasteful 867
obnoxious 898
– and defensive alliance 712
– to ears polite 579
offer *proposal* 763
– the alternative 609
– a choice 609
– of marriage 902
– oneself 763
– up prayers 990
– sacrifice 990
– for sale 796
offering *gift* 784
burnt – 990
sin – 952
offertory *gift* 784
worship 990
rite 998
off-hand *soon* 132
inattentive 458
careless 460
spontaneous 612
office *doing* 170
room 191
business 625
mart 799
worship 900
do one's – 772
good –s 724, 906
hold – 693
kind –s 906
do an ill – 907
man in – 694
officer *director* 694
commander 745
constable 965
offices
kitchen &c. 191
official *certain* 474
true 494
business 625
man in office 694
authoritative 737
master 745
servant 746
officialism 739
officiate
business 625
act 680
conduct 692
religious 998
officio, ex –
officer 694
authority 737
duly 924
officinal 613
officious 682
offing 196, 341
offscourings 645, 653
offset
compensation 30
offspring 167
offshoot *adjunct* 39
part 51
effect 154
offspring 167
offspring *effect* 154
posterity 167
offuscate 421, 426
often *repeated* 104
frequent 136
most – 613

– to be met with 136
ogee 847
Ogham 590
ogive 215
ogle *look* 441
desire 865
rude 895
endearment 902
ogpu 696
ogre *bugbear* 860
evil-doer 913
demon 980
oil *lubricate* 332
grease 355, 356
pour – on
relieve 834
– on the troubled waters 174, 714
– lamp 423
– stove 386
oilcloth 223
oiled *drunk* 959
oilskin 386
oil-painting 556
oily *smooth* 255
greasy 355
servile 886
courteous 894
flattery 933
oinomania 959
ointment
grease 356
remedy 662
O.K. 488
old 124
of – 122
– age 128
die of – age 729
– bachelor 904
– clothes 225
– fashioned 851
– fogey 501, 857
– joke 842
– maid *cards* 840
spinster 904
– man *veteran* 130
husband 903
– man of the sea 706
– Nick 978
– school 124
obstinate 606
habit 613
pay off – scores 718
– song
repetition 104
trifle 643
cheap 815
– stager
veteran 130
actor 599
proficient 700
– story
repetition 104
stale news 532
love 897
– times 122
one's – way 613
– woman *fool* 501
wife 903
Oldbuck 122
olden 124
older 128
oldest inhabitant
not in memory of – 137
old-fashioned 124, 851
oldness 124
oleagine 356
oleaginous 355
oleomargarine 356
oleum addere camino 35, 173
olfactory 398
olid 401
oligarch 745
oligarchy 737
olio 41
olive-branch
infant 129
offspring 167
pacification 723
olive-green 435
olla podrida 41
Olympiad 720
Olympus 981
ombre 840
ombres chinoises 448
omega *end* 67
omelet 298
omen 512
ominate 511
ominous
predicting 511
indicating 550
danger 665
hopeless 859
omission
incomplete 53
exclusion 55
neglect 460
failure 732
non-observance 773
guilt 947
omitted 2, 187
omne tulit punctum 731
omnibus 272
omnifarious 81
omnific 168
omniform 81
omnigenous 81
omnipotence 157, 976
omnipresence 186, 976
omniscience 490, 976
omnium gatherum
mixture 41
confusion 59
assemblage 72
omnivorous
eating 298
desire 865
gluttony 957
omphalos 68
on *forwards* 282
– account of 155
– all accounts 52
– that account 155
– approval 463
– an average 29
– the brink of 32
– the cards 152
– foot *duration* 106
event 151
doing 170
– the fire 730
– all fours 13, 23
– the other hand 30
– one's head 218
– the increase 35
– a large scale 31
– these lines 627
– the move 264
– the nail 118
– no account 32
– no occasion 107
– a par 27
– the part of 9
– the point of 111
– the present occasion 118
– trial 463
– the whole 50
on dit 532, 588
once *past* 119, 122
seldom 137
at – 113, 132
– for all *final* 67
infrequency 137
tell one - 527
determine - 604
choose 609
– in a blue moon 137
– more 90, 104
– over 457
– upon a time
time 106
different time 119
formerly 122
– in a way 137
Ondine 979
one *identical* 13
whole 50
unity 87
somebody 372
married 903
all – to 823
at – with *agree* 23
concur 178
concord 714
make – of 186
neither – nor the other 610
of – accord 488
– and all
whole 50
general 78
unanimous 488
from – to another
transfer 783
– thing with another 476
– of the best 948
– bone and one flesh 903
– consent 178, 488
– of these days 121
– fell swoop 113, 173
– fine morning 106
– and a half 87
– horse 643
– idea 481
– jump 113
– leg in the grave 160
as – man 488, 709
– mind 178, 488
– by one
separately 44
respectively 79
unity 87
both the – and the other 89
the – or the other 609
– over the eight 959
– and the same 13
on – side 217, 236
– step 840
– in ten thousand 648, 948
– at a time 87

– or two 100
with – voice 488
– in a way 83
– way or another 627
at – with
agree 23
concur 178
concord 714
one-eyed 443
oneirocritic 524
oneiromancy 511
oneness 13
onerous *bad* 649
difficult 704
burdensome 706
troublesome 830
oneself 13
have all to – 777
kill – 361
take merit to – 884
take upon –
will 600
undertake 676
talk to – 589
true to – 604*a*
be – again 660
one-sided
misjudging 481
wrong 923
dishonourable 940
onion 393
onlooker 444
only *small* 32
simple 42
single 87
imperfect 651
if – 865
– think 870
– yesterday 123
only-begotten 87
onomancy 511
onomatopœia 560, 564
onset *beginning* 66
attack 716
onslaught 716
ontology 1
onus *burden* 706
duty 926
– probandi
uncertainty 475
doubt 485
onward 282
onychomancy 511
onyx 847
oof 800
ooze *emerge* 295
flow 348
semiliquid 352
– out
disclosure 529
opacity 426
opal 847
opalescent 427, 440
opaque 426
open *begin* 66
expand 194
unclose 260
manifest 525
reveal 529
frank 543
artless 703
break – 173
lay – 226
lay oneself – to 177
leave the matter – 705
pry – 173
throw – 296
– and above board 703, 939
– air 220, 338
– arms *willing* 602
friendship 888
social 892
courtesy 894
– the ball 62, 66
– a case 476
– country 344
in – court 525, 531
– a discussion 476
– to discussion 475
– the door to
cause 153
facilitate 705
permit 760
with – doors 531
– enemy 891
– eyes *see* 441
attention 457
discovery 480*a*
expectation 507
inform 527
undeceive 529
teach 537
predetermination 611
wonder 870
– fire 716
– house 892
– into
conversion 144
river 348
– the lips 529
– the lock 480*a*
– market 799
– one's mind 529
– order 194
– one's purse-strings 809
– question 461, 475
– rupture 713
– sesame 260, 550, 631, 993
– the sluices 297
– space 180
– to suspicion 485
– to *liable* 177
facile 705
– the trenches 716
– up *begin* 66
disclose 529
– to the view 446
– war 722, 889
– the wound 824
opening
beginning 66
opportunity 134
space 180
gap 198
aperture 260
open-handed 809, 816
open-hearted
veracious 543
artless 703
liberal 816
honourable 939
open-mouthed
cry 411
expectation 507
speak 582
loquacious 584
desire 865
wonder 870
opera *music* 415
poetry 597
drama 599
– glass 445
– hat 225
– house 599
opéra bouffe 599
operculum 261
operæ pretium est 646
operandi, modus 627, 692
operate *cause* 153
produce 161
act 170
work 680
– upon *motive* 615
operation
[*see* operate]
arithmetical – 85
in – 680
put in – 677
surgical – 662
operative
acting 170
workman 690
operator
surgeon 662
doer 690
operculated 261
operculum 223
operetta 415
operose 686, 704
ophicleide 417
ophiology 368
ophiomancy 511
ophthalmia 443
ophthalmic 441
opiate 174
opine 484
opiniative 481
opiniator 606
opinion 484
give an – 480
have too high an – of oneself 880
popular – 488
system of –s 484
wedded to an – 606
opinionate 481, 606
opinionated 474
self– 880
opiniâtre 481
opinionist 474, 606
opitulation 707
opium *soothe* 174
deaden sense 376
bane 663
opium-eater 683
oppidan 188
oppilation 706
opponent **710,** 891
opportune
well-timed 134
expedient 646
opportunism 605, 646
opportunity 134
lose an – 135
oppose *contrary* 14
counteract 179
evidence 468
clash 708
opposite 14
– scale 30
– side 237
opposition
[*see* oppose] **708**
the – 710
oppositionist 710
oppress *molest* 649
severe 739
malevolence 907
oppressed with

melancholy 837
oppressive *hot* 382
painful 830
oppressor 739, 913
opprobrium 874
oppugnation 708, 719
optative 865
optical 441
– instruments 445
– lantern 448
optician 445
optics *light* 420, 445
optics *sight* 441
optimacy 875
optimates 875
optime! 931
optimism 482, 858
optimist 858
flatterer 935
option 609
optional 600
optometer 445
optometry 445
opulence 803
opuscule 593
or *yellow* 436
orange 439
alternative 609
oracle 500, 513
Oracle, Sir –
positive 474
vanity 880
blusterer 887
oracular
answering 462
ambiguous 475
wise 498
prediction 511
oral *information* 527
voice 580
speech 582
– communication 588
– evidence 467
orange *round* 249
colour 439
orangery 371
orarium 999
oration 582
funeral – 363
orator 582
oratorio 415
oratory
speaking 582
place of prayer 1000
orb *region* 181
circle 247
luminary 423
eye 441
sphere of action 625
– of day *sun* 318
luminary 423
– of night 318
orbicular 247
orbit *circle* 247
heavens 318
path 627
orchard 371
orchestra
music 415
musicians 416
instruments 417
theatre 599
orchestral 415
orchestrate 60, 413, 416
orchestration 413
orchestrelle 417
ordain
command 741
commission 755
due 924
legal 963
God 976
church 995
ordained *due* 924
clergy 996
ordeal
experiment 463
trouble 828
sorcery 992
– of battle 722
order
regularity 58
arrangement 60
class 75
record 551
requisition 630
direct 693
command 741
money 800
rank 873
quality 875
decoration 877
law 963
at one's – 743
call to – 932
in – 620
keep in – 693
money – 800
out of – 651
put in – 60
recur in regular – 138
set in – 60
set one's house in – 673
standing – 613
in working – 673
– of the day
conformity 82
events 151
habit 613
plan 626
command 741
pass to the – of the day 624
orderless 59
orderly
regular 58, 80
arrange 60
conformable 82
servant 746
– of succession 63
– of things 80
orders, holy – 995
in – 996
ordinal 998
ordinance
command 741
law 963
rite 998
ordinary *usual* 82
meal 298
habitual 613
imperfect 651
ugly 846
simple 849
in – *store* 636
lie in – 681
– condition
rule 80
– course of things 613
ordinate 466
ordination
measurement 466
command 741
commission 755
church 995
rite 998
ordnance 727
ordonnance 963
ordure 653
ore 635
ore rotundo 577
oread 979
orectic 865
organ *music* 417
voice 580
instrument 633
internal –s 221
– point 413
organic *state* 7
structural 329
protoplastic 357
– change 146
– chemistry 357
– remains 357
dead 329
organism 329
organist 416
organization 60
production 161
structure 329
animated nature 357
organize
arrange 60
produce 161
plan 626
organized hypocrisy 544
organology 329
orgasm 173
orgies 954
oriel *recess* 191
corner 244
window 260
chapel 1000
Orient 236, 420
orifice
beginning 66
opening 260
oriflamme 550
Origenism 984
origin 66, 153
derive its – 154
original
dissimilar 18
not imitated 20
model 22
initial 66
individual 79
exceptional 83
cause 153
invented 515
unaccustomed 614
laughing-stock 857
return to – state 660
originality 600
want of – 843
originate *begin* 66
cause 153
invent 515
– in 154
originator 164
originative 168
Orion's belt 318
orismology 562, 564
orison *request* 765
worship 990
orlop deck 211
ormolu
sham 545
ornament 847
Ormuzd 979
ornament

in writing **577**
adornment **847**
glory 873
excess of – 851
ornamental art 847
painting 556
ornate
- *writing* 577
ornamental 847
ornavit, nihil tetigit quod non – 850
orniscopy 511
ornithology 368
ornithomancy 511
orotundity 577
orphan 893
Orpheus 416
orpiment 436
orrery 318
orthodox
conformable 82
- *religion* 983a
– dissenter 984
orthodoxy **983a**
orthoepy 562, 580
orthogonal 212
orthography 561
orthology 494
orthometry 466, 597
orthopædy 662
orthopraxy 662
orts *remnants* 40
useless 645
(*trifles* 643)
oryctology
minerals 358
organic remains 368
oscillation
change 149
motion **314**
centre of – 222
oscitancy
opening 260
sleepy 683
osculation
contact 199
endearment 902
Osiris 979
Osmanli 984
osmose 302
Ossa on Pelion 72, 319, 549
osseous 323
ossify 323
ossuary 363
ostensible
appearance 448
probable 472
manifest 525
plea 617
ostentation **882**
osteology 329
ostiary
doorkeeper 263
mouth 260
estuary 343
ostler 370, 746
ostracize *exclude* 55
eject 297
banish 893
censure 932
punish 972
ostrich, stomach of an – 957
Othello's occupation's gone 757
other 15, 37
do unto –s as we would men should do unto us 942
enter into the feelings of –s 906
every – 138
put oneself in the place of –s 942
the – day 123
– extreme 14
– side of the shield 468
– than 18
– things to do 683
– time 119
just the – way 14
in – words 522
otherwise 18
otia fecit, Deus nobis hæc – 840
otiose 683
otium cum dignitate 685
ottar, otto 400
ottoman 215
oubliette
ambush 530
prison 752
ough! 874
ought:
– to be 922, 926
ouï-dire 532
ouija board 992
ounce *weight* 319
ourselves 372
oust *eject* 297
dismiss 756
deprive 789
out *exterior* 220
in error 495
come – 446
go – *egress* 295
cool 385
play – 729
send – 297
time – of joint 735
waters – 337
– at elbows 874
– at heels 804
– of [*see below*]
– and out 52
– in one's reckoning 495
– upon it
malediction 908
censure 932
– with it
disclose 529
obliterate 552
out of *motive* 615
insufficient 640
get well – 671
– breath 688
– cash 804
– character 24
– whole cloth 544
– the common 83
– conceit with 867
– countenance
disrepute 874
humbled 879
– danger 664
– date
anachronism 115
old 124
ill-timed 135
unfashionable 851
– one's depth
deep 208
shortcoming 304
difficult 704
rash 863
– doors 220, 338
turn – doors 297
– employ 681
– favour 867
– focus 447
– gear
disorder 59
powerless 158
unprepared 674
– hand *soon* 132
completed 729
– harness 748
– health 655
– hearing 196, 419
– humour
discontent 832
anger 900
– a job 681
– joint
disorder **59**
impotent 158
evil 619
– luck 735
– one's mind **503**
– order
disorder 59
unconformity **83**
imperfect 651
– patience 825
– the perpendicular 217
– place
disorder 59
unconformable **83**
displaced 185
inexpedient 647
– pocket *loss* 776
poverty 804
debt 806
– one's power 471
– print 552
– all proportion **31**
– the question
impossible 471
dissent 489
rejection 610
refusal 764
hopeless 859
undue 925
– reach 196, 471
– one's reckoning
uncertain 475
error 495
inexpectation **508**
disappointment 509
– repair 659
– repute 874
– season 135
– shape 243
put – sight
invisible 447
neglect 460
conceal 528
– sorts *disorder* **59**
dejection 837
– the sphere of 196
– spirits 837
– one's teens 131
– tune
unmusical 414
imperfect 651
spoiled 659
discord 713
– the way
irrelevant 10
exceptional 83
absent 187
distant 196
ridiculous 853

secluded 893
get – the way 623
go – one's way 629
– one's wits 824
– work 681
– the world
dead 360
secluded 893
outbalance 30, 33
outbid 794
outbrave 885
out-brazen 885
outbreak
beginning 66
violence 173
egress 295
discord 713
attack 716
revolt 742
passion 825
outburst
violence 173
egress 295
revolt 825
outcast
unconformable 83
pariah 876
secluded 893
bad man 949
outcome *effect* 154
egress 295
produce 775
outcry *noise* 411
complaint 839
censure 932
outdo *superior* 33
transcursion 303
activity 682
cunning 702
conquer 731
outdoor 220
outer 220
outermost 220
outface 885
outfit 225, 673
outflank *flank* 236
defeat 731
outgate 295
outgeneral 731
outgo 303
outgoing 295
outgoings 809
outgrow 194
outgrowth 154
out-Herod 33, 173
outhouse 191
outing 266
outjump
transcursion 303
repute 873
outlander 57
outlandish
foreign 10
extraneous 57
irregular 83
barbarous 851
ridiculous 853
outlast 110
outlaw *irregular* 83
secluded 893
reprobate 949
outlawry 964
outlay 809
outleap 303
outlet *opening* 260
egress 295
outline *contour* 230
form 240
features 448
sketch 554
painting 556
plan 626
outlines
rudiments 66
principles 596
outlive 110, 141
outlook *view* 448
outstare 885
outlying
remaining 40
exterior 220
outmanœuvre
trick 545
defeat 731
outnumber 102
outpost
distant 196
circumjacent 227
front 234
outpouring
egress 295
information 527
abundance 639
output *egress* 295
produce 775
outrage
violence 173
evil 619
badness 649
injury to 659
malevolence 907
disrespect 929
guilt 947
outrageous
excessive 31
violent 173
scandalous 874
outrance: à –
great 31
complete 52
violent 173
guerre – 722
outrank 33, 62
outré
exceptional 83
exaggerate 549
ridiculous 853
outre mer 196
outreach 545
outreckon 482
outride 303
outrider 64
outrigger
support 215
boat 273
outright 52
outrival
superior 33
surpass 303
fame 873
outrun 303
– the constable
debt 806
prodigal 818
outscourings 653
outset 66, 873
outshine 873, 874
outside
extraneous 57
exterior 220
appearance 448
– the gates 893
mere – 544
– car 272
clean the – of the platter
ostentation 882
outsider 57, 893
outskirts 196, 227
outspan 292
outspeak 582
outspoken *say* 582
artless 703
be – *censure* 932
outspread 202
outstanding
remaining 40
outside 220
– debt 806
– feature 642
outstare 885
outstep 303
outstretched 202
with – arms 894
outstrip 303
outtalk 584
outvie 720, 873
outvote 731
outward 220
– bound 295
outweigh 33, 175
outwit 545, 731
outwork
defence 717
outworn 124
oval 247
ovate 247
ovation 883
oven 386
like an – *hot* 382
over *more* 33
remainder 40
end 67
past 122
high 206
too much 641
all – *completed* 729
all – with
destroyed 162
dead 360
failure 732
adversity 735
danger – 664
get – 660
fight one's battles – again 594
hand – 783
make – 784
set – 755
turn – 218
– and above
superior 33
added 37
remainder 40
redundance 641
– again 104
– against 237
– the border 196
– head and ears
complete 52
height 206
feeling 821
– the hills and far away 196
– the mark 33
– one's head 208, 641
– the way 237
overabound 641
overact *bustle* 682
affect 855
overalls 225
over-anxiety 865
overarch 223
overawe *sway* 737
intimidate 860
respect 928
overbalance
unequal 28
compensation 30
superior 33
overbear 175
overbearing 885
overboard, throw –

eject 297
reject 610
disuse 678
abrogate 756
relinquish 782
overborne 732, 749
overburden
redundant 641
bad 649
fatigue 688
overcast *cloudy* 353
dark 421
dim 422
over-cautious 864
overcharge
exaggerate 549
style 577
redundance 641
dearness 814
overcoat 225
overcolour 549
overcome
prevail 175
induce 615
conquer 731
sad 837
disgraced 874
tipsy 959
– an obstacle 731
over-confident 486, 863
over-credulous 486
over-curious 455
overdate 115
overdecorated 846
over-distension 194
overdo
redundance 641
bustle 682
affectation 855
overdose 641
overdraft 808
overdraw
exaggerate 549
misrepresent 555
prodigal 818
over-due 115, 133
over-eager 865
overeat oneself 957
over-estimation 482
overfatigued 688
overfed 957
overfeed 641
overflow *stream* 348
redundance 641
– with gratitude 916
overgo 303
overgorged 869, 957
overgrown *much* 31
large 192
expanded 194
overhang *high* 206
overhanging
destiny 152
over-hasty 901
overhaul *count* 85
attend to 457
inquire 461
censure 932
overhead 206
overhear *hear* 418
be informed 527
overindulgence 957
overjoyed 827
overjump 303
overlap 225, 303
overlay *cover* 223
exaggerate 549
excess 641
overdo 682
hinder 706
– with ornament
writing 577
overleap 303
over-liberal 818
overlie 223
overload
redundance 641
hinder 706
overlook *slight* 458
neglect 460
superintend 693
forgive 918
disparage 929
bewitch 992
overlooked
not to be – 642
overlooker 694
overlord 745
overlying 206
overmaster 731
overmastery 821
overmatch
unequal 28
superior 33
strength 159
conquer 731
over-measure 641
overmuch 641
over-night 122
– bag 191
over-officious 682
overpaid 816
overpass
exceed 33
transgress 303
overpersuade 615
overplay 855
overplus 40, 641
overpoise 179
overpower
subdue 731
emotion 824
overpowering
strong 159
overpraise
over-rate 482
exaggerate 549
flatter 933
overprize 482
overrate 482
overreach *pass* 303
deceive 545
baffle 731
overreckon 482
over-refinement 477
over-religious 955
override
superior 33
influence 175
pass 303
hinder 706
defeat 731
authority 737
severity 739
abrogate 756
over-righteous 988
overrule 737, 756
overruling
important 642
overrun
presence 186
spread 194
redundance 641
despoil 659
over-running
printing 591
over-scrupulous 939
overseas 57
oversee 693
overseer 694
over-sensitive 822
overset *invert* 218
level 308
subvert 731
overshadow
darken 421
repute 873
disrepute 874
overshoes 225
overshoot the mark
go beyond 303
exaggerate 549
overdo 682
clumsy 699
oversight
inattention 458
error 495
superintendence 693
failure 732
overskip 303
oversleep 683
overspent 688
overspread
disperse 73
be present 186
cover 223
overstate 549
overstep 303
overstock 641
overstrain
extol 482
fatigue 688
oversupply 641
overt 525
– act 680
overtake 292
overtaken
tipsy 959
overtask, **overtax** 679, 688
overthrow
undo 145
destroy 162
level 308
confute 479
vanquish 731
overthrown
vanquished 732
overthwart 708
overtired 688
overtone 413
overtop 31, 33, 206
overture
precursor 64
music 415
peace 723
offer 763
request 765
overturn
destroy 162
invert 218
level 308
confute 479
overvalue 482
overweening
excess 641
rash 863
pride 878
conceit 880
insolence 885
overweigh
exceed 33
influence 175
overrate 482
overwhelm
ruin 162
redundant 641

affect 824
overwhelmed
defeated 732
subjection 749
overwhelming
strong 159
wonderful 870
over-wise 880
overwork 679, 688
overwrought
exaggerated 549
emotion 824
affectation 855
over-zealous 825
oviform 249
ovo, in – 153
ovoid 247, 249
ovule 247
owe 806
– it to oneself 926
owing *debt* 806
– to *effect* 154
attribution 155
owl *fool* 501
–'s light 422
–s to Athens 641
own *assent* 488
divulge 529
possess 777
property 780
come by one's – 775
condemned out of one's – mouth 479
consult one's – pleasure 943
hold one's – 737
know one's – mind 604
not know one's – interest 699
not know one's – mind 605
will of one's – 604
of one's – accord 600, 602
pay in one's – coin 718
look with one's – eyes 459
– flesh and blood 11
throw a stone in one's – garden
clumsy 699
retaliation 718
take the law into one's – hands 722, 964
out of one's – head 600
after one's – heart 897
look after one's – interest 943
stand in one's – light 699
act on one's – responsibility 738
at one's – risk 926
have one's – way
will 600
easy 705
succeed 731
authority 737
freedom 748
– oneself in the wrong 950
owner *possessor* 779
without an – 777*a*
ownership
property 780
ox 366, 373
hot enough to roast an – 382
oxidation 659
oxymoron 24
oyer and terminer, court of – 966
O yes 531
Oyez! *hear* 418
publication 531

P

P:
mind one's –'s and Q's
care 459
polite 894
duty 926
pabulum 298, 316
mental – 454
pace *walk* 264
journey 266
measure 466
permission 760
keep – with
concur 178
velocity 274
put through one's –s 525
show one's –s
ostentation 882
– tanti nominis 928
– up and down 266
pachydermatous 376, 823
pacific 172, 721
pacification 723
pacificism 721
pacify 174
pack *arrange* 60
assemblage 72
locate 184
squeeze 195
prepare 673
burden 706
send –ing 297
– of nonsense 643
– off *depart* 293
eject 297
– up 229
package
assemblage 72
location 184
packer 673
packet
assemblage 72
ship 273
pack-horse 271
pack-saddle 215
pack-thread 205
pact 23, 769
Pactolus 803
pad *thicken* 194
line 224
horse 271
soft 324
expatiate 573
tablet 590
padding *lining* 224
stopper 263
soft 324
words 573
paddle *walk* 266
row 267
oar 633
– one's own canoe
conduct 692
free 748
– steamer 273
paddock 232
padishah 745
padlock 45, 752
put a – on one's lips 585
padre 996
padrone 745
pæan
rejoicing 838
celebration 883
gratitude 916
approbation 931
worship 990
paganism 984
page
numeration 85
printing 591
book 593
attendant 746
wedding 903
– proof 591
pageant 448, 882
paginate 85
pagoda 206, 1000
pah 717
pail 191
paillard 962
paillasse 215
pain *physical* - 378
moral - 828
penalty 974
painfulness 830
painfully *very* 31
painim 984
painless 827
pains 686
get for one's – 973
take – 686
– and penalties 974
painstaking
active 682
laborious 686
paint *coat* 223
colour 428
deceive 545
delineate 556
ornament 847
– the lily 641
paintable 845
painter *rope* 45
artist 559
painting 556
pair *similar* 17
combine 48
couple 89
– off *average* 29
marry 903
pair-oar 273
pairs *cards* 840
pal 711, 890
palace 189
bishop's – 1000
floating – 273
Paladin 717, 726
hero 861
palæocrystic 124
palæology [*see* paleology &c.]
palæstra
school 542
arena 728
palais de vérité 703
palanquin 272
palatable 394, 829
palatal *letter* 561
palate 390
tickle the – 394

palatial *palace* 189
ostentatious 882
palatinate 181
palatine 745
Palatine Court 966
palaver
unmeaning 517
speech 582
loquacity 584
colloquy 588
council 696
pale *stake* 45
region 181
inclosure 232
limit 233
dim 422
colourless 429
emotion 821
frightened 860
turn –
lose colour 429
emotion 821
fear 860
– of the church 995
– its ineffectual fire
dim 422
out of repute 874
pale-faced 429
paleography
past 122
philology 560
paleology *past* 122
language 560
paleontology 368
paleozoic 124
palestric 686, 720
paletot 225
palette 556
palfrey 271
palimpsest 147, 528
palindrome
inversion 218
neology 563
paling 232, 752
palingenesia 163
palingenesis 660
palinode 597
palinody 607
palisade
wall 212
defence 717
prison 752
pall *covering* 223
mantle 225
funeral 363
disgust 395
insignia 747
weary 841
dislike 867
satiety 869
canonicals 999
palladium
safety 664
Pallas 979
pall-bearer 363
pallet *support* 215
painter's - 556
palliament 225
palliate
moderate 174
mind 658
relieve 834
extenuate 937
palliative 174
remedy 662
pallid 429
pallium 999
pall-mall 840
pallone 840
pallor 429
palm
measure of length 200
trophy 733
steal 791
laurel 877
bear the – 873
grease the –
induce 615
give 784
itching – 865
win the – 731
– off, – upon 545
– tree 367
palmated 257
palmer
traveller 268
clergy 996
palmist 513
palmistry 511
palmy
prosperous 734
pleasant 829
– days
prosperous 734
pleasure 827
palpable
material 316
tactile 379
obvious 446
manifest 525
– obscure 421
palpation 379
palpitate
tremble 315
colour 440
emotion 821
fear 860
palsy
impotence 158
physical insensibility 376
disease 655
mental insensibility 823
palter
falsehood 544
shift 605
elude 773
paltry *small* 32
unimportant 643
mean 940
paludal 345
pampas 344
pamper 902, 954, 957
pamphlet 531, 593
pamphleteer 595
Pan 979
pan 191
panacea 662
panache 256, 847
panama *hat* 225
panary 636
pancake 298
pandar [*see* pander]
Pandean pipes 417
pandect
knowledge 490
dissertation 595
compendium 596
code 963
pandemonium 59, 404, 982
inhabitants of – 978
pandemic 657
pander *pimp* 962
– to *instrument* 631
help 707
flatter 933
pandiculation
expansion 194
opening 260
sleepy 683
Pandour 726
Pandora's box 619
bottom of 858
paned 440
panegyric 931
panegyrize 482
panel *list* 86
layer 204
partition 228
accused 938
jury 967
sliding – 545
panelling 847
pang 378, 828
Pangloss 492
panguid 355
panhandle 765, 767, 876
panic 860
panier 225
Panjandrum 875
pannel 215
pannikin 191
pannier 191
panoply 717, 727
panopticon 752
panorama 448, 556
panoramic 78, 446
– view 441
pansophy 490
pant *heat* 382
fatigue 688
emotion 821
– for 865
pantaloon
old man 130
pantomimist 599
buffoon 844
pantaloons 225
pantechnicon 272, 636
pantheism 984
Pantheon 979, 1000
panther 861
pantile 223, 350
pantologist 492, 700
pantology 490
pantomime 550, 599
pantry 191, 636
pants 225
panurgy 698
pap 250, 354
papa *father* 166
Papa *pope* 996
papacy 984, 995
papal 995
paper *cover* 223
white 430
writing 590
book 593
security 771
exist only on – 4
– credit 805
– money 800
– pellet 643
– war 476, 720
Paphian 954, 961
papilla 250
papistry 984
papoose 129
pappous 256
papula 250
papulose 250
papyrus 590
par 27
above – 648

below – *low* 207
imperfect 651
– excellence 33
– nobile fratrum
alike 17
friends 890
de – le roi 737
– parenthèse 134
– pari refero 718
– value 812
parable
metaphor 521
teaching 537
description 594
parabola *curve* 245
parabolic
metaphorical 521
paracentesis 297
parachronism 115
parachute
balloon 273
means of safety 666
– light 423
Paraclete 976
parade *procession* 69, 266
walk 189
ostentation 882
paradigm 22, 567
Paradise *bliss* 827
heaven 981
in – 827
parados 717
paradox
absurdity 497
obscurity 519
difficulty 704
paradoxical 475, 519
paraffin 356
paragon
perfect 650
glory 873
good man 948
paragram
ambiguous 520
neology 563
paragraph *part* 51
phrase 566
article 593
paraleipsis 460
parallax 196
parallel
similarity 17
imitate 19
harmonious 178
- *position* 216
symmetry 242
draw a – 464
none but himself can be his – 873
run – 178
parallelism 216
agreement 23
parallelogram 244
parallelopiped 244
paralogism 477
paralogize 477
paralysis
impotence 158
physical insensibility 376
disease 655
moral insensibility 823
paralyse 158, 376, 823
paramount
supreme 33
important 642
authority 737
lord – *master* 745
possessor 779
– estate 780
paramour 897
paranoia 503, 504
parapet 717
paraph 550
paraphernalia
machinery 633
belonging 780
paraphrase
imitation 19
copy 21
synonym 522
phrase 566
paraphrast 524
paraphrastic 19, 522
parasite *auxiliary* 711
servile 886
flatterer 935
parasitic
subjection 749
grasping 789
servile 886
parasol *covering* 223
shade 424
paratus:
in utrumque –
resolved 604
ready 673
semper – 673
parboil 384
parbuckle 633
Parcæ 601
parcel *part* 51
group 72
part and – 56
– out *arrange* 60
allot 786
parcels
property 780
parcere subjectis 740, 914
parch *dry* 340
heat 382
bake 384
parched with thirst 865
parchment
writing 590
security 771
parcity 819
pardi 535
pardon 506, 918
beg – 952
– me 489
pardonable 937
pare *cut* 38
reduce 195
peel 204
divest 226
– down
shorten 201
paregoric 662
parenchyma 316, 329
parent 166
– ship 726
parentage 11, 166
parenthesis
discontinuity 70
inversion 218
interjacence 228
by way of – 134
parenthetical
irrelative 10
pargeting 847
parhelion 423
pari passu 27, 120
Pariah
outlaw 83
commonalty 876
outcast 893
parian
sculpture 557
parietal 236
parietes 224
paring 32
parish 181
bring to the – 804
come upon the – 804
– council 696
parishioner 997
paritor 965
parity 17, 27
park *house* 189
plain 344
trees 367
artillery 727
pleasure ground 840
– paling 232
parkway 627
parlance 582
in common – 576
parlante 415
parlementaire 534, 723
parler:
facon de – 521
– à tort et à travers
illogical 477
nonsense 497
parley *talk* 588
conference 695
mediation 724
parliament 696
parliamentary securities 802
parlour 191
parlour-maid 746
parlous 665
Parnassus 597
parochial 181, 189
prejudiced 481
parody
imitation 19
copy 21
misinterpret 523
misrepresent 555
travesty 856
parole *speech* 582
on – *restraint* 751
prisoner 754
promise 768
Parolles 887
paronomasia
neology 563
ornament 577
paronymous 562
paroxysm
violence 173
agitation 315
emotion 825
anger 900
parquetry 440
Parr, Old – 130
parricide 361
parrot
imitation 19
repetition 104
loquacity 584
repeat as a – 505
parry *confute* 479
avert 623
defend 717
pars magna fui, quorum – 690

parse 461, 567
Parsee 984
parsimony 819
parson 996
parsonage 1000
part *divide* 44
portion **51**
diverge 291
music 413
book 593
rôle 599
function 625
duty 926
act a – *action* 680
take an active – 682
bear – in 709
component – 56
fractional – 100*a*
in – *a little* 32
for my – 79
on the – of 707
play a – in 175
principal – 642
take the – of 709
take – with 709
take a – in 680
take no – in 623
– company
disjunction 44
avoid 623
quarrel 713
– and parcel 56
– by part 51
–song 415
– of speech 567
– with 782, 784
partake 778
– of the sacrament 998
parte, ex – 481
parterre *level* 213
cultivation 371
Parthis mendacior 544
parti pris 611
partial *unequal* 28
incomplete 51
special 79
misjudging 481
unjust 923
– shadow 422
partiality
preponderance 33
desire 865
friendship 888
love 897
partially 32, 51
partible 44
particeps criminis 690, 711
participate 709, 778
– in *be a doer* 680
participation 778
participator 690
particle 32, 330
parti-coloured 440
particular *item* 51
event 151
attentive 457
careful 459
exact 494
capricious 608
odd 851
fastidious 868
in – 79
– account 594
– estate 780
particularize
special 79
describe 594
particularly 31, 33
particulars 79, 594
partie carrée 892
parting 44
partisan
auxiliary 711
weapon 727
friend 890
sympathizer 914
partisanship
warped judgment 481
co-operation 709
partiality 923
partition *wall* 228
allot 786
partlet 366
partly 51
partner
companion 88
auxiliary 711
sharer 778
friend 890
spouse 903
sleeping – 683
partnership
party 712
join – with 709
parts *intellect* 450
skill 698
wisdom 498
parturition 161
parturiunt montes 482, 509
party *assemblage* 72
special 79
person 372
association **712**
sociality 892
– spirit
warped judgment 481
cooperation 709
wrong 923
– to *action* 680
agent 690
co-operate 709
– to a suit 969
– wall 228
parva componere magnis 464
parvenu
new 123
successful 734
vulgar 851
low-born 876
parvitude 193
pas *precedence* 62
term 71
precession 280
rank 873
– de quatre 840
– seul 840
pas si bête 498
paschal 998
pasha 875
pashalic 737
pashaw 745
pasigraphie 560
pasigraphy 590
pasquinade 934
pass *conjuncture* 8
be superior 33
course 109
lapse 122
happen 151
interval 198
defile 203
move 264
transfer 270
move through 302
exceed 303
vanish 449
way 627
difficulty 704
thrust 716
passport 760
gratuity 815
- *as property* 783, 784
barely – 651
let it – 460
make a – at 716
pretty – 704
– away
cease to exist 2
end 67
transient 111
past 122
cease 142
die 360
– by *course* 109
inattention 458
neglect 460
disrespectful 929
– comprehension 519
– current 484
– an examination 648, 873
– the eyes over 457
– the fingers over 379
– into one's hand 785
– through one's hands 625
– into 144
– judgment 480
– a law 963
– in the mind 451
– muster
conform to 82
sufficient 639
good 648
approbation 931
barely – muster 651
– under the name of 564
– off *be past* 122
egress 295
– off for 544
– on 282
– an opinion 480
– to the order of the day 624
– out of 295
– over
exclude 55
cross 302
give 784
forgive 918
exemption 927*a*
– over to 709
– and repass 302, 314
– in review 457, 461
– the Rubicon 609
– sentence on 971
– time *exist* 1
time 106
do nothing 681
– one's time in 625
– to 144
– through
event 151
motion 302
– one's word 768
passable *small* 32

unimportant 643
imperfect 651
pretty 845
passado 716
passage [*see* pass]
part 51
conversion 144
street 189
corridor 191
opening 260
navigation 267
moving through 302
music 413
- *in a book* 593
action 680
cut a – 260
force a – 302
– of arms 720
passant, en –
transit 270
incidentally 621
pass-book 811
passe: mot de – 550
passé
antiquated 124
aged 128
spoiled 659
passed away 122
passementerie 847
passenger 268
– train 272
passe-partout
key 260
instrument 631
passer by 444
passer le temps, pour – 681
passeront pas, ilsne 717
passe-temps 840
passim
dispersed 73
place 182
situation 183
passing *very* 31
transient 111
– bell 363
– strange 870
– word 527
passion
emotion 820, 821
excitability 825
pain 828
desire 865
love 897
anger 900
ruling – 606
Passion-week 998
passionate
warm 825
irascible 901
passionless 823
passive *inert* 172
inaction 681
obedient 743
inexcitable 826
– resister 489
passivity 172, 989
pass-key 631
Passover 998
passport
indication 550
instrumentality 631
order 741
permission 760
pass-word
answer 462
sign 550
military 722
past 122
danger – 664
insensibility to the – 506
obliteration of the – 506
thing of the – 124
– bearing 830
– comprehension 519
– cure 859
– dispute 474
– praying for 945
– one's prime 128
– recollection 506
– work
useless 645
impaired 659
paste *attach* 43
cement 45
to cement 46
pulp 354
sham 545
tinsel 847
scissors and – 609
pastel 556
pasteurize 652
pasticcio 21, 41
pastil 400
pastime 840
pastor 996
pastoral
bucolic 370
music 415
poem 597
religious 995
sermon 998
pastorale 415
pastry *food* 298
sweets 396
pasturage
meadow 344
herbage 367
pasture *food* 298
pasty *tart* 298
like paste 352
pat *pertinent* 23
strike 276
(*expedient* 646)
– on the back
induce 615
comfort 834
encourage 861
approve 931
– on the cheek 902
– on the head
endearment 902
Patagonian 206
patch *small* 32
change 140
region 181
blemish 848
– up *restore* 660
compromise 774
patchwork
mixture 41
discontinuous 70
variegation 440
pate *summit* 210
brain 450
patefaction 260
patella 191
paten 191
patent *open* 260
manifest 525
licence 760
property 780
– medicine 662
pater 166
– patriæ 912
patera *cup* 191
sacramental 998
paterfamilias 166
paternal
father 166
benevolent 906
– domicile 189
paternity 166
paternoster 990
path *direction* 278
way 627
cross the – 706
secret – 530
pathetic 830
pathless
spacious 180
closed 261
difficult 704
pathognomonic 550
pathology 655, 662
pathos 821
pathoscopic 820
pathway 627
patience
perseverance 604a
endurance 826
cards 840
patient *sick* 655
patisserie 298
patois 563
patriæ: amor – 910
pater – 912
patriarch
family 11
veteran 130
ancestors 166
priest 996
patriarchal
ancient 124
ancestral 166
patriarchate 737
patrician 875
patrilineal 11, 166
patrimony 780
patriot 910
patrol *walk* 266
safeguard 664
(*warning* 668)
patrolman 664
patron
auxiliary 711
customer 795
friend 890
benefactor 912
patronage
influence 175
aid 707
authority 737
patronize 693, 707
patronymic 564
patten 225, 998
patter *strike* 276
sound 407
meaningless 517
talk 584
stage 599
patterer 582
pattern *model* 22
perfection 650
ornament 847
– after 19
patte de
– mouche 590
– velours 544, 545
patulous 194
patty 298
pauciloquy 585
paucity *small* 32
few 103
scanty 640
paughty 878
Paul Jones 792

Paul Pry
curious 455
prattle 588
paulo post futurum 121
paunch 191, 250
pauper 804
pause
discontinue 70
cease 142
quiescence 265
doubt 485
irresolution 605
repose 687
pauvre diable 804
pavanne 840
pave 223
– the way 705
pavé, on the – 961
pavement *base* 211
covering 223
path 627
pavilion 189
paving 211
paviour 673
pavor 860
paw *touch* 379
retention 781
– the ivories 416
pawky 702
pawl 45
pawn 771
pawnbroker 787
pax *hush!* 403
– in bello 723
– vobiscum 894
pay *paint* 223
profitable 775
defray 807
expend 809
income 810
punish 972
remunerate 973
in one's –
servant 746
hired 795
– in advance 809
– attention to 457
– back 718
– down 807
– dues 924
– in full 807
– homage
submission 725
worship 990
– the debt of nature 360
– no attention &c. to 458, 460
– through the nose 814
– off 718
– off old scores 919
– old debts 807
– out 200, 972
– in one's own coin 718
– the penalty 952
– the piper 707
– regard to 484
– one's respects 894
– too much 814
– a visit 892, 894
– one's way
defray 807
economy 817
paymaster 801
payment 807
remuneration 973
paynim 984
pays, mal du –
regret 833
sociality 892
pea 249
peace
silence 403
concord 714
amity 721
at – 714
commission of the – 965
justice of the – 967
keep the –
moderation 174
concord 714
make – 723
make – with 831
Prince of – 976
speak – 831
peaceable
moderate 174
peaceably, get on – 736
peaceful
inexcitable 826
peace-maker 714
mediator 724
contented 831
peace-offering
pacification 723
mediation 724
gift 784
atonement 952
peach 529
peach-coloured 434
peacock
variegation 440
beauty 845
proud 878
vain 880
gaudy 882
jackdaw in –'s feathers 701
pea-green 435
pea-jacket 225
peak *height* 206
summit 210
sharp 253
sicken 655
peaked 253
peaky 203
peal *loud* 404
roll 407
music 415
– of bells 407, 417
– of laughter 838
pearl *type* 591
goodness 648
ornament 847
glory 873
mother-of– 440
cast –s before swine 638
pearly
semitransparent 427
colour 428
white 430
grey 432
variegated 440
pear-shape 249
peasant 876
peat 388
pebble *little* 193
hard 323
– dash 223
peccability 945
peccable 947
peccadillo 947
peccant *bad* 649
unclean 653
diseased 655
– humour 653, 655
peccavi 950
peck *much* 31
multitude 102
eat 298
– at *censure* 932
– of troubles
difficulty 704
adversity 735
pain 828
peckish 865
Pecksniff 548
pectinated 253
peculate 791
peculator 792
peculiar 79, 83
peculiarly 31, 33
pecuniary 800
pecunious 803
pedagogic 537
pedagogue
scholar 492
teacher 540
pedantic 855
pedagogy 537
pedal 633
– note 408
– point 416
pedant *scholar* 492
pedantic
half-learned 491
- *style* 577
affected 855
pedantry 481
peddle *meddle* 683
hawk 796
peddler 796, 797
peddling
trifling 643
miserly 819
pederero 727
pedestal 215
place on a – 307, 931
pedestrian 268
pedicel 215
pedicle 215
pedigree 69, 166
pediment 210, 215
pedlar 797
–'s French 563
pedometer 200
peduncle 214
peek 441
peel *layer* 204
skin 223
uncover 226
– off *separate* 44
peeler 664
peel-house 717
peep 441
– behind the curtain 461
– of day 125
– into the future 510
– out 446, 529
peep-hole 260
peep-show 448, 840
peer *equal* 27
pry 441
inquire 461
lord 875
– out 446
peerless *supreme* 33
first rate 648
glorious 873
virtuous 944
peeved 900

peevish 895, 901
peg *grade* 71
hang 214
project 250
drink 298, 959
come down a – 306
let down a – 308
not stir a – 265, 681
– away 682
– to hang on 617
– on *journey* 266
– out *die* 360
Pegasus 271
pegomancy 511
pegs *legs* 266
peignoir 225
peindre, fait à – 845
peine forte et dure 974
pejorative 483
pelagic 341
pelerine 225
pelf *gain* 775
property 780
money 803
pelisse 225
Pelion, Ossa on – 72, 319
pellet 249, 727
paper – 643
pellicle 204, 223
pell-mell 59
pellucid 425
pelote 249
pelt *skin* 223
dress 225
throw 276
attack 716
punish 972
peltry 223
pemmican 298
pen *inclosure* 232
write 590
writer 593
restrain 751
imprison 752
ready – 569
slip of – 495, 568
stroke of the –
write 590
authority 737
command 741
– in hand 590
– and ink 590
– name 565
draw the – through 552
penal 972
– servitude 972
– settlement 752
penalty **974**
extreme – 972
penance 952, 974
do – 998
penates, lares et – 189, 991
penchant
willing 602
desire 865
love 897
pencil *bundle* 72
- *of light* 420
write 590
pencil-drawing 556
pencraft 590
pendant *match* 17
flag 550
ornament 847
pendency *time* 106
hanging **214**
pendente lite 106
uncertain 475
lawsuit 969
pendule 114
pendulous 214, 314
pendulum 114, 214
motion of a – 314
Penelope, work of – 645, 730
penetralia 221
– mentis 450, 820
penetrate
ingress 294
passage 302
sagacity 498
– the soul 824
penetrated with 484, 821
penetrating
sagacious 498
feeling 821
– glance 441
penfold 232
peninsula 342
penitence **950**
penitentiary 752, 996
pen-knife 253
penman 590
inspired – 985
penmanship 590
pennant 550
pennate 267
penniless 804
pennon 550
penny 800
not have a – 804
cost a pretty – 814
turn a – 775
no – no paternoster 812
in for a – in for a pound 768
– dreadful 594
– trumpet 410
– whistle 410
penny-a-liner 534, 593
penny-a-lining 573
pennyweight 319
penny-wise 819
– and pound foolish *caprice* 608
waste 638
prodigal 818
pennyworth 812
penology 972
penscript 590
pensée, arrière – 528
penseroso 837
pensile 214
pension *income* 810
pensioner
student 541
servant 746
receiver 785
pensive 451, 837
penstock 350
pent up 751
– in one's memory 505
pentagon 98, 244
pentahedron 244
pentameter 98, 597
Pentateuch 98, 985
Pentecost 998
Penthesilean 861
penthouse 189, 191
pentile 223
penultimate 67
penumbra 421
penurious 819
penury 804
peon 726
people
kinsfolk 11
multitude 102
inhabit 186
mankind 372
commonalty 876
laity 997
pep 171
– up 171
pepastic 662
pepper *pungent* 392
condiment 393
attack 716
– and salt 432, 440
peppercorn 643
– rent 815
peppery
irascible 901
peptic 662
per 631
– contra
contrariety 14
counter-evidence 468
opposition 708
– procuratio 755
– saltum 70, 113
– se 87
peradventure 470
peragrate 266
perambulate 266
perambulator
measure of length 200
vehicle 272
perceivable 446
perceive
be sensible of 375
see 441
know 490
percentage 84, 813
perceptible 446
perception 453, 490
perceptive 375
perch *location* 184
abide 186
habitation 189
length 200
height 206
support 215
– up 307
perchance 156, 470
percipience 450
percolate 295, 348
percolator 191
percursory 458
percussion 276
centre of – 222
percussive 277
perdition
destruction 162
ruin 732
loss 776
perdre son Latin 704
perdrix, toujours – 841
perdu 528
enfant – 859, 863
perdurable 110
perdy 535
peregrination 266
peregrinator 268
peremptory
assertion 535

firm 604
authoritative 737
rigorous 739
compulsory 744
duty 926
– denial 536
– refusal 764
perennial
continuous 69
diuturnal 110
- *plants* 367
perennius, ære – 873
pererration 266
perfect
great 31
entire 52
excellent 650
complete 729
perfection 650
bring to – 729
perfervidum ingenium 682
perfidy 874, 940
perflate 349
perforate 260
perforator 262
perforce 601, 744
perform
produce 161
do 170
- *music* 416
action 680
achieve 729
fulfil 772
– a circuit 629
– a duty 926
– the duties of 625
– a function 644
– an obligation 772
– a part 599, 680
– a service 998
performable 470
performance
[*see* perform]
effect 154
performer
musician 416
stage-player 599
agent 690
affectation 855
perfume 400
perfunctory 53, 460
pergola 191
perhaps 470, 514
peri 845, 979
periapt 993
pericranium 450
periculous 665
peridot 847
perihelion 197
peril 665
at your – 909
take heed at one's – 668
perilepsis 476
perimeter 230
period *end* 67
point 71
- *of time* 106, **108**
recurrence 138
at fixed –s 138
well rounded –s 577, 578
periodical
recurring 138
book 593
periodicity 138
peripatetic 266, 268
periphery 230
periphrase 566, 573
periplus 267
periscope 441, 445
periscopic 446
– lens 445
perish
cease to exist 2
be destroyed 162
die 360
decay 659
– with cold 383
– with hunger 956
perishable 111
perissology 573
peristaltic 248
peristyle 189
periwig 225
perjured 940
perjurer 548
perjury 544
perk *dress* 225
– up *elevate* 307
revive 689
perked up
proud 878
perky 880
perlustration 441
permanence
durability 110
unchanging **141**
unchangeable 150
permanent
habitual 613
permeable 260
permeate
insinuate 228
pervade 186
pass through 302
–d with 613
permissible 760
permission 760
permissive 760
permit 760
permitting
weather &c. – 469, 470
permutation
numerical - 84
change 140
interchange 148
pernicious 649
pernicity 274
perorate
diffuse style 573
peroration
sequel 65
end 67
speech 582
perpend *think* 451
perpendicular 212
perpension
attention 457
perpetrate 680
– a pun &c. 842
perpetrator 690
perpetua, esto – 928, 931
perpetual 112
frequent 136
– curate 996
– motion 467
perpetuate 112
continue 143
establish 150
perpetuity 69, **112**
perplex *derange* 61
distract 458
uncertainty 475
bother 830
perplexed 59, 248
perplexity
disorder 59
uncertainty 475
unintelligibility 519
difficulty 704
perquisite 775, 973
perquisition 461
perron 627
perscrutation 461
persecute
oppress 649
annoy 830
malevolence 907
perseverance 143, 604a
Persides 215
persiflage 842, 856
persifleur 844
persist *duration* 106
permanence 141
continue 143
persevere 604*a*
persistence
diuturnity 110
person 3, 372
without distinction of –s 922
persona grata 890, 899
personable 845
personæ, dramatis – 599, 690
personage 372
personal
[*see* person]
special 79
subjective 317
– narrative 594
– property 780
– remarks 932
– security **771**
personality
[*see* personal]
discourtesy 895
disrespect 929
censure 932
detraction 934
personalty 780
personate 19, 554
personify 521, 554
personnel 56, 590
perspective
view 448
expectation 507
painting 556
aerial – 428
in – 200
perspicacity
sight 441
intelligence 498
fastidiousness 868
perspicuity
intelligibility 518
style **570**
perspiration 295, 299
in a – 382
perstringe 457
persuadable 602
persuade *belief* 484
induce 615
persuasibility
willingness 602
persuasion
class 75
opinion 484
teaching 537
inducement 615
religious – 983
persuasive
reasoning 476
pert

vain 880
insolent 885
discourteous 895
pertain to
relate to 9
included under 76
power 157
belong 777
property 780
duty 926
perte de vue, à – 196, 447
pertinacity 604*a*
pertinent 9, 23
pertingent 199
perturbation
derange 61
ferment 171
agitation 315
emotion 821
excitation 824, 825
fear 860
pertusion 260
peruke 225
peruse 539
pervade
influence 175
extend 186
affect 821
– the soul 824
pervading spirit 820
perverse
obstinate 606
difficult 704
churlish 895
sulky 901*a*
perversion
sophistry 477
misinterpretation 523
misteaching 538
falsehood 544
untruth 546
injury 659
impiety 988
pervert 144, 607
[*see* perversion]
perverted 495
pervestigation 461
pervicacious 606
pervigilium 682
pervious 260
pessimism
overrate 482
underrate 483
dejection 837
hopeless 859
pessimist
[*see* pessimism]
coward 862
pessomancy 511
pessoribus orti 876
pest 663, 830
pester 830
pest-house 662
pestiferous 657
pestilence 655
pestle 330
pet *love* 897
favourite 899
anger 900
fondle 902
flatter 933
– lamb 366
petal 367
petard 727
hoist on one's own – 718, 732
Peter to pay Paul:
borrow of – 788
rob – *steal* 791
wrong 923
–'s pence 784, 809
peter out 142
petit maître 854
petite dame 962
petitio principii 477
petition 765, 969, 990
petitioner 767
petrel *warning* 668
petrify *dense* 321
hard 323
freeze 385
thrill 824
affright 860
astonish 870
petrol 388
petroleum 356
pétroleuse 384
petronel 727
petticoat *dress* 225
woman 374
– government
authority 737
pettifogger 968
pettifogging
sophistry 477
deception 545
litigious 713
dishonourable 940
pettish 901
petto, in –
mental 450
thought of 454
concealed 528
intention 620
petty *little* 32, 193
unimportant 643
– cash 800, 811
– jury 967
– larceny 791
– officer 745
– sessions 966
– treason 742
petulance 885, 901
petulant
- *language* 574
peu de chose 643
peu s'en faut 32
pew *cell* 191
church 1000
pewter 41
phaeton 272
Phaëthon 423
phalanx 712, 726
phantasm
unsubstantiality 4
illusion 443
appearance 448
imagination 515
phantasmagoria 448
phantasy 453, 515
phantom *unreal* 4
fallacy of vision 443
imaginary 515
pharisaical 544, 988
Pharisee 548, 988
pharmacy 662
pharos 550
phase *aspect* 8
transition 144
form 240
appearance 448
have many –s 149
assume a new – 144
view in all its –s 461
phasis 448
phasma 443
phenomenon
event 151
appearance 448
prodigy 872
phial 191
Phidias 559
philander 902
philanthropy 784, 906, 910
Philip drunk to Philip sober, appeal from – 658
philippic 932
Philistine 491, 876
philologist 492
philology 560
philomath 492
philomel 416
philosopher 492, 500
–'s stone
impossibility 471
perfect 650
remedy 662
wealth 803
philosophical
thoughtful 451
calm 826
philosophy
calmness 826
knowledge 490
Moral – 450
– of the Mind 450
philtre 993
phiz *face* 234
look 448
phlebotomy
ejection 297
remedy 662
Phlegethon 982
phlegm *viscid* 352
insensibility 823
phlegmatic
indifferent 866
phlogiston 382
pho! 497
Phœbus *sun* 318
luminary 423
phœnix
exception 83
reproduction 163
paragon 650
restoration 660
phonate 402
phonetic
sound 402
voice 580
speech 582
– spelling 561
phonics 402
phonograph 417, 418
phonography
sound 402
letter 561
writing 590
phonology 562
Phosphor 423
phosphorescence 420, 423
phosphorus 423
photo-engraving 558
photograph 17
photographer 559
photography 445
light 420
representation 554

photogravure 558
photolysis 49
photometer 445
photosphere 318
photostat 553
phrase *part* **51**
music **413**
language **566**
phrasemonger 577
phraseology 569
phrenetic 503
phrenitis 503
phrenology 450
phrenotypics 505
Phryne 962
phthisozoics 361
phylacteric
sorcery **992**
phylactery
maxim **496**
spell **993**
physic
cure **660**
remedy **662**
physical 316
– education
material **316**
teaching **537**
– force
strength **159**
compulsion **744**
– nature 3
– pleasure **377**
– pain **378**
– science 316
physician
remedy **662**
advice **695**
Physics 316
physiognomy
face **234**
appearance **448**
interpret **522**
Physiology
organization **357**
life **359**
Vegetable – 369
physique
strength **159**
animality **364**
phytivorous 298
Phytology 369
pi 591
piacere, al – 600
piacular 952
pianino 417
pianissimo 415
pianist 416
piano *gentle* **174**
music **415**
– organ 417
– player 417
pianoforte 417
pianola 417
piazza 189, 191
pibroch *music* **415**
war **722**
pica 591
picaresco, gusto – 945
picaroon 792
piccolo 410, 417
pick *axe* **253**
eat **298**
select **609**
best **648**
clean **652**
gain **775**
– a-back 215
– the brains of 461
– holes
censure **932, 934**
– the lock 480*a*
– me up 662
– out *extract* 301
select **609**
– to pieces
separate **44**
destroy **162**
find fault **932**
– a quarrel 713
– one's steps 459
– up *learn* 539
get better **658**
gain **775**
– one's way 675
pickaninny 129
pickaxe 253
picked 648
– men 700
pickeer 791
pickeerer 792
Pickelhaube
armour **717**
picket *join* **43**
locate **184**
fence **229**
guard **668**
defence **717**
soldiers **726**
restrain **751**
imprison **752**
torture **972**
– boat 273
pickings 775, 793
pickle *condition* **7**
macerate **337**
pungent **392**
condiment **393**
preserve **670**
difficulty **704**
have a rod in – 673
pickle-herring 844
pickpocket 792
abuse like a – 932
pickthank *busy* **682**
servile **886**
flatterer **935**
picnic *food* **298**
participation **778**
amusement **840**
picquet 840
pictorial
painting **556**
beauty **845**
picture
appearance **448**
representation **554**
painting **556**
description **594**
– to oneself 515
picture-gallery 556
picture-theatre 599
picturesque
painting **556**
beauty **845**
piddle *dawdle* **683**
piddling *trivial* **643**
pidgin English 563
pie *food* **298**
sweet **396**
printing **591**
piebald 440
piece *adjunct* **39**
bit **31**
painting **556**
drama **599**
cannon **727**
coin **800**
courtesan **962**
fall to –s 162
go to –s 162
in –s 330
of a – 42
pull to –s 162
give a – of advice 695
– of good fortune 618
– of music 415
– of news 532
– out 52
– together 43
– of work 713
make a – of work about 642
pièce
– justificative 467
– de résistance 298
piecemeal 51
pied *variegated* **440**
pied de la lettre, au – 494
pie-poudre, court of – 966
pier 189, 666
pierce
perforate **260**
bodily pain **378**
chill **385**
hurt **649**
wound **659**
affect **824**
mental pain **830**
– the head 410
– the heart 830
piercer 262
piercing *cold* **383**
loud **404**
shrill **410**
intelligent **498**
feeling **821**
– eye 441
– pain 378
pier-glass 445
Pierian spring 597
pierre fendre, à – 383
Pierrot 599
pietas 998
piété, mont de – 787
pietism 988
pietist 987, 988
piety 987
pig *animal* **366**
sensual **954***a*
– in a poke
uncertain **475**
chance **621**
rash **863**
– together **72**
pigeon
dupe **547**
steal **791**
gorge de – 440
pigeon-hearted 862
pigeon-hole 191, 260
piggin 191
piggish 954
pig-headed 499, 606
pigment 428
pigmy 193
pignoration 771
pignus 771
pig-sticking 361
pigsty 653
pigtail 214
pigwidgeon 193, 980
pike *hill* **206**
sharp **253**

highway 627
weapon 727
pikeman 726
pikestaff *tall* 206
plain 525
pilaster
support 215
projection 250
ornament 847
pile *stake* 45
heap 72
edifice 161
post 215
velvet 256
money 800
funeral – 363
– up 549, 641
pile-driver 276
pilfer *steal* 791
pilferer 792
pilgarlic
outcast 893
pilgrim 268, 996
pilgrimage 266, 676
pill *sphere* 249
medicine 662
bitter – 735
pillage 659, 791
pillager 792
pillar *stable* 150
lofty 206
support 215
monument 551
tablet 590
–s of Hercules 550
– of the state &c. 873
from – to post
transfer 270
agitation 315
irresolute 605
circuit 629
pillion 215
pillory 975
pillow
support 215
soft 324
consult one's –
temporize 133
reflect 451
pilot *mariner* 269
inform 527
guide 693
director 694
pilot-balloon 463
pilot-boat 273
pilot-officer 745
pilot-jacket 225
pilous 256
pimp 962
pimple 250, 848
pin *fasten* 43
fastening 45
locate 184
sharp 253
axis 312
trifle 643
might hear a – drop 403
point of a – 193
not a – to choose 27, 609*a*
– down 744, 751
– one's faith upon 484
– oneself upon 746, 886
pinafore 225
pince-nez 445
pincers 781
pinch *emergency* 8
contract 195
pain 378
chill 385
need 630
difficulty 704
adversity 735
grudge 819
hurt morally 830
at a – 630, 704
jack at a – 711
where the shoe –s 830
– of snuff 643
pinchbeck 545, 847
pinched [*see* pinch]
thin 203
poor 804
– with hunger 865
pinching 383, 819
Pindaric 597
pine *disease* 655
dejection 837
suffer in mind 828
– away 837
– for 865
pinery 371
ping-pong 840
pinguid 355
pin-hole 260
pinion *fasten* 43
wing 267
instrument 633
restrain 751
fetter 752
pink *notch* 257
pierce 260
thrust 276
colour 434
perfection 650
glory 873
pink of *beauty* 845
– fashion 852
– perfection 650
– politeness 894
pinnace 273
pinnacle 210
pinocle 840
pin-prick 180*a*
pins *legs* 266
– and needles
bodily pain 378
numb 381
mental pain 828
pinscher 366
Pinto, Fernam Mendez – 548
pioneer
precursor 64
leader 234
teacher 540
prepare 673
pious 987
– fraud 546, 988
pip 747
pipe *tube* 260
conduit 350
vent 351
tobacco 392
sound 410
cry 411
music 416, 417
weep 839
no – no dance 812
– one's eye 839
– of peace 721, 723
pipeclay *habit* 613
strictness 739
piper 416
pay the – 707, 807
piping – hot 382
– time 721, 734
pipkin 191
piquant
pungent 392
- *style* 574
impressive 821
piquante, sauce – 393, 829
pique *fly* 267
excite 824
pain 830
hate 898
anger 900
– oneself
pride 878
piqueerer 792
piquet 717, 726
pirate 773, 791, 792
pirogue 273
pirouette 218, 312
turn a – 607
Pisa, tower of – 271
pis-aller 147
piscatorial 366
pisces natare docere 538, 641
pisciculture 370
piscina 350, 1000
pish! *absurd* 497
trifling 643
excitable 825
irascible 901
piste 551
Pistol 887
pistol 727
pistol-shot 197
piston 263
pit *deep* 208
hole 252
opening 260
extract 301
grave 363
theatre 599
danger 667
bottomless – 982
– of Acheron 982
– against 708, 713
– against one another 464
pit-a-pat
agitation 315
rattle 407
feeling 821
excitation 824
pitch *degree* 26
term 71
location 184
height 206
summit 210
erect 212
throw 284
descent 306
depression 308
reel 314
resin 356*a*
musical - 413
black 431
absolute – 416
– of one's breath 411
– dark 421
– into *attack* 716
contend 720
punish 972
– overboard 782
– one's tent 292
– and toss 621
– upon *reach* 292
discover 480*a*
choose 609
get 775

pitched battle 720
pitcher 191
pitchfork 272, 284
rain –s 348
pitch-pipe 417
piteous 830
piteously *much* 31
pitfall 545, **667**
pith *gist* 5
strength 159
interior 221
centre 222
meaning 516
important part 642
pithless 158
pithy *meaning* 516
concise 572
vigorous 574
pitiable *bad* 649
painful 830
contemptible 930
pitied, to be – 828
pitiful
unimportant 643
bad 649
disrepute 874
pity 914
pitiless 914a
revengeful 919
pittance
quantity 25
dole 640
allotment 786
income 810
pitted 848
pituitous 352
pity 914
express – **915**
what a –
regret 833
lament 839
for –'s sake 914
pivot *junction* 43
cause 153
support 215
axis 222, 312
pix *box* 191, 998
assay 463
pixy 980
pizzicato 415
placable 918
placard 531
placate 723, 918
place
circumstances 8
order 58
arrange 60
term 71
situation **182,** 183
locate 184
abode 189
office 625
rank 873
give – to 623
have – 1
in – 183
in – of 147
make a – for 184
out of – 185
take – 151
– to one's credit 805
– itself 58
– in order 60
– upon record 551
– under
include 76
placebit, decies repetita – 829
placebo 933
place-hunter 767
placeman 758
placet 488, 741
placid 826
placket 260
plagiarism
imitation 19
borrowing 788
theft 791
plagiarist 792
Plagiary, Sir Fretful – 901
plagiedral 217
plague *disease* 655
pain 828
worry 830
plague-spot 657
plaguy 704, 830
plaid *shawl* 225
variegation 440
plaidoyer 476
plain
horizontal 213
country **344**
obvious 446
meaning 518
manifest 525
style 576
artless 703
ugly 846
simple 849
speak –ly 576
tell one –ly 527
– English 576
– dealing 543
– interpretation 522
– question 461
– sailing 705
– sense 498
– speaking 525, 703
– terms
intelligible 518
interpreted 522
language 576
– truth 494
– words 703
plainness 576
plainsong 990
plain-spoken 525, 703
plaint 411, 839
plaintiff 938
plaintive 839
plaisance
[*see* pleasance]
plaisanterie 842
plaister 223
plait 219, 258
plan *itinerary* 266
information 527
representation 554
scheme **626**
according to – 82
planchette 992
plane *horizontal* 213
flat 251
smooth 255
fly 267
aeroplane 273
soar 305
inclined – 633
planet *world* 318
luminary 423
fate 601
planet-struck
adversity 735
wonder 870
planimeter 466
planish 255
plank *board* 204
programme 626
path 627
safety 666
plant *place* 184
insert 300
vegetable 367
agriculture 371
trick 545
tools 633
property 780
– a battery 716
– a dagger in the breast 830
– oneself 184
– a thorn in the side 830
plantation
location 184
agriculture 371
estate 780
planter 188
planter ses choux, aller – 893
plaque 204
plash *lake* 343
stream 348
sound 405, 408
plashy 345
plasm 22
plasma 847
plasmic 240
plaster *cement* 45
covering 223
remedy 662
– up *repair* 660
plastered 959
plastic *alterable* 149
form 240
soft 324
– **arts 557**
plastron 717
plat *weave* 219
ground 344
plate *dish* 191
layer 204
covering 223
flat 251
food 298
engraving 558
– layer 690
– printing 558, 591
plateau 213, 344
plated 545
platform
horizontal 213
support 215
stage 542
scheme 626
arena 728
– orator 582
platinum blond 430
platitude 517, 843
Platonic
contemplative 451
inexcitable 826
chaste 960
– bodies 244
Platonism 451
platoon 726
– fire 716
platter 191
layer 204
flat 251
clean the outside of the – 544
plaudit 931
plausible
probable 472

sophistical 477
false 544
approbation 931
flattery 933
vindication 937
play *operation* 170
influence 175
scope 180
oscillation 314
music 416
drama 599
use 677
action 680
freedom 748
amusement 840
at – 840
bring into – 677
full – 175
full of – 836
in – 842
– along with 709
– one's best card 686, 698
– of colours 440
– at cross purposes 59, 523
– a deep game 702
– the deuce 825
– the devil 907
– one false
disappoint 509
falsehood 544
deception 545
– fast and loose
falsehood 544
irresolute 605
tergiversation 607
caprice 608
– on the feelings 824
– first fiddle 642, 873
– the fool
folly 499
clumsy 699
amusement 840
ridiculous 853
ridicule 856
– for *chance* 621
– a game
pursue 622
conduct 692
pastime 840
– the game 939
– into the hands of 709
– havoc 659
– hide and seek 528, 623
– a joke 853
give – to the imagination 515
– of light 420
– the monkey 499
– off 545
– a part
false 544
drama 599
action 680
– one's part 625, 692
– second fiddle 34, 749
– one a trick 509, 545
– tricks with 699, 702
– truant 623
– upon 545, 856
– with 460
– upon words
misinterpret 523
neology 563
wit 842
play-boy 818
play-day 840
played out
end 67
fatigue 688
completion 729
failure 732
player
musician 416
actor 599
– piano 417
playfellow 890
playful 836
– imagination 515
playground 728, 840
play-house 599
playmate 890
playsome 836
plaything
trifle 643
toy 840
make a – of 749
playwright 599
plea
defence 462
argument 476
excuse **617**
vindication 937
lawsuit 969
plead *argue* 467
plea 617
beg 765
– one's cause 937
– guilty 950
pleader *lawyer* 968
pleading, special – 477
pleadings 969
pleasance 189, 840
pleasant
agreeable 829
amusing 840
witty 842
make things –
deceive 545
induce 615
please 829
flatter 933
pleasantry 840, 842
please 829
as you – 743
do what one –s 748
if you –
obedience 743
consent 762
request 765
– oneself 943
pleasurableness **829**
pleasure
physical - **377**
will 600
moral - **827**
dissipation 954
at – 600
at one's – 737
during – 108*a*
give – 829
man of – 954*a*
make a toil of – 682
take one's – 840
will and – 600
with –
willingly 602
pleasure-giving 829
pleasure-ground
demesne 189
amusement 840
pleat 258
plebeian 851, 876
plébiscite 480, 609
plectrum 417
plectuntur Achivi 739
pledge *affirmation* 535
promise 768
security 771
borrow 788
drink to 883, 894
hold in – 771
take the – 958
– oneself 768
– one's word 768
pledget 263, 662
Pleiades 72, 318
plenary 31, 52
plenipotent 157
plenipotentiary
consignee 758
deputy 759
plentitude 639
in the – of power 159
plenty
multitude 102
sufficient 639
– to do 682
plenum *substance* 3
matter 316
pleonasm
repetition 104
diffuseness 573
redundance 641
plerophory 484
plethora 641
plexal 219
plexus 219
pliable 324
pliant *soft* 324
irresolute 605
facile 705
servile 886
plicature 258
pliers 301, 781
plight *state* 7
promise 768
security 771
evil – 735
– one's faith 902
– one's troth 768, 902
plighted love 897, 902
Plimsoll mark 466
plinth 211, 215
plod *journey* 266
slow 275
persevere 604*a*
work 682
– along 143
plodding 604*a*, 682
dull 843
plot - *of ground* 181
plain 344
story 594
plan 626
realty 780
the – thickens
assemblage 72
plough *furrow* 259
agriculture 371
– the ground 673
– in 228
– the waves 267
– one's way 266
ploughboy

commonalty 876
ploughman 371
ploughshare 253
pluck *cheat* 545
resolution 604
persevere 604a
reject 610
take 789
steal 791
courage 861
– up courage 861
– a crow with 932
– out 301
plug 261, 263
– along 143
plum *number* 98
sweet 396
money 800
plumage 256
plumb *vertical* 212
close 261
measure 466
plumber 690
plumb-line 212
plum-coloured 437
plume *feather* 256
ornament 847
borrowed –s 545
– oneself 878
plume
coup de – 590
nom de – 565
plumigerous 256
plummet 208, 212
plumose 256
plump
instantaneous 113
fat 192
plunge 310
unexpected 508
– down 306
– upon 292
plumper
expansion 194
vote 609
plunder 791, 793
plunderer 792
plunge
revolution 146
insert 300
dive 306, **310**
immerse 337
hurry 684
– into difficulties **704**
– into dissipation 954
– headlong 684
– into 676
– in medias res 576, 604
– into sorrow 830
plunged
– in debt 806
– in grief 828
plunger 621
plurality **100**
plus 37
plus fours 225
plush 256
Pluto 979, 982
realms of – 982
Plutocracy 803
plutonic 382
Plutus 803
pluvial 348
ply *layer* 204
fold 258
use 677
exert 686
request 765
– one's task 680
– one's trade 625
– a trade 794
Plymouth Brother 984
p.m. 114, 126
pneumatics 334, 338
pneumatology 450
pneumatoscopic 317
poach 791, 964
poacher 792
poachy 345
pock 250
pocket *place* 184
pouch 191
diminutive 193
receive 785
take 789
money 800
treasury 802
brook 826
button up one's – 808
out of – 776, 806
touch the – 800
– the affront 725, 918
pocket-book 551
pocket-handkerchief 225
pocket-money 800
pocket-pistol
bottle 191
pococurante 823, 866
pocula, inter – 959
pod 191, 223
podestà **967**
podgy 201
poem 597
book of –s 593
pœnitentiæ, locus –
pity 914
forgive 918
vindicate 937
repent 950
poesy 597
poet 597
poetaster 597, 855
poetic *style* 574
poetic frenzy 515
poetry **597**
pogrom 361
poignancy
physical energy 171
pain 378
pungency 392
feeling 821
point *condition* **8**
degree 26
small 32
end 67
term 71
poignancy **171**
no magnitude 180a
place 182
speck 193
sharp 253
topic 454
mark 550
vigour 574
intention 620
wit 842
punctilio 939
at the – of 197
come to the –
special 79
attention 457
reasoning 476
plain language 576
culminating – 210
disputed – 713
from all –s 180
full of – 574
give –s to 27
go straight to the – 278
in – *relative* 9
agreeing 23
conformable 82
knotty – 704
make a – of
resolution 604
contention 720
compulsion 744
conditions 770
due 924
honour 939
nice – 697
on the – of **111**, 121
to the – **572**, 642
– an antithesis 578
– at *direction* 278
direct attention 457
intend 620
discourtesy **895**
disrespect 929
censure 932
– of attack **716**
at the – of the bayonet 173
– of the compass 278
– of convergence 74
– of death 360
– in dispute 461
– of etiquette 852
in – of fact 1
– the finger of scorn 930
– of honour 939
– of land 250
– a moral 537
– out **155**, **457**, 527
– to – race 720
at the – of the sword
violence 173
severity 739
compulsion 744
– to *attribute* 155
direction 278
probable 472
predict 511
mean 516
– of view 441, **448**
point d'appui 215
point-blank
direct 278
plain language 576
refusal 764
point-champain 874
pointed
great 31
sharp 253
affirmation 535
marked 550
concise 572
language **574**
pointedly
intention 620
pointer *dog* 366
indicator 550

pointless 843
poise 27, 319, 852
mental – 498
poison 659, 663
– gas 722, 727
poisoned 655
commend the – chalice 544
poisonous 657, 665
poke
pocket 191
pig in a –
uncertain 475
chance 621
dawdle 683
rash 863
– at 276, 716
– the fire 384
– fun at 856
– one's nose in 682
– out *project* 250
poker 386
cards 840
polacca 273
polacre 273
polar 210
cold 383
– co-ordinates 466
polarization 420
polariscope 445
polarity
duality 89
counteraction 179
contraposition 237
pole *measure of length* 200
tall 206
summit 210
axis 222
punt 267
rotation 312
greasy – 840
opposite –s 237
from – to pole 180
pole-axe 727
polecat 401
pole-star 550, 693
polemic
discussion 476
discord 713
contention 720
combatant 726
polemoscope 445
police 965
– court 966
– magistrate 967
policeman 664, 965
policy 626, 692
polish *smooth* 255
rub 331
furbish 658
beauty 845
ornament 847
taste 850
politeness 894
– off *finish* 729
Polish bank 840
polished
- *language* 578
fashionable 852
polite 894
polisson 949
polite 894
offensive to ears – 579
– literature 560
– society 852
politic *wise* 498
cunning 702
cautious 864
body –
mankind 372
government 737
political economy 692
politician
director 694
proficient 700
politics 702
polity *conduct* 692
authority 737
duty 926
polka 840
poll 85, 609
– tax 812
pollard 193, 201
tree 367
Poll-parrot 584
pollute *soil* 653
corrupt 659
disgrace 874
pollution
disease 655
vice 945
Pollyanna 858
polo 840
polonaise 840
poltroon 862
polyandry 903
polychord 417
polychromatic 428, 440
polychrome 440, 556
polygamy 903
polygastric 191
polyglot 522, 560
polygon
buildings 189
figure 244
polygraphy 590
polylogy 573
polymorphic 81
polyphonism 580
polypus 250
polyscope 445
polysyllable 561
polytheism 984
pomade 356
pomatum 356
pommel
support 215
round 249
beat 972
Pomona 369
pomp 882
pom-pom 727
pomposity 882
pompous
language 577
poncho 225
pond 343, 636
fish – 370
ponder 451
ponderable 316, 319
ponderation 319, 480
ponderous 319
- *style* 574, 579
dull 843
pondus fumo, dare – 481
poniard 727
pons asinorum 519, 704
pontifical 995
pontificals 999
pontificate 995
pontiff 996
pontoon
vehicle 272
boat 273
way 627
pony 271
poodle 366
pooh, pooh!
unimportance 643
contempt 930
pool *lake* 343
combination 709
prize 775
billiards 840
poop 235
poor *weak* 160
- *reasoning* 477
- *style* 575
insufficient 640
trifling 643
indigent 804
unhappy 828
cut a – figure 874
– hand 701
– head 499
– house 189
– man 804
– in spirit 881
– stick 501
– thing 914
poorly 160, 655
– off 804
poor-spirited 862
pop *noise* 406
unexpected 508
– at 716
– in *ingress* 294
insertion 300
– off *die* 360
– a question 461
– the question
request 765
endearment 902
– upon *arrive* 292
discover 480a
Pope
infallibility 474
priest 996
Popedom 995
Pope Joan 840
Popery 984
pop-gun *trifle* 643
popinjay 854
poplar *tall* 206
poppy *sedative* 174
populace 876
popular
in demand 865
celebrated 873
favourite 897
approved 931
– opinion 488
popularis, aura – 873
popularize
render intelligible 518
facilitate 705
make pleasant 829
populate 184
population 188, 372
populi, vox –
publication 531
election 609
authority 737
populous
crowded 72
multitude 102
presence 186
porcelain
baked 384
sculpture 557

porch *entrance* 66
lobby 191
mouth 231
opening 260
church 1000
porcupine 253, 901
pore *opening* 260
egress 295
conduit 350
– over *look* 441
apply the mind 457
learn 539
porism 461, 480
pornographic 961
porous 260
porpoise 192
porridge 298
porringer 191
port *abode* 189
sinistral 239
gait 264
arrival 292
carriage 448
harbour 666
in – 664
make – 666
– admiral 745
– fire 388
– wine 959
portable *small* 193
transferable 270
light 320
portage 270
portal *entrance* 66
mouth 231
opening 260
portative 193, 270
portcullis 706, 717
let down the – 666
porte-monnaie 802
portend 511
portent 512
portentous
prophetic 511
fearful 860
porter *janitor* 263
carrier 271, 690
porterage 270
portfolio *case* 191
book 593
magazine 636
direction 693
insignia 747
porthole 260
portico 66, 191
portion 51, 786
– out 786
portly 192
portmanteau 191
– word 572
portrait 554
portrait painting 556
portrait painter 559
portraiture 554, 556
portray 19, 554
portreeve 745, 965
posada 189
pose *situation* 183
form 240
puzzle 475
difficulty 704
affectation 855
– as 554
strike a – 855
posited 184
position
circumstances 8
term 71
situation 183
proposition 514
assertion 535
– in society 873
positive *real* 1
great 31
strict 82
certain 474
narrow-minded 481
belief 484
unequivocal 518
assertion 535
obstinate 606
absolute 739
philosophie – 316
– colour 428
– degree 31
– fact 474
– quantity 84
positivism 984, 989
posnet 191
posology 662
posse 72, 712
in – 470
– comitatûs
collection 72
army 726
authority 737
jurisdiction 965
possess 777
– knowledge 490
– the mind 484
– oneself of 789
– the soul 824
– a state 7
possessed with a devil 503
possession 777, 780
sorcery 992
come into – 775, 783
in one's – 777
person in – 779
put one in – of 527
remain in – of the field 731
possessor 779
posset 298
possibility
chance 156
liability 177
may be 470
property 780
– upon a possibility 475
possidetis, uti –
possession 777
retention 781
post *fastening* 45
situation 183
location 184
support 215
transmit 270
swift 274
publish 531
mail 534
beacon 550
record 551
employment 625
accounts 811
stigmatize 874
punish 972
at one's –
persist 604a
prepared 673
on duty 926
sign – 550
stand like a – 265
– hoc ergo propter hoc 477
drive from – to pillar 704
postal order 800
postboy 268
post-card 592
postcenal 117
post-chaise 272
postcibal 117
post-date 115
post-diluvial 117
postfix 37
postprandial 117
post-war 117
poster 531
posterior
in order 63
in time 117
in space 235
posteriority 117
posterity 121, 167
hand down to – 551, 873
postern *portal* 66
back 235
opening 260
post-existence 152
post-graduate 492
– student 541
post-haste
swift 274
haste 684
rash 863
post-horse 271
posthumous 117, 133
– fame 873
postilion 268, 694
postliminious 117, 133
postman 534
post-meridiem 126
post-mortem 360, 363
postnate 117
post-obit 360, 363
post-office 534
– order 800
– red 434
postpone 133
postscript 39, 65
postulant
asking 765
petitioner 767
nun 996
postulate 496
reasoning 476
supposition 514
postulation
supposition 514
request 765
posture
circumstance 8
situation 183
form 240
posture-master 599, 844
posy *motto* 550
poem 597
flowers 847
pot *much* 31
mug 191
heat 384
saucepan 386
preserve 670
death in the – 657
go to – 162, 732
keep the – boiling 143, 682
make the – boil 775
le – au lait
imagination 515

hope 858
potable 298
potage 298
potager 191
potation 298, 959
pot-bellied 194
pot-companion 890
potency 157
potent 157, 159
potentate 745
potential
inexistent 2
potentiality 157, 470
pother *disorder* 59
feeling 821
excitement 825
annoyance 830
pot-herbs 393
pot-hooks 590
pot-house 189
pot-hunter 767
potion
beverage 298
medicine 662
cordial 392
pot-luck *eating* 298
chance 621
non-preparation 674
take – with 892
Potosi 803
pot-pourri
mixture 41
fragrance 400
music 415
pottage 298
pottering 682, 683
pottery *baked* 384
art 557
pottle 191
potulent 298, 959
pot-valiant 959
potwalloper 876
pouch 191
poudre:
qui n'a pas inventé la – 501, 701
jeter de la – aux yeux 442
poultice *pulp* 354
remedy 662
relief 834
poultry 298, 366
pounce upon
unexpected 508
attack 716
seize 789
pound *inclose* 232
weight 319
bruise 330
imprison 752
– together 41
poundage 813
pounds, shillings, and pence 800
pour *emerge* 295
stream 348
sufficient 639
it never rains but it –s 641
– out blood like water 361
– a broadside into 716
– forth *eject* 297
speak 582
loquacity 584
– forth like water 818
– in *converge* 290
ingress 294
sufficiency 639
– on *lavish* 784
– with rain 348
– water into a sieve 638, 818
– out 295, 297
pourboire 784
pourparler
interlocution 588
advice 695
council 696
pout *project* 250
sad 837
discourteous 895
irate 900
sulky 901a
poverty
insufficiency 640
unimportance 643
indigence **804**
– of intellect 499
powder 330
cosmetics 847
food for – 726
gun– 727
smell – 722
keep one's – dry 673
– and shot 727
waste – 638
not worth – 645
powdered
variegated 440
powdering
ornament 847
power
much 31, 102
numerical 84
efficacy **157**
loud 404
- *of style* **574**
authority 737
do all in one's – 686
give – 760
in the – of
authority 737
subjection 749
literary – 569
– of attorney 755
– behind the throne 694
– of money 800
powerful 159, 171
– voice 580
powerless 158, 160
powers that be 745
pow-wow 588, 696
pox 655
praam 273
practicable 470, 644
practical
acting 170
expedient 646
executive 692
– joke
absurdity 497
deception 545
ridicule 856
disrespect 929
– knowledge 698
practically
intrinsically 5
practice
arithmetic 85
training 537
habit 613
conduct 692
in – *prepared* 673
skilled 698
put in – *use* 677
action 680
conduct 692
complete 729
out of – 699
– of medicine 662
practise *train* 537
use 677
act 680
– at the bar 968
– on one's credulity 545
– upon
experiment 463
deceive 545
practised
skilled 698
– eye 700
– hand 700
practitioner
medical - 662
doer 690
præcognita 467
prænomen 564
prætor 967
Pragmatic Sanction 769
pragmatical 855, 880
pragmatism 677
prahu 273
prairie *space* 180
plain 344
vegetation 367
praise *thanks* 916
commendation 931
worship 990
praiseworthy 931, 944
prame 273
prance 266, 315
prandial 298
prank *caprice* 608
amusement 840
adorn 847
prate 584
prattle 582, 584
pravity 945
praxis
grammar 567
action 680
Praxiteles 559
pray 765, 990
prayer 765, 990
house of – 1000
prayer-book 998
preach *teach* 537
speak 582
predication 998
– to the winds 645
– to the wise 538
preacher
teacher 540
priest 996
preachment 998
preadamite 124, 130
preamble 64
preapprehension 481
prebend 995
prebendary 996
precarious
transient 111
uncertain 475
dangerous 665
precatory 765
precaution
care 459
expedient 626

safety 664
preparation 673
precede
superior 33
- *in order* 62
- *in time* 116
- *in motion* 280
precedence 873
precedent
[*see* precede]
prototype 22
precursor 64
habit 613
legal decision 969
follow -s 82
precentor 694, 996
precept *adage* 496
maxim **697**
order 741
permit 760
preceptor 540
precession 62, **280**
précieuse ridicule 855
precinct *region* 181
place 182
environs 227
boundary 233
precious *great* 31
excellent 648
valuable 814
beloved 897
– metals 800
– stone 648, 847
precipice
vertical 212
slope 217
dangerous 667
on the verge of a – 665
precipitancy 684, 863
precipitate
early 132
sink 308
consolidate 321
refuse 653
haste 684
rash 863
– oneself 306
precipitous 217
précis 596
precise *exact* 494
preciosity 578
precisely
literally 19
assent 488
precisianism
affectation 855
heterodoxy 984
over-religious 988
preclude 55, 706
precocious
early 132
immature 674
pert 885
rude 895
precognition
forethought 490
knowledge 510
preconceived idea 481
preconception 481
preconcert 611, 626
preconcertation 673
precursor
- *in order* 62, 64
- *in time* 116
predict 511
predatory 789, 791
predecessor 64
predeliberation 510, 611
predella 215
predesigned 611
predestination
fate 152
necessity 601
predetermination 611
Deity 976
predetermination **611**
predial
land 342
agriculture 371
manorial 780
predicament 8, 75
predicate
affirm 535
preach 998
prediction **511**
predilection
bias 481
affection 820
desire 865
predispose 615, 673
predisposed
willing 602
predisposition 176, 820
predominant 175, 737
predominate 33
pre-eminent 33, 873
pre-emption 795
preen 847
pre-engage 132
pre-engagement 768
pre-establish 626
pre-examine 461
pre-exist 1, 116
preface 62, 64
prefect 745, 759
prefecture 737
prefer *choose* 609
– a claim 969
– a petition 765
preference 62
preferment
improvement 658
ecclesiastical - 995
prefigure 511
prefix 62, 64
letter 561
pre-glacial 124
pregnable 158
pregnant
producing 161
productive 168
predicting 511
- *style* 572
important 642
– with meaning 516
prehensile 789
prehension 789
pre-historic 124
pre-instruct 537
prejudge 481
prejudicate 481
prejudice
misjudge 481
evil 619
detriment 659
prejudicial 481, 649
prelacy 995
prelate 996
prelation 609
prelection 537, 582
prelector 540
preliminaries:
settle – 673
– of peace 723
preliminary 62, 64
prelude 62, 64
beginning 66
music 415
premature 132, 674
premeditate 611, 620
prémices 154
premier 694, 759
– pas 66
premiership 693
premise *prefix* 62
precede 116
announce 511
premises
precursor 64
prior 116
ground 182
evidence **467**
logic 476
premium
debt 806
receipt 810
reward 973
at a – 814
premonish 668
premonitory 511, 668
Premonstratensian 996
premonstration
appearance 448
prediction 511
manifestation 525
premunire 742, 974
prendre la balle au bond 134
prenotion
misjudgment 481
foresight 510
prensation 789
prentice 541
prenticeship 539
preoccupancy
possession **777**
preoccupation
inattention 458
preoption 609
preordain 152, 601
preparation **673**
music 413
instruction 537
in – 730
in course of – 626
preparatory
preceding 62
prepare the way
facilitate 705
prepared *expectant* 507
ready 698
preparing
destined **152**
prepense
spontaneous 600
predetermined 611
intended 620
malice – 907
prepollence 157
preponderance
superiority 33
influence 175
dominance 737
prepossessed
obstinate 606

prepossessing 829
prepossession
prejudice 481
possession 777
preposterous
great 31
absurd 497
exaggerated 549
ridiculous 853
undue 925
prepotency 157
pre-Raphaelite 122, 124, 556
pre-require 630
pre-resolve 611
prerogative 737, 924
presage 511, 512
presbyopia 443
presbyter 996
Presbyterian 984
presbytery 995, 996, 1000
prescience 510
prescious 511
prescribe *direct* 693
advice 695
order 741
entitle 924
enjoin 926
prescript 697, 741
prescription
remedy 662
prescriptive *old* 124
unchanged 141
habitual 613
due 924
presence
in space **186**
appearance 448
breeding 894
in the – of
near 197
real – 998
saving one's – 928
– of God 981
– of mind 826, 864
presence-chamber 191
present
- *in time* 118
- *in space* 186
offer 763
give 784
church preferment 995
at – 118
these –s 590, 592
– arms 894, 928
– a bold front 861
– a front 719
– itself *event* 151
visible 446
thought 451
– oneself
presence 186
offer 763
courtesy 894
– to the mind 457, 505
– time **118**
instant 113
– to the view 448
presentable 852
presentation 883, 894
presentiment
instinct 477
prejudgment 481
foresight 510
presently 132
presentment
information 527
law proceeding 969
preservation
continuance 141
conservation **670**
Divine attributes 976
preserve *sweets* 396
preserver 664
preshow 511
preside 693, 737
presidency 737
president 694, 745
press *crowd* 72
closet 191
weight 319
public - 531
printing 591
book 593
move 615
compel 744
offer 763
solicit 765
go to – 591
under – of 744
writer for the – 593
– of business 682
– one hard 716
– in 300
– on *course* 109
progression 282
haste 684
– into the service 677, 707
– out 301
press-agent 599
pressed: hard – **704**
– for time 684
press-gang 965
pressing *need* 630
urgent 642
pressure *power* 157
influence 175
weight 319
urgency 642
exertion 686
adversity 735
centre of – 222
high – 824
work under – 684
Prester John 515
prestidigitation 545
prestidigitator 548
prestige *bias* 481
authority 737
fascination 865
fame 873
prestigiation 545
prestissimo 415
presto
instantly 113
music 415
prestriction 442
presumable 472
presume
misjudge 481
believe 484
suppose 514
hope 858
pride 878
presumption
[*see* presume]
probability 472
expectation 507
rashness 863
arrogance 885
unlawfulness 925
presumptive
probable 472
supposed 514
due 924
heir – 779
– evidence
evidence 467
probability 472
presumptuous 885
presuppose
misjudge 481
suppose 514
presurmise 510, 514
pretence
imitation 19
falsehood 544
untruth 546
excuse 617
ostentation 882
boast 884
pretend *assert* 535
simulate 544, 546
pretended 545
pretender
deceiver 548
braggart 884
unentitled 925
pretending 544
pretension
ornament 577
affectation 855
due 924
pretentious
affected 855
vain 880
ostentatious 882
boasting 884
undue 925
preterite 122
preterition **122**
preterlapsed 122
pretermit 460
preternatural 83
preterperfect 122
pretext 546, 617
pretty
much 31
imperfectly 651
beautiful 845
– fellow 501
– good 651
– kettle of fish, pass &c. 59, 704
– well *much* 31
little 32
trifling 643
preux chevalier 939
prevail *exist* 1
superior 33
general 78
influence 175
habit 613
succeed 731
– upon 615
prevailing 78
– taste 852
prevalence
[*see* prevail]
prevaricate 544
prévenance 894
prevenient 62, 132
prevention
prejudice 481
hindrance 706
– of waste 817
preventive 55
preventorium 656
previous 116
move the – question 624
not within –

experience 137
prevision 510
pre-war 116
prewarn 668
prey *food* 298
quarry 620
booty 793
victim 732, 828
fall a – to
be defeated 732
subjection 749
– to grief 828
– to melancholy 837
– on the mind
excite 824
regret 833
fear 860
– on the spirits 837
price
consideration 147
value 648
money **812**
reward 973
at any – 604*a*
beyond – 814
cheap at the – 815
of great –
good 648
dear 814
have one's – 812
price-current 812
priceless
valueless 645
dear 814
prick *sharp* 253
hole 260
sting 378
sensation of touch 380
incite 615
mental suffering 830
kick against the –s
useless 645
resistance 719
– up one's ears
hear 418
curiosity 455
attention 457
expect 707
prickle 253, 380
pride
ornament 847
loftiness **878**
take a – in 878
prie-dieu 215
priest 996
priestcraft 995
priesthood 995, 996
priest-ridden 988, 995
prig *steal* 791
puppy 854
affected 855
blusterer 887
priggish 855, 880
prim *affected* 855
fastidious 868
proud 878
prima: – donna
actress 599
important 642
proficient 700
– facie *sight* 441
appearance 448
probable 472
- *meaning* 516
manifest 525
primacy
superiority 33
celebrity 873
church 995
primary
original 20
cause 153
important 642
– colour 428
– education 537
primarily 66
primate 996
primates 875
prime
primeval 124
early 132
teach 537
important 642
excellent 648
prepare 673
in one's – 131
in the – of manhood 159
– cost *price* 812
cheap 815
– of life *youth* 127
adolescence 131
– and load 673
– minister 694
– of the morning 125
– mover 153
– number 84
prime constituent 1
primed
skilled 698
tipsy 959
primer 542
primeval 124
– forest 367
primigenous 124
primitive 124, 153
– colour 428
primogenial 66
primogeniture
old 124
age 128
posterity 167
primordial 20, 124, 153
primordinate 124
primrose-coloured 436
primum:
– mobile 153, 615
primus inter pares 33
prince
perfection 650
master 745
nobility 875
– of darkness 978
princely
authoritative 737
liberal 816
famous 873
noble 875
generous 942
princeps
facile – 33
princess 745, 875
principal
important 642
director 694
– part 31, 50
principality 181, 780
principally 33
principia 66, 496
principiis obstare 673
principle
intrinsic 5
rule 80
cause 153
element 316
idea 453
reasoning 476
tenet 484
maxim 496
motive 615
probity 939
on – 615
want of – 945
principled, high- 939
prink 847, 882
print *copy* 21
mark 550
engraving 558
letter-press 591
out of – 552
printer 591
printing 531, **591**
– telegraph 553
prior
- *in order* 62
- *in time* 116
clergy 996
priori reasoning, a – 476
priority **116**, 234
priory 1000
Priscian's head, break – 568
prism
angularity 244
optical 445
see through a – 443
prismatic
colour 428
variegated 440
prison **752**
cast into – 751
in – 754
prisoner **754**, 938
take – 751, 789
prison-house
secrets of the – 529, 533
pristine 20, 122
prithee 765
prittle-prattle 588
private *special* 79
hidden 528
secluded 893
to gain some – ends 943
in – 528
keep – 881
talk to in – 586, 588
– road 627
– soldier 726
privateer 726, 792
privateering 791
privately 881
privation 776, 804
privative 789
privilege
freedom 748
permission 760
exemption 777*a*
due 924
privity 490
privy *hidden* 528
latrines 653
– to 490
Privy Council 696
prize *good* 618
palm 733
gain 775
booty 793

receipt 810
love 897
approve 931
reward 973
win the – 731
– open 173
prizer 767
prize-fighter 726
prize-fighting 720
prizeman 700
pro: – and con 476, 615
– formâ 82
– hâc vice
special 79
present time 118
occasion 134
seldom 137
– rata 23
– re natâ
circumstances 8
relation 9
special 79
occasion 134
conditions 770
– tanto 26, 32
– tempore 111
proa 273
probability 156, **472**
probable 858
probate 771
Probate Court 966
probation
trial 463
demonstration 478
probationary 463, 675
probationer 541
probative 478
probatum est 478, 931
probe *depth* 208
perforator 262
investigate 461
measure 466
probity **939**
problem *topic* 454
question 461
enigma 533
problematical 475
proboscis 250
procacity
insolence 885
rudeness 895
irascibility 901
procedure
method 627
action 680
conduct 692
proceed *time* 109
advance 282
– from 154
– with 692
proceeding
incomplete 53
event 151
action 680
not finished 730
course of – 692
proceedings 551
proceeds *gain* 775
money 800
receipts 810
procerity 206
procès-verbal
record 551
law proceeding 969
process
projection 250
conduct 692
legal – 963
– engraving 558
– of time 109
in – of time 117
procession
continuity 69
march 266
ceremony 882
processional
rite 998
prochronism 115
proclaim 531
proclivity 176, 820
proconsul 759
proconsulship 737
procrastination 133, 460, 683
procreant 168
procreate 161, 168
procreator 166
procrustean 82
– law 80
Procrustes:
stretch on the bed of – 27
proctor *teacher* 540
officer 694, 965
consignee 758
lawyer 968
proctorship 693
procumbent 213
procurator 694
procuration 170, 755
procure *cause* 153
induce 615
get 775
buy 795
procuress 962
procurement 170
prod 276
prodigal 641, 818
prodigality **818**
prodigious 31, 870
prodigy 83, **872**
– of learning 700
prodition 940
prodrome 64
produce
increase 35
cause 153
effect 154
create 161
prolong 200
show 525
stage 599
fruit 775
merchandise 798
– itself 446
producer **164**
product
multiple 84
effect 154
harvest 636
gain 775
finished – 154
production 54, **161**
[*and see* produce]
productive
cause 153
power 157
inventive 515
profitable 775
productiveness **168**
proem 64
proemial
preceding in order 62
beginning 66
profane
desecrate 679
impious 988
laical 997
– swearing 908
profanum vulgus 876
profession
assertion 535
pretence 546
business 625
promise 768
enter a – 625
– of faith 484, 983
professional 700
– mourner 363, 839
professor 492, 540, 700
professorship 542
proffer 763
proficient
knowledge 490
skill 698
adept **700**
proficuous 644
profile
outline 230
side 236
appearance 448
portraiture 556
profit
increase 35
advantage 618
utility 644
acquisition 775
– by *use* 677
– sharing 778
profitable
useful 644
good 648
gainful 775
profitless 645
profligacy 945
profluent
progressive 282
stream 348
profound
great 31
deep 208
learned 490
wise 498
sagacious 702
feeling 821
– attention 457
– knowledge 490
– secret 533
profundis, de – 839, 950
profuse
diffuse style 573
redundant 641
prodigal 818
profusion 102, 639
prog 298
progenerate 161
progenitive 163
progenitor 166
progeny 167
prognosis 510, 511, 522, 655
prognostic 511, 512
prognosticate 511
prognostication 507
programme
catalogue 86
publication 531
plan 626
progress
growth 144
motion 264
advance 282

in – *incomplete* 53, 730
make – 282
in mid – 270
– of science 490
– of time 109
progression
gradation 58
series 69
numerical – 84
motion 282
progressive
continuous 69
course 109
advancing 282
improving 658
prohibition 761
exclusion 55
stoppage 706
teetotalism 953, 958
project *bulge* 250
impel 284
intend 620
plan 626
projectile 727
projection *map* 554
projector
lantern 423
film 445
designer 626
prolation 580, 582
prole, sine – 169
prolegomena 64
prolepsis 64, 115
proletarian 876
prolific 168
prolix 573
prolocutor
interpreter 524
teacher 540
speaker 582
prologue
precursor 64
drama 599
prolong
protract 110
late 133
continue 143
lengthen 200
prolongation 63, 143
prolusion 64
prom 892
promenade 266
display 882
on pier 189
Promethean 359
prominent
convex 250
manifest 525
important 642
eminent 873
prominently 31, 33
promiscuous
mixed 41
irregular 59
indiscriminate 465a
casual 621
promise
predict 511
engage 768
hope 858
keep one's – 939
keep – to ear and break to hope 545
– oneself 507, 858
promissory 768
– note 771, 800
promontory
height 206
projection 250
land 342
promote 153, 658, 707
promoter 626
promotion 658
prompt *early* 132
remind 505
tell 527
induce 615
active 682
advise 695
– memory 505
prompter
drama 599
motive 615
adviser 695
promptuary 636
promulgate 531
– a decree 741
pronation and supination 218
prone
horizontal 213
proneness
tendency 176
disposition 820
prôner 882, 931
prôneur 935
prong 91
pronounce
judge 480
assert 535
voice 580
speak 582
pronounced 525
pronouncement 531
pronunciamento 531
pronunciation 580
pronunciative 535
proof *hard* 323
insensible 376
test 463
demonstration 478
printing 591
draft 626
ocular – 446
– against
strong 159
resolute 604
safe 664
defence 717
resistance 719
insensible 823
prop 215, 707
propædeutics 537
propagable 168
propaganda 537, 542
propagandism 537
propagandist 540, 996
propagate
produce 161
be productive 168
publish 531
propel 284
propellant 727
propeller 267, 312
propend 602
propendency
predetermination 611
inclination 820
propense 602
propension 820
propensity 176, 820
proper *special* 79
expedient 646
handsome 845
due 924
– name 564
in its – place 58
show a – spirit 939
the – thing 926
– time 134
properties
theatrical – 225, 599
property *power* 157
possessions 780
wealth 803
property-man 599
prophecy 511
prophet 513, 996
false –s 986
in the name of the – figs! 497
prophetic 511, 985
Prophets, the – 985
prophylactic
healthful 656
remedy 662
preservative 670
hindrance 706
prophylaxis 670
propinquity 197
propitiate
pacify 723, 724
calm 826
content 831
love 897
pity 914
forgive 918
atone 952
worship 990
propitious
timely 134
beneficial 648
helping 707
prosperous 734
auspicious 858
proplasm 22
proportion
relation 9
degree 26
mathematical 84
symmetry 242
style 578
allotment 786
proportionate
agreeing 23
proportions 180, 192
proposal *plan* 626
propose
suggest 514
broach 535
intend 620
offer 763
offer marriage 902
– a question 461
proposition
supposition 454
reasoning 476
project 626
suggestion 514
offer 763
propound 514, 535
– a question 461
propriâ personâ
in – *speciality* 79
presence 186
proprietary 779
proprietor 779
proprietorship 780
propriety

agreement 23
elegance 578
expedience 646
fashion 852
right 922
duty 926
proprio motu 600
props 599
propter hoc 155
propugn
resist 717
vindicate 937
propulsion **284**
propylon 66
prore 234
prorogue 133
proruption 295
prosaic *usual* 82
- *style* 575, 576
dull 843
prosaism *prose* 598
proscenium
front 234
theatre 599
proscribe
interdict 761
banish 893
curse 908
condemn 971
prose
diffuse style 573
prate 584
not verse **598**
– run mad 577, 597
– writer 598
prosecute
pursue 622
act 680
accuse 938
arraign 969
– an inquiry 461
prosecutor 938
proselyte
convert 144, 607
learner 541
proselytism 537
proser 841
prosody 597
prosopopœia 521
prospect
futurity 121
view 448
probability 472
expectation 507
landscape painting 556
good – 858
in – *intended* 620
prospective 121
prospector 463
prospectus *list* 86
foresight 510
compendium 596
scheme 626
prosper 618
prosperity **734**
prospicience 510
prosternation
dejection 837
servility 886
prostitute
corrupt 659
misuse 679
impure 961
courtesan 962
prostrate
powerless 158
destroyed 162
low 207
horizontal 213
depress 308
laid up 655
exhausted 688
dejected 837
servile 886
fall – 306
– oneself
servile 886
obeisance 928
worship 990, 991
prostration
[*see* prostrate]
submission 725
pain 828
prosy 841, 843
prosyllogism 476
protagonist
actor 599
proficient 700
protasis
precursor 64
beginning 66
maxim 496
protean 149
protect *safe* 664
protected cruiser 726
protective 717
protection
influence 175
defence 717
restrain 751
protector 664, 717
master 745
keeper 753
protectorate 737, 780
protégé *servant* 746
friend 890
proteiform 149
protein 298
semiliquid 352
organic 357
protervity 901
protest *dissent* 489
assert 535
deny 536
refuse 764
deprecate 766
not observe 773
not pay 808
counter – 468
enter a – 766
under – 603, 744
– against 708, 932
protestant 489, 764
Protestant 984
protested bills 808
Proteus 149
prothesis 1000
prothonotary 553
protocol *scheme* 626
compact 769
protogram 572
protoplasm
prototype 22
material 316
organization 357
protoplast 22
prototype **22**
prediction 511
prototypal 20
protozoon 366
protract *time* 110
late 133
lengthen 200
diffuse style 573
protreptical 615
protrude 250
protuberance 250
protypify 511
proud 873, 878
– flesh 250
prove
arithmetic 85
turn out 151
try 463
demonstrate 478
affect 821
– one's case
vindication 937
– true 494
provender 298, 637
proverb 496
proverbe *acting* 599
proverbial 490
provide
furnish 637
– against
prepare 673
– against a rainy day 817
provided
conditionally 8
qualification 469
supposition 514
well – 639
– for 803
providence
foresight 510
preparation 673
divine government 976
Providence 976
special – 711
waiter on – 683, 831
provident
careful 459
wise 498
prepared **673**
providential
opportune 134
fortunate 734
province
department **75**
region 181
abode 189
office 625
provincial
[*see* province]
prejudiced 481
vulgar 851
provincialism
neology 563
provision *food* 298
supply **637**
preparation 673
wealth 803
– merchant 637
provisional
uncertain 475
circumstances 8
temporary 111
preparing 673
provisions
conditions 770
proviso 469, 770
provisory 111
provoke *cause* 153
incite 615
excite 824
vex 830
anger 900
– desire 865
– hatred 898
provoquant 824
provost *master* 745
deputy 759
prow 234
prowess 861
prowl *walk* 266
lurk 528
– after 622

proximate
next 63
near 197
– cause 153
proximity *near* 197
adjacent 199
proximo 121
proximus ardet
danger 665, 667
proxy 634, 759
prude *affected* 855
chaste 960
prudent
careful 459
wise 498
economical 817
cautious 864
prudery 855, 868
prudish 739
prune
take away 38
lop 201, 371
repair 658
prunes and prisms 855
prunello, leather or – 643
prurience 865, 961
Prussian blue 438
Prussic acid 663
pry *look* 441
curiosity 455
inquire 461
– into the future 510
Prytaneum 931
psalm 415, 990
psalm-book 998
psalmody 415, 998
psalter 998
psaltery 417
psephomancy 511
pseudo 17, 545
pseudoblepsis 443
pseudonym 565
pseudo-revelation 986
pseudoscope 445
pshaw
trifling 643
excitement 825
psychiatry 662
psychical 450
psycho-analysis 662
psychological moment 824
Psychology 450
Psychomancy 511
psycho-therapy 662
ptisan 662
ptomaine poisoning 663
puberty 127
pubescent 131
public, general – 372
make – 531
– enemy 891
– good 644
– opinion 488
– press 531
– school 542
– spirit 910
– welfare 910
publican 637
publication 531
production 161
book 593
public-house 189
go to the – 959
publicist 593, 595, 968
publicity 531
publicly rumoured 532
publico, pro bono – 644, 910
publish 531
– the banns 765, 903
publisher 593
puce 433, 437
pucelage *youth* 127
celibacy 904
purity 960
Puck 980
play – 699
pucker *fold* 258
anger 900
in a – 824
pudder
disorder 59
pudding *food* 298
soft 324
pulpy 354
sweets 396
in – time 132
Pudding, Jack – 599
puddle 343
pudicity 960
pudor, proh – 874
puerile *boyish* 129
foolish 499
feeble 575
trifling 643
puerperal 161
puff *inflate* 194
wind 349
tartlet 396
exaggerate 482
advertisement 531
pant 688
boast 884
praise 931
flatter 933
– of smoke 330
– out 194
– up *vanity* 880
puffed up
exaggerated 482
pride 878
puffer 935
puffery 884
puffy 194
pug *short* 201
dog 366
pugilist 726
pugh! 643
pugilism 720
pugilist 726
pugilistic 720
pugnacity 720, 901
puisné
posterior 117
young 127
puissant 157, 159
puke 297
pukka 494
pulchritude 845
pulcinella 599, 844
pule *cry* 411, 412
weep 839
pull *superiority* 33
influence 175
row 267
draw 285
printing 591
a long and a strong – 709
strong – 636
– the check string 142
– different ways 713
– down 162, 308
– about one's ears 308
– in 751
– an oar 680
– out 301
– to pieces
separate 44
destroy 162
censure 932
detract 934
– upon the purse 814
– by the sleeve 505
– the strings 631
– through 660, 707
– together 709
– towards 288
– up *stop* 142
rest 265
root out 301
reprimand 932
accuse 969
– the wires 693
pulled down 160, 688
pullet 129
pulley 633
Pullman car 272
pullulate
produce 161
multiply 168
grow 194
pulmonary 349
pulmotor 349
pulp 354
pulpiness 354
pulpit *rostrum* 542
church 1000
the – 996
pulsate
periodic 138
oscillate 314
agitate 315
pulsation
feeling 821
pulse [*see* pulsate]
vegetable 367
feel the –
inquire 461
test 463
pulsion 276
pultaceous 354
pulverize 330
destroy 162
dust 358
pulverulence 330
pulvil 400
pummel
[*see* pommel]
pump *shoe* 225
water supply 348
inquire 461
– up 349
pump-room
house 189
remedy 662
pun *similarity* 17
absurdity 497
ambiguity 520
wit 563, 842
punce 276
punch *mould* 22
perforate 260
perforator 262

nag 271
strike 276
beverage 298
engrave 558
vigour 574
Punch *buffoon* 844
– and Judy 599, 840
punchbowl
vessel 191
hollow 252
tippling 959
puncheon
vessel 191
perforator 262
punchinello 599
punctated 440
punctilio 852
punctilious
exact 494
observant 772
ostentation 882
scrupulous 939
puncto 882
punctual *early* 132
periodical 138
exact 494
observance 772
scrupulous 939
punctuation 567
puncture 260
pundit
learned man 492, 500
lawyer 968
pungency
physical energy 171
taste 392
pungent *taste* 392
odour 398
vigour 574
feeling 821
wit 842
Punica fides 940
punishment **972**
punition 972
punk 962
punkah 349
punnet 191
punster 844
punt 267, 273
punter 621
puny 193
pup *infant* 129
give birth 161
dog 366
pupil 541
- of the eye 441
pupilage *youth* 127
learning 539
pupillari, in statu – 541
puppet *little* 193
dupe 547
effigy 554
auxiliary 711
tool 746
make a – of 737
be the – of 749
puppet-show 599, 840
puppy *dog* 366
fop 854
braggart 884
blusterer 887
puppyism 855
pur: – sang 875
Purana 986
purblind 443, 481
purchase
support 215
acquisition 775
buy **795**
purchase-money 147
purchaser 795
purdah 374, 530
pure *simple* 42
true 494
truthful 543
- style 576, 578
clean 652
artless 703
- taste 850
honourable 939
virtuous 944
innocent 946
chaste 960
devout 987, 990
– accent 580
– colour 428
– and simple 42
purée 298
purely 31, 32
purgation
cleansing 652
atonement 952
purgative 652
purgatory
suffering 828
atonement 952
hell 982
purge *cast out* 297
clean 652
atone 952
purification 998
purify 652, 658
puris naturalibus, in – 226
purist *style* 578
affected 855
Pharisee 988
Puritan 984, 988
puritanical
strict 739
affected 855
ascetic 955
purity **960**
[*see* pure]
purl *drink* 298
stream 348
faint sound 405
music 416
purlieus 197, 227
purloin 791
purple
violet **437**
insignia **747**
– and fine linen 377
purport 516, 600
purpose 620
at cross –s 523
infirm of – 605
to little or no – 645
on – 620
serve a – 644
to some – 731
tenacity of – 604*a*
purposeless 621
purpure 437
purr 412
purse 800, 802
long – 803
put into one's – 785
– up 195
purse-bearer 801
purse-proud 878
purser 801
purse strings:
draw the – 808
open the – 809
pursuant to 620
pursue *continue* 143
follow 281
aim 622
– a course 680
– an inquiry 461
– the tenor of one's way 625, 881
pursuer 622
pursuit **622**
pursuivant 534
pursy 194
purulent 653
purvey 637
purview 620
pus 653
Puseyite 984
push *exigency* **8**
impel 276
progress 282
propel 284
essay 675
activity 682
haste 684
come to the – **704**
– aside 460, 929
– forward 682, 707
– from 289
– to the last 133
– on *haste* 684
– out *eject* 297
pushing 282, 284, 682
pusillanimity 862
puss 366
play – in the corner 148
pussy-foot 528, 958
pustule 250, 848
put *place* 184
fool 501
cards 840
clown 876
neatly – **578**
– across 484
– about
turn back 283
go round 311
publish 531
– aside
exclude 55
inattention 458
neglect 460
disuse 678
– away
- thought 452
relinquish 782
divorce 905
– back
turn back 283
deteriorate 659
restore 660
– before 527
– by 636
– a case 82, 514
– in commission 755
– a construction on 522
– on the cuff 806
– down
destroy 162
record 551
conquer 731
compel 744
pay 807
humiliate 874
– an end to **67**

end 67
stop 142
destroy 162
- *oneself* 361
– in force
complete 729
compel 744
– forth
expand 194
suggest 514
publish 531
assert 535
- *a question* 461
- *strength* 686
– forward
suggest 514
publish 531
ostentation 882
– one's hand to 676
– the horses to 673
– in [*see below*]
– to inconvenience 647
– a mark upon 457
– one's nose out of joint 33
– off *late* 133
divest 226
depart 293
plea 617
– on *clothe* 225
deceive 544
hasten 684
affect 855
– out [*see below*]
– on paper 551
– over 484, 731
– a question 461
– right 660
– the saddle on the right horse 155
– the seal to 729, 769
– to [*see below*]
– together *join* 43
combine 48
assemble 161
– one's trust in 484
– up [*see below*]
– upon 545, 649
put in *arrive* 292
insert 300
– an affidavit 535
– hand 676
– one's head 514
– mind 505
– motion 264
– order 60
– the place of 147
– one's pocket 785
– practice 692
– remembrance 505
– shape 60
– trim 60, 673
– the way of 470
– a word 582, 588
put out
destroy 162
outside 220
extinguish 385
darken 421
distract the attention 458
uncertain 475
difficult 704
discontent 832
– of countenance 874
oneself – of court
sophistry 477
bungling 699
– of gear 158
– of one's head 458
– of joint 61
– of one's misery 914
– to nurse 707
– of order 59
put to *attribute* 155
request 765
– the blush 879
– death 361
– the door 261
– it 704
– one's oath 768
– press 591
– the proof 463
– the question 830
– the rack 830
– rights 60
– sea 293
– shame 874
– silence 581
– the sword 361
– task 677
– use 677
– the vote 609
put up *assemble* 72
locate 184
store 636
– to auction 796
– for 865
– a petition } 765
– a prayer } 990
– for sale 796
– a shutter 424
– the sword 723
– to 615
– with 147, 826
putative
attributed 155
believed 484
supposed 514
putid 643
putrefy 653
putrescence 49
putrid 653
putsch 742
puttee 225
putter 683
putting the weight 840
putty 45
puzzle *uncertain* 475
conceal 528
enigma 533
– out 522
puzzled 475, 533
puzzle-headed 499
puzzling 519
pyæmia 655
pyjamas 225
Pylades and Orestes 890
pylon 206
pyramid *heap* 72
height 206
point 253
pyramids
billiards 840
pyre 363
pyriform 249
pyrology 382
pyromaniac 384, 504, 913
pyromancy 511
pyrometer 389
pyrotechnics 423
pyrotechny 382
Pyrrhic victory 814
pyrrhonism 487, 989
Pythagorean 953
Pythia *oracle* 513
Python, -ess 513
pyx *vessel* 191, 998
temple 1000

Q

Q-boat 726
Q.C. 968
Q.E.D. 478
quack *cry* 412
imposter 548
quackery
falsehood 544
want of skill 699
affectation 855
quacksalver 548
quad 189
quadragesima 956
quadrangle
four-sided 95
precinct 182
house 189
angular 244
quadrant 244, 247
quadrate with 23
quadratic 95
quadrature
four 95
angle 244
quadrennial 95
quadrible 96
quadrifid 97
quadriga 95, 272
quadrilateral
sides 236
angles 244
quadrille 840
quadripartition 97
quadrisection 97
quadrivalent 95
quadroon 41
quadruped 366
quadruplet 95
quadruplex 96
quadruplication 96
quære 461
quaff 298
– the bitter cup 828
quaggy 345
quagmire
marsh 345
dirty 653
difficult 704
quail 860, 862
quaint *odd* 83
pretty 845
ridiculous 853
quake *oscillate* 314
shake 315
cold 383
fear 860
quakery 826, 855
Quakerism 984
qualification
[see qualify]
power 157
modification 469
skill 698
discount 813
qualify *change* 140
modify 469

deny 536
teach 537
qualis ab incepto 141
qualities
character 820
quality nature 5
power 157
tendency 176
nobility 875
qualm disbelieve 485
unwilling 603
fear 860
qualms of conscience 950
quamdiu se bene gesserit 108a
quand même
compensating 30
opposed 708
quandary 475, 704
quantity 25, 31, 102
quantum amount 25
allotment 786
– mutatus 140
– sufficit 639
quaquaversum 278
quarantine 664, 751
qua re 461
quarrel 24, 713
– with one's bread and butter
bungling 699
discontent 832
quarrelsome 901
quarry object 620
mine 636
quart 97
quarter cut up 44
fourth 95
quadrisection 97
period 108
region 181
locate 184
abode 189
side 236
direction 278
forbearance 740
money 800
give – 914
give no –
kill 361
severe 739
pitiless 914a
revenge 919
– of a hundred 98
– upon 184
quarter-day 138
quarter-deck 210
quarterly
periodical 531
quartermaster 637
quartern 95
quarteron 41
quarters abode 189
take up one's – 184
quarter sessions 966
quarter-staff
contention 720
weapon 727
quartet four 95
music 415
quartic 95
quarto 593
quartz 323
quash 162, 756
quasi similar 17
supposed 514
quassia 395
quaternity 95
quatrain 597
quatrefoil 95
quaver oscillate 314
shake 315
sound 407
music 413, 416
fear 860
quay 189, 666
edge 231
quean 962
queasiness 867
queasy 868
queen 745
Queen's – Bench
prison 752
court 966
– counsel 968
– English 560
– evidence 529
– highway 627
Queensberry rules 922
queer 83, 853
– fish 857
quell destroy 162
moderate 174
quiescence 265
subdue 731
quench destroy 162
cool 385
dissuade 616
gratify 829
satiate 869
quenchless 865
querimonious 839
querist 461
quern 330
querulous
complaining 839
fastidious 868
irritable 901
query 461, 485
quest 461
question
inquiry 461
doubt 485
deny 536
in – event 151
topic 454
inquiry 461
danger 665
pop the – 902
put to the – 830
– at issue 461
questionable
uncertain 475
doubtful 485
disreputable 874
dishonest 939
questionary 461
questioner 455
questionist 541
questionless
certain 474
questionnaire 461
questor 801
queue 65, 214
quib 856
quibble
sophistry 477
unmeaning 517
equivocation 520
falsehood 544
wit 842
verbal –
absurdity 497
quick transient 111
rapid 274
alive 359
intelligent 498
active 682
skilful 698
feeling 821
irascible 901
cut to the – 824
probe to the – 461
sting to the – 830, 900
to the – 375, 822
touch to the – 822, 824
– ear 418
– eye 441
– as a flash 113
– succession 136
– time 274
– as thought 113
quicken work 170
violence 173
come to life 359
promote 707
excite 824
quickening power 170
quickly soon 132
quicksands 667, 704
quick-scented 398
quickset hedge 232
quicksilver
changeable 149
energy 171
velocity 274
quick-witted 842
quid 392
– pro quo
compensation 30
substitution 147
interchange 148
error 495
retaliation 718
barter 794
wit 842
reward 973
– valeant humeri quid ferre recusant 157
quiddity
existence 1
essence 5
quibble 477
wit 842
quidnunc 455
quiescence 265
quiet calm 174
rest 265
silence 403
dissuade 616
leisure 685
inexcitability 826
keep – 681
– life 721
quieta non movere
continuance 143
quiescence 265
inaction 681
quietism
quiescence 265
insensibility 823
irreligion 989
quietly modest 881
get on – 736
quietude 826
quietus death 360
failure 732
acquittal 970
give a – 361
receive its – 756
quill 590
quill-driver 590
quillet 477
quills

– upon the fretful porcupine 256
quilt *covering* 223
variegated 440
quinary 98
quincunx 98
quinquarticular 99
quinquennium 108
quinquesection 99
quinquifid 99
quint 98
quintain 620, 840
quintal 319
quinteron 41
quintessence 5
quintet 98, 415
quintuple 98
quinze 840
quip
amusement 840
wit 842
ridicule 856
disrespect 929
quire *singers* 416
paper 593
church 1000
quirk
sophistry 477
misjudgment 481
caprice 608
amusement 840
wit 842
quirt 975
quis custodiet istos custodes? 459
quit *depart* 293
relinquish 624
pay 807
– claim 927*a*
– one's hold 782
– of 776, 782
– scores 807
qui-tam 969
quite 52
– another thing 10, 18
– the reverse 14
– the thing 23
quits *equal* 27
atonement 952
be – with
retaliation 718
pay 807
quittance
security 771
payment 807
forgiveness 918
atonement 952
reward 973
quiver
receptacle 191
oscillation 314
agitation 315
shiver 383
store 636
feeling 821
fear 860
in a – 821, 824
– with rage 900
qui-vive 669
on the – 459
Quixote, Don – 504, 863
Quixotic 515, 863
Quixotism 825
quiz 856, 857
quizzical 853
quo animo 620
quoad minus 30
quod *prison* 752
in – 754
quodlibet
inquiry 461
sophism 477
wit 842
quoits 840
quondam 122
quorum 696
quot homines tot sententiæ 489, 713
quota
quantity 25
contingent 786
expenditure 809
furnish its – 784
quotation
imitation 19
conformity 82
price 812
– marks 550
quote 82
evidence 467
quoth 535, 582
quotidian 138
quotient 84
quotum 25

R

Ra 423, 979
R's, three – 537
rabbet 43
Rabbi 996
Rabbist 984
rabbit
productive 168
rabble 72, 876
rabid *insane* 502
emotion 821
eager 865
angry 900
rabies 503
raccroc 156
race *relation* 11
sequence 69
kind 75
lineage 166
run 274
stream 348
conduit 350
pungency 392
course 622
business 625
haste 684
career 692
opposition 708
contention 720
run a – 720
run in a – 680
run one's – 729
one's – is run 360
– prejudice 481
race-course 728
racehorse
horse 271
swift 274
racing car 272
rack *receptacle* 191
frame 215
cloud 353
physical pain 378
purify 652
moral pain 828
torture 830
punish 972
instrument of torture 975
on the – 507
– one's brains
thought 451
imagination 515
–rent 810
go to – and ruin 735
racket
agitation 315
loud 404
roll 407
scheme 626
discord 713
racket-court 840
racketeer 913
racketeering 361, 792
racketing 682, 840
rackets 840
rackety *loud* 404
raconteur 594
racy *strong* 171
pungent 392
- *style* 574
feeling 821
raddle *weave* 219
raddled *tipsy* 959
radiance *light* 420
beauty 845
radiant
diverging 291
glorious 873
– heat 420
radiate 73, 291
radiation 420
radiator 386
radical
essential 5
complete 52
algebraic root 84
cause 153
important 642
reformer 658
party 712
– change 146
– cure 662
– reform 658
radically 31
radication 613
radio 532
radio-active 171
radio-activity 420
radio-graph 421, 554
radiogram
wireless 532
X-ray 554
radiometer 445
radiomicrometer 389
radiophone 418
radio star 899
radiotelegraph 534
radiotelephone 534
radium 423
radius 200, 202
radix 153
radoter 499
radoteur 501
raff 653, 876
raffle 156
Raffles
thief 792
raft 273
rafter 215
rag 32
tease 830, 856, 929
ragamuffin 876
rage *violence* 173
influence 175
excitement 824, 825
fashion 852
desire 865

wrath 900
the battle –s 722
ragged 226
ragoût 41, 298
rag-picker 876
rags *clothes* 225
useless 645
do to – 384
tear to – 162
worn to – 659
ragtime 415, 473
raid 716, 791
rail *inclosure* 232
prison 752
– at 932
– in
circumscribe 229
restrain 751
railing 232
raillerie, ne pas entendre – 900
raillery 856
railway 627
– speed 274
– station 292
raiment 225
rain *stream* 348
sufficient 639
– or shine 474, 604
rainbow 440
raincoat 225
rainless 340
rains but it pours, never – 641
rainy day 735
provide against a – 673, 817
rainy season 348
raise *increase* 35
produce 161
erect 212
elevate 307
excite 824
– alarm 860
– anger 900
– one's banner 722
– a cry 531
– a dust 682
– expectations 858
– the finger 550
– funds 775
– one's head
improve 658
refresh 689
prosperity 734
repute 873
– ghosts 992
– hope 511
– a hue and cry
against 932
– a laugh 840
– the mask 529
– money 788
– a question 461, 485
– a report 531
– a siege 723
– the spirits 836
– spirits from the dead 992
– a storm 173
– troops 722
– up 212, 824
– the voice 411
– one's voice 535, 932
– the wind 775, 788
raised *convex* 250
raison:
– d'être 620
– de plus 467
raj 737
rajah 745
rajpoot 726
rake *drag* 285
gardening 371
clean 652
profligate 949
intemperance 954
libertine 962
– out 301
– up *collect* 72
extract 301
recall 505
excite 824
– up evidence 467
rake-hell 949, 962
raking-fire 716
rakish
intemperate 954
licentious 961
rallentando 415
rally *arrange* 60
improve 658
restore 660
ridicule 856
encourage 861
– round *order* 58
co-operate 709
rallying: – cry 550, 861
– point 74
ram *impulse* 276
sheep 366
male 373
man-of-war 726
milk the – 645
– down 261, 321
– in 300
Ramadan 956, 998
ramage 367
ramble *stroll* 266
wander 279
folly 499
delirium 503
digress 573
rambler 268
rambling 139
ramification *part* 51
bisection 91
posterity 167
filament 205
symmetry 242
divergence 291
rammer 263, 276
ramose 242
ramp *slope* 217
climb 305
leap 309
rampage 173
rampant
violent 173
prevalent 175
vertical 212
raised 307
free 748
vehement 825
licentious 961
rampart 717
ramrod 263
ramshackle 665
ranch 780
rancid 401, 653
rancour 907, 919
randan 273
random *casual* 156
carriage 272
uncertain 475
aimless 621
talk at –
sophistry 477
exaggerate 549
loquacity 584
- *experiment* 463
chance 621
range *extent* 26
collocate 60
series 69
term 71
class 75
space 180
distance 196
roam 266
direction 278
stove 386
freedom 748
out– 196
long – 196
within – 197
–finder 200
– itself 58
– under, – with 76
ranger
director 694
keeper 753
thief 792
rank *have place* 1
degree 26
thorough 31
collocate 60
row 69
term 71
vegetation 365
fetid 401
estimate 480
bad 649
soldiers 726
glory 873
nobility 875
man of – 875
– and file
continuity 69
soldiers 726
commonalty 876
– marks 747
rankle *unclean* 653
corrupt 659
painful 830
animosity 900
malevolence 907
revenge 919
ranks
fill up the – 660
risen from the – 876
ransack *seek* 461
deliver 672
plunder 791
price 812
atonement 952
– one's brains 451, 515
ransom 672
rant
unmeaning 517
exaggeration 549
diffuse style 573
turgescence 577
speech 582
acting 599
excitement 825
boasting 884
ranter *talker* 584
false piety 988
rantipole 458
rap *blow* 276
sound 406
trifle 643
money 800
not worth a – 804
– on the knuckles

angry 900
censure 932
punish 972
– out *affirm* 535
voice 580
speak 582
– out oaths 885, 908
rapacity
taking 789
stealing 791
avarice 819
greed 865
rape 791, 961
– oil 356
rapid 274
– slope 217
– strides
progress 282
velocity 274
– succession 136
rapids 348
rapier 727
rapine 791
rapparee 792
rappel 722
rapping, spirit – 992
rapport 9
rapports, sous tous les – 494
rapprochement 714, 888
rapscallion 949
rapt *attention* 457
inattention 458
emotion 821
– in thought 451
raptorial 789, 791
rapture 827, 897
rapturous 827
rara avis
exceptional 83
good 648
famous 873
rare *exceptional* 83
few 103
infrequent 137
light 322
excellent 648
raree show 448, 840
rarefaction 194, 322
rari nantes 103
rarity 322
rasa, tabula – 552
rascal 941, 949
rascality 940
rase *obliterate* 552
rash
skin disease 655
reckless 863
rasher 204
rashness 863
rasp 330, 331
rasper *difficult* 704
rasure 552
rat *recant* 607
smell a –
discover 480a
doubt 485
rataplan 407
rat-a-tat 407
ratchet 253
rate *degree* 26
motion 264
measure 466
estimation 480
price, tax 812
abuse 932
at a great – 274
rath *early* 132
fort 717
rather 32, 643
have – 609
– good 651
have – not 867
ratification
confirm 467
affirm 488
consent 762
compact 769
ratio *relation* 9
degree 26
proportion 84
apportionment 786
ratiocination 476
ration *quantity* 25
food 298
provisions 637
allotment 786
short –s 956
rational
- *quantity* 84
intellectual 450
judicious 498
sane 502
rationale *cause* 153
attribution 155
answer 462
interpretation 522
rationalism 476, 989
rationalization 60
rats in the upper story 503
rattan 975
ratten 158
rattle *noise* 407
music 417
prattle 584
death – 360
watchman's – 669
– on 584
rattle-snake 913
rattle-traps 780
rattling 836
– pace 274
raucity 405, 410
raucous *hoarse* 581
ravage 162, 659
ravages of time 659
rave *madness* 503
excitement 824, 825
– against 932
ravel *untwist* 60
derange 61
entangle 219
difficulty 704
ravelin 717
ravelled 59
raven *black* 431
hoarse 581
gorge 957
– for 865
ravening 173, 865
ravenous 789, 865
raver 504
ravine *interval* 198
narrow 203
dike 259
channel 350
raving *mad* 503
feeling 821
excitement 824, 825
ravish *seize* 789
please 829
ravished
pleased 827
ravishment 824
raw *immature* 123
sensitive 378
cold 383
colour 428
unprepared 674
unskilled 699
– head and bloody bones 860
– levies 726
– material 635
raw-boned 203
ray 420
– of comfort 831
rayah 745
rayless 421
raze 162
– to the ground 308
razor 253
cut a whetstone with a – 638
misuse 679
unskilful 699
keen as a – 821
razzia
destruction 162
attack 716
plunder 791
re, in – 9
reabsorb 296
reach *degree* 26
equal 27
distance 196
fetch 270
arrive at 292
river 348
deceive 545
grasp 737
take 789
within – *near* 197
possible 470
– the ear
hearing 418
information 527
– of thought 498
– to *distance* 196
length 200
reach-me-down 673
reaction
compensation 30
reversion 145
counteraction 179
recoil 277
restoration 660
reactionary 145, 607
reactionist 710
read 522, 539
well – 490
– a lecture 537
readable 578
reader *teacher* 540
printer 591
clergyman 996
readership 542
readily 705
reading
speciality 79
knowledge 490
interpretation 522
learning 539
– glass 445
– in 995
reading-desk 1000
readjust 23, 27
readmit 296
ready
expecting 507
willing 602
useful 644
prepare 673

active 682
skilful 698
cash 800
get - 673
make - 673
- to burst forth 825
- made 673
- memory 505
- money 800
- pen 569
- to sink 824
- wit 842
reaffirm 535
reagent 463
real *existing* 1
substantial 3
- *number* 84
true 494
- estate 780
- property 780
- security 771
realism 494
realistic 17
realize
speciality 79
intellect 450
think 451
discover 480a
believe 484
conceive 490
imagine 515
accomplish 729
acquire 775
sell 796
really *wonder* 870
realm *region* 181
people 372
government 737
property 780
realness 1
realty 780
ream 593
reamer 262
reanimate
reproduce 163
life 359
resuscitate 660
reap *shorten* 201
agriculture 371
take 789
- the benefit of
be better for 658
- and carry 775
- the fruits
succeed 731
acquire 775
reward 973
- where one has not sown 923
- the whirlwind
product 154
failure 732
reappear
repetition 104
reproduce 163
visible 446
restore 660
rear *sequel* 65
end 67
bring up 161
erect 212
back 235
elevate 307
teach 537
in the - 281
- its head
manifest 525
- one's head
pride 878
rear-admiral 745
reason *cause* 153
intellect 450
thought 451
argue 476
wisdom 498
motive 615
by - of 615
feast of - 588
in - *moderate* 174
right 922
listen to - 498
stand to -
certain 474
proof 478
manifest 525
what's the - ? 461
without rhyme or - 615a
- in a circle 477
- why 153, 615
reasonable
moderate 174
probable 472
judicious 498
sane 502
cheap 815
right 922
- prospect 472
reasoner 476
reasoning 476
reasonless 499
reasons 476
reassemble 72
reassert 535
reassure 858, 861
reasty 401, 653
reave 789
rebate
subtract 38
decrement 40a
moderate 174
discount 813
rebeck 417
rebel 742
rebellion 715, 742
rebellow 412
rebirth 660
reboation 412
rebound 277, 283
rebours, à -
reversion 145
regression 283
difficult 704
rebuff *recoil* 277
resist 719
repulse 732
refuse 764
discourtesy 895
censure 932
rebuild 660
rebuke 932
rebus 533
rebut *answer* 462
counter evidence 468
confute 479
deny 536
rebutter 462, 969
recalcitrant 719, 742
recalcitrate 277, 719
recalescence 382
recall
recollect 505
recant 607
cancel 756
- to life 660
recant *deny* 536
retract 607
resign 756
recapitulate
enumerate 85
repeat 104
describe 594
summarize 596
recast
revolution 146
scheme 626
recede 283, 287
- into the shade 874
receipt
scheme 626
prescription 662
precept 697
security 771
payment 807
- *of money* 810
- in full 807
receive *include* 76
admit 296
belief 484
assent 488
acquire 775
take in 785
take 789
- *money* 810
welcome 892, 894
- Christ 987
received *known* 490
habitual 613
- maxim 496
receiver
vessel 191
treasurer 801
official - 967
- of stolen goods 792
receiving 785
recension 85
recent 122, 123
receptacle 191
reception
comprehension 54
inclusion 76
arrival 292
ingestion 296
interview 588
receiving 785
welcome 892, 894
warm - 892
reception-room 191
recess
receptacle 191
corner 244
regression 283
ambush 530
vacation 687
retirement 893
recesses
interior 221
secret - of one's heart 820
recession
motion from 287
Rechabite 958
réchauffé *copy* 21
repetition 104
food 298
made hot 384
restored 660
recherché 648, 852
recidivation
regression 283
relapse 607, 661
recipe *remedy* 662
precept 697
recipient 191, 785
reciprocal 12, 84
reciprocate
correlation 12
interchange 148

assent 488
concord 714
retaliate 718
reciprocity 709
recision 38
recital 415
recitativo 415
recite
enumerate 85
speak 582
narrate 594
reck 459
reckless
careless 460
defiant 715
rash 863
recklessly profuse 818
reckon *count* 85
– among 76
– upon 484, 507
– with 807
– without one's host
unskilful 699
fail 732
rash 863
reckoning
numeration 85
measure 466
expectation 507
payment 807
accounts 811
reward 973
day of – 919
out of one's – 704
reclaim *restore* 660
command 741
due 924
atonement 952
reclaimed
penitent 950
recline *lie flat* 213
depress 308
repose 687
– on 215
recluse 893
recognition
[see recognize]
courtesy 894
thanks 916
means of – 550
recognizable 446, 518
– by 550
recognizance 771
recognize *see* 441
attention 457
discover 480a
assent 488
know 490
remember 505
understand 518
permit 760
recognized
influential 175
customary 613
– maxim 496
recoil *reaction* 179
repercussion 277
reluctance 603
shun 623
from which reason –s 471
– at *hate* 898
– from *dislike* 867
recollect 505
recommence 66
recommend 695, 931
– itself
approbation 931
recompense 790, 973
reconcile *agree* 23
pacify 723
content 831
forgive 918
– oneself to 826
recondite 519, 528
recondition 660, 790
reconnaissance 441
reconnoitre 441, 461
reconsideration 451
on – 658
reconstitute 660
reconstruct 660
reconvert 660
record 551
break the – 33
court of – 966
gramophone – 551
recorder 553
judge 967
recount 594
recoup 30, 790
recourse 677
recovery
improvement 658
reinstatement 660
getting back 775
restitution 790
– of strength 689
recreant
coward 862
base 940
knave 941
vicious 945
bad man 949
recreation 840
recrement 653
recriminate 932
recrimination 938
recrudescence 661
recruit *strength* 159
learner 541
provision 637
health 654
repair 658
reinstate 660
refresh 689
aid 707
auxiliary 711
soldier 726
beat up for –s 673, 707
rectangle 244
rectangular 212, 244
rectify
straighten 246
improve 658
re-establish 660
rectilinear 246
rectitude 939, 944
rector 694, 996
rectorship 995
rectory 1000
rectus in curiâ 946
reculer pour mieux sauter 673, 702
reculons, à – 283
recumbent 213, 217
recuperation 790
recuperative 660
recur
repeat 104
frequent 136
periodic 138
– to the mind 505
– to 677
recure 660
recursion 292
recurvity 245
recusant
dissenting 489
denying 536
disobedient 742
refusing 764
impenitent 951
heterodox 984
red 434
paint the town – 840
turn – *feeling* 821
– book *list* 86
– coat 726
– cross 662
– flag 669
– hot *great* 31
violent 173
hot 382
emotion 821
excited 824
– letter 550, 883
–letter day
important 642
rest 687
amusement 840
celebration 883
– light 669
– rag to a bull 900
– republican 742
– tape 613
– tapist 694
– and yellow 439
redact 590, 658
redan 717
redargue 479
red cap 271
redden *colour* 434
humble 879
angry 900
reddition
interpretation 522
restitution 790
redeem
compensate 30
substitute 147
reinstate 660
deliver 672
regain 775
restore 790
pay 807
atone 952
– from oblivion 505
– one's pledge 772, 926
Redeemer 976
redemption
[see redeem]
liberation 750
duty 926
salvation 976
red-handed
murder 361
in the act 680
guilty 947
redict 905
redingote 225
redintegrate 660
redintegratio amoris 607
redivivus 660
redness 434
redolence
odour 398
fragrance 400
redouble
increase 35
duplication 90

repeat 104
– one's efforts 686
redoubt 717
redoubtable 860
redound to
conduce 176
– one's honour
glory 873
approbation 931
honour 939
redress *restore* 660
remedy 662
reward 973
red-tape 694, 739
reduce *lessen* 36
- *in number* 103
weaken 160
contract 195
shorten 201
lower 308
subdue 731
discount 813
– to ashes 384
– to demonstration 478
– to a mean 29
– to order 60
– to poverty 804
– to powder 330
– the speed 275
– in strength 160
– to subjection 749
– to *convert* 144
– to writing 551
reduced [*see* reduce]
impoverished 804
– to the last extremity 665
– to a skeleton 659
– to straits 704
reductio ad absurdum 476, 479
reduction
[*see* reduce]
arithmetical 85
conversion 144
at a – 815
– of temperature 385
redundance
diffuseness 573
too much **641**
redundancy 104
reduplication 19, 90
re-echo *imitate* 19
repeat 104
resonance 408
reechy 653
reed *weak* 160
pan 590
arrow 727

trust to a broken – 699
– instrument 417
reef *slacken* 275
shoal 346
danger 667
take in a – 664
double – topsails 664
reefer 269
reek *gas* 334
vaporize 336
liquid 337
hot 382
fester 653
reeking 339, 653
reel *rock* 314
agitate 315, 851
dance 840
– back *yield* 725
re-embody
junction 43
combination 48
re-enter 245
re-entrant angle 244
re-establish 660
re-estate 660
refashion 163
refect
strengthen 159
refection
meal 298
refreshment 689
(*restoration* 660)
refectory 191
refer to *relate* 9
include 76
attribute 155
cite 467
allude 521
take advice 695
referable 9, 155
referee
judgment 480
judge 967
reference
[*see* refer]
referendary 967
referendum 480, 609
ad – 461, 605
referrible 9, 155
refine *clean* 652
– upon 658
refined *colour* 428
fashionable 852
refinement
discrimination 465
wisdom 498

elegance 578, 845
improvement 658
taste 850
over– 477
refit 660
reflect *imitate* 19
think 451
– dishonour 874
– light 420
– upon *censure* 932
reflecting 498
reflection 408, 453
light 420
reflector *mirror* 445
reflex *copy* 21
recoil 277
regressive 283
reflexion 21, 277
refluence *recoil* 277
regress 283
reflux *decrease* 36
recoil 277
regress 283
current 348
refocillate
strengthen 159
refresh 689
reform *convert* 144
improve 658
reformatory 542, 752
reformer 658
refound 144
refraction
deviation 279
light 420
fallacy of vision 443
refractory
obstinate 606
difficult 704
mutinous 742
ill-tempered 901a
refrain *poetry* 597
avoid 623
do nothing 681
temperate 953
– from laughter 837
– from voting 609a
repetition 104
refresh
strengthen 159
cool 385
refit 658
restore 660
recruit 689
relieve 834
– the memory 505

refreshing 377, 829
refreshment
food 298
recruiting **689**
delight 827
refrigeration
anæsthetic 376
making cold **385**
refrigerator **387**
reft 44
refuge **666**
refugee 268, 623
refulgence 420
refund 807
refurbish 673
refusal **764**
pre-emption 795
refuse *remains* **40**
useless 645
not consent 764
– assent 489
– to associate with 893
– to believe 487
– to hear 460
refute 479
refuted 495
regain 775
– breath 689
regal 737
regale *feast* 298
physical pleasure 377
refresh 689
pleasing 829
amusement 840
regalia 747
regality 737
regard
relation 9
view 441
attention **457**
judge 480
credit 873
love 897
respect 928
approbation 931
have – to 457
merit – 642
pay – to
believe 484
honour 873
– as 484
regardful 457, 459
regardless 458, 823
regards 894, 928
regatta 720, 840
regency 755
regenerate
reproduce **163**
restore 660

piety 987
regeneration
divine function 976
baptismal – 998
regent 745, 759
regicide 361
régime
circumstances **8**
conduct 692
authority 737
ancien – 875
regimen *diet* 298
remedy 662
conduct 692
regiment 72, 726
regimentals 225
region 181
register
arrange **60**
list 86
chronicle 114
record 551, 553
registrar 553
registration 551
registry 114
règle: en – 924
regnant 175, 737
regni, anno – 106
regorge 790
regrade 283
regrate 777
regrater 797
regression 283
regret 833, 950
express – 952
regretted, to be – 833
reguerdon 973
regular
uniform **16**
complete **52**
order 58
arrangement 60
rule 80
conformity 82
periodic 138
symmetric 242
habitual 613
by – intervals 58
– return 138
regulars 726
regulate
adjust **23**
arrange **60**
direct 693
regulated by
conformity 82
regulation 697, 963
regurgitate
return 283
flow 348
restore 790
rehabilitate 660, 790
rehearse
repeat **104**
try 463
describe 594
drama 599
prepare 673
Reichsrath 696
reign 175, 737
– of terror 739, 860
reimburse 790, 807
rein 752
– in 275, 751
reincarnation 163
reindeer 271
re infectâ 304, 681
reinforce
strengthen 159
restore 660
aid 707
reinforced concrete 635
reinforcement
addition **37**
adjunct **39**
materials 635
provision 637
aid 707
reinless 738
reins [*see* rein]
direction 693
give the – to
facilitate 705
lax 738
permit 760
hold the – 693
take the – 737
give – to the imagination 515
reinstall 660
reinstate 660, 790
reinvest 790
reinvigorate 658, 689
Reis Effendi 694
reiterate 104
reject
exclude **55**
eject 297
refuse 764
rejected
hateful 898
rejection 610
rejoice *exult* 838
amuse 840
– the heart
gratify 829
cheer 836
– in 827
– in the name of 564
rejoicing 838
rejoin *assemble* 72
arrive 292
rejoinder
answer 462
law pleadings 969
rejuvenescence 660
rekindle
ignite 384
excite 824
relapse
turn back **145**, 283
fall back **661**
relate *narrate* 594
– to *refer* 9
related *kin* **11**
relation 9
kin 11
narrative 594
relationship 9
relative 11, 464
– position
relativity 9
relator
accuser 938
relax *loose* 47
weaken 160
moderate 174
slacken speed 275
soften 324
inactive 683
repose 687
misrule 738
liberate 750
relent 914
– one's efforts 681
– the mind 452
relaxation
[*see* relax]
amusement 840
dereliction 927
relaxed *weak* 160
relay 635, 636
release *death* 360
deliverance 672
liberate 750
exempt 760
from engagement **768a**
security 771
restore 790
repay 807
forgive 918
exempt 927*a*
discharge 970
deed of – 923
relegate *banish* 55
transfer 270
remove 297
relent *moderate* **174**
soften 324
pity 914
relentless
resolute 604
severe 739
wrathful 900
malevolent 907
revenge 919
impenitent 951
relessee
possessor 779
receiver 785
relevancy 9, 23
relevé 298
reliable 474
reliance
confidence 484
hope 858
relic *remainder* 40
reminiscence 505
token 551
relics *corpse* 362
sacred 998
relict 40, 905
relief
prominence **250**
aid 707
comfort **834**
bas - 250, 557
in strong – 446, 525
relieve *improve* **658**
aid 707
comfort 834
relievo 250, 557
religieuse 996
religion 983, 987
under the mask of – 988
religionist 988
religious
honourable 939
theological 983
pious 987
over– 955
– education 537
– persuasion 983
– sects 984
religiously exact 494
relinquish 757
+ hope 859
– life 360
– property 782
– a purpose 624
recant 607
relinquishment 624, 782

reliquary 191, 998
reliquiæ 362
relish *pleasure* 377
savour 390
condiment 393
savoury 394
delight 827
desire 865
relive 660
relucent 420
reluct 720
reluctance
dissuasion 616
unwilling 603
dislike 867
reluctation 719
relume 384, 420
rely 484, 858
rem acu tetigisti 23
remain *be left* 40
endure 106
long time 110
continue 141
be present 186
stand 265
– firm 150
– on one's hands 641
– in one's mind 505
– neuter 605
– in possession of the field 731
remainder 40
estate 780
in – *posterior* 117
remainder-man 779
remains
remainder 40
corpse 362
vestige 551
organic – 357
remand *defer* 133
order 741
remanet 40
remark *observe* 457
affirmation 535
worthy of – 642
remarkable
great 31
exceptional 83
important 642
remarry 903
Rembrandtesque 160
remediable, remedial 660, 662
remediless 859
remedy 660, 662
remembrance 505
remembrances 894
rememoration 505
remigration
regression 283
arrival 292
egress 295
remind 505
that -s me 134
reminiscence 505
remise 927*a*
remiss
neglectful 460
reluctant 603
idle 683
lax 738
remission
cessation 142
moderation 174
laxity 738
forgiveness 918
exemption 927*a*
remit
[*see* remission]
– one's efforts 681
remittance 807
remittent
periodic 138
remitter 790
remnant 40
remodel
convert 144
revolutionize 146
improve 658
remonstrance 616, 766, 932
remora *cohere* 46
hindrance 706
remorse 950
remorseless 919
remote 10, 196
– age 122
– cause 153
– future 121
remotest idea, not have – 491
remotion 270
remount 147
remove *subduct* 38
term 71
displace 185
transfer 270
recede 287
depart 293
dinner 298
extract 301
school 541
– the mask 529
removedness
distance 196
remugient 412
remunerate 973
remunerative 644, 775
renaissance 660
renascence 660
renascent 163
rencounter
contact 199
meeting 292
fight 720
rend 44
– the air 404, 411, 839
– the heart-strings 830
render *convert* 144
interpret 522
give 784
restore 790
– an account
inform 527
describe 594
– *hors de combat* 645
– a service 644
rendering
covering 223
rendezvous 72, 74
rendition
interpretation 522
restore 790
renegade
convert 144
turncoat 607
fugitive 623
apostate 941
renew *twice* 90
repeat 104
reproduce 163
recollect 505
improve 658
restore 660
– one's strength 689
reniform 245
renitence
counteraction 179
hardness 323
elasticity 325
unwillingness 603
resistance 719
renitency
light 420
renounce
recant 607
relinquish 624
resign 757
abnegate 764
- *property* 782
repudiate 927
renovare dolorem, infandum – 833
renovate 163, 660
renovated *new* 123
renown 873
renownless 874
rent *tear* 44
fissure 198
hire 788
purchase 795
rental 810
renter 188, 779
rent-free 815
rent-roll 780, 810
rents *houses* 189
renunciation
[*see* renounce]
exemption 927*a*
reorganize
order 60
convert 144
improve 658
restore 660
repair
mend 658
make good 660
refresh 689
out of – 659
– to 266
reparation
[*see* repair]
compensation 30
restitution 790
atonement 952
reward 973
repartee 462, 842
reparteeist 844
repartition 786
repass, pass and – 314
repast 298
repatriation 790
repay 790, 807, 973
repeal 756
repeat *imitate* 19
duplication 90
iterate 104
reproduce 163
affirm 535
– by rote 505
repeated 104, 136
repeater
watch 114
fire-arm 727
repel *repulse* 289
deter 616
defend 717
resist 719
refuse 764
give pain 830
disincline 867
banish 893
excite hate 898
repent 950
repercussion 277

répertoire 599
repertory 636
repetend
arithmetical 84
iteration 104
repetition 19, **104**
repine
pain 828
discontent 832
regret 833
sad 837
replace
substitute 147
locate 184
restore 660
replenish 52, 637
repletion
filling 639
redundance 641
satiety 869
replevin
recovery 775
borrow 788
restore 790
replica 21
replication
answer 462
law pleadings 969
reply 462, 937
répondre en Normand 544
report *noise* 406
judgment 480
inform 527
publish 531
news 532
rumour 532
record 551
statement 594
good – 873
through evil report and good – 604*a*
– progress 527
reporter
informant 527
messenger 534
recorder 553
journalist 593, 758
reports *law* 969
repose
quiescence 265
leisure 685
rest 687
– confidence in 484
– on *support* 215
evidence 467
– on one's laurels 142
reposit 184
repository 636
repostum, manet alta mente – 919
repoussé 250
reprehend 932
reprehensible 945, 947
represent *similar* 17
imitate 19
exhibit 525
intimate 527
declare 535
denote 550
delineate 554
commission 755
deputy 759
– to oneself 515
representation [*see* represent]
copy 21
portrait **554**
drama 599
representative
typical 79
commissioner 758
deputy 759
– government 737
– of the people 696
– of the press
messenger 534
writer 593
repress 751
– one's feelings 826
– a smile 837
reprieve
respite 133, 970
deliverance 672
release 750
pardon 918
reprimand 932
reprint
copy 21
repetition 104
reproduce 163
reprisal
retaliation 718
resumption 789
reprise 40*a*
reproach
disgrace 874
blame 932
accusation 938
reprobate
disapproved 932
vicious 945
bad man 949
sinner 988
reprobation 932, 988
reproduce
imitate 19
repeat 104
renovate 163
reproduction [*see* reproduce] 21, **163**
reproductive 163
reproof 932
reprover 936
reptile
animal 366
servile 886
knave 941
miscreant 949
republic
country 181
people 372
government 737
– of letters 560
republican
party 712
government 737
commonalty 876
republicanism 737
repudiate
exclude 55
deny 489
reject 610
abrogate 756
violate 773
not pay 808
evade 927
repugn 719
repugnance
incongruity 24
resistance 719
dislike 867
hate 898
repulse *recoil* 277
repel 289
resist 719
failure 732
refusal 764
repulsion 157, **289**
repulsive [*see* repulse]
unsavoury 395
painful 830
ugly 846
disliked 867
discourteous 895
hateful 898
repurchase 795
reputable 873, 939
reputation 873
repute 873
request **765**
in – 630
– permission **760**
requiem 839
requies, nec mora nec – 682
requiescat in pace 363, 723
require
need 630
insufficient 640
exact 741
compel **744**
price 812
due 924
duty 926
– explanation 519
requirement **630**
requisite 630
requisition 741, 765
put in – *use* 677
order 741
requital
retaliation 918
gratitude 916
punishment 972
reward 973
reredos 1000
res ipsa loquitur – 525
rescind *cut off* 44
abrogate 756
refuse 764
rescission 44, 756
rescript *answer* 462
transcript 590
letter 592
order 741, 963
rescriptive 761
rescue *preserve* **670**
deliver 672
aid 707
research 461
– student 541
reseat 660
resection 44
reseda 435
resemblance **17, 21**
resent 900
resentful 901
resentment **900**
reservation
location 184
concealment 528
mental – 477, 528
equivocation 520
untruth 546
with a – 38, 770
reservatory 191, 636
reserve
concealment 528
silence 585

choose 609
store 636
disuse 678
retain 781
shyness 881
in – *destined* 152
prepared 673
– forces 726
– oneself 881
reservoir 636
re-shape 140
resiance 189
resiant 186
reside 1, 186
residence 189
resident
consignee 758
present 186
inhabitant 188
residentiary 186, 188
clergy 996
residue 40
residuum
remainder **40**
dregs 653
commonalty 876
resign 757, 782
– one's being 364
– one's breath 360
– oneself 725, 826
resignation [*see* resign]
submission 725
obedience 743
abdication **757**
renunciation 782
endurance 826
humility 879
resile 277
resilience
regression 283
elasticity 325
resin **356a**
resipiscence 950
resist *oppose* 179
withstand 719
disobey 742
refuse 764
resistance 719
résistance, pièce de – 298
resister
passive – **710**
resisting
tenacious 327
resistless 159, 601
resolute 604, 861
resolution
decomposition 49
conversion 144
music 413
topic 454
investigation 461
mental energy **604**
intention 620
scheme 626
courage 861
resolvable into 27, 144
resolve *change* 140
liquefy 335
investigate 461
discover 480a
interpret 522
determine 604
predetermine 611
intend 620
– into elements 49
– into *convert* 144
resonance 402, **408**
resorb 296
resort *assemble* 72
focus 74
dwelling 189
converge 290
last – 601
– to *be present* 186
travel 266
employ 677
resound *loud* 404
ring 408
– praises 931
resourceful 698
resources
means 632
property 780
wealth 803
respect *relation* 9
observe 772
fame 873
salutation 894
deference **928**
have – to 9
in no – 536
with – to 9
respectability
mediocrity 736
repute 873
probity 939
respectable
unimportant 643
respectful 928
– distance 623, 864
respective 79, 786
respectless 458
respects 894, 928
resperse 73
respicere finem 510
respire *breathe* 349
live 359
refresh 689
respite
intermission 106
defer 133
pause 142
deliver 672
repose 687
reprieve 970
resplendent
luminous 420
splendid 845
respond *accord* 23
answer 462
feel 821
respondent 462
accused 938
response
answer 462, **587**
concord 714
feeling 821
friendship 888
worship 990
responsible 177, 926
responsibility
upon one's own – 600
responsive 375
rest *remainder* 40
pause 141
cessation 142
support 215
quiescence 265
death 360
silence 403
music 413
inaction 681
repose 687
at – *repose* 687
content 831
home of – 189
set at –
answer 462
ascertain 474
complete 729
compact 769
set one's mind at – *calm* 826
set the question at – 478, 480
– assured 484, 858
– on *support* 215
– on one's oars 142, 687
– satisfied 831
– and be thankful 681, 687
– upon
evidence 467
confide 484
– with *duty* 926
restaurant 189
– car 272
restaurateur **637**
restful 265
resting place
support 215
quiet 265
arrival 292
restitution **790**, 660
restive *averse* 603
obstinate 606
disobedient 742
refusal 764
perverse 901*a*
restless
changeable 149
moving 264
agitated 315
active 682
excited 825
fearful 860
restoration **660**
restorative
salubrious 656
remedial 662
relieving 834
restore *reinstate* 660
refresh 689
return 790
– equilibrium 27
– harmony 723
– to health 654
restrain 616, 706, 751
restrainable 743
restrained 751
restraint 578, **751**
self – 826, 953
restrict *hinder* 706
restrain 751
prohibit 761
restringency 751
result *remainder* 40
follow 117
effect 154
conclusion 480
completion 729
resultant 48, 154
resume *begin* 66
repeat 104
change 140
restore 660
take 789
résumé 596
resupination 213
resurgence 163, 660
resurrection
reproduction 163
restoration 660
heaven 981

resuscitate
reproduce 163
reinstate 660
retable 215
retail *distribute* 73
inform 527
barter 794
sell 796
retailer 797
retain *stand* 150
keep 781
– the memory of 505
– one's reason 502
retainer 746
retake 789
retaliation 718, 919
retard *later* 133
slower 275
hinder 706
retch 297
retection 529
retention 781
retentive 781
– memory 505
reticence 528
reticle 219
reticulation 219, 248
reticule 191
retiform 219
retina 441
retinue *followers* 65
series 69
servants 746
retire *move back* 283
recede 287
resign 757
modest 881
seclusion 893
– into the shade
inferior 34
decrease 36
– from sight
disappear 449
hide 528
retiring
concave 252
- *colour* 438
retold 104
retort
receptacle 191
vaporizer 336
boiler 386
answer 462
confutation 479
retaliation 718
wit 842
retouch *restore* 660
retoucher 559
retrace 505
– one's steps 607
retract
recant 607
annul 756
abjure 757
violate 773
retreat
resort 74
withdraw 187
abode 189
regression 283
recede 287
ambush 530
refuge 666
escape 671
give way 725
beat a – 623
retreating
concave 252
retrench *subduct* 38
shorten 201
lose 789
economize 817
retribution
retaliation 718
payment 807
punishment 972
reward 973
retrieve *restore* 660
acquire 775
retriever *dog* 366
retroaction
counteraction 179
recoil 277
regression 283
retroactive
past 122
retrocession
regression 283
recession 287
retrograde
moving back 283
deteriorated 659
relapsing 661
retrogression
regression 283
deterioration 659
relapse 661
retrospection
past 122
thought 451
memory 505
retroussé 245
retroversion 218
retrude 289
return *list* 86
repeat 104
periodic 138
reverse 145
recoil 277
regression 283
arrival 292
answer 462
report 551
relapse 661
appoint 755
profit 775
restore 790
proceeds 810
reward 973
in –
compensation 30
– the compliment
interchange 148
retaliate 718
– to the original state 660
–ed prodigal 950
– thanks 916, 990
return game 104
return match 104
reunion *junction* 43
réunion
assemblage 72
concord 714
lieu de – 74
point de – 74
social – 892
revamp 140
revanche, en – 718
reveal 529
– itself 446
reveille 550
réveiller le chat qui dort, ne pas – 668, 864
revel 840, 954
– in *enjoy* 377
revelation
disclosure 480a, 529
theological 985
Revelations 985
reveller 840
drunkard 959
revelling 59, 838
revendicate
claim 741
acquisition 775
due 924
revenge 919
breathe – 900
revenons à nos moutons 283, 660
revenue 632, 810
reverberate 277, 408
reverberatory 386
revere *love* 897
respect 928
piety 987
reverence *title* 877
respect 928
piety 987
clergy 996
reverenced 500
reverend 877, 996
reverent 987, 990
reverential 928
reverie
train of thought 451
inattention 458
imagination 515
reversal 218, 607
reverse *contrary* 14
inversion 218
- *of a medal* 235
contraposition 237
adversity 735
abrogate 756
cards 840
– of the shield 468
reverseless 150
reversible 605
reversion
[see reverse]
posterity 117
return 145
possession 777
property 780
succession 783
remitter 790
reversioner 779
revert *repeat* 104
return 145
turn back 283
revest 790
– to 457
revest 790
revet 223
reviction 660
review *consider* 457
inquiry 461
judge 480
recall 505
periodical 531
dissertation 595
compendium 596
entertainment 599
revise 658
parade 882
reviewer 480, 595
revile 932, 988
reviler 936
revise *copy* 21
consider 457
printing 591
plan 626
improve 658
revising barrister 967

revision, under – 673
revisit 186
revival
reproduction 163
restoration 660
worship 990
revivalist 996
revive
reproduce 163
improve 658
resuscitate 660
excite 824
revivify
reproduce 163
life 359
improve 658
resuscitate 660
revocable 605
revoir, au – 293
revoke 607, 756
revolt *resist* 719
disobey 742
shock 830
disapproval 932
– against *hate* 898
– at the idea
dissent 489
revolting
painful 830
revolution
periodicity 138
change 146
rotation 312
disobedience 742
revolutionize 140, 146
revolve
[*see* revolution]
– in the mind 451
revolver 727
revue 599
intimate – 599
revulsion
reversion 145
revolution 146
inversion 218
recoil 277
reward 973
reword 104
Reynard
animal 366
cunning 702
rez-de-chaussée 191, 207
rhabdology 85
rhabdomancy 511
Rhadamanthus 967, 982
rhapsodical
irregular 139
imaginary 515
rhapsodist
fanatic 504
rhapsody
discontinuity 70
music 415
nonsense 497
fancy 515
poetry 597
rhetoric *speech* 582
flowers of – 577
rheum
excretion 299
fluidity 333
water 337
rhino 800
rhinoceros hide 376, 823
rhomb 244
rhumb 278
rhyme
similarity 17
verse 597
without – or reason
absurd 497
caprice 608
motiveless 615a
rhymeless 598
rhymester 597
rhythm
periodicity 138
melody 413
elegance 578
verse 597
rhythmical
- *style* 578
Rialto 799
rib *support* 215
ridge 250
wife 903
ribald *vulgar* 851
disreputable 874
impure 961
riband
[*see* ribbon]
ribbed 259
ribbon *tie* 45
filament 205
record 551
decoration 877
–s *reins* 752
handle the – 693
ribroast 972
rich *savoury* 394
colour 428
language 577
abundant 639
wealthy 803
beautiful 845
ornament 847
– man 803
riches 803
richesses, embarras de – 641, 803
richly *much* 31
– deserve 924
rick 72, 636
rickety *weak* 160
ugly 846
imperfect 651
rickshaw 272
ricochet 277
ricordo, non mi – 506
rid *deliver* 672
get – of *eject* 297
liberation 750
loose 776
relinquish 782
riddance 672, 776, 782
good – 776
riddle *arrange* 60
sieve 260
secret 533
clean 652
ride *get above* 206
move 266
break in 370
– at anchor 265
– full tilt at 622, 716
– hard 274
– one's hobby 622
– rough shod
violence 173
severity 739
insolence 885
illegality 964
– out the storm 664
– and tie
periodicity 138
journey 266
– the whirlwind 604, 737
rideau, lever de – 599
ridentem dicere verum 836, 842
rider *appendix* 39
equestrian 268
rideret Heraclitus 853
ridge *narrow* 203
height 206
prominence 250
ridicule 856, 929
ridiculous
absurd 497
foolish 499
trifling 643
grotesque 853
ridiculousness 853
riding *district* 181
journey 266
ridotto 840, 892
rifacimento 104, 660
rife *existence* 1
general 78
influence 175
riff-raff *dirt* 653
commonalty 876
bad folk 949
rifle *musket* 727
plunder 791
– shot 406
rifled cannon 727
rifleman 726
rifler 792
rifles 726
rifle-shooting 840
rift 44, 198
– within the lute 651, 713
rig *dress* 225
prepare 673
frolic 840
strumpet 962
– the market 794
run the – upon 929
rigadoon 840
rigging *ropes* 45
gear 225
instrument 633
riggish 961
right *dextral* 238
straight 246
true 494
property 780
just 922
privilege 924
duty 926
honour 939
virtuous 944
bill of – 969
by – 924
have a – to 924
set – *inform* 527
disclose 529
that's – 931
– about
[*see below*]
– ahead 234
– angle 212
– ascension 466
– away 133
step in the – direction 644
– hand [*see below*]
– itself 660

– and left 180, 227, 236
– line 246
– man in the right place 23
in one's – mind 498, 502
hit the – nail on the head 480*a*, 698
– owner 779
keep the – path 944
in the – place 646
– thing to do 926
– as a trivet 650
– word in the right place 578
right about: to the – 283
go to the – **311**, 607
send to the –
eject 297
reject 610
refuse 764
turn to the – **218**, 279
right hand
power 157
dextrality 238
help 711
not let the – know what the left is doing 528
– of friendship 888
righteous 944
the – 987
– overmuch 988
Righteousness:
Lord our – 976
Sun of – 976
rightful 922
– owner 779
rightly served, be – 972
right-minded 939, 944
rights 748
put to – 660
set to – 60
stand on one's – 748
rigid *regular* **82**
hard 323
exact 494
severe 739
rigmarole **517**, **573**
rigor 383
– mortis 360
rigorous *exact* 494
severe 739
revengeful 919
rigour 494, 739
Rigsdag 696
rigueur
de – 744
rile *annoy* 830
hate 898
anger 900
rilievo *convex* 250
sculpture 557
rill 348
rim 231
rime *chink* **198**
frost 283
rimer 262
rimple 258
rind 223
ring
fastening **45**
pendency 214
circle 247
loud 404
resonance 408
test 463
combination 709
clique 712
arena 728, 840
badge 747
rub the – 992
have the true – 494
– the changes
repeat 104
change 140
changeable 149
– in the ear 404
in a – fence 229, 232
– with the praises of 931
– the tocsin 669
– up 527
ringleader
director 694
mutineer 742
ringlet 247, 256
rink 840
rinse 652
rinsings 653
riot *confusion* 59
derangement 61
violence 173
discord 713
resist 719
mutiny 742
run – *activity* 682
excitement 825
intemperance 954
– in *pleasure* 377
rioter 742
riotous 173
rip 949, 962
– open 260
– up *tear* 44
recall the past 505
excite 824
Rip van Winkle 130
riparian 342
ripe 673
– age *old* 128
ripen *perfect* 650
improve 658
prepare 673
complete 729
– into 144
rippet 713
riposte 462
ripple *ruffle* 256
shake 315
water 348
murmur 405
ripuarian 342
rire, pour – 853
rise *grow* 35
begin 66
slope 217
progress 282
ascend 305
stir 682
revolt 742
– again 660
– in arms 722
– from 154
– to the occasion 612
– in price 814
– up *elevation* 307
– in the world 734
risible 838, 853
rising [*see* **rise**]
– of the curtain 66, 448
– generation 127, 167
– ground
height 206
slope 217
worship the – sun 886
risk *chance* 621
danger 665
invest 787
at any – 604
risqué 961
rissole 298
risum teneatis amici? 853
rite 963, **998**
funeral – 363
ritornello 64, 104
ritual
ostentation **882**
rite 998
ritualism 984
rival
emulate **648**
oppose 708
opponent 710
compete 720
combatant 726
outshine 873
rivalry *envy* **921**
rive 44
rivel 258
river **348**
rivet 43, 45
– the attention 457, 824
– the eyes upon 441
– in the memory 505
– the yoke **739**
riveted *firm* 150
rivulet 348
rixation 713
Ro 560
road *street* 189
direction 278
way 627
on the –
transference 270
progression 282
approach 286
on the high – to 278
– to ruin
destruction 162
danger 665
adversity 735
road-book 266
roads *lake* 343
roadstead 184
abode 189
refuge 666
roadster 271
roadway 627
roam 266
roan *horse* **271**
colour 433
roar *violence* 173
wind 349
sound 404, **407**
bellow 411, **412**
laugh 838
weep 839
roaring *great* 31
– trade 731, 734
roast *heat* 384
ridicule 856
rib – 972

- and boiled 298
- an ox 883
rob 354, 791
robber 792
robbery 791
robe 225, 999
robes - of state 747
Robin Goodfellow 980
Robinson
say Jack - 132
Robot 554
robust *strong* 159, 654
roc 83
rocaille 853
rock *firm* 150
oscillate 314
hard 323
land 342
safety 664
danger 667
build on a - 150
founded on a - 664
split upon a - 732
- ahead 665
-bound coast 342
- oil 356
rocket *rapid* 274
rise 305
light 423
signal 550
arms 727
fireworks 840
go up like a - and come down like the stick 732
rocking-chair 215
rococo 124, 853
rod *support* 215
measure 466
scourge 975
divining 993
kiss the - 725
sounding - 208
- of empire 747
- in pickle
prepared 673
accusation 938
punishment 972
scourge 975
rodeo 720, 840
rodomontade
exaggeration 482
unmeaning 517
boast 884
roe 366, 374
Roentgen rays 420
rogation
request 765

worship 990
rogue *cheat* 548
knave 941
scamp 949
-'s march 297
roguery 940
roguish
playful 840
Roi le veut, le - 741
roister 885
roisterer 887
Roland for an Oliver
retaliation 718
revenge 919
barter 794
rôle *drama* 599
business 625
plan 626
conduct 692
roll *list* 86
fillet 205
convolution 248
rotundity 249
make smooth 255
move 264
fly 267
rotate 312
rock 314
flow 348
sound **407**
record 551
money 800
strike off the - 756, 972
- along 312
- in the dust 731
- on the ground 839
- of honour 86
- in 639, 641
- on 109
- into one 43
- in riches 803
- up 312
- up in 225
- in wealth 803
roll-call 85
roller *fillet* 45
round 249
clothing 255
rotate 312
roller-coaster 840
rollers *billows* 348
rollick 836
rollicker 838
rollicking
frolicsome 836
blustering 885
rolling: - pin 249

- stock 272
- stone 312
Rolls: Master of the -
recorder 553
judge 967
- Court 966
Roman candle 840
Roman Catholic 984
romance
music 415
absurdity 497
imagination 515
untruth 546
fable 594
Romanism 984
romantic
imaginative 515
art 556
sensitive 822
romanticism 515
Romanus sum, civis - 924
Romany 563
Rome: Church of 984
do at - as the Romans do 82
romp *violent* 173
game 840
rondeau *music* 415
poem 597
rondel 597
rondoletto 597
rood *area* 180
cross 998
- loft 1000
roof 189, 223
roofless 226
rook 791, 792
rookie 726
rookery *nests* 189
dirt 653
room *occasion* 134
space 180
lodge 186
chamber 191
plea 617
assembly - 840
in the - of 147
make - for
opening 260
respect 928
roommate 890
rooms
lodgings 189
roomy 180
roost 189
rule the - 737
rooster 366

root *algebraic* - 84
cause 153
place 184
abide 186
base 211
etymon 562
lie at the - of 642
pluck up by the -s 301
strike at the - of 716
take -
influence 175
locate 184
habit 613
- and branch 52
cut up - and branch 162
- out *eject* 297
extract 301
discover 480a
rooted
old 124
firm 150
located 184
habit 613
deep - 820
- antipathy 867
- belief 484
rope *fastening* 45
cord 205
freedom 748
scourge 975
give - enough 738
-'s end 975
- of sand
incoherence 47
weakness 160
impossible 471
- way 627
rope-dancer 700
rope-dancing 698
ropy 352
roquelaure 225
roric 339
rosâ, sub - 528
rosary 990, 998
Roscius 599
rose *pipe* 350
fragrant 400
red 434
beauty 845
bed of -s 377, 734
couleur de -
red 434
good 648
prosperity 734
hope 858
under the - 528
welcome as the -s in May 829, 892

roseate *red* 434
hopeful 858
rose-coloured
hope 858
Rosetta stone 522
rosette 847
rose-water
moderation 174
flattery 933
not made with –
704
Rosicrucian
sect 984
sorcerer 994
rosin *rub* 331
resin 356a
Rosinante 271
roster 86
rostrum *beak* 234
pulpit 542
rosy 434
– wine 959
rosy-cheeked 845
rot *decompose* 49
absurdity 497
rubbish 517
putrefy 653
disease 655
decay 659
rota 86, 138
Rotarian 892
rotate 138
rotation 312
periodicity 138
rote, by – 505
know – 490
learn – 539
rôti 298
rôtisserie 189
rotogravure 531, 558
rotten *weak* 160
bad 649
foul 653
decayed 659
– at the core
deceptive 545
diseased 655
– borough 893
rotulorum, custos – 553
rotund 249
rotunda 189
rotundity 249
roturier 876
roué 949
rouge 434, 847
rouge-et-noir 621
rough *violent* 173
shapeless 241
uneven 256
pungent 392
unsavoury 395
sour 397
sound 410
unprepared 674
fighter 726
ugly 846
low fellow 876
bully 887
churlish 895
evil-doer 913
bad man 949
cut up – 900
– copy *writing* 590
unprepared 674
– diamond
uncouth 241
unprepared 674
artless 703
vulgar 851
commonalty 876
good man 948
– draft 626
– guess 514
– it 686
– sea 348
– side of the tongue 932
– and tumble 59
– weather 173, 349
rough-cast 256
covering 223
shape 240
scheme 626
unpolished 674
rough-hew 240, 673
roughly
nearly 197
rough-neck 876, 887
roughness 256
rough-rider 268
roughshod over, ride – 739
roulade 415
rouleau
assemblage 72
cylinder 249
money 800
roulette 621, 840
round *series* 69
revolution 138
- of a ladder 215
curve 245
circle 247
rotund 249
music 415
fight 720
all – 227
bring – 660
come –
periodic 138
recant 607
persuade 615
dizzy – 312
get – 660
go – 311
go one's –s 266
go the –
publication 531
make the – of 311
run the – of 682
go the same – 104
turn – *invert* 218
retreat 283
revolve 311
– assertion 535
– a corner 311
– dance 840
– game 840
– hand 590
– like a horse in a mill 613
– of the ladder 71
– number 84, 102
in – numbers 29, 197
– pace 274
– of pleasures 377, 840
– robin
information 527
petition 765
censure 932
– and round 138, 312
– sum 800
– terms 566
– trot 274
– up 370
– of visits 892
round about
circumjacent 227
deviation 279
circuit 311
amusement 840
– phrases 573
– way 279
rounded periods 577, 578
roundelay 597
rounders 840
round-house 752
roundlet 247
round-shouldered 243
roup 796
rouse 615, 824
– oneself 682
rousing 171
rout *crowd* 72
agitation 315
overcome 731
discomfit 732
rabble 876
assembly 892
put to the – 731
– out 652
route 627
en – 270
en – for 282
routine
uniform 16
order 58
rule 80
periodic 138
custom 613
business 625
rove *travel* 266
deviate 279
rover *traveller* 268
pirate 792
roving commission 475
row *disorder* 59
series 69
violence 173
street 189
navigate 267
discord 713
– in the same boat 88
rowdy *vulgar* 851, 876
blusterer 887
bad man 949
rowel 253, 615
rower 269
rowlock 215
royal 737
– blue 438
– highness 877
– road 627, 705
Royal Academician 559
royalist 737
royaliste que le roi, plus 33
royalty 737
Rt. Hon. 877
ruade *impulse* 276
attack 716
ruat cœlum 908
rub *friction* 331
touch 379
difficulty 704
adversity 735
painful 830
– off corners 82
– down *lessen* 195
powder 330
– down with an oaken towel 972

- one's eyes 870
- one's hands 838
- up the memory 505
- off 552
- on *slow* 275
progress 282
inexcitable 826
- out 552
- up 658
- up the wrong way 713
rubadub 407
rubber 325
whist 840
rubber boots 225
rubber hose 975
rubber-stamp 82
rubbish
absurdity 497
unmeaning 517
trifling 643
useless 645
rubble 645
rube 876
rubescence 434
Rubicon *limit* 233
pass the -
begin 66
cross 303
choose 609
rubicund 434
rubify 434
rubigo 653
rubric 550, 697, 998
rubricate
redden 434
ruby *red* 434
gem 648
ornament 847
ruck 29, 258
in the - 235
rucksack 191
ructation 297
rudder 273, 693
rudderless 158
ruddle 434
ruddy *red* 434
beautiful 845
rude *violent* 173
shapeless 241
ignorant 491
inelegant 579
ugly 846
vulgar 851
uncivilized 876
uncivil 895
disrespect 929
- health 654
rudera 645
rudiment 66, 153
rudimental 193, 674
rudimentary 66
rudiments 490, 542
rudis indigestaque moles 59, 241
rue *bitter* 395
regret 833
repent 950
rueful 830, 837
ruff 225
ruffian 876
blusterer 876
maleficent 913
scoundrel 949
ruffianism 851, 907
ruffle *disorder* 59
derange 61
roughen 256
fold 258
feeling 821
excite 824, 825
pain 830
anger 900
rufous 434
rug 215, 223
Rugby
football 840
rugged
shapeless 241
rough 256
difficult 704
ugly 846
churlish 895
rugose 256
ruin *destruction* 162
evil 619
failure 732
adversity 735
poverty 804
ruined
bankrupt 808
hopeless 859
ruinous
painful 830
ruins *remains* 40
rule *mean* 29
regularity **80**
influence 175
length 200
measure 466
decide 480
custom 613
precept 697
government 737
law 963
absence of - 699
as a - 613
by - 82
golden - 697
obey -s 82
- of three 85
- of thumb
experiment 463
unreasoning 477
essay 675
unskilled 699
ruler 745
ruling 697, 969
- passion 606, 820
rum *liquor* 298
queer 853
- running 964
rumba 840
rumble 407
ruminate
chew 298
think 451
rummage 461
rummer 191
rumour 531, 532
rump 235
rumple
disorder 59
derange 61
roughen 256
fold 258
rumpus
confusion 59
violence 173
discord 713
run *generality* 78
repetition 104
continuance 106, 143
course 109
eventuality 151
motion 264
speed 274
sequence 281
liquefy 335
flow 348
habit 613
smuggle 791
contraband 964
have a - 852, 873
have - of 748
near - 197
ordinary - 29
race is - 729
time -s 106
- abreast 27
- after 622, 873
- against 276, 708, 716
- at 716
- away 623
- away with 789, 791
- away with a notion
misjudge 481
credulous 486
- back 283
- a chance
probable 472
chance 621
- counter to 468, 708
- its course
course 109
complete 729
past 122
- into danger 665
- into debt 806
- down
underestimate 483
pursue 622
bad 649
finished 678
attack 716
depreciate 932
detract 934
- dry 638, 640
- the eye over 441, 539
- the fingers over 379
- foul of 276
- the gauntlet 861
- on in a groove 613
- hard *danger* 665
difficult 704
success 731
- in the head 451, 505
- high *great* 31
violent 173
- in *introduce* 228
- into
conversion 144
insert 300
- low 36
- of luck 156, 734
- mad 503, 825
- mad after 865
- like mad 274
- of the mill 29
- amuck
violent 173
kill 361
mad 503
attack 716
- on 143
- out *end* 67
course 109
past 122
antiquated 124
egress 295
prodigal 818
- out on 573
- over *count* 85

- *in the mind* 451
examine 457
describe 594
synopsis 596
overflow 641
- in pairs 17
- parallel 178
- into port 664
- a race *speed* 274
conduct 692
contend 720
- in a race
act 680
he that -s may read 525
- a rig 840
- the rig upon 929
- riot *violent* 173
exaggerate 549
redundance 641
active 682
disobey 742
intemperance 954
- a risk 665
- rusty 603
- to seed 128, 659
- smooth 705, 734
- a tilt at 716, 720
- of things 151
- through
uniform 16
influence 175
be present 186
kill 361
expend 809
prodigal 818
- up *increase* 35
build 161
- up an account
credit 805
debt 806
charge 812
- up bills 808
- upon 630
- upon a bank 808, 809
- to waste 638
- wild 173
run-about 272
runagate
fugitive 623
disobey 742
bad man 949
runaway 623
rundle *circle* 247
convolution 248
rotundity 249
rundlet 191
Runes *writing* 590
poetry 597
spell 993
rung 215
runnel 348
runner *branch* 51
courier 268
messenger 534
running
continuous 69
the mind - upon 451
the mind - upon other things 458
- account 811
- commentary 595
- fight 720
- hand 590
- over 641
- water 348
runnion 949
runt 193
rupture
disjunction 44
quarrel 713
rural 189, 371
- dean 996
ruralist 893
rus in urbe 189, 893
ruse 545, 702
Rush, Friar 980
rush *crowd* 72
violence 173
velocity 274
water 348
plant 367
trifle 643
haste 684
make a - at 716
- to a conclusion 481, 486
- on destruction 863
- in medias res 604
- into print 591
- upon 622
rushlight *dim* 422
candle 423
rusk 298
Russe, montagne - 840
russet
brown 433
red 434
Russian
- ballet 840
- bath 386, 652
rust *red* 434
decay 659
canker 663
inaction 683
moth and - 659
- of antiquity 122
rustic
village 189
agricultural 371
vulgar 851
clown 876
rusticate
punish 972
seclude 893
rusticity
impolite 895
rusticus expectat dum defluat amnis 858
rustle 405, 407, 409
rustling 791
rusty *dirty* 653
decayed 659
sluggish 683
unskilful 699
sulky 901a
run - *averse* 603
rut *rule* 80
furrow 259
habit 613
in a - 16
ruth 914
ruthless
savage 907
pitiless 914a
revengeful 919
rutilant 420
ruttish 961
ryot *servant* 746
possessor 779
commonalty 876

S

sabaoth 726
sabbatarian
ascetic 955
sectarian 984
false piety 988
ritualistic 998
Sabbath *rest* 687
rite 998
sabbatism 988
Sabellianism 984
Sabianism 984
sable 223, 431
sabot 225
sabotage 162, 742
sabre 361, 727
sabreur *slayer* 361
soldier 726
sabulous 330
sac 191
- de nuit 225
sacatra 83
saccharine 396
saccular 191
sacerdotal 995
sacerdotalism 988
sachel 191
sachem 745
sachet 400
sack *bag* 191
discharge 297, 756
gain 775
take 789
plunder 791
give the - to 297
sackbut 417
sackcloth and ashes
lament 839
atonement 952
ascetic 955
rite 998
sacrament 998
sacrarium 1000
sacred
dignified 873
holy 976
revelation 985
piety 987
sacrifice
destroy 162
gift 784
atonement 952
worship 990
idolatry 991
at any - 604
fall a - 828
make a - 942
make the supreme - 361
self - 942
sacrificed 732
sacrilege 988
sacring bell 550, 998
sacristan 996
sacristy 1000
sacrosanct
honourable 873
inviolable 924
holy 976
sad *great* 31
grey 432
bad 649
painful 830
dejected 837
- disappointment 509
- dog 949
- times 735
- work 699
sadden 830, 837
sadder and wiser man 950

saddle 215
in the – 673
– on 37, 43
– on the right horse
discovery 480a
skill 698
right 922
fair 939
– with *add* 37
attribute 155
quarter on 184
clog 706
impose a duty 926
accuse 938
– on the wrong horse 495, 699
– up 293
saddle-bags 191
Sadducee 984
sadness, in – 535
safe *cupboard* 191
hiding place 530
secure 664
treasury 802
cautious 864
– conduct 631
– conscience 926, 946
– deposit 636
– keeping 670
– and sound 654
on the – side 864
safety 664
– bicycle 272
– curtain 599
– first 664, 864
– match 388
– valve 666
saffron *colour* 436
sag 214, 217, 245
saga 594
sagacious 498, 510
sage 498, **500**
– maxim 496
saggar 386
sagittal 253
sagittary 83
sagum 225
Sahara 169
sahib 373, 745, 875
saick 273
said *preceding* 62
repeated 104
prior 116
it is – 532
thou hast – 488
more easily – than done 704
sail *navigate* 267
ship 273
set out 293
easy – 174
full – 274
press of – 274
shorten – 275
take in – 174
take the wind out of one's –s 706
too much – 863
under – 267
– before the wind 734
– near the wind 698
– too near the wind 863
sailing: plain – 705
– vessel 273
sailor 269
fair weather – 701
saint *angel* 977
revelation 985
piety 987
false piety 988
tutelary – 664
Saint Monday 840
saintly 944, 987
sais quoi, je ne – 563
sake:
for the – of 615, 707
for goodness – 765
salaam
bow 308
submit 725
courtesy 894
respect 928
salacity 961
salad 41
– oil 356
salade 717
salamander 386
salariat 875
salary 973
sale **796**
bill of – 771
for – *offer* 763
barter 794
saleable 796
salebrosity 256
salesman 797
salient
projecting 250
sharp 253
manifest 525
important 642
– angle 244
– points 642
saline 392
saliva 299, 332
salivate 297
salle-à-manger 191
sallet 717
sallow
colourless 429
yellow 436
sally *issue* 293
attack 716
wit 842
sally-port 295, 717
salmagundi 41
salmi 298
salmon-coloured 434
saloon 189, 191
salt *sailor* 269
pungent 392
condiment 393
importance 642
preserve 670
money 800
wit 842
below the – 876
worth one's – 644
– of the earth 648, 948
– water 341
saltation 309
saltatory 315
saltimbanco 548
saltpetre 392, 727
saltum, per – 315
salubrity **656**
salutary 656
salutatory 582
salute
allocution 586
celebration 883
courtesy 894
kiss 902
respect 928
salutiferous [*see* salutary]
salva:
– res est 664
– sit reverentia 928
salvable 946
salvage
acquisition 775
tax 812
discount 813
reward 973
salvation
preservation 670
deliverance 672
religious 976
piety 987
work out one's – 990
salve *unguent* 356
remedy 662
relieve 834
salver 191
salvo *exception* 83
explosion 406
qualification 469
plea 617
attack 716
excuse 937
– of artillery
celebration 883
Samaritan, good – 906, 912
same 13
all the – to 823
in the – boat 709
in the – breath 113, 120
go over the – ground 104
of the – mind 488
on the – tack 709
adds up to the – thing 27
at the – time **30**, 120
sameness 16
samiel 349
samisen 417
Sammael 978
samovar 191
sampan 273
sample 82, 463
Samson 159
sana, mens – 502
– in corpore sano 827
sanation 660
sanative 662
sanatorium 662
sanctification 976
sanctify 926, 987
sanctimony 988
sanction
permission 760
dueness 924
approbation 931
sanctitude 987
sanctity 987
sanctuary 666, 1000
sanctum 191
– sanctorum
abode 189
privacy 893
temple 1000
sand *powder* 330
-bag 727
built upon – **665**
-dance 840
sow the – 645

sandal 225
sand-blind 442
Sandemanian 984
sand-paper 255
sands *danger* 667
– on the seashore
multitude 102
sand-storm 330
sandwich-wise 228
sandy *yellow* 436
sane 502
sangar 717
sang-froid
insensibility 823
inexcitability 826
presence of mind 864
sangrail 998
sanguinary 361
sanguine *red* 434
hopeful 858
– expectation 507, 858
– imagination 515
sanhedrim 696, 995
sanies 333
sanitaire, cordon – 670
sanitarian 656
sanitarium 656, 662
sanitary 656
sanity *mental* **502**
bodily - 654
sans 187
– cérémonie 888, 892
– facon
simple 849
modest 881
social 892
– pareil 33
– peur et sans reproche
perfect 650
heroic 873
honourable 939
– souci
insensible 823
pleasure 827
content 831
sans-culotte 742, 876
Santa Claus 784
santé, maison de – 662
santon 893, 996
sap *essence* 5
destroy 162
excavate 252
juice 333
damage 659
attack 716
– the foundations 162, 659
sapid 390
sapient 498
sapless 160, 340
sapling 129, 367
saponaceous 355
saporific 390
sapper 252, 726
sappers and miners
preparers 673
Sapphic 597
sapphire *blue* 438
gem 847
sappy
young 127
juicy 333
foolish 499
sarà sarà, che – 601
saraband 840
sarcasm
disrespect 929
censure 932
detraction 934
sarcastic 856, 895
sarcoma 250
sarcophagus 363
sarculation 103
sard 847
Sardanapalus 954*a*
sardonic 932, 934
– grin
laughter 838
ridicule 856
discontent 932
sardonyx 847
sark 225
sartorial 225
Sarum, old – 893
sash 247
Satan **978**
satanic
malevolent 907
vicious 945
diabolic 978
satchel 191
sate 869
satellite
companion 88
follower 281
heavenly body 318
auxiliary 711
servant 746
satiate 957
satiety
sufficient 639
pleasant 829
cloy 869
satin 255
satire 521, 856, 932
satirical 546, 932
detraction 934
satirist 936
satis: jam – 869
– superque 641
satisfaction
[see satisfy]
duel 720
pleasure 827
atonement 952
hail with – 931
satisfactorily 618
satisfactory 648
satisfy *answer* 462
convince 484
sufficient 639
consent 762
observance 772
pay 807
gratify 829
content 831
satiate 869
reward 973
– an obligation 926
– oneself 484
satrap 745
saturate *fill* 52
moisten 339
satiate 869
Saturn 979
saturnalia
disorder 59
games 840
intemperance 954
Saturnian 829, 946
– age 734
Saturnia regna 734, 827
saturnine 837
satyr *ugly* 846
libertine 962
demon 980
sauce *adjunct* 39
mixture 41
food 298
condiment 393
impertinence 885
abuse 908
– boat 191
pay – for all 807
sauce piquante 829
sauce-box 887
saucer 191
– eyes 441
saucepan 191
saucy 885, 895
saunter 133, 266, 275
sausage 298
saute aux yeux, cela – 525
sauvage 893
sauve qui peut
run away 623
alarm 669
haste 684
cowardice 862
savage *violent* 173
vulgar 851
brave 861
boorish 876
angry 900
malevolent 907
evil-doer 913
savanna 344
savant 490, 492
save *subduct* 38
exclude 55
except 83
store 636
preserve 670
deliver 672
economize 817
God – 990
– one's bacon 671
– and except 83
– money 817
– the necessity 927*a*
– us 707
save-all 817
saving 817
– clause 469
– one's presence 928
savings 636, 817
saviour 912
Saviour 976
savoir: – faire 698, 852
– gré 916
– vivre *skill* 698
fashion 852
sociality 892
savour 390
– of *resemble* 17
– of the reality 780
savouriness **394**
savourless 391
savoury 394
saw *cut* 44
jagged 257
maxim 496
– the air
gesture 550
sawbuck 800
sawder, soft –
flattery 933
sawdust 330
sawney 501

sax-horn 417
Saxon
style 576, 578
saxophone 417
say *nearly* 32
assert 535
speak 560, 582
you don't – so 870
go without –ing 525
have one's – 535, 582
that is to – 522
what do you – to that 870
– by heart 505
– no 489
– nothing 585
– to oneself 589
– one's prayers 990
– what comes uppermost 612
saying 496, 535
sbirro 965
scabbard 191
throw away the –
resolution 604
war 722
scabby 940
scabrous 256
scaffold
support 215
preparation 673
execution 975
scagliola 545
scalawag 193
scald *burn* 384
poet 597
scale *transcend* 31
portion 51
series 69
term 71
slice 204
skin 223
mount 305
weigh 319
gamut 413
measure 466
hold the –s 480
turn the –
reversion 145
influence 175
counter evidence 468
motive 615
hold the –s even 922
–s of justice 922
– the heights 305
– the walls 716
–s falling from the eyes 441, 529
scalene 243
scallop 248, 257
scalp 226
scalpel 253
scamble 44
scamp *neglect* 460
shirk 603
rascal 949
scamped *sham* 545
scamper *speed* 274
– off 623
scampish 945
scan *see* 441
attend to 457
inquire 461
know 490
prosody 597
scandal *news* 532
obloquy 934
scandaleuse, chronique – 934
scandalize 932
scandal-monger 532
scandalous 874, 945
scandalum magnatum
infamy 874
detraction 934
accusation 938
scandent 305
scansion 597
scant *small* 32
few 103
little 193
narrow 203
insufficient 640
scantling *model* 22
scrap 32
dimensions 192
scanty [*see* scant]
scape 671
scapegoat 147, 952
scapegrace 863, 949
Scapin 548, 941
scapulary 999
scar *shore* 342
record 551
blemish 848
scarab 993
scaramouch 844
scarce
few 103, 137, 640
make oneself – 187, 623
scarcely 32
– any 103
– anything 643
– ever 137
scarcity 103
scare 860
scarecrow 846, 860
scarf 225, 999
scarfskin 223
scarify *notch* 257
torment 830
scarlet 434
– Lady 984
scarp *oblique* 217
defence 717
scathe 649, 659
scatheless 650
scatter *derange* 61
disperse 73
diverge 291
– to the winds
destroy 162
confute 479
scatterbrained 458, 503
scatterling 268
scavenger 652
scenario 594, 626
scene
appearance 448
painting 559
drama 599
excitement 825
– of action 728
look behind the –s 461
scene-painter 559
scene-painting 556
scenery 448, 599
scenic 599, 882
– railway 840
scenography 556
scent *smell* 398
discovery 480a
disbelieve 485
knowledge 490
sign 550
trail 551
get – of 527
put on a new – 279
on the – 622
throw off the – 623
on the right – 462
– from afar 510
scent-bag 400
scent-bottle 400
scented 400
scentless 399
sceptre 747
sway the – 737
schedule 86
schematist 626
scheme *draft* 554
plan 626
schemer 626
scherif 745, 875
scherzo 415
schesis 7
schism *dissent* 489
discord 713
heterodoxy 984
schismless 983a
schistose 204
scholar 492, 541
scholarly 539
scholarship
knowledge 490
learning 539
distinction 873
scholastic
knowledge 490
teaching 537
learning 539
school 542
scholiast 492, 522
scholium 496, 522
school
herd 72
multitude 102
system of opinions 484
knowledge 490
teaching 537
academy 542
painting 556
go to – 539
send to – 537
schoolboy 129, 541
familiar to every – 490
schooldays 127
schoolfellow 541
schoolgirl 129, 541
schoolman 492, 983
schoolmaster 540
– abroad 490, 537
schoolroom 191
schooner 273
schottische 840
sciatica 378
science 490, 698
scientific *exact* 494
scientist 476, 492
scimitar 727
scintilla *small* 32
spark 420, 423
scintillate 446, 873
scintillation
heat 382
light 420
wit 842
scintillula forsan, latet – 858
sciolism 491

sciolist 493
sciomachy 497
Sciomancy 511
scion *part* 51
child 129
posterity 167
scire: – facias 461
– quid valeant humeri 698
scission 44
scissors 253
– and paste 609
scissure 198
sclerotics 195
scobs 330
scoff *ridicule* 856
deride 929
impiety 988
– at *despise* 930
censure 932
scold *shrew* 901
malediction 908
censure 932
scollop 248, 257
sconce *top* 210
candlestick 423
brain 450
defence 717
mulct 974
scone 298
scoop
depression 252
perforator 262
scooter 272
scope *degree* 26
opportunity 134
extent 180
meaning 516
freedom 748
scorch
rush 274
heat 382, 384
scorching
violent 173
score
music 60, 415
count 85
list 86
twenty 98
notch 257
furrow 259
mark 550
success 731
credit 805
debt 806
accounts 811
on the – of
relation 9
motive 615
scores *many* 102
scoriæ *ash* 384
dirt 653
scorify 384
scoring board 551
scorn 930
scorpion
painful 830
evil-doer 913
(*bane* 663)
chastise with –s 739
scorse 794
scot *reward* 973
scot free *free* 748
cheap 815
exempt 927*a*
escape –
escape 671
let off – 970
scotch *notch* 257
injure 659
– the snake
maim 158
insufficient 640
non-completion 730
– the wheel 706
scotomy 443
Scotsman
canny 702
Scotticism 563
scoundrel 913, 949
scour *run* 274
rub 331
clean 652
– the country 266
– the plain 274
scourge *bane* 663
painful 830
punish 972
instrument of punishment **975**
– of the human race 913
scourings 645
scout 234
observer 444
feeler 463
messenger 534
reject 610
warship 726
servant 746
watch 664
warning 668
disrespect 929
disdain 930
(*looker* 444)
(*underrate* 483)
(*ridicule* 856)
scow 273
scowl
complain 839
frown 895
anger 900
sullen 901*a*
disapprobation 932
scrabble
unmeaning 517
scribble 590
scrag 32, 203
scraggy *lean* 193, 203
rough 256
scramble
confusion 59
climb 305
pursue 622
haste 684
difficulty 704
contend 720
seize 789
scranch 330
scrannel 643
scrap 32, 720
– of paper 158, 940
scrap-book 596
scrape *subduct* 38
reduce 195
pulverize 330
abrade 331
mezzotint 558
difficulty 704
mischance 732
bow 894
– together
assemble 72
acquire 775
scraper 652
scratch *groove* 259
abrade 331
mark 550
daub 555
draw 556
write 590
hurt 619
wound 649
come to the – 720, 861
mere – 209
old – 978
up to the – 861
without a – 654, 670
– the head 461
– out 552
scrawl 590
scrawny 203
screak 411
scream *cry* 411, 839
screech 411, 412
screech owl 412
screed 582, 593
screen *sift* 60
sieve 260
shade 424
cinema 448
hide 528
hider 530
side-scene 599
clean 652
safety 664
shelter 666
defence 717
– from sight 442
screw *fasten* 43
fastening 45
distort 243
oar 267
rotation 312
instrument 633
miser 819
put on the – 739, 744
– one's courage to the sticking place 861
– loose *insane* 503
imperfect 651
unskilful 699
hindrance 706
attack 713
– up *fasten* 43
strengthen 159
prepare 673
– up the eyes 443
screw-driver 633
screwed
drunk 959
screw-steamer 273
scribble 517, 590
scribbler 593
scribe *recorder* 553
writer 590, 593
priest 996
–s and Pharisees 988
scribendi, cacoëthes – 580
scrimshanker 603
scrimmage 713, 720
scrimp *short* 201
insufficient 640
stingy 819
scrip 191
script 590, 599
scripta, lex – 963
scriptæ, literæ – 590
scriptural 983*a*
Scripture
certain 474
revelation 985
scrivener *writer* 590
lawyer 968

scroll 86, 551
scrub *rub* 331
bush 367
clean 652
dirty person 653
commonalty 876
scrubby *small* 193
trifling 643
stingy 819
disreputable 874
vulgar 876
shabby 940
scruff 235
scruple
small quantity 32
weight 319
doubt 485
reluctance 603
probity 939
scrupulous
careful 459
incredulous 487
exact 494
reluctant 603
fastidious 868
punctilious 939
scrutator 461
scrutiny 457, 461
scrutoire 191
scud *sail* 267
speed 274
shower 348
cloud 353
– under bare poles 704
scuffle 720
scull *row* 267
brain 450
scull-cap 225
scullery 191
scullion 746
sculpsit 558
sculptor 559
sculpture 240, **557**
scum *dirt* 653
– of the earth 949
– of society 876
scupper 350
scurf 653
scurrilous
ridicule 856
malediction 908
disrespect 929
detraction 934
scurry 274, 684
scurvy
insufficient 640
unimportant 643
base 940
wicked 945
scut 235
scutcheon
standard 550
honour 877
scutiform 251
scuttle *destroy* 162
receptacle 191
speed 274
– along *haste* 684
Scylla and Charybdis, between –
danger 665
difficulty 704
Scyllam, incidit in – 699
scythe *pointed* 244
sharp 253
'sdeath! *wonder* 870
anger 900
disapprobation 932
se non è vero è ben trovato 546
sea *multitude* 102
ocean 341
at – 341
uncertain 475
erroneous 495
go to – 293
on the high –s 341
heavy – 315
the seven –s 341
– of doubt 475
– of troubles
difficulty 704
adversity 735
seaboard 342
seafarer 269
seafaring 267, 273
sea-fight 720
sea-girt 346
sea-going 267, 341
sea-green 435
seal
matrix 22
close 261
evidence 467
mark 550
resolve 604
complete 729
compact 769
security 771
break the – 529
under – 769
– the doom of 162
– one's infamy 940
– the lips 585
– of secrecy 528
– up *restrain* 751
sealed:
one's fate is – 601
hermetically – 261
– book
ignorance 491
unintelligible 519
secret 533
sealing-wax 356
seals *insignia* 747
sealskin 223
seam 43
sea-maid 979
sea-man 269
seamanship 692, 698
sea-mark 550
seamless 50
seamstress 225, 690
seamy side 651
séance 525, 696
sea-piece 556
seaplane 273, 726
sea-port 666
sear *dry* 340
burn 384
deaden 823
– and yellow leaf 128, 659
search *inquire* 461
searching
severe 739
painful 830
searchless 519
searchlight 423, 726
seared conscience 951
searing 830
seascape 556
sea-serpent 83
seaside 342
season *mix* 41
time 106
pungent 392
accustom 613
preserve 670
prepare 673
seasonable 23, 134
seasoning 393
seasons 138
seat *place* 183
locate 184
abode 189
support 215
posterior 235
parliament 693
country – 189
judgment – 966
– of government 737
– of war 728
seated, firmly – 150
seaway 180
seaweed 367
seaworthy 273, 664
sebaceous 355
secant 219
secede *dissent* 489
relinquish 624
disobey 742
seceder
heterodox 984
secern 297
seclusion **893**
second
duplication 90
– *of time* 108
instant 113
– *in music* 413, 415
abet 707
play or sing a – 416
– best 651, 732
– childhood 128, 499
– crop 168, 775
– edition 104
play – fiddle
obey 743
subject 749
disrepute 874
– nature 613
– to none 33
one's – self 17
– rate 659
– sight
foresight 510
sorcery 992
– thoughts
sequel 65
thought 451
improvement 658
– youth 660
secondary
inferior 34
following 63
imperfect 651
deputy 759
– education 537
– evidence 467
– school 542
seconder 711
second-hand
imitation 19
old 124
deteriorated 659
received 785
secondly 90
second-rate 651
secret *key* 522
latent 526
hidden 528
riddle **533**

in the – 490
keep a – 585
– motive 615
– passage 627, 671
– place 530
– writing 590
secrétaire 191
secretary
recorder 553
writer 590
director 694
auxiliary 711
servant 746
consignee 758
– of state 694
– of the treasury 801
secrete *excrete* 297
conceal 528
secretion 299
secretive 528
sect 75
religious – 983, 984
sectarian
dissent 489
ally 711
heterodox 984
sectary 489
section *division* 44
part 51
class 75
chapter 593
troops 726
sector *part* 51
circle 247
secula seculorum, in – 112
secular
centenary 98
periodic 138
laity 997
– education 537
secularism 984
secundum artem 82, 698
secure *fasten* 43
bespeak 132
belief 484
safe 664
restrain 751
engage 768
gain 775
confident 858
– an object 731
securities 802–805
security *safety* 664
pledge 771
hope 858
lend on – 787
Sedan
disaster 162
sedan chair 272
sedate
thoughtful 451
calm 826
grave 837
sedative 174, 662
sedentary 265
sedge 367
sedile 1000
sediment *dregs* 653
sedimentary 40
sedition 742
seduce *entice* 615
love 897
debauch 961
seducer 962
seduction 829, 865
sedulous 682, 865
see *view* 441
look 457
believe 484
know 490
bishopric 995
we shall – 507
– after 459
– daylight 480*a*
– double 959
– fit 600, 602
– at a glance 498
– justice done 922
– life 840
– the light
born 359
published 531
– service 722
– sights 455
– through 480*a*, 498
– to *attention* 457
care 459
direction 693
– one's way
foresight 510
intelligible 518
skill 698
easy 705
seed *small* 32
cause 153
posterity 167
grain 330
run to – *age* 128
lose health 659
sow the – 673
seedling 129
seed-plot 168, 371
seed-time of life 127
seedy *weak* 160
disease 655
deteriorated 659
exhausted 688
needy 804
seeing that 8, 476
seek *inquire* 461
pursue 622
offer 763
request 765
– safety 664
seek-sorrow 837
seel 217
seem 448
as it –s good to 600
seeming 448
seemingly 472
seemless 846, 925
seemliness 926
seemly
expedient 646
handsome 845
due 924
seep 295
seer *veteran* 130
madman 504
oracle 513
sorcerer 994
see-saw 12, 314
seethe *wet* 339
hot 382
make hot 384
excitement 824
seething caldron 386
segar 392
segment 44, 51
segnitude 683
s'égosiller 411
segregate
not related 10
separate 44
exclude 55
segregated
incoherent 47
seigneur, grand –
pride 878
insolence 885
seignior 745, 875
seigniority
authority 737
possession 777
property 780
seigniory 737
seine net 232
seisin 777, 780
seismic 314
seismograph 553
seismometer 276, 314
seize 789, 791
– an opportunity 134
seized with
disease 655
feeling 821
seizure 925
sejunction 44
seldom 137
select *choose* 609
good 648
self 13, 79
–abasement 879
–accusing 950
–admiration 880
–applause 880
–appointed task 602
–assertion 885
–called 565
–command 604, 864
–communing 451
–complacency 836, 880
–confidence 880
–conquest 604
–conscious 855
–consultation 451
–contained 52
–control 604
–conviction
belief 484
penitent 950
condemned 971
–counsel 451
–deceit *error* 495
–deception 486
–defence 717
–delusion 486
–denial
disinterested 942
temperance 953
penance 990
–discipline 990
–effacement 879, 942
–esteem 880
–evident 474, 525
–examination 990
–existing 1
–government 748
–help 698
–immolation 991
–indulgence
selfishness 943
intemperance 954
–interest 943
–knowledge 881
–love 943
–luminous 423
–mastery 604
–opinioned 481
–possession

sanity 502
resolution 604
inexcitability 826
caution 864
–praise 880
–preservation 717
–reliance
resolution 604
hope 858
courage 861
–reproach 950
–respect 878
–restraint 953
–sacrifice 942
–satisfied 880
–seeking 943
–styled 565
–sufficient 880
–taught 490
–tormentor 837
–will 606
selfishness 943
self-same 13
sell *convince* 484
absurdity 497
deception 545
untruth 546
sale 796
– for 812
– one's life dearly 719, 722
– off 796
– oneself 940
– out 796
seller 796
selon les règles 82
selvedge 231
semaphore 550
semblance
similarity 17
imitation 19
copy 21
probability 472
wear the – of
appearance 448
semeiology 522
semeiotics 550
semester 108
semi- 91
semi-barbarian 913
semibreve 413
semicircle 247
semicircular 245
semicolon 142
semi-diaphanous 427
semi-fluid 352
semi-liquidity 352
semi-lunar 245
seminal 153
seminary 542
semination 673
semi-opaque 427
semi-pellucid 427
semiquaver 413
semitone 413
semi-transparency 427
sempervirent 110
sempiternal 112
sempstress 225, 690
senary 98
senate 696
senate-house 966
senator 695, 696
senatorship 693
senatus consultum 741
send 270, 284
– adrift 597
– away
repel 289
eject 297
refuse 764
– for 741
– forth 284, 531
– a letter to 592
– off 284
– out *eject* 297
– packing 289
commission 755
– word 527
senescence 128
seneschal
director 694
master 745
servant 746
seneschalship 737
senile 128
senility 158, 659
senior *age* 128
student 541
master 745
seniores priores 62, 280
seniority 124, 128
sennight 108
señor 373, 877
señora 374
sensation
physical sensibility 375
emotion 821
wonder 870
sensational 574, 824
sensation drama 599
sensations of touch 380
sense 498, 516
deep – 821
horse – 498
in no – 565
accept in a particular – 522
– of duty 926
senseless
insensible 376
absurd 497
foolish 499
unmeaning 517
senses
external - 375
intellect 450
sanity 502
sensibility 375, 822
sensible
material 316
wise 498
sensitive 375, 822
sensorial 821
sensorium 450
sensual 377, 954
sensualist 954a
sensuous
sensibility 375
pleasure 377
feeling 821
sentence
decision 480
maxim 496
affirmation 535
phrase 566
condemnation 971
sententious 572, 574
sentient 375, 821
sentiment 453
sentimental
sensitive 822
affected 855
sentinel } 263
sentry } 263
guardian 664
watch 668
keeper 753
separate *disjoin* 44
exclude 55
bisect 91
diverge 291
divorce 905
– the chaff from the wheat
discriminate 465
select 609
– into elements 49
– maintenance 905
separation 44
separatist 489, 984
sepia 433
seposition 44, 55
sepoy 726
sept *kin* 11
class 75
clan 166
Septentrional 237
septet 415
septic 655, 657
septicæmia 655
septuagenarian 98
Septuagint 985
septum 228
sepulchral
interment 363
resonance 408
stridor 410
hoarse 581
sepulchre 363
whited – 545
sepulture 363
sequacious 63
sequacity *soft* 324
tenacity 327
sequel 65, 117
sequela 65, 154
sequence
- *in order* 63
- *in time* 117
motion 281
logical – 476
sequent 63
sequester 789, 974
sequestered 893
sequestrate
seize 789
condemn 971
confiscate 974
sequin 847
serac 383
seraglio 961
seraph 948, 977
seraphic
blissful 829
virtuous 944
pious 987
seraphina 417
seraskier 745
sere and yellow leaf 128
serein 339, 348
serenade *music* 415
compliment 894
endearment 902
serene
pellucid 425
calm 826
content 831
imperturbable 871
– highness 877
serf *slave* 746
clown 876
serfdom 749
sergeant 745

serial
continuous 69
periodic 138
book 593
seriatim
in order 58
continuously 69
each to each 79
slowly 275
series 69, 84
sérieux, take au – 843
serio-comic 853
serious *great* 31
resolved 604
important 642
dejected 837
seriously 535
serjeant:
common – 967
-at-law 968
sermon *lesson* 537
speech 582
dissertation 595
pastoral 998
funeral – 363
sermonizer 584
seroon 72
serosity 333, 337
serpent
tortuous 248
snake 366
hiss 409
wind instrument 417
wise 498
deceiver 548
cunning 702
evil-doer 913
knave 941
demon 949
the old – 978
great sea – 515
serpentine 248
serrated 244, 257
serried 72, 321
serum 333, 337
servant *instrumentality* 631
help 711
retainer 746
– of all work 690
serve *benefit* 618
business 625
utility 644
aid 707
warfare 722
obey 743
servant 746
– an apprenticeship 539
– faithfully 743
– loyally 743
– notice 527
– out 972
– one right
retaliation 718
right 922
punish 972
– as a substitute 147
– one's turn 644
– with a writ 969
service *good* 618
utility 644
use 677
warfare 722
servitude 749
worship 990
rite 998
hold – 363
at one's – 763
press into the – 677
render a – 644, 906
serviceable 644, 648
serviette 652
servile 749, 876, 886
servitor 746
servitorship 749
servitude 749
penal – 972
sesame, open – 260
watchword 550
spell 993
sesqui- 87
sesquipedalia verba 577
sesquipedalian 200
sess 812
sessile 46
session *council* 696
sessions *law* 966
sestet 597
set
condition 7
join 43
coherence 46
group 72
class 75
firm 150
tendency 176
place 184
form 240
sharpen 253
direction 278
go down 306
dense 321
stage 599
habit 613
prepare 673
gang 712
impose 741
make a dead – at 716
– about 66, 676
– abroach 73
– one's affections on 897
– afloat 153, 531
– against
oppose 708
quarrel 713
hate 898
angry 900
– against one another 464
– agoing
impulse 276
propulsion 284
aid 707
– apart
separate 44
exclude 55
select 609
– aside
displace 185
disregard 458
neglect 460
negative 536
reject 610
disuse 678
annul 756
refuse 764
not observe 773
relinquish 782
dereliction 927
– one's back up 878
– before
inform 527
choice 609
– before oneself 620
– by 636
– one's cap at 897, 902
– on a cast 621
– down [*see below*]
– by the ears 898
– at ease 831
– an example
model 22
motive 615
– the eyes on 441
– one's face against
oppose 708
refuse 764
disapprove 932
– the fashion
influence 175
authority 737
fashion 852
– fast 704
– on fire
ignite 384
excite 824
– on foot 66
– foot on 294
– forth *show* 525
assert 535
describe 594
– forward 293
– free 750
– going
[*see* – agoing]
– one's hand to 467
– one's heart upon 604, 865
– at hazard 665
– in *begin* 66
rain 348
– on its legs 150
– on one's legs 159, 660
– in motion 264, 677
– to music 416
– at naught
make light of 483
reject 610
oppose 708
defy 715
disobey 742
not observe 773
dereliction 927
– no store by 483, 930
– off
compensation 30
depart 293
improve 658
discount 813
adorn 845
display 882
– on 615
– in order 60
– out *arrange* 60
begin 66
depart 293
decorate 845
display 882
– over 755
– phrase 566
– a price 85, 812
– purpose 620
– at rest *end* 67
answer 462
adjudge 480
complete 729
compact 769

– right
inform 527
disclose 529
teach 537
reinstate 660
vindicate 937
– to rights 60
– sail 293
– the seal on 729
– one's seal to 467
– store by 642
– straight 246, 723
– the table in a roar 840
– one's teeth 604
– terms
manifest 525
phrase 566
style 574
– a trap for 545
– to 720, 722
– in towards 286
– up
printing 54
originate 153
strengthen 159
produce 161
upright 212
raise 307
successful 731
prosperous 734
– up shop 676
– upon
resolved 604
attack 716
desirous 865
– too high a value upon 482
– watch 459
– one's wits to work *think* 451
imagine 515
plan 626
– to work
undertake 676
impose 741
set-back 735
set down
record 551
unseat 756
humiliate 879
slight 929
censure 932
give one a –
confute 479
– as 484
– for 484
– a cause for hearing 969
– to 155
– in writing 551

setaceous 256
seton 662
setose 256
sett *lease* 771, 787
settee 215
setter 366
settle *regulate* 60
establish 150
be located 184
bench 215
come to rest 265
subside 306
kill 361
decide 480
choose 609
vanquish 731
consent 762
compact 769
pay 807
– accounts 807, 811
– down 131
stability 150
moderate 174
locate oneself 184
– into 144
– matters 723
– preliminaries 673
– property 781
– the question 478
– to sleep 683
– upon *give* 784
– with 807, 972
settled [*see* settle]
characteristic 5
ended 67
account – 811
– opinion 484
– purpose 620
settlement [*see* settle]
location 184
colony 188
dregs 653
compact 769
deed 771
property 780
strict – 781
settler 188
settlor 784
seven 98
–league boots 274, 992
wake the – sleepers 404
seventy 98
sever 38, 44
several *special* 79
plural 100
many 102

– times 104
severalize 465
severally 44, 79
severalty 44
severance 38
severe
energetic 171
symmetry 242
exact 494
- *style* 576
harsh 739
painful 830
simple 849
critical 932
severely *very* 31
severity 739
sew 43
sewage 299, 653
sewed up
drunk 959
sewer 350, 653
sewerage 652, 653
sewer-gas 663
sewing-silk 205
sex *kind* 75
women 374
fair – 374
sexagenarian 98, 130
sexagenary 99
sextant 217, 244, 247
sextet 98
sextodecimo 593
sexton 363, 996
sextuple 98
seyyid 745
sforzando 415
shabbiness 34
shabby *trifling* 643
deteriorated 659
stingy 819
mean 874
disgraceful 940
shabby-genteel 851
shack 189
shackle
fastening 45
hinder 706
restrain 751
fetter 752
shade *degree* 26
small quantity 32
manes 362
darkness 421
shadow 424
colour 428
conceal 528
screen 530
paint 556
ghost 980

eye – 443
in the – 528, 874
shadow of a – 32, 422
throw into the –
surpass 303
conceal 528
glory 873
throw all else into the – 642
thrown into the – 34, 874
under the – of 664
without a – of doubt 474
shades:
– below 982
– of death 360
– of difference 15
– of evening 422
shading 421
– off 26
shadow
unsubstantial 4
copy 21
small 32
accompaniment 88
thin 203
be behind 235
sequence 281
dark 421
shade 424
pursue 461, 622
dream 515
demon 980
fight with a – 699
follow as a – 281
partial – 422
without a – of turning 141
worn to a –
thin 203
worse for wear 659
– of coming events 511
– forth *dim* 422
predict 511
metaphor 521
represent 554
may your – never be less
courtesy 894
respect 928
approbation 931
take the – for the substance
credulous 486
mistake 495
unskilful 699

under the – of
one's wing 664
shadowy 4, 447
shady 874
shaft *deep* 208
frame 215
pit 260
missile 284
axis 312
air-pipe 351
handle 633
weapon 727
shaggy 256
shagreen 223
shah 745
shake *totter* 149
weak 160
vibrate 314
agitation 315
shiver 383
trill 407
music 416
dissuade 616
injure 659
impress 821
excited 824
fear 860
– one's faith 485
– hands
pacification 723
friendship 888
courtesy 894
forgive 918
– the head
dissent 489
deny 536
refuse 764
disapprove 932
– off 297
– off the yoke 750
– to pieces 162
– one's sides 838
– up 315
shakedown *bed* 215
shakes, no great –
643, 651
shako 225, 717
shaky *weak* 160
in danger 665
fearful 860
shallop 273
shallow
not deep 32, 209
ignorant 491
ignoramus 493
foolish 499
trifling 643
– pretext 617
– profundity 855
shallow-brain 501
shallowness 209
shallow-pated 499
shallows
danger 667
sham *imitation* 19
falsehood 544
deception 545,
546
– fight 720
shaman 994
shamanism 992
shamble 275, 315
shambles 361
shame
disrepute 874
wrong 923
censure 932
chastity 960
cry – upon 932
false – 855
for – 874
sense of – 879
– the devil 939
to one's – be it
spoken 874
shamefaced 881
shameful
disgraceful 874
profligate 945
shameless
bold 525
impudent 885
profligate 945
indecent 961
shampoo 652
shandredhan 272
shanghai 791
shank *support* 215
instrument 633
Shanks's mare 266
shanty 189
shape 240, 448
– one's course
direction 278
pursuit 622
conduct 692
– out a course 626
shapeless 241, 846
shapely 242, 845
shard 51
share
part 51
participate 778
allotted portion
786
– and share alike
778
shareholder 778
shark 792
sharp
energetic 171
violent 173
acute 253
sensible 375
pungent 392
- *sound* 410
musical tone 413
intelligent 498
active 682
clever 698
cunning 702
feeling 821
painful 830
rude 895
censorious 932
look – 459, 682
– appetite 865
– contest 720
– ear 418
– eye 441
– fellow 682, 700
– frost 383
– look-out 459,
507
– pain 378
– practice
cunning 702
severity 739
improbity 940
– set 865
sharpen
[see sharp]
excite 824
– one's tools 673
– one's wits 537
sharpener 253
sharper 792
sharpness 253
sharpshooter 726
sharpshooting 716
Shaster 986
shatter *disjoin* 44
disperse 73
render powerless
158
destroy 162
shatter-brained 503
shattered 160, 688
shave *reduce* 195
shorten 201
layer 204
smooth 255
cut 44
lie 546
close – 671
shaved 226
shaving *small* 32
layer 204
filament 205
shave-tail 726, 745
shawl 225
shawm 417
shay 272
she 374
sheaf 72
shear *reduce* 195
shorten 201
sheep 370
take 789
shears 253
sheath 191, 223
sheathe 225
moderate 174
– the sword 723
sheathing 223
sheave 633
shed *scatter* 73
building 189
divest 226
emit 297
give 784
– blood 361
– light upon 420
– a lustre on 873
– tears 839
Shedim 980
sheen 420
sheep 366
sheep-dog 366
sheep-fold 232
sheepish 881
sheep's eye, cast a –
desire 865
modest 881
endearment 902
sheer *simple* 42
complete 52
deviate 279
– off *avoid* 623
sheet *layer* 204
covering 223
paper 593
come down in –s
rain 348
white – 952
winding – 363
– of fire 382
of water 343
sheet-anchor
safety 664, 666
hope 858
sheet-lightning 423
sheik *ruler* 745, 875
lover 897
priest 996
shelf 215, 667
on the –
powerless 158
disused 678
inaction 681
shell *cover* 223
coffin 363
bombard 716
bomb 727

-burst 404
-shock 655
- out 784, 807, 809
shellac 356*a*
shellback 269
shell-fish 366
shelter 664, 666
- oneself under plea of 617
sheltie 271
shelve *defer* 133
locate 184
slope 217
neglect 460
disuse 678
shelving beach 217
shend 659
shepherd *tender of sheep* 370
director 694
pastor 996
Shepherd, the Good - 976
shepherd's dog 366
Sheppard, Jack - 792
shere 32
sheriff 745, 965
Shetland pony 271
shew [*see* show]
shibboleth 550
shield
heraldry 550
safety 664
buckler 666
defend 717
scutcheon 877
look only at one side of the - 481
reverse of the - 235, 468
under the - of 664
shift *change* 140
convert 144
substitute 147
changeable 149
chemise 225
move 264
transfer 270
deviate 279
prevaricate 546
plea 617
cunning 702
last - 601
make a - with 147, 677
put to one's -s 704, 804
- one's ground 607
- off *defer* 133
- for oneself 692, 748
left to - for oneself 893
- one's quarters 264
- the scene 140
- to and fro 149
shifting [*see* shift]
transient 111
- sands 149
- trust or use 783
shiftless 674, 699
shillelagh 727
shilling 800
cut off with a - 789
- shocker 594
shilly-shally 605
shimmer 420
shimmy
dance 840
shindy 720
shine *light* 420
beauty 845
glory 873
take the - out of 874
- in conversation 588
- forth 873
- upon
illumine 420
aid 707
shingle 330
shingled
hair 53
shingles 223
shining [*see* shine]
- light *sage* 500
Shintoism 984
shiny 420
ship *lade* 190
transfer 270
vessel 273
take - 267, 293
one's - coming in 803
- of the line 726
shipboard, on - 273
ship-load 31, 190
shipman 269
shipmate 890
shipment
contents 190
transfer 270
shippen 189
shipping 273
shipshape *order* 58
conformity 82
skill 698
shipwreck
destruction 162
vanquish 731
failure 732
shire 181
shirk 603, 623, 742
shirker 862
shirt 225
Shiva 979
shive 32, 204
shiver
small piece 32
divide 44
destroy 162
filament 205
shake 315
brittle 328
cold 383
fear 860
go to -s 162
- in one's shoes 860
shivery *brittle* 328
powdery 330
shoal
assemblage 72
multitude 102
shallow 209
shoals *danger* 667
surrounded by -
difficulty 704
shoat 366
shock *sheaf* 72
violence 173
concussion 276
agitation 315
unexpected 508
disease 655
discord 713
affect 821
move 824
pain 828
give pain 830
dislike 867
scandalize 932
shocking *bad* 649
painful 830
ugly 846
vulgar 851
fearful 860
disreputable 874
hateful 898
in a - temper 901*a*
shockingly *much* 31
shod 225
shoddy 645
shoe *support* 215
dress 225
hindrance 706
stand in the -s of
commission 755
deputy 759
where the - pinches
badness 649
difficulty 704
opposition 708
sensibility 822
painful 830
shoemaker 225
shofle 272
shoful 792
shog 173
shoneen 855
shoot
offspring 167
expand 194
dart 274
propel 284
kill 361
sprout 365, 367
pain 378
execute 972
teach the young idea to - 537
- ahead 282
- ahead of 303
- at 716
- out beams 420
- up *increase* 35
prominent 250
shooting
[*see* shoot]
chase 622
- pain 378
- star 318, 423
shooting-coat 225
shop 795, 799
keep a - 625, 794
shut up - *end* 67
cease 142
relinquish 624
rest 687
smell of the - 851
shopkeeper 797
shoplifter 792
shoplifting 791
shopman 797
shopmate 890
shopping 794, 795
shore
support 215
border 231
land 342
buttress 717
hug the - 286
on - 342
- up 215, 670
shoreless 180
shorn *cut short* 201
deprived 776

- of its beams 422, 874
- lamb 828
short
not long 201
brittle 328
concise 572
uncivil 895
come - of, fall - of
inferior 34
shortcoming 304
insufficient 640
in - 572, 596
- allowance 640
- answer 895
- breath 688
- by 201
- of cash 804
- commons
insufficiency 640
fasting 956
- circuit 279, 628
- cut *straight* 246
mid-course 628
- distance 197
- life and merry 840
- measure 53
at - notice 111, 132
- of *small* 32
inferior 34
subtraction 38
incomplete 53
shortcoming 304
insufficient 640
- sea 348
make - work of
destroy 162
active 682
haste 684
complete 729
conquer 731
punish 972
shortage 53
shortcoming
inequality 28
inferiority 34
motion short of 304
non-completion 730
deficiency 945
shorten 201
- sail 275
shorthand 590
short-handed 651
shorthorn 366
short-lived 111
shortly *soon* 132
shortness 201

for - sake 572
shorts 225
short-sighted
myopic 443
misjudging 481
foolish 499
short-story 594
short-winded 160, 688
short-witted 499
shot *missile* 284
report 406
variegated 440
guess 514
war material 722, 727
price 812
reward 973
bad - 701
exchange -s 720
good - 700
have a - at 716
like a - 113
off like a - 623
pistol - 406
random - 463, 621
round - 727
- in the locker 632
not have a - in one's locker 804
- and shell 722
shot-free 815
shot-gun 727
should be:
no better than she - 961
what - 922
shoulder
support 215
projection 250
shove 276
broad -ed 159
cold - 289
have on one's -s 625
on the -s of
high 206
elevated 307
instrumentality 631
shrug the -s [*see* shrug]
rest on the -s of 926
rub -s with nobility 852
take upon one's -s 676
- arms 673
- a musket 722
- to shoulder 709, 712
- to the wheel 604, 676
shoulder-knot 847
shoulder-strap 747
shout
loud 404
cry 411
rejoice 838
shove 276
give a - to
aid 707
shovel
receptacle 191
transfer 270
vehicle 272
fire-iron 386
cleanness 652
put to bed with a - 363
- away 297
shovel-hat 999
show *visible* 446
appear 448
draw attention 457
evidence 467
demonstrate 478
manifest 525
entertainment 599
parade 882
dumb - 550
make a - 544
mere - 544
peep- 840
- off 525
- one's cards 529
- cause 527
- one's colours, 550
- one's face
presence 186
manifest 525
disclose 529
- fight *defy* 715
attack 716
defend 717
brave 861
- forth 525
- in front 303
- one's cards 529
- one's hand 529
- a light pair of heels 623
- itself 446
- of 17, 472
- off 882, 884
- one's teeth 715
- up *visible* 446
manifest 525
ridicule 856

degrade 874
censure 932
accuse 938
shower
assemblage 72
rain 348
- bath 386
- down
abundance 639
- down upon 784, 816
showman 524
showy *colour* 428
beauty 845
ornament 847
fashion 852
vulgar 851
ostentatious 882
shrapnel 727
shred 32, 205
shredder 260
shrew 901
shrewd
knowing 490
wise 498
cunning 702
shriek 410, 411
shrievalty 965
shrieve 965
shrift
confession 529
absolution 952
shriftless 951
shrill 410, 411
shrimp 193
shrine 363, 1000
receptacle 191
shrink
decrease 36
shrivel 195
go back 283, 287
unwilling 603
avoid 623
sensitive 822
- from *fear* 860
dislike 867
hate 898
shrive 952, 998
shrivel 195
shrivelled *thin* 203
shroud *cover* 225
funeral 363
hide 528
safety 664
defend 717
-ed in mystery 519
shrouds 45
Shrove Tuesday 998
shrub *plant* 367

plantation 371
shrug *sign* 550
– the shoulders
dissent 489
submit 725
discontent 832
dislike 867
contempt 930
disapprobation 932
shrunk 193, 195
shudder *cold* 383
fear 860
make one –
painful 830
– at *aversion* 867
hate 898
shuffle *mix* 41
derange 61
change 140
interchange 148
changeable 149
move slowly 275
agitate 315
falsehood 544
untruth 546
irresolute 605
recant 607
dance 840
improbity 940
– the cards
begin again 66
change 140
chance 621
prepare 673
patience and – the cards 826
– off *run away* 623
– off this mortal coil 360
– on 266
shuffler 548
shun 623, 867
shunt 270, 279
shunted
shelved 460
shut 261
– the door 761
– the door in one's face 764
– the door upon 893
– one's ears 419, 487
– the eyes 442
– one's eyes to
not attend to 458
neglect 460
not believe 487
permit 760
not observe 773
– the gates of mercy 914*a*
– in 751
– oneself up 893
– out 55, 761
– up shop *end* 67
cease 142
silence 403
relinquish 624
repose 687
– up *close* 261
confute 479
imprison 751
shutter 424
shuttle 314
shuttlecock 605
shy *deviate* 279
draw back 283
propel 284
avoid 623
fearful 860
cowardly 862
modest 881
fight – of 623
have a – at 716
– of belief 487
– cock 862
– of *doubtful* 485
unwilling 603
cautious 864
dislike 867
Shylock 787
Siamese twins 89
sib 11
Siberia 383
sibi gladio hunc jugulo, suo – 718
sibilation *hiss* 409
disrespect 929
disapprobation 932
Sibyl *oracle* 513
ugly 846
Sibylline 511
– leaves 513
sic *imitation* 19
exact 494
si – omnes! 948
– transit gloria mundi 111
– volo sic jubeo 600
– vos non vobis 791
siccity 340
sick *ill* 655
make one – 830, 867
visitation of the – 998
– at heart 837
– of *weary* 841
dislike 867
satiated 869
in –ness and in health 604
sick-chamber 655
sicken *nauseate* 395
disease 655
pain 830
weary 841
disgust 867
sickener
too much 641
sickle 244, 253
sickly *weak* 160
sick-room 655
side
consanguinity 11
edge 231
laterality 236
party 712
ostentation 882
at one's – 197
on every – 227
on one – 243
on one's – 714
look only at one – of the shield 481
pass from one – to another 607
take up a – 476
wrong – up 218
– by side
accompaniment 88
near 197
laterality 236
party 712
from – to side 314
– with *aid* 707
co-operate 709
concord 714
side-arms 727
side-blow 702
sideboard 191
side-car 272
side-dish 298
side-drum 417
side-kick 890
side issue 643
sideling 279
sidelong 236
sideration 158
sidereal 318
– time 114
siderite 288
Sideromancy 511
side-saddle 215
side-scene 599
sideslip 267
sidesman 996
side-track 287
sidewalk 627
sideways 217, 236
side-wind
oblique 217
circuit 629
cunning 702
sidle *oblique* 217
lateral 236
deviate 279
siege 716
lay – to 716
state of – 722
siege-train 727
siesta 683
sieve *sort* 60
perforate 260
clean 652
memory like a – 506
pour water into a – 638, 818
stop one hole in a – 819
sift *simplify* 42
sort 60
inquire 461
discriminate 465
clean 652
– the chaff from the wheat 609
sigh 405, 839
– for 865
sighing like furnace 902
sight *much* 31
multitude 102
vision 441
appearance 448
ugly 846
prodigy 872
at – 132, 441
dim – 443
in – 446
in – of 197, 441
in plain – 525
keep in – 457
within – of shore 858
sightless
blind 442
invisible 447
ugly 846
sightly 845
sights, see – 455
sightseeing 441
sightseer 444, 455
sigil *seal* 550
evidence 769
sigmoidal 248
sign *attest* 467

omen 512
indication 550
record 551
write 590
compact 769
prodigy 872
give – of 525
make no – 585
– of the cross 998
–s of the times
indication 550
omen 512
warning 668
–s of the zodiac 318
signal *great* 31
sign 550
important 642
give the – 741
– of distress 669
signalize
indicate 550
glory 873
celebrate 883
signally 31
signal oil 356
signal-post 668
signature
mark, identification 550
writing 590
compact 769
security 771
sign-board 550
signet
mark, identification 550
sign of authority 747
compact 769
writer to the – 968
significant 642
[*see* signify]
evidence 467
important 642
signifies, what – 643
signify
forebode 511
mean 516
inform 527
signior 875
sign-manual 550, 590
signor 373, 877
signora 374
sign-painter 559
sign-painting 555
sign-post 550
signum, ecce – 550
sike 348
silence *disable* 158
no sound 403
confute 479
latency 526
concealment 528
aphony 581
taciturn 585
check 731
silencer 405, 408
silentio, sub –
silent 403
inattention 458
latent 526
silhouette
outline 230, 448
shadow 421
portrait 556
siliquose 191
silk 255, 324
– gown
barrister 968
– hat 225
make a – purse out of a sow's ear 471
silken repose 687
silkiness 954
sill 215
silly
credulous 486
imbecile 499
insane 503
silo 636
silt *deposit* 321
dirt 653
silvan 367
silver *bright* 420
white 430
grey 432
money 800
bait with a – hook 615
german – 545
– lining of the cloud 858
– wedding 883
silver certificate 800
silver-toned 413
silviculture 371
simagrée 855
similarity 17
– of form 240
simile
similarity 17
comparison 464
metaphor 521
similitude 17, 21
simmer
agitation 315
boil 382, 384
excitement 824
simmering 825
simoleon 800
Simon Pure
the real – 494
Simon, Simple – 501, 547
Simon Stylites 893
simony 964
simoon 349, 382
simper *smile* 838
affectation 855
simple *mere* 32
unmixed 42
credulous 486
ignorant 493
silly 499
- *language* 576
herb 662
artless 703
unadorned 849
– meaning 516
simple-hearted 543
simpleness 42
Simple Simon 501, 547
simpleton 501
simplex munditiis 849
simplicity
[*see* simple] 849
ignorance 491
simplify
[*see* simple]
elucidate 518
simply 32, 87
more – 522
simulacrum 19
simulate
resemble 17
imitate 19
cheat 544
simultaneous 120
sin 945, 947
sinapism 662
since *under the circumstances* 8
after 117
cause 155
reason 476
sincere
veracious 543
ingenuous 703
feeling 821
sine 217
sine: – curâ 831
– die 107, 133
– ictu 158
– quâ non
required 630
important 642
condition 770
sinecure 681
no – 682
sinew 159
sunewless 158
sinews of war 800
sinful 945
sing *bird* 412
resonance 408
music 416
voice 580
poetry 597
rejoice 838
– Io triumphe 884
– out 411
– praises
approve 931
worship 990
– in the shrouds 349
– small 879
singe 382, 384
singer 416
single *unmixed* 42
unit 87
secluded 893
unmarried 904
ride at – anchor 863
– combat 720
– entry
– file 69
– out 609
single-handed
one 87
easy 705
unassisted 706
single-minded 703
singleness
[*see* single]
– of heart 703, 939
– of purpose 604*a*, 703
single-stick 720
singlet 225
Sing Sing 752
sing-song 414, 892
singular *special* 79
exceptional 83
one 87
singularly *very* 31
sinister *left* 239
bad 649
vicious 945
bar –
imperfect 651
disrepute 874
sinistrality 239
sinistromanual 239
sinistrous

left-handed 239
sullen 901a
sink *disappear* 4
destroy 162
descend 306
lower 308
submerge 310
neglect 460
conceal 528
cloaca 653
fatigue 688
vanquish 731
fail 732
adversity 735
invest 787
pain 828
depressed 837
– back 661
– of corruption 653
– into the grave 360
– of iniquity 945
– in the mind
thought 451
memory 505
excite 824
– money 809
– into oblivion 506
– or swim
certainty 474
perseverance 604a
sinking
heart – 837
– fund 802
sinless 946
sinned against than sinning, more – 946
sinner 949
Sinn Fein 742
sin-offering 952
sinuous 243, 248
sinus 252
sip *small* 32
drink 298
siphon 350
sippet 298
sir *man* 373
title 877
– Oracle 887
sirdar 745
sire 166
siren
sea-nymph 341
loud sound 404
musician 416
seducing 615
warning 668
alarm 669
evil-doer 913
demon 980
sorcerer 994
song of the –s 615
– strains 415
sirene *musical instrument* 417
siriasis 503
sirius 423
sirocco *wind* 349
heat 382
sirrah! 949
sister *kin* 11
likeness 17
nurse 662
nun 996
sisterhood
party 712
frail – 962
sisterly 906
sisters:
weird – 994
– three 601
sistrum 417
Sisyphus, task of –
useless 645
difficult 704
sit 308
– down *settle* 184
lie 213
stoop 308
– in judgment
adjudge 480
jurisdiction 965
lawsuit 969
– on 215
– on thorns
annoyance 828
fear 860
site 183, 780
sith 476
sitting [*see* sit]
incubation 673
convocation 696
– up *late* 133
work 686
sitting-room 191
situ, in – 183, 265
situation
circumstances 8
place 183
location 184
business 625
out of a – 185
Siva 979
six 98
– of one and half-a-dozen of the other 27
sixes and sevens, at – 59, 713
sixty 98
sizar 746
size *degree* 26
magnitude 31
glue 45
arrange 60
dimensions 192
viscid 352
– up 480
sizzle 409
sjambok 975
skat 840
skate
locomotion 266
vehicle 272
skating 840
skean 727
skedaddle 623
skeel 191
skein 219
tangled – 59
skeleton
remains 40
essential part 50
thin 203
support 215
corpse 362
plan 626
reduced to a – 659
– in the closet 649, 830
– at the feast 837
skelter 276
skepticism
doubt 485
incredulity 487
irreligion 989
sketch
form 240
represent 554
paint 556
describe 594
plan 626
sketcher 559
sketchy
incomplete 53
feeble 575
unfinished 730
skew 217
-bald 440
skewer 45
ski 266, 272
-running 840
-joring 840
-jumping 840
skiagraphy 421, 554, 556
skid *support* 215
hindrance 706
skies:
exalt to the – 873
praise to the – 933
skiff 273
skill 698
acquisition of – 539
game of – 840
skillet 191
skilly 298
skim *move* 266
navigate 267
rapid 274
neglect 460
summarize 596
skimp 460, 819
skimpy 640
skin *outside* 220
tegument 223
peel 226
swindle 791
fleece 814
wet to the – 339
with a whole – 670
without – 822
mere – and bone 203
– a flint 471, 819
– over 660
skin-deep
shallow 32, 209
external 220
skinned: thick- 376
thin- 375
skinny 203, 223
skip *jump* 309
neglect 460
rejoice 838
skipjack
prosperous 734
low-born 876
skipper
sea captain 269
captain 745
skippingly 70
skips, by – 70
skirmish 720
skirmisher 726
skirt
appendix 39
pendent 214
dress 225
surrounding 227
edge 231
side 236
– dance 840
skirting 231
skirts of:
hang upon the – *sequence* 281
on the – *near* 197
skit *ridicule* 856
detraction 934

prostitute 962
skittish
capricious 608
excitable 825
timid 862
bashful 881
skittle sharper 792
skittles 840
skiver 253
skulk 528, 862
skull 450
skull-cap 225
skunk 401
skurry 684
sky *summit* 210
world 318
air 338
necessity 601
sky-aspiring 865
sky-blue 438
sky-lark 305
sky-larking 840
sky-light 260
sky-line 196
sky-pilot 996
sky-rocket 305
sky-scraper 206, 210
slab *layer* 204
support 215
flat 251
viscous 352
record 551
slabber *slaver* 297
unclean 653
slack *loose* 47
weak 160
inert 172
slow 275
cool 385
fuel 388
neglectful 460
unwilling 603
insufficient 640
inactive 683
lax 738
slacken
loosen 47
moderate 174
repose 687
hinder 706
one's pace 275
slacker 460, 603, 623, 927
slag *embers* 384
inutility 645
dirt 653
slake *quench* 174
gratify 829
satiate 869
– one's appetite
intemperance 954
slam 276, 406
– the door in one's face
oppose 708
refuse 764
slammerkin 653
slander 934
slanderer 936
slang 560, 563, 908
slant 217
slap *instantly* 113
strike 276
censure 932
punish 972
– in the face
opposition 708
attack 716
anger 900
disrespect 929
disapprobation 932
– the forehead 461
slap-dash 684
slash 44, 308
slashing *style* 574
slate
writing tablet 590
election 609
disparage 932
clean the – 918
– loose *mad* 503
slate-coloured 432
slates *roof* 223
slattern
disorder 59
dirty 653
bungler 701
vulgar 851
slatternly 699
slaughter 361
slaughter-house 361
slave *instrumentality* 631
toil 686
servant 746
a – to 749
– trade 795
slaver *ship* 273
slobber 297
dirt 653
flatter 933
slavery 686, 749
slavish 749, 886
slay 361
sleave 59
sled 272
sledge 272
sledge-hammer 276
with a – 162, 686
sleek 255, 845
sleep 683
last – 360
rock to – 174
send to – 841
not have a wink of – 825
– with one eye open 459
– at one's post 683
– upon 133, 451
– walker 268
– walking 266
sleeper *support* 215
wake the seven –s 404
sleeping partner 683
sleepless 682
sleepy 683
sleet 383
sleeve *skein* 219
dress 225
hang on the – of 746
wear one's heart upon his – 525, 703
in one's – 528
laugh in one's – 838, 856
sleeveless 499, 608
– errand 645, 699
sleigh 272
sleight *skill* 698
– of hand 545
slender *small* 32
thin 203
trifling 643
– means 804
sleuth 527
– hound 913
slew round 312
slice *cut* 44
piece 51
layer 204
slick 682, 698
slicker 225
slide *elapse* 109
smooth 255
pass 264
locomotion 266
descend 306
– back 661
– in 228
– into 144
sliding 840
sliding-panel 545
sliding-rule 85
slight *small* 32
slender 203
rare 322
neglect 460
disparage 483
feeble 575
trifle 643
dereliction 927
disrespect 929
contempt 930
slight-made 203
slily
surreptitiously 544
craftily 702
slim 203
cunning 702
slime *viscous* 352
dirt 653
sling *hang* 214
project 284
weapon 727
slink *hide* 528
cowardice 862
– away *avoid* 623
disrepute 874
slip *small* 32
elapse 109
child 129
strip 205
petticoat 225
descend 306
error 495
workshop 691
fail 732
false coin 800
vice 945
guilt 947
give one the – 671
let – *liberate* 750
lose 776
relinquish 782
– away 187, 623
– cable 623
– the collar 671, 750
– 'twixt cup and lip 509
let – the dogs of war 722
– in (*or* – into) 294
– the memory 506
– on 225
– out 187
– over *neglect* 460
– of the pen 568
– of the tongue
solecism 568
stammering 583
– through the fingers *miss an opportunity* 135
escape 671

fail 732
slipper 225
hunt the – 840
slippery
transient 111
smooth 255
greasy 355
uncertain 475
vacillating 607
dangerous 665
facile 705
faithless 940
– ground 667
slipshod 575
slipslop
absurdity 497
solecism 568
weak language 575
slit *divide* 44
chink 198
furrow 259
slither 264
sliver 32
slobber *drivel* 297
slop 337
dirt 653
sloe *black* 431
slog 143
slogan 722
sloop 273
-of-war 726
slop *spill* 297
water 337
dirt 653
slope *oblique* 217
run away 623
sloppy *moist* 339
marsh 345
- *style* 575
slops *clothes* 225
slosh 337, 653
slot 44, 260
sloth 683
slouch *low* 207
oblique 217
move slowly 275
inactive 683
slouching *ugly* 846
slough
quagmire 345
dirt 653
difficulty 704
adversity 735
– of Despond 859
sloven *untidy* 59
bungler 701
slovenly *untidy* 59
careless 460
- *style* 575
dirty 653
awkward 699
vulgar 851
slow *tardy* 133
inert 172
moderate 174
motion 275
inactive 683
wearisome 841
dull 843
by – degrees 26
– movement
music 415
march in – time 275
– as molasses in January 275
be – to
unwilling 603
not finish 730
refuse 764
slow-coach 701
slowness **275**
sloyd 537
slubber 653
slubberdegullion 876
sludge 653
slug *slow* 275
inaction 681
inactivity 683
bullet 727
sluggard 275, 683
sluggish 172, 823, 843
sluice *limit* 233
egress 295
river 348
conduit 350
open the –s 297
slum 653
slumber 683
slump 304
slur *blemish* 848
stigma 874
gloss over 937
reproach 938
– over *neglect* 460
slight 483
slush *marsh* 345
semiliquid 352
dirt 653
slut *untidy* 59
female 374
dirty 653
unchaste 962
sly *stealthy* 528
cunning 702
smack
small quantity 32
mixture 41
boat 273
impulse 276
taste 390
thud 406
kiss 902
strike 972
– the lips
pleasure 377
taste 390
savoury 394
rejoice 838
– of *resemble* 17
small
– *in degree* 32
– *in size* 193
become – 195
feel – 879
of – account 643
esteem of – account 930
– arms 727
– beer 643, 880, 930
– coin 800
– chance 473
– fry 193, 643, 876
– matter 643
– number 103
– part 51
– pica 591
in the – hours 125
on a – scale 32, 193
– talk 588
small-bore 727
small-clothes 225
smaller 34, 195
smallness **32**
smalls 225
smalt 438
smart *pain* 378
active 682
clever 698
feel 821
grief 828
witty 842
pretty 845
ornamental 847
– pace 274
– saying 842
– under 821
smarten 847
smart-money 973
smash 162, 732
smasher 792
smatch 390
smatterer 493
smattering 491
smear *cover* 223
soil 653
blemish 848
smell 398
bad – 401
– of the lamp
ornate style 577
prepared 673
– powder 722
smell-feast 886
smelling-bottle 400
smelt *heat* 384
prepare 673
smicker 838
smile 836, 838
raise a – 840
– at 856
– of contempt 930
– of fortune 734
– upon *aid* 707
courtesy 894
endearment 902
smirch 431, 653
smirk 838
smite *maltreat* 649
excite 824
afflict 830
punish 972
smith 690
smithereens 162
smitten *love* 897
– with *moved* 615
smock 225, 258
smock-faced 862
smock-frock 225
smoke
dust 330
vapour 336
heat 382
tobacco 392
discover 480a
suspect 485
unimportant 643
dirt 653
cure 670
disrespect 929
end in –
shortcoming 304
failure 732
– the calumet of peace 723
–ed glasses 424
– screen 424
– stack 260
smoking hot 382
smoking-jacket 225
smoking-room 191
smoky *opaque* 426
dirty 653
smooth *uniform* 16
calm 174
flattery 213, 251
not rough 255
easy 705
– the bed of death

707, 906
– down 174
– over 174
– the ruffled brow of care 834
– sailing 705
– water *easy* 705
– the way 705
smooth-bore 727
smoothly, go on – *prosperous* 734
smoothness 255
smooth-tongued 544, 933
smother
repress 174
kill 361
stifle sound 581
restrain 751
smoulder *inert* 172
burn 382
latent 526
smous 796, 797
smudge 431, 653, 848
smug *affected* 855
smuggle
introduce 228
steal 791
illegal 964
smuggler 792
smut
dirt 653
impurity 961
smutch 431
snack
small quantity 32
food 298
snacks, go – 778
snaffle 752
snag *projection* 250
sharp 253
danger 667
hindrance 706
snail *slow* 275
snake *undulation* 248
serpent 366
hissing 409
miscreant 913
scotch the – 640
– in the grass
hidden 528
deceiver 548
bad 649
source of danger 667
evil-doer 913
knave 941
snake-like
convoluted 248
snap *break* 44
eat 298
brittle 328
noise 406
rude 895
– at *seize* 789
bite 830
censure 932
– of the fingers
trifle 643
– one's fingers at
defy 715
insolence 885
despise 930
– the thread 70
– up *seize* 789
– one up
censure 932
–shot 554
snap-dragon 840
snappish 901
snare *deception* 545
snarl *growl* 412
rude 895
angry 900
threaten 909
snatch
small quantity 32
seize 789
– at *pursue* 622
seize 789
– a grace beyond the reach of art 845
– from one's grasp 789
– from the jaws of death 662, 672
– from under one's nose 702
– a verdict 545, 702
snatches, by – 70
sneak *hide* 528
coward 862
servile 886
base 940
knave 941
bad man 949
– off, – out of 623
sneer *disparage* 929
contempt 930
blame 932
sneeze *blow* 349
snuffle 409
– at *despise* 930
sneezed at, not to be – 642
snick 32, 51
snicker 838
sniff *blow* 349
odour 398
discovery 480a
sniffle 349
snigger *laugh* 838
ridicule 856
disrespect 929
sniggle 545
snip
small quantity 32
cut 44
short 201
tailor 225
sniping 716
snippet 32
snip-snap 713
snip-snap-snorem 840
snivel *weep* 839
snivelling
servile 886
snob *vulgar* 851
plebeian 876
servile 886
snobbishness
flattery 933
snood
headdress 225
circle 247
snooker 840
Snooks, Mr. – 876
snooze 683
snore 411, 683
snort 411, 412
snout 250
snow *ship* 273
ice 383
white 430
snow-ball 72
snow-blindness 443
snow-drift 72
snow-shoe 272
snow-storm 383
snozzle 250
snub *short* 201
hinder 706
cast a slur 874
humiliate 879
bluster 885
censure 932
snub-nosed 243
snuff *blow* 349
pungent 392
odour 398
up to – 698, 702
go out like the – of a candle 360
– out 162, 421
– up 296, 398
snuff-colour 433
snuffing, want – *pert* 885
snuffle *blow* 349
hiss 409
stammer 583
hypocrisy 988
snuffy 653
snug *closed* 261
comfortable 377
safe 664
prepared 673
content 831
secluded 893
keep – 528, 893
make all – 673
snuggery 189
snugness 827
so *similar* 17
very 31
therefore 476
method 627
– be it 488, 762
– far so good 618
– let it be 681
– much the better 831, 838
– much the worse 832, 835
– to speak 17, 521
soak *immerse* 300
water 337
moist 339
drunkenness 959
– up 340
So-and-so, Mr. – *neology* 563
soap *lubricate* 332
oil 356
cleanser 652
soapy *unctuous* 355
servile 886
flattery 933
soar *great* 31
height 206
fly 267
rise 305
sob 839
sober *moderate* 174
wise 498
sane 502
style 576
grave 837
temperate 953
abstinent 958
– down 174, 502
humility 879
in – *sadness*
affirmation 535
– senses 502
– truth *fact* 494
sober-minded 502
calm 826
humble 879

sobriety 958
sobriquet 565
sob sister 534
so-called 545, 565
soc *jurisdiction* **965**
socage 777
soccer 840
sociable
carriage **272**
sociality 892
social *mankind* **372**
sociable 892
– circle 892
– evil 961
– gathering 892
– science 910
socialism
government 737
participation 778
philanthropy 910
socialist 712
sociality 892
society
mankind 372
party 712
fashion 852
sociality 892
position in – 873
Socinianism 984
sociology 910
sock *hosiery* **225**
drama 599
socket 191, 252
socle 215
Socratic method 461
sod 344
beneath the – 363
sodality 712, 888
sodden 339, 384
sofa 215
Sofi 984, 996
soft *stop!* **142**
weak 160
moderate 174
smooth 255
not hard 324
moist 339
marsh 345
silence! 403
- *sound* 405
dulcet 413
credulous 486
silly 499
lenient 740
tender 822
timid 862
own to the – impeachment 529
– music 415
– pedal 405
– sawder 617, 933
– soap 356, 933
– tongue, – words 894
soften [*see* soft]
moderate 174
relieve 834
pity 914
palliate 937
softening of the brain 158
softer sex 374
soft-hearted 914
softling 160
softness 324
persuasibility 615
soft-spoken 894
soggy 339
soho
attention 457
parley 586
hunting 622
soi-disant
asserting 535
pretender 548
misnomer 565
vain 880
boastful 884
soil *region* **181**
land 342
dirt 653
deface 846
till the – 371, 673
soirée 892
sojourn 186, 189
sojourner 188
soke 181
solace *relief* **834**
recreation 840
– oneself with *pleasure* 827
solar 318
– system 318
– time 114
solatium 973
sold to the devil 949
soldan [*see* sultan]
solder *join* **43**
cement 45
cohere 46
soldier 726
soldier-like 722, 861
sole *alone* **87**
base 211
support 215
feme – 904
solecism 568
soleil, coup de –
hot 384
mad 503
solemn
affirmation 535
important 642
grave 837
glorious 873
ostentatious 882
religious 987
worship 990
– mockery 882
– silence 403
solemnity *rite* **998**
solemnization 883
sol-fa 416
solfeggio 415
solicit *induce* **615**
request 765
desire 865
– the attention 457
solicitor *agent* **758**
petitioner 767
lawyer 968
solicitous 865
solicitude *care* **459**
pain 828
anxiety 860
desire 865
solid *complete* **52**
dense 321
certain 474
learned 490
exact 494
wise 498
persevering 604a
solvent 803
– angle 244
solidarity
party 712
solidify 321
soliloquy 589
solitaire *game* **840**
hermit 893
solitary } *alone* 87
solitude } *alone* 87
secluded 893
solmization 416
solo 87, 415
– dance 840
Solomon } *wise* 498
Solon } *wise* 498
sage 500
solstice 125, 126
soluble *fluid* **333**
liquefy 335
solus 87
solution
liquefaction 335
answer 462
explanation 522
– of continuity 70
solve *liquefy* **335**
discover 480a
unriddle 522
solvent
liquefier 335
monied 803
somatics 316
sombre *dark* **421**
black 431
grey 432
sad 837
sombrero 225
some *indefinite quantity* 25
small quantity 32
more than one 100
–body *person* 372
important or distinguished 642
in – degree
degree 26
small 32
at – other time 119
in – place 182
– ten or a dozen 102
– time ago 122
– time or other 119
somehow or other
cause 155
instrument 631
somersault 218
something *thing* **3**
small degree 32
matter 316
– else 15
– like 17
– or other 475
sometimes 136
somewhat
a little 32
a trifle 643
somewhere 182
– about 32
somnambulism
walking 266
trance 515
somnambulist
walker 268
dreamer 515
somniferous
sleepy 683
weary 841
somnolence 683
son 167
Son, God the – 976
sonant 402
letter 561
sonata 415
Sonderbund 769

song *music* 415
poem 597
death – 360, 839
love– 597
for a mere – 815
no – no supper 812
old – 643
songster 416
soniferous 402
sonnet 597
sonneteer 597
sonorous *sound* 402
loud 404
language 577
sons of:
– Belial 988
– God 977
Soofeeism 984
soon *transient* 111
future 121
early 132
too – for 135
sooner: – or later
another time 119
future 121
– said than done 704
soot 431, 653
sooth 511
in good – 543
soothe
allay 174
relieve 834
flatter 933
soothing
faint sound 405
– syrup 174
soothsay 511
soothsayer 513, 994
soothsaying 511
sop
small quantity 32
food 298
fool 501
inducement 615
reward 973
– to Cerberus 458
– in the pan 615
soph 492, 541
Sophi 745, 996
sophism 477, 497
sophist *scholar* 492
dissembler 548
sophister 492
student 541
sophistical 477
sophisticate *mix* 41
debase 659
sophisticated
spurious 545
sophistry 477

sophomore 541
soporific 683, 841
soporous 683
soprano 410, 416
sorbet 298
sorcerer **994**
sorcery **992**
sordes 653
sordet 417
sordid *stingy* 819
covetous 865
sordine 417
sore
bodily pain 378
disease 655
mental suffering 828, 830
discontent 832
anger 900
– as a boil 901*a*
– place 822
– subject 830, 900
sorely *very* 31
s'orienter 278
sorites 476
sorority 712
sorrel 433, 434
sorrow 828
give – words 839
sorry *trifling* 643
grieved 828
mean 876
make a – face 874
cut a – figure 874
be – for 750, 914
in a – plight 732
– sight 830, 837
sort *degree* 26
arrange 60
kind 75
– with
sociality 892
sortable } *agreement* 23
sortance }
sortes
chance 156, 621
– Virgilianæ
sorcery 992
sortie 716
sortilege
prediction 511
sorcery 992
sortilegy 621
sortition 621
sorts, out of –
ill-health 655
sulky 901*a*
S.O.S. 669, 707
so-so *small* 32
trifling 643

imperfect 651
sostenuto 415
sot *fool* 501
drunkard 959
sot à triple étage 501
sotto voce
faint sound 405
conceal 528
voiceless 581
sou *money* 800
qui n'a pas le – 804
soubrette 599, 746
sough *conduit* 350
noise 405
cloaca 653
soul *essence* 5
person 372
intellect 450
genius 498
affections 820
cure of –s 995
flow of – 588
not a – 187
not dare to say one's – is his own *subjection* 749
fear 860
– of wit 572
have one's whole – in his work 686
soulless 683, 823
soul-mate 903
soul-sick 837
soul-stirring 821, 824
sound *great* 31
conformable 82
stable 150
strong 159
fathom 208
bay 343
noise **402**
investigate 461
measure 466
true 494
wise 498
sane 502
good 648
perfect 650
healthy 654
solvent 803
orthodox 983*a*
catch a – 418
safe and – 654, 670
– the alarm
indication 550

warning 668
alarm 669
fear 860
– asleep 683
full of – and fury
unmeaning 517
insolent 885
– the horn 416
– of limb 654
– locator 726
– mind 502
– the praises of 931
– the note of preparation 673
– reasoning 476
– a retreat 283
– sleep 683
– a trumpet
publish 531
alarm 669
– of wind 654
sounding: big – 577
– brass 517
sounding-board 417
soundings 208
soundless
unfathomable 208
silent 403
soup 298, 352
soupçon 32, 41
soufflé 298
sour *acid* 397
discontented 832
embitter 835
uncivil 895
sulky 901
– grapes
impossible 471
excuse 617
– the temper 830
source *beginning* 66
cause 153
sourdet 417
sourdine 417
à la – *noiseless* 405
concealed 528
sourdough 463
soured 832
sourness **397**
sous tous les rapports 52
souse 310, 337
South *direction* 278
North and –
opposite 237
Southern
antipodes 237
– Cross 318
souvenir 505

sovereign
superior **33**
all-powerful 159
authorities 737
ruler 745
– contempt 930
– remedy 662
Soviet 696, 737
sow *scatter* 73
pig 366
agriculture 371
female 374
get the wrong – by the ear
misjudgment 481
error 495
mismanage 699
fail 732
– broadcast 818
– dissension 713, 898
– the sand 645
– the seed
prepare 673
– the seeds of
cause 153
teach 537
– one's wild oats
improve 658
amusement 840
vice 945
intemperance 954
sozzled 959
spa *town* 189
sanatorium 662
space *distribute* 60
time 106
extension **180**
musical 413
celestial –s 318
wide open –'s 180
spaddle 272
spade 272
call a – a spade
plain language 576
straightforward 703
spade-husbandry 371
spahi 726
span *join* 43
link 45
duality 89
time 106
transient 111
distance 196
near 197
length 200
short 201
measure 466
– new 124
spangle *spark* 420
ornament 847
spaniel *dog* 366
servile 886
spanish fly 171
spank *swift* 274
flog 972
spanking *large* 192
– pace 274
spanner 633
spar *beam* 214
quarrel 713
contend 720
spare *extra* 37
small 193
meagre 203
refrain 623
store 636
scanty 640
redundant 641
disuse 678
inaction 681
relinquish 782
give 784
economy 817
exempt 927*a*
temperate 953
enough and to – 639
not a moment to – 682
to – 641
– diet 956
– no expense 816
– no pains 686
– room 180
– time 685
spared: be –
live 359
it cannot be – 630
sparge 337
spargefaction
scatter 73
wet 337
sparing [*see* spare]
small 32
economy 817
parsimony 819
temperate 953
with a – hand 819
with no – hand 639
– of praise 932
– of words 585
spark *small* 32
heat 382
light 420
luminary 423
wag 844
fop 854
as the –s fly upwards *habit* 613
sparkle
bubble 353
glisten 420
sparkling
vigorous 574
excitement 824
cheerful 836
wit 842
beauty 845
with – eyes 827
sparse 73
sparsity 103
Spartacus 742
spartan 739
spasm
sudden change 146
violence 173
agitation 315
pain 378
spasmodic
discontinuous 70
irregular 139
changeable 149
violent 173
spat 225, 713
spate 348
spathic 204
spatter *dirt* 653
spatterdash 225
spatula 191, 272
spavined 655
spawn *produce* 161
offspring 167
dirt 653
spay 38, 158
speak 560, 580, 582
– one fair 894
– for 937
– ill of 932, 934
– for itself 518, 525
– low 581
– of *meaning* 516
publish 531
speak 582
– out *make manifest* 525
artless 703
– softly 581
– to 586
– up 411
– up for 937
– volumes 467
– well of 931
speakeasy 189, 964
speaker
interpreter 524
chairman 694
speakie 964
speaking: much – 584
way of – 521
– likeness 554
on – terms 888
speaking-trumpet 418
spear 260, 727
– shaped 253
spearman 726
special 79
– correspondent 593
special pleader 968
special pleading
sophistry 477
speciali gratiâ 760
specialist 662, 700
speciality **79**
specialty
security 771
specie 800
species *kind* 75
appearance 448
human – 372
specific *special* 79
remedy 662
– gravity 321
specification 594
specify
particularize 79
tell 527
name 564
specimen 82
specious
probable 472
sophistical 477
beauty 845
flattering 933
pardonable 937
speck 32
speckle 440, 848
spectacle
appearance 448
prodigy 872
show 882
drama 599
spectacles 445
look through rose coloured – 523
spectacular 882
spectator 444
spectral 4, 980
spectre
fallacy of vision 443
ugly 846
ghost 980
spectroscope
light 420
colour 428

optical instrument 445
spectrum
colour 428
variegation 440
optical illusion 443
speculate
view 441
think 451
suppose 514
chance 621
essay 675
traffic 794
speculation
experiment 463
cards 840
speculative 463, 514
speculum 445
veluti in – 446
sped *completed* 729
speech 582
figure of – 521
parts of – 567
speechify 582
speechless 403, 581
speechmaker 582
speed
velocity 274
activity 682
haste 684
help 707
succeed 731
with breathless – 684
God – 731, 906
speedily *soon* 132
speedometer 200, 274, 553
speedway 840
speer 455, 461
spell *period* 106
influence 175
read 539
letter 561
necessity 601
motive 615
exertion 686
charm 993
cast a – 992
wonder 870
knurr and – 840
– for 865
– out *interpret* 522
spell-bound 601, 615
spence 636
spencer 225
spend *effuse* 297
waste 638
give 784
purchase 795
expend 809
– freely 816
– time 106
– time in 683
– one's time in 625
spender 818
spendthrift 818
spent 160, 688
spermaceti 356
spermatic 168
spermatize 168
spero, dum spiro – 858
spes sibi quisque 604
spew 297
sphacelus 655
sphere *rank* 26
domain 75
space 180
region 181
ball 249
world 318
business 625
– of influence 181, 780
spheroid 249
spherule 249
sphery 318
Sphinx *monster* 83
oracle 513
ambiguous 520
riddle 533
spial 668
spice
small quantity 32
mixture 41
pungent 392
condiment 393
spiced 390
spicilegium 72, 596
spick and span 123
spiculate 253
spiculum 253
spicy 400, 824
spigot 263
spike *sharp* 253
pierce 260
plug 263
– guns 158, 645
spikebit 262
spikenard 356
spill *filament* 205
stopper 263
shed 297
splash 348
match 388
waste 638
lavish 818
– blood 722
– and pelt 59
spin *flying* 267
rotate 312
pluck 610
– out *protract* 110
late 133
prolong 200
diffuse style 573
– the wheel 140
– a long yarn 549
spindle 312
spindling 203
spindle-shanks 203
spindle-shaped 253
spindrift 353
spine 222, 253
spinel 847
spinet *copse* 367
harpsichord 417
spinney 367
spinner of yarns 594
spinosity
unintelligible 519
discourtesy 895
sullenness 901*a*
spinous *prickly* 253
spinster 374, 904
spiracle 351
spiral 248
spire *height* 206
convolution 248
peak 253
soar 305
spirit *essence* 5
immateriality 317
fuel 388
intellect 450
meaning 516
vigorous language 574
activity 682
affections 820
courage 861
ghost 980
bad – 980
keep one's – up
hope 858
with life and – 682
unclean – 978
– away 791
– up 615, 824
Spirit, the Holy – 976
spirited
language 574
active 682
sensitive 822
cheerful 836
brave 861
generous 942
spiritless
insensible 823
sad 837
cowardly 862
spirit-level 213
spiritoso *music* 415
spirit-rapping 992
spirits *drink* 298, 959
cheer 836
spirit-stirring 824
spiritual
immaterial 317
psychical 450
heterodoxy 984
divine 976
pious 987
– director 996
– existence 987
spiritualism
immateriality 317
intellect 450
sorcery 992
spiritualize 317
reasoning 476
spirituel 842
spirt *eject* 297
stream 348
haste 684
exertion 686
spirtle *disperse* 73
splash 348
spissitude 321, 352
spit *pointed* 253
perforate 260
eject 297
rotate 312
rain 348
– fire *irascible* 901
spite 907
in – of
disagreement 24
notwithstanding 30
counteraction 179
opposition 708
in – of one's teeth
unwilling 603
compulsion 744
spiteful 898, 907
hating 898
spittle 299
spittoon 191
splanchnology 329
splash *affuse* 337
stream 348
spatter 653
parade 882
make a –
fame 873

display 882
-board 666
splay 291
-footed 243
spleen
melancholy 837
hatred 898
anger 900
sullen 901*a*
harbour – 907
spleenless 906
splendour
bright 420
beautiful 845
glorious 873
display 882
splenetic 837, 901*a*
splice *join* 43
cross 219
interjacent 228
repair 660
– the main brace
tipsy 959
spliced, be –
marriage 903
splint 215
splinter
small piece 32
divide 44
filament 205
brittle 328
split *divide* 44
discontinuity 70
bisect 91
brittle 328
divulge 529
quarrel 713
fail 732
portion 786
laugh 838
– the difference 29, 774
– the ears 404
– the head 410
– hairs
discriminate 465
sophistry 477
fastidiousness 868
– upon a rock 732
– one's sides 838
splutter *energy* 171
spit 297
stammer 583
haste 684
spoil *vitiate* 659
hinder 706
lenity 740
plunder 791
booty 793
deface 846
satiate 869
– sport 706
– trade 708
spoiled child 869, 899
– of fortune 734
spoiler 792
spoke *radius* 200
tooth 253
obstruct 706
put a – in one's wheel *render powerless* 158
hinder 706
spokesman 524, 582
spolia opima 793
spoliate 791
spoliative 793
spondee 597
spondulics 800
sponge *moisten* 339
dry 340
pulp 354
clean 652
despoil 791
hanger on 886
drunkard 959
apply the –
obliterate 552
non-payment 808
– out 552
sponging-house 752
spongy *porous* 252
soft 324
marshy 345
sponsion 771
sponsor
witness 467
security 771
be – for
promise 768
obligation 926
sponsorship 771
spontaneous
voluntary 600
willing 602
impulsive 612
spontoon 727
spoof 545
spook 980
spool 312
spoon
receptacle 191
ladle 272
bill and coo 902
born with a silver – in one's mouth 734
Spoonerism 218, 853
spoonful 25, 32
spoon-like 252
spoon-meat 298
spoony *foolish* 499
lovesick 902
spoor 551
sporadic 73, 137, 657
spore 330
sport *killing* 361
chase 622
amusement 840
show off 882
in – *pastime* 840
humour 842
the – of 749
– of fortune 735
sporting *killing* 361
contention 720
amusement 840
– dog 366
sportive 836, 840
sports 686
sportsman 361, 622, 840
sportulary 784, 785
sportule 784
sporule 330
spot *place* 182
discover 480*a*
mark 550
dirt 653
blemish 848
blot 874
on the –
instantly 113
present time 118
soon 132
in one's presence 186
spotless *perfect* 650
clean 652
innocent 946
spot light 423, 599
spots in the sun, see – *fastidious* 868
spotted
variegated 440
damaged 659
spousal 903
spouse 88, 903
spouseless 904
spout *egress* 295
flow out 348
conduit 350
speak 582
act 599
pawn 771, 787, 788
sprag 215
sprain 158, 160
sprat to catch a:
– herring 794
– whale 699
sprawl *length* 200
horizontal 213
descend 306
spray *sprig* 51
vaporizer 336
foam 353
spread *enlarge* 35
disperse 73
broadcast 78
expanse 180
expand 194
diverge 291
feast 298
publish 531
– abroad 531
– canvas 267
– out 194
– sail 267
– a shade 421
– to 196
– the toils 545
spree 840
spretæ injuria formæ *ugly* 846
disrespect 929
detraction 934
sprig *branch* 51
child 129
shillelagh 727
sprightly 836, 842
spring *early* 125
source 153
strength 159
velocity 274
recoil 277
fly 293
leap 309
elasticity 325
rivulet 348
instrument 633
store 636
-s of action 615
– back 277
– to one's feet 307
– from 154
– a leak 651, 659
– a mine
destroy 162
unexpected 508
attack 716
– a project 626
– up *begin* 66
event 151
grow 194
ascend 305
visible 446
hot – 382
– upon 789

spring balance 319
springe 545
spring-gun 545
spring tide
greatness 31
increase 35
completeness 52
youth 127
high 206
low 207
wave 348
water 337
springy 325
sprinkle *add* 37
mix 41
scatter 73
wet 337
rain 348
variegate 440
baptize 998
sprinkler 348, 385
sprinkling
small quantity 32
sprint 274
sprit *sprout* 167
support 215
sprite 979, 980
sprout *grow* 35
germinate 161
offspring 167
expand 194
– from *result* 154
spruce 652, 845
– up 847
sprue 653
sprung 651, 659
spry 682, 836
spud 272
spume 353
spun out 110, 573
spunk 861
spur
pointed 250
sharp 253
incite 615
hasten 684
win –s *succeed* 731
glory 873
on the – of the moment
instantly 113
now 118
soon 132
opportune 134
impulse 612
– gearing 633
the – of necessity 745
spurious
erroneous 495
false 544
deceptive 545
illegitimate 925
spurlos versenkt 2, 449
spurn *reject* 55
disdain 930
spurred 253
spurt
transient 111
swift 274
gush 348
impulse 612
haste 684
exertion 686
sputa 299
sputter *emit* 297
splash 348
stammer 583
spy *see* 441
spectator 444
inquire 461
informer 527
emissary 534
watcher 664
warning 668
spy-glass 445
squab *large* 192
short 201
broad 202
bench 215
squabble 713
squad 72, 726
squadron 726
– leader 745
squalid 653, 846
squall *violent* 173
wind 349
cry 411
quarrel 713
squalor 653
squamous 204, 223
squander *waste* 638
misuse 679
lose 776
prodigal 818
square
congruous 23
compensate 30
four 95
limited space 182
houses 189
perpendicular 212
form 244
sparring 720
justice 924
honourable 939
make all – 660
on the – 939
– accounts
pay 807
account 811
– dance 840
– deal 922
– the circle 471
– inches 180
– peg into a round hole 699
– up 556
– with 23
– yards 180
square-toes 857
squash *destroy* 162
flatten 251
blow 276
soft 324
marsh 345
semiliquid 352
hiss 409
game 840
squashy 345, 352
squat 308
locate oneself 184
little 193
short 201
thick 202
low 207
squatter 188
squaw *woman* 374
wife 903
squeak, **squeal** 411, 412
squeamish 655
unwilling 603
fastidious 868
squeasy 868
squeezable 762
squeeze
contract 195
condense 321
embrace 894
squeeze out 301, 784
squelch 162
squib *sound* 406
lampoon 856, 934
squiffy 959
squilgee 652
squint
peephole 260
look 441
defective sight 443
squirarchy 875
squire *aid* 707
attendant 746
gentry 875
– of Dames 897
squirm 315
squirrel 274, 682
squirt 297, 348
S.S.C. 968
stab *pierce* 260
kill 361
pain 378, 649, 828
injure 659
stabilimetre 150
stabilizator 150
stability 16, 150
stable *firm* 150
house 189
lock the – door when the steed is stolen
too late 135
useless 645
bungling 699
– equilibrium 150
staccato 415
stack 72, 636
staddle 215
stade 252
stadium 728, 840
stadtholder 745
staff *support* 215
music 413
measure 466
signal 550
council 696
party 712
weapon 727
chief 745
retinue 746
pastoral – 999
– of life 298
– of office 747
– officer 745
stag *deer* 366
male 373
defaulter 808
stage *degree* 26
term 71
time 106
position 183
layer 204
platform 215
forum 542
drama 599
arena 728
come upon the – 446
on the – 525, 599
go off the – 293
revolving – 599
– business 599
– coach 272
– craft 599
– direction 697
– effect 882
– hand 599
– manager 599
– name 565
– play 599
– player 599

– struck 599
– whisper 580
stager *player* 599
doer 690
old – 130
stagger *slow* 275
totter 314, 821
agitate 315
unexpected 508
dissuade 616
affect 824
astonish 870
– belief *doubt* 485
– like a drunken man 605
staggers 315
stagirite 850
stagnant 265
stagnation 681
stagy 599, 855
staid *wise* 498
calm 826
grave 837
stain *paint* 223
colour 428
dirt 653
spoil 659
blemish 848
disgrace 874
– paper *writing* 590
stained, travel- 266
stainless *clean* 652
honourable 939
innocent 946
stair 305, 627
stake *fastening* 45
wager 621
danger 665
security 771
property 780
lay down 807
execution 975
at – *intended* 620
in danger 665
the – *agony* 828
burn at the – 384
stalactite 224
stalagmite 224
stale *old* 124
insipid 391
deteriorated 659
– flat and unprofitable 645
– news 532
stale-mate 27, 731
stalk *stem* 153
support 215
walk 266
– abroad
generality 78
pursue 622
proud 878
stalking-horse
ambush 530
plea 617
stall *cease* 142
abode 189
receptacle 191
support 215
play-house 599
mart 799
churchdom 995
cathedral 1000
finger– 223
stallion 271, 373
stalwart 159, 192
stamina 159, 604*a*
stammel 434
stammering 583
stamp
character 7
prototype 22
kind 75
form 240
mark 550
engraving 558
complete 729
security 771
– the foot
anger 900
– in the memory 505
– out 162, 385
stampede 860
stanch - *a flow* 348
persevering 604*a*
health 654
reinstate 660
stanchion 215
stanchless 825
stand *exist* 1
rank 71
long time 110
permanent 141
support 215
quiescence 265
difficulty 704
resistance 719
brook 821
patience 826
brave 861
at a – 681
come to a – 704
make a – 708, 719
take one's –
resolve 604
resist 719
due 924
take one's – upon
reasoning 476
affirm 535
plea 617
– aghast 870
– aloof 623, 681
– of arms 727
– at attention 507
– the brunt 717
– by *near* 197
aid 707
defend 717
– a chance 470, 472
– committed 754
– at ease 458
– to one's engagement 772
– fair for 472
– fire 861
– firm 150, 719
– first 66
– for *indicate* 550
deputy 759
candidate 763
– forth 446
– one's ground
preserved 670
resist 719
– the hazard of the die 621
– one in 812
– in need of 630
– no nonsense 604
– off 287, 623
– on 215
– out *project* 250
visible 446
obstinate 606
– over 133
– the proof 648
– to reason
proof 478
manifest 525
right 922
– on one's rights 748
– in the shoes of 147
– one in good stead 644
– still *remain* 141
stop 265
difficulty 704
– the test 494, 648
– up [*see below*]
– upon *pride* 878
– upon one's rights 924
– in the way of 706
– well in the opinion of 931
stand up 212, 307
– against 719
– fight 720
– for 931, 937
– to 459
standard *model* 22
degree 26
mean 29
rule 80
measure 466
flag 550
good 648
perfect 650
gold – 800
standard-bearer 726
standardize 22, 60, 466
standing *footing* 8
degree 26
long time 110
permanence 141
situation 183
note 873
– army 726
– dish *rule* 80
permanent 141
– jest *wit* 842
– order 613, 963
– type 591
– water 343
stand-pipe 348, 385
stand-point 183, 441
Stannary Court 966
stanza 597
staple
fastening 45
whole 50
peg 214
texture 329
material 635
trade 794
mart 799
– commodity 798
star *luminary* 423
actor 599
destiny 601
badge 747
ornament 847
glory 873
noble 875
decoration 877
– in the ascendant
success 731
prosperity 734
– of fashion 852
– it *drama* 599
fame 873
display 882
– shell 423
– trap 599
starboard 238

starch *stiff* 323
viscid 352
affected 855
proud 878
Star Chamber 966
starched
ostentatious 882
stare *look* 441
curiosity 455
wonder 870
make one – 870
– out of countenance
humiliate 879
insolent 885
discourteous 895
– one in the face
destiny 152
manifest 525
Death –s one in the face 360
stare super antiquas vias
continue 143
habit 613
preservation 670
inaction 681
star-gazing 318
staring 446
stark *very* 31
sheer 32
complete 52
hard 323
– blind 442
– naked 226
stark staring 31
manifest 525
– mad 503
starlight 422
starlike
pointed 253
starry 318
stars [*see* star]
worlds 318
bless one's – 916
– in the firmament
multitude 102
– and stripes 550
start *begin* 66
sudden change 146
arise 151
impulse 276
move 284
depart 293
leap 309
unexpected 508
suggest 514
crack 659
offer 763
fear 860
wonder 870
get the –
precede 280
success 731
give a – to 276
have the –
prior 116
early 132
get before 280
– afresh 66
– a doubt 485
– game 622
– off 293
– a question 461
– up *project* 250
arise 305
appear 446
starting: – hole
plea 617
– point
departure 293
reasoning 476
eyes – out of one's head 870
startle *doubt* 485
unexpected 508
excite 824
fear 860
wonder 870
startling 508
startlish 825
starts, by fits and – 608
starvation 640, 956
starve *cold* 383, 385
poverty 804
parsimony 819
fast 956
starveling *thin* 203
insufficient 640
poor 804
state *condition* 7
speciality 79
nation 372
inform 527
affirm 535
government 737
realm 780
ostentation 882
robes of – 747
secretary of – 694
– of affairs 151
–'s evidence 529
– of facts
description 594
lawsuit 969
– paper 551
– room 191
– of siege 722
statecraft 693
stated periods, at – 138
stately *grand* 873
proud 878
pompous 882
statement 535, 594
statemonger 694
state prison 752
states-general 696
statesman 694
statesmanlike 698
statesmanship 692, 693
static 404
Statics *strength* 159
gravity 319
station *degree* 26
term 71
place 182
situation 183
locate 184
rank 873
stationary
permanent 141
quiescent 265
stationery 590
station-house 752
statist 694
statistics 85, 86
statu:
in – pupillari 127
in – quo 141, 660
statuary 557, 559
statue 554
still as a – 265
stature 206
status *position* 8
terms 71
situation 183
repute 873
status quo
past 122
unchanged 145
restoration 660
– ante bellum 145
statute 697, 963
staunch *health* 654
reinstate 660
honest 939
– belief 484
stave *music* 413, 415
contention 720
– in *concave* 252
hole 260
– off 133, 706
stay *remain* 106
wait 133
continue 141
stop 142
dwell 186
support 215
not move 265
prevent 706
– away 187
– one's hand
cease 142
relinquish 624
rest 687
– at home 893
stayed [*see* staid]
stays *corset* 225
stead 644
in the – of
substitution 147
commission 755
deputy 759
stand one in good – 644
steadfast *stable* 150
persevering 604a
– belief 484
– thought 457
steady *uniform* 16
regular 80
periodic 138
stable 150
persevering 604a
unexcitable 826
cautious 864
steal 791
– along 275, 528
– away 623
– on the ear 405
– a march
prior 116
early 132
precede 280
deceive 545
active 682
cunning 702
– upon one 508
stealing 791
stealth 528
do good by – &c. 881
stealthy 528
cunning 702
caution 864
steam *navigate* 267
gas 334
vaporize 336
bubbles 353
under – 267
under sail and – 274
– car 272
– up 171
get the – up 673
steamboat 273
steam-hammer to crack a nut
waste 638

redundance 641
misuse 679
steamer 273
- track 343
stearine 356
steed 271
steel *strong* 159
sharp 253
hard 323
sword 727
harden the sensibility 823
- gray 432
- the heart 951
- helmet 717
- oneself 604
steeled against 604, 823
steel-engraving 558
steelyard 319
steep *height* 206
cliff 212
slope 217
soak 337
steeped in
- iniquity 945
- misery 828
steeple 206, 253
steeple-chase
swift 274
pursuit 622
contest 720
steer *beast* 366
mate 373
direct 693
- clear 279, 623
- one's course 692
- for 278
steerage 278, 693
steersman 269, 694
steganographic 526
steganography
unintelligible 519
hidden 528
writing 590
stellar 318
stellated 253
stelography 590
St. Elmo's fire 423
stem *origin* 153
ancestor 166
front 234
oppose 708
- to stern 200
- the tide 142, 719
- the torrent 731
stench 401
stencil 556
stenographer 553, 746
stenography 590
stentor *cry* 411
stentorian *loud* 404
step *degree* 26
term 71
support 215
motive 264, 266
measure 466
expedient 626
act 680
dance the back – 283
but a – 197
take a decisive – 609
not stir a – 265
–dance 840
– forward 282
– in *mediate* 724
– into *acquire* 775
– on *be supported by* 215
– in the right direction 644
– into the shoes of
sequence 63
posteriority 117
substitution 147
– short 275
– by step
degree 26
order 58
seriatim 69
slowly 275
– of time 109
steppe 180, 344
stepping-stone
link 45
way 627
instrument 631
resource 666
preparation 673
steps *way* 627
bend one's –
travel 266
direction 278
flight of – 305
retrace one's – 283
take – *plan* 626
prepare 673
conduct 692
tread in the – of 281
stercoraceous 653
stereography 591
stereometry 466
stereopticon 445
stereoscope 445
stereoscopic 446
stereotype *copy* 21
mark 550
engraving 558
printing 591
stereotyped
uniform 16
stable 150
habit 613
sterile 169, 645, 732
sterilize 652
sterling *true* 494, 944
– coin 800
stern *rear* 235
severe 739
discourteous 895
– necessity 601, 603
– truth 494
sternmost 235
sternutation
sneeze 349
sound 409
sternway 267
stertorous 402, 580
stet 150
– pro ratione voluntas 600
stethoscope 418
stevedore 271, 613, 690
stew *food* 298
heat 382
cook 384
difficulty 704
emotion 821
excitement 825
annoyance 828
bagnio 961
in a – *angry* 900
steward 637
director 694
agent 758
treasurer 801
stewardship 692, 693
stewpan 386
stichomancy 511
stick *adhere* 46
cease 142
staff 215
stab 260
remain quiet 265
fool 501
bungler 701
weapon 727
scourge 975
dirty end of the – 699
give the – to 972
– at *doubt* 485
averse 603
– fast *firm* 150
difficulty 704
– in one's gizzard 830, 900
– in 300
– law 972
– in the mud 304, 732
– at nothing
resolve 604
active 682
rash 863
– out 250
– to 143, 604*a*
– in the throat
hoarse 581
not say 585
dislike 867
– up 212, 307, 791
– up for *aid* 707
applaud 931
vindicate 937
stickle 603, 616
– for 720, 794
stickler 606
severity 739
sticky
cohering 46
viscid 352
stiff *rigid* 323
style 579
severe 739
coactive 751
ugly 846
affected 855
haughty 878
pompous 882
– breeze 349
stiffen 323
stiff-necked 606
stiffness
stability 150
stifle *kill* 361
silence 403
conceal 528
stifled
faint sound 405
stifling *hot* 382
stigmatize 874
censure 932
accuse 938
stile *way* 627
hindrance 706
help a lame dog over a – 707
stiletto 262, 727
still
on the other hand 30
moderate 174
not moving 265
vaporization 336
furnace 386

silent 403
– less 467
– life *matter* 316
painting 556
– more
superior 33
evidence 467
– small voice 405
in – water 714
still-born 360, 732
stillroom 636
stillicidium 348
stilted
elevated 307
- *style* 577
ridiculous 853
affected 855
boasting 884
stilts *support* 215
on – *high* 206
elevated 307
hyperbolical 549
proud 878
boasting 884
stimulant 662
stimulate
energy 171
violence 173
incite 615
excite 824
stimulating
suggestive 514
stimulus 615
sting *pain* 378
tingle 380
poison 663
excite 824
mental suffering 830
anger 900
stinging
pungent 392
stingo 298
stingy 819
stink 401
– in the nostrils
unpleasant 830
dislike 867
hate 898
stink-bomb 727
stink-pot 401
stint *degree* 26
limit 233
scanty 640
begrudge 819
stintless 639
stipend *salary* 973
stipendiary
subject 749
receiving 785
magistrate 967
stipple
variegate 440
painting 556
engraving 558
stipulate 769, 770
– for 720
stipule 51
stir *energy* 171
move 264
agitation 315
excite 375
activity 682
jail 752
emotion 824
make a – 642, 682
– about 682
– the blood 824, 900
– up dissension 713
– the embers 163, 824
– the feelings 824
– the fire 384
– a question 461, 476
– one's stumps 266, 682
– up *mix* 41
violent 173
excite 824
stirps *kin* 11
source 153
paternity 166
stirring *events* 151
important 642
active 682
– news 532
stirrup
support 215
with a foot in the – 293
stirrup-cup 293, 959
stitch *junction* 43
pain 378
work 680
– in time 132
– of work 686
stive 384
stiver 800
stoat 401
stoccado 717
stock *kinship* 11
quantity 25
origin 153
paternity 166
collar 225
soup 298
fool 501
habitual 613
materials 635
store 636
property 780
merchandise 798
money 800
in – 777
laughing – 857
lay in a – 637
take – *inspect* 457
accounts 811
– exchange 799
– still 265
– in trade
means 632
store 636
property 780
merchandise 798
– with 637
stockade 717
stocked, well – 639
stock exchange 621
stock-farm 370
stocking 225
hoard 800
stock-jobbing 794
stock operator 621
stocks *prison* 752
funds 802
punishment 975
on the –
business 625
preparation 673
incomplete 730
– and stones 316, 823
stocky 201
stodge 957
stoicism
insensibility 823
inexcitability 826
disinterested 942
temperance 953
stoke 388
stoker 268
stole 999
stolen: – away 671
– goods 793
stolid 499, 843
stomach *pouch* 191
taste 390
brook 826
desire 865
not have the – to 603
turn the – 830
– of an ostrich 957
stomacher 225
stone *heavy* 319
dense 321
hard 323
kill 361
lithography 558
material 635
attack 716
weapon 727
punish 972
corner – 642
go down like a – 310
cast the first – at 938
heart of – 823, 907
key– 642
musical –s 417
no – unturned 461, 686
philosopher's – 662
precious – 648
stepping – 627
throw a – at
attack 716
censure 932
accuse 938
throw –s at 907
tomb– 363
mark with a white – 642
throw a – in one's own garden 699
– dead 360
– of Sisyphus 645
stone-blind 442
stone-coloured 432
stone-deaf 419
stone's throw 197
stoneware 384
stony 323
stony-hearted 907, 919
stooge 711, 746, 886
stook 72
stool 215
between two –s 704
– of repentance 950
– pigeon 527, 548
stoop *slope* 217
lower 308
humble 879
servile 886
dishonourable 940
– to conquer 702
stop *end* 67
cease 142
close 261
rest 265
silent 403
danger 665
inaction 681
hinder 706
prohibit 761

put a – to 142
– the breath 361
– the ears 419
– a flow 348
– a gap 660
– the mouth 479, 581
– payment 808
– press news 532
– short 142, 265
– short of 304
– the sound 408*a*
– up 261
– the way 706
stopcock 263
stopgap
substitute 147
stopper 263
stoppage
cessation 142
hindrance 706
stopper 263
stopping place 292
store *store* 184
stock **636**
shop 799
in – *destiny* 152
preparing 673
lay in a – 637
set – by 642, 931
set no – 483
– of knowledge 490
– in the memory 505
store-house 636
store-keeper 636
store-ship 273, 726
storied 594
storm *crowd* 72
convulsion 146
violence 173
agitation 315
wind 349
danger 667
attack 716
passion 825
anger 900
ride the – 267
take by –
conquer 731
seize 789
– brewing 665
– in a teacup
overrate 482
exaggerate 549
unimportance 643
storthing 696
story *rooms* 191
layer 204
news 532
lie 546
history 594
the old – 897
as the – goes 532
story-teller 548, 594
stot 366
stound 870
stoup *cup* 191
altar 1000
stour 59
stout *strong* 159
large 192
drink 298
stout-hearted 861
stove *fireplace* 386
– in 252
stow *locate* 184
pack close 195
store 636
stowage 180, 184
stowaway 528, 673
strabism 443
straddle 266, 607
Stradivarius 417
strafe 972
straggle 266, 279
straggler 268
straggling 44, 59
straight
vertical 212
rectilinear 246
direction 278
all – *rich* 803
solvent 807
– course 628
– descent 167
– face 837
– sailing 705
straighten 246
– up 60
straightforward 278
truthful 543
artless 703
honourable 939
straightness 246
straight shot 278
straightway 132
strain *race* 11
weaken 160
operation 170
violence 173
percolate 295
transgress 303
sound 402
melody 415
overrate 482
exaggerate 549
style 569
poetry 597
voice 580
clean 652
effort 686
fatigue 688
– in the arms 902
– one's eyes 441, 507
– at a gnat and swallow a camel 608
– one's invention 515
– the meaning 523
– every nerve 686
– a point
go beyond 303
exaggerate 549
not observe 773
undue 925
– the throat 411
strait
interval 198
water 343
difficulty 704
straitened
poor 804
strait-handed 819
strait-jacket 752
strait-laced
severe 739
restraint 751
fastidious 868
haughty 878
strait-waistcoat 751, 752
strake 205
stramash 720
strand *thread* 205
shore 231, 342
stranded
stuck fast 150
in difficulty 704
failure 732
pain 828
strange
unrelated 10
exceptional 83
ridiculous 853
wonderful 870
– bedfellows 713
– to say 870
strangely *much* 31
stranger 57
a – to 491
strangle
render powerless 158
contract 195
kill 361
strap *fasten* 43
fastening 45
restraint 752
punish 972
instrument of punishment 975
strappado 972
strapping
mighty 31
strong 159
pace 274
big 192
strapwork 847
stratagem
deception 545
plan 626
artifice 702
strategic *plan* 626
artifice 702
strategist
planner 626
director 694
proficient 700
strategy 692, 722
strath 252
strathspey 840
stratification 204, 329
stratocracy 737
stratosphere 338
stratum 204
stratus 353
straw *scatter* 73
light 320
unimportant 643
care not a – 866, 930
catch at –s
overrate 482
credulous 486
misuse 679
unskilful 699
hope 858
rash 863
the eyes drawing –s 683
in the – 161
man of –
unsubstantial 4
cheat 545
insolvent 808
low person 876
not worth a – 643, 645
– to show the wind 463
straw-coloured 436
straw-hat 225
stray *dispersion* 73
exceptional 83
random 156
wanderer 268
deviate 279
streak *intrinsicality* 5

long 200
narrow 203
furrow 259
light 420
stripe 440
mark 550
streaked 219, 440
stream *assemble* 72
move 264
– *of fluid* 347
– *of water* 348
– *of air* 349
– *of light* 420
abundance 639
against the – 708
with the –
conformity 82
progression 282
assent 488
facility 705
concord 714
fashion 852
servility 886
– of events 151
– of time 109
streamer *flag* 550
streaming 47, 73
streamlet 348
street 189, 627
man in the – 876
streets:
in the open – 525
on the – 961
street-walker 962
strength
quantity 25
degree 26
greatness 31
vigour 159
energy 171
tenacity 327
animality 364
put all one's – into 686
lose – 655
tower of – 717
– of mind 604
strengthen 35
strengthless 160
strenuous
persevering 604a
active 682
exertion 686
Strephon and Chloe 902
stress *emphasis* 580
requirement 630
importance 642
strain 686
difficulty 704
by – of 601

lay – on 476
– of circumstances
compulsion 744
– of weather 349
stretch *expanse* 180
expand 194
extend 200
exaggerate 549
exertion 686
encroach 925
at a – 69
mind on the – 451
on the – 686
upon the – 457
– away to 196
– forth one's hand 680, 789
– of the imagination 515, 549
– the meaning 523
– a point 83, 303
exaggerate 549
severity 739
permit 760
not observe 773
undue 925
exempt 927a
– to *distance* 196
length 200
stretcher 215, 272
strew 73
striæ, striated 259, 440
stricken *pain* 828
terror– 860
be – by 655
– in years 128
strict
in conformity 82
exact 494
severe 739
conscientious 939
orthodox 983a
– inquiry 461
– interpretation 522
– search 461
– settlement 780
strictly speaking
literally 19
exact 494
interpreted 522
stricture
constriction 203
hindrance 706
censure 932
stride *distance* 196
motion 264
walk 266
strident 410
strides: make – 282

rapid – 274
stridor 410
strife 713, 720
strigil 652
strike *operate* 170
hit 276
resist 719
disobey 742
impress 824
beat 972
– at 716
– a balance
equalize 27
mean 29
pay 807
– a bargain 769, 794
– a blow *act* 680
– dumb *dumb* 581
excitement 824
wonder 870
humble 879
– the eye 457
– the first blow 716
– one's flag 725
– hard 171
– all of a heap 824, 860
– home 171
– in with
imitate 19
assent 488
cooperate 709
– the iron while it is hot 134
– a light 384, 420
– the lyre 416
– the mind 457
– out something new 146, 515
– off *exclude* 55
– one 451
– out *exclude* 55
destroy 162
invent 515
obliterate 552
scheme 626
– off the roll 756, 972
– at the root of 162
– root 150
– sail 275
– tents 293
– terror 860
– up 416
– with wonder 870
striker 927
striking 525
– likeness 554

strikingly
greatly 31
string *tie* 43
ligature 45
continuity 69
filament 205
musical note 413
– together 60, 69
stringed instruments 417
stringent
energetic 171
authoritative 737
strict 739
compulsory 744
strings: *music* 417
leading – 541
pull the – 175, 693
two – to one's bow 632
stringy 205, 327
strip *adjunct* 39
narrow 203
filament 205
divest 226
take 789
rob 791
stripe *length* 200
variegation 440
mark 550
badge 747
blow 972
stripling 129
stripped *poor* 804
strive *endeavour* 675
exert 686
contend 720
– against 720
stroke *impulse* 276
touch 379
mark 550
evil 619
expedient 626
disease 655
action 680
success 731
painful 830
at a – 113
good – 626
– of death 360
– of the pen
writing 590
command 741
– of policy 626
– of time 113
– of work 686
– the wrong way 256
stroll 266
strolling player 599

strong *great* 31
powerful 159
energetic 171
tough 327
taste 390
pungent 392
fetid 401
healthy 654
feeling 821
wonderful! 870
smell – of 398
– accent 580
– argument 476
by a – arm 744
– box 802
with a – hand
resolution 604
exertion 686
severity 739
– language 574
– pull 686
– point 476
strong-headed 498
stronghold
refuge 666
defence 717
prison 752
strong-minded 498, 861
strong-scented 398
strong-willed 604
strop 253
strophe 597
strow 73
struck [*see* stricken, strike]
awe– 860
– down 732
– all of a heap
emotion 821
wonder 870
humbled 879
– with *love* 897
structural *state* 7
structure
production 161
form 240
texture 329
organization 357
struggle *exert* 686
difficulty 704
contend 720
strum 416, 517
strumpet 962
strung
highly – 825
strut *walk* 266
pride 878
parade 882
boast 884
– and fret one's hour upon a stage 359, 599
strychnine 663
stub 40, 550
stubbed 201
stubble *remains* 40
useless 645
stubborn
strong 159
hard 323
obstinate 606
resistance 719
stubby 201
stucco 45, 223
stuck [*see* stick]
– fast 150, 704
be – on 897
stuck-up 878
stud *hanging-peg* 214
knob 250
horses 271
studded *many* 102
spiked 253
variegated 440
student 541
stud-farm 370
studied
predetermined 611
studio *room* 191
painting 556
workshop 691
studious
thoughtful 451
docile 539
intending 620
study *copy* 21
room 191
thought 451
attention 457
research 461
learning 539
painting 556
intention 620
retreat 893
brown – 515
stuff *substance* 3
contents 190
expand 194
line 224
matter 316
texture 329
absurdity 497
unmeaning 517
material 635
trifle 643
overeat 957
such – as dreams are made of 515
– gown 968
– in 300
– the memory with 505
– and nonsense
unsubstantial 4
absurdity 497
unmeaning 517
– up *close* 261
hoax 545
stuffed
redundancy 641
stuffing *contents* 190
lining 224
stopper 263
stuffy 321, 382
stultified 732
stultify oneself 699
stultiloquy 497
stumble *fall* 306
flounder 315
error 495
unskilful 699
failure 732
– on *chance* 156
discover 480*a*
stumbling-block
difficulty 704
hindrance 706
stump
remainder 40
trunk 51
walk 266
drawing 556
speak 582
stir your –s
active 682
worn to the – 659
– along *slow* 275
stump orator 582, 887
stumpy *short* 201
stun *physically*
insensible 376
loud 404
deafen 419
unexpected 508
morally insensible 823
affect 824
astonish 870
stung [*see* sting]
– to the quick 824
stunt *shorten* 201
performance 680
stunted 193, 195
insufficient 640
stupe 834
stupefaction 826
stupefy
- *physically* 376
- *morally* 823
astonish 870
stupendous
great 31
large 192
wonderful 870
stupid
unsubstantial 4
misjudging 481
credulous 486
unintelligent 499
tiresome 841
dull 843
stupor
insensibility 823
wonder 870
stupration 961
sturdy *strong* 159
persevering 604*a*
– beggar 767, 792
stutter 583
sty *house* 189
enclosure 232
dirt 653
Stygian *dark* 421
diabolic 945
infernal 982
cross the – ferry
die 360
– shore
death 360
style *state* 7
time 114
painting 556
graver 558
name 564
diction 569
writing 590
beauty 845
fashion 852
stylet
awl 262
dagger 727
stylist 578
Stylites, Simon – 893
stylographic pen 590
stylography 590
stylus 590
styptic 397
Styx 982
suasible 602
suasion 615
suave mari magno 664
suaviter in modo 826, 894
suavity 894
sub 34
– spe rati 475
subacid 397

subaction 330
subahdar 745
subalpine 206
subaltern
inferior 34
soldier 726
officer 745
servant 746
plebeian 876
subaqueous 208
subastral 318
subaudition 527
subcommittee 696
subconscious 317
subcontrary 237
subcutaneous 221
subdean 996
subdichotomy 91
subdititious 147
subdivide 44
subdivision
part 51
class 75
military 726
realty 780
subdolous 702
subdominant 413
subdual 731
subduction **38**
subdue *calm* 174
succeed 731
subdued
morally 826
sub-editor 593
subitaneous 113
subito 113
subjacent 207
subject *dominate* 175
liable 177
topic 454
meaning 516
servant 746
enthral 749
– of dispute 713
– to examination 461
– of inquiry 461
– of thought 454
– to 469, 475
subjection **749**
subjective
intrinsic 5
immaterial 317
intellectual 450
subjoin 37
subjugate 731, 749
subjugation 732, 824
subjunctive 37
sublapsarian 984
sublation 38
sublevation 307
sub-lieutenant 745
sublimate
elevate 307
lighten 320
vaporize 336
sublime *high* 206
language 574
beauty 845
glory 873
magnanimous 942
from the – to the ridiculous 853
subliminal 317
sublineation 550
sublunary 318
submarine
deep 208
ship 273
warship 726
– chaser 726
– warfare 722
submediant 413
submerge
destroy 162
immerse 300
plunge 310
steep 337
submersible 273, 726
submersion 208
subministration 707
submission **725**
obedience 743
submissive
tractable 705
enduring 826
humble 879
submit to arbitration 774
submonish 695
submultiple 84
subordinate
inferior 34
unimportant 643
subject 749
subordination 58
suborn 615, 795
subpœna 741, 969
subreption
falsehood 544
acquisition 775
subrogation 147
subscribe
assent 488
aid 707
agree to 769
give 784
subscript 39, 65
subscription
gift 784
subsequent
- *in order* 63
- *in time* 117
subserviency
servility 886
subservient
instrumental 631
aid 707
subject 749
subside 36, 306
subsidiary *aid* 707
servant 746
subsidy
assistance 707
gift 784
pay 809
subsist *exist* 1
continue 141
live 359
subsistence 298
subsoil 221, 342
substance
existence 1
thing 3
quantity 25
inside 221
matter 316
texture 329
important part 642
wealth 803
in – 596
man of – 803
substantial
existing 1
hypostatic 3
material 316
dense 321
true 494
– meaning 516
substantiality **3**
substantially
intrinsically 5
– true 494
substantiate 467, 924
substantive 1, 3
substitute
inferior 34
change 147
means **634**
deputy 759
substitution **147**
substratum
substance 3
layer 204
base 211
support 215
interior 221
materiality 316
substructure 211
subsultory 315
subsume 54
subtend 237
subterfuge 617
sophistry 477
lie 546
cunning 702
subterranean 208
subtile *light* 320
rare 322
- *texture* 329
subtilize *rarefy* 322
sophistry 477
subtle *slight* 32
light 320
cunning 702
– point 704
– reasoning 476
subtlety 477, 498
subtraction
subduction 38
arithmetic 85
taking 789
subtrahend 38, 84
suburb *town* 189
near 197
environs 227
subvention
support 215
aid 707
gift 784
subversion 146
subvert *destroy* 162
invert 218
depress 308
subway 627
– train 272
succedaneum 147
succeed *follow* 63
posterior 117
success 731
transfer 783
– to *acquire* 775
succès d'estime 873
success **731**
succession
sequence 63
continuity 69
repetition 104
posteriority 117
transfer 783
in quick – 136
in regular – 138
– of ideas 451
– of time 109
successless 732
successor 65, 117
succinct 572

succour 707
succubus 980
succulent
nutritive 298
juicy 333
semiliquid 352
succumb
fatigue 688
yield 725
fail 732
succussion 315
such: – as 17
– being the case 8
– like 17
– a one 372
suchwise 8
suck
draw off 297
drink 298
take 789
– in 296
– the blood of 789
sucker 260, 547
suckle 707
suckling *infant* 129
suction *force* 157
reception 296
sudary 652
sudation 299
sudatory 386
sudden
transient 111
instantaneous 113
soon 132
unexpected 508
– burst 508
– death 360
– and quick in quarrel 901
– thought 612
sudorific 382
suds *froth* 353
in the – 704, 837
sue *demand* 765
go to law 969
suet 356
suffer *physical pain* 378
disease 655
allow 760
feel 821
endure 826
moral pain 828
– for 972
– punishment 972
sufferance, tenant on – 779
suffice 639
sufficiency 639
suffix *adjunct* 39
sequence 63
sequel 65
letter 561
sufflation 349
suffocate *kill* 361
excess 641
suffocating 382, 401
suffocation 361
suffragan 996
suffrage 609
suffragette 742
suffusion
mixture 41
feeling 821
blush 879
sugar 396
sugar-loaf 253
suggest *suppose* 514
inform 527
influence 615
advise 695
– itself 451, 515
– a question 461
suggestio falsi 546
suggestion 626, 695
suggestive
reminder 505
significant 516
descriptive 594
bawdy 961
sui generis 83
suicidal 162
suicide *killing* 361
suisse *beadle* 996
Suisse, point d'argent point de – 812
suit *accord* 23
series 69
class 75
clothes 225
expedient 646
petition 765
courtship 902
follow – 19
law– 969
love– 897
– the action to the word 550
– the occasion 646
do – and service 743
suit case 191
suitable 23, 646
– season 134
suite *sequel* 65
series 69
escort 88
retinue 746
– of rooms 189, 191
suitor
petitioner 767
lover 897
lawsuit 969
sulcated 259
sulky *carriage* 272
obstinate 606
discontented 832
dejected 837
sullen 901a
sullen
obstinate 606
gloomy 837
discourteous 895
sulky 901a
sullenness 901a
sully 653, 874
sulphur 388
– coloured 436
sultan 745
sultry 382
sum *number* 84
money 800
– and substance
meaning 516
synopsis 596
important part 642
– total 800
– up *reckon* 85
description 594
compendium 596
sumless 105
summation 37, 85
summary
transient 111
early 132
short 201
concise 572
compendious 596
illegal 964
– of facts 594
summer *season* 125
support 215
heat 382
Indian – 125
St. Luke's – 125
St. Martin's – 125
– lightning 423
– time 114
summer-house 191
summerset 218
summit *top* 210
summon 741, 969
– up 505, 824
– up courage 861
summum:
– bonum 618, 827
– jus 922
sump *base* 211
pool 343
slough 345
store 636
cess 653
sumpter-horse 271
sumptuary 800, 809
sumptuous 882
sum-total 50
sun 318
luminary 423
glory 873
bask in the – 377
going down of the – 126
farthing candle to the – 645
under the – 180, 318
as the – at noonday *bright* 420
certain 474
plain 525
– oneself 384
Sun:
– of Righteousness 976
sunbeam 420
–s from cucumbers 471
sunburn *heat* 384
sunburnt *brown* 433
Sunday:
– Monday &c. 138
–'s best 847, 882
– school 542
sunder 44
sundial 114
sundown 126
sundry 102
sunk [*see* sink]
deep 208
– fence 717
– in iniquity 945
– in oblivion 506
sunken rocks 667
sunless 421
sunlight 420
sunny *warm* 382
luminous 420
cheerful 836
sunny side 829
view the – 858
– of the hedge 734
sun-painting 556
sunrise 125
sunset 126
at – 133
sunshade 223, 424
sunshine *light* 420
prosperity 734
happy 827
cheerful 836
sunstroke 384, 503
sun-up 125

suo: – periculo 926
– sibi gladio hunc jugulo
absurdity 479
retaliation 718
sup *small quantity* 32
feed 298
– full of horrors 828
super *theatrical* 599
superable 470
superabound 641
superadd 37
superannuated 128
superb 845
supercargo 694
supercherie 545
supercilious
proud 878
insolent 885
disrespectful 929
scornful 930
superdreadnought 726
supereminence 648, 873
supererogation 641, 645
superexaltation 873
superexcellence 648
superfetation 37, 168
superficial
shallow 209
outside 220
misjudging 481
ignorant 491
– extent 180
superficies 220
superfine 648
superfluitant 305
superfluity 40, 641
superfluous 645
superhuman 650, 976
superimpose 223
superimposed 206
superincumbent 206, 319
superinduce
change 140
cause 153
produce 161
superintend 693
superintendent 694
superior *greater* 33
- *in size* 194
important 642
good 648
director 694
superiority **33**
superjunction 37
superlative 33
superlatively good 648
superman 33
supernal 206, 210, 981
supernatant 206, 305
supernatural 976, 980
– aid 707
supernumerary
adjunct 39
theatrical 599
reserve 636
redundant 641
superpose 37, 223
supersaturate 641
superscription 550, 590
supersede
substitute 147
disuse 678
relinquish 782
supersensible 317
superstition
credulity 486
error 495
religion 984
superstratum 220
superstructure 729
supertax 812
supertonic 413
supervacaneous 641
supervene
extrinsic 6
be added 37
succeed 117
happen 151
supervise 693
supervisor 694
supination 213
supine
horizontal 213
inverted 218
sluggish 683
mentally torpid 823
suppeditate 637
supper 298
supplant 147
supple *soft* 324
servile 886
supplement
addition 37
adjunct 39
completion 52
publication 531
book 593
suppletory 37
suppliant 765, 767
supplicate *beg* 765
pity 914
worship 990
supplies
materials 635
aid 707
money 800
supply *store* 636
provide 637
give 784
– aid 707
– deficiencies 52
– the place of 147
– and transport 726
support *perform* 170
sustain **215**
evidence 467
preserve 670
aid 707
feel 821
endure 826
vindicate 937
– life 359
supporter 711
–s *heraldic* 550
suppose 514
supposing 469
supposition **514**
supposititious 546
suppress
destroy 162
conceal 528
silent 581
restrain 751
suppression of truth 544
suppuration 653
suppute 85
supralapsarian 984
supramundane 939
supremacy 33, 737
supreme 33
summit 210
authority 737
in a – degree 31
Supreme Being 976
surbate 659
surbated 688
surcease 142
surcharge 641
– and falsify 811
surcingle 45
surcoat 225
surd *number* 84
deaf 419
silent letter 561
sure *certain* 474
belief 484
safe 664
make – against 673
make – of
inquire 461
take 789
you may be – 535
to be – *assent* 488
on – ground 664
security 771
sure-footed
careful 459
skilful 698
cautious 864
surely 488, 602, 870
sureness 474
surety 474, 664
surf 348, 353
surface *outside* 220
texture 329
below the – 526
lie on the – 518, 525
skim the – 460
Surface, Joseph – 548
surfeit 641, 869
surge *swarm* 72
swell 305
rotation 312
wave 348
surgeon 662
surgery 662
surgit amari aliquid 651
surly *gruff* 895
sullen 901a
unkind 907
surmise 514
surmount *be superior* 33
tower 206
transcursion 303
ascent 305
– a difficulty
overcome 731
surmountable 470
surname 564
surpass
be superior 33
grow 194
go beyond 303
outshine 873
surplice 999
surplus 40, 641
surplusage 641
surprint 550
surprise
non-expectation

508
unprepared 674
wonder 870
surprisingly 31
surrebutter &c.
answer 462
pleadings 969
surrender 725, 782
– one's life 360
surreptitious
furtive 528
deceptive 545
untrue 546
surrogate 759
surround 227, 229
surroundings 227
amidst such and such – 183
sursum corda 990
surtax 812
surtout *coat* 225
surveillance
care 459
direction 693
under – 938
survene 151
survey 441, 466
surveyor 85, 694
survive *remain* 40
long time 110
permanent 141
susceptibility
power 157
tendency 176
liability 177
sensibility 375
motive 615
impressibility 822
irascibility 901
suscipient 785
suscitate *cause* 153
produce 161
stir up 173
excite 824
suspect *doubt* 485
suppose 514
suspected 938
suspectless 484
suspend *defer* 133
discontinue 142
hang 214
suspended animation 823
suspender 45, 214
suspense
cessation 142
uncertainty 475
expectation 507
irresolution 605
in – *inert* 172
suspension
cessation 142
hanging 214
music 413
– of arms 723
suspicion *doubt* 485
incredulity 487
knowledge 490
supposition 514
fear 860
under – 938
suspiration 839
sustain
continue 143
strength 159
perform 170
support 215
preserve 670
aid 707
endure 821
sustained note 413
sustenance 298
sustentation
[*see* sustain]
food 298
susurration 405
sutler 637, 797
suttee *killing* 361
arson 384
unselfishness 942
idolatry 991
suture 43
suum cuique 780, 922
suzerain 745
suzerainty 737
swab *dry* 340
clean 652
lubber 701
swaddle *clothe* 225
restrain 751
swaddling clothes,
in – *infant* 129
subjection 749
swag *hang* 214
lean 217
curve 245
drop 306
oscillate 314
booty 793
ostentation 887
swag-bellied 194
swage 174
swagger
pride 878
boast 884
bluster 885
swaggerer 887
swain *man* 373
rustic 876
lover 897
swale 659
swallow *gulp* 296
eat 298
believe 484
credulous 486
brook 826
– the bait 547, 602
– flight 274
– the leek 607, 725
– up *destroy* 162
use 677
take 789
– hook, line and sinker 602
– whole 465*a*, 484
swallow-tail coat 225
swamp *destroy* 162
marsh 345
defeat 731
swamped
failure 732
swampy *moist* 339
swank 845, 882, 884
swan-pan 85
swan-song 360
swap *exchange* 148
blow 276
sward 344
swarm *crowd* 72
multitude 102
climb 305
sufficiency 639
redundance 641
swarthy 431
swash *affuse* 337
spurt 348
swashbuckler 726, 887
swashy 339
swastika 621, 993
swat 276
swath 72
swathe *fasten* 43
clothe 225
restrain 751
sway *power* 157
influence 175
lean 217
oscillate 314
agitation 315
induce 615
authority 737
– to and fro 149
sweal 659
swear *affirm* 535
promise 768
curse 908
just enough to –
by 32
– at 908
– by *believe* 484
– false 544
– a witness 768
sweat *exude* 295
excretion 299
heat 382
exertion 686
fatigue 688
cold – 860
in a – 382
– of one's brow 686
sweater 225
Swedenborgian 984
Swedish dance 840
sweep *space* 180
curve 245
oar 267
rapid 274
bend 279
clean 652
dirty fellow 653
steal 791
make a clean – of 297
– along 264
– away
destroy 162
eject 297
abrogate 756
relinquish 782
– the chords 416
– off 297
– out 297, 652
– of time 109
sweeper 652
mine– 726
sweeping *whole* 50
complete 52
general 78
– change 146
sweepings
useless 645
dirt 653
sweepstakes 775, 810
sweet
saccharine 396
melodious 413
colour 428
clean 652
agreeable 829
lovely 897
look – upon
desire 865
love 897
endearment 902
– smell 400
– tooth 865, 868

– wine 396
– words 894
sweeten 396, 829
sweetheart 897
sweetmeat 396
sweetness 396
sweets 298, 396
sweet-scented 400
swell *increase* 35
expand 194
wave 348
sound 404
emotion 821
fop 854
nobility 875
swagger 885
extol 931
ground – 315
– over 250
– with rage 900
– the ranks of 37
– out
diffuse style 573
swelling
expansion 194
prominence 250
- *style* 577
excitement 824
swell-mob 792
swelter 382
swerve *change* 140
deviate 279
demur 603
tergiversation 607
swift 274
swig 298, 959
swill *dirt* 653
drink 298
intemperance 954
drunkenness 959
swim *navigate* 267
float 305
light 320
– against the stream 704
– in *pleasure* 377
abundance 639
– with the stream 82, 683
– with the tide 734
swimming 840
- *eyes* 443
- *head* 503
– belt 666
– pool 652, 840
swimmingly
easily 705
success 731
prosperity 734
swindle 545, 791
swindler 548, 792
swine 366
cast pearls before – 638
– of Epicurus 954*a*
swineherd 746
swing
operation 170
space 180
hang 214
oscillate 314
freedom 748
amusement 840
full – 682, 731
give full – 705
have one's – 738
– the lead 544
swinge 972
swingeing *great* 31
swinish 954, 957
– multitude 876
swink 686
swipe 276
swirl 312
swish 409
switch *shunt* 279
flog 972
rod 975
switchback 840
Swithin, reign of St. – 348
swivel *hinge* 312
cannon 727
swivel-eye 443
swollen 194, 878
swoon 158, 688
swoop 274
descend 306
seize 789
at one fell – 173
swop 794
sword *weapon* 727
draw the – } 722
flesh one's – } 722
measure –s 720, 722
at the point of the – 722, 889, 898
severity 739
compulsion 744
subjection 749
put to the – 361
– of Damocles 667
– in hand
prepare 673
war 722
turn –s into ploughshares 723
– of state 747
swordsman 726
Sybarite 954*a*
sybaritism 954
sycophancy 933
sycophant 886, 935
syenite *blue* 438
syllable 561
breathe not a – 528
syllabus 86, 596
syllogism 476
sylph 979
sylvan 367
symbol
copy 21
mathematical - 84
sign 550
symbolize 526, 550
represent 554
symmetrical 80
symmetry
equality 27
order 58
conformity 82
centrality 222
regular form 242
style 578
beauty 845
want of – 846
sympathizer
partisan 890
sympathy
concord 714
friendship 888
love 897
kindness 906
pity 914
condolence 915
symphonious 413
symphony
overture 64
music 415
concord 714
symphysis 43
symposium 72, 840, 892
symptom 550, 668
symptomatology 522
synagogue 1000
synchronism 120
synchysis 218
syncopation 415
syncope
impotence 158
musical 413
rhetoric 572
fatigue 688
syncretic 61
syncretism 24, 984
syndic 745, 967
syndicate 696, 712
synecdoche 521
synod 696, 995
synonym
identity 13
meaning 516
interpretation 522
term 564
synonymous 13
synopsis
arrangement 60
list 86
compendium 596
synovia 332, 356
syntagma 60
syntax 567
synthesis
combination 48
composition 54
reasoning 476
synthesize 54
syntony 23, 120
syringe 337, 348
syrup 352, 396
system *order* 58
rule 80
plan 626
– of knowledge 490
– of opinions 484
systematize 60, 626
systole 195
syzygy 199

T

T, to a – 494
tab 39, 550, 747
tabard 225
tabby *mottled* 440
gossip 588
tabefaction 195
tabernacle 189, 1000
house 189
temple 1000
tabescent 195
tabid *shrunk* 195
thin 203
disease 655
deteriorated 659
table
arrangement 60
list 86
defer 133
layer 204
support 215
flat 251
repast 298

writing 590
on the – 626, 673
turn the –s 218, 468
under the –
hidden 528
drunk 959
– of the Lord 1000
– the motion 624
tableau *list* 86
appearance 448
painting 556
theatrical 599
table-cloth 652
table d'hôte 298
table-land 231, 344
tablet *layer* 204
flat 251
record 551
writing 590
remedy 662
table-talk 532, 588
tablets of the memory 505
table-turning 992
tabloid 531, 662
taboo 761, 992
tabor 417
tobouret 215
tabret 417
tabula rasa
inexistence 2
absence 187
ignorance 491
obliterated 552
facility 705
tabulate 60, 69
tabulation 551
tachometer 274
tachygraphy 590
tachy case 191
tacit 526
taciturnity 585
Tacitus
concise style 572
tack *join* 43
nails 45
change course 140
sharp 253
direction 278
turn 279
food 298
way 627
go upon another – 607
wrong – 732
– to *add* 37
tackle
fastening 45
gear 633
try 675
undertake 676
manage 693
tacky 352
tact *touch* 379
discrimination 465
wisdom 498
skill 698
taste 850
want of – 851
tactful 894
tactician 700
tactics 692, 722
tactless 895
tactile &c. 379
tadpole 129
tædium vitæ 837, 841
tag *small* 32
addition 37
adjunct 39
fastening 45
sequel 65
end 67
point 253
sheep 366
– after 281
tagrag and bobtail 876
tail *sequel* 65
end 67
pendent 214
back 235
aircraft 273
estate – 780
turn – 623
– off *decrease* 36
tail-coat 225
tailor 225, 690
tailoring 225, 882
tail-piece *sequel* 65
rear 235
engraving 558
ornament 847
tail-race 350
taint
imperfection 651
dirt 653
decay 659
disgrace 874
tainted 401, 655
taintless 652
taj 225
take *eat* 298
believe 484
know 490
understand 518
succeed 731
receive 785
appropriate 789
captivate 829
give and – 718
– a back 508, 870
– an account of 85
– action 680
– advice 695
– after 17
– aside 586
– away
annihilate 2
subtract 38
remove 185
seize 789
– back again 790
– a back seat 34
– by [*see below*]
– the cake 33
– care 668, 864
– care of 459, 664
– no care of 460
– off 293
– one's chance 621, 675
– one's choice 609
– things as they come 683, 826
– comfort 831, 834
– the consequences 154
– coolly 826
– a course 692
– its course 143, 151
– no denial 606, 744
– a disease 655
– down
swallow 298
depress 308
record 551
write 590
dismantle 681
humiliate 874
censure 932
– easily 826
– effect 151, 170
– an ell 885
– exception 932
– one's fancy 829, 865
– fire 384
– flight 623
– from 38, 789
– for [*see below*]
– the good the gods provide 831
– heart 831, 836
– to heart 828, 832
– heed 864
– a hint 498
– hold of 46, 789
– hold of the mind 484
– ill 832
– in [*see below*]
– an infection 655
– no interest in 823
– into [*see below*]
– it 484, 514
– the lead 62
– a leaf out of another's book 19
– a lease 788
– leave of 624
– a liberty 748
– away life 361
– a likeness 554
– measures 626
– money 810
– no note of 460
– no note of time 115
– notice 457
– one's oath 535
– off [*see below*]
– oneself off 293
– on [*see below*]
– one with another 29
– out 301, 552
– over 783
– part with 709
– pattern by 19
– a peep 441
– pen in hand 590
– to pieces 44, 681
– place 151
– the place of 147
– possession of 789
– precedence 33, 62
– its rise 66, 154
– root 150, 184
– the shine out of 33
– ship 267
– steps 673, 680
– stock 85
– time
duration 106
late 133
leisure 685
– time by the forelock 132
– to *habit* 613
pursuit 622
use 677
like 827
desire 865
love 897
– on trust 484

– a turn 140
– up [*see below*]
– upon oneself 676, 768
– warning 668
– wing 293
– one at one's word 769
take by
– the button 586
– the hand 707
– surprise 508, 674
take for 484
– better or for worse 609
– gospel 486
– granted 484
take in *include* 54
shorten 201
admit 296
understand 518
deceive 545
receive money 785
– good part
be calm 826
be pleased 827
content 831
– hand *teach* 537
undertake 676
aid 707
– an idea 498
– sail 275
take into
– account
include 76
discriminate 465
qualify 469
– consideration 451
– custody 751
– one's head 514, 608
take off *mimic* 19
destroy 162
remove 185
divest 226
depart 293
discount 813
ridicule 856
– one's hands 785
– the hat 894
take on
attempt 675
discontent 832
melancholy 837
– credit 484
– trust 484
take up
elevate 307
inquire 461
dissent 595
choose 609
undertake 676
befriend 707
arrest 751
borrow 788
censure 932
– arms 722
– a case 476
– one's abode 184
– the cudgels 716, 720
– an inquiry 461
– money 788
– one's pen 590
– with
attention 457
use 677
content 831
taken, be –
die 360
– ill 655
– with 897
taker 789
taking 789
infectious 657
in a – *pained* 828
angry 900
talapoin 996
talbotype 556
tale
counting 85
narrative 594
thereby hangs a – 526
twice-told –
diffuse style 573
weary 841
tale-bearer 532
talent 698
bury one's – in a napkin 528
not put one's – in a napkin 878
talionis, lex – 718, 922
taliped 243
talisman 747, 993
talismanic 992
talk
unsubstantial 4
rumour 532
speak 582
conversation 588
small – 588
– big *boast* 884
insolent 885
threat 909
– glibly 584
– nonsense 497
– of *signify* 516
publish 531
intend 620
– to oneself 589
– oneself out of breath 584
– over
confer 588
persuade 615
– to in private 586
– at random
illogical 477
loquacity 584
– together 588
– against time
time 106
protract 110
inaction 681
– of the town
gossip 588
fame 873
talkative 582, 584
talked of 873
talkies 599, 840
talking, fine –
over-estimation 482
tall 206
– hat 225
– talk 884
tallage 812
tallies 85
tallow 356
– candle 423
tallow-faced 429
tally *agree* 23
list 85, 86
sign 550
credit 805
– with *conform* 82
tally-ho 622
tally-man 797
talma 225
Talmud 985
talons
authority 737
claws 781
talus 217
tam-o'-shanter 225
tambourine 417
tame *inert* 172
moderate 174
domesticate 370
teach 537
feeble 575
subjugate 749
insensible 823
calm 826
tameless
violent 173
malevolent 907
Tammany 940
tamp 261, 276
tamper with
alter 140
seduce 615
injure 659
meddle 682
tan *colour* 433
tandem
at length 200
vehicle 272
tang *taste* 390
bane 663
tangent 199
angle 217
fly off at a –
deviate 279
diverge 291
excitable 825
tangere ulcus 505
tangible
material 316
touch 379
exact 494
sufficient 639
useful 644
tangle 61, 219
tangled 59, 704
weave a – web 704
tango 840
tank *pool* 343
reservoir 636
armoured vehicle 726
tankard 191
tanker 273
tant: – mieux 838
– s'en faut 489
– soit peu 32
tantalize *balk* 509
induce 615
desire 865
tantalizing
exciting 824
Tantalus: torment of – 507, 865
tantamount 27, 516
tantæne animis cœlestibus iræ 900
tantara 407
tantas componere lites 723
tanti 642
tantivy *speed* 274
tantrums 900
tap *open* 260
plug 263
hit 276
let out 295, 297
sound 406
turn on the – 297
tap-dance 840

tape *string* 205
measure 466
– machine 553
taper *contract* 195
narrow 203
candle 423
– to a point 253
tapestry 556, 847
tapinois, en – 528
tapis: on the –
event 151
topic 454
intention 620
plan 626
tap-root 153
taps 550
tapster 746
tar *cover* 223
sailor 269
pitch 356a
– and feather 929, 972
taradiddle 546
tarantass 272
tarantella 840
tarboosh 225
tardiloquence 583
tardy 133, 275
tare 40a
– and tret 813
tares 645
targe 717
target 620
shield 717
tariff 812
tarmac 635
tarn 343
tarnish
discoloration 429
soil 653
deface 848
disgrace 874
tarpaulin 223
tarry *remain* 110, 265
later 133
continue 141
– for *expect* 507
tart *pastry* 298, 396
acid 397
rude 895
irascible 901
harlot 962
tartan 440
tartane 273
Tartar *choleric* 901
catch a – *dupe* 547
unskilful 699
retaliation 718
tartar *dirt* 653
– emetic 663
Tartarus 982
Tartufe
hypocrisy 544
deceiver 548
impiety 988
task *lesson* 537
business 625
put to use 677
fatigue 688
command 741
hard – 704
set a – 741
take to – 932
– the memory 505
taskmaster 694
tass 191
tassel 847
taste *sapidity* **390**
experience 821
good taste **850**
man of – 850
to one's – *savoury* 394
pleasant 829
love 897
tasteful 850
tasteless *insipid* 391
tasty 394, 850
tâtonner 463
tatter
small quantity 32
tatterdemalion 876
Tattersalls 799
tatters *garments* 225
tear to – 162
tatting 847
tattle 588
tattler 532, 588
tattoo
drumming 407
mottled 440
summons 741
taught [*see* teach]
fastened 43
taunt 929, 938
tauromachy 720
taut 43
tautology 104, 573
tavern 189
tawdry 851
tawny 433, 436
tax *inquire* 461
employ 677
fatigue 688
command 741
compel 744
request 765
accounts 811
impost 812
discount 813
accuse 938
– one's energies 686
– the memory 505
taxi 266
taxi-cab 272
taxi-driver 268
taxidermy 368
taxis 60
taxonomy 60
tazza 191
Te Deum 990
te fabula narratur, de – *retaliate* 718
condemn 971
tea 298
teach 537
– one's grandmother 641, 885
– one his place 879
teachable 539
teacher **540,** 673
teaching **537**
false – 538
teacup, storm in a –
overrate 482, 549
exaggerate 549
teagown 225
team *assemblage* 69, 72
teamster 694
tea-party 892
tea-pot 191
tear *separate* 44
violence 173
move rapidly 274
excite 825
weeping 839
– away from 789
– oneself away 623
– asunder one's bonds 750
– one's hair 839
– out 301
– to pieces
separate 44
destroy 162
– up *destroy* 162
tear-gas 663, 727
tearful 839
tearing passion 825
tears: draw – 830
shed – 839
– in one's eyes
excited 824
sad 837
tease *annoy* 830
spite 907
teaser *difficult* 704
teasing 830
teat 250
tea-table talk 588
technic 698
technica, memoria – 505
technical
conformable 82
workmanlike 698
– college 542
– education 537
– knowledge 698
– school 542
– term 564
technicality
special 79
cant term 563
formulary 697
technique 556, 698
technocracy 698
technology 698
techy 901
tedious 841
while away the – hours 681
tedium 841
teem
produce 161
productive 168
abound 639
– with *multitude* 102
teemful 168
teeming *crowd* 72
teemless 169
'teens 98
in one's – 127, 129
teeter 314
teeth 330, 781
armed to the – 673, 717, 722
between the – 405
cast in one's – 938
chattering of – 383
have cut one's eye – 698
in the – of 704, 708
grind one's – 900
the run of one's – 815
set one's – 604
show one's – 900
in spite of one's – 708, 744
make one's – chatter 385, 860
set the – on edge
scrape 331
sour 397
stridor 410
pain the feelings

830
tee 66
teetotalism 953, 958
teetotum 312, 840
teg 366
tegument 223
teind 99
teinoscope 445
tekel upharsin 668
telautograph 553
telegram 532
telegraph
velocity 274
messenger 534
signal 550
– boy 534
by – *haste* 684
telegraphone 553
telegraphy
publication 531
teleology 620
telemeter 200
telepathy 992
telephone 418
inform 527
messenger 534
telescope 445
– word 572
telescopic 196
telesis 658
telesm 993
tell *count* 85
influence 175
evidence 467
inform 527
speak 582
describe 594
succeed 731
let me – you 535
who can – 475
– one's beads 990, 998
– the cause of 522
– fortunes 511
– how 155
– a lie 544
– a piece of one's mind 529
– of 467
– off 85
– one plainly 527
– its own tale 518
– tales
disclose 529
– the truth 543
teller *treasurer* 801
– of tales 594
telling 175
graphic 518
important 642
exciting 824
with – effect 171, 175
telltale *news* 532
indicator 550
knave 941
telluric 318
telum imbelle 158
temerity 863
temper *nature* 5
state 7
moderate 174
elasticity 323
pliability 324
modify 469
prepare 673
affections 820
irascibility 901
command of – 826
lose one's – 900
out of – 901*a*
trial of – 824
– the wind to the shorn lamb 834
tempera 556
temperament
nature 5
tendency 176
musical 413
affections 820
temperance 174, 953
temperate
[*see* temperance]
mild 826
temperature 382
increase of – 384
reduction of – 385
tempest
violence 173
agitation 315
wind 349
excitement 825
tempestivity 134
tempest-tossed 824
tempestuous 59
Templar 996
Good – 958
temple *house* 189
side 236
church 1000
– of the Holy Ghost 983*a*
templet 22
tempora:
O –! O mores!
lament 839
disreputable 874
disapprobation 932
improbity 940
vice 945
– mutantur 140
temporal
transient 111
laical 997
lords – and spiritual 875
temporality 997
temporary 111
temporize
protract 110
defer 133
cunning 702
temporizer 943
tempt *entice* 615
attempt 675
desire 865
– fortune 621, 675
– Providence 863, 885
tempter 615
Satan 978
voice of the – 615
temulency 959
ten 98
– to one 472
– thousand 98
tenable 664
tenacity
coherence 46
toughness **327**
memory 505
resolution 604
obstinacy 606
retention 781
avarice 819
courage 861
– of life 359
– of purpose 604*a*
tenaculum 781
tenancy 777
tenant
present 186
occupier 188
possessor 779
tenantless
absence 187
seclusion 893
tenax propositi 204, 939
tend *conduce* 176
- *animals* 370
aid 707
serve 631, 746
– towards 278
tendence 749
tendency **176**
tender *slight* 32
ship 273
soft 324
painful **378**
colour 428
war vessel 726
offer 763
susceptible 822
affectionate 897
compassionate 914
– age 127
– conscience 926
– heart
susceptible 822
kind 906
compassionate 914
– mercies [ironical]
badness 649
severity 739
cruelty 907
– passion 897
– one's resignation 757
– to 707
tenderfoot 57, 541
tendon 45
tendril *fastening* 45
offshoot 51
infant 129
filament 205
convoluted 248
plant 367
tenebrious 421
tenebrosity 421
tenement 189, 780
– of clay 362
tenet *belief* 484
tenner 800
tennis 840
– ground 213
tenor *course* 7
degree 26
direction 278
high note 410
singer 416
violin 417
meaning 516
pursue the noiseless – of one's way 881
tense *hard* 323
tensile 325
tension 159, 200
tensure 200
tent *abode* 189
covering 223
pitch one's –
locate 184
arrive 292
tentacle 781
tentative 463, 675
tente d'abri 223
tented field 722

tenter-hook 214
on –s 507
tenth 99
tenths
tithe 812
tent-pegging 840
tents, O Israel, to your – 722
tenue, en grande – 847, 882
tenuity
smallness 32
thinness 203
rarity 322
tenuous
shadowy 4
tenure
possession 777
property 780
due 924
tepee 189
tepefaction 384
Tephramancy 511
tepid 382
tepidarium 386
ter quaterque beatus 827
teratology
unconformity 83
distortion 243
altiloquence 577
boasting 884
tercentenary 98, 138, 883
terceron 41
terebration 260
teres atque rotundus 249
in seipso – 650
tergiversation 283, 607
term *end* 67
place in series 71
period of time 106
limit 233
word 562
name 564
lease 780
termagant 901
terminal 67, 233, 292
terminate 67, 292
limit 233
termination 154
termine, mezzo – 628
terminology 562
terminus *end* 67
limit 233
arrival 292
termless 105
terms [*see* term]
circumstances 8
reasoning 476
pacification 723
conditions 770
bring to – 723
come to –
assent 488
pacify 723
submit 725
consent 762
compact 769
couch in – 566
on friendly – 888
in no measured – 574
ternary 93
ternion 92
Terpsichore 416, 840
terra: – cotta
baked 384
sculpture 557
– firma
support 215
land 342
safety 664
– incognita 491
terrace *houses* 189
level 213
terrain 181
terraqueous 318
terre verte 435
terrene 318, 342
terrine 191
terrestrial 318
terrible 860
terribly *greatly* 31
terrier *list* 86
auger 262
dog 366
terrific 31, 830, 860
terrify 860
territorial *land* 342
soldier 726
territory 181, 780
terror 860
King of –s 360
reign of – 739, 828
terrorem, in – 860, 909
terrorism 860
insolence 885
terrorist
coward 862
blusterer 887
evil-doer 913
terse 572
tertian *periodic* 138
tertiary *three* 92
tertium quid
dissimilar 18
mixture 41
combination 48
unconformable 83
tesselated 440, 847
tesseræ
mosaic 440
counters 550
test 463
testa, voce di – 410
testament 771
Testament 985
tester *bedstead* 215
sixpence 800
testify 467, 550
testimonial 551
testimony 467
testy 901
tetanus 315
tetchy 901
tête: – baissée 863
– exaltée 503
– montée 503, 825
–à-tête *two* 89
near 197
confer 588
tether *fasten* 43
locate 184
restrain 751
means of restraint 752
go beyond the length of one's – 738
tethered *firm* 150
tetrachord 413
tetractic 95
tetrad 95
tetrahedral 95
tetrahedron 244
tetrarch 745
text *prototype* 22
topic 454
meaning 516
printing 591
–book 542, 596
textile 219, 329
textuary 983*a*, 985
texture *mixture* 41
roughness 256
fabric 329
Thais 962
Thalia 599
Thalmud 985
Thames on fire
set the – 471
never set the – 501, 701
thane *nobility* 875
thank 916
no – you 764
– one's stars 838
– you for nothing 917
thankful 916
rest and be – 265, 831
thankless
painful 830
ungrateful 917
thank-offering 916, 990
thanks to 155
thanksgiving
gratitude 916
worship 990
that 79
– is 118
– is to say 79
– being so 8
at – time 119
thatch *roof* 223
thaumatrope 445
thaumaturgist 994
thaumaturgy 992
thaw *melt* 335
heart 382
heating 384
calm the mind 826
pity 914
Thearchy
authority 737
Deity 976
theatre
spectacle 441
school 542
drama 599
arena 728
amusement 840
tribunal 966
théâtre: coup de –
appearance 448
prodigy 872
display 882
jeu de – 448, 872
nom de – 565
theatrical 599
affected 855
ostentatious 882
Theban, learned – 492
theca 223
thé dansant 840
theft 775, 791
theism 984, 987
theistic *of God* 976
theme *topic* 454
dissertation 595
Themis 922
then *time* 106
therefore 476
thence

caused by 155
departure 293
therefore 476
thenceforward 121
theocracy 976, 995
theodolite 217, 244
theogony 983
theologicum, odium –
misjudgment 481
false piety 988
churchdom 995
theology 983
theomancy 511
theopathy 987
theopneustic 985
theorbo 417
theorem
topic 454
maxim 496
supposition 514
theoretical 514
theorize 155, 514
theory
attribution 155
knowledge 490
supposition 514
theosophy 983, 984
therapeutics 655, 662
therapy 662
there 183, 186
thereabouts
almost 32
place 183
near 197
thereafter 117
thereby 631
– hangs a tale 154
therefore
attribution 155
reasoning 476
motive 615
therein 221
thereof 9
theretofore 116
thereupon 106, 117
therewith
accompanying 88
means 632
theriac 662
thermal 382
thermion 330
thermogenic 382
thermology 382
thermometer
heat 389
thermopile 389
thermoscope 389
Thersites 936
thesaurus 802
list 86
book 593
words 562
store 636
thesis *theme* **454**
proposition 514
dissertation 595
Thespian 599
Thetis 341
theurgist 994
theurgy 992
thews and sinews 159
thick *crowded* **72**
numerous 102
broad 202
dense 321
semiliquid 352
turbid 426
dirty 653
friends 888
come – 102
in the – of
middle 68
imbedded 228
action 680
lay it on –
cover 223
redundance 641
flattery 933
– of the action 682
– of the fray 722
through – and thin 173, 604*a*
thick-coming
many 102
repeated 104
frequent 136
– fancies 515
thicken 35
thickens, the plot – 682
thicket 367
thick-head 501
thickness 202, 204
thick-ribbed 159
– ice 383
thickset *short* **201**
broad 202
dense 321
thick-skinned 376, 823
thick-skull 499, 501
thief 792
set a – to catch a thief 791
like a – in the night
unexpected 508
concealment 528
dishonourable 940
thievery 791
thieves' Latin 563
thimble
receptacle 191
defence 717
thimbleful 25, 32
thimblerig 545
thimblerigger 792
thin *subduct* **38**
few 103
small 193
narrow 203
rare 322
scanty 640
– end of the wedge 66
– out 371
thing *substance* **3**
matter 316
just the – 924
the – 926
– to do 625
– of naught 4
know a – or two 698
things
events 151
clothes 225
chattels 780
as – go 613
thingumbob 563
think 451, 484
only – 870
reason to – 472
– aloud 589, 703
– better of 607, 658
– fit 600, 602
– highly 931
– ill 932
– likely 472
– no more of
inattention 458
forgive 918
– of *intend* 620
– out 457
as one –s proper 600
– twice 605, 864
– upon
remember 505
thinker 500
thinking principle 450
thinness 203
thin-skinned
physically sensible 375
morally sensitive 822
fastidious 868
irascible 901
third 93
trisection 94
music 413
– degree 461
– heaven 981
– part 94
– person 664
– power 92
thirdly 93
thirst 865
– for knowledge 455
thirsty soul 959
thirteen 98
thirty-nine articles 983*a*
thirty-one
cards 840
this 79
– that or the other 15
at – time of day 118
thistle *prickly* **253**
thistle-down 320
thither 278
thole 821
– pin 215
Thompson sub-machine gun 727
thong *fastening* **45**
scourge 975
Thor 979
thorn *sharp* **253**
bane 663
painful 830
plant a – 830
spiteful 907
– in the flesh 663, 830
– in the side
badness 649
bane 663
annoyance 830
thorns: sit on –
physical pain 378
moral pain 828
fear 860
on – for 865
thorny 253, 704
thorough 52
thorough-bass 413, 415
thorough-bred
intrinsic 5
horse 271
skill 698
fashionable 852
thoroughfare 260,

627
thorough-going 52
thoroughly, do –
729
thorough-paced 31
thorp 189
though
compensation 30
qualification 469
opposition 708
thought *little* 32
reflection 451
idea 453
give a – to 457
not to be – of
610, 761
organ of – 450
quick as – 274
seat of – 450
subject of – 454
want of – 458
who would have –
it? 508
– of 454
thoughtful 451, 498
thoughtless
incogitant 452
inattentive 458
careless 460
improvident 674
thoughts:
– that breathe 574
– elsewhere 458
thousand 98, 102
one in a – 648,
948
thralldom 749, 751
thrash 972
Thraso 887
Thrasonic 884, 885
thread
arrange 60
series 69
weak 160
filament 205
pass through 302
not have a dry –
339
hang by a – 665
life hangs by a –
360
worn to a – 659
– one's way 266,
302
threadbare 226, 659
threadpaper 203
threat 909
threaten
future 121
destiny 152
danger 665

threatening
warning 668
unhopeful 859
three 93
– in one and one
in – 976
sisters – 601
go through – hundred and sixty
degrees 311
– sheets in the
wind 959
times three
number 98
approbation 931
threefold 93
three-score 98
– years and ten
128
three-tailed
bashaw
master 745
nobility 875
threne 839
threnody 839
thresh 972
– out 461
threshold
beginning 66
edge 231
at the – *near* 197
– of an inquiry 461
thrice 93
– happy 827
–told tale 573
thrid 302
thrift
prosperity 734
gain 775
economy 817
thriftless 818
thrill
physical pain 378
touch 380
feeling 821
excitation 824
thrilling
pleasing 829
painful 830
thrive 734
throat *opening* 260
pipe 350, 351
cut the – 361
force down the –
739
stick in one's –
581, 585
take by the – 789
throb 315, 821
throbbing: – heart
860

– pain 378
throe
revolution 146
violence 173
agitation 315
physical pain 378
agony 828
birth– 161
throne *abode* 189
seat 215
emblem of authority 747
ascend the – 737
occupy the – 737
power behind
the – 526
– of God 981
throng 72
throttle
render powerless
158
close 261
kill 361
seize 789
– down 275
through
owing to 154
viâ 278
by means of 631
get – 729
go – one 824
wet – 339
– thick and thin
complete 52
violence 173
perseverance 604a
throughout 50, 52
– the world 180
throw *impel* 276
propel 284
exertion 686
– oneself into the
arms of 666
– away *reject* 610
waste 638
relinquish 782
– back 145
– cold water on
616
– of the dice 156
– doubt upon 485
– down 162, 308
– oneself at the
feet of 725
– good money
after bad 818
– in 228
– off [*see below*]
– open 260, 296
– out [*see below*]
– over *destroy* 162

– overboard
exclude 55
destroy 162
eject 297
abrogate 756
– on paper 590
– away the scabbard 722
– into the shade
superior 33
lessen 36
surpass 303
important 642
– a tub to catch a
whale 545
– up [*see below*]
– a veil over 528
throw off 297
– all disguise 529
– one's guard 508
– the mask 529
– the scent
misdirect 538
avoid 623
throw out 284, 297
eject 297
– a feeler 379
– of gear
disjoin 44
derange 61
– a hint 527
– a suggestion 514
throw up *eject* 297
resign 757
– one's cap 884
– the game 624
throwing stick 727
thrown out 704
thrum 416
thrush 416
thrust *push* 276
attack 716
– in *insert* 300
(*interpose*) 228
– one's nose in 682
– out 55
– down one's
throat 744
– upon 784
thud 406, 408a
thug *murderer* 361
thief 792
thumb *touch* 379
bite the – 929
one's fingers all –s
699
rule of –
experiment 463
unreasoning 477
essay 675
twiddle one's –

681
under one's –
authority 737
subjection 749
– over 539
– screw 975
Thumb, Tom – 193
thump
beat 276
thud 406
non-resonance 408a
punish 972
thumping *great* 31
big 192
thunder
violence 173
noise 404
prodigy 872
threaten 909
look black as – 832, 900
– against 908, 932
– of applause 931
– forth 531
– at the top of one's voice 411
–s of the Vatican 908
thunderbolt
weapon 727
prodigy 872
thunder-clap 508, 872
thundering *great* 31
big 192
thunderstorm 173
thunderstruck 870
thurible 400, 998
thurifer 996
thuriferous 400
thurification
fragrance 400
rite 998
thus *circumstance* 8
therefore 476
– far *little* 32
limit 233
thwack 276, 972
thwart
across 219
harm 649
obstruct 706
oppose 708
cross 830
thwarted 732
tiara *insignia* 747
ornament 847
canonicals 999
Tib's eve 107
tick *graze* 199, 379
oscillation 314
sound 407
mark 550
credit 805
go on – 806
– off *record* 551
ticker 553
ticket 86, 550, 609
ticket of leave 760
– man 754, 949
tickle *touch* 380
please 829
amuse 840
– the fancy 829, 840
– the ivories 416
– the palate 394
– the palm 784, 807
ticklish
uncertain 475
dangerous 665
difficult 704
tidal wave 348, 667
tid-bit 648, 829
tide *ocean* 341
wave 348
abundance 639
prosperity 734
against the – 708
drift with the – 705
go with the – 82
high &c. – 348
stem the – 708
swim with the – 734
turn of the – 210
– of events 151
– over *time* 106
defer 133
safe 664
inaction 681
succeed 731
– of time 109
tidings 532
tidy *orderly* 58
arrange 60
good 648
clean 652
pretty 845
– up 60
tie *relation* 9
equality 27
fasten 43
fastening 45
neckcloth 225
security 771
obligation 926
nuptial – 903
ride and – 266
–s of blood 11
– down
hinder 706
compel 744
restrain 751
– the hands 158, 751
– oneself 768
– up *restrain* 751
condition 770
entail 771
tie-beam 45
tied up
busy 135
in debt 806
tier *continuity* 69
layer 204
tierce 92
– and carte 716
tiff 713, 900
tiffin 298
tiger *violent* 173
servant 746
courage 861
savage 907
evil-doer 913
bad man 949
tight *fast* 43
closed 261
smart 845
drunk 959
– grasp 739
– hand 739
– rope dancing 698
keep a – hand on 751
on one's – ropes 878
tighten 43, 195
tight-fisted 819
tights 225
tightwad 819
tigress 374
tike 876
tilbury 272
tile *roof* 223
hat 225
– loose *insane* 503
till *up to the time* 106
coffer 191
cultivate 371
treasury 802
– doomsday 112
– now 122
– the soil 673
tiller
instrument 633
money-box 802
– of the soil
agriculture 371
clown 876
tilt *slope* 217
cover 223
propel 284
fall 306
contention 720
full – *direct* 278
active 682
haste 684
ride full – at 622, 716
run a – at 716
– over 218
– up 307
– with 720
tilth 371, 775
tilting at the ring 840
tilt-yard 728
timber *trees* 367
materials 635
timbre 413
timbrel 417
time 106
instant 113
leisure 685
against – 684
at –s 136
behind the –s 124
course of – 109
doing –
imprisonment 751
employ one's – in 625
glass of – 106
in – *course* 109
early 132
destiny 152
measure – 114
no – *instantly* 113
soon 132
no – to lose 630, 684
no – to spare 684
ravages of – 659
slow – 275
take – *slow* 275
inaction 681
inactive 683
true – 113
waste – 683
– and again 104
– has been 122
– being 118
– to come 121
– of day 113
– drawing on 121
– enough 132
– gone by 135
– hanging on one's hands

inaction 681
leisure 685
weariness 841
– immemorial 122
– of life
duration 106
now 118
age 128
– out of mind 122
– to spare 685
– after time 104
– up 111, 134
– was 122
there being –s when 136
timeful 134
time-honoured
old 124
repute 873
respected 928
time-keeper 114
time-recorder 553
timeless 135
timelessness 112
timely 132, 134
timeo Danaos 485, 864
timeous 134
time-piece 114
time-pleaser 607
timetable 266
times *present* 118
events 151
hard – 735
many – 136
– out of number 104
time-serving
tergiversation 607
cunning 702
servility 886
improbity 940
selfishness 943
time-worn *old* 124
age 128
deteriorated 659
timid *fearful* 860
cowardly 862
humble 881
timist 607
Timocracy 803
Timon of Athens
wealth 803
seclusion 893
misanthrope 911
timorous [*see* timid]
tin *preserve* 670
money 800
– hat 717
tinct 428
tinctorial 428
tincture
small quantity 32
mixture 41
colour 428
tinctured
disposition 820
tinder *fuel* 388
irascible 901
tine 253
tinge
small quantity 32
mix 41
colour 428
tingent 428
tingle *pain* 378
touch 380
emotion 821
make the ears – 900
tink 408
tinker
repair 660
tinkle
faint sound 405
resonance 408
tinkling cymbal 517
tinnient 408
tinsel *glitter* 420
sham 545
ornament 847
frippery 851
tinsmith 690
tint 428
tintamarre 404
tintinnabulary 408
tiny 32, 193
– bit 32
tip *end* 67
summit 210
cover 223
give 784
reward 973
on –toe *high* 206
expect 507
– off 527
– the wink 550
tip-cat 840
tippet 214, 225
tipple 298, 959
tippler 959
tipstaff 965
tipsy 959
tip-top 210, 648
tirade 582, 932
tire *dress* 225
fatigue 688
worry 830
weary 841
tiré à quatre épingles 850
tirer d'affaire 672
se – 731
Tiresias 513
tiresome [*see* tire]
Tisiphone 173, 900
tissue *whole* 50
assemblage 72
matted 219
texture 329
tit *small* 193
pony 271
tit for tat 718
Titan 159, 980
Titania 979
titanic 192
titbit 298, 394, 829
tithe *tenth* 99
tax 812
tithing 181
titillate 840, 865
titillation 377, 380
titivate 847
title
indication 550
name 564
printing 591
right to property 780
distinction 877
right 924
titled 875
title-deed 771
title-page 66
titter 838
tittle 32
to a – 494
tittle-tattle 532, 588
titubancy 583
titubate 306, 732
titular 562, 564
tmesis 218
T.N.T. 727
to *direction* 278
lie – 681
– all intents and purposes 27, 52
– a certain degree 32
– come 121, 152
– the credit of 805
– crown all 33, 642
– do 59
– the end of the chapter 52
– the end of time 112
– and fro 12, 314
– the full 52
– a great extent 31
– the letter 19
– a man 78
– the point 23
– the purpose 23
– a small extent 32
– some extent 26
– be sure 488
– this day 118
– wit 79
toad 649, 846
– under a harrow 378
toad-eater 886, 935
toad-eating
flattery 933
toadstool 367
toady 886
toast *roast* 384
celebrate 883
tobacco 392
toboggan 272, 840
toby *jug* 191
toccata 415
tocsin 669
tod 319
to-day 118
toddle 266, 275
toddy 298
toe 211
on the light fantastic 309, 840
toes turn up the – *die* 360
toff 854
toffee 396
toga 225, 747
assume the – virilis 131
together 88, 120
come – 290
get – 72
hang – 709
lay heads – 695
– with 37, 88
toggery 225
toil
activity 682
exertion 686
– of a pleasure 682
–s *trap* 545
toilet 225
– water 400
toilette 225
en grande – 847
toilsome 686, 704
toilworn 688
token 550
give – 525
– of remembrance 505
told, do what one is – 743
tolderolloll 838

Toledo 727
tolerable
a little 32
trifling 643
pretty good 648
not perfect 651
satisfactory 831
tolerably, get on – 736
toleration
laxity 738
lenity 740
permission 760
feeling 821
calmness 826
benevolence 906
toll *sound* 407
tax 812
– the knell 363
tollbooth
prison 752
market 799
tomahawk 727
tomb 363
lay in the – 363
– of the Capulets 506
tombé des nues 83, 870
tombola 156
tomboy 129, 851
tombstone 363
tom-cat 373
tome 593
tomentous 256
tomfool 501
tomfoolery
absurdity 497
amusement 840
wit 842
ostentation 882
Tom Noddy 501
Tommy Atkins 726
tommy-gun 727
to-morrow 121
– and to-morrow 104, 109
tompion 263
tomtit 193
Tom Thumb 193
tom-tom 417, 722
ton *weight* 319
fashion 852
-s of money 800
tonality 413, 420
tone *state* 7
strength 159
tendency 176
sound 402
music 413
colour 428
blackness 431
painting 556
method 627
disposition 820
give a – to 852
– down
moderate 174
darken 421
discolour 429
– in with 714
– of voice 580
tone poem 415
toney 852
tongs
fire-irons 386
retention 781
tongue
projection 250
taste 390
language 560
bite the – 392
bridle one's – 585
give – 404, 580
hold one's – 403
slip of the –
error 495
solecism 568
stammering 583
on the tip of one's –
near 197
forget 506
latent 526
speech 582
wag the – 582
– cleave to the roof of one's mouth 870
have a – in one's head 582
– of land 342
– running loose 584
keep one's – between one's teeth 585
tongueless 581
tongue-tied 581
tonic
musical note 413
healthy 656
medicine 662
– sol fa 415
tonicity 159
tonnage 192
tonsillectomy 662
tonsils 351
tonsure 999
tonsured 226
tontine 810
tony 501
Tony Lumpkin 876
too
also 37
excess 641
– bad
disreputable 874
wrong 923
censure 932
– clever by half 702
in a – great degree 31
– far 641
– hot to hold one 830
– late 133
– late for 135
– little 640
– many 641
– much [*see below*]
– soon 132
– soon for 135
– true 833, 839
too much
redundance 641
intemperance 954
have – of 869
make – of 482
– for 471
– of a good thing 869
tool *instrument* 633
steer 693
catspaw 711
ornament 847
servile 886
edge – 253
mere – 690
toot 406
tooth *fastening* 45
projection 250
sharp 253
roughness 256
notch 257
texture 329
taste 390
sweet –
desire 865
fastidious 868
– and nail
violence 173
exertion 686
attack 716
– paste &c. 652
toothache 378
toothed 253
toothsome 394
top *supreme* 33
summit 210
roof 223
spin 312
sleep like a – 683
fool to the – of one's bent 545
go over the – 861
– to bottom 52
– coat 225
– hat 225
at the – of the heap 210
– of the ladder 873
at the – of one's speed 274
from – to toe 200
at the – of the tree 210, 873
at the – of one's voice 404, 411
toparchy 737
topaz 436, 847
top-boot 225
tope *tomb* 363
trees 367
drink 959
temple 1000
topee 225
toper 959
top-full 52
top-gallant mast, 206, 210
top-heavy
unbalanced 28
inverted 218
dangerous 665
tipsy 959
Tophet 982
topiary 847
topic 454
– of the day 532
topical 183
top-mast 206
topmost 210
topography 183
topographer 466
topple
unbalanced 28
perish 162
decay 659
– down *fall* 306
– over 28, 306
topsail schooner 273
topsawyer 642, 700
top sergeant 745
topsy-turvy 14, 218
toque 225
tor 206
torch 388, 423
apply the – 824
light the – of war 722
– of Hymen 903

Tories 712
torment
physical 378
moral 828, 830
place of – 982
Tormes, Lazarillo de – 941
torn [*see* tear]
discord 713
tornado 312, 349
torpedo *bane* 663
sluggish 683
weapon 727
evil-doer 913
– boat 726
– boat destroyer 726
– plane 276
torpid, torpor
inert 172
inactive 683
insensible 823
torque 847
torrefy 384
torrent
violence 173
rapid 274
flow 348
rain in –s 348
torrid 382
torsion 248
torso 50
tort 925, 947
tort et à travers, à –
disagreement 24
absurdity 497
resolution 604
tortious 925
tortile 248
tortive 248
tortoise 275
tortoise-shell 440
tortuous
twisted 248
dishonourable 940
torture
physical 378
moral 828, 830
cruelty 907
punishment 972
– a question 476
torvity 901*a*
toss *derange* 61
throw 284
oscillate 314
agitate 315
– in a blanket 929
– the caber 840
– the head
pride 878
insolence 885
contempt 930
– off *drink* 298
– overboard 610
– on one's pillow 825
– up 156, 621
tosspot 959
tot *child* 129
tot homines, tot sententiæ 15
total 50, 84
sum – 800
– abstinence 953, 955
– eclipse 421
totalisator 621
totality 52
totally 52
totidem verbis 19, 494
totient 84
toties quoties 136
totis viribus 686
totitive 84
toto: in – 52
– cœlo 52
totter
changeable 149
weak 160
limp 275
oscillate 314
agitate 315
decay 659
danger 665
– to its fall 162
touch *relate to* 9
small quantity 32
mixture 41
contact 199
sensation **379, 380**
music 416
test 463
indication 550
act 680
receive 785
excite 824
pity 914
– and go
instant 113
soon 132
changeable 149
easy 705
– the guitar 416
– the hat 894
– the heart 824
– on 516
– to the quick 822
– up 658
– upon 595
in – with 9
touched *crazy* 503
tainted 653
compassion 914
– in the wind 655
– with *feeling* 821
touching 830
touchstone 463
touchwood
fuel 388
irascible 901
touchy 901
tough *coherent* 46
tenacious 327
difficult 704
toujours perdrix
repetition 104
weary 841
satiety 869
toupee 256
tour 266
tour de force
skill 698
stratagem 702
display 882
touring car 272
tourist 268
tournament 720
tourniquet 263
tournure 230, 448
belle – 845
tous les rapports, sous – 494
tousle 61
tout *solicit* 765
tout: – au contraire 14
– court 265
– ensemble 50
– le monde 78
touter *agent* 758
solicitor 767
eulogist 935
tow 285
take in – *aid* 707
towage 812
towardly 705
towards 278
draw – 288
move – 286
towel *clean* 652
flog 972
tower
stability 150
edifice 161
abode 189
height 206
soar 305
defence 717
– of strength
strong 159
influential 175
safety 664
towering *great* 31
furious 173
large 192
high 206
– passion 900
– rage 900
town *city* 189
fashion 852
man about – 854
on the – 961
all over the – 532
talk of the – 873
– council 696
town-hall 189, 966
township 181
townsman 188
fellow – 892
town-talk 532, 588
toxic 657
toxicology 663
toxophilite 284
toy *trifle* 643
amusement 840
fondle 902
toy-dog 366
toy-shop 840
trabant 717
tracasserie 713
trace *inquire* 461
discover 480*a*
mark 550
record 551
delineate 554
– back 122
– out 480*a*
– to 155
– up 461
tracery
lattice 219
curve 245
ornament 847
traces *harness* 45
trachea 351
tracing 21
track *trace* 461
record 551
way 627
cover up one's –s 528
in one's –s 113
racing – 840
– meet 840
– racing 728
trackless
space 180
difficult 704
– trolley 272
tract *region* 181
book 593
dissertation 595

– of time 109
tractable
malleable 324
willing 602
easy 705
tractarian 984
tractile
traction **285**
soft 324
traction **285**
tractor 271
trade *exchange* 148
business 625
traffic 794
drive a – 625
learn one's – 539
tricks of the – 702
two of a – 708
– with 794
trader 797
trade-mark 550
tradesman 797
trade-publication 531
trade-union 712
trade-wind 349
tradition *old* 124
description 594
custom 613
traduce 934
traducer 936
traffic 794
tragedian 599
tragedy
drama 599
evil 619
tragic *drama* 599
tragical 830
tragi-comedy 599
tragi-comic 853
trail *sequel* 65
pendent 214
slow 275
follow 281
traction 285
odour 398
inquiry 461
record 551
highway 627
follow in the – of 281
– of a red herring 615, 706
train *sequel* 65
series 69
pendent 214
vehicle 272
sequence 281
traction 285
- *animals* 370
teach 537
accustom 613
prepare 673
bring in its – 615
in – 673
in the – of 281, 746
lay a – 626, 673
put in – 673
siege – 727
– de luxe 272
– of reasoning 476
– of thought 451
train-band 726
train-bearer 746
train-ferry 273
trained 698
trainer 673
- *of horses* 268
- *of animals* 370
teacher 540
training
education 537
– college 542
train-oil 356
traipse 275
trait *speciality* 79
appearance 448
mark 550
description **594**
traitor
disobedient 742
knave 941
enemy 891
trajection 297
trajectory 627
tra-la-la 838
tralatitious 521
tralineate 279
tralucent 425
tram 272
trammel *hinder* 706
restrain 751
fetter 752
cast –s off 750
tramontane
foreign 57
distant 196
wind 349
outlandish 851
tramp *stroll* 266
stroller 268
idler 683
vagabond 876
on the – 264
trample
– in the dust
destroy 162
prostrate 308
– out 162
– under foot
vanquish 731
not observe 773
disrepute 874
insolence 885
dereliction 927
contempt 930
– upon 649, 739
tramway 627
trance *insensibility* 376
dream 515
sleep 683
lethargy 823
tranquil *calm* 174
quiet 265
peaceful 721
calmness 871
– mind 826
tranquillize
moderate 174
pacify 723
soothe 826
transact *act* 680
conduct 692
– business 625
– business with 794
transaction 151, 625, 680, 769
transactions 551
transalpine 196
transanimation 140
transatlantic 196
transcalency 384
transcend *great* 31
superior 33
go beyond 303
transcendency 641
transcendent 33, 873
transcendental 78, 519
transcendentalism 450
transcolate 295
transcribe 19, 590
transcript 21, 590
transcursion **303**
transept 1000
transfer
copy 21
displace 185
- *of things* 270
- *of property* **783**
transference **270**
transfiguration
change 140
divine - 998
transfix 260
transfixed *firm* 150
transform 140
transformation
scene 599
transfuse 41, 270
– the sense of 522
transgress
go beyond 303
infringe 773
violate 927
sin 945
transgression 947
transi de froid 383
transient 111, 149
transientness **111**
transilience 146, 303
transit
conversion 144
motion 264
transference 270
- *circle* 244
transit gloria mundi, sic – 735, 874
transition 144, **270**
transitional 140
transitory 111
transitu, in –
transient **111**
journey 266
transference **270**
translate
interpret 522
promote 995
translator 524
translation
transference 270
resurrection 981
translocation 270
translucence 425
transmarine 196
transmigration 140, 144
transmission
moving 270
passage 302
- *of property* 783
transmit light 425
transmogrify 140
transmutation 140, 144
transom 215
transparency **425**
transparent
transmitting light 425
obvious 518
transpicuous
transmitting light 425
obvious 518
transpierce 260
transpire

evaporate 336
appear 525
be disclosed 529
transplace 270
transplant 270
transplendent 420
transpontine 196
transport
transfer 270
ship 273
war vessel 726
excitement 825
delight 827
please 829
punish 972
– of love 897
– plane 273
transpose
exchange 148
displace 185
invert 218
transfer 270
- *music* 413
transubstantiation
change 140
sacrament 998
transude 295, 302
transume 140
transumption 270
transverse 217, 219
tranter 271
trap *closure* 261
gig 272
snare 545
stage – 599
pitfall 667
fall into a – 547, 699
lay a – for 545
trapan 545
trap bat and ball 840
trap-door
opening 260
snare 545
pitfall 667
trapes 701
trappings
adjunct 39
clothes 225
equipment 633
ornament 847
Trappist 996
traps
clothes 225
baggage 780
trash
unmeaning 517
trifling 643
useless 645
trashy – style 575

traulism 583
traumatic 662
travail 161, 686
trave 215
travel 266
– out of the record 477
traveller 268
bagman 758
tricks upon –s 545, 702
–'s tale 546, 549
travelling bag 191
traverse *move* 266
pass 302
negative 536
obstruct 706
travesty
imitate 19, 21
misinterpret 523
misrepresent 555
ridicule 856
travis 215
trawl 285, 463
trawler 273
tray 191
treacherous 907, 940
– memory 506
treachery 545, 940
treacle 352, 396
tread 264, 266
– the beaten track 82, 613
– the boards 599
– down 739, 879
– on the heels of 281
– a path 266, 622
– the stage 599
– in the steps of 19
– under foot
destroy 162
subjection 749
disrepute 874
insolence 885
contempt 930
– upon 649
treadle 633
treadmill 975
treason 742, 940
treasure *cherish* 897
store 636
goodness 648
money 800
– trove 618
– up in the memory 505
treasurer 801
treasury 802
– note 800

treat *physical pleasure* 377
manage 692
bargain 769
delight 827, 829
amusement 840
– of 595
– oneself to 827
– well 906
treatise 593, 595
treatment
painting 556
conduct 692
ill – 649
medical – 662
treaty 769
treble
three 93
shrill 410
childish – 581
tree *pedigree* 166
plant 367
gallows 975
top of the – 210
up a – 704
as the – falls 151
– of knowledge 490
treenail 45
trefoil 92
trek 266
trellis 219
tremble
fluctuate 149
weakness 160
shake 315
cold 383
emotion 821
fear 860
make one – 860
trembling:
– in the balance 475, 665
– to its fall 162
tremblingly alive 822
tremendous 31, 830, 860
tremendously 31
tremolo 415
tremor
agitation 315
emotion 821
fearful 860
tremulous
agitated 315
– *voice* 583
irresolute 605
fear 860
trench *moat* 232
furrow 259

concavity 252
defence 717
– mortar 727
– on *near* 197
trespass 303
moral trespass 925
trenchant
energetic 171
assertive 535
concise style 572
vigorous language 574
important 642
emotion 821
discourteous 895
censure 932
trench-coat 225
trencher *plate* 191
layer 204
trenches, open the – 716
trend *tendency* 176
bend 278
deviate 279
trennel 45
trepan 260
snare 545
borer 262
trephine 260, 262
trepidation
agitation 315
emotion 821
excitement 825
fear 860
tres juncta in uno 92
trespass
go beyond 303
vice 945
guilt 947
tress 256
trestle 215
trevet 215
[*and see* **trivet**]
trews 225
trey 92
triad 92
triagonal 244
trial *inquiry* 461
experiment 463
essay 675
difficulty 704
adversity 735
suffering 828, 830
lawsuit 969
punishment 972
– of temper 824
triality 92
trialogue 588
triangle 92, 244

music 417
punishment 975
triangular duel 720
triarchy 737
tribe *race* 11
assemblage 72
class 75
clan 166
tribulation 828
tribunal 966
tribune
rostrum 542
judge 967
tributary *river* 348
giving 784
tribute
compensation 30
donation 784
money paid 809
reward 973
pay – to 928, 931
trice 113, 633
– up 43
in a – 113
trichotomy 94
trichroism 440
trick *deception* 545
trait 550
habit 613
contrivance 626
skill 698
artifice 702
- *at cards* 775
play –s
bungle 699
cunning 702
amusement 840
ridicule 856
– of fortune 509
– out 847, 851
–s of the trade 702
trickery *deceit* 545
finery 851
trickle 295, 348
trickster
deceiver 548
cunning 702
rogue 792
tricksy *cheery* 836
pretty 845
ornamented 847
tricolour
variegated 440
flag 550
tricycle 272
trident 92, 341
triennial
periodical 138
plant 367
triennium 92
trifid 94
trifle *small* 32
neglect 460
folly 499
unimportant 643
not to be –d with 744
not stick at –s 604
– time away 683
– with *neglect* 460
deceive 545
disrespect 929
trifler 460, 501
trifling 499, 643
wit 842
triforium 1000
triform 92
trifurcate 94
trigamy 903
trigger 633
draw the – 722
Trigger, Sir Lucius O' – 887
trigon 244
trigonometry 244
trihedral 93
trilateral 236, 244
trilogistic 93
trilogy 93
drama 599
trill *stream* 348
sound 407
music 416
trillion 98
trim *state* 7
adjust 27
dress 225
form 240
lie 544
waver 605
change sides 607
clean 652
beautify 845
adorn 847
scold 932
flog 972
in – order 58
trimmer *fickle* 607
apostate 941
selfish 943
trimming
border 231
ornament 847
dishonesty 940
trinal 92
trine 93
trinitrotoluene 727
trinity 92
– Sunday 998
Trinity, Holy – 976
trinket 643, 847
Trinkgeld 784
trinal 93
trinomial 92
trio *three* 92
music 415
triolet 597
trip *jaunt* 266
run 274
fall 306
leap 309
mistake 495
bungle 699
fail 732
vice 945
guilt 947
– up *deceive* 545
overthrow 731
tripartition 94
triplane 273
triple 93
– crown 747, 999
triplet *three* 92
verse 597
triplex 93
triplication 93
triplicity 93
tripod 215
tripos 461
tripotage 588
tripping [*see* trip]
style 578
nimble 682
caught – 491
trippingly on the tongue 584
Triptolemus 371
trireme 273
trisection 94
triste 837
tristful 837
trisulcate
trisected 94
furrow 259
trite
known 490
conventional 613
– saying 496
tritheism 984
Triton *sea* 341
– among the minnows
superior 33
huge 192
important 642
trituration 330
trium literarum, homo – 792
triumph
success 731
trophy 733
exult 838
celebrate 883
boast 884
triumvirate 92, 737
triune 92
Triune God 976
trivet 215, 386
right as a – 650, 924
trivia 643
trivial
unmeaning 517
trifling 643
useless 645
troat 412
trocar 262
trochaic 597
trochee 597
trochilic 312
trodden: down– 749
well – 613, 677
Troglodyte 893
troika 92
troll
roll 312
fairy 980
trollop 962
trolley 272
– omnibus 272
trombone 417
tronk 752
troop 72, 726
raise –s 722
– carrier
aeroplane 726
trooper 726
lie like a – 544
swear like a – 908
troop-ship 726
trop, de – 641
trope 521
Trophonius, cave of – 837
trophy 551, 733
tropical 382
troposphere 338
trot 266, 274
– out 525, 882
troth *belief* 484
veracity 543
promise 768
by my – 535
plight one's – 902
trothless 544, 940
trotters 266
trottoir 627
troubadour 597
trouble *disorder* 59
derange 61
exertion 686
difficulty 704

adversity 735
pain 828
painful 830
bring into – 649
get into – 649, 732
in – 619, 735
take – 686
– one's head about 682
– one for 765
– oneself 686
troubled waters, fish in – 704
troublesome 686, 704, 830
troublous 59, 173
– times 713
trough *hollow* 252
trench 259
conduit 350
trounce 932, 972
troupe 72
trousers 225
trousseau 225
trouvaille 775
trouvère 597
trover 775, 964
trow *think* 451
believe 484
know 490
trowel 191
troy-weight 319
truant *absent* 187
runaway 623
idle 682
apostate 941
truce *cessation* 142
deliverance 672
peace 721
pacification 723
flag of – 724
trucidation 361
truck *summit* 210
vehicle 272
barter 794
truck driver 268
truck farm 371
truckle to
submit 725
servile 886
flatter 933
truckle-bed 215
truck-load 31
truckman 268
truculent 907
trudge 266, 275
truditur dies die 109
true *real* 1
straight 246
assent 488
accurate 494
veracious 543
faithful 772
honourable 939
orthodox 983a
– bill
vindicate 937
accuse 938
lawsuit 969
see in its – colours 480a
– meaning 516
– to nature 17
– to oneself 604a
– saying 496
– to scale 494
true-hearted 543, 939
true-love 897
true-lover's knot 897, 902
true-penny 939
truism *axiom* 496
unmeaning 517
trull 962
truly *very* 31
assent 488
really 494
indeed 535
trump *perfect* 650
honourable 939
good man 948
turn up –s 731
– card *device* 626
success 731
– up *falsehood* 544
accuse 938
trumped up 468, 545, 546
trumpery 517, 643
trumpet *music* 417
war cry 722
boast 884
flourish of –s
ostentation 882
celebration 883
boasting 884
ear– 418
penny –
skill 410
sound of –
alarm 669
speaking – 418
– blast 404
– call 550, 741
– forth 531
trumpeter
musician 416
messenger 534
boaster 884
trumpet-toned 410
trumpet-tongued 404, 531
truncate 201, 241
truncated 53
truncheon
weapon 727
staff of office 747
instrument of punishment 975
trundle 284, 312
trunk *whole* 50
origin 153
paternity 166
box 191
trunk-hose 225
trunnion
support 215
projection 250
truss *tie* 43
pack, packet 72
support 215
trust
belief 484
combination 709
property 780
credit 805
hope 858
– to a broken reed 699
– to the chapter of accidents 621
trustee
consignee 758
possessor 779
treasurer 801
trustful 484
trustless 940
trustworthy
certain 474
belief 484
- *memory* 505
veracious 543
honourable 939
truth
exactness 494
veracity 543
probity 939
arrive at the – 480a
in – *certainly* 474
love of – 543
of a – 535, 543
prove the – of 937
religious – 983a
speak the – 529, 543
in very – 543
Truth, Spirit of – 976
truthless 544
trutination 319
try *experiment* 463
adjudge 480
endeavour 675
use 677
lawsuit 969
– a case 967
– a cause 480
– conclusions
discuss 476
quarrel 713
contend 720
– one's hand 675
– one's luck 621
– one 704
– out 463
– the patience 830
– a prisoner 967
– one's temper 824
– one's utmost 686
trying 688, 704
tryst 892
trysting-place 74
tsar [*see* czar]
tu quoque 718
– argument
counter-evidence 468
confutation 479
accuse 938
tub 191
– thumper 582
– to a whale 545, 617
tuba 417
tubam trepidat, ante – 860, 862
tubby 202
tube 260
test – 144
tubercle 250
tuberculous 655
tuberosity 250
tubman 968
tubular 260
tubulated 260
tubule 260
tuck *fold* 258
dagger 727
– in *locate* 184
eat 298
insert 300
tucker 225
tuft *collection* 72
rough 256
tufted 256
tuft-hunter 886, 943
tuft-hunting 886, 933
tug *ship* 273
pull 285

effort 686
– of war 720, 722
athletic sport 840
tuition 537
tulip *variegated* 440
gaudy 882
tumble *derange* 61
destruction 162
fall 306
agitate 315
fail 732
rough and – 59
– down 665
tumbler *athlete* 159
glass 191
actor 599
buffoon 844
tumbrel 272
tumefaction 194
tumid
expanded 194
- *style* 577
tumour
expansion 194
prominence 250
tumult *disorder* 59
agitation 315
revolt 742
emotion 825
tumultuous 59, 173
tumulus 363
tun *receptacle* 191
large 192
drunkard 959
tunable 413
tund 972
tundra 344
tune 402, 415
in – 413
out of –
unmusical 414
imperfect 651
deteriorated 659
put in –
prepare 673
concord 714
to the – of
quantity 25
payment 807
price 812
– up 416
tuneful *music* 413
poetry 597
– nine 416, 597
tuneless 414
tunic 225
tunicle 999
tuning-fork 417
tunnage 192
tunnel *concave* 252
opening 260

passage 627
tup 366, 373
turban 225
turbary 267
turbid 426, 653
turbinated 248, 312
turbine 153
turbulence
violence 173
agitation 315
excitation 825
turbulent 59
Turcism 984
tureen 191
turf *lawn* 344
grass 367
fuel 388
gambling 621
races 720
race-course 728
amusement 840
turgid
expanded 194
- *style* 577
redundant 641
ostentatious 882
Turk
polygamist 903
grand – 745
'bear like the – no rival near the throne' 878
turkey-trot 840
Turkish bath 386, 652
turlupinade 842
turmoil
confusion 59
violence 173
agitation 315
turn *state* 7
crisis 134
period of time 138
change 140
tendency 176
form 240
curve 245
blunt 254
stroll 266
deviate 279
circuition 311
rotate 312
aptitude 698
affections 820
emotion 821
dance 840
nausea 867
by –s 138, 148
come in its – 138
each in its – 148
meet one at

every – 641
take a favourable – 658
give one a –
aid 707
excite 824
do a good – 648, 906
ill – 907
in – 58, 138
one's luck –s 735
serve one's – 644
to a – 494
take a wrong – 732
– about 148
– to account 677, 775
– adrift 73, 297
– aside *change* 140
deviate 279
hinder 706
– one's attention from 458
– away *eject* 297
not look 442
avoid 623
dismiss 756
relinquish 782
– back 145, 283
– one's back upon
oppose 708
refuse 764
disrespect 929
contempt 930
– the brain 503
– of the cards 156
– colour 821
– a corner
go round 311
succeed 731
– the corner 140, 658
– a deaf ear to
deaf 419
refuse 764
– down 258
– of expression 566
– the eyes upon 441
– for 698
– from *repent* 950
– to good account 658
– one's hand to 625
– the head
induce 615
excite 824
astonish 870
vanity 880
hate 898

– on one's heel
avoid 623
discourtesy 895
– the house out of window 713
– in *go to bed* 683
– inside out 529
– into
conversion 144
translate 522
- *money* 796
- *ridicule* 856
– of mind 820
– the mind to 457
– off 972
– on the tap 297
– the other cheek 725
– out *become* 144
happen 151
exterior 220
clothes 225
carriage 272
eject 297
strike 719
- *well* 731
- *ill* 732
dismiss 756
display 882
– over [*see below*]
– a penny 775
– round
inversion 218
revolve 311
rotate 312
recant 607
- *one's little finger* 737
– the scale
unequal 28
superior 33
change 140
reverse 145
cause 153
counter-evidence 468
induce 615
– the stomach 395, 867
– the tables 14, 718
– of the table 156
– tail *go back* 283
run away 623
cowardice 862
– the tide 145
– of the tide 145, 218
– topsy turvy 61, 218
– and turn about

148, 149
- turtle 218
- and twist 248
- under 258
- up [*see below*]
- upon
depend upon 154
retaliate 718
turn over *give* 784
invert 218
entrust 755
- the leaves 457, 539
- in the mind 451
- a new leaf
change 140
improve 658
repent 950
- to 270
turn up *happen* 151
chance 156
visible 446
unexpected 508
- one's eyes
wonder 870
hypocrisy 988
- one's nose at
aversion 867
fastidious 868
contempt 930
turn-coat 605, 607
turnover 298
turned of 128
turning-point
crisis 8
end 67
occasion 134
reversion 145
cause 153
summit 210
limit 233
turnkey 753
turnpike 706
- road 627
turnscrew 633
turnspit 366
turnstile 553, 706
turpentine and beeswax 255
Turpin, Dick - 792
turpitude 874, 940
turquoise *blue* 438
jewel 847
turret 206
turret-ship 726
turtle *savoury* 394
turtle-doves 897
tush *silence* 403
taciturn 585
trifling 643
tusk 253
tussle 720
tussock 256
tut [*see* **tush**]
censure 932
tutelage
teaching 537
learning 539
safety 664
subjection 749
tutelary *safety* 664
- genius
auxiliary 711
god 979
- god 664
- saint 890, 912
tutor *cultivate* 375
teach 537
teacher 540
tutus, cavendo - 664
tuyère 386
twaddle
absurd 497
unmeaning 517
diffuseness 573
talk 584
twain 89
in - 44
twang *taste* 390
pungency 392
sound 402
stridor 410
music 416
voice 583
twattle
[*see* **twaddle**]
tweak 378
- the nose 830
tweed 219
tweedle *touch* 379
music 416
tweedledum and tweedledee 415
tweeny 746
tweezers 781
twelfth 99
twelve 98
twentieth century 118
twenty &c. 98
- shillings in the pound 803
twice 90
twice-told tale 104, 841
twiddle 379
twig 51
hop the - 360
twilight
morning 125
evening 126
dusk 422
- sleep 376
twill *crossing* 219
convolution 248
fold 258
twin *similar* 17
accompanying 88
two 89
duplicate 90
twine *string* 205
intersect 219
convolution 248
- round 43, 227
twinge 378, 828
twinkle
instantaneous 113
light 420
dimness 422
twinkling of an eye, in the - 113
twins 89
twire 315
twirl *convolute* 248
revolve 311
rotate 312
twist *join* 43
thread 205
oblique 217
crossing 219
distort 243
convolution 248
deviate 279
bend 311
prejudice 481
insanity 503
fault 651
appetite 865
twit *deride* 856
disrespect 929
censure 932
accuse 938
twitch *pull* 285
shake 315
pain 378
mental - 828
twitter
agitation 315
cry 412
music 416
emotion 821
excitement 824
'twixt 228
two 89
kill - birds with one stone 682
make - bites of a cherry 629, 956
- dozen 98
- meanings 520
in - places at once 471
game at which - can play 718
- score 98
fall between - stools 732
- strings to one's bow 632
- or three 100
- of a trade 708
unable to put - words together 583
two-bits 800
two-edged 253
two-faced 544
twofold 90
twopenny-half-penny 643
two-sided 90
two-step 840
Tyburn tree 975
tycoon 745
tyg 191
tyke 876
tymbal 417
tympani 417
tympanum 210, 418
tympany 194
type *essential* 5
similarity 17
pattern 22
class 75
form 240
prediction 511
metaphor 521
indication 550
letter 561
printing 591
heavy - 550
- script 21
- writing 590
typhoon 349
typical *special* 79
conformable 82
metaphorical 521
significant 550
typist 590
typify 511
typography 591
tyranny 739
tyrant *severe* 739
ruler 745
evil-doer 913
tyre 230
tyro *ignoramus* 493
learner 541

U

uberrima fides 484
uberty 168
ubiety 186

ubiquity 186
U-boat 726
Ucalegon, proximus ardet – 667
udder 191
ugh! 867
ugliness **846**
ugly 846
– customer *source of danger* 667
evil-doer 913
bad man 949
– duckling 948
call by – names 932
take an – turn 732
uhlan 726
ukase 741
ukulele 417
ulcer *disease* 655
care 830
ulema 967, 996
uliginous 352
ullage 53, 190
ulster 225
ulterior
additional 37
extraneous 57
- *in time* 121
- *in space* 196
– motive 615
ultima ratio 744
– regum 722
ultima Thule 196
ultimate 67
ultimately 121, 133, 151
ultimatum
definite 474
intention 620
requisition 630
terms 770
ultimo 122
ultra 31, 33
– vires 925
ne plus – 729
– crepidam 471
ultramarine 438
ultramontane
foreign 57
distant 196
heterodox 984
church 995
ultramundane 196
ultra-violet rays 420
ululation **412**, 839
Ulysses 702
umbilicus 222
umbra 421
magni nominis – 659
umbrage *shade* 424
hatred 898
take – *anger* 900
umbrageous 421
umbrella
covering 223
shade 424
protection 666
umpire
judgment 480
mediator 724
judge 967
unâ voce 488
unabashed
bold 861
vain 880
insolent 885
unabated 31
unable 158
– to say 'No' 605
unacceptable 830
unaccommodating
disagreeing 24
disagreeable 830
discourteous 895
sulky 901*a*
unaccompanied 87
unaccomplished 730
unaccountable
exceptional 83
unintelligible 519
irresponsible 927*a*
arbitrary 964
unaccustomed
unusual 83
unused 614
unskilful 699
unachievable 471
unacknowledged 489, 917
unacquainted 491
unacquired 777*a*
unadmonished 665
unadorned 576, 849
beauty – 845
unadulterated 42, 494, 652
unadventurous 864
unadvisable 647
unadvised 665, 699
unaffected
genuine 494
sincere 543
– *style* 578
obstinate 606
artless 703
insensible 823
simple 849
taste 850
unafflicted 831
unaided *weak* 160
unalarmed 861
unalienable 924
unallayed 159
unallied 10
unallowable 923
unallowed 925
unalloyed 42
– happiness 827
– truth 494
unalluring 866
unalterable 150
unaltered 13, 150
unamazed 871
unambiguous 518
unambitious 866
unamiable 907
unanimated 823
unanimity 23, 488, 714
unannexed 44
unanswerable
demonstrative 478
irresponsible 927*a*
arbitrary 964
unanswered 478
unanticipated 508
unappalled 861
unappareled 226
unapparent 526
unappeasable 173
unappetizing 395
unapplied 678
unappreciated 483
unapprehended 491
unapprehensive 861
unapprized 491
unapproachable
great 31
infinite 105
distant 196
unapproached 33
unappropriated 782
unapproved 932
unapt
incongruous 24
important 158
unskilful 699
unarmed 158
unarranged 59, 674
unarrayed 849
unascertained 475, 491
unasked 602, 766
unaspiring 866, 881
unassailable 664
unassailed 748
unassembled 73
unassisted 160, 706
– eye 441
unassociated 44
unassuming 881
unatoned 951
unattached 44
unattackable 664
unattainable 471
unattained 732
unattempted 623
unattended 87
– to 460
unattested 468
unattracted
indifferent 866
unattractive 866
unauthenticated
unproved 468
uncertain 475
error 495
unauthoritative 475
unauthorized
prohibited 761
undue 925
lawless 964
unavailing 645, 732
unavenged 918
unavoidable 474, 601
unavowed 489
unawakened 683
unaware 491, 508
take –s 674
unawed 861
unbalanced 28
unbar 750
unbearable 830
unbeaten 123
unbeauteous 846
unbecoming
incongruous 24
disreputable 874
undue 925
dishonourable 940
– a gentleman 895
unbefitting 24, 925, 940
[*see* unbecoming]
unbegotten 2
unbeguile 527, 529
unbegun 67, 674
unbelief 485, 989
unbeloved 898
unbend
straighten 246
repose 687
– the mind 452
unbending 323
unbenevolent 907
unbenign 907
unbeseeming 851, 940

unbesought 766
unbetrayed 939
unbewailed 932
unbiassed 498, 748
unbidden 600, 742
unbigoted 498
unbind 44, 750
unblamable 946
unblamed 946
unblemished 650, 946
unblenching 861
unblended 42
unblest 735, 932
– with 777*a*
unblown 674
uncommenced 67
unblushing
proud 878
vain 880
imprudent 885
unboastful 881
unbodied 317
unboiled 674
unbolt 750
unbookish 491
unborn 2, 152
unborrowed 787, 788
unbosom oneself 529
unbought
not bought 796
honorary 815
honourable 939
unselfish 942
unbound 748, 927*a*
unbounded 105
unbrace 160, 655
unbreathed 526
unbred 895
unbribed 939, 942
unbridled
violent 173
lax 738
free 748
unbroken
entire 50
continuous 69
preserved 670
unviolated 939
unbruised 50
unbuckle 44
unburden
– one's mind 529
unburdened 705
unburied 362
unbusinesslike 699
unbuttoned 748
uncalculating 863
uncalled for
redundant 641
useless 645
not used 678
uncandid 544, 907
uncanny 846, 980
uncanonical 984
uncared for
neglected 460
indifference 866
disliked 867
hated 898
uncase 226
uncaught 748
uncaused 156
unceasing 112
uncensured 931
unceremonious 880, 895
uncertain
irregular 139
not certain 475
doubtful 485
in an – degree 32
uncertainty 475
unchain 44, 750
unchained 748
unchallenged 488, 924
unchangeable 150, 604*a*
unchanged 16, 141
unchanging 5
uncharitable 907
unchartered 925, 964
unchaste 961
unchastised 970
unchecked 748
uncheckered 141
uncheerful 837
unchivalric 940
unchristian 984, 989
uncial 590
uncinated 244
uncircumscribed 180
uncircumspect 460
uncivil 851, 895
uncivilized 876, 895
unclaimed 748
unclassical 851
uncle *kin* 11
my –'s
pawnshop 787
unclean 653
– spirit 978, 980
uncleanness 653
unclipped 50
unclog 705, 750
unclose 260, 750
unclothe 226
unclouded 420, 446
unclubbable 893
unclutch 790
uncoif 226
uncoil 313
uncoloured
achromatic 429
true 494
uncombed 653, 851
uncombined
simple 42
incoherent 47
uncomeatable 471
uncomely 846
uncomfortable 828, 830
uncommenced 67
uncommendable
blamable 932
bad 945
guilt 947
uncommensurable 24
uncommon 31, 83, 137
uncommonly 31
uncommunicated 781
uncommunicative 528
uncompact 322
uncompassionate 914*a*
uncompelled 748
uncomplaisant 764
uncompleted
incomplete 53
unfinished 730
failure 732
uncomplying 742, 764
uncompounded 42
uncompressed 320, 322
uncompromising
conformable 82
severe 739
unconcealable 525
unconceived
uncreated 2
unintelligible 519
unconcern 823, 866
unconcocted 674
uncondemned 970
unconditional
complete 52
free 748
permission 760
consent 762
release 768*a*
unconducive 175*a*
unconfined 748
unconfirmed 475
unconformity
disagreement 24
irregularity 83
unconfused
methodical 58
clear 518
unconfuted 478, 494
uncongealed 333
uncongenial 24, 657
unconnected
irrelative 10
disjointed 44
discontinuous 70
illogical 477
unconquerable
strong 159
persevering 604*a*
– will 604
unconquered 719
unconscientious 940
unconscionable
excessive 31
unprincipled 945
unconscious
ignorant 491
insensible 823
unconsenting 603, 764
unconsidered 452
unconsolable 837
unconsolidated 47
unconsonant 24
unconspicuous 447
unconstitutional 925, 964
unconstrained 748, 880
unconsumed 40
uncontested 474
uncontradicted 488
uncontrite 951
uncontrollable
violent 173
necessity 601
emotion 825
uncontrolled
free 748
excitability 825
uncontroverted 488
unconventional 83, 614
unconversant 491, 699
unconverted
dissenting 489
irreligious 989

unconvinced 489
uncooked 674
uncopied 20
uncork 750
uncorrupted 939
uncounted 475
uncouple 44
uncourteous 895
uncourtly 851, 895
uncouth
- *style* 579
ugly 846
vulgar 851
uncover
denude 226
open 260
disclose 529
bow 894
uncreated 2
uncritical 931
uncropped 50
uncrown 756
unction
emotion 821, 824
divine functions 976
piety 987
extreme – 998
lay the flattering – to one's soul 834, 858
unctuous *oily* 355, 894
flattering 933
hypocritical 988
unctuousness 355
unculled
unused 678
relinquished 782
unculpable 946
uncultivated
vulgar 851
ignorant 491
unprepared 674
uncurbed 748
uncurl 246
uncustomary 83
uncut 50
undamaged (648)
undamped 340
undated
without date 115
waving 248
undaunted 861
undazzled 498
undebauched 939
undeceive 527, 529
undeceived 490
undecided
inquiring 461
uncertain 475
irresolute 605
leave – 609*a*
undecipherable 519
undecked 849
undecomposed 42
undefaced 845
undefended 725
undefiled
honest 939
innocent 946
chaste 960
undefinable
uncertain 475
unmeaning 517
unintelligible 519
undefined
invisible 447
uncertain 475
undeformed 845
undemolished 50
undemonstrable 485
undemonstrated 475
undemonstrative 826
undeniable 474, 478
undeplored 898
undepraved 939
undeprived 781
under *less* 34
below 207
subject to 749
range – 76
– advisement 454
– age 127
– agent 758
– arrest 751
– breath 405
– the conditions 8
– one's control 743
– cover
covered 223
hidden 528
safe 664
– the domination of 737
– one's eyes 446
– foot [*see below*]
– full strength 651
– the head of 9
– lock and key 664
– the mark 34
– press of 744
– protest 489, 744
– restraint 751
– the rule of 737
– seal 467
– subjection 749
– the sun 1
– way 282
underbid 794
underbreath 405
underbred 851
underclothing 225
undercurrent
cause 153
stream 348, 349
latent 526
opposing 708
underestimation 483
underfed 640
underfoot 207
tread – 739
undergo 151
– a change 144
– pain 828
undergraduate 541
underground
low 207
deep 208
latent 526
hidden 528
underhand 526, 528
– dealing 528
underhung 250
underived 20
underlessee 779
underlet 787
underlie 207, 526
underline
mark 550
emphatic 642
underling
servant 746
clown 876
undermine
weaken 158
burrow 252
damage 659
stratagem 702
hinder 706
undermost 211
underneath 207
undernourished 640
underpaid 817
underpin 215
underplot 626
underprop 215
underrate 483
underreckon 483
undersell 796
underset 215
undershot 250
undersign 467
undersized 193
understand
know 490
intelligible 518
latent 526
be informed 527
give one to – 572
– by 516, 522
– one another 709, 714
understanding
agreement 23
intellect 450
intelligence 498
come to an – 488
intelligible 518
agree 714
pacification 723
compact 769
good – 714, 888
by a mutual – 526
with the – 469
understate 483
understood
meaning 516
implied 526
customary 613
understrapper 746
understudy 634
undertake
endeavour 676
promise 768
undertaker 363
undertaking 625, 676
undertone 405
undertow 348
undervalue 483
underwood 367
underwrite
promise 768
compact 769
insurance 771
underwriter 758
undescribed 83
undeserved 925
undeserving of belief 485
undesigned 621
undesigning 703
undesirable 647, 830
undesired 830, 866
undesirous 866
undespairing 858
undestroyed
existing 1
whole 50
persisting 141
undetermined
chance 156
inquiry 461
uncertain 475
unintelligible 519
irresolute 605
undeveloped 526

undeviating
uniform 16
unchanged 150
straight 246
direct 278
persevering 604*a*
undevout 989
undigested 674
undignified 940
undiminished 31, 35, 50
undirected 279, 621
undiscernible 447, 519
undiscerning
blind 442
inattentive 458
undisciplined 608
undisclosed 526, 528
undiscoverable 519
undiscovered 526
undiscriminating 465*a*
undisguised
true 494
manifest 525
sincere 543
undismayed 861
undisposed of 678, 781
undisputed 474
undissembling 543
undissolved
entire 50
dense 321
undistinguishable 465*a*
undistinguished 465*a*
undistorted 246, 494
undistracted 457
undisturbed
quiescent 265
repose 685
unexcited 826
undivided 50, 52
undo *untie* 44
reverse 145
destroy 162
neutralize 179
not do 681
undoing *ruin* 735
undone *failure* 732
adversity 735
pained 828
hopeless 859
undoubted 474
undubitably 488
undraped 226
undreaded 861
undreamt of 452
undress *clothes* 225
nude 226
simple 849
undressed 226, 674
undried 339
undrilled 674
undrooping 604*a*
undueness 925
undulate 248, 314
unduly 32
undutiful 945
undying 112, 150
une aile, ne battre que d' – 683
unearned 925
unearth *eject* 297
disinter 363
inquire 461
discover 480*a*
unearthly
immaterial 317
Deity 976
demon 980
heavenly 981
pious 987
uneasy 828
uneatable 395
unedifying 538
uneducated 491, 674
unembarrassed 705, 852
unembodied 317
unemotional 823
unemployed 678, 681
unencumbered 705, 927*a*
unendeared 898
unending 112
unendowed 158
– with reason 450*a*
unendurable 830
unenjoyed 841
unenlightened 491, 499
unenslaved 748
unenterprising 864
unentertaining 843
unenthralled 748
unentitled 925
unenvied 929, 930
unequal 28, 139
inequitable 923
– to 640
unequalled 33
unequipped 674
unequitable 923
unequivocal
great 31
sure 474
clear 518
unerring
certain 474
tone 494
innocent 946
unessayed 678
unessential 643
unestablished 185
uneven *diverse* 16*a*
unequal 28
irregular 139
rough 256
uneventful 643
unexact 495
unexaggerated 494
unexamined 460
unexampled 83
unexceptionable
good 648
legitimate 924
innocent 946
unexcitable 826
unexcited 823, 826
unexciting 174
unexecuted 730
unexempt 177
unexercised 674, 678
unexerted 172
unexhausted 159, 639
unexpanded 195, 203
unexpected
exceptional 83
inexpectation 508
unexpensive 815
unexplained
not known 491
unintelligible 519
latent 526
unexplored
neglected 460
ignorant 491
unseen 526
unexposed 526
unexpressed 536
unexpressive 517
unextended 317
unextinguished 173, 382
unfaded 428
unfading 112
unfailing 141
unfair *false* 544
unjust 923
dishonourable 940
unfaithful 940
unfaltering 604*a*
unfamiliar 83
unfashionable 83, 851
unfashioned 241, 674
unfasten 44
unfathomable
infinite 105
deep 208
mysterious 519
unfavourable
out of season 135
hindrance 706
obstructive 708
– chance 473
unfeared 861
unfeasible 471
unfed 640, 956
unfeeling 376, 823
unfeigned 543
unfelt 823
unfeminine
manly 373
vulgar 851
unfertile 169
unfetter 750
unfettered 748
unfinished 53, 730
unfit
inappropriate 24
impotence 158
inexpedient 647
unskilful 699
wrong 923
undue 925
unfitted
not prepared 674
unfix 44
unfixed 149
unflagging 604*a*
unflammable 385
unflattering 494, 703
unfledged
young 127, 129
unprepared 674
unflinching
firm 604
persevering 604*a*
brave 861
unfold
straighten 246
evolve 313
interpret 522
manifest 525
disclose 529
– a tale 594
unforbidden 760
unforced 602, 748
unforeseen 508

unforfeited 781
unforgettable 505
unforgiving 919
unforgotten 505
unformed 241, 674
unfortified
pure 42
powerless 158
unfortunate
ill-timed 135
failure 732
adversity 735
unhappy 828
– woman 962
unfounded 546
unfrequent 137
unfrequented 893
unfriended
powerless 158
secluded 893
unfriendly
opposed 708
hostile 889
malevolent 907
unfrock 756, 972
unfrozen 382
unfruitful 169
unfulfilled 773, 925
unfurl
unfold 313
– a flag 525, 550
unfurnished 640, 674
ungainly 846, 895
ungallant 895
ungarnished 849
ungathered 678
ungenerous 819, 943
ungenial 657
ungenteel 851, 895
ungentle 173, 895
ungentlemanly
vulgar 851
rude 895
dishonourable 940
ungifted 499
unglorified 874
unglue 47
ungodly 989
ungovernable
violent 173
disobedient 742
passionate 825
ungoverned 748
ungraceful
- *language* 579
ugly 846
vulgar 851
ungracious 895, 907
ungrammatical 568
ungranted 764
ungrateful 917
ungratified 832
ungrounded
unsubstantial 4
erroneous 495
ungrudging 816
unguarded
neglected 460
spontaneous 612
unprepared 674
in an – moment
unexpectedly 508
unguem, ad – 494, 650
unguent 356
unguibus et rostro 686
unguided
ignorant 491
impulsive 612
unskilled 699
unguilty 946
unhabitable 187
unhabituated 614
unhackneyed 614
unhallowed 988, 989
unhand 750
unhandseled 123
unhandsome 940
unhandy 699
unhappy
adversity 735
pain 828
dejected 837
make – 830
unharbored 185
unhardened
tender 914
innocent 946
penitent 950
unharmonious 24, 414
unharness 750
unhatched 674
unhazarded 664
unhealthy 655, 657
unheard of
exceptional 83
improbable 473
ignorant 491
wonderful 870
unheated 383
unheed, -ed 460
unheeding 458
unhesitating
belief 484
resolved 604
unhewn 241, 674
unhindered 748
unhinge 61, 158
unhinged
impotent 158
insane 503
failure 732
unhitch 44
unholy 989
unhonoured 874
unhook (44)
unhoped 508
unhorsed 732
unhostile 888
unhouse 297
unhoused 185
unhurt 670
unicorn
monster 83
carriage 272
unideal *existing* 1
no thought 452
true 494
unification 48, 87
uniform
homogeneous 16
simple 42
orderly 58
regular 80
dress 225
symmetry 242
livery 550
uniformity 16
unilluminated 421
unimaginable 471, 473
wonderful 870
unimaginative 576, 843, 871
unimagined 1, 494
unimitated 20
unimpaired 670
unimpassioned 826
unimpeachable
certain 474
true 494
due 924
approved 931
innocent 946
unimpeached 931, 946
unimpeded 705, 748
unimportance 643
unimpressed 838
unimpressible 823
unimproved 659
unincreased 36
unincumbered
easy 705
exempt 927a
uninduced 616
uninfected 652
uninfectious 656
uninflammable 385
uninfluenced
obstinate 606
unactuated 616
free 748
uninfluential 172, 175a
uninformed 491
uningenuous 544
uninhabit, -able, -ed 187, 893
uninitiated 491, 699
uninjured
perfect 650
healthy 654
preserved 670
uninjurious 656
uninquisitive 456
uninspired 823
uninstructed 491
unintellectual 452, 499
unintelligent 499
unintelligibility 519
unintelligible 519
- *style* 571
render – 538
unintentional
necessary 601
undesigned 621
uninterested 456, 841, 843
unintermitting
unbroken 69
durable 110
continuing 143
persevering 604a
uninterrupted
continuous 69
perpetual 112
unremitting 143
unintroduced 893
uninured 614
uninvented 526
uninvestigated 491
uninvited 893
uninviting 830
union
agreement 23
junction 43
combination 48
concurrence 178
workhouse 189
party 712
concord 714
marriage 903
unionist 712
union-jack 550
union-pipes 417
unique
dissimilar 18

original 20
exceptional 83
alone 87
unirritating 174
unison
agreement 23
melody 413
concord 714
unit 51, 87
Unitarian 984
unite *join* 43
combine 48
assemble 72
concur 178
converge 290
party 712
– one's efforts 709
– in pairs 89
– with 709
united 46, 714
unity *identity* 13
uniformity 16
whole 50
complete 52
single 87
concord 714
– of time 120
Unity, Trinity in – 976
universal 78
– Church 983*a*
– favourite 899
universality 52
universe 318
university 542
– education 537
– extension 537
go to the – 539
unjust *wrong* 923
impious 988
unjustifiable
wrong 923
inexcusable 938
wicked 945
unjustified 923
undue 925
unkempt
unclean 653
vulgar 851
unkennel *eject* 297
disclose 529
unkind 907
–est cut of all 828
unknightly 940
unknit (44)
unknowable 519
unknowing 491
unknown
ignorant 491
latent 526
– to fame
inglorious 874
low-born 876
– quantities 491
unlaboured
- *style* 578
unprepared 674
unlace (44)
unlade 297
unladylike
vulgar 851
rude 895
unlamented
hated 898
disapproved 932
unlatch 44, 750
unlawful
undue 925
illegal 964
unlearn 506
unlearned 491
unleavened 674
unless
circumstances 8
except 83
qualification 469
unlettered 491
– Muse 579
unlicensed 761
unlicked
unprepared 674
vulgar 851
clownish 876
– cub
youngster 129
shapeless 241
unmannerly 895
unlike 18
unlikely 473
unlikeness 15
unlimber 323
unlimited
great 31
infinite 105
free 748
– space 180
unliquefied 321
unlively 837, 843
unload
displaced 185
eject 297
disencumber 705
unlock *unfasten* 44
discover 480*a*
unlooked for 508
unloose
unfasten 44
liberate 750
unloved 898
unlovely 846
unlucky
inopportune 135
bad 649
unfortunate 735
in pain 830
unmade 2
unmaimed 654
unmake 145
unman
mutilate 38
render powerless 158
madden 837
frighten 860
unmanly
effeminate 374
dishonourable 940
unmanageable
unwieldy 647
perverse 704
unmanned
dejected 837
cowardly 862
unmannered 895
unmannerly 895
unmarked 460
unmarred 654, 670
unmarried 904
unmask 529
unmatched
different 15
dissimilar 18
unparalleled 20
unmeaningness 517
unmeant 517
unmeasured
infinite 105
undistinguished 465*a*
abundant 639
unmeditated 612
unmeet 925
unmellowed 674
unmelodious 414
unmelted 321
unmentionable 874
–s 225
unmentioned 526
unmerciful 914*a*
unmerited 925
unmethodical 59
unmindful
inattentive 458
neglectful 460
ungrateful 917
unmingled 42
unmissed 460
unmistakable
certain 474
intelligible 518
manifest 525
unmitigable 173
unmitigated
great 31
complete 52
violent 173
unmixed 42
unmolested 664, 831
unmoneyed 804
unmoral 823
unmourned 898
unmoved
quiescent 265
obstinate 606
insensible 823
unmusical 414
– voice 581
unmuzzled 748
unnamed 565
unnatural
exceptional 83
affected 855
spiteful 907
unnecessary
redundant 641
useless 645
inexpedient 647
unneeded 645
unneighbourly 895
unnerved
powerless 158
weak 160
dejected 837
unnoted } 460
unnoticed } 874
unnumbered 105
unnurtured 674
uno saltu 113
unobeyed 742
unobjectionable
good 648
pretty good 651
innocent 946
unobnoxious 648
unobscured 420
unobservant 458
unobserved 460
unobstructed 705, 748
unobtainable 471
unobtained 777*a*
unobtrusive 881
unoccupied
vacant 187
unthinking 452
doing nothing 681
inactive 683
untenanted 893
unoffended
enduring 826
humble 879
unofficial 964
unoften 137

unopened 261
unopposed 709
unorganized 674
- matter 358
unornamental 846
unornamented
- *style* 576
simple 849
unorthodox 984
unostentatious 881
unowed 807
unowned 782
unpacific 713, 722
unpacified 713
unpack
unfasten 44
take out 297
unpaid *debt* 806
honorary 815
the great -
magistracy 967
- worker 602
unpalatable 395, 830
unparagoned
supreme 33
best 648
perfect 650
unparalleled
unimitated 20
supreme 33
exceptional 83
unpardonable 938, 945
unparliamentary language 895, 908
unpassable 261
unpassionate 826
unpatriotic 911
unpeaceful 720, 722
unpeople
emigration 297
banishment 893
unperceived
neglected 460
unknown 491
unperformed 730
unperjured 543, 939
unperplexed 498
unpersuadable 606
unpersuaded 616
unperturbed 826
unphilosophical 499
unpierced 261
unpin (44)
unpitied 932
unpitying 914*a*
unplaced 185
unplagued 831
unpleasant 830
unpleasing 830
unpoetical 598, 703
unpolished
rough 256
inelegant 579
unprepared 674
vulgar 851, 876
rude 895
unpolite 895
unpolluted
good 648
perfect 650
unpopular 830, 867
unpopularity 898
unportioned 804
unpossessed 777*a*
unpractical 699
unprecedented 83, 137
unprejudiced 498, 748
unpremeditated
impulsive 612
undesigned 621
unprepared 674
unprepared 508, 674
unprepossessed 498
unprepossessing 846
unpresentable 851
unpretending 881
unprevented 748
unprincipled 945
unprivileged 925
unprized 483
unproclaimed 526
unproduced 2
unproductive 645
unproductiveness 169
unproficiency 699
unprofitable
unproductive 169
useless 645
inexpedient 647
bad 649
unprolific 169
unpromising 859
unprompted 612
unpronounceable 519
unpronounced 526
unpropitious
ill-timed 135
opposed 708
hopeless 859
unproportioned 24
unprosperous 735
unprotected 665
unproved 477
unprovided
scanty 640
unprepared 674
unprovoked (616)
unpublished 526
unpunctual
tardy 133
untimely 135
irregular 139
unpunished 970
unpurchased 796
unpurified 653
unpurposed 621
unpursued 624
unqualified
incomplete 52
impotent 158
certain 474
unprepared 674
inexpert 699
unentitled 925
- truth 494
unquelled 173
unquenchable
strong 159
desire 865
unquenched
violence 173
heat 382
unquestionable 474
unquestionably 488
unquestioned 474, 488
unquiet
motion 264
agitation 315
excitable 825
unravel *untie* 44
arrange 60
straighten 246
evolve 313
discover 480*a*
interpret 522
disembarrass 705
unreached 304
unread 491
unready 674
unreal
not existing 2
erroneous 495
imaginary 515
unreasonable
impossible 471
illogical 477
misjudging 481
foolish 499
exorbitant 814
unjust 923
unreclaimed 951
unrecognizable 146,
unreconciled 713
unrecorded 552
unrecounted 55
unreduced 31
unrefined 851
unreflecting 458
unreformed 951
unrefreshed 688
unrefuted 478, 494
unregarded
neglected 460
unrespected 929
unregenerate 988
unregistered 552
unreined 748
unrelated 10
unrelenting 914*a*, 919
unreliable
uncertain 475
irresolute 605
dangerous 665
unrelieved 835
unremarked 460
unremembered 506
unremitting
continuous 69
continuing 110
unvarying 143
persevering 604*a*
unremoved 184
unremunerated 808
unrenewed 141
unrepealed 141
unrepeated 87, 103
unrepentant 951
unrepining 831
unreplenished 640
unrepressed 173
unreproached 946
unreproved 946
unrequited 806, 917
unresented 918
unresenting 826
unreserved
manifest 525
veracious 543
artless 703
unresisted 743
unresisting 725
unresolved 605
unrespected 929
unrest 149, 264
unrestored 688
unrestrained
capricious 608
unencumbered 705
free 748
unrestricted
undiminished 31

free 748
unretracted 535
unrevenged 918
unreversed 143
unrevoked 143
unrewarded 806, 917
unrhymed 598
unriddle 480*a*, 529
unrig 645
unrighteous 945
unrip 260
unripe
young 127
sour 397
immature 674
unrivalled 33
unroll *evolve* 313
display 525
unromantic 494
unroot 301
unruffled
calm 174
quiet 265
unaffected 823
placid 826
unruly *violent* 173
obstinate 606
disobedient 742
unsaddle 756
unsafe 665
unsaid 526
unsaleable
useless 645
selling 796
cheap 815
unsaluted 929
unsanctified 988, 989
unsanctioned 925
unsated 865
unsatisfactory
inexpedient 647
bad 649
displeasing 830
discontent 832
unsatisfied 832, 865
unsavouriness 395
unsay *recant* 607
unscanned 460
unscathed 654
unschooled 491
unscientific 477
unscoured 653
unscriptural 984
unscrupulous 940
unseal 529
unsearched 460
unseasonable 24, 135
unseasoned 614, 674
unseat 756
unseemly
inexpedient 647
ugly 846
vulgar 851
undue 925
vicious 945
unseen
invisible 447
neglected 460
latent 526
unseldom 136
unselfish 942
unseparated 46
unserviceable 645
unsettle *derange* 61
unsettled
mutable 149
displaced 185
uncertain 475
– in one's mind 503
unsevered 50
unsex 146
unshaded 525
unshaken 159
– belief 484
unshapely 846
unshapen 241
unshared 777
unsheathe
– the sword 722
unsheltered 665
unshielded 665
unshifting 143
unship 185, 297
unshocked 823
unshorn 50
unshortened 200
unshrinking 604, 861
unsifted 460
unsightly 846
unsinged 670
unskilfulness 699
unslaked 865
unsleeping 604*a*, 682
unsmooth 256
unsociable 893
unsocial 893
unsoiled 652
unsold 777
unsoldierlike 862
unsolicitous 866
unsolved 526
unsophisticated
simple 42
genuine 494
artless 703
unsorted 59
unsought
avoided 623
unrequested 766
unsound
illogical 477
erroneous 495
deceptive 545
imperfect 651
– mind 503
unsown 674
unsparing
abundant 639
severe 739
liberal 816
with an – hand 818
unspeakable 31, 870
unspecified 78
unspent 678
unspied 526
unspiritual 316, 989
unspoiled 648
unspotted
clean 652
beautiful 845
innocent 946
unstable 218
changeable 149
uncertain 475
irresolute 605
precarious 665
– equilibrium 149
unstaid 149
unstained
clean 652
honourable 939
unstatesmanlike 699
unsteadfast 605
unsteady
mutable 149
irresolute 605
in danger 665
unstinted 639
unstinting 816
unstirred 823, 826
unstopped
continuing 143
open 260
unstored 640
unstrained
turbid 653
relaxed 687
– meaning 516
unstrengthened 160
unstruck 823
unstrung 160
unstudied 460
unsubject 748
unsubmissive 742
unsubservient
useless 645
inexpedient 647
unsubstantial 4
weak 160
rare 322
erroneous 495
imaginary 515
unsubstantiality 4
unsuccessful 732
unsuccessive 70
unsuitable
incongruous 24
(*inexpedient* 647)
– time 135
unsullied *clean* 652
honourable 939
(*guiltless* 946)
unsung 526
unsupplied 640
unsupported
weak 160
(*unassisted* 706)
– by evidence 468
unsuppressed 141
unsurmountable 471
unsurpassed 33
unsusceptible 823
unsuspected
latent 526
unsuspecting
belief 484
hopeful 858
unsuspicious
belief 484
artless 703
hope 858
unsustainable 495
unsweet 395
unswept 653
unswerving
straight 246
direct 278
persevering 604*a*
unsymmetric 83
unsymmetrical 59, 243
unsystematic 59
untainted *pure* 652
healthy 654
honourable 939
untalked of 526
untamed 851, 907
untarnished 939
untasted 391
untaught 491, 674
untaxed 815
unteach 538
unteachable 499,

699
untenable
powerless 158
illogical 477
undefended 725
untenanted 187, 893
unthanked 917
unthankful 917
unthawed 321, 383
unthinkable 471
unthinking
unconsidered 452
involuntary 601
unthought of 452, 460
unthreatened 664
unthrifty
unprepared 674
prodigal 818
unthrone 756
untidy 59, 653
untie 44, 750
– the knot 705
until 106
– now 118
untilled 674
untimely 135
– end 360
untinged 42
untired 689
untiring 604*a*
untitled 876
untold
countless 105
uncertain 475
latent 526
secret 528
untouched
disused 678
insensible 823
untoward
ill-timed 135
bad 649
unprosperous 735
unpleasant 830
untraced 526
untracked 526
untractable 606, 699
untrained
unaccustomed 614
unprepared 674
unskilled 699
untrammelled 705, 748
untranslatable 523
untranslated 523
untravelled 265
untreasured 640
untried *new* 123
not decided 461
untrimmed 674, 849
untrodden *new* 123
impervious 261
not used 678
untroubled 174, 721
untrue 495, 546
untrustworthy
uncertain 475
erroneous 495
danger 665
dishonourable 940
untruth 544, 546
untunable 414
unturned 246
untutored
ignorant 491
unprepared 674
artless 703
untwine 313
untwist 313
unused
new 123
unaccustomed 614
unskilful 699
unusual 83
unusually *very* 31
unutterable 31, 519, 870
unvalued
underrated 483
undesired 866
disliked 898
unvanquished 748
unvaried
continuing 143
- *style* 575, 576
unvarnished
true 494
- *style* 576
unreserved 703
simple 849
– tale 494, 543
unvarying 16, 143
unveil 525, 529
unventilated 261
unveracious 544
unversed 491
unvexed 831
unviolated 939
unvisited 893
unwakened 683
unwarlike 862
unwarmed 383
unwarned 508, 665
unwarped judgment 498
unwarrantable 923
unwarranted
illogical 477
undue 925
illegal 964
unwary 460
unwashed 653
great – 876
unwatchful 460
unwavering 604*a*
unweakened 159
unwearied
persevering 604*a*
indefatigable 682
refreshed 689
unwedded 904
unweeded garden 674
unweeting 491
unweighed 460
unwelcome 830, 893
unwell 655
unwept 831
unwholesome 657
unwieldy
large 192
heavy 319
cumbersome 647
difficult 704
ugly 846
unwilling 489
unwillingness 603
unwind *evolve* 313
unwiped 653
unwise 499
unwished 866
unwithered 159
unwitting
ignorant 491
involuntary 601
unwittingly 621
unwomanly 373
unwonted 83, 614
unworldly 939
unworn 159
unworshipped 929
unworthy
shameful 874
vicious 945
– of belief 485
– of notice 643
unwrap 246
unwrinkled 255
unwritten
latent 526
obliterated 552
spoken 582
– law 697, 963
unwrought 674
unyielding
tough 323
resolute 604
obstinate 606
resisting 719
up
aloft 206
vertical 212
effervescing 353
excited 824
the game is – 735
prices looking – 814
time – 111
– in arms
prepared 673
active 682
opposition 708
attack 716
resistance 719
warfare 722
– and at them 716
– and doing 682
– and down 314
– on end 212
– in 698
– to [*see below*]
all – with
destruction 162
failure 732
adversity 735
up to
time 106
power 157
knowing 490
skilful 698
brave 861
– the brim 52
– date 123
– one's ears 641
– one's eyes 641
– the mark
equal 27
sufficient 639
good 648
due 924
– snuff 702
– this time
time 106
past 122
Upas tree 663
upbear 215, 307
upbraid 932
upcast 307
upgrow 206
upgrowth 194, 305
upheaval 146
upheave 307
uphill
acclivity 217
ascent 305
laborious 686
difficult 704
uphoist 307
uphold

continue 143
support 215
evidence 467
aid 707
praise 931
upholder 488, 711
upholstery 633
uplands 180, 206, 344
uplift 307, 658
upon:
– my honour 535
– oath 535
– which 117, 121
upper 206
– boxes, – circle 599
– classes 875
– hand
influence 175
success 731
sway 737
– story
summit 210
intellect 450
wisdom 498
– ten thousand 875
be on one's –'s 804
uppermost 210
say what comes – 612
– in the mind
thought 451
topic 454
attention 457
– in one's thoughts
memory 505
upraise 307
uprear 307
upright
vertical 212
honest 939
uprise 305
uprising 742
uproar
disorder 59
violence 173
noise 404
uproarious 825
uproot 301
ups and downs of life 151, 735
upset *destroy* 162
invert 218
throw down 308
defeat 731
excite 824
disconcert 874
– the apple cart 732
upshot *result* 154
judgment 480
completion 729
upside down 218
upstairs 206
upstart
new 123
prosperous 734
plebeian 876
upturn 218
upwards 206
– of 33, 100
uranology 318
urban 189
urbane 894
urbis conditæ, anno – 106
urceole 998
urchin
child 129
small 193
wretch 949
imp 980
urge *violence* 173
impel 276
incite 615
hasten 684
beg 765
urgent
required 630
important 642
haste 684
request 765
urn *vase* 191
funereal 363
heater 386
cinerary – 363
usage 613, 677
usance 806
use *habit* 613
waste 638
utility 644
employ 677
property 780
make good – of 658
in – 677
be of – to *aid* 707
benevolence 906
– one's discretion 600
– one's endeavour 675
– a right 924
– up 677
used to 613
used up
deteriorated 659
disuse 678
fatigue 688
weary 841
satiated 869
useful 644
render – 677
useless 645
user, right of – 780
usher
guard 263
receive 296
teacher 540
servant 746
courtesy 894
wedding 903
– in *precedence* 62
begin 66
procession 280
announce 511
– into the world 161
usque ad nauseam 841
U.S.S. 726
ustulation 384
usual
general 78
ordinary 82
customary 613
usufruct 677
usurer
lender 787
merchant 797
credit 805
miser 819
usurious 819
usurp *assume* 739
seize 789
illegal 925
– authority 738
usurpation
insolence 885
usurper 737
usury 806
utensil 191, 633
uti possidetis
permanence 141
possession 777
retention 781
utilitarian 677, 910
utility 644
general – *actor* 599
utilize 677
utmost 33
do one's – 686
– height 210
in one's – need 735
deserted in one's – need 893
Utopia 515, 858
utricle 191
utter *extreme* 31
distribute 73
disclose 529
publish 531
speak 580, 582
money 800
utterly 52
uttermost 31
to the – parts of the earth 180, 196
uxorious 897

V

va sans dire, cela – 474, 525
vacant *void* 4
absent 187
thoughtless 452
unmeaning 517
scanty 640
– hour 685
– mind *folly* 499
vacate *displace* 185
absent 187
depart 293
resign 757
vacation 687
vaccine 366
vache 191
vacillate
changeable 149
undulate 314
waver 605
vacuity 187
vacuous
unsubstantial 4
absent 187
vacuum 187
– cleaner 652
vade mecum 527, 542
vadium 771
væ victis! *war* 722
threat 909
vagabond
wanderer 268
low person 876
rogue 949
vagabondage 266
vagary
absurdity 497
imagination 515
whim 608
antic 840
vagrant
changeable 149
roving 266
traveller 268

deviating 279
vague
unsubstantial 4
uncertain 475
unreasoning 477
unmeaning 517
obscure 519
- *language* 571
– suggestion 514
vail *panel* 228
donation 784
reward 973
vain *unreal* 2
unprofitable 645
unvalued 866
conceited 880
in – *failure* 732
labour in –
come short 304
useless 645
fail 732
take a name in – 895
– attempt 732
use – efforts 645
– expectation 509
vainglorious
haughty 878
vain 880
boasting 884
vaivode 745
valance 231
vale 252
– of years 128
valeat quantum 467
valediction 293, 894
valedictory 293
valentine 902
valet 631, 746
valet
– de chambre 746
– de place 524, 527
valetudinarian 655, 656
Valhalla 981
valiant 861
valid *confirmed* 150
powerful 157
strong 159
true 494
sufficient 639
– reasoning 476
valise 191
valley 252
– of the shadow of death 360
vallum 717
valoir, se faire – 884
valorem, ad – 812
valour 861
valuable 644, 648
value *colour* 428
measure 466
estimate 480
importance 642
utility 644
goodness 648
price 812
approbation 931
of priceless – 814
set a – upon 482
– received 810
–s *painting* 556
valueless 645
valve *stop* 263
conduit 350
safety – *safety* 664
refuge 666
escape 671
vamp *change* 140
music 416
– up *improve* 658
restore 660
prepare 673
vampire 913, 980
vampirism 789, 992
van *beginning* 66
front 234
wagon 272
in the – 234
precession 280
van-courier 64
Vandal
destroyer 165
vulgar 851
commonalty 876
evil-doer 913
vandalism 851
vandyke 257
Vandyke brown 433
vane *wind* 349
indication 550
vanguard 234
vanish
unsubstantial 4
transient 111
disappear 449
vanishing 32, 193
vanity *useless* 645
conceit 880
- bag 191
Vanity Fair 852
vanquish 731
vantage ground
superiority 33
power 157
influence 175
height 206
vapid *insipid* 391
- *style* 575
vaporization 336
vaporous
imaginary 515
opaque 426
vapour *gas* 334
bubbles 353
fancy 515
boast 884
insolence 885
– bath 386, 652
vapourer 887
vapours
dejection 837
variable 149, 605
variance
difference 15
disagreement 24
discord 713
at – *enmity* 889
at – with 489
variant 15
variation
difference 15
diverseness 20a
number 84
chance 140
music 415
varied 15
variegated 16*a*, 440
variegation 440
variety
difference 15
class 75
multiformity 81
exception 83
entertainment 599
variform 81
various 15, 102
– places 182
– times 119
varlet 949
varnish
overlay 223
resin 356*a*
sophistry 477
falsehood 544
painting 556
decorate 847
excuse 937
vary *differ* 15
dissimilar 18
variation 20*a*
change 140
fluctuate 149
vascular *cells* 191
holes 260
pipes 350
vase 191
vassal 746
vassalage 749
vast *great* 31
spacious 180
large 192
– learning 490
vasty deep 341
vat 191
Vatican 995, 1000
thunders of the – 908
vaticination 511
vatum, genus irritabile – 901
vaudeville 599, 840
vault
cellar 191
curve 245
leap 309
tomb 363
store 636
– of heaven 318
vaulted 245, 252
vaulting 33, 865
vaunt 884
vaurien 949
vavasour
possessor 779
nobleman 875
V.C. 733
vection 270
Vedas 986
vedette 668
Vedidad 986
veer
change 140
deviate 279
go back 283
change intention 607
vegetability 365
vegetable 367
– kingdom 367
– life 365
– oil 356
– physiology 369
vegetarian 298, 953
vegetate 365
exist 1
grow 194
stagnate 265
inactive 681, 683
insensible 823
vegetation 365
vehemence
violence 173
feeling 821
emotion 825
vehement
- *language* 574
vehicle
carriage 272
instrument 631
veil *covering* 225
shade 424

concealment 526, 527
conceal 528
ambush 530
behind the – 360
draw aside the – 529
take the – 893, 995
veiled
uncertain 475
invisible 447
concealed 528
vein *temper* 5
tendency 176
thin 203
thread 205
channel 350
humour 602
mine 636
affections 820
in the – 602
not in the – 603
veined 440
veldt 344
velis et remis 274
velitation 720
velleity 600
vellicate 315
vellicating 392
vellum 590
veloce *music* 415
velocipede 272
velocity 264, 274
angular – 244
veluti in speculum 17
velvet 255, 256
pleasure 377
on – *easy* 705
venal *price* 812
stingy 819
dishonest 940
selfish 943
venation 622
vend 796
vendee 795
vender 796
vendetta 919
vendible 796
venditation 884
vendor 796
veneer 204, 223
venenation 659
venerable *old* 124
aged 128
sage 500
respected 928
veneration
respect 928
piety 987
venereal disease 655
venery *killing* 361
hunting 622
impurity 961
venesection
ejection 297
remedy 662
Venetian blinds 351
vengeance 919
cry to heaven for – 923
with a – 31, 173
vengeful 919
veni vidi vici 731
venial 937
veniam petimusque damusque vicissim 918
venienti occurrere morbo 673
venison 394
venom 663, 907
venomous *bad* 649
poisonous 657
rude 895
maleficent 907
vent *opening* 260
egress 295
air-pipe 351
disclose 529
escape 671
sale 796
find – *egress* 295
passage 302
publish 531
escape 671
give – to 297, 529
– one's rage 900
– one's spleen 900
venter 191
ventiduct 351
ventilate
begin 66
air 338
wind 349
discuss 595
– a question 461, 476
ventilator 349, 351
ventosity 349
vent-peg
stopper 263
safety 666
escape 671
ventre
– à terre 274
danse du – 840
ventricle 191
ventriloquism 580
venture
chance 621
danger 665
try 675
courage 861
I'll – to say 535
venturesome
undertaking 677
brave 861
rash 863
venue 74, 183
Venus *woman* 374
planet 423
beauty 845
love 897
goddess 979
veracity 543
verandah 191
verbal 562
– intercourse 582, 588
– quibble 497, 842
verbatim
imitation 19
exact 494
words 562
verbiage
unmeaning 517
words 562
diffuse 573
verbis:
totidem – 494
– ad verbera 720
verborum, copia –
diffuse 573
eloquence 582
loquacious 584
verbosity
words 562
diffuse 573
loquacity 584
verboten 761
verbum sapienti 527
verdant 367, 435
verd-antique 435
verdict
opinion 480
lawsuit 969
snatch a – 545, 702
verdigris 435
verditer 435
verdure 367, 435
verecundiam, argumentum ad – 874, 939
verecundity 879, 881
veredical 543
Verein 712
verge
tendency 176
near 197
edge 231
limit 233
direction 278
verger 996
veriest 31
verification 463, 771
verify 463
evidence 467
demonstrate 478
find out 480a
verily *truly* 494
verisimilitude 472
veritable 494
veritas, nuda – 494
vérité, palais de – 703
verity 494
verjuice 397
vermicular
convoluted 248
worm 366
vermiform 248
vermilion 434
vermin
animal 366
unclean 653
base 876
vernacular
native 188
internal 221
language 560
habitual 613
vernal 123, 125
vernier
minuteness 193
– *scale* 466
vero, vitam impendere – 535, 939
verrons, nous – 507
versatile 149
verse *division* 51
poetry 597
versed in 490
versicolour 440
versify 597
version *change* 140
special 79
interpretation 522
versus 278, 708
vert 435
vertebral 222
vertebrate 366
vertex 210
verticality 212
verticity 312
vertigo
rotation 312

delirium 503
verve
imagination 515
vigorous language 574
energy 682
feeling 821
very 31
- best 648
- image 554
- many 102
- minute 113
- much 31
- picture 17
- small 32
- thing
identity 13
agreement 23
exact 494
- true 488
- well 831
Véry light 423
vesicle *cell* 191
covering 223
globe 249
vesicular 191, 260
vespers 126, 990
vespertine 126
vessel
receptacle 191
tube 260
ship 273
vest *place* 184
dress 225
- in *belong to* 777
give 784
Vesta 979
vesta *match* 388
vestal 960
vested *fixed* 150
legal 963
- in *located* 184
- interest
given 780
due 924
vestibule 66, 191
vestige 551
vestigia:
veteris - flammæ 505, 613
- nulla retrorsum 282, 604*a*
vestment 225, 999
vestry *council* 696
churchdom 995
church 1000
vesture 225
vesuvian
match 388
veteran *old* 130
adept 700

warrior 726
veterinary art 370
veteris vestigia flammæ 505, 613
veto 761
vetturino 694
vex 830, 898
vexata quæstio 704, 713
vexation 828, 830
- of spirit 828
discontent 832
resentment 900
vexatious 830
vexed question 704, 713
vi et armis
violence 173
exertion 686
compulsion 744
viâ 278, 627
viable 359
via lactea 318
viaduct 627
vial 191
vials:
- of hate 898
- of wrath 900
viands 298
viaticum
provision 637
rite 998
vibrate 314
- between two extremes 149
vibrato 415
vibratory 149
vibroscope 314
vicar *deputy* 759
clergyman 996
- of Bray 607, 886
vicarage 1000
vicariate 995
vicarious 147
vicarship 995
vice *deputy* 759
holder 781
wickedness 945
vice versâ
reciprocal 12
contrary 14
interchange 148
vice-admiral 745
Vice-Chancellor 967
-'s Court 966
vicegerency 755
vicegerent 758, 759
vice-president 694
vice-regal 759

viceroy
governor 745
deputy 759
vicesimal 98
vicinage 197
vicinism 145
vicinity 197, 227
vicious 173, 945
render - 659
- reasoning 477
vicissitude 149
Vickers gun 727
victim *dupe* 547
defeated 732
sufferer 828
victimize *kill* 361
deceive 545
injure 649
baffle 731
victis, væ - 722, 909
victor 731
victoria
carriage 272
Victoria Cross 733
victory 731
victual *provide* 637
victuals 298
videlicet 79, 522
viduage 905
viduity 905
vie *good* 648
- with 720
vielle 417
view
sight 441
appearance 448
attend to 457
opinion 484
landscape painting 556
intention 620
bring into - 525
come into - 446
commanding - 441
in - *visible* 446
intended 620
expected 507
keep in - 457
on - 448
present to the - 448
with a - to 620
- as 484
- in a new light 658
viewer 444
viewless 447
view-point 441
vigesimal 98
vigil *care* 459
vigilance *care* 459

wisdom 498
activity 682
caution 864
vigils *worship* 990
vignette 558, 594, 847
vigour *strength* 159
energy 171
style 574
resolution 604
health 654
activity 682
viking 792
vile *valueless* 643
bad 649
painful 830
disgraceful 874
plebeian 876
dishonourable 940
vicious 945
vilify *shame* 874
malediction 908
censure 932
detract 934
vilipend
disrespect 929
censure 932
detract 934
vilipendency 930
villa 189
village 189
- talk 588
villager 188
villain
servant 746
serf 876
knave 941
rascal 949
villainous 649, 945
- saltpetre 727
villainy 940
villein [*see* villain]
villenage 749, 777
villi 256
villous 256
vim 171
vin: - d'honneur 292, 894
not think - ordinaire of oneself 880
vinaigrette 400
vincible 158
vincture 43
vinculo matrimonii, separatio a - 905
vinculum 45
- matrimonii 903
vindicate 467, 937
- a right 924
vindication 937

vindicator 919
vindictive 901, 919
vine 367
- grower 371
vinegar 397
- aspect 846
vinery 191
vineyard 371, 691
vingt et un 840
vintage 371, 636
vintner 637
viol 417
violate
disobey 742
non-observance 773
undue 925
dereliction 927
ravish 961
- a law 83
- the law 964
- a usage 614
violence 173
arbitrary 964
do - to *bad* 649
non-observance 773
undue 925
violent 173
excitable 825
- death 360, 361
in a - degree 31
lay - hands on 789
violet 437
violin 417
violinist 416
violoncello 417
viper *snake* 366
bane 663
evil-doer 913
bad man 949
- in one's bosom 667
virago 901
virent 435
vires acquirit eundo
increase 35
energy 171
velocity 274
virescence 435
Virgilianæ, sortes - 621
virgin *new* 123
girl 129
woman 374
spinster 904
good 948
pure 960
- forest 367
- soil
ignorance 491
untilled 674
the - Mary 977
virginals 417
virginibus puerisque 960
viribus, totis - 686
viridity 435
virile
adolescent 131
strong 159
manly 373
virtu 850
article of - 847
virtual 2, 5
- image 443
virtue *power* 157
courage 861
goodness 944
purity 960
by - of 157, 631
in - of 737
make a - of necessity *no choice* 609*a*
skill 698
submit 725
compromise 774
bear 826
virtueless 945
virtuoso 416, 850
virtuous 944, 960
virulence
energy 171
noxiousness 649
insalubrity 657
discourtesy 895
anger 900
malevolence 907
virulent 932
virum volitare per ora 531
virus 655, 663
vis:
- comica 842
- conservatrix 670
- inertiæ
power 157
inertness 172
insensibility 823
- medicatrix 660, 662
- mortua 157
- a tergo 284
- viva 157
visa 488
visage 234, 448
vis-à-vis *front* 234
opposite 237
carriage 272
viscera 221
viscid 352
viscount 875
viscous 352
vise 781
Vishnu 979
visibility 446
visible 446
be - 448
become - 448
darkness - 421
- radiation 420
vision *sight* 441
phantasm 443
dream 515
spectre 980
organ of - 441
visionary
inexistence 2
unsubstantial 4
impossible 471
imaginary 515
heterodox 984
visionless 442
visit *arrival* 292
social 892
courtesy 894
- upon 972
pay a surprise - 674
visitation
disease 655
adversity 735
suffering 828
-s of Providence 976
- of the sick 998
visiting:
- card 550
on - terms 888, 892
visitor *incomer* 294
director 694
friend 890
visor 530
vista
convergence 260
sight 441
appearance 448
expectation 507
visual 441
- organ 441
vitability 359
vitæ, elixir - 662
vital *life* 359
important 642
vitality
stability 150
strength 159
life 359
vitalize 359
vitals 221
vitam impendere vero 535, 939
vitamines 298
vitiate 659
vitiated 655
viticulture 371
vitreous 323, 425
vitrify 323
vituperate 908, 932
vituperator 936
viva! 873, 931
vivace *music* 415
vivacious
active 682
sensitive 822
cheerful 836
vivamus, dum vivimus - 840
vivandière 797
vivarium 370
vivâ voce 582
vive *glory be to* 873
on the qui - 824
vivendi
modus - 723
- causa 359
vivid *energetic* 171
sensibility 375
light 420
colour 428
distinct 518
- memory 505
vivify 159, 359
vivisection 378
vixen *fox* 366
female 374
shrew 901
viz. [*see* videlicet]
vizier *director* 694
mask 530
shield 717
deputy 759
vizor 530
vobis, sic vos non - 791
vocable 562
vocabulary 562
vocal 415, 580
- training 537
vocalist 416
vocalize 580
vocation 625
voce, sotto - 581
vociferation
loud 404
cry 411
voice 580
vogue *custom* 613
fashion 852
fame 873
vogue la galère

persevere 604*a*
amusement 840
voice *sound* 402
cry 411
judgment 480
promulgate 531
affirmation 535
express 566
human - 580
speak 580
choice 609
give one's – for 488
raise one's – 411, 582
still small –
faint sound 405
conscience 926
want of – 581
warning – 668
– against 489, 708
– of the charmer 933
make one's – heard 175
– of the tempter 615
voiced 561
voiceless 581
void *unsubstantial* 4
absence 187
emit 297
null and – 964
– of foundation 546
– of suspicion 484
voidance 297
voiturette 272
voiturier 268
volplane 267
volant 267
volapuk 560
volatile *light* 320
gaseous 334
vaporizable 336
irresolute 605
capricious 608
volatility 111
vol-au-vent 298
volcanic
violent 173
heat 382
burnt 384
excitable 825
volcano
violence 173
heat 382
furnace 386
pitfall 667
on a – 665
volitant 267
volitare per ora, virum – 531
volitation 267
volition 600
volley
collection 72
violence 173
report 406
attack 716
volonté, à – 600
volo sic jubeo, sic – 600, 741
volt 466
voltaic electricity 157
volte face 283
voltigeur 726
volto sciolto i pensieri stretti, il – 544
voluble 584
volume *great* 31
part 51
bulk 192
book 593
speak –s
evidence 467
intelligible 518
inform 527
– of smoke 330
voluminous 573, 641
voluntary *overture* 64, 415
will 600
willing 602
donation 784
voluntas, stet pro ratione – 600
volunteer *will* 600
willing 602
endeavour 676
combatant 726
offer 763
voluptas, sua cuique – 865
voluptuary 954*a*, 962
voluptuous
pleasure 377
delightful 829
intemperate 954
impure 961
volutation 312
volute 248
vomit 297
vomitory 260, 295
voodoo 992, 994
voracious *desire* 865
glutton 957
vortex *rotation* 312
agitation 315
river 348
danger 667
vorticist 556
votary
auxiliary 711
devotee 865
vote 535, 609
– for 488
voting machine 553
votis, hoc erat in – 865
votive 768
– offering 990
vouch *assert* 535
– for 467
voucher
evidence 467
indication 550
security 771
payment 807
vouchsafe
permit 760
consent 762
ask 765
condescend 879
vow *affirmation* 535
promise 768
worship 990
take –s 995
vowel 561
vox:
– faucibus hæsit
voiceless 581
fear 860
wonder 870
– populi
assent 488
publication 531
choice 609
– et præterea nihil
unsubstantial 4
powerless 158
unmeaning 517
vain 880
boasting 884
voyage 267
voyager 268
vraisemblance 472
vue d'œil, à – 132, 446
Vulcan 690, 979
vulgar *inelegant* 579
low born 876
– tongue 560
vulgarian 851
vulgarity
want of refinement 851
Vulgate 985
vulgus, ignobile – 475, 876
vulnerable 665
vulnerary 662
vulnus:
æternum servans sub pectore – 919
immedicabile – 619
vulpine 702
vulture 739, 913

W

wabble *slow* 275
oscillate 314
wad 263
wadding *lining* 224
stopper 263
soft 324
waddle 275
wade 267
– in blood 361
– through
learn 539
exertion 686
waddle 314
wafer *cement* 45
thin 203
lamina 204
waft *transfer* 270
blow 349
wafted, be – 267
wag *oscillate* 314
agitate 315
joker 844
– on *journey* 266
progression 282
wage war 722
wager 621
– of battle 722
– of law 467
wages 973
waggery *wit* 842
waggish 836, 853
waggle 314, 315
wagon 272
wagoner 268
wagonette 272
wagon-load 31
waif 618, 782
waifs and estrays 73, 268
wail 412, 839
wain 272
wainscot 211, 224
waist 203
waistcoat 225
put in a strait – 751

wait 133, 681
lie in – for 530
– for 507
– impatiently 133
– on *accompany* 88
aid 707
– to see how the wind blows 607
– upon *serve* 746
call on 894
waiter *servant* 746
– on Providence
neglect 460
inactive 683
content 831
waiting 507
be kept – 133
waiting-maid 746
waitress 746
waits 416
waive *defer* 133
not choose 609a
not use 678
waiwode 745
wake *sequel* 65
rear 235
funeral 363
trace 551
excite 824
amusement 840
in the – of 281
enough to – the dead 404
– the thoughts 457
– up 824
wakeful
careful 459
active 682
Walhalla 981
walk *region* 181
lane 189
move 266
business 625
way 627
conduct 692
arena 728
– one's chalks 293, 623
– the earth 359
– of life 625
–ed off one's legs 688
– off with 791
– over the course 705, 731
– in the shoes of 19
walker 268
walking gentleman 599
wall *vertical* 212
parietes 224
inclosure 232
refuge 666
obstacle 706
defence 717
prison 752
driven to the – 704
go to the –
destruction 162
die 360
fail 732
pushed to the – 601
take the – 873, 878
wooden –s 726
–eyed 442
– in 229, 751
wallah 746
wallet 191
wallop 315
wallow *low* 207
plunge 310
rotate 312
– in 377, 641
– in the mire 653
– in riches 803
– in voluptuousness 954
wallsend 388
Wall-street 799
– slang 563
waltz 415, 840
wamble
vacillate 149
oscillate 314
dislike 867
wampum 800
wan 429, 837
wand *sceptre* 747
magic 993
wave a – 992
wander *move* 264
journey 266
deviate 279
delirium 503
the attention –s 458
wanderer 268
wandering
exceptional 83
– Jew 268
wane
decrease 36
age 128
contract 195
decay 659
one's star on the – 735
wax and – 140
wangle 943
want
inferiority 34
shortcoming 304
requirement 630
insufficiency 640
poverty 804
desire 865
wanted 187
wanting
incomplete 53
absent 187
imbecile 499
found –
imperfect 651
disapproval 932
guilt 947
wantless 639
wanton
unconformable 83
capricious 608
unrestrained 748
amusement 840
rash 863
impure 961
wapentake 181
war 722
at – 24, 720
at – with 708, 722
declare – 713
man of – 726
seat of – 728
– correspondent 534, 593
– of words 588, 720
warble 416
war-cry *alarm* 669
defiance 715
war 722
ward *part* 51
parish 181
safety 664
asylum 666
dependent 746
restraint 751
watch and – 459, 753
– off 706, 717
war-dance 715
warden
guardian 664
master 745
deputy 759
warder
perforator 262
porter 263
guardian 664
keeper 753
wardmote 966
wardrobe 191, 225
ward-room 191
war-drum 417
wardship 664
ware
warning 668
merchandise 798
warehouse 636, 799
warfare 722
discord 713
war-horse 726
warlike 722
warlock 994
warm
violent 173
hot 382
make hot 384
red 434
orange 439
wealthy 803
ardent 821
excited 824
angry 900
irascible 901
flog 972
– bath 386
– the blood 824
– the cockles of the heart 829
– imagination 515
– man 803
– reception
repel 717
welcome 892
– up 658, 660
– work 686
warm-hearted
feeling 821
sensibility 822
friendship 888
benevolence 906
warming 384
warming-pan
locum tenens 147
heater 386
preparation 673
warmth
vigorous language 574
warn *dissuade* 616
caution 668
– off 761
warning *omen* 512
dissuasion 616
caution 668
give – *dismiss* 678
relinquish 782
– voice *alarm* 668
warp *change* 140
tend 176
contract 195

distort **243**
navigate **267**
deviate 279
prejudice 481
deteriorate 659
– and weft 329
war-paint 673
war-path 722
on the – 716
warped 651
warped notion 495
warrant
evidence 467
protest 535
order 741
permit 760
promise 768
security 771
money order 800
justify 937
death – *die* 360
kill 361
condemn 971
I'll – you 535
– officer 745
warranted 924
warranty
permission 760
promise 768
security 771
sanction 924
warren 168
free – 815
warrior 726
warship 726
wart 250
wary 864
wash *cover* 223
water 337
marsh 345
colour 428
paint 556
cleanse 652
– down 298
– one's hands of
relinquish 624
depute 757
refuse 764
part with 782
dereliction 927
– out
discolour 429
obliterate 552
deteriorate 659
– up 659
washer 247
washerwoman 652
washhouse 386, 652
washy *weak* 160
unmeaning 517
feeble style 575

wasp *narrow* 203
bring a –'s nest about one's ears 735
waspish 173, 901
wassail
beverage 298
feast 840
drunkenness 954
wastage 40*a*
waste *decrease* 36
decrement 40*a*
destroy 162
unproductive 169
space 180
contract 195
plain 344
consumption **638**
useless 645
spoiled 659
misuse 679
loss 776
prodigality 818
run to – 641, 659
watery – 341
– away 655
– time 683
wasted 160, 659
wasteful 818
waste-paper 158, 645
– basket 191, 645
– bonds 808
waste-pipe 350
waster 460
waste-thrift 818
wasting, wide – 649
wastrel 268, 893
Wat Tyler 742
watch *clock* 114
observe 441
attend to 457
take care of 459
expect 507
guardian 664
warning 668
keeper 753
death – *death* 360
warning 668
on the – 459, 507
– for 507
– out for 668
– over 664
– and pray 673
– and ward 459, 753
watch-dog 664, 753
watchet 438
watch-fire 550
watchful 459
watch-glass 191

watch-house 752
in the – 938
watchman
guardian 664
sentinel 668
keeper 753
watch-tower
view 441
signal 550
warning 668
watchword
sign 550
military 722
water **337**
transparent 425
keep one's head above – 664
back – 283
cast one's bread upon the –s 638
throw cold – on 174
depth of – 208
of the first – 648
great –s 341
hold – 478, 494
land covered with – 343
pour forth like – 818
make one's mouth – 507
running – 348
walk the –s 267
pour – into a sieve 638
– bearer, carrier 348
water-colour 556
watercourse 350
water-cure 662
water-dog 361
water-drinker 958
watered
variegated 440
waterfall 348
water-glass 556
water-gruel 160
watering
– cart 348
– place 189
– pot 348
waterless 340
water-logged
powerless 158
danger 665
hindrance 706
waterman 269
water-pipe 350
water-polo 840
waterproof

dress 225
dry 340
protection **664**
waters
– of bitterness 830
– of oblivion 506
watershed 210
water-spaniel 366
waterspout 348
water-tight 261, 340
waterworks 350
watery *wet* 337
moist 339
– eyes 839
– grave 360
wattle 219
wave *sinuous* 248
oscillate **314**
hair 847
- *of water* 348
[*and see* waive]
brain – 498
– a banner 550
– a wand 992
waver
changeable 149
doubt 485
irresolute 605
waverer 605
waves 341
buffet the –
navigate 267
difficult 704
oppose 708
lash the – 645
plough the – 267
wax *increase* **35**
become 144
expand 194
soft 324
lubrication 332
viscid 352
substance 356
close as – 528
– and wane 140
– candle 423
waxwork 554
waxy *unctuous* 355
irate 900
way *degree* 26
space 180
habit 613
method 627
in a bad – 655
by – of 278, 627
by the –
in transitu 270
accidental 621
fall in the – of 186
fight one's – 622, 722

find its – 302
gather – 267
get into the – of 613
go one's – 293
go your – 297
let it have its – 681
it must have its – 601
have one's own – 748
in a – 828, 900
in the – *near* 197
in the – of 706, 708
make – 302
make one's –
journey 266
progression 282
passage 302
prosperity 734
make – for
substitution 147
opening 260
turn aside 279
avoid 623
facilitate 705
courtesy 894
on the – 282
place in one's – 763
put in the – of 470, 537
see one's – 490
show the – 693
under – *move* 264
sail 267
progression 282
depart 293
wing one's – 267
– in 294
long – off 196
have – on 267
– out 295
– of speaking 521
– of thinking 484
not know which – to turn 475
Way, the – 976
wayfarer 268
wayfaring 266
waylay 545, 702
wayless 261
ways 692
in all manner of – 278
– and means 632, 800
wayward
changeable 149
obstinate 606
capricious 608
sullen 901*a*
waywode 745
wayworn 266, 688
wayzgoose 840
weak *feeble* 160
water 337
insipid 391
illogical 477
foolish 499
- *style* 575
irresolute 605
trifling 643
lax 738
compassionate 914
vicious 945
– point 477, 651
expose one's – point 479
– side 499, 945
weaken
decrease 36, 38
enfeeble 160
refute 468
weaker vessel 374
weak-headed 499
weak-hearted 862
weak-kneed 725
weakness 160
– of the flesh 945
weal 618
common – 644
weald 367
wealth 780, 803
wean 484, 614
– from 616
– one's thoughts from 506
weanling 129
weapon 727
weaponless 158
wear *decrease* 36
clothes 225
deflect 279
use 677
– away *cease* 142
deteriorate 659
– the breeches 737
– off 142, 614
– on 109
– out 659, 688
– and tear
decrease 36
waste 638
injury 659
exertion 686
weariness 841
wearing 841
– apparel 225
wearisome
laborious 686
fatiguing 688
painful 830
weary *fatigue* 688
painful 828
sad 837
ennuyant 841
– flat, stale, and unprofitable 843
– waste 344
– Willie 876
weasand 260, 351
weasel asleep, catch a – 471, 682
weather 338
keep one's – eye open 864
rough – 173, 349
– the storm
stability 150
recover 660
safe 664
succeed 731
weather permitting 469, 470
weather-beaten
weak 160
damaged 659
fatigue 688
weather-bound 751
weathercock
changeable 149
wind 349
indication 550
fickle 607
weathered 659
weather-gauge 338
weather-glass 338
weather-proof 654, 664
weatherwise 338
foresight 510
weave *produce* 161
interlace 219
– a tangled web 704
weazen 193
web
complexity 59
intersection 219
texture 329
wed 48, 903
wedded: – pair 903
– to *belief* 484
habit 613
loving 897
– to an opinion
misjudgment 481
obstinacy 606
wedding 903
– breakfast 892
– day 883
wedge *join* 43
angular 244
sharp 253
instrument 633
thin edge of the –
begin 66
insinuate 228
cunning 702
– in 228
wedged in 751
wedlock 903
wee 193
weed *exclude* 55
few 103
plant 367
agriculture 371
cigar 392
trifle 643
clean 652
– out 297, 301
weeds *dress* 225
useless 645
mourning 839
widowhood 905
weedy 203, 643
week 108
weekly 138
– paper 531
ween *judge* 480
believe 484
know 490
weeny 32
weep 839, 914
weet 480, 490
weetless 491
weft, warp and – 329
weigh *influence* 175
lift 307
heavy 319
ponder 451
under – [*see* way]
– anchor 293
– carefully 465
– down 649, 749
– on the heart 830
– heavy on 649
– on the mind
regret 833
dejection 837
fear 860
– with 615
weighed and found wanting 34, 932
weighing machine 319
weight
influence 175
gravity 319

importance 642
short – 53
attach – to 484
carry – 175
drag – 706
have – 467
throw one's – into the scale 175
weightless 320
weights and measures 466
weighty
style 574
weir *conduit* 350
hindrance 706
weird 860
demon 980
mystic 992
spell 993
– sisters 994
welcome
arrival 292
grateful 829
friendly 888
sociality 892
reception 894
weld 43, 46
welfare 734
welkin 318, 338
make the – ring 404
well *much* 31
origin 153
deep 208
welcome 292
exude 295
pool 343
flow 348
assent 488
good 618
store 636
healthy 654
spa 662
act – 944
all's – 664
drop a bucket into an empty – 645
get – 660
go on – 734
let – alone 265, 681
inaction 681
think – of 931
treat – 906
turn out – 731
work – 731
– and good
assent 488
consent 762
content 831
– done! 931

– enough 32, 651
– out 295
– over 641
– up in 698
– with 888
well-a-day 839, 870
well-advised 498
well-affected 888
well-behaved 852, 894
well-being 734, 827
well-beloved 897
well-born 875
well-bred 852
well-composed 845
well-defined
visible 446
exact 494
predetermined 611
well-disposed 707
well-doing 944
well-favoured 845
well-fed 192
well-formed 845
well-founded
existent 1
probable 472
certain 474
- *belief* 484
true 494
well-grounded
existent 1
informed 490
- *hope* 858
well-informed 490
Wellington boots 225
well-intentioned 906, 944
well-knit 159
well-known 490, 613
well-made 845
well-mannered 894
well-marked 446
well-meaning 906
well-meant 906
well-met 894
well-natured 906
well-nigh 32, 197
well-off 734, 803
well-proportioned 845
well-provided 639
well-regulated
order 58
conformity 82
circumspect 864
well-set 242
well-spent

successful 731
virtuous 944
well-tasted 394
well-timed 134
well-to-do 734, 803
well-turned periods 578
well-weighed 611
well-wisher 890, 906
welsher 792, 808
welt 321
welter 310, 312
– in one's blood 361
wem 848
wen 250
wench *girl* 129
woman 374
impure 962
wenching 961
wend 266
were, as you – 660
werewolf 980
Wesleyan 984
West *lateral* 236
direction 278
go – *die* 360
Westminster
superior courts of – 966
wet 337, 339
– blanket
dissuade 616
hindrance 706
sadden 837
weary 841
dull 843
just enough to – one's feet 209
– one's whistle 298, 959
wether 366
whack 276
out of – 59
whacking 31, 192
whale *large* 192
sprat to catch a – 699
tub to a – 545, 617
whalebone 325
whaler 273
whallop 972
whap 276
wharf *houses* 189
workshop 691
mart 799
wharfage 812
what 461, 870
know –'s what
discriminate 465

intelligent 498
skill 698
– d'ye call 'em 563
– on earth 83
–'s his name 563
– next 455
and – not 81
– is the reason? 461
– signifies 643
–'s up 461
– in the world 83, 870
whatever 78
– may happen 474
wheal 250
wheat
winnow the chaff from the – 609
wheedle
coax 615
endearment 902
flatter 933
wheel *circle* 247
deviate 279
turn back 283
circuition 311
rotation 312
rack 975
break on the – 378, 972
get the – out of the rut 672
paddle – 267
scotch the – 706
stern – 267
– about 279
– and axle 633
– of Fortune
changeable 149
chance 156, 621
rotation 312
necessity 601
– round 218, 607
wheelbarrow 272
wheel-chair 272
wheelman 268
wheels within wheels 59, 633
wheel-work 633
wheeze 349, 409
whelm 641
whelp *infant* 129
produce 161
dog 366
rogue 949
when *inquiry* 461
in the time – 106
whence
attribution 155
departure 293

inquiry 461
reasoning 476
where 186, 461
– am I? 870
whereabouts 183, 197
whereas 9, 476
whereby 631
wherefore
attribution 155
inquiry 461
reasoning 476
motive 615
wherein 221
whereness 186
whereupon 106, 121
wherever 180, 182
wherewith 632, 800
wherret 830
wherry 273
whet *sharpen* 253
meal 298
incite 615
excite 824
take a –
tipple 959
– the appetite 865
– the knife 673
whether or not 609
whetstone, cut a – with a razor 638
which:
at – time 119
know – is which 465
whiff 349, 825
whiffle 349
Whig 712
while *time* 106
in a – 132
worth – 646
– away time
inaction 681
pastime 840
– speaking of 9, 134
whilom 122
whilst 106
whim *fad* 481
fancy 515
caprice 608
wit 842
desire 865
whimper 839
whimsey 515, 865
whimsical [*see* whim] 853
whimwham 608, 643
whin 367
whine 411, 839
whinyard 727
whip *collect* 72
coachman 268
strike 276
stir up 315
urge 615
hasten 684
director 694
flog 972
scourge 975
– and spur 274
– away 293
– hand 731, 737
– in 300
– on 684
– off 293
– up 789
whipcord 205
whipper-in 694
whippersnapper 129
whipping-post 975
whipster 129
whir *rotate* 312
sound 407
whirl *rotate* 312
flurry 825
whirligig 312
whirlpool *rotate* 312
agitation 315
water 348
danger 667
whirlwind
disorder 59
agitation 315
wind 349
reap the –
product 154
fail 732
ride the –
resolution 604
authority 737
whisk *rapid* 274
circuition 311
agitation 315
– off 297
whisker 256
whisket 191
whisky
vehicle 272
drink 298
whisper
faint sound 405
tell 527
conceal 528
stammer 583
stage – 580
– about
disclose 529
publish 531
– in the ear
voice 580
whist *hush* 403
cards 840
whistle *wind* 349
hiss 409
play music 416
musical instrument 417
clean as a –
thorough 52
perfect 650
neatly 652
pay too dear for one's –
inexpedient 647
unskilful 699
dear 814
police – 669
wet one's –
drink 298
tipple 959
– at 930
– for *request* 765
desire 865
– jigs to a milestone 645
– for want of thought
inaction 681
whit *small* 32
whit-leather 327
Whit-Monday 840
white 430
– of the eye 441
– feather 862
– flag 723
– frost 383
– heat 382
– horses 348
– lie *equivocal* 520
concealment 528
untruth 546
plea 617
– liver 862
– as a sheet 860
– slave 962
stand in a – sheet 952
mark with a – stone 642, 931
whitechapel
vehicle 272
Whitefriars 996
whiteness 430
whitewash
cover 223
whiten 430
cleanse 652
ornament 847
justify 937
acquit 970
whitewashed
get – 808
whitewasher 935
white wings 652
whitey-brown 433
whither
tendency 176
direction 278
inquiry 461
whitlow 655
whittle 44, 253
whittled
drunk 959
Whitsuntide 998
whiz 409
who 461
– goes there? 669
– would have thought? 508, 870
whoa! 265
whole *entire* 50
healthy 654
make – 660
as a – 50
on the – 476, 480
go the – hog 729
the – time 106
– truth
truth 494
disclosure 529
veracity 543
wholesale
large scale 31
whole 50
abundant 639
trade 794
wholesome 656
wholly 50, 52
whoop 411
war – 715, 722
whop *flog* 972
whoopee 840
whopper *lie* 546
whopping *huge* 192
whore 962
whoredom 961
whoremonger 962
whorl 248
why *cause* 153
attribution 155
inquiry 461
indeed 535
motive 615
– not 868
wibble-wabble 314
wick 388, 423
wicked 945
the – *bad men* 949
impious 988
the – one 978
wicker 219
wicket 66, 260

wide 202
- apart 15
-awake *hat* 225
intelligent 498
- away 196
- berth 748
- of the mark
distance 196
deviation 279
error 495
- of *distant* 196
- open 194, 260
- of the truth 495
- world 180, 318
in the - world 180
widen 194
- the breach 713, 900
wide-spread
great 31
dispersed 73
space 180
expanded 194
widow 905
widowhood 905
width 202
wield
brandish 315
handle 379
use 677
- authority 737
- the sword 722
wieldy 705
wife 903
wig 225
wigging 932
wiggle 315
wight 373
wigwam 189
wild 851
unproductive 169
violent 173
plain 344
inattentive 458
mad 503
shy 623
unskilled 699
excited 824, 825
untamed 851
rash 863
angry 900
licentious 954
run - 825
- animals 366
- beast *fierce* 173
evil-doer 913
- goose chase
caprice 608
useless 645
unskilful 699
- imagination 515
sow one's - oats
grow up 131
improve 658
amusement 840
vice 945
intemperance 954
Wild, Jonathan -
thief 792
bad man 949
wilderness
disorder 59
unproductive 169
space 180
solitude 893
wild-fire 382
spread like -
violence 173
influence 175
expand 194
publication 531
wile 545, 702
wilful
voluntary 600
obstinate 606
will
volition 600
resolution 604
testament 771
gift 784
at - 600
at one's own sweet - 608
have one's own - 600, 748
make one's - 360
tenant at - 779
- be 152
- for the deed 774, 937
- of Heaven 601
- he nil he 601
- power 600
- and will not 605
- you 765
Will o' the wisp
luminary 423
imp 980
willing or unwilling 601
willingness 602
willow 839
willy-nilly 601, 744
wilted 659
wily 702
wimble 262
wimple 225
win 731, 775
- the affections 897
- golden opinions 931
- the heart 829
- laurels 873
- out 33
- over *belief* 484
induce 615
content 831
wince
bodily pain 378
emotion 821
excitement 825
mental pain 828
flinch 860
winch 307, 633
wind *convolution* [*see below*]
velocity 274
blast 349
life 359
against the - 278, 708
before the - 278, 734
cast to the -s
repudiate 610
disuse 678
not observe 773
relinquish 782
close to the - 278
fair - 705
to the four -s 180
get - 531
get the - up 860
see how the - blows
direction 278
experiment 463
foresight 510
fickle 607
in the - 151, 152
lose - 688
sail near the -
direction 278
skill 698
sharp practice 940
outstrip the - 274
preach to the -s 645
raise the - 775
scatter to the -s 756
see where the - lies 698
short -ed 688
sport of -s and waves 315
sound of - and limb 654
take the - out of one's sails
render powerless 158
hinder 706
defeat 731
touched in the - 655
what's in the - ? 461
- ahead 708
- bag 584
in the -'s eye 278
- the horn 416
hit between - and water 659
- and weather permitting
qualification 469
possibility 470
wind *blast* [*see above*]
convolution 248
deviate 279
circuition 311
- round the heart 897
- up *strengthen* 159
prepare 673
complete 729
- *accounts* 811
windbag 884
wind instruments 417
wind-bound 706
windfall 618
wind-gauge 349
wind-gun 727
winding 248, 311
winding-sheet 363
windings and turnings 248
wind-jammer 273
windlass 307, 633
windless 688
windmill 312
tilt at -s 638
window 260
make the -s shake
loud noise 404
- dressing 544
wind-pipe 351
wind-up 67
windward, to - 236, 278
windy 349
wine 298, 959
put new - into old bottles 699
look upon the - when it is red 953
wine-bibbing 959
wine-cooler 387
wineglass 191

wing *extension* 39
part 51
side 236
fly 267
side-scene 599
instrument 633
refuge 666
army 726
clip the –s 275
lend –s to 707
on the –
motion 264
flying 267
transference 270
departure 293
take – *journey* 266
fly 267
depart 293
under the – of
safe 664
with –s *active* 682
– one's flight 293
– one's way 267
on the –s of the wind 274
wing-commander 745
winged *swift* 274
wink 443, 550
tip the – 550, 527
– at
be blind to 442
disregard 458
neglect 460
permit 760
forgive 918
– of sleep 683
winning [*see* win]
pleasing 829
courteous 894
lovable 897
winnings 775
winnow *sift* 42
exclude 55
inquire 461
pick 609
clean 652
– the chaff from the wheat 465
winsome 829, 836
winter 126, 383
– of our discontent 832
– garden 840
– sports 840
wintry 126
wipe *dry* 340
clean 652
disrespect 929
flog 972
give one a –
rebuke 932
– away 552
– the eyes
relieve 834
– off old scores 807, 952
– the tears 914
wire *ligature* 45
filament 205
telegraph 527, 534
pull the –s 693
wire-drawn
long 200
wireless 531
– telegram 532
– telegraph 534
– telephone 534
wire-puller 526, 694
wire-worm 913
wiry *strong* 159
wis 514
wisdom 498
have cut one's – teeth 698
worldly – 864
wise
intelligent 498
sage 500
manner 627
in such – 8
word to the – 695
– in one's own conceit 880
– after the event 135
– man 500
– maxim 496
dine not –ly but too well 953
wiseacre 493, 500,
wiser, nobody the – 528
wish *will* 600
intention 620
desire 865
do what one –es 748
– at the bottom of the Red Sea 832
– the father to the thought
misjudge 481
credulous 486
hope 858
desire 865
– joy 896
– well 906
wishing-cap 993
wish-wash
unmeaning 517
wishy-washy
languid 160
insipid 391
feeble style 575
unimportant 643
wisket 191
wisp 72
wistful
thought 451
care 459
feeling 821
desire 865
wit *intellect* 450
wisdom 498
humour 842
humorist 844
mother – 498
soul of – 572
to – 522
at one's –'s end 475, 704
witch *oracle* 513
ugly 846
sorceress 994
– doctor 994
witchcraft 992
witchery
attraction 615
pleasing 829
sorcery 992
witching time 126, 421
witenagemote 696
with *added* 37
mixed 41
ligature 45
accompanying 88
means 632
go – 178
– all its parts 52
– regard to 9
– a vengeance 31, 52
– a witness 31
withal
in addition 37
accompanying 88
enough 639
withdraw
subduct 38
absent 187
turn back 283
recede 287
depart 293
– from
recant 607
relinquish 624
dislike 867
withe 45
wither 195, 659
– one's hopes 837
withered *weak* 160
disease 655
withering
harsh 739
painful 830
contempt 930
censure 932
withers 250
– unwrung 159, 823
withhold *hide* 528
restrain 751
prohibit 761
retain 781
stint 819
– one's assent 764
within 221
derived from – 5
place – 221
keep – 221
– an ace 32
– bounds
small 32
shortcoming 304
restraint 751
– call 197
– compass
shortcoming 304
temperate 953
– the mark 304
– one's memory 505
– reach 197, 705
without *unless* 8
subduction 38
exception 83
absence 187
exterior 220
circumjacent 227
exemption 777*a*
derived from – 6
not be able to do – 630
– alloy 827
– ballast 605, 863
– ceasing 136
– ceremony 881
– charge 815
– fear of contradiction 535
– a dissentient voice 488
– end 105, 112
– exception 16
– excuse 945
– fail 474, 604*a*
– God 989
– a leg to stand on 158
– limit 105
– measure 105

– notice 508
– number 105
– parallel 33
– a rap 804
– reason 499
– regard to 10
– reluctance 602
– reserve 525
– rhyme or reason 615*a*
– a shadow of turning 141
– stint 639
– warning 508
withstand 708, 719
withy 45
witless 491
witling 501, 844
witness [*see* 441]
spectator 444
evidence 467
voucher 550
call to – 467
witness-box 966
wits 450
live by one's –
deceive 545
skill 698
cunning 702
steal 791
dishonourable 940
set one's – to work
think 451
invent 515
plan 626
all one's – about one
care 459
intelligence 498
skill 698
one's – gone a woolgathering 458
witsnapper 844
witticism 842
wittingly 620
wittol 962
wive 903
wiveless 904
wizard *sage* 500
proficient 700
sorcerer 994
wizen *wither* 195
throat 260
woad 438
wobble 605
woe 828
– betide 908, 914
– is me 839
– to 908
woebegone 828, 837
woeful 649, 830
woefully *very* 31
wold 344
wolf *ravenous* **865**
cry – *false* **544**
alarm 669
fear 860
hold the – by the ears **704**
keep the – from the door **359**
unable to keep the – from the door 804
– at the door 667, 804
– and the lamb 923
– in sheep's clothing 548, **941**
woman 131, **374**
– of the town 962
woman-hater 911
womanhood 131, 374
womanish 160
womanly
adolescent **131**
feminine **374**
womb *cause* 153
interior 221
– of time 121, 152
wonder
exception 83
astonishment **870**
prodigy 872
do –s 682, 731
for a – 870
nine days' – 643
not – **507**
– whether
uncertain 475
ignorant 491
suppose 514
–s of the world 872
wonderfully 31
wonder-working 870
wondrous 870
wont *habitual* 613
won't do, it – 932
woo 865, 902
wood *trees* 367
material **635**
not out of the – 665, **704**
take to the –s 666
woodcut 558
woodcutter 371
wooded, well- 256
wooden 635
– horse 975
– spoon 493
– walls 717, 726
wood engraving 558
woodlands 367
wood-note 412
wood pavement 255
woody 367
wooer 897
woof
warp and – 329
wool *flocculent* 256
warm 382
much cry and little – 482
woolgathering 458
woolly 255, 256
woolpack *cloud* 353
woolsack
pillow 215
authority **747**
tribunal 966
word *maxim* 496
intelligence 532
assertion **535**
vocable **562**
phrase 566
command 741
promise **768**
give the – 741
good as one's –
veracious 543
complete 729
probity 939
in a – 572
keep one's – 939
man of his – 939
not a – to say 585, 879
pass– 550
put in a – 582
take at one's – 484, 762
upon my – 535
watch– 722
– and a blow
hasty 684
contentious 720
irascible 901
– of command
indication 550
military 722
command 741
– in the ear 527, 586
– of honour 768
– it 566
– of mouth 582
– to the wise
intelligible 518
advice 695
– for word **19, 494**
Word *Deity* **976**
– of God 985
word-catcher 936
wordiness 573, 584
wording **569**
wordless 581
word-play
equivocal **520**
neology **563**
wit 842
words *quarrel* 713
bandy – 588
bitter – **932**
choice of – **569**
command of – 574
express by – 566
flow of – 582, 584
mere – **477, 517**
no – can paint 872
play of – **842**
put into – 566
war of – 588, 720
– that burn 574
– painting 515
– with 932
wordy 573
work
product 154
operation 170
pass and repass 302
book 593
business 625
use **677**
action 680
exertion 686
ornament 847
at –
in operation 170
business 625
doing 680
active 682
earth– 717
field– 717
hard – 686, 704
piece of –
importance 642
discord 713
stick to – 604*a*
stitch of – 686
stroke of – 686
– of art 845, 847
– a change 140
– a cure 662
– of fiction 594
– for 707
– hard 686, 704
– ill 732
– in 228
– out *conduct* 692

complete 729
-room 191
- out one's salvation 990
- against time 684
- up [*see below*]
- upon
influence 175
incite 615
excite 824
- one's way
progress 282
ascent 305
exertion 681
succeed 731
- well 705, 731
- wonders 682, 731
work up
prepare 673
use 677
excite 824
- into *form* 240
- into a passion 900
workable 470
work-a-day 625, 682
worker 690
workhouse 691
working *acting* 170
active 682
- bee 690
- man 690
- order 673
- towards 176
workman 690
workmanlike 698
workmanship 161, 680
works
board of - 696
good - 906
- of the mind 451
workshop 691
workwoman 690
world *great* 31
events 151
space 180
universe 318
mankind 372
fashion 852
all the - over 180
citizen of the - 910
come into the - 359
for all the - 615
give to the - 531
knowledge of the - 698
man of the -
proficient 700
fashion 852
not for the - 489, 764
organized - 357
Prince of this - 978
rise in the - 734
throughout the - 180
- to come 152
follow to the -'s end 743
- forgetting by the world forgot 893
as the - goes 613
- of good 618, 648
a - of 102
- and his wife 102
- without end 112
worldling 943, 988
worldly 943, 989
world-wide
great 31
universal 78
space 180
world-wisdom
skill 698
caution 864
selfishness 943
worm *small* 193
spiral 248
animal 366
bane 663
- in 228
- oneself
ingress 294
love 897
- out 480a
- that never dies 982
- one's way 275, 302
worm-eaten 659
worms, food for - 362
wormwood
gall and - 395
worn *weak* 160
damage 659
fatigue 688
well- *used* 677
- out 659, 841
worry
vexation 828
tease 830
harass 907
worse 659, 835
- for wear 160
worship *title* 877
servility 886
religious 990
demon - 991
idol - 991
fire - 991
his - 967
place of - 1000
- Mammon 803
- the rising sun 886
worshipful 873
worst *defeat* 731
do one's - 659, 907
do your - 715, 909
have the - of it 732
make the - of 482
worst come to the - *certain* 474
bad 649
hopeless 859
worsted 205
worth *value* 644
goodness 648
possession 777
price 812
virtue 944
penny - 815
what one is - 780
- a great deal 803
- the money 815
- much 803
- one's salt 644
- while 646
worthless
trifling 643
useless 645
profligate 945
worthy
famous 873
virtuous 944
good 948
- of 924
- of belief 484
- of blame 932
- of notice 642
- of remark 642
wot 490
would: - fain 865
- that! 865
would-be *pert* 885
usurping 925
wound *evil* 619
injure 659
pain 830
anger 900
keep the - green 919
- the feelings 830
- up 704
woven fabrics 219
wowser 988
wrack 162
go to - and ruin
perish 162
fail 732
bankrupt 804
wraith 980
wrangle
disagreement 24
reason 476
quarrel 713
contend 720
wrangler
reasoner 476
scholar 492
opponent 710
wrap 223, 225
wrapped in
attention 457
- clouds 528
- self 943
- thought 458
wrapper 223, 225
inclosure 232
wraprascal 225
wrath 900
wreak *violent* 173
harsh 739
- one's anger 919
- one's malice on 907
wreath *woven* 219
circle 247
trophy 733
ornament 847
honour 877
wreathe *weave* 219
wreathy 248
wreck
remainder 40
destruction 162
damage 659
defeat 732
wrecker 792
wrench *disjoin* 44
draw 285
extract 301
twist 311
tool 633
seize 789
wrest *distort* 243
- from 789
- the sense 523
wrestle 720
wrestler 726
wretch *sufferer* 828
sinner 949
wretched
unimportant 643
bad 649
unhappy 828
wretchedly

small 32
wriggle 314, 315
- into 294
- out of 671
wright 690
wring *twist* 248
pain 378
clean 652
torment 830
- from
extract 301
compel 744
take 789
- one's hands 839
- the heart 830
wringing wet 339
wrinkle *fold* 258
hint 527
wrinkled 128
wrist 781
wristband 225
writ 741, 969
Writ, Holy - 985
write *compose* 54
style 569
writing 590
- down *record* 551
- music 416
- off 624
- out 590
- prose 598
- to 592
- upon 595
- word 527
writer 590, 593
dramatic - 599
pen of a ready - 569
- to the Signet 968
writhe *distort* 243
agitate 315
pain 378
writing 590, 593
put in - 551
- in cipher 590
written, it is - 601
wrong *error* 495
evil 619
injury 649
spite 907
improper 923
vice 945
go - 732
in the - *error* 495, 923
own oneself in the - 950
- box 699, 704
wrong 923
- course 945
begin at the - end 699
- in one's head 503
in the - place 647
- side out 145, 218
- side up 218
- side of the wall 665
- sow by the ear 699, 732
- step 732
wrong-doer 949
wrong-doing 945
wrongful 923
wrong-headed 481
wrought:
highly -
prepared 673
complete 729
- iron 323
- out 729
- up *excited* 824
angry 900
wry 217, 243
- face *pain* 378
discontent 832
lamentation 839
ugly 846
disapproval 932
wynd 189
wyvern 83

X

X-rays 420, 554
xanthic 436
Xanthippe 901
xebec 273
xenogenesis 161
xerophagy 956
xylography 558
xylophone 417
x, y, z 491

Y

yacht 273
yachting 267
yachtsman 269
yager 726
Yahoo 876
yammer 839
yap 412
yard *abode* 189
length 200
enclosure 232
workshop 691
yardarm to yard-arm 197
yare 682
yarn *filament* 205
story 532
untruth 546
exaggeration 549
mingled - 41
spin a long - 549
diffuse style 573
yarr 412
yashmak 225
yataghan 727
yaup 411
yaw 279
yawl *ship* 273
cry 412
yawn *open* 260
sleepy 683
tired 688
weary 841
yawning *gulf* 198, 260
yclept 564
yea *more* 33
assent 488
yean 161
year 106, 108
- in and - out 104
since the - one 124
all the - round 110
- after year 104
tenant from - to year 779
yearling 129
yearly 138
yearn 828, 837
- for *desire* 865
pity 914
yearning *love* 897
years 128
in - 128
tenant for - 779
- ago 122
come to - of discretion 131
- old 128
yeast *leaven* 320
bubbles 353
yell *cry* 411
scream 839
yellow 436
- flag 668
- streak 862
- and red 439
yellow-eyed 920
yellowness 436
yelp 412
yeoman 371, 373
- of the guard 726
-'s service 644
yeomanry 726
yerk *strike* 276
yes 488, 762
yes-man 886
yesterday *past* 122
of - *new* 123
yet *in compensation* 30
exception 83
time 106
prior 116
past 122
qualification 469
yeux doux, faire les - 902
yield *soft* 324
harvest 636
submit 725
consent 762
resign 782
furnish 784
gain 810
price 812
- assent 488, 762
- one's breath 360
- to despair 859
- up the ghost 360
- the palm 34, 879
- to temptation 615
yielding *soft* 324
facile 705
submissive 725
yodel 580
yoicks 622
yoke *join* 43
vinculum 45
couple 89
subject 749
means of restraint 752
rivet the - 739
yokel 701, 876
yokemate 903
yonder 79, 196
yore 122
Yorkshireman 702
you: - don't say so 870
-'re another 718
young 127
- man *lover* 897
younger generation 127
youngster 129
younker 129
youth 127, 129
Yule log 388

Z

Zadkiel 513
zambo 41
Zamiel 978

zany 501
zeal *eagerness* 602
activity 682
feeling 821
desire **865**
zealot *bigot* 474
obstinate 606
active 682
zealotry 606
zebra 440
zemindar 779
zemindary 780
zemstvo 696
zenana 374, 961
Zendavesta 986
zenith 31, 210
in the – **873**
zephyr 349
Zeppelin 273, 726
Zerdhusht 986
zero 4, 101
– hour 66
zest 394, 827
zetetic 461
Zeus 979
zigzag *oblique* 217
angle 244
deviating 279
oscillating 314
circuit 629
ornament 847
Zimmermann
disciple of – 893
zinc
– white 430
zincography 558
zircon 847
zither 412
zocle 215
zodiac *zone* **230**
worlds **318**
zodiacal light **423**
Zoilus 936
Zollverein 712, 769
zonam perdidit 804
zone *region* 181
layer 204
belt 230
circle **247**
Zoo 370
zoography 368
zoohygiantics 370
zoolatry 991
zoological 366
– garden **370**
zoology 368
zoom 305
zoonomy 368
zoophorous 210
zoophyte 366
zootomy 368
Zoroaster 986
Zoroastrianism 984
zouave 726
zounds 870, 900
zymotic 655, **657**